SCOTT McCLOUD

THE SCULPTOR

:01
First Second
NEW YORK

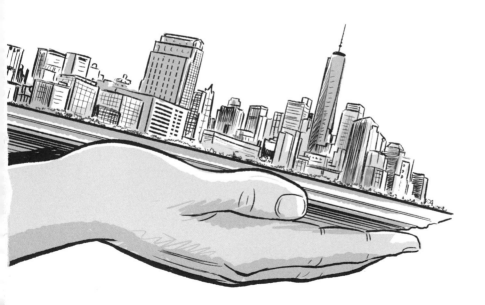

First Second

New York

Text and art copyright © 2015 by Scott McCloud

Published by First Second
First Second is an imprint of Roaring Brook Press, a division of
Holtzbrinck Publishing Holdings Limited Partnership
175 Fifth Avenue, New York, New York 10010
All rights reserved

Cataloging-in-Publication Data is on file at the Library of Congress.

ISBN 978-1-59643-573-5

First Second books may be purchased for business or promotional use.
For information on bulk purchases please contact Macmillan Corporate and
Premium Sales Department at (800) 221-7945 x5442 or by email
at specialmarkets@macmillan.com.

First edition 2015
Book design by Colleen AF Venable and John Green

Printed in China

10 9 8 7 6 5 4 3 2 1

For the Girl in the Hat

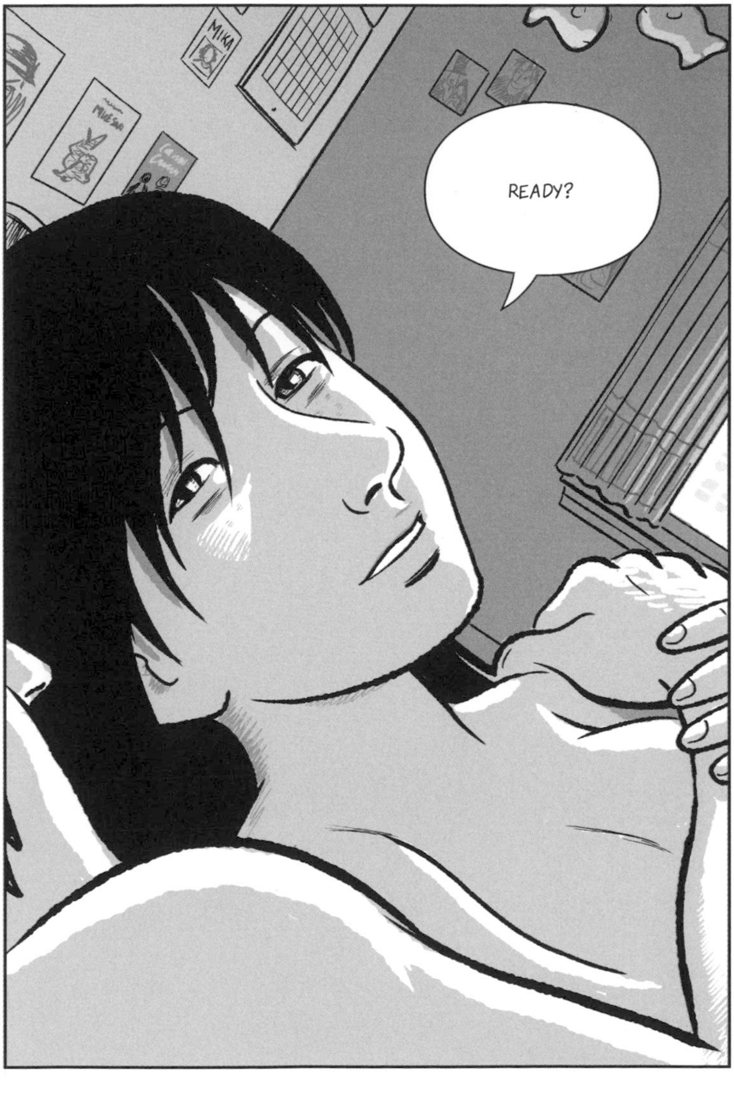
READY?

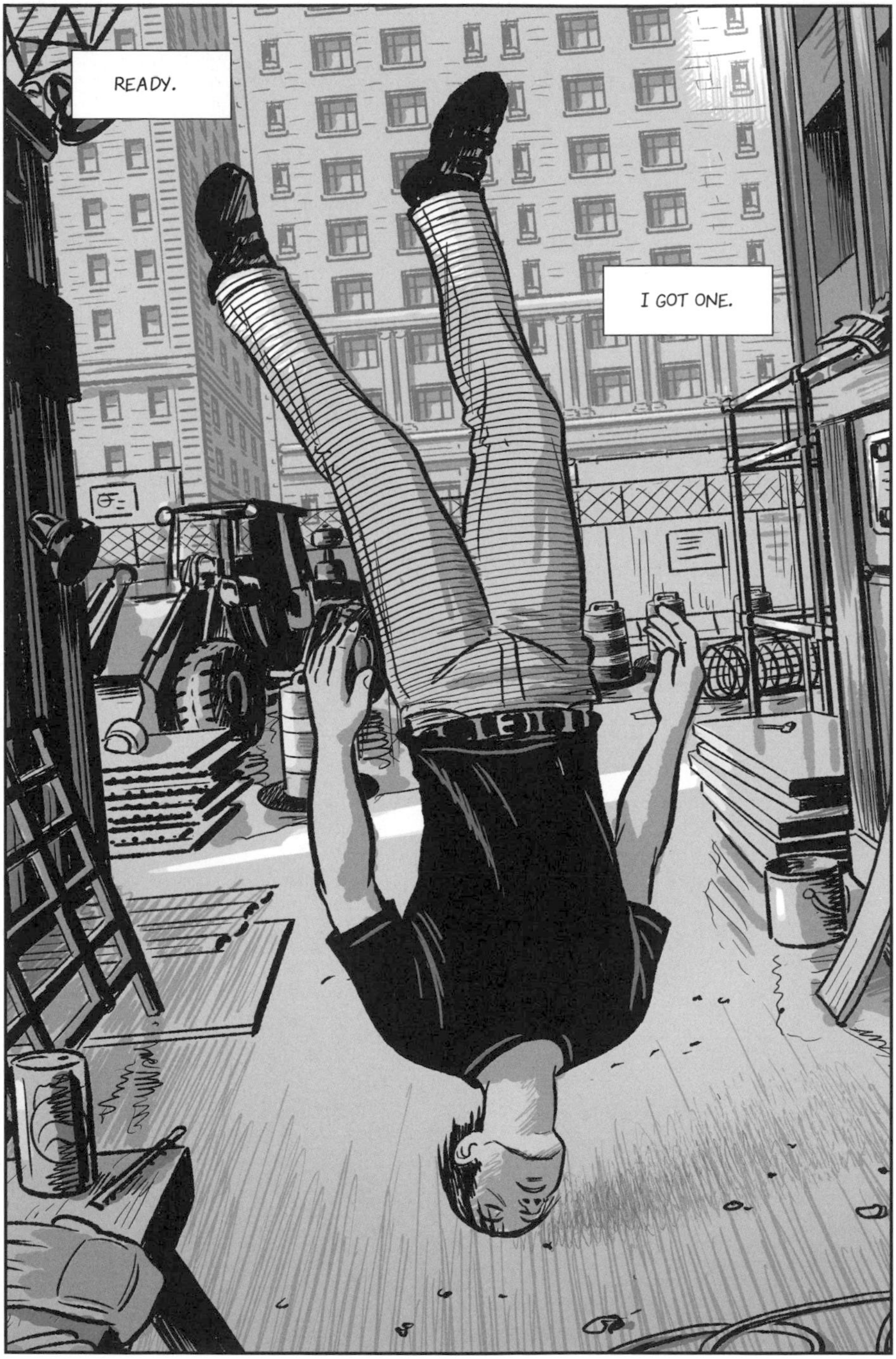
READY.
I GOT ONE.

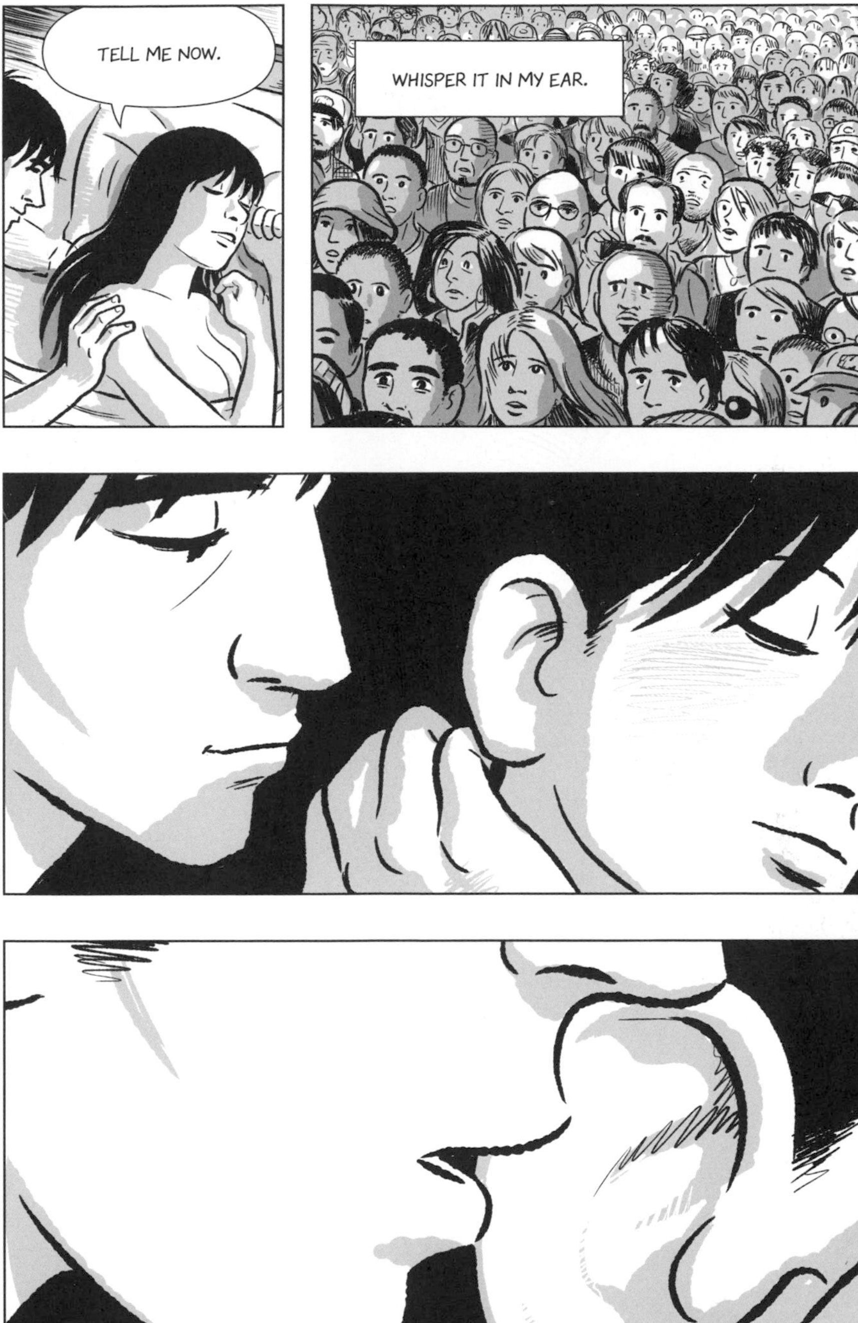
TELL ME NOW.
WHISPER IT IN MY EAR.

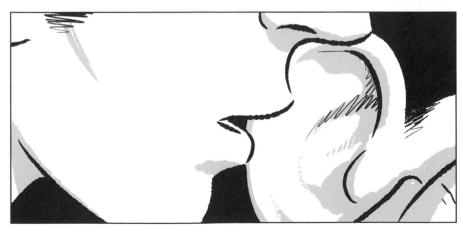

1.

THE OTHER DAVID SMITH

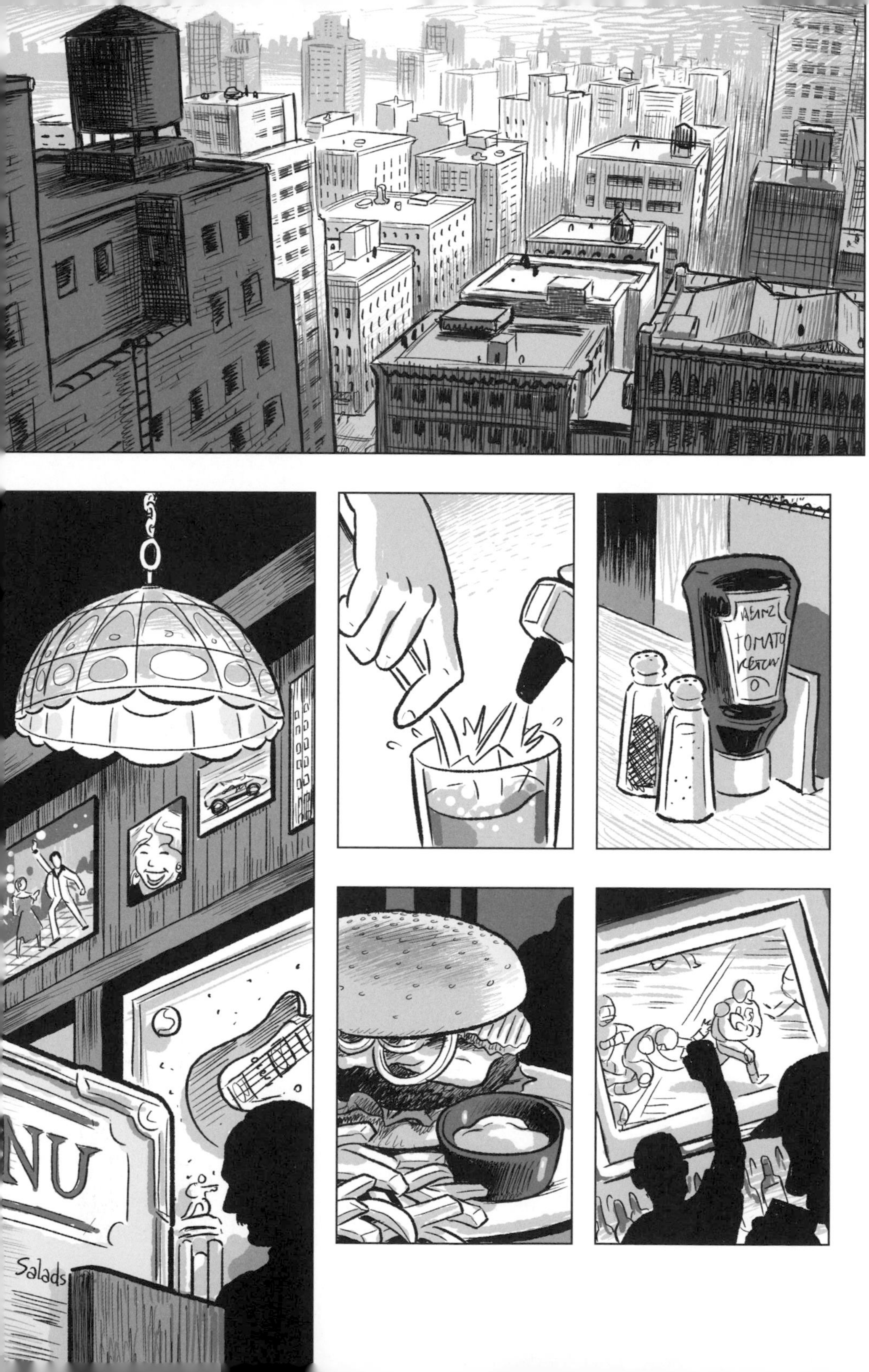
TOMATO
NU
Salads

ME, SIR.
EXCUSE ME?
SIR?

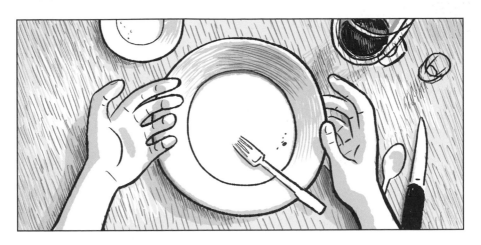

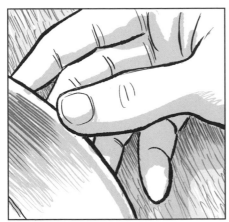

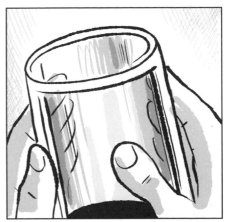

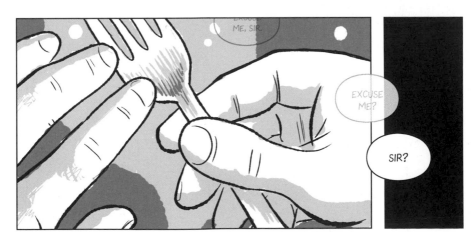

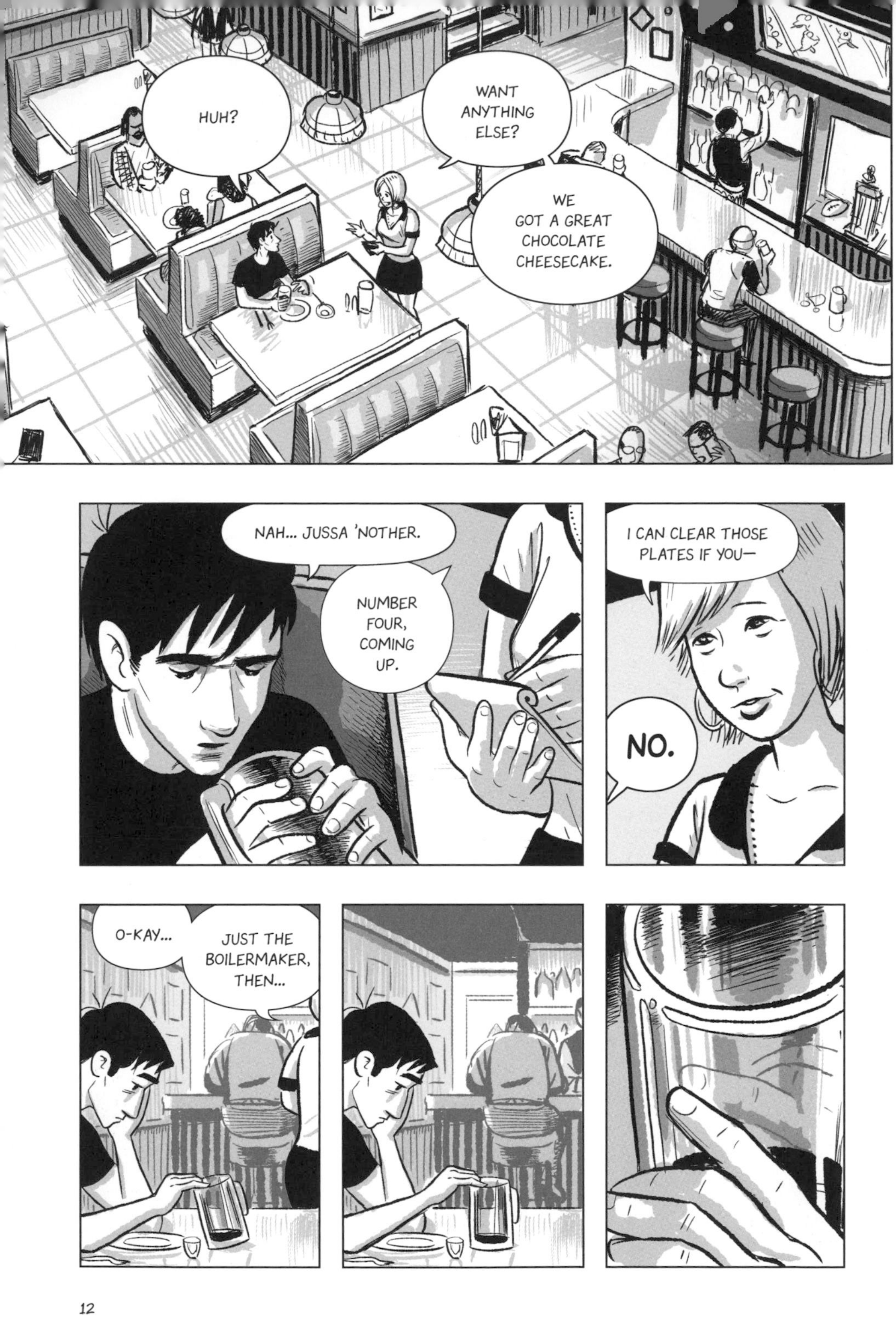
WANT ANYTHING ELSE?
HUH?
WE GOT A GREAT CHOCOLATE CHEESECAKE.
NAH... JUSSA 'NOTHER.
NUMBER FOUR, COMING UP.
I CAN CLEAR THOSE PLATES IF YOU—
NO.
O-KAY...
JUST THE BOILERMAKER, THEN...

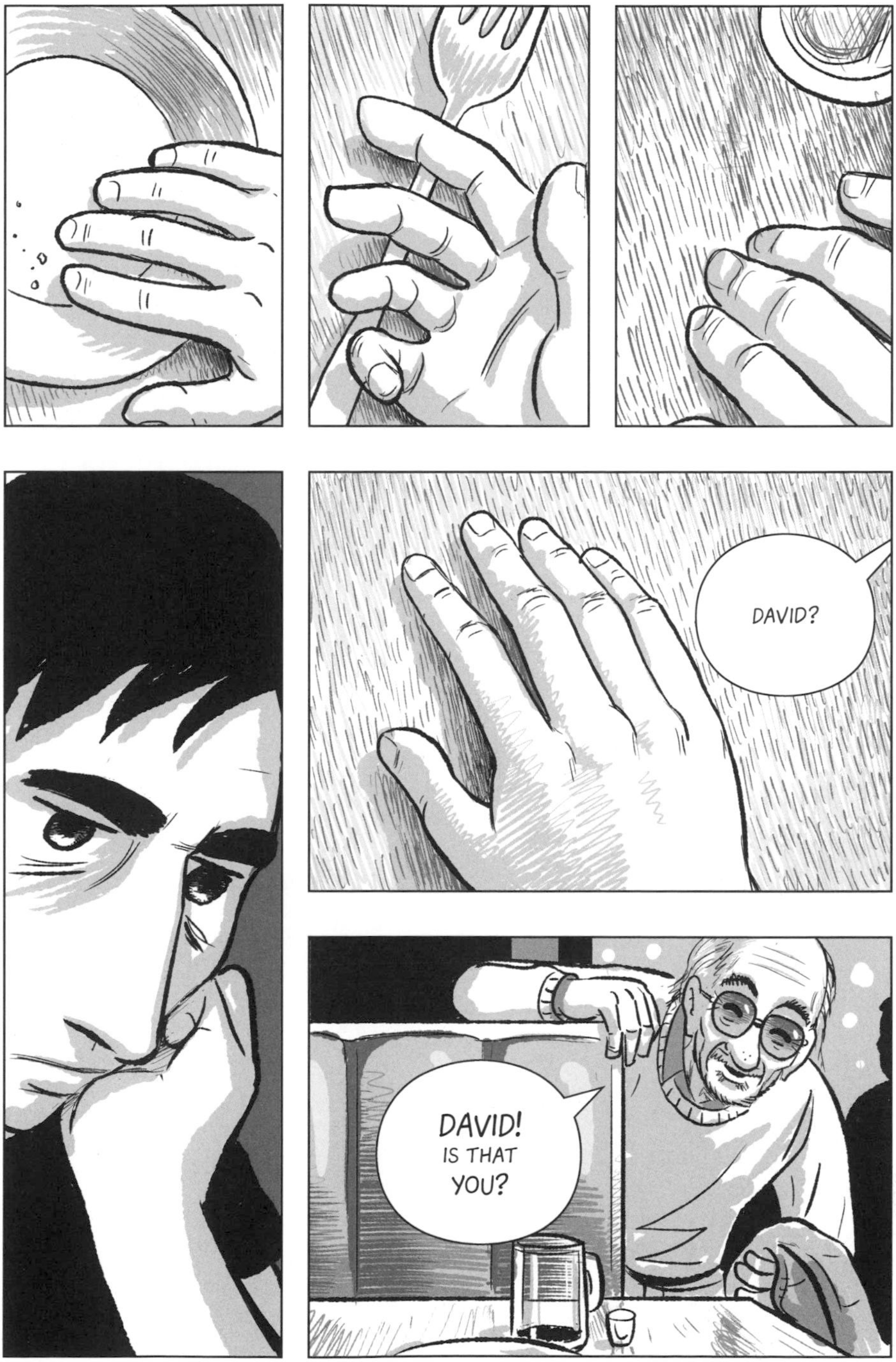
DAVID?
DAVID! IS THAT YOU?

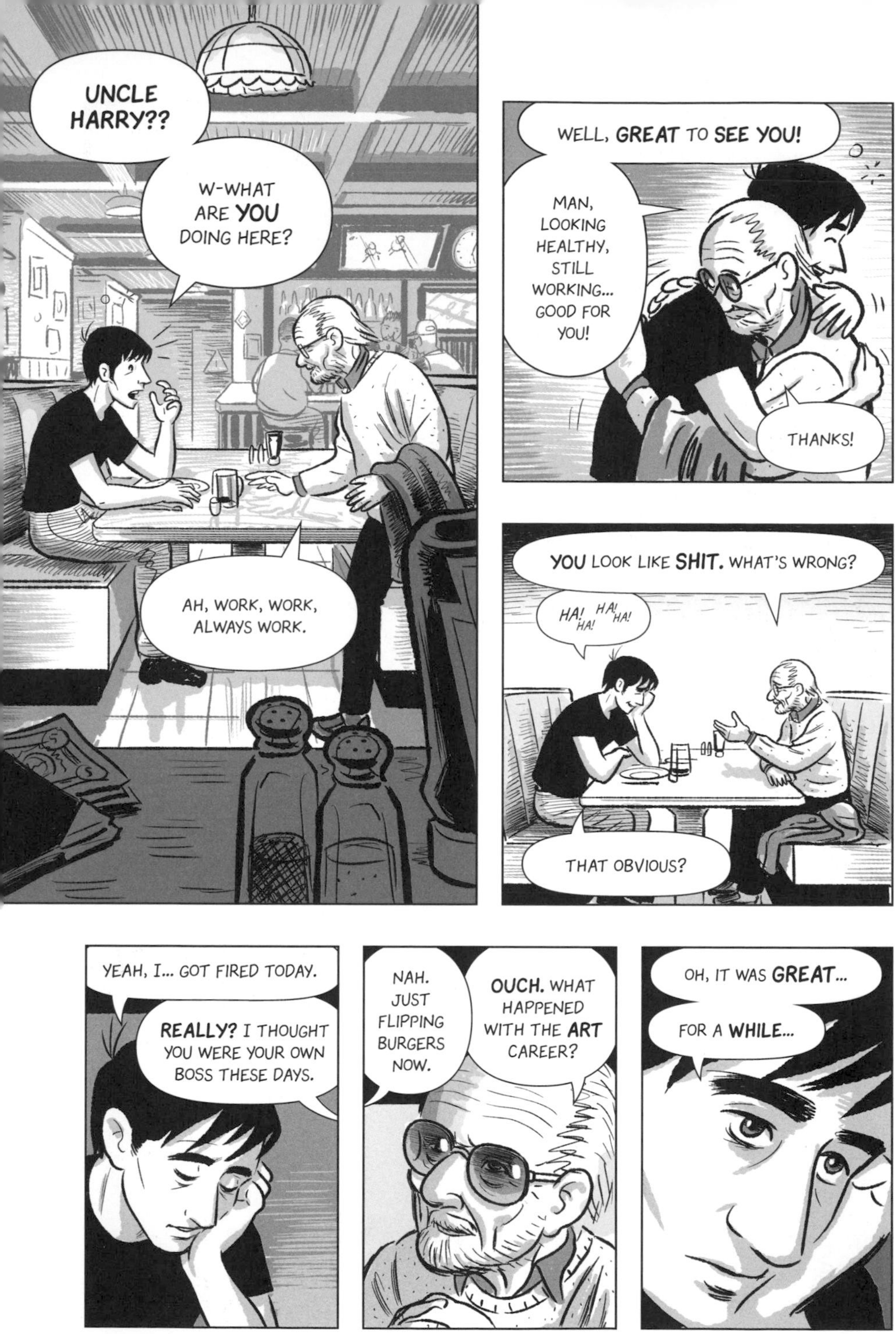
UNCLE HARRY??
W-WHAT ARE YOU DOING HERE?
AH, WORK, WORK, ALWAYS WORK.
WELL, GREAT TO SEE YOU!
MAN, LOOKING HEALTHY, STILL WORKING... GOOD FOR YOU!
THANKS!
YOU LOOK LIKE SHIT. WHAT'S WRONG?
HA! HA! HA! HA!
THAT OBVIOUS?
YEAH, I... GOT FIRED TODAY.
REALLY? I THOUGHT YOU WERE YOUR OWN BOSS THESE DAYS.
NAH. JUST FLIPPING BURGERS NOW.
OUCH. WHAT HAPPENED WITH THE ART CAREER?
OH, IT WAS GREAT...
FOR A WHILE...

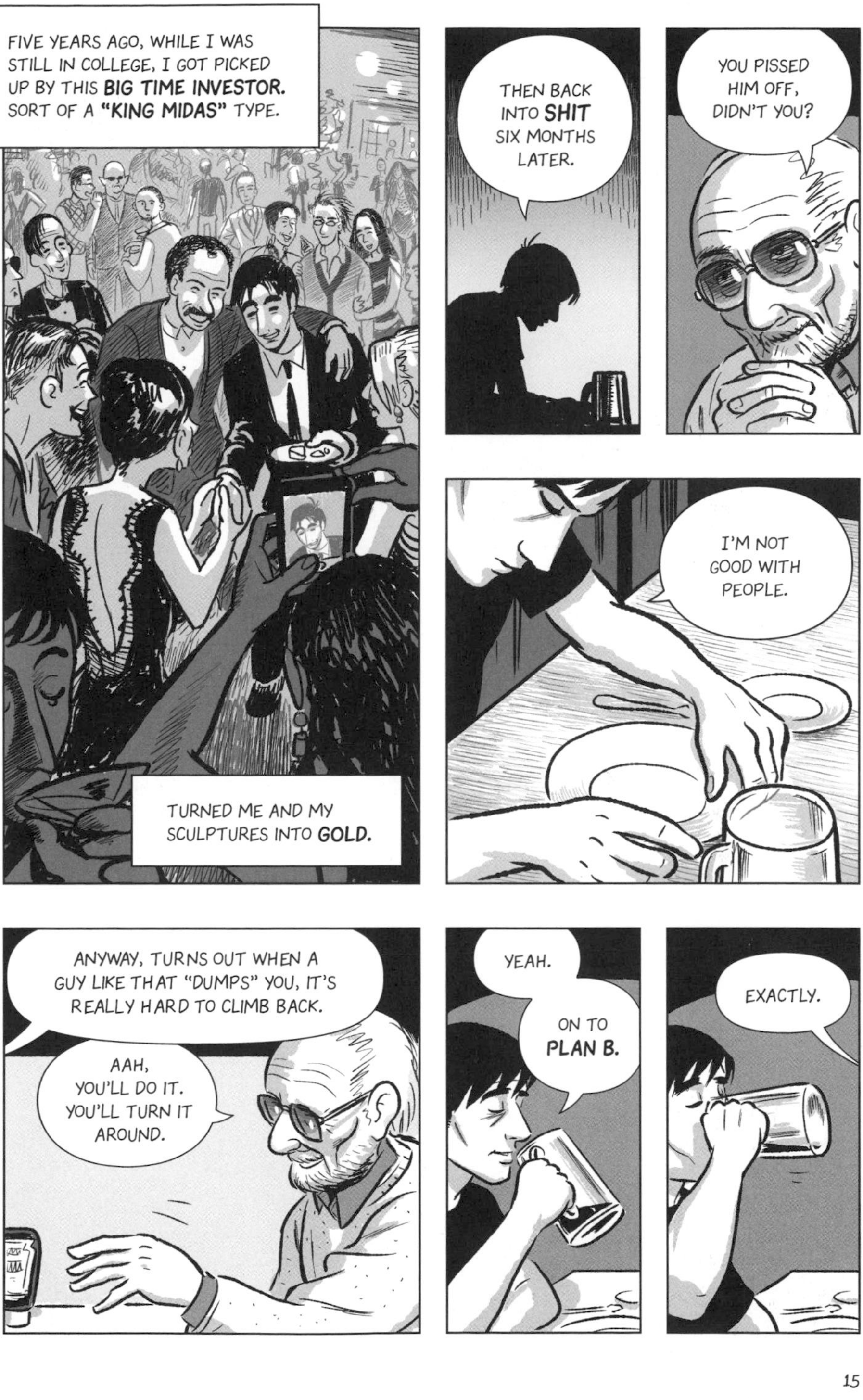
FIVE YEARS AGO, WHILE I WAS STILL IN COLLEGE, I GOT PICKED UP BY THIS BIG TIME INVESTOR. SORT OF A "KING MIDAS" TYPE.
TURNED ME AND MY SCULPTURES INTO GOLD.
THEN BACK INTO SHIT SIX MONTHS LATER.
YOU PISSED HIM OFF, DIDN'T YOU?
I'M NOT GOOD WITH PEOPLE.
ANYWAY, TURNS OUT WHEN A GUY LIKE THAT "DUMPS" YOU, IT'S REALLY HARD TO CLIMB BACK.
AAH, YOU'LL DO IT. YOU'LL TURN IT AROUND.
YEAH.
ON TO PLAN B.
EXACTLY.

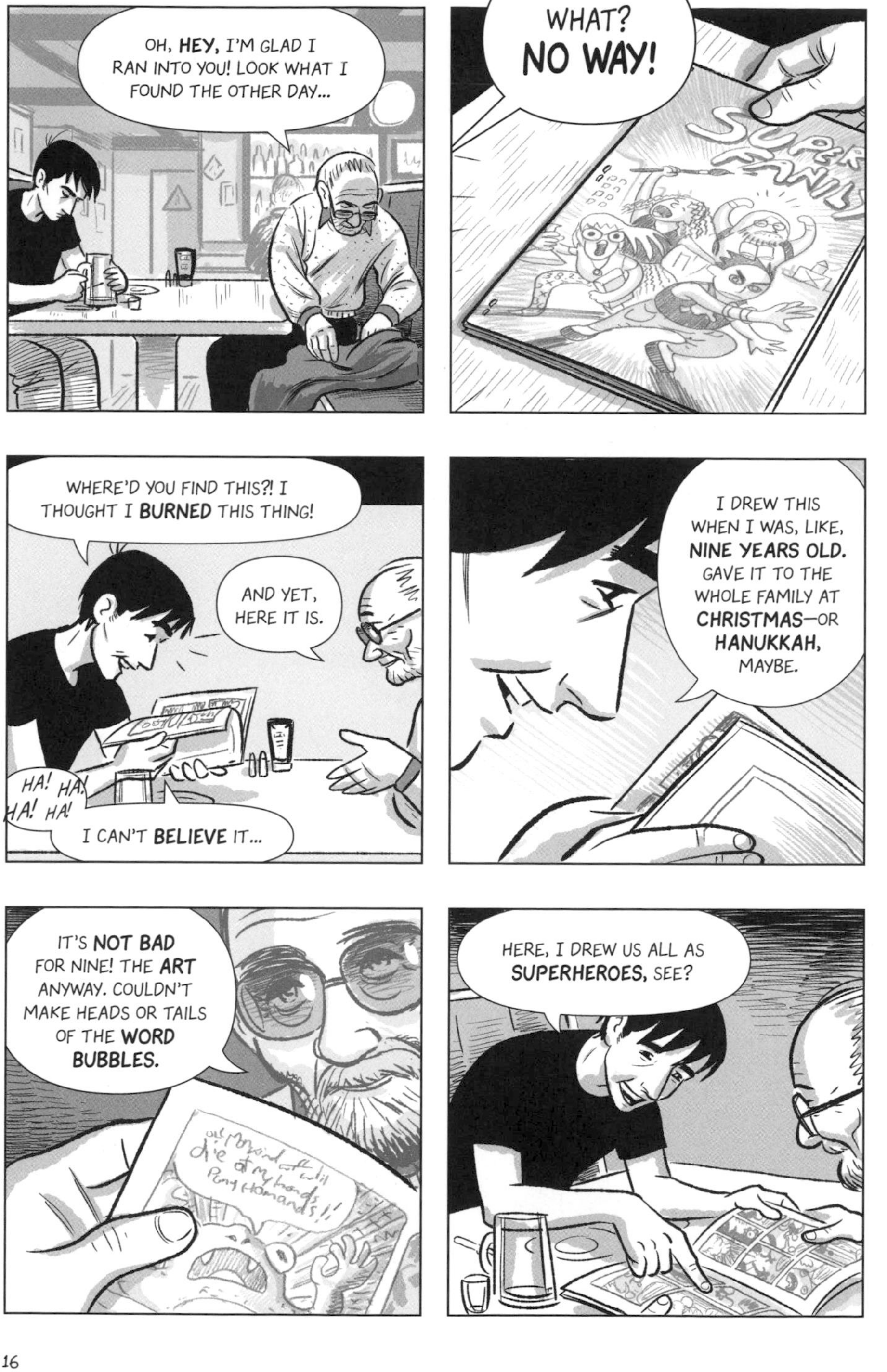
OH, **HEY,** I'M GLAD I RAN INTO YOU! LOOK WHAT I FOUND THE OTHER DAY...
WHAT? **NO WAY!**
WHERE'D YOU FIND THIS?! I THOUGHT I **BURNED** THIS THING!
AND YET, HERE IT IS.
HA! HA! HA! HA!
I CAN'T **BELIEVE** IT...
I DREW THIS WHEN I WAS, LIKE, **NINE YEARS OLD.** GAVE IT TO THE WHOLE FAMILY AT **CHRISTMAS**—OR **HANUKKAH,** MAYBE.
IT'S **NOT BAD** FOR NINE! THE **ART** ANYWAY. COULDN'T MAKE HEADS OR TAILS OF THE **WORD BUBBLES.**
HERE, I DREW US ALL AS **SUPERHEROES,** SEE?

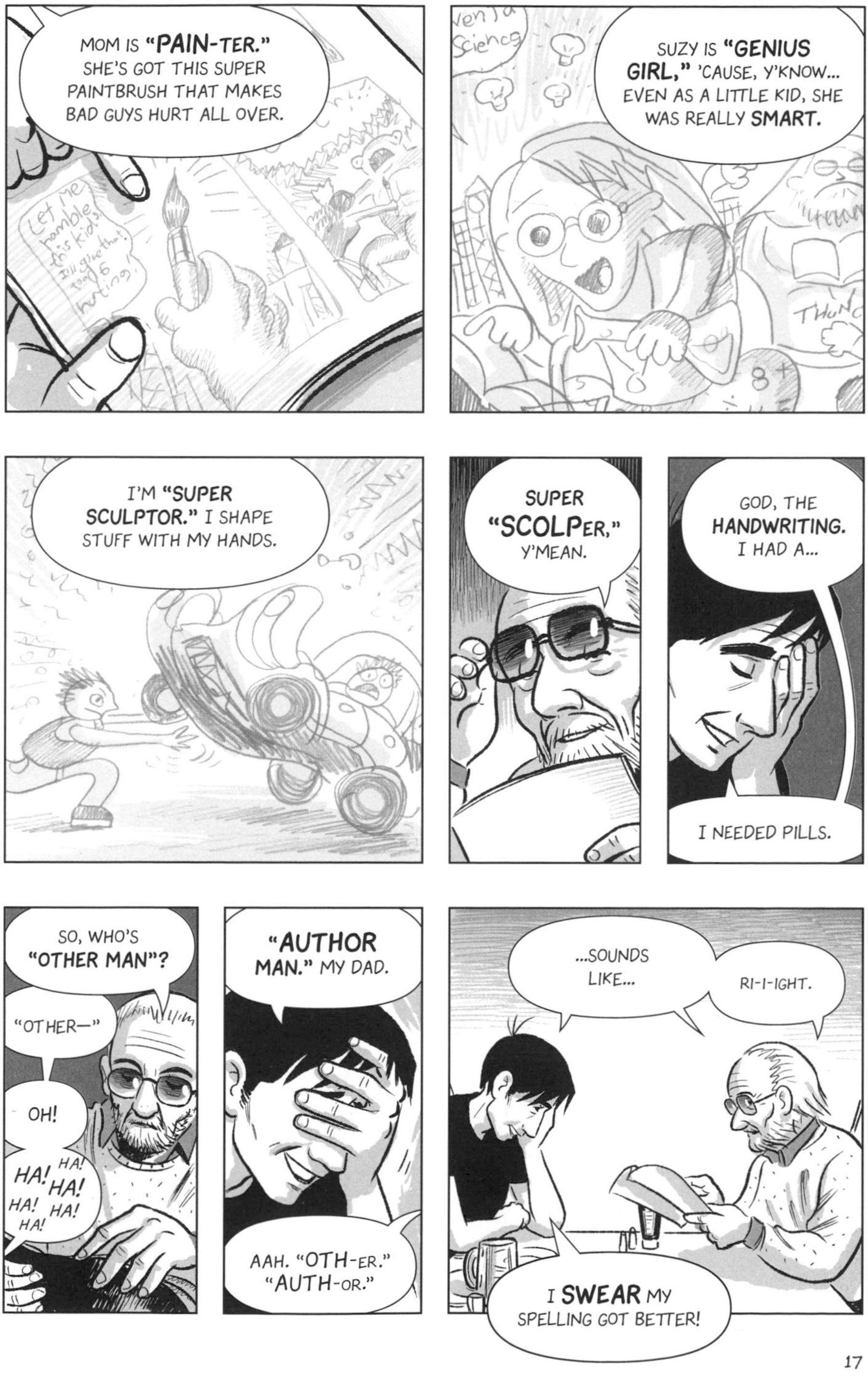
MOM IS "PAIN-TER." SHE'S GOT THIS SUPER PAINTBRUSH THAT MAKES BAD GUYS HURT ALL OVER.
SUZY IS "GENIUS GIRL," 'CAUSE, Y'KNOW... EVEN AS A LITTLE KID, SHE WAS REALLY SMART.
I'M "SUPER SCULPTOR." I SHAPE STUFF WITH MY HANDS.
SUPER "SCOLPer," Y'MEAN.
GOD, THE HANDWRITING. I HAD A...
I NEEDED PILLS.
SO, WHO'S "OTHER MAN"?
"OTHER—"
OH!
HA! HA! HA! HA! HA! HA!
"AUTHOR MAN." MY DAD.
AAH. "OTH-er." "AUTH-or."
...SOUNDS LIKE...
RI-I-IGHT.
I SWEAR MY SPELLING GOT BETTER!

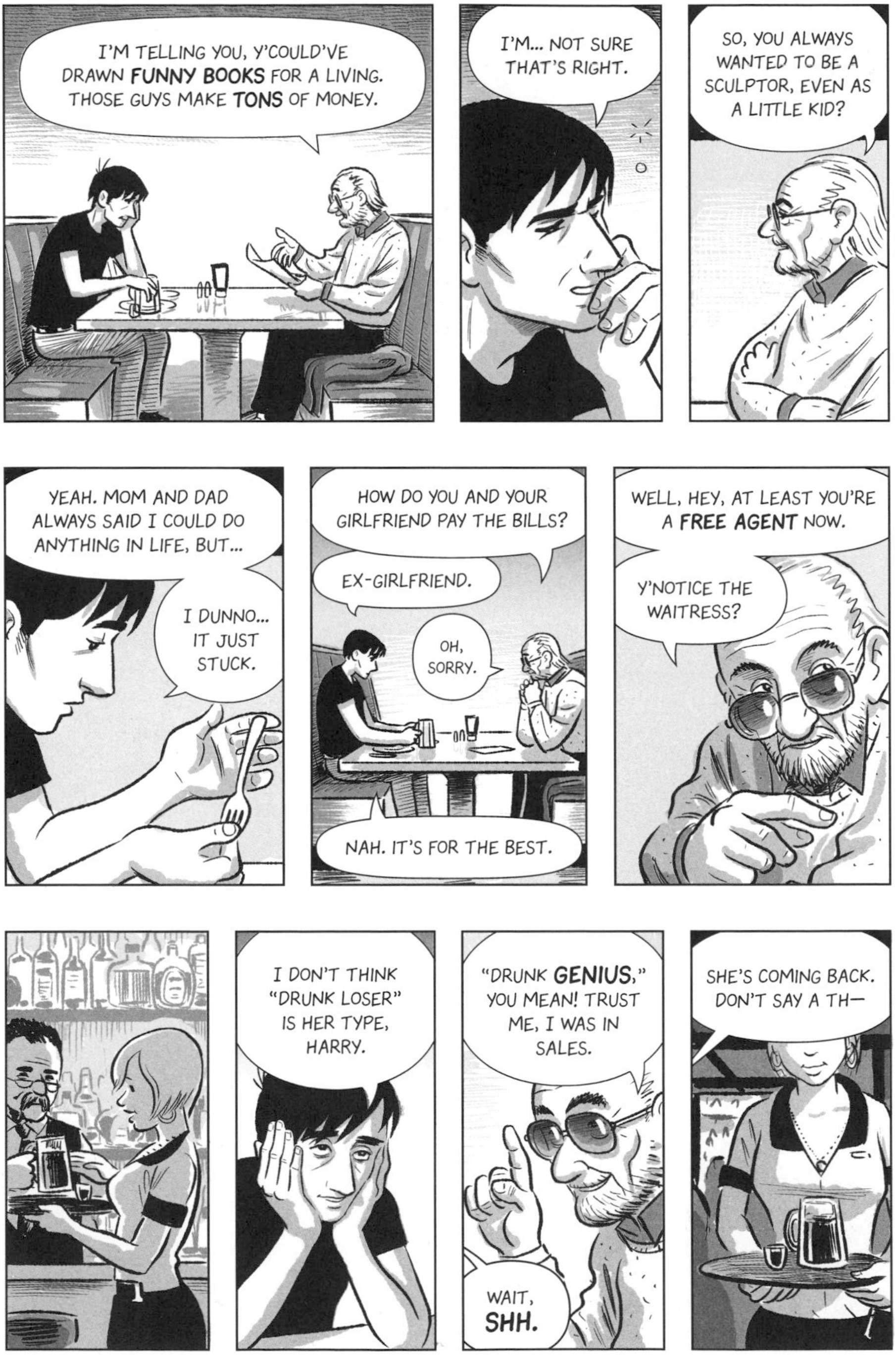
I'M TELLING YOU, Y'COULD'VE DRAWN **FUNNY BOOKS** FOR A LIVING. THOSE GUYS MAKE **TONS** OF MONEY.
I'M... NOT SURE THAT'S RIGHT.
SO, YOU ALWAYS WANTED TO BE A SCULPTOR, EVEN AS A LITTLE KID?
YEAH. MOM AND DAD ALWAYS SAID I COULD DO ANYTHING IN LIFE, BUT...
I DUNNO... IT JUST STUCK.
HOW DO YOU AND YOUR GIRLFRIEND PAY THE BILLS?
EX-GIRLFRIEND.
OH, SORRY.
NAH. IT'S FOR THE BEST.
WELL, HEY, AT LEAST YOU'RE A **FREE AGENT** NOW.
Y'NOTICE THE WAITRESS?
I DON'T THINK "DRUNK LOSER" IS HER TYPE, HARRY.
"DRUNK **GENIUS**," YOU MEAN! TRUST ME, I WAS IN SALES.
WAIT, **SHH.**
SHE'S COMING BACK. DON'T SAY A TH—

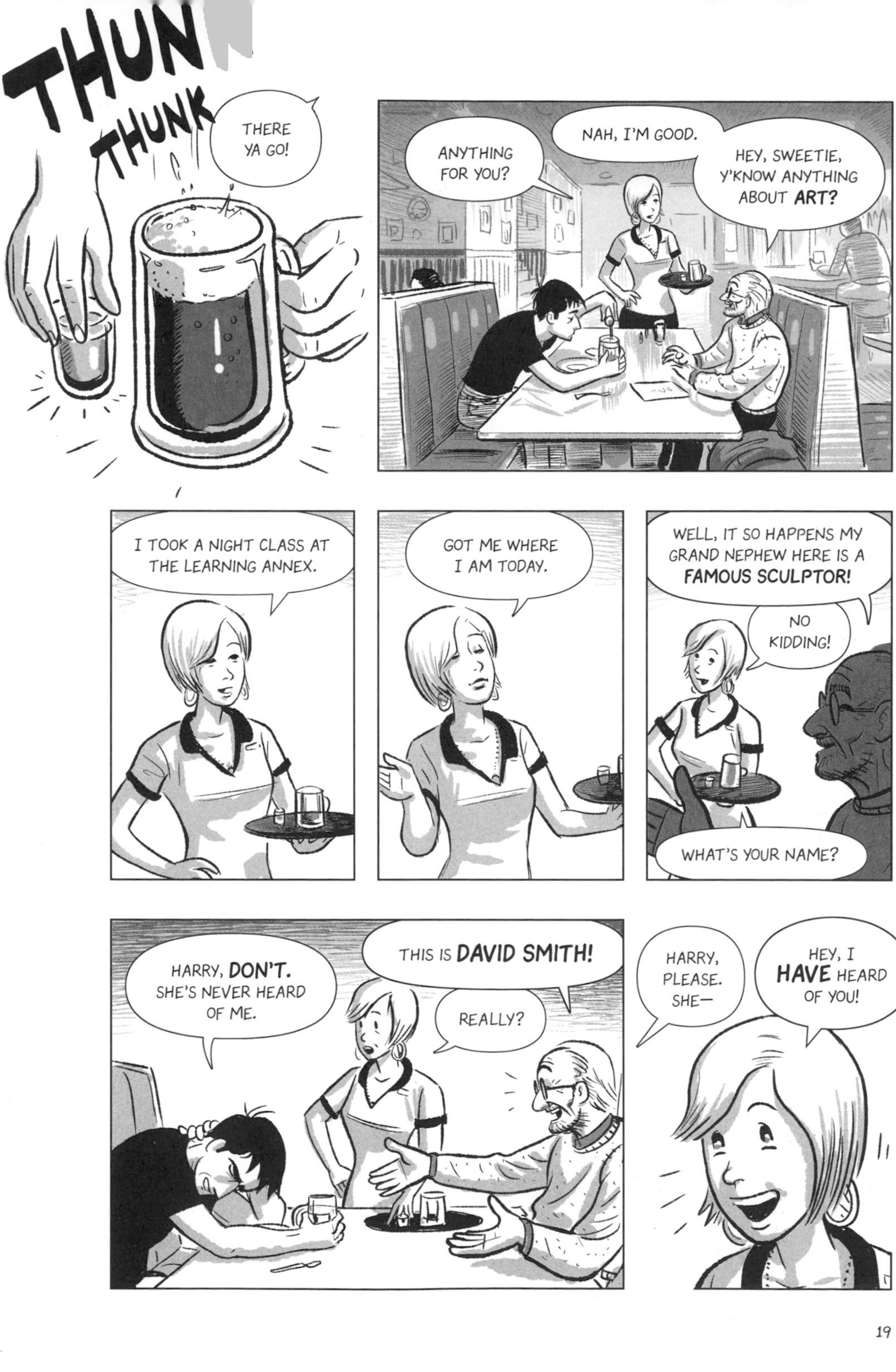
THUNK
THUNK
THERE YA GO!
ANYTHING FOR YOU?
NAH, I'M GOOD.
HEY, SWEETIE, Y'KNOW ANYTHING ABOUT **ART?**
I TOOK A NIGHT CLASS AT THE LEARNING ANNEX.
GOT ME WHERE I AM TODAY.
WELL, IT SO HAPPENS MY GRAND NEPHEW HERE IS A **FAMOUS SCULPTOR!**
NO KIDDING!
WHAT'S YOUR NAME?
HARRY, **DON'T.** SHE'S NEVER HEARD OF ME.
THIS IS **DAVID SMITH!**
REALLY?
HARRY, PLEASE. SHE—
HEY, I **HAVE** HEARD OF YOU!

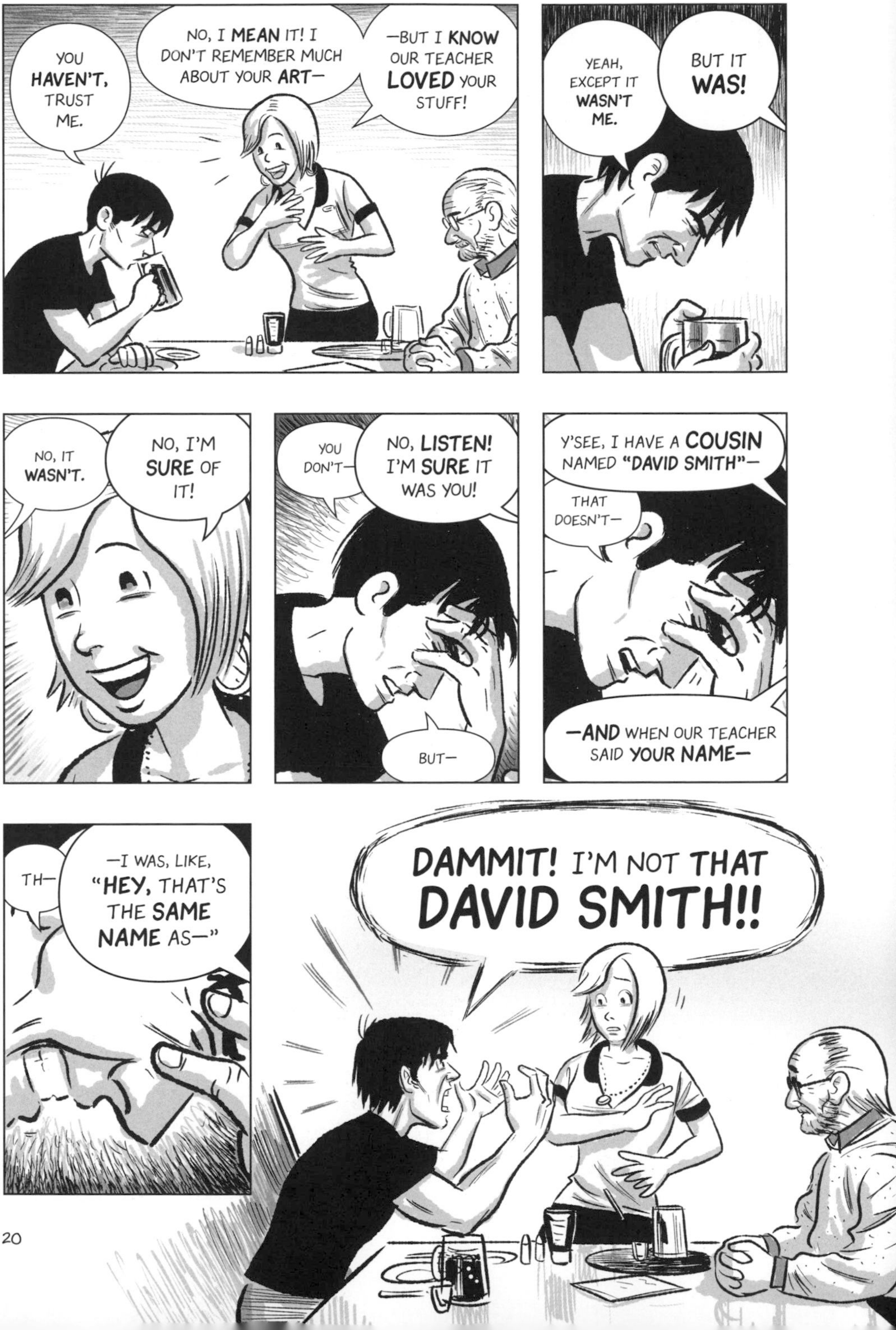
YOU HAVEN'T, TRUST ME.
NO, I MEAN IT! I DON'T REMEMBER MUCH ABOUT YOUR ART—
—BUT I KNOW OUR TEACHER LOVED YOUR STUFF!
YEAH, EXCEPT IT WASN'T ME.
BUT IT WAS!
NO, IT WASN'T.
NO, I'M SURE OF IT!
YOU DON'T—
NO, LISTEN! I'M SURE IT WAS YOU!
BUT—
Y'SEE, I HAVE A COUSIN NAMED "DAVID SMITH"—
THAT DOESN'T—
—AND WHEN OUR TEACHER SAID YOUR NAME—
TH—
—I WAS, LIKE, "HEY, THAT'S THE SAME NAME AS—"
DAMMIT! I'M NOT THAT DAVID SMITH!!

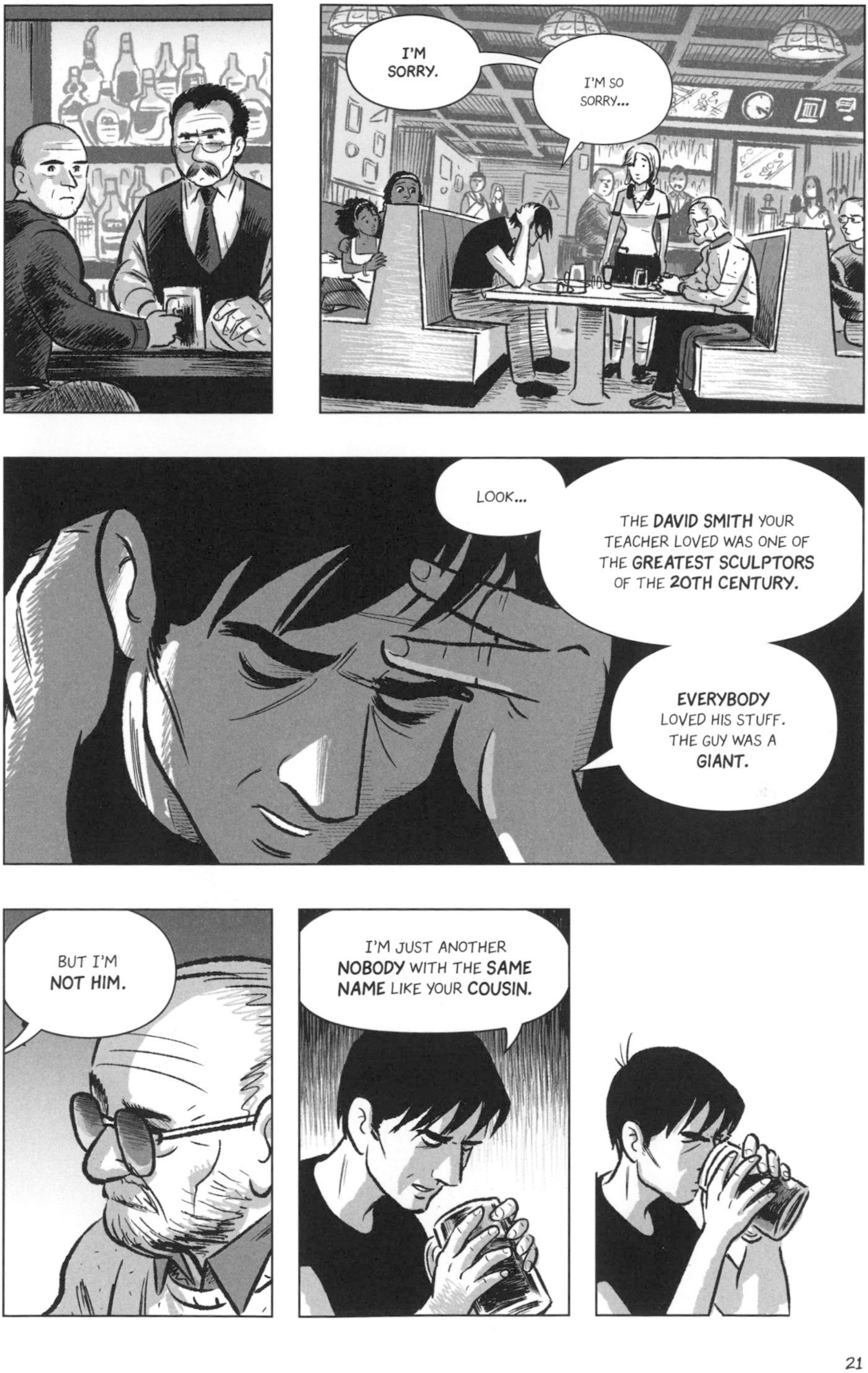
I'M SORRY.
I'M SO SORRY...
LOOK...
THE DAVID SMITH YOUR TEACHER LOVED WAS ONE OF THE GREATEST SCULPTORS OF THE 20TH CENTURY.
EVERYBODY LOVED HIS STUFF. THE GUY WAS A GIANT.
BUT I'M NOT HIM.
I'M JUST ANOTHER NOBODY WITH THE SAME NAME LIKE YOUR COUSIN.

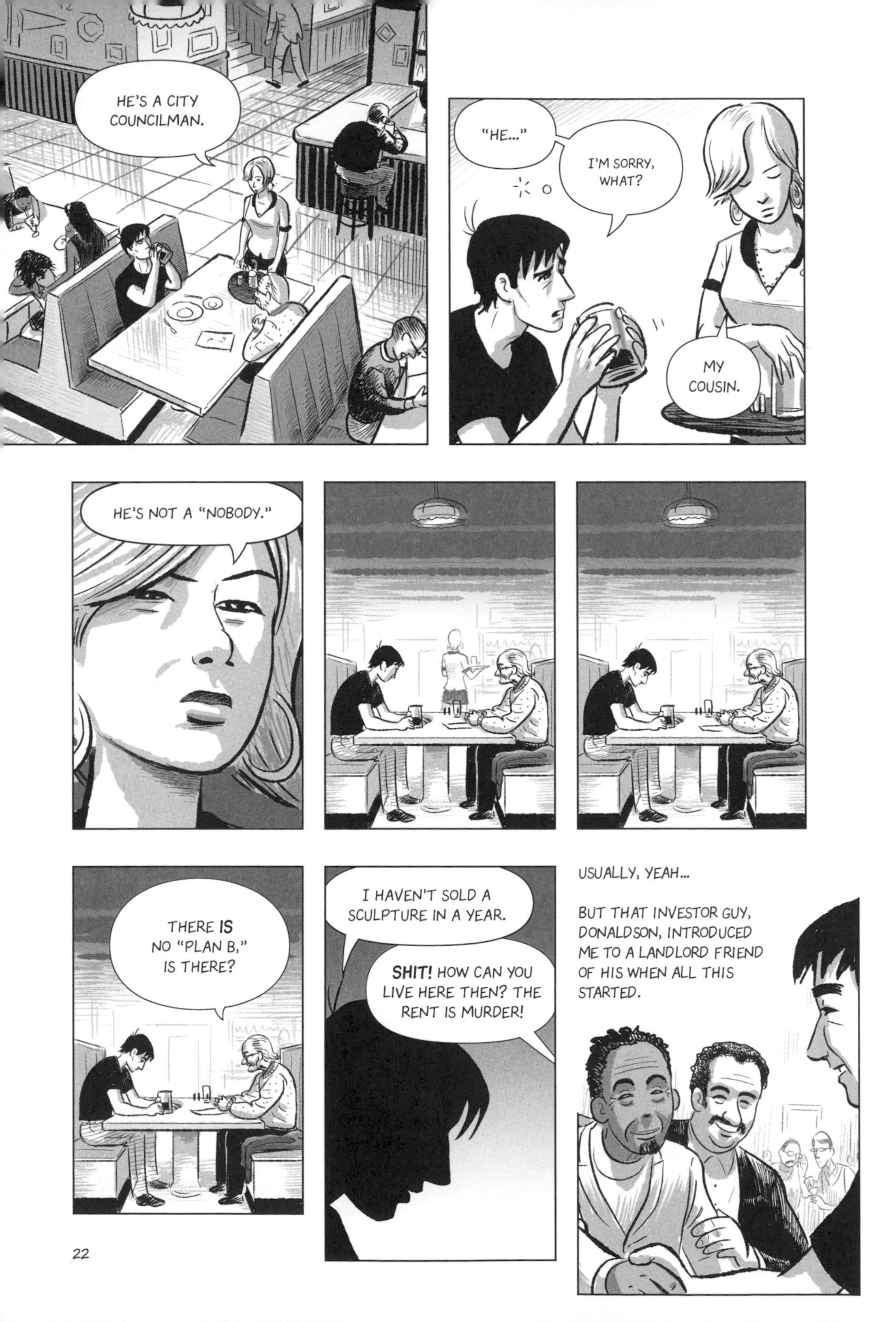

HE'S A CITY COUNCILMAN.
"HE..."
I'M SORRY, WHAT?
MY COUSIN.
HE'S NOT A "NOBODY."
THERE **IS** NO "PLAN B," IS THERE?
I HAVEN'T SOLD A SCULPTURE IN A YEAR.
SHIT! HOW CAN YOU LIVE HERE THEN? THE RENT IS MURDER!
USUALLY, YEAH...
BUT THAT INVESTOR GUY, DONALDSON, INTRODUCED ME TO A LANDLORD FRIEND OF HIS WHEN ALL THIS STARTED.

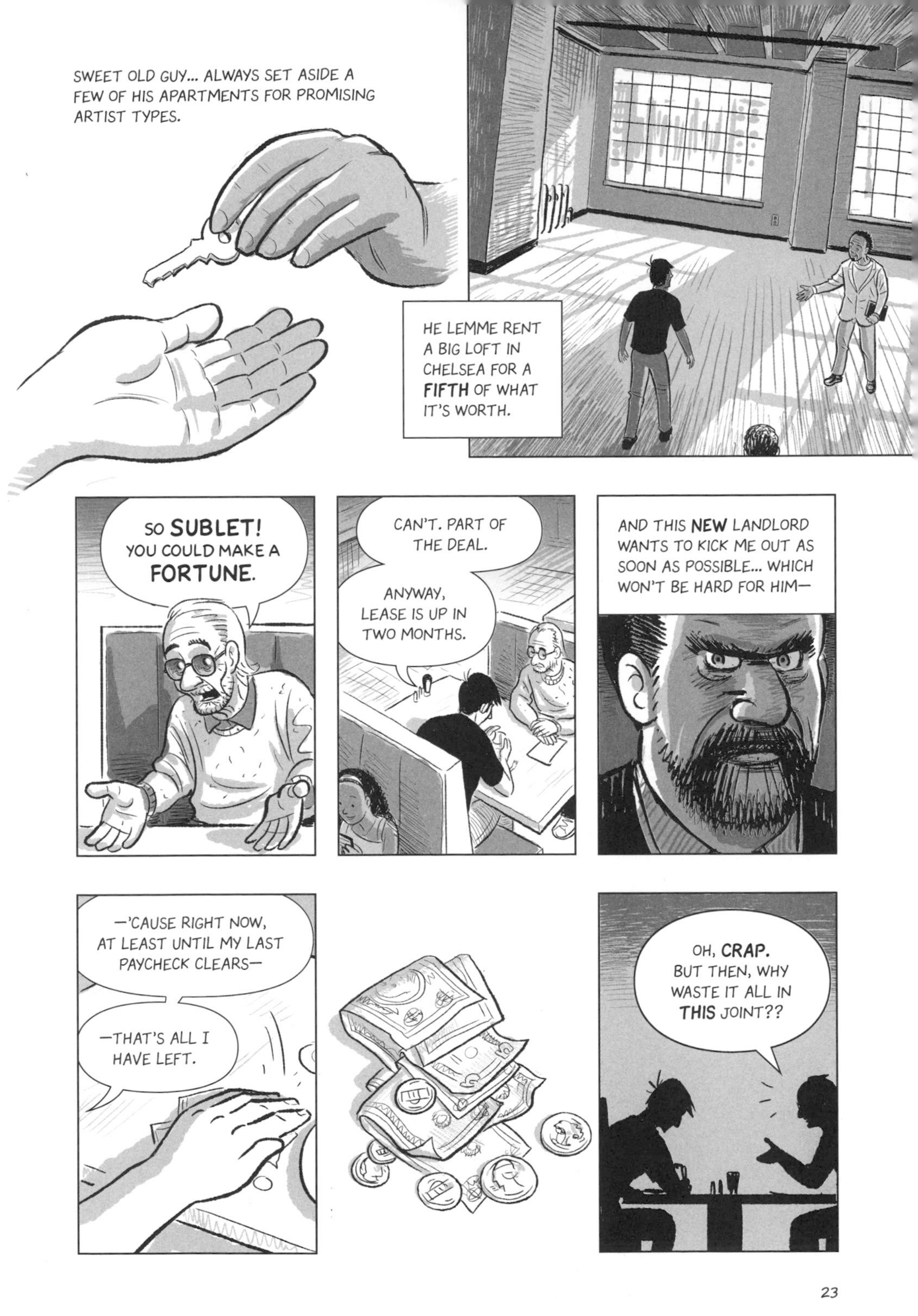
SWEET OLD GUY... ALWAYS SET ASIDE A FEW OF HIS APARTMENTS FOR PROMISING ARTIST TYPES.
HE LEMME RENT A BIG LOFT IN CHELSEA FOR A FIFTH OF WHAT IT'S WORTH.
SO SUBLET! YOU COULD MAKE A FORTUNE.
CAN'T. PART OF THE DEAL.
ANYWAY, LEASE IS UP IN TWO MONTHS.
AND THIS NEW LANDLORD WANTS TO KICK ME OUT AS SOON AS POSSIBLE... WHICH WON'T BE HARD FOR HIM—
—'CAUSE RIGHT NOW, AT LEAST UNTIL MY LAST PAYCHECK CLEARS—
—THAT'S ALL I HAVE LEFT.
OH, CRAP. BUT THEN, WHY WASTE IT ALL IN THIS JOINT??

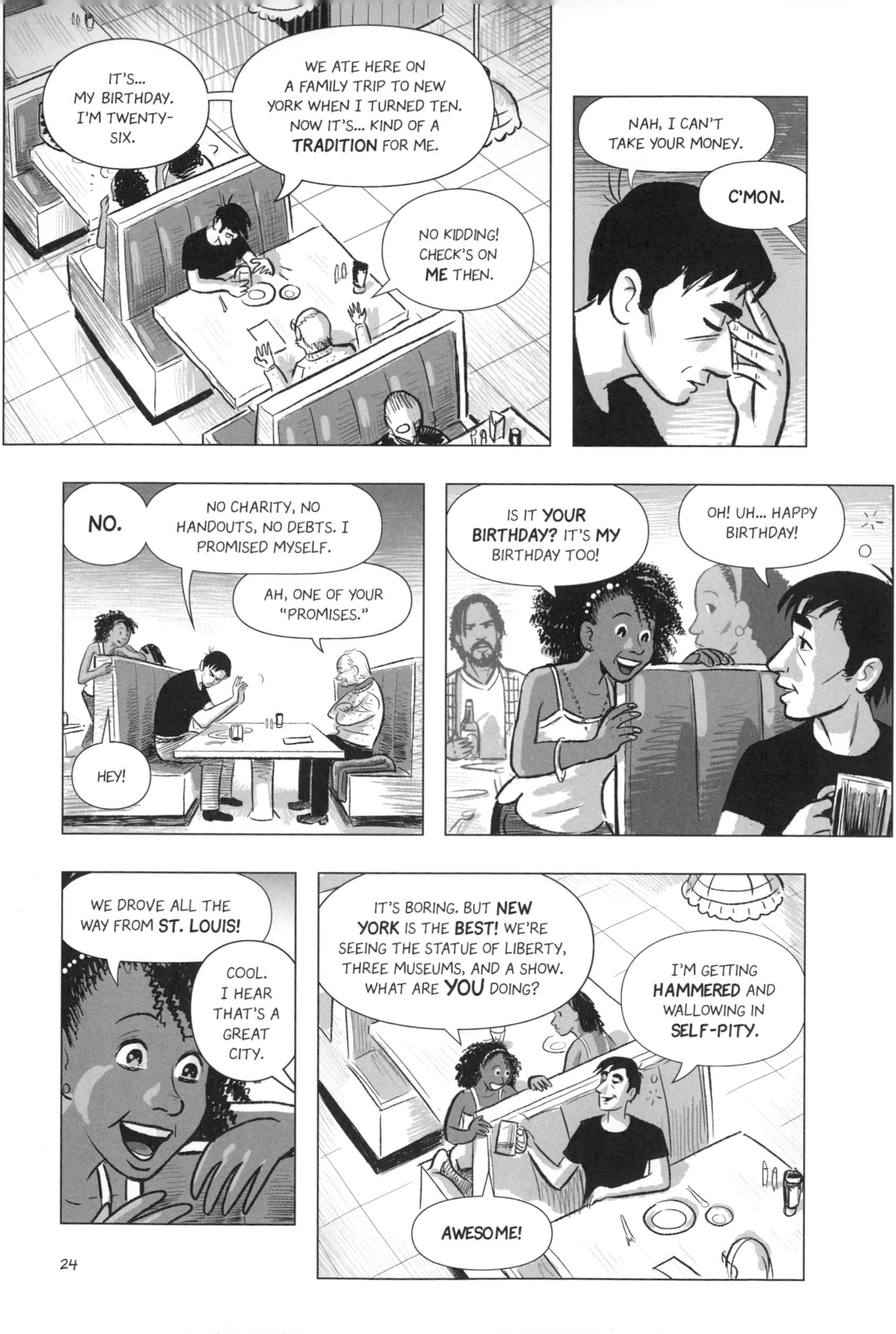
IT'S... MY BIRTHDAY. I'M TWENTY-SIX.
WE ATE HERE ON A FAMILY TRIP TO NEW YORK WHEN I TURNED TEN. NOW IT'S... KIND OF A **TRADITION** FOR ME.
NO KIDDING! CHECK'S ON **ME** THEN.
NAH, I CAN'T TAKE YOUR MONEY.
C'MON.
NO.
NO CHARITY, NO HANDOUTS, NO DEBTS. I PROMISED MYSELF.
AH, ONE OF YOUR "PROMISES."
HEY!
IS IT **YOUR BIRTHDAY?** IT'S **MY** BIRTHDAY TOO!
OH! UH... HAPPY BIRTHDAY!
WE DROVE ALL THE WAY FROM **ST. LOUIS!**
COOL. I HEAR THAT'S A GREAT CITY.
IT'S BORING. BUT **NEW YORK** IS THE **BEST!** WE'RE SEEING THE STATUE OF LIBERTY, THREE MUSEUMS, AND A SHOW. WHAT ARE **YOU** DOING?
I'M GETTING **HAMMERED** AND WALLOWING IN **SELF-PITY.**
AWESOME!

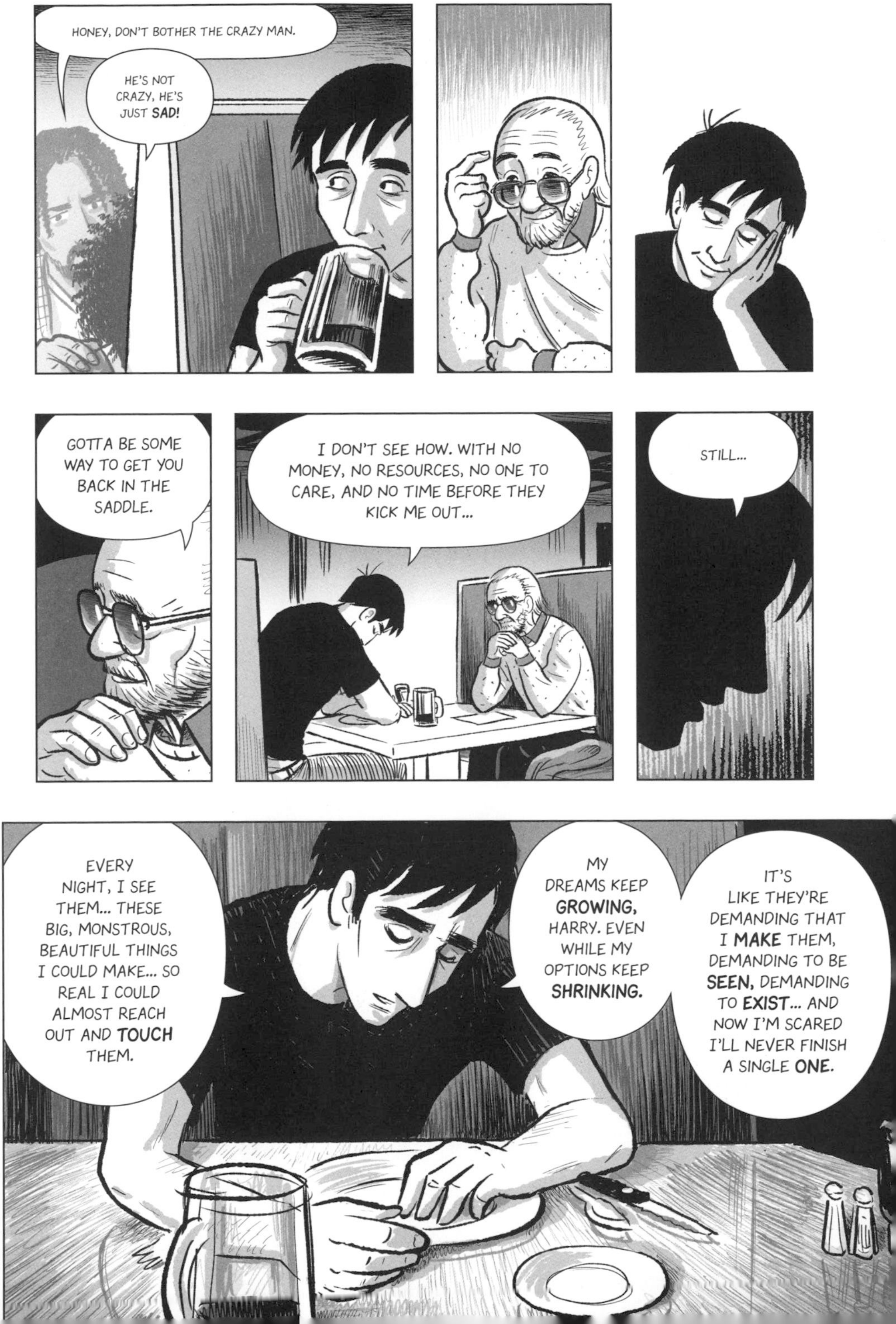
HONEY, DON'T BOTHER THE CRAZY MAN.
HE'S NOT CRAZY, HE'S JUST **SAD!**
GOTTA BE SOME WAY TO GET YOU BACK IN THE SADDLE.
I DON'T SEE HOW. WITH NO MONEY, NO RESOURCES, NO ONE TO CARE, AND NO TIME BEFORE THEY KICK ME OUT...
STILL...
EVERY NIGHT, I SEE THEM... THESE BIG, MONSTROUS, BEAUTIFUL THINGS I COULD MAKE... SO REAL I COULD ALMOST REACH OUT AND **TOUCH** THEM.
MY DREAMS KEEP **GROWING,** HARRY. EVEN WHILE MY OPTIONS KEEP **SHRINKING.**
IT'S LIKE THEY'RE DEMANDING THAT I **MAKE** THEM, DEMANDING TO BE **SEEN,** DEMANDING TO **EXIST...** AND NOW I'M SCARED I'LL NEVER FINISH A SINGLE **ONE.**

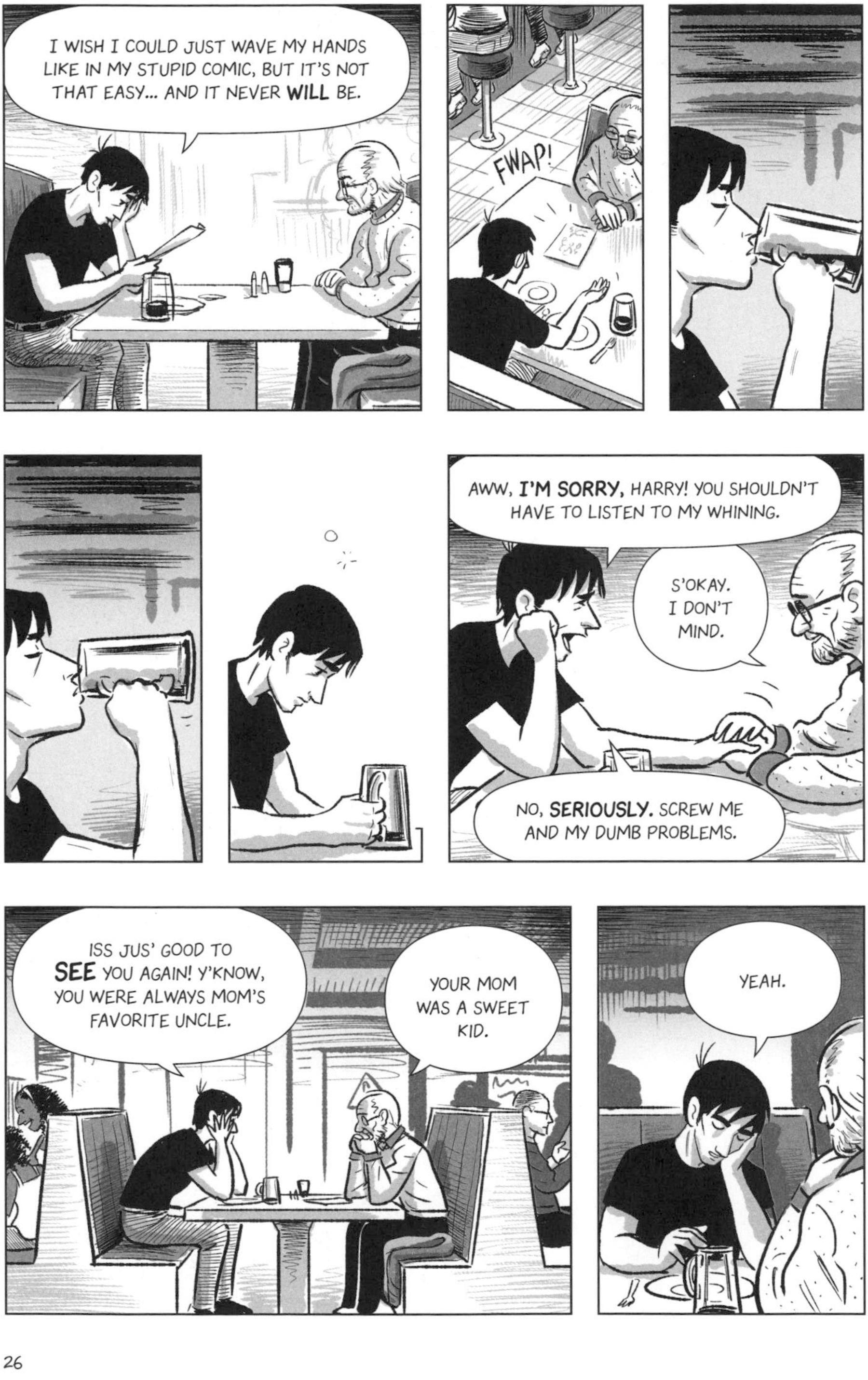
I WISH I COULD JUST WAVE MY HANDS LIKE IN MY STUPID COMIC, BUT IT'S NOT THAT EASY... AND IT NEVER WILL BE.
FWAP!
AWW, I'M SORRY, HARRY! YOU SHOULDN'T HAVE TO LISTEN TO MY WHINING.
S'OKAY. I DON'T MIND.
NO, SERIOUSLY. SCREW ME AND MY DUMB PROBLEMS.
ISS JUS' GOOD TO SEE YOU AGAIN! Y'KNOW, YOU WERE ALWAYS MOM'S FAVORITE UNCLE.
YOUR MOM WAS A SWEET KID.
YEAH.

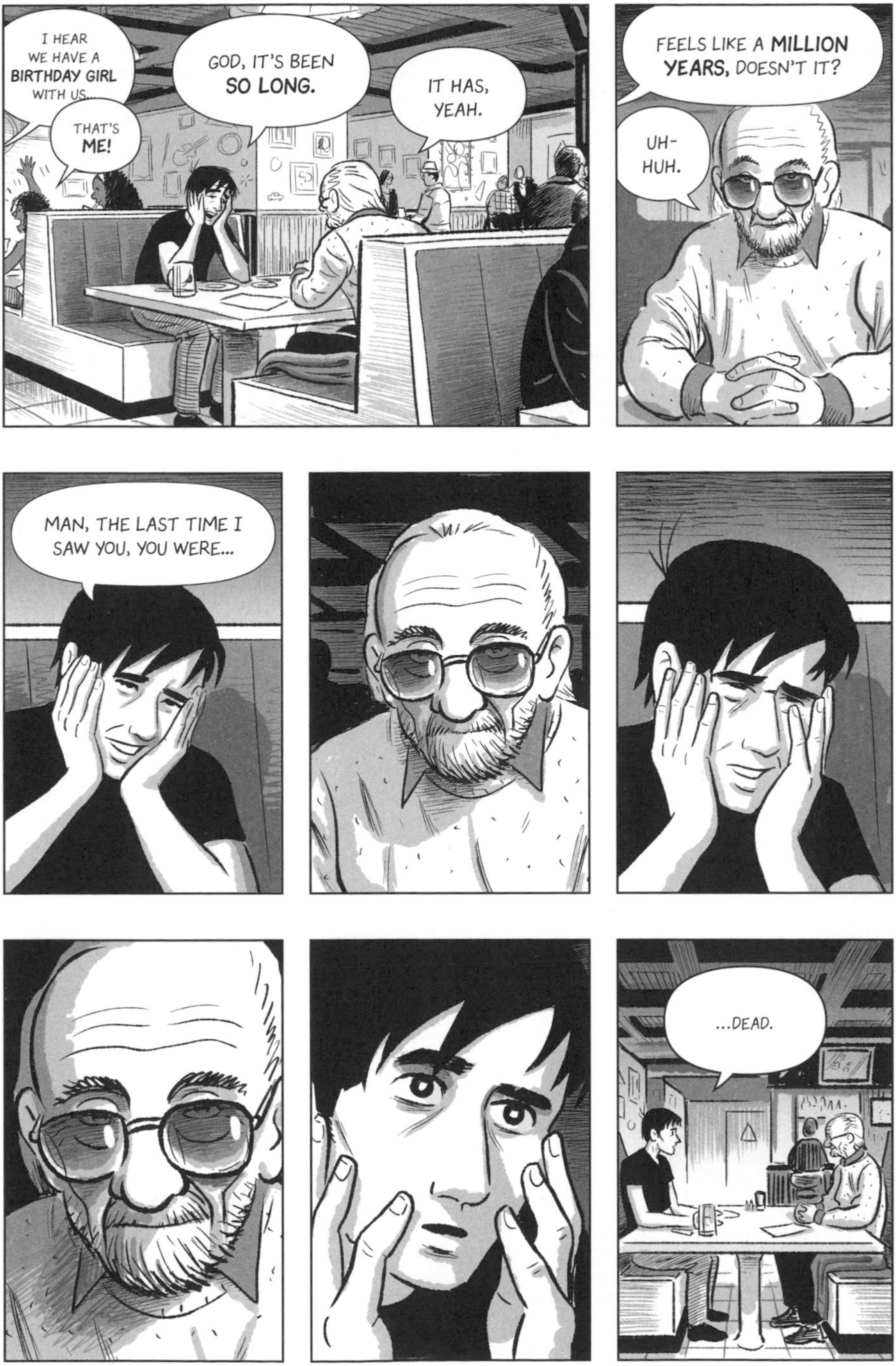
I HEAR WE HAVE A BIRTHDAY GIRL WITH US...
THAT'S ME!
GOD, IT'S BEEN SO LONG.
IT HAS, YEAH.
FEELS LIKE A MILLION YEARS, DOESN'T IT?
UH-HUH.
MAN, THE LAST TIME I SAW YOU, YOU WERE...
...DEAD.

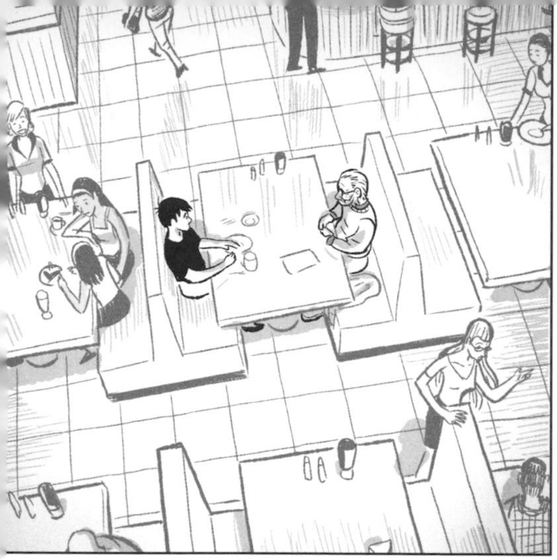

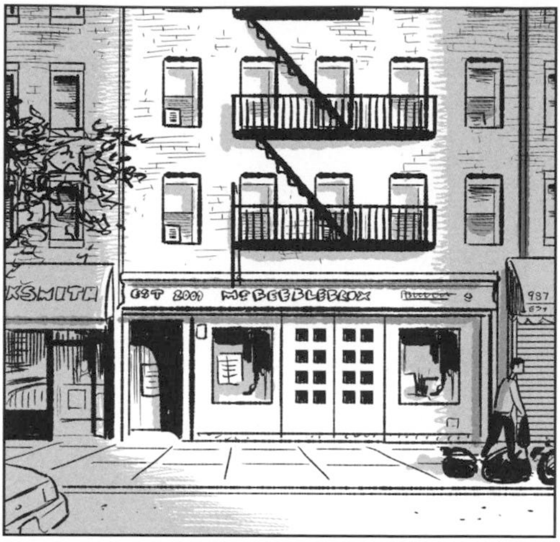

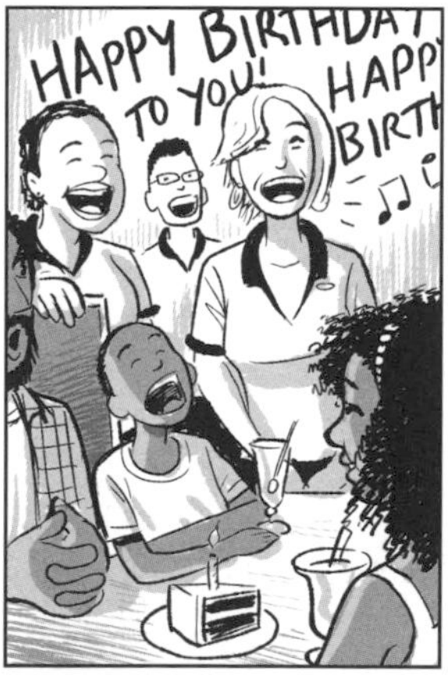
HAPPY BIRTHDAY TO YOU! HAPPY BIRTH

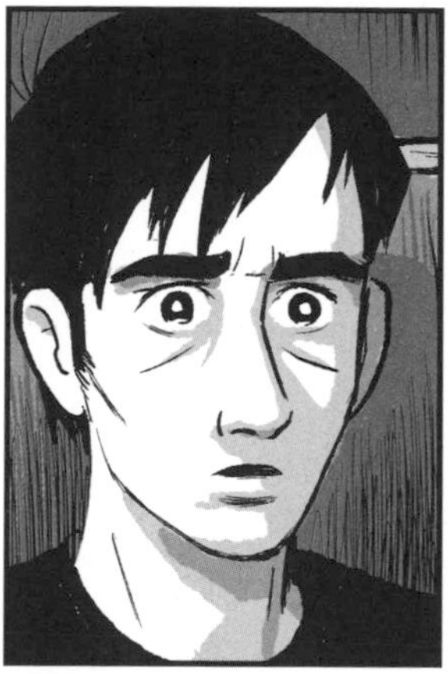

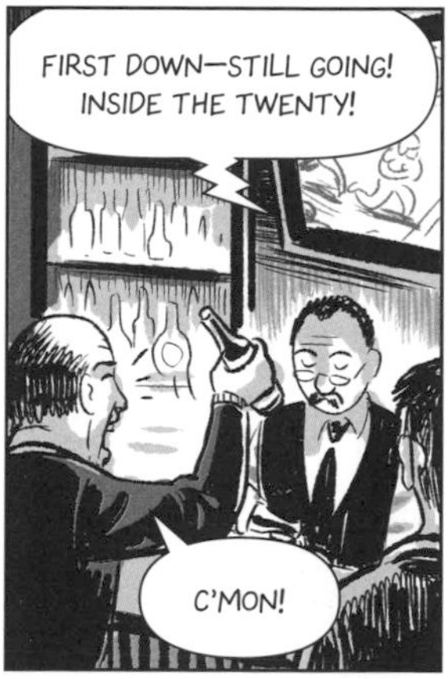
FIRST DOWN—STILL GOING! INSIDE THE TWENTY!
C'MON!

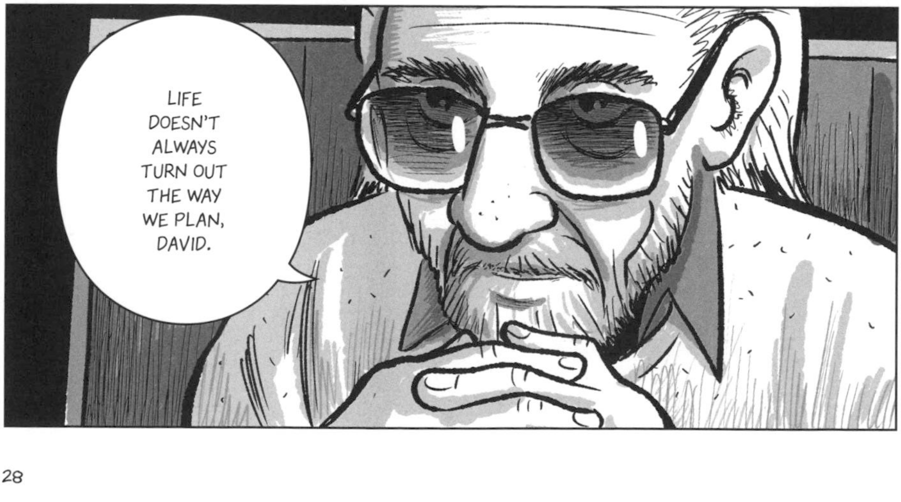
LIFE DOESN'T ALWAYS TURN OUT THE WAY WE PLAN, DAVID.

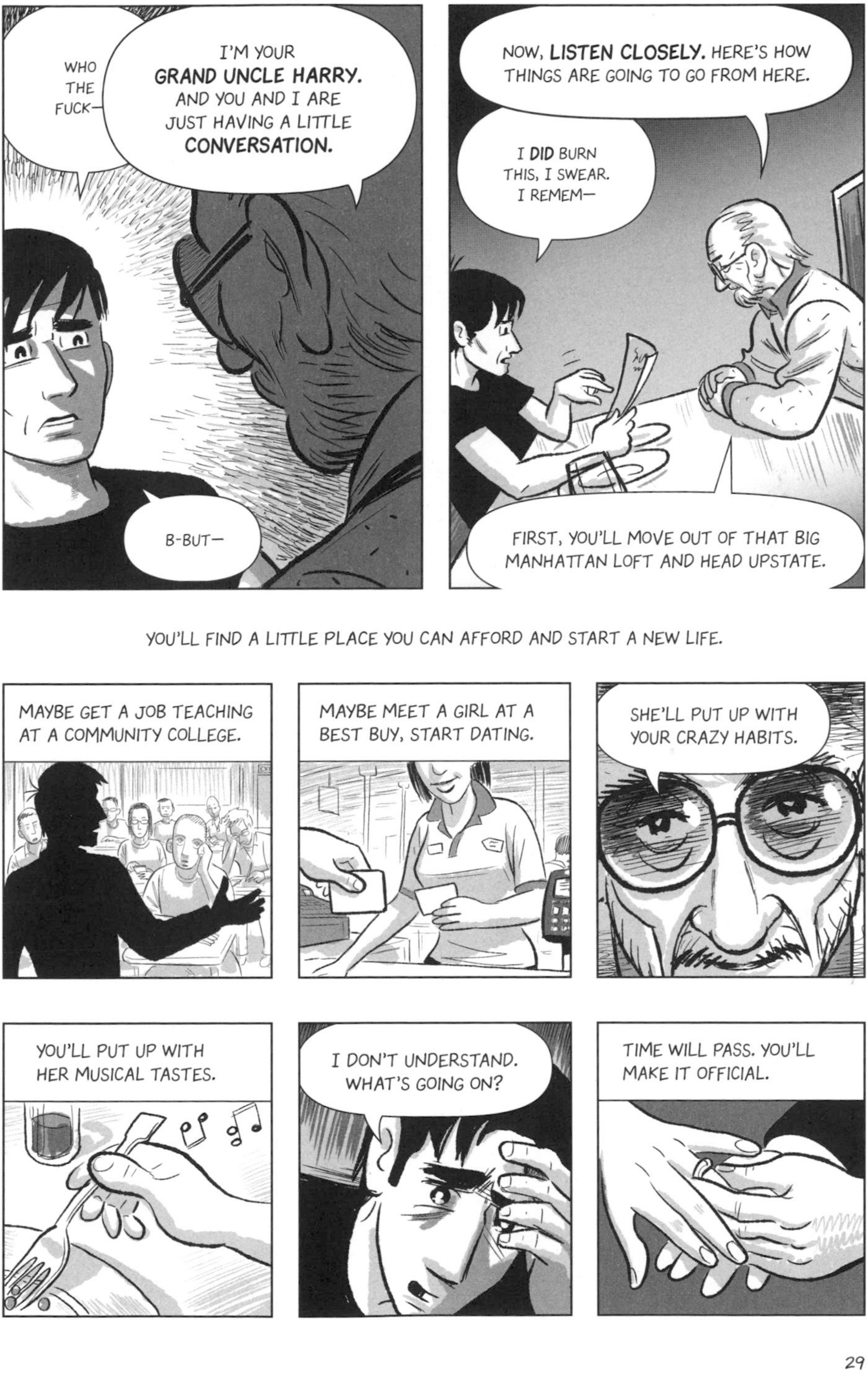
WHO THE FUCK—
I'M YOUR **GRAND UNCLE HARRY.** AND YOU AND I ARE JUST HAVING A LITTLE **CONVERSATION.**
B-BUT—
NOW, **LISTEN CLOSELY.** HERE'S HOW THINGS ARE GOING TO GO FROM HERE.
I **DID** BURN THIS, I SWEAR. I REMEM—
FIRST, YOU'LL MOVE OUT OF THAT BIG MANHATTAN LOFT AND HEAD UPSTATE.
YOU'LL FIND A LITTLE PLACE YOU CAN AFFORD AND START A NEW LIFE.
MAYBE GET A JOB TEACHING AT A COMMUNITY COLLEGE.
MAYBE MEET A GIRL AT A BEST BUY, START DATING.
SHE'LL PUT UP WITH YOUR CRAZY HABITS.
YOU'LL PUT UP WITH HER MUSICAL TASTES.
I DON'T UNDERSTAND. WHAT'S GOING ON?
TIME WILL PASS. YOU'LL MAKE IT OFFICIAL.

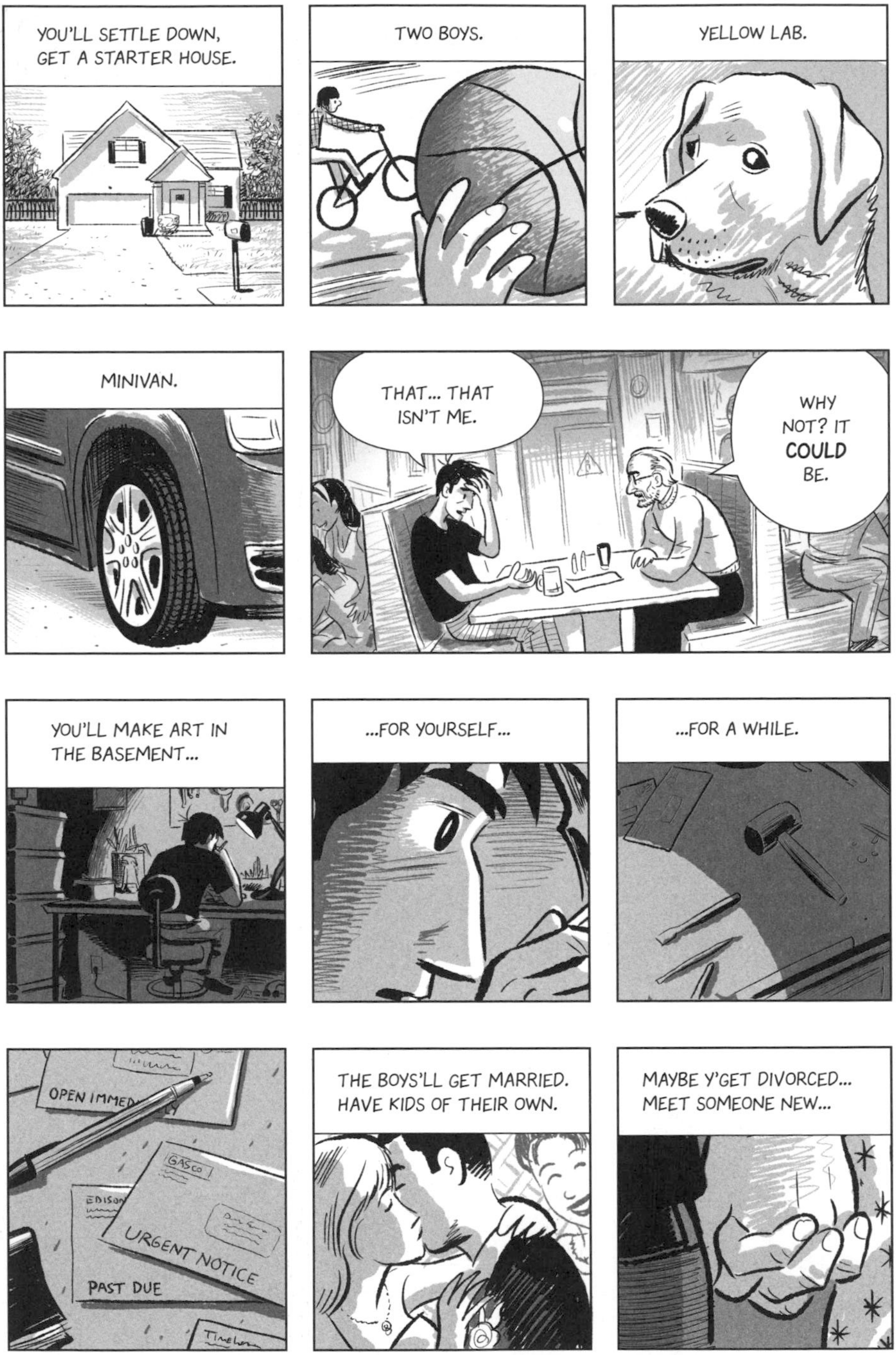
YOU'LL SETTLE DOWN, GET A STARTER HOUSE.
TWO BOYS.
YELLOW LAB.
MINIVAN.
THAT... THAT ISN'T ME.
WHY NOT? IT **COULD** BE.
YOU'LL MAKE ART IN THE BASEMENT...
...FOR YOURSELF...
...FOR A WHILE.
URGENT NOTICE
PAST DUE
THE BOYS'LL GET MARRIED. HAVE KIDS OF THEIR OWN.
MAYBE Y'GET DIVORCED... MEET SOMEONE NEW...

AND YEAH, YOU'LL WONDER WHAT COULD HAVE BEEN.
BUT LESS, AS THE YEARS GO BY.

"JUST WASN'T MEANT TO BE," YOU'LL SAY.

AND THERE'LL BE GOOD TIMES ALONG THE WAY.

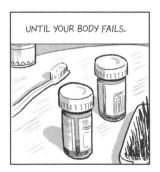

SWEET MEMORIES.

UNTIL IT STARTS TO WIND DOWN.

UNTIL YOUR BODY FAILS.

UNTIL YOU DON'T RECOGNIZE THE WORLD AROUND YOU.

UNTIL IT'S TIME TO GO.

THAT... ISN'T ME. IT **CAN'T** BE.

WHY NOT? IT'S A DECENT LIFE. FOOD, SEX, RUNNING WATER, A ROOF...

NOT TO MENTION **LOVE** AND **FAMILY.** THOSE AREN'T SMALL THINGS.

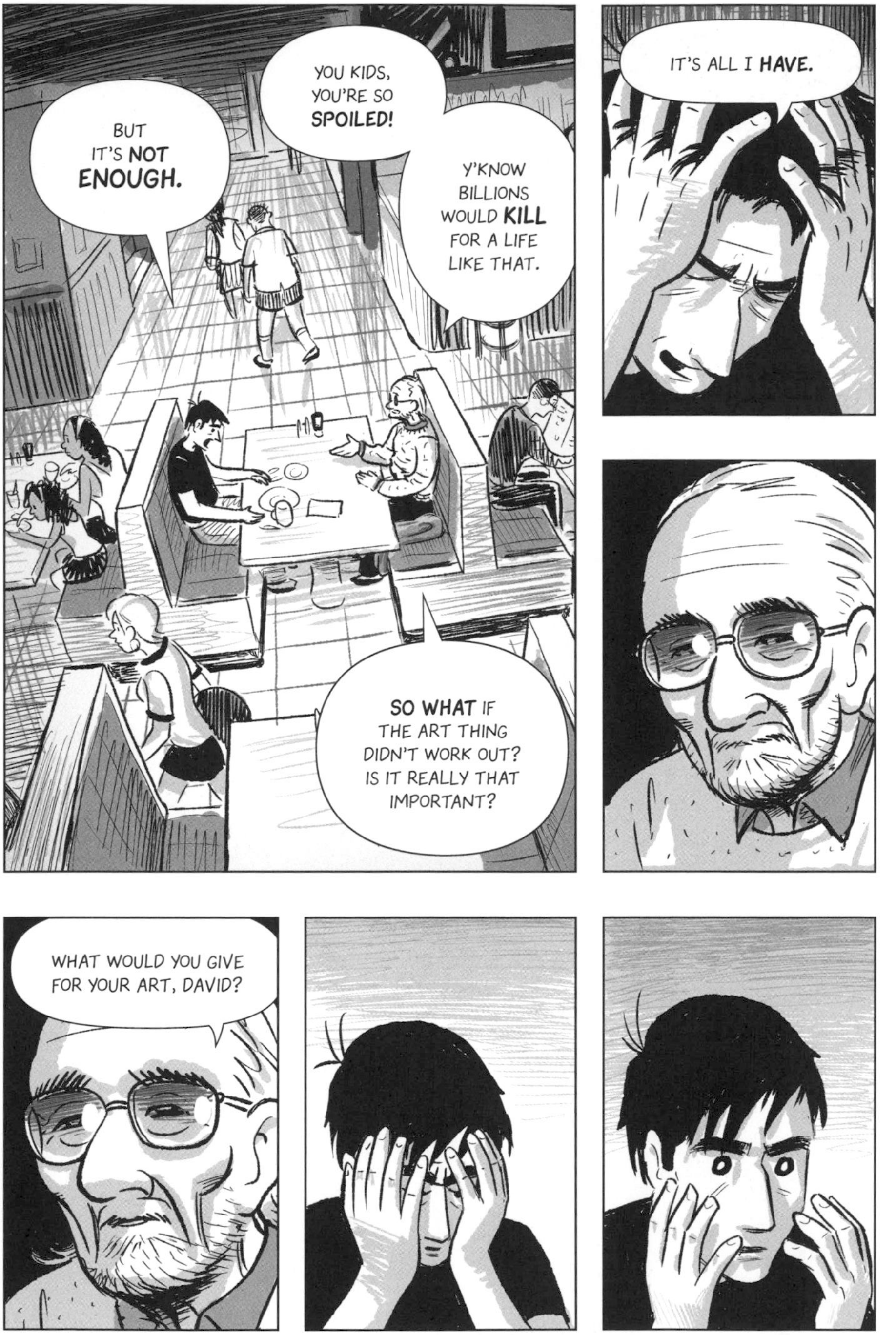
BUT IT'S **NOT ENOUGH.**
YOU KIDS, YOU'RE SO **SPOILED!**
Y'KNOW BILLIONS WOULD **KILL** FOR A LIFE LIKE THAT.
SO WHAT IF THE ART THING DIDN'T WORK OUT? IS IT REALLY THAT IMPORTANT?
IT'S ALL I **HAVE.**
WHAT WOULD YOU GIVE FOR YOUR ART, DAVID?

I'D GIVE MY **LIFE**.

LEMME HAVE YOUR HAND.

WHY?

JUST FOR A SECOND. TRY TO HOLD STILL.

I GOTTA **SHOW** YOU SOMETHING.

SHOW ME **WHAT?**

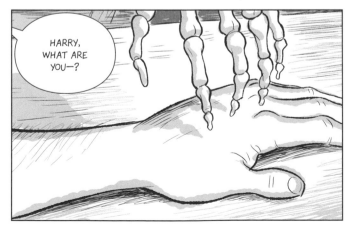

HARRY, WHAT ARE YOU—?

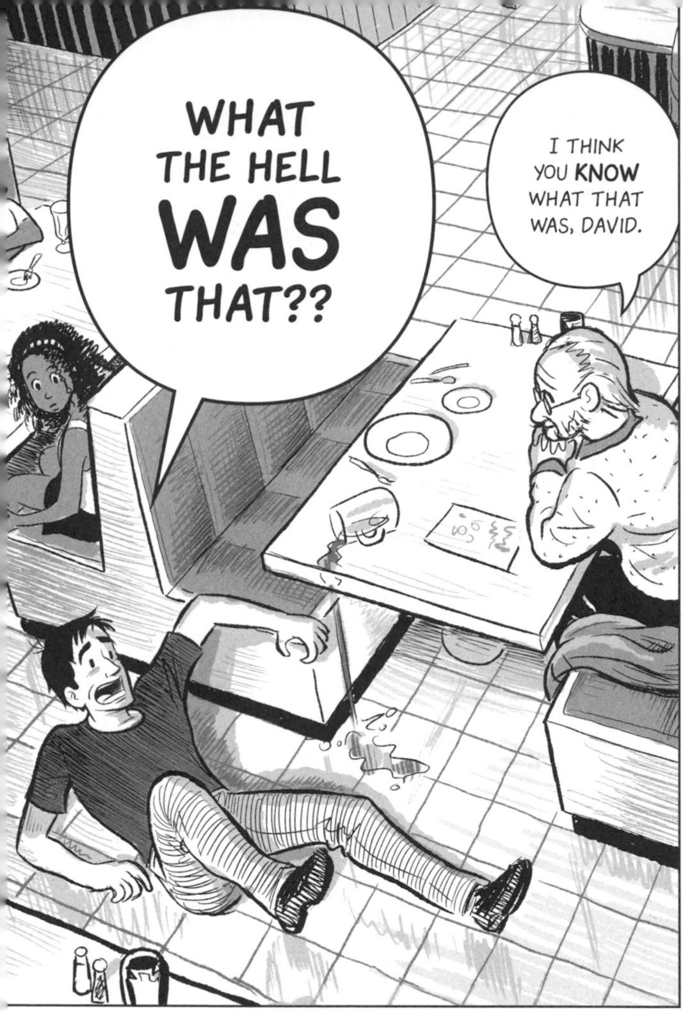
WHAT THE HELL WAS THAT??
I THINK YOU KNOW WHAT THAT WAS, DAVID.

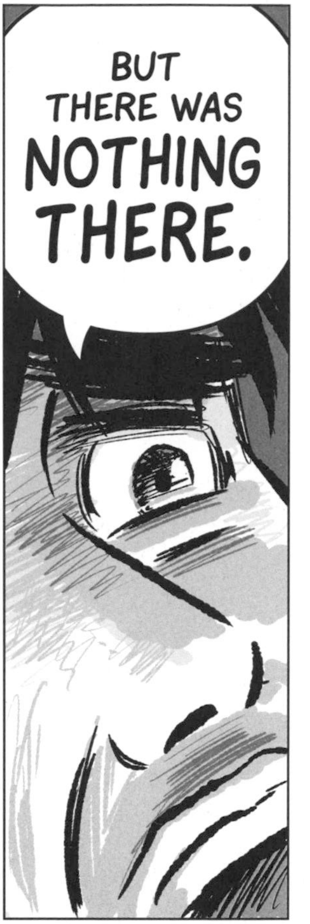
BUT THERE WAS NOTHING THERE.

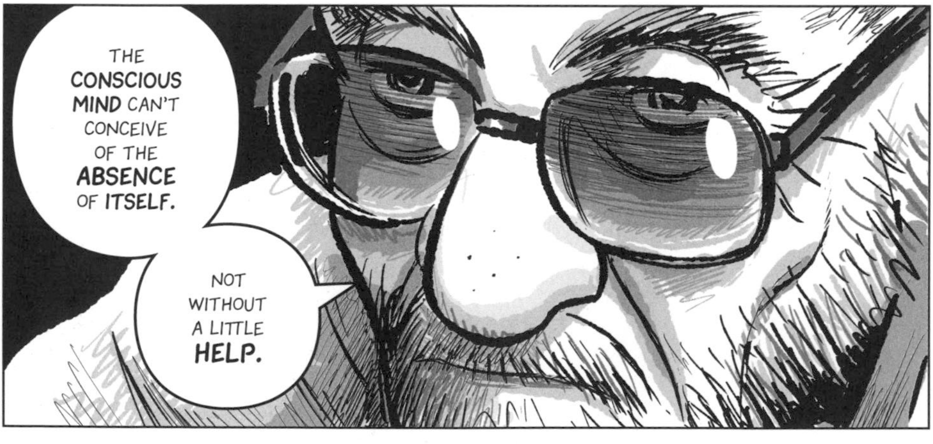
THE CONSCIOUS MIND CAN'T CONCEIVE OF THE ABSENCE OF ITSELF.
NOT WITHOUT A LITTLE HELP.

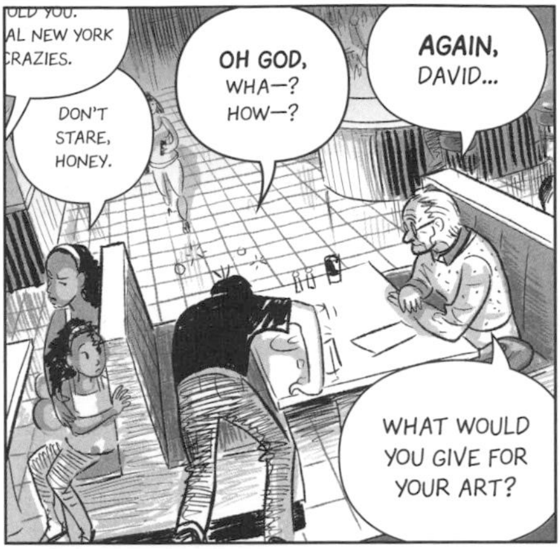
OLD YOU. AL NEW YORK RAZIES.
DON'T STARE, HONEY.
OH GOD, WHA—? HOW—?
AGAIN, DAVID...
WHAT WOULD YOU GIVE FOR YOUR ART?

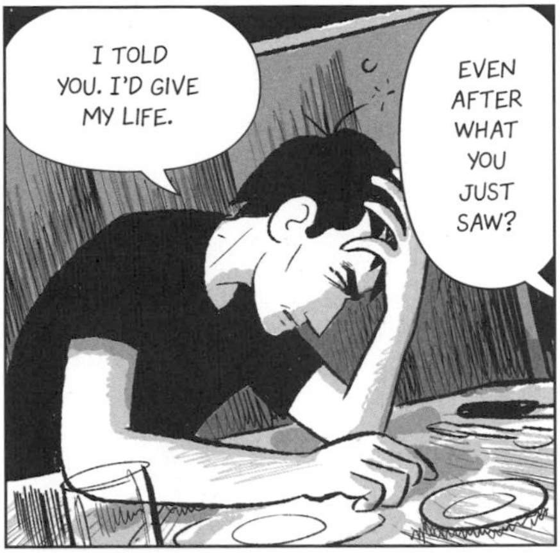
I TOLD YOU. I'D GIVE MY LIFE.
EVEN AFTER WHAT YOU JUST SAW?

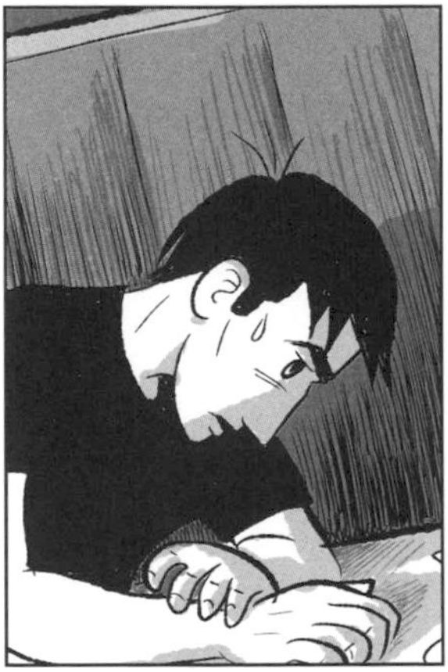

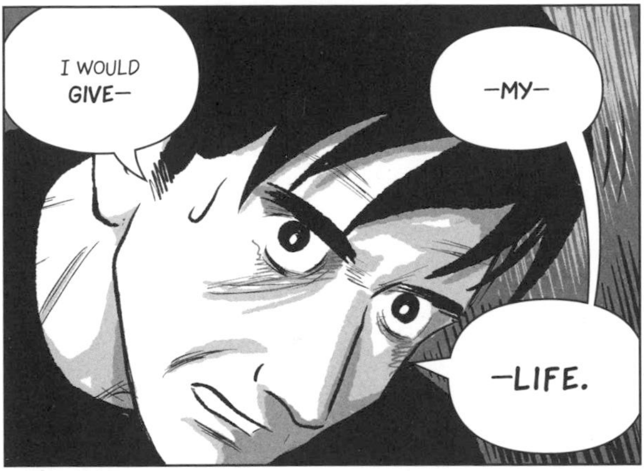
I WOULD GIVE—
—MY—
—LIFE.

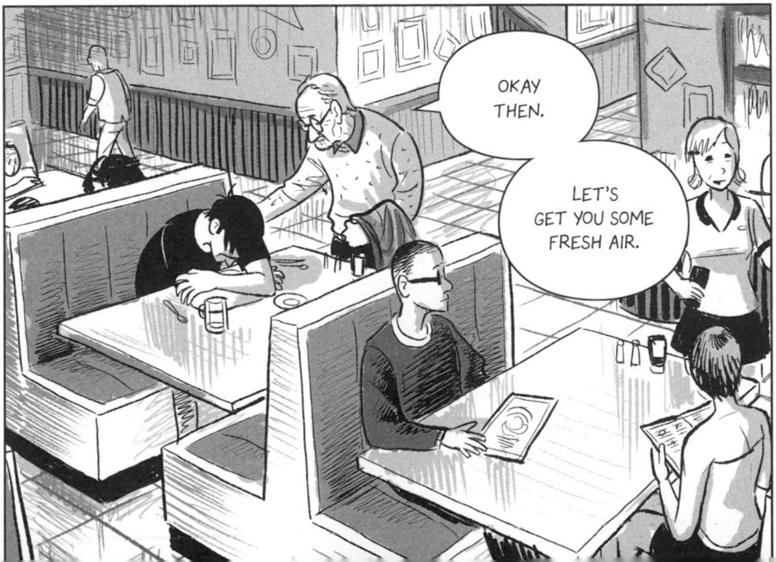
OKAY THEN.
LET'S GET YOU SOME FRESH AIR.

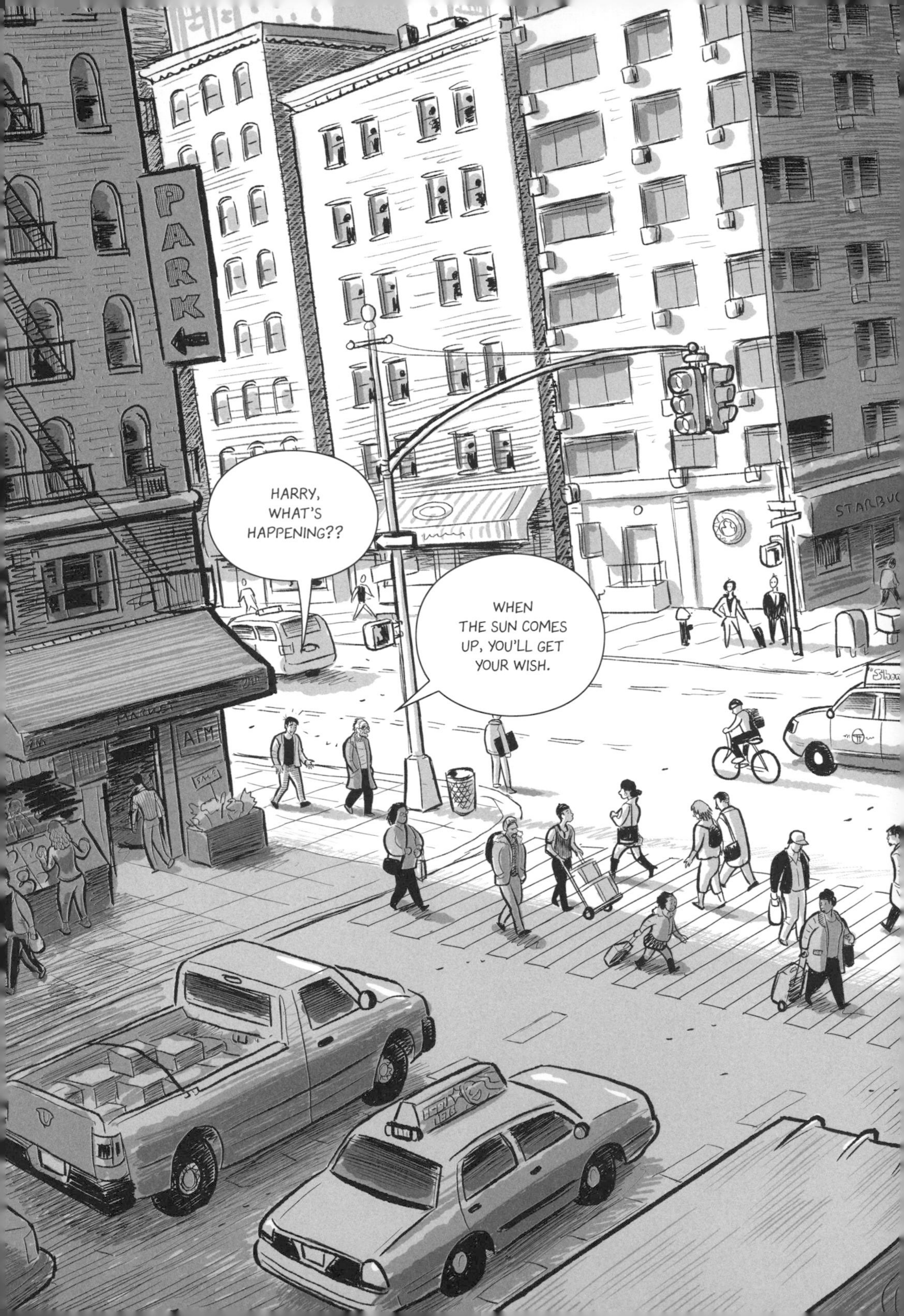
HARRY, WHAT'S HAPPENING??
WHEN THE SUN COMES UP, YOU'LL GET YOUR WISH.

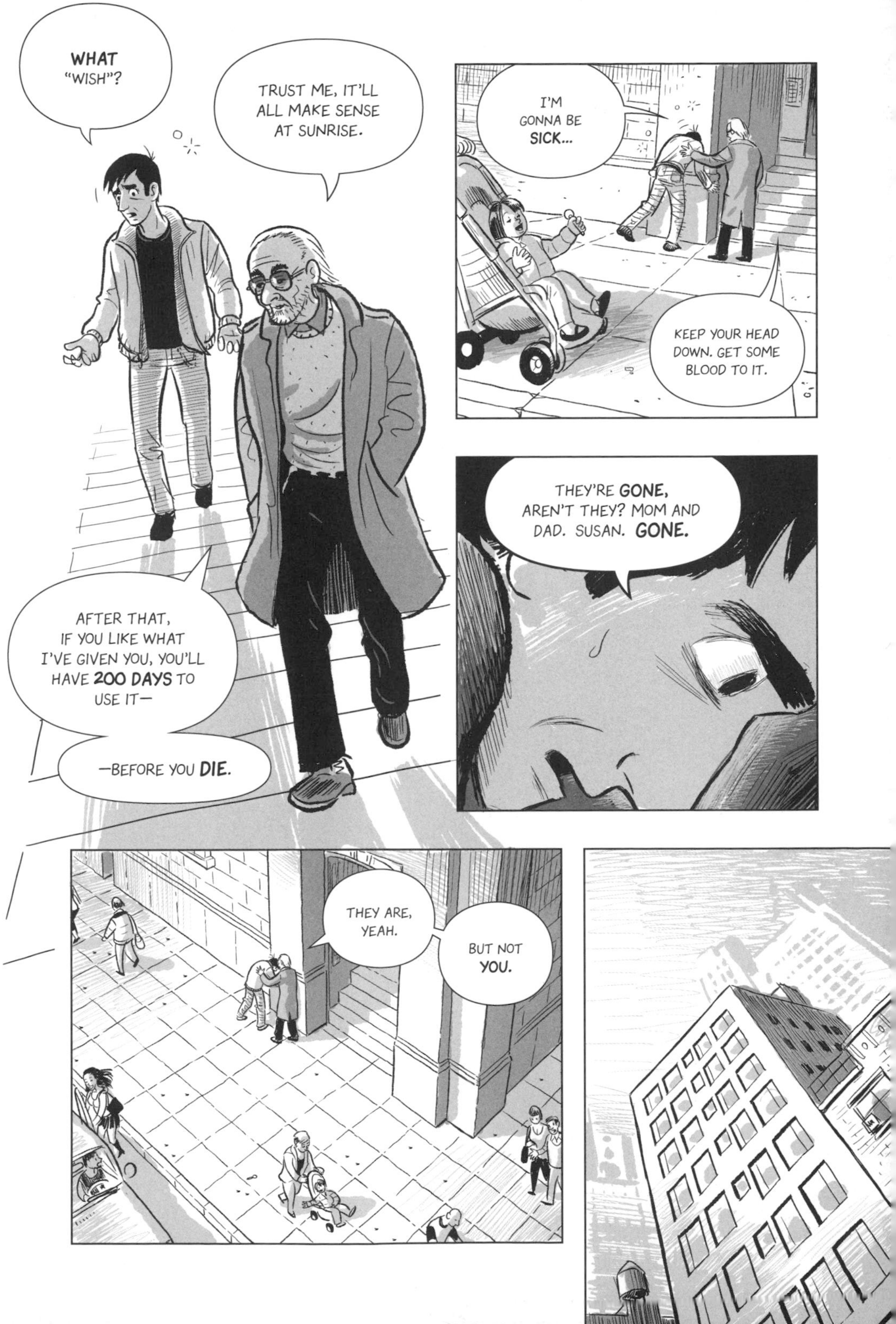
WHAT "WISH"?
TRUST ME, IT'LL ALL MAKE SENSE AT SUNRISE.
I'M GONNA BE SICK...
KEEP YOUR HEAD DOWN. GET SOME BLOOD TO IT.
AFTER THAT, IF YOU LIKE WHAT I'VE GIVEN YOU, YOU'LL HAVE 200 DAYS TO USE IT—
—BEFORE YOU DIE.
THEY'RE GONE, AREN'T THEY? MOM AND DAD. SUSAN. GONE.
THEY ARE, YEAH.
BUT NOT YOU.

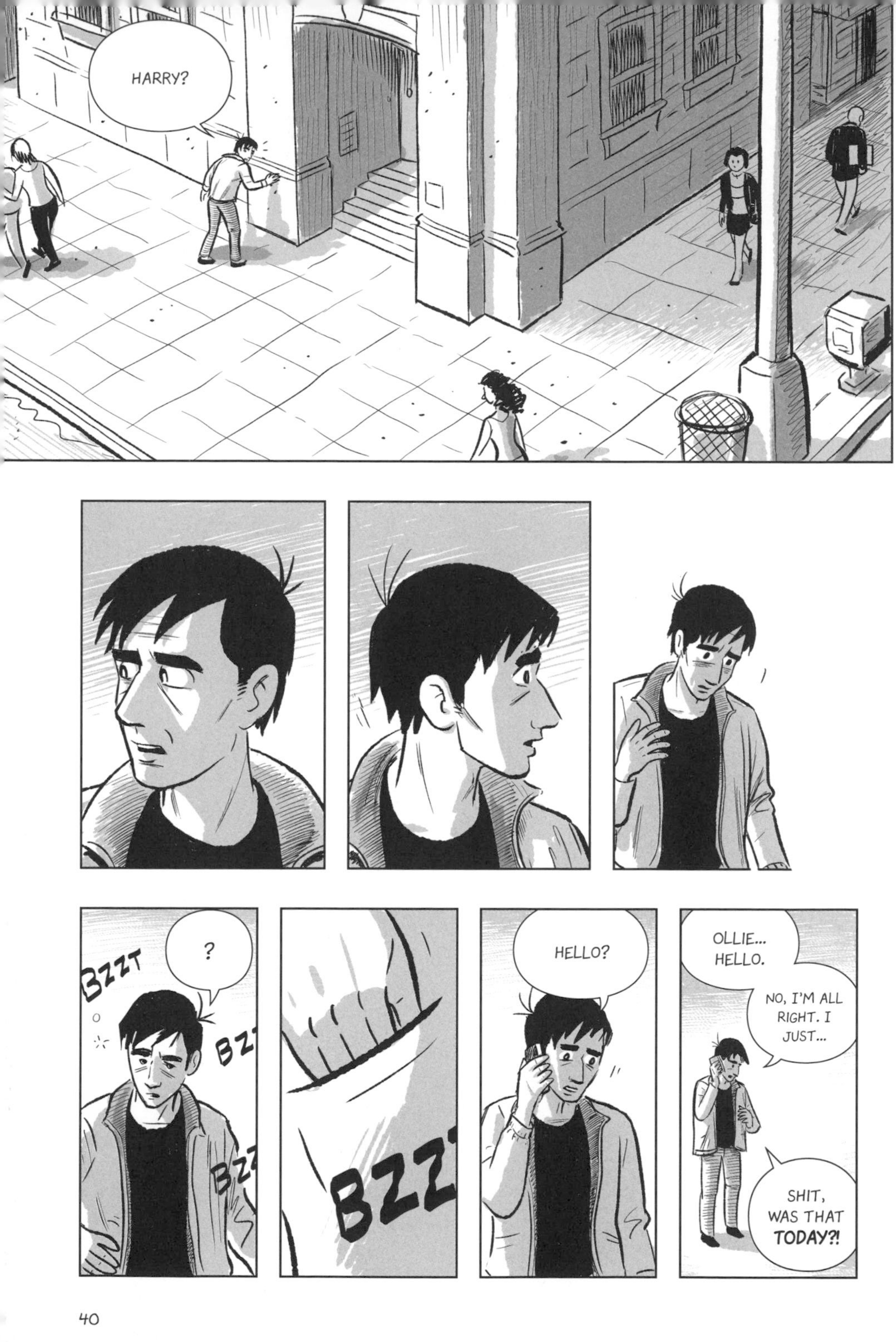
HARRY?
?
BZZT
BZZ
BZZ
BZZT
HELLO?
OLLIE... HELLO.
NO, I'M ALL RIGHT. I JUST...
SHIT, WAS THAT **TODAY?!**

NO, I... I'M MAYBE TEN BLOCKS FROM THERE.

NO, REALLY, I'M OKAY.

SEE YOU SOON. BYE.

I'M OKAY.

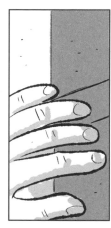

I'M OKAY.

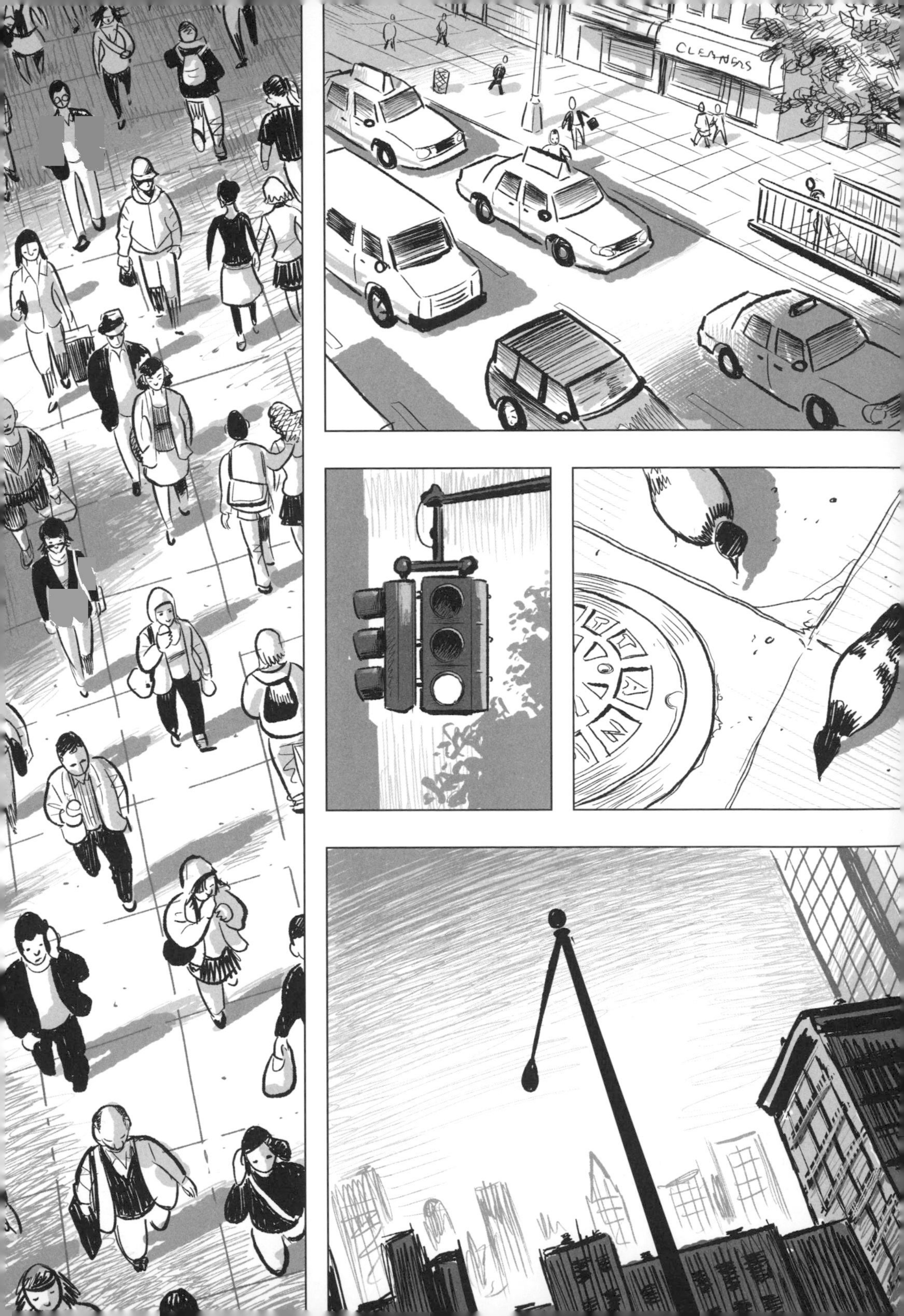
CLEANERS

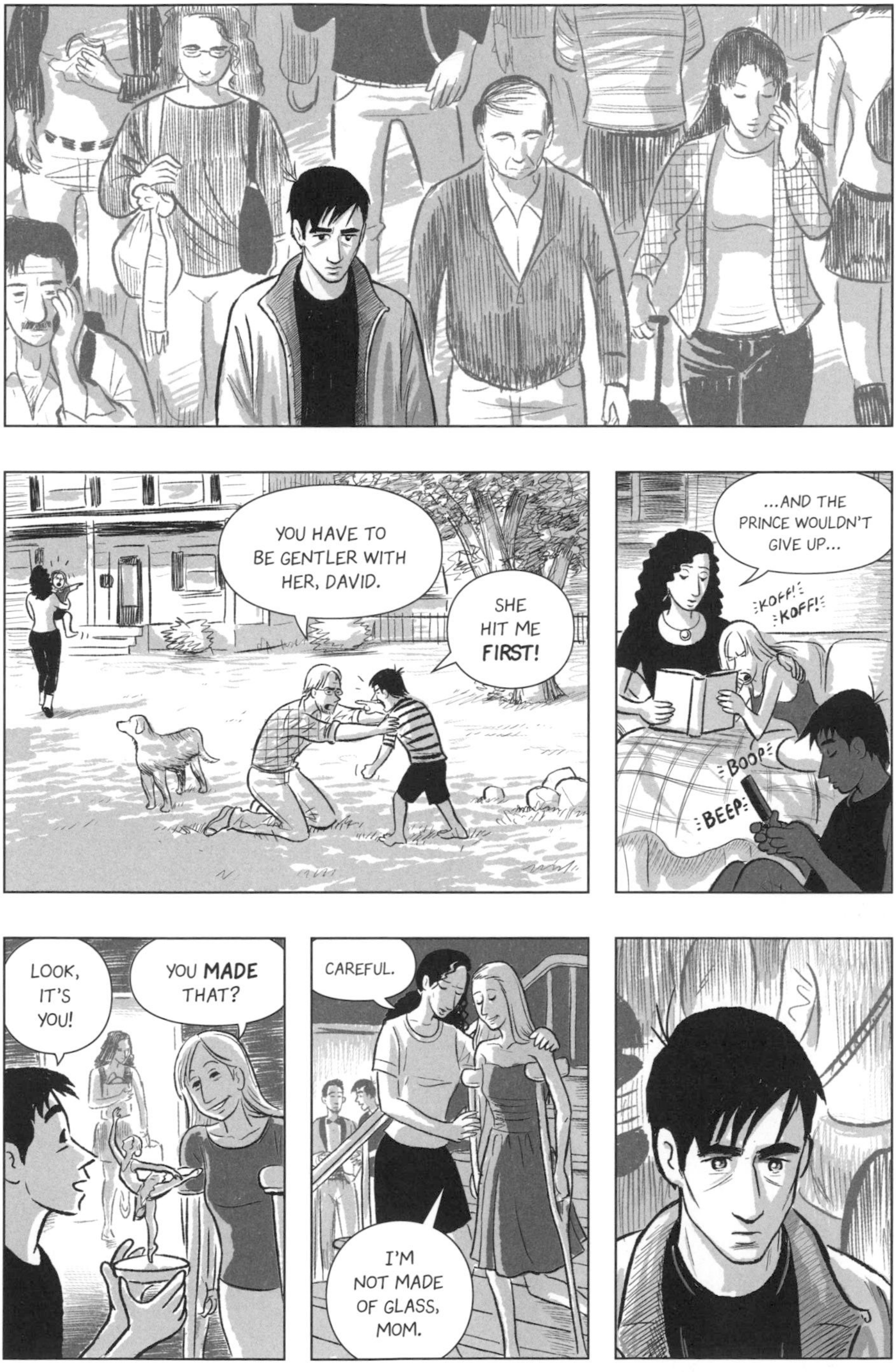
YOU HAVE TO BE GENTLER WITH HER, DAVID.
SHE HIT ME FIRST!
...AND THE PRINCE WOULDN'T GIVE UP...
KOFF! KOFF!
BOOP
BEEP
LOOK, IT'S YOU!
YOU MADE THAT?
CAREFUL.
I'M NOT MADE OF GLASS, MOM.

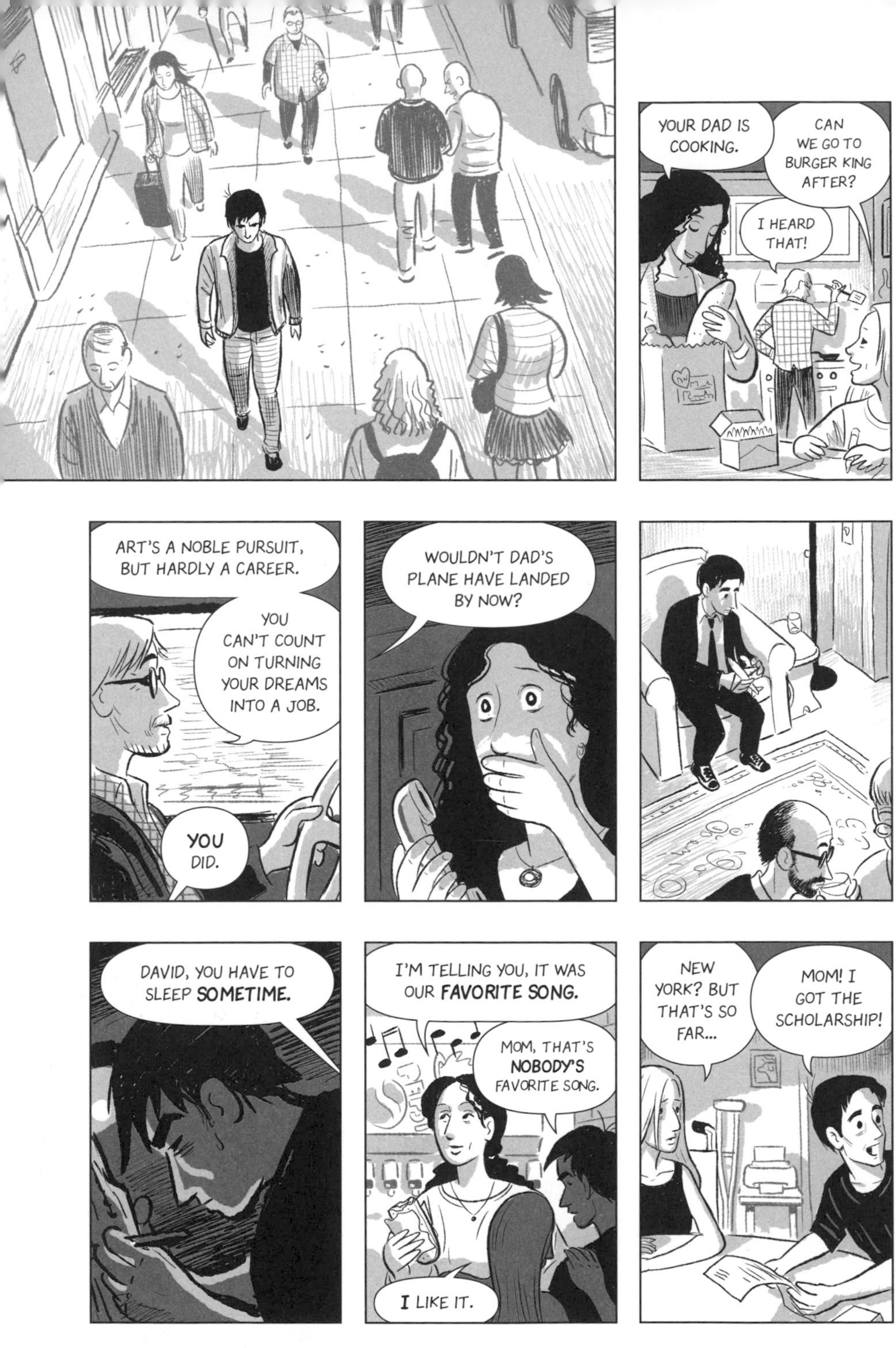
YOUR DAD IS COOKING.
CAN WE GO TO BURGER KING AFTER?
I HEARD THAT!
ART'S A NOBLE PURSUIT, BUT HARDLY A CAREER.
YOU CAN'T COUNT ON TURNING YOUR DREAMS INTO A JOB.
YOU DID.
WOULDN'T DAD'S PLANE HAVE LANDED BY NOW?
DAVID, YOU HAVE TO SLEEP SOMETIME.
I'M TELLING YOU, IT WAS OUR FAVORITE SONG.
MOM, THAT'S NOBODY'S FAVORITE SONG.
I LIKE IT.
MOM! I GOT THE SCHOLARSHIP!
NEW YORK? BUT THAT'S SO FAR...

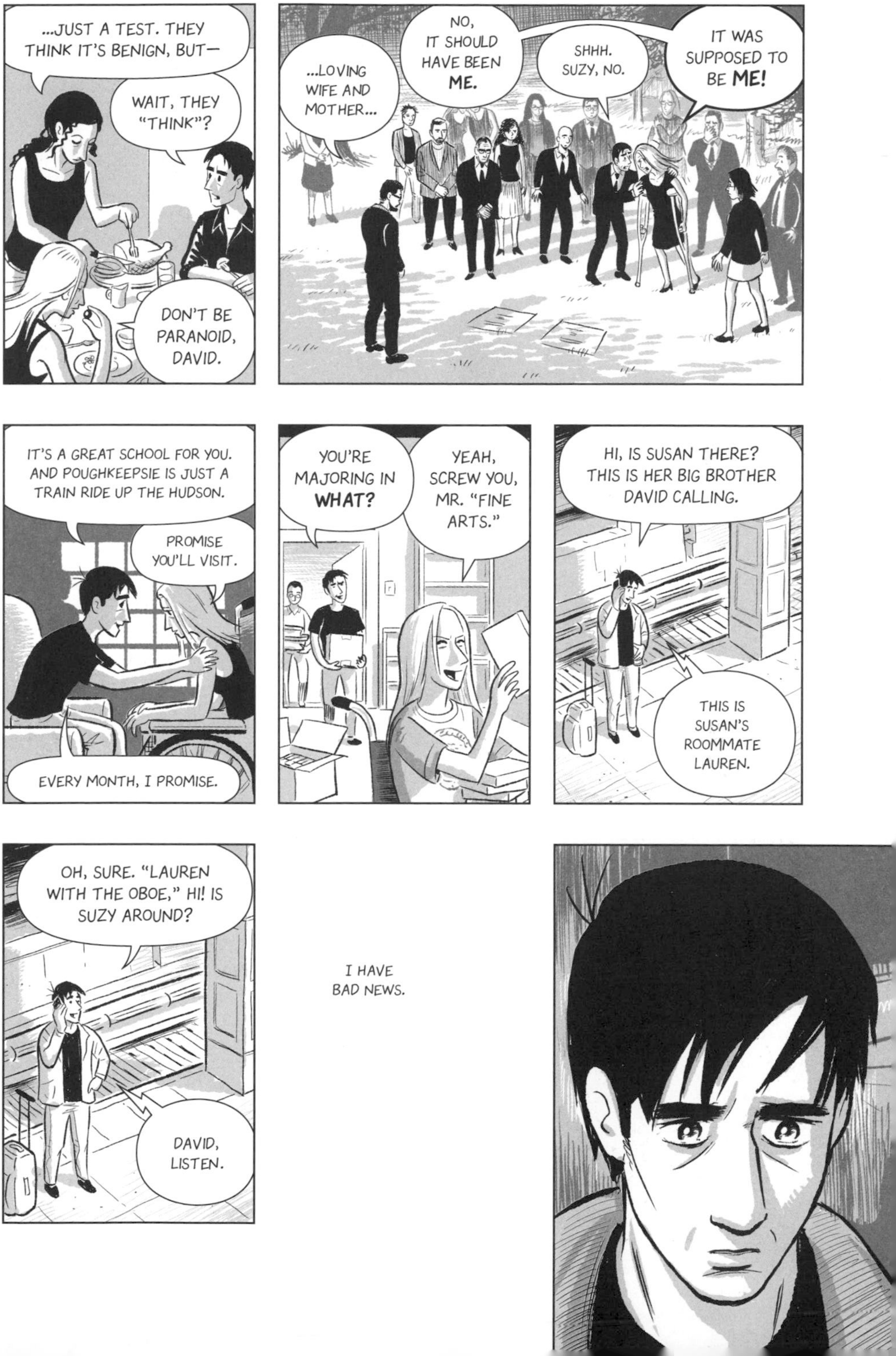
...JUST A TEST. THEY THINK IT'S BENIGN, BUT—
WAIT, THEY "THINK"?
DON'T BE PARANOID, DAVID.
...LOVING WIFE AND MOTHER...
NO, IT SHOULD HAVE BEEN ME.
SHHH. SUZY, NO.
IT WAS SUPPOSED TO BE ME!
IT'S A GREAT SCHOOL FOR YOU. AND POUGHKEEPSIE IS JUST A TRAIN RIDE UP THE HUDSON.
PROMISE YOU'LL VISIT.
EVERY MONTH, I PROMISE.
YOU'RE MAJORING IN WHAT?
YEAH, SCREW YOU, MR. "FINE ARTS."
HI, IS SUSAN THERE? THIS IS HER BIG BROTHER DAVID CALLING.
THIS IS SUSAN'S ROOMMATE LAUREN.
OH, SURE. "LAUREN WITH THE OBOE," HI! IS SUZY AROUND?
DAVID, LISTEN.
I HAVE BAD NEWS.

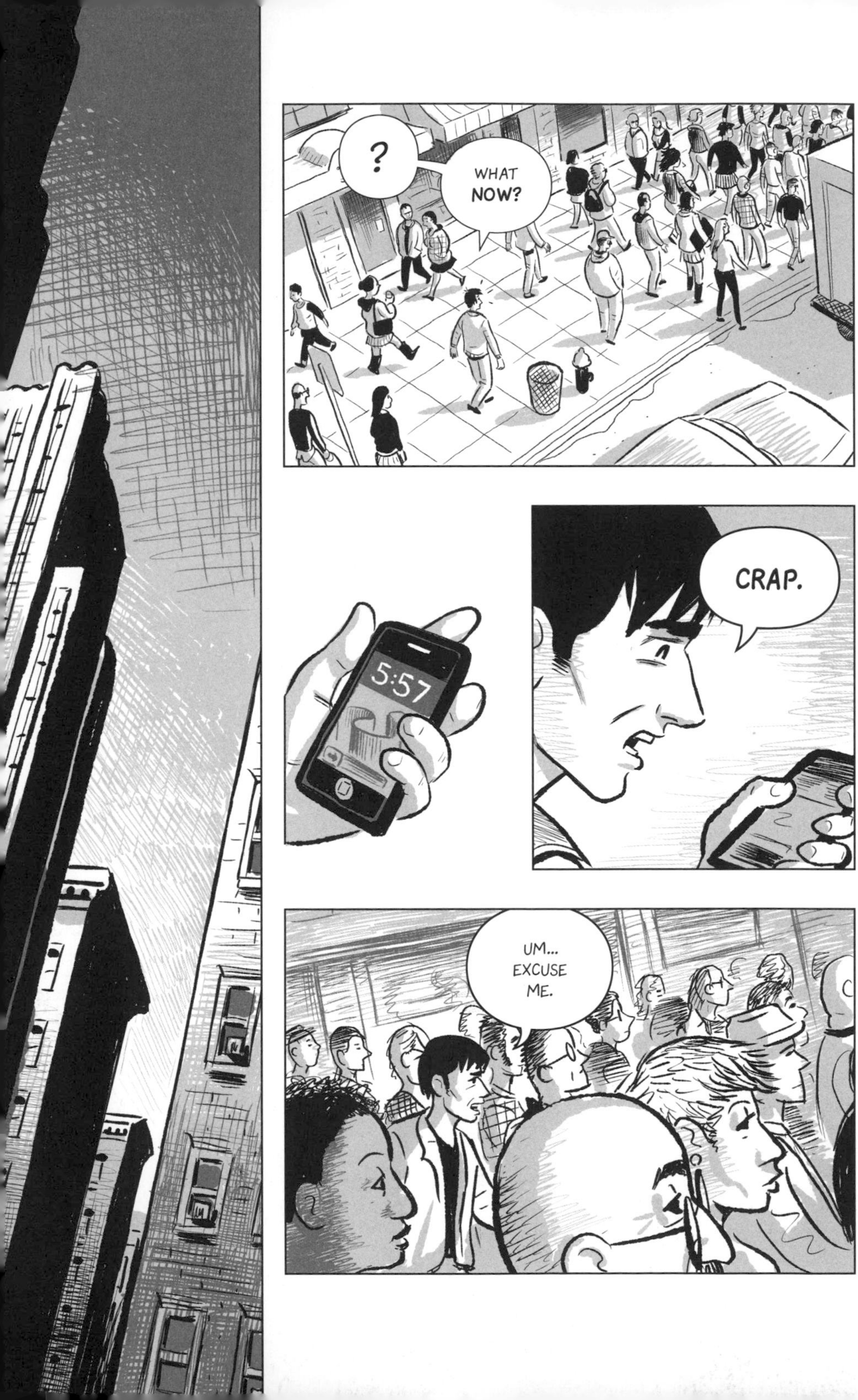
?
WHAT NOW?
5:57
CRAP.
UM... EXCUSE ME.

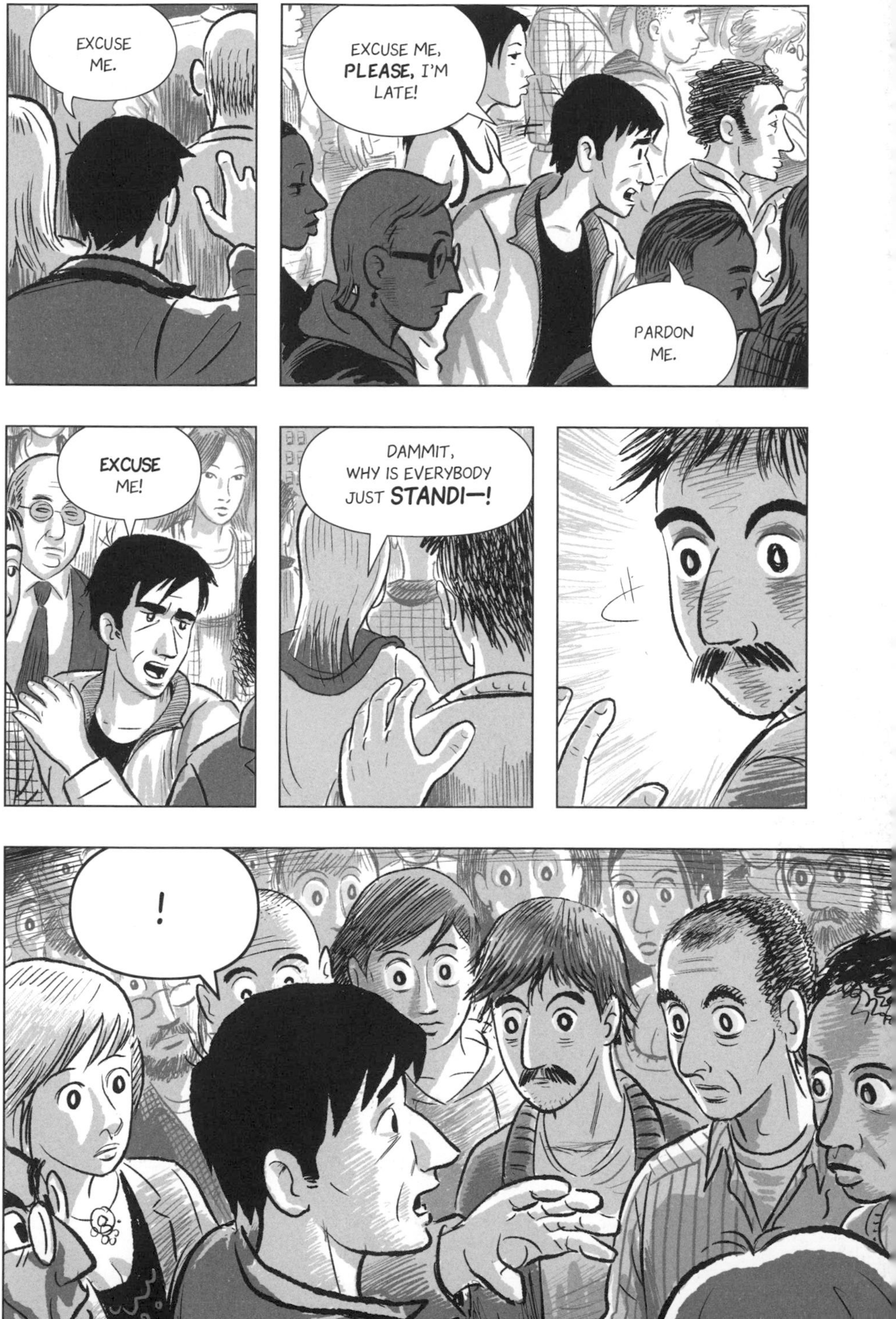
EXCUSE ME.
EXCUSE ME, **PLEASE,** I'M LATE!
PARDON ME.
EXCUSE ME!
DAMMIT, WHY IS EVERYBODY JUST **STANDI—!**
!

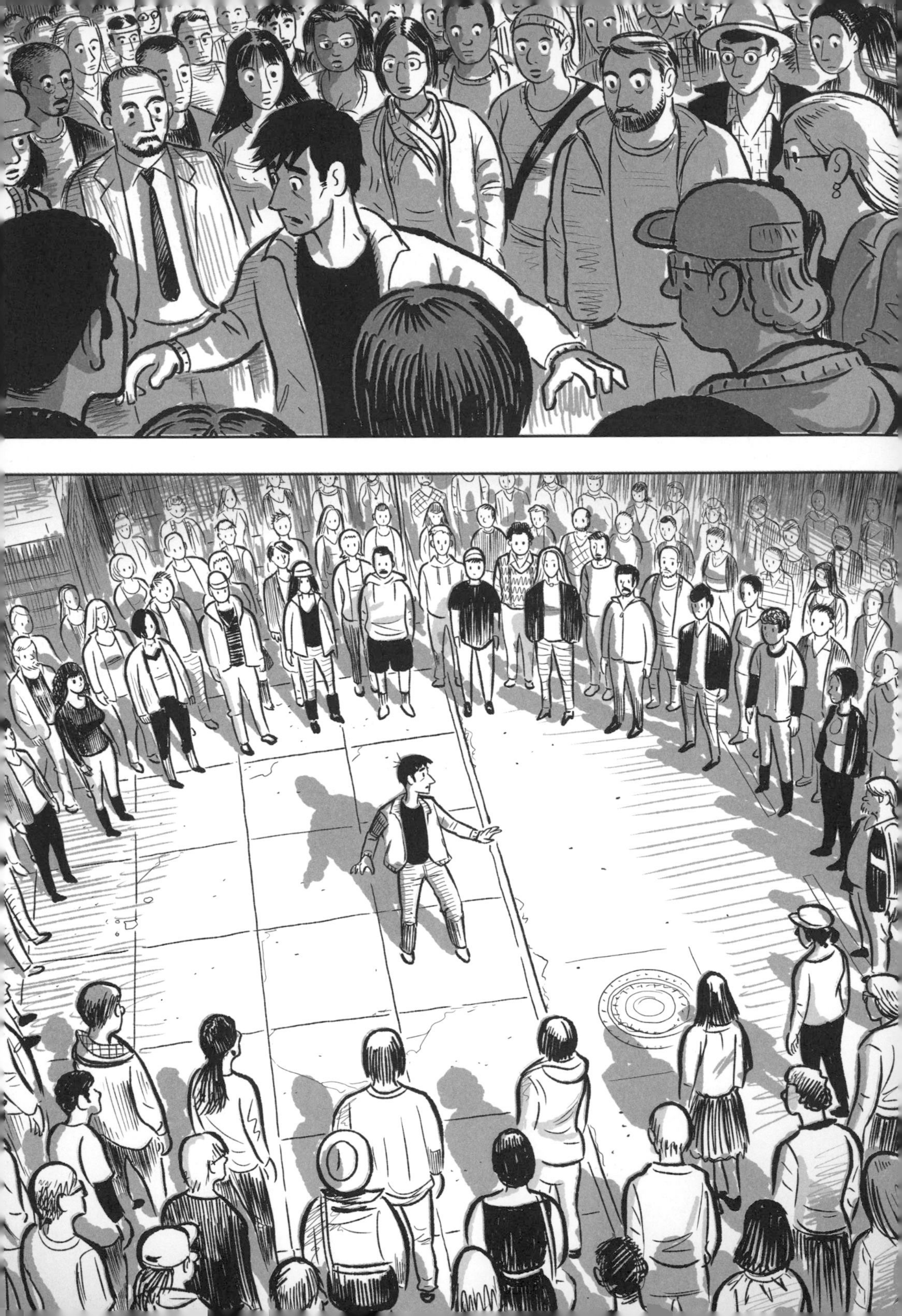

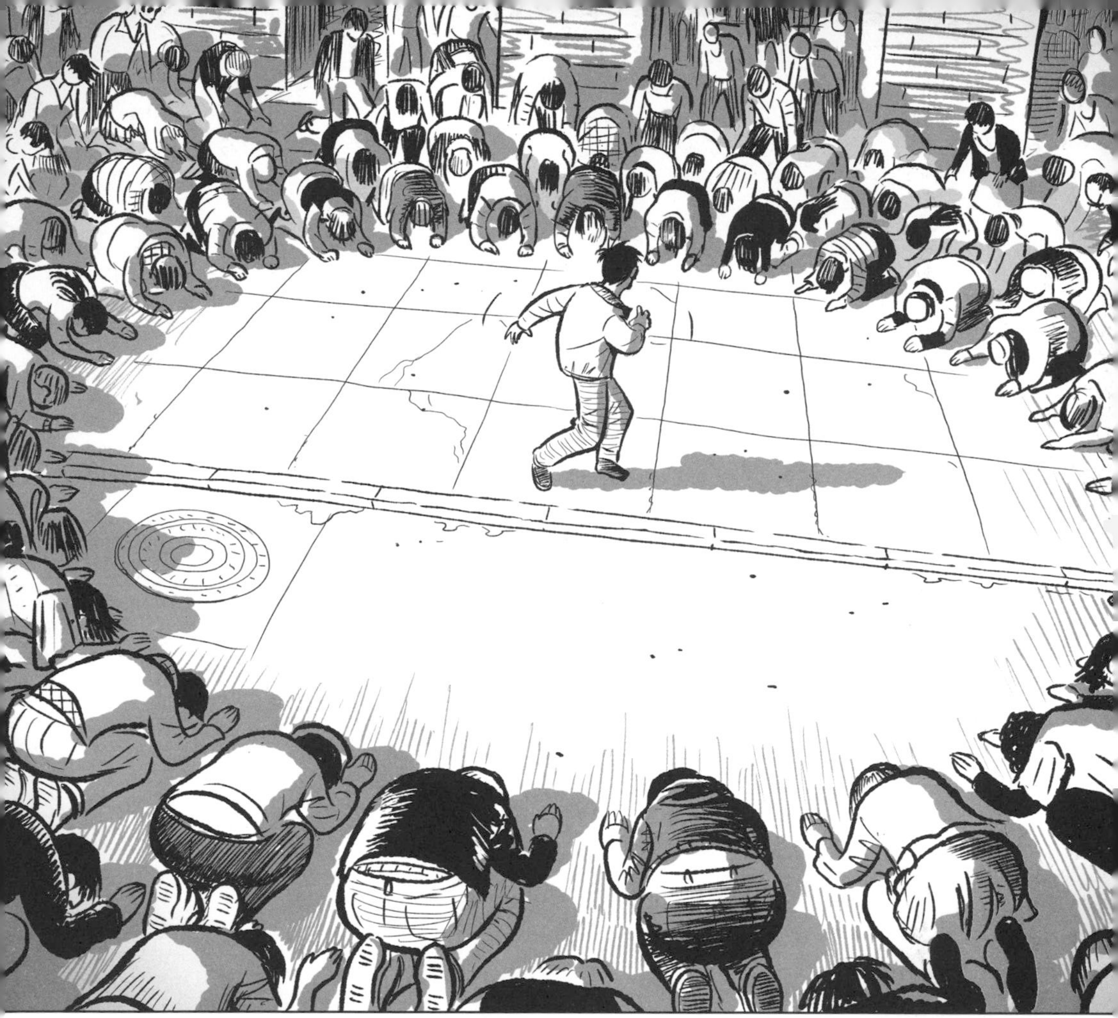

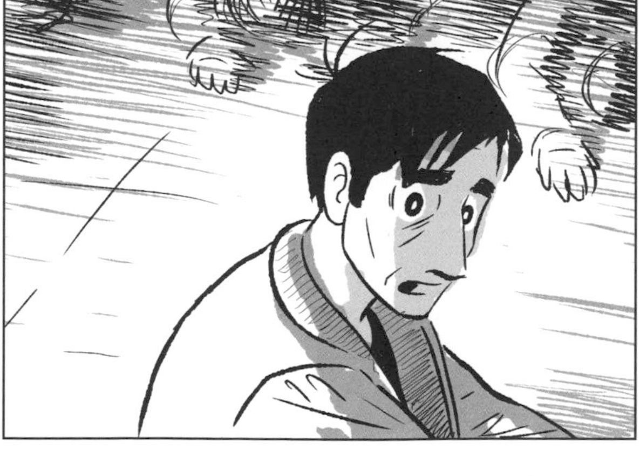

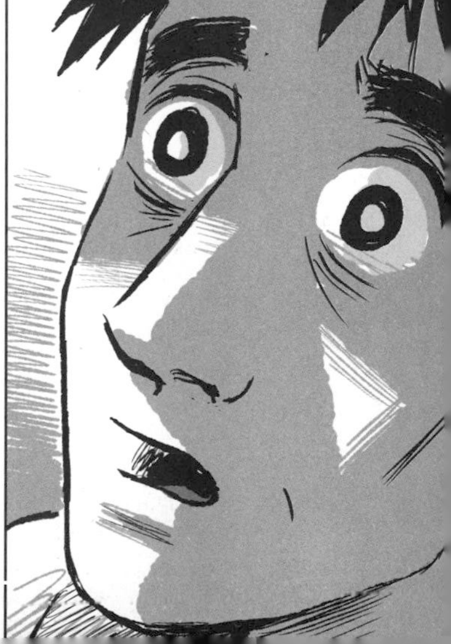

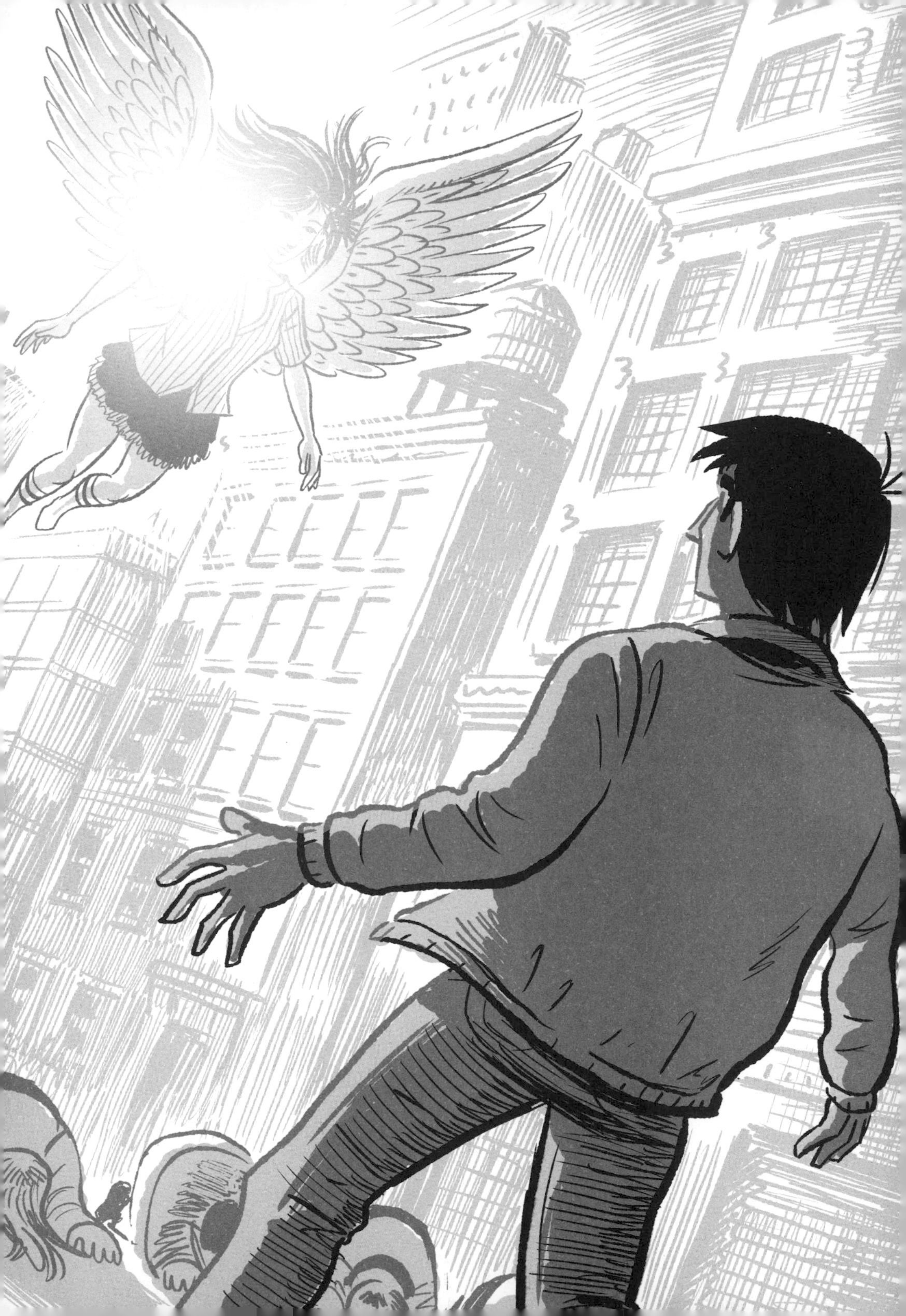

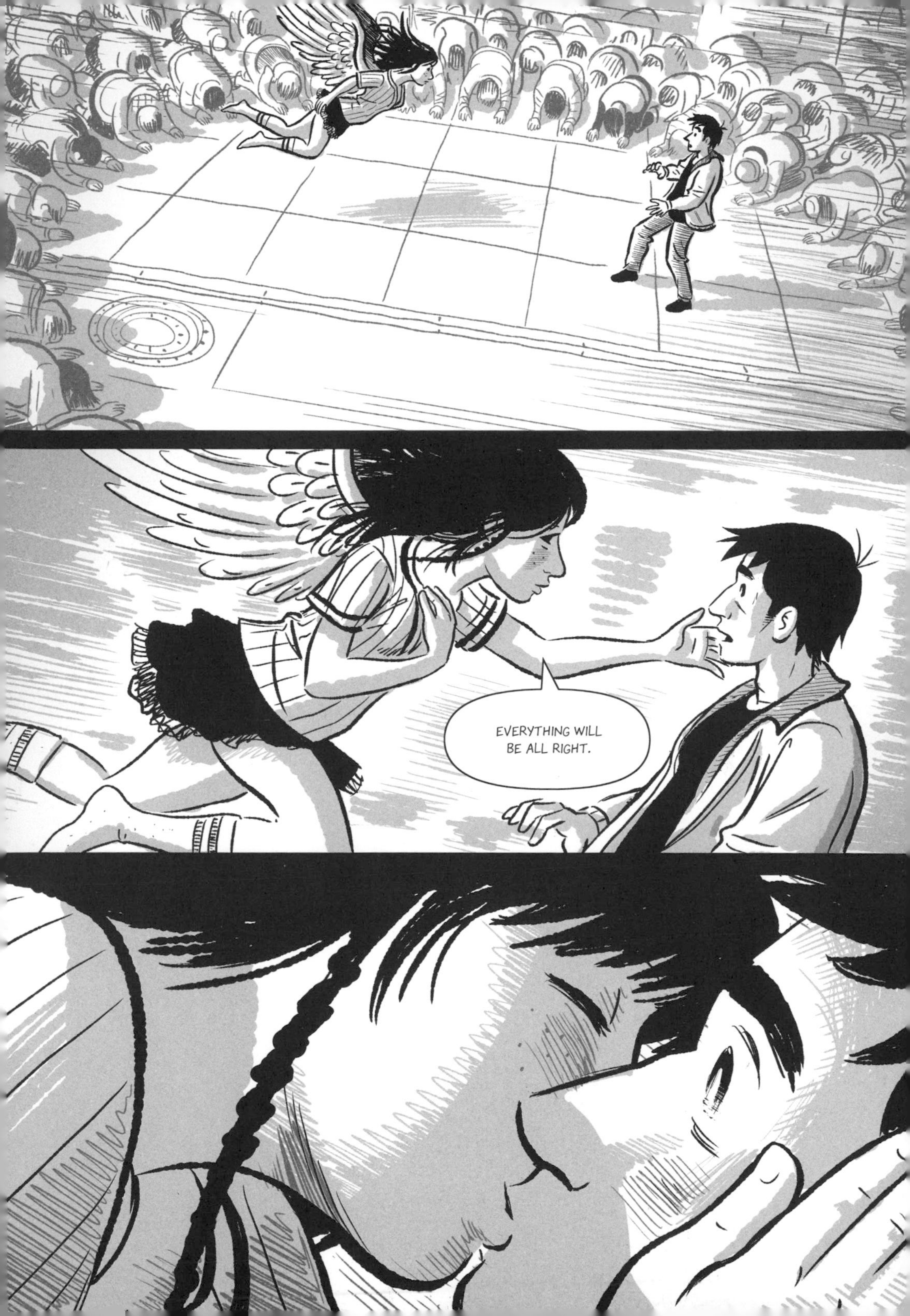
EVERYTHING WILL BE ALL RIGHT.

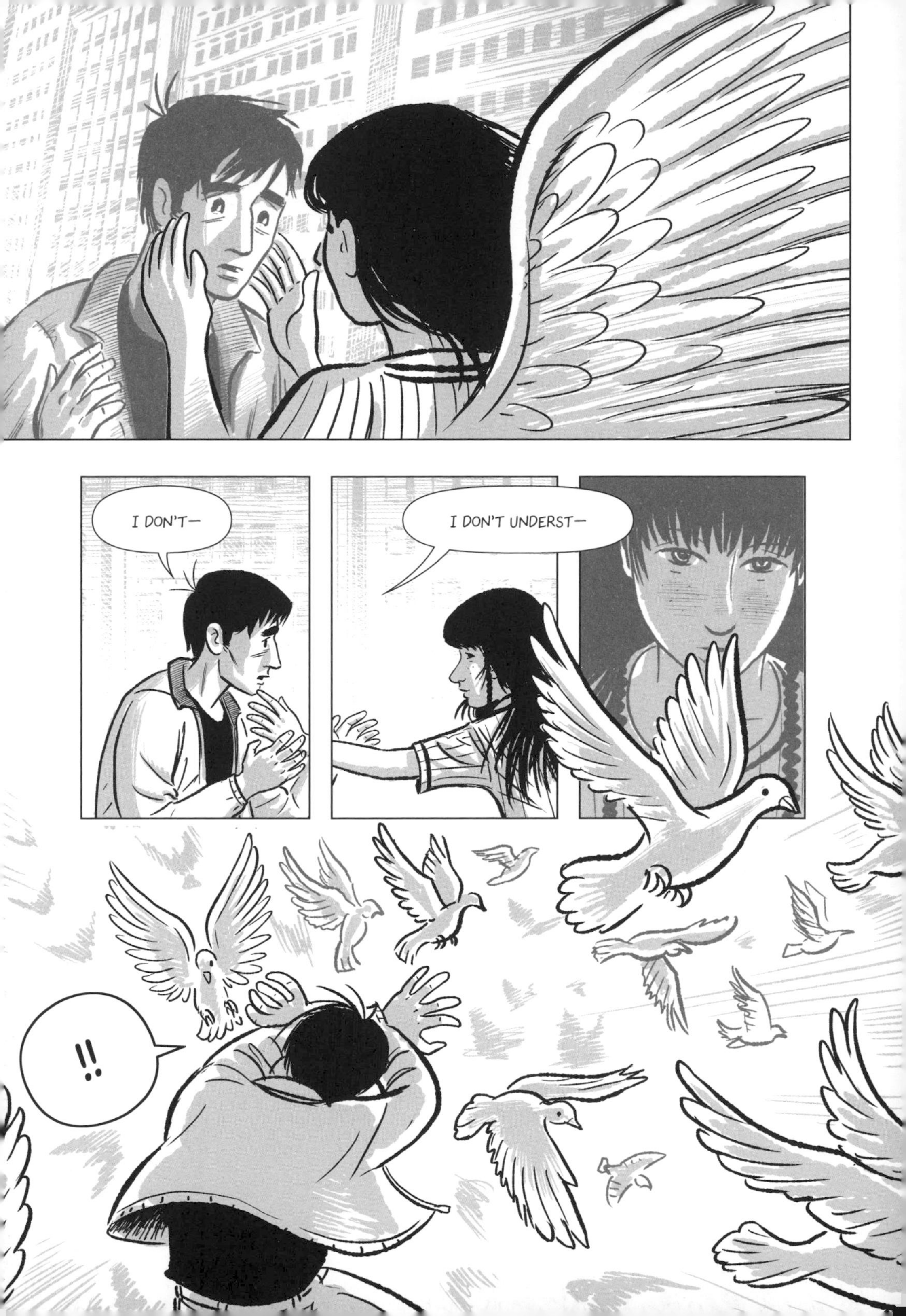
I DON'T—
I DON'T UNDERST—
!!

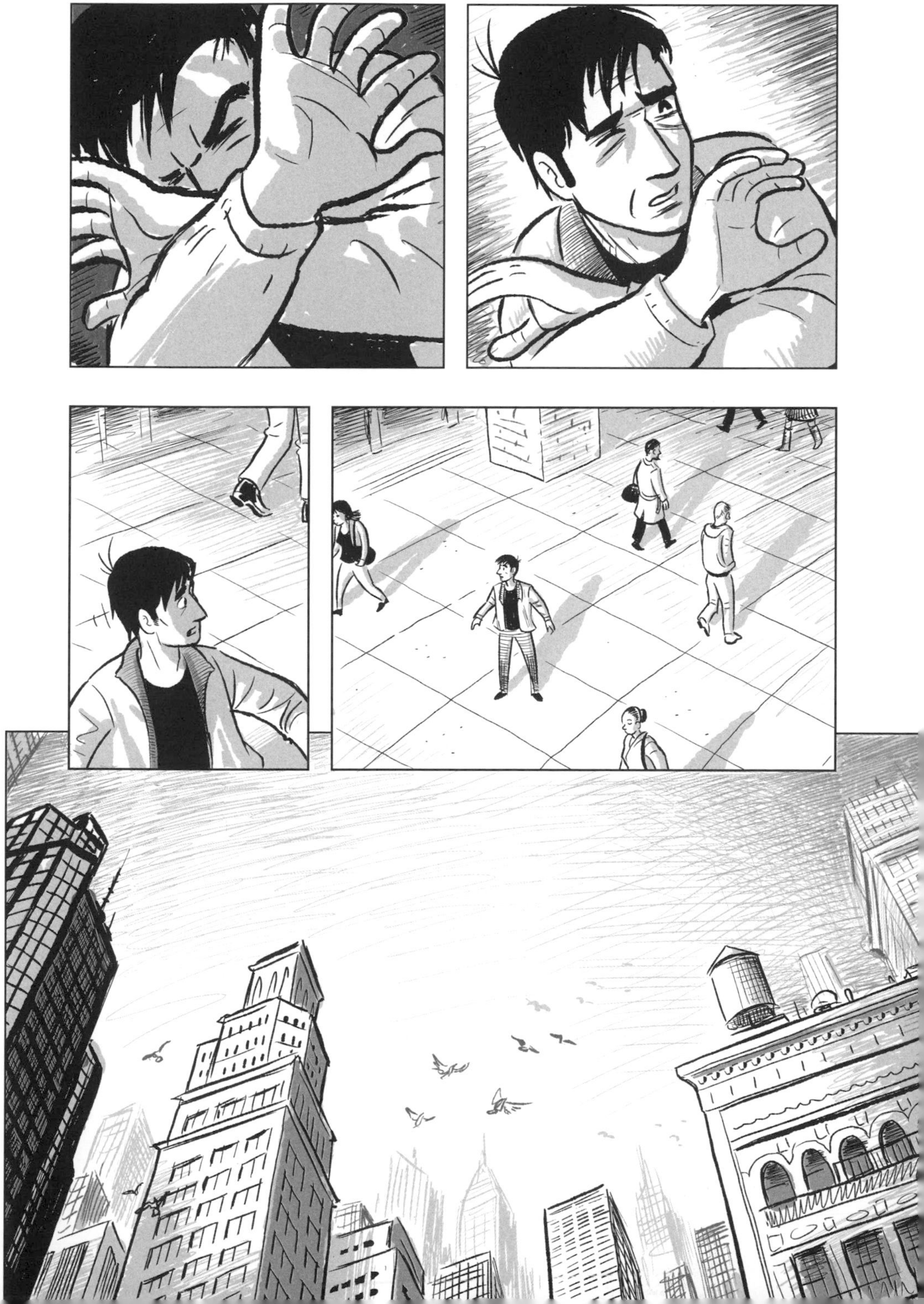

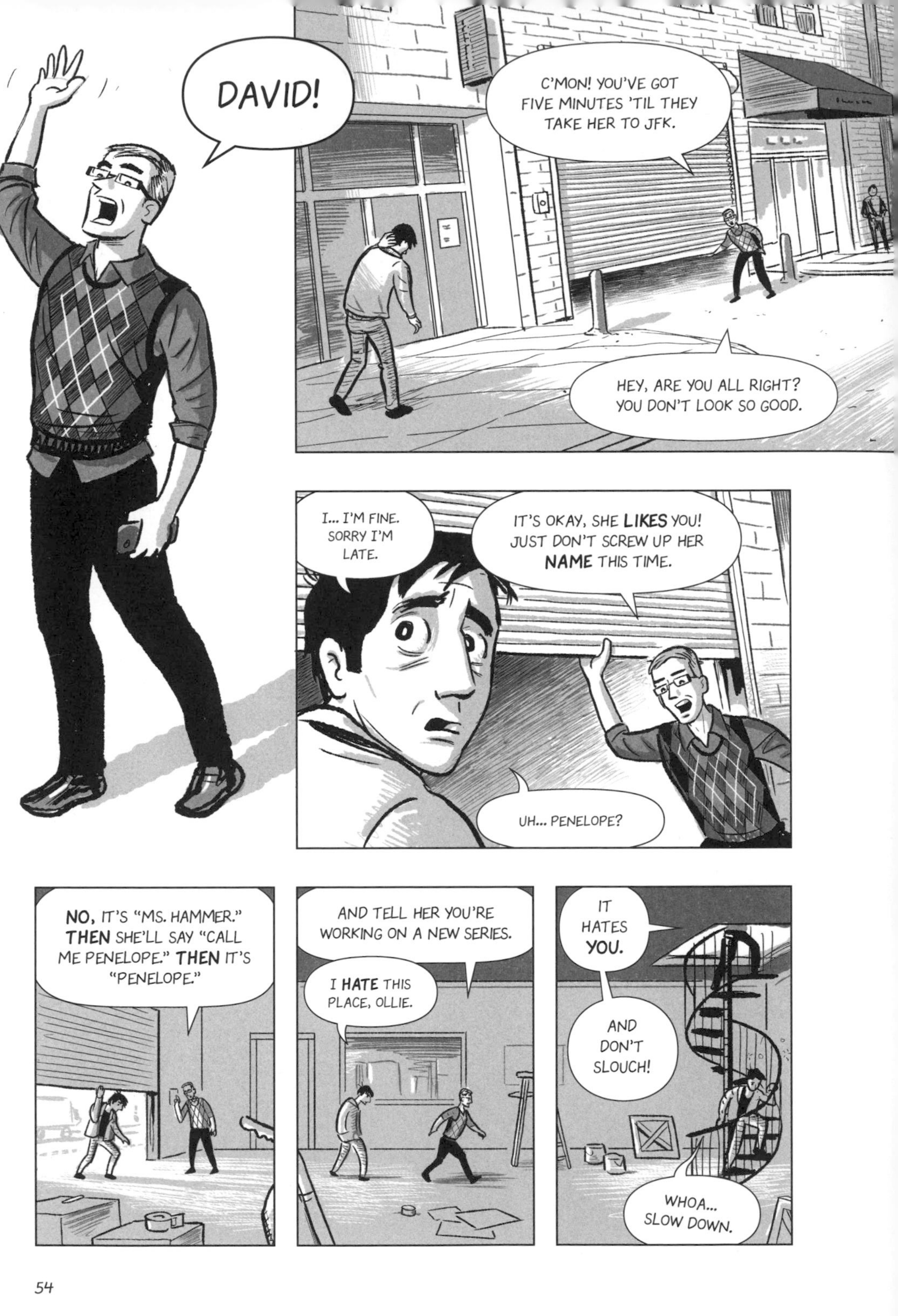
DAVID!
C'MON! YOU'VE GOT FIVE MINUTES 'TIL THEY TAKE HER TO JFK.
HEY, ARE YOU ALL RIGHT? YOU DON'T LOOK SO GOOD.
I... I'M FINE. SORRY I'M LATE.
IT'S OKAY, SHE LIKES YOU! JUST DON'T SCREW UP HER NAME THIS TIME.
UH... PENELOPE?
NO, IT'S "MS. HAMMER." THEN SHE'LL SAY "CALL ME PENELOPE." THEN IT'S "PENELOPE."
AND TELL HER YOU'RE WORKING ON A NEW SERIES.
I HATE THIS PLACE, OLLIE.
IT HATES YOU.
AND DON'T SLOUCH!
WHOA... SLOW DOWN.

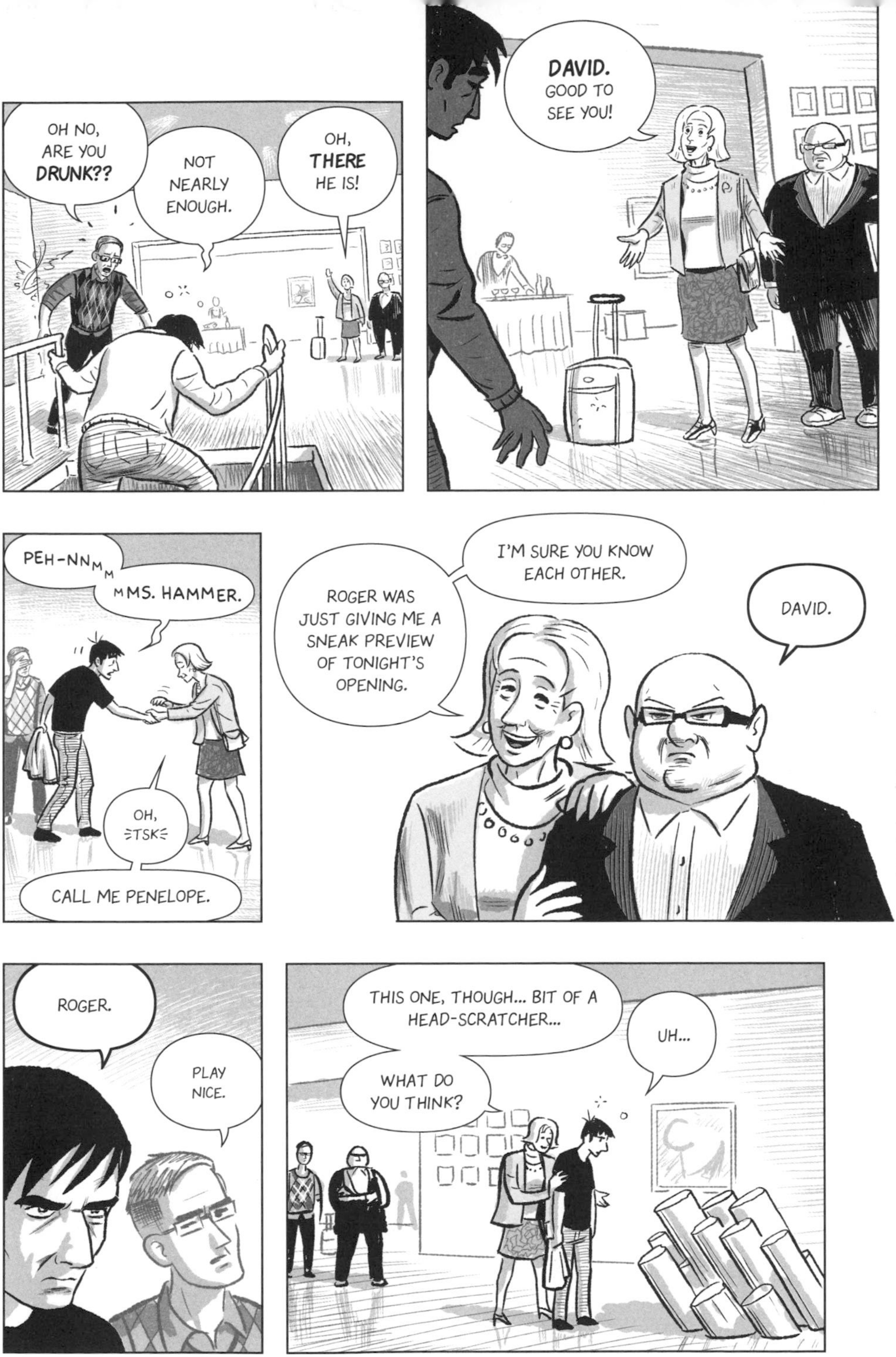
OH NO, ARE YOU DRUNK??
NOT NEARLY ENOUGH.
OH, THERE HE IS!
DAVID. GOOD TO SEE YOU!
PEH-NNMM MMS. HAMMER.
OH, ≠TSK≠
CALL ME PENELOPE.
ROGER WAS JUST GIVING ME A SNEAK PREVIEW OF TONIGHT'S OPENING.
I'M SURE YOU KNOW EACH OTHER.
DAVID.
ROGER.
PLAY NICE.
THIS ONE, THOUGH... BIT OF A HEAD-SCRATCHER...
WHAT DO YOU THINK?
UH...

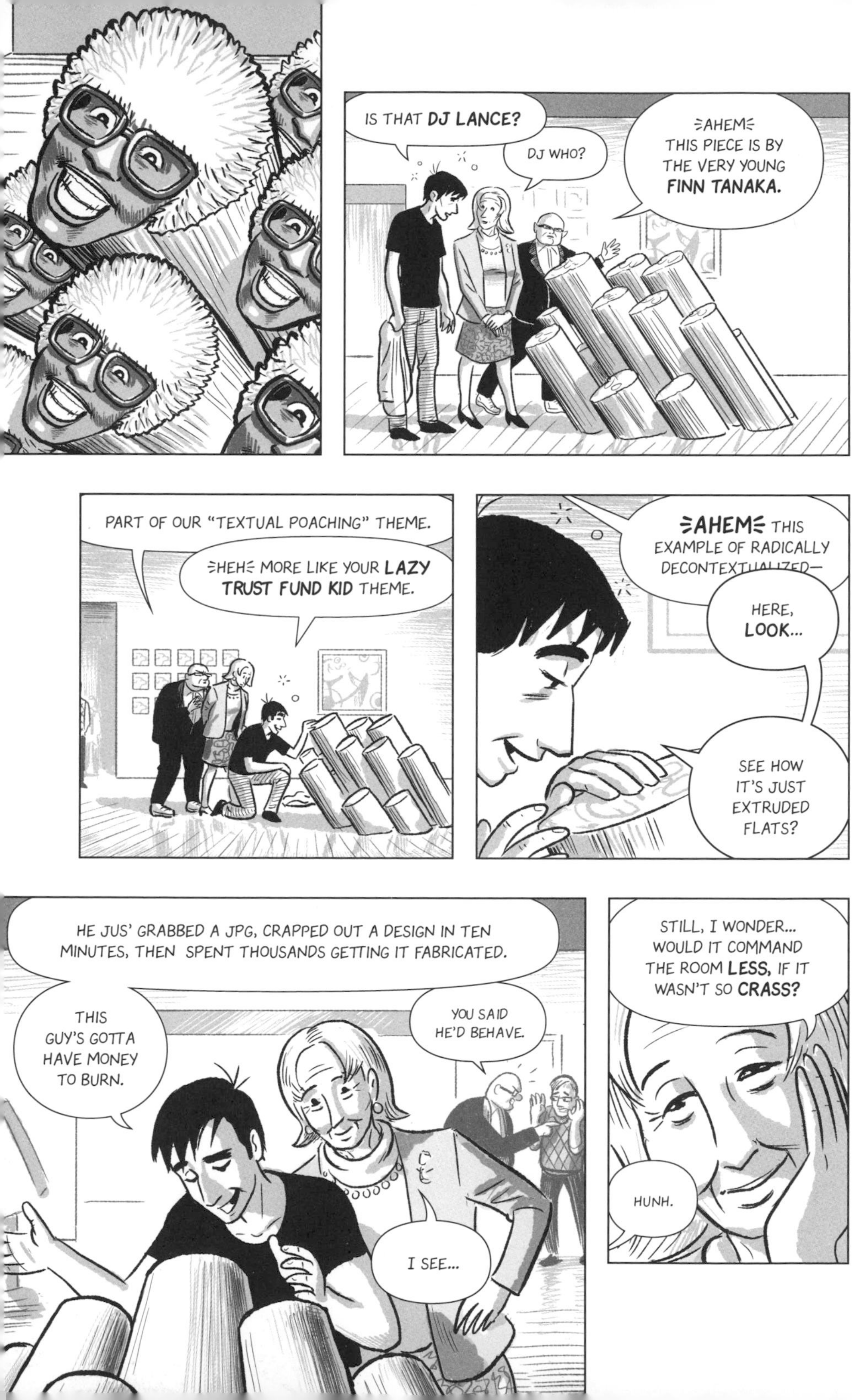
IS THAT DJ LANCE?
DJ WHO?
=AHEM= THIS PIECE IS BY THE VERY YOUNG FINN TANAKA.
PART OF OUR "TEXTUAL POACHING" THEME.
=HEH= MORE LIKE YOUR LAZY TRUST FUND KID THEME.
=AHEM= THIS EXAMPLE OF RADICALLY DECONTEXTUALIZED—
HERE, LOOK...
SEE HOW IT'S JUST EXTRUDED FLATS?
HE JUS' GRABBED A JPG, CRAPPED OUT A DESIGN IN TEN MINUTES, THEN SPENT THOUSANDS GETTING IT FABRICATED.
THIS GUY'S GOTTA HAVE MONEY TO BURN.
YOU SAID HE'D BEHAVE.
I SEE...
STILL, I WONDER... WOULD IT COMMAND THE ROOM LESS, IF IT WASN'T SO CRASS?
HUNH.

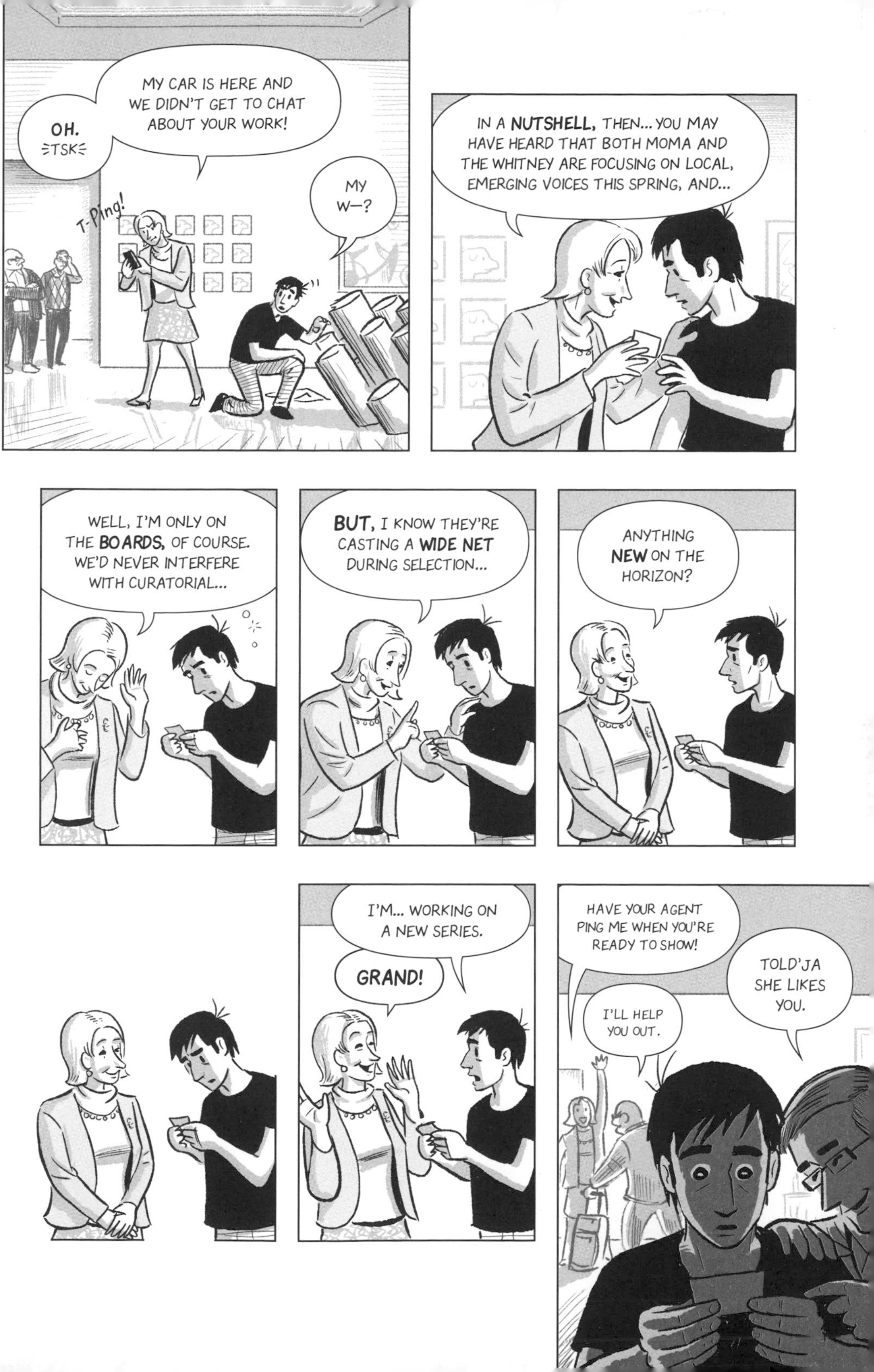
OH. TSK
MY CAR IS HERE AND WE DIDN'T GET TO CHAT ABOUT YOUR WORK!
T-Ping!
MY W—?
IN A NUTSHELL, THEN... YOU MAY HAVE HEARD THAT BOTH MOMA AND THE WHITNEY ARE FOCUSING ON LOCAL, EMERGING VOICES THIS SPRING, AND...
WELL, I'M ONLY ON THE BOARDS, OF COURSE. WE'D NEVER INTERFERE WITH CURATORIAL...
BUT, I KNOW THEY'RE CASTING A WIDE NET DURING SELECTION...
ANYTHING NEW ON THE HORIZON?
I'M... WORKING ON A NEW SERIES.
GRAND!
HAVE YOUR AGENT PING ME WHEN YOU'RE READY TO SHOW!
I'LL HELP YOU OUT.
TOLD'JA SHE LIKES YOU.

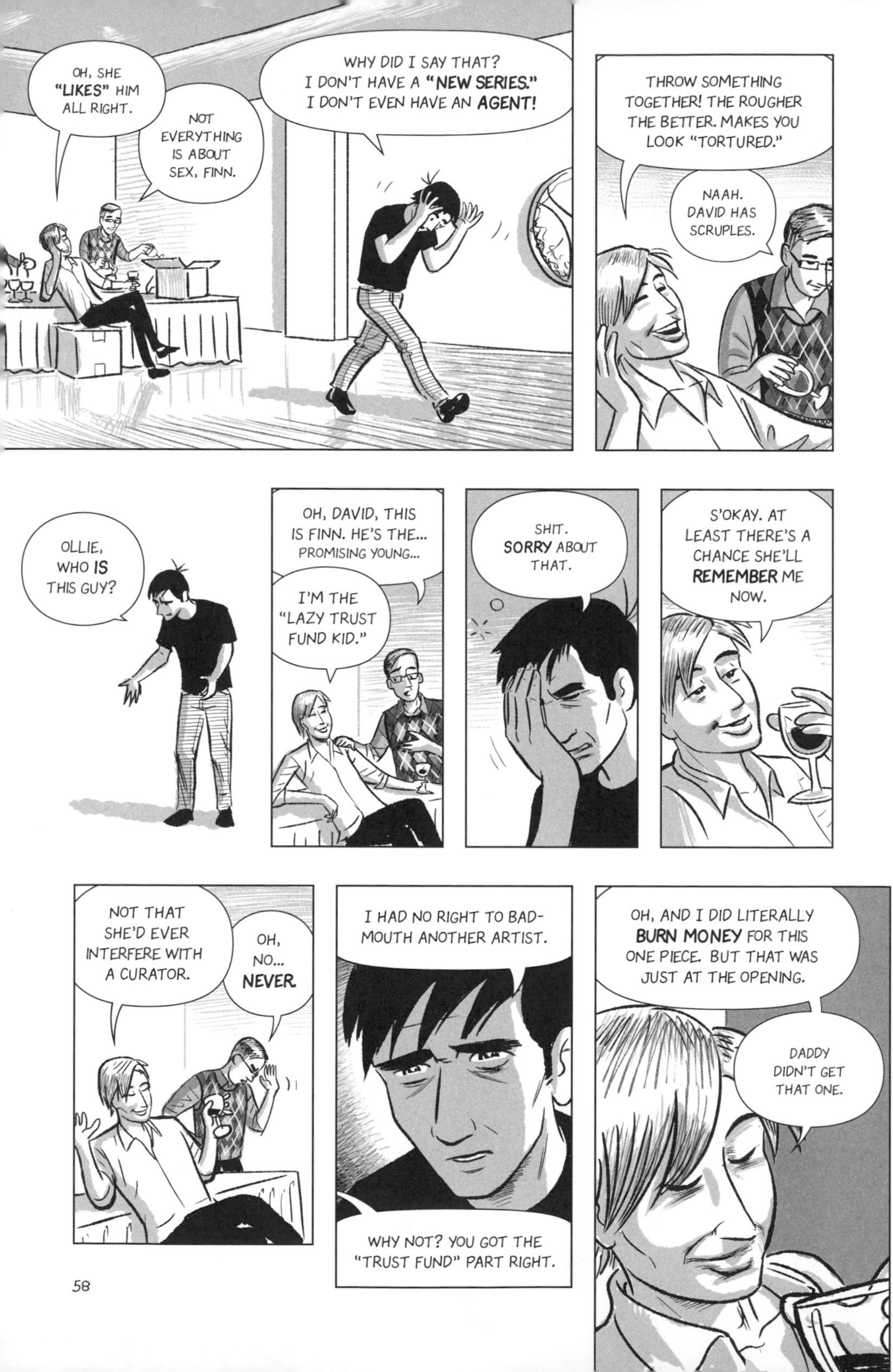

OH, SHE "LIKES" HIM ALL RIGHT.
NOT EVERYTHING IS ABOUT SEX, FINN.
WHY DID I SAY THAT? I DON'T HAVE A "NEW SERIES." I DON'T EVEN HAVE AN AGENT!
THROW SOMETHING TOGETHER! THE ROUGHER THE BETTER. MAKES YOU LOOK "TORTURED."
NAAH. DAVID HAS SCRUPLES.
OLLIE, WHO IS THIS GUY?
OH, DAVID, THIS IS FINN. HE'S THE... PROMISING YOUNG...
I'M THE "LAZY TRUST FUND KID."
SHIT. SORRY ABOUT THAT.
S'OKAY. AT LEAST THERE'S A CHANCE SHE'LL REMEMBER ME NOW.
NOT THAT SHE'D EVER INTERFERE WITH A CURATOR.
OH, NO... NEVER.
I HAD NO RIGHT TO BAD-MOUTH ANOTHER ARTIST.
WHY NOT? YOU GOT THE "TRUST FUND" PART RIGHT.
OH, AND I DID LITERALLY BURN MONEY FOR THIS ONE PIECE. BUT THAT WAS JUST AT THE OPENING.
DADDY DIDN'T GET THAT ONE.

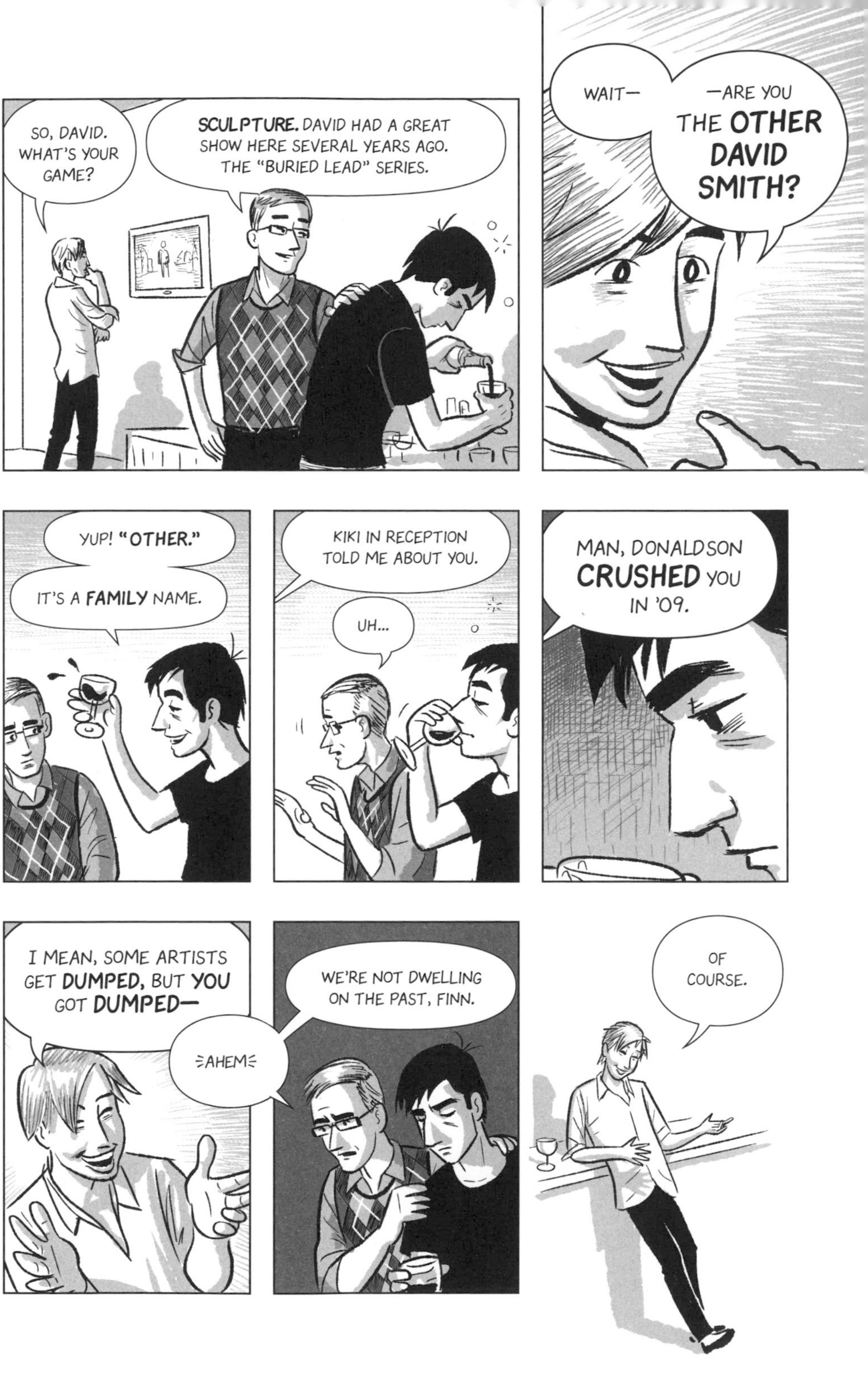
SO, DAVID. WHAT'S YOUR GAME?
SCULPTURE. DAVID HAD A GREAT SHOW HERE SEVERAL YEARS AGO. THE "BURIED LEAD" SERIES.
WAIT—
—ARE YOU THE OTHER DAVID SMITH?
YUP! "OTHER."
IT'S A FAMILY NAME.
KIKI IN RECEPTION TOLD ME ABOUT YOU.
UH...
MAN, DONALDSON CRUSHED YOU IN '09.
I MEAN, SOME ARTISTS GET DUMPED, BUT YOU GOT DUMPED—
WE'RE NOT DWELLING ON THE PAST, FINN.
AHEM
OF COURSE.

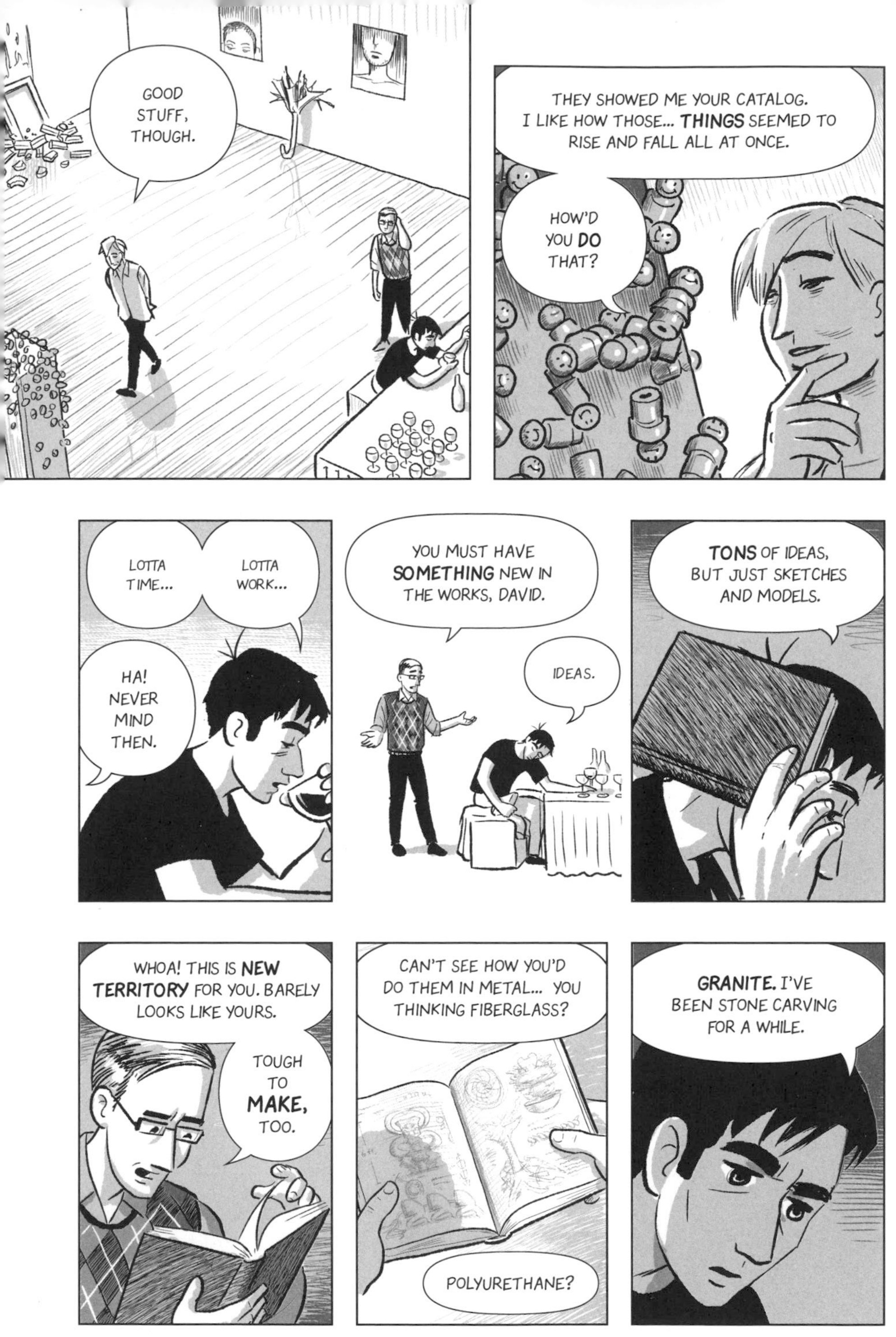
GOOD STUFF, THOUGH.
THEY SHOWED ME YOUR CATALOG. I LIKE HOW THOSE... **THINGS** SEEMED TO RISE AND FALL ALL AT ONCE.
HOW'D YOU **DO** THAT?
LOTTA TIME...
LOTTA WORK...
HA! NEVER MIND THEN.
YOU MUST HAVE **SOMETHING** NEW IN THE WORKS, DAVID.
IDEAS.
TONS OF IDEAS, BUT JUST SKETCHES AND MODELS.
WHOA! THIS IS **NEW TERRITORY** FOR YOU. BARELY LOOKS LIKE YOURS.
TOUGH TO **MAKE,** TOO.
CAN'T SEE HOW YOU'D DO THEM IN METAL... YOU THINKING FIBERGLASS?
POLYURETHANE?
GRANITE. I'VE BEEN STONE CARVING FOR A WHILE.

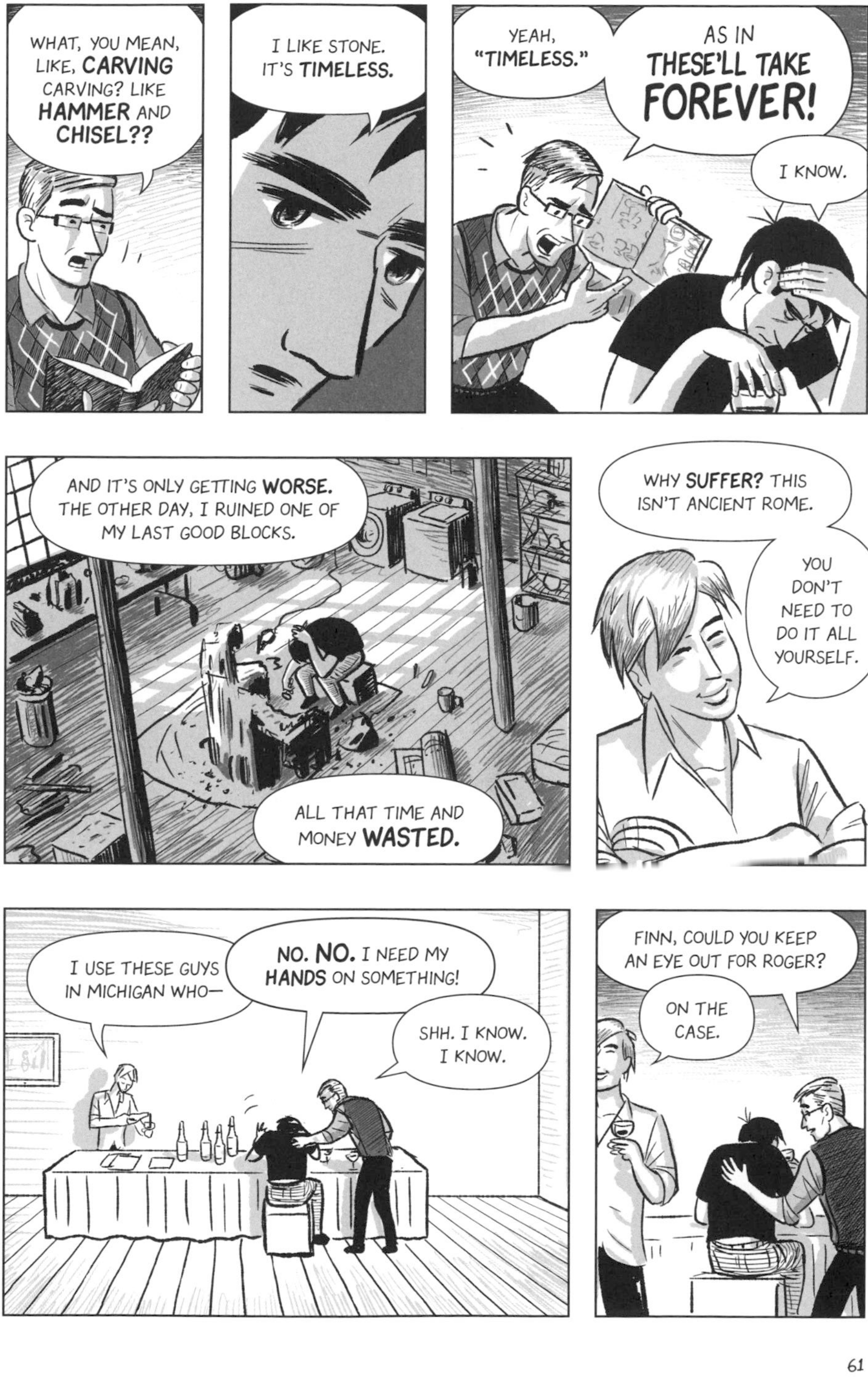
WHAT, YOU MEAN, LIKE, CARVING CARVING? LIKE HAMMER AND CHISEL??
I LIKE STONE. IT'S TIMELESS.
YEAH, "TIMELESS."
AS IN THESE'LL TAKE FOREVER!
I KNOW.
AND IT'S ONLY GETTING WORSE. THE OTHER DAY, I RUINED ONE OF MY LAST GOOD BLOCKS.
ALL THAT TIME AND MONEY WASTED.
WHY SUFFER? THIS ISN'T ANCIENT ROME.
YOU DON'T NEED TO DO IT ALL YOURSELF.
I USE THESE GUYS IN MICHIGAN WHO—
NO. NO. I NEED MY HANDS ON SOMETHING!
SHH. I KNOW. I KNOW.
FINN, COULD YOU KEEP AN EYE OUT FOR ROGER?
ON THE CASE.

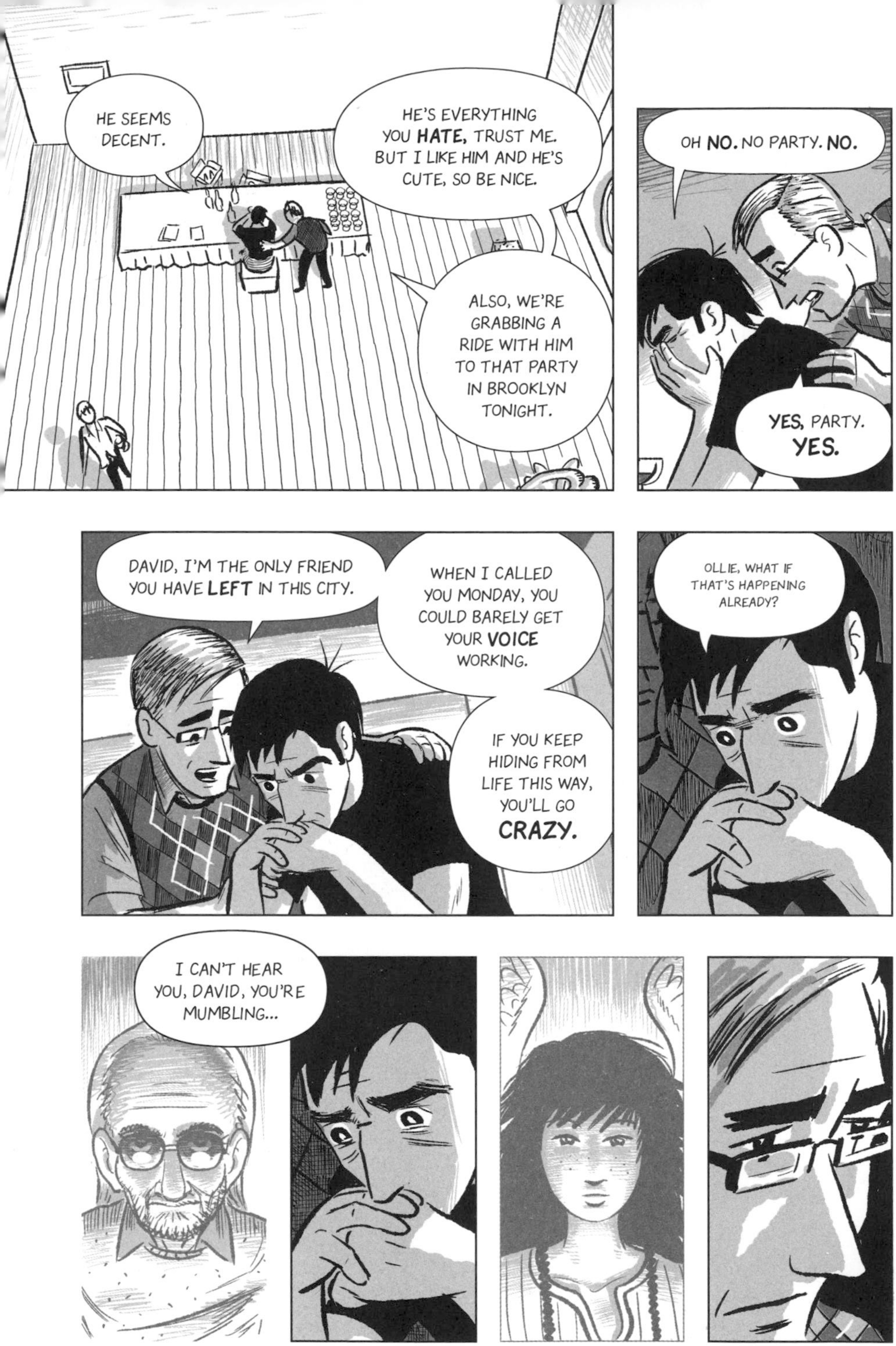

HE SEEMS DECENT.
HE'S EVERYTHING YOU **HATE,** TRUST ME. BUT I LIKE HIM AND HE'S CUTE, SO BE NICE.
ALSO, WE'RE GRABBING A RIDE WITH HIM TO THAT PARTY IN BROOKLYN TONIGHT.
OH **NO.** NO PARTY. **NO.**
YES, PARTY. **YES.**
DAVID, I'M THE ONLY FRIEND YOU HAVE **LEFT** IN THIS CITY.
WHEN I CALLED YOU MONDAY, YOU COULD BARELY GET YOUR **VOICE** WORKING.
IF YOU KEEP HIDING FROM LIFE THIS WAY, YOU'LL GO **CRAZY.**
OLLIE, WHAT IF THAT'S HAPPENING ALREADY?
I CAN'T HEAR YOU, DAVID, YOU'RE MUMBLING...

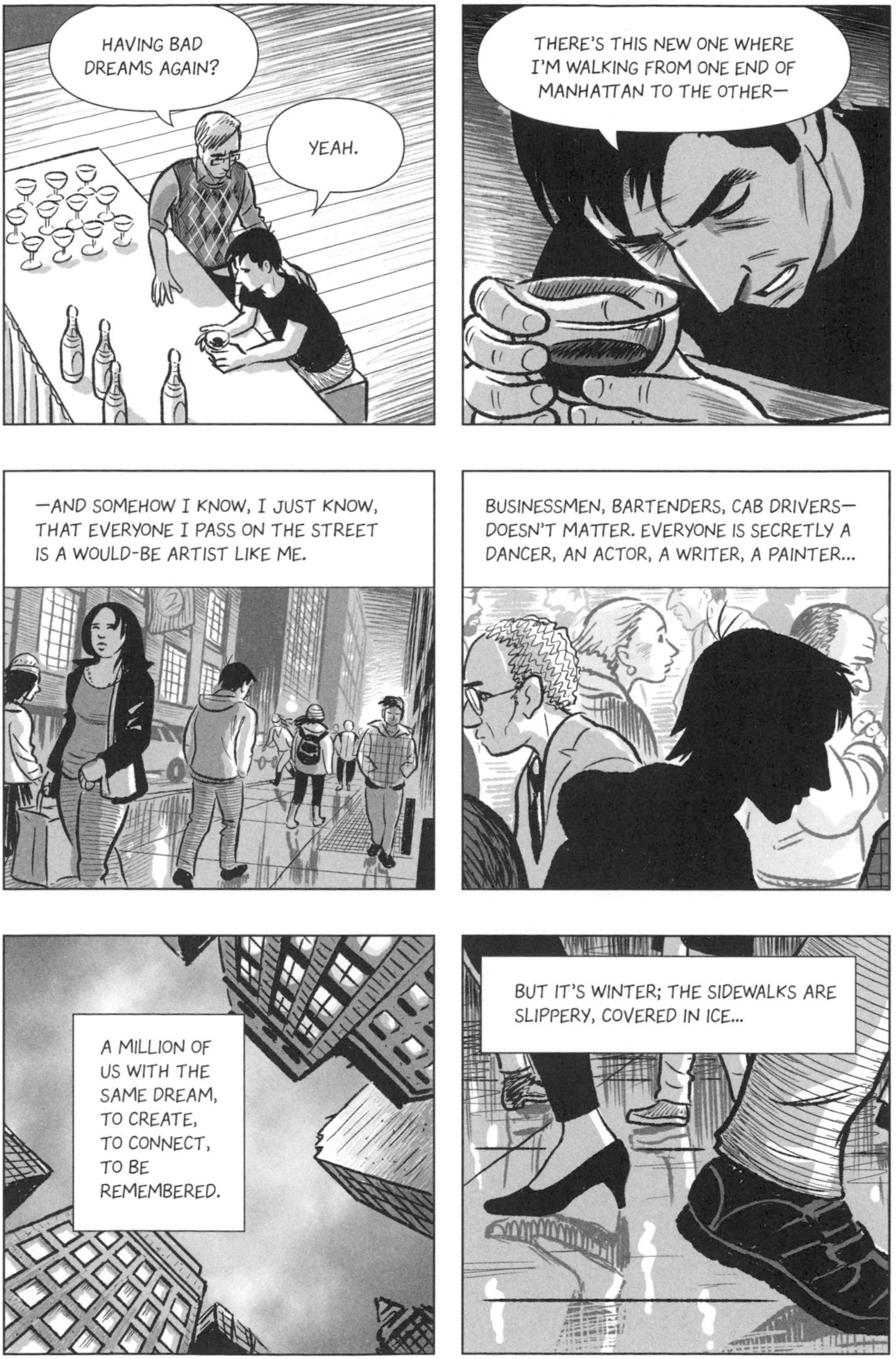
HAVING BAD DREAMS AGAIN?
YEAH.
THERE'S THIS NEW ONE WHERE I'M WALKING FROM ONE END OF MANHATTAN TO THE OTHER—
—AND SOMEHOW I KNOW, I JUST KNOW, THAT EVERYONE I PASS ON THE STREET IS A WOULD-BE ARTIST LIKE ME.
BUSINESSMEN, BARTENDERS, CAB DRIVERS— DOESN'T MATTER. EVERYONE IS SECRETLY A DANCER, AN ACTOR, A WRITER, A PAINTER...
A MILLION OF US WITH THE SAME DREAM, TO CREATE, TO CONNECT, TO BE REMEMBERED.
BUT IT'S WINTER; THE SIDEWALKS ARE SLIPPERY, COVERED IN ICE...

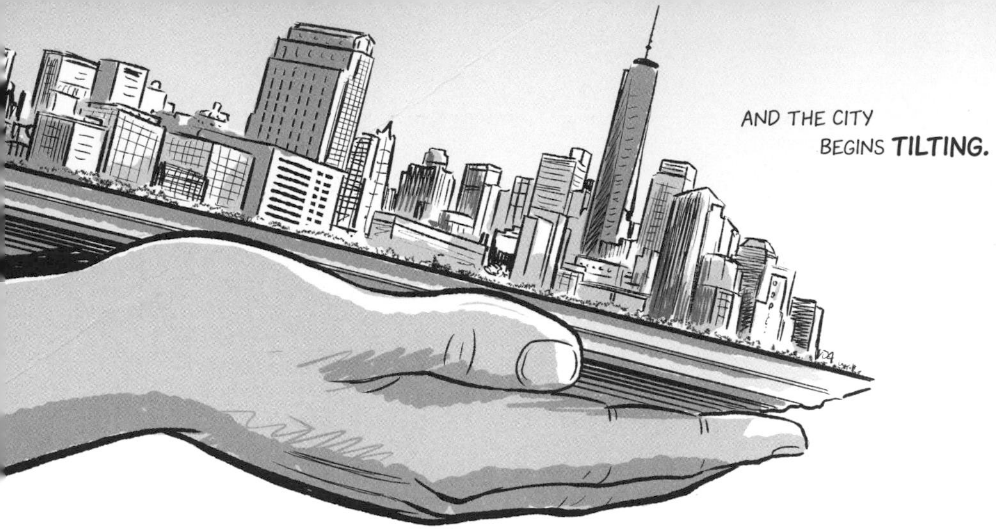
AND THE CITY
BEGINS **TILTING.**

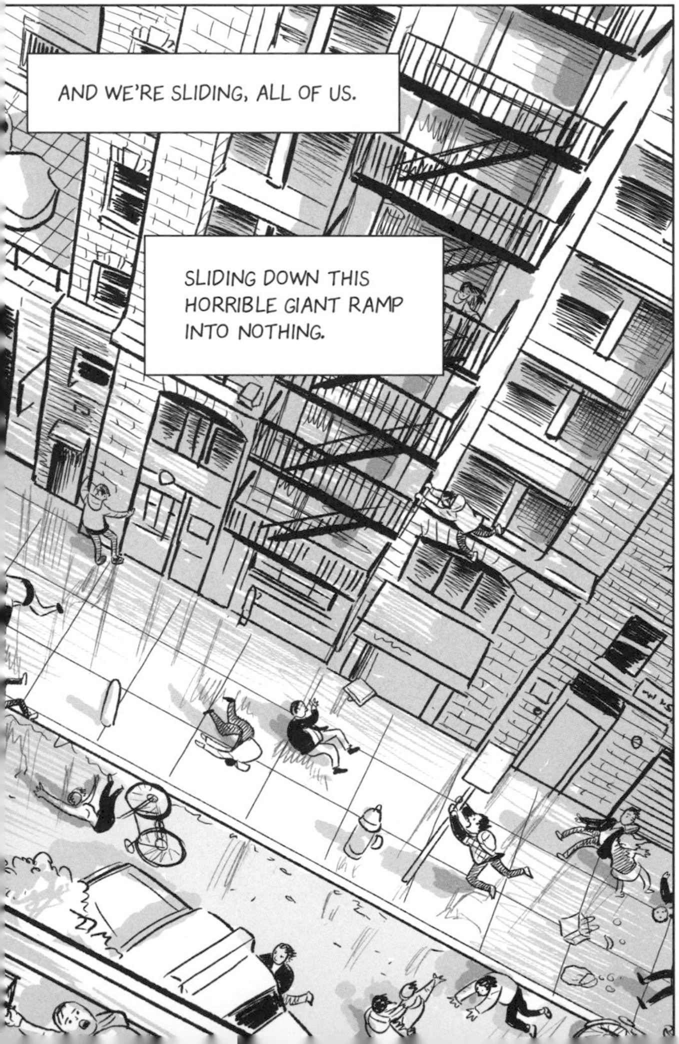
AND WE'RE SLIDING, ALL OF US.
SLIDING DOWN THIS HORRIBLE GIANT RAMP INTO NOTHING.

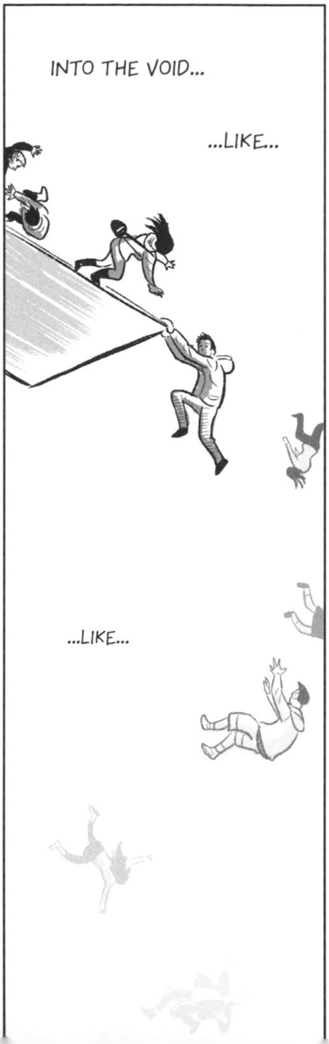
INTO THE VOID...
...LIKE...
...LIKE...

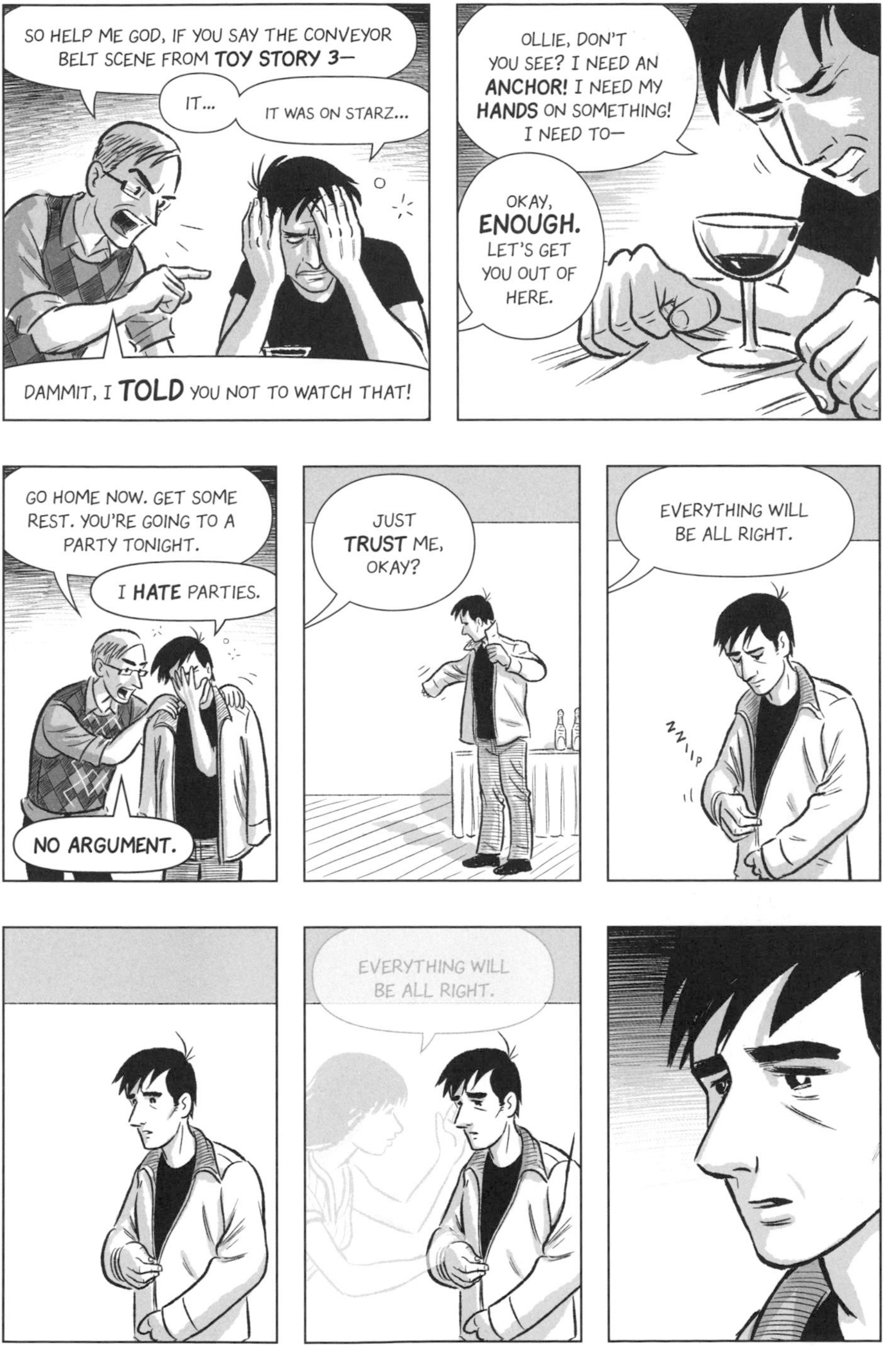
SO HELP ME GOD, IF YOU SAY THE CONVEYOR BELT SCENE FROM TOY STORY 3—
IT...
IT WAS ON STARZ...
DAMMIT, I TOLD YOU NOT TO WATCH THAT!
OLLIE, DON'T YOU SEE? I NEED AN ANCHOR! I NEED MY HANDS ON SOMETHING! I NEED TO—
OKAY, ENOUGH. LET'S GET YOU OUT OF HERE.
GO HOME NOW. GET SOME REST. YOU'RE GOING TO A PARTY TONIGHT.
I HATE PARTIES.
NO ARGUMENT.
JUST TRUST ME, OKAY?
EVERYTHING WILL BE ALL RIGHT.
ZZIIP
EVERYTHING WILL BE ALL RIGHT.

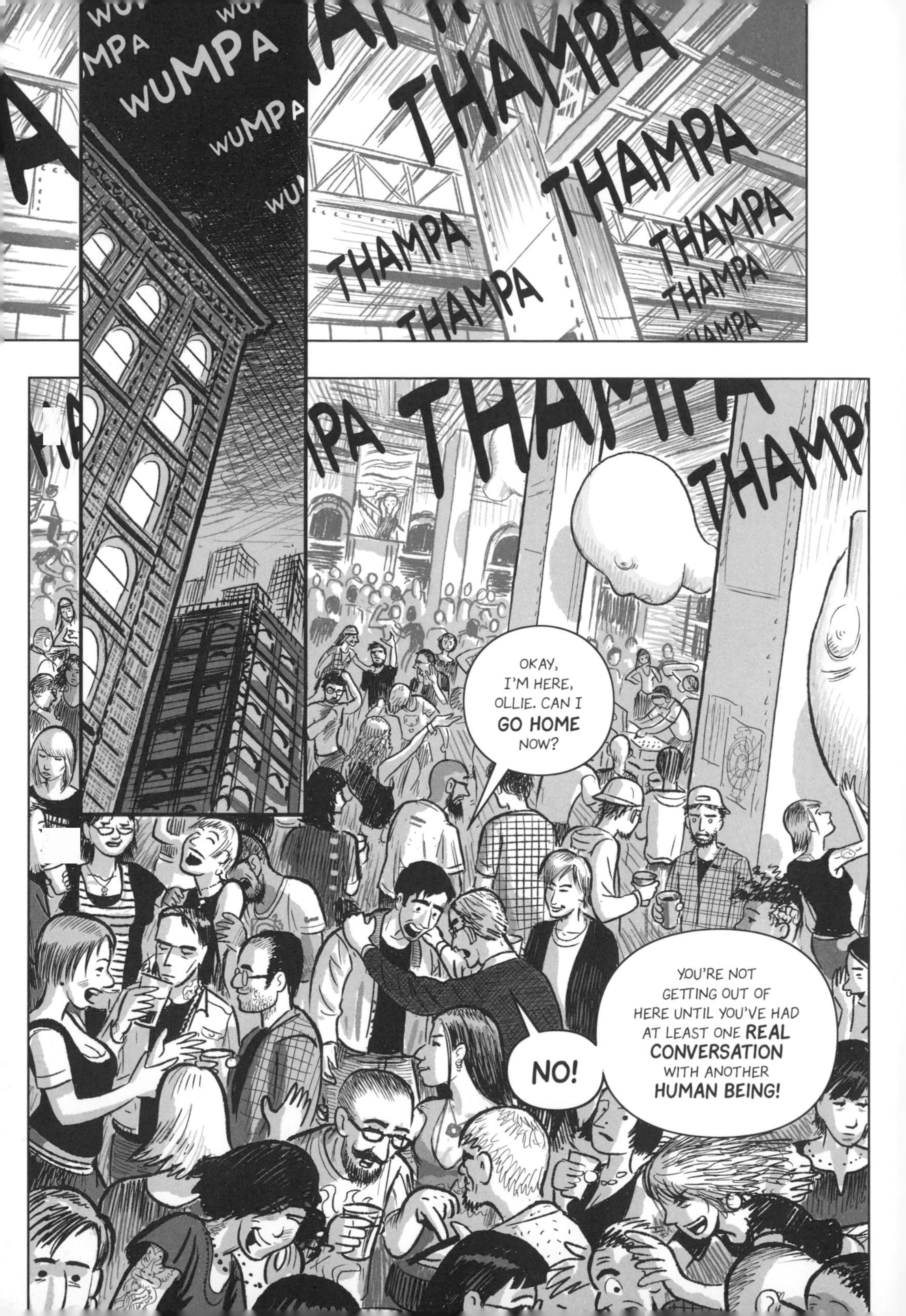
WUMPA
WUMPA
WUMPA
WUMPA
THAMPA
THAMPA
THAMPA
THAMPA
THAMPA
THAMPA
THAMPA
THAMPA
THAMPA
OKAY, I'M HERE, OLLIE. CAN I GO HOME NOW?
NO!
YOU'RE NOT GETTING OUT OF HERE UNTIL YOU'VE HAD AT LEAST ONE REAL CONVERSATION WITH ANOTHER HUMAN BEING!

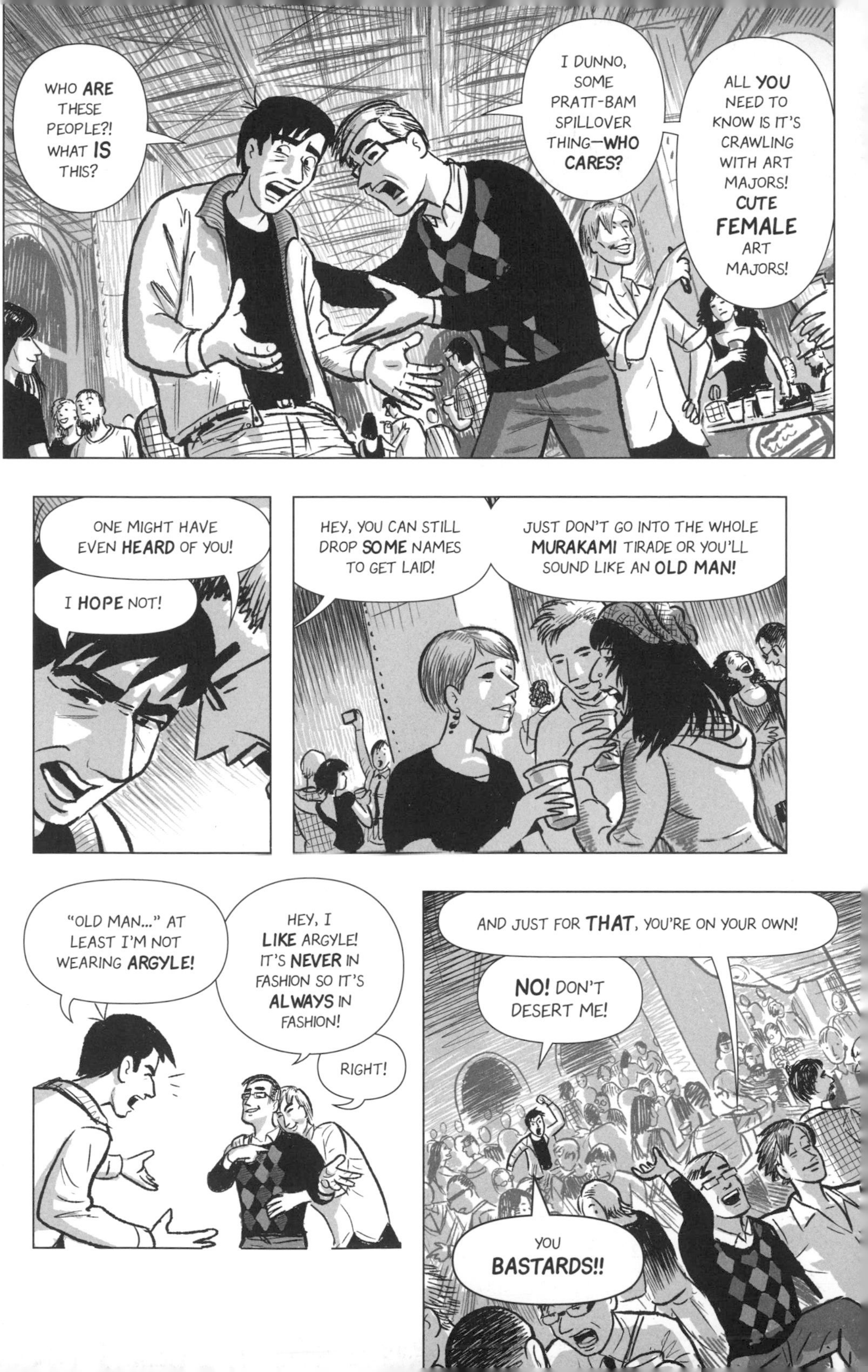
WHO **ARE** THESE PEOPLE?! WHAT **IS** THIS?
I DUNNO, SOME PRATT-BAM SPILLOVER THING—**WHO CARES?**
ALL **YOU** NEED TO KNOW IS IT'S CRAWLING WITH ART MAJORS! **CUTE FEMALE** ART MAJORS!
ONE MIGHT HAVE EVEN **HEARD** OF YOU!
I **HOPE** NOT!
HEY, YOU CAN STILL DROP **SOME** NAMES TO GET LAID!
JUST DON'T GO INTO THE WHOLE **MURAKAMI** TIRADE OR YOU'LL SOUND LIKE AN **OLD MAN!**
"OLD MAN..." AT LEAST I'M NOT WEARING **ARGYLE!**
HEY, I **LIKE** ARGYLE! IT'S **NEVER** IN FASHION SO IT'S **ALWAYS** IN FASHION!
RIGHT!
AND JUST FOR **THAT**, YOU'RE ON YOUR OWN!
NO! DON'T DESERT ME!
YOU **BASTARDS!!**

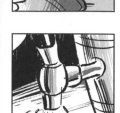

AND WE ALL GOT TO MEET **LEE BONTECOU!**

WHA— I'M SORRY, WHO? **WHAT?!**

...AGENT FOR MY PAIN

FUCK L.A. AFTER SUNDANCE, WE WON'T HAVE TO...

...WELL I HEA SHE'S SLEEP WITH THE

...AND THIS IS WHY MURAKAMI ALWAYS GETS A FREE P—

OH! THERE THEY ARE! **WAIT UP,** YOU GUYS!

ATED A EAL BUZZ AUSTIN

C'MON, FINN... ...SERIOUSLY... ...YOU REALLY DOING IT...

...RE SLEEPING ...ARGYLE BOY TONIGHT?

...INFLUENCE WITH ROGER AND THAT GALLERY HE RUNS IS A...

?

...EALLY USE HIM...

...UMP HIM AS SOON AS MY ...OW GOES UP...

...THINK HE'S COMING BACK.

THERE YOU ARE!

OLLIE, LISTEN! I THINK FINN IS TAKING ADVANTAGE OF YOU!

I HOPE SO! HE'S COMING BACK TO MY PLACE!

NO, THE GALLERY! HE'S USING YOU TO GET TO ROGER!

YOU'RE IMAGINING THINGS, DAVID! PLEASE DON'T SPOIL THIS, OKAY?

WHOAH! DIZZY...

I KNOW YOU WON'T ACCEPT CAB FARE, BUT I GOT YOU A RIDE WITH THE GUY BRINGING THE SPEAKERS BACK.

HE'LL BE BACK IN A HALF HOUR. HERE'S HIS NAME, JUST ASK AROUND.

OLLIE, YOU'RE MAKING A MISTAKE! FINN IS JUST—

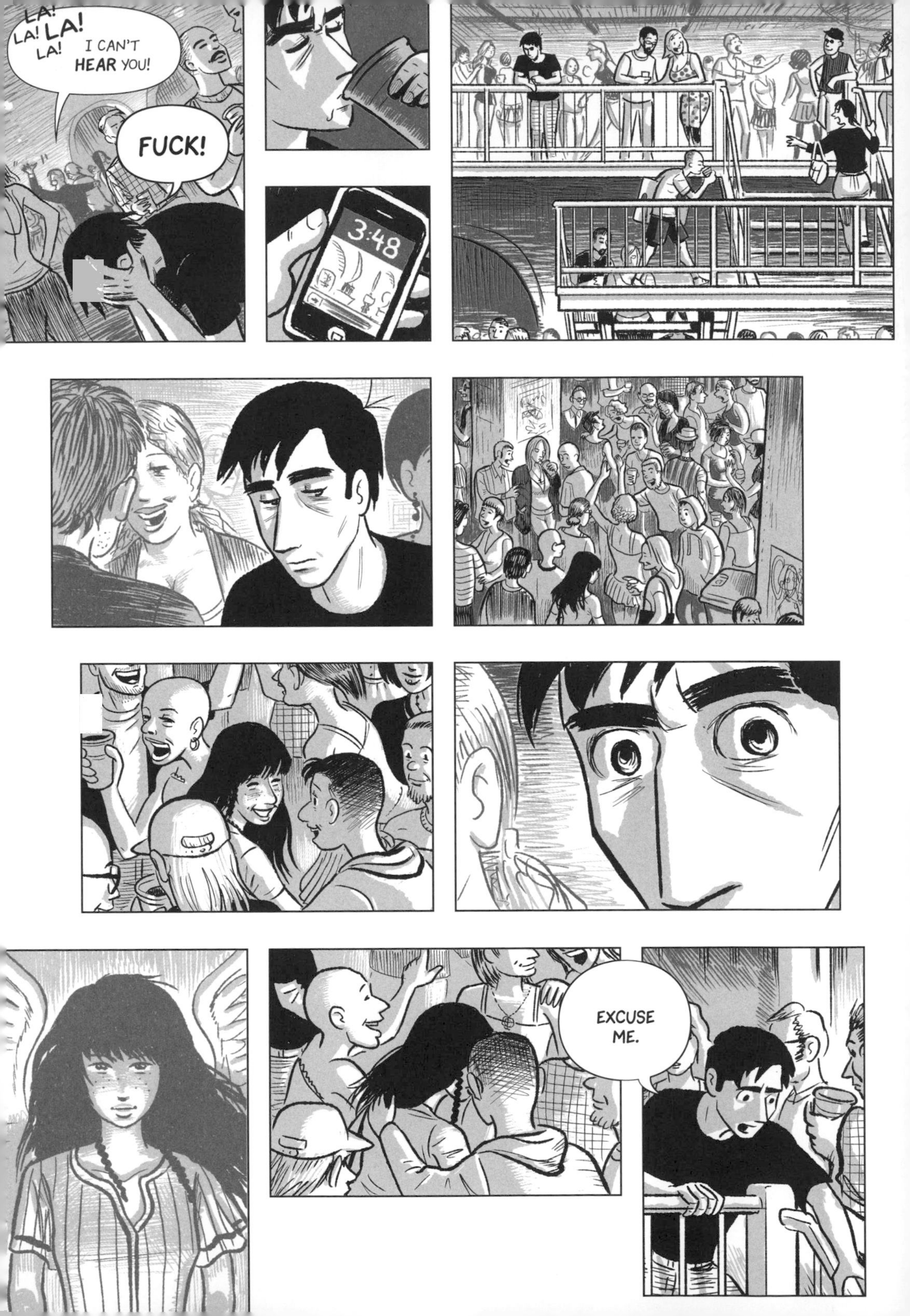

LA! LA! LA! LA! I CAN'T HEAR YOU!
FUCK!
3:48
EXCUSE ME.

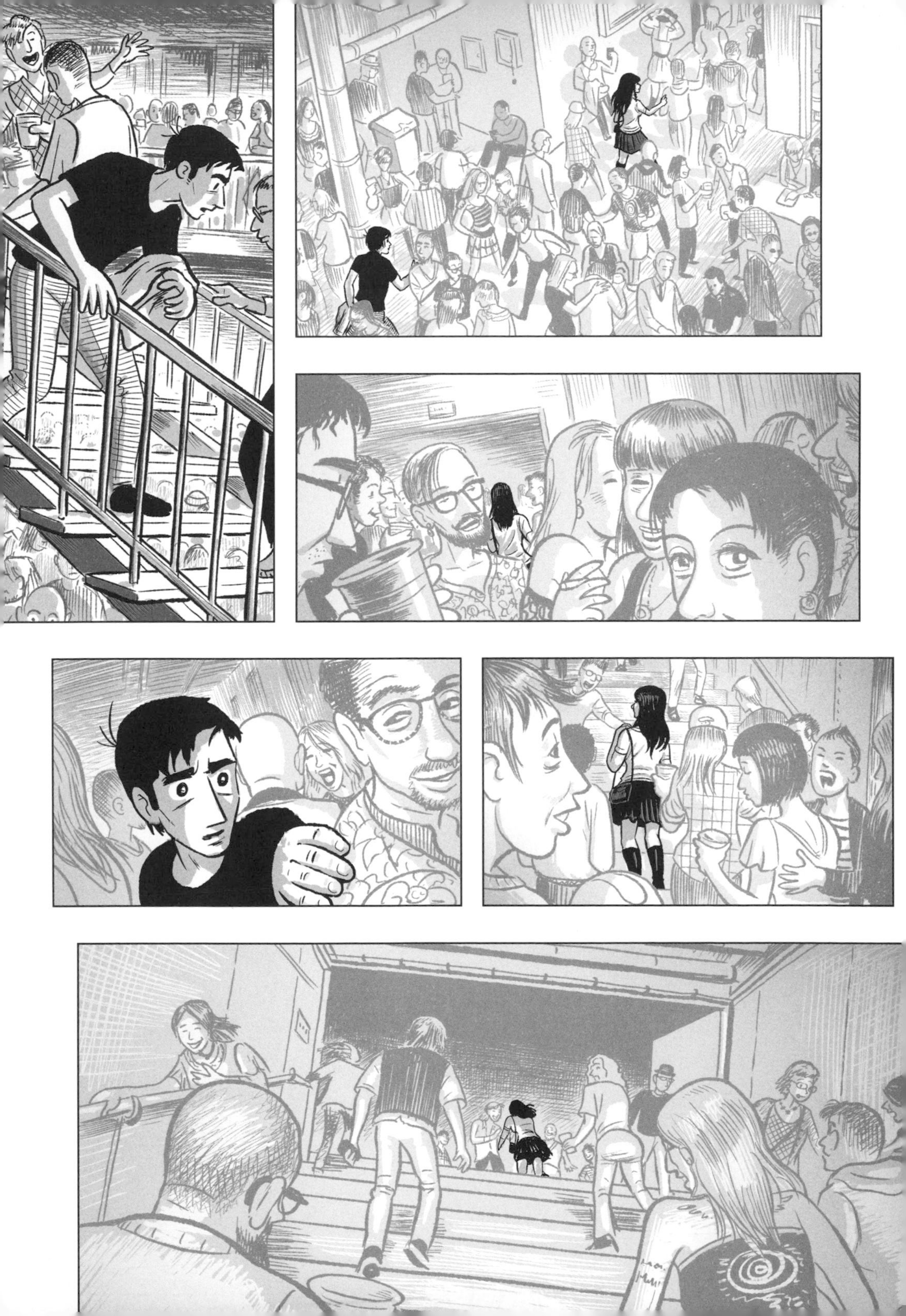

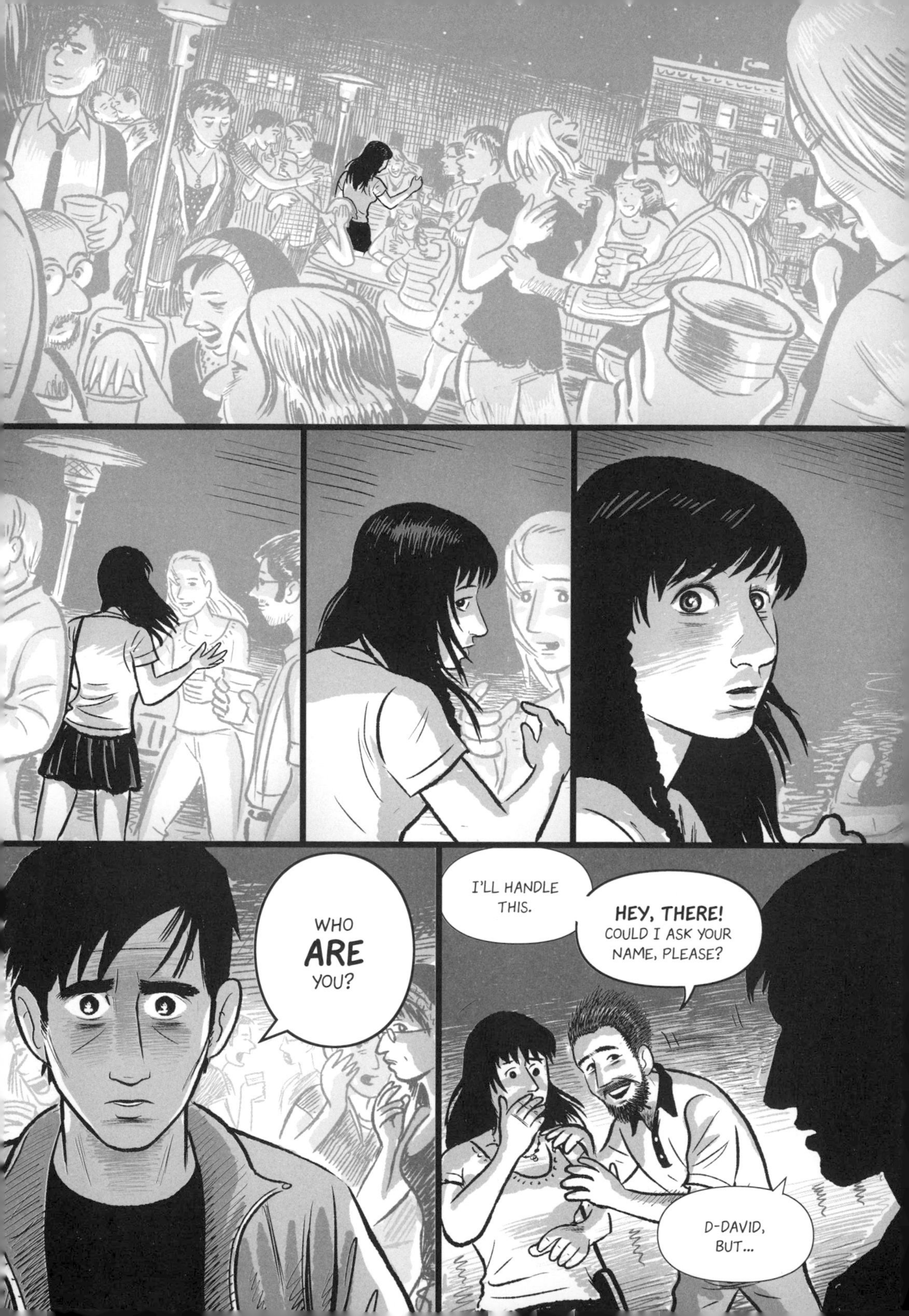
WHO ARE YOU?
I'LL HANDLE THIS.
HEY, THERE! COULD I ASK YOUR NAME, PLEASE?
D-DAVID, BUT...

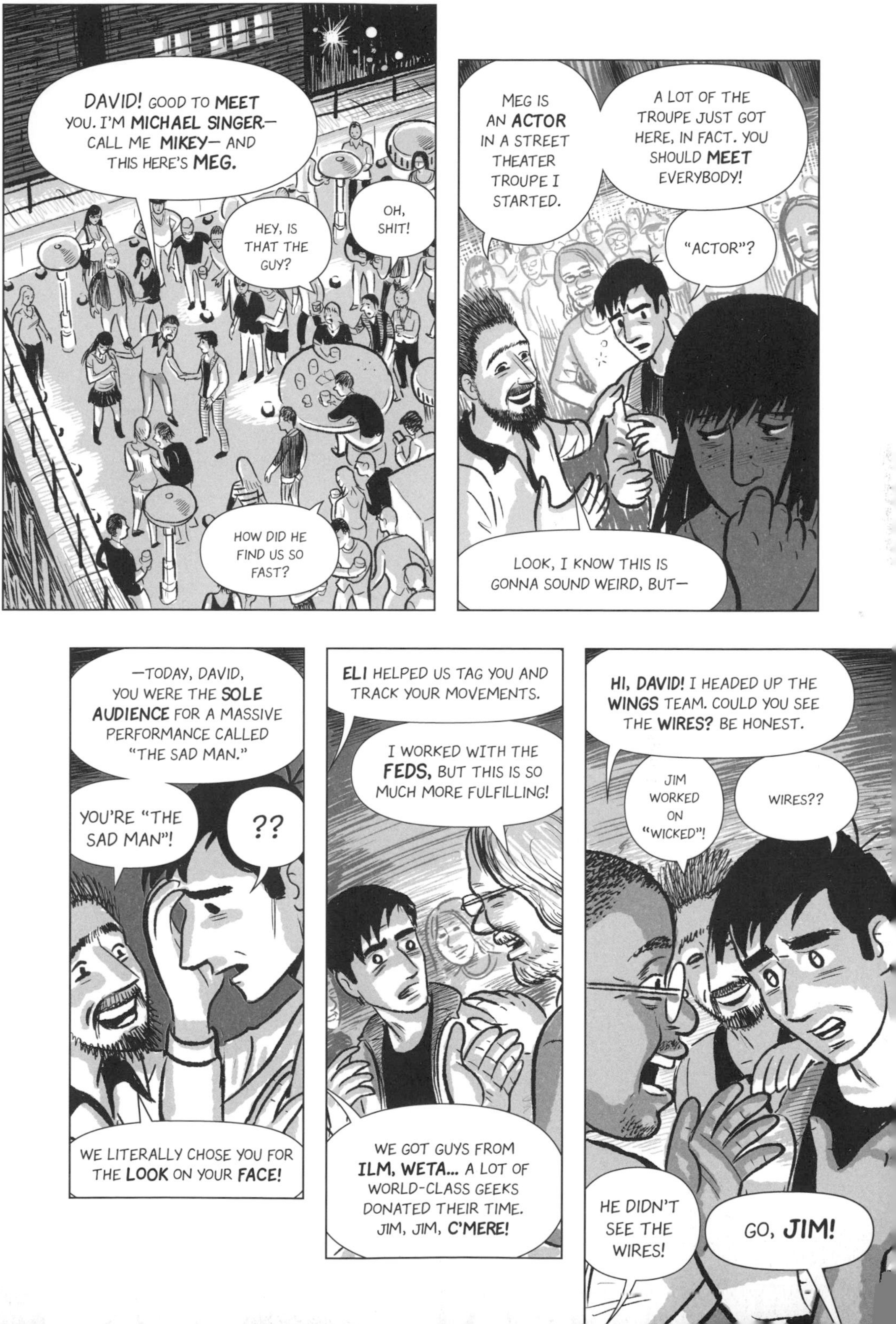
DAVID! GOOD TO MEET YOU. I'M MICHAEL SINGER— CALL ME MIKEY— AND THIS HERE'S MEG.
HEY, IS THAT THE GUY?
OH, SHIT!
HOW DID HE FIND US SO FAST?
MEG IS AN ACTOR IN A STREET THEATER TROUPE I STARTED.
A LOT OF THE TROUPE JUST GOT HERE, IN FACT. YOU SHOULD MEET EVERYBODY!
"ACTOR"?
LOOK, I KNOW THIS IS GONNA SOUND WEIRD, BUT—
—TODAY, DAVID, YOU WERE THE SOLE AUDIENCE FOR A MASSIVE PERFORMANCE CALLED "THE SAD MAN."
YOU'RE "THE SAD MAN"!
??
WE LITERALLY CHOSE YOU FOR THE LOOK ON YOUR FACE!
ELI HELPED US TAG YOU AND TRACK YOUR MOVEMENTS.
I WORKED WITH THE FEDS, BUT THIS IS SO MUCH MORE FULFILLING!
WE GOT GUYS FROM ILM, WETA... A LOT OF WORLD-CLASS GEEKS DONATED THEIR TIME. JIM, JIM, C'MERE!
HI, DAVID! I HEADED UP THE WINGS TEAM. COULD YOU SEE THE WIRES? BE HONEST.
JIM WORKED ON "WICKED"!
WIRES??
HE DIDN'T SEE THE WIRES!
GO, JIM!

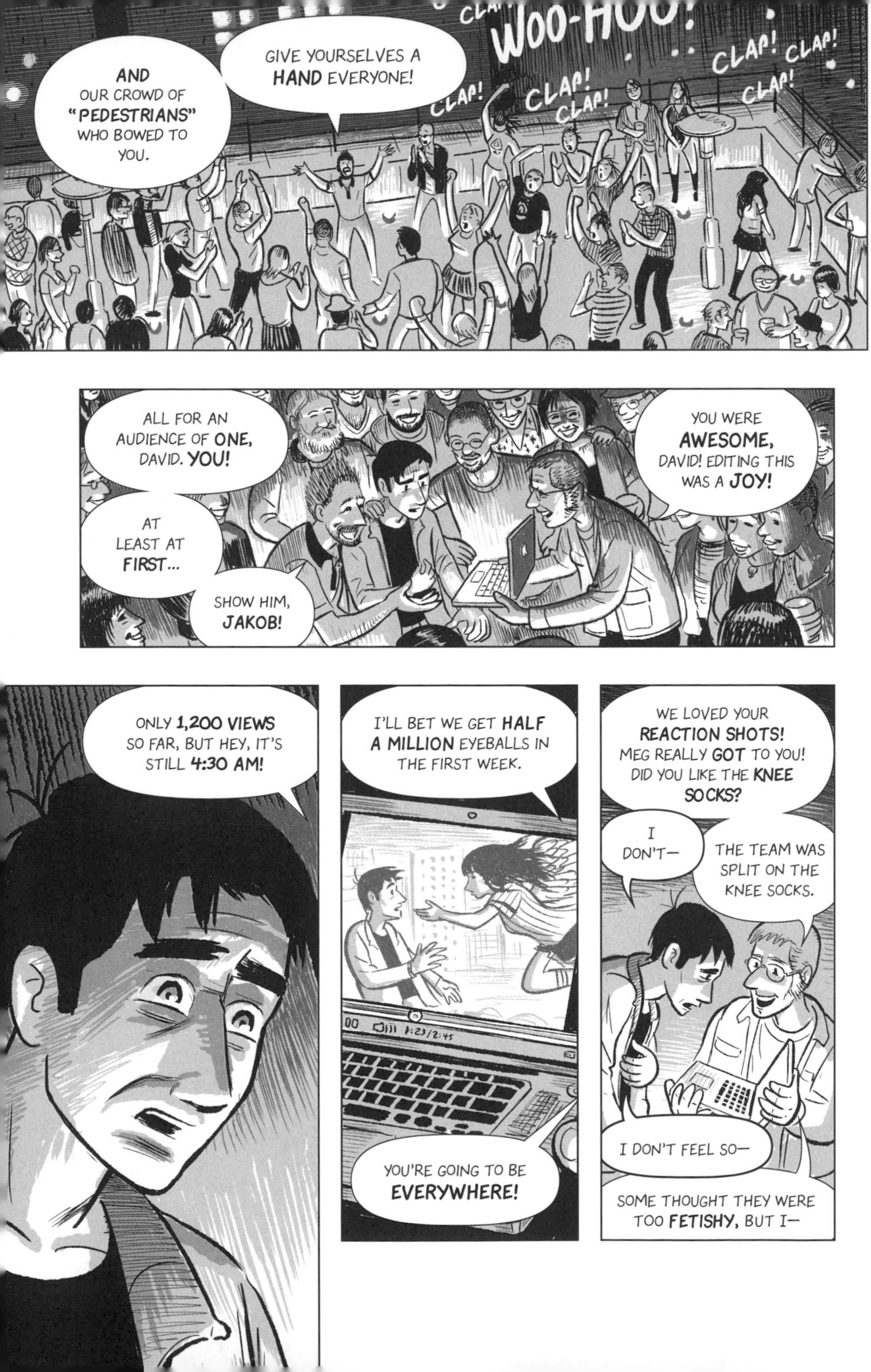
CLAP!
WOO-HOO!
AND OUR CROWD OF "PEDESTRIANS" WHO BOWED TO YOU.
GIVE YOURSELVES A HAND EVERYONE!
CLAP!
CLAP! CLAP!
CLAP! CLAP!
CLAP!
ALL FOR AN AUDIENCE OF ONE, DAVID. YOU!
AT LEAST AT FIRST...
SHOW HIM, JAKOB!
YOU WERE AWESOME, DAVID! EDITING THIS WAS A JOY!
ONLY 1,200 VIEWS SO FAR, BUT HEY, IT'S STILL 4:30 AM!
I'LL BET WE GET HALF A MILLION EYEBALLS IN THE FIRST WEEK.
1:23/2:45
YOU'RE GOING TO BE EVERYWHERE!
WE LOVED YOUR REACTION SHOTS! MEG REALLY GOT TO YOU! DID YOU LIKE THE KNEE SOCKS?
I DON'T—
THE TEAM WAS SPLIT ON THE KNEE SOCKS.
I DON'T FEEL SO—
SOME THOUGHT THEY WERE TOO FETISHY, BUT I—

BLARRR!!

HOLY SHIT!

NO! NOT THE MACBOOK! NOT THE MACBOOK!

OH MY GOD!

HA! HA!

ᴇHGKᴇ YOU **SICK BASTARDS!!** WHAT HAVE YOU DONE TO ME??

DAVID, **PLEASE!** WE'RE NOT YOUR ENEMY.

DUDE, SERIOUSLY, **CALM DOWN!**

OH NO...

IT'S NOT STARTING!

IT'S **NOT** STARTING!

TAP! TAP! TAP!

GET OFF ME!

DAVID, PLEASE!

OKAY, **CALM DOWN** BUDDY

SHIT, HE'S FLIPPING OUT!

I HAD A **REASON** TO BE **SAD,** YOU **ASSHOLES!!**

CALM DOWN!

OW!

HEY!

HE HIT **BOBBY!**

—POWER-TRIPPING, MANIPULATIVE...

FUCK YOU! FUCK YOU!

PICKED A CRAZY ONE!

LET GO OF ME!

THAT' ENOUG

GET HIM **OUT OF HERE!**

OUT! NOW!!

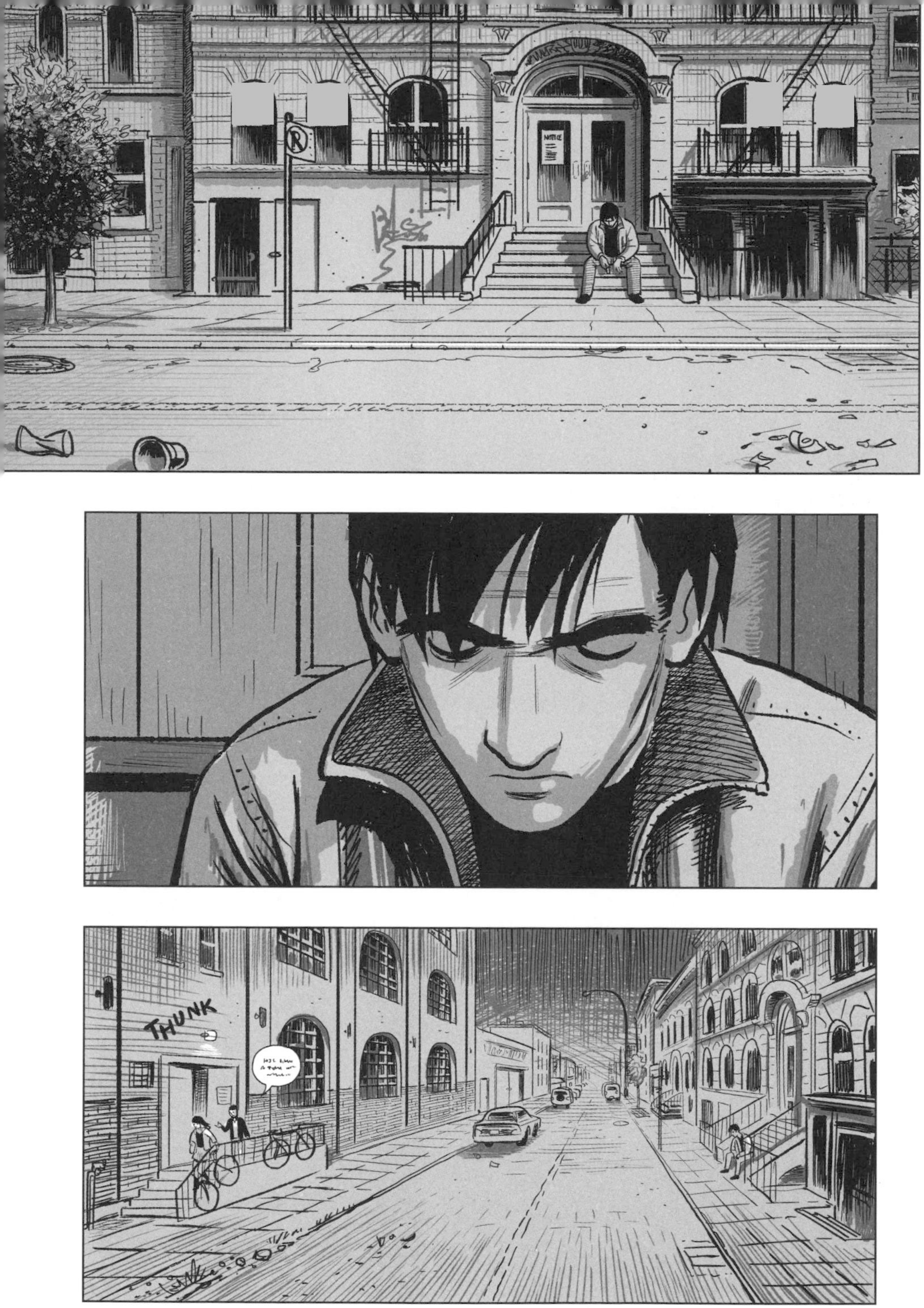
NOTICE
THUNK

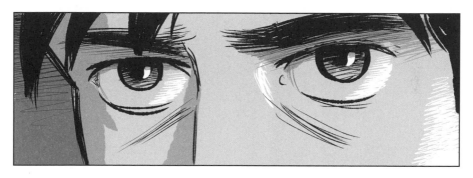

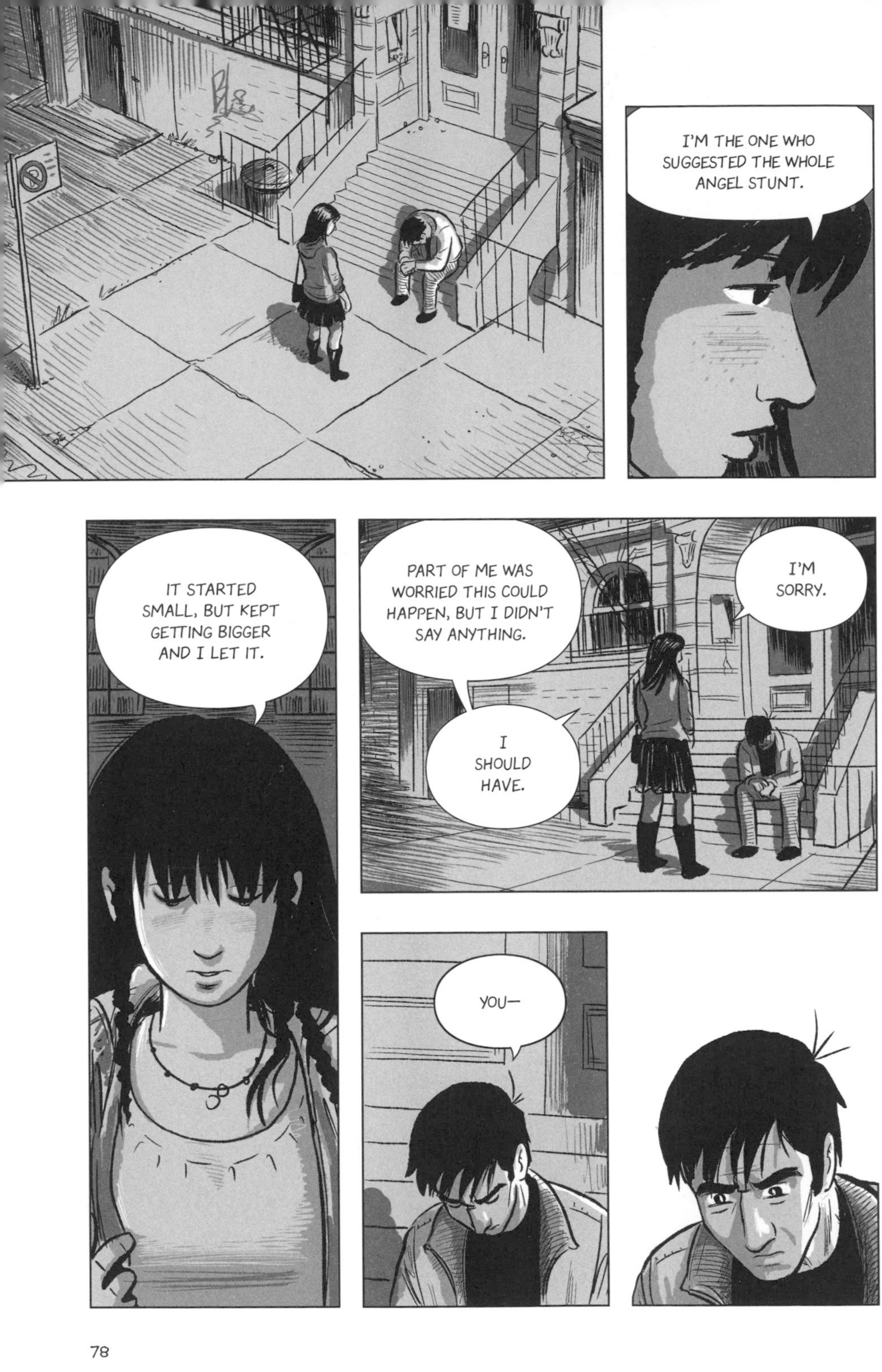
I'M THE ONE WHO SUGGESTED THE WHOLE ANGEL STUNT.
IT STARTED SMALL, BUT KEPT GETTING BIGGER AND I LET IT.
PART OF ME WAS WORRIED THIS COULD HAPPEN, BUT I DIDN'T SAY ANYTHING.
I SHOULD HAVE.
I'M SORRY.
YOU—

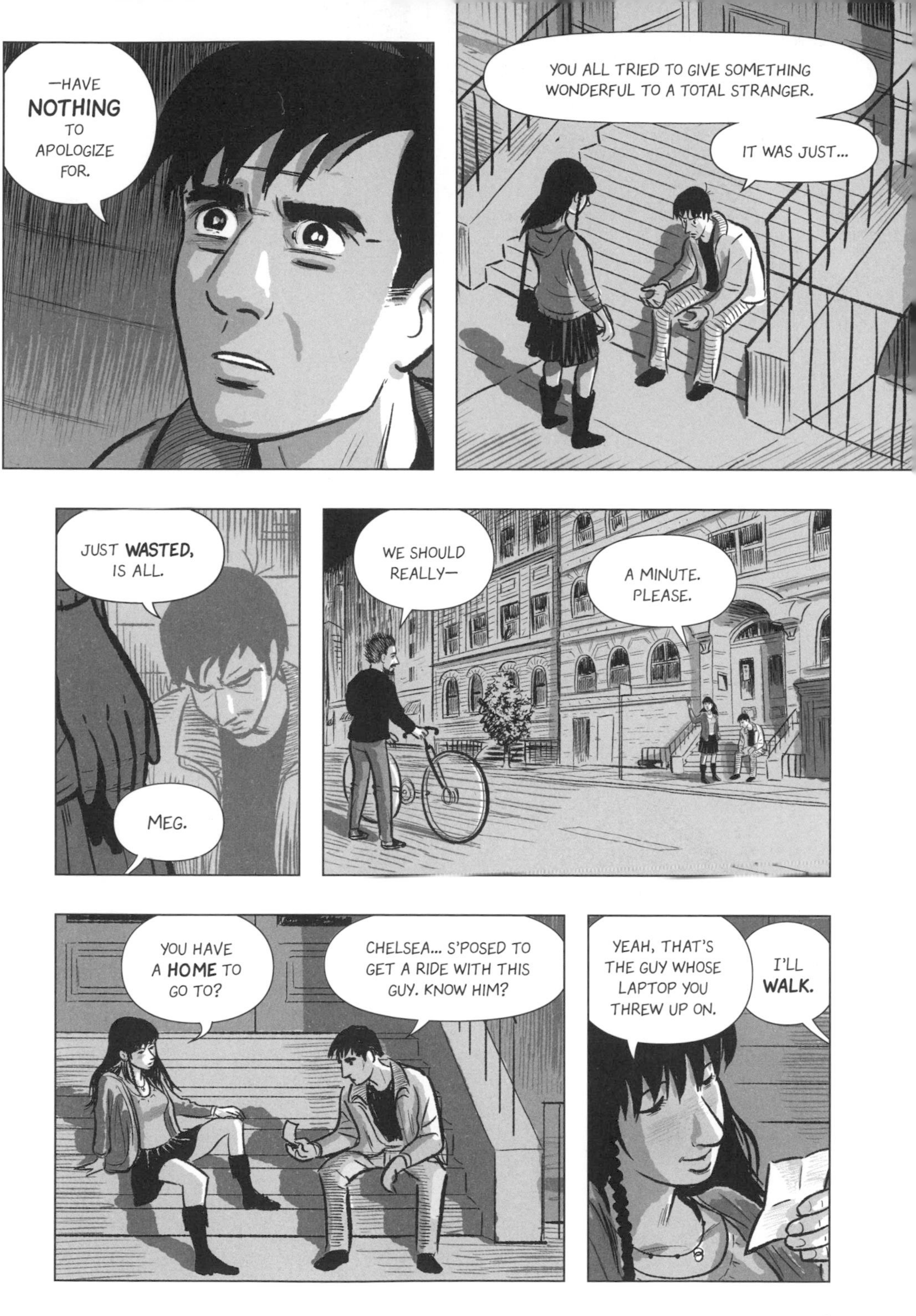
—HAVE NOTHING TO APOLOGIZE FOR.
YOU ALL TRIED TO GIVE SOMETHING WONDERFUL TO A TOTAL STRANGER.
IT WAS JUST...
JUST WASTED, IS ALL.
MEG.
WE SHOULD REALLY—
A MINUTE. PLEASE.
YOU HAVE A HOME TO GO TO?
CHELSEA... S'POSED TO GET A RIDE WITH THIS GUY. KNOW HIM?
YEAH, THAT'S THE GUY WHOSE LAPTOP YOU THREW UP ON.
I'LL WALK.

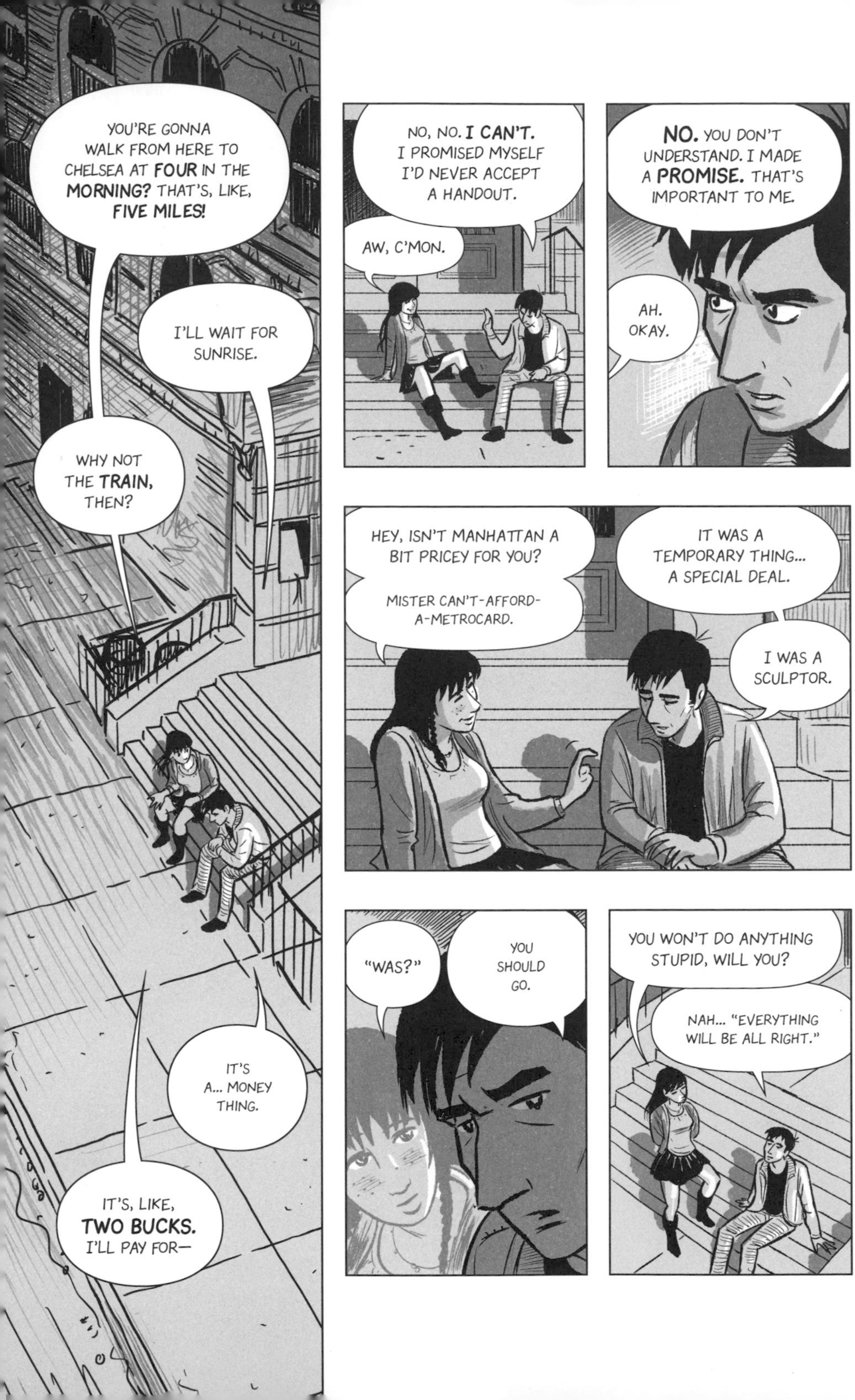
YOU'RE GONNA WALK FROM HERE TO CHELSEA AT FOUR IN THE MORNING? THAT'S, LIKE, FIVE MILES!
I'LL WAIT FOR SUNRISE.
WHY NOT THE TRAIN, THEN?
IT'S A... MONEY THING.
IT'S, LIKE, TWO BUCKS. I'LL PAY FOR—
NO, NO. I CAN'T. I PROMISED MYSELF I'D NEVER ACCEPT A HANDOUT.
AW, C'MON.
NO. YOU DON'T UNDERSTAND. I MADE A PROMISE. THAT'S IMPORTANT TO ME.
AH. OKAY.
HEY, ISN'T MANHATTAN A BIT PRICEY FOR YOU?
MISTER CAN'T-AFFORD-A-METROCARD.
IT WAS A TEMPORARY THING... A SPECIAL DEAL.
I WAS A SCULPTOR.
"WAS?"
YOU SHOULD GO.
YOU WON'T DO ANYTHING STUPID, WILL YOU?
NAH... "EVERYTHING WILL BE ALL RIGHT."

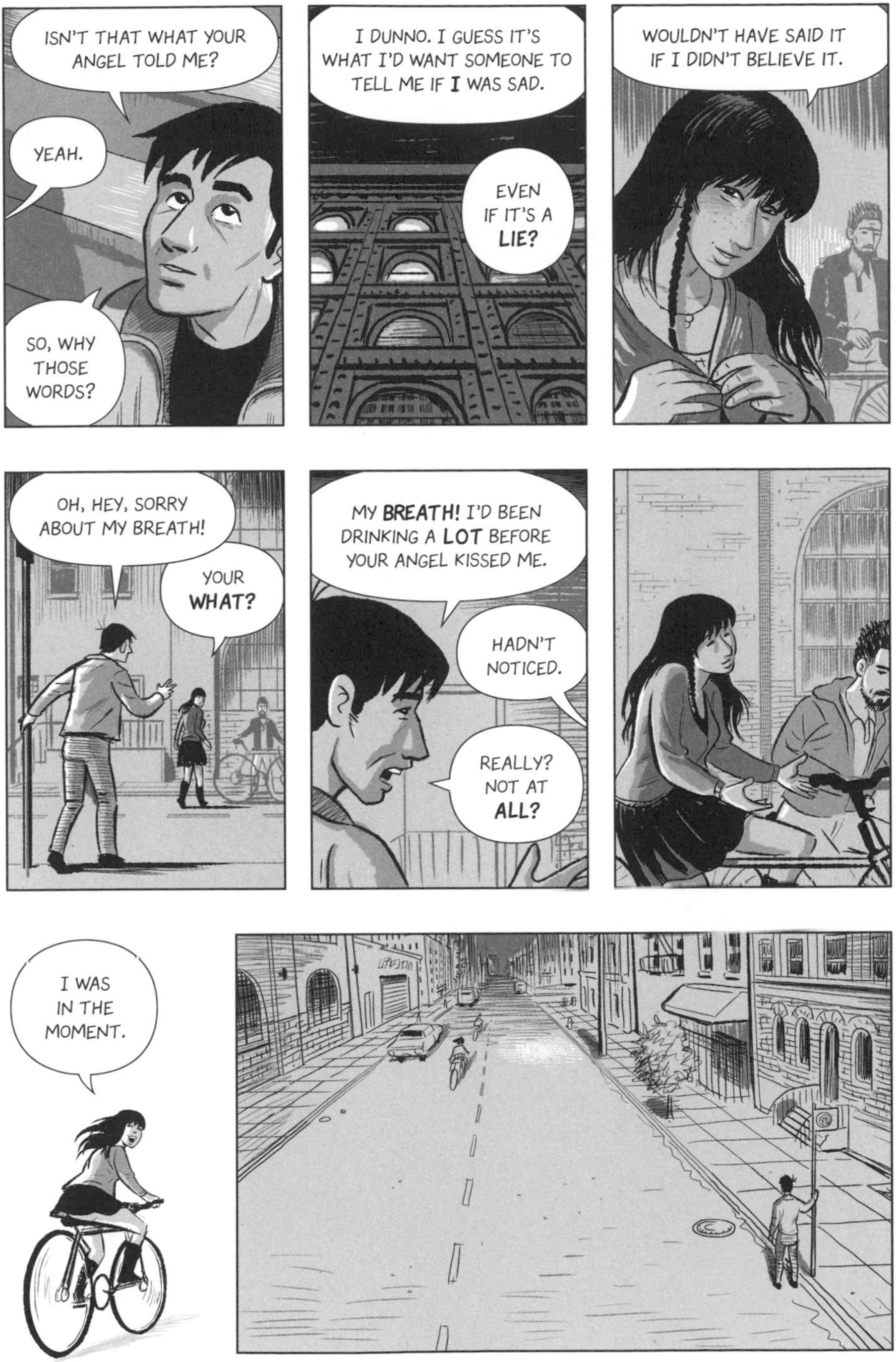
ISN'T THAT WHAT YOUR ANGEL TOLD ME?
YEAH.
SO, WHY THOSE WORDS?
I DUNNO. I GUESS IT'S WHAT I'D WANT SOMEONE TO TELL ME IF **I** WAS SAD.
EVEN IF IT'S A **LIE?**
WOULDN'T HAVE SAID IT IF I DIDN'T BELIEVE IT.
OH, HEY, SORRY ABOUT MY BREATH!
YOUR **WHAT?**
MY **BREATH!** I'D BEEN DRINKING A **LOT** BEFORE YOUR ANGEL KISSED ME.
HADN'T NOTICED.
REALLY? NOT AT **ALL?**
I WAS IN THE MOMENT.

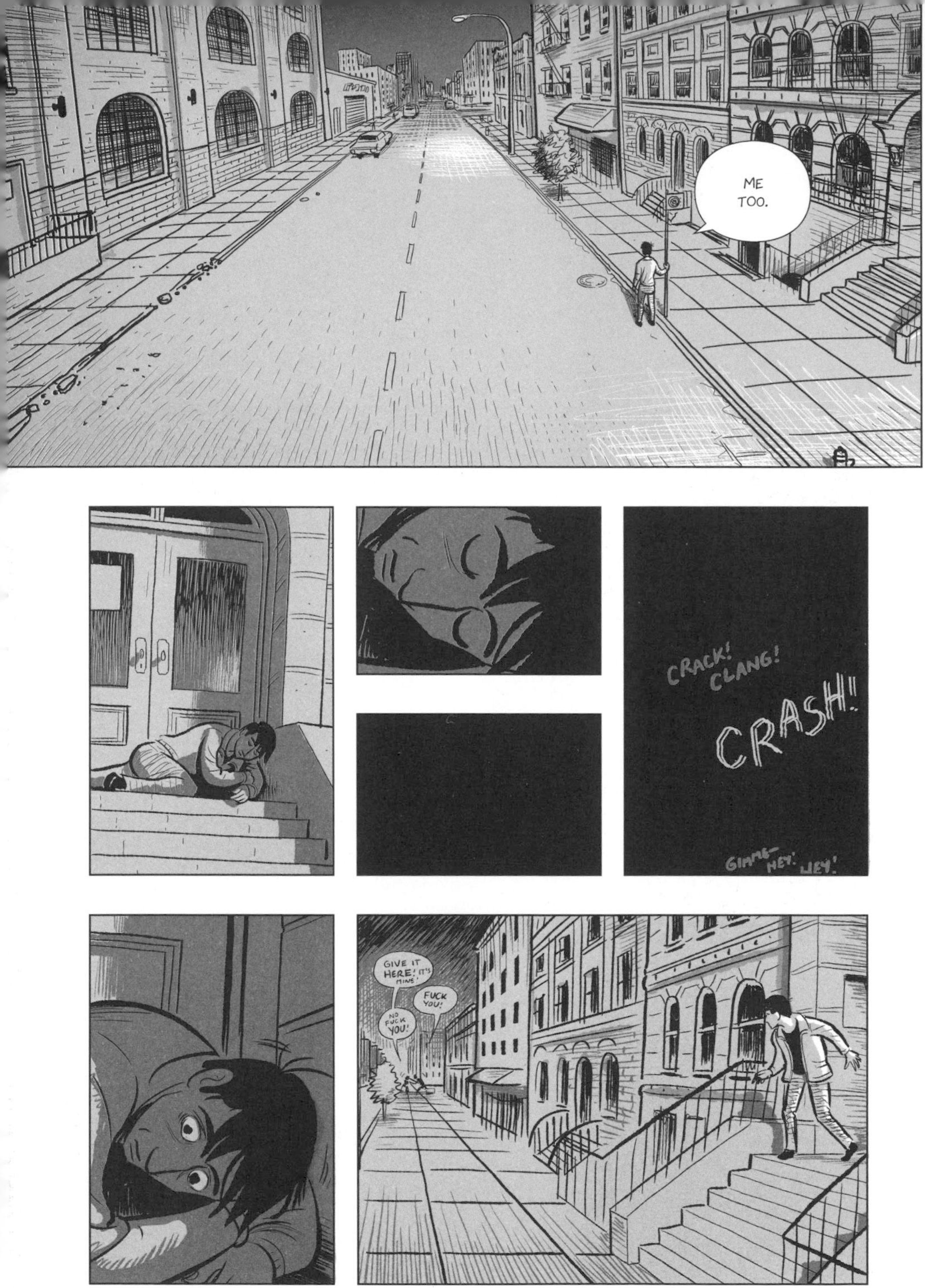
ME TOO.
CRACK! CLANG!
CRASH!!
GIMME—
HEY!
HEY!
GIVE IT HERE! IT'S MINE!
FUCK YOU!
NO FUCK YOU!

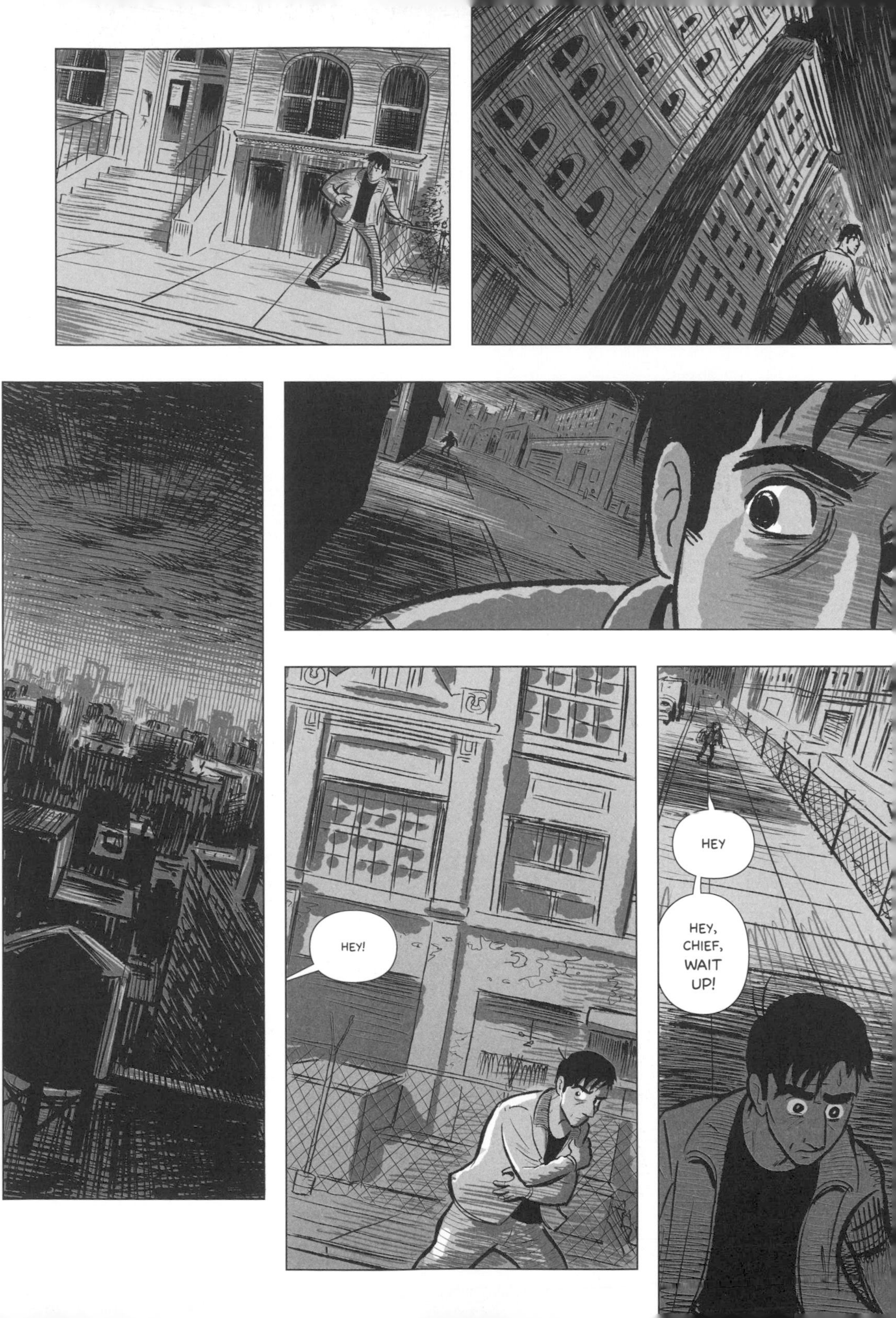
HEY!
HEY
HEY, CHIEF, WAIT UP!

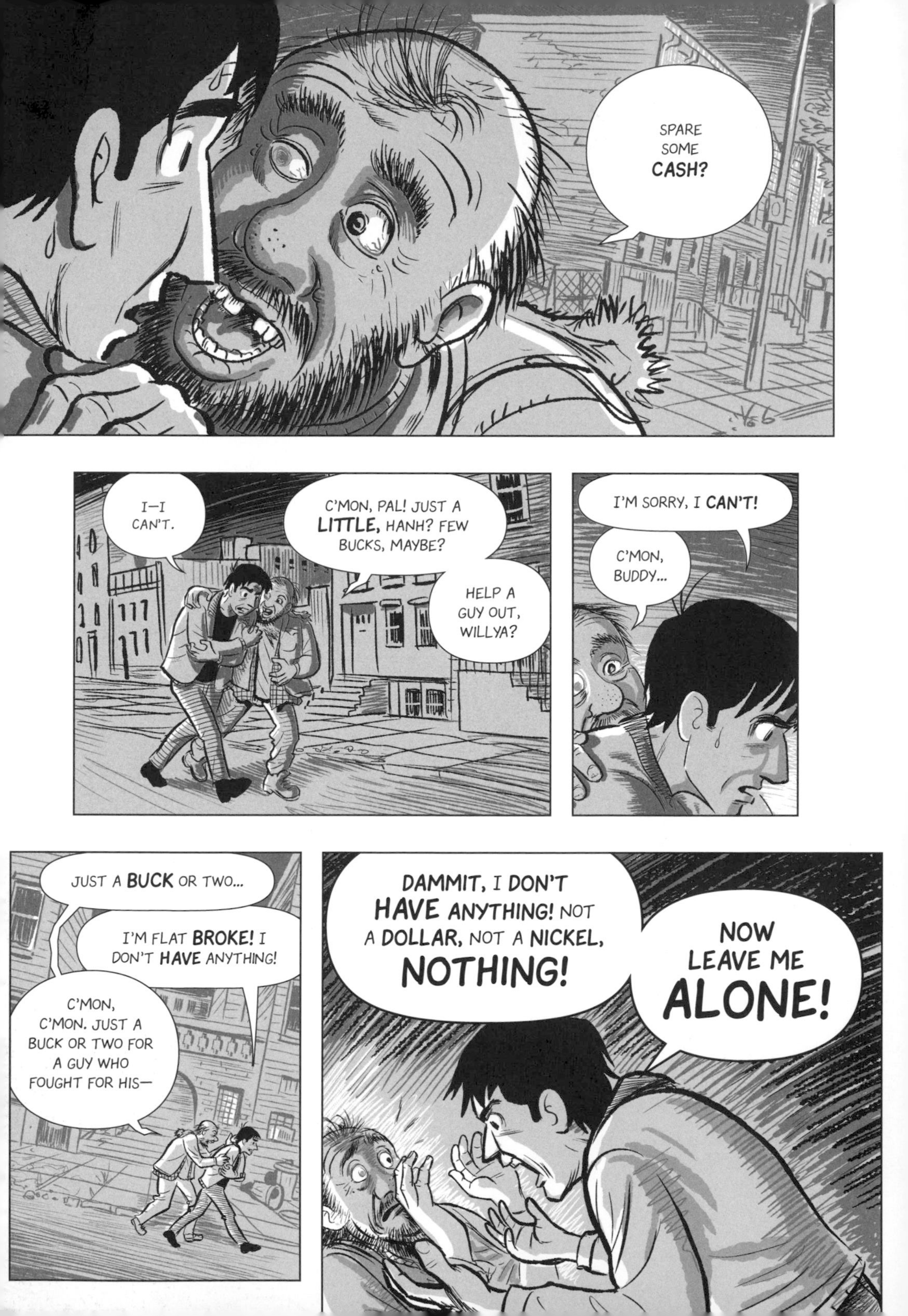
SPARE SOME CASH?
I—I CAN'T.
C'MON, PAL! JUST A LITTLE, HANH? FEW BUCKS, MAYBE?
HELP A GUY OUT, WILLYA?
I'M SORRY, I CAN'T!
C'MON, BUDDY...
JUST A BUCK OR TWO...
I'M FLAT BROKE! I DON'T HAVE ANYTHING!
C'MON, C'MON. JUST A BUCK OR TWO FOR A GUY WHO FOUGHT FOR HIS—
DAMMIT, I DON'T HAVE ANYTHING! NOT A DOLLAR, NOT A NICKEL, NOTHING!
NOW LEAVE ME ALONE!

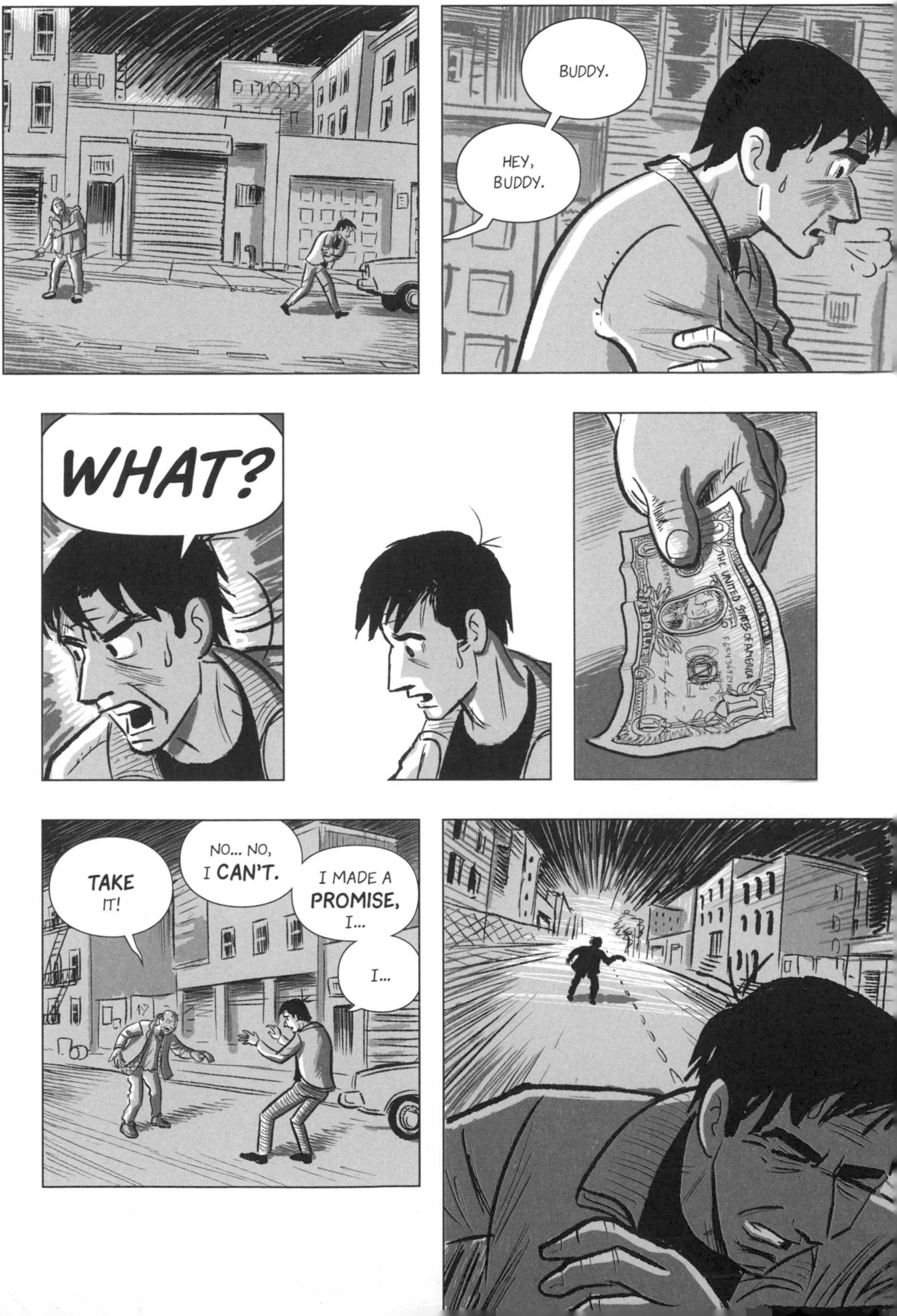
HEY, BUDDY.
BUDDY.
WHAT?
TAKE IT!
NO... NO, I CAN'T.
I MADE A PROMISE, I...
I...

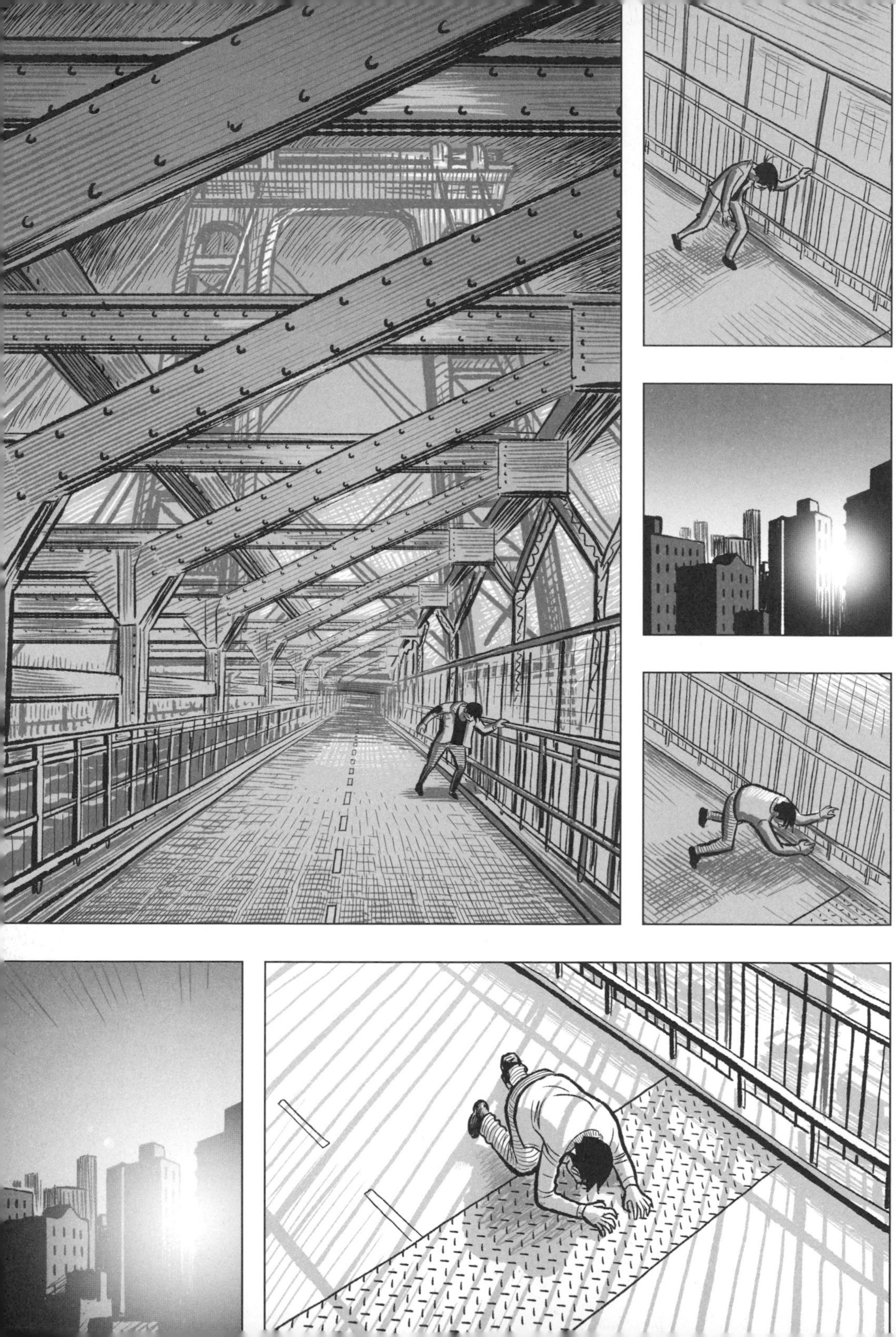

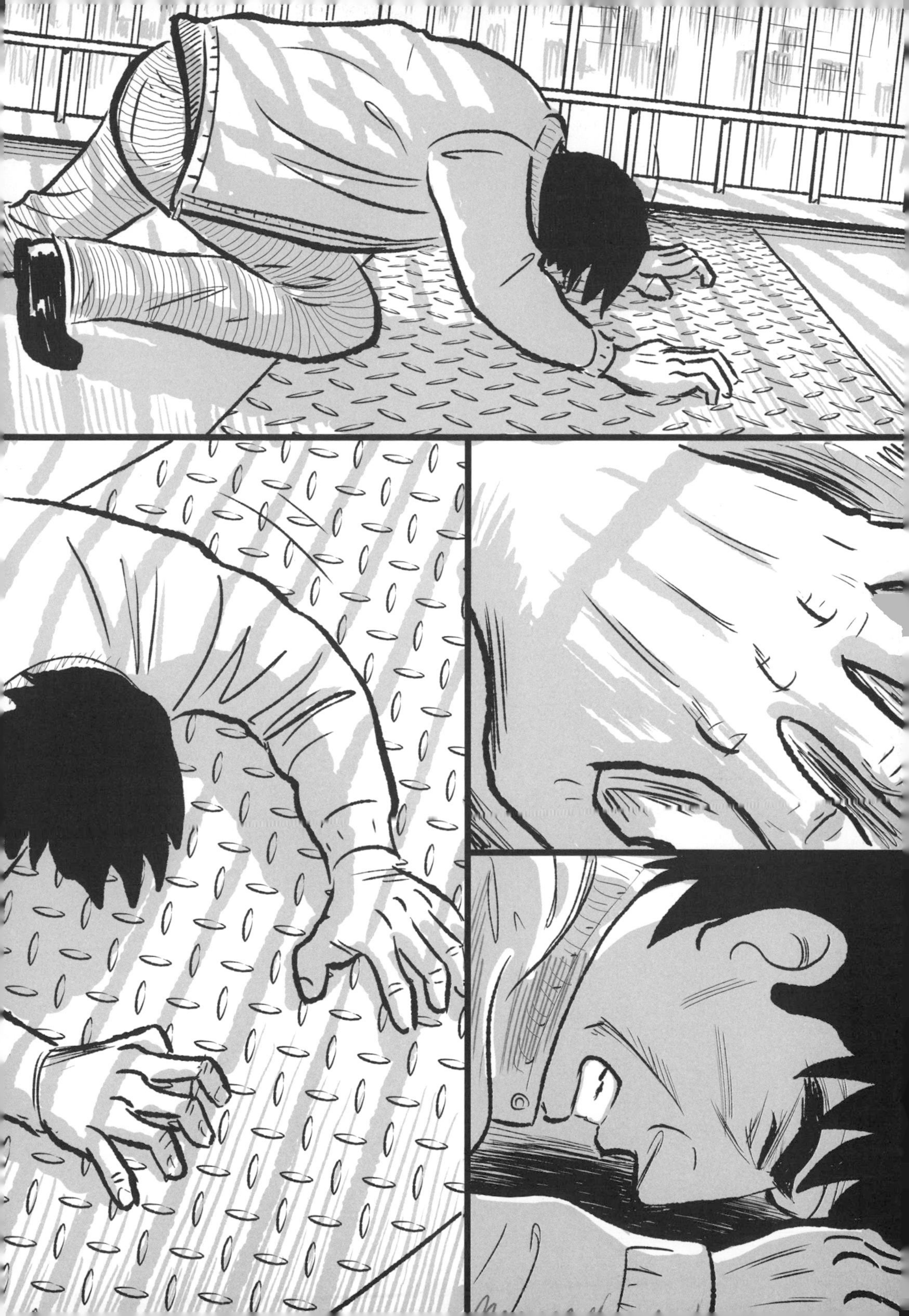

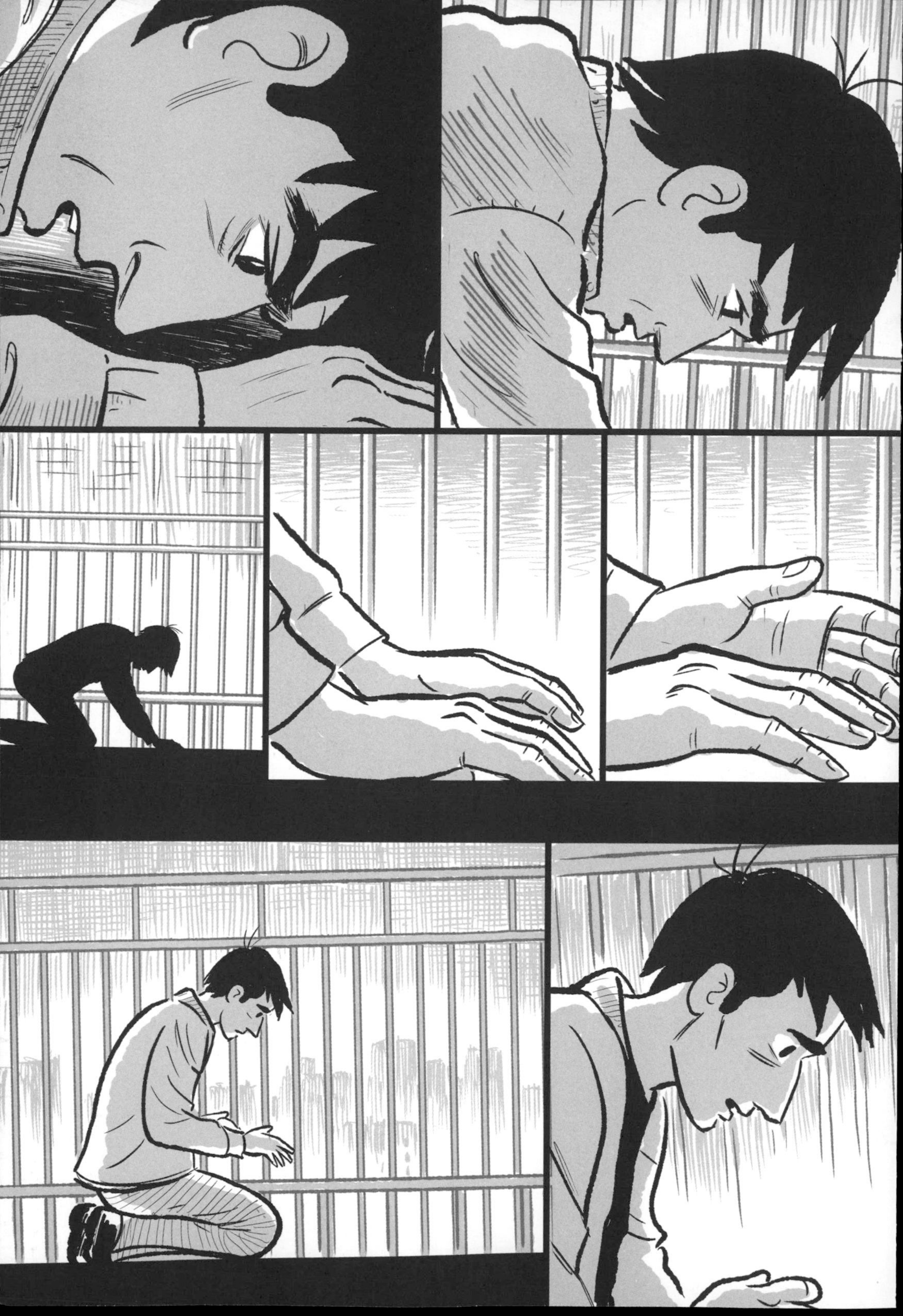

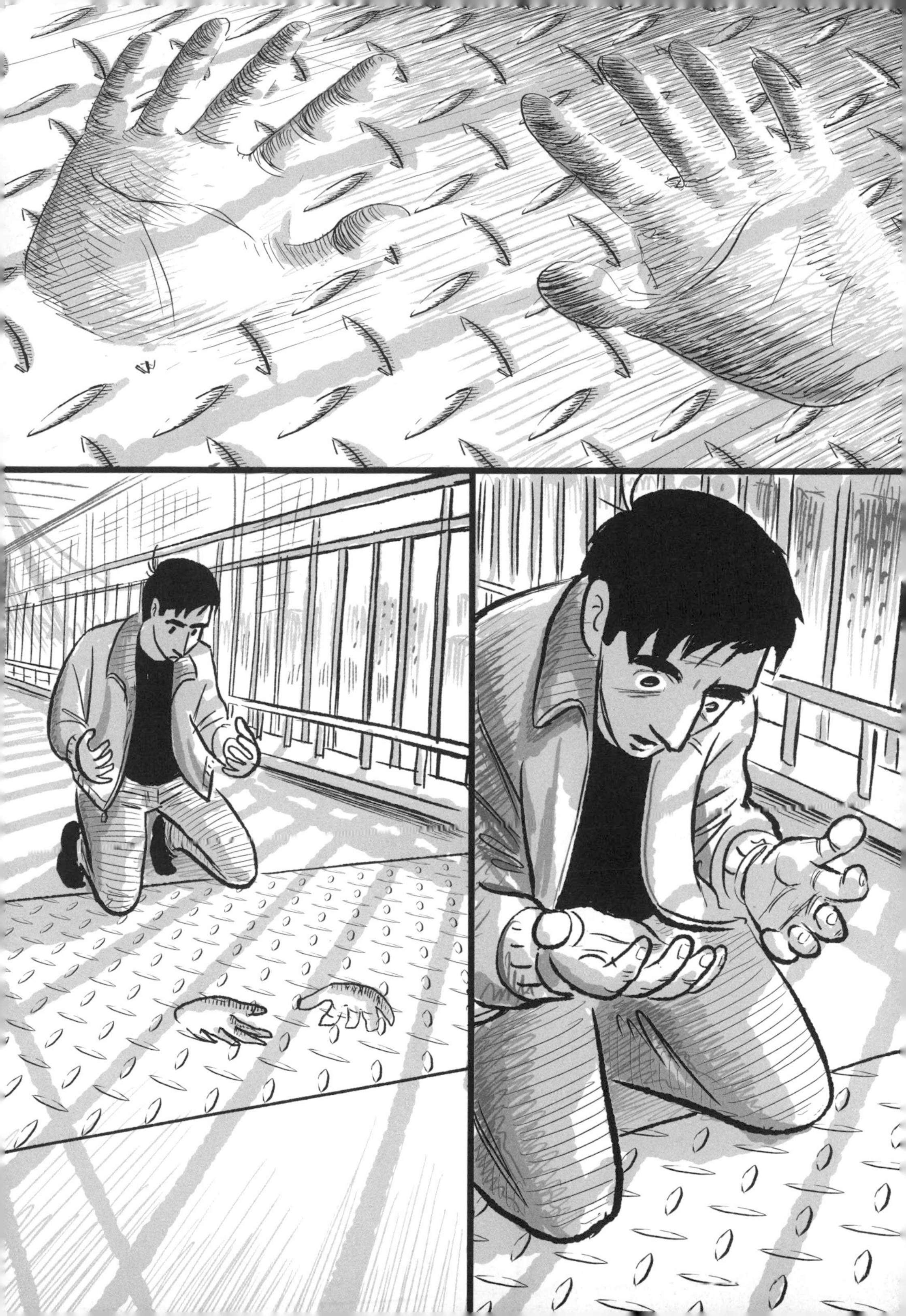

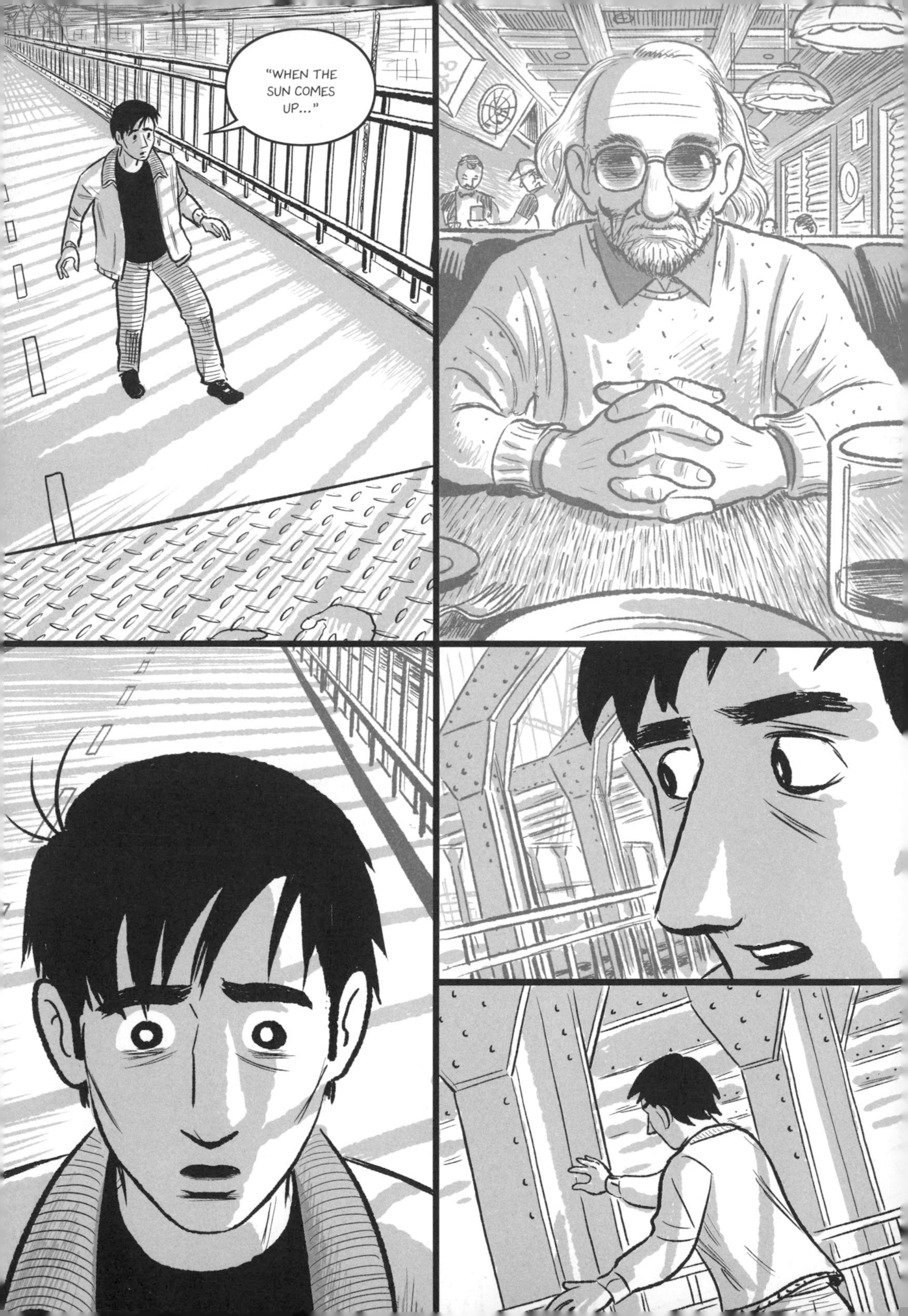
"WHEN THE SUN COMES UP..."

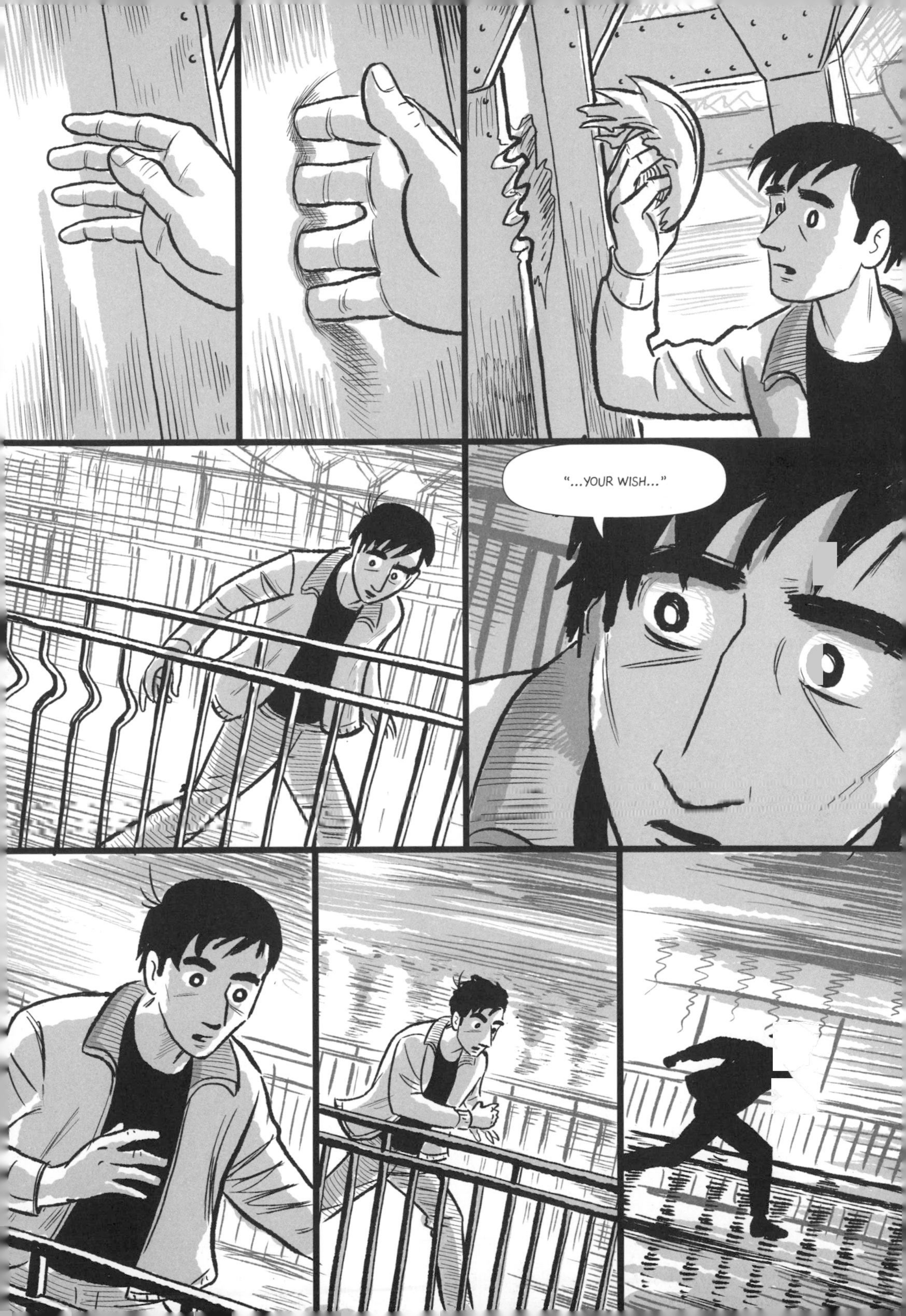
"...YOUR WISH..."

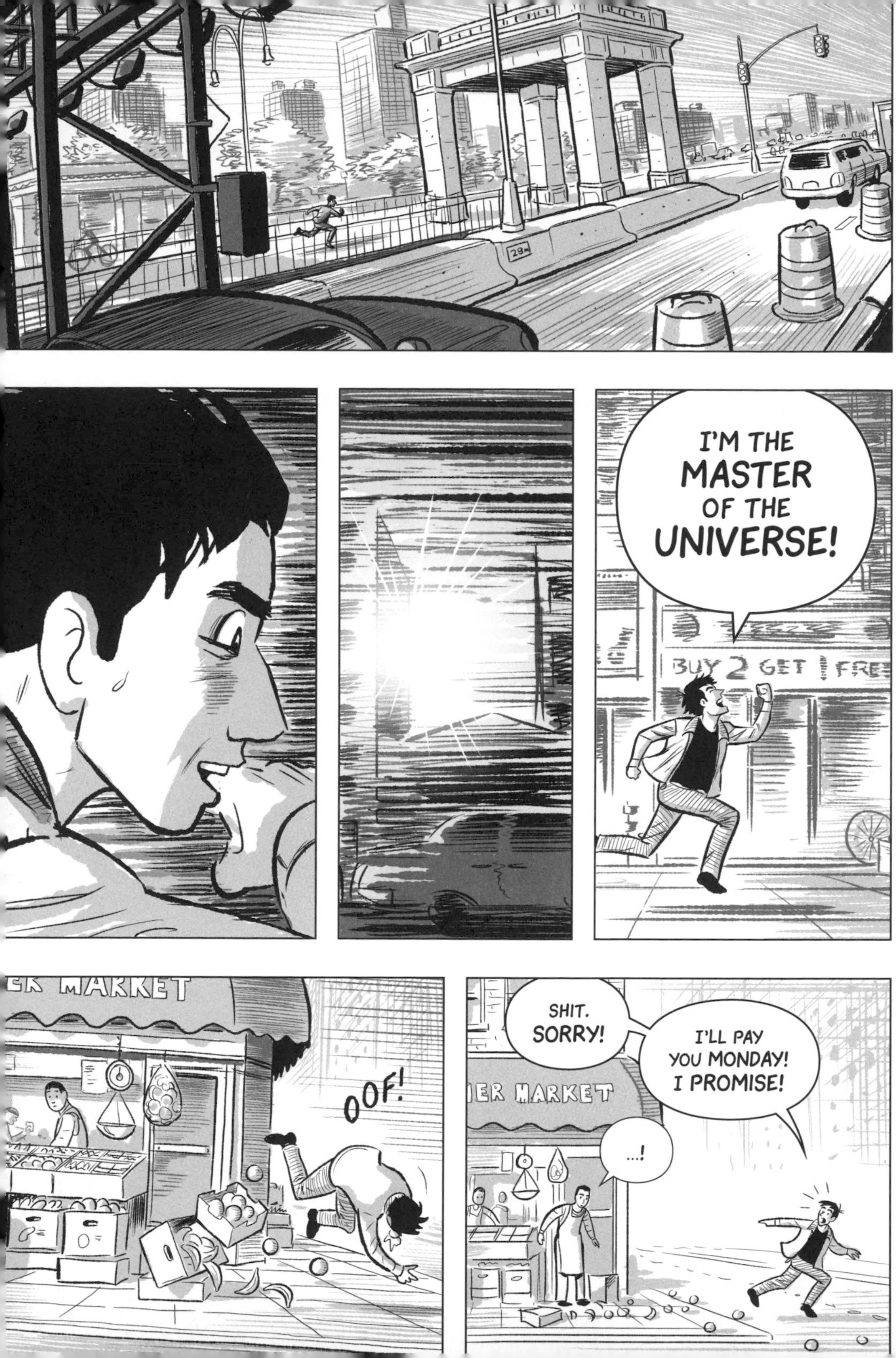
28N
I'M THE MASTER OF THE UNIVERSE!
BUY 2 GET 1 FRE
ER MARKET
OOF!
SHIT. SORRY!
I'LL PAY YOU MONDAY! I PROMISE!
ER MARKET
...!

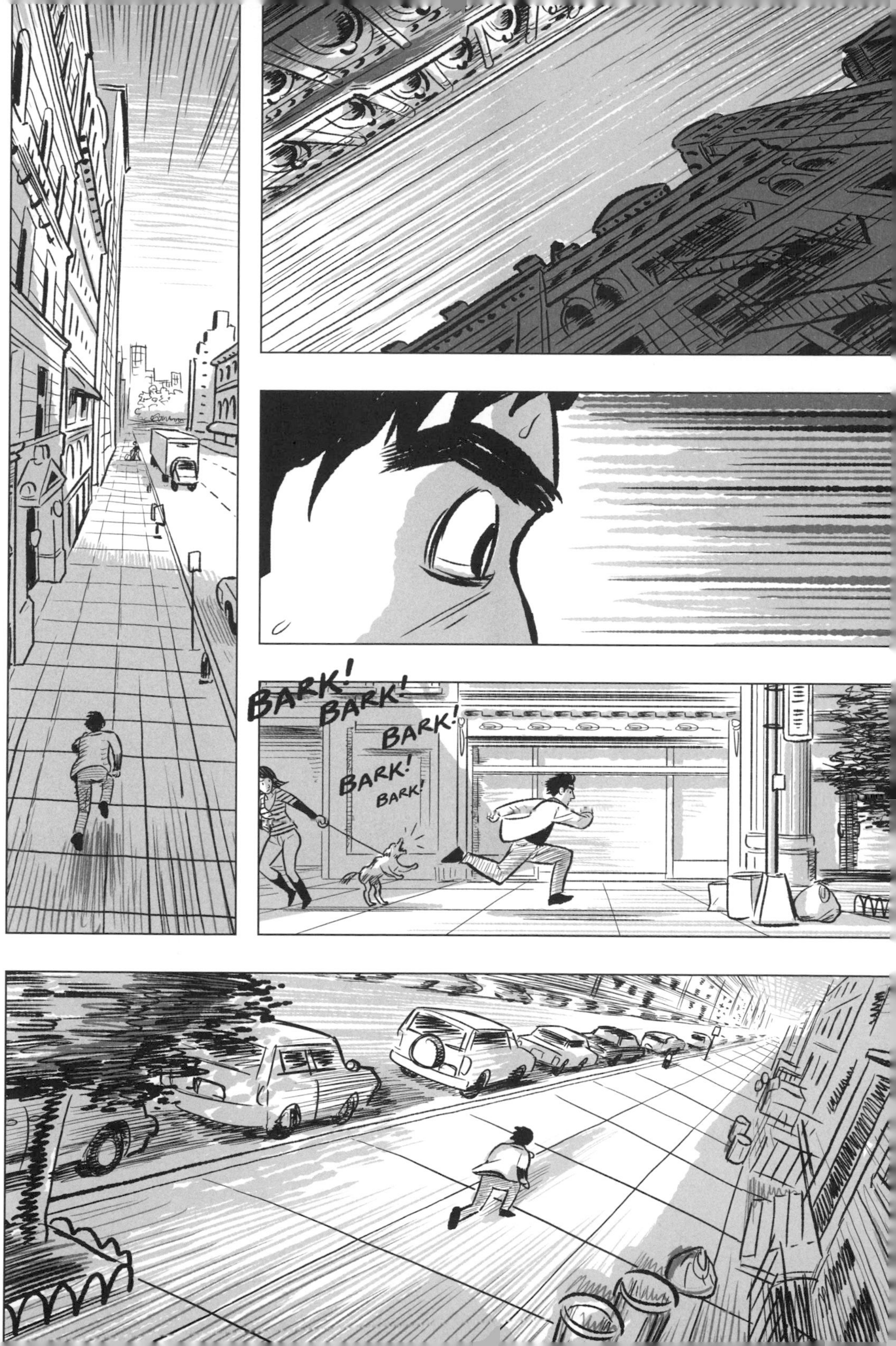
BARK!
BARK!
BARK!
BARK!
BARK!

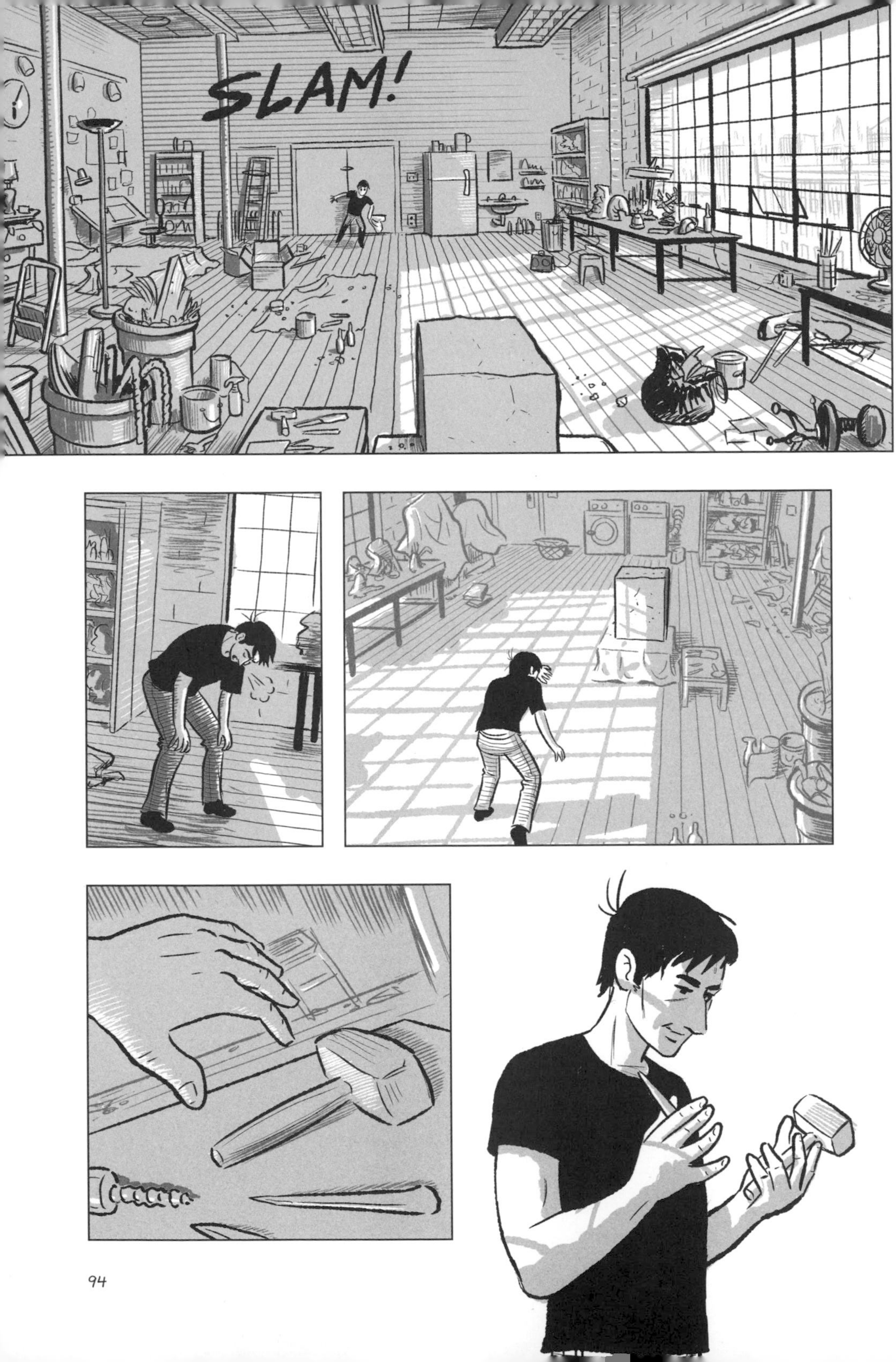
SLAM!

GRANITE...

YOU STUBBORN
OLD BASTARD.

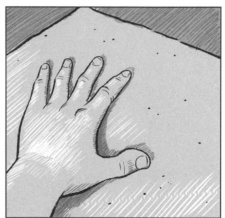

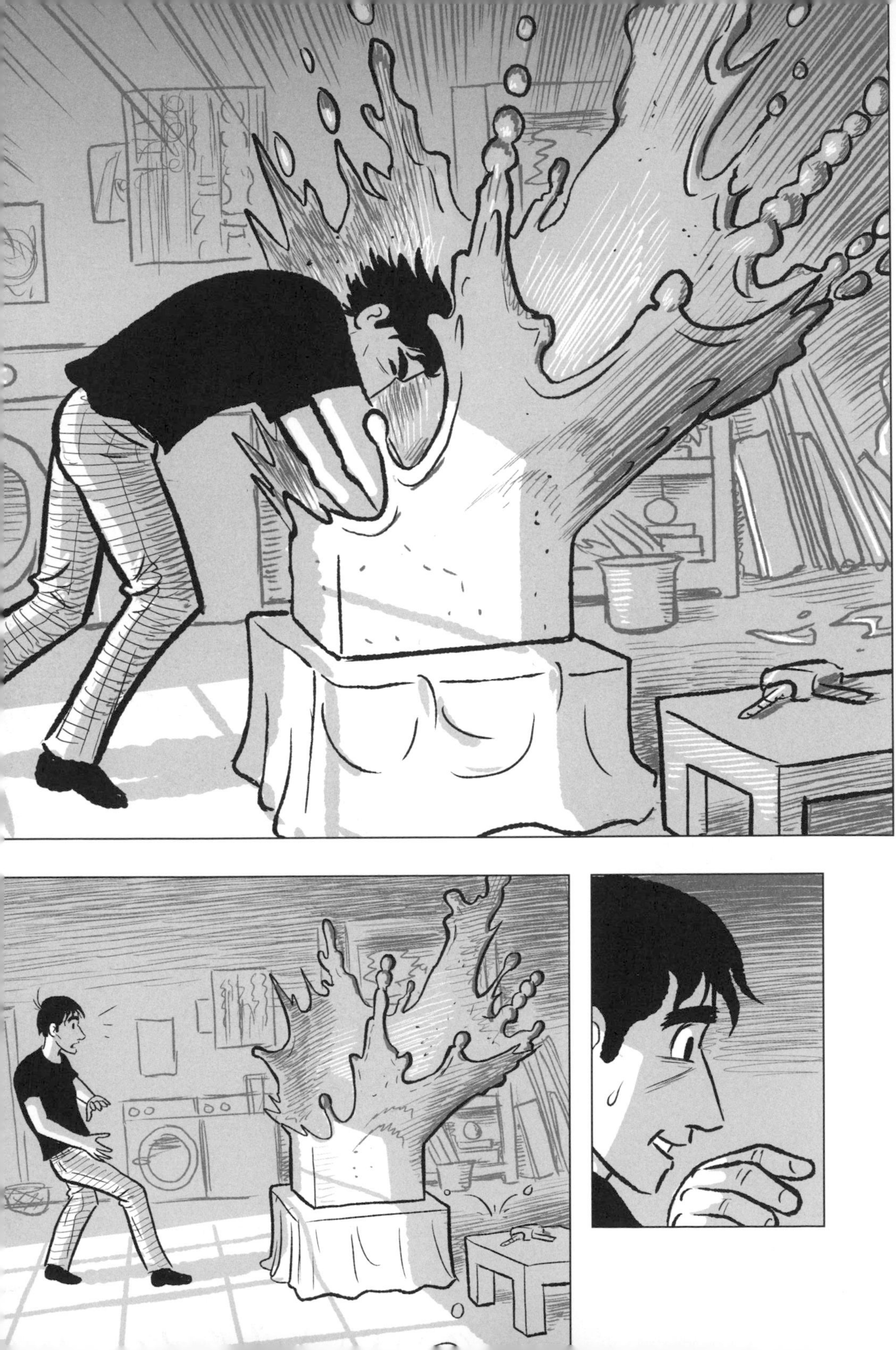

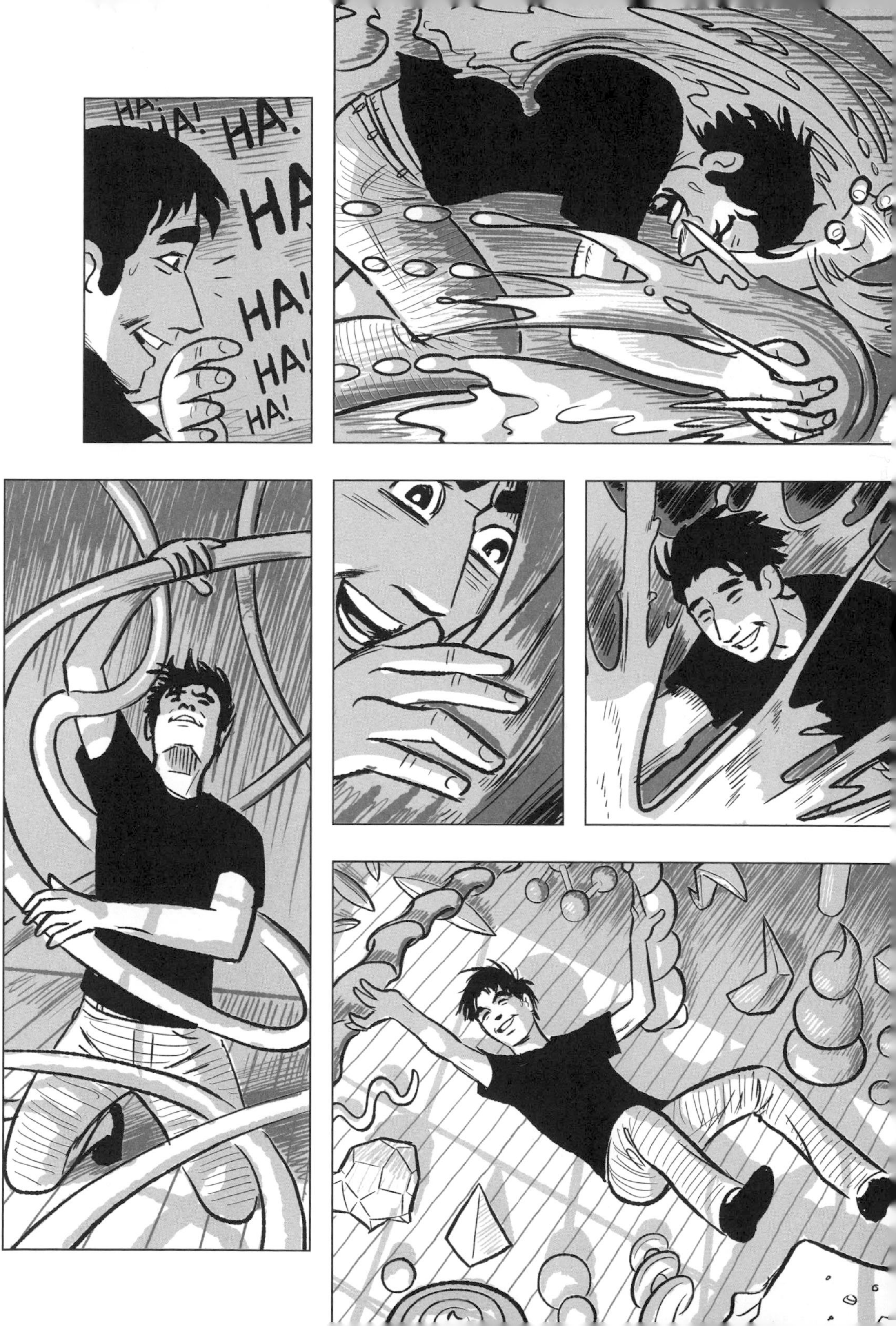
HA! HA! HA!
HA!
HA!
HA!
HA!

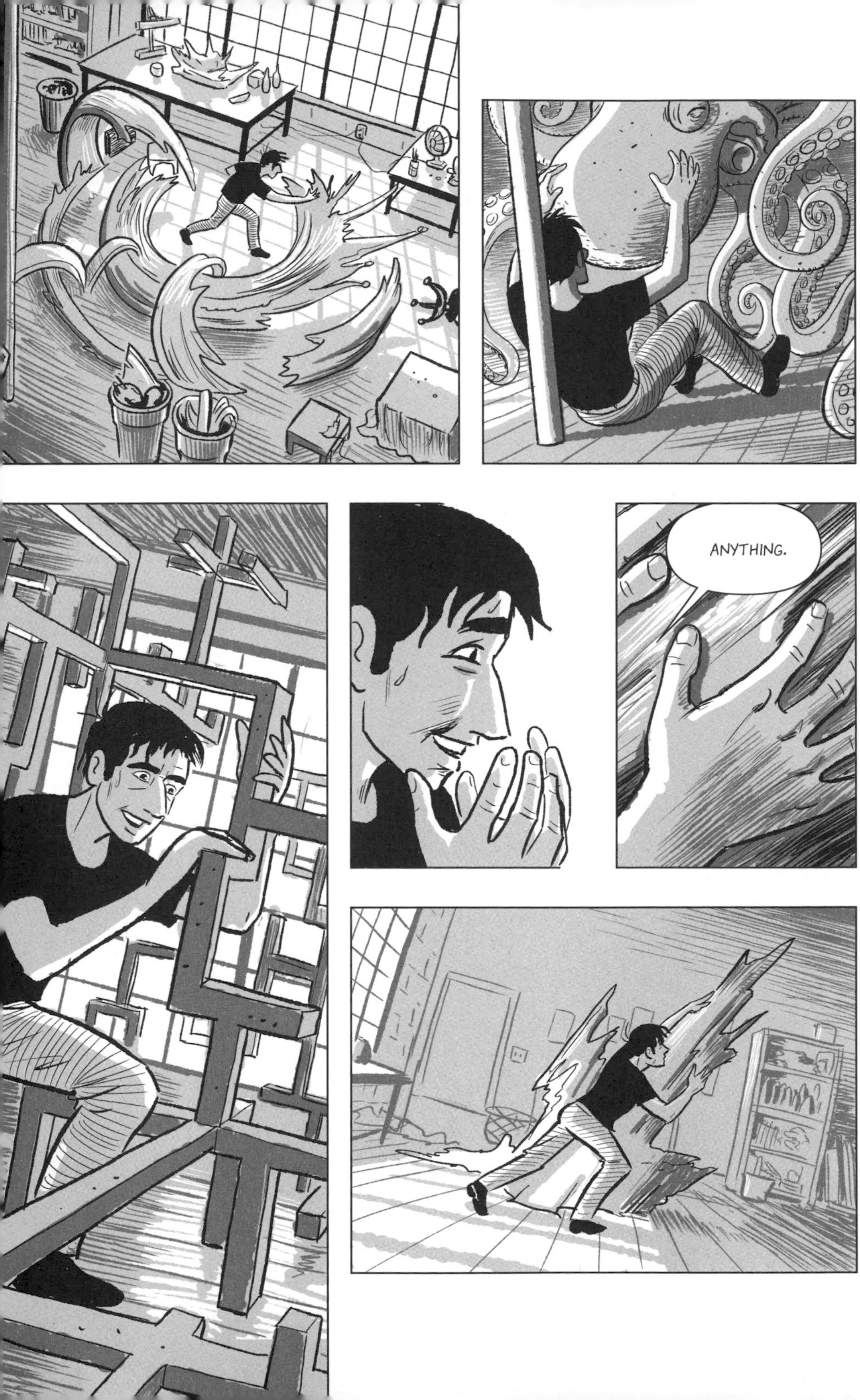
ANYTHING.

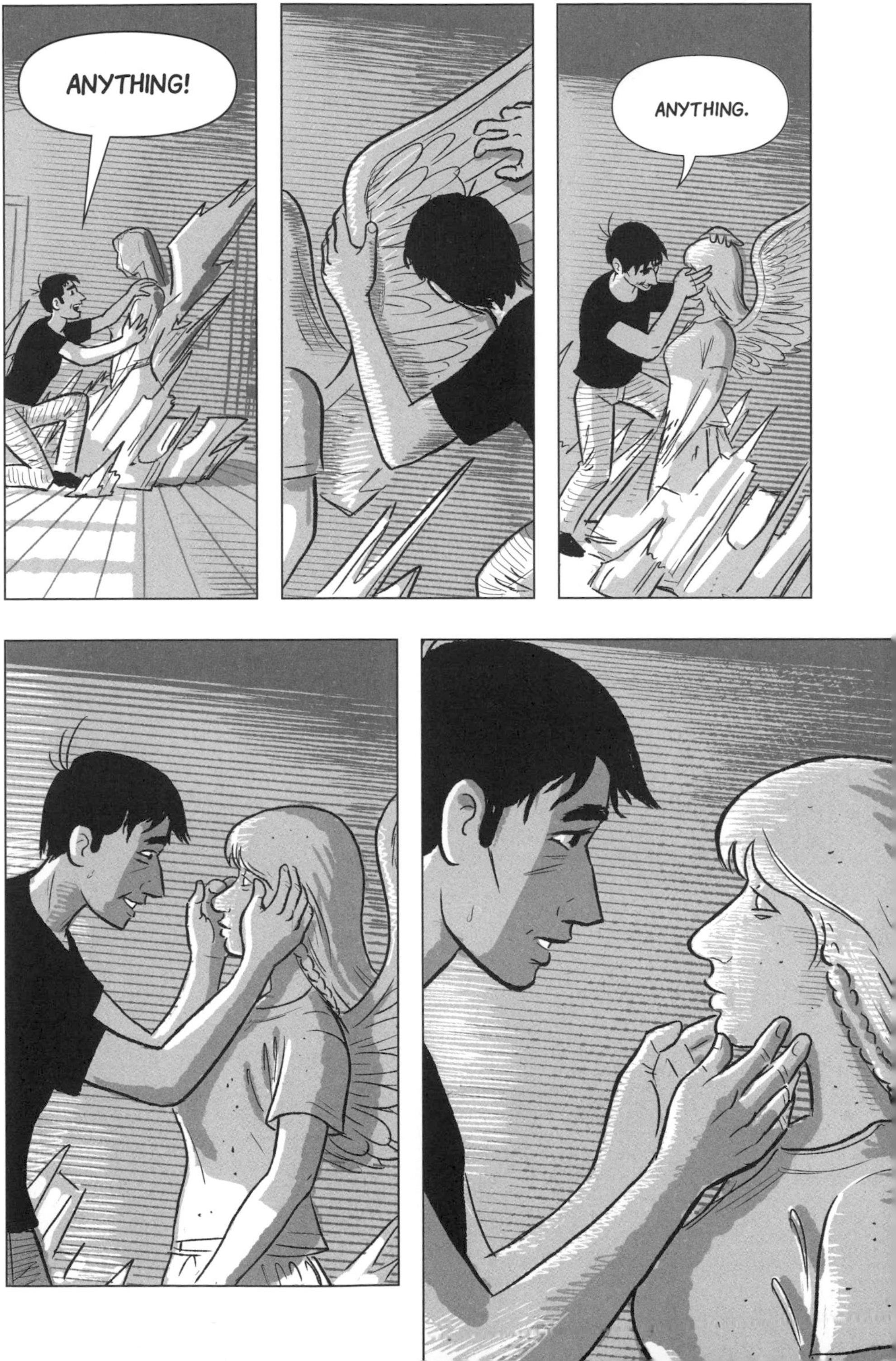
ANYTHING!
ANYTHING.

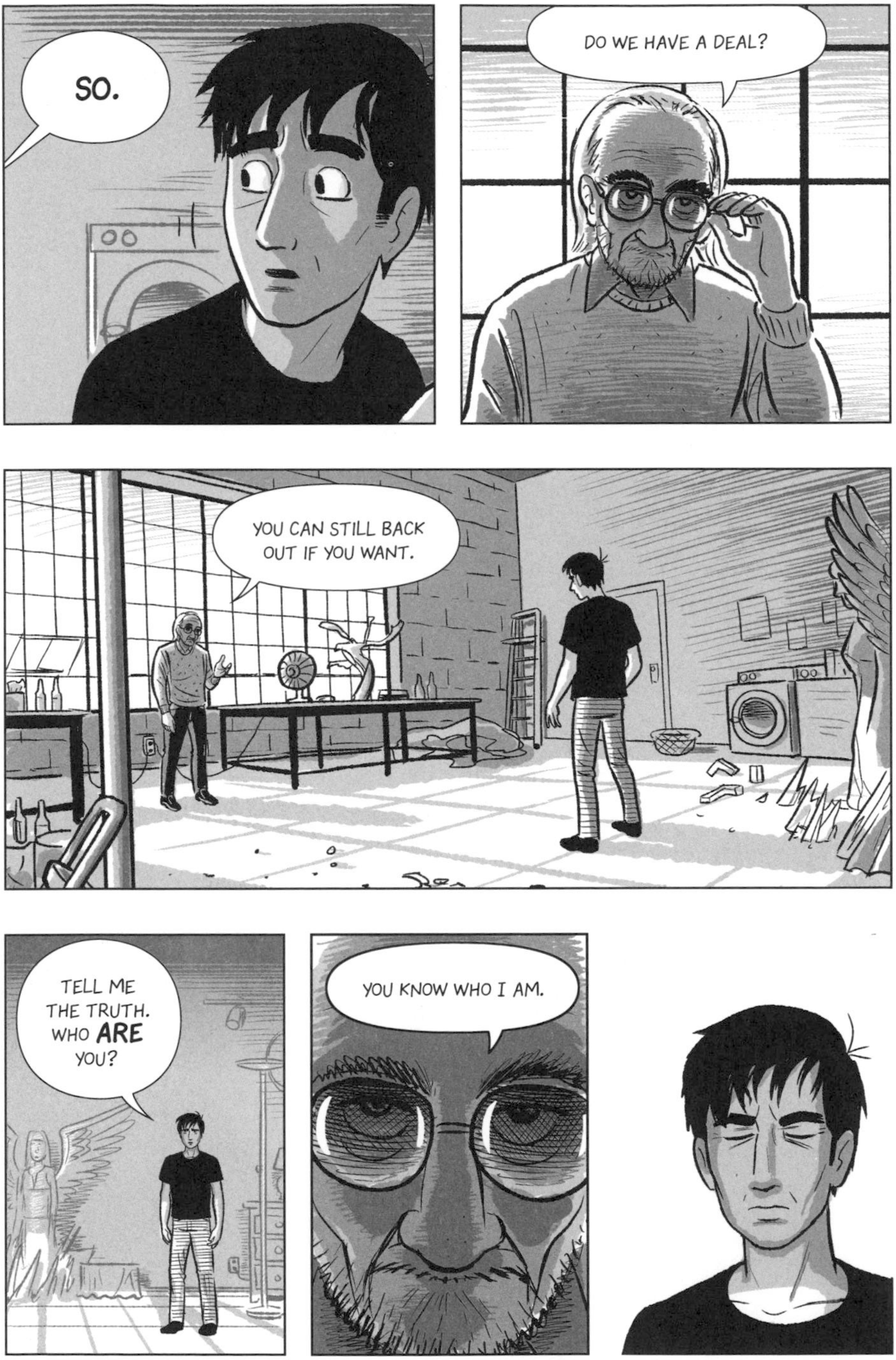
SO.
DO WE HAVE A DEAL?
YOU CAN STILL BACK OUT IF YOU WANT.
TELL ME THE TRUTH. WHO **ARE** YOU?
YOU KNOW WHO I AM.

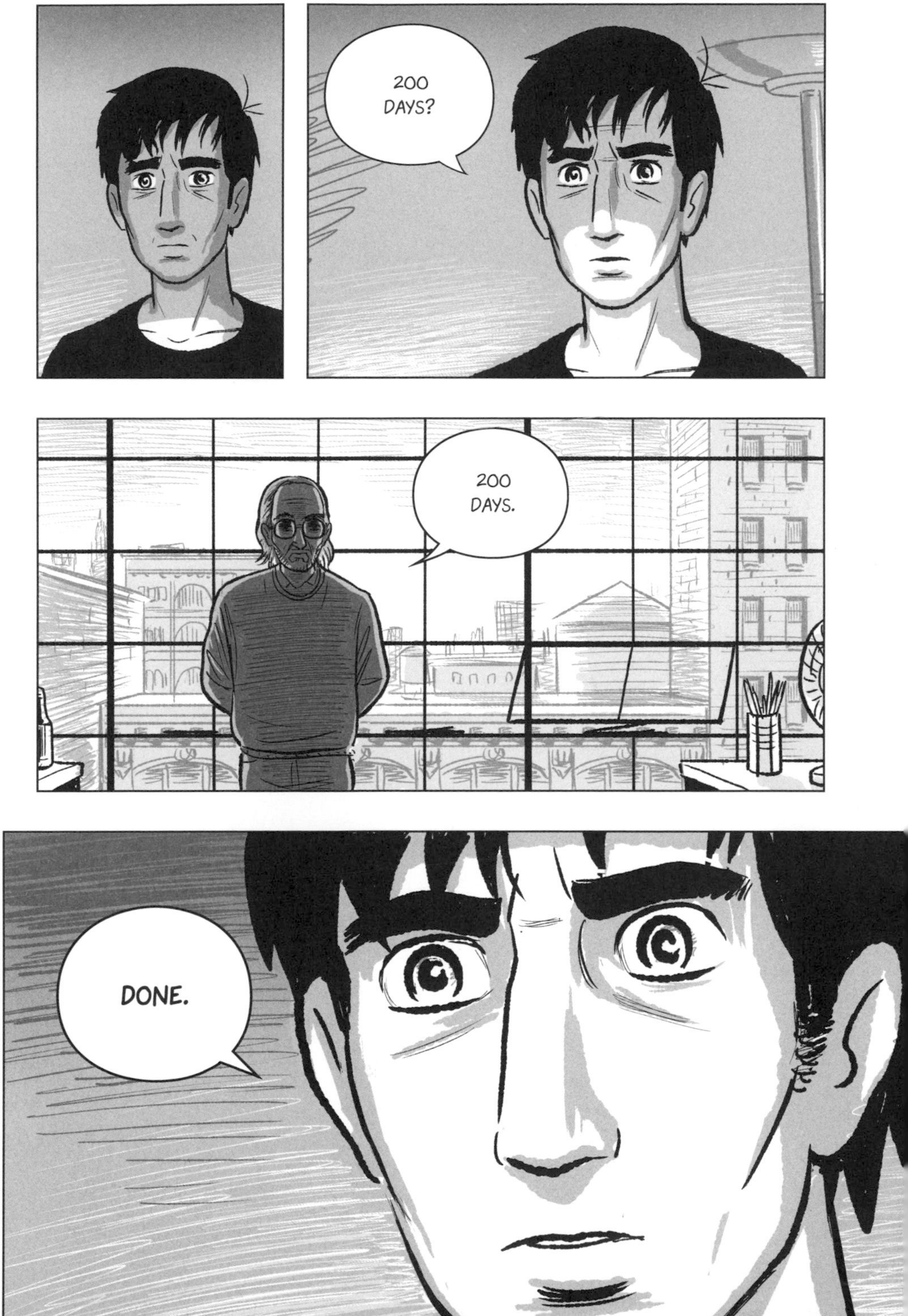
200 DAYS?
200 DAYS.
DONE.

2.

ALL OR NOTHING

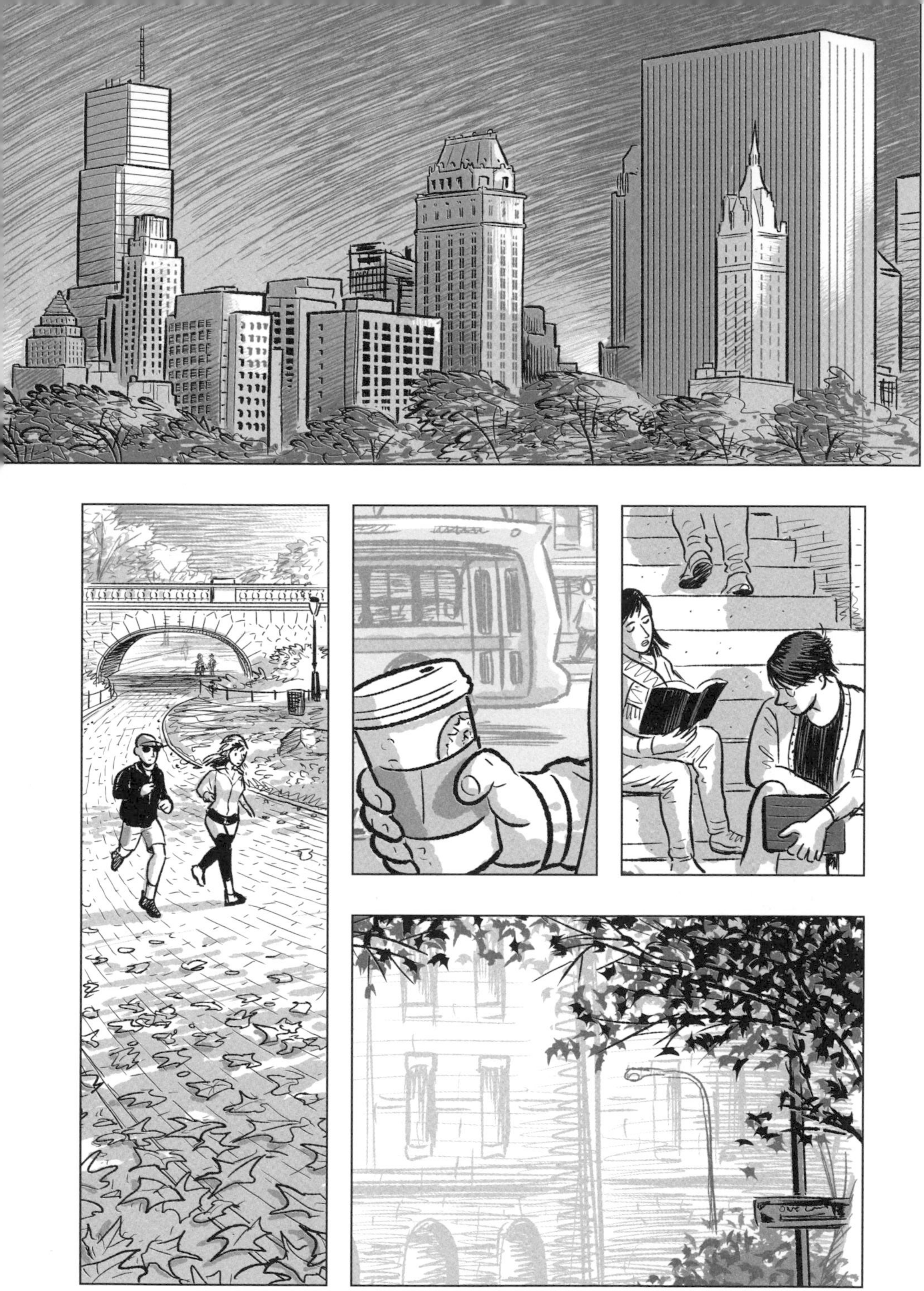

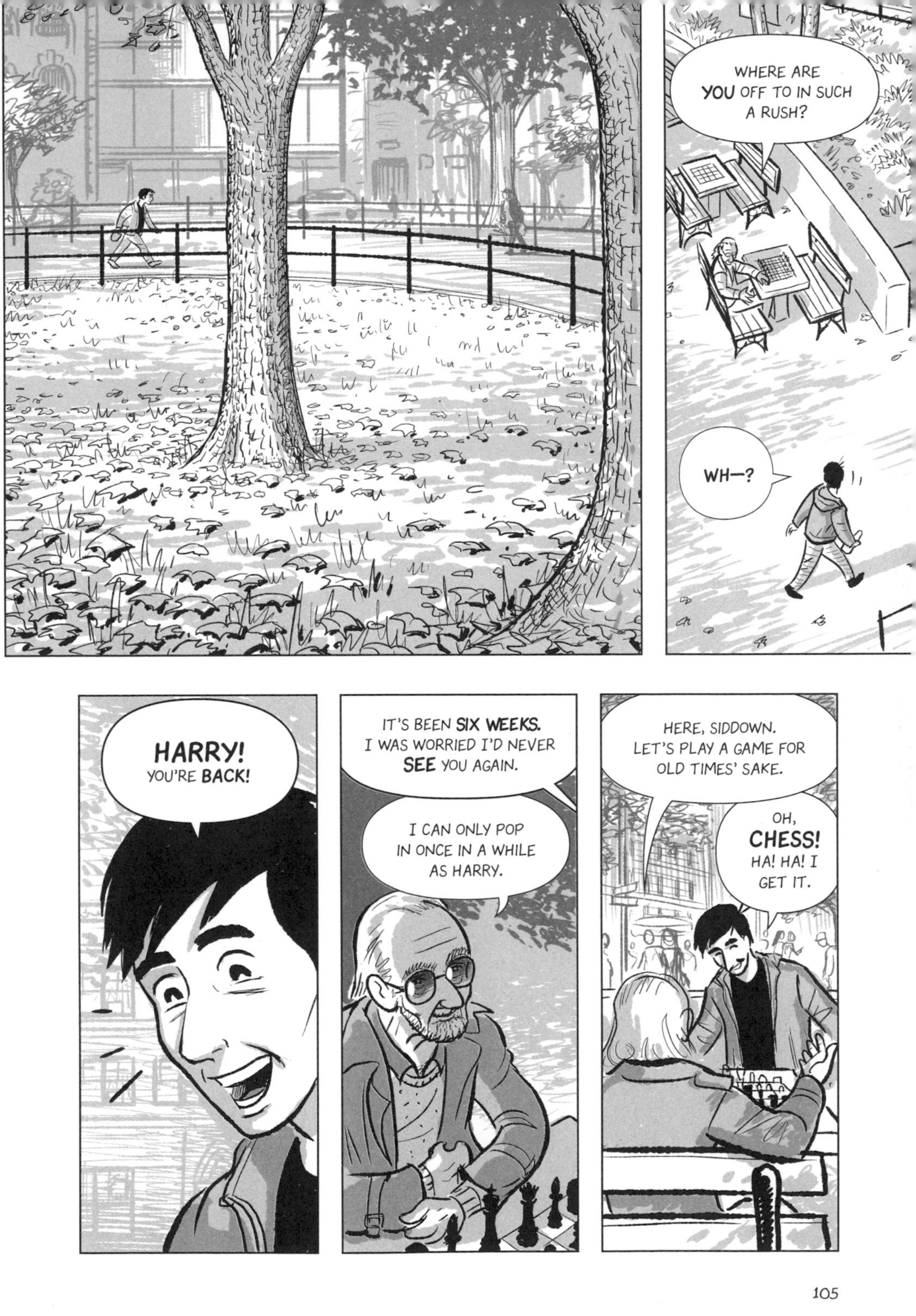
WHERE ARE YOU OFF TO IN SUCH A RUSH?
WH—?
HARRY! YOU'RE BACK!
IT'S BEEN SIX WEEKS. I WAS WORRIED I'D NEVER SEE YOU AGAIN.
I CAN ONLY POP IN ONCE IN A WHILE AS HARRY.
HERE, SIDDOWN. LET'S PLAY A GAME FOR OLD TIMES' SAKE.
OH, CHESS! HA! HA! I GET IT.

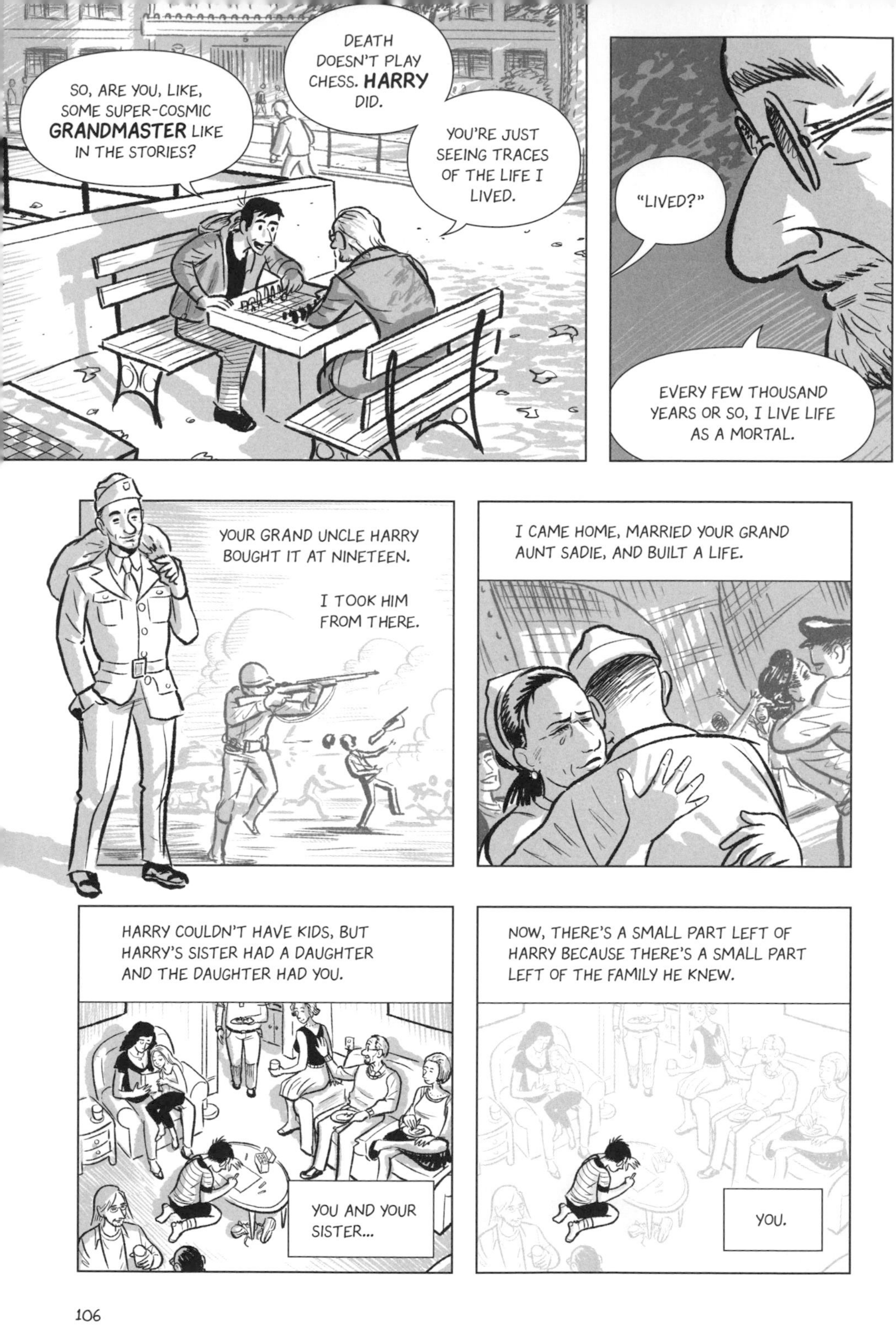
SO, ARE YOU, LIKE, SOME SUPER-COSMIC **GRANDMASTER** LIKE IN THE STORIES?
DEATH DOESN'T PLAY CHESS. **HARRY** DID.
YOU'RE JUST SEEING TRACES OF THE LIFE I LIVED.
"LIVED?"
EVERY FEW THOUSAND YEARS OR SO, I LIVE LIFE AS A MORTAL.
YOUR GRAND UNCLE HARRY BOUGHT IT AT NINETEEN.
I TOOK HIM FROM THERE.
I CAME HOME, MARRIED YOUR GRAND AUNT SADIE, AND BUILT A LIFE.
HARRY COULDN'T HAVE KIDS, BUT HARRY'S SISTER HAD A DAUGHTER AND THE DAUGHTER HAD YOU.
YOU AND YOUR SISTER...
NOW, THERE'S A SMALL PART LEFT OF HARRY BECAUSE THERE'S A SMALL PART LEFT OF THE FAMILY HE KNEW.
YOU.

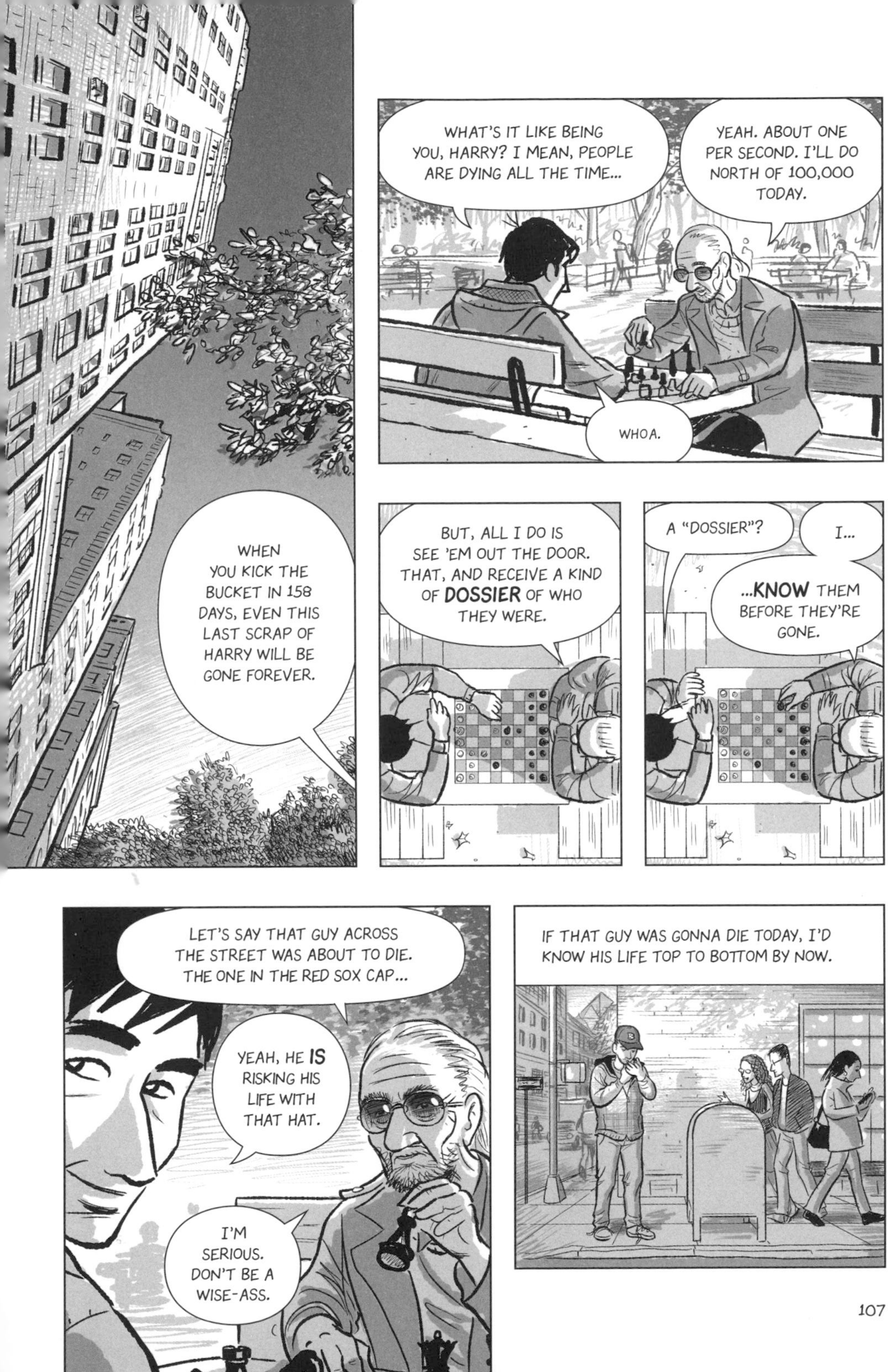
WHEN YOU KICK THE BUCKET IN 158 DAYS, EVEN THIS LAST SCRAP OF HARRY WILL BE GONE FOREVER.
WHAT'S IT LIKE BEING YOU, HARRY? I MEAN, PEOPLE ARE DYING ALL THE TIME...
YEAH. ABOUT ONE PER SECOND. I'LL DO NORTH OF 100,000 TODAY.
WHOA.
BUT, ALL I DO IS SEE 'EM OUT THE DOOR. THAT, AND RECEIVE A KIND OF **DOSSIER** OF WHO THEY WERE.
A "DOSSIER"?
I...
...**KNOW** THEM BEFORE THEY'RE GONE.
LET'S SAY THAT GUY ACROSS THE STREET WAS ABOUT TO DIE. THE ONE IN THE RED SOX CAP...
YEAH, HE **IS** RISKING HIS LIFE WITH THAT HAT.
I'M SERIOUS. DON'T BE A WISE-ASS.
IF THAT GUY WAS GONNA DIE TODAY, I'D KNOW HIS LIFE TOP TO BOTTOM BY NOW.

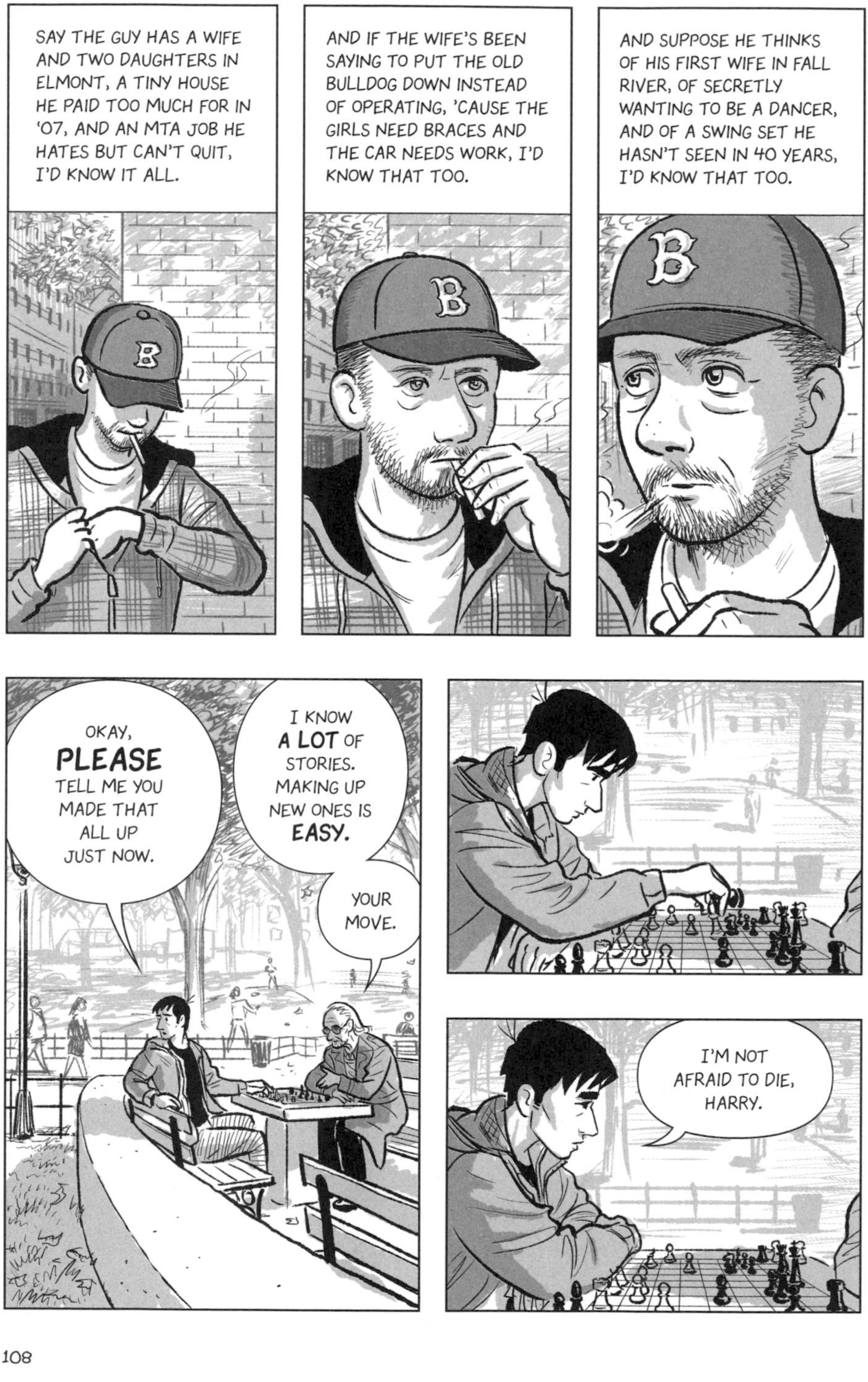
SAY THE GUY HAS A WIFE AND TWO DAUGHTERS IN ELMONT, A TINY HOUSE HE PAID TOO MUCH FOR IN '07, AND AN MTA JOB HE HATES BUT CAN'T QUIT, I'D KNOW IT ALL.
AND IF THE WIFE'S BEEN SAYING TO PUT THE OLD BULLDOG DOWN INSTEAD OF OPERATING, 'CAUSE THE GIRLS NEED BRACES AND THE CAR NEEDS WORK, I'D KNOW THAT TOO.
AND SUPPOSE HE THINKS OF HIS FIRST WIFE IN FALL RIVER, OF SECRETLY WANTING TO BE A DANCER, AND OF A SWING SET HE HASN'T SEEN IN 40 YEARS, I'D KNOW THAT TOO.
OKAY, **PLEASE** TELL ME YOU MADE THAT ALL UP JUST NOW.
I KNOW **A LOT** OF STORIES. MAKING UP NEW ONES IS **EASY.**
YOUR MOVE.
I'M NOT AFRAID TO DIE, HARRY.

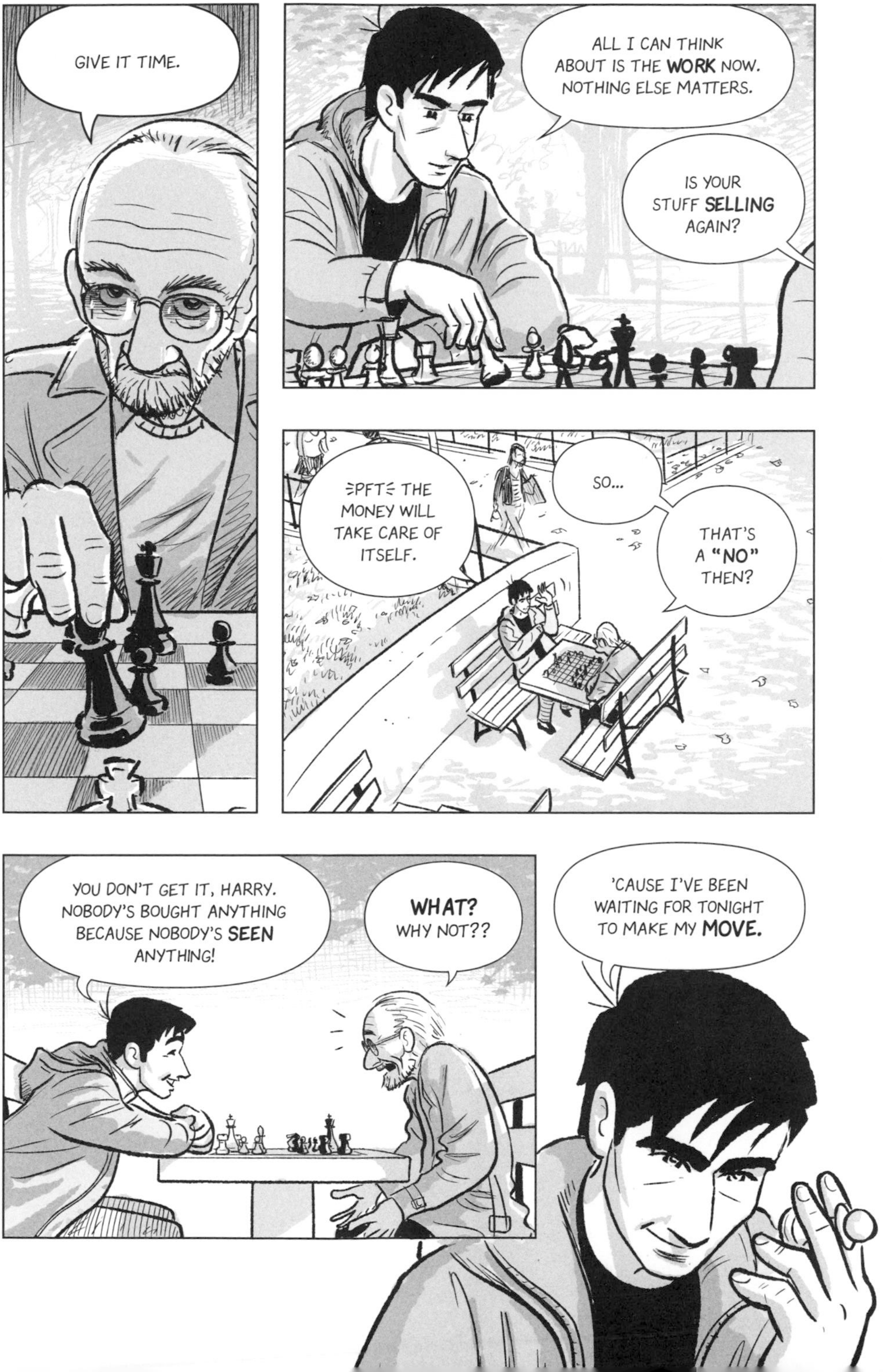
GIVE IT TIME.
ALL I CAN THINK ABOUT IS THE **WORK** NOW. NOTHING ELSE MATTERS.
IS YOUR STUFF **SELLING** AGAIN?
⇌PFT⇌ THE MONEY WILL TAKE CARE OF ITSELF.
SO...
THAT'S A **"NO"** THEN?
YOU DON'T GET IT, HARRY. NOBODY'S BOUGHT ANYTHING BECAUSE NOBODY'S **SEEN** ANYTHING!
WHAT? WHY NOT??
'CAUSE I'VE BEEN WAITING FOR TONIGHT TO MAKE MY **MOVE.**

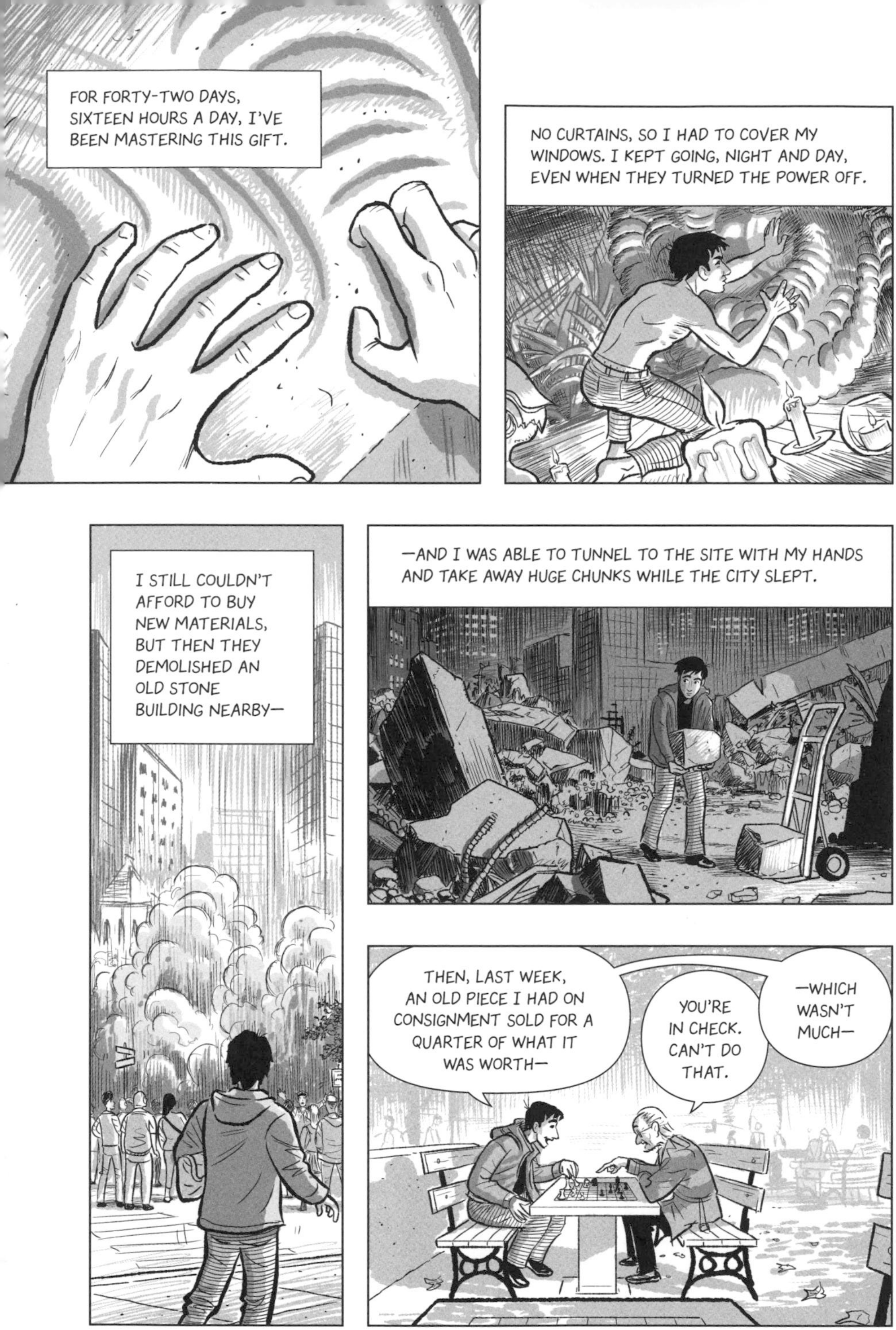
FOR FORTY-TWO DAYS, SIXTEEN HOURS A DAY, I'VE BEEN MASTERING THIS GIFT.
NO CURTAINS, SO I HAD TO COVER MY WINDOWS. I KEPT GOING, NIGHT AND DAY, EVEN WHEN THEY TURNED THE POWER OFF.
I STILL COULDN'T AFFORD TO BUY NEW MATERIALS, BUT THEN THEY DEMOLISHED AN OLD STONE BUILDING NEARBY—
—AND I WAS ABLE TO TUNNEL TO THE SITE WITH MY HANDS AND TAKE AWAY HUGE CHUNKS WHILE THE CITY SLEPT.
THEN, LAST WEEK, AN OLD PIECE I HAD ON CONSIGNMENT SOLD FOR A QUARTER OF WHAT IT WAS WORTH—
YOU'RE IN CHECK. CAN'T DO THAT.
—WHICH WASN'T MUCH—

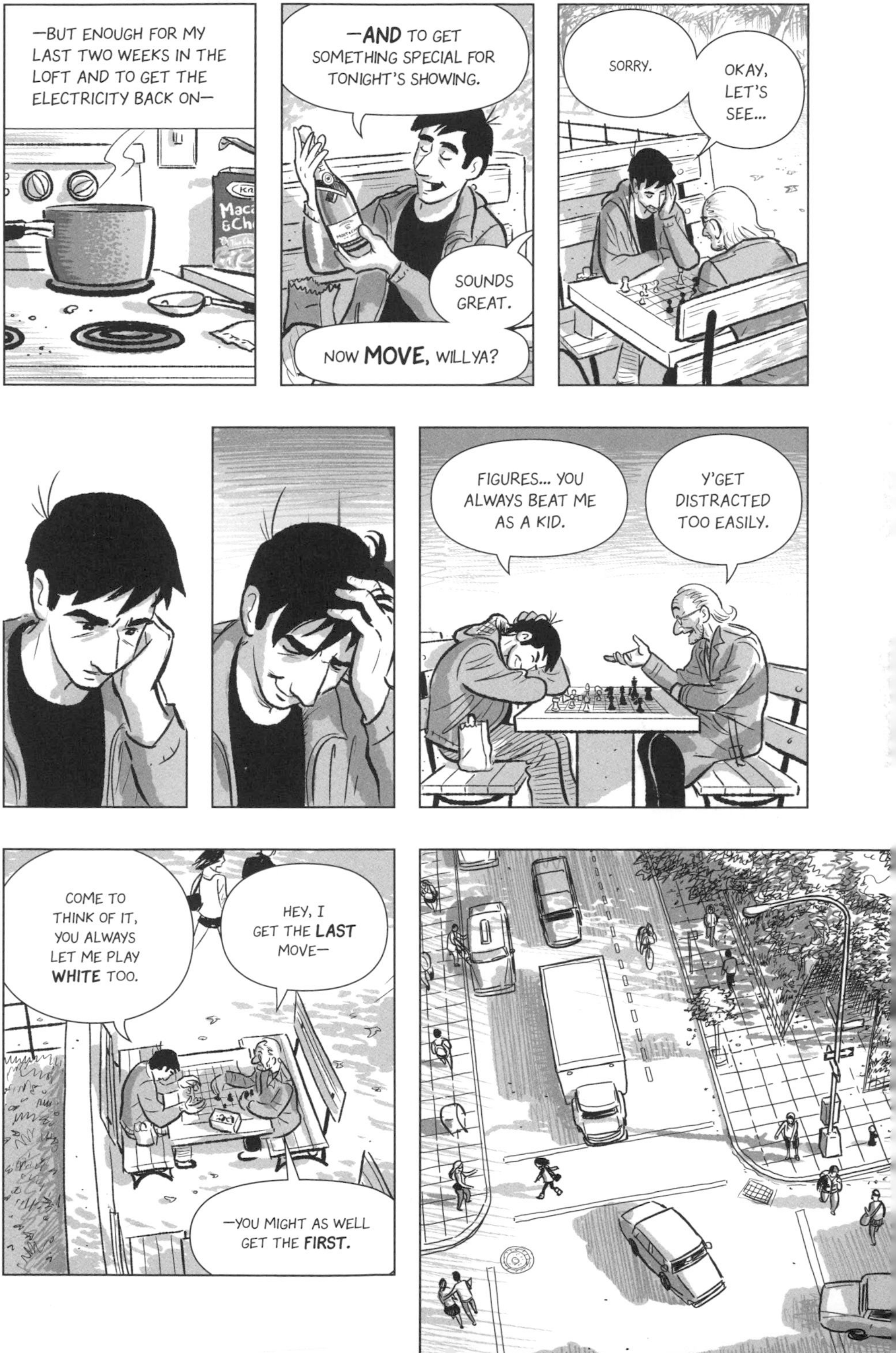
—BUT ENOUGH FOR MY LAST TWO WEEKS IN THE LOFT AND TO GET THE ELECTRICITY BACK ON—
—**AND** TO GET SOMETHING SPECIAL FOR TONIGHT'S SHOWING.
SOUNDS GREAT.
NOW **MOVE**, WILLYA?
SORRY.
OKAY, LET'S SEE...
FIGURES... YOU ALWAYS BEAT ME AS A KID.
Y'GET DISTRACTED TOO EASILY.
COME TO THINK OF IT, YOU ALWAYS LET ME PLAY **WHITE** TOO.
HEY, I GET THE **LAST** MOVE—
—YOU MIGHT AS WELL GET THE **FIRST**.

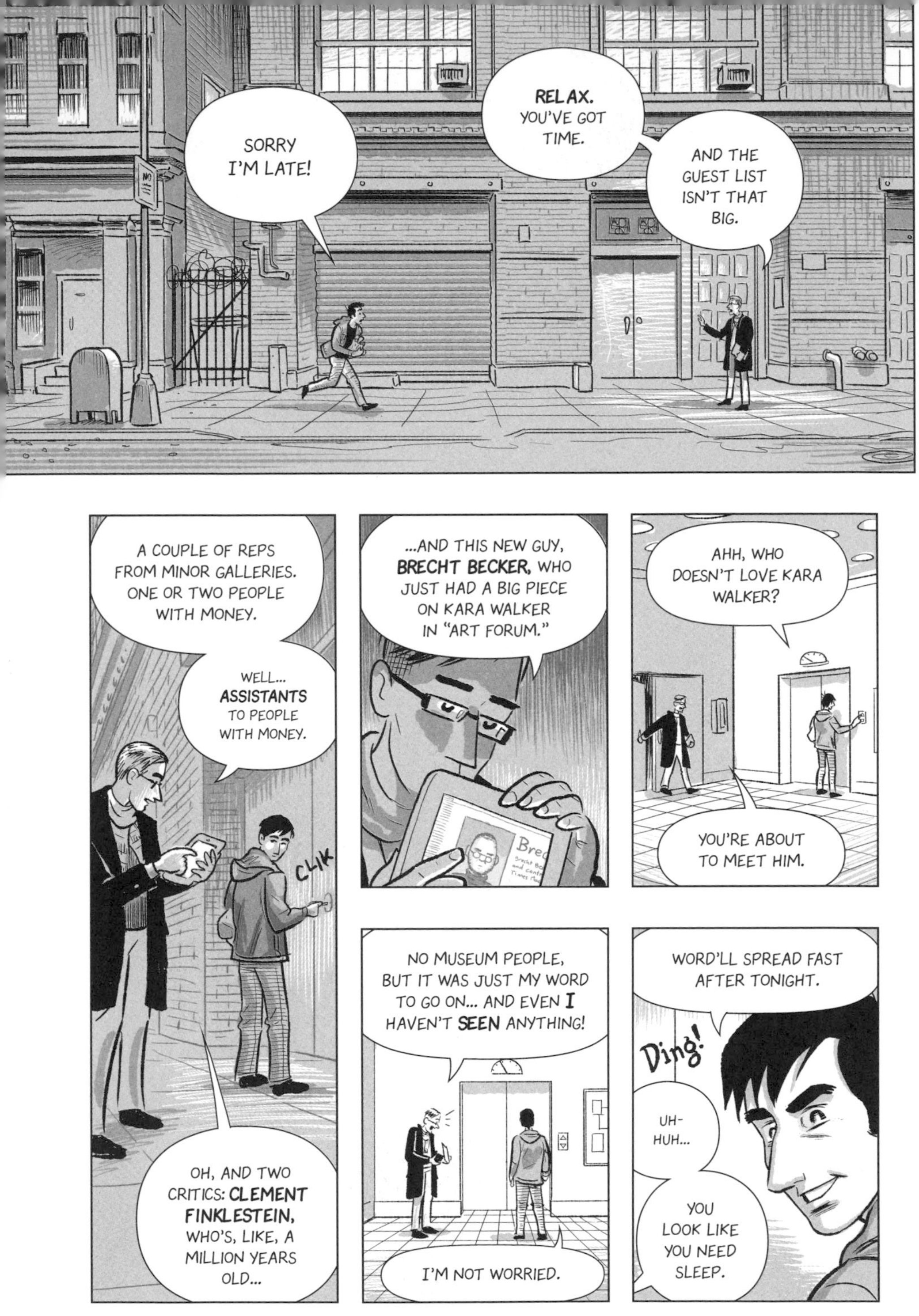
SORRY I'M LATE!
RELAX. YOU'VE GOT TIME.
AND THE GUEST LIST ISN'T THAT BIG.
A COUPLE OF REPS FROM MINOR GALLERIES. ONE OR TWO PEOPLE WITH MONEY.
WELL... ASSISTANTS TO PEOPLE WITH MONEY.
CLIK
OH, AND TWO CRITICS: CLEMENT FINKLESTEIN, WHO'S, LIKE, A MILLION YEARS OLD...
...AND THIS NEW GUY, BRECHT BECKER, WHO JUST HAD A BIG PIECE ON KARA WALKER IN "ART FORUM."
AHH, WHO DOESN'T LOVE KARA WALKER?
YOU'RE ABOUT TO MEET HIM.
NO MUSEUM PEOPLE, BUT IT WAS JUST MY WORD TO GO ON... AND EVEN I HAVEN'T SEEN ANYTHING!
I'M NOT WORRIED.
WORD'LL SPREAD FAST AFTER TONIGHT.
Ding!
UH-HUH...
YOU LOOK LIKE YOU NEED SLEEP.

SO, DID YOU CALL PENELOPE HAMMER?

YEAH.

SHE'S IN MILAN, BUT SHE ASKED THIS GUY **HARRIS** TO STOP BY.

Ding!

OOH... HARRIS HAS CLOUT, BUT HE'S A **MONEY** GUY.

HEY, I COULD USE A **LITTLE** MONEY.

NO, I MEAN HE STARTED IN INVESTING, NOT ART.

WOULDN'T KNOW A BRANCUSI FROM A BARBELL. JUST "BUYS WITH HIS EARS."

HE'LL HEAR PLENTY FROM THE OTHERS, I'M SURE.

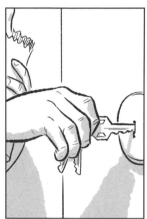

OKAY, SO FAR, IT LOOKS LIKE A REALLY DARK ROOM...

YEAH, YEAH. LET ME JUST FIND THE SWITCH...

CLICK

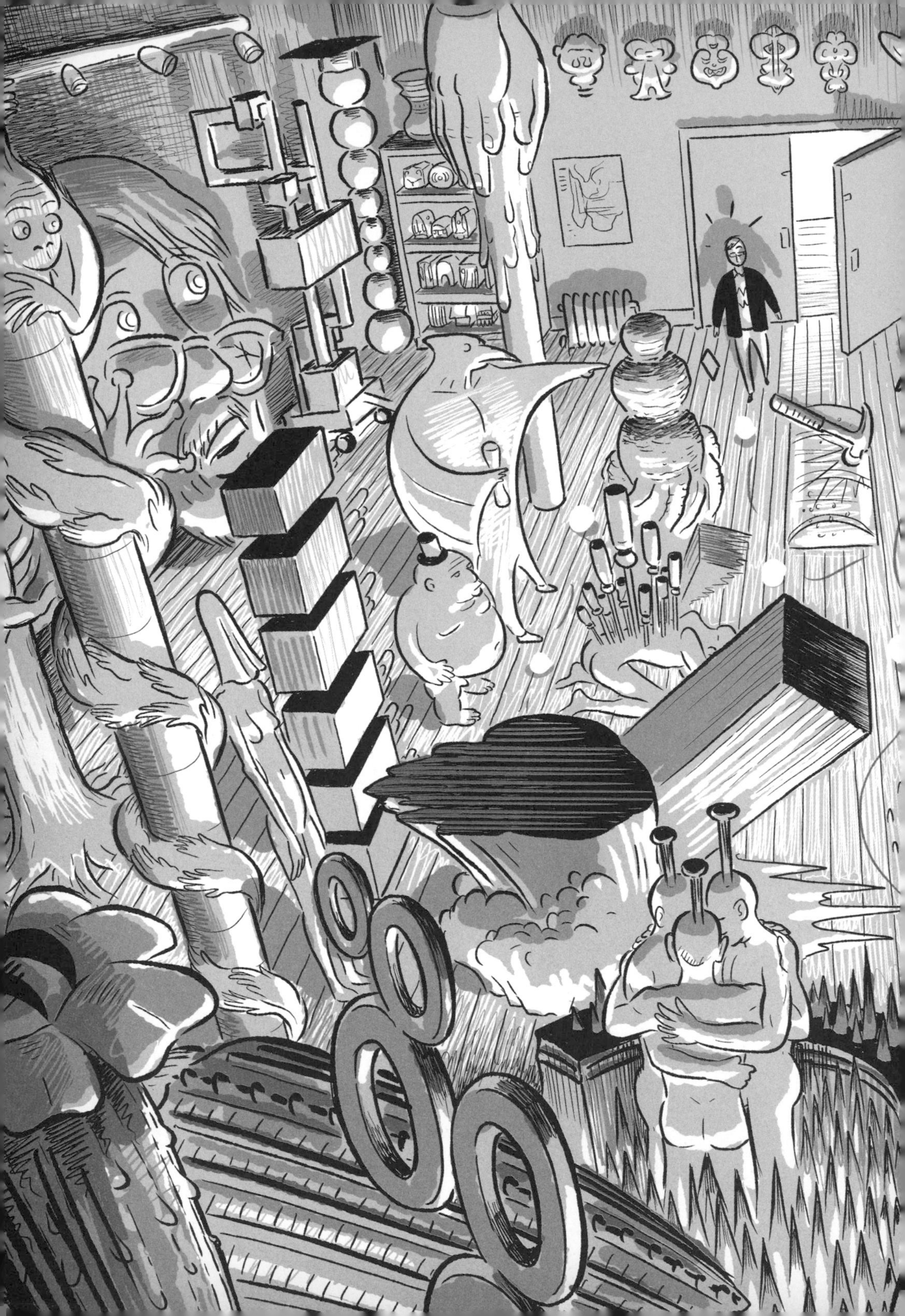

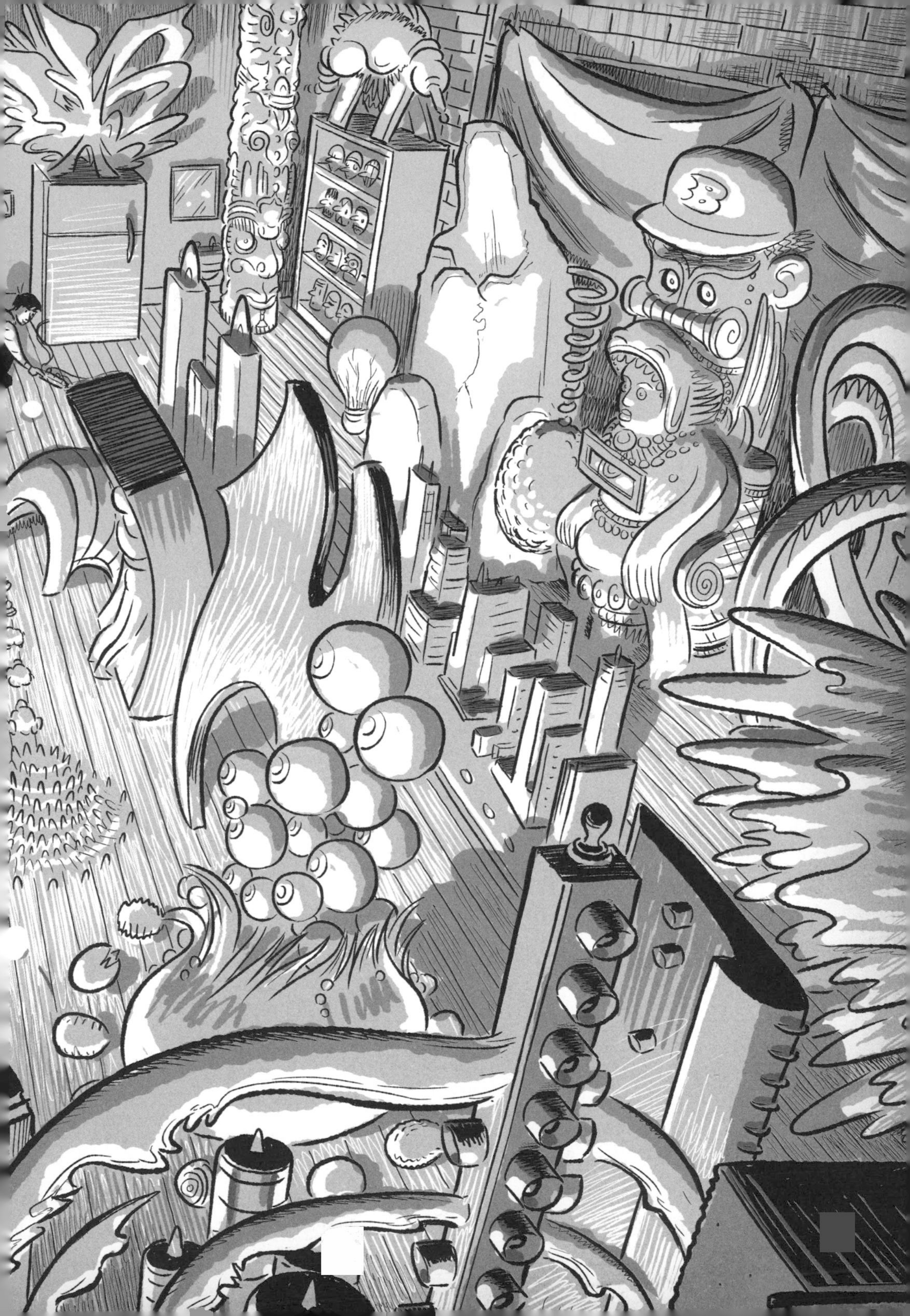

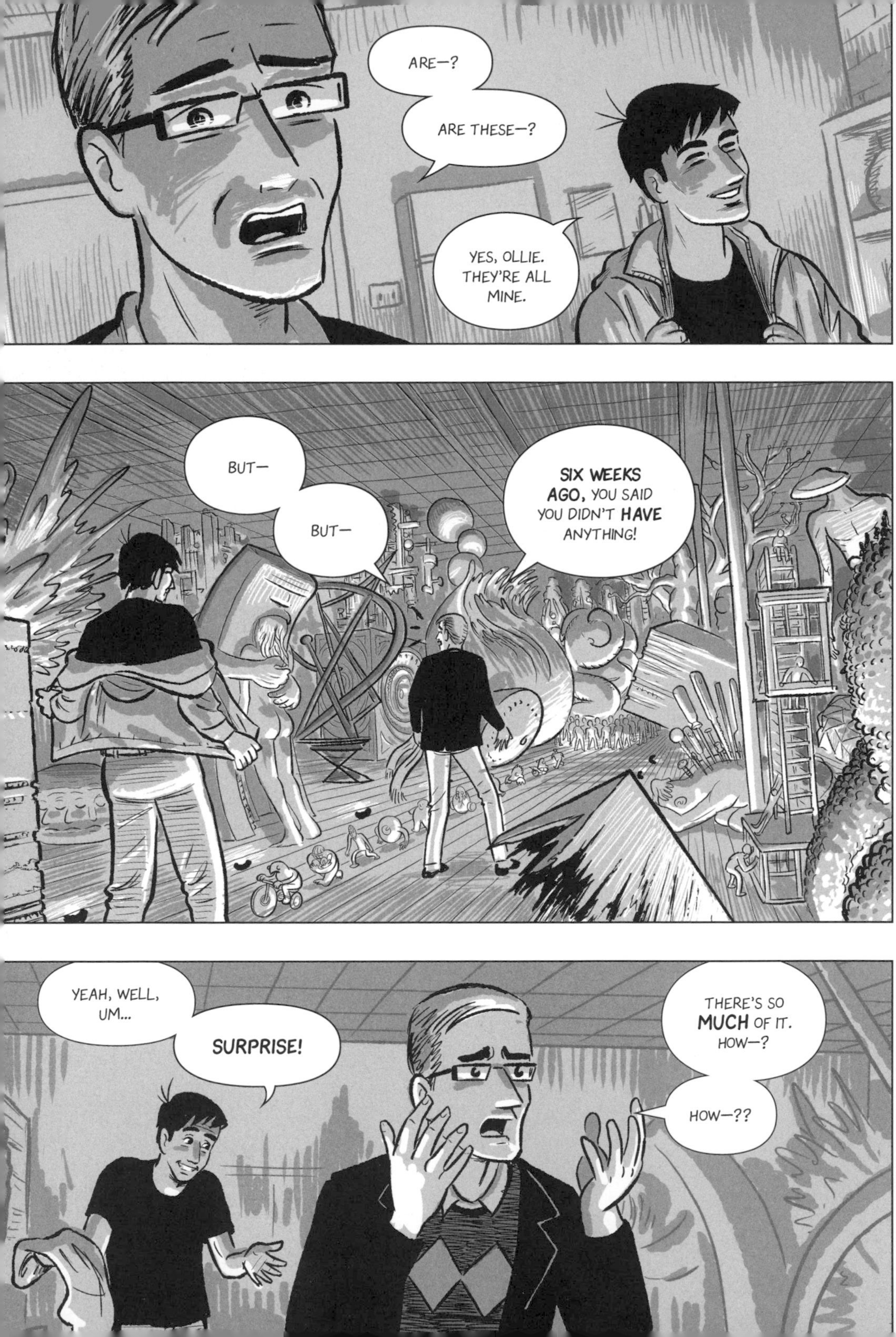

ARE—?
ARE THESE—?
YES, OLLIE. THEY'RE ALL MINE.
BUT—
BUT—
SIX WEEKS AGO, YOU SAID YOU DIDN'T **HAVE** ANYTHING!
YEAH, WELL, UM...
SURPRISE!
THERE'S SO **MUCH** OF IT. HOW—?
HOW—??

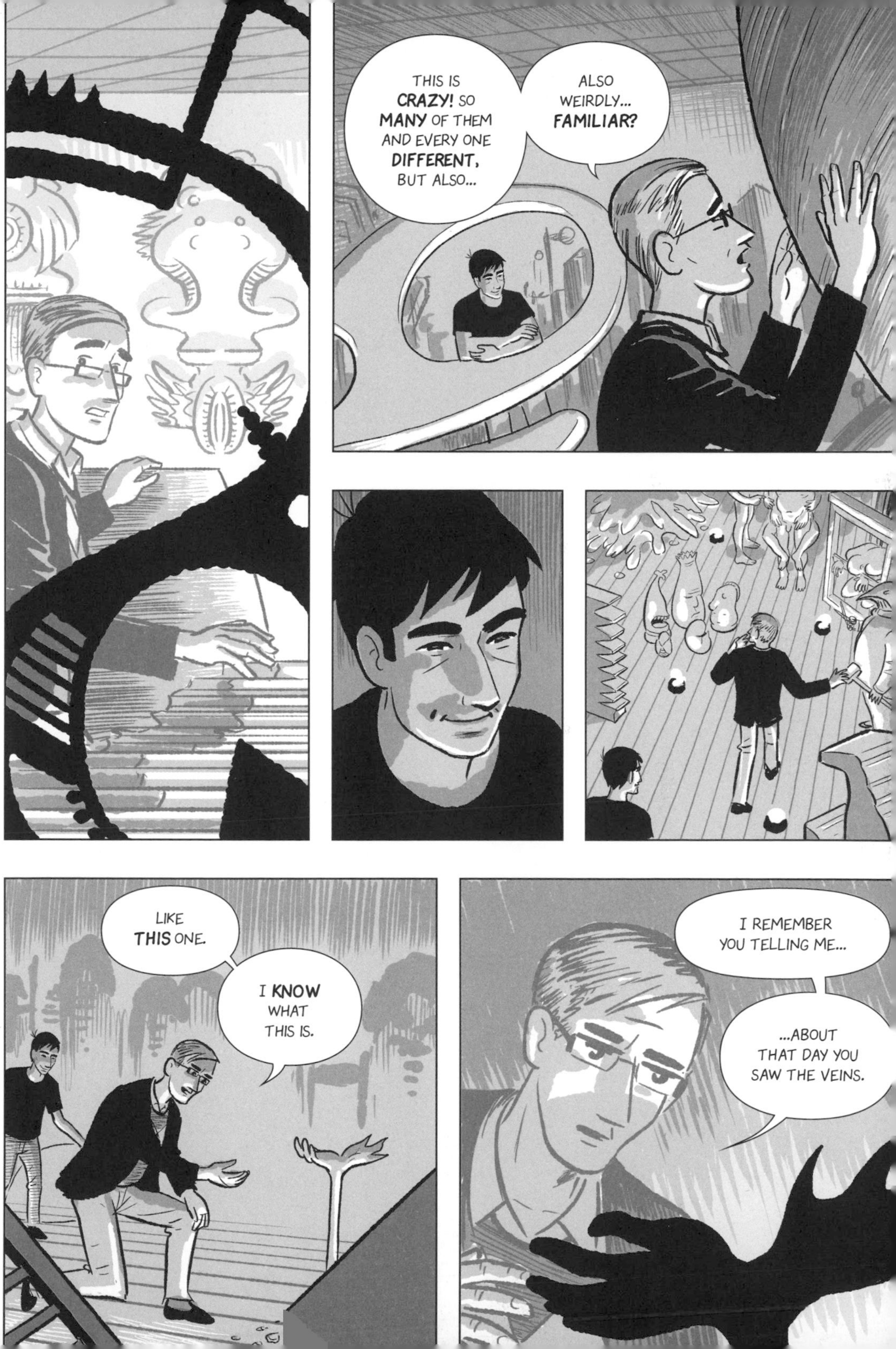
THIS IS CRAZY! SO MANY OF THEM AND EVERY ONE DIFFERENT, BUT ALSO...
ALSO WEIRDLY... FAMILIAR?
LIKE THIS ONE.
I KNOW WHAT THIS IS.
I REMEMBER YOU TELLING ME...
...ABOUT THAT DAY YOU SAW THE VEINS.

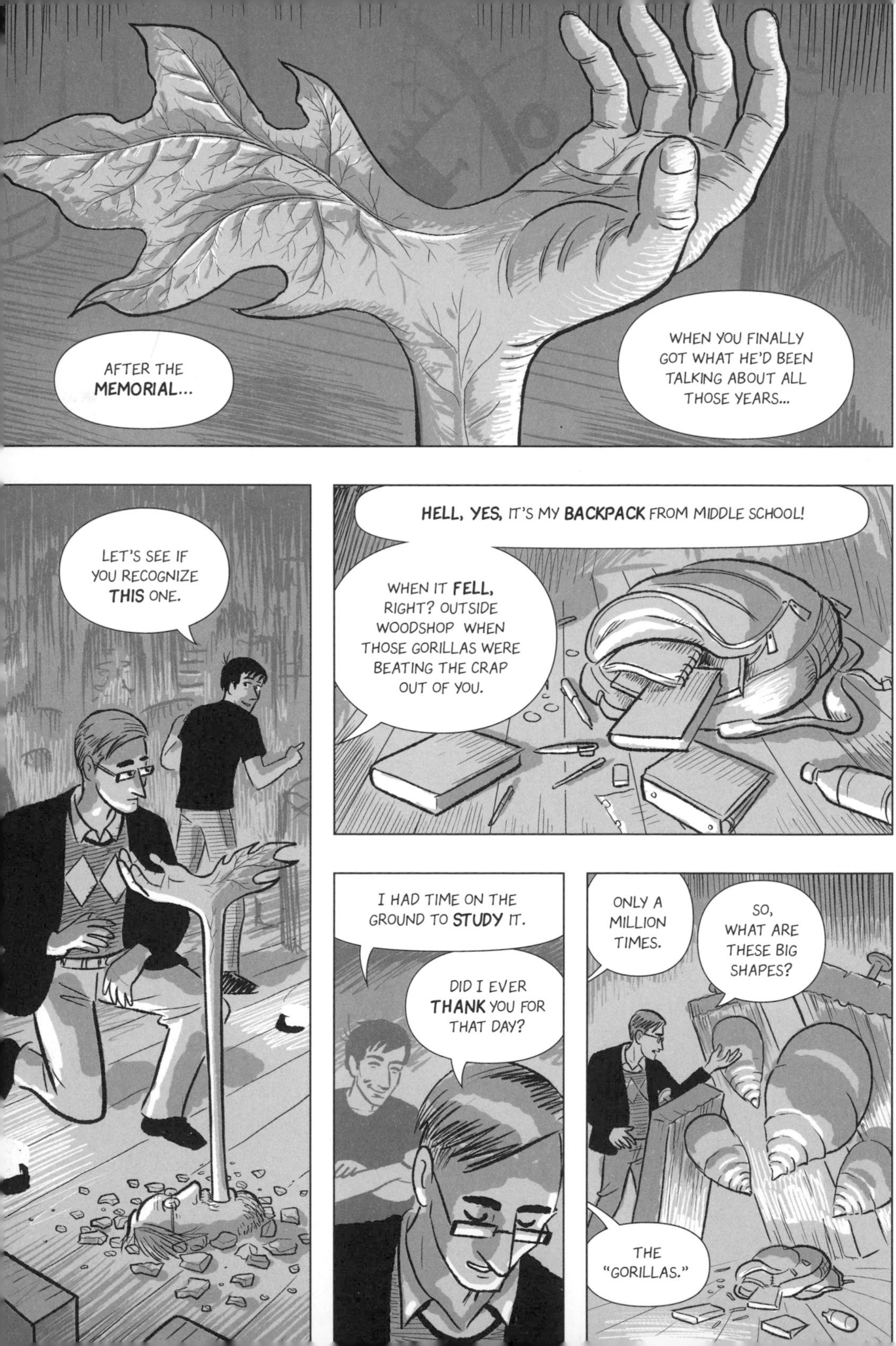
AFTER THE MEMORIAL...
WHEN YOU FINALLY GOT WHAT HE'D BEEN TALKING ABOUT ALL THOSE YEARS...
LET'S SEE IF YOU RECOGNIZE THIS ONE.
HELL, YES, IT'S MY BACKPACK FROM MIDDLE SCHOOL!
WHEN IT FELL, RIGHT? OUTSIDE WOODSHOP WHEN THOSE GORILLAS WERE BEATING THE CRAP OUT OF YOU.
I HAD TIME ON THE GROUND TO STUDY IT.
DID I EVER THANK YOU FOR THAT DAY?
ONLY A MILLION TIMES.
SO, WHAT ARE THESE BIG SHAPES?
THE "GORILLAS."

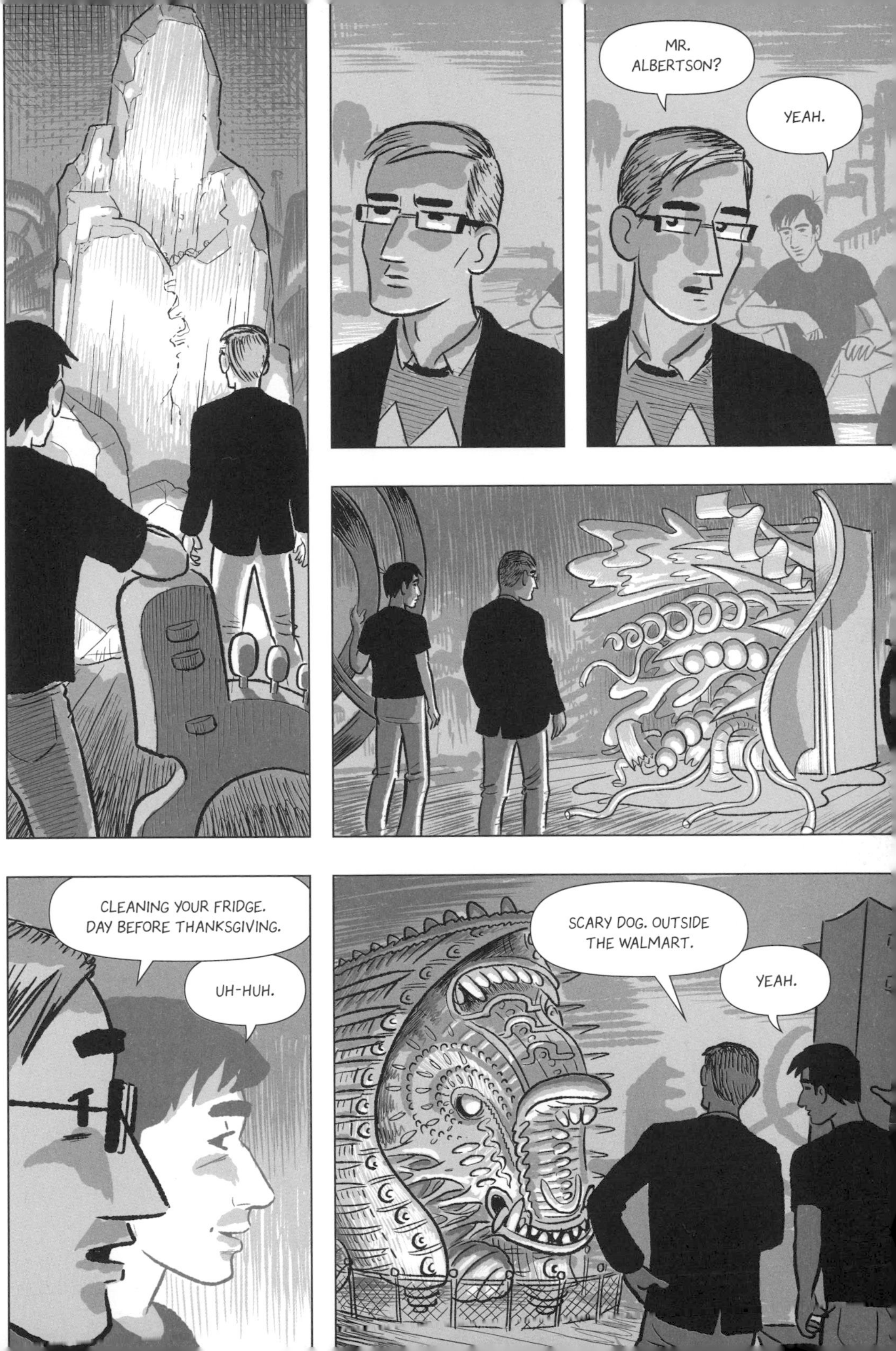
MR. ALBERTSON?
YEAH.
CLEANING YOUR FRIDGE. DAY BEFORE THANKSGIVING.
UH-HUH.
SCARY DOG. OUTSIDE THE WALMART.
YEAH.

JESUS, THE **FLOORBOARDS** ARE SAGGING! SOME OF THESE MUST WEIGH A **TON**.

AND JUST FOR THESE LITTLE, TEMPORARY... **MOMENTS** OF YOURS.

THEY WERE NEVER LITTLE TO **ME**.

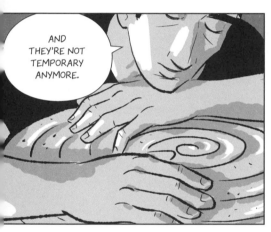

AND THEY'RE NOT TEMPORARY ANYMORE.

THESE CAN'T **ALL** BE SPECIFIC MEMORIES, RIGHT? I MEAN, SOME OF THIS STUFF LOOKS PRETTY **ABSTRACT**.

SCHOOL FIELD TRIP. ART MUSEUM. YOU WERE HOME WITH CHICKEN POX.

THEY HAD THIS **RODIN** ON LOAN, AND THERE WAS THIS TINY PART OF IT AROUND THE COLLAR BONE I KEPT STARING AT.

THE BUS ALMOST LEFT WITHOUT ME.

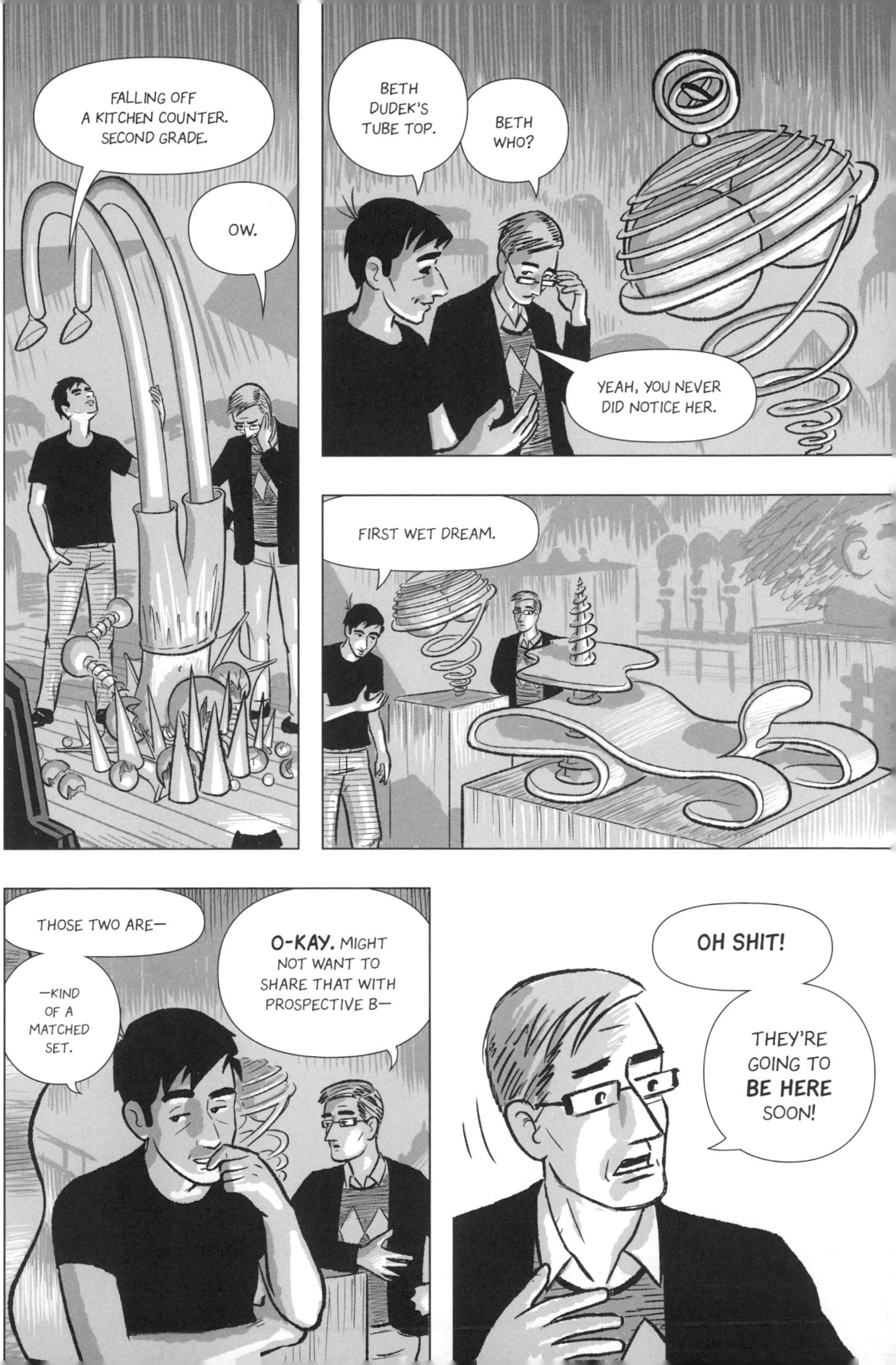
FALLING OFF A KITCHEN COUNTER. SECOND GRADE.
OW.
BETH DUDEK'S TUBE TOP.
BETH WHO?
YEAH, YOU NEVER DID NOTICE HER.
FIRST WET DREAM.
THOSE TWO ARE—
—KIND OF A MATCHED SET.
O-KAY. MIGHT NOT WANT TO SHARE THAT WITH PROSPECTIVE B—
OH SHIT!
THEY'RE GOING TO **BE HERE** SOON!

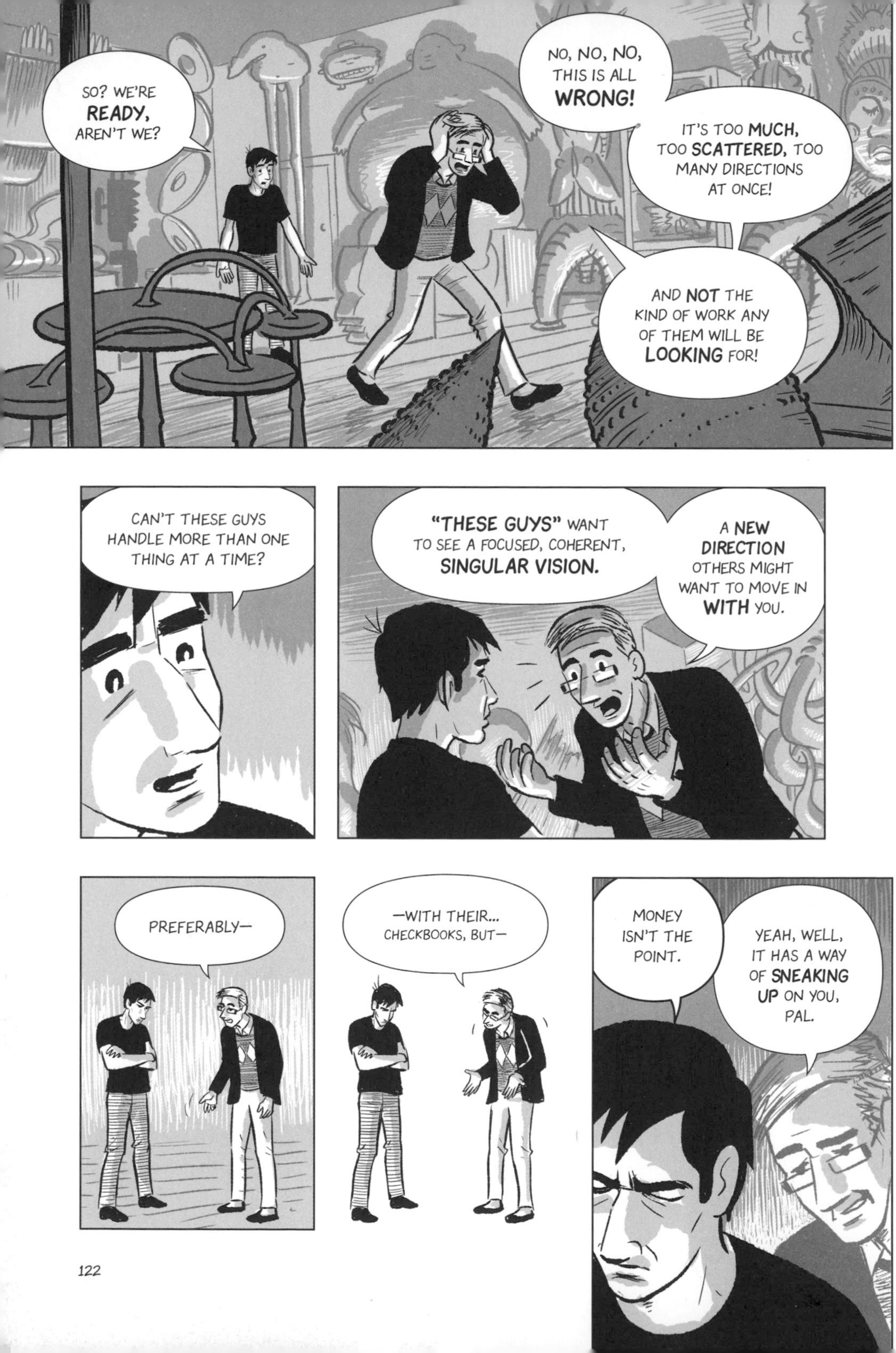
SO? WE'RE **READY,** AREN'T WE?
NO, NO, NO, THIS IS ALL **WRONG!**
IT'S TOO **MUCH,** TOO **SCATTERED,** TOO MANY DIRECTIONS AT ONCE!
AND **NOT** THE KIND OF WORK ANY OF THEM WILL BE **LOOKING** FOR!
CAN'T THESE GUYS HANDLE MORE THAN ONE THING AT A TIME?
"THESE GUYS" WANT TO SEE A FOCUSED, COHERENT, **SINGULAR VISION.**
A **NEW DIRECTION** OTHERS MIGHT WANT TO MOVE IN **WITH** YOU.
PREFERABLY—
—WITH THEIR... CHECKBOOKS, BUT—
MONEY ISN'T THE POINT.
YEAH, WELL, IT HAS A WAY OF **SNEAKING UP** ON YOU, PAL.

LOOK,
WE CAN JUST
RESCHEDULE.

OLLIE,
I...

NO BUTS!
I'LL SAY YOU
GOT **SICK.**

OR
MUGGED OR
WHATEVER...
LEAVE IT
TO ME.

WE CAN PARCEL IT
OUT, FIND FIVE OR SIX
OF THE MORE AUSTERE,
CRYPTIC PIECES.

NOTHING WITH
A FACE. THAT ISN'T
WORKING FOR YOU.

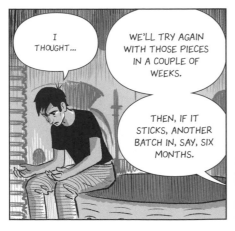

I
THOUGHT...

WE'LL TRY AGAIN
WITH THOSE PIECES
IN A COUPLE OF
WEEKS.

THEN, IF IT
STICKS, ANOTHER
BATCH IN, SAY, SIX
MONTHS.

I THOUGHT
IF I JUST GAVE
IT EVERYTHING
I HAD...

TRUST ME, YOU
CAN STILL SALVAGE
THIS, BUT YOU NEED
TO PLAY TO YOUR
STR—

SUZY??

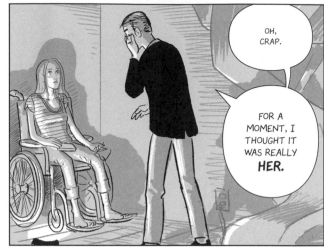

OH, CRAP.

FOR A MOMENT, I THOUGHT IT WAS REALLY **HER.**

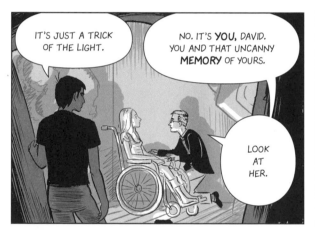

IT'S JUST A TRICK OF THE LIGHT.

NO. IT'S **YOU**, DAVID. YOU AND THAT UNCANNY **MEMORY** OF YOURS.

LOOK AT HER.

THE HAIR. THE BLOUSE.

GOD, THE VEINS ON HER WRIST.

AND THAT LOOK ON HER FACE...

WHEN...?

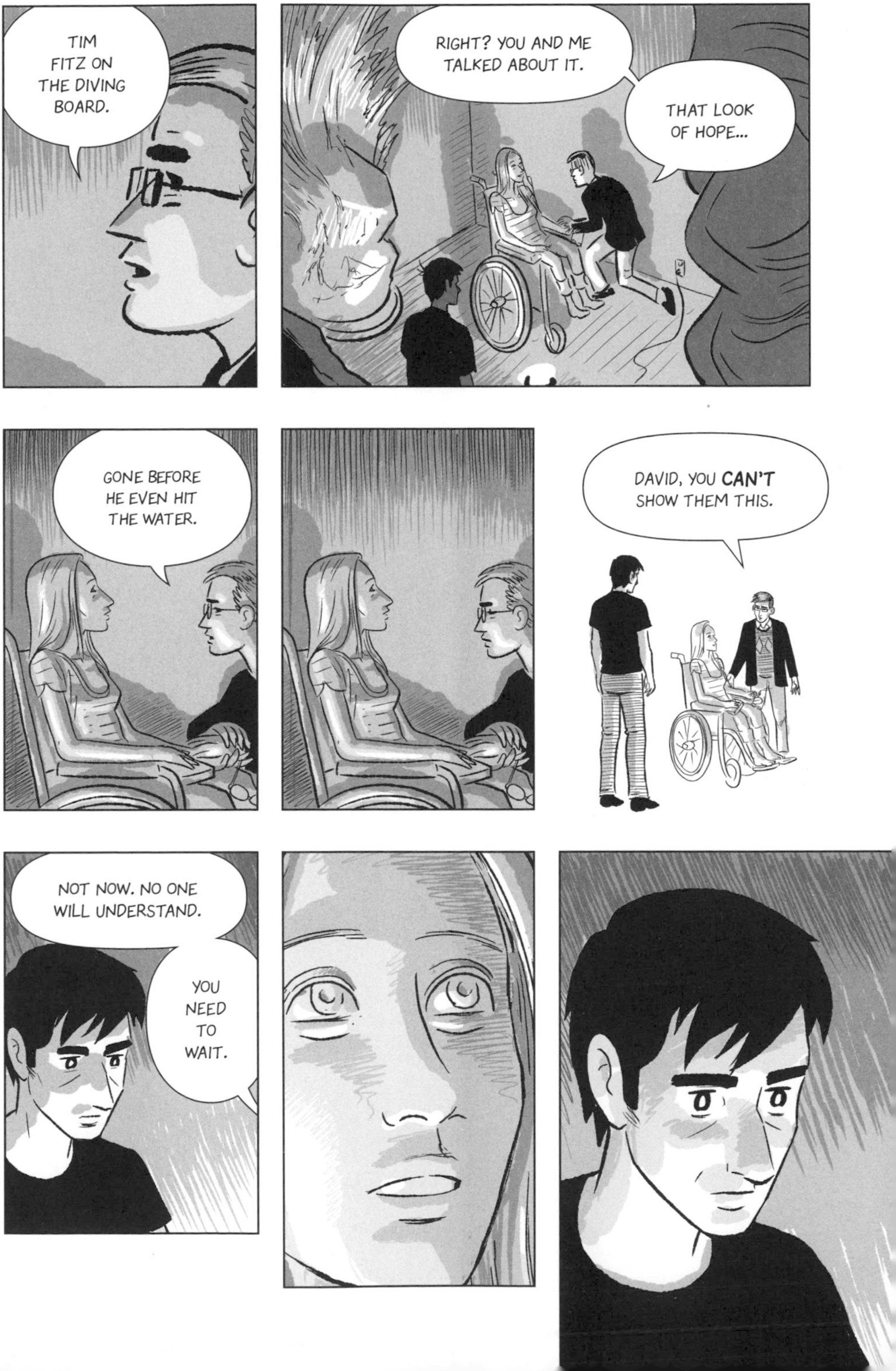
TIM FITZ ON THE DIVING BOARD.
RIGHT? YOU AND ME TALKED ABOUT IT.
THAT LOOK OF HOPE...
GONE BEFORE HE EVEN HIT THE WATER.
DAVID, YOU **CAN'T** SHOW THEM THIS.
NOT NOW. NO ONE WILL UNDERSTAND.
YOU NEED TO WAIT.

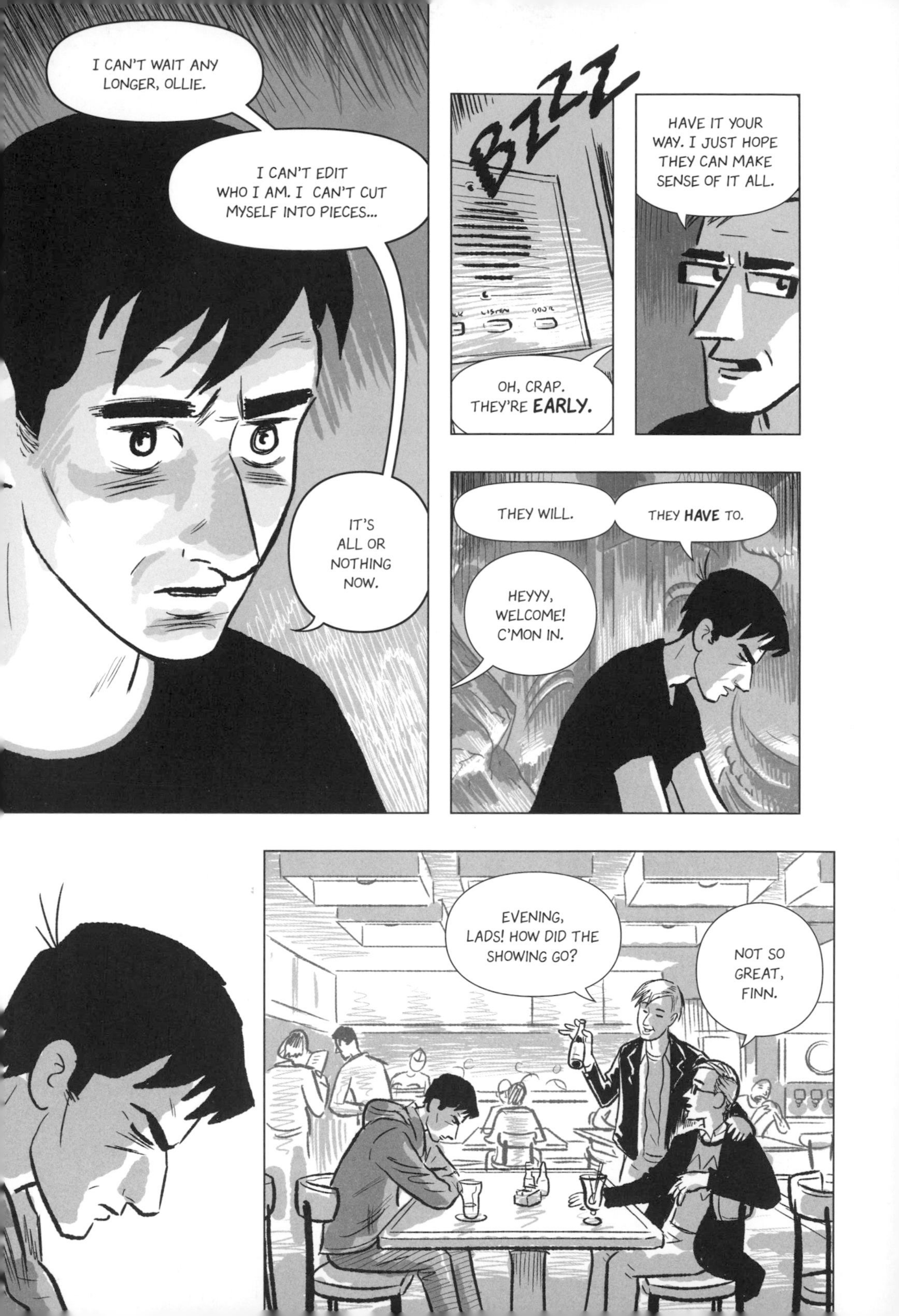
I CAN'T WAIT ANY LONGER, OLLIE.
I CAN'T EDIT WHO I AM. I CAN'T CUT MYSELF INTO PIECES...
IT'S ALL OR NOTHING NOW.
BZZZ
OH, CRAP. THEY'RE **EARLY.**
HAVE IT YOUR WAY. I JUST HOPE THEY CAN MAKE SENSE OF IT ALL.
THEY WILL.
THEY **HAVE** TO.
HEYYY, WELCOME! C'MON IN.
EVENING, LADS! HOW DID THE SHOWING GO?
NOT SO GREAT, FINN.

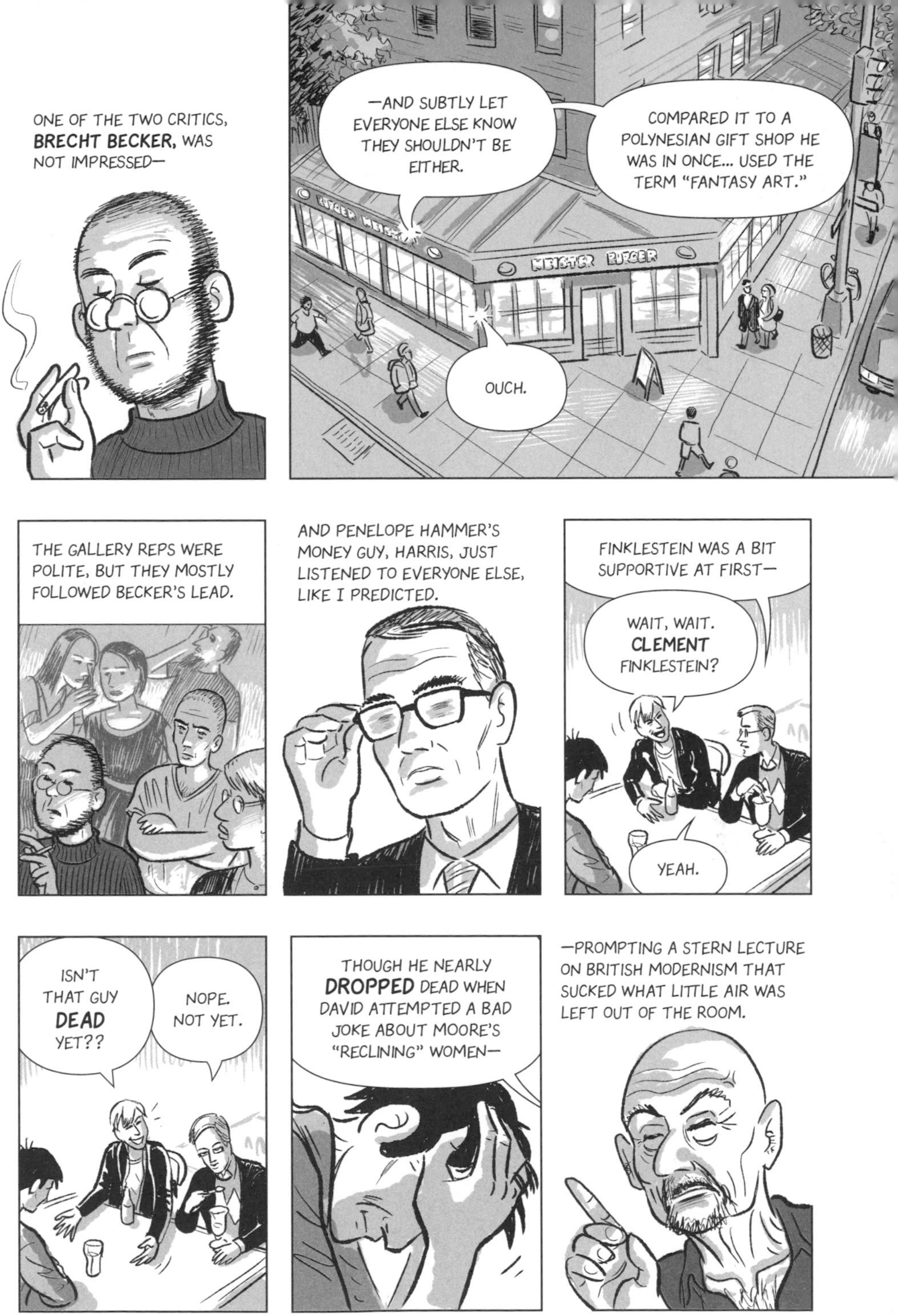

ONE OF THE TWO CRITICS, **BRECHT BECKER,** WAS NOT IMPRESSED—
COMPARED IT TO A POLYNESIAN GIFT SHOP HE WAS IN ONCE... USED THE TERM "FANTASY ART."
—AND SUBTLY LET EVERYONE ELSE KNOW THEY SHOULDN'T BE EITHER.
MEISTER BURGER
OUCH.
THE GALLERY REPS WERE POLITE, BUT THEY MOSTLY FOLLOWED BECKER'S LEAD.
AND PENELOPE HAMMER'S MONEY GUY, HARRIS, JUST LISTENED TO EVERYONE ELSE, LIKE I PREDICTED.
FINKLESTEIN WAS A BIT SUPPORTIVE AT FIRST—
WAIT, WAIT. **CLEMENT** FINKLESTEIN?
YEAH.
ISN'T THAT GUY **DEAD** YET??
NOPE. NOT YET.
THOUGH HE NEARLY **DROPPED** DEAD WHEN DAVID ATTEMPTED A BAD JOKE ABOUT MOORE'S "RECLINING" WOMEN—
—PROMPTING A STERN LECTURE ON BRITISH MODERNISM THAT SUCKED WHAT LITTLE AIR WAS LEFT OUT OF THE ROOM.

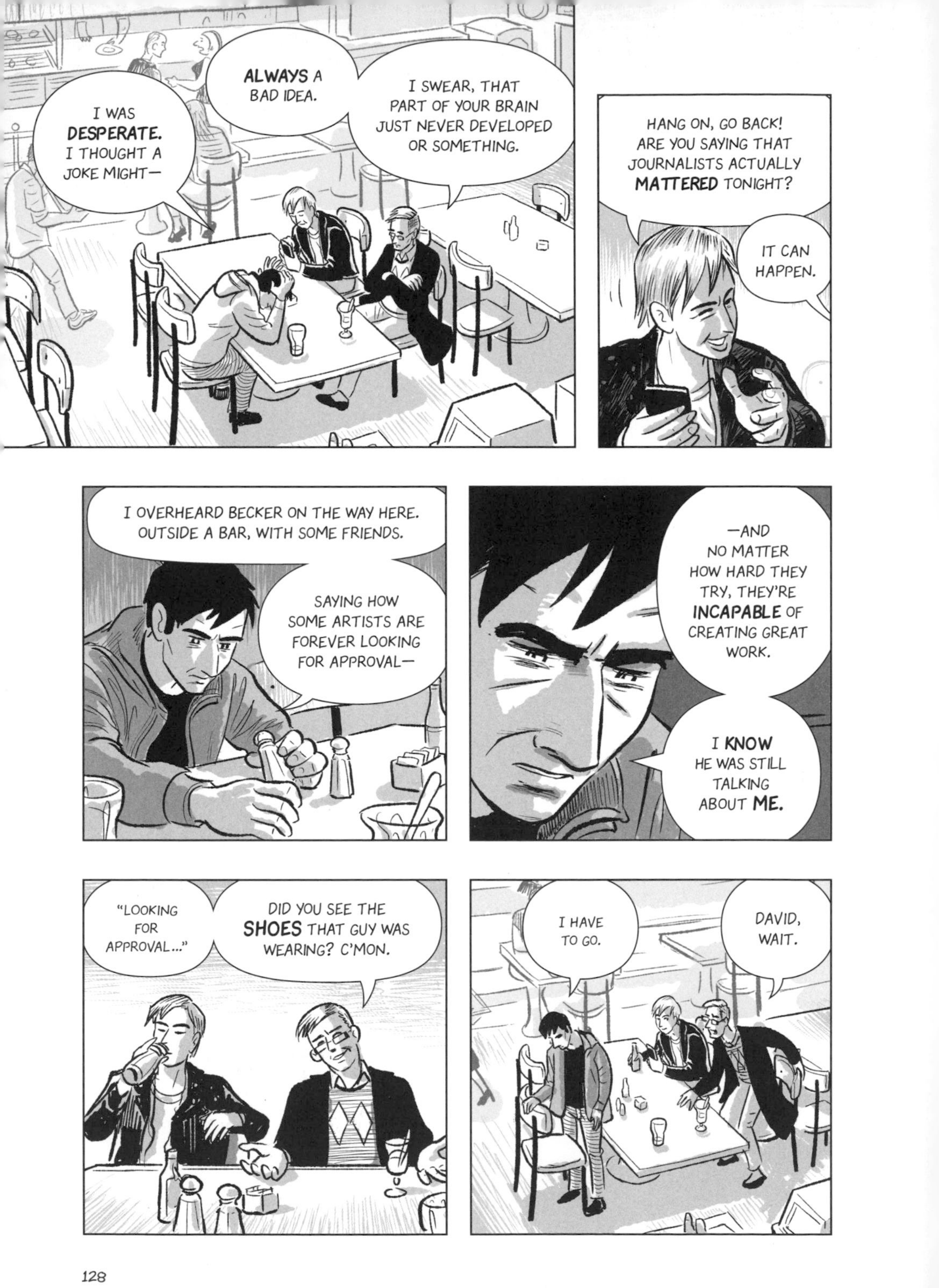
I WAS DESPERATE. I THOUGHT A JOKE MIGHT—
ALWAYS A BAD IDEA.
I SWEAR, THAT PART OF YOUR BRAIN JUST NEVER DEVELOPED OR SOMETHING.
HANG ON, GO BACK! ARE YOU SAYING THAT JOURNALISTS ACTUALLY MATTERED TONIGHT?
IT CAN HAPPEN.
I OVERHEARD BECKER ON THE WAY HERE. OUTSIDE A BAR, WITH SOME FRIENDS.
SAYING HOW SOME ARTISTS ARE FOREVER LOOKING FOR APPROVAL—
—AND NO MATTER HOW HARD THEY TRY, THEY'RE INCAPABLE OF CREATING GREAT WORK.
I KNOW HE WAS STILL TALKING ABOUT ME.
"LOOKING FOR APPROVAL..."
DID YOU SEE THE SHOES THAT GUY WAS WEARING? C'MON.
I HAVE TO GO.
DAVID, WAIT.

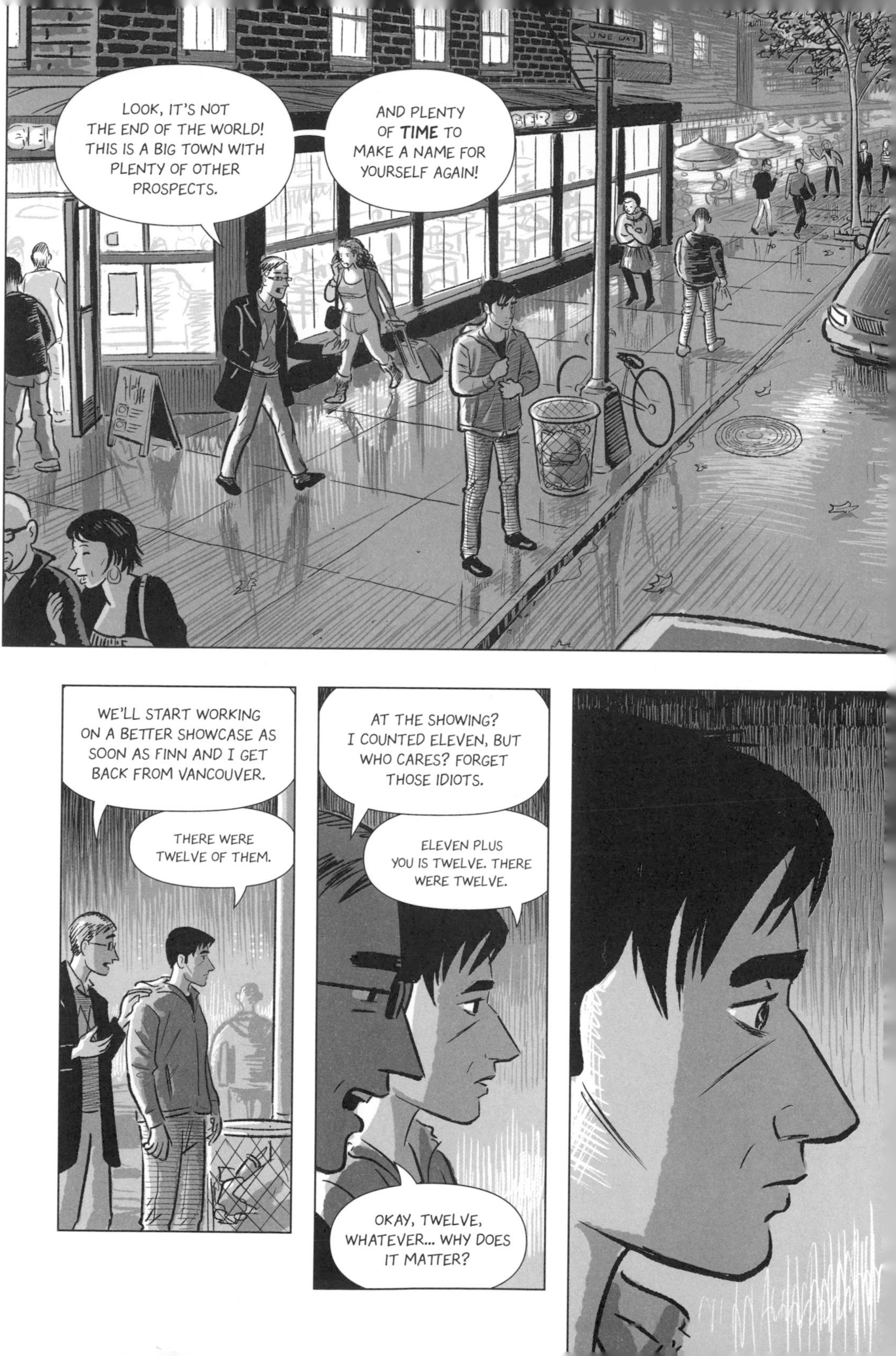
ONE WAY
LOOK, IT'S NOT THE END OF THE WORLD! THIS IS A BIG TOWN WITH PLENTY OF OTHER PROSPECTS.
AND PLENTY OF **TIME** TO MAKE A NAME FOR YOURSELF AGAIN!
WE'LL START WORKING ON A BETTER SHOWCASE AS SOON AS FINN AND I GET BACK FROM VANCOUVER.
THERE WERE TWELVE OF THEM.
AT THE SHOWING? I COUNTED ELEVEN, BUT WHO CARES? FORGET THOSE IDIOTS.
ELEVEN PLUS YOU IS TWELVE. THERE WERE TWELVE.
OKAY, TWELVE, WHATEVER... WHY DOES IT MATTER?

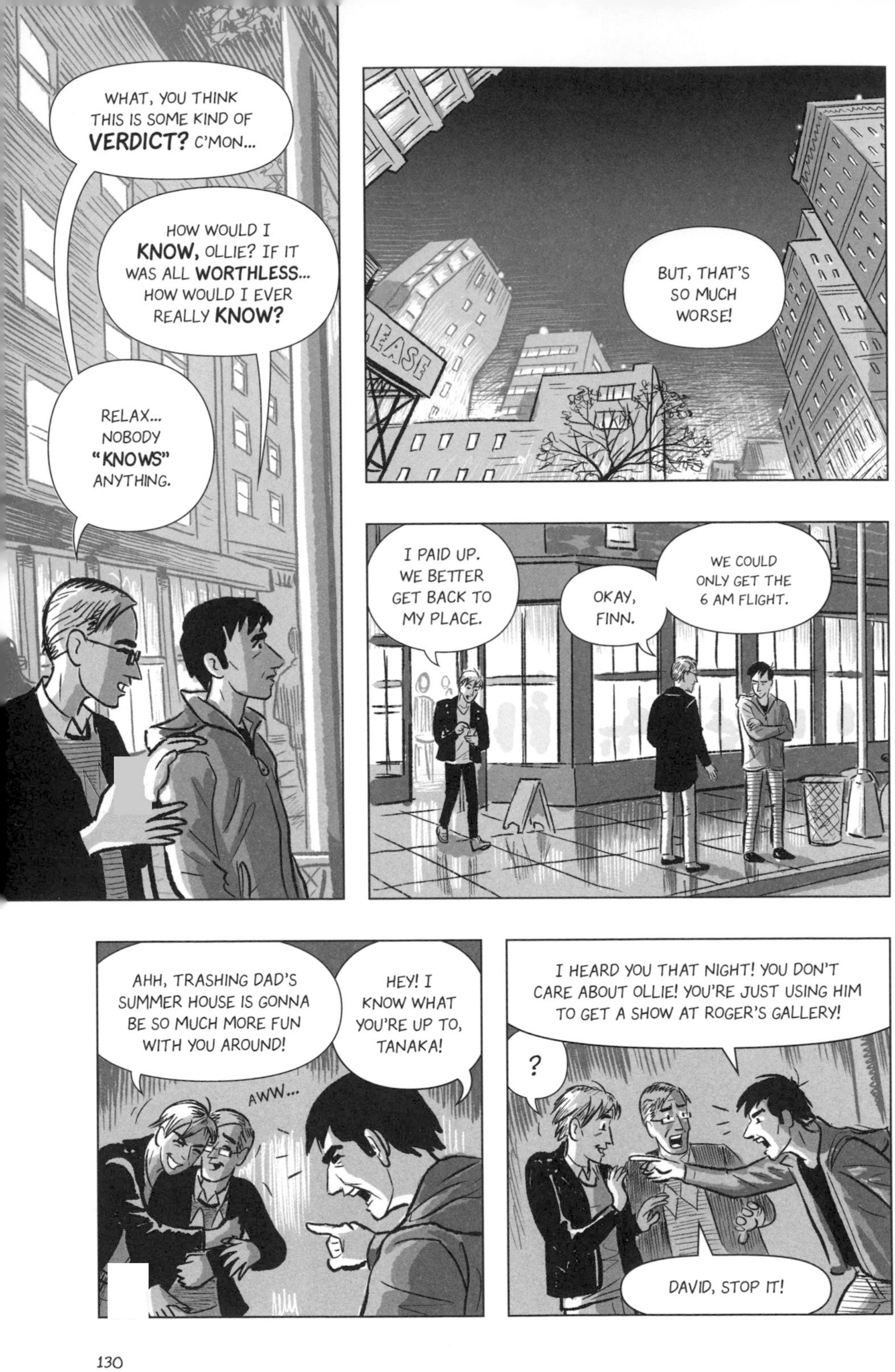
WHAT, YOU THINK THIS IS SOME KIND OF **VERDICT?** C'MON...
HOW WOULD I **KNOW,** OLLIE? IF IT WAS ALL **WORTHLESS...** HOW WOULD I EVER REALLY **KNOW?**
RELAX... NOBODY **"KNOWS"** ANYTHING.
BUT, THAT'S SO MUCH WORSE!
LEASE
I PAID UP. WE BETTER GET BACK TO MY PLACE.
OKAY, FINN.
WE COULD ONLY GET THE 6 AM FLIGHT.
AHH, TRASHING DAD'S SUMMER HOUSE IS GONNA BE SO MUCH MORE FUN WITH YOU AROUND!
HEY! I KNOW WHAT YOU'RE UP TO, TANAKA!
AWW...
I HEARD YOU THAT NIGHT! YOU DON'T CARE ABOUT OLLIE! YOU'RE JUST USING HIM TO GET A SHOW AT ROGER'S GALLERY!
?
DAVID, STOP IT!

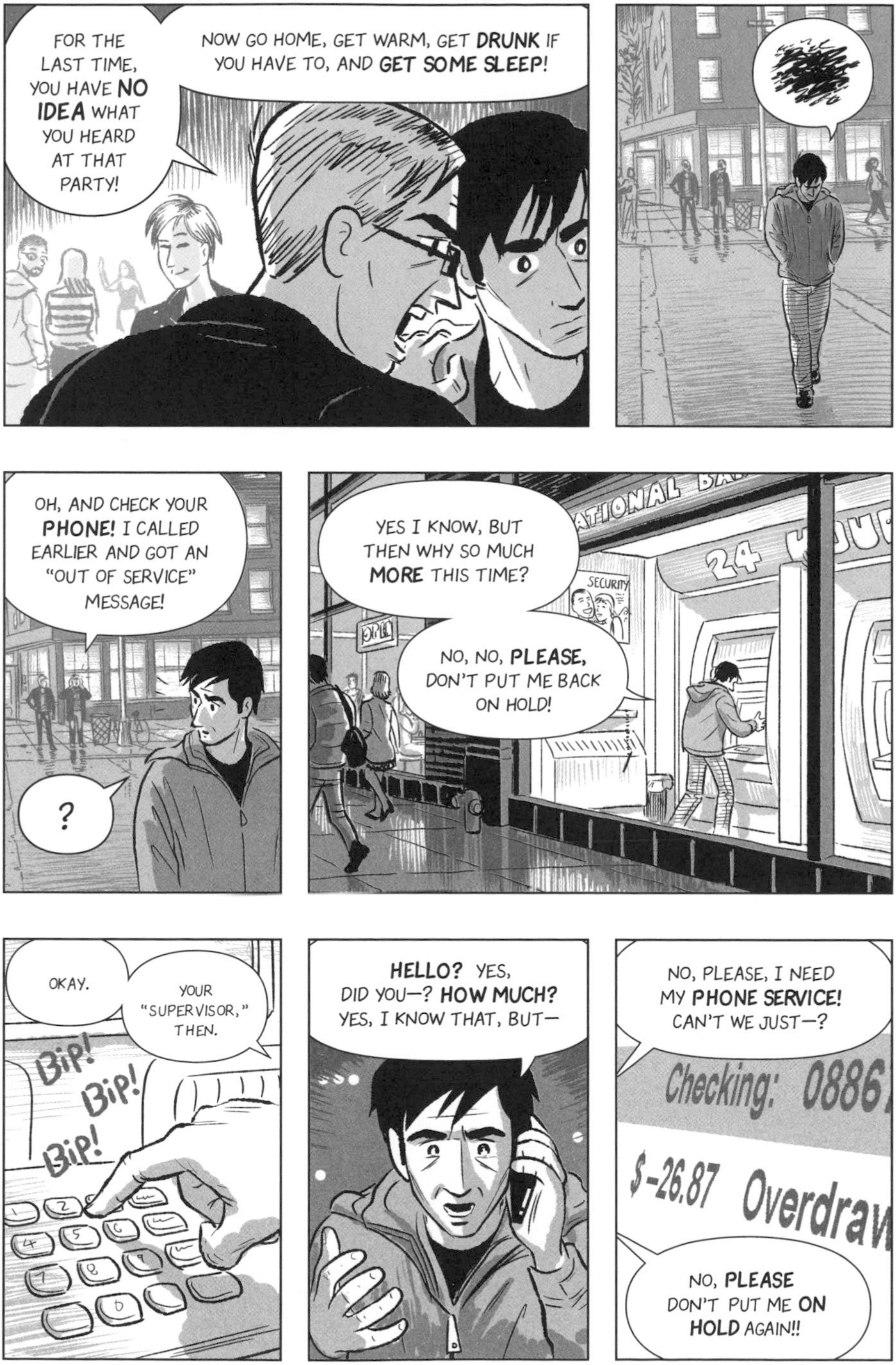
FOR THE LAST TIME, YOU HAVE **NO IDEA** WHAT YOU HEARD AT THAT PARTY!
NOW GO HOME, GET WARM, GET **DRUNK** IF YOU HAVE TO, AND **GET SOME SLEEP!**
OH, AND CHECK YOUR **PHONE!** I CALLED EARLIER AND GOT AN "OUT OF SERVICE" MESSAGE!
?
NATIONAL BA
24 HOU
OPEN
SECURITY
YES I KNOW, BUT THEN WHY SO MUCH **MORE** THIS TIME?
NO, NO, **PLEASE,** DON'T PUT ME BACK ON HOLD!
OKAY.
YOUR "SUPERVISOR," THEN.
Bip!
Bip!
Bip!
HELLO? YES, DID YOU—? **HOW MUCH?** YES, I KNOW THAT, BUT—
NO, PLEASE, I NEED MY **PHONE SERVICE!** CAN'T WE JUST—?
Checking: 0886
$ -26.87 Overdraw
NO, **PLEASE** DON'T PUT ME **ON HOLD** AGAIN!!

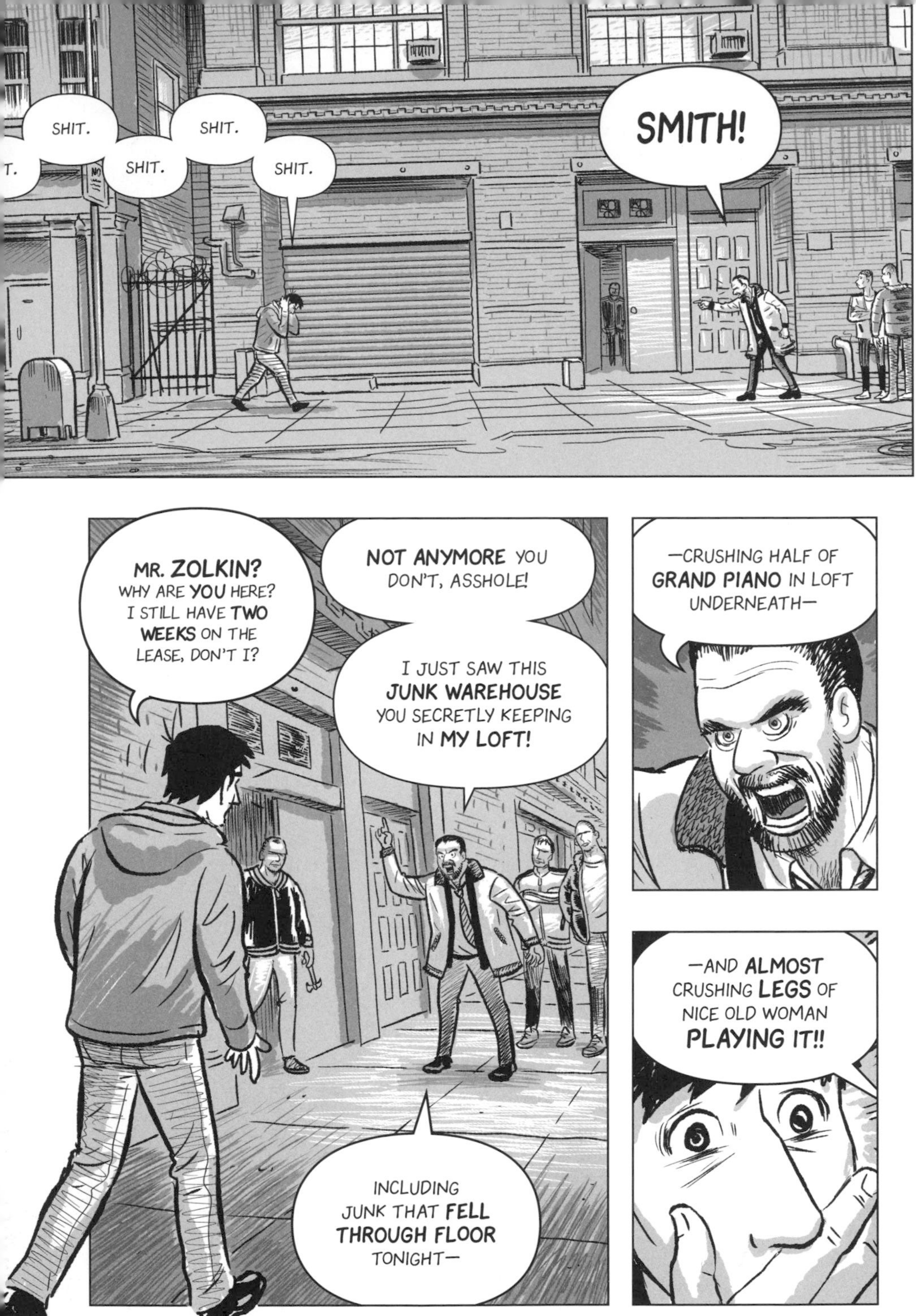
SHIT.
SHIT.
SHIT.
SHIT.
SMITH!
MR. ZOLKIN? WHY ARE YOU HERE? I STILL HAVE TWO WEEKS ON THE LEASE, DON'T I?
NOT ANYMORE YOU DON'T, ASSHOLE!
I JUST SAW THIS JUNK WAREHOUSE YOU SECRETLY KEEPING IN MY LOFT!
INCLUDING JUNK THAT FELL THROUGH FLOOR TONIGHT—
—CRUSHING HALF OF GRAND PIANO IN LOFT UNDERNEATH—
—AND ALMOST CRUSHING LEGS OF NICE OLD WOMAN PLAYING IT!!

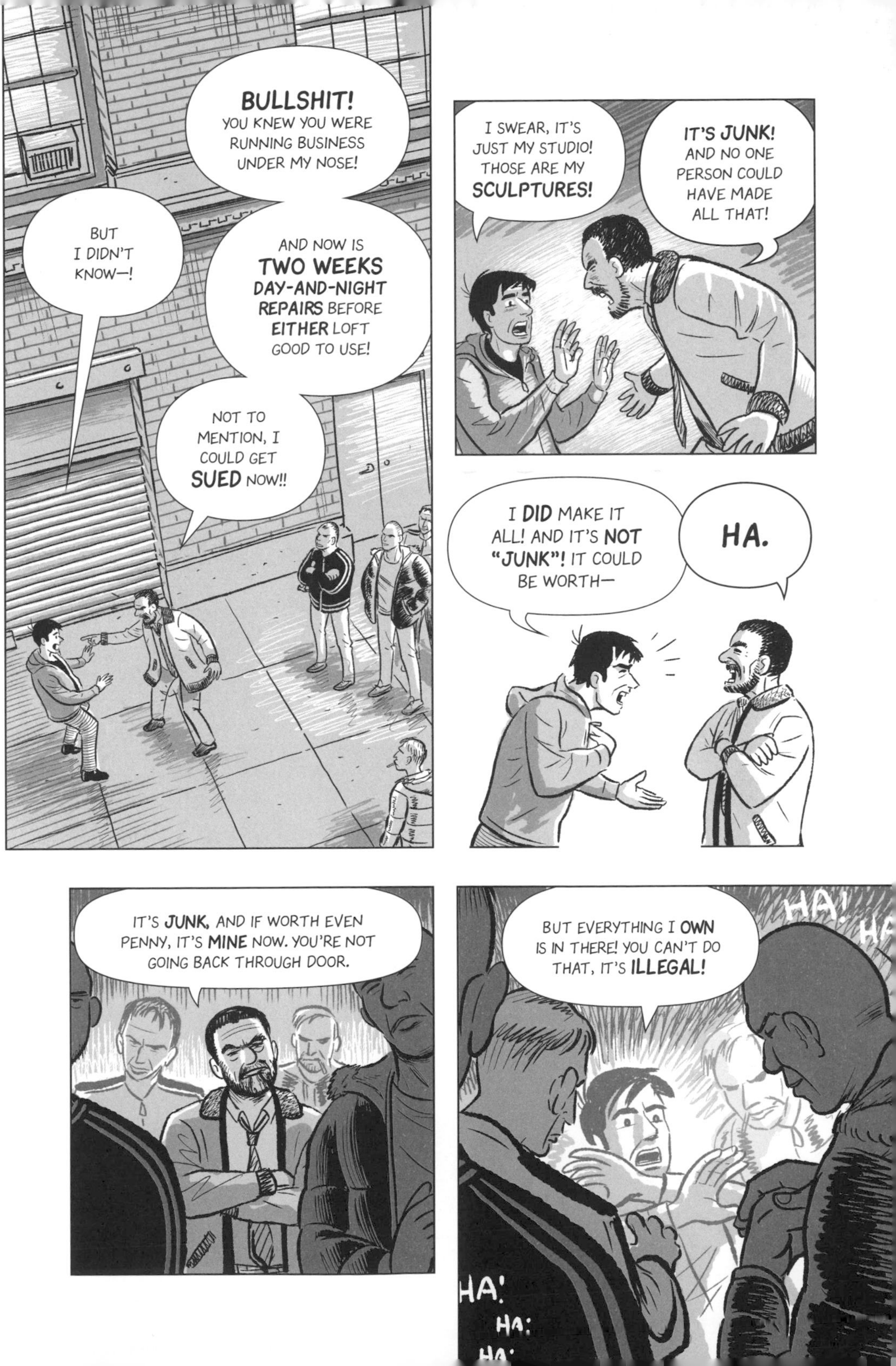
BULLSHIT! YOU KNEW YOU WERE RUNNING BUSINESS UNDER MY NOSE!
BUT I DIDN'T KNOW—!
AND NOW IS TWO WEEKS DAY-AND-NIGHT REPAIRS BEFORE EITHER LOFT GOOD TO USE!
NOT TO MENTION, I COULD GET SUED NOW!!
I SWEAR, IT'S JUST MY STUDIO! THOSE ARE MY SCULPTURES!
IT'S JUNK! AND NO ONE PERSON COULD HAVE MADE ALL THAT!
I DID MAKE IT ALL! AND IT'S NOT "JUNK"! IT COULD BE WORTH—
HA.
IT'S JUNK, AND IF WORTH EVEN PENNY, IT'S MINE NOW. YOU'RE NOT GOING BACK THROUGH DOOR.
BUT EVERYTHING I OWN IS IN THERE! YOU CAN'T DO THAT, IT'S ILLEGAL!
HA!
HA!
HA!
HA!

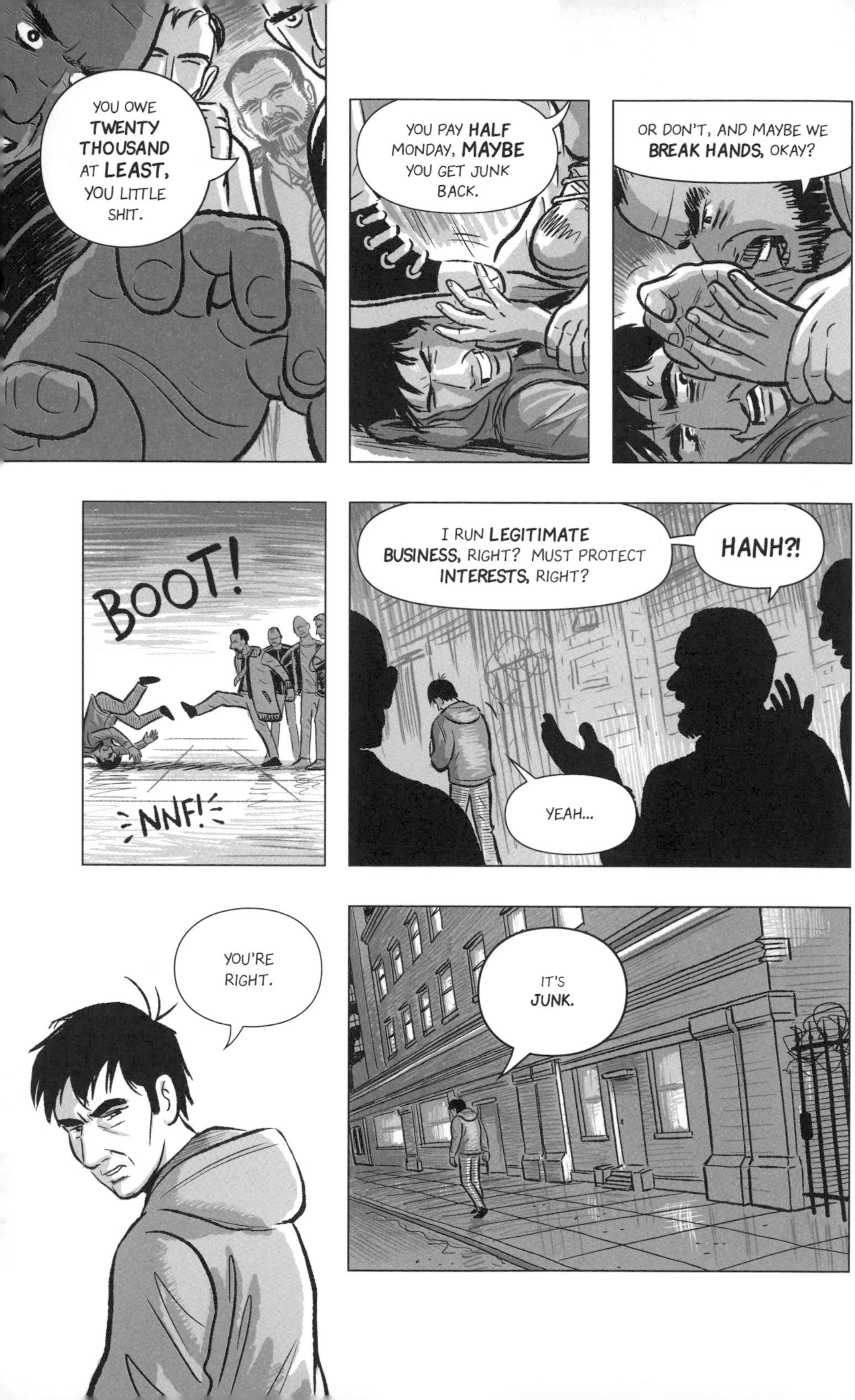
YOU OWE TWENTY THOUSAND AT LEAST, YOU LITTLE SHIT.
YOU PAY HALF MONDAY, MAYBE YOU GET JUNK BACK.
OR DON'T, AND MAYBE WE BREAK HANDS, OKAY?
BOOT!
NNF!
I RUN LEGITIMATE BUSINESS, RIGHT? MUST PROTECT INTERESTS, RIGHT?
HANH?!
YEAH...
YOU'RE RIGHT.
IT'S JUNK.

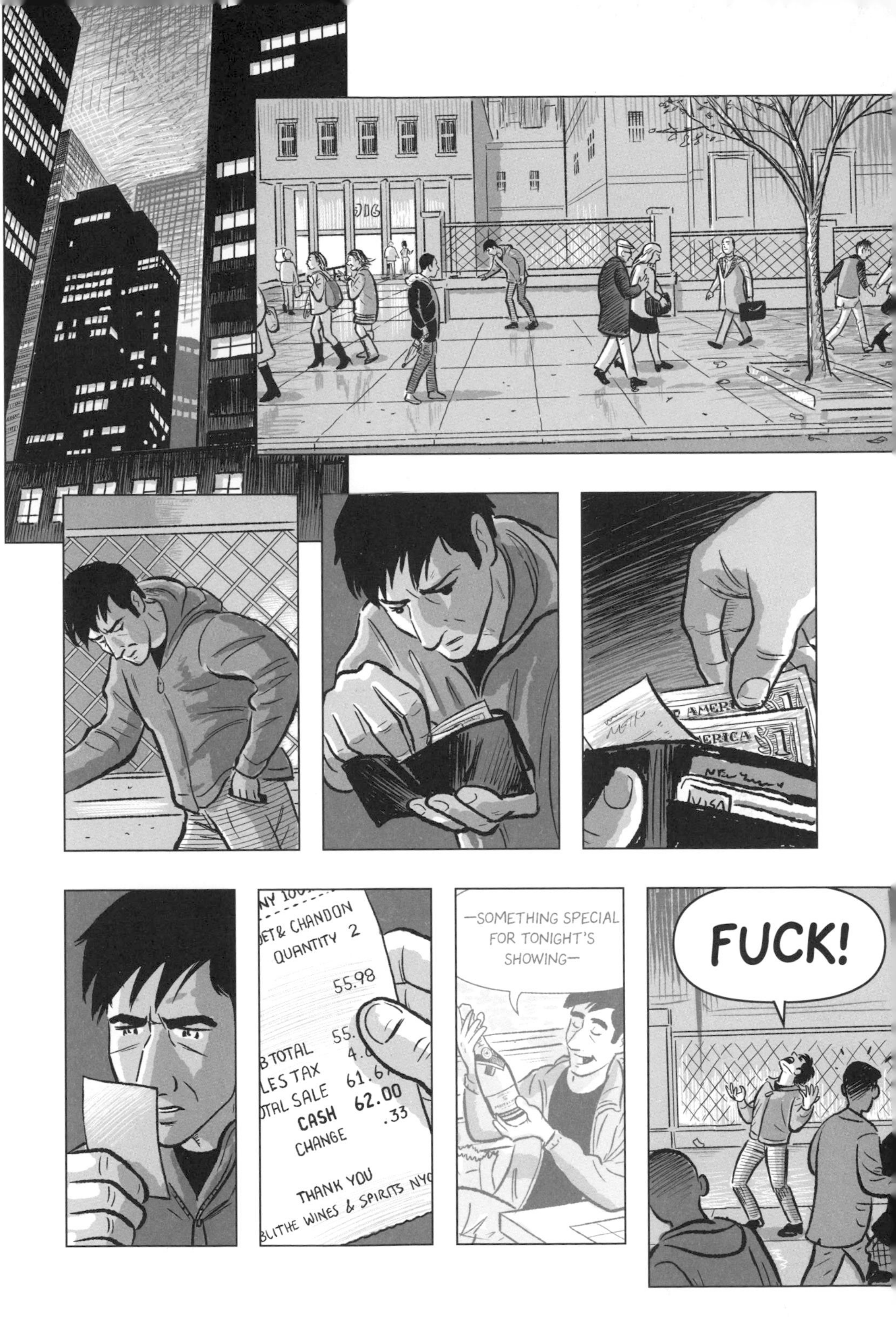
NY 100
ET& CHANDON
QUANTITY 2
55.98
B TOTAL 55.
LES TAX 4.
TAL SALE 61.6
CASH 62.00
CHANGE .33
THANK YOU
BLITHE WINES & SPIRITS NYC
—SOMETHING SPECIAL FOR TONIGHT'S SHOWING—
FUCK!

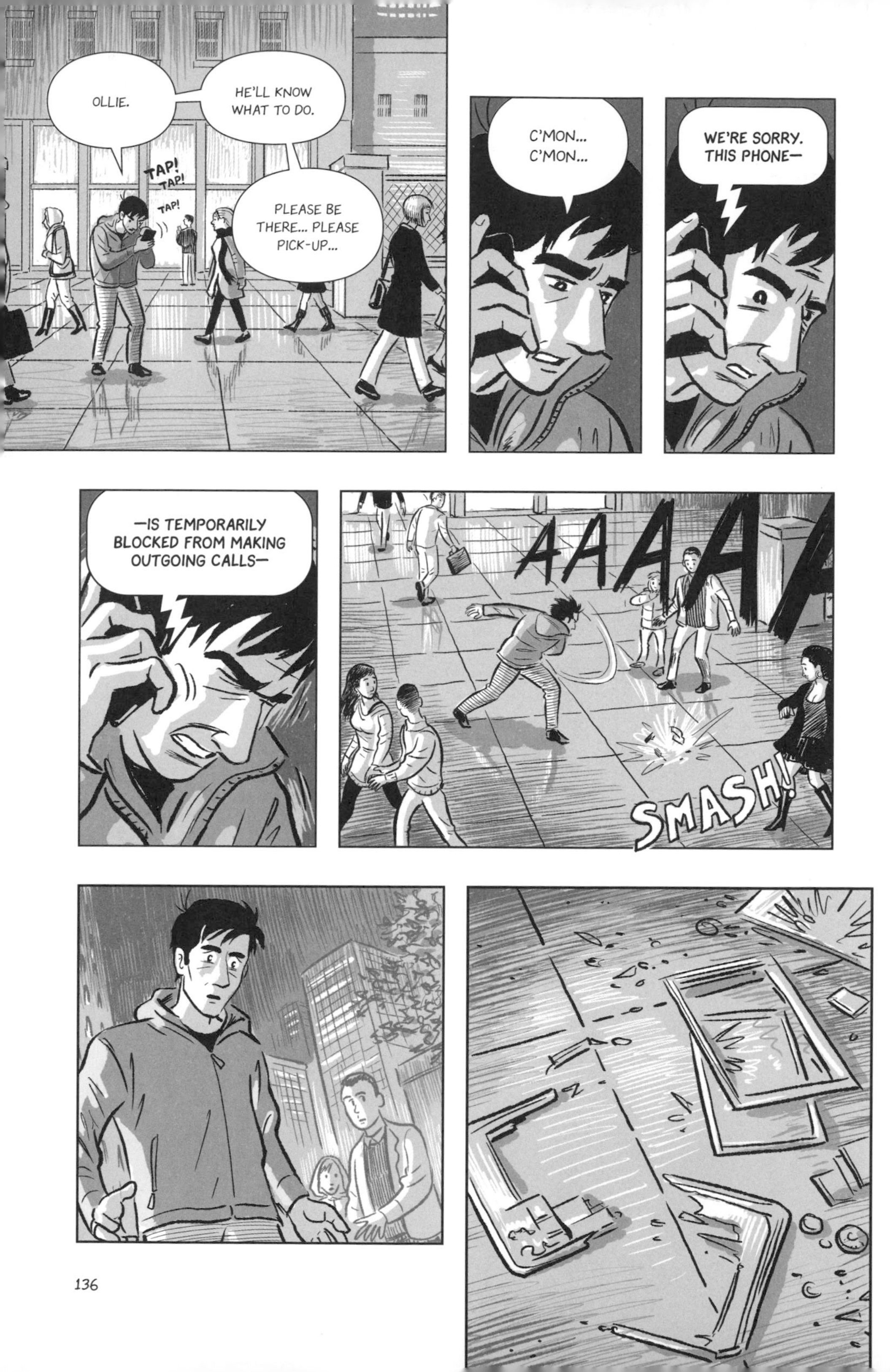
OLLIE.
HE'LL KNOW WHAT TO DO.
TAP! TAP! TAP!
PLEASE BE THERE... PLEASE PICK-UP...
C'MON... C'MON...
WE'RE SORRY. THIS PHONE—
—IS TEMPORARILY BLOCKED FROM MAKING OUTGOING CALLS—
AAAAA
SMASH!

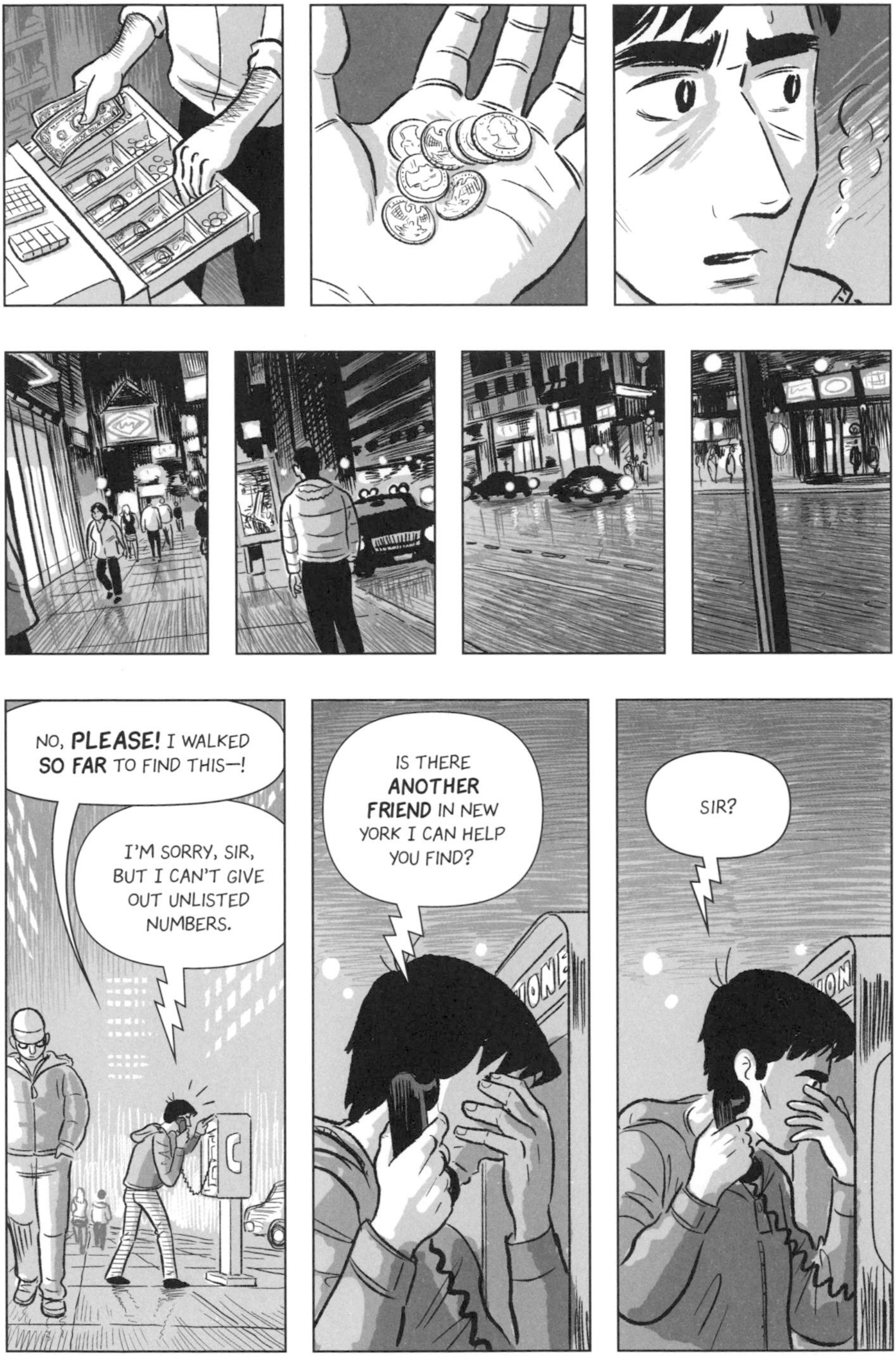
NO, PLEASE! I WALKED SO FAR TO FIND THIS—!
I'M SORRY, SIR, BUT I CAN'T GIVE OUT UNLISTED NUMBERS.
IS THERE ANOTHER FRIEND IN NEW YORK I CAN HELP YOU FIND?
SIR?

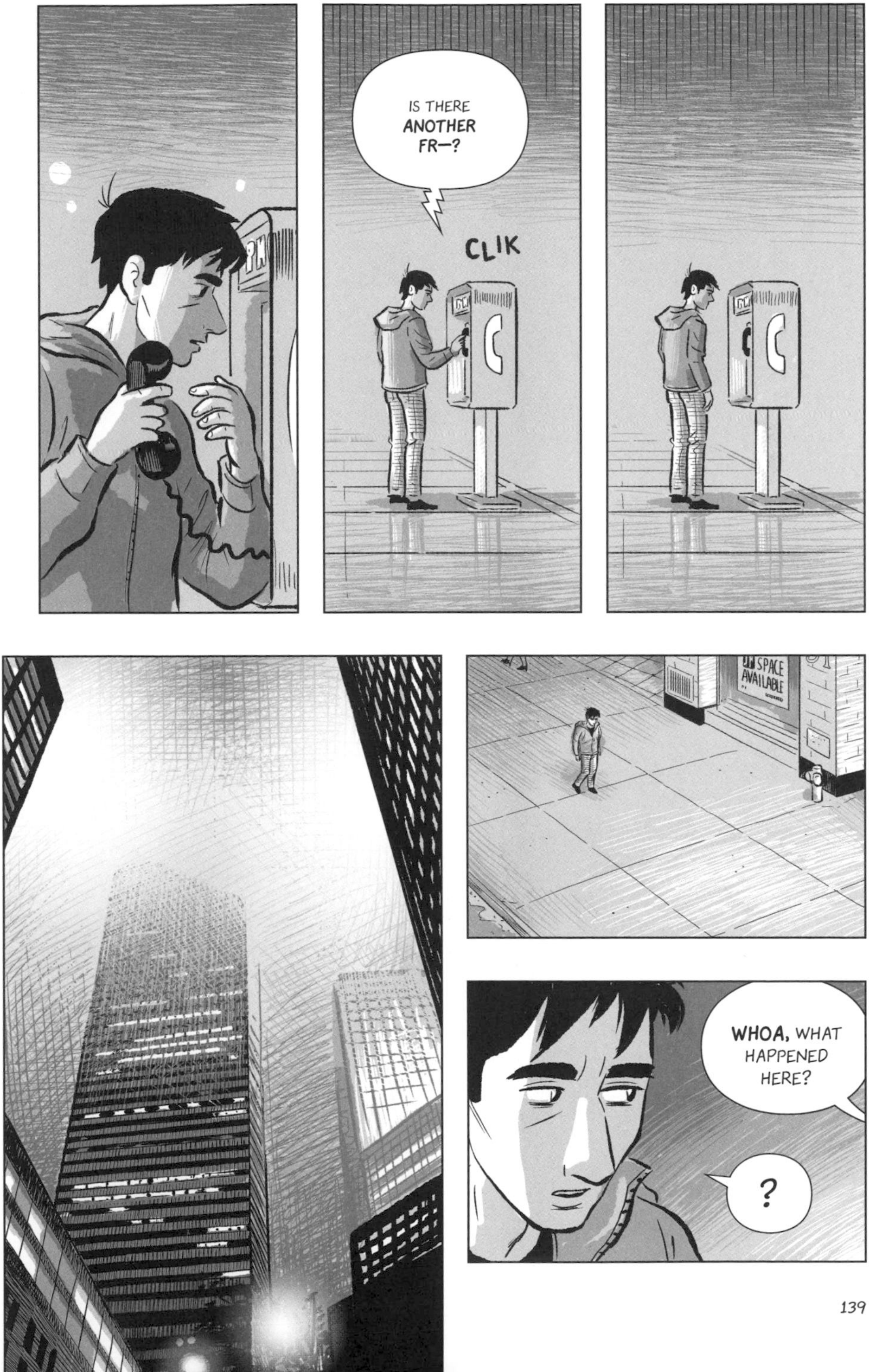
IS THERE ANOTHER FR—?
CLIK
SPACE AVAILABLE
WHOA, WHAT HAPPENED HERE?
?

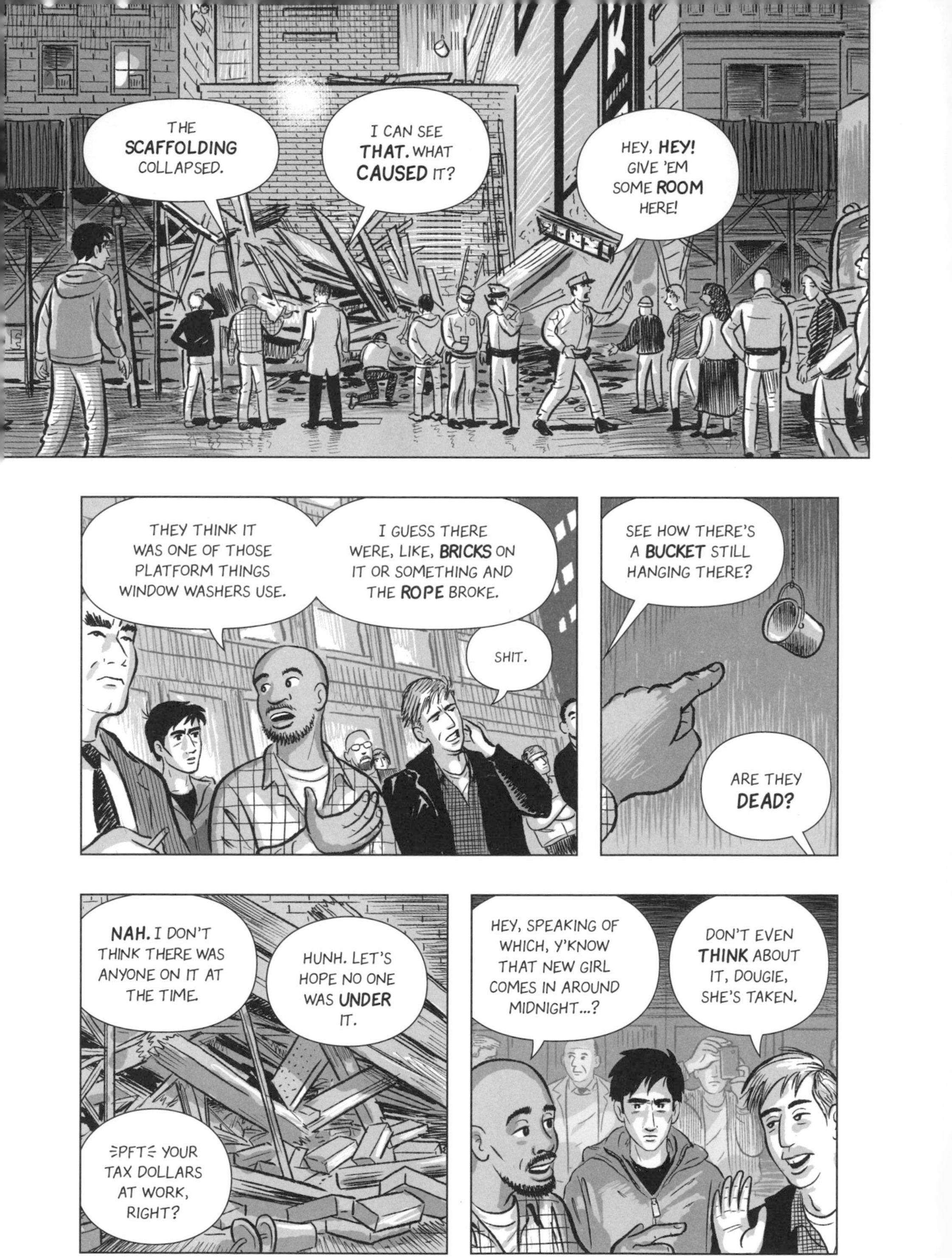
THE SCAFFOLDING COLLAPSED.
I CAN SEE THAT. WHAT CAUSED IT?
HEY, HEY! GIVE 'EM SOME ROOM HERE!
THEY THINK IT WAS ONE OF THOSE PLATFORM THINGS WINDOW WASHERS USE.
I GUESS THERE WERE, LIKE, BRICKS ON IT OR SOMETHING AND THE ROPE BROKE.
SHIT.
SEE HOW THERE'S A BUCKET STILL HANGING THERE?
ARE THEY DEAD?
NAH. I DON'T THINK THERE WAS ANYONE ON IT AT THE TIME.
HUNH. LET'S HOPE NO ONE WAS UNDER IT.
≡PFT≡ YOUR TAX DOLLARS AT WORK, RIGHT?
HEY, SPEAKING OF WHICH, Y'KNOW THAT NEW GIRL COMES IN AROUND MIDNIGHT...?
DON'T EVEN THINK ABOUT IT, DOUGIE, SHE'S TAKEN.

I SAW HER GETTING INTO HECTOR'S CAR AFTER WORK THIS MORNING.

SO? MAYBE THEY'RE CARPOOLING.

NAH, SHE LIVES IN QUEENS. ANYWAY, IT WASN'T CASUAL.

WOW, THAT GUY SWOOPS IN TOO FAST.

YOU HAD A WEEK. SHOULD HAVE MADE YOU MOVE SOONER.

WHAT "MOVE?" I COULDN'T HAVE BOUGHT HER MORE THAN A HOT DOG 'TIL I PAID RENT, ANYWAY.

NEITHER COULD HECTOR, BUT HE'S GOT WHEELS AND A PLACE HE CAN WARM UP.

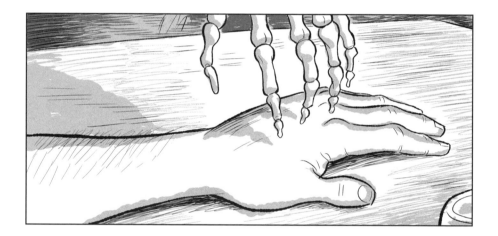

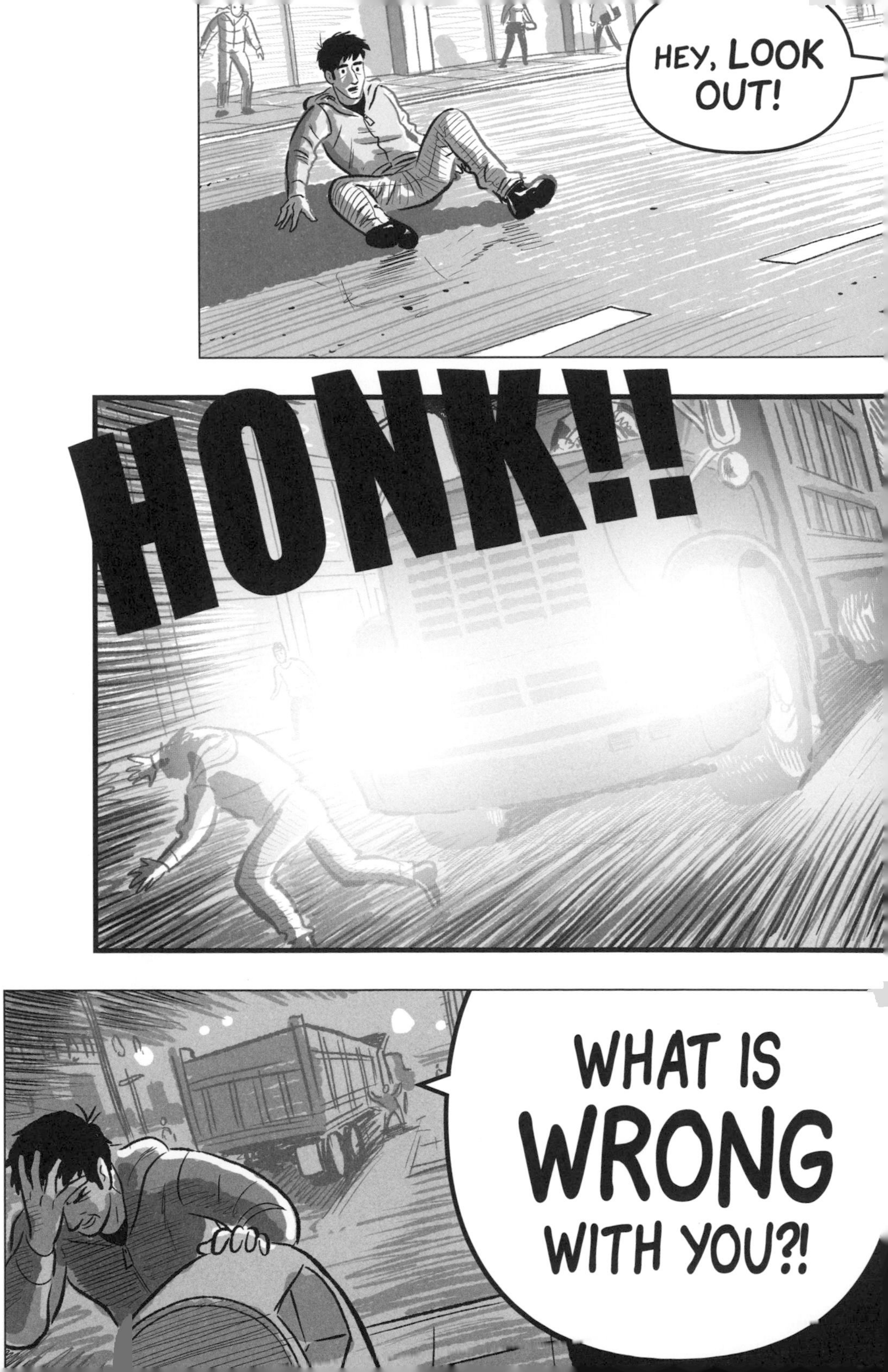
HEY, LOOK OUT!
HONK!!
WHAT IS WRONG WITH YOU?!

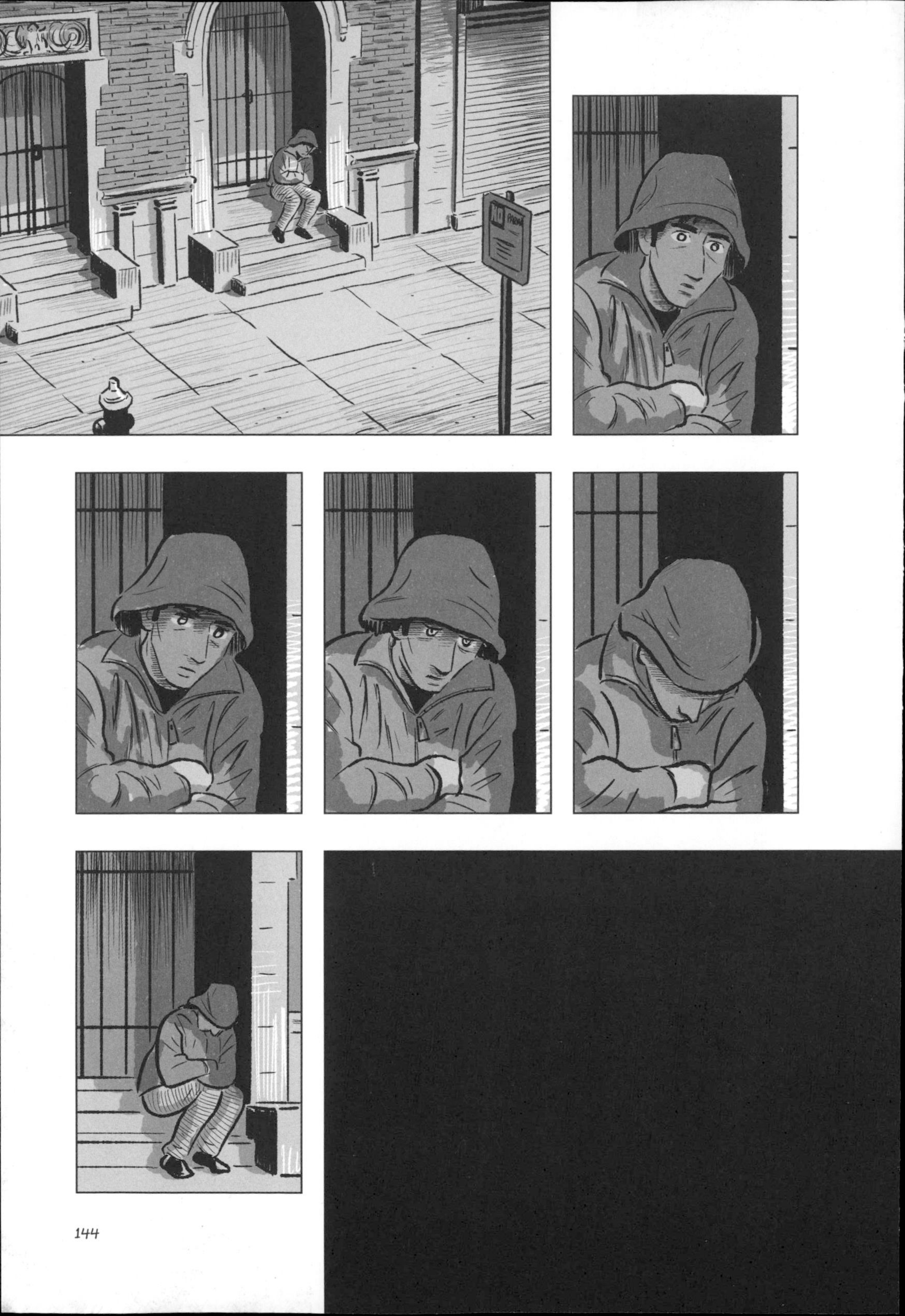

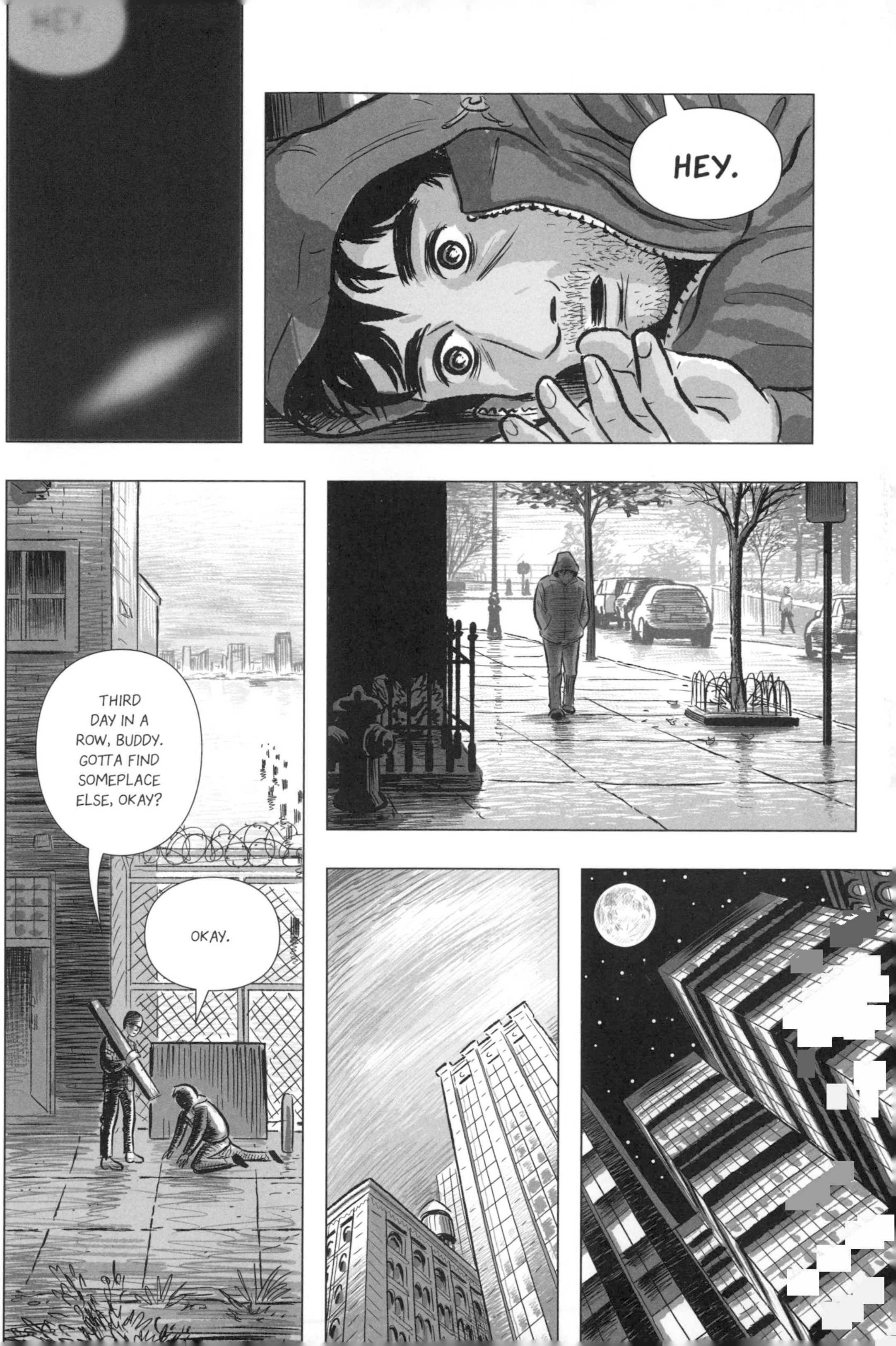
HEY.
THIRD DAY IN A ROW, BUDDY. GOTTA FIND SOMEPLACE ELSE, OKAY?
OKAY.

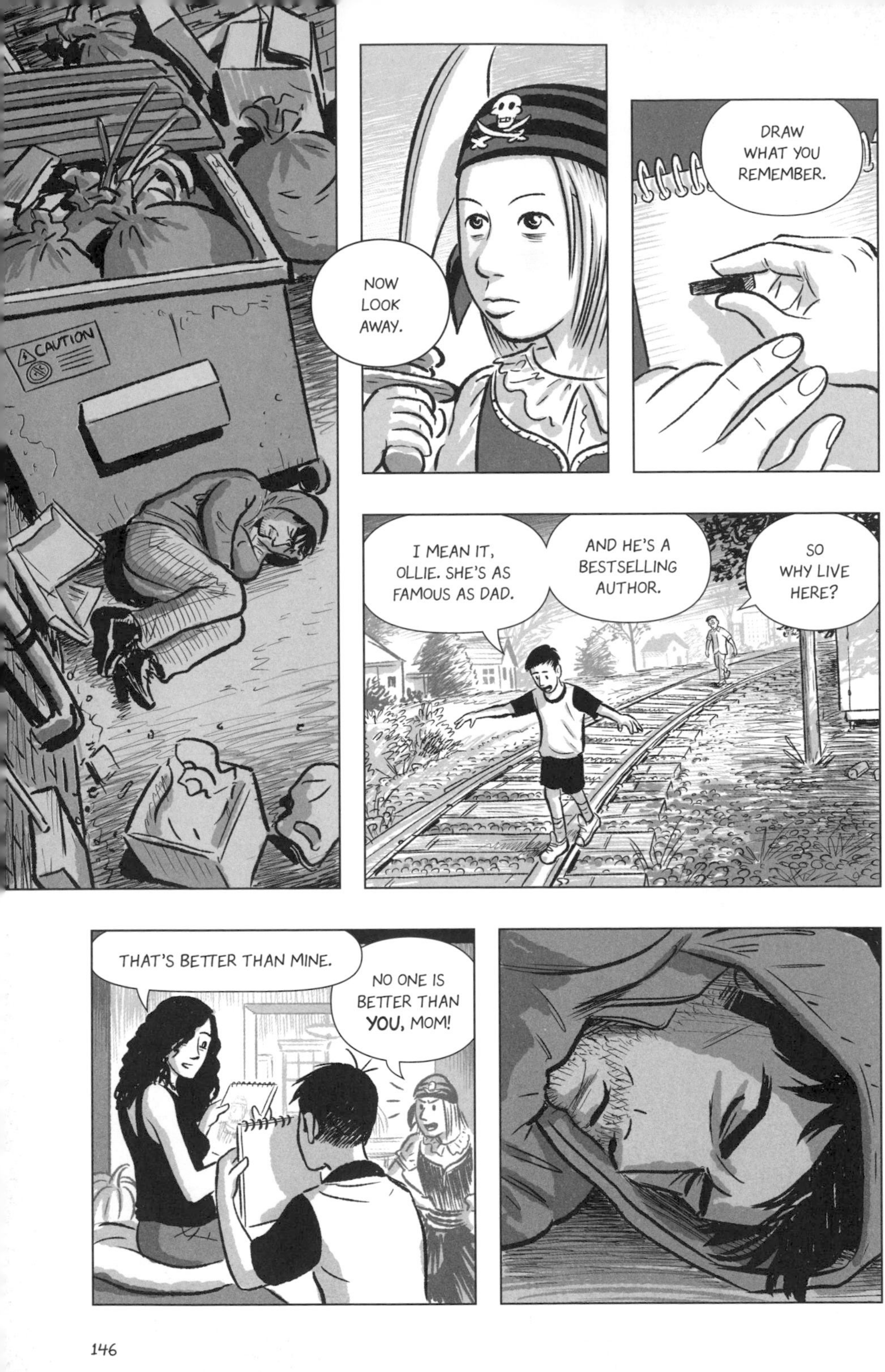
NOW LOOK AWAY.
DRAW WHAT YOU REMEMBER.
I MEAN IT, OLLIE. SHE'S AS FAMOUS AS DAD.
AND HE'S A BESTSELLING AUTHOR.
SO WHY LIVE HERE?
THAT'S BETTER THAN MINE.
NO ONE IS BETTER THAN **YOU**, MOM!

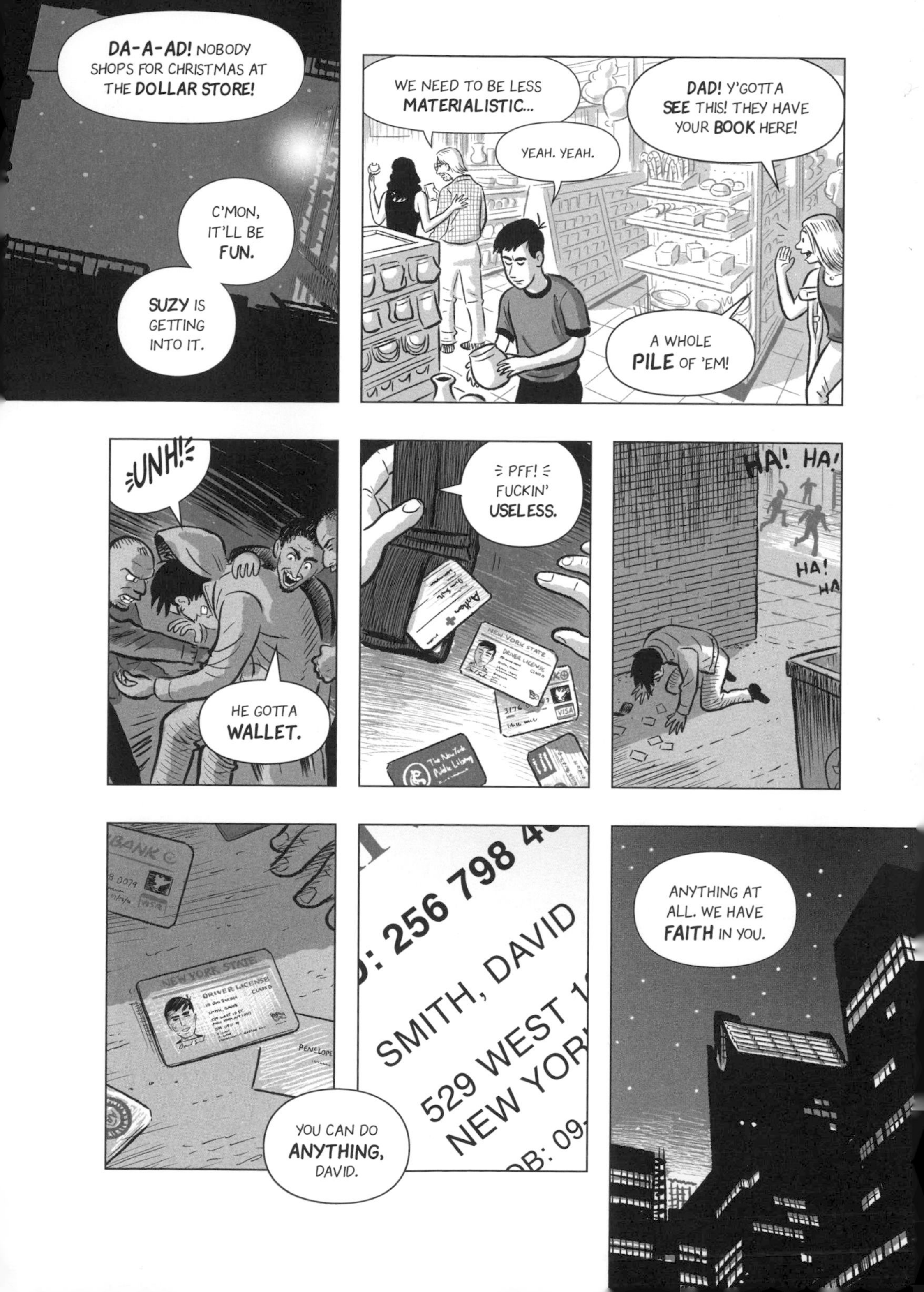
DA-A-AD! NOBODY SHOPS FOR CHRISTMAS AT THE DOLLAR STORE!
C'MON, IT'LL BE FUN.
SUZY IS GETTING INTO IT.
WE NEED TO BE LESS MATERIALISTIC...
YEAH. YEAH.
DAD! Y'GOTTA SEE THIS! THEY HAVE YOUR BOOK HERE!
A WHOLE PILE OF 'EM!
UNH!
HE GOTTA WALLET.
PFF! FUCKIN' USELESS.
NEW YORK STATE
DRIVER LICENSE
VISA
HA! HA!
HA!
HA
NEW YORK STATE
DRIVER LICENSE
PENELOPE
: 256 798 4
SMITH, DAVID
529 WEST 1
NEW YOR
OB: 09-
YOU CAN DO ANYTHING, DAVID.
ANYTHING AT ALL. WE HAVE FAITH IN YOU.

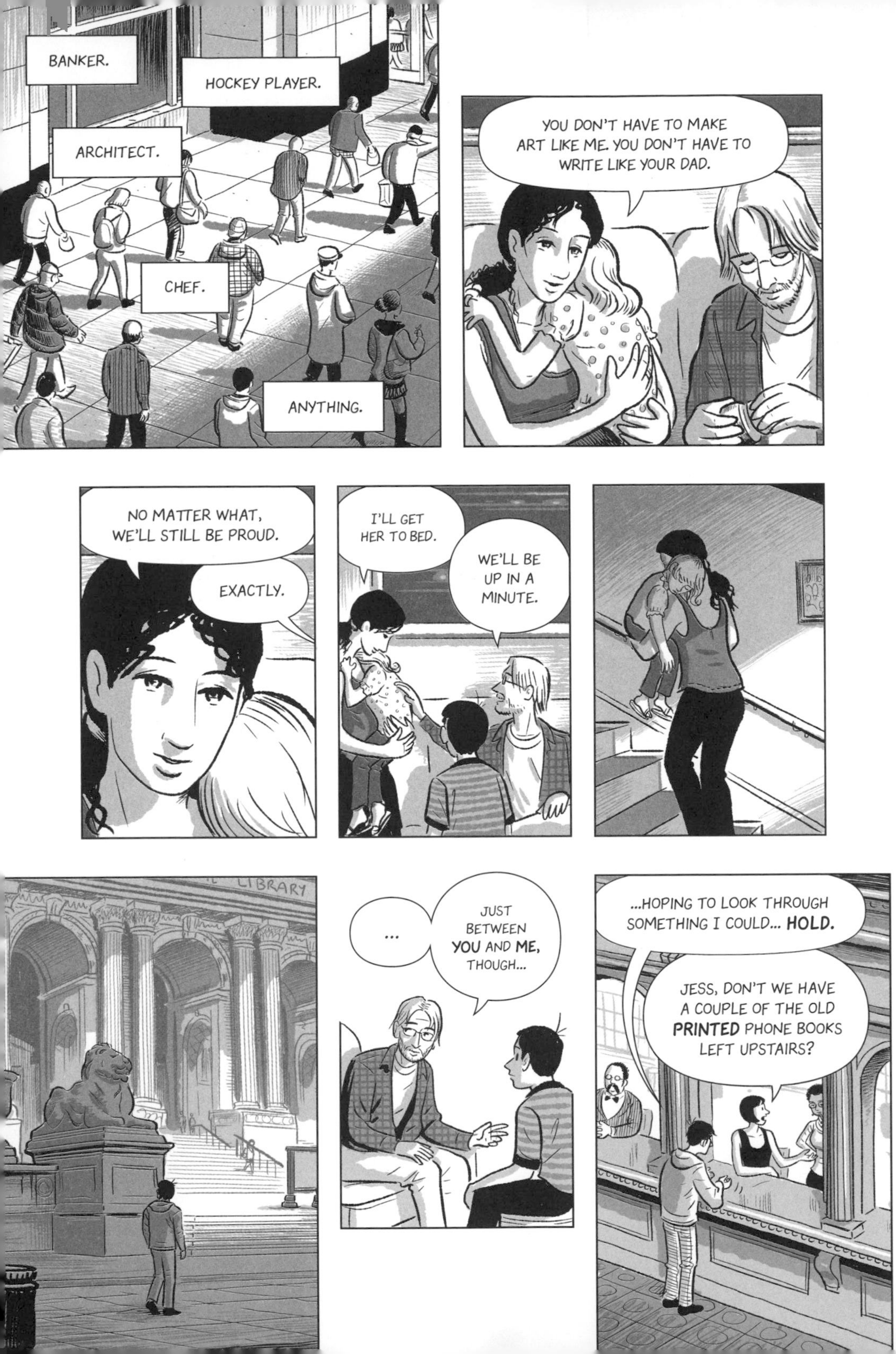
BANKER.
HOCKEY PLAYER.
ARCHITECT.
CHEF.
ANYTHING.
YOU DON'T HAVE TO MAKE ART LIKE ME. YOU DON'T HAVE TO WRITE LIKE YOUR DAD.
NO MATTER WHAT, WE'LL STILL BE PROUD.
EXACTLY.
I'LL GET HER TO BED.
WE'LL BE UP IN A MINUTE.
LIBRARY
...
JUST BETWEEN **YOU** AND **ME,** THOUGH...
...HOPING TO LOOK THROUGH SOMETHING I COULD... **HOLD.**
JESS, DON'T WE HAVE A COUPLE OF THE OLD **PRINTED** PHONE BOOKS LEFT UPSTAIRS?

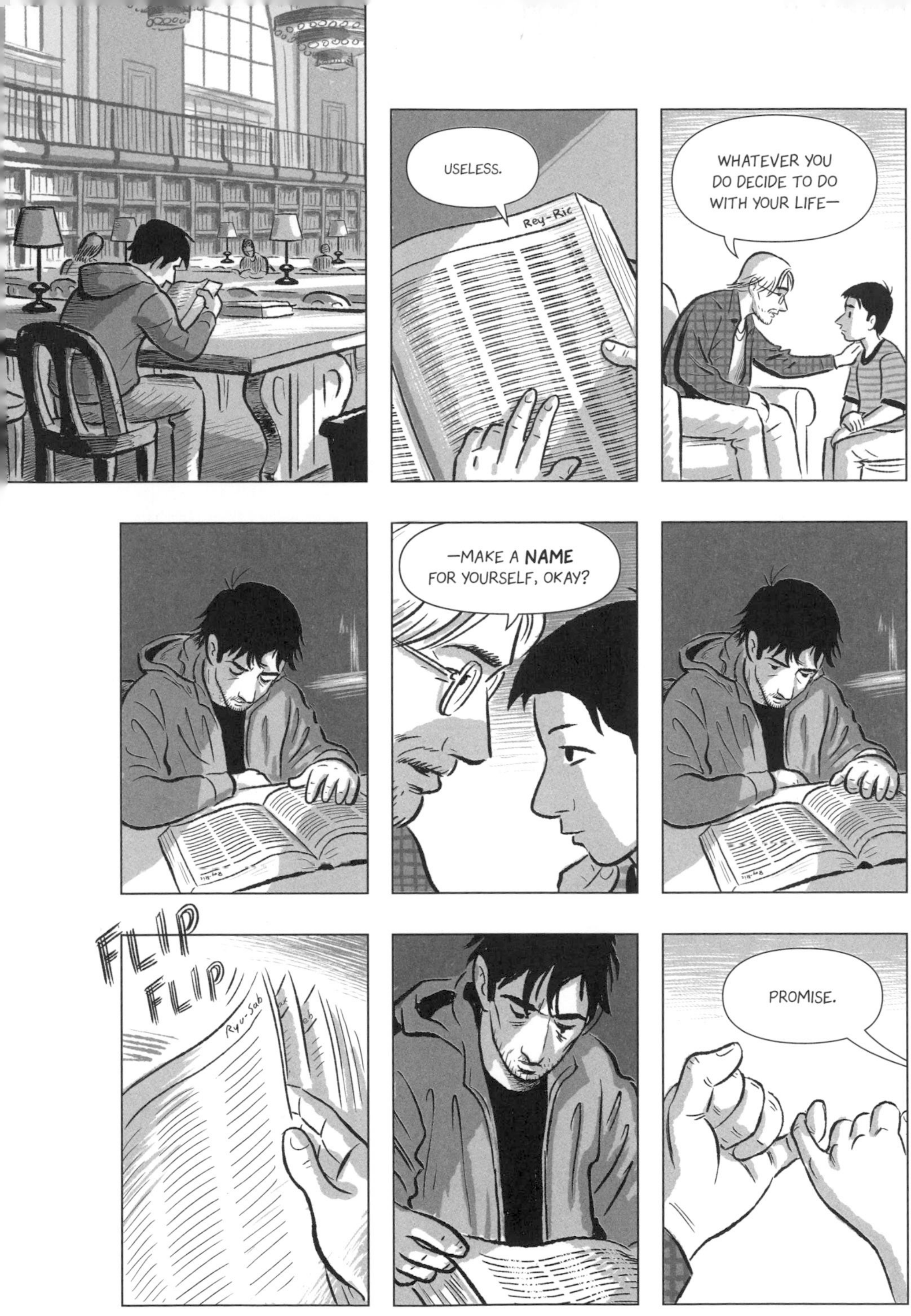
USELESS.
Rey-Ric
WHATEVER YOU DO DECIDE TO DO WITH YOUR LIFE—
—MAKE A **NAME** FOR YOURSELF, OKAY?
FLIP FLIP
Ryu-Sab
PROMISE.

Smith David 27 Avenue C........................ 50
Smith David 2025 Bway.......................... 58
Smith David 2130 Bway.......................... 72
Smith David 3333 Bway.......................... 28
Smith David 265 Cabrini Blvd.................. 56
Smith David 292 Convent Av.................... 49
Smith David 180 Edgcmbe Av.................... 28
Smith David 708 Grenwch Av.................... 80
Smith David 90 La Salle........................ 74
Smith David 531 Main Rsvlt Isl................ 83
Smith David 177 Nagle Av....................... 94
Smith David 30 Park Av......................... 68
Smith David 89 Park Av......................... 68
Smith David 1175 Park Av....................... 34
Smith David 55 Perry........................... 67
Smith David 626 Riv Dr......................... 28
Smith David 40 St Nicholas Pl................. 86
Smith David 15 Sheridan Sq.................... 24
Smith David 80 Thompson....................... 33
Smith David 107 Thompson...................... 96
Smith David 424 West End Av................... 72
Smith David 1540 York Av...................... 73
Smith David 160 1 Av........................... 25
Smith David 1964 1 Av.......................... 72
Smith David 2070 1 Av.......................... 86
Smith David 1905 2 Av.......................... 83
Smith David 380 3 Av........................... 68
Smith David 1428 5 Av.......................... 86
Smith David 3856 10 Av......................... 56
Smith David 230 E 15........................... 67
Smith David 321 W 24........................... 98
Smith David 427 W 26........................... 56
Smith David 141 E 56........................... 75
Smith David 429 E 65........................... 24
Smith David 235 E 82........................... 83
Smith David 200 E 84........................... 28
Smith David 355 E 86........................... 72
Smith David 50 E 89............................ 72
Smith David 310 E 90........................... 41
Smith David 215 E 102.......................... 34
Smith David 324 E 108.......................... 83
Smith David 15-19 W 110....................... 87
Smith David 236 W 114.......................... 66
Smith David 523 W 135.......................... 86
Smith David 526 W 147.......................... 36
Smith David 310 W 148.......................... 86
Smith David 231 W 149.......................... 92
Smith David 648 W 158.......................... 56
Smith David 708 W 171.......................... 78
Smith David 605 W 182.......................... 92
Smith David A 280 Mott........................ 26
Smith David A 2 Peter Cooper Rd............. 23
Smith David B 45 Wadsworth Terr............. 43
Smith David D 1385 York Av.................. 86
Smith David F 111 4 Av....................... 47
Smith David H 451 E 14....................... 50
Smith David H 366 W 46....................... 75

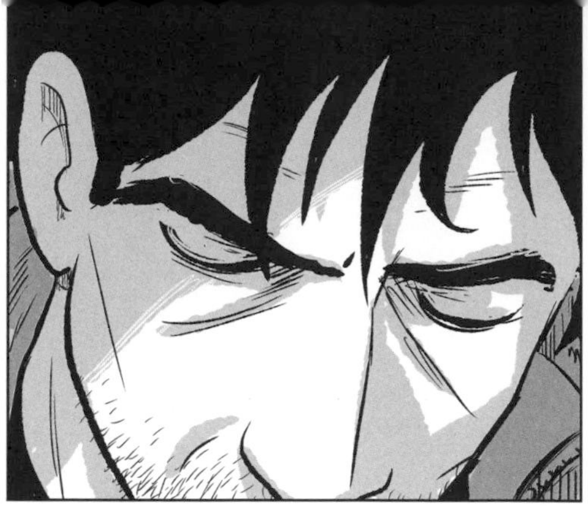

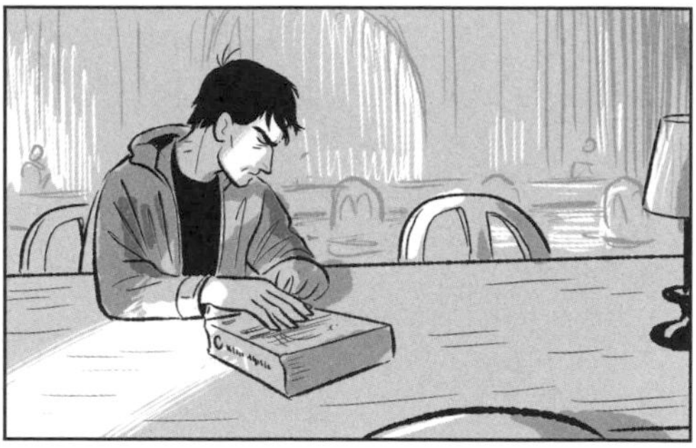

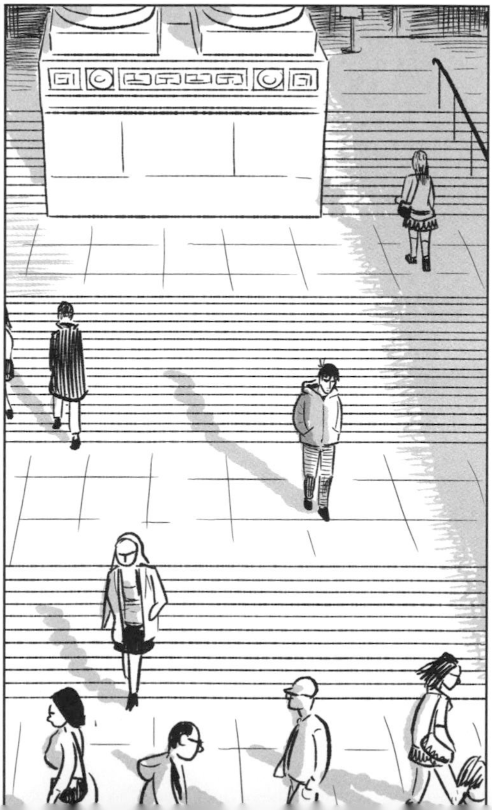

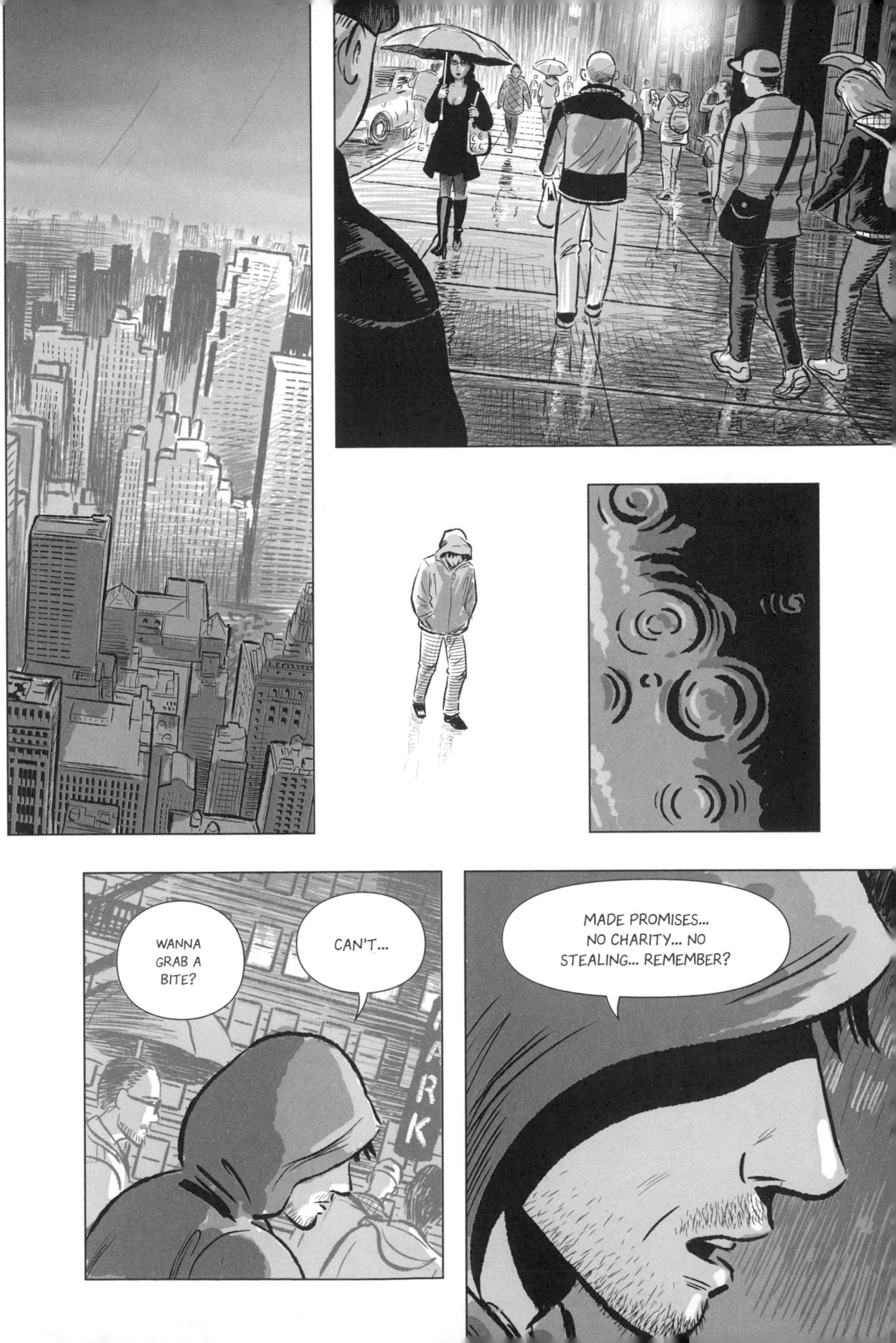
WANNA GRAB A BITE?
CAN'T...
MADE PROMISES... NO CHARITY... NO STEALING... REMEMBER?

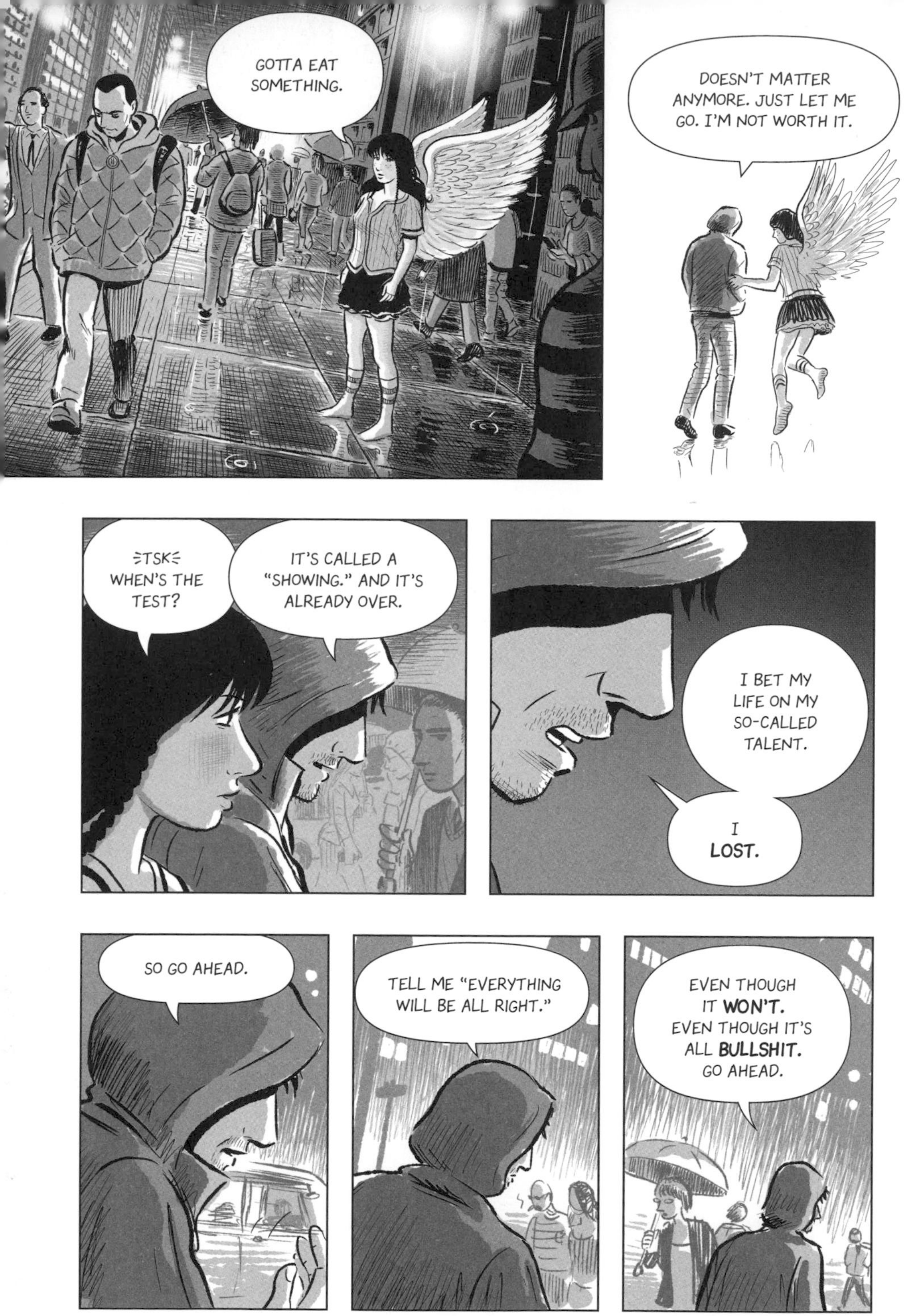

GOTTA EAT SOMETHING.
DOESN'T MATTER ANYMORE. JUST LET ME GO. I'M NOT WORTH IT.
≡TSK≡ WHEN'S THE TEST?
IT'S CALLED A "SHOWING." AND IT'S ALREADY OVER.
I BET MY LIFE ON MY SO-CALLED TALENT.
I **LOST.**
SO GO AHEAD.
TELL ME "EVERYTHING WILL BE ALL RIGHT."
EVEN THOUGH IT **WON'T.** EVEN THOUGH IT'S ALL **BULLSHIT.** GO AHEAD.

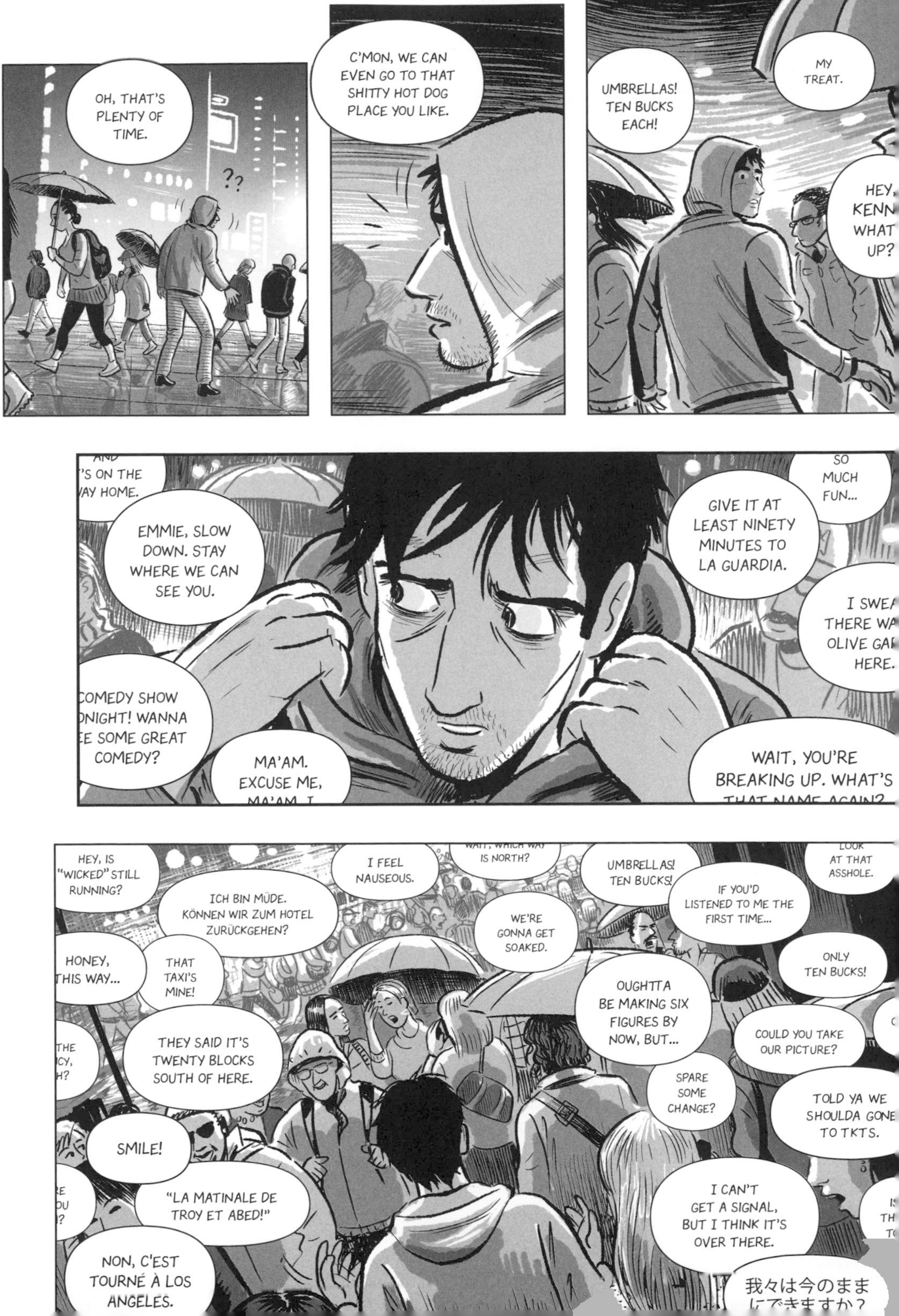
OH, THAT'S PLENTY OF TIME.
??
C'MON, WE CAN EVEN GO TO THAT SHITTY HOT DOG PLACE YOU LIKE.
UMBRELLAS! TEN BUCKS EACH!
MY TREAT.
HEY, KENN WHAT UP?
'S ON THE WAY HOME.
EMMIE, SLOW DOWN. STAY WHERE WE CAN SEE YOU.
GIVE IT AT LEAST NINETY MINUTES TO LA GUARDIA.
SO MUCH FUN...
I SWEA THERE WA OLIVE GAR HERE.
COMEDY SHOW ONIGHT! WANNA EE SOME GREAT COMEDY?
MA'AM. EXCUSE ME,
WAIT, YOU'RE BREAKING UP. WHAT'S
HEY, IS "WICKED" STILL RUNNING?
ICH BIN MÜDE. KÖNNEN WIR ZUM HOTEL ZURÜCKGEHEN?
I FEEL NAUSEOUS.
IS NORTH?
UMBRELLAS! TEN BUCKS!
AT THAT ASSHOLE.
IF YOU'D LISTENED TO ME THE FIRST TIME...
WE'RE GONNA GET SOAKED.
HONEY, THIS WAY...
THAT TAXI'S MINE!
ONLY TEN BUCKS!
OUGHTTA BE MAKING SIX FIGURES BY NOW, BUT...
THEY SAID IT'S TWENTY BLOCKS SOUTH OF HERE.
COULD YOU TAKE OUR PICTURE?
SPARE SOME CHANGE?
TOLD YA WE SHOULDA GONE TO TKTS.
SMILE!
"LA MATINALE DE TROY ET ABED!"
I CAN'T GET A SIGNAL, BUT I THINK IT'S OVER THERE.
NON, C'EST TOURNÉ À LOS ANGELES.
我々は今のままにできますか？

BE THERE LATE ALL THIS WEEK.

FRONT POCKET, I KNOW...

I LOVE YOU TOO, STUPID.

WE COULD SEE IT NOW AND DO A LATE DINNER.

SOMEWHERE WARM AND DRY...

HOW MUCH ELECTRICITY D'YA THINK IT USES?

HE GET COLD?

OKAY, BUT I'M GOING TO NEED CAFFEINE FIRST.

KOCH WOULD'VE NEVER PUT UP WITH THAT.

I'M GONNA RUIN THESE SHOES.

IS THAT A TARGET OR AN AD FOR TARGET?

DON'T STARE AT THE COWBOY, TIMMY.

OOH! THINK THEY HAVE THE CHOCOLATE CREME FILLED?

WHO

STARTS N TEN.

I DIDN'T SAY IT MADE YOU LOOK FAT!

DON'T LIKE THOSE CLOUDS.

THIS WAY...

CAN WE GO BACK TO THE HOTEL NOW?

USE ME, RRY.

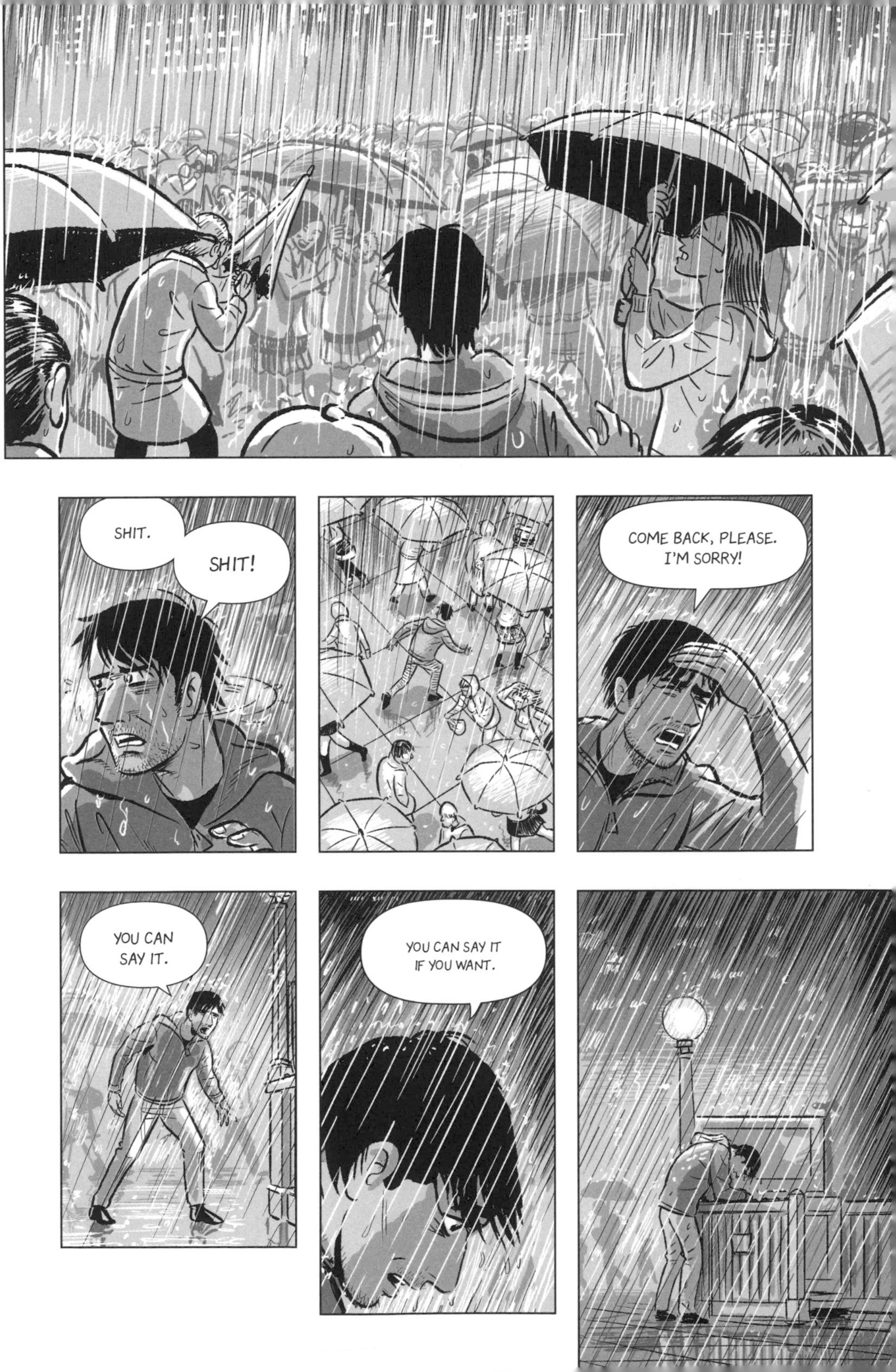
SHIT.
SHIT!
COME BACK, PLEASE. I'M SORRY!
YOU CAN SAY IT.
YOU CAN SAY IT IF YOU WANT.

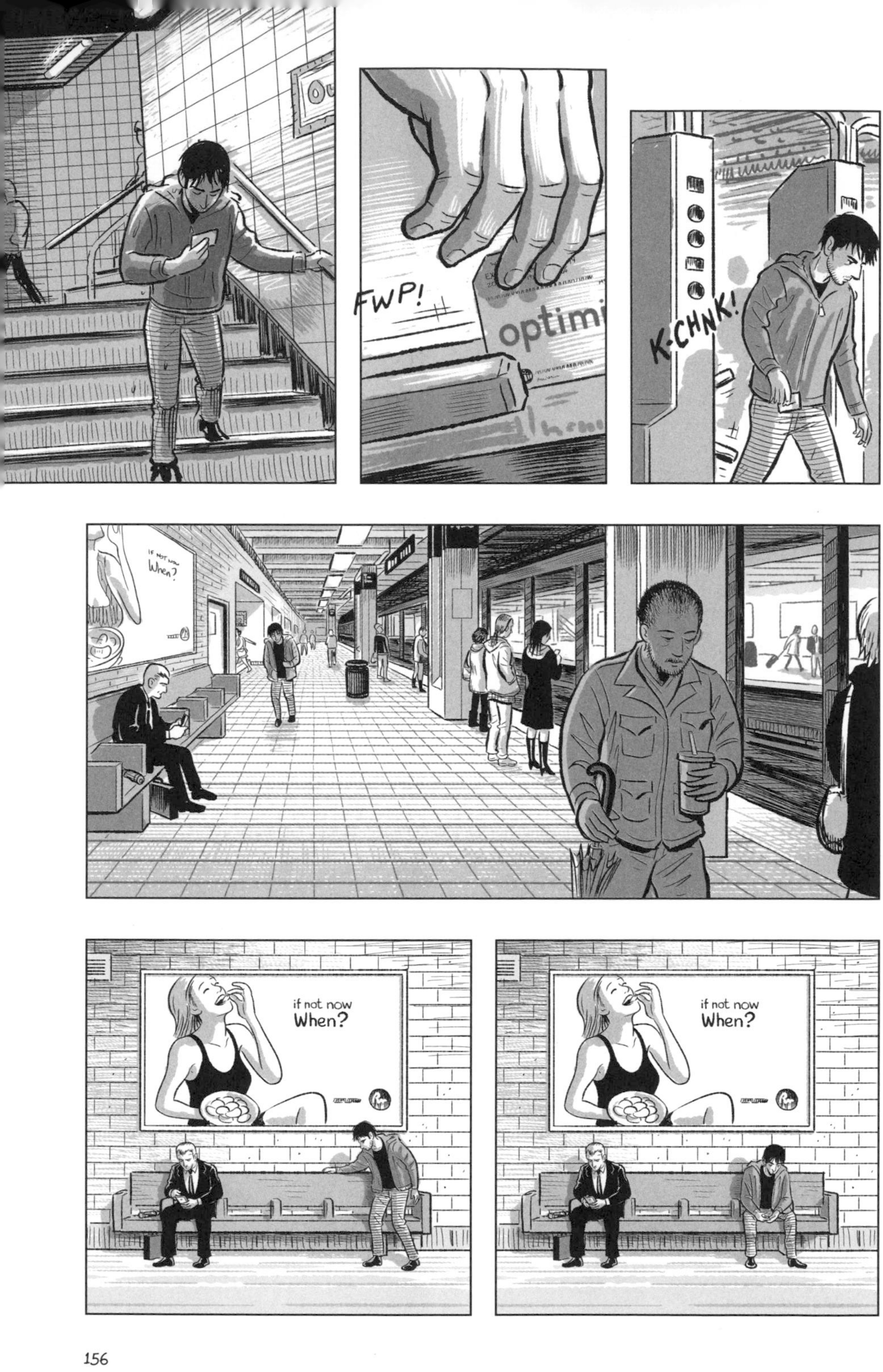
FWP!
optimi
K-CHNK!
if not now
When?
if not now
When?
if not now
When?

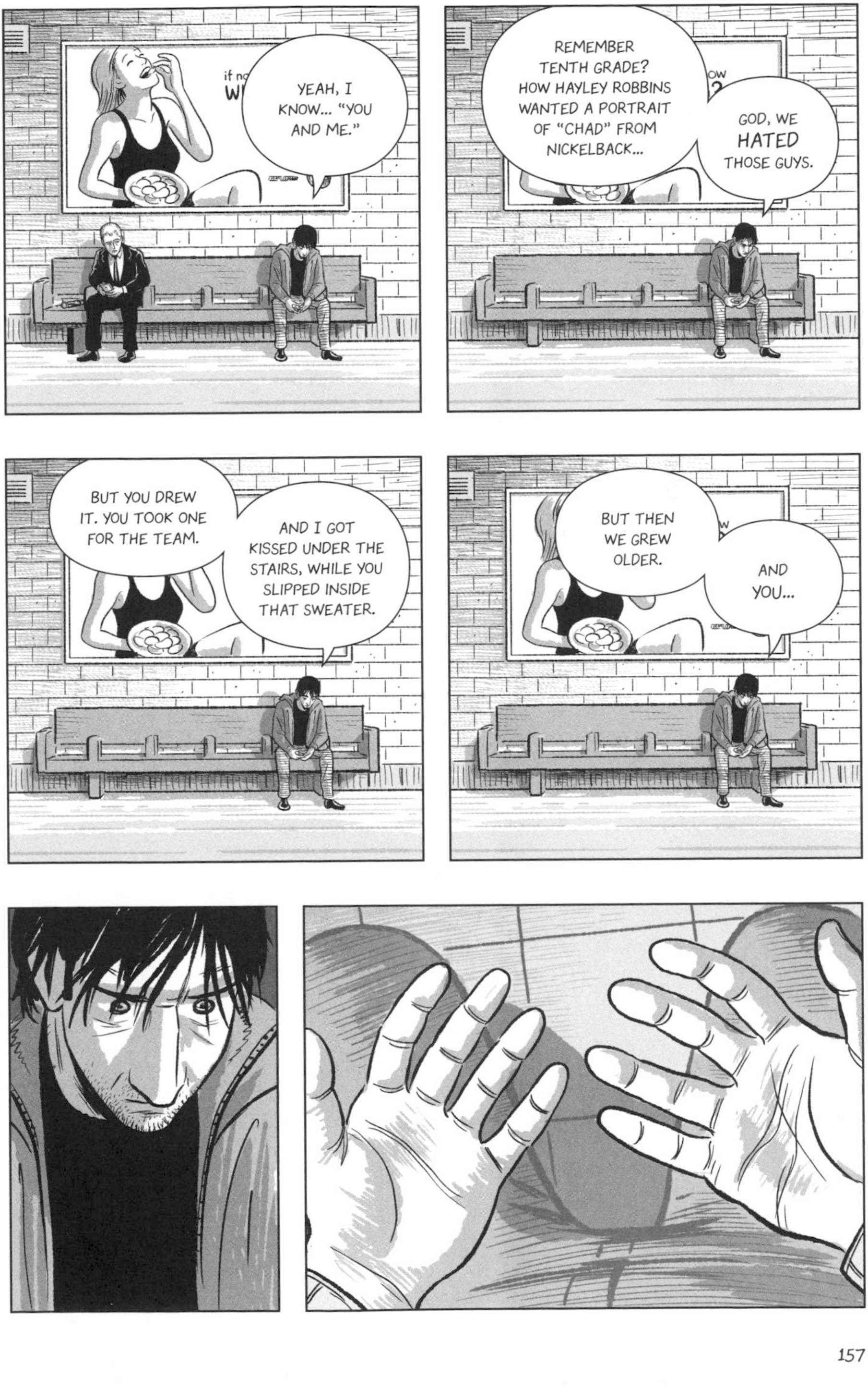

YEAH, I KNOW... "YOU AND ME."
REMEMBER TENTH GRADE? HOW HAYLEY ROBBINS WANTED A PORTRAIT OF "CHAD" FROM NICKELBACK...
GOD, WE HATED THOSE GUYS.
BUT YOU DREW IT. YOU TOOK ONE FOR THE TEAM.
AND I GOT KISSED UNDER THE STAIRS, WHILE YOU SLIPPED INSIDE THAT SWEATER.
BUT THEN WE GREW OLDER.
AND YOU...

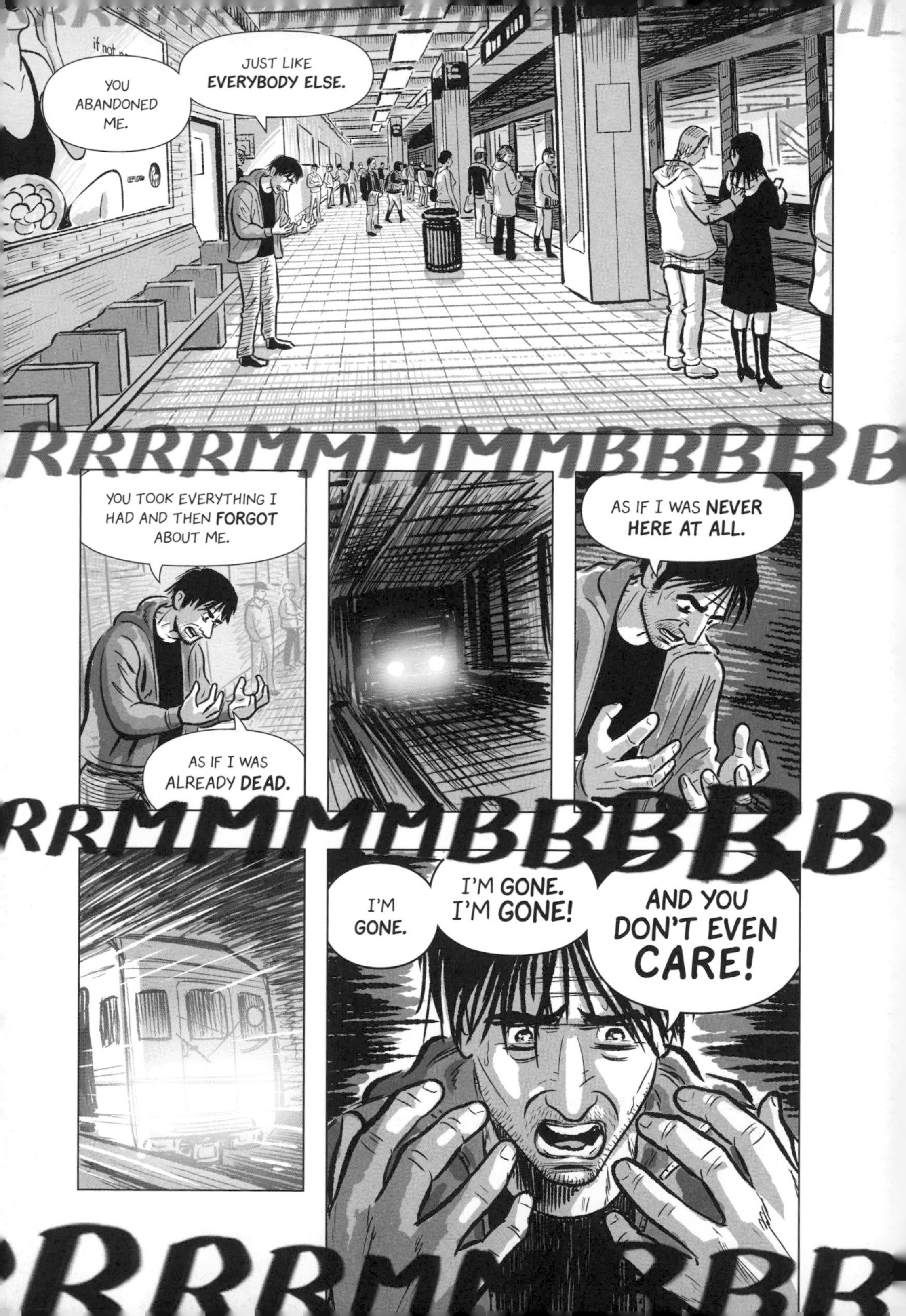

YOU ABANDONED ME.
JUST LIKE EVERYBODY ELSE.
RRRRMMMMMBBBBB
YOU TOOK EVERYTHING I HAD AND THEN FORGOT ABOUT ME.
AS IF I WAS ALREADY DEAD.
AS IF I WAS NEVER HERE AT ALL.
RRMMMMBBBBB
I'M GONE.
I'M GONE. I'M GONE!
AND YOU DON'T EVEN CARE!
RRRRMMRBBB

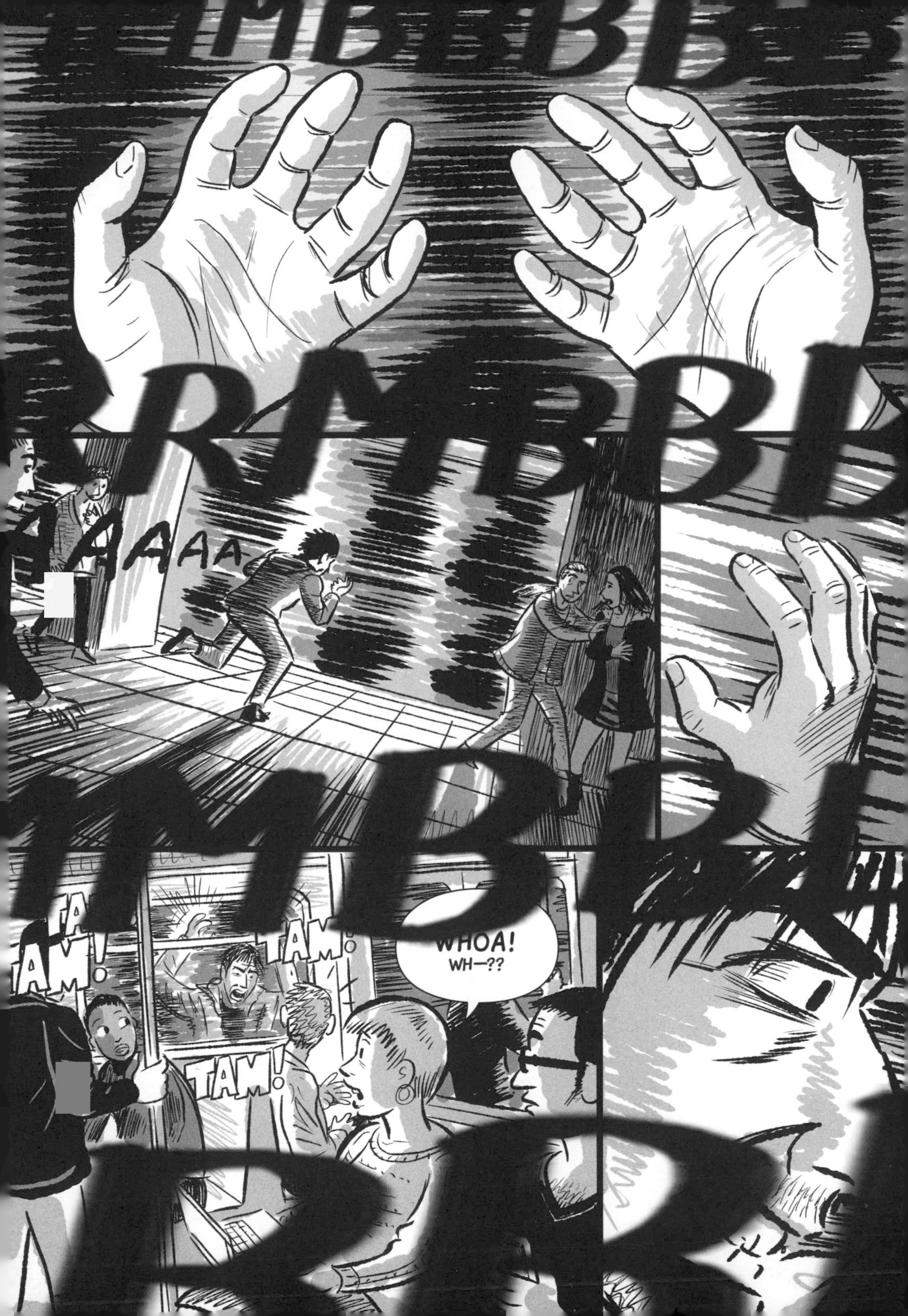
RMBBB
RMBBB
AAAAA
TAM!
TAM!
TAM!
TAM!
WHOA!
WH—??

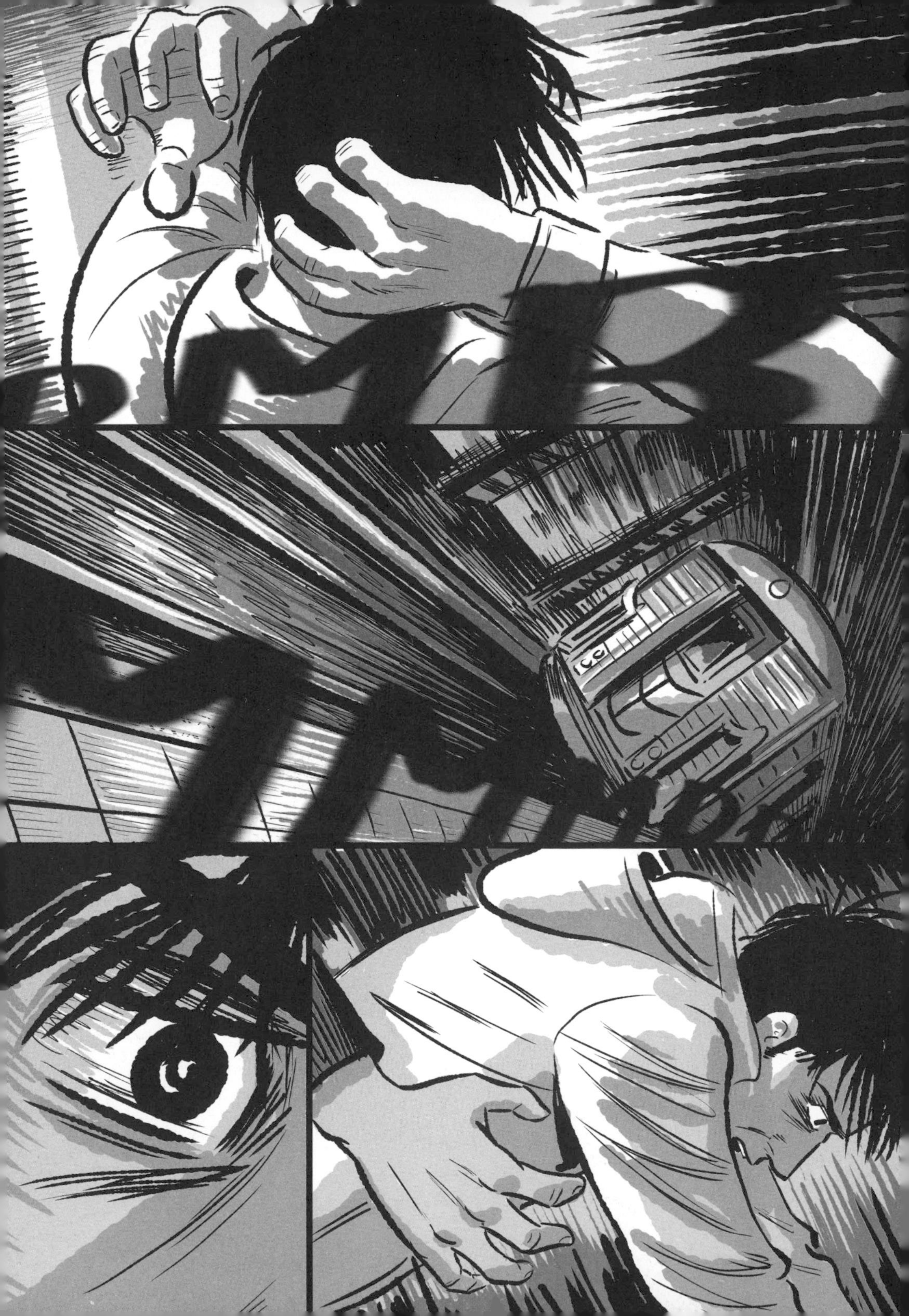

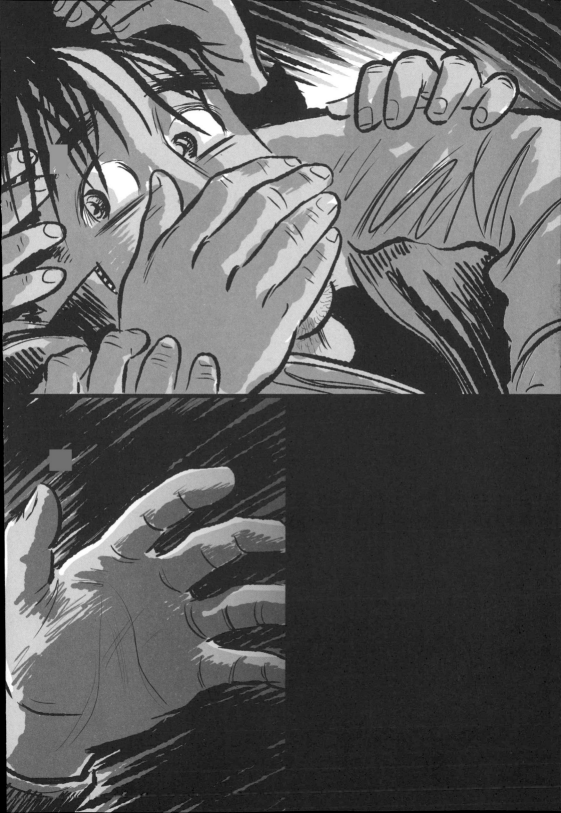

3.

THE PROMISE

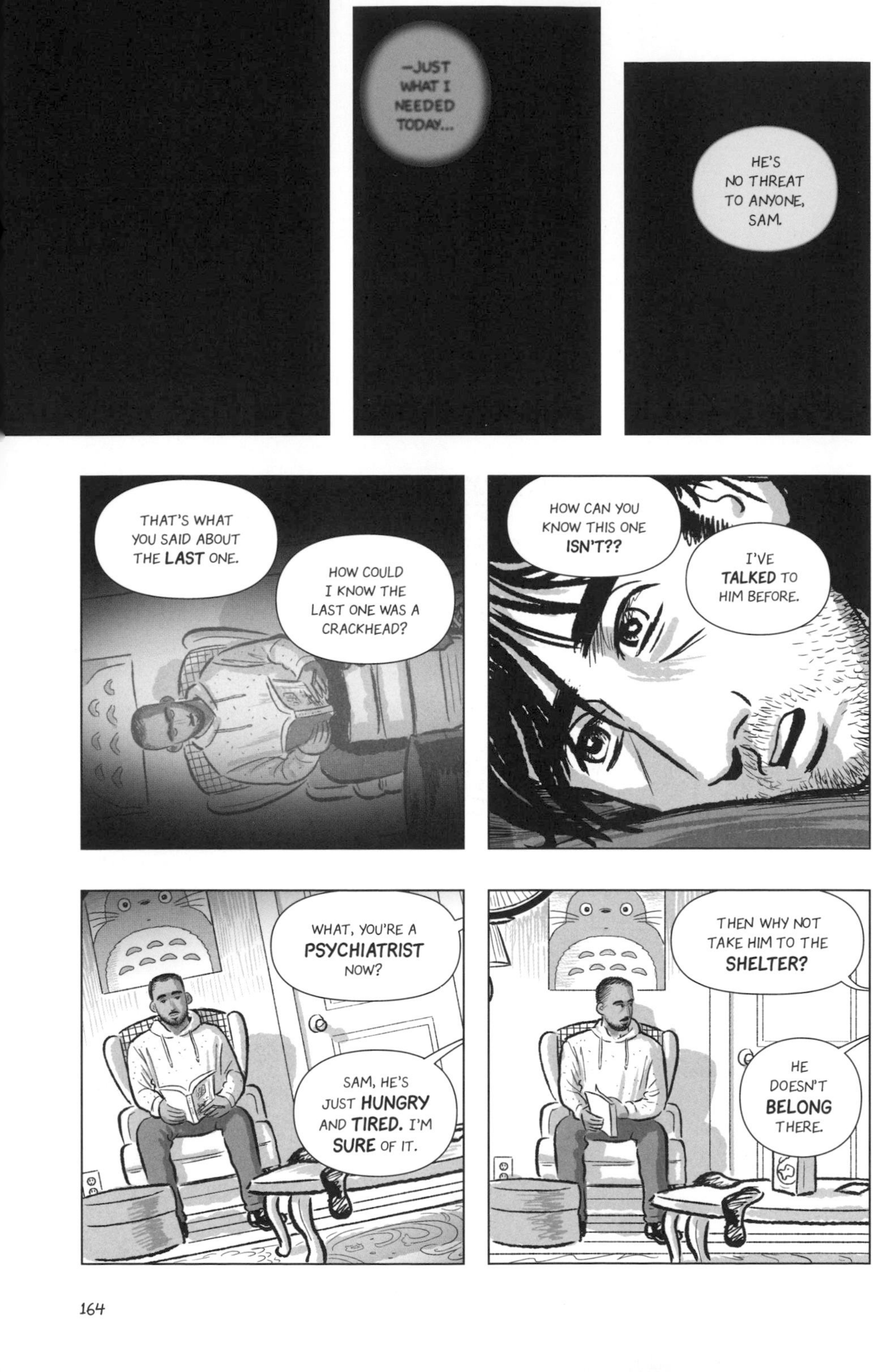
—JUST WHAT I NEEDED TODAY...
HE'S NO THREAT TO ANYONE, SAM.
THAT'S WHAT YOU SAID ABOUT THE LAST ONE.
HOW COULD I KNOW THE LAST ONE WAS A CRACKHEAD?
HOW CAN YOU KNOW THIS ONE ISN'T??
I'VE TALKED TO HIM BEFORE.
WHAT, YOU'RE A PSYCHIATRIST NOW?
SAM, HE'S JUST HUNGRY AND TIRED. I'M SURE OF IT.
THEN WHY NOT TAKE HIM TO THE SHELTER?
HE DOESN'T BELONG THERE.

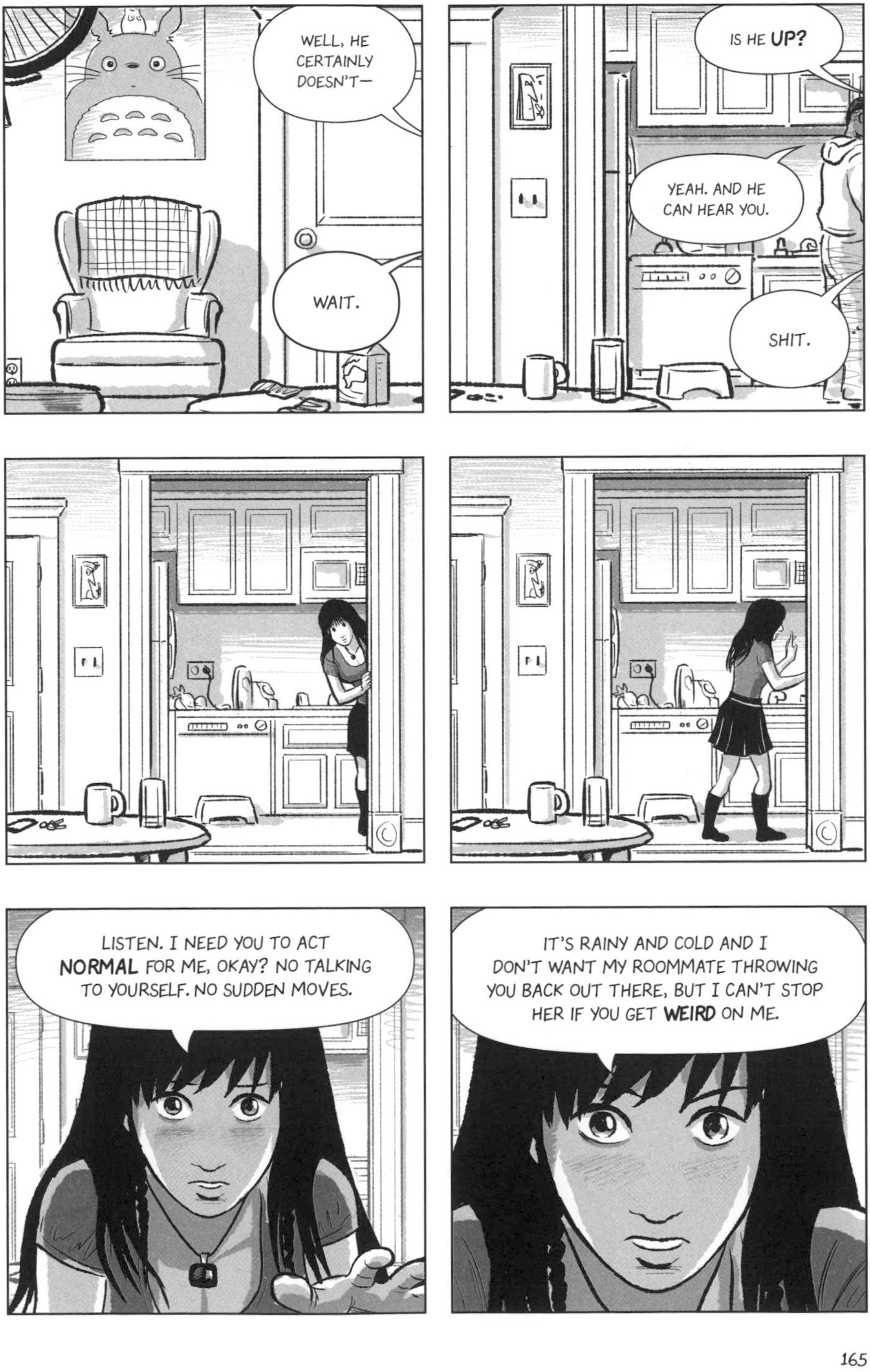
WELL, HE CERTAINLY DOESN'T—
WAIT.
IS HE **UP?**
YEAH. AND HE CAN HEAR YOU.
SHIT.
LISTEN. I NEED YOU TO ACT **NORMAL** FOR ME, OKAY? NO TALKING TO YOURSELF. NO SUDDEN MOVES.
IT'S RAINY AND COLD AND I DON'T WANT MY ROOMMATE THROWING YOU BACK OUT THERE, BUT I CAN'T STOP HER IF YOU GET **WEIRD** ON ME.

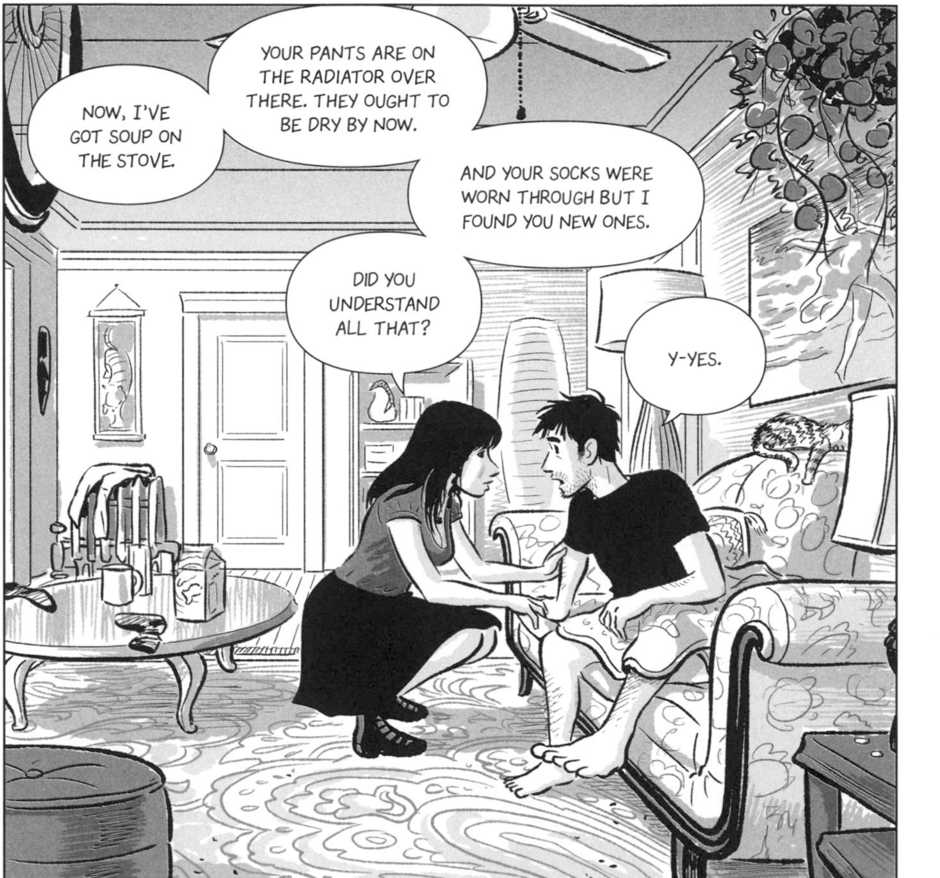
NOW, I'VE GOT SOUP ON THE STOVE.
YOUR PANTS ARE ON THE RADIATOR OVER THERE. THEY OUGHT TO BE DRY BY NOW.
AND YOUR SOCKS WERE WORN THROUGH BUT I FOUND YOU NEW ONES.
DID YOU UNDERSTAND ALL THAT?
Y-YES.

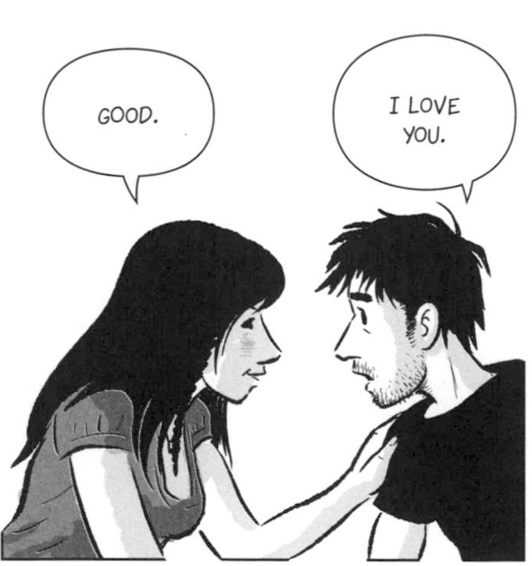
GOOD.
I LOVE YOU.

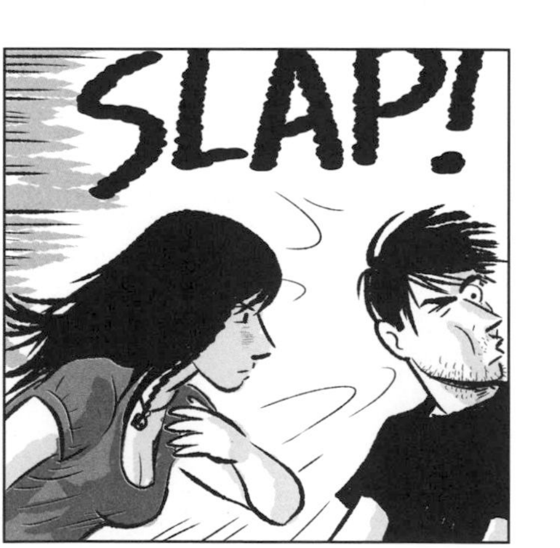
SLAP!

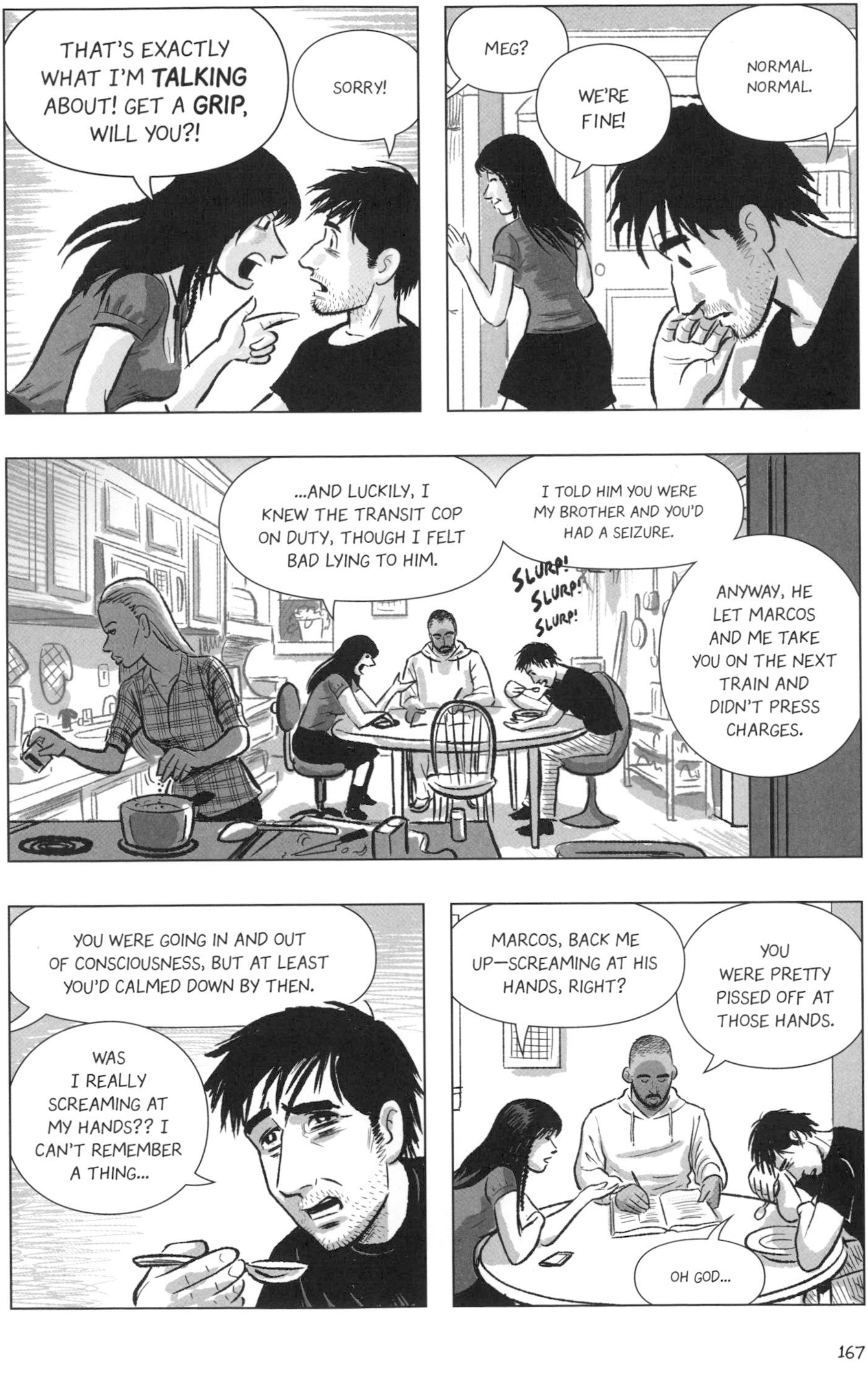
THAT'S EXACTLY WHAT I'M **TALKING** ABOUT! GET A **GRIP**, WILL YOU?!
SORRY!
MEG?
WE'RE FINE!
NORMAL. NORMAL.
...AND LUCKILY, I KNEW THE TRANSIT COP ON DUTY, THOUGH I FELT BAD LYING TO HIM.
I TOLD HIM YOU WERE MY BROTHER AND YOU'D HAD A SEIZURE.
SLURP! SLURP! SLURP!
ANYWAY, HE LET MARCOS AND ME TAKE YOU ON THE NEXT TRAIN AND DIDN'T PRESS CHARGES.
YOU WERE GOING IN AND OUT OF CONSCIOUSNESS, BUT AT LEAST YOU'D CALMED DOWN BY THEN.
WAS I REALLY SCREAMING AT MY HANDS?? I CAN'T REMEMBER A THING...
MARCOS, BACK ME UP—SCREAMING AT HIS HANDS, RIGHT?
YOU WERE PRETTY PISSED OFF AT THOSE HANDS.
OH GOD...

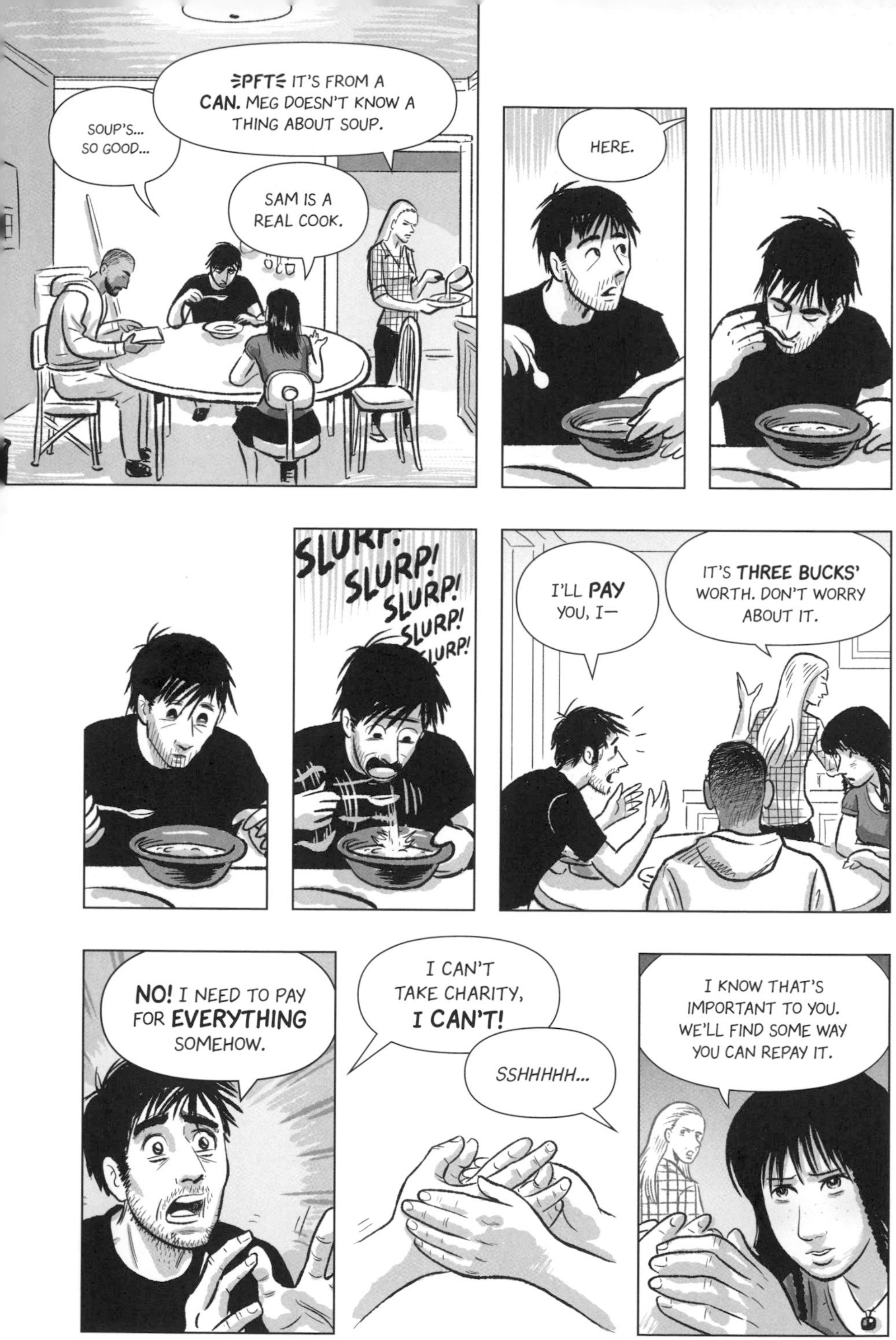
SOUP'S... SO GOOD...
≡PFT≡ IT'S FROM A CAN. MEG DOESN'T KNOW A THING ABOUT SOUP.
SAM IS A REAL COOK.
HERE.
SLURP!
SLURP!
SLURP!
SLURP!
SLURP!
I'LL PAY YOU, I—
IT'S THREE BUCKS' WORTH. DON'T WORRY ABOUT IT.
NO! I NEED TO PAY FOR EVERYTHING SOMEHOW.
I CAN'T TAKE CHARITY, I CAN'T!
SSHHHHH...
I KNOW THAT'S IMPORTANT TO YOU. WE'LL FIND SOME WAY YOU CAN REPAY IT.

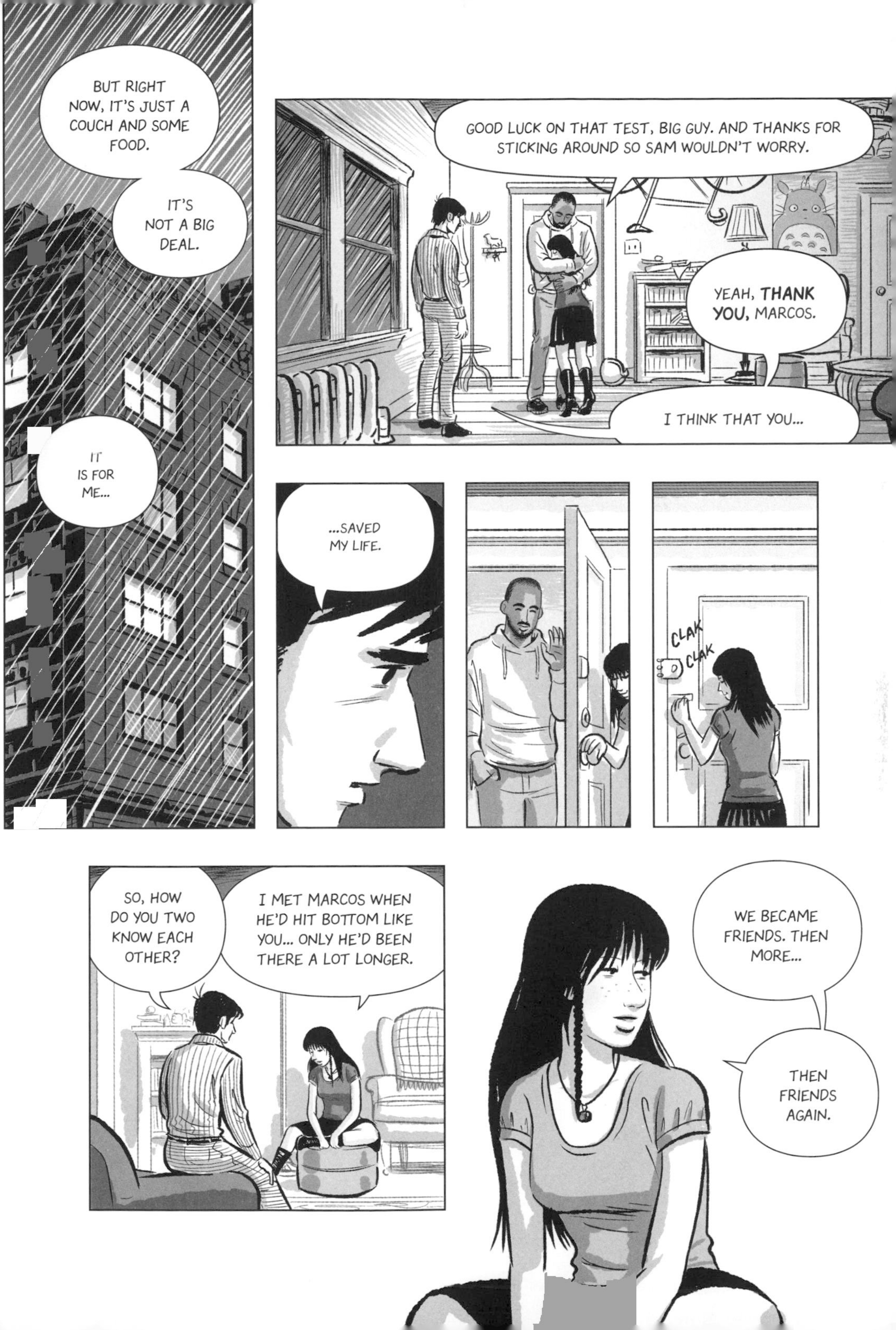
BUT RIGHT NOW, IT'S JUST A COUCH AND SOME FOOD.
IT'S NOT A BIG DEAL.
IT IS FOR ME...
GOOD LUCK ON THAT TEST, BIG GUY. AND THANKS FOR STICKING AROUND SO SAM WOULDN'T WORRY.
YEAH, **THANK YOU,** MARCOS.
I THINK THAT YOU...
...SAVED MY LIFE.
CLAK
CLAK
SO, HOW DO YOU TWO KNOW EACH OTHER?
I MET MARCOS WHEN HE'D HIT BOTTOM LIKE YOU... ONLY HE'D BEEN THERE A LOT LONGER.
WE BECAME FRIENDS. THEN MORE...
THEN FRIENDS AGAIN.

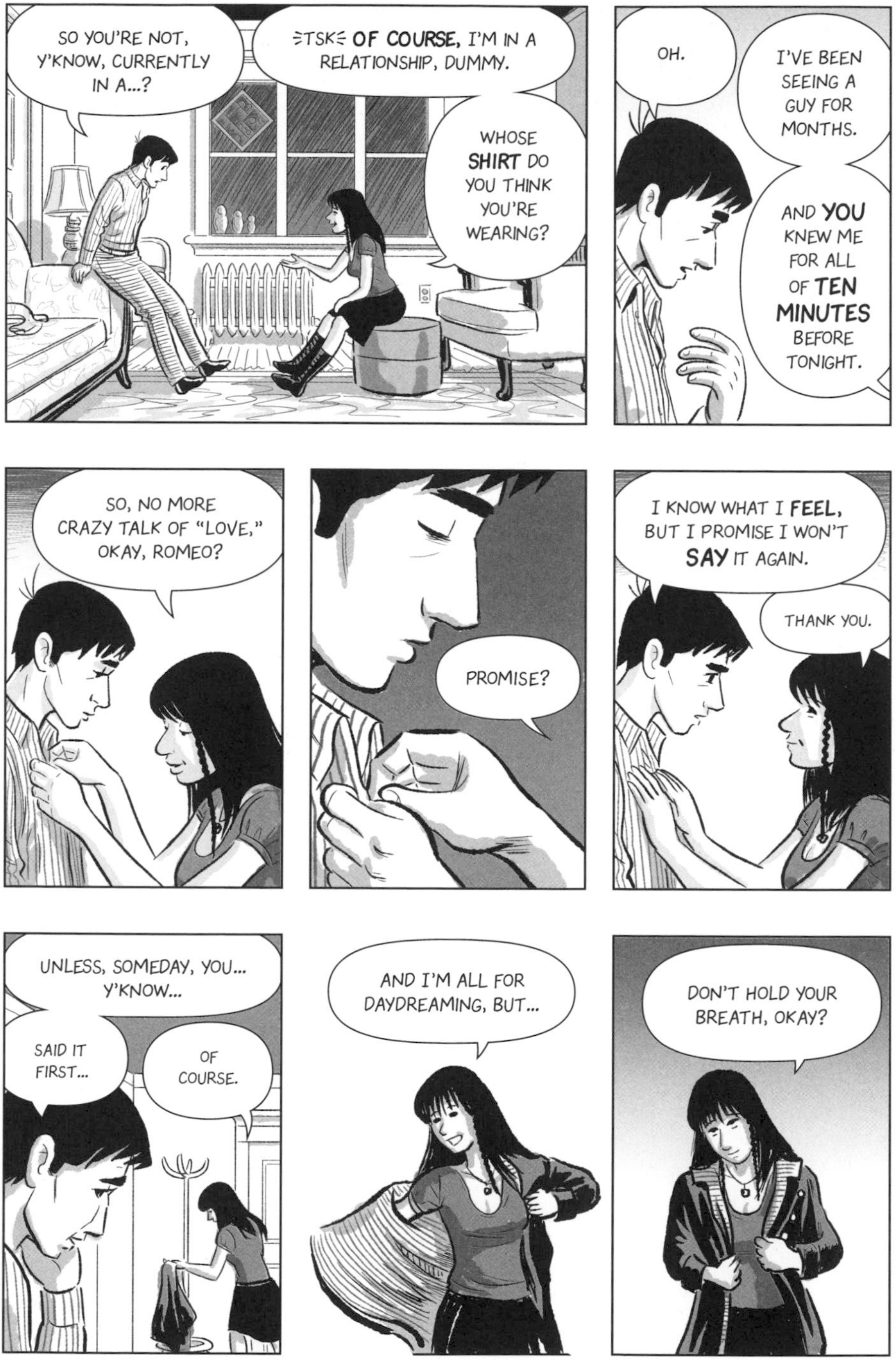
SO YOU'RE NOT, Y'KNOW, CURRENTLY IN A...?
≑TSK≑ OF COURSE, I'M IN A RELATIONSHIP, DUMMY.
WHOSE SHIRT DO YOU THINK YOU'RE WEARING?
OH.
I'VE BEEN SEEING A GUY FOR MONTHS.
AND YOU KNEW ME FOR ALL OF TEN MINUTES BEFORE TONIGHT.
SO, NO MORE CRAZY TALK OF "LOVE," OKAY, ROMEO?
PROMISE?
I KNOW WHAT I FEEL, BUT I PROMISE I WON'T SAY IT AGAIN.
THANK YOU.
UNLESS, SOMEDAY, YOU... Y'KNOW...
SAID IT FIRST...
OF COURSE.
AND I'M ALL FOR DAYDREAMING, BUT...
DON'T HOLD YOUR BREATH, OKAY?

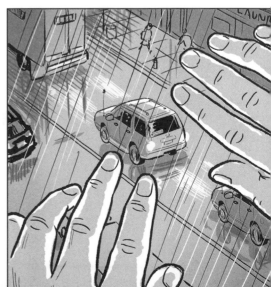

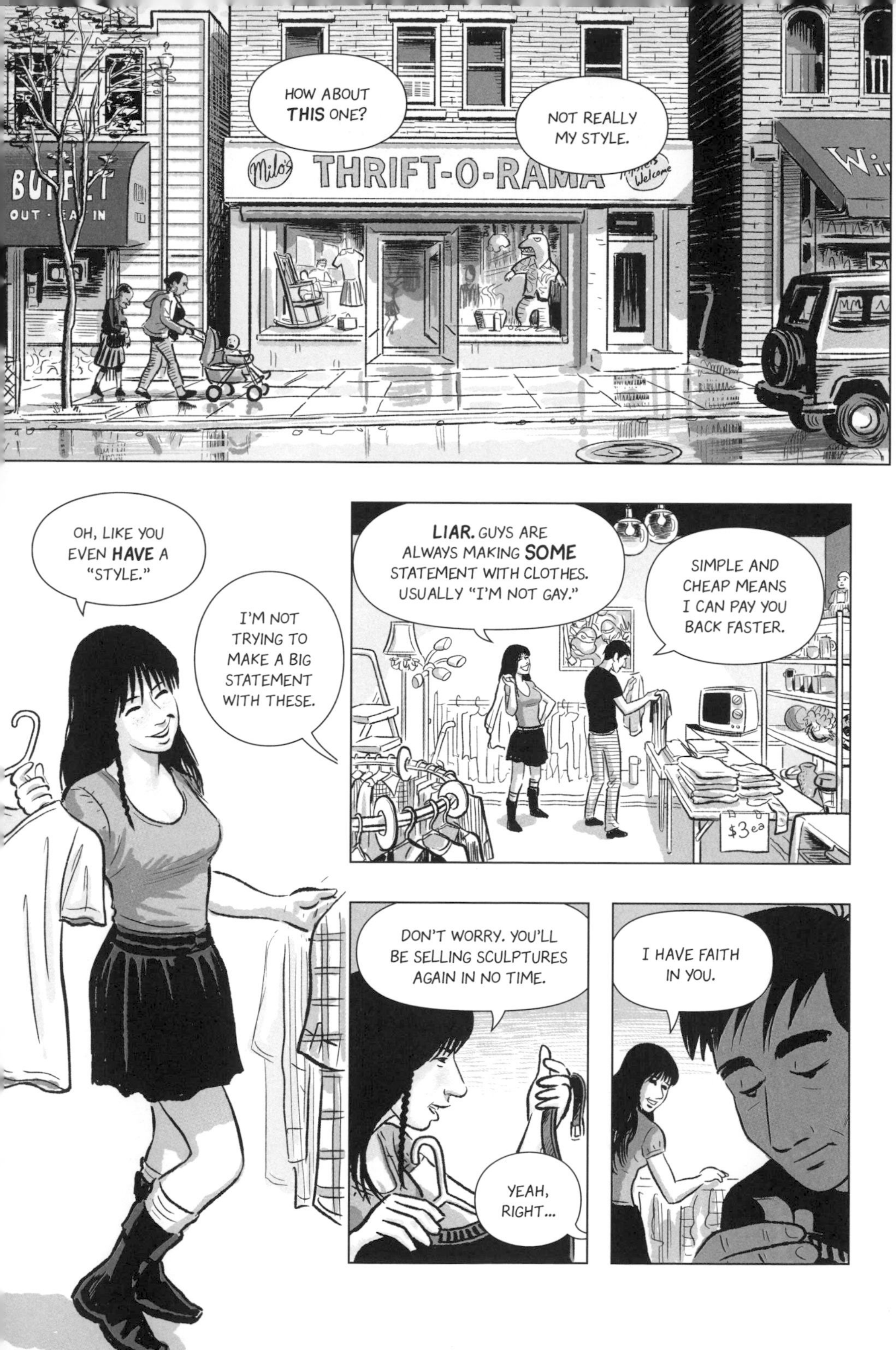
HOW ABOUT THIS ONE?
NOT REALLY MY STYLE.
BUFFET
OUT · EAT IN
Milo's
THRIFT-O-RAMA
OH, LIKE YOU EVEN HAVE A "STYLE."
I'M NOT TRYING TO MAKE A BIG STATEMENT WITH THESE.
LIAR. GUYS ARE ALWAYS MAKING SOME STATEMENT WITH CLOTHES. USUALLY "I'M NOT GAY."
SIMPLE AND CHEAP MEANS I CAN PAY YOU BACK FASTER.
$3ea
DON'T WORRY. YOU'LL BE SELLING SCULPTURES AGAIN IN NO TIME.
YEAH, RIGHT...
I HAVE FAITH IN YOU.

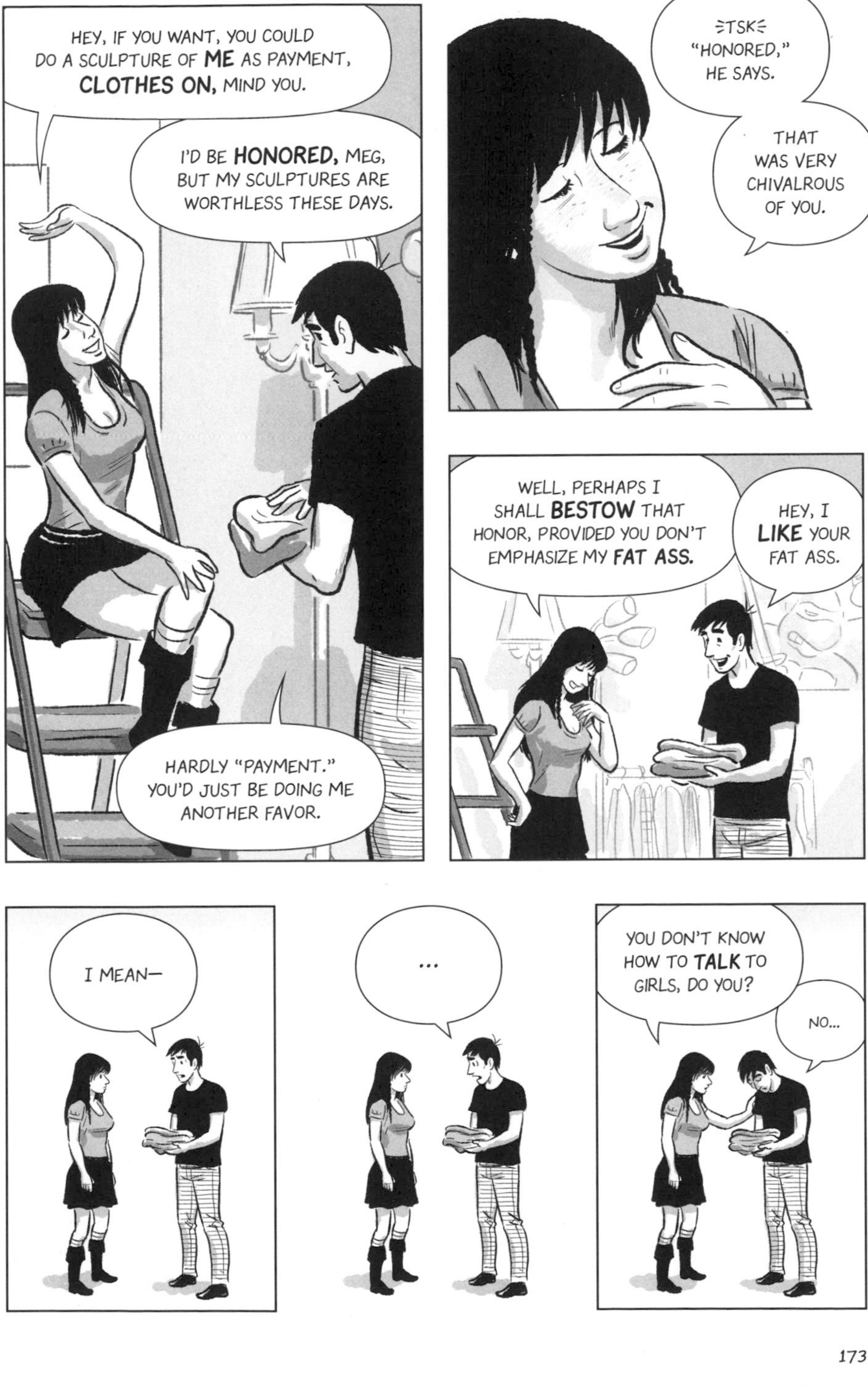
HEY, IF YOU WANT, YOU COULD DO A SCULPTURE OF **ME** AS PAYMENT, **CLOTHES ON,** MIND YOU.
I'D BE **HONORED,** MEG, BUT MY SCULPTURES ARE WORTHLESS THESE DAYS.
HARDLY "PAYMENT." YOU'D JUST BE DOING ME ANOTHER FAVOR.
⚞TSK⚟ "HONORED," HE SAYS.
THAT WAS VERY CHIVALROUS OF YOU.
WELL, PERHAPS I SHALL **BESTOW** THAT HONOR, PROVIDED YOU DON'T EMPHASIZE MY **FAT ASS.**
HEY, I **LIKE** YOUR FAT ASS.
I MEAN—
...
YOU DON'T KNOW HOW TO **TALK** TO GIRLS, DO YOU?
NO...

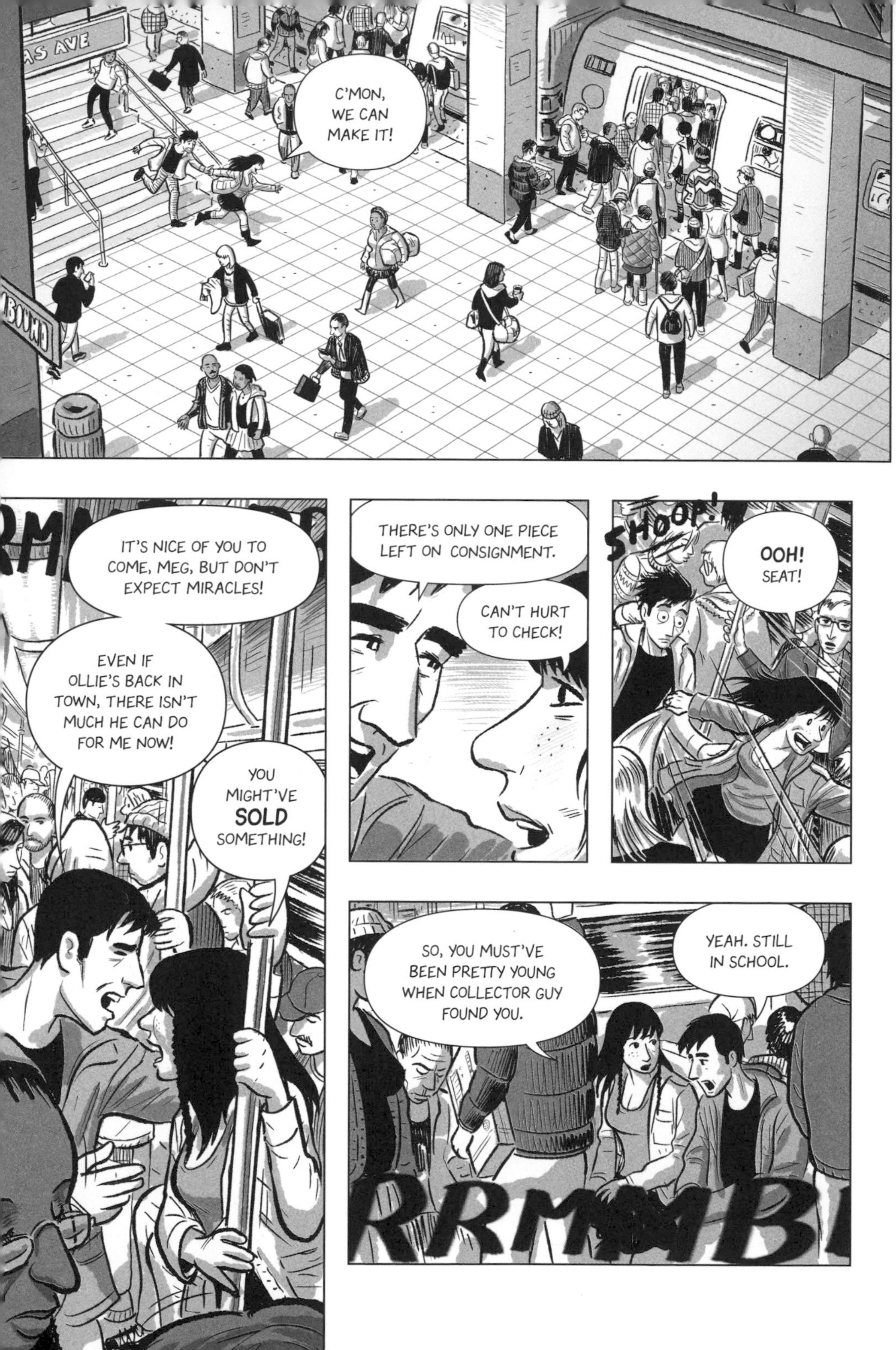
C'MON, WE CAN MAKE IT!
IT'S NICE OF YOU TO COME, MEG, BUT DON'T EXPECT MIRACLES!
EVEN IF OLLIE'S BACK IN TOWN, THERE ISN'T MUCH HE CAN DO FOR ME NOW!
YOU MIGHT'VE **SOLD** SOMETHING!
THERE'S ONLY ONE PIECE LEFT ON CONSIGNMENT.
CAN'T HURT TO CHECK!
SHOOP!
OOH! SEAT!
SO, YOU MUST'VE BEEN PRETTY YOUNG WHEN COLLECTOR GUY FOUND YOU.
YEAH. STILL IN SCHOOL.
RRMMBL

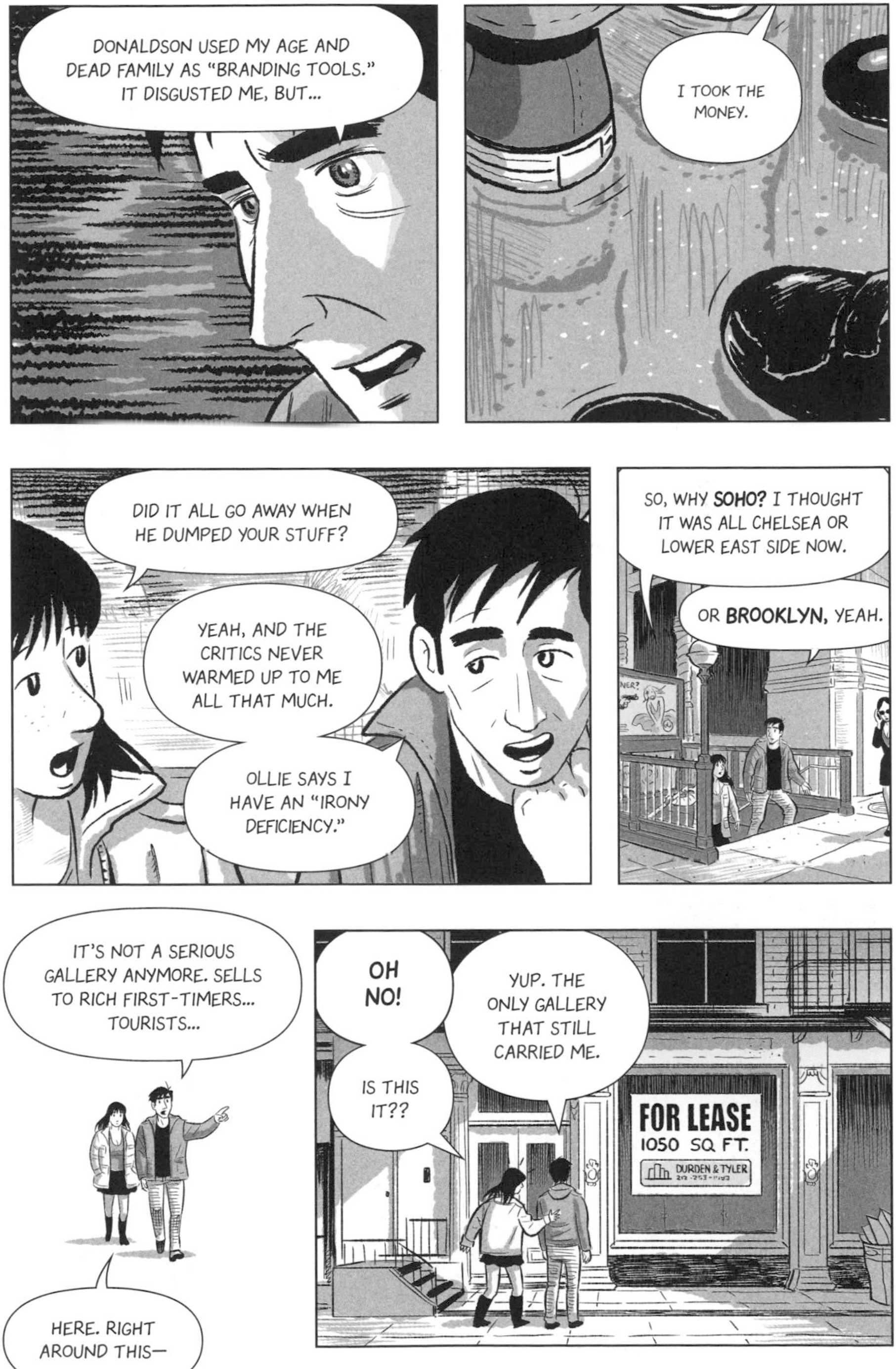
DONALDSON USED MY AGE AND DEAD FAMILY AS "BRANDING TOOLS." IT DISGUSTED ME, BUT...
I TOOK THE MONEY.
DID IT ALL GO AWAY WHEN HE DUMPED YOUR STUFF?
YEAH, AND THE CRITICS NEVER WARMED UP TO ME ALL THAT MUCH.
OLLIE SAYS I HAVE AN "IRONY DEFICIENCY."
SO, WHY **SOHO?** I THOUGHT IT WAS ALL CHELSEA OR LOWER EAST SIDE NOW.
OR **BROOKLYN,** YEAH.
IT'S NOT A SERIOUS GALLERY ANYMORE. SELLS TO RICH FIRST-TIMERS... TOURISTS...
HERE. RIGHT AROUND THIS—
OH NO!
IS THIS IT??
YUP. THE ONLY GALLERY THAT STILL CARRIED ME.
FOR LEASE
1050 SQ FT.
DURDEN & TYLER

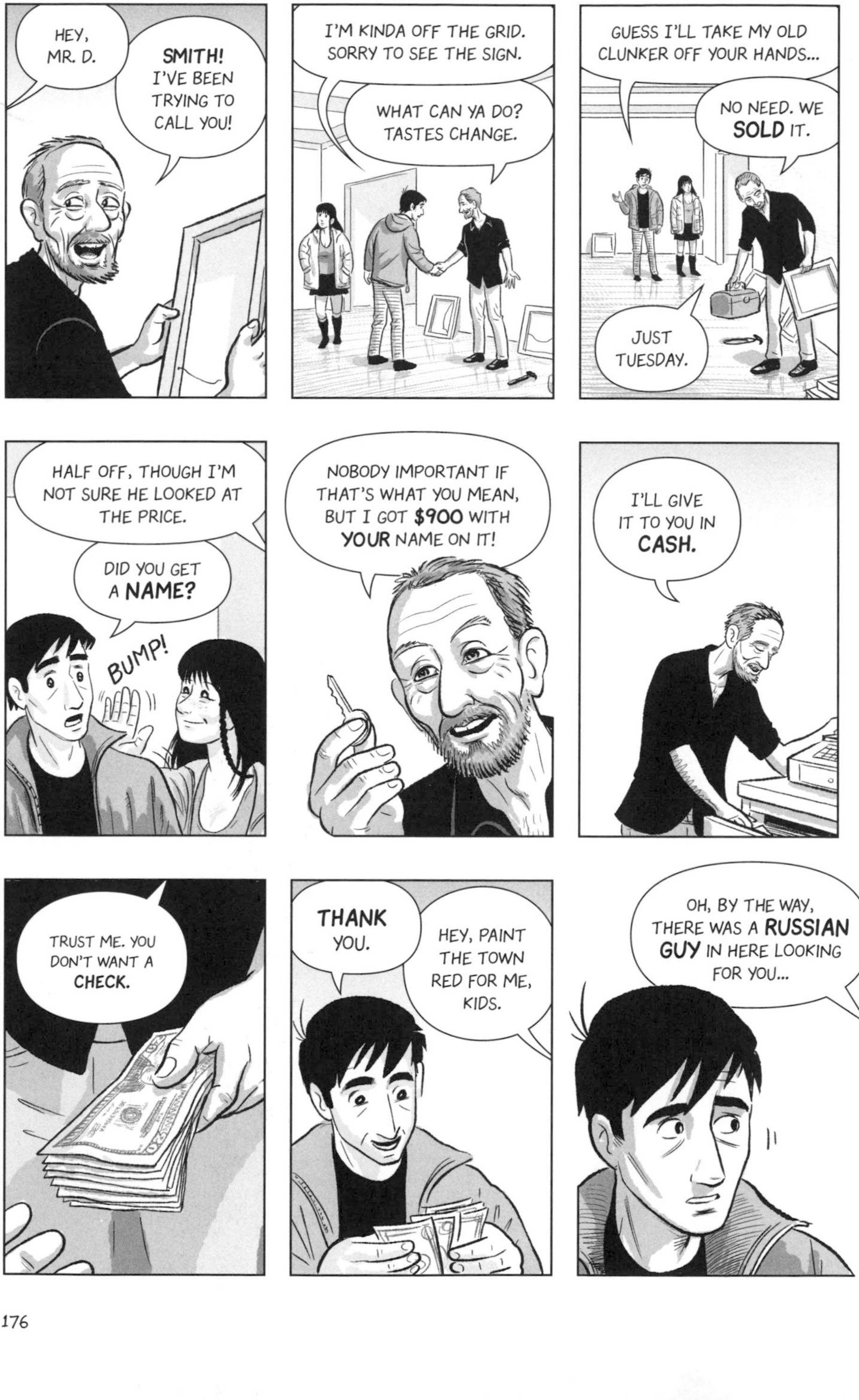
HEY, MR. D.
SMITH! I'VE BEEN TRYING TO CALL YOU!
I'M KINDA OFF THE GRID. SORRY TO SEE THE SIGN.
WHAT CAN YA DO? TASTES CHANGE.
GUESS I'LL TAKE MY OLD CLUNKER OFF YOUR HANDS...
NO NEED. WE SOLD IT.
JUST TUESDAY.
HALF OFF, THOUGH I'M NOT SURE HE LOOKED AT THE PRICE.
DID YOU GET A NAME?
BUMP!
NOBODY IMPORTANT IF THAT'S WHAT YOU MEAN, BUT I GOT $900 WITH YOUR NAME ON IT!
I'LL GIVE IT TO YOU IN CASH.
TRUST ME. YOU DON'T WANT A CHECK.
THANK YOU.
HEY, PAINT THE TOWN RED FOR ME, KIDS.
OH, BY THE WAY, THERE WAS A RUSSIAN GUY IN HERE LOOKING FOR YOU...

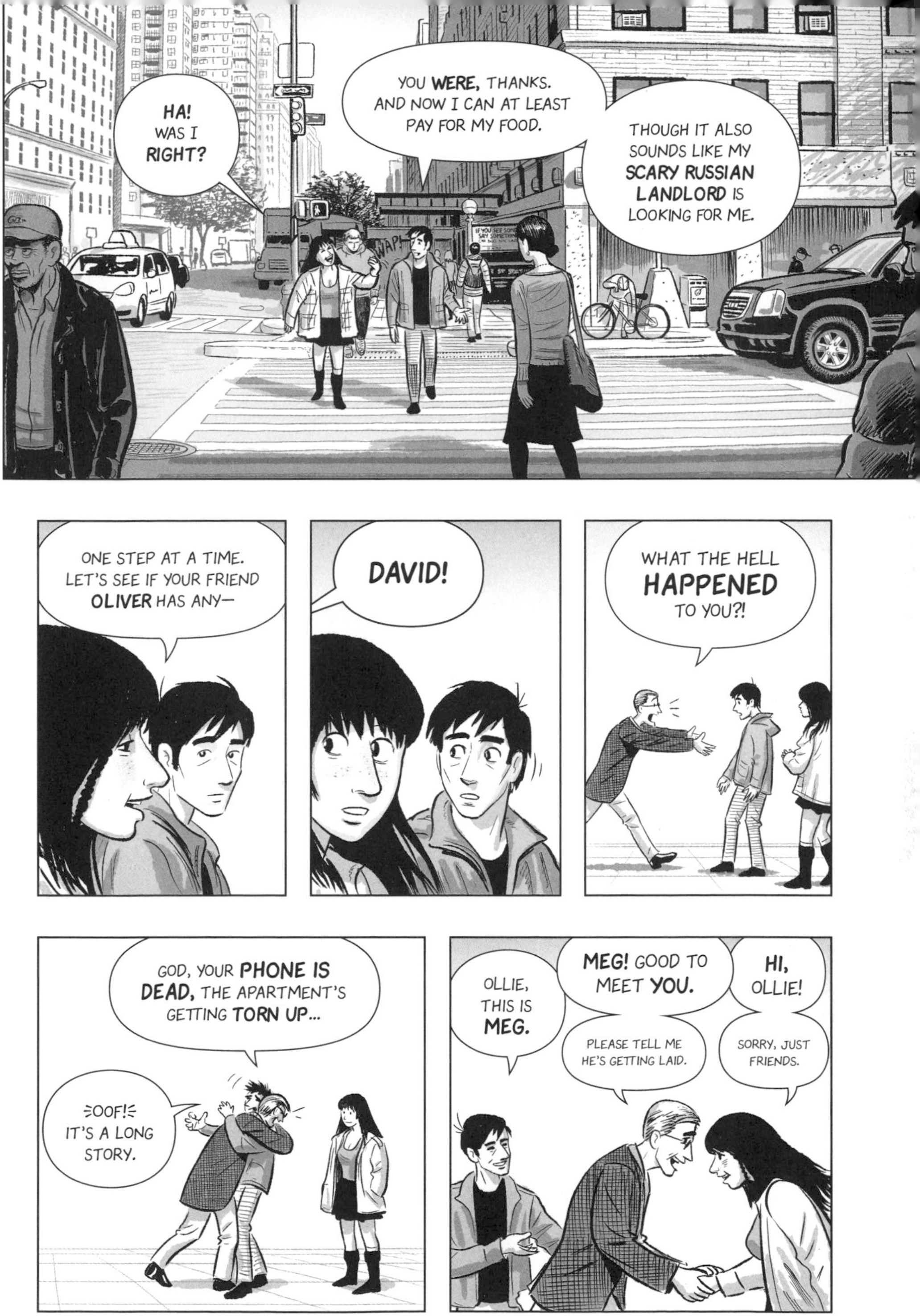
HA! WAS I RIGHT?
YOU WERE, THANKS. AND NOW I CAN AT LEAST PAY FOR MY FOOD.
THOUGH IT ALSO SOUNDS LIKE MY SCARY RUSSIAN LANDLORD IS LOOKING FOR ME.
ONE STEP AT A TIME. LET'S SEE IF YOUR FRIEND OLIVER HAS ANY—
DAVID!
WHAT THE HELL HAPPENED TO YOU?!
GOD, YOUR PHONE IS DEAD, THE APARTMENT'S GETTING TORN UP...
OOF! IT'S A LONG STORY.
OLLIE, THIS IS MEG.
MEG! GOOD TO MEET YOU.
HI, OLLIE!
PLEASE TELL ME HE'S GETTING LAID.
SORRY, JUST FRIENDS.

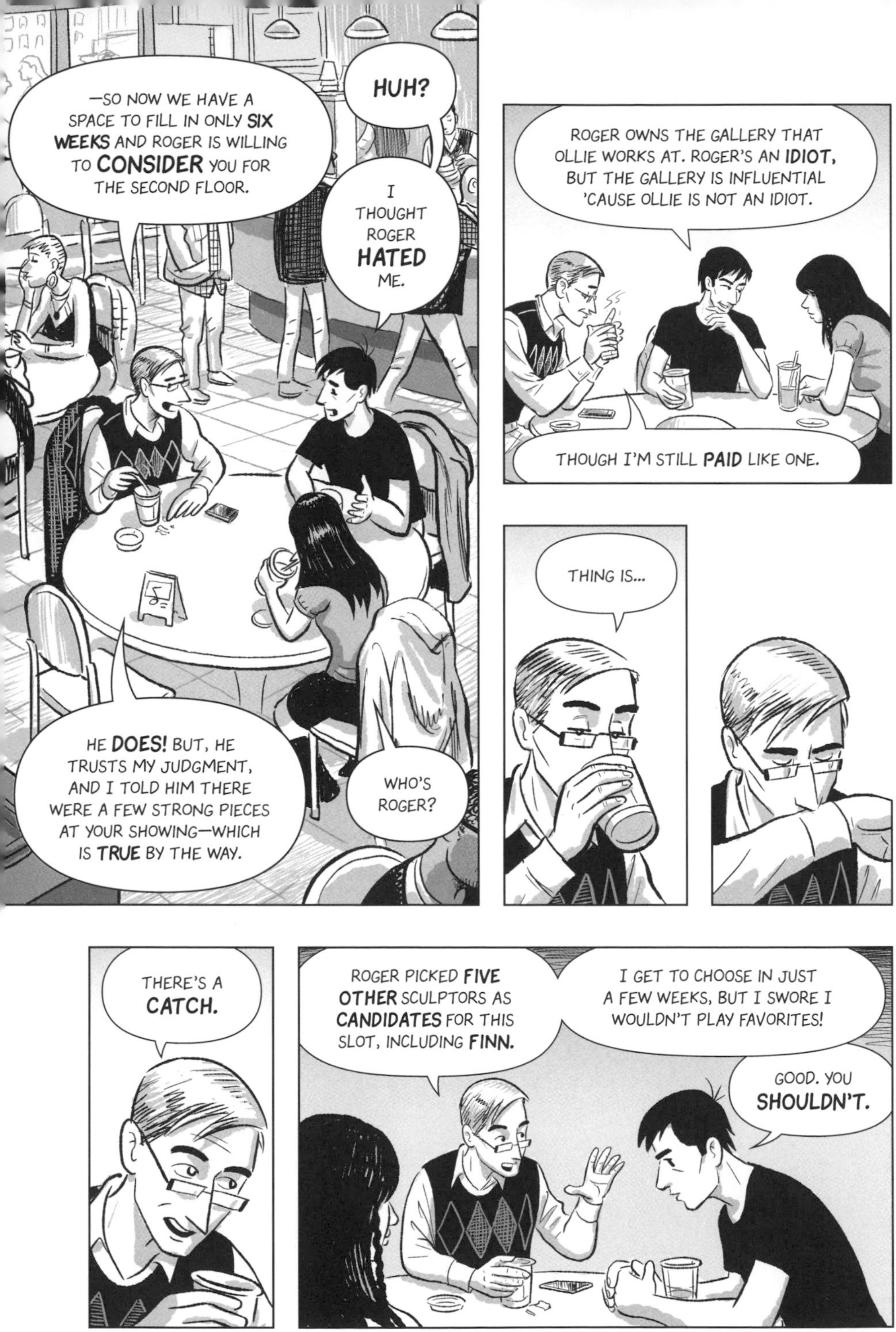
—SO NOW WE HAVE A SPACE TO FILL IN ONLY SIX WEEKS AND ROGER IS WILLING TO CONSIDER YOU FOR THE SECOND FLOOR.
HUH?
I THOUGHT ROGER HATED ME.
HE DOES! BUT, HE TRUSTS MY JUDGMENT, AND I TOLD HIM THERE WERE A FEW STRONG PIECES AT YOUR SHOWING—WHICH IS TRUE BY THE WAY.
WHO'S ROGER?
ROGER OWNS THE GALLERY THAT OLLIE WORKS AT. ROGER'S AN IDIOT, BUT THE GALLERY IS INFLUENTIAL 'CAUSE OLLIE IS NOT AN IDIOT.
THOUGH I'M STILL PAID LIKE ONE.
THING IS...
THERE'S A CATCH.
ROGER PICKED FIVE OTHER SCULPTORS AS CANDIDATES FOR THIS SLOT, INCLUDING FINN.
I GET TO CHOOSE IN JUST A FEW WEEKS, BUT I SWORE I WOULDN'T PLAY FAVORITES!
GOOD. YOU SHOULDN'T.

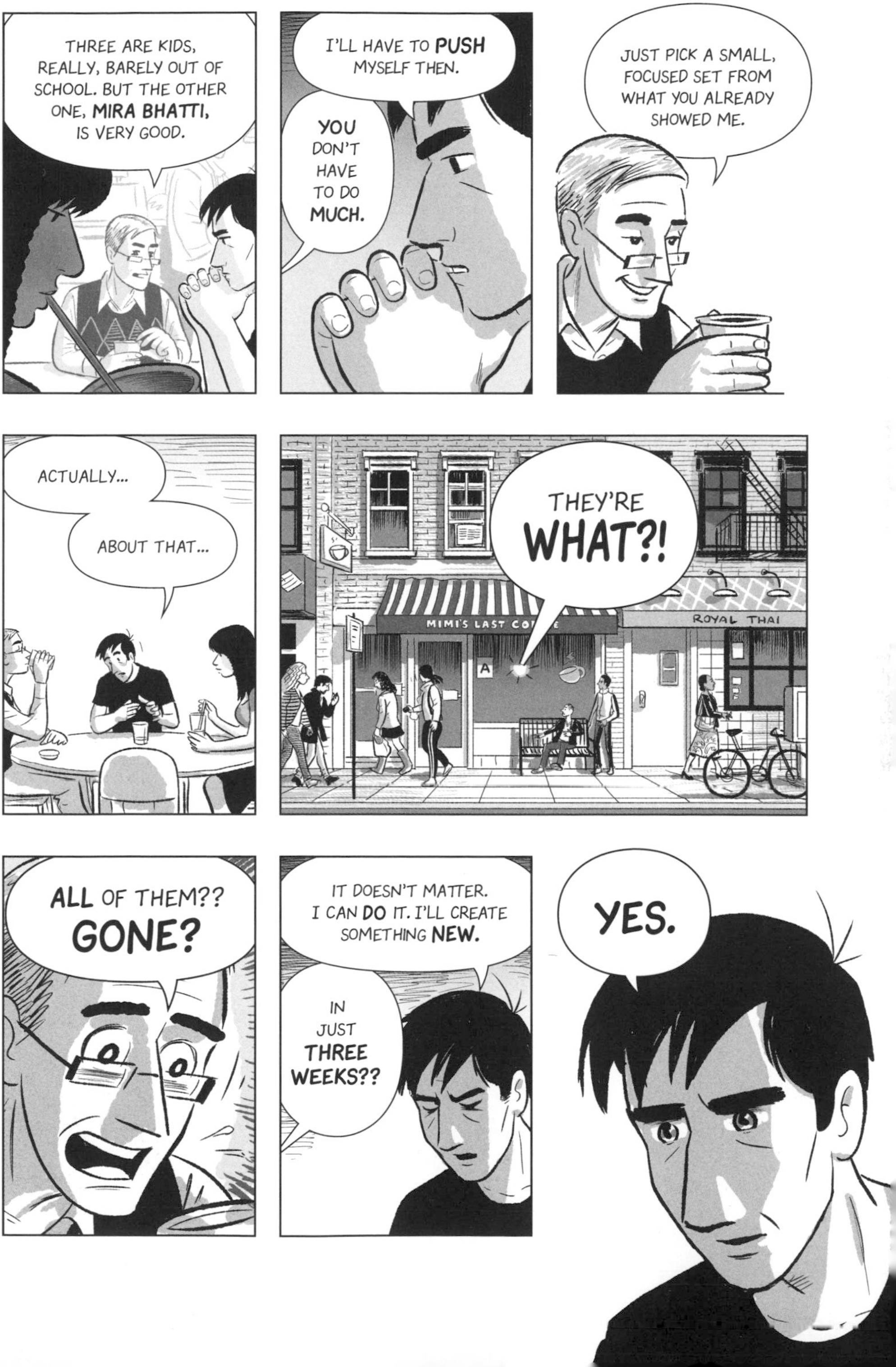
THREE ARE KIDS, REALLY, BARELY OUT OF SCHOOL. BUT THE OTHER ONE, MIRA BHATTI, IS VERY GOOD.
I'LL HAVE TO PUSH MYSELF THEN.
YOU DON'T HAVE TO DO MUCH.
JUST PICK A SMALL, FOCUSED SET FROM WHAT YOU ALREADY SHOWED ME.
ACTUALLY...
ABOUT THAT...
THEY'RE WHAT?!
MIMI'S LAST CO
ROYAL THAI
ALL OF THEM?? GONE?
IT DOESN'T MATTER. I CAN DO IT. I'LL CREATE SOMETHING NEW.
IN JUST THREE WEEKS??
YES.

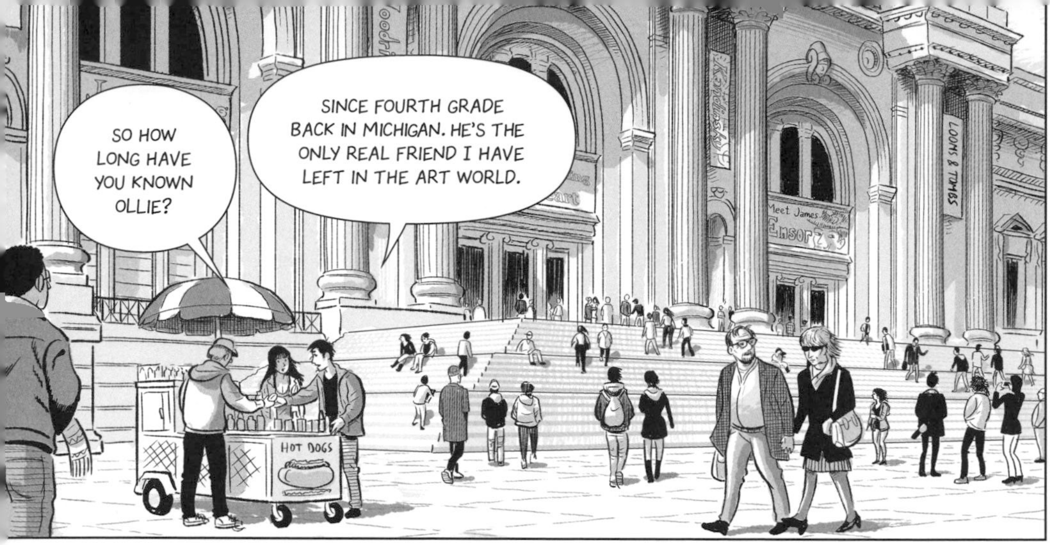
SO HOW LONG HAVE YOU KNOWN OLLIE?
SINCE FOURTH GRADE BACK IN MICHIGAN. HE'S THE ONLY REAL FRIEND I HAVE LEFT IN THE ART WORLD.
LOOMS & TOMBS
Meet James Ensor
HOT DOGS

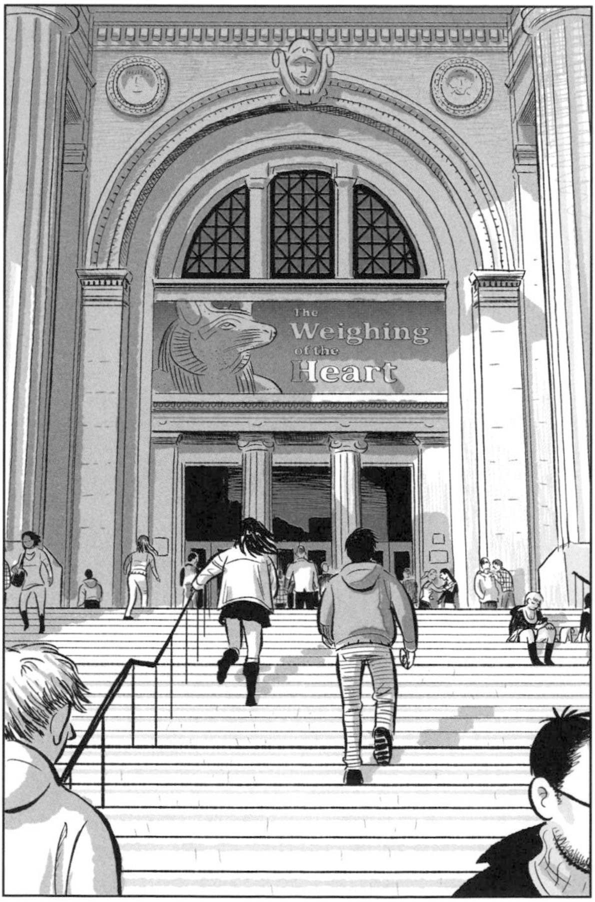
The Weighing of the Heart

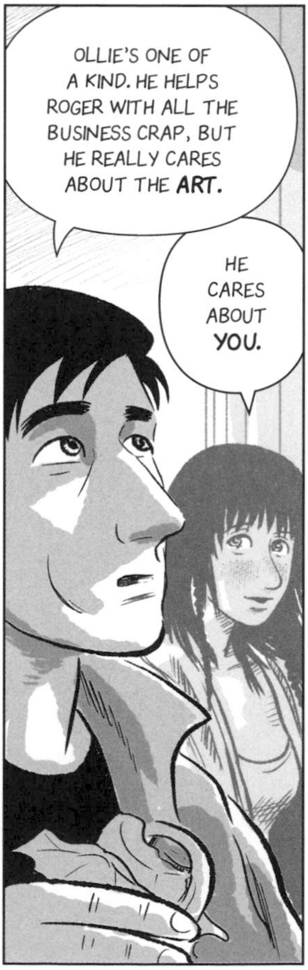
OLLIE'S ONE OF A KIND. HE HELPS ROGER WITH ALL THE BUSINESS CRAP, BUT HE REALLY CARES ABOUT THE **ART**.
HE CARES ABOUT **YOU**.

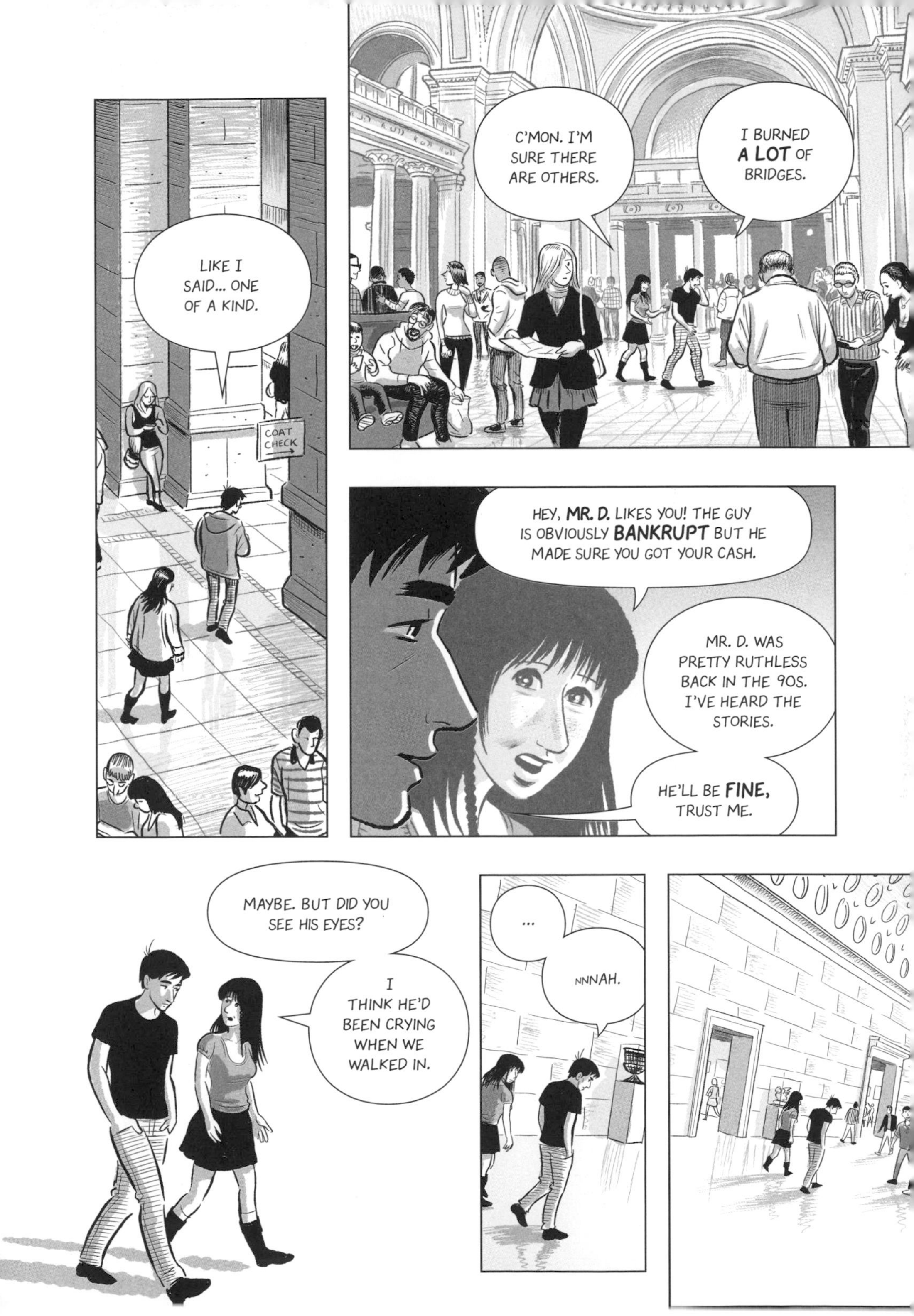
LIKE I SAID... ONE OF A KIND.
C'MON. I'M SURE THERE ARE OTHERS.
I BURNED A LOT OF BRIDGES.
HEY, MR. D. LIKES YOU! THE GUY IS OBVIOUSLY BANKRUPT BUT HE MADE SURE YOU GOT YOUR CASH.
MR. D. WAS PRETTY RUTHLESS BACK IN THE 90S. I'VE HEARD THE STORIES.
HE'LL BE FINE, TRUST ME.
COAT CHECK
MAYBE. BUT DID YOU SEE HIS EYES?
I THINK HE'D BEEN CRYING WHEN WE WALKED IN.
...
NNNAH.

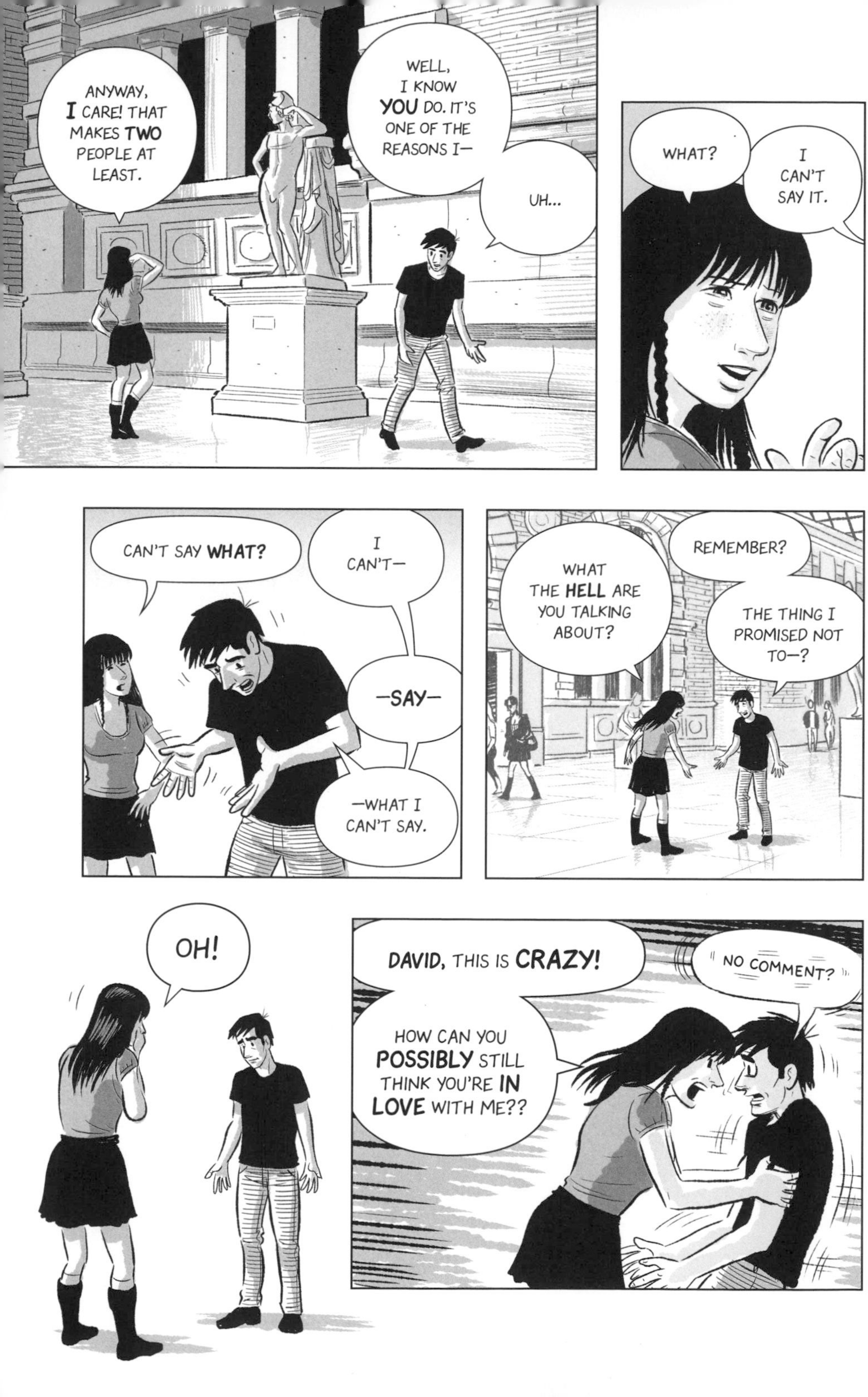
ANYWAY, I CARE! THAT MAKES TWO PEOPLE AT LEAST.
WELL, I KNOW YOU DO. IT'S ONE OF THE REASONS I—
UH...
WHAT?
I CAN'T SAY IT.
CAN'T SAY WHAT?
I CAN'T—
—SAY—
—WHAT I CAN'T SAY.
WHAT THE HELL ARE YOU TALKING ABOUT?
REMEMBER?
THE THING I PROMISED NOT TO—?
OH!
DAVID, THIS IS CRAZY!
HOW CAN YOU POSSIBLY STILL THINK YOU'RE IN LOVE WITH ME??
NO COMMENT?

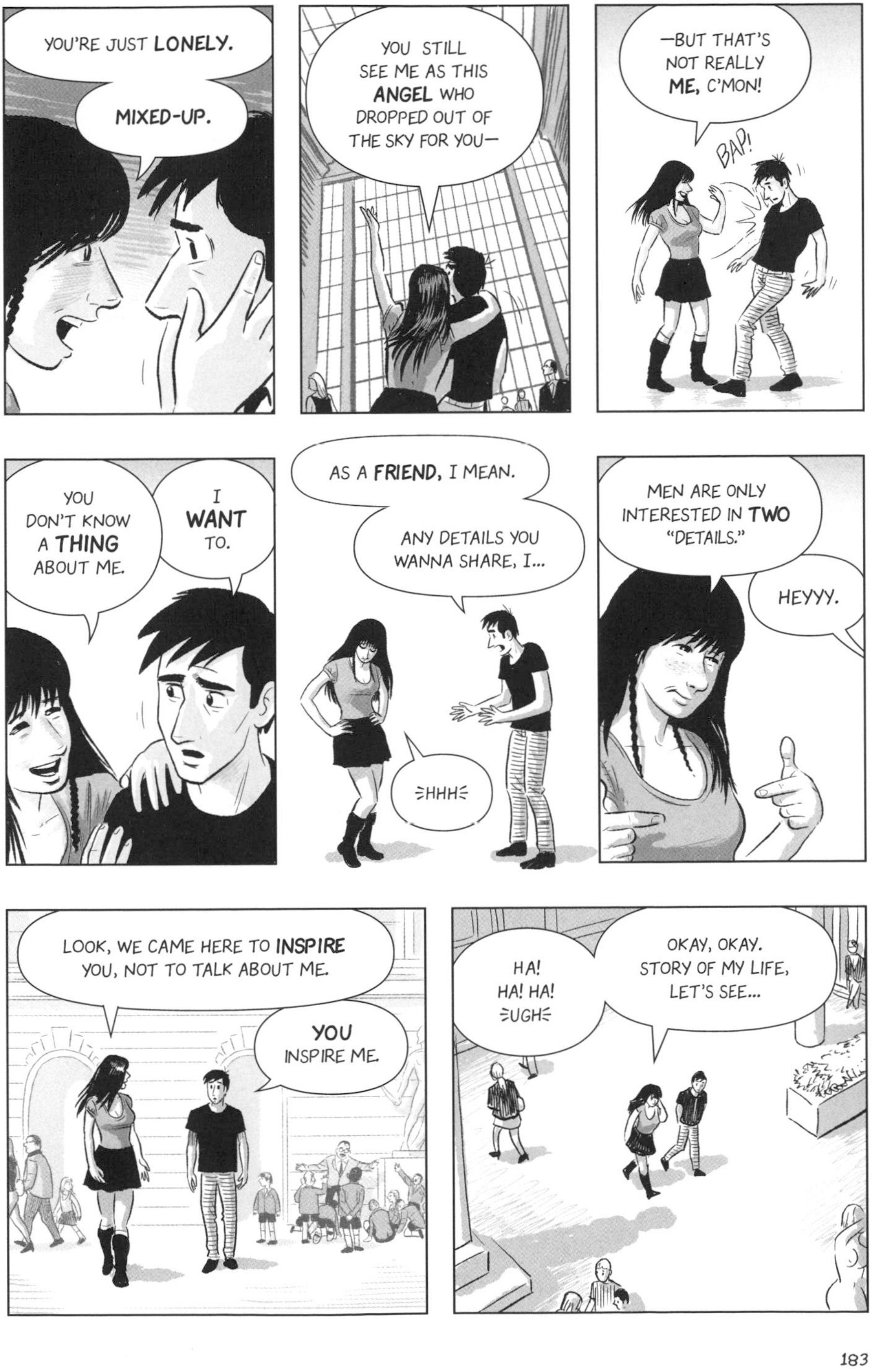
YOU'RE JUST LONELY.
MIXED-UP.
YOU STILL SEE ME AS THIS ANGEL WHO DROPPED OUT OF THE SKY FOR YOU—
—BUT THAT'S NOT REALLY ME, C'MON!
BAP!
YOU DON'T KNOW A THING ABOUT ME.
I WANT TO.
AS A FRIEND, I MEAN.
ANY DETAILS YOU WANNA SHARE, I...
HHH
MEN ARE ONLY INTERESTED IN TWO "DETAILS."
HEYYY.
LOOK, WE CAME HERE TO INSPIRE YOU, NOT TO TALK ABOUT ME.
YOU INSPIRE ME.
HA! HA! HA! UGH
OKAY, OKAY. STORY OF MY LIFE, LET'S SEE...

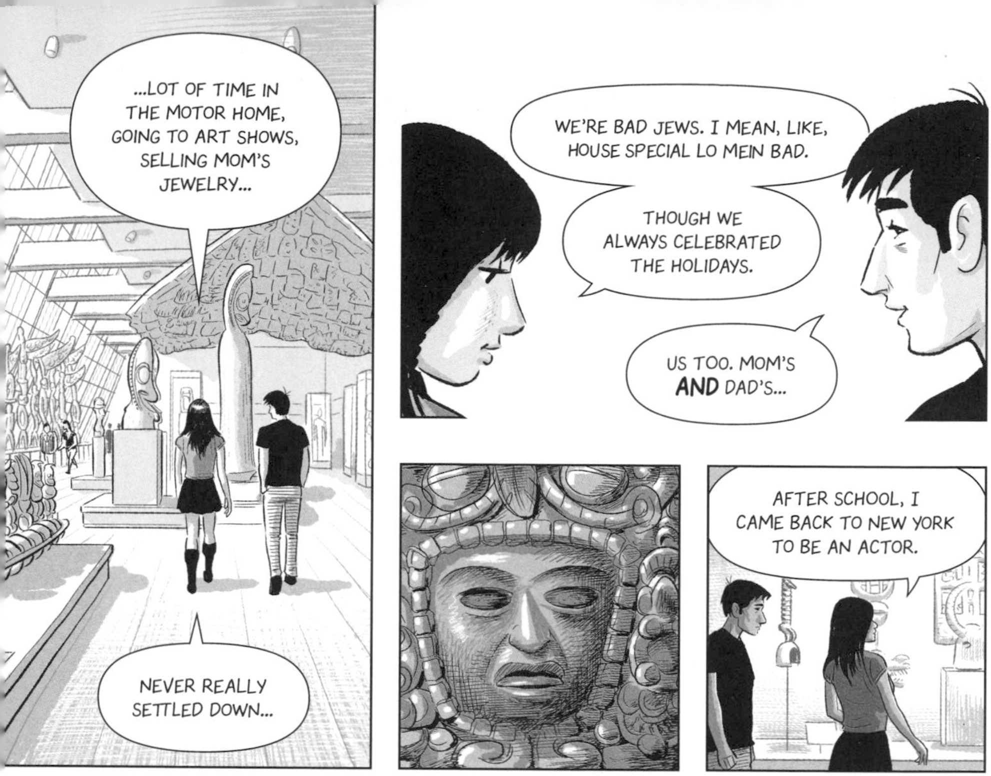
...LOT OF TIME IN THE MOTOR HOME, GOING TO ART SHOWS, SELLING MOM'S JEWELRY...
NEVER REALLY SETTLED DOWN...
WE'RE BAD JEWS. I MEAN, LIKE, HOUSE SPECIAL LO MEIN BAD.
THOUGH WE ALWAYS CELEBRATED THE HOLIDAYS.
US TOO. MOM'S **AND** DAD'S...
AFTER SCHOOL, I CAME BACK TO NEW YORK TO BE AN ACTOR.

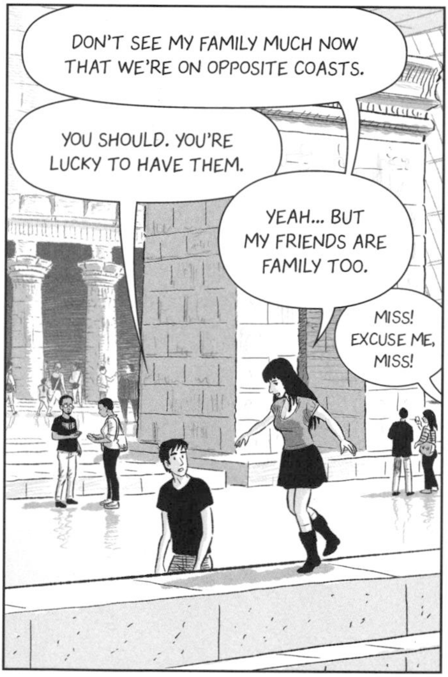
DON'T SEE MY FAMILY MUCH NOW THAT WE'RE ON OPPOSITE COASTS.
YOU SHOULD. YOU'RE LUCKY TO HAVE THEM.
YEAH... BUT MY FRIENDS ARE FAMILY TOO.
MISS! EXCUSE ME, MISS!

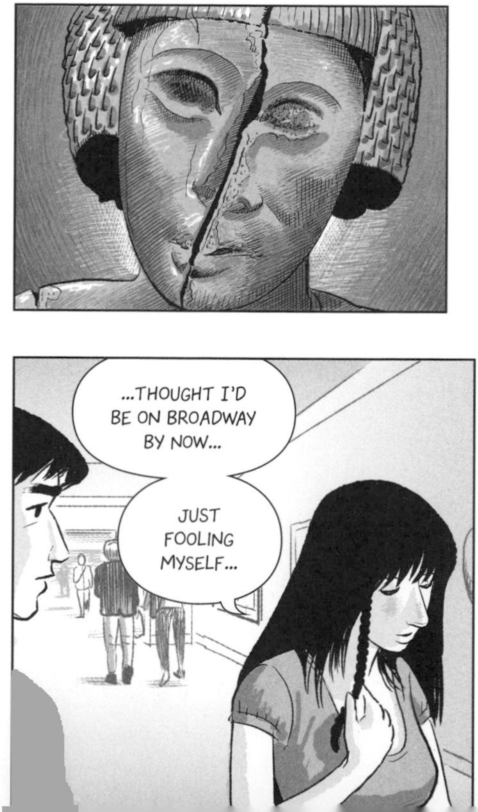
...THOUGHT I'D BE ON BROADWAY BY NOW...
JUST FOOLING MYSELF...

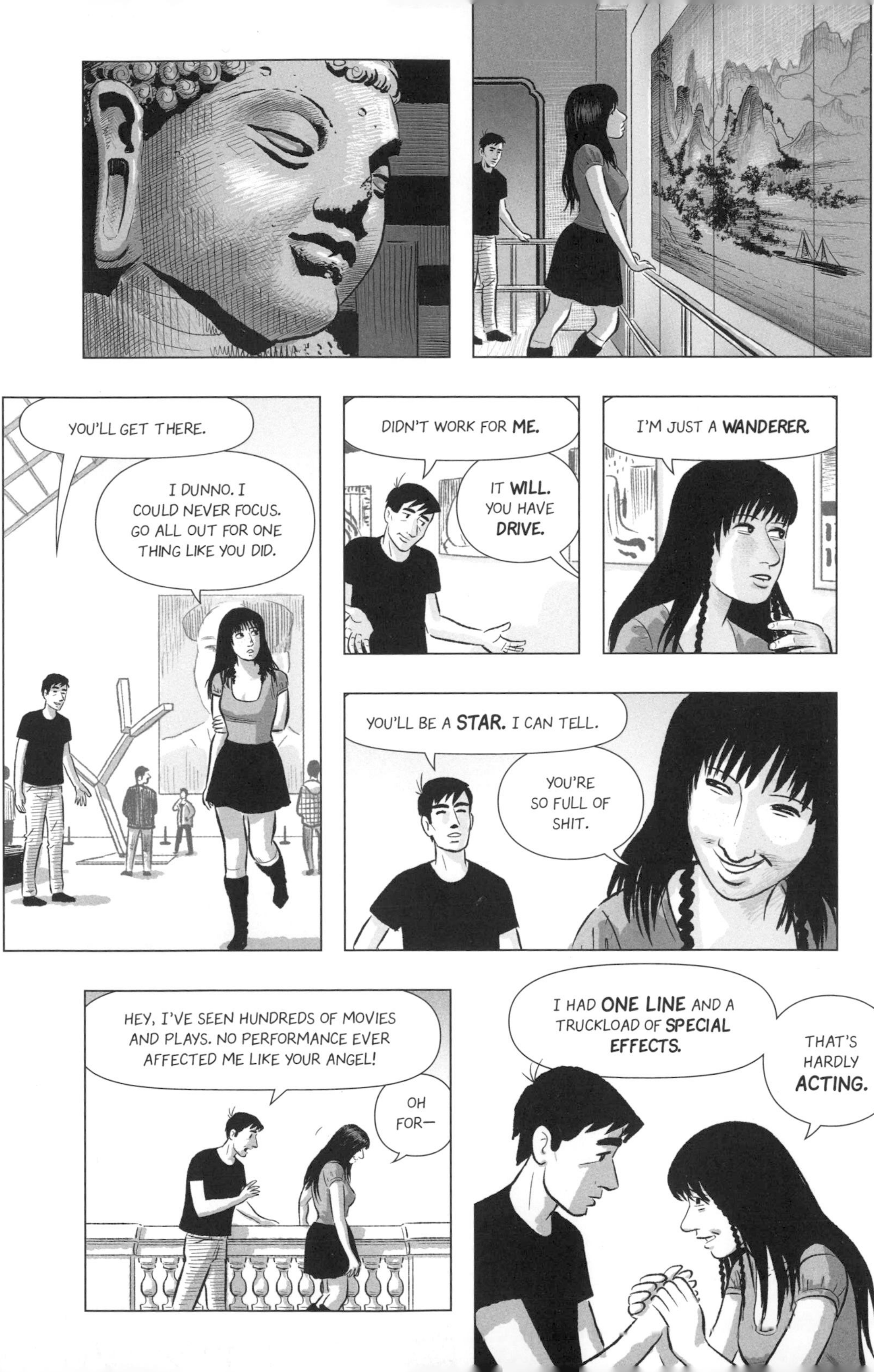
YOU'LL GET THERE.
I DUNNO. I COULD NEVER FOCUS. GO ALL OUT FOR ONE THING LIKE YOU DID.
DIDN'T WORK FOR ME.
IT WILL. YOU HAVE DRIVE.
I'M JUST A WANDERER.
YOU'LL BE A STAR. I CAN TELL.
YOU'RE SO FULL OF SHIT.
HEY, I'VE SEEN HUNDREDS OF MOVIES AND PLAYS. NO PERFORMANCE EVER AFFECTED ME LIKE YOUR ANGEL!
OH FOR—
I HAD ONE LINE AND A TRUCKLOAD OF SPECIAL EFFECTS.
THAT'S HARDLY ACTING.

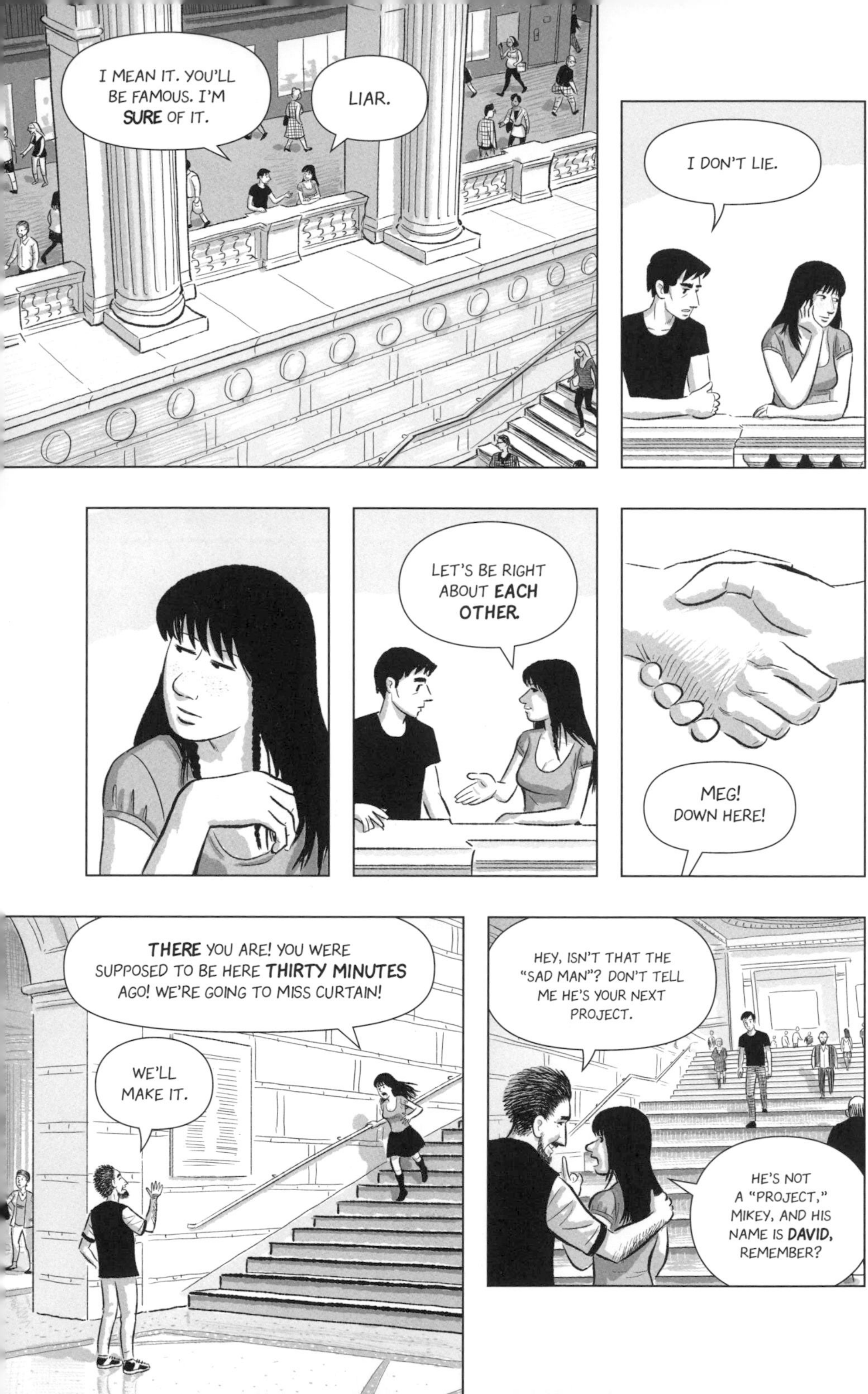
I MEAN IT. YOU'LL BE FAMOUS. I'M SURE OF IT.
LIAR.
I DON'T LIE.
LET'S BE RIGHT ABOUT EACH OTHER.
MEG! DOWN HERE!
THERE YOU ARE! YOU WERE SUPPOSED TO BE HERE THIRTY MINUTES AGO! WE'RE GOING TO MISS CURTAIN!
WE'LL MAKE IT.
HEY, ISN'T THAT THE "SAD MAN"? DON'T TELL ME HE'S YOUR NEXT PROJECT.
HE'S NOT A "PROJECT," MIKEY, AND HIS NAME IS DAVID, REMEMBER?

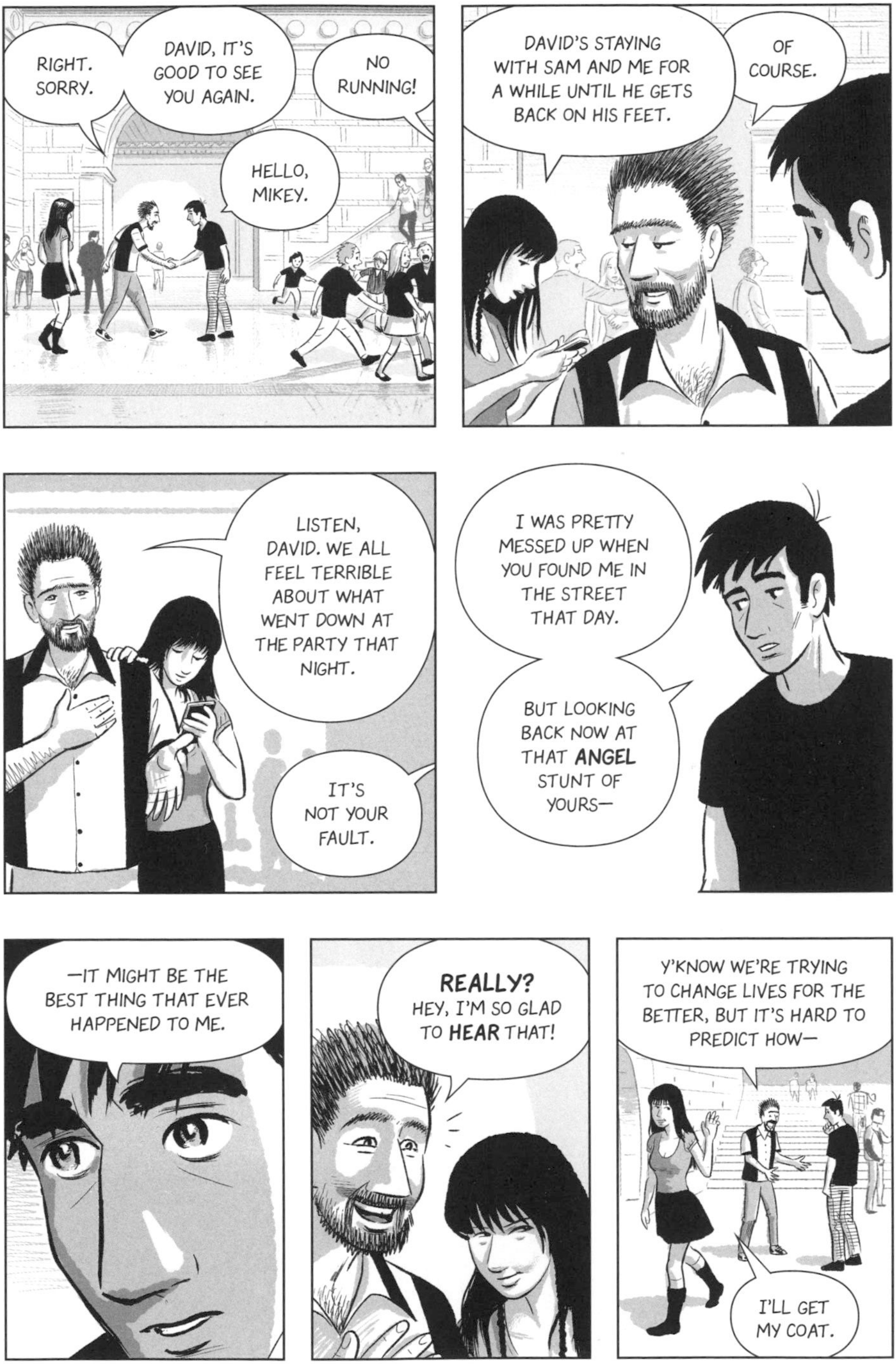
RIGHT. SORRY.
DAVID, IT'S GOOD TO SEE YOU AGAIN.
NO RUNNING!
HELLO, MIKEY.
DAVID'S STAYING WITH SAM AND ME FOR A WHILE UNTIL HE GETS BACK ON HIS FEET.
OF COURSE.
LISTEN, DAVID. WE ALL FEEL TERRIBLE ABOUT WHAT WENT DOWN AT THE PARTY THAT NIGHT.
IT'S NOT YOUR FAULT.
I WAS PRETTY MESSED UP WHEN YOU FOUND ME IN THE STREET THAT DAY.
BUT LOOKING BACK NOW AT THAT **ANGEL** STUNT OF YOURS—
—IT MIGHT BE THE BEST THING THAT EVER HAPPENED TO ME.
REALLY? HEY, I'M SO GLAD TO **HEAR** THAT!
Y'KNOW WE'RE TRYING TO CHANGE LIVES FOR THE BETTER, BUT IT'S HARD TO PREDICT HOW—
I'LL GET MY COAT.

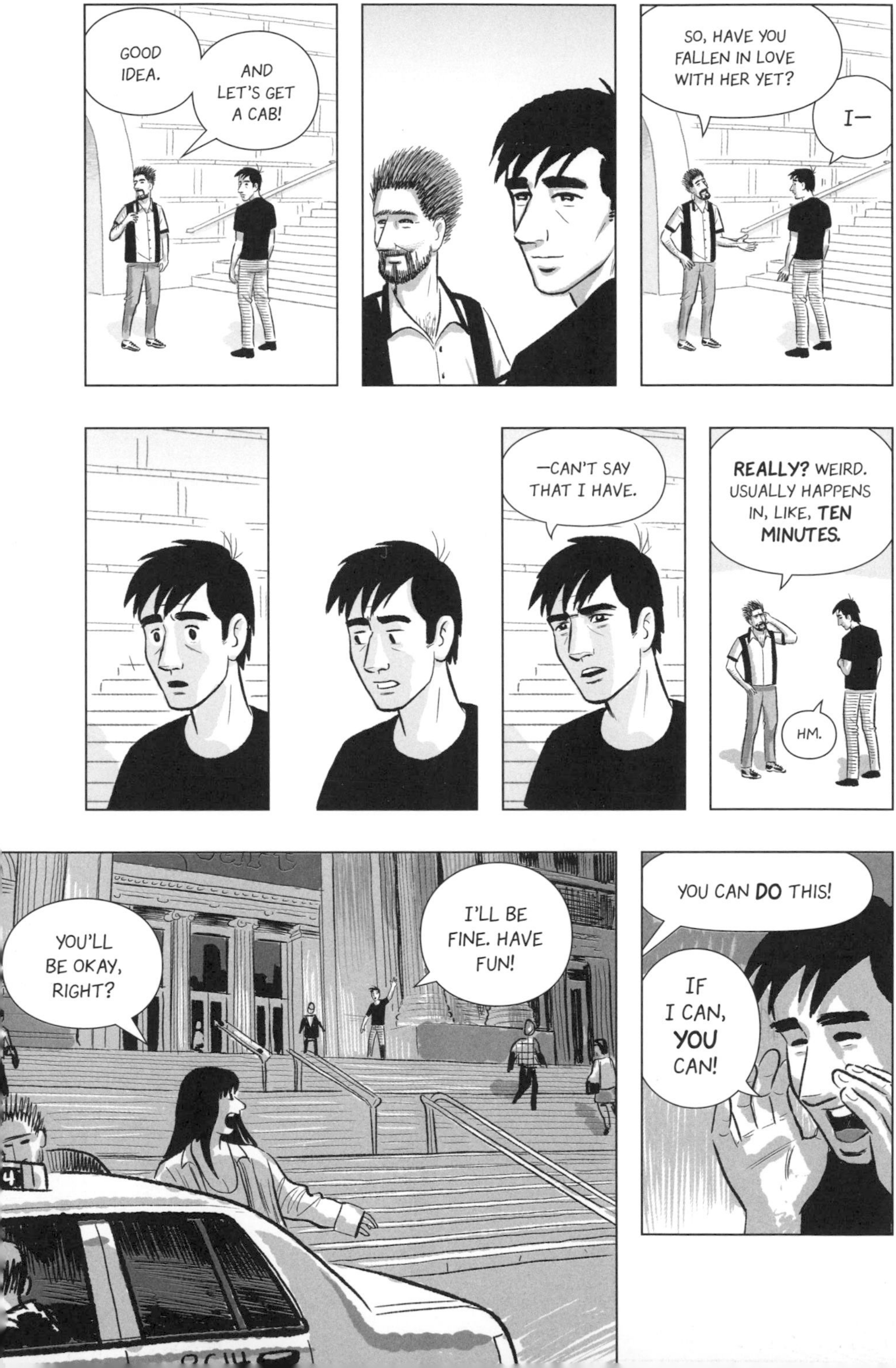
GOOD IDEA.
AND LET'S GET A CAB!
SO, HAVE YOU FALLEN IN LOVE WITH HER YET?
I—
—CAN'T SAY THAT I HAVE.
REALLY? WEIRD. USUALLY HAPPENS IN, LIKE, **TEN MINUTES.**
HM.
YOU'LL BE OKAY, RIGHT?
I'LL BE FINE. HAVE FUN!
YOU CAN **DO** THIS!
IF I CAN, **YOU** CAN!

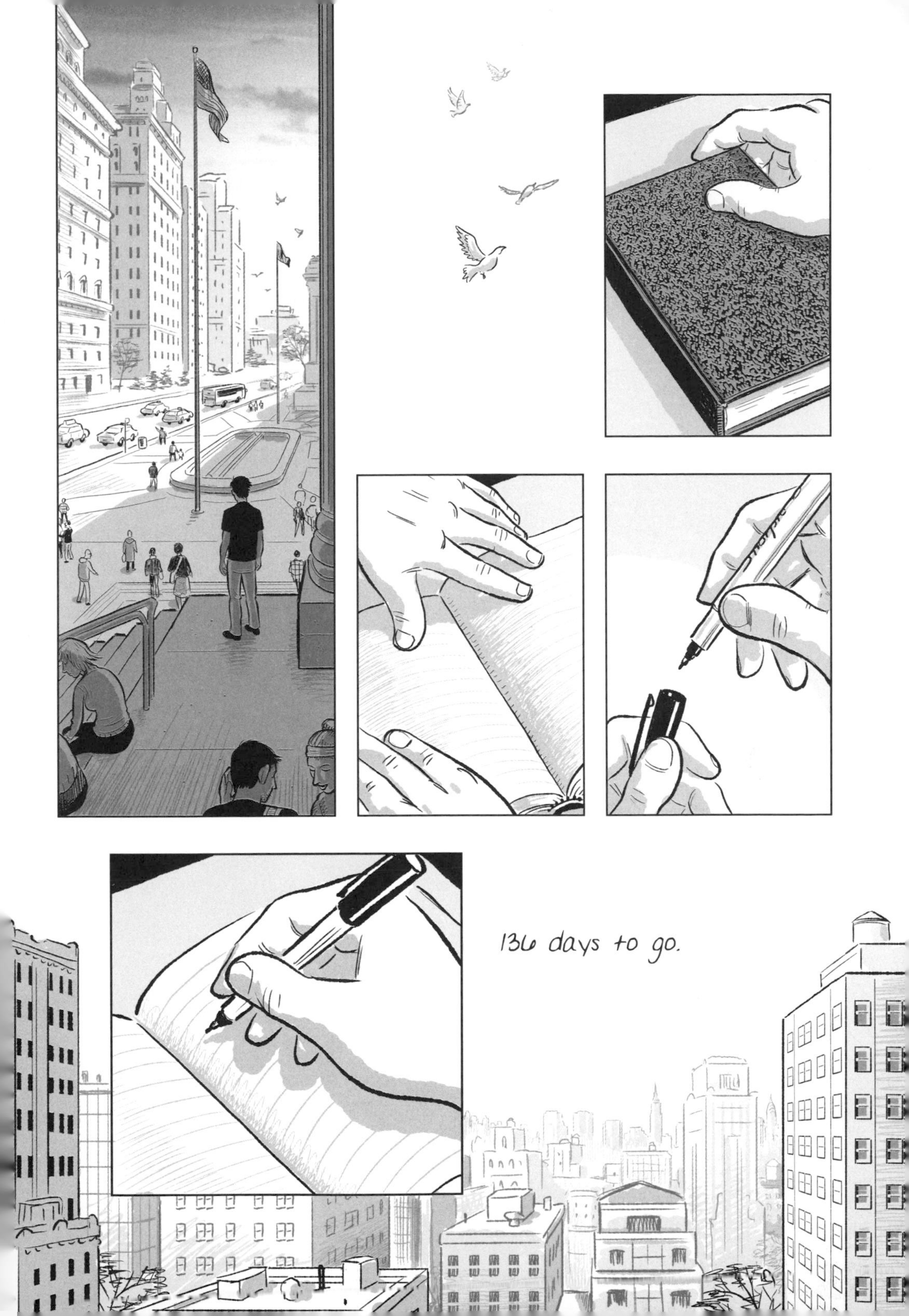
136 days to go.

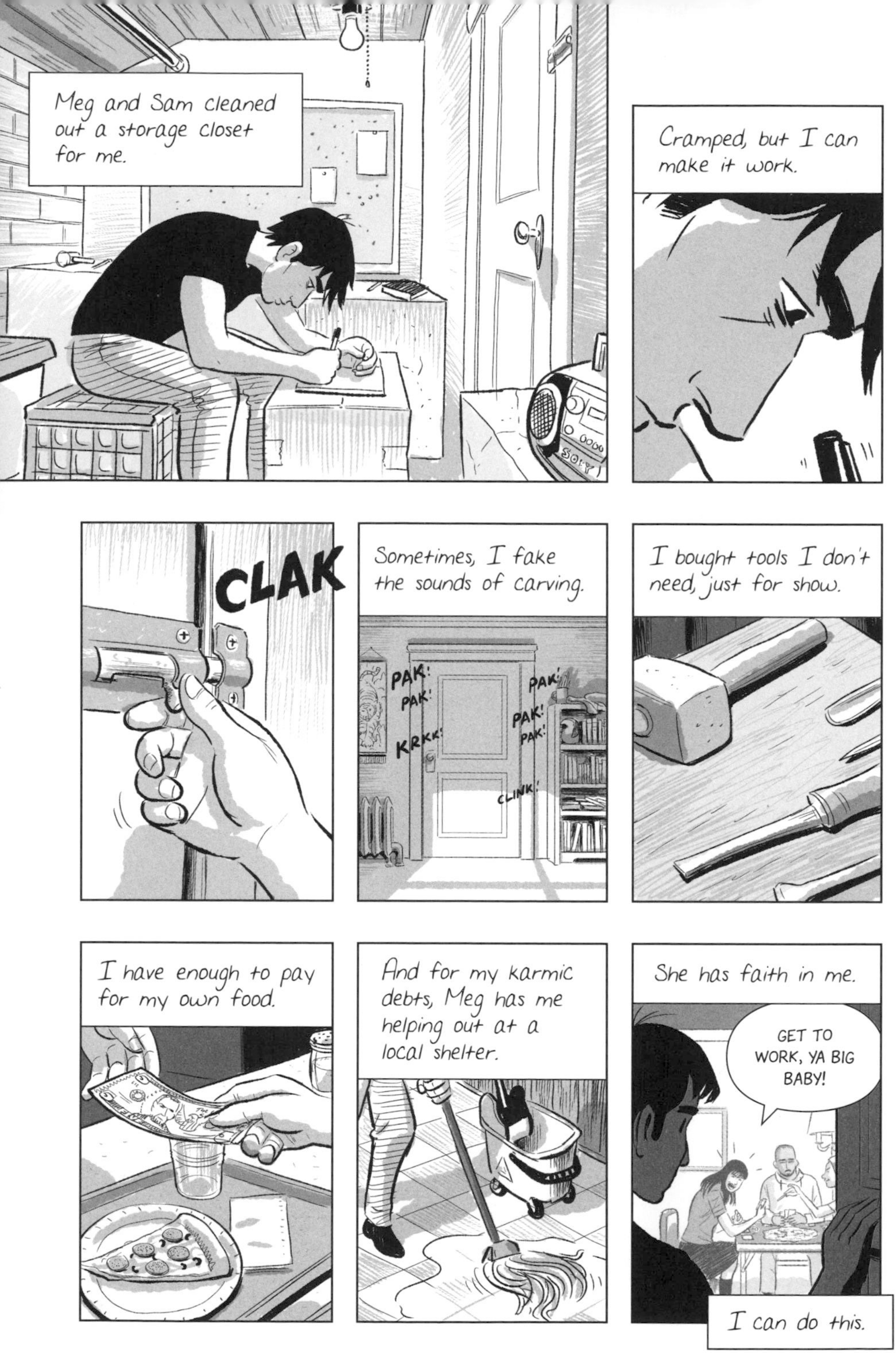
Meg and Sam cleaned out a storage closet for me.
SONY
Cramped, but I can make it work.
CLAK
Sometimes, I fake the sounds of carving.
PAK!
PAK!
KRKK!
PAK!
PAK!
PAK!
CLINK!
I bought tools I don't need, just for show.
I have enough to pay for my own food.
And for my karmic debts, Meg has me helping out at a local shelter.
She has faith in me.
GET TO WORK, YA BIG BABY!
I can do this.

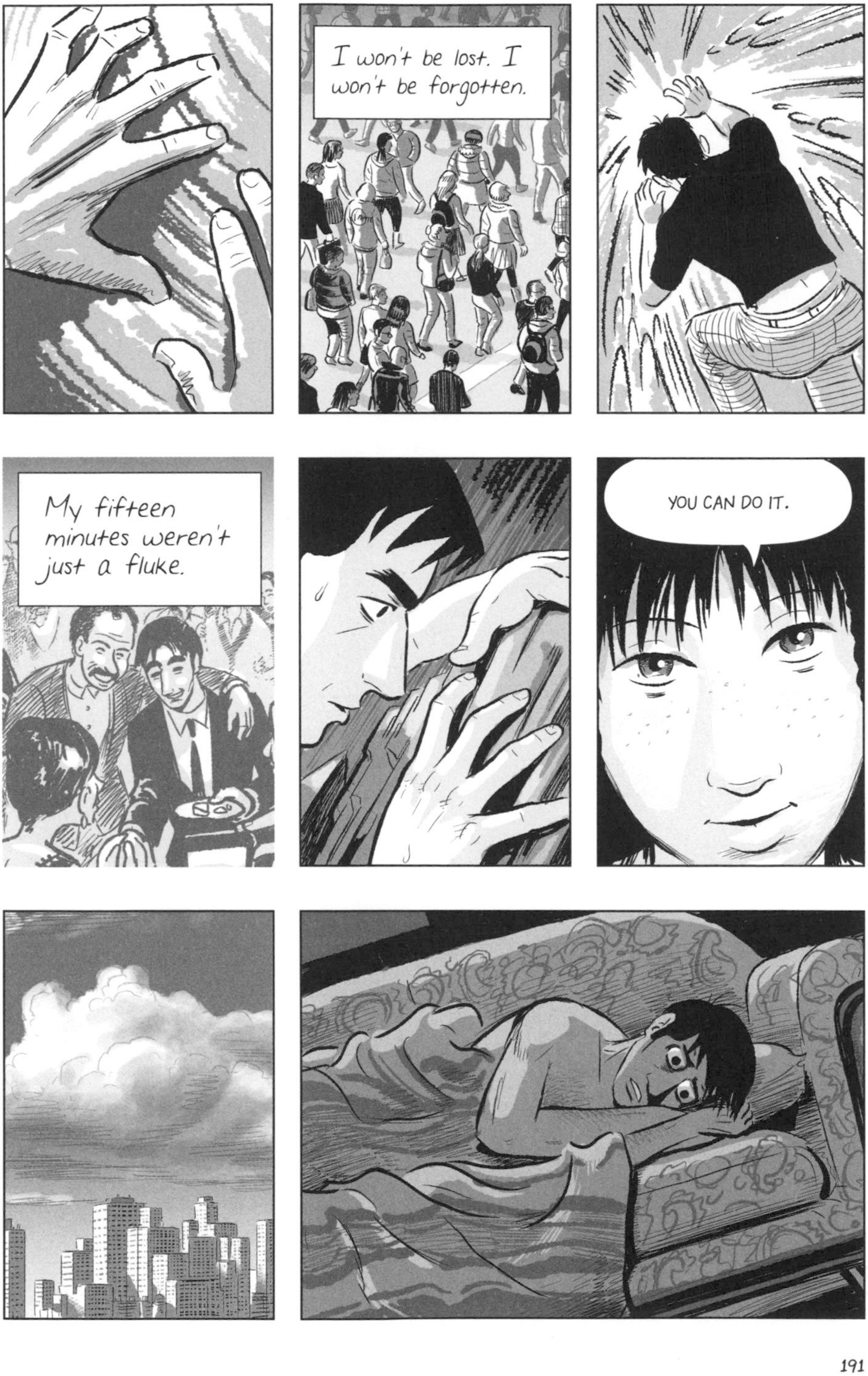
I won't be lost. I won't be forgotten.
My fifteen minutes weren't just a fluke.
YOU CAN DO IT.

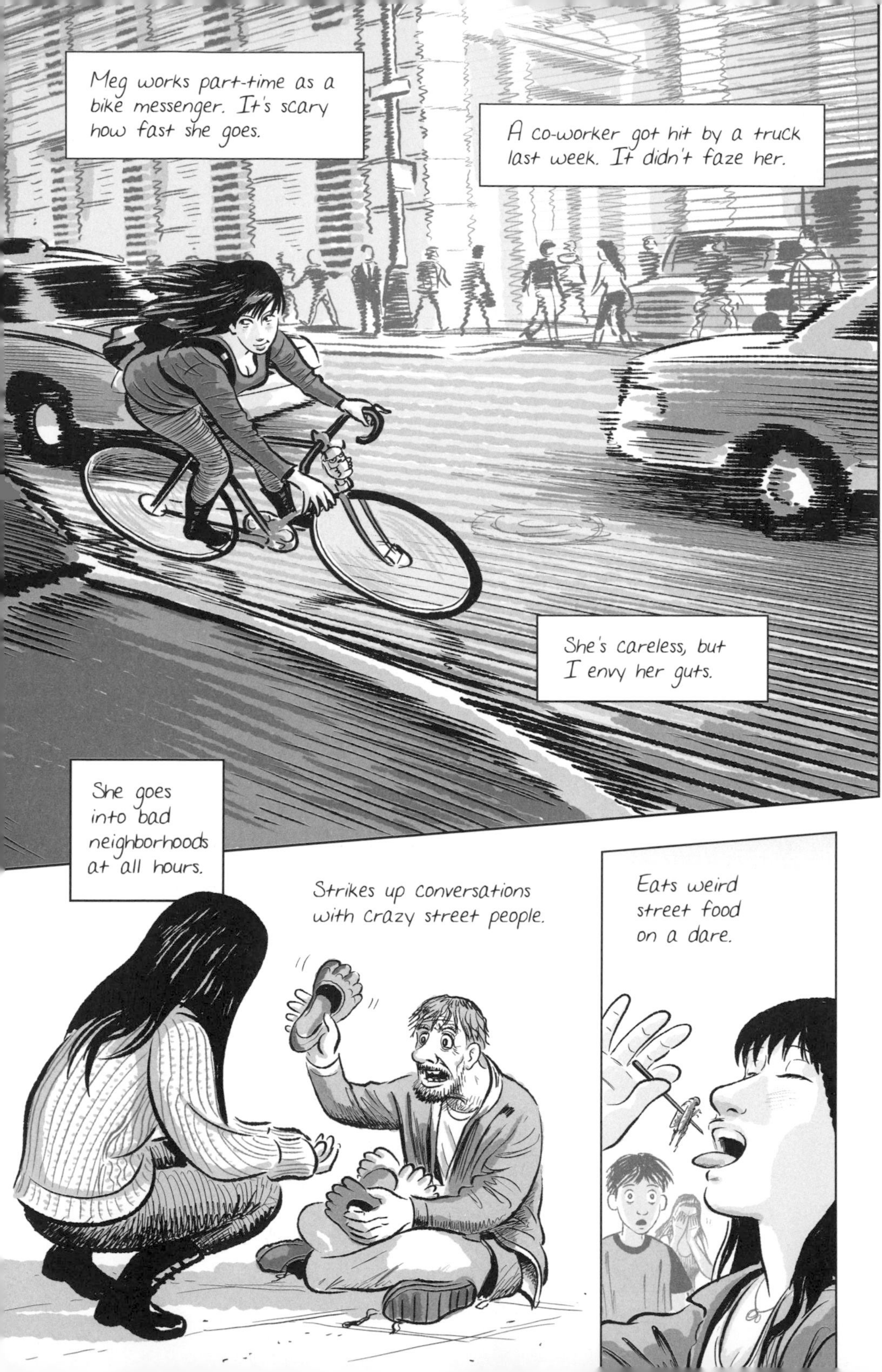
Meg works part-time as a bike messenger. It's scary how fast she goes.
A co-worker got hit by a truck last week. It didn't faze her.
She's careless, but I envy her guts.
She goes into bad neighborhoods at all hours.
Strikes up conversations with crazy street people.
Eats weird street food on a dare.

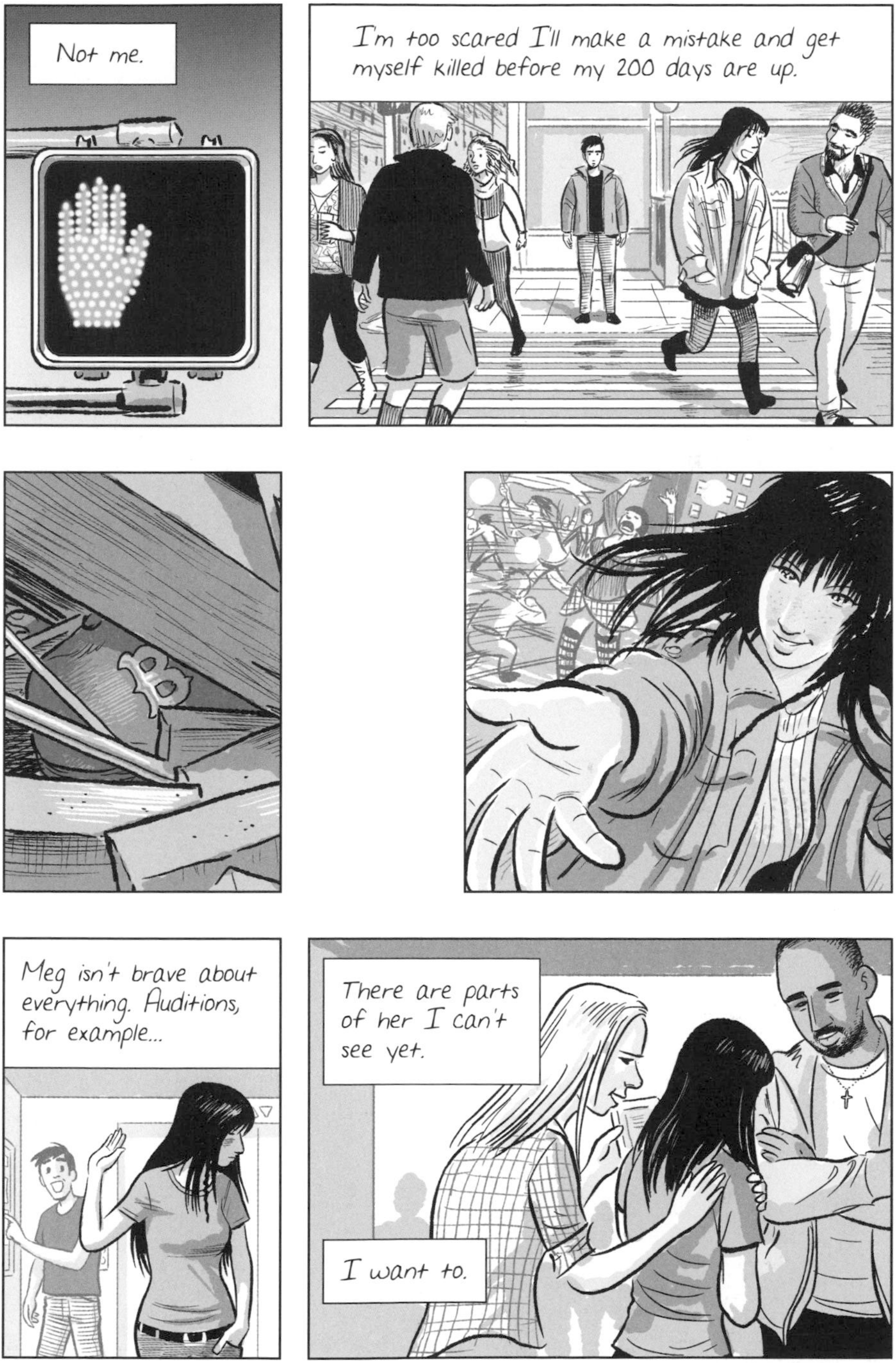
Not me.
I'm too scared I'll make a mistake and get myself killed before my 200 days are up.
Meg isn't brave about everything. Auditions, for example...
There are parts of her I can't see yet.
I want to.

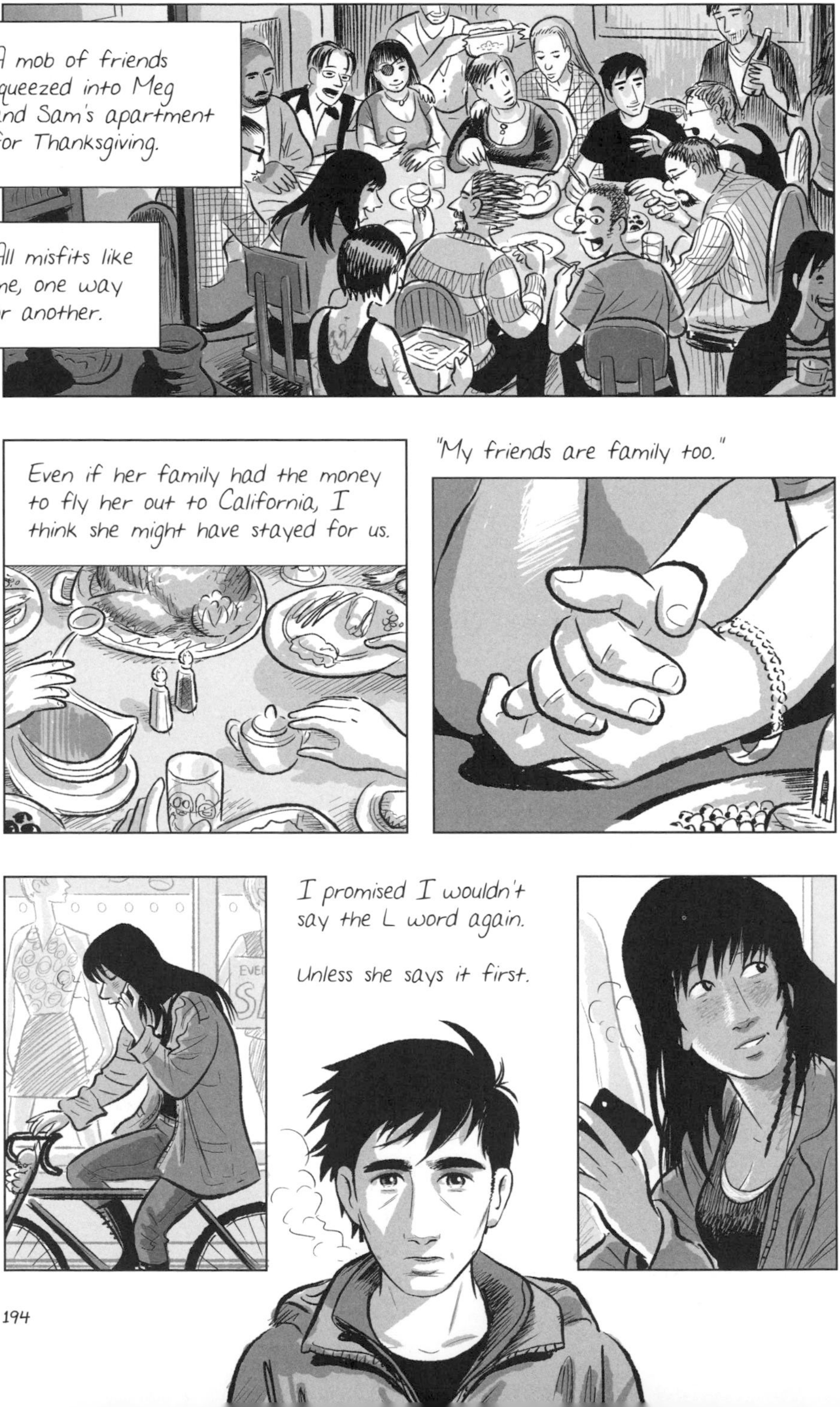
A mob of friends squeezed into Meg and Sam's apartment for Thanksgiving.
All misfits like me, one way or another.
Even if her family had the money to fly her out to California, I think she might have stayed for us.
"My friends are family too."
I promised I wouldn't say the L word again.
Unless she says it first.

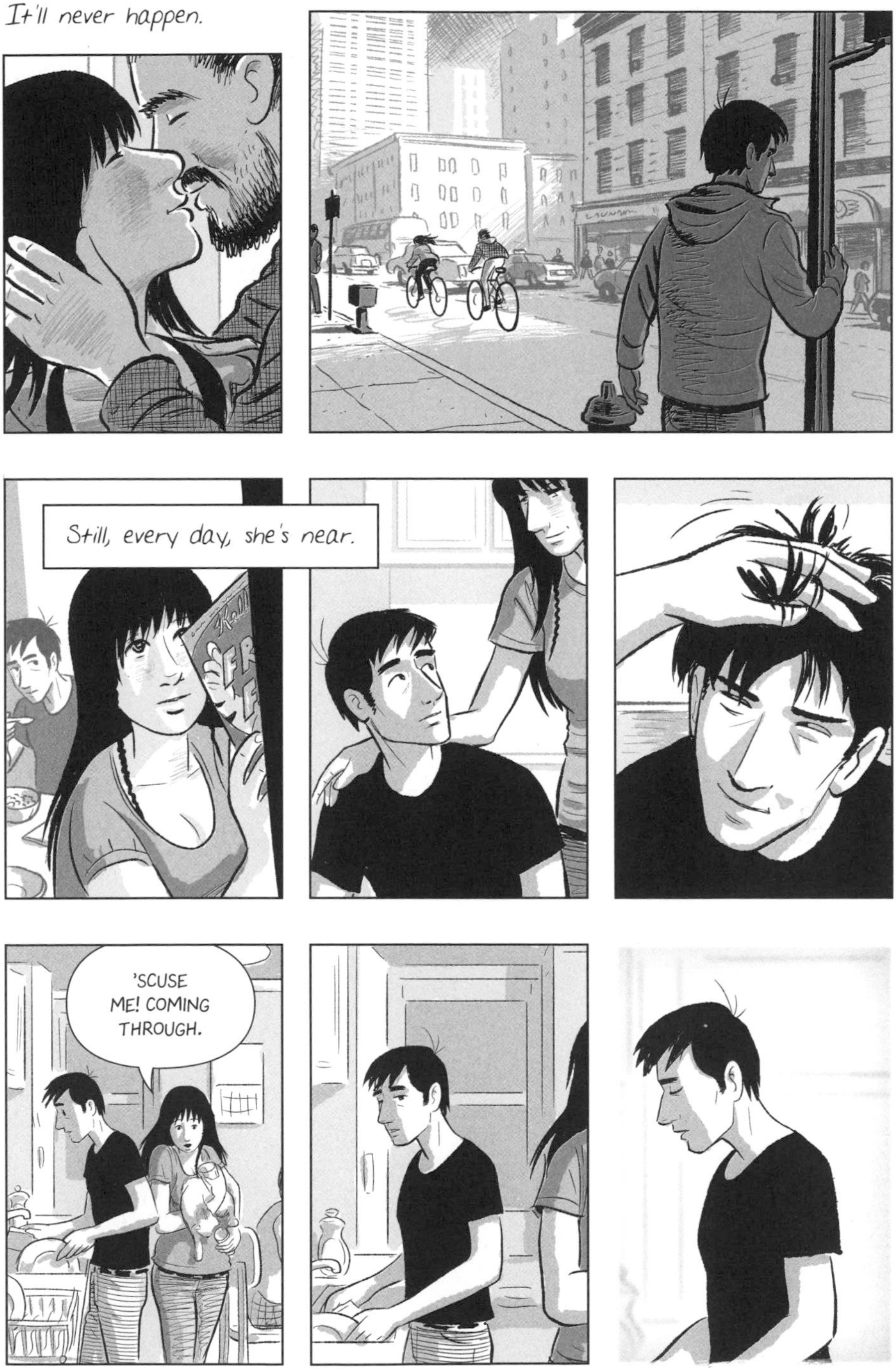
It'll never happen.
Still, every day, she's near.
'SCUSE ME! COMING THROUGH.

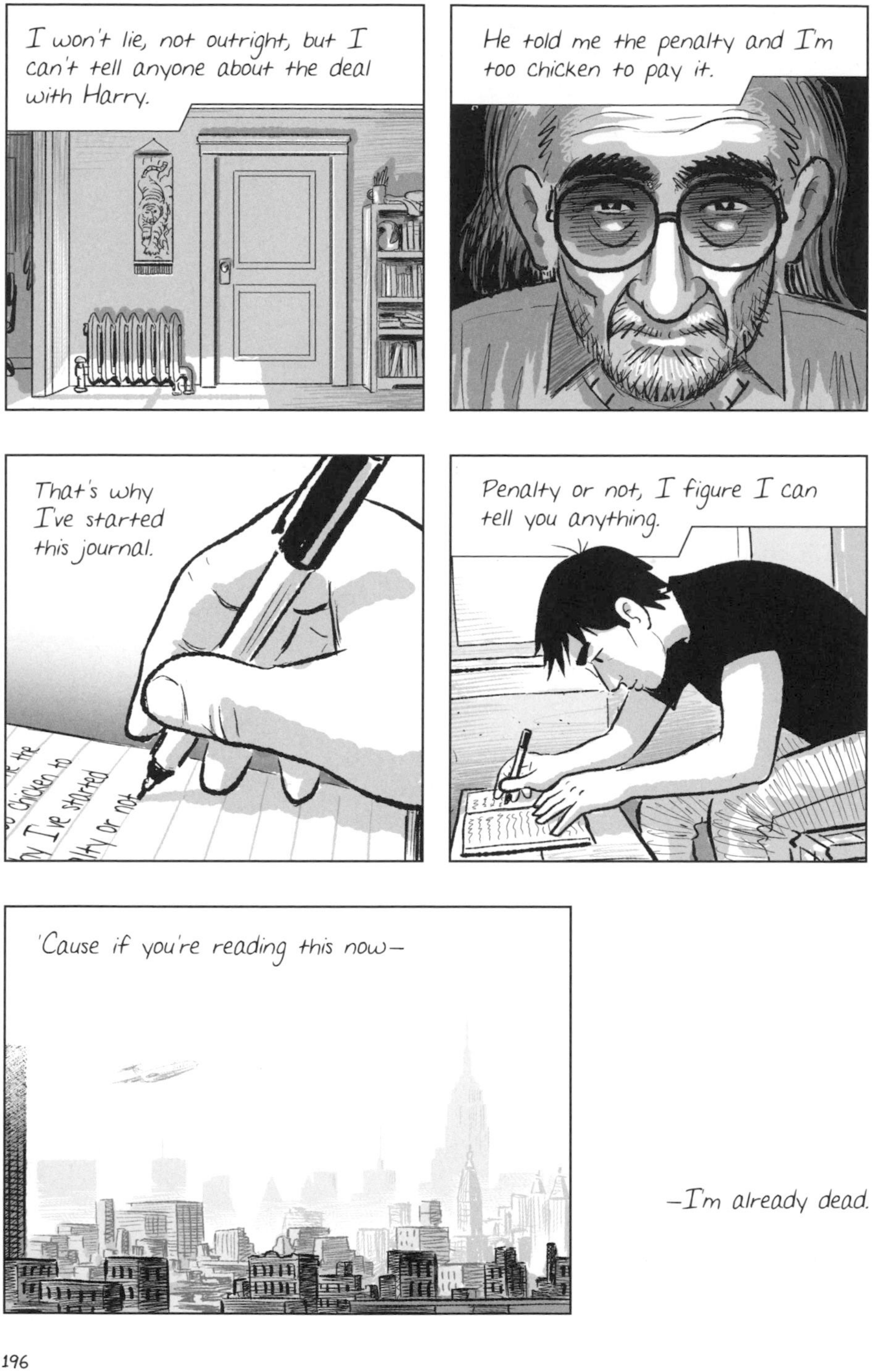
I won't lie, not outright, but I can't tell anyone about the deal with Harry.
He told me the penalty and I'm too chicken to pay it.
That's why I've started this journal.
Penalty or not, I figure I can tell you anything.
'Cause if you're reading this now—
—I'm already dead.

THURS
BINGO
7:30

SAT SUN
YOU C NT TAK
IT WI H YOU

CLAP! CLAP!
CLAP! CLAP!
CLAP!
CLA
CLA

CLAP! CLAP!
CLAP! CLAP
CLAP!
CLAP!

WOO!

CLAP! CLAP! CLAP!
CLAP! CLA

ZIPPER EMERGENCY! SHE'LL BE OUT IN A MINUTE.

TELL HER SHE WAS AWESOME!

SERIOUSLY, THE SISTER ISN'T A BIG ROLE, BUT SHE JUST **NAILED** IT!

SHE DID.

SHE'S SUCH A JOY TO WATCH.

SHE IS.

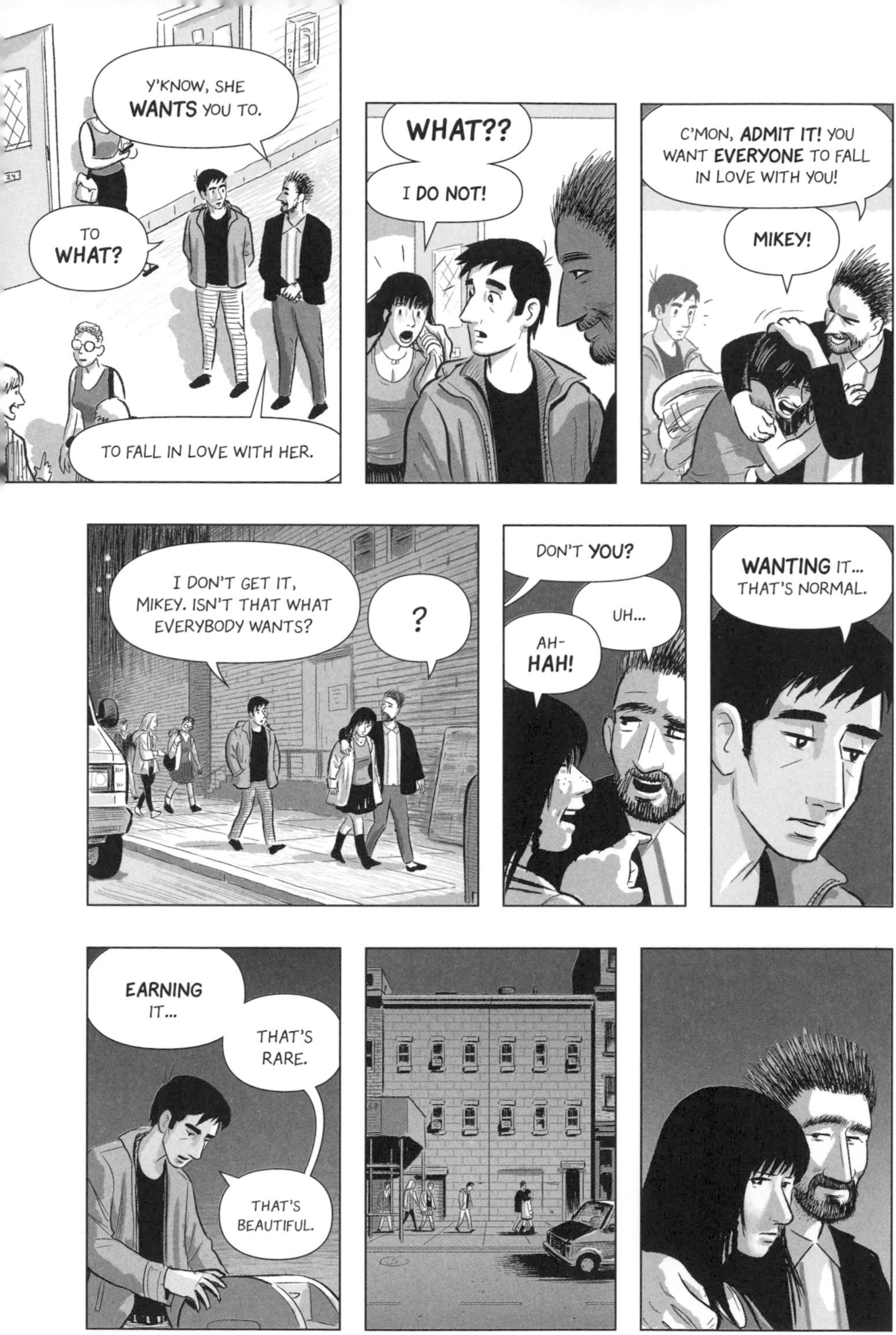
Y'KNOW, SHE WANTS YOU TO.
TO WHAT?
TO FALL IN LOVE WITH HER.
WHAT??
I DO NOT!
C'MON, ADMIT IT! YOU WANT EVERYONE TO FALL IN LOVE WITH YOU!
MIKEY!
I DON'T GET IT, MIKEY. ISN'T THAT WHAT EVERYBODY WANTS?
?
DON'T YOU?
UH...
AH-HAH!
WANTING IT... THAT'S NORMAL.
EARNING IT...
THAT'S RARE.
THAT'S BEAUTIFUL.

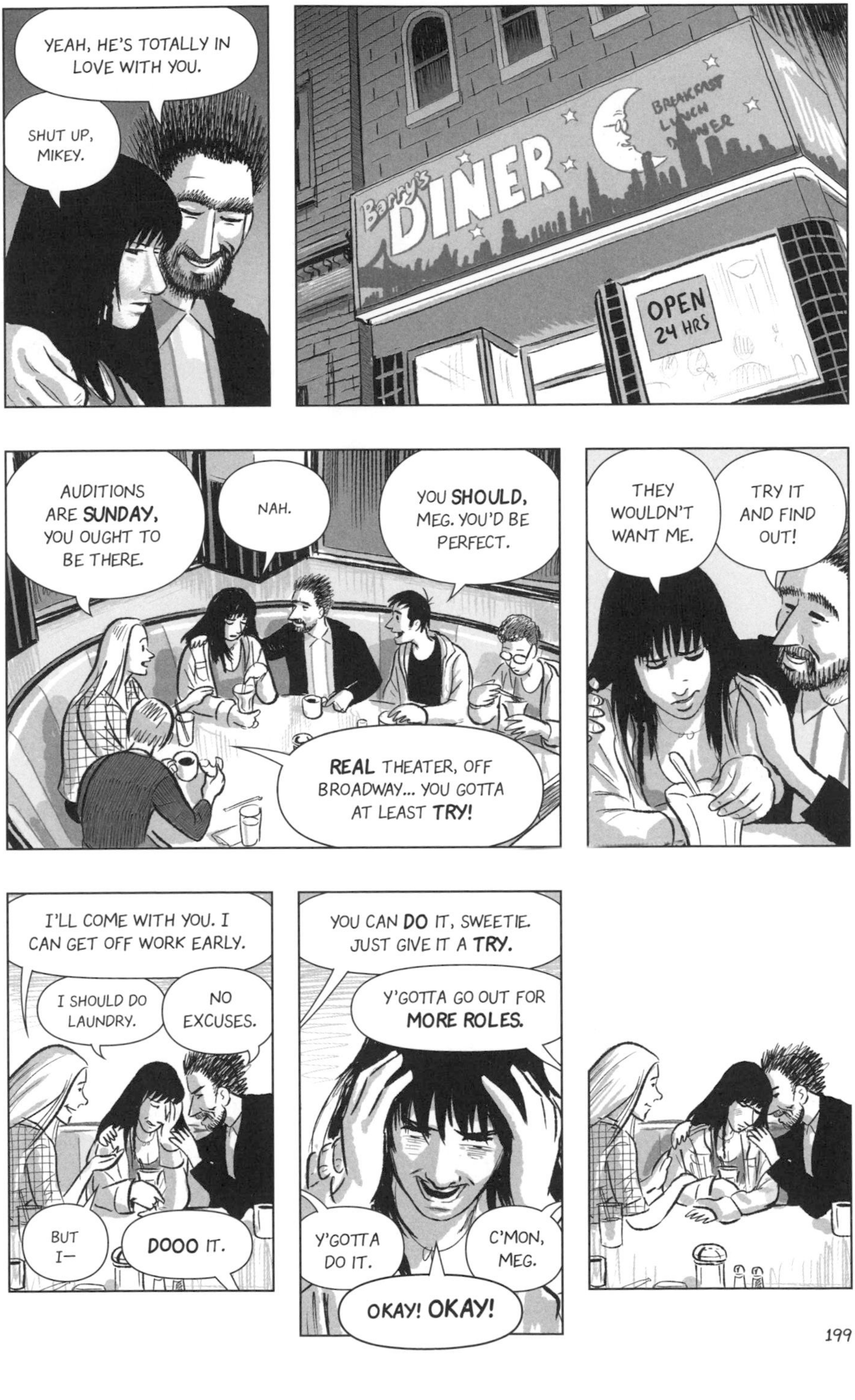
YEAH, HE'S TOTALLY IN LOVE WITH YOU.
SHUT UP, MIKEY.
Barry's DINER
BREAKFAST LUNCH DINNER
OPEN 24 HRS
AUDITIONS ARE SUNDAY, YOU OUGHT TO BE THERE.
NAH.
YOU SHOULD, MEG. YOU'D BE PERFECT.
REAL THEATER, OFF BROADWAY... YOU GOTTA AT LEAST TRY!
THEY WOULDN'T WANT ME.
TRY IT AND FIND OUT!
I'LL COME WITH YOU. I CAN GET OFF WORK EARLY.
I SHOULD DO LAUNDRY.
NO EXCUSES.
BUT I—
DOOO IT.
YOU CAN DO IT, SWEETIE. JUST GIVE IT A TRY.
Y'GOTTA GO OUT FOR MORE ROLES.
Y'GOTTA DO IT.
C'MON, MEG.
OKAY! OKAY!

124 days to go. I'm looking at my competition.

Mira Bhatti is showing us a series of miniature interiors she made by hand.

Mira lives in Queens with her 7-year-old son from a bad marriage. She's 36, but just getting her degree.

She's been making her boxes for years in relative obscurity. Each one is its own little world.

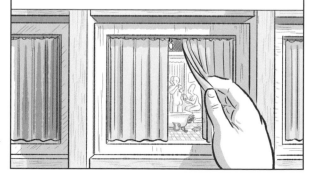

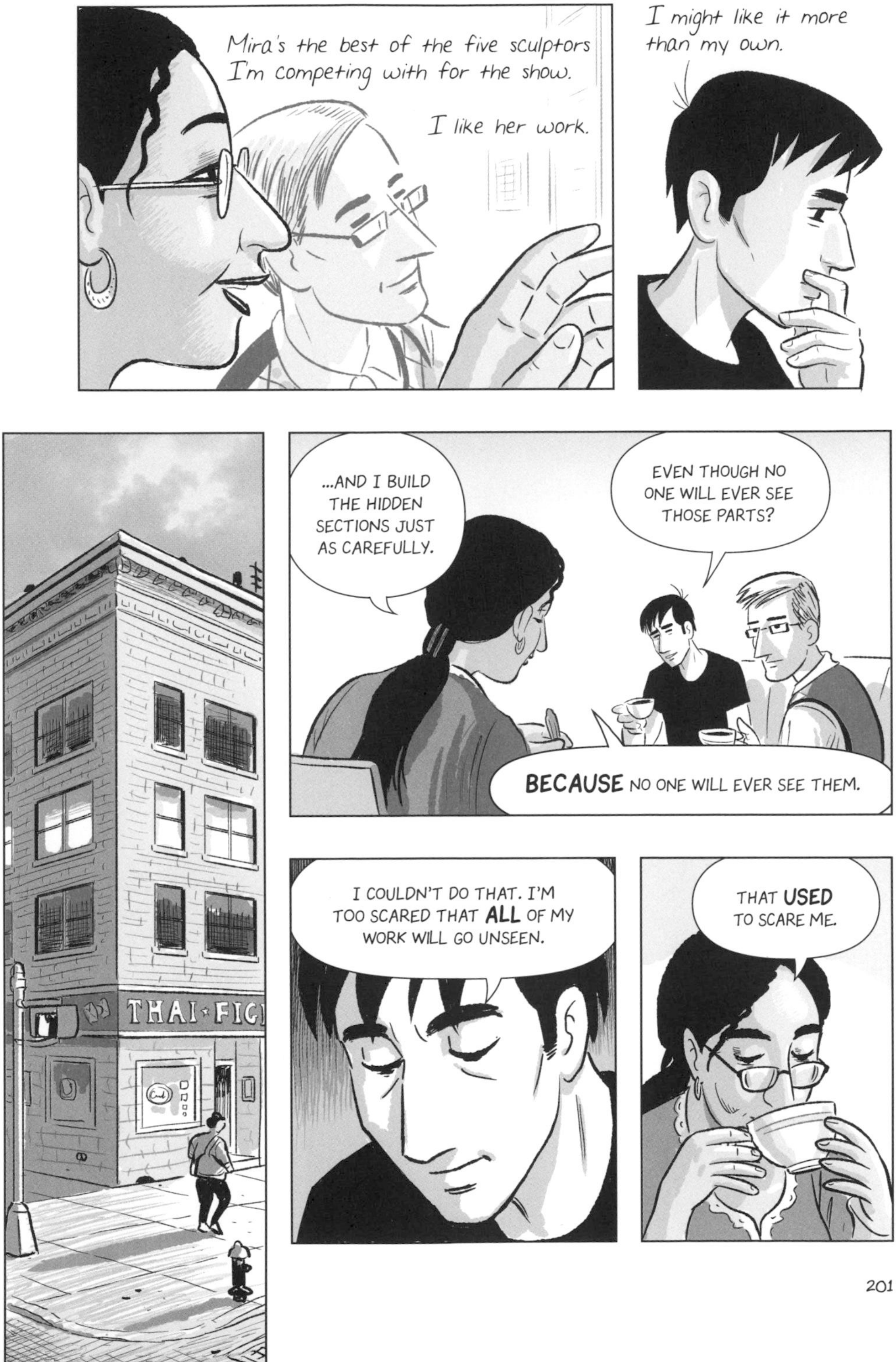
Mira's the best of the five sculptors I'm competing with for the show.
I like her work.
I might like it more than my own.
...AND I BUILD THE HIDDEN SECTIONS JUST AS CAREFULLY.
EVEN THOUGH NO ONE WILL EVER SEE THOSE PARTS?
BECAUSE NO ONE WILL EVER SEE THEM.
THAI★FIG
I COULDN'T DO THAT. I'M TOO SCARED THAT ALL OF MY WORK WILL GO UNSEEN.
THAT USED TO SCARE ME.

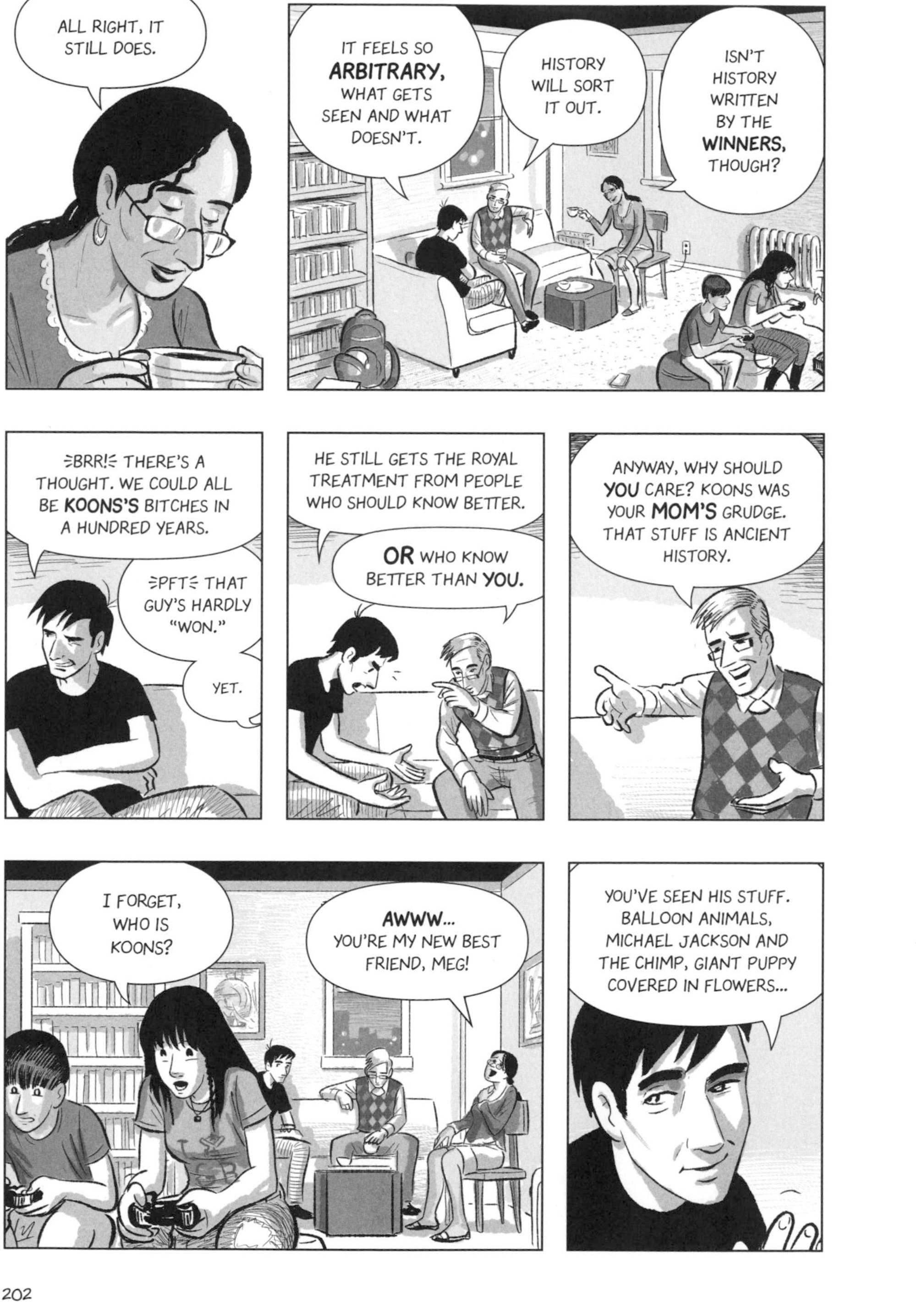
ALL RIGHT, IT STILL DOES.
IT FEELS SO **ARBITRARY,** WHAT GETS SEEN AND WHAT DOESN'T.
HISTORY WILL SORT IT OUT.
ISN'T HISTORY WRITTEN BY THE **WINNERS,** THOUGH?
⋛BRR!⋚ THERE'S A THOUGHT. WE COULD ALL BE **KOONS'S** BITCHES IN A HUNDRED YEARS.
⋛PFT⋚ THAT GUY'S HARDLY "WON."
YET.
HE STILL GETS THE ROYAL TREATMENT FROM PEOPLE WHO SHOULD KNOW BETTER.
OR WHO KNOW BETTER THAN **YOU.**
ANYWAY, WHY SHOULD **YOU** CARE? KOONS WAS YOUR **MOM'S** GRUDGE. THAT STUFF IS ANCIENT HISTORY.
I FORGET, WHO IS KOONS?
AWWW... YOU'RE MY NEW BEST FRIEND, MEG!
YOU'VE SEEN HIS STUFF. BALLOON ANIMALS, MICHAEL JACKSON AND THE CHIMP, GIANT PUPPY COVERED IN FLOWERS...

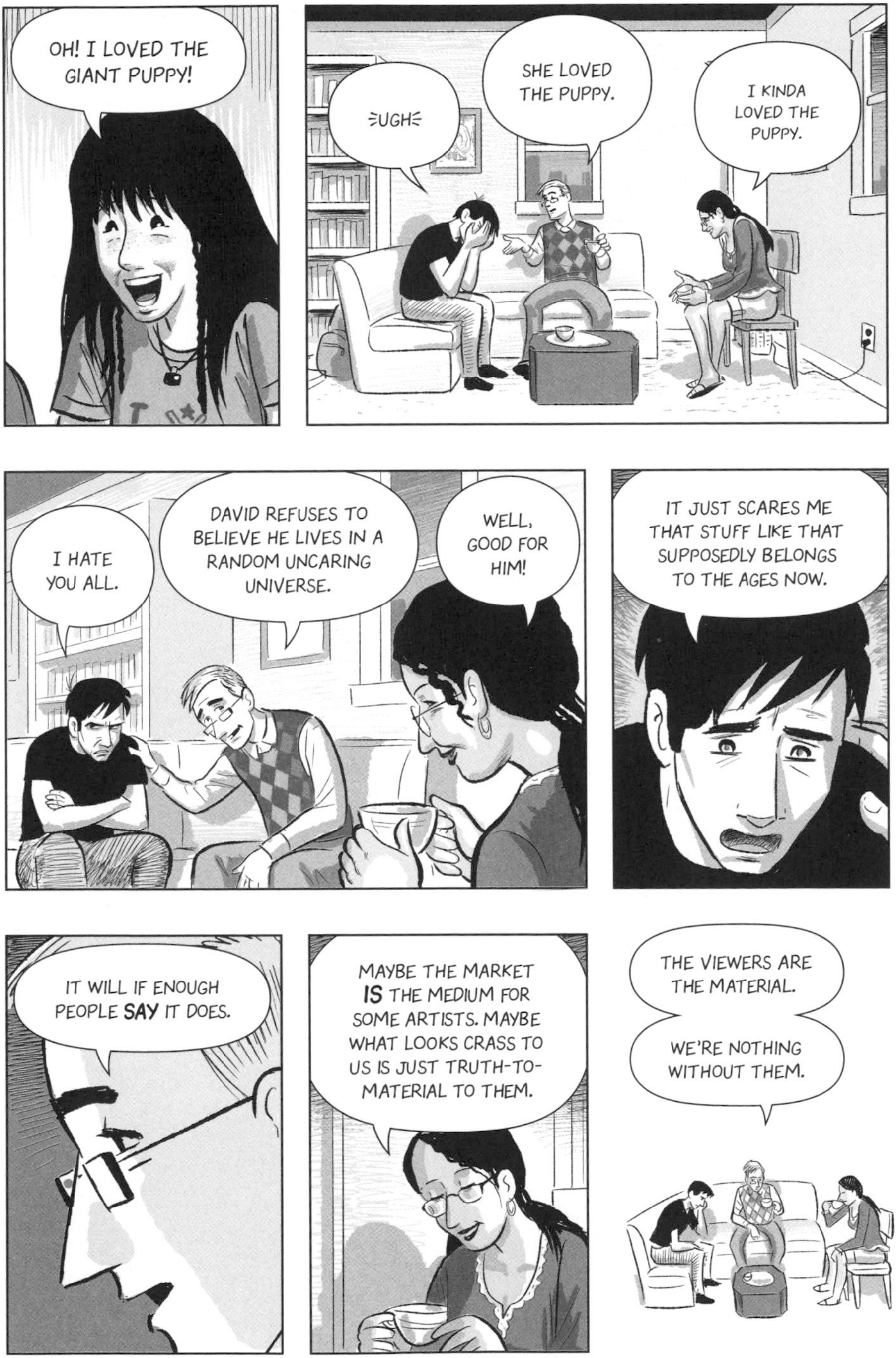
OH! I LOVED THE GIANT PUPPY!
UGH
SHE LOVED THE PUPPY.
I KINDA LOVED THE PUPPY.
I HATE YOU ALL.
DAVID REFUSES TO BELIEVE HE LIVES IN A RANDOM UNCARING UNIVERSE.
WELL, GOOD FOR HIM!
IT JUST SCARES ME THAT STUFF LIKE THAT SUPPOSEDLY BELONGS TO THE AGES NOW.
IT WILL IF ENOUGH PEOPLE SAY IT DOES.
MAYBE THE MARKET IS THE MEDIUM FOR SOME ARTISTS. MAYBE WHAT LOOKS CRASS TO US IS JUST TRUTH-TO-MATERIAL TO THEM.
THE VIEWERS ARE THE MATERIAL.
WE'RE NOTHING WITHOUT THEM.

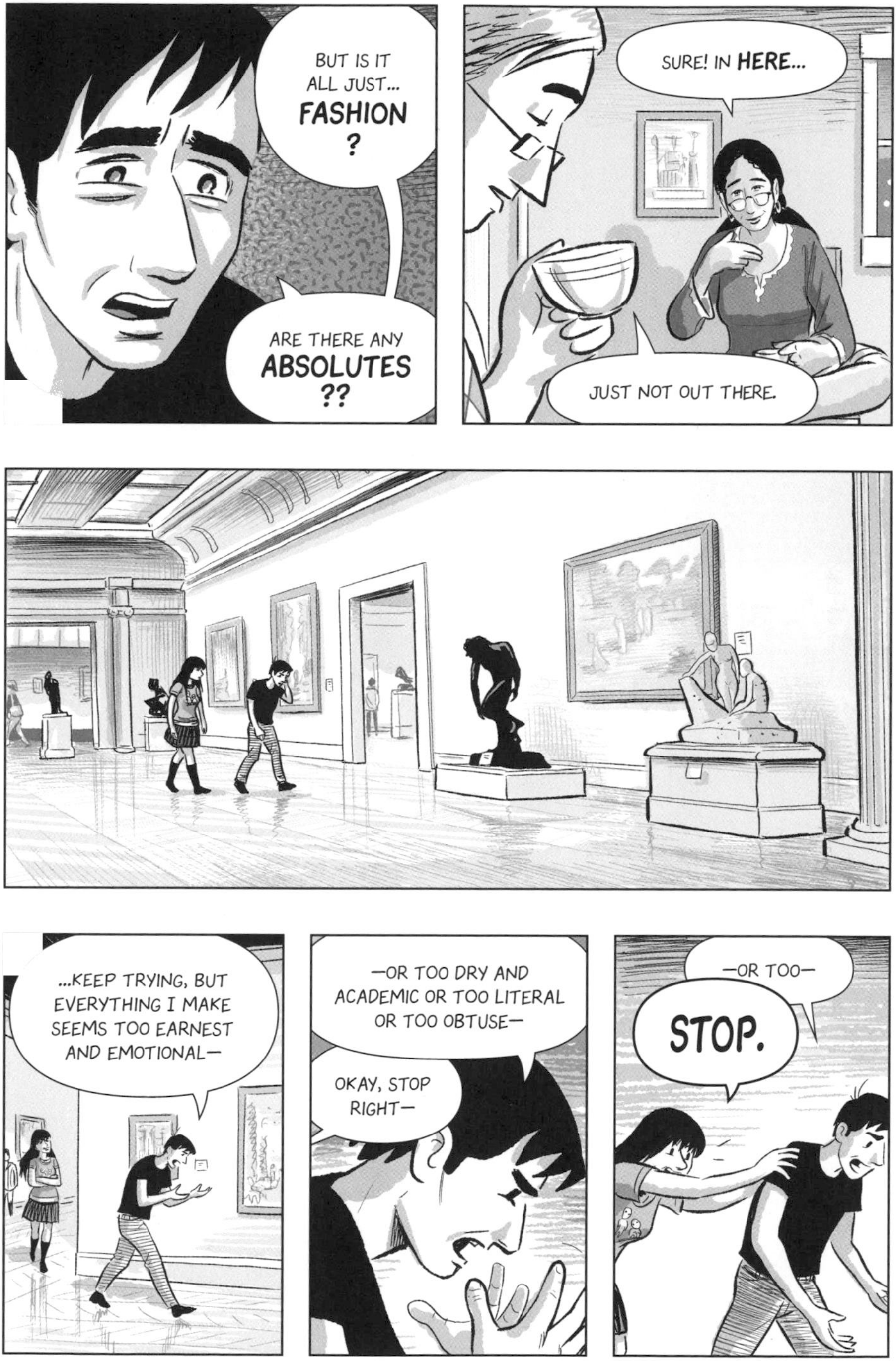
BUT IS IT ALL JUST... FASHION ?
ARE THERE ANY ABSOLUTES ??
SURE! IN HERE...
JUST NOT OUT THERE.
...KEEP TRYING, BUT EVERYTHING I MAKE SEEMS TOO EARNEST AND EMOTIONAL—
—OR TOO DRY AND ACADEMIC OR TOO LITERAL OR TOO OBTUSE—
OKAY, STOP RIGHT—
—OR TOO—
STOP.

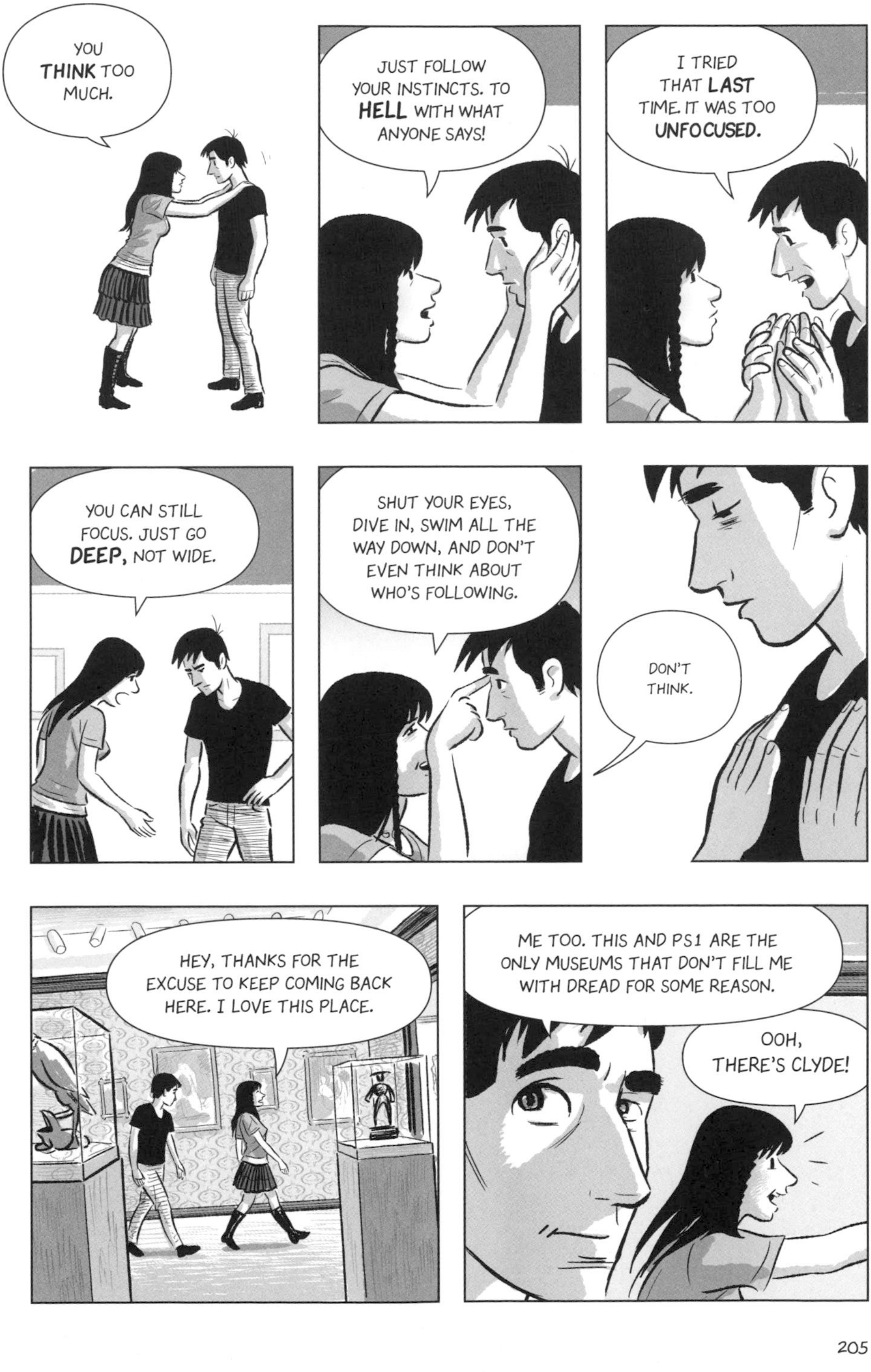
YOU **THINK** TOO MUCH.
JUST FOLLOW YOUR INSTINCTS. TO **HELL** WITH WHAT ANYONE SAYS!
I TRIED THAT **LAST** TIME. IT WAS TOO **UNFOCUSED.**
YOU CAN STILL FOCUS. JUST GO **DEEP,** NOT WIDE.
SHUT YOUR EYES, DIVE IN, SWIM ALL THE WAY DOWN, AND DON'T EVEN THINK ABOUT WHO'S FOLLOWING.
DON'T THINK.
HEY, THANKS FOR THE EXCUSE TO KEEP COMING BACK HERE. I LOVE THIS PLACE.
ME TOO. THIS AND PS1 ARE THE ONLY MUSEUMS THAT DON'T FILL ME WITH DREAD FOR SOME REASON.
OOH, THERE'S CLYDE!

WE USED TO TAKE THE TRAIN DOWN ON MY BIRTHDAY EVERY YEAR, BACK WHEN WE LIVED IN PEEKSKILL.

MY SISTERS AND I ALWAYS FOUND THIS GUY FIRST.

WE CALLED HIM "CLYDE." NOBODY REMEMBERS WHY.

BUT IT WAS IMPORTANT THAT EACH OF US SAY "GOOD MORNING" TO CLYDE BEFORE OUR DAY COULD GET STARTED.

BECAUSE OF THE TIME ON THE ROAD, THE WHOLE FAMILY HAD TRADITIONS THAT NONE OF OUR FRIENDS SEEMED TO UNDERSTA

WE DIDN'T STA PUT IN ANY ONE PLACE LONG ENOU TO HAVE THAT KI OF LINK WITH TH OPLE WE MET

NEW YORK THAT I MADE THE NDS OF FRIENDS THAT WERE A

WE'RE ALL CONNECTED...

206

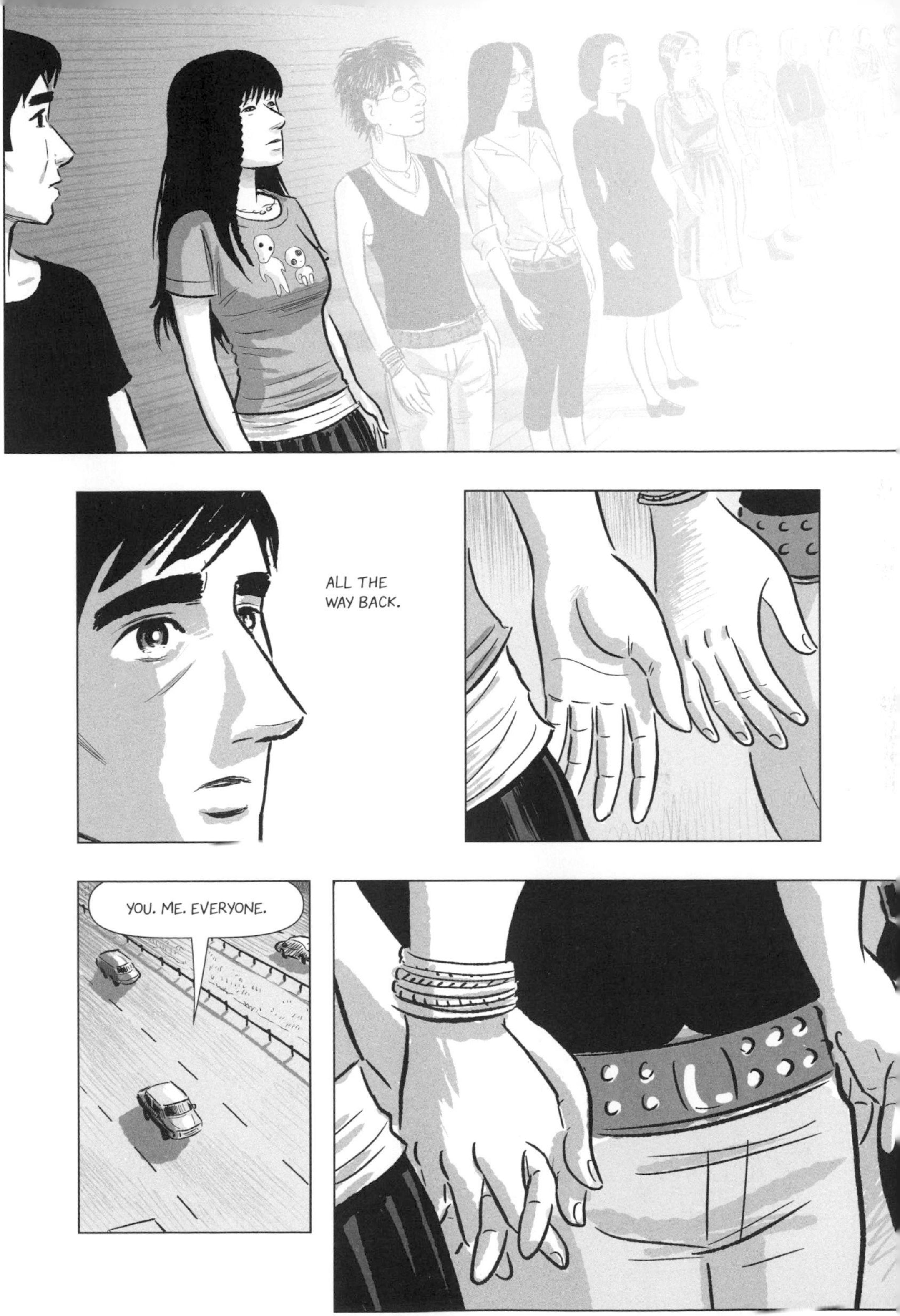
ALL THE WAY BACK.
YOU. ME. EVERYONE.

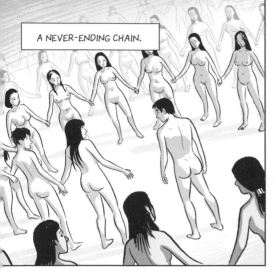

A NEVER-ENDING CHAIN.

BUT I COULD END MINE, COULDN'T I?

YOU COULD, BUT YOU WON'T WANT TO—

—WHEN THE TIME COMES.

≡AHEM≡

UH...

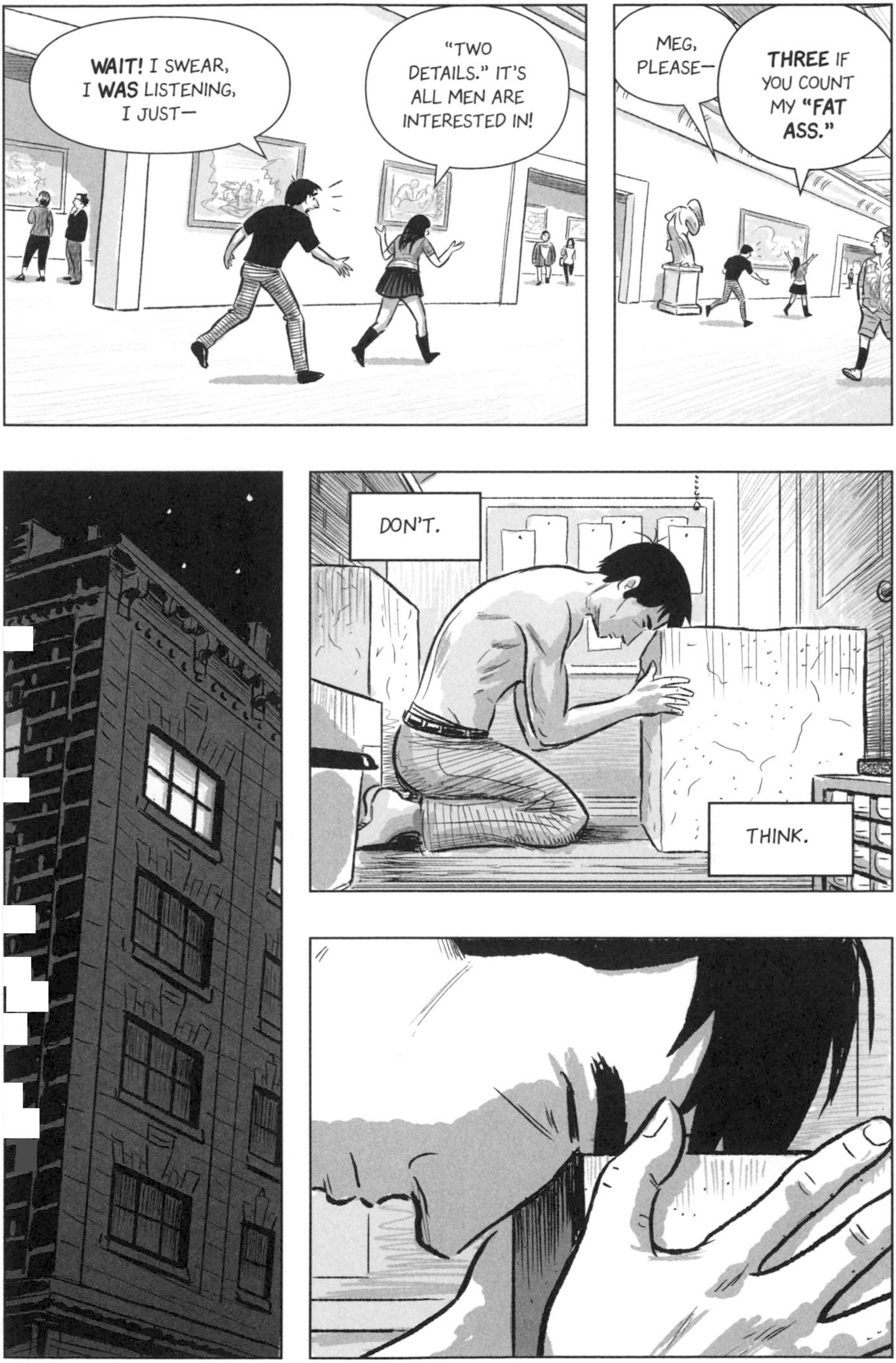
WAIT! I SWEAR, I WAS LISTENING, I JUST—
"TWO DETAILS." IT'S ALL MEN ARE INTERESTED IN!
MEG, PLEASE—
THREE IF YOU COUNT MY "FAT ASS."
DON'T.
THINK.

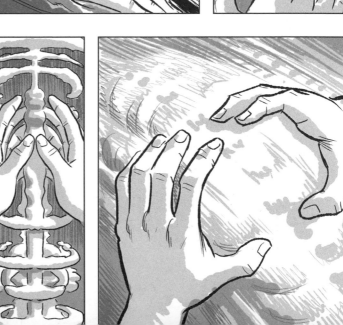

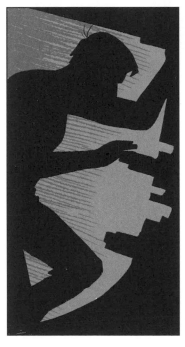
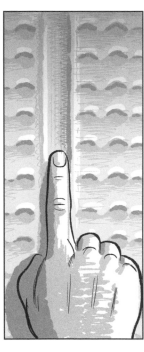
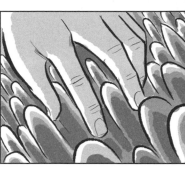

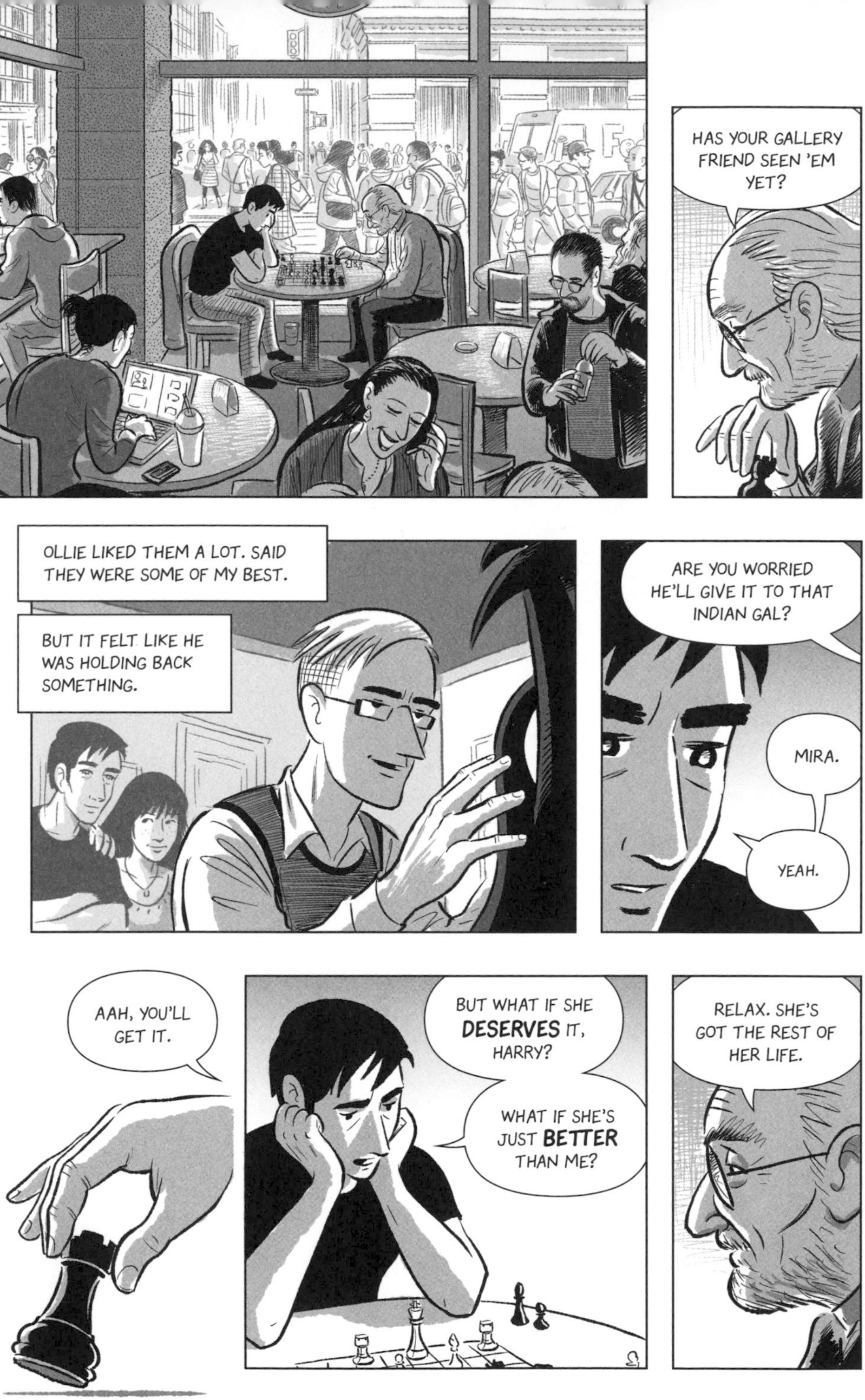
HAS YOUR GALLERY FRIEND SEEN 'EM YET?
OLLIE LIKED THEM A LOT. SAID THEY WERE SOME OF MY BEST.
BUT IT FELT LIKE HE WAS HOLDING BACK SOMETHING.
ARE YOU WORRIED HE'LL GIVE IT TO THAT INDIAN GAL?
MIRA.
YEAH.
AAH, YOU'LL GET IT.
BUT WHAT IF SHE **DESERVES** IT, HARRY?
WHAT IF SHE'S JUST **BETTER** THAN ME?
RELAX. SHE'S GOT THE REST OF HER LIFE.

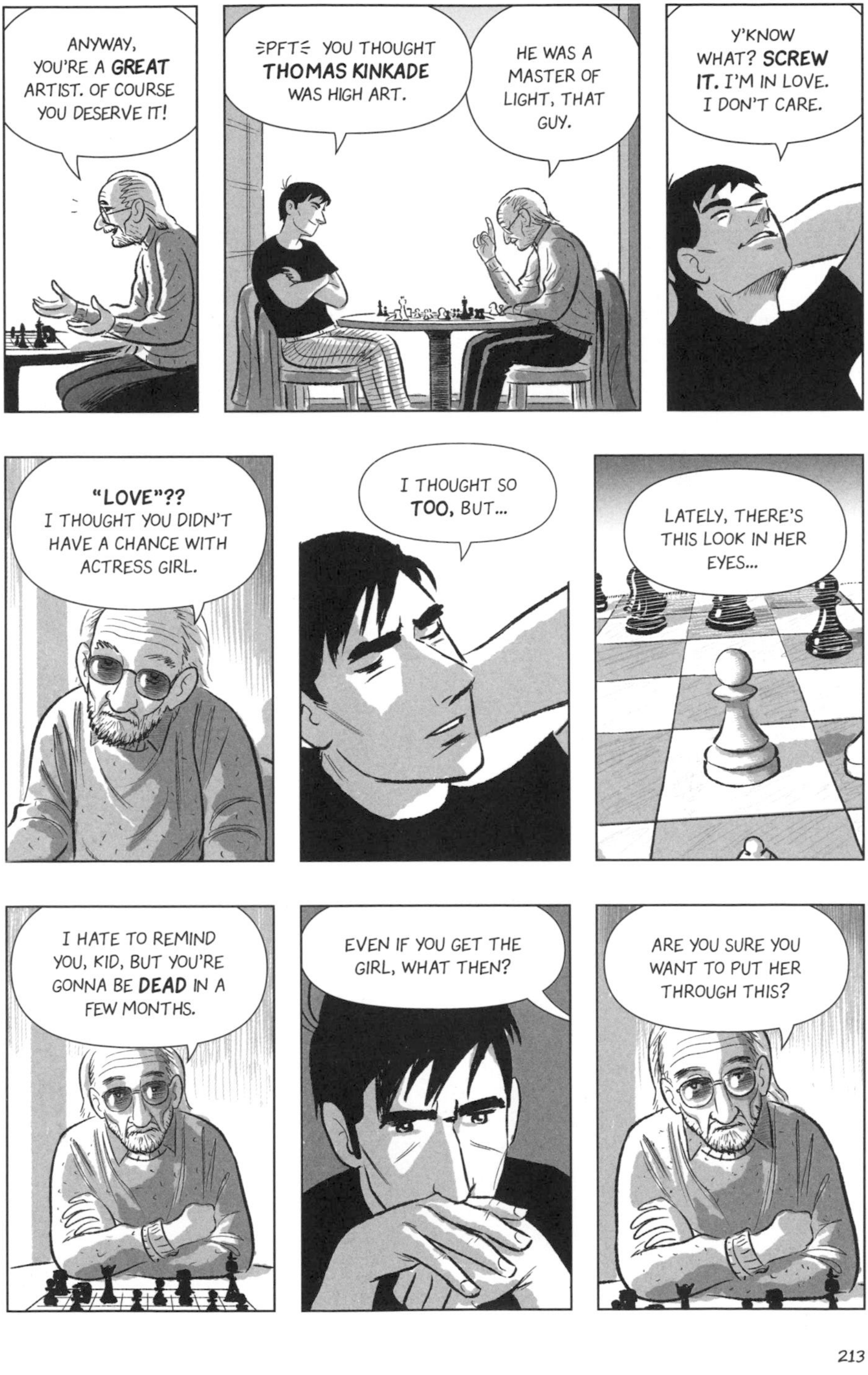
ANYWAY, YOU'RE A **GREAT** ARTIST. OF COURSE YOU DESERVE IT!
=PFT= YOU THOUGHT **THOMAS KINKADE** WAS HIGH ART.
HE WAS A MASTER OF LIGHT, THAT GUY.
Y'KNOW WHAT? **SCREW IT.** I'M IN LOVE. I DON'T CARE.
"LOVE"?? I THOUGHT YOU DIDN'T HAVE A CHANCE WITH ACTRESS GIRL.
I THOUGHT SO **TOO,** BUT...
LATELY, THERE'S THIS LOOK IN HER EYES...
I HATE TO REMIND YOU, KID, BUT YOU'RE GONNA BE **DEAD** IN A FEW MONTHS.
EVEN IF YOU GET THE GIRL, WHAT THEN?
ARE YOU SURE YOU WANT TO PUT HER THROUGH THIS?

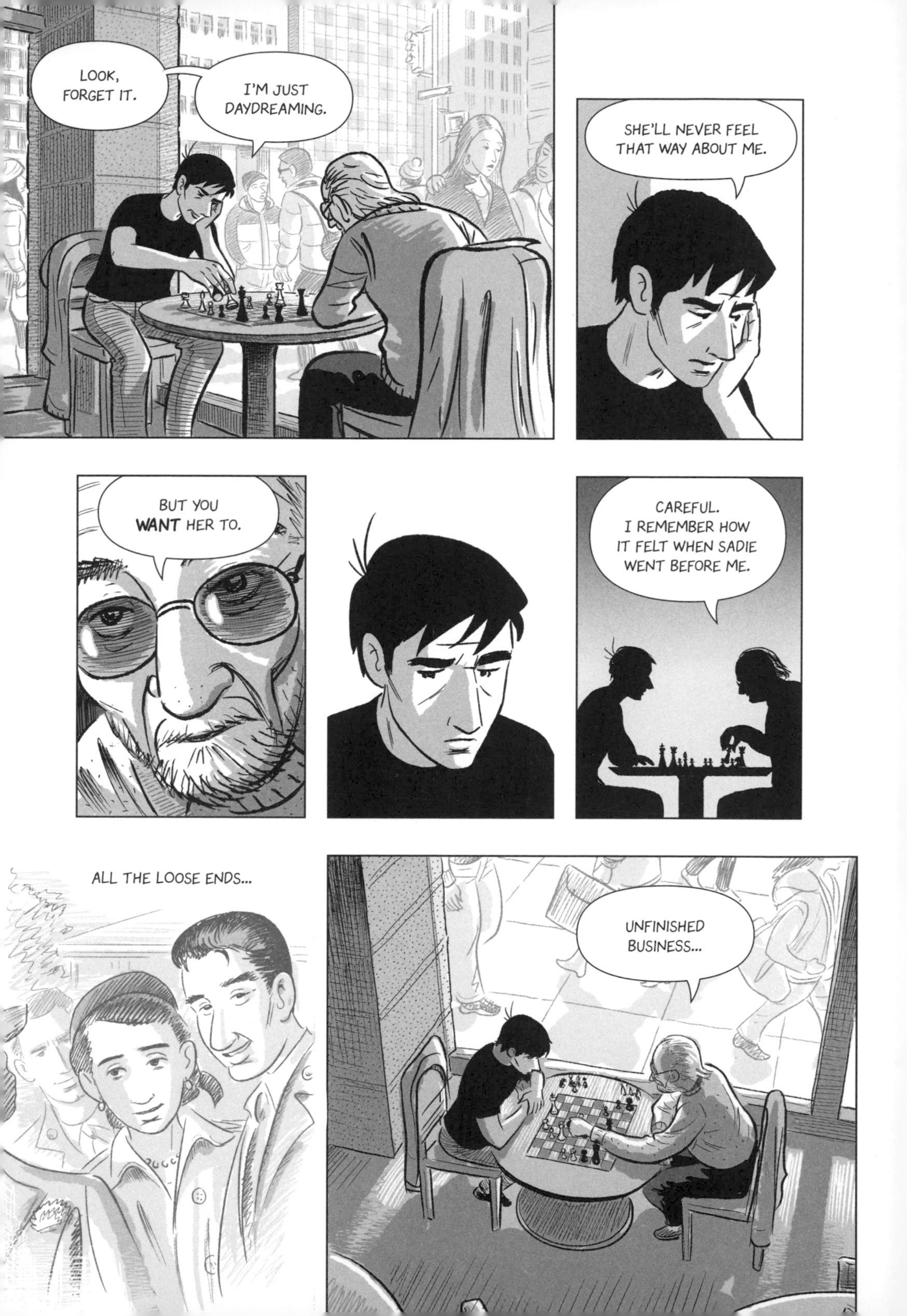
LOOK, FORGET IT.
I'M JUST DAYDREAMING.
SHE'LL NEVER FEEL THAT WAY ABOUT ME.
BUT YOU **WANT** HER TO.
CAREFUL. I REMEMBER HOW IT FELT WHEN SADIE WENT BEFORE ME.
ALL THE LOOSE ENDS...
UNFINISHED BUSINESS...

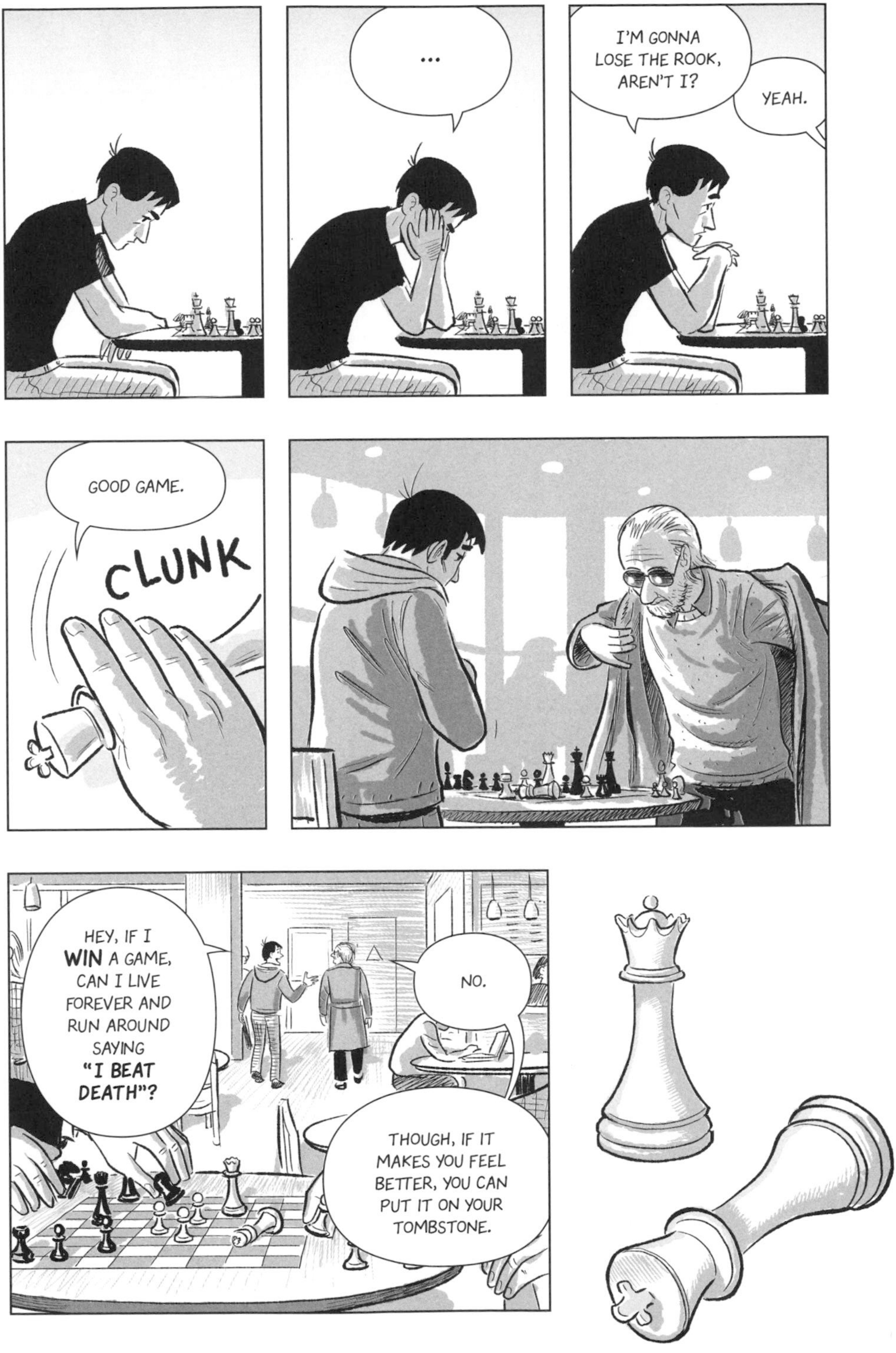
...
I'M GONNA LOSE THE ROOK, AREN'T I?
YEAH.
GOOD GAME.
CLUNK
HEY, IF I **WIN** A GAME, CAN I LIVE FOREVER AND RUN AROUND SAYING **"I BEAT DEATH"**?
NO.
THOUGH, IF IT MAKES YOU FEEL BETTER, YOU CAN PUT IT ON YOUR TOMBSTONE.

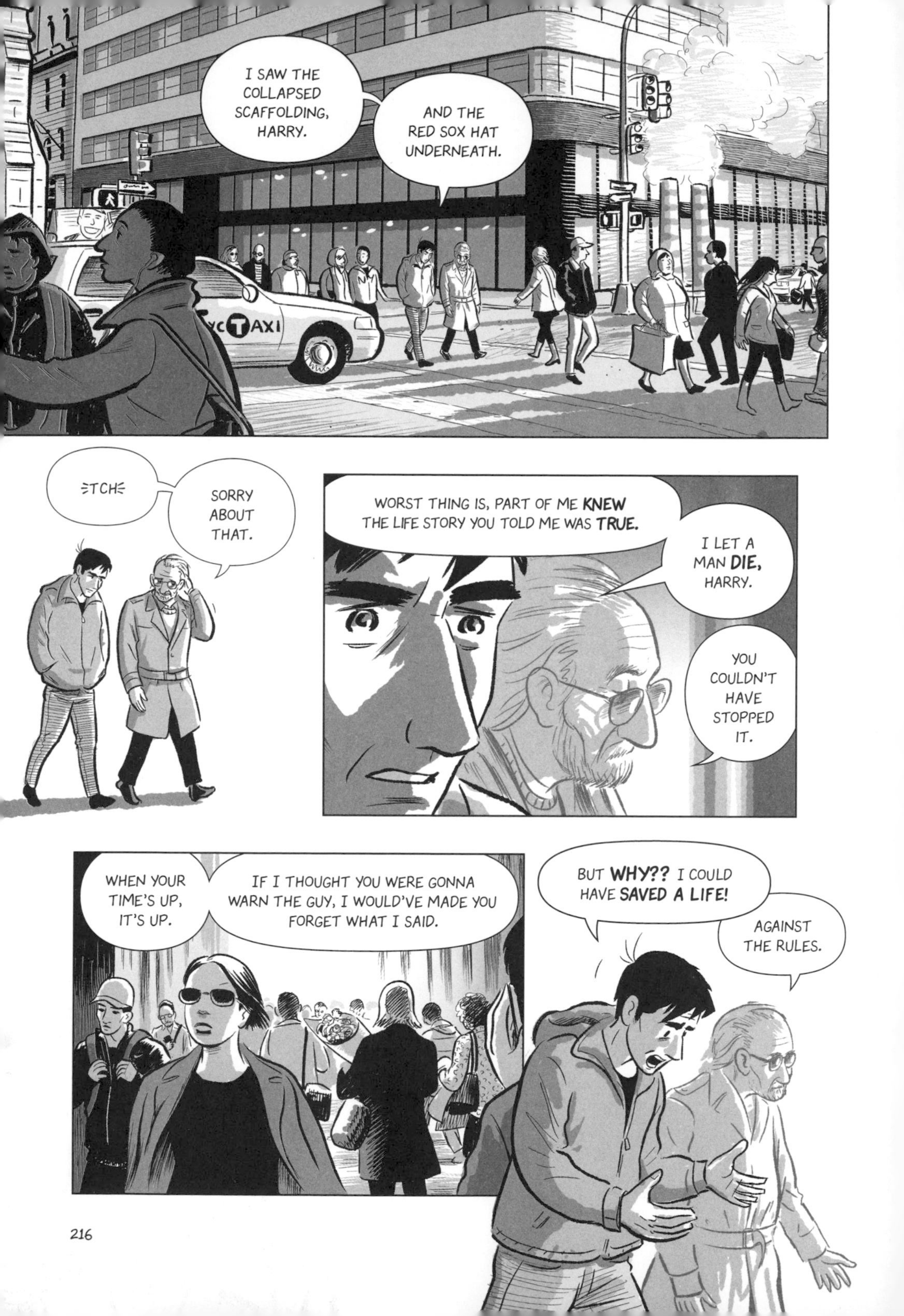
I SAW THE COLLAPSED SCAFFOLDING, HARRY.
AND THE RED SOX HAT UNDERNEATH.
NYC TAXI
TCH
SORRY ABOUT THAT.
WORST THING IS, PART OF ME **KNEW** THE LIFE STORY YOU TOLD ME WAS **TRUE.**
I LET A MAN **DIE,** HARRY.
YOU COULDN'T HAVE STOPPED IT.
WHEN YOUR TIME'S UP, IT'S UP.
IF I THOUGHT YOU WERE GONNA WARN THE GUY, I WOULD'VE MADE YOU FORGET WHAT I SAID.
BUT **WHY??** I COULD HAVE **SAVED A LIFE!**
AGAINST THE RULES.

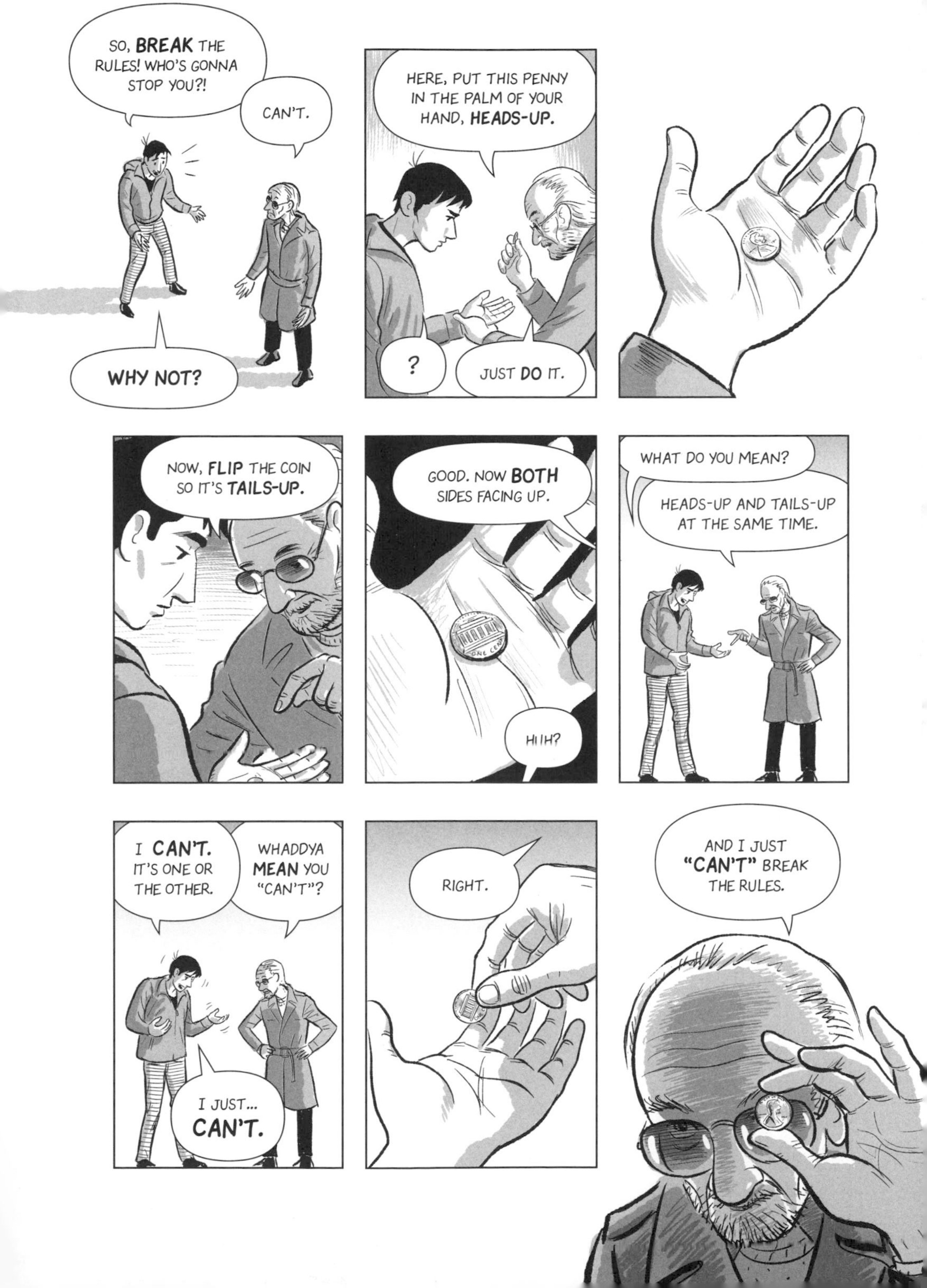
SO, BREAK THE RULES! WHO'S GONNA STOP YOU?!
CAN'T.
WHY NOT?
HERE, PUT THIS PENNY IN THE PALM OF YOUR HAND, HEADS-UP.
?
JUST DO IT.
NOW, FLIP THE COIN SO IT'S TAILS-UP.
GOOD. NOW BOTH SIDES FACING UP.
HUH?
WHAT DO YOU MEAN?
HEADS-UP AND TAILS-UP AT THE SAME TIME.
I CAN'T. IT'S ONE OR THE OTHER.
WHADDYA MEAN YOU "CAN'T"?
I JUST... CAN'T.
RIGHT.
AND I JUST "CAN'T" BREAK THE RULES.

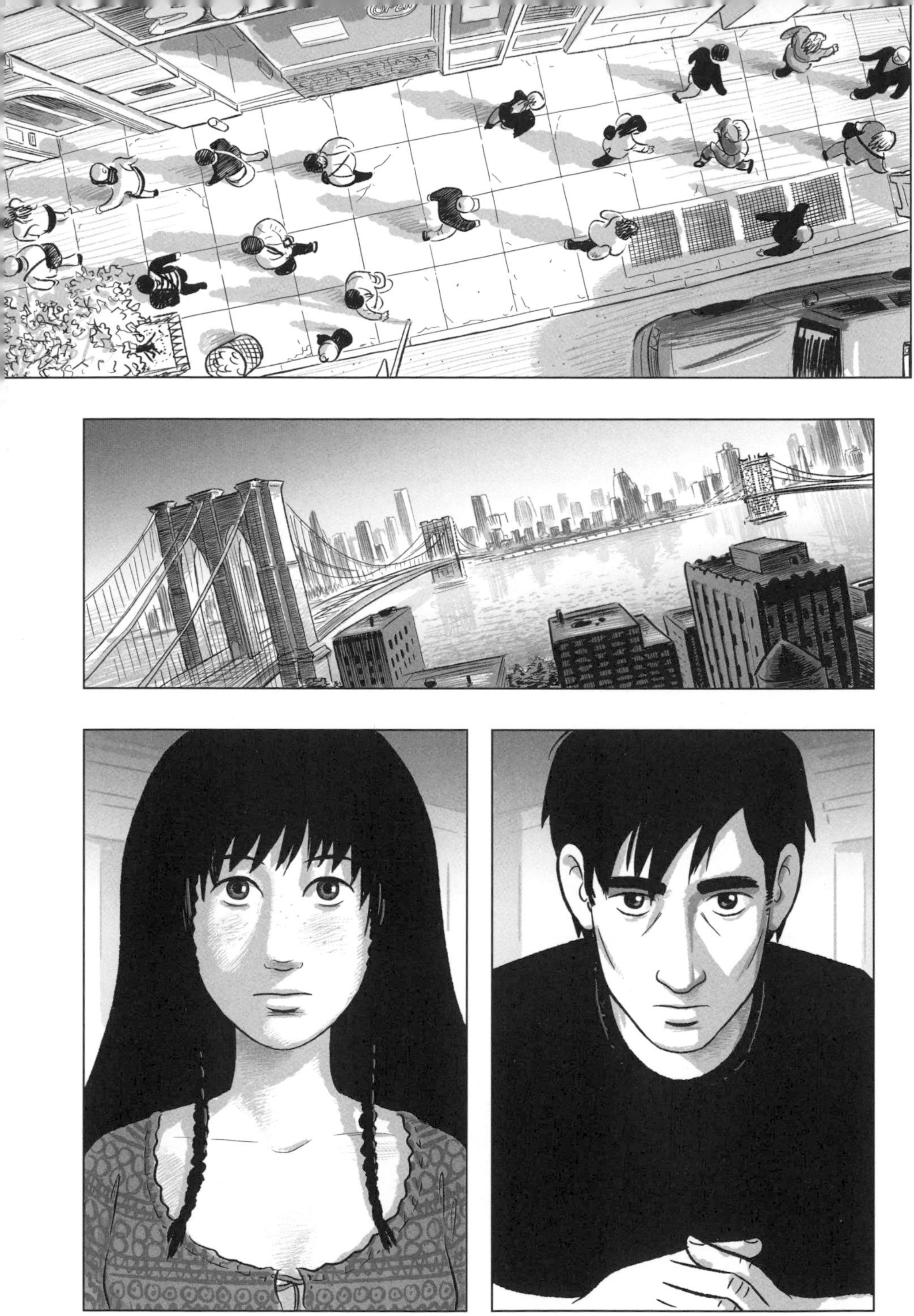

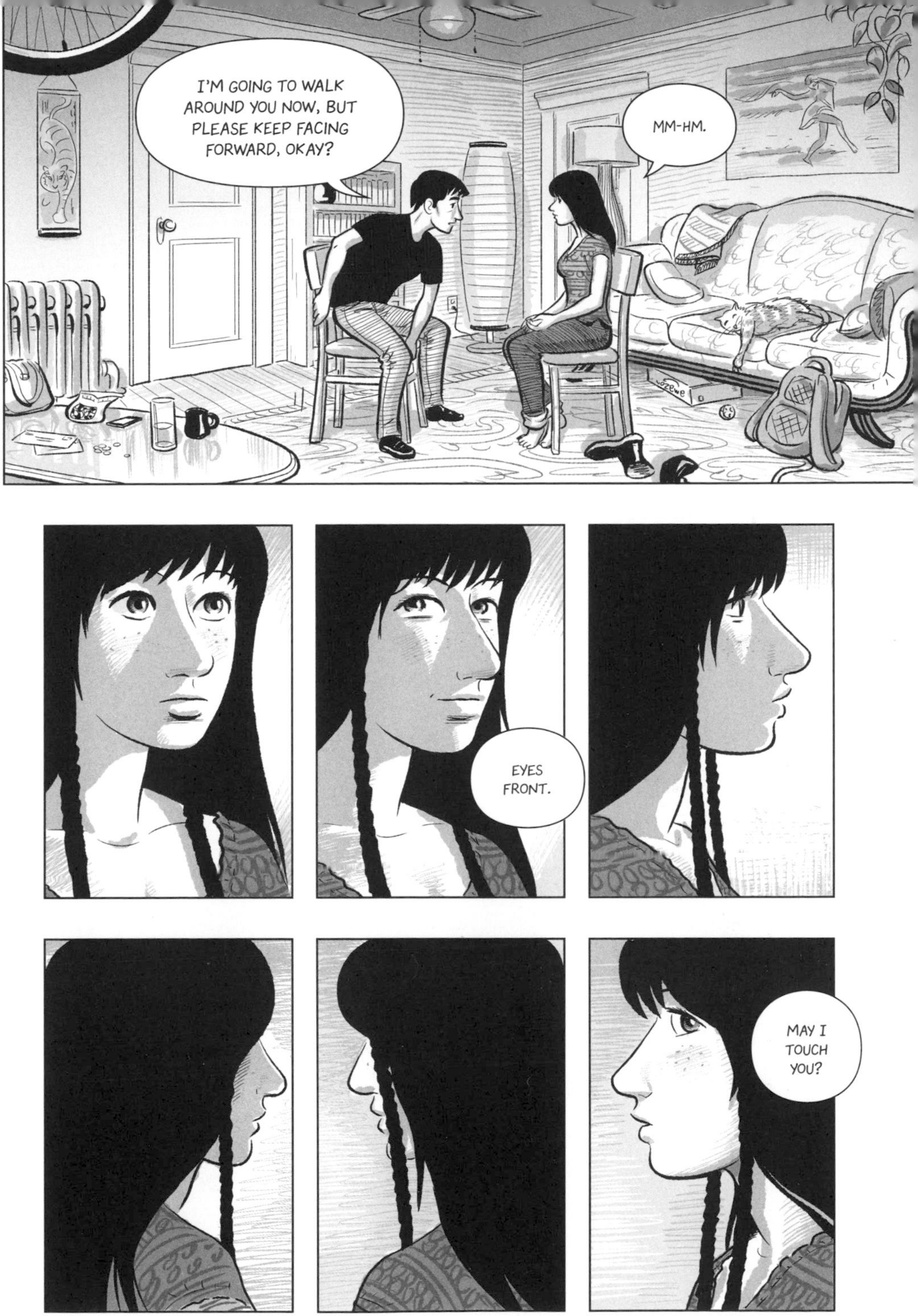
I'M GOING TO WALK AROUND YOU NOW, BUT PLEASE KEEP FACING FORWARD, OKAY?
MM-HM.
EYES FRONT.
MAY I TOUCH YOU?

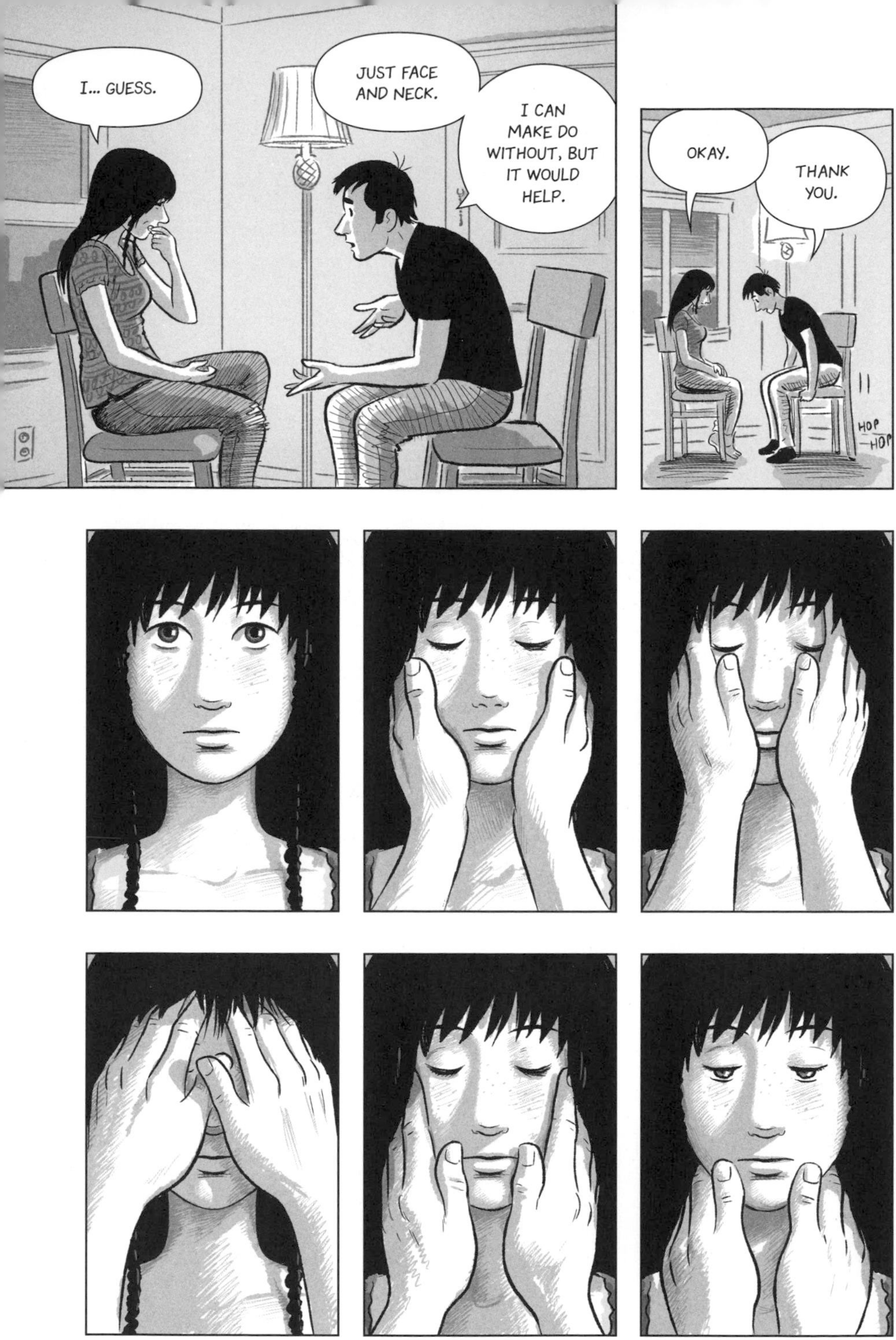
I... GUESS.
JUST FACE AND NECK.
I CAN MAKE DO WITHOUT, BUT IT WOULD HELP.
OKAY.
THANK YOU.
HOP HOP

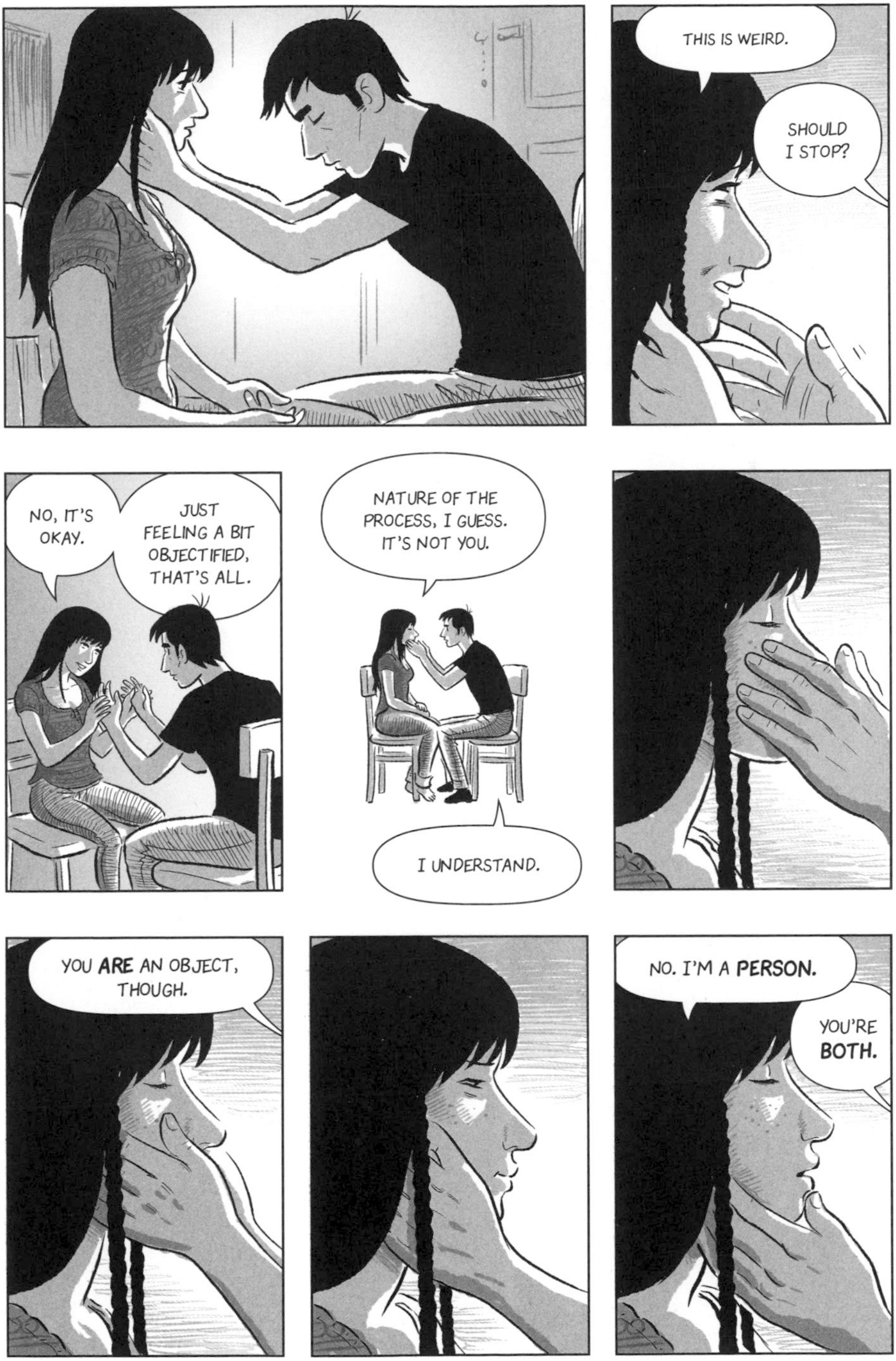

THIS IS WEIRD.
SHOULD I STOP?
NO, IT'S OKAY.
JUST FEELING A BIT OBJECTIFIED, THAT'S ALL.
NATURE OF THE PROCESS, I GUESS. IT'S NOT YOU.
I UNDERSTAND.
YOU **ARE** AN OBJECT, THOUGH.
NO. I'M A **PERSON.**
YOU'RE **BOTH.**

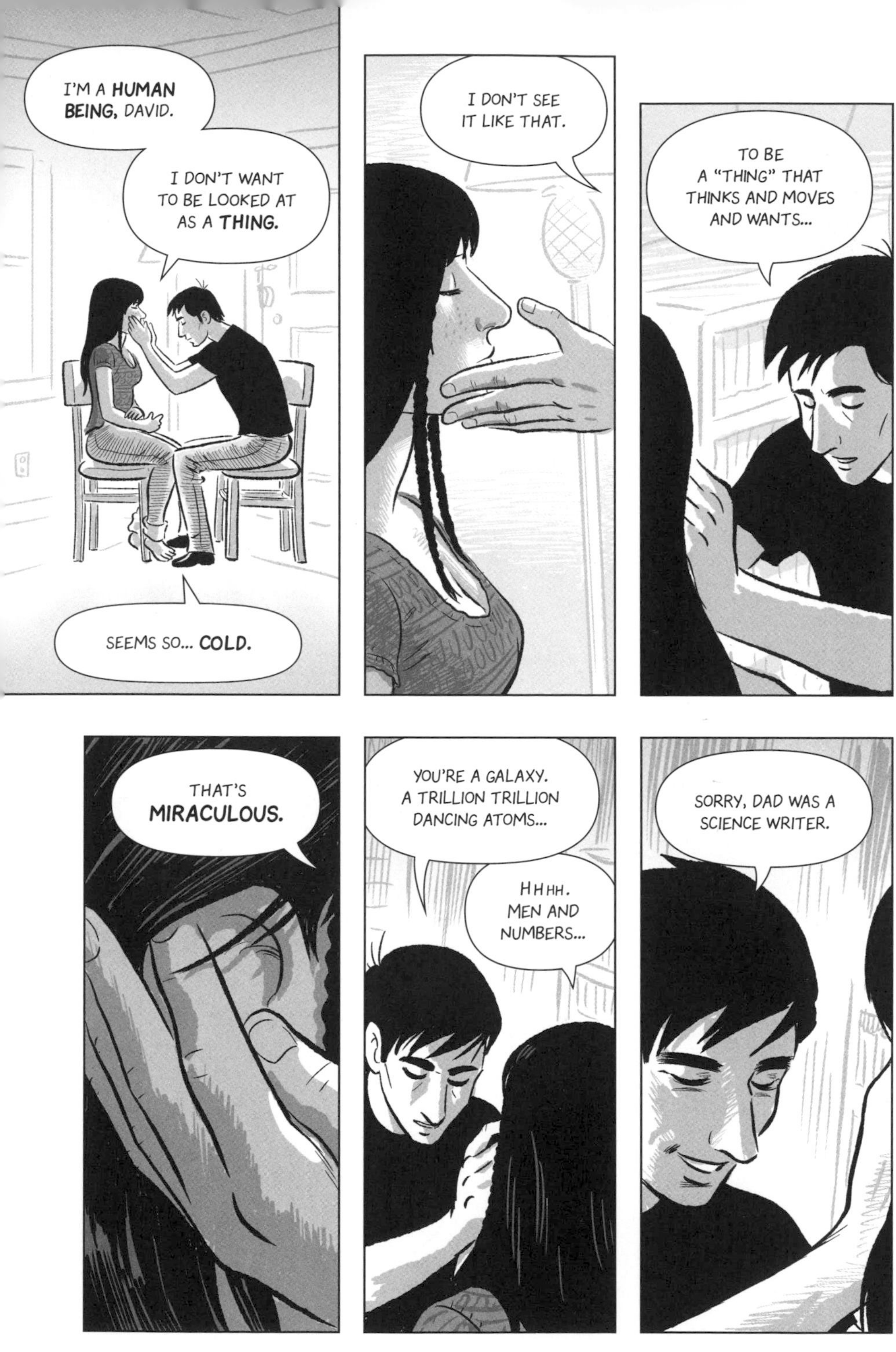
I'M A **HUMAN BEING,** DAVID.
I DON'T WANT TO BE LOOKED AT AS A **THING.**
SEEMS SO... **COLD.**
I DON'T SEE IT LIKE THAT.
TO BE A "THING" THAT THINKS AND MOVES AND WANTS...
THAT'S **MIRACULOUS.**
YOU'RE A GALAXY. A TRILLION TRILLION DANCING ATOMS...
HHHH. MEN AND NUMBERS...
SORRY, DAD WAS A SCIENCE WRITER.

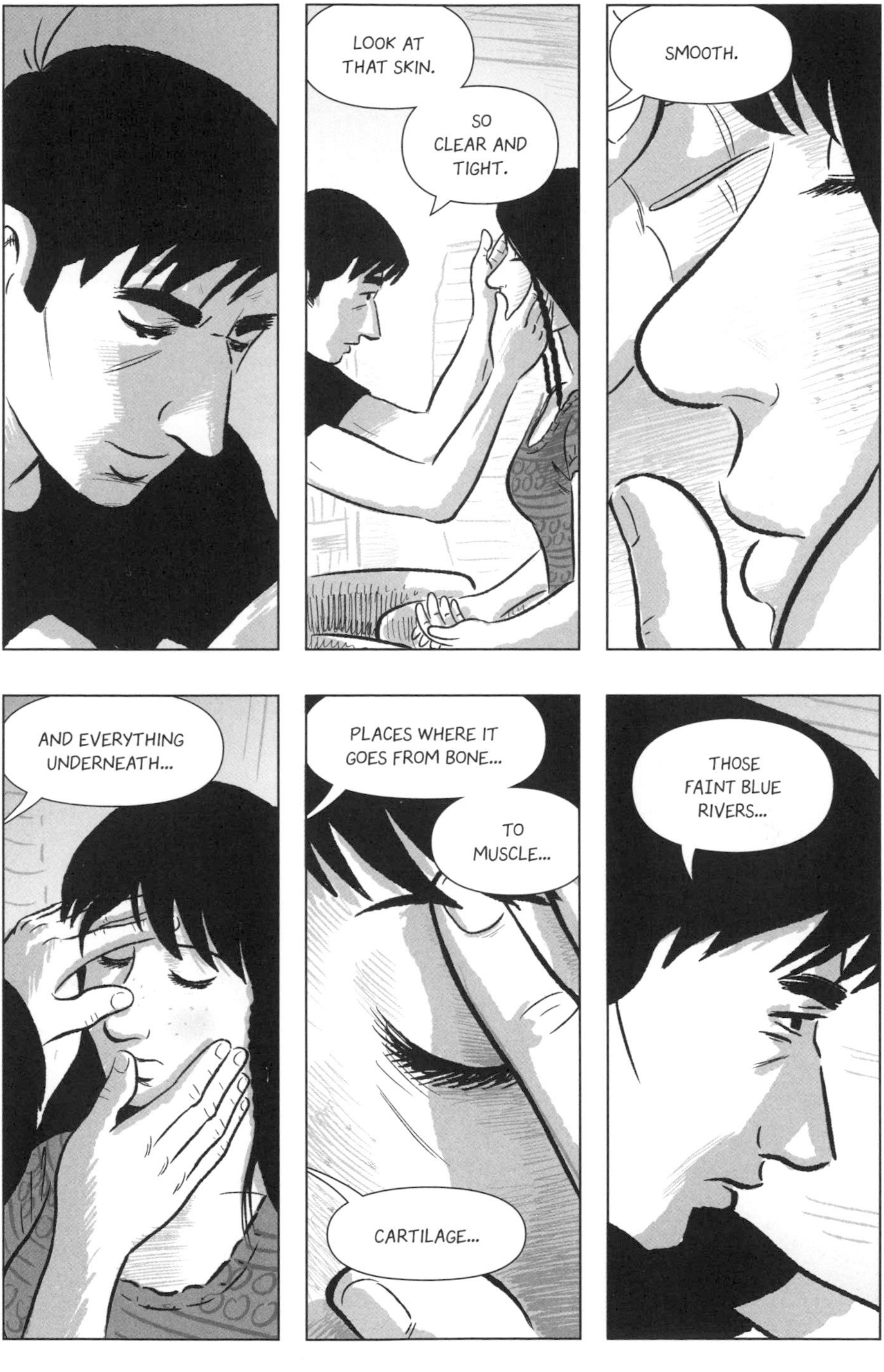
LOOK AT THAT SKIN.
SO CLEAR AND TIGHT.
SMOOTH.
AND EVERYTHING UNDERNEATH...
PLACES WHERE IT GOES FROM BONE...
TO MUSCLE...
CARTILAGE...
THOSE FAINT BLUE RIVERS...

THERE.

FEEL THAT
PRESSURE.

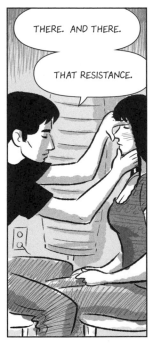

THERE. AND THERE.

THAT RESISTANCE.

SO
SOLID.

CLOSE.

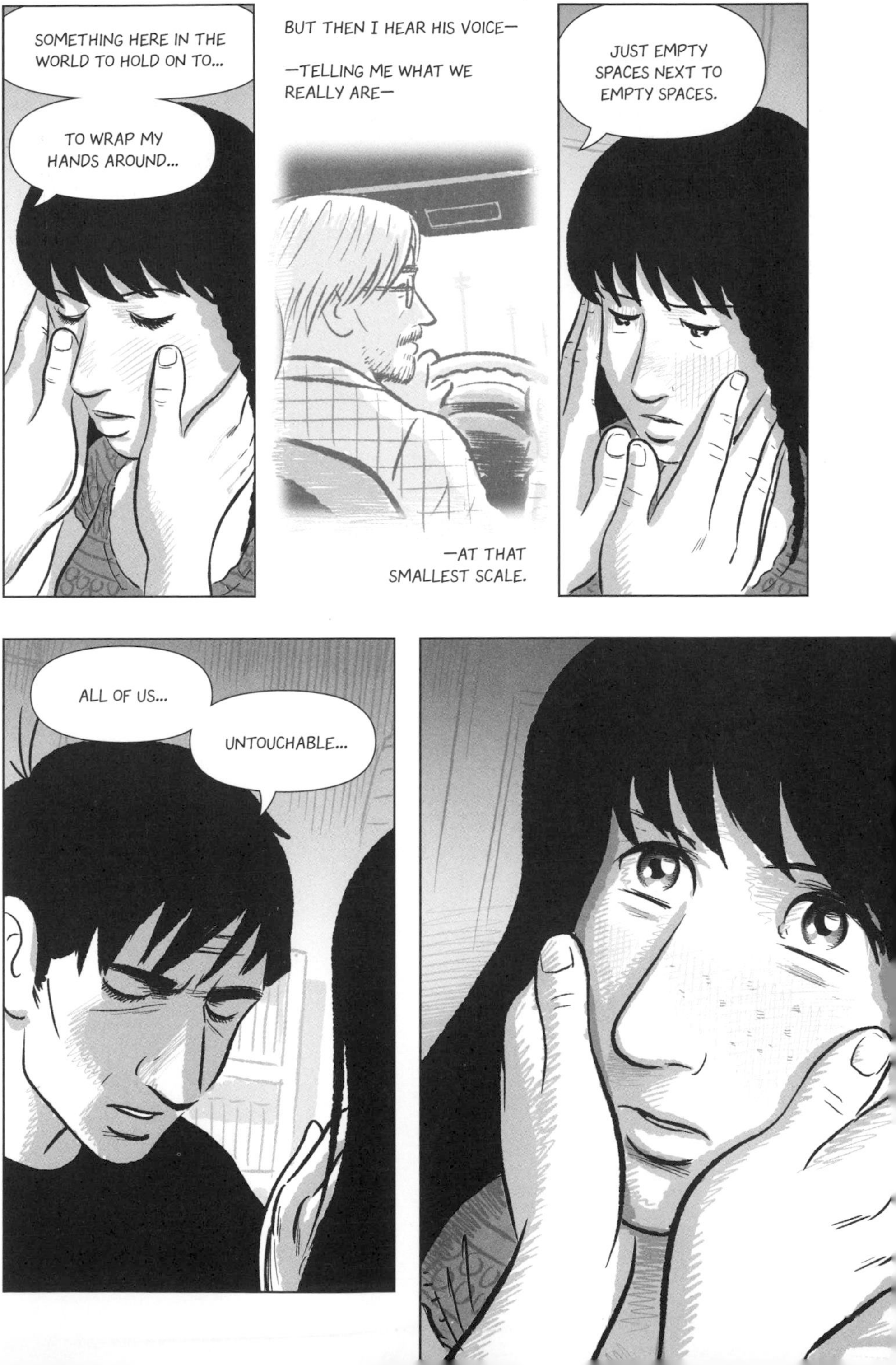
SOMETHING HERE IN THE WORLD TO HOLD ON TO...
TO WRAP MY HANDS AROUND...
BUT THEN I HEAR HIS VOICE—
—TELLING ME WHAT WE REALLY ARE—
—AT THAT SMALLEST SCALE.
JUST EMPTY SPACES NEXT TO EMPTY SPACES.
ALL OF US...
UNTOUCHABLE...

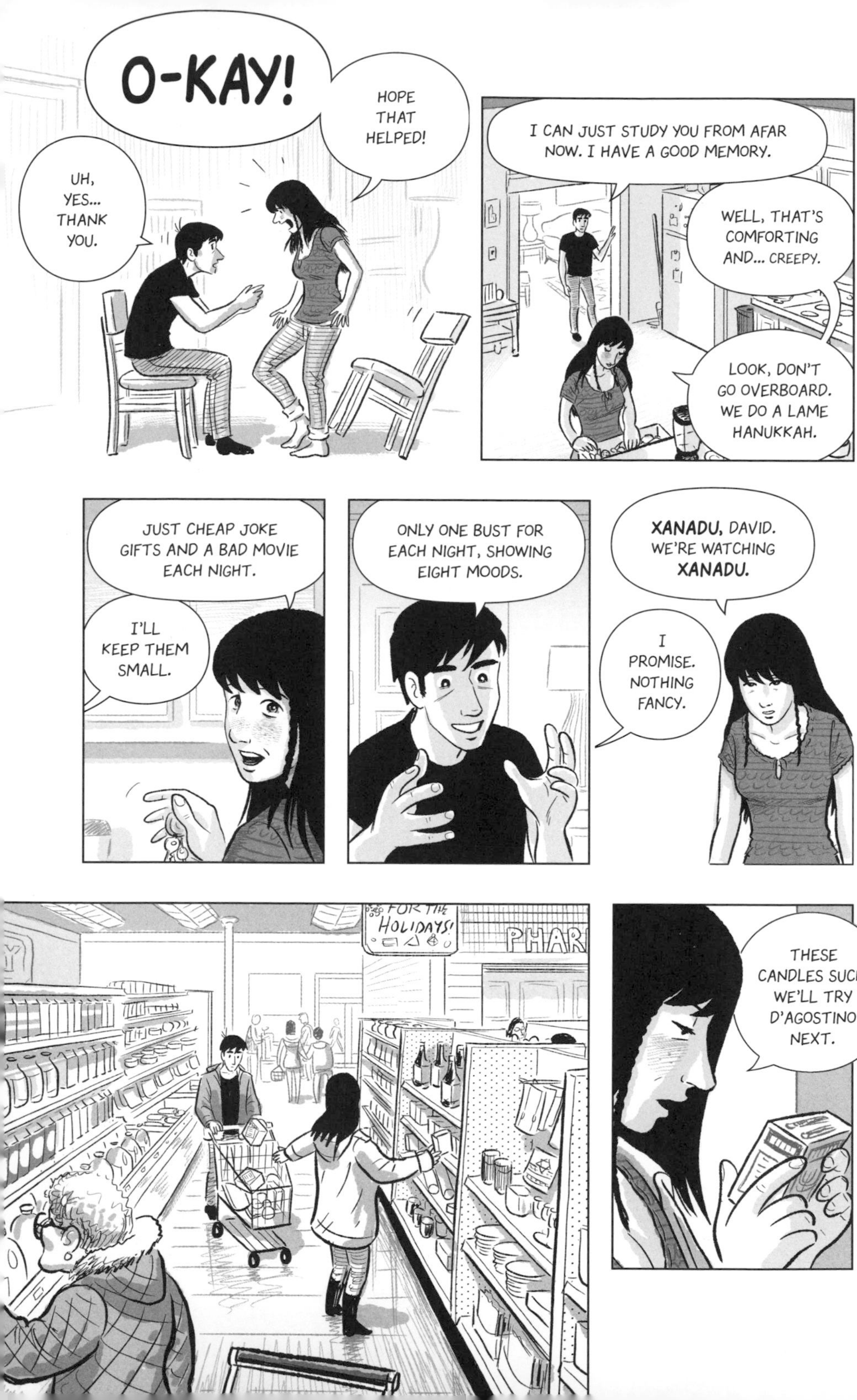
O-KAY!
HOPE THAT HELPED!
UH, YES... THANK YOU.
I CAN JUST STUDY YOU FROM AFAR NOW. I HAVE A GOOD MEMORY.
WELL, THAT'S COMFORTING AND... CREEPY.
LOOK, DON'T GO OVERBOARD. WE DO A LAME HANUKKAH.
JUST CHEAP JOKE GIFTS AND A BAD MOVIE EACH NIGHT.
I'LL KEEP THEM SMALL.
ONLY ONE BUST FOR EACH NIGHT, SHOWING EIGHT MOODS.
XANADU, DAVID. WE'RE WATCHING XANADU.
I PROMISE. NOTHING FANCY.
FOR THE HOLIDAYS!
PHAR
THESE CANDLES SUCK. WE'LL TRY D'AGOSTINO NEXT.

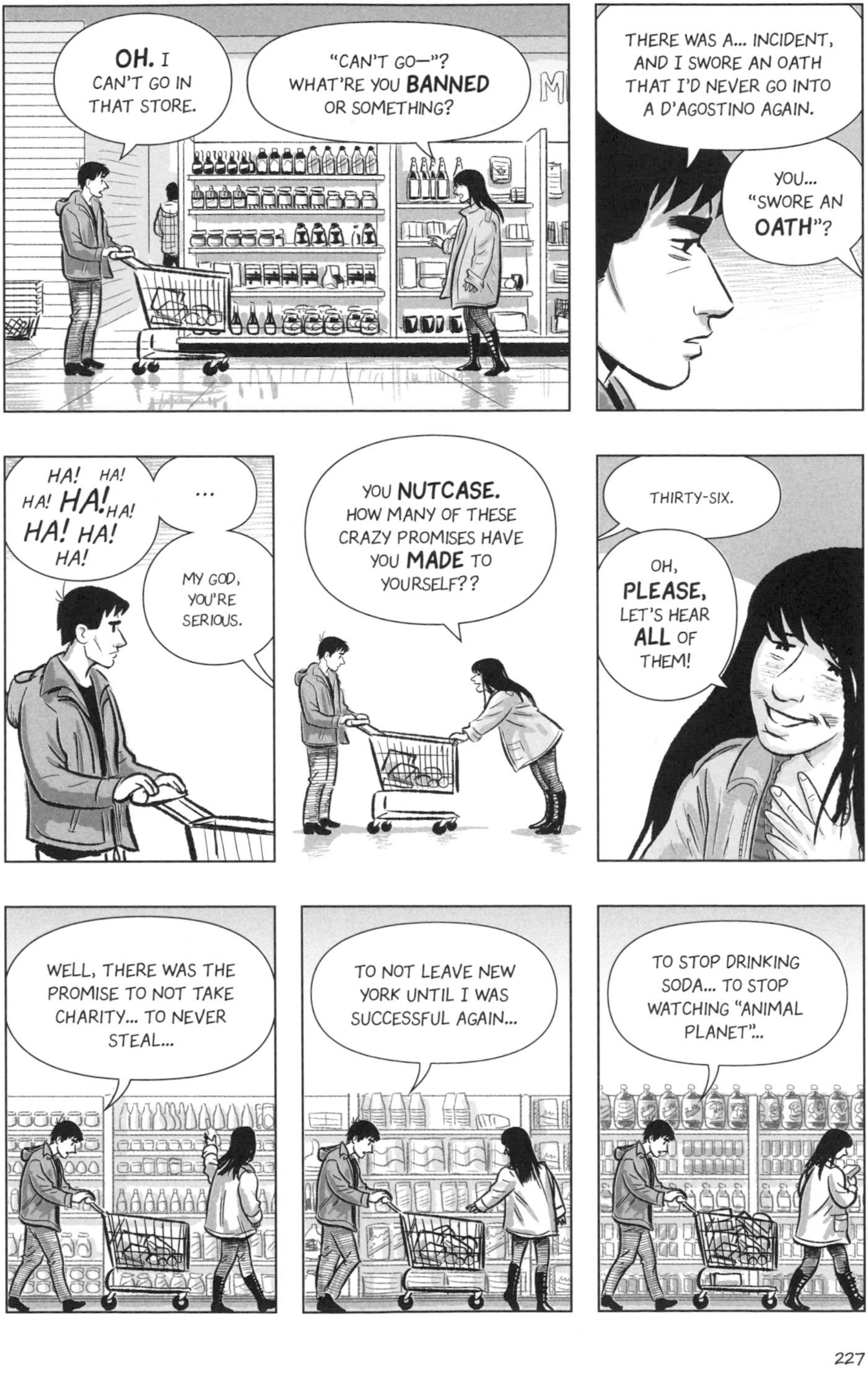
OH. I CAN'T GO IN THAT STORE.
"CAN'T GO—"? WHAT'RE YOU BANNED OR SOMETHING?
THERE WAS A... INCIDENT, AND I SWORE AN OATH THAT I'D NEVER GO INTO A D'AGOSTINO AGAIN.
YOU... "SWORE AN OATH"?
HA! HA! HA! HA! HA! HA! HA! HA!
...
MY GOD, YOU'RE SERIOUS.
YOU NUTCASE. HOW MANY OF THESE CRAZY PROMISES HAVE YOU MADE TO YOURSELF??
THIRTY-SIX.
OH, PLEASE, LET'S HEAR ALL OF THEM!
WELL, THERE WAS THE PROMISE TO NOT TAKE CHARITY... TO NEVER STEAL...
TO NOT LEAVE NEW YORK UNTIL I WAS SUCCESSFUL AGAIN...
TO STOP DRINKING SODA... TO STOP WATCHING "ANIMAL PLANET"...

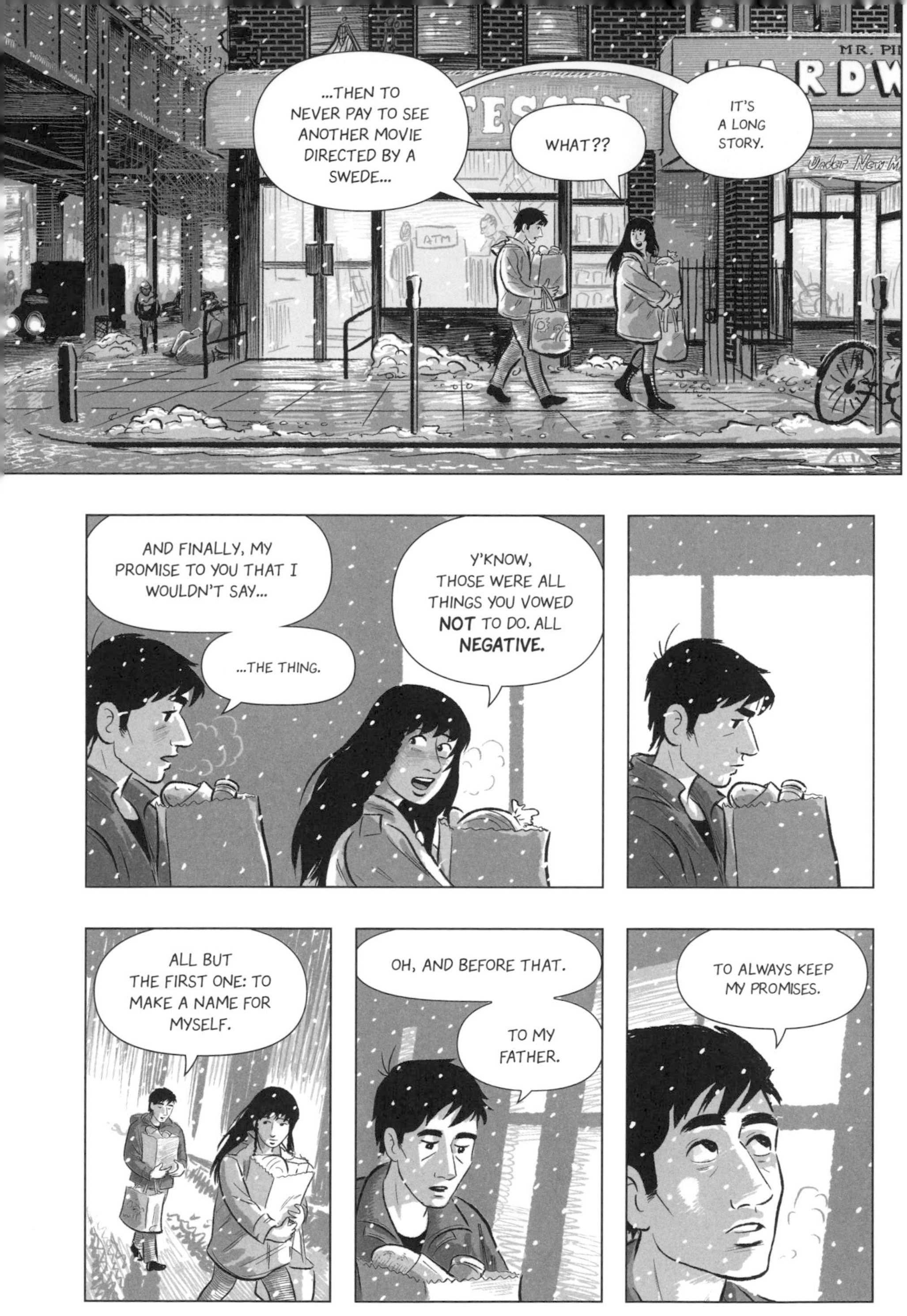
...THEN TO NEVER PAY TO SEE ANOTHER MOVIE DIRECTED BY A SWEDE...
WHAT??
IT'S A LONG STORY.
MR. PI
ARDW
ATM
AND FINALLY, MY PROMISE TO YOU THAT I WOULDN'T SAY...
...THE THING.
Y'KNOW, THOSE WERE ALL THINGS YOU VOWED **NOT** TO DO. ALL **NEGATIVE.**
ALL BUT THE FIRST ONE: TO MAKE A NAME FOR MYSELF.
OH, AND BEFORE THAT.
TO MY FATHER.
TO ALWAYS KEEP MY PROMISES.

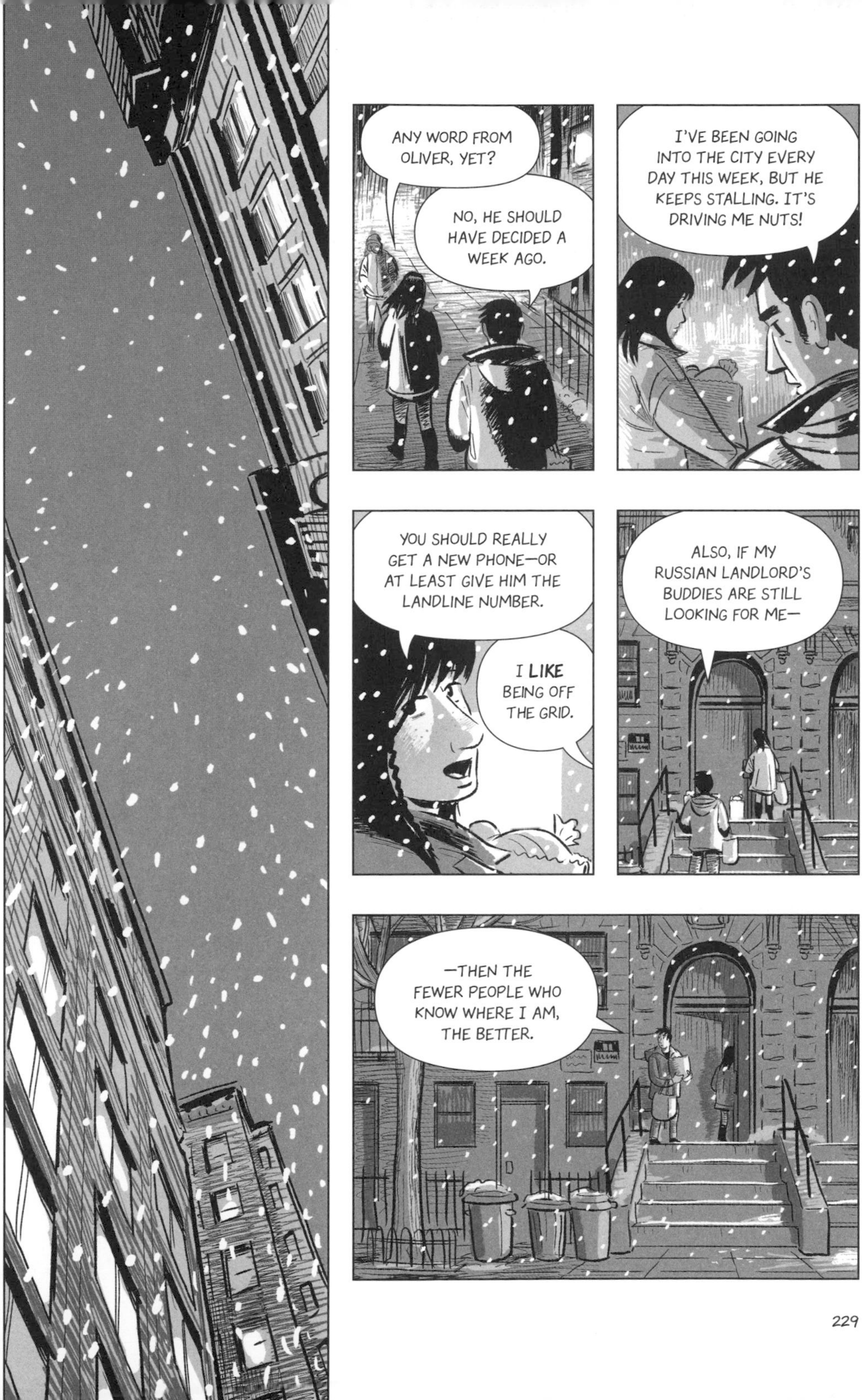
ANY WORD FROM OLIVER, YET?
NO, HE SHOULD HAVE DECIDED A WEEK AGO.
I'VE BEEN GOING INTO THE CITY EVERY DAY THIS WEEK, BUT HE KEEPS STALLING. IT'S DRIVING ME NUTS!
YOU SHOULD REALLY GET A NEW PHONE—OR AT LEAST GIVE HIM THE LANDLINE NUMBER.
I **LIKE** BEING OFF THE GRID.
ALSO, IF MY RUSSIAN LANDLORD'S BUDDIES ARE STILL LOOKING FOR ME—
—THEN THE FEWER PEOPLE WHO KNOW WHERE I AM, THE BETTER.

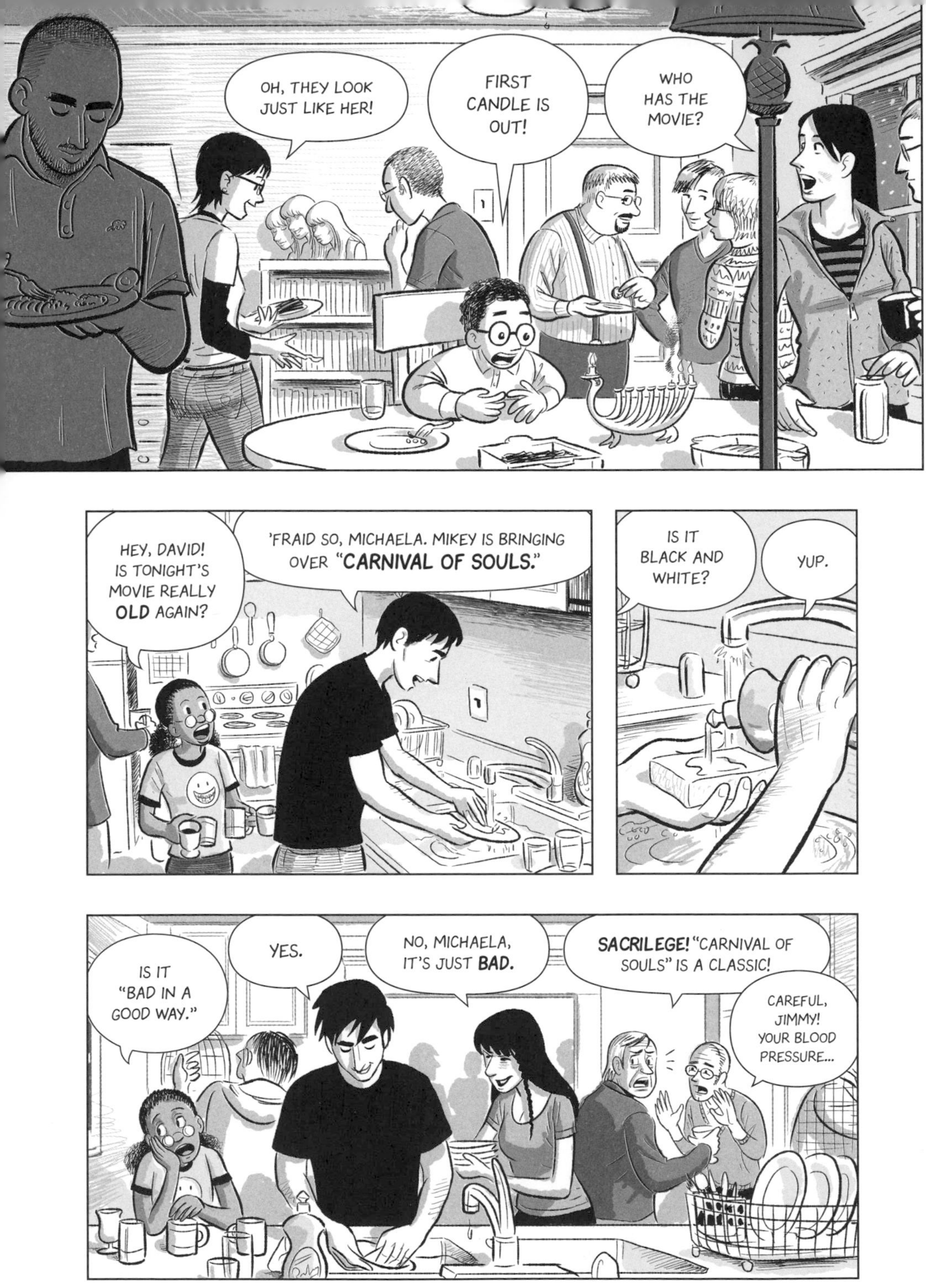
OH, THEY LOOK JUST LIKE HER!
FIRST CANDLE IS OUT!
WHO HAS THE MOVIE?
HEY, DAVID! IS TONIGHT'S MOVIE REALLY OLD AGAIN?
'FRAID SO, MICHAELA. MIKEY IS BRINGING OVER "CARNIVAL OF SOULS."
IS IT BLACK AND WHITE?
YUP.
IS IT "BAD IN A GOOD WAY."
YES.
NO, MICHAELA, IT'S JUST BAD.
SACRILEGE! "CARNIVAL OF SOULS" IS A CLASSIC!
CAREFUL, JIMMY! YOUR BLOOD PRESSURE...

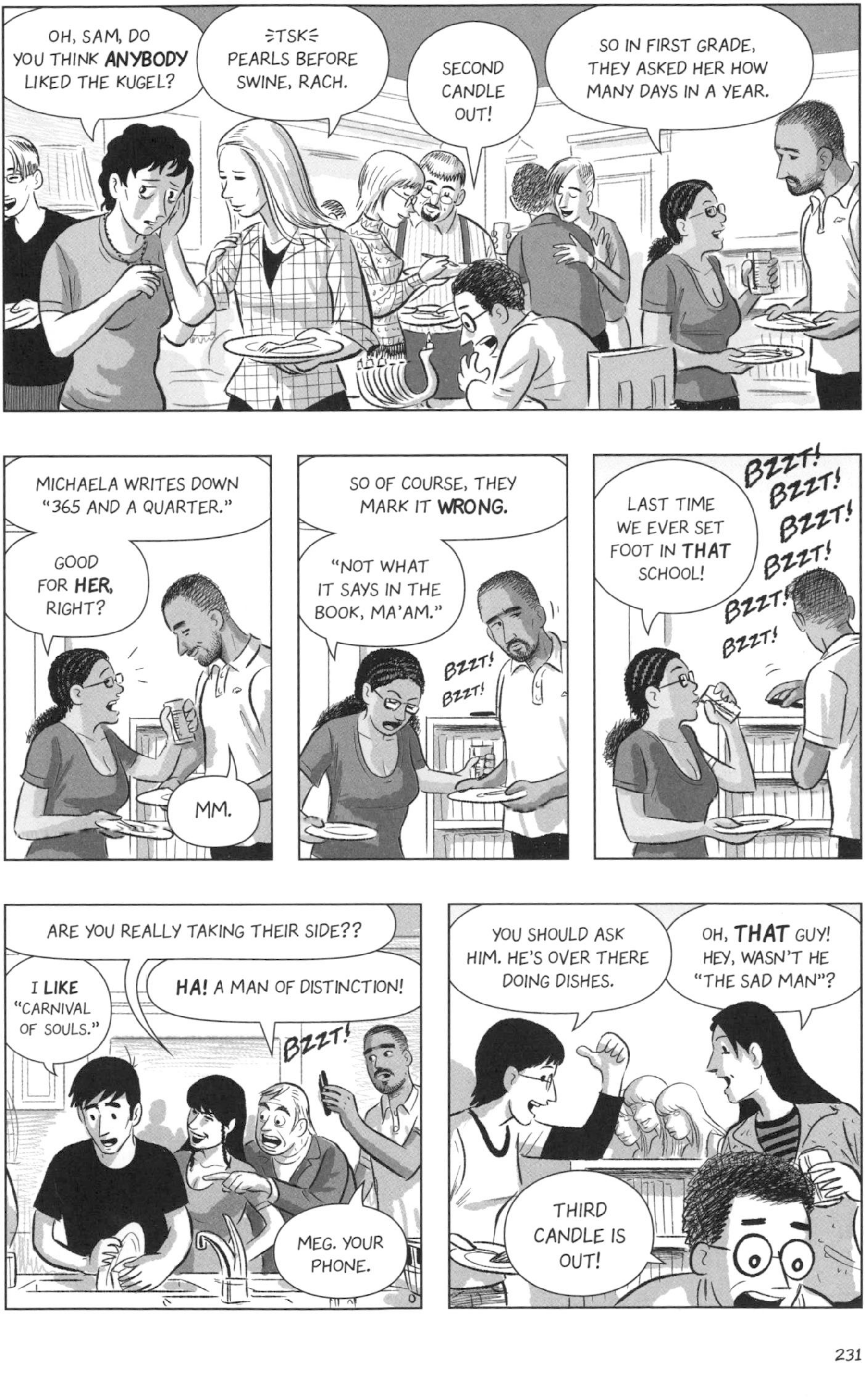

OH, SAM, DO YOU THINK **ANYBODY** LIKED THE KUGEL?
TSK
PEARLS BEFORE SWINE, RACH.
SECOND CANDLE OUT!
SO IN FIRST GRADE, THEY ASKED HER HOW MANY DAYS IN A YEAR.
MICHAELA WRITES DOWN "365 AND A QUARTER."
GOOD FOR **HER,** RIGHT?
MM.
SO OF COURSE, THEY MARK IT **WRONG.**
"NOT WHAT IT SAYS IN THE BOOK, MA'AM."
BZZT! BZZT!
LAST TIME WE EVER SET FOOT IN **THAT** SCHOOL!
BZZT! BZZT! BZZT! BZZT! BZZT! BZZT!
ARE YOU REALLY TAKING THEIR SIDE??
I **LIKE** "CARNIVAL OF SOULS."
HA! A MAN OF DISTINCTION!
BZZT!
MEG. YOUR PHONE.
YOU SHOULD ASK HIM. HE'S OVER THERE DOING DISHES.
OH, **THAT** GUY! HEY, WASN'T HE "THE SAD MAN"?
THIRD CANDLE IS OUT!

WELL, SURE. MAYBE AFTER TONIGHT WE... WAIT, WHAT DO YOU MEAN?

HEY, DAVID, THIS IS KATIE FROM DOWNSTAIRS.

I **LOVE** THE **BUSTS!** I'VE SEEN MEG **MAKE** THOSE FACES.

OH, UH... THANK YOU.

YOU REALLY DOING **EIGHT?**

I HOPE TO, YEAH.

THAT'S SO SWEET!

DID YOU PLAN THEM OUT? IS THERE A DAY FOR **ANGRY?**

Y'KNOW, I'VE BARELY **SEEN** MEG ANGRY.

WHAT?? MIKEY, ARE YOU SERIOUS?? THAT'S **TOO LATE!!**

OKAY, THAT WAS FREAKY.

NO! I TOLD YOU! EVERYBODY IS **HERE** ALREADY!

WANNA TAKE NOTES?

THIS IS THE **THIRD NIGHT** IN A **ROW,** MIKEY! YOU SAID I COULD **COUNT** ON YOU THIS TIME!

NO, I'M SORRY, MIKEY. THAT'S NOT ENOUGH. NO. **NO!** YOU WANT TO MAKE IT UP? REALLY?! THEN **STOP** ACTING LIKE JUST ANOTHER JERK—

—WHO **NEVER KEEPS HIS PROMISES!**

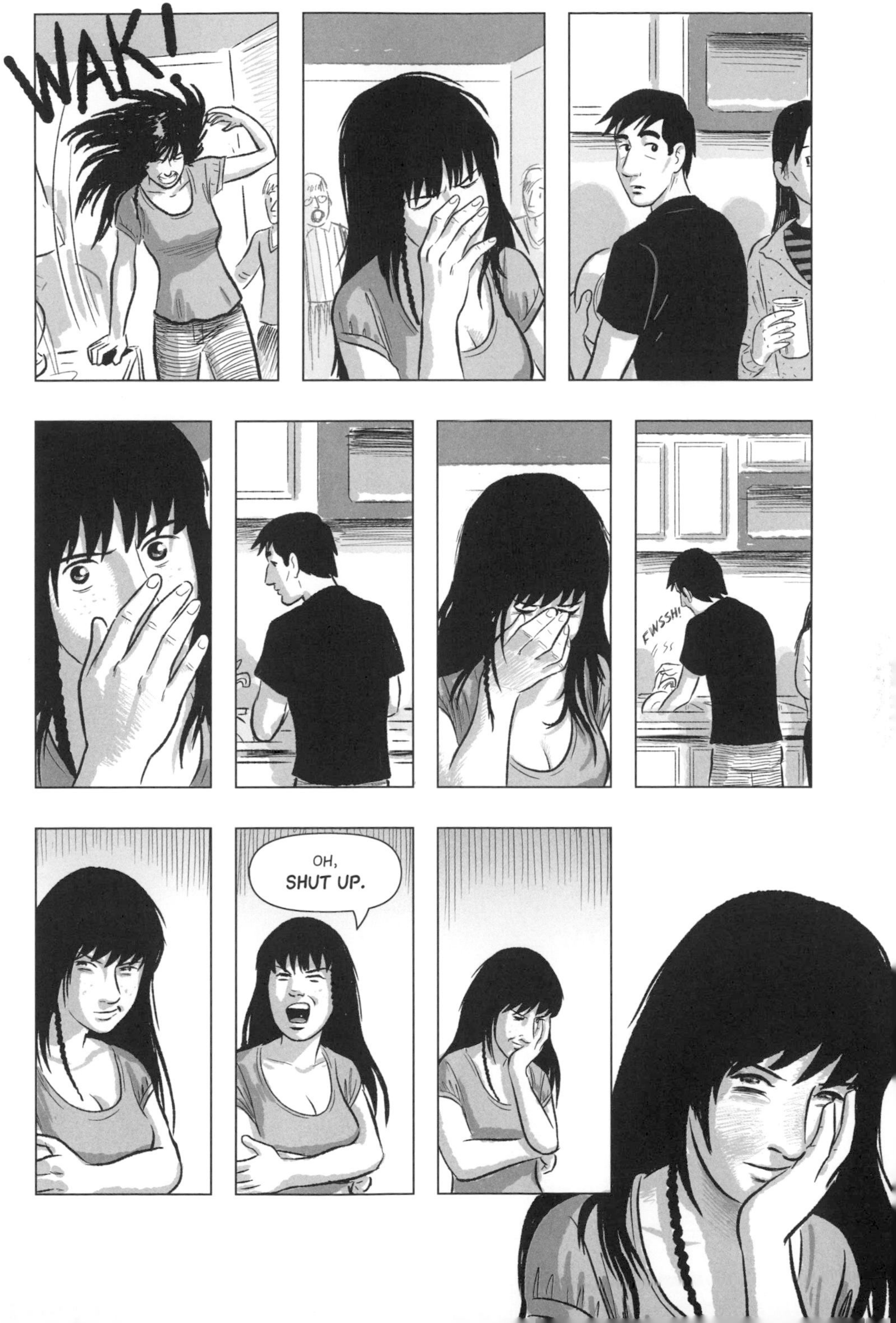
WAK!
FWSSH!
OH,
SHUT UP.

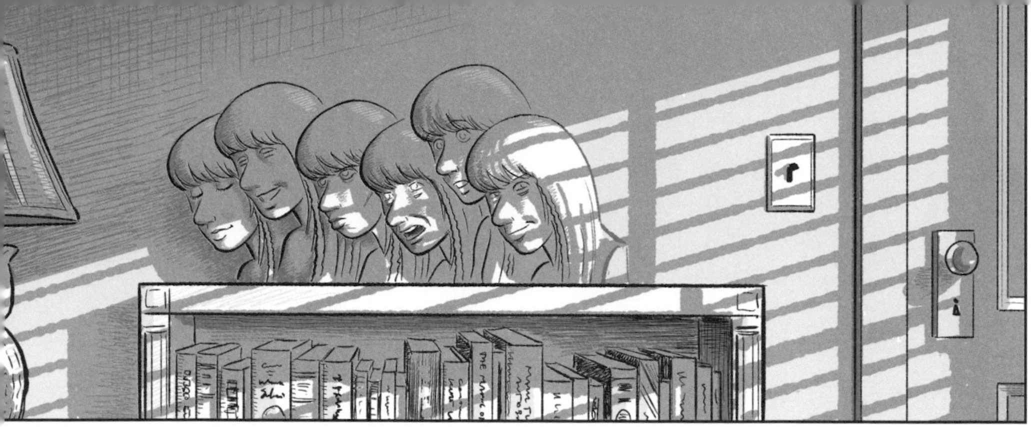

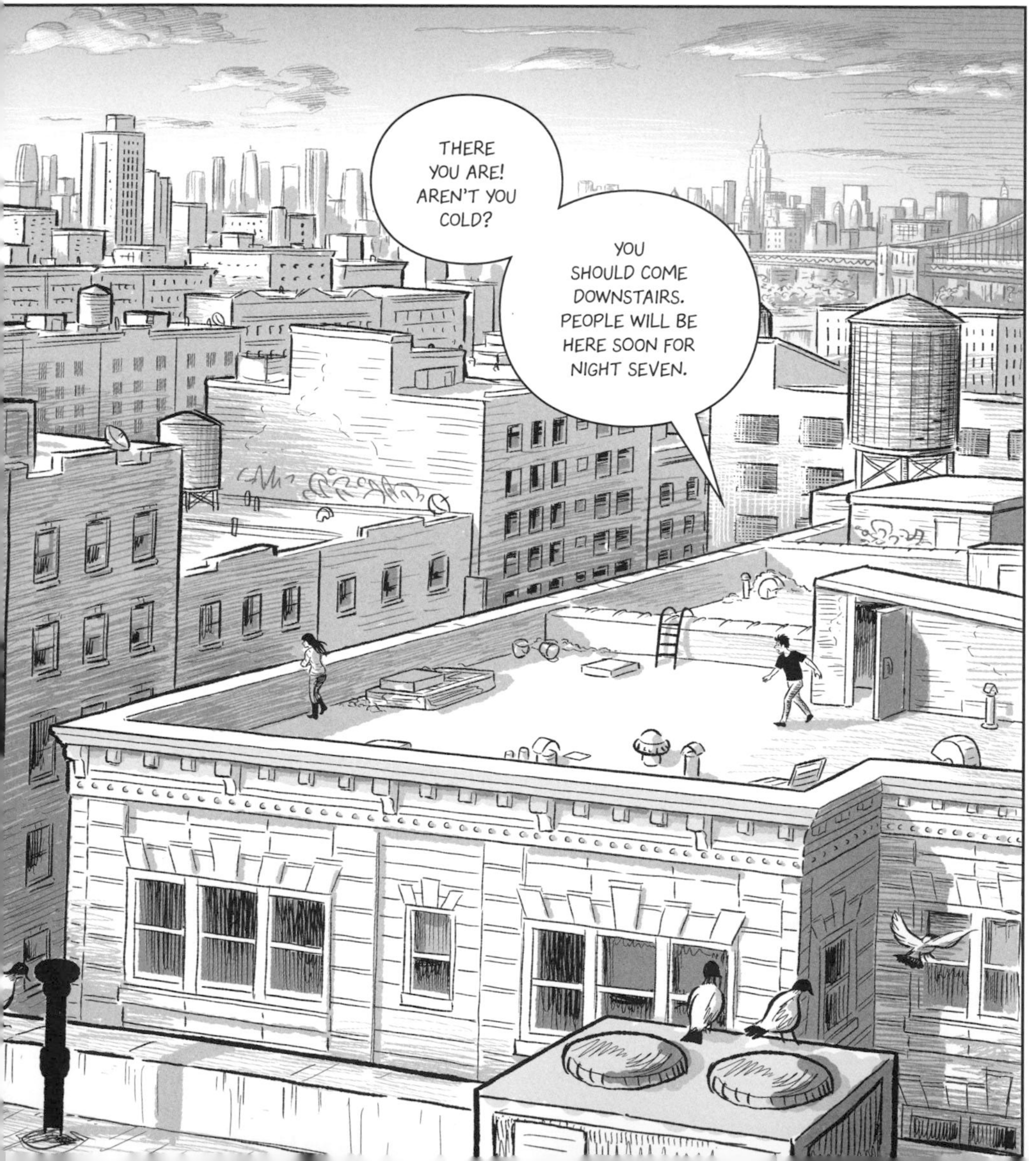
THERE YOU ARE! AREN'T YOU COLD?
YOU SHOULD COME DOWNSTAIRS. PEOPLE WILL BE HERE SOON FOR NIGHT SEVEN.

IS IT TRUE THAT TO SCULPT A PERSON OUT OF A STONE BLOCK—

—YOU JUST CHIP AWAY EVERYTHING THAT ISN'T THEM?

ARE YOU READING THIS?

MAYBE.

YOU KNOW THIS BOOK IS FOR TEN-YEAR-OLDS, RIGHT?

MICHAELA LEFT IT LAST NIGHT. SHE SUGGESTED I "READ UP" ON YOU.

SERIOUSLY, THOUGH, IS THAT A FAIR SUMMARY OF WHAT YOU GUYS DO?

IT'S... ONE WAY TO LOOK AT ONE **KIND** OF SCULPTURE, BUT THE WORD CAN MEAN ALMOST **ANYTHING** THESE DAYS.

CLOTH, HAIR, FOUND OBJECTS... AND THERE ARE LOTS OF TRADITIONAL METHODS...

LIKE **GIACOMETTI** HERE.

HE STARTED WITH WIRE-FRAMES, THEN ADDED BITS OF WET PLASTER AND CAST THE RESULTS IN BRONZE.

Al... Giaco...

Sculptures come in all shapes and sizes just like people do. Some are fat, some are skinny, som... some are short...

SO, HE WAS **ADDING** INSTEAD OF TAKING AWAY?

YOU COULD SAY THAT.

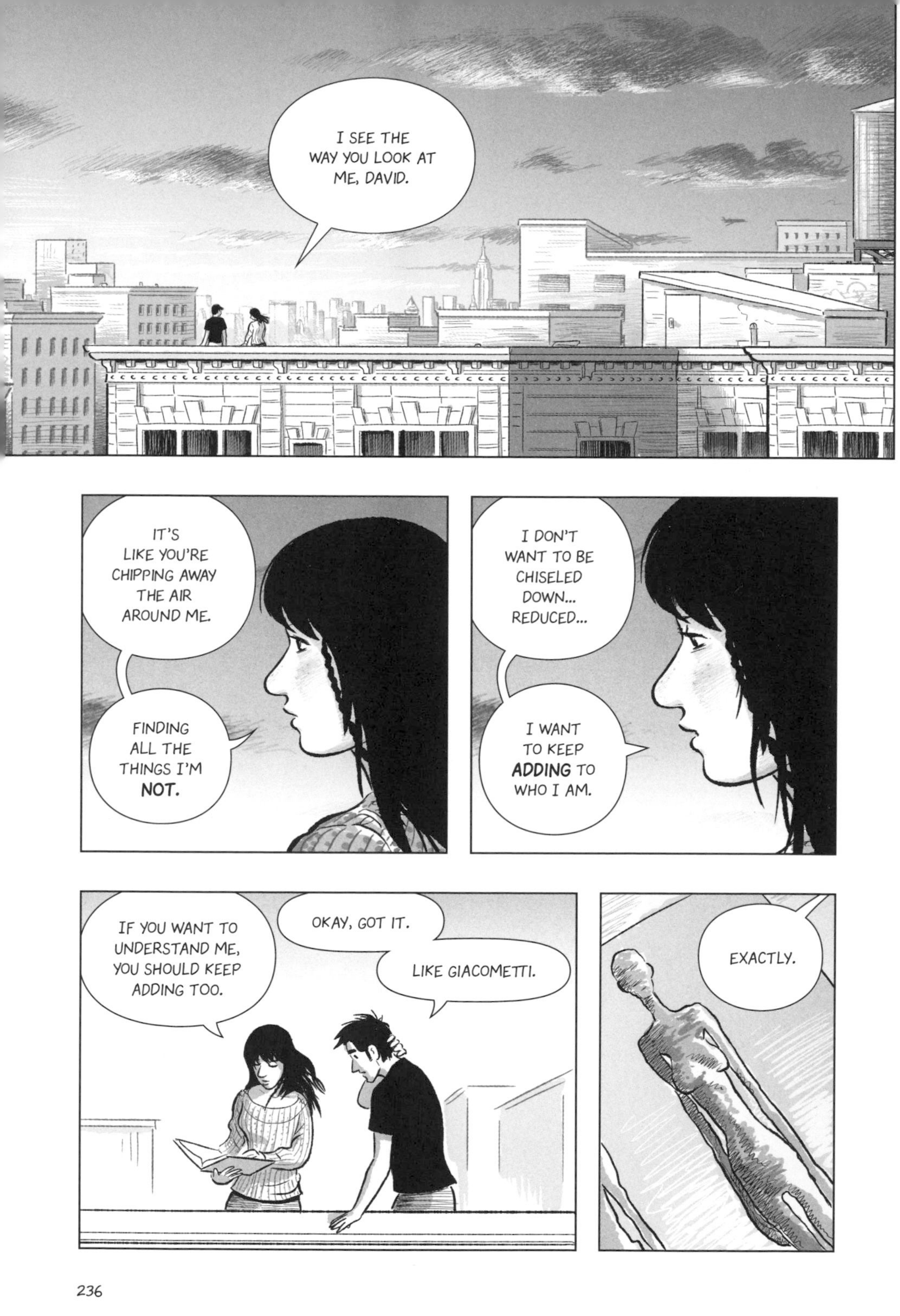
I SEE THE WAY YOU LOOK AT ME, DAVID.
IT'S LIKE YOU'RE CHIPPING AWAY THE AIR AROUND ME.
FINDING ALL THE THINGS I'M **NOT.**
I DON'T WANT TO BE CHISELED DOWN... REDUCED...
I WANT TO KEEP **ADDING** TO WHO I AM.
IF YOU WANT TO UNDERSTAND ME, YOU SHOULD KEEP ADDING TOO.
OKAY, GOT IT.
LIKE GIACOMETTI.
EXACTLY.

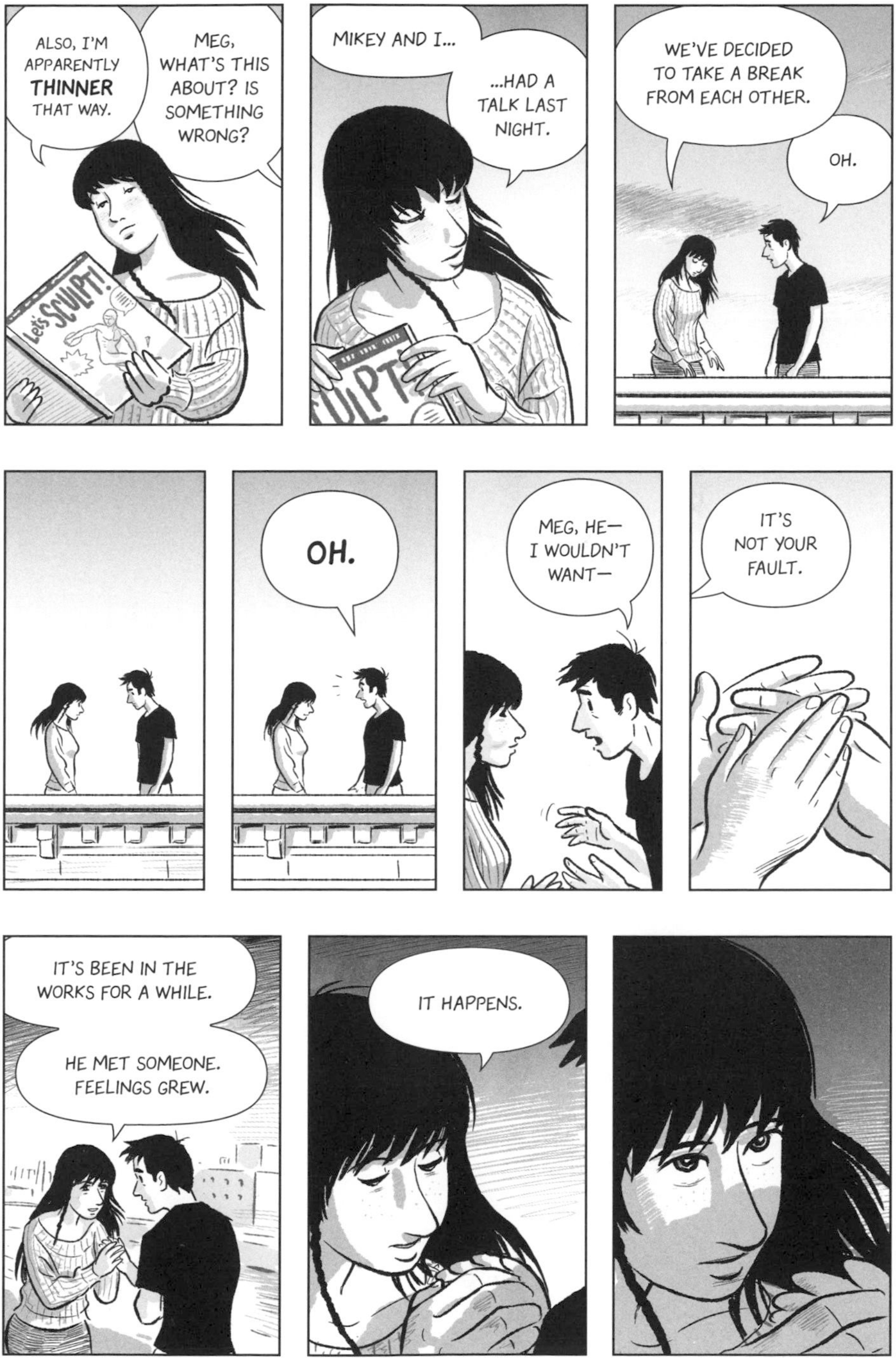
ALSO, I'M APPARENTLY **THINNER** THAT WAY.
MEG, WHAT'S THIS ABOUT? IS SOMETHING WRONG?
Let's SCULPT!
MIKEY AND I...
...HAD A TALK LAST NIGHT.
WE'VE DECIDED TO TAKE A BREAK FROM EACH OTHER.
OH.
OH.
MEG, HE— I WOULDN'T WANT—
IT'S NOT YOUR FAULT.
IT'S BEEN IN THE WORKS FOR A WHILE.
HE MET SOMEONE. FEELINGS GREW.
IT HAPPENS.

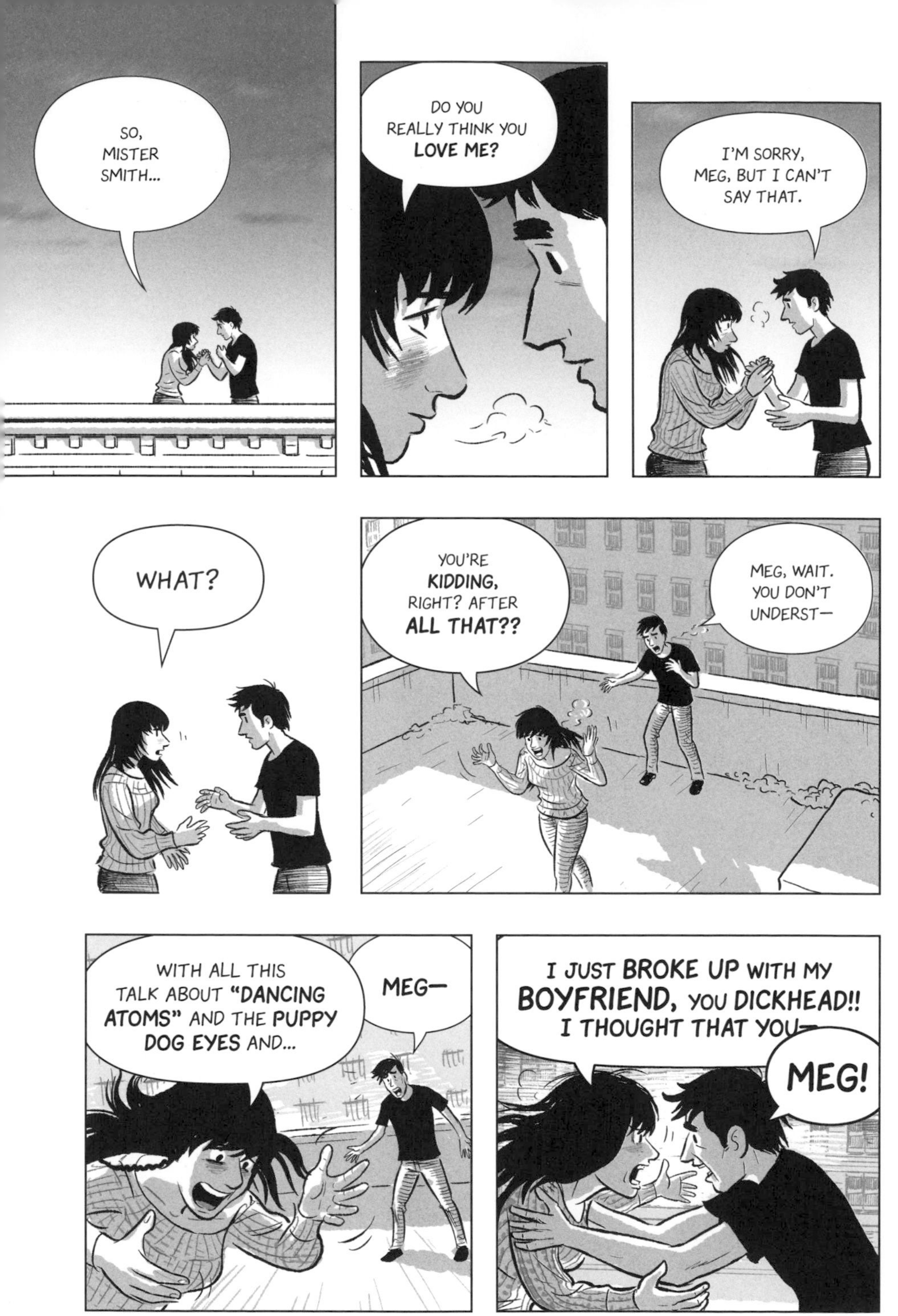
SO, MISTER SMITH...
DO YOU REALLY THINK YOU LOVE ME?
I'M SORRY, MEG, BUT I CAN'T SAY THAT.
WHAT?
YOU'RE KIDDING, RIGHT? AFTER ALL THAT??
MEG, WAIT. YOU DON'T UNDERST—
WITH ALL THIS TALK ABOUT "DANCING ATOMS" AND THE PUPPY DOG EYES AND...
MEG—
I JUST BROKE UP WITH MY BOYFRIEND, YOU DICKHEAD!! I THOUGHT THAT YOU—
MEG!

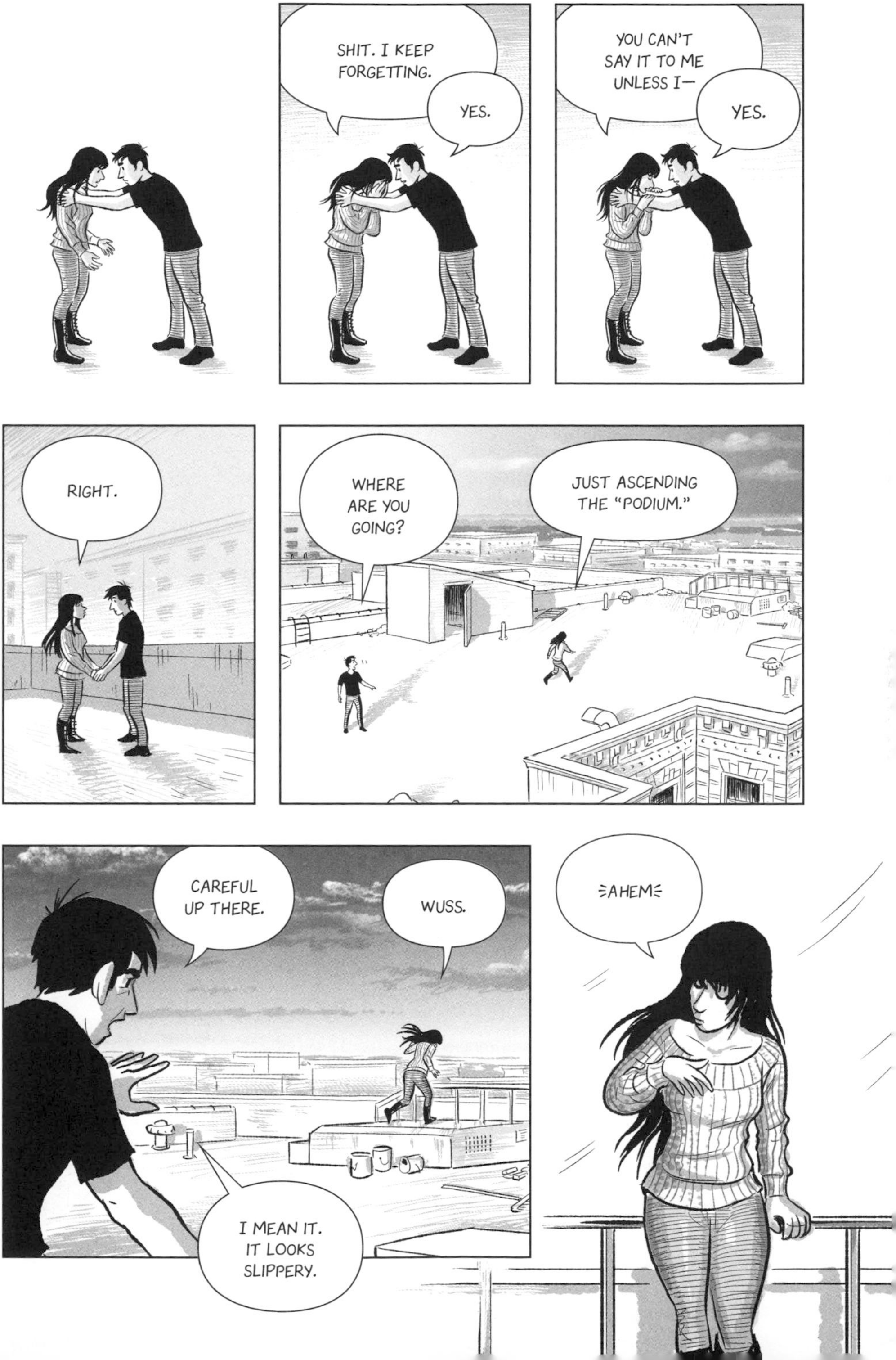
SHIT. I KEEP FORGETTING.
YES.
YOU CAN'T SAY IT TO ME UNLESS I—
YES.
RIGHT.
WHERE ARE YOU GOING?
JUST ASCENDING THE "PODIUM."
CAREFUL UP THERE.
WUSS.
I MEAN IT. IT LOOKS SLIPPERY.
AHEM

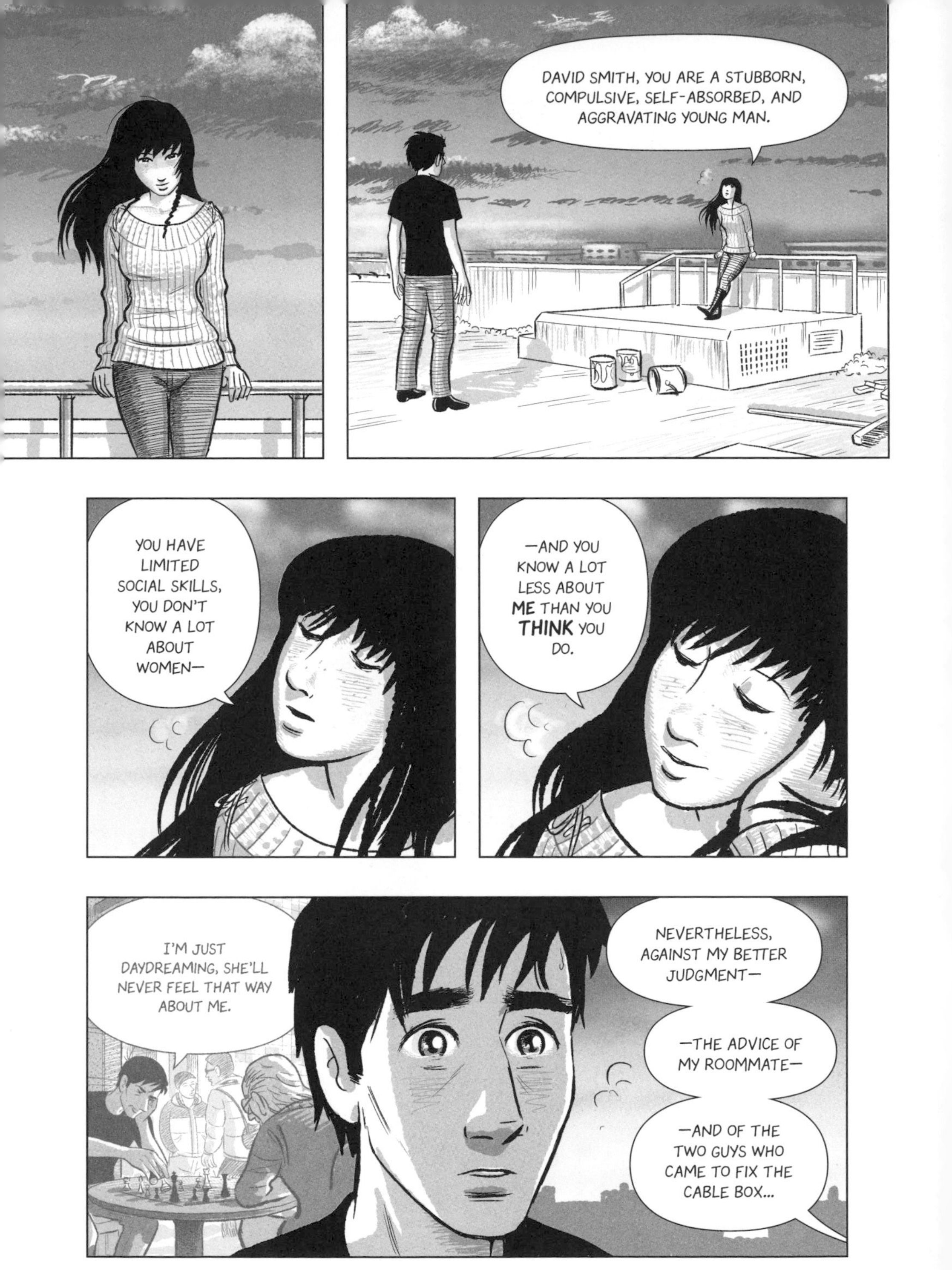
DAVID SMITH, YOU ARE A STUBBORN, COMPULSIVE, SELF-ABSORBED, AND AGGRAVATING YOUNG MAN.
YOU HAVE LIMITED SOCIAL SKILLS, YOU DON'T KNOW A LOT ABOUT WOMEN—
—AND YOU KNOW A LOT LESS ABOUT **ME** THAN YOU **THINK** YOU DO.
I'M JUST DAYDREAMING, SHE'LL NEVER FEEL THAT WAY ABOUT ME.
NEVERTHELESS, AGAINST MY BETTER JUDGMENT—
—THE ADVICE OF MY ROOMMATE—
—AND OF THE TWO GUYS WHO CAME TO FIX THE CABLE BOX...

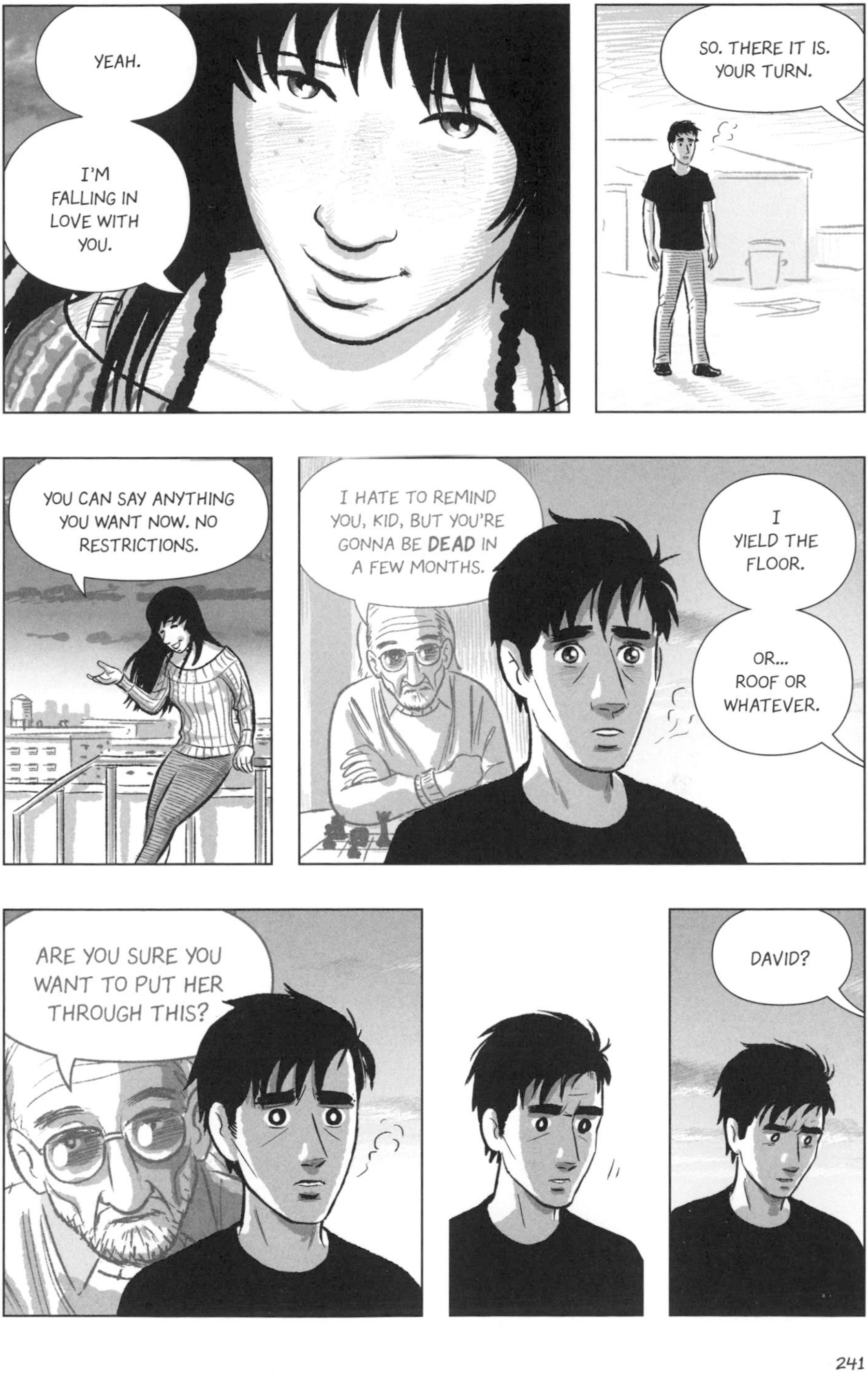
YEAH.
I'M FALLING IN LOVE WITH YOU.
SO. THERE IT IS. YOUR TURN.
YOU CAN SAY ANYTHING YOU WANT NOW. NO RESTRICTIONS.
I HATE TO REMIND YOU, KID, BUT YOU'RE GONNA BE DEAD IN A FEW MONTHS.
I YIELD THE FLOOR.
OR... ROOF OR WHATEVER.
ARE YOU SURE YOU WANT TO PUT HER THROUGH THIS?
DAVID?

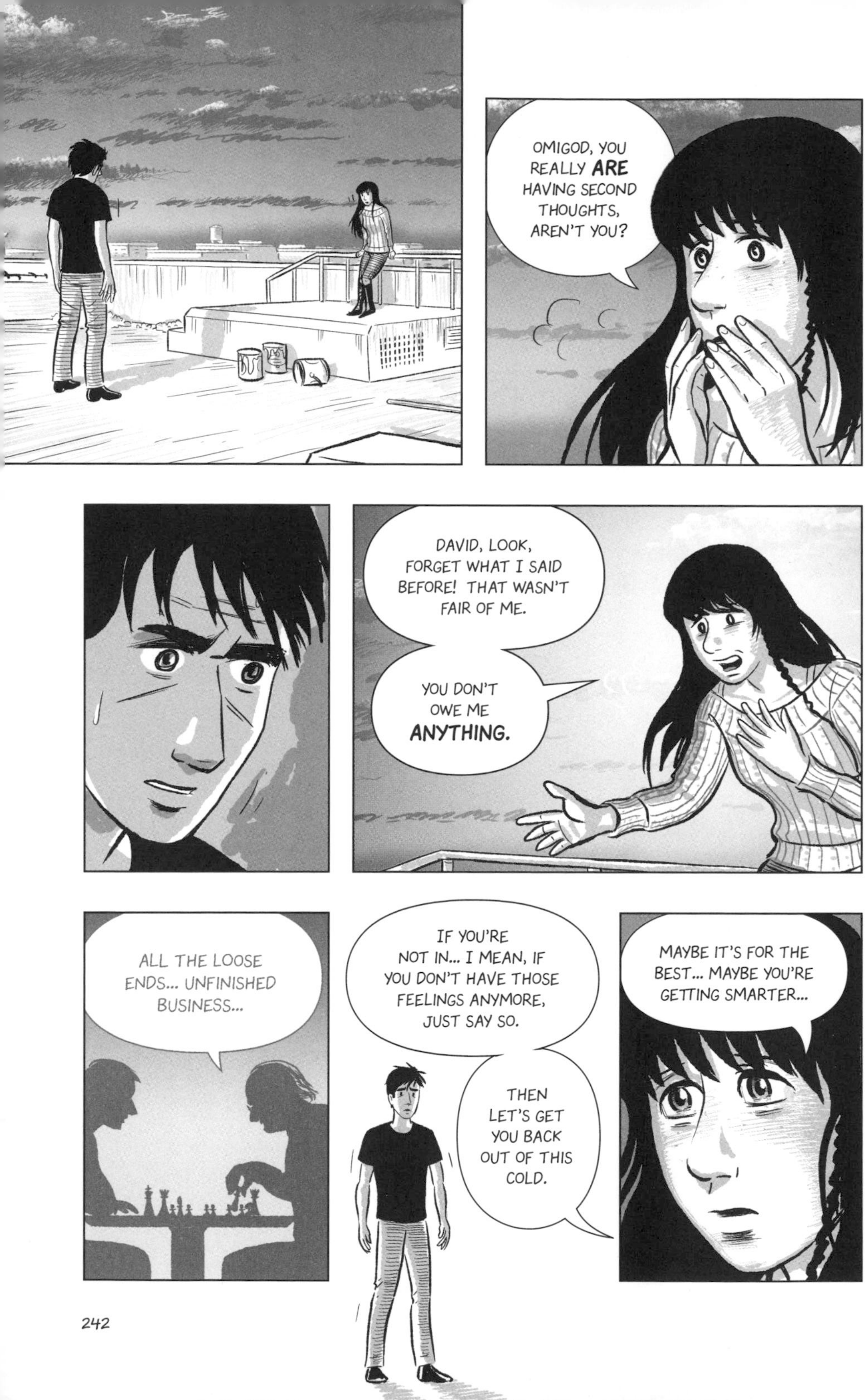
OMIGOD, YOU REALLY **ARE** HAVING SECOND THOUGHTS, AREN'T YOU?
DAVID, LOOK, FORGET WHAT I SAID BEFORE! THAT WASN'T FAIR OF ME.
YOU DON'T OWE ME **ANYTHING.**
ALL THE LOOSE ENDS... UNFINISHED BUSINESS...
IF YOU'RE NOT IN... I MEAN, IF YOU DON'T HAVE THOSE FEELINGS ANYMORE, JUST SAY SO.
THEN LET'S GET YOU BACK OUT OF THIS COLD.
MAYBE IT'S FOR THE BEST... MAYBE YOU'RE GETTING SMARTER...

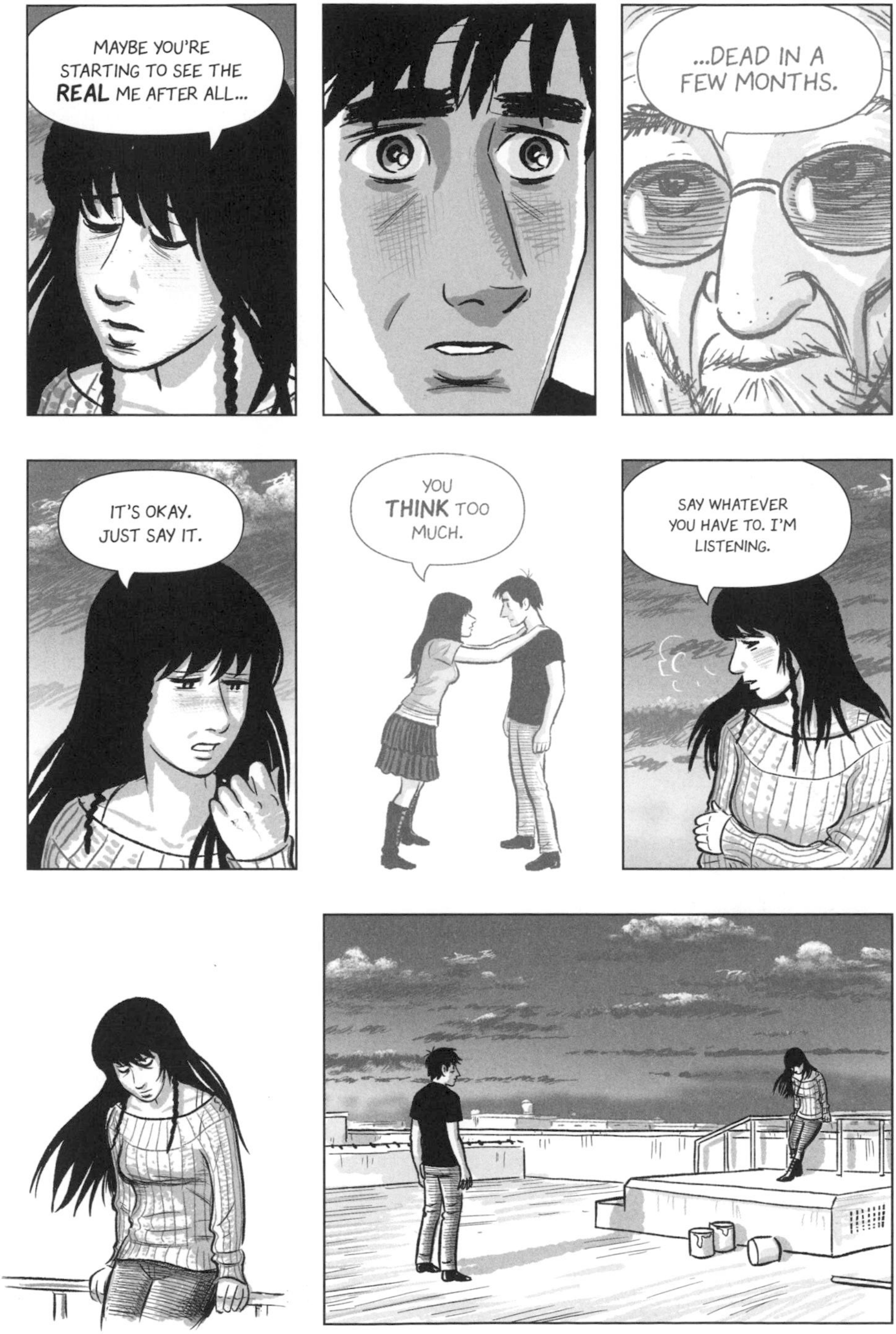
MAYBE YOU'RE STARTING TO SEE THE REAL ME AFTER ALL...
...DEAD IN A FEW MONTHS.
IT'S OKAY. JUST SAY IT.
YOU THINK TOO MUCH.
SAY WHATEVER YOU HAVE TO. I'M LISTENING.

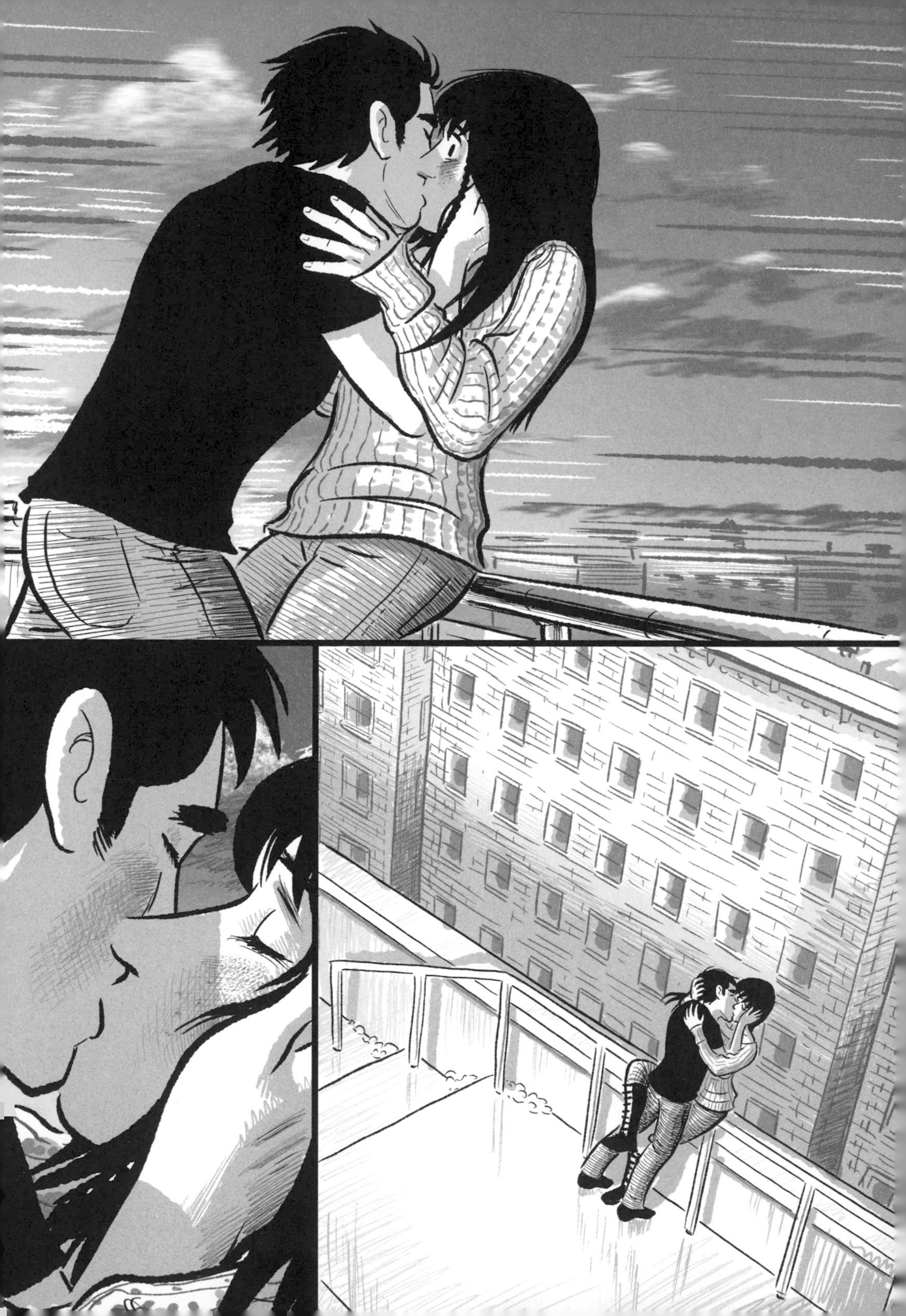

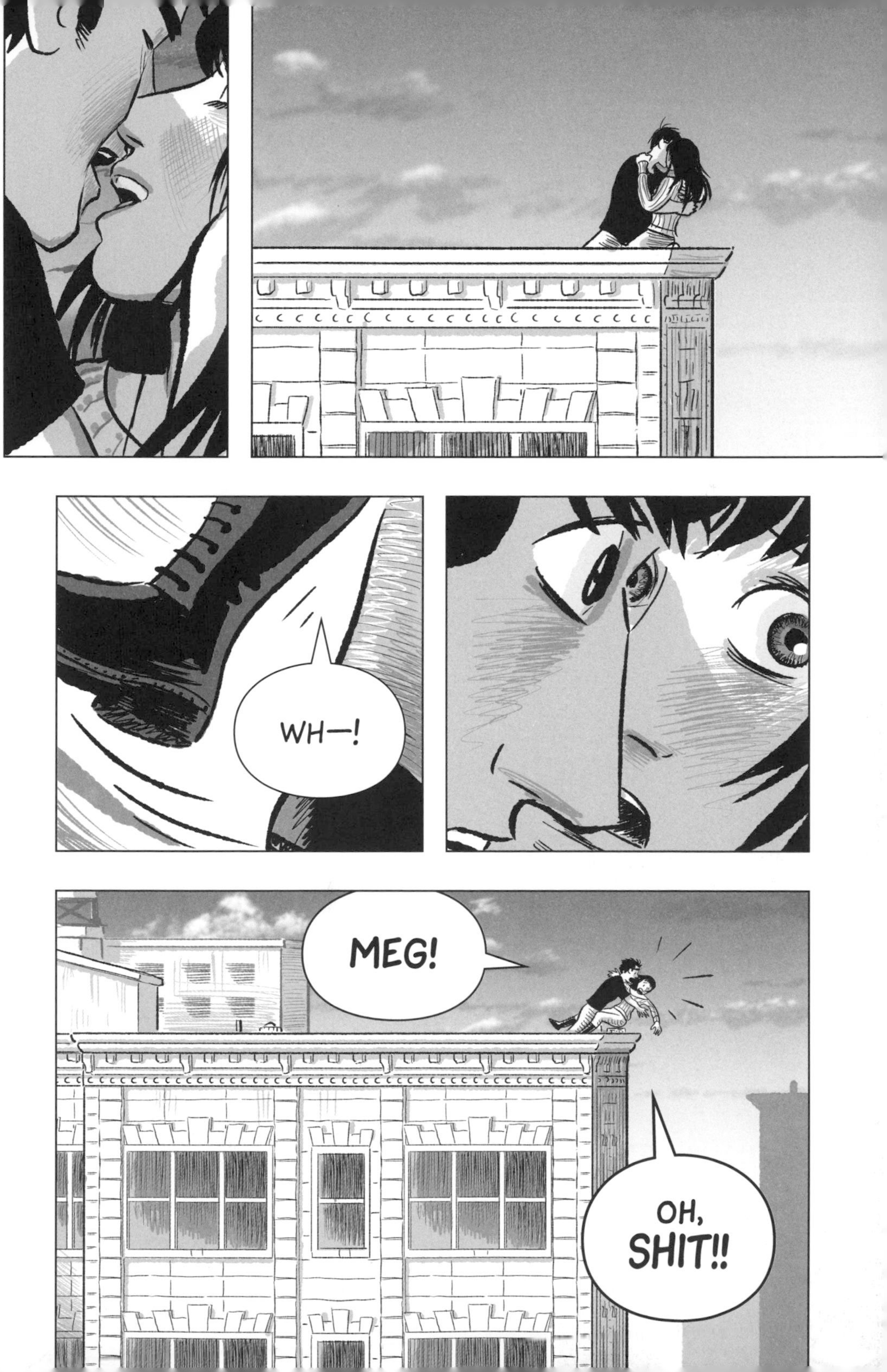
WH—!
MEG!
OH, SHIT!!

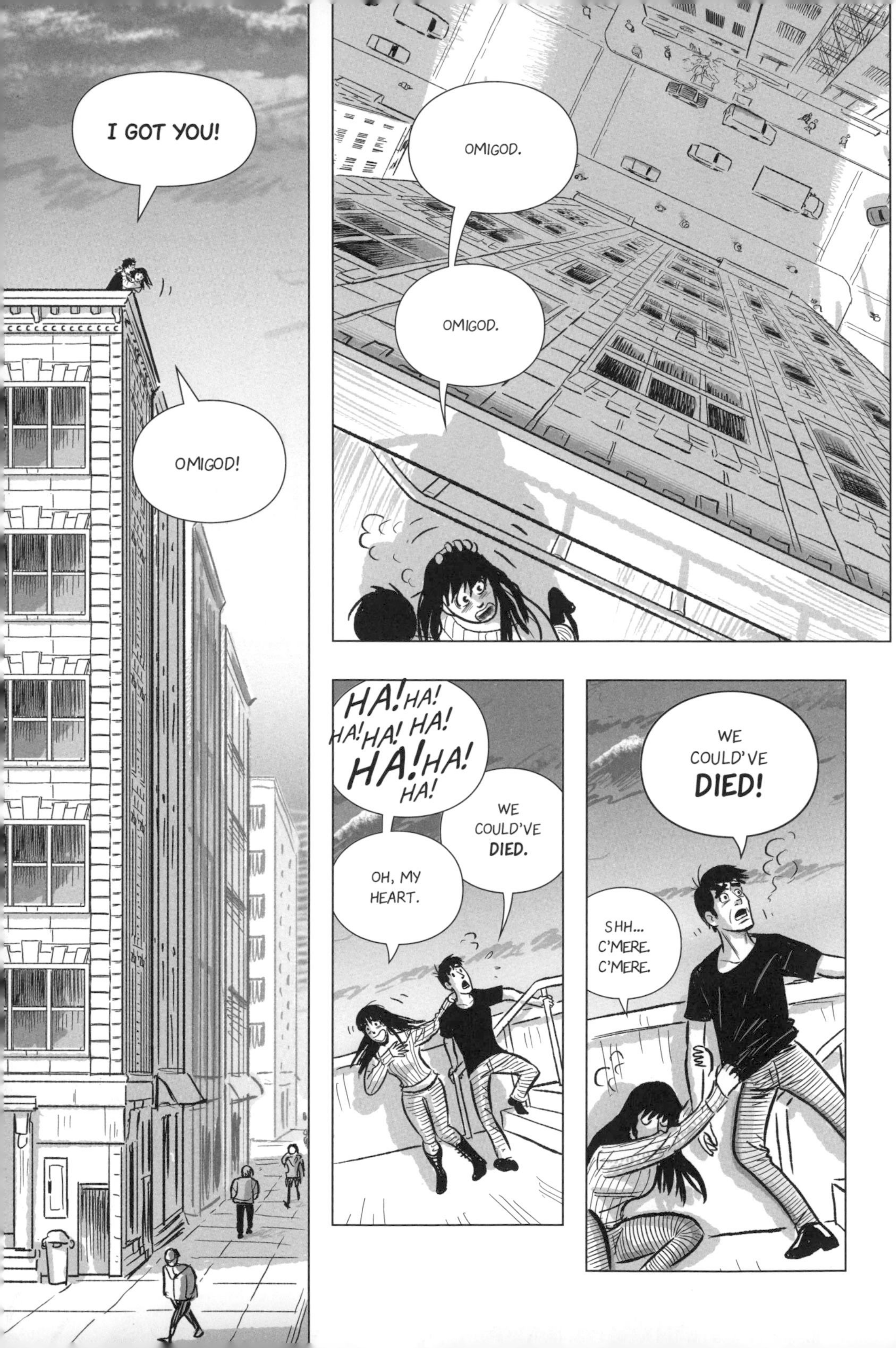
I GOT YOU!
OMIGOD!
OMIGOD.
OMIGOD.
HA! HA! HA! HA! HA! HA! HA! HA!
WE COULD'VE DIED.
OH, MY HEART.
WE COULD'VE DIED!
SHH... C'MERE. C'MERE.

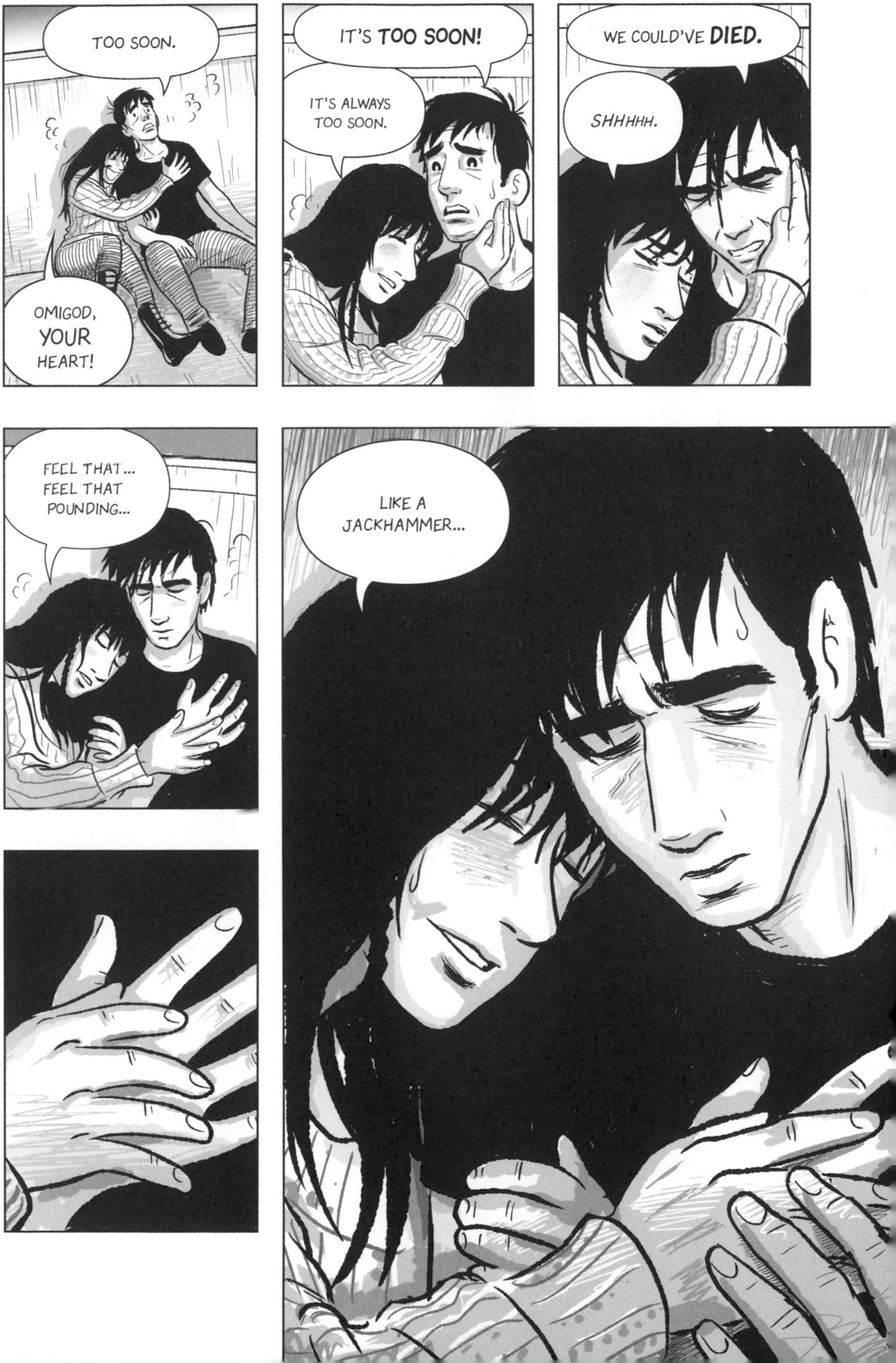

TOO SOON.
OMIGOD, YOUR HEART!
IT'S TOO SOON!
IT'S ALWAYS TOO SOON.
WE COULD'VE DIED.
SHHHHH.
FEEL THAT... FEEL THAT POUNDING...
LIKE A JACKHAMMER...

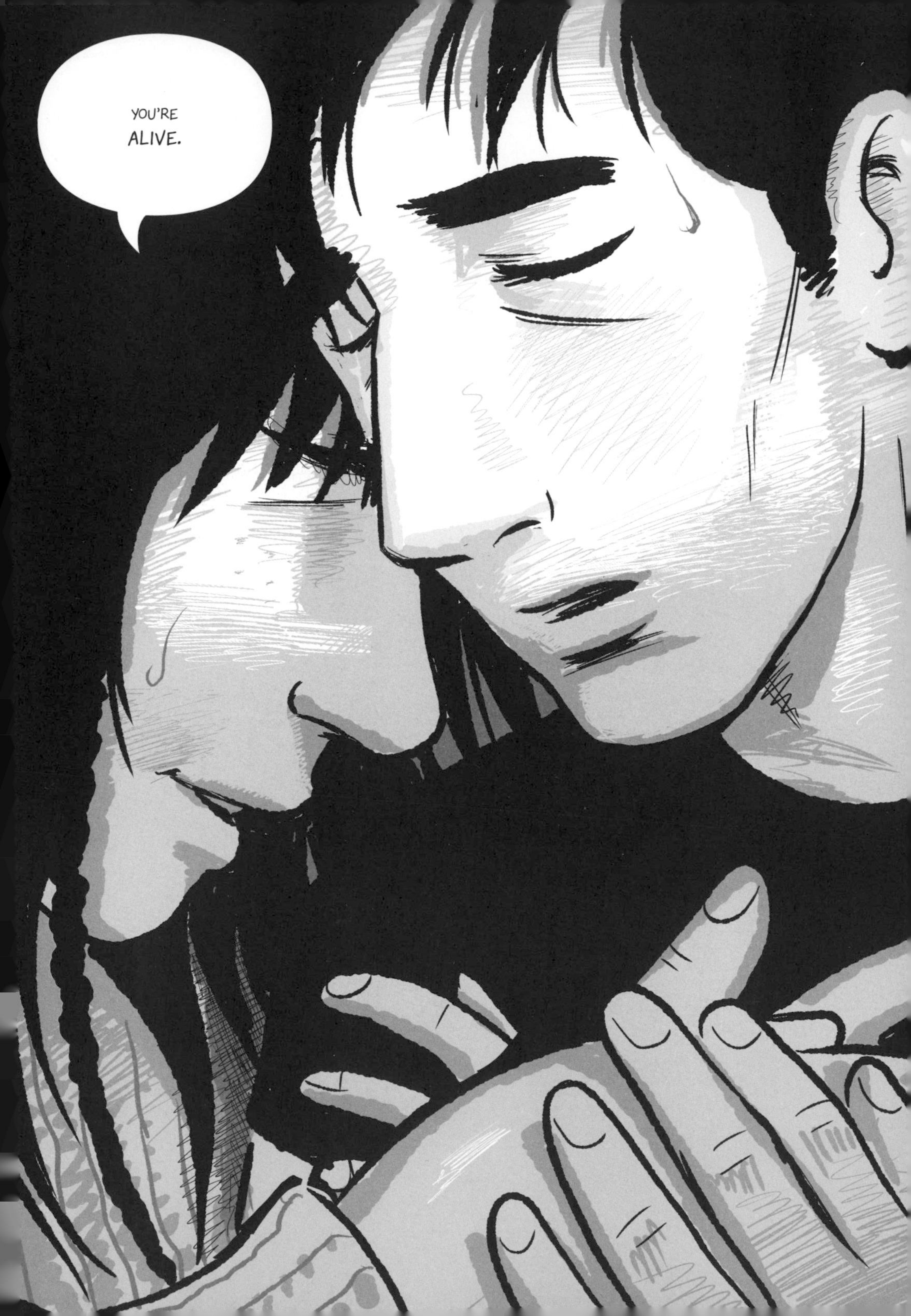
YOU'RE ALIVE.

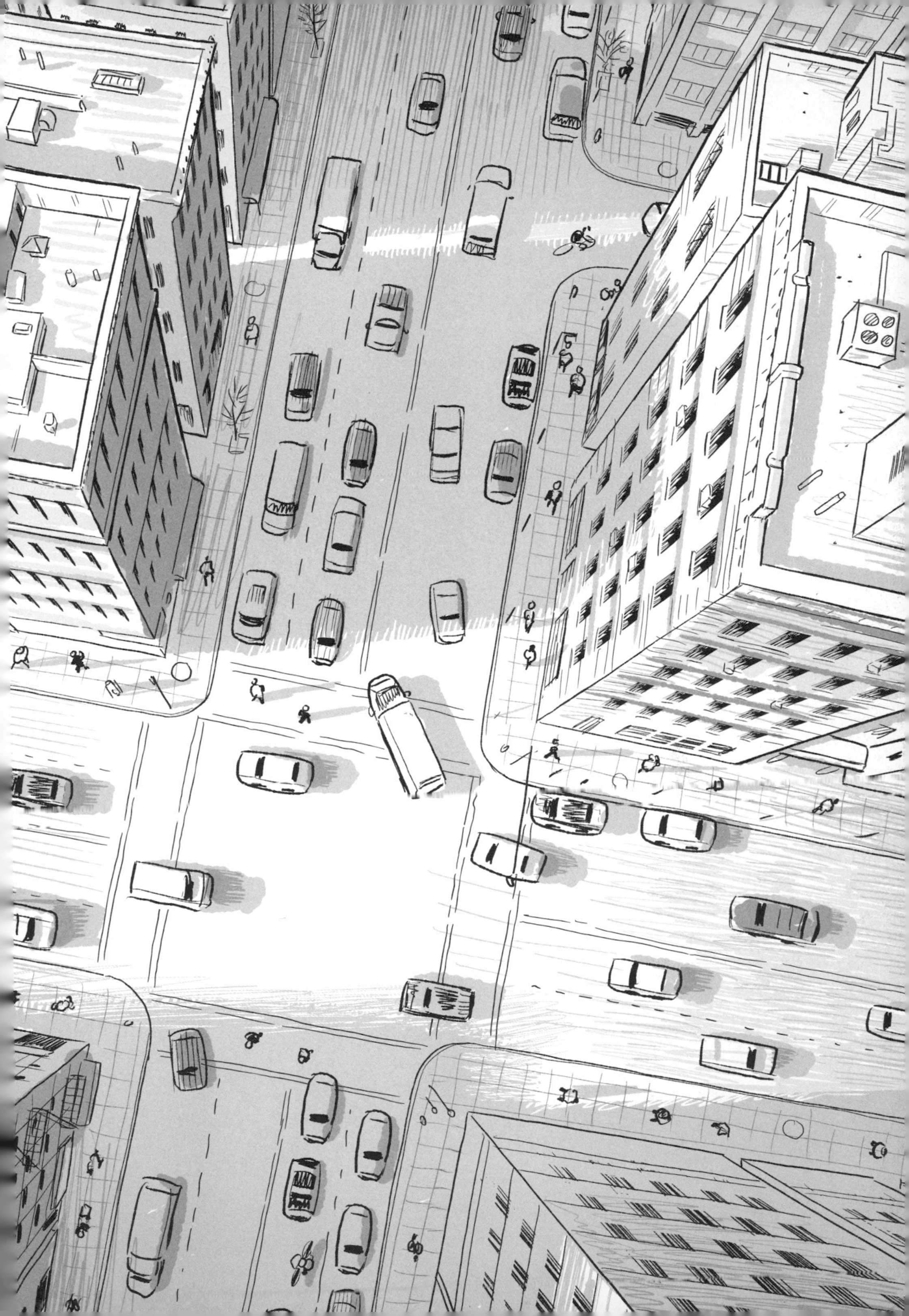

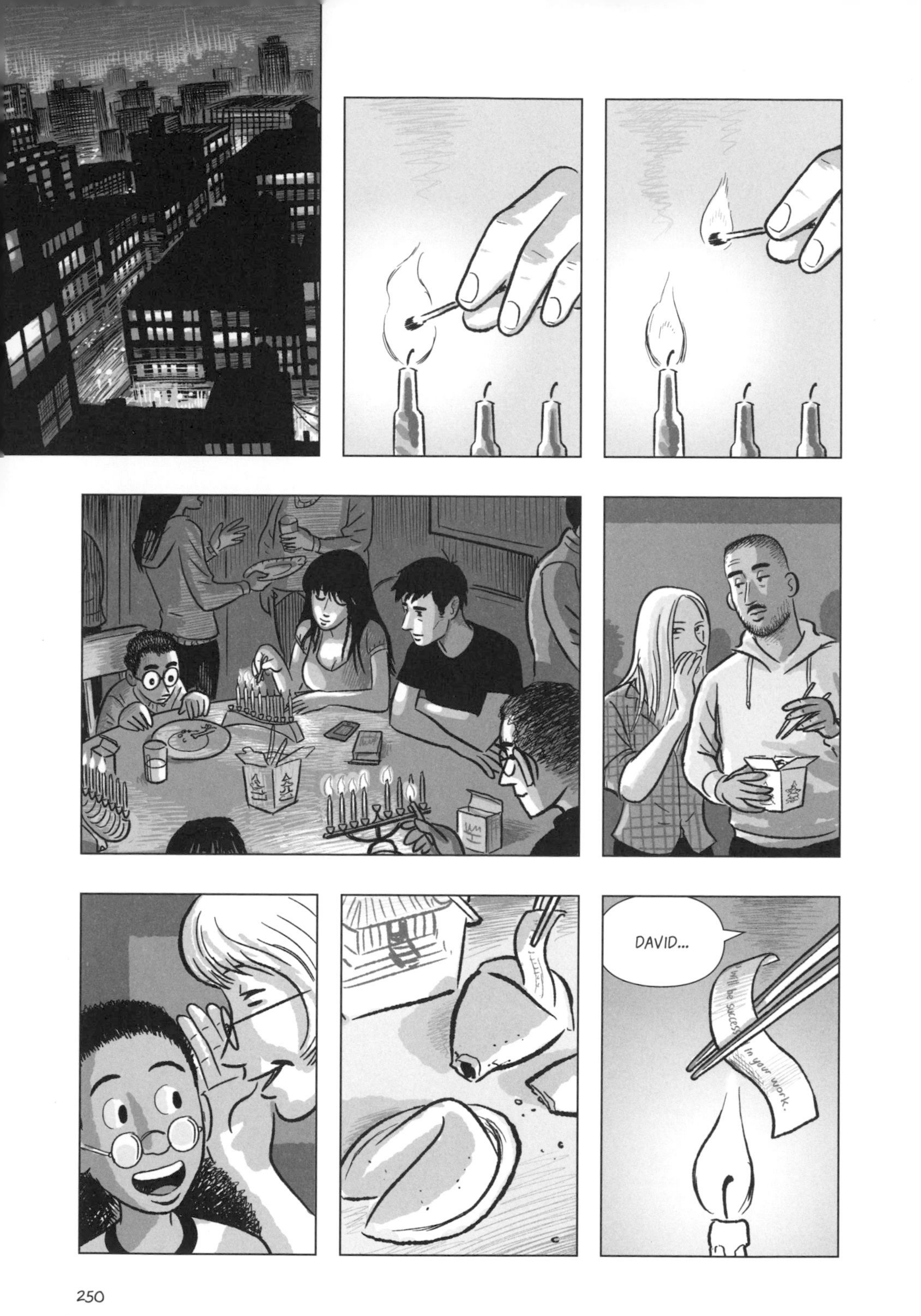
DAVID...
will be success
in your work.

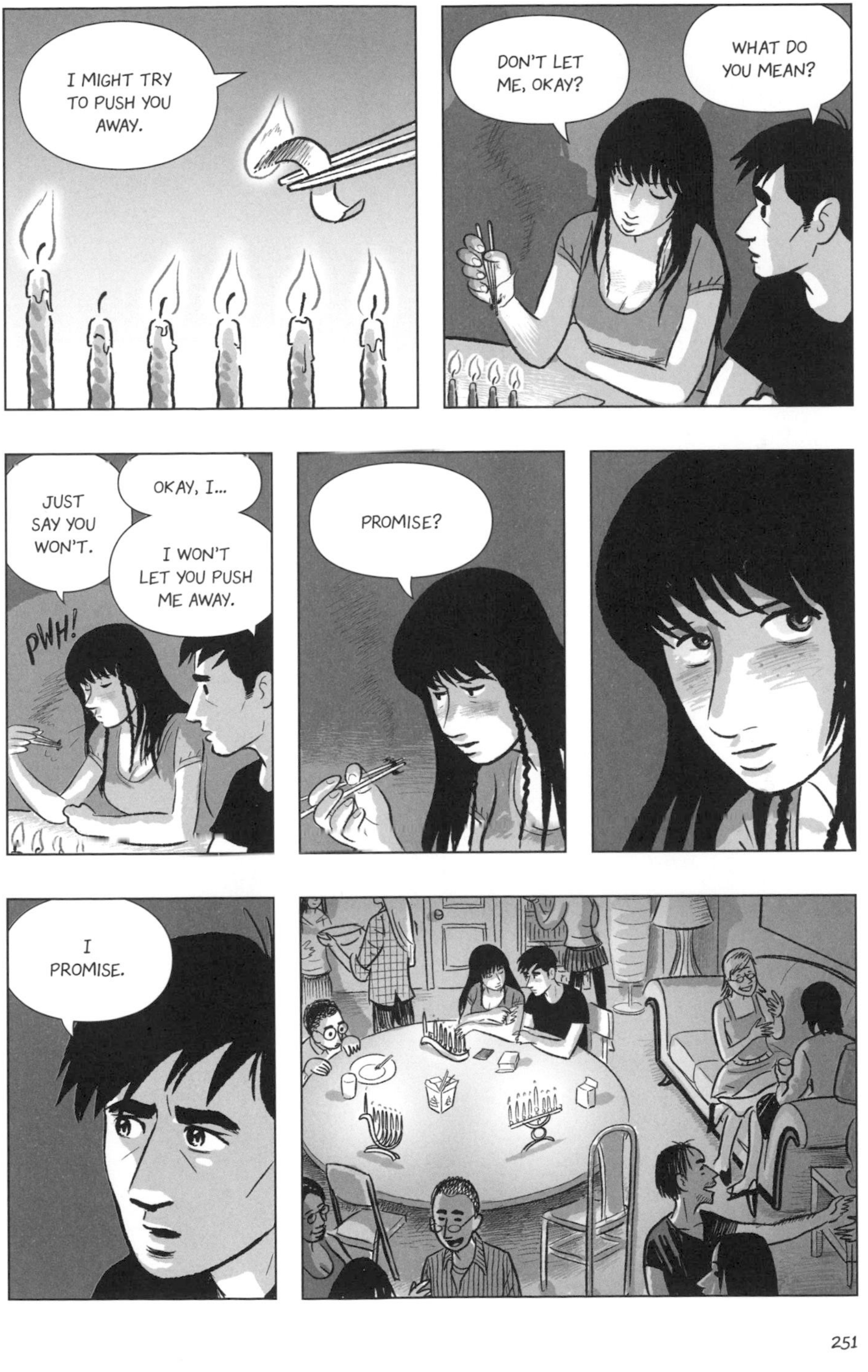
I MIGHT TRY TO PUSH YOU AWAY.
DON'T LET ME, OKAY?
WHAT DO YOU MEAN?
JUST SAY YOU WON'T.
OKAY, I...
I WON'T LET YOU PUSH ME AWAY.
PWH!
PROMISE?
I PROMISE.

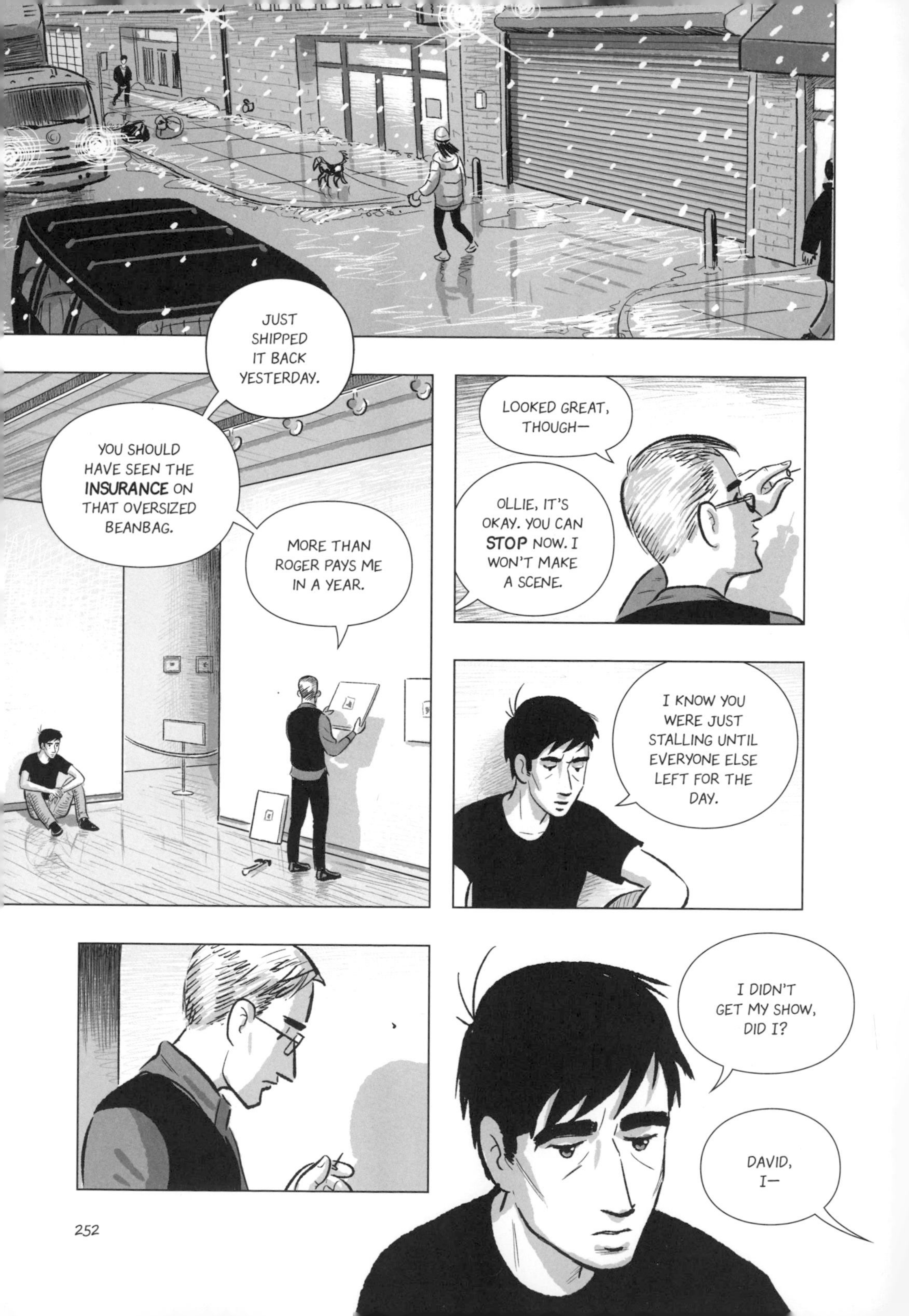
JUST SHIPPED IT BACK YESTERDAY.
YOU SHOULD HAVE SEEN THE **INSURANCE** ON THAT OVERSIZED BEANBAG.
MORE THAN ROGER PAYS ME IN A YEAR.
LOOKED GREAT, THOUGH—
OLLIE, IT'S OKAY. YOU CAN **STOP** NOW. I WON'T MAKE A SCENE.
I KNOW YOU WERE JUST STALLING UNTIL EVERYONE ELSE LEFT FOR THE DAY.
I DIDN'T GET MY SHOW, DID I?
DAVID, I—

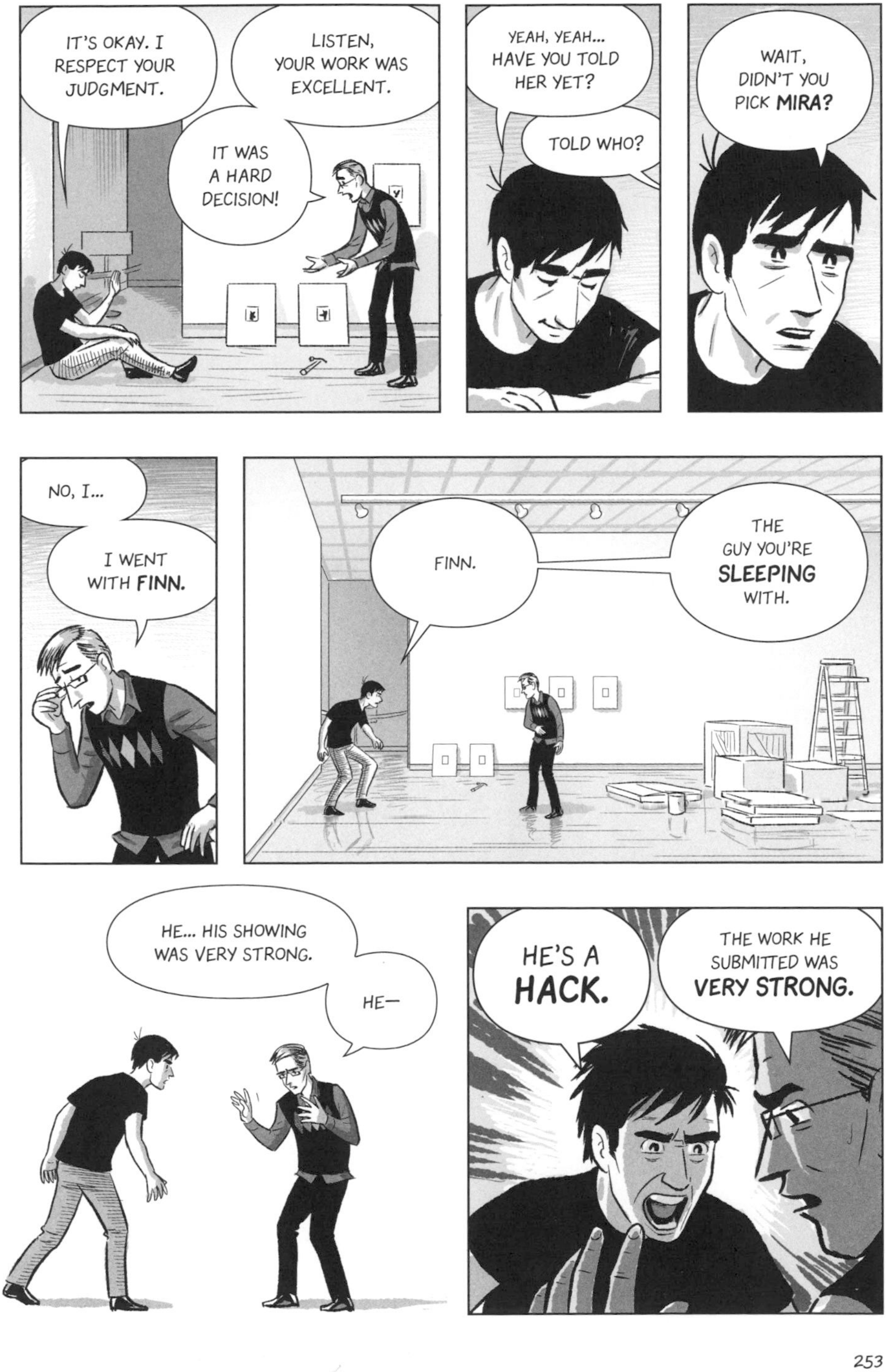
IT'S OKAY. I RESPECT YOUR JUDGMENT.
LISTEN, YOUR WORK WAS EXCELLENT.
IT WAS A HARD DECISION!
YEAH, YEAH... HAVE YOU TOLD HER YET?
TOLD WHO?
WAIT, DIDN'T YOU PICK **MIRA?**
NO, I...
I WENT WITH **FINN.**
FINN.
THE GUY YOU'RE **SLEEPING** WITH.
HE... HIS SHOWING WAS VERY STRONG.
HE—
HE'S A **HACK.**
THE WORK HE SUBMITTED WAS **VERY STRONG.**

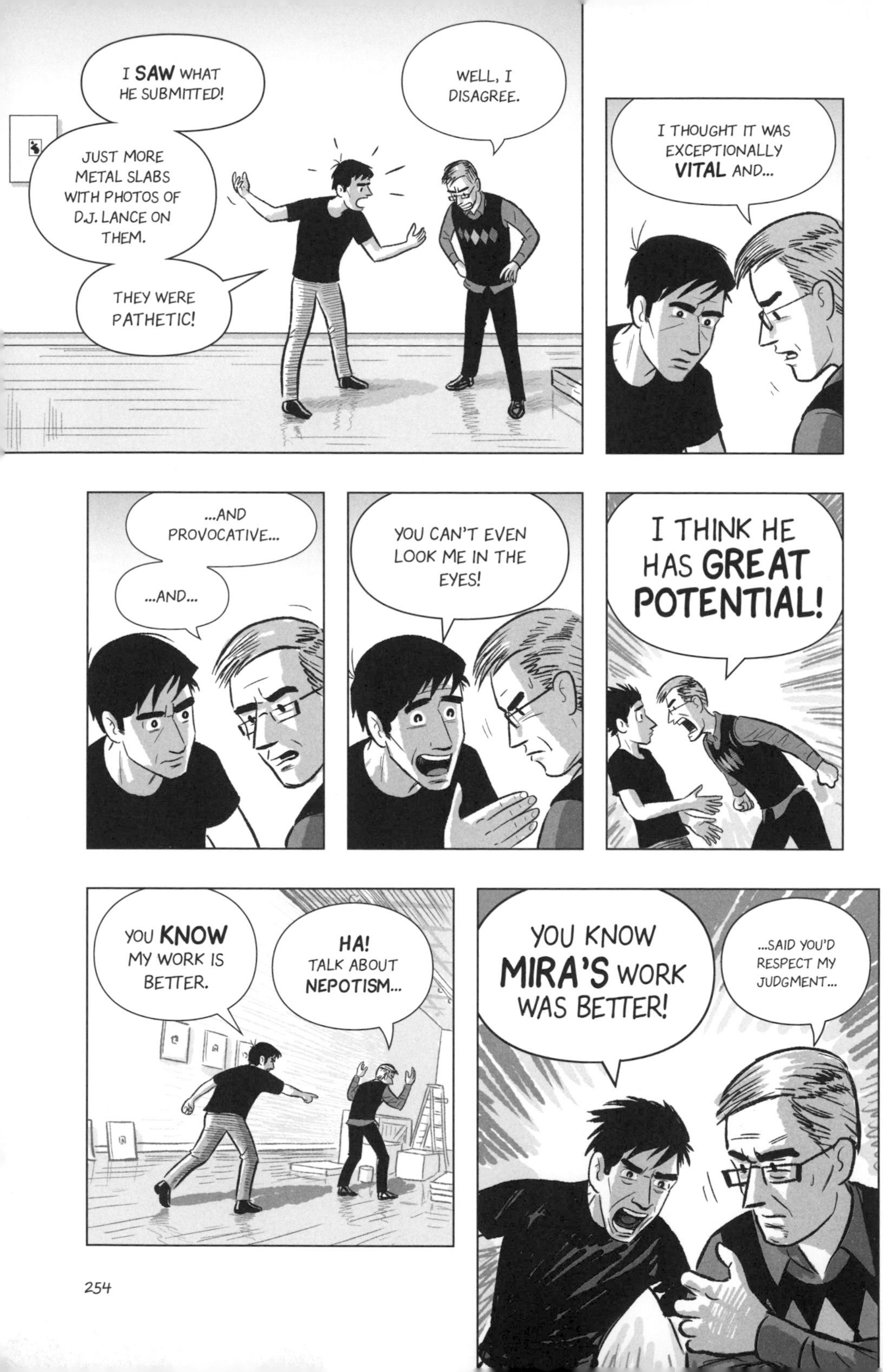

I SAW WHAT HE SUBMITTED!
JUST MORE METAL SLABS WITH PHOTOS OF D.J. LANCE ON THEM.
THEY WERE PATHETIC!
WELL, I DISAGREE.
I THOUGHT IT WAS EXCEPTIONALLY VITAL AND...
...AND PROVOCATIVE...
...AND...
YOU CAN'T EVEN LOOK ME IN THE EYES!
I THINK HE HAS GREAT POTENTIAL!
YOU KNOW MY WORK IS BETTER.
HA! TALK ABOUT NEPOTISM...
YOU KNOW MIRA'S WORK WAS BETTER!
...SAID YOU'D RESPECT MY JUDGMENT...

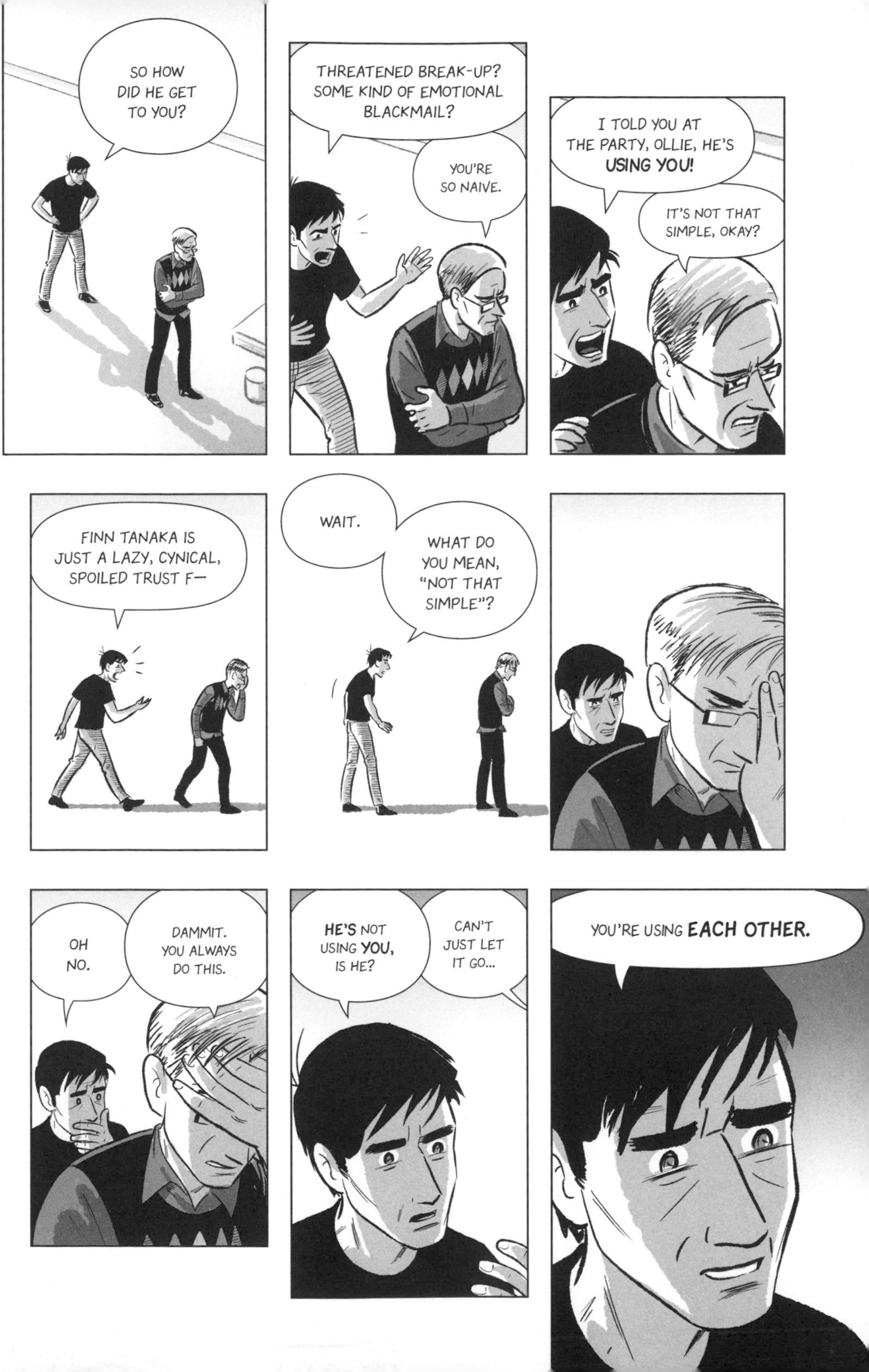
SO HOW DID HE GET TO YOU?
THREATENED BREAK-UP? SOME KIND OF EMOTIONAL BLACKMAIL?
YOU'RE SO NAIVE.
I TOLD YOU AT THE PARTY, OLLIE, HE'S USING YOU!
IT'S NOT THAT SIMPLE, OKAY?
FINN TANAKA IS JUST A LAZY, CYNICAL, SPOILED TRUST F—
WAIT.
WHAT DO YOU MEAN, "NOT THAT SIMPLE"?
OH NO.
DAMMIT. YOU ALWAYS DO THIS.
HE'S NOT USING YOU, IS HE?
CAN'T JUST LET IT GO...
YOU'RE USING EACH OTHER.

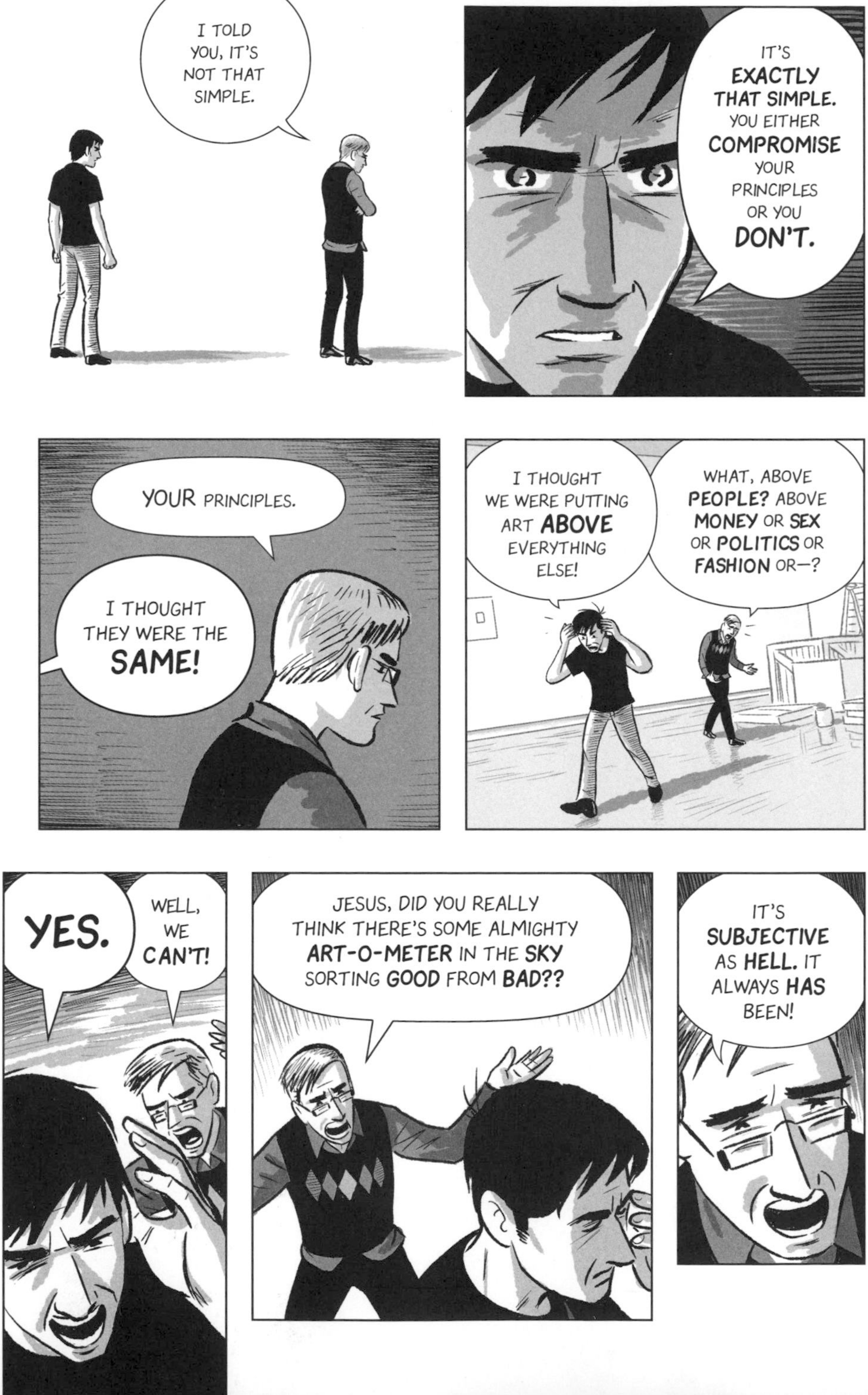
I TOLD YOU, IT'S NOT THAT SIMPLE.
IT'S EXACTLY THAT SIMPLE. YOU EITHER COMPROMISE YOUR PRINCIPLES OR YOU DON'T.
YOUR PRINCIPLES.
I THOUGHT THEY WERE THE SAME!
I THOUGHT WE WERE PUTTING ART ABOVE EVERYTHING ELSE!
WHAT, ABOVE PEOPLE? ABOVE MONEY OR SEX OR POLITICS OR FASHION OR—?
YES.
WELL, WE CAN'T!
JESUS, DID YOU REALLY THINK THERE'S SOME ALMIGHTY ART-O-METER IN THE SKY SORTING GOOD FROM BAD??
IT'S SUBJECTIVE AS HELL. IT ALWAYS HAS BEEN!

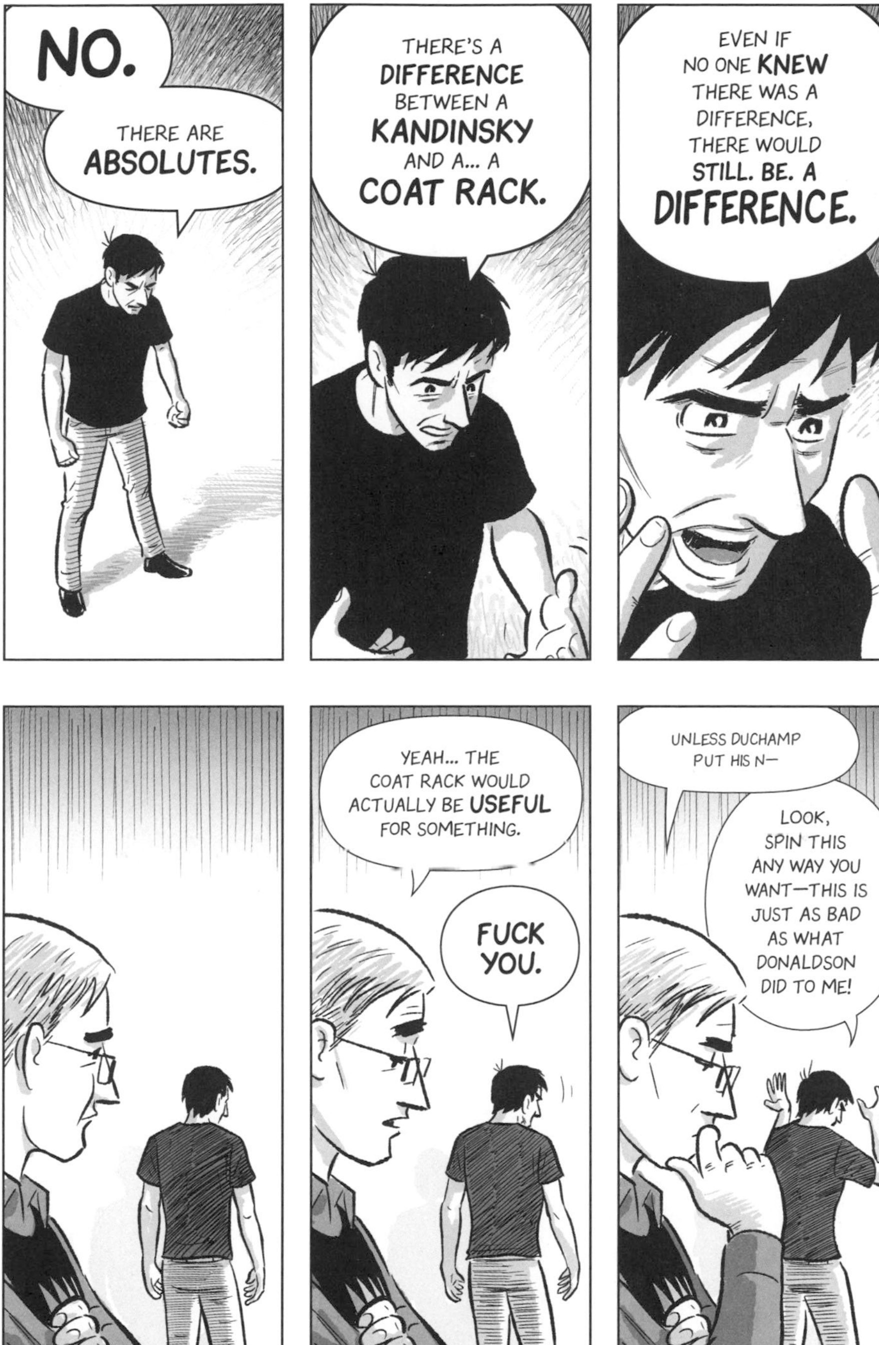
NO.
THERE ARE ABSOLUTES.
THERE'S A DIFFERENCE BETWEEN A KANDINSKY AND A... A COAT RACK.
EVEN IF NO ONE KNEW THERE WAS A DIFFERENCE, THERE WOULD STILL. BE. A DIFFERENCE.
YEAH... THE COAT RACK WOULD ACTUALLY BE USEFUL FOR SOMETHING.
FUCK YOU.
UNLESS DUCHAMP PUT HIS N—
LOOK, SPIN THIS ANY WAY YOU WANT—THIS IS JUST AS BAD AS WHAT DONALDSON DID TO ME!

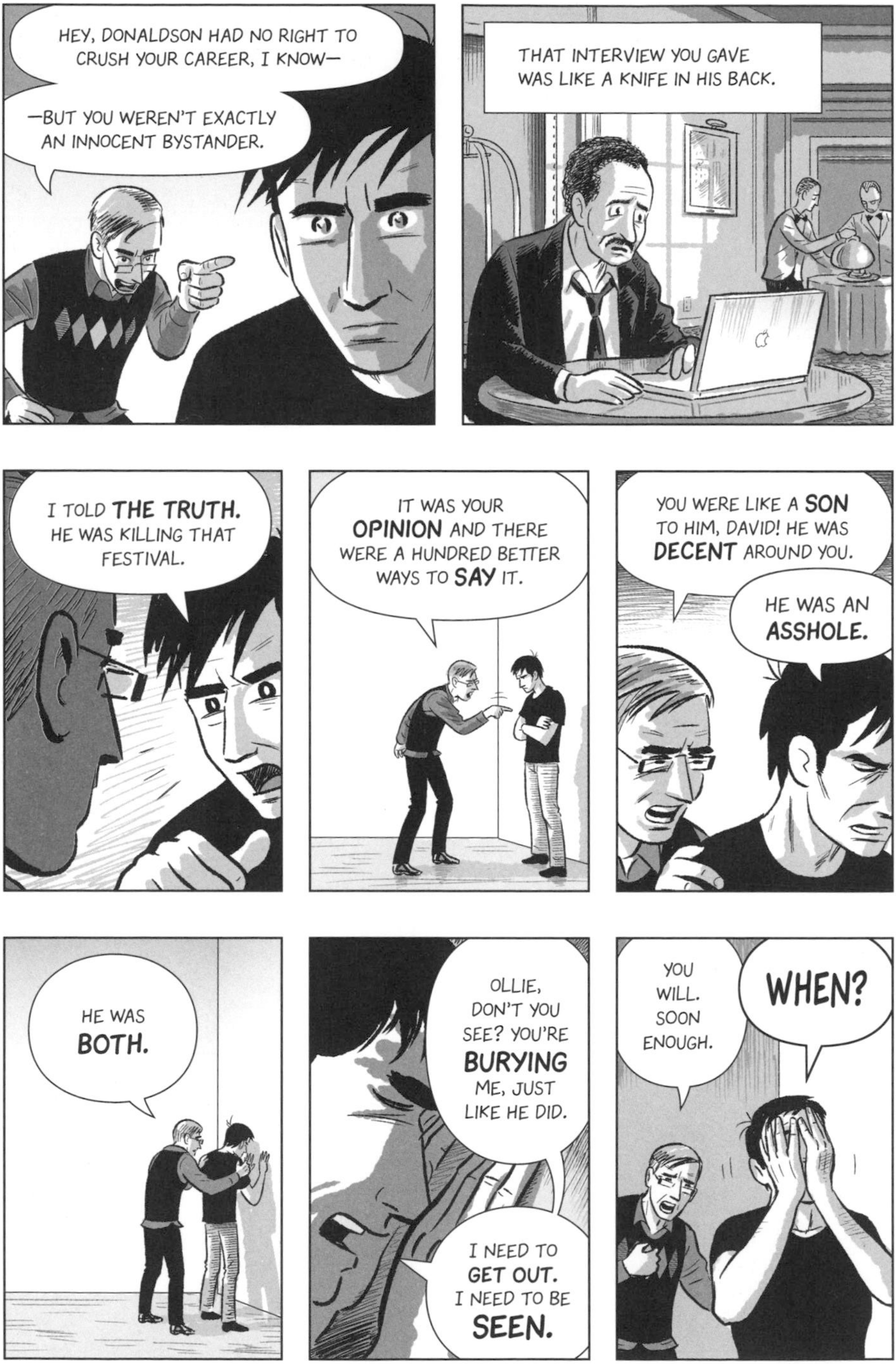
HEY, DONALDSON HAD NO RIGHT TO CRUSH YOUR CAREER, I KNOW—
—BUT YOU WEREN'T EXACTLY AN INNOCENT BYSTANDER.
THAT INTERVIEW YOU GAVE WAS LIKE A KNIFE IN HIS BACK.
I TOLD THE TRUTH. HE WAS KILLING THAT FESTIVAL.
IT WAS YOUR OPINION AND THERE WERE A HUNDRED BETTER WAYS TO SAY IT.
YOU WERE LIKE A SON TO HIM, DAVID! HE WAS DECENT AROUND YOU.
HE WAS AN ASSHOLE.
HE WAS BOTH.
OLLIE, DON'T YOU SEE? YOU'RE BURYING ME, JUST LIKE HE DID.
I NEED TO GET OUT. I NEED TO BE SEEN.
YOU WILL. SOON ENOUGH.
WHEN?

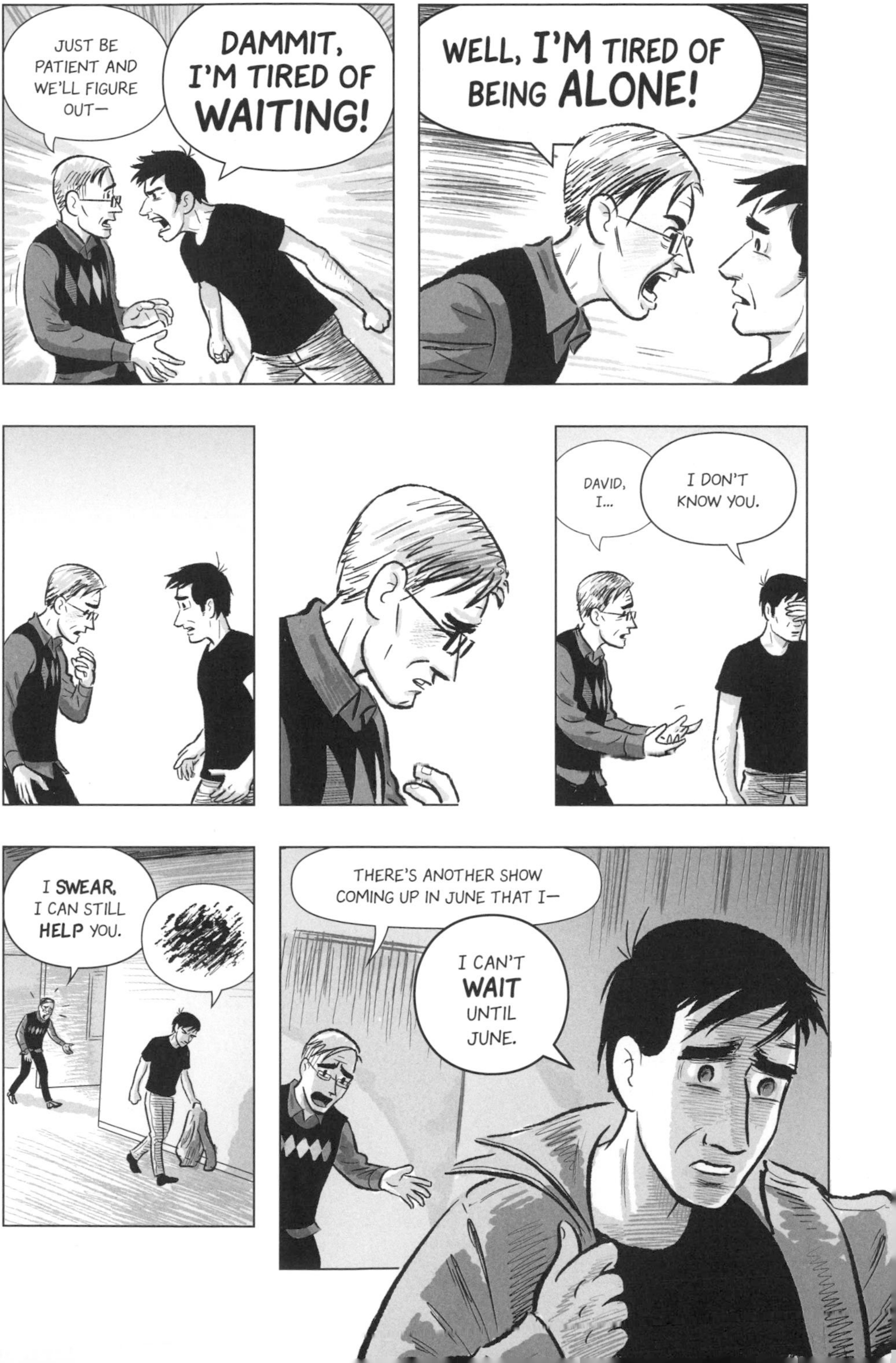
JUST BE PATIENT AND WE'LL FIGURE OUT—
DAMMIT, I'M TIRED OF WAITING!
WELL, I'M TIRED OF BEING ALONE!
DAVID, I...
I DON'T KNOW YOU.
I SWEAR, I CAN STILL HELP YOU.
THERE'S ANOTHER SHOW COMING UP IN JUNE THAT I—
I CAN'T WAIT UNTIL JUNE.

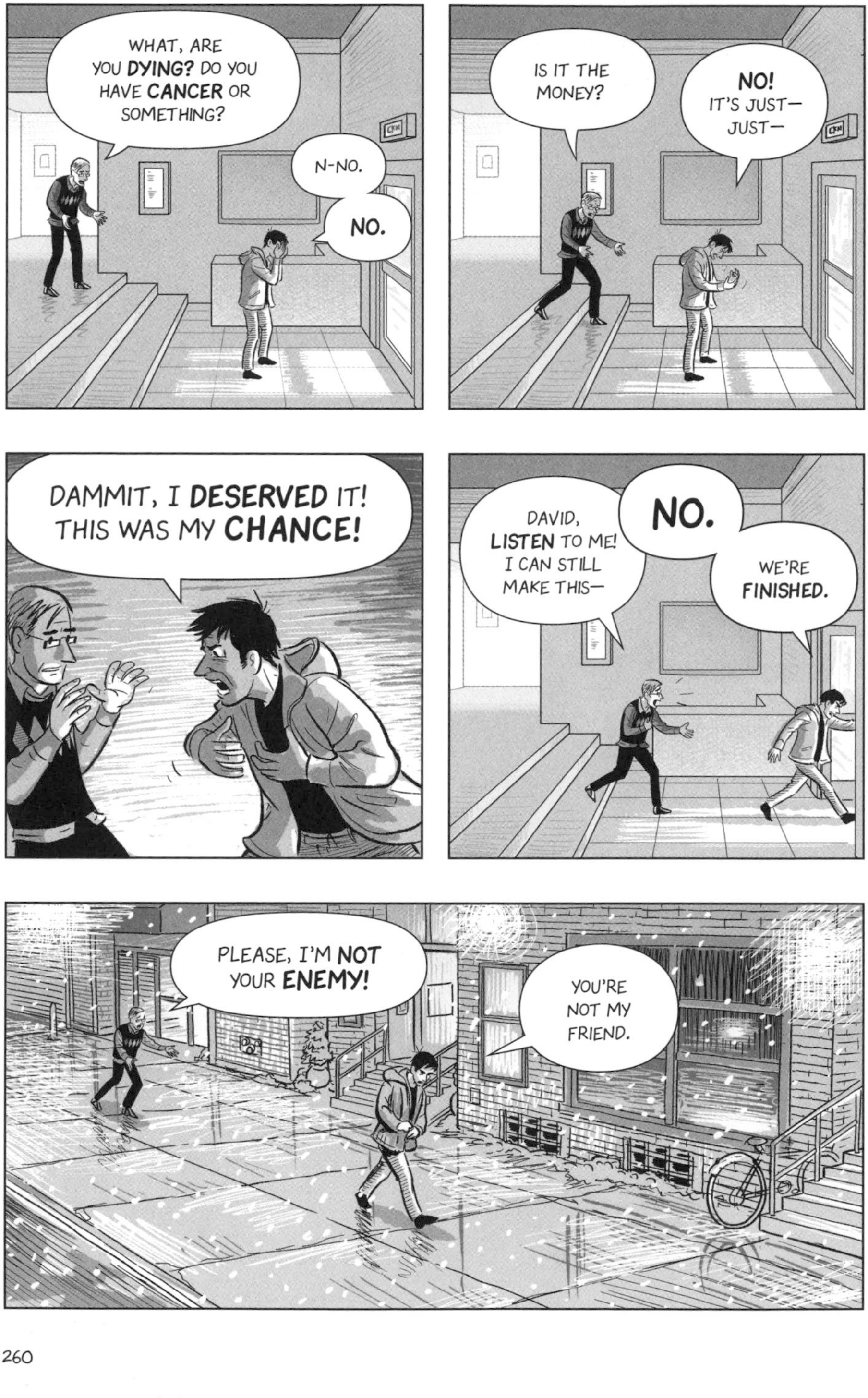
WHAT, ARE YOU DYING? DO YOU HAVE CANCER OR SOMETHING?
N-NO.
NO.
IS IT THE MONEY?
NO! IT'S JUST— JUST—
DAMMIT, I DESERVED IT! THIS WAS MY CHANCE!
DAVID, LISTEN TO ME! I CAN STILL MAKE THIS—
NO.
WE'RE FINISHED.
PLEASE, I'M NOT YOUR ENEMY!
YOU'RE NOT MY FRIEND.

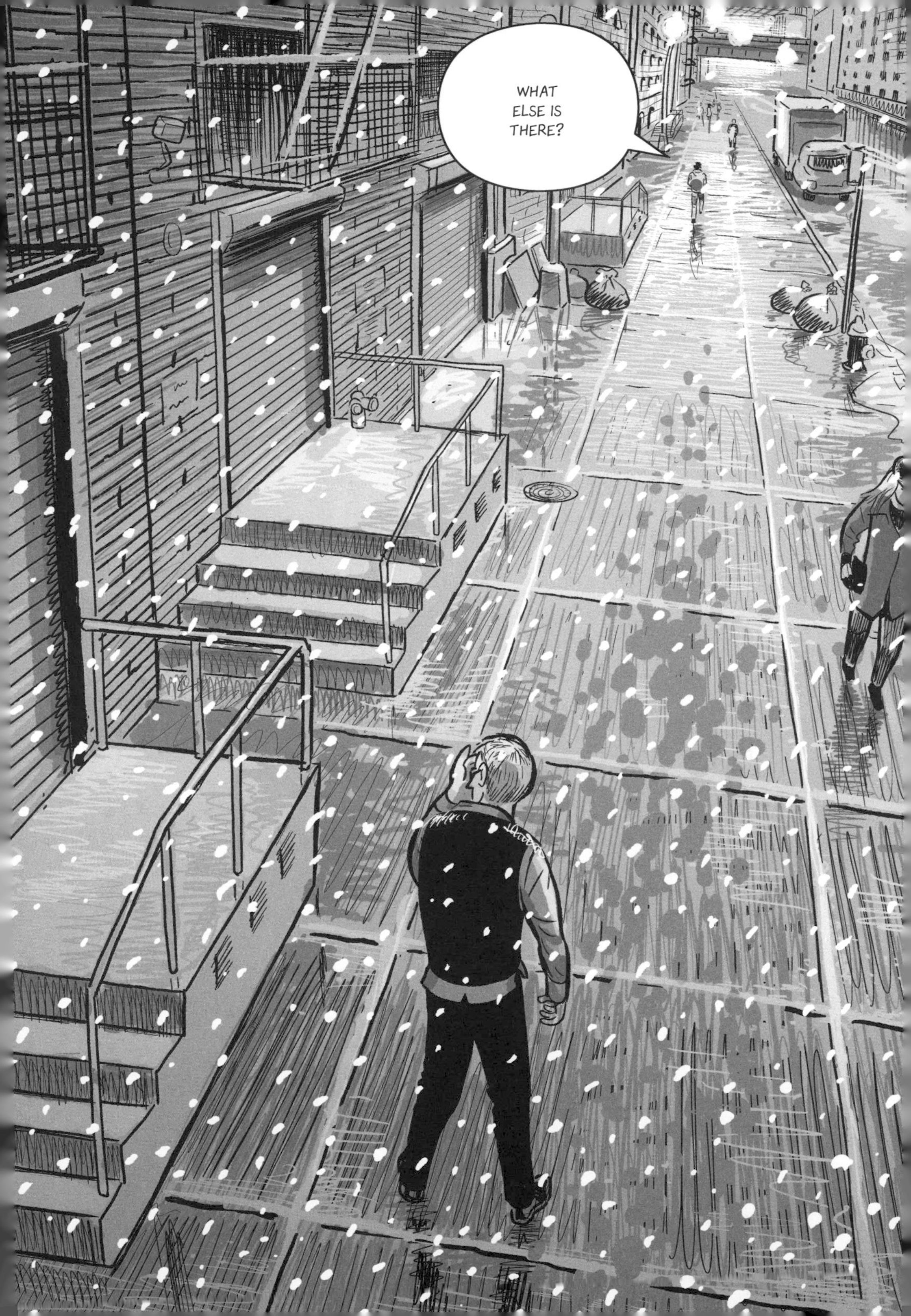
WHAT ELSE IS THERE?

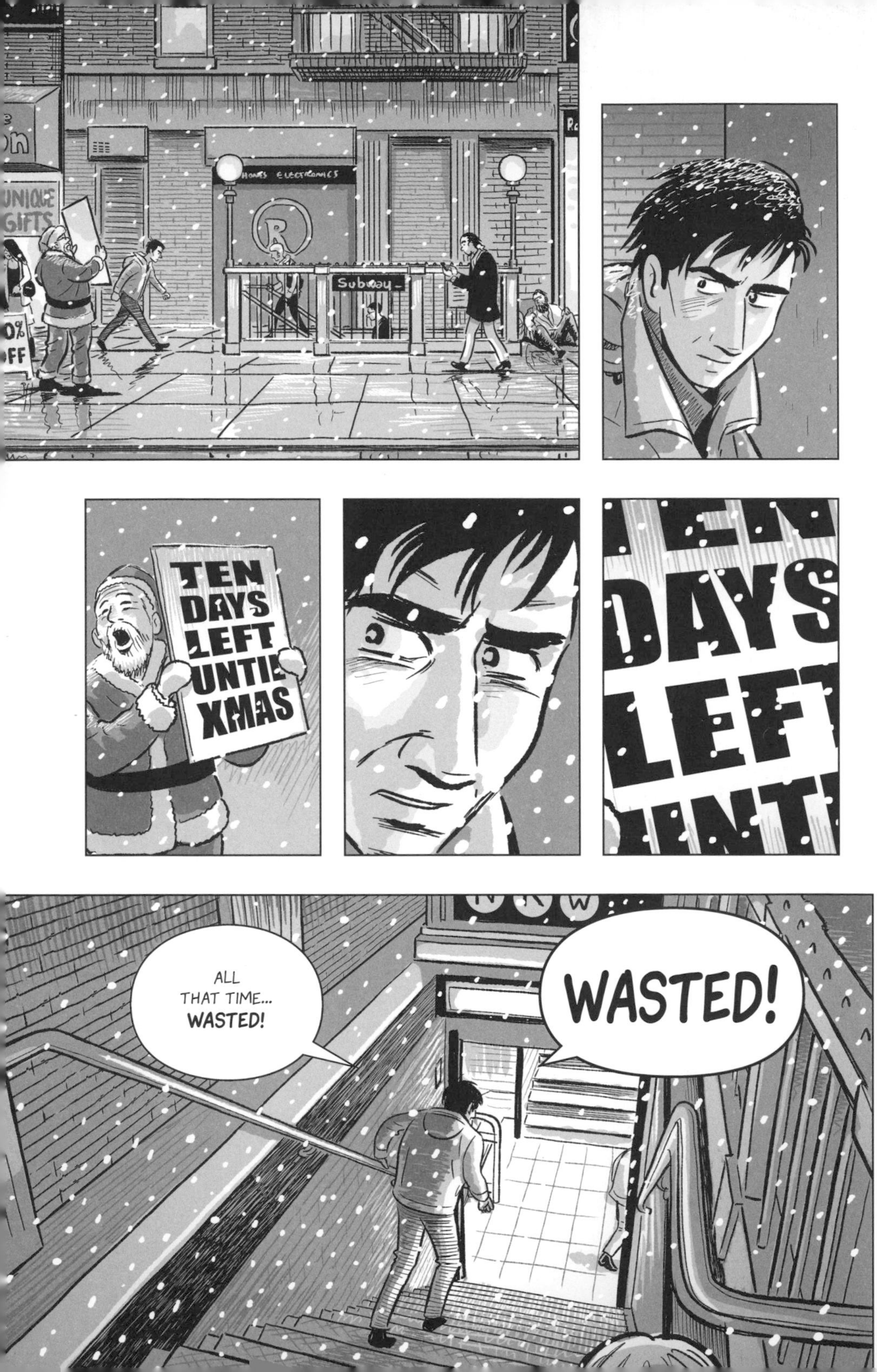
UNIQUE GIFTS
PHONES ELECTRONICS
Subway
TEN DAYS LEFT UNTIL XMAS
ALL THAT TIME... WASTED!
WASTED!

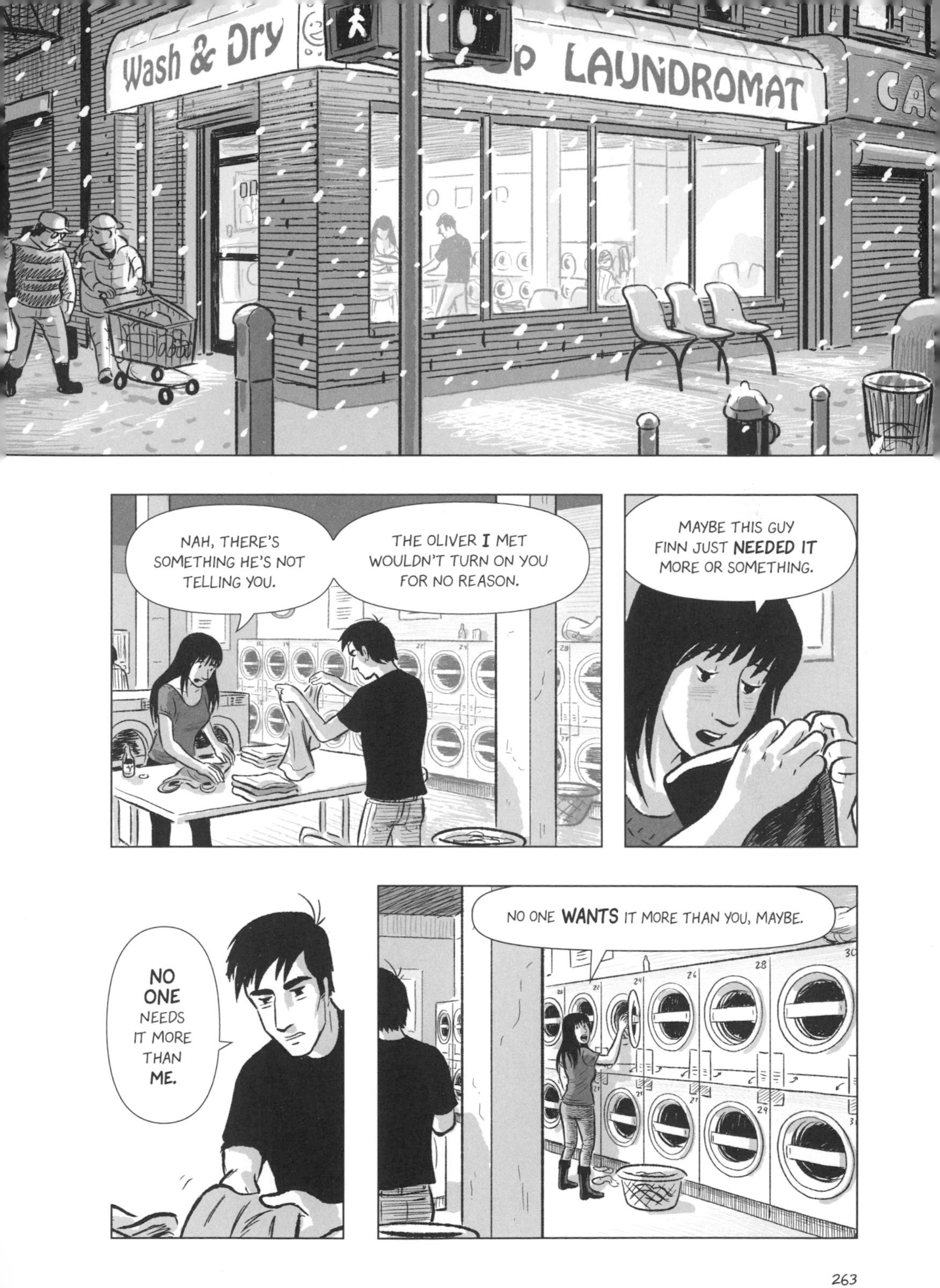
Wash & Dry
LAUNDROMAT
NAH, THERE'S SOMETHING HE'S NOT TELLING YOU.
THE OLIVER **I** MET WOULDN'T TURN ON YOU FOR NO REASON.
MAYBE THIS GUY FINN JUST **NEEDED IT** MORE OR SOMETHING.
NO ONE NEEDS IT MORE THAN **ME.**
NO ONE **WANTS** IT MORE THAN YOU, MAYBE.

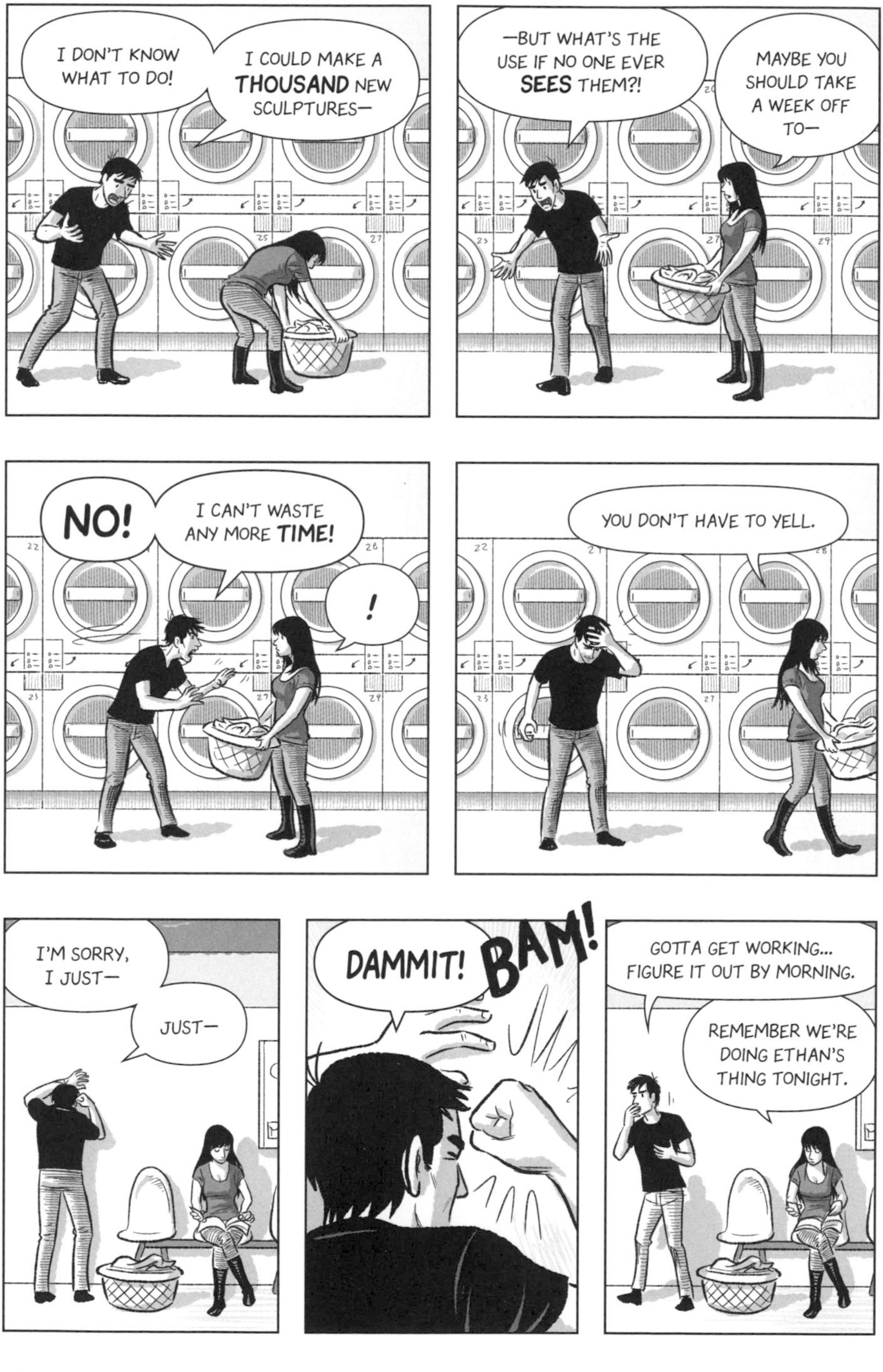
I DON'T KNOW WHAT TO DO!
I COULD MAKE A **THOUSAND** NEW SCULPTURES—
—BUT WHAT'S THE USE IF NO ONE EVER **SEES** THEM?!
MAYBE YOU SHOULD TAKE A WEEK OFF TO—
NO!
I CAN'T WASTE ANY MORE **TIME**!
!
YOU DON'T HAVE TO YELL.
I'M SORRY, I JUST—
JUST—
DAMMIT!
BAM!
GOTTA GET WORKING... FIGURE IT OUT BY MORNING.
REMEMBER WE'RE DOING ETHAN'S THING TONIGHT.

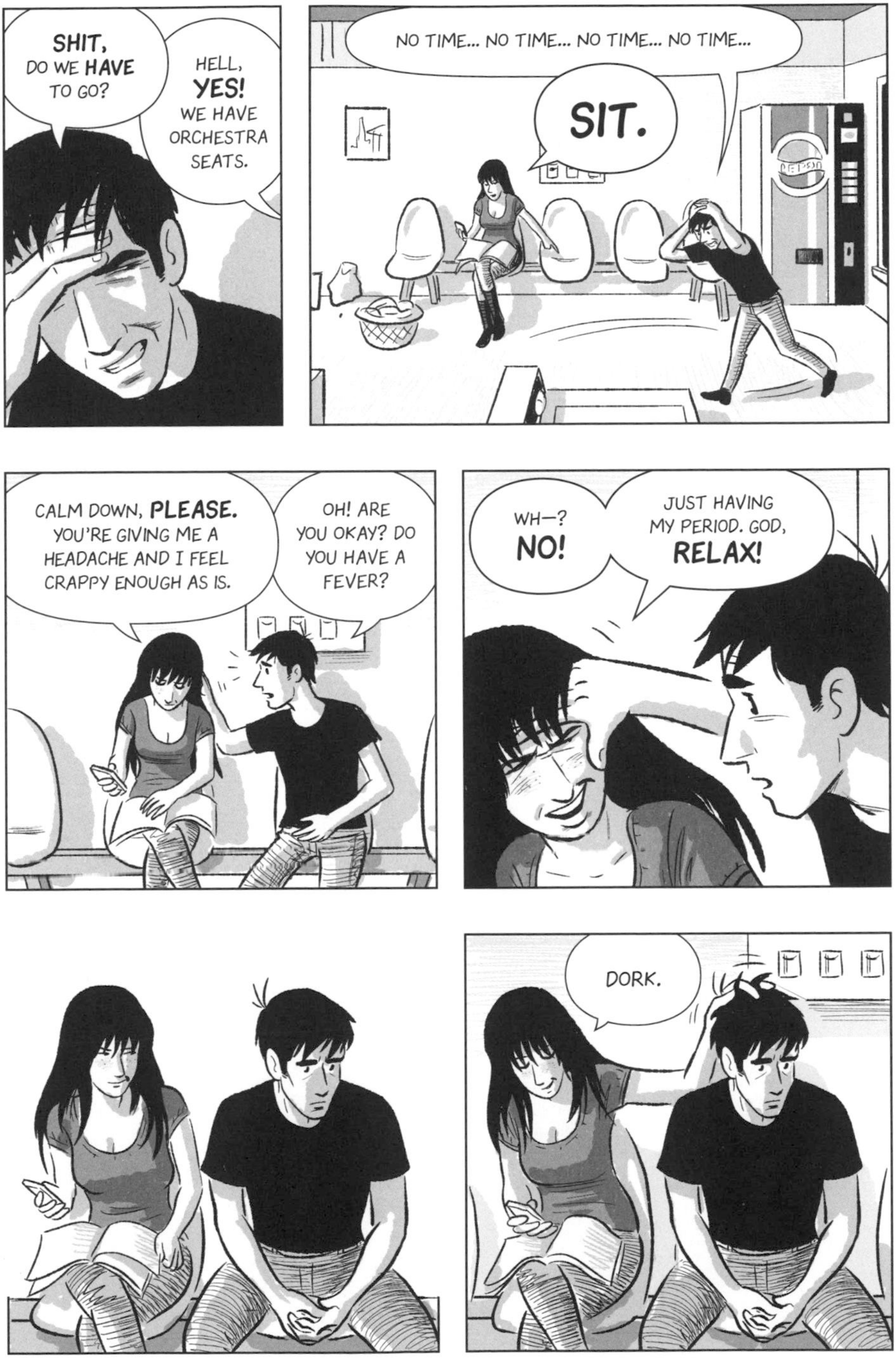
SHIT, DO WE HAVE TO GO?
HELL, YES! WE HAVE ORCHESTRA SEATS.
NO TIME... NO TIME... NO TIME... NO TIME...
SIT.
CALM DOWN, PLEASE. YOU'RE GIVING ME A HEADACHE AND I FEEL CRAPPY ENOUGH AS IS.
OH! ARE YOU OKAY? DO YOU HAVE A FEVER?
WH—? NO!
JUST HAVING MY PERIOD. GOD, RELAX!
DORK.

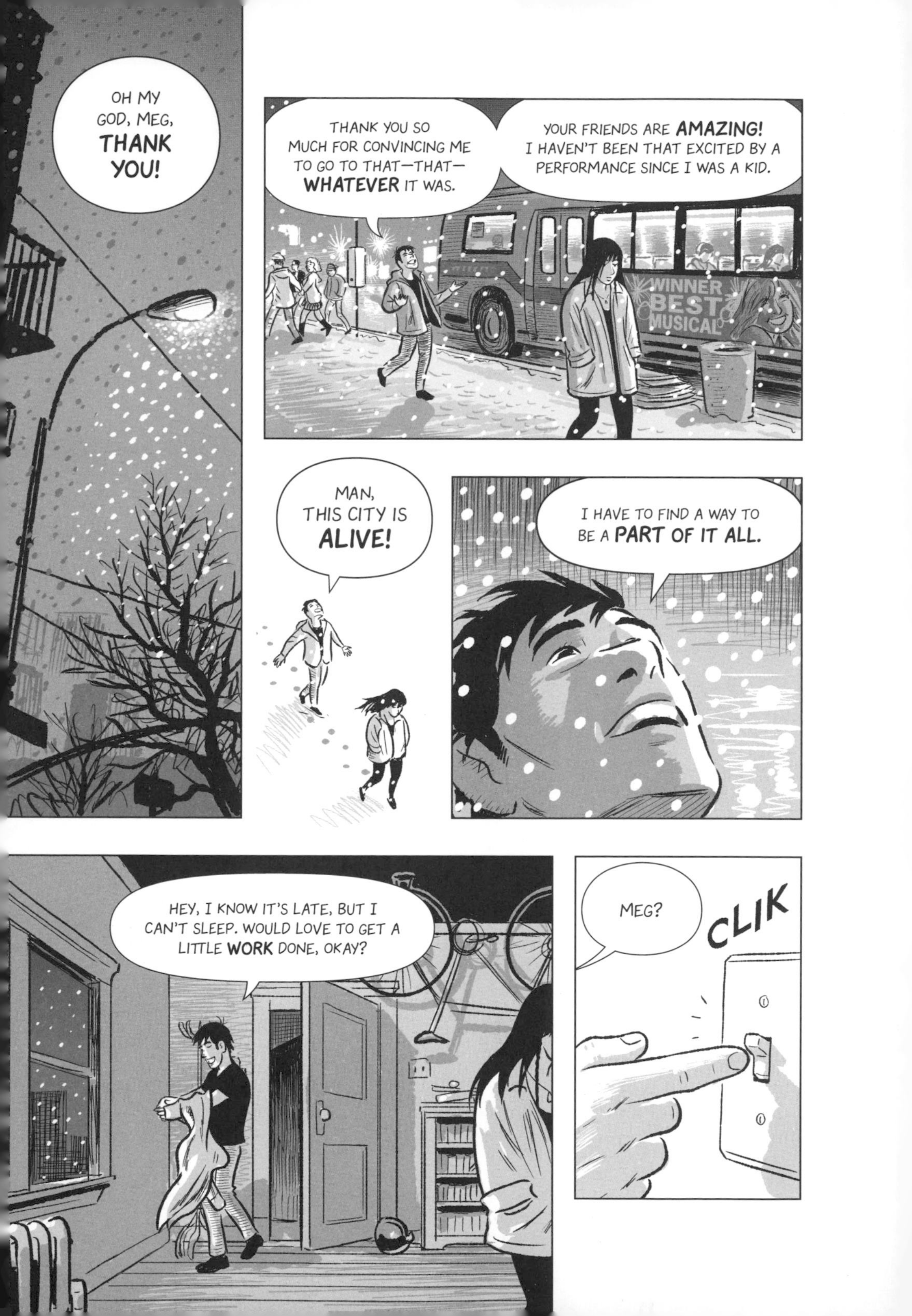
OH MY GOD, MEG, **THANK YOU!**
THANK YOU SO MUCH FOR CONVINCING ME TO GO TO THAT—THAT—**WHATEVER** IT WAS.
YOUR FRIENDS ARE **AMAZING!** I HAVEN'T BEEN THAT EXCITED BY A PERFORMANCE SINCE I WAS A KID.
WINNER BEST MUSICAL
MAN, THIS CITY IS **ALIVE!**
I HAVE TO FIND A WAY TO BE A **PART OF IT ALL.**
HEY, I KNOW IT'S LATE, BUT I CAN'T SLEEP. WOULD LOVE TO GET A LITTLE **WORK** DONE, OKAY?
MEG?
CLIK

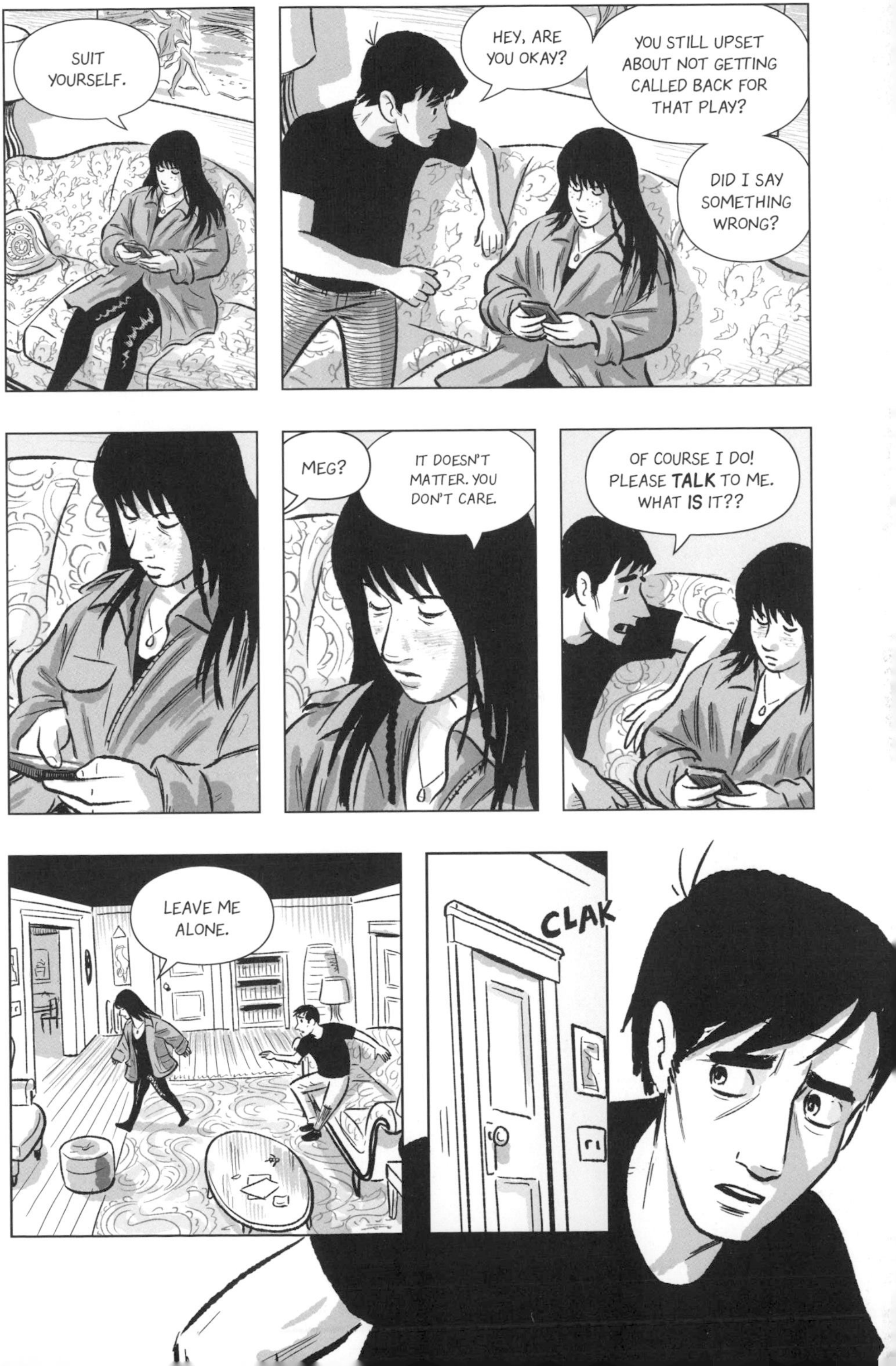
SUIT YOURSELF.
HEY, ARE YOU OKAY?
YOU STILL UPSET ABOUT NOT GETTING CALLED BACK FOR THAT PLAY?
DID I SAY SOMETHING WRONG?
MEG?
IT DOESN'T MATTER. YOU DON'T CARE.
OF COURSE I DO! PLEASE **TALK** TO ME. WHAT **IS** IT??
LEAVE ME ALONE.
CLAK

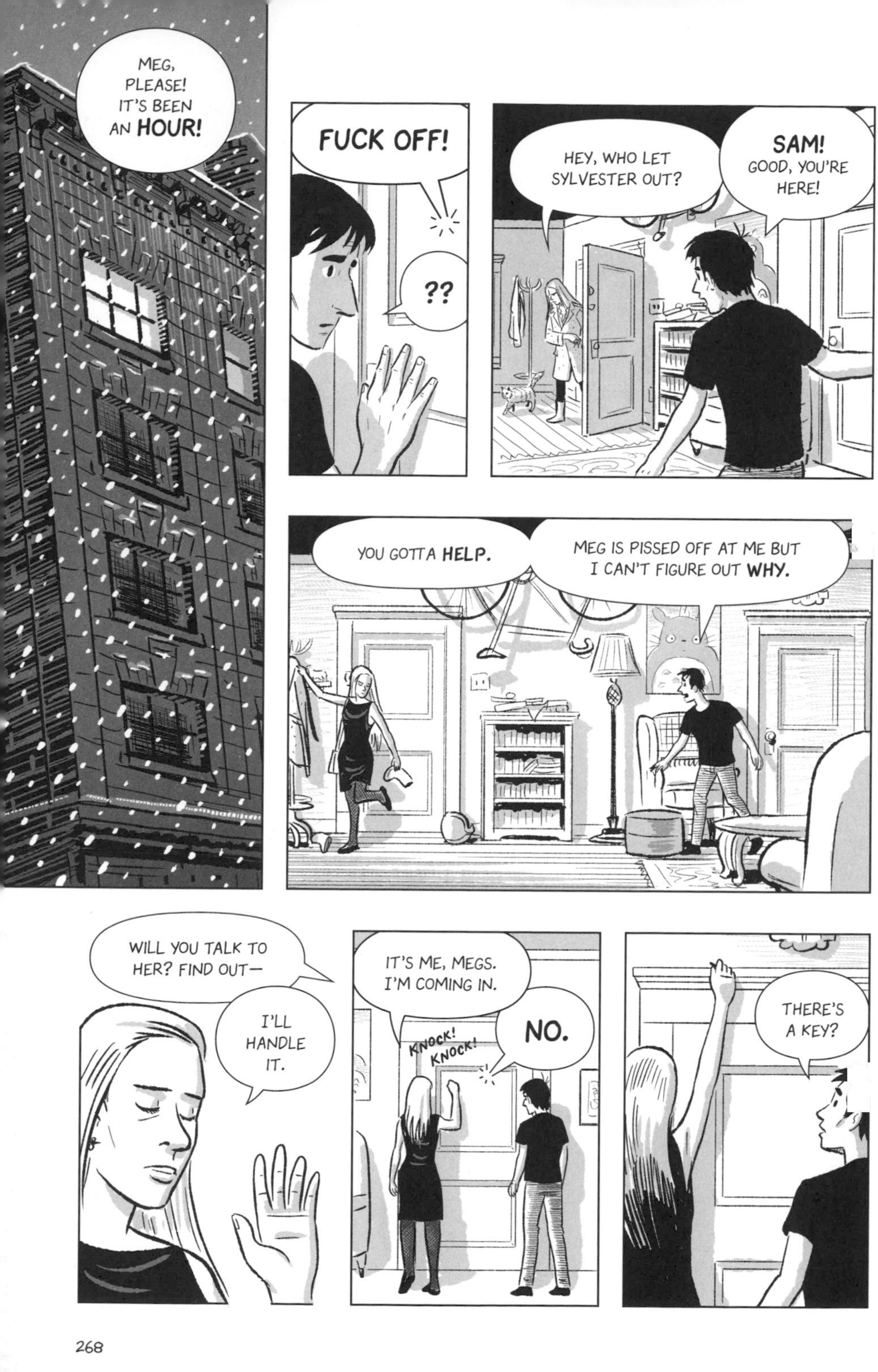
MEG, PLEASE! IT'S BEEN AN HOUR!
FUCK OFF!
??
HEY, WHO LET SYLVESTER OUT?
SAM! GOOD, YOU'RE HERE!
YOU GOTTA HELP.
MEG IS PISSED OFF AT ME BUT I CAN'T FIGURE OUT WHY.
WILL YOU TALK TO HER? FIND OUT—
I'LL HANDLE IT.
IT'S ME, MEGS. I'M COMING IN.
KNOCK! KNOCK!
NO.
THERE'S A KEY?

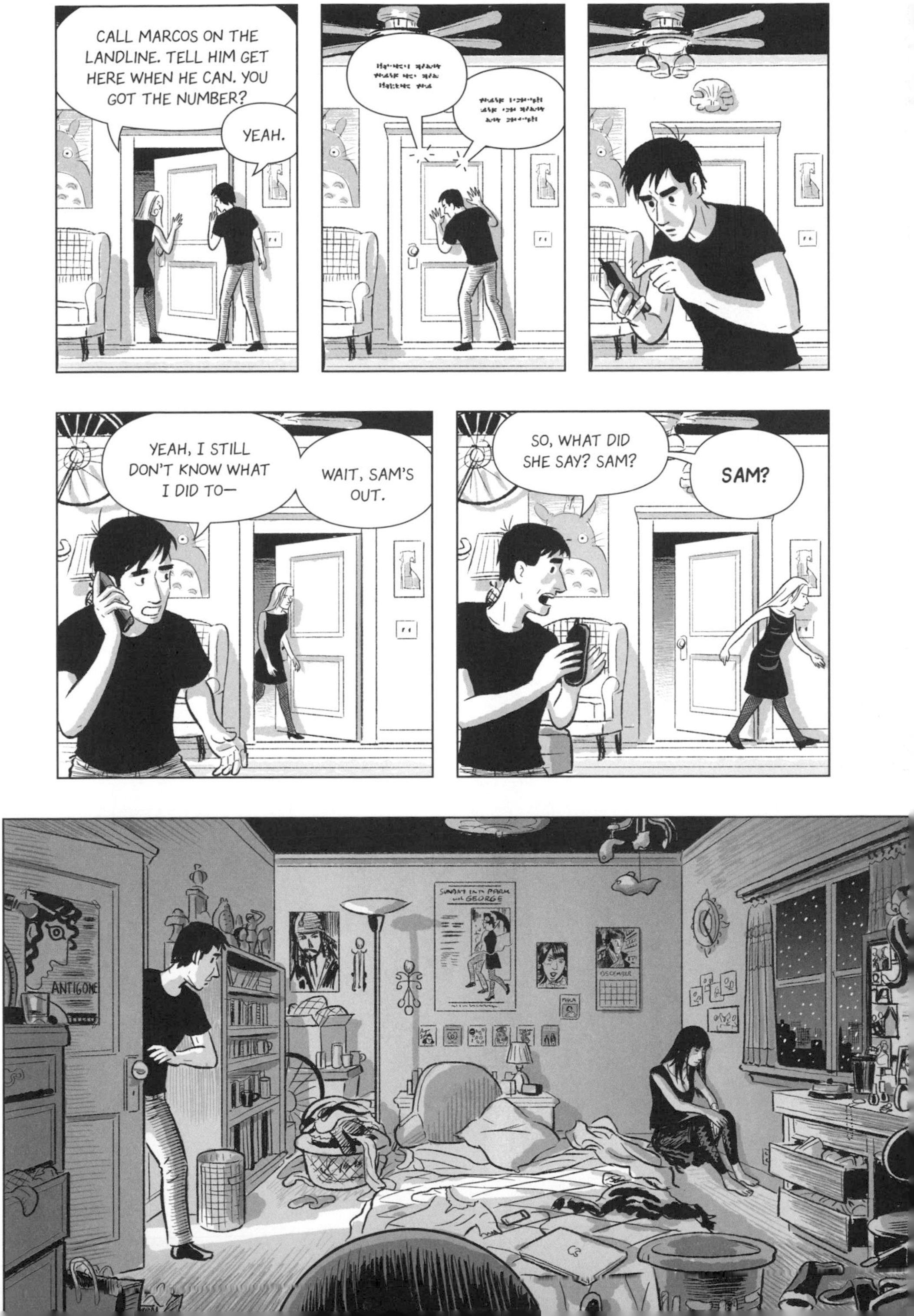
CALL MARCOS ON THE LANDLINE. TELL HIM GET HERE WHEN HE CAN. YOU GOT THE NUMBER?
YEAH.
YEAH, I STILL DON'T KNOW WHAT I DID TO—
WAIT, SAM'S OUT.
SO, WHAT DID SHE SAY? SAM?
SAM?
ANTIGONE
DECEMBER

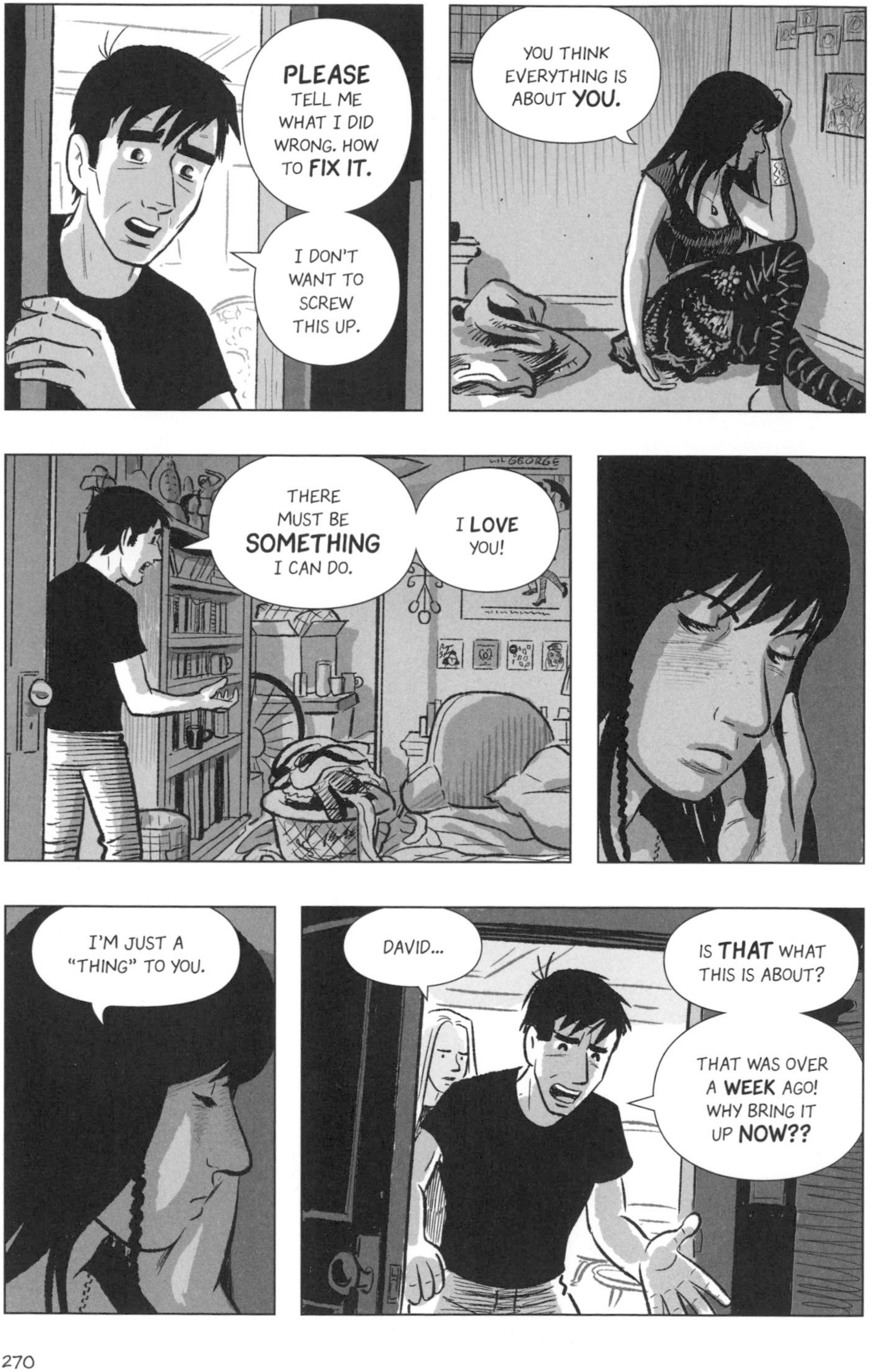
PLEASE TELL ME WHAT I DID WRONG. HOW TO FIX IT.
I DON'T WANT TO SCREW THIS UP.
YOU THINK EVERYTHING IS ABOUT YOU.
THERE MUST BE SOMETHING I CAN DO.
I LOVE YOU!
I'M JUST A "THING" TO YOU.
DAVID...
IS THAT WHAT THIS IS ABOUT?
THAT WAS OVER A WEEK AGO! WHY BRING IT UP NOW??

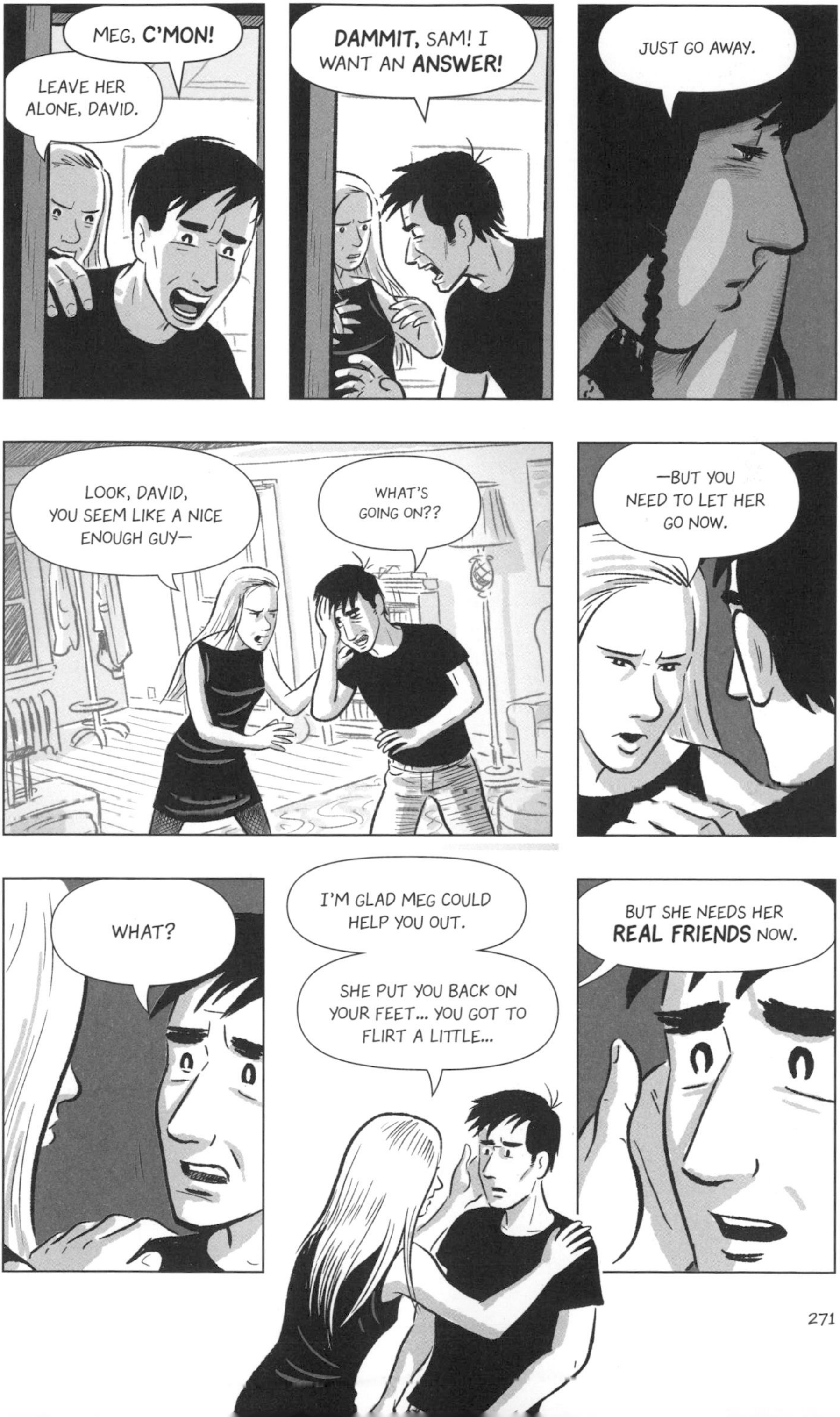
MEG, C'MON!
LEAVE HER ALONE, DAVID.
DAMMIT, SAM! I WANT AN ANSWER!
JUST GO AWAY.
LOOK, DAVID, YOU SEEM LIKE A NICE ENOUGH GUY—
WHAT'S GOING ON??
—BUT YOU NEED TO LET HER GO NOW.
WHAT?
I'M GLAD MEG COULD HELP YOU OUT.
SHE PUT YOU BACK ON YOUR FEET... YOU GOT TO FLIRT A LITTLE...
BUT SHE NEEDS HER REAL FRIENDS NOW.

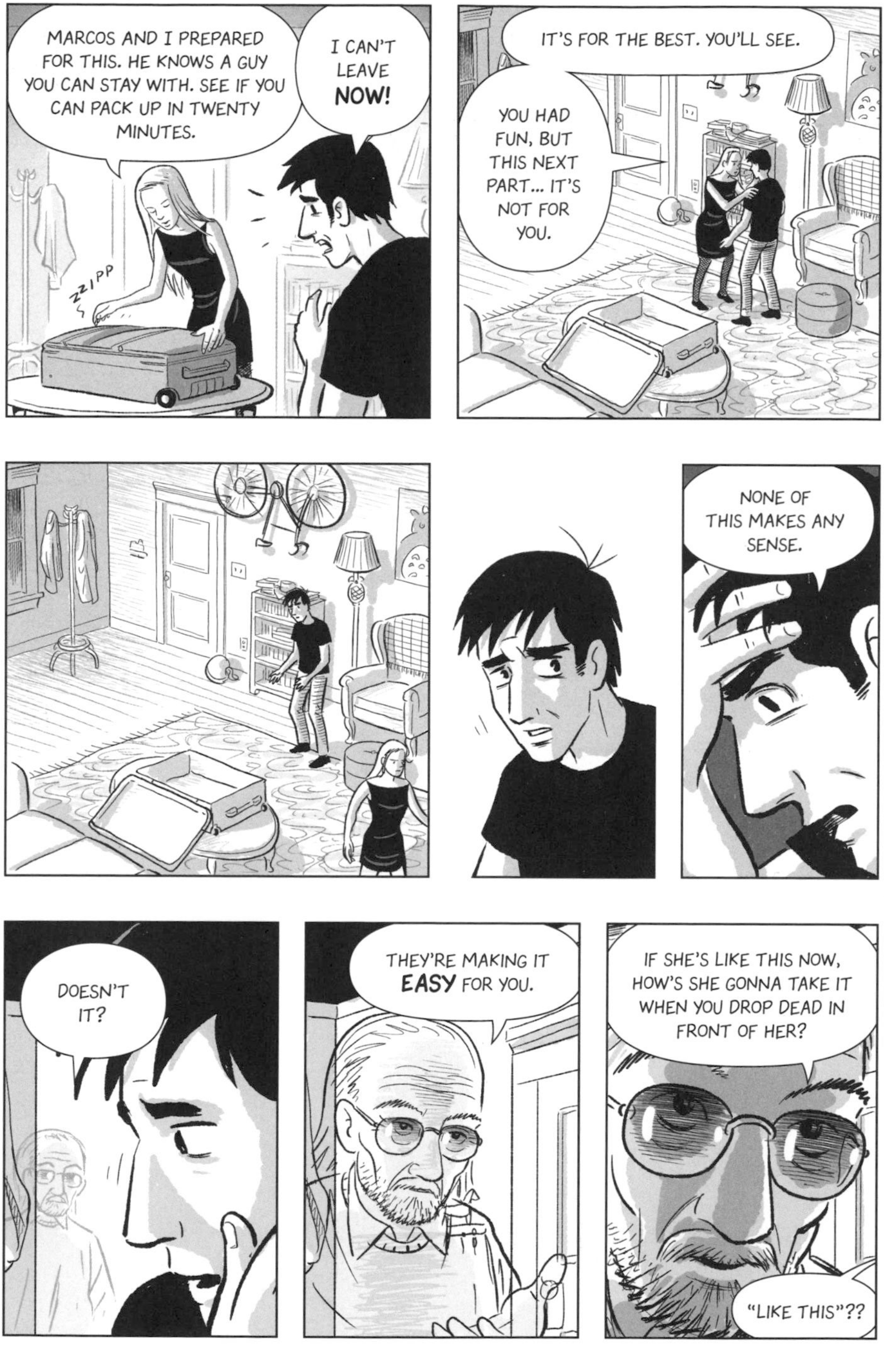
MARCOS AND I PREPARED FOR THIS. HE KNOWS A GUY YOU CAN STAY WITH. SEE IF YOU CAN PACK UP IN TWENTY MINUTES.
I CAN'T LEAVE **NOW!**
ZZIPP
IT'S FOR THE BEST. YOU'LL SEE.
YOU HAD FUN, BUT THIS NEXT PART... IT'S NOT FOR YOU.
NONE OF THIS MAKES ANY SENSE.
DOESN'T IT?
THEY'RE MAKING IT **EASY** FOR YOU.
IF SHE'S LIKE THIS NOW, HOW'S SHE GONNA TAKE IT WHEN YOU DROP DEAD IN FRONT OF HER?
"LIKE THIS"??

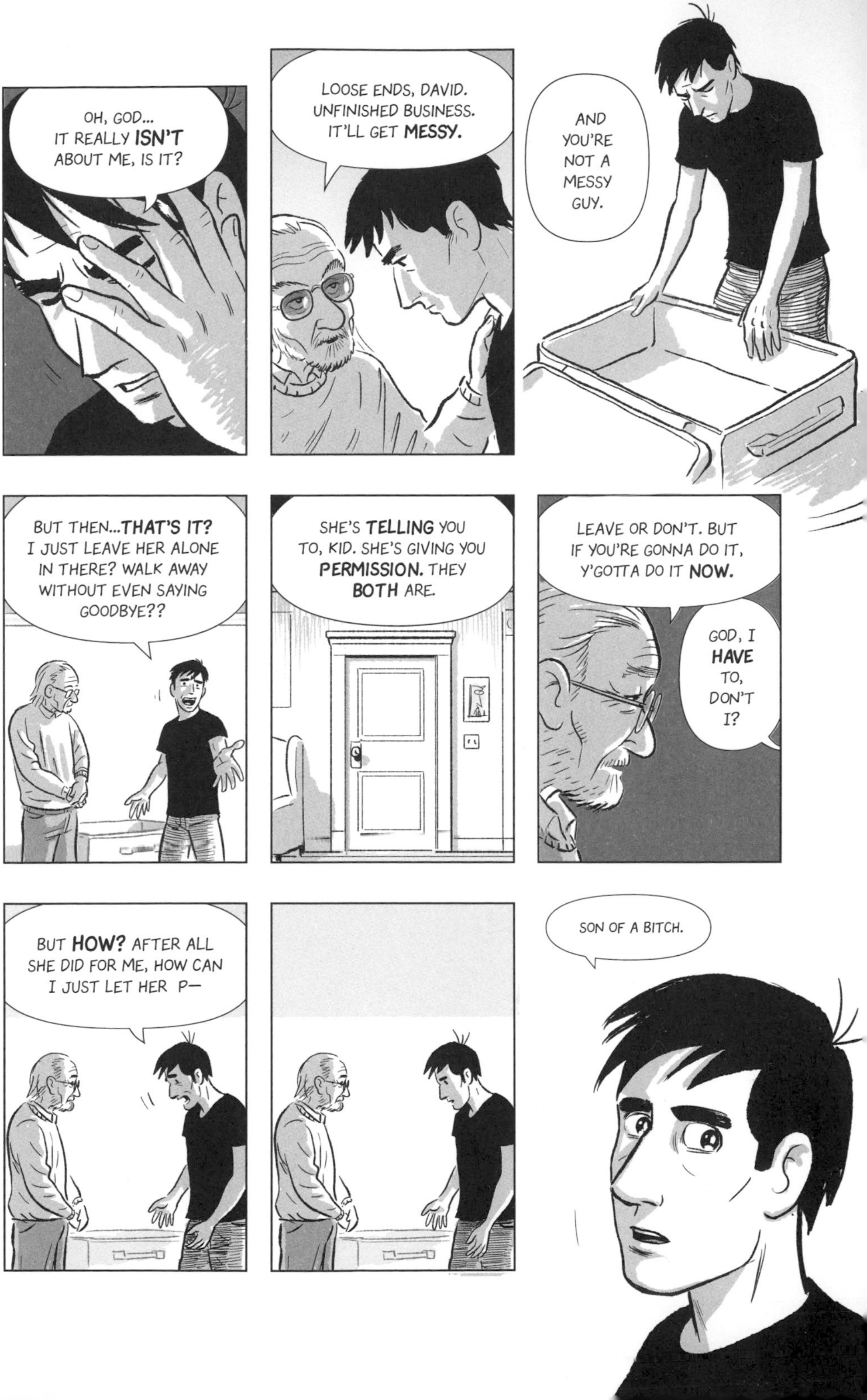
OH, GOD... IT REALLY ISN'T ABOUT ME, IS IT?
LOOSE ENDS, DAVID. UNFINISHED BUSINESS. IT'LL GET MESSY.
AND YOU'RE NOT A MESSY GUY.
BUT THEN...THAT'S IT? I JUST LEAVE HER ALONE IN THERE? WALK AWAY WITHOUT EVEN SAYING GOODBYE??
SHE'S TELLING YOU TO, KID. SHE'S GIVING YOU PERMISSION. THEY BOTH ARE.
LEAVE OR DON'T. BUT IF YOU'RE GONNA DO IT, Y'GOTTA DO IT NOW.
GOD, I HAVE TO, DON'T I?
BUT HOW? AFTER ALL SHE DID FOR ME, HOW CAN I JUST LET HER P—
SON OF A BITCH.

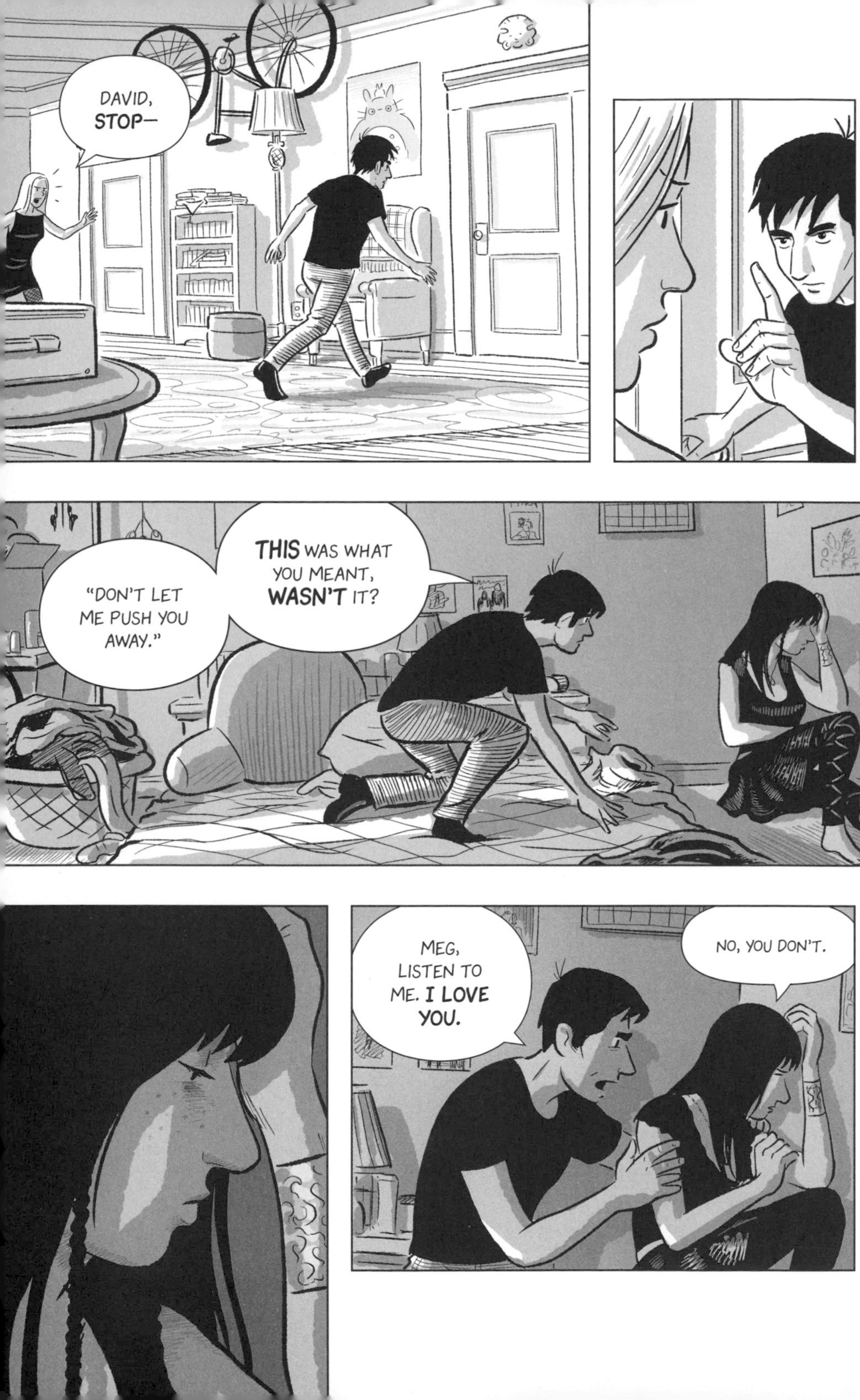
DAVID, **STOP—**
“DON’T LET ME PUSH YOU AWAY.”
THIS WAS WHAT YOU MEANT, **WASN’T** IT?
MEG, LISTEN TO ME. **I LOVE YOU.**
NO, YOU DON’T.

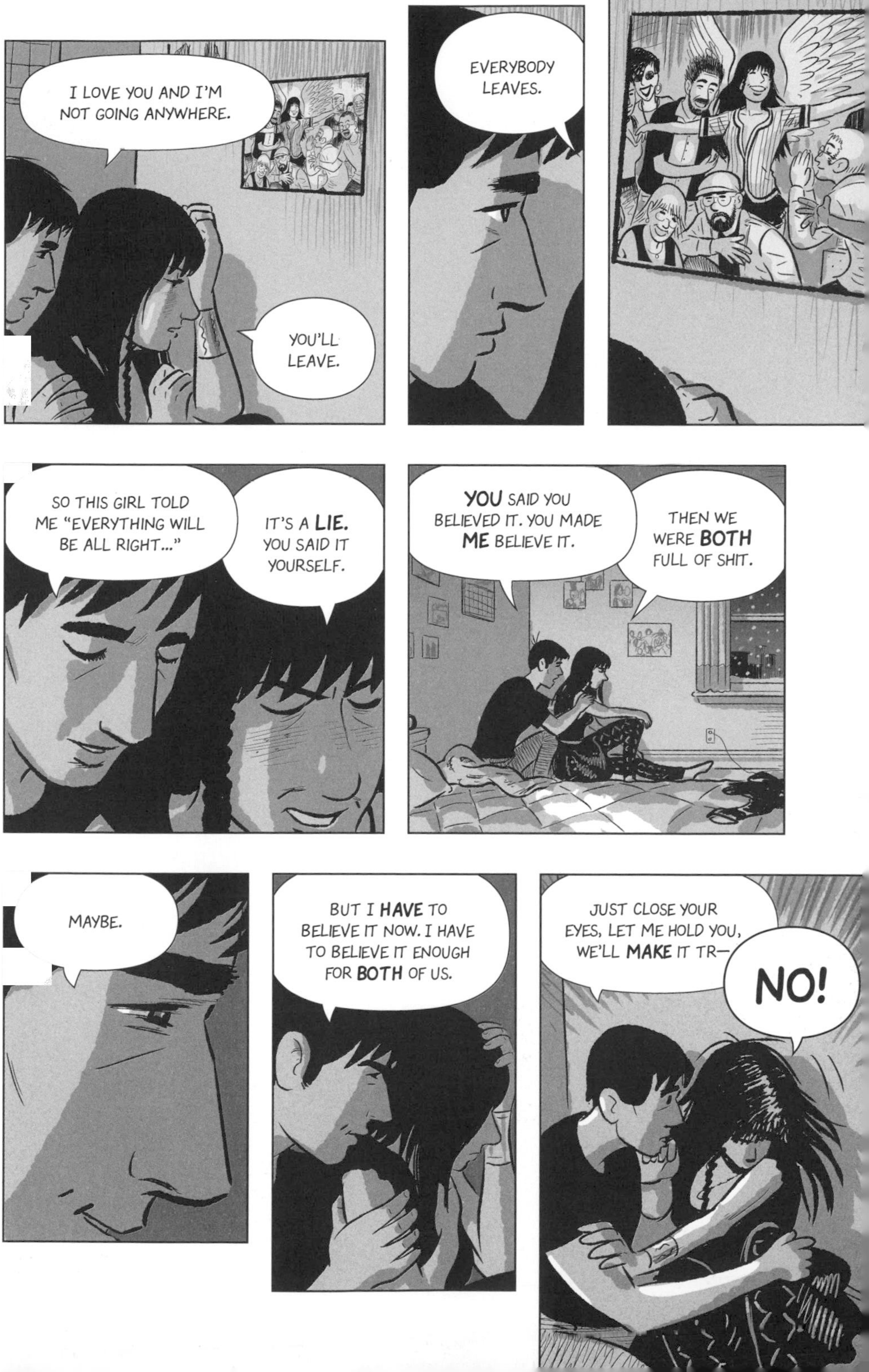
I LOVE YOU AND I'M NOT GOING ANYWHERE.
YOU'LL LEAVE.
EVERYBODY LEAVES.
SO THIS GIRL TOLD ME "EVERYTHING WILL BE ALL RIGHT..."
IT'S A **LIE.** YOU SAID IT YOURSELF.
YOU SAID YOU BELIEVED IT. YOU MADE **ME** BELIEVE IT.
THEN WE WERE **BOTH** FULL OF SHIT.
MAYBE.
BUT I **HAVE** TO BELIEVE IT NOW. I HAVE TO BELIEVE IT ENOUGH FOR **BOTH** OF US.
JUST CLOSE YOUR EYES, LET ME HOLD YOU, WE'LL **MAKE** IT TR—
NO!

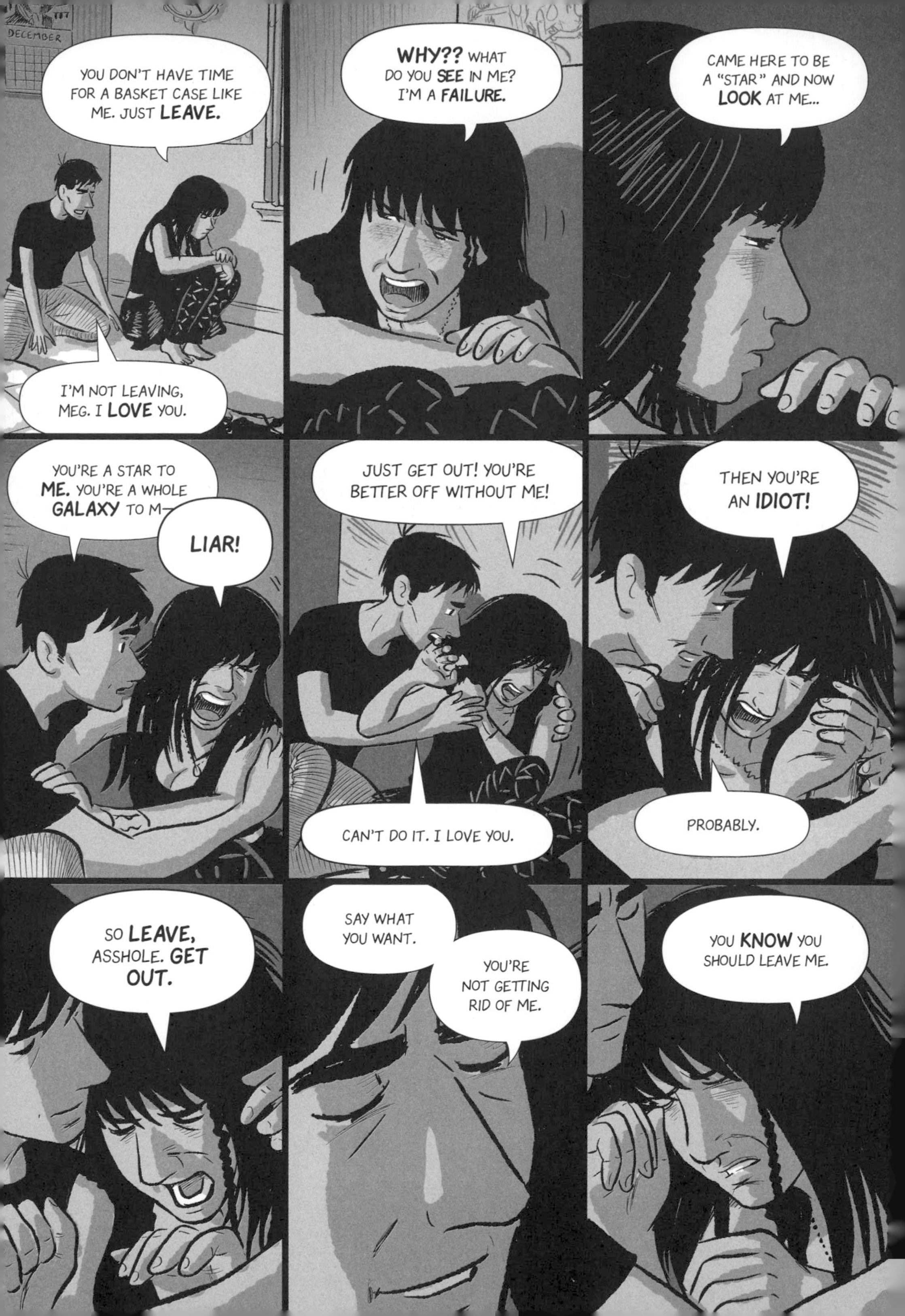
YOU DON'T HAVE TIME FOR A BASKET CASE LIKE ME. JUST **LEAVE.**
I'M NOT LEAVING, MEG. I **LOVE** YOU.
WHY?? WHAT DO YOU **SEE** IN ME? I'M A **FAILURE.**
CAME HERE TO BE A "STAR" AND NOW **LOOK** AT ME...
YOU'RE A STAR TO **ME.** YOU'RE A WHOLE **GALAXY** TO M—
LIAR!
JUST GET OUT! YOU'RE BETTER OFF WITHOUT ME!
CAN'T DO IT. I LOVE YOU.
THEN YOU'RE AN **IDIOT!**
PROBABLY.
SO **LEAVE,** ASSHOLE. **GET OUT.**
SAY WHAT YOU WANT.
YOU'RE NOT GETTING RID OF ME.
YOU **KNOW** YOU SHOULD LEAVE ME.

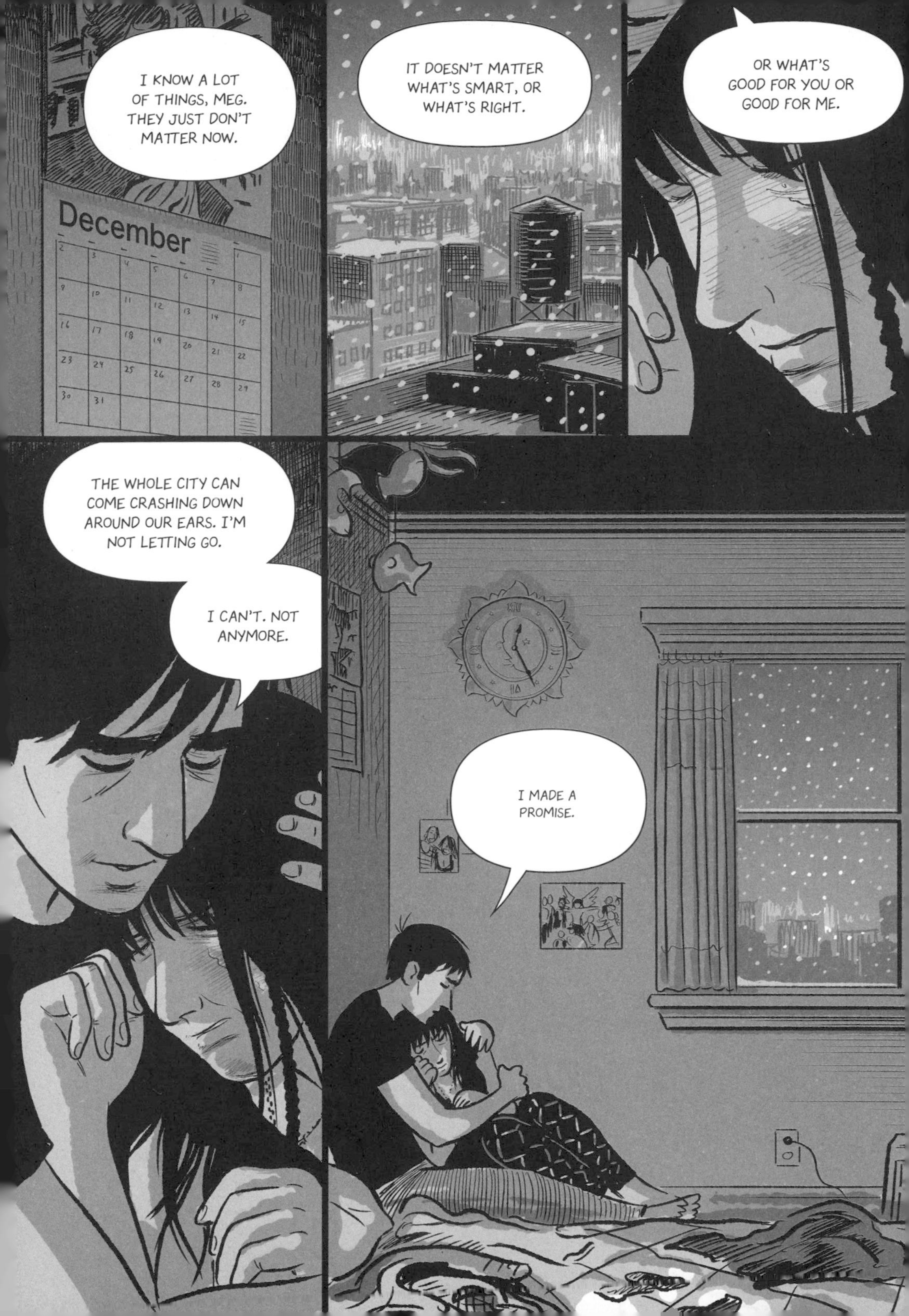
I KNOW A LOT OF THINGS, MEG. THEY JUST DON'T MATTER NOW.
December
IT DOESN'T MATTER WHAT'S SMART, OR WHAT'S RIGHT.
OR WHAT'S GOOD FOR YOU OR GOOD FOR ME.
THE WHOLE CITY CAN COME CRASHING DOWN AROUND OUR EARS. I'M NOT LETTING GO.
I CAN'T. NOT ANYMORE.
I MADE A PROMISE.

4.

DEADLINE

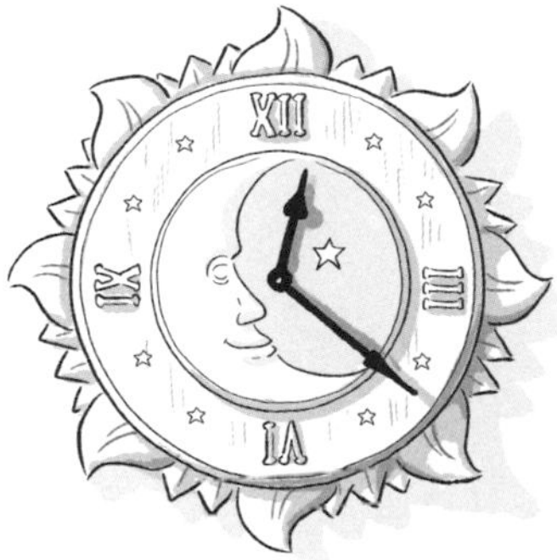
XII
III
VI
IX

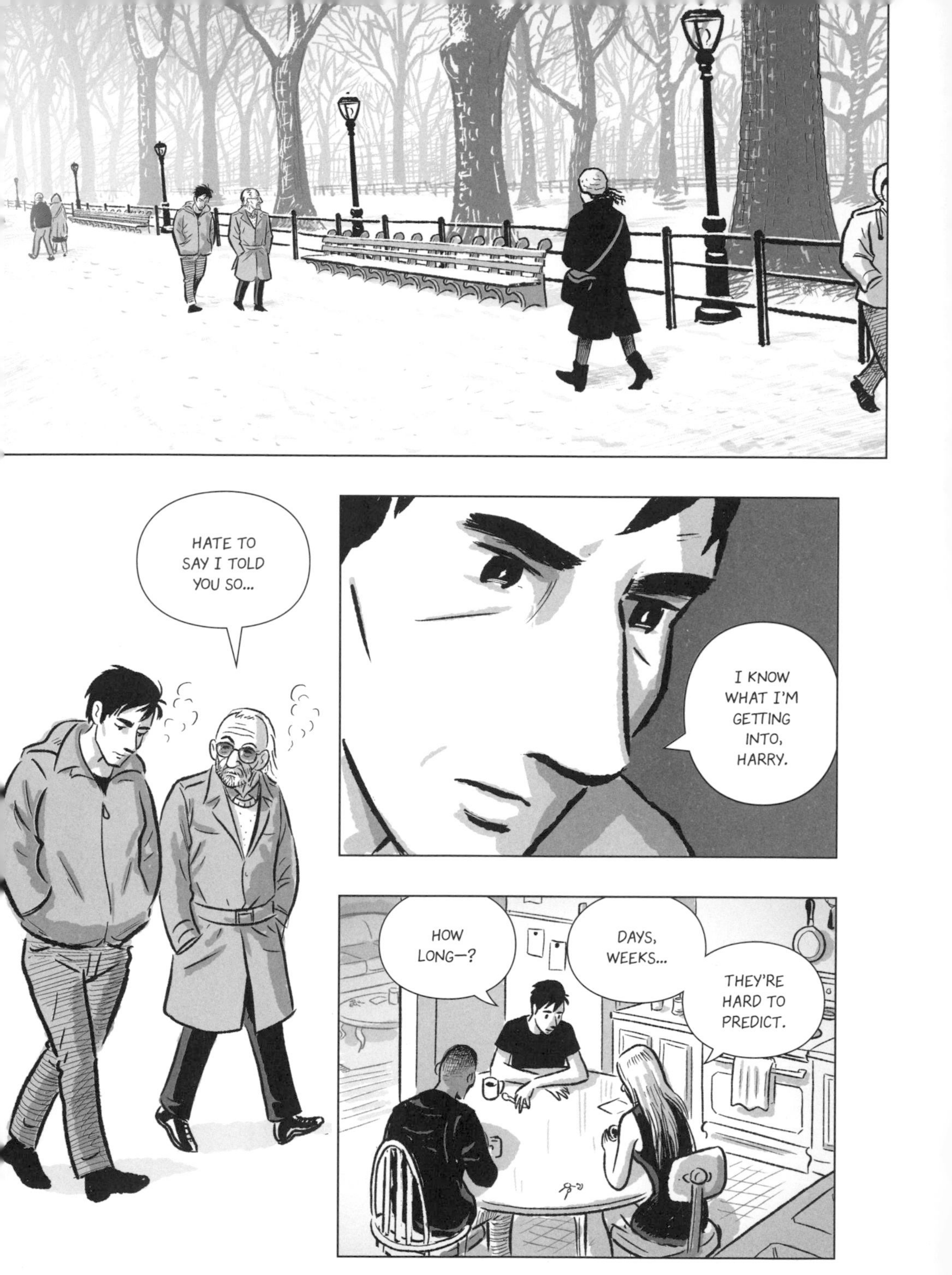
HATE TO SAY I TOLD YOU SO...
I KNOW WHAT I'M GETTING INTO, HARRY.
HOW LONG—?
DAYS, WEEKS...
THEY'RE HARD TO PREDICT.

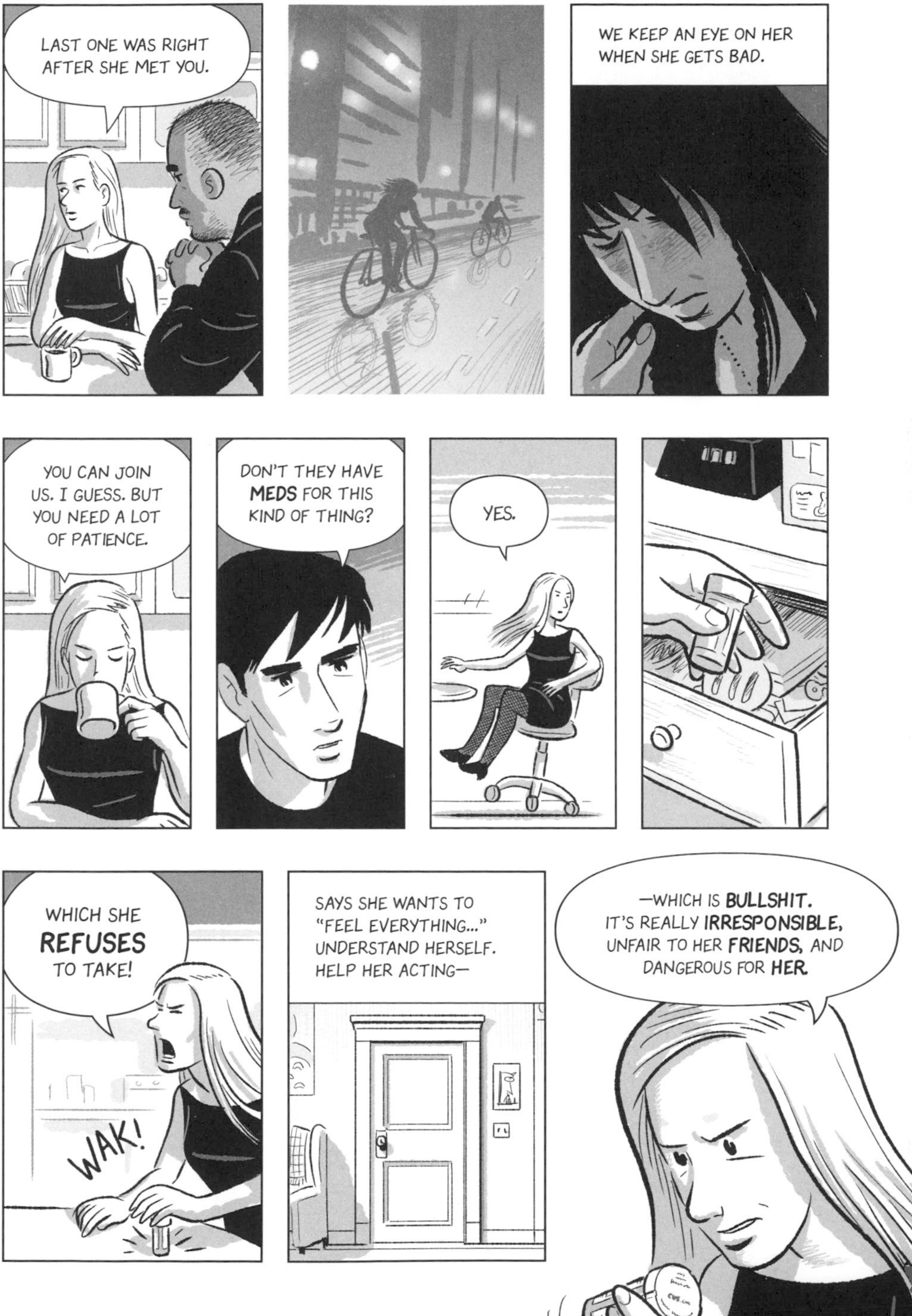
LAST ONE WAS RIGHT AFTER SHE MET YOU.
WE KEEP AN EYE ON HER WHEN SHE GETS BAD.
YOU CAN JOIN US. I GUESS. BUT YOU NEED A LOT OF PATIENCE.
DON'T THEY HAVE **MEDS** FOR THIS KIND OF THING?
YES.
WHICH SHE **REFUSES** TO TAKE!
WAK!
SAYS SHE WANTS TO "FEEL EVERYTHING..." UNDERSTAND HERSELF. HELP HER ACTING—
—WHICH IS **BULLSHIT.** IT'S REALLY **IRRESPONSIBLE,** UNFAIR TO HER **FRIENDS,** AND DANGEROUS FOR **HER.**

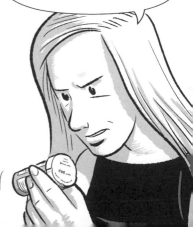

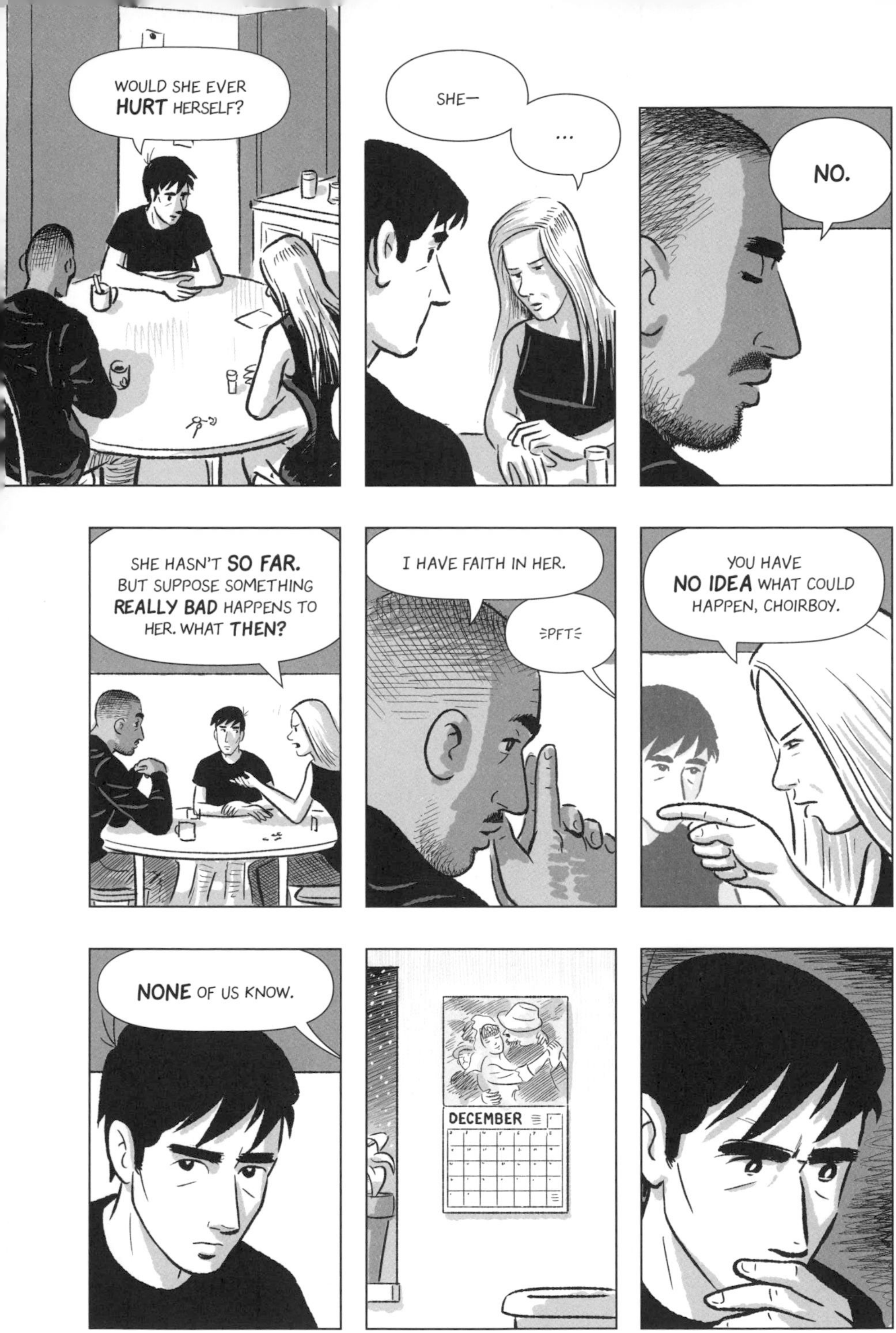
WOULD SHE EVER **HURT** HERSELF?
SHE—
...
NO.
SHE HASN'T **SO FAR.** BUT SUPPOSE SOMETHING **REALLY BAD** HAPPENS TO HER. WHAT **THEN?**
I HAVE FAITH IN HER.
PFT
YOU HAVE **NO IDEA** WHAT COULD HAPPEN, CHOIRBOY.
NONE OF US KNOW.
DECEMBER

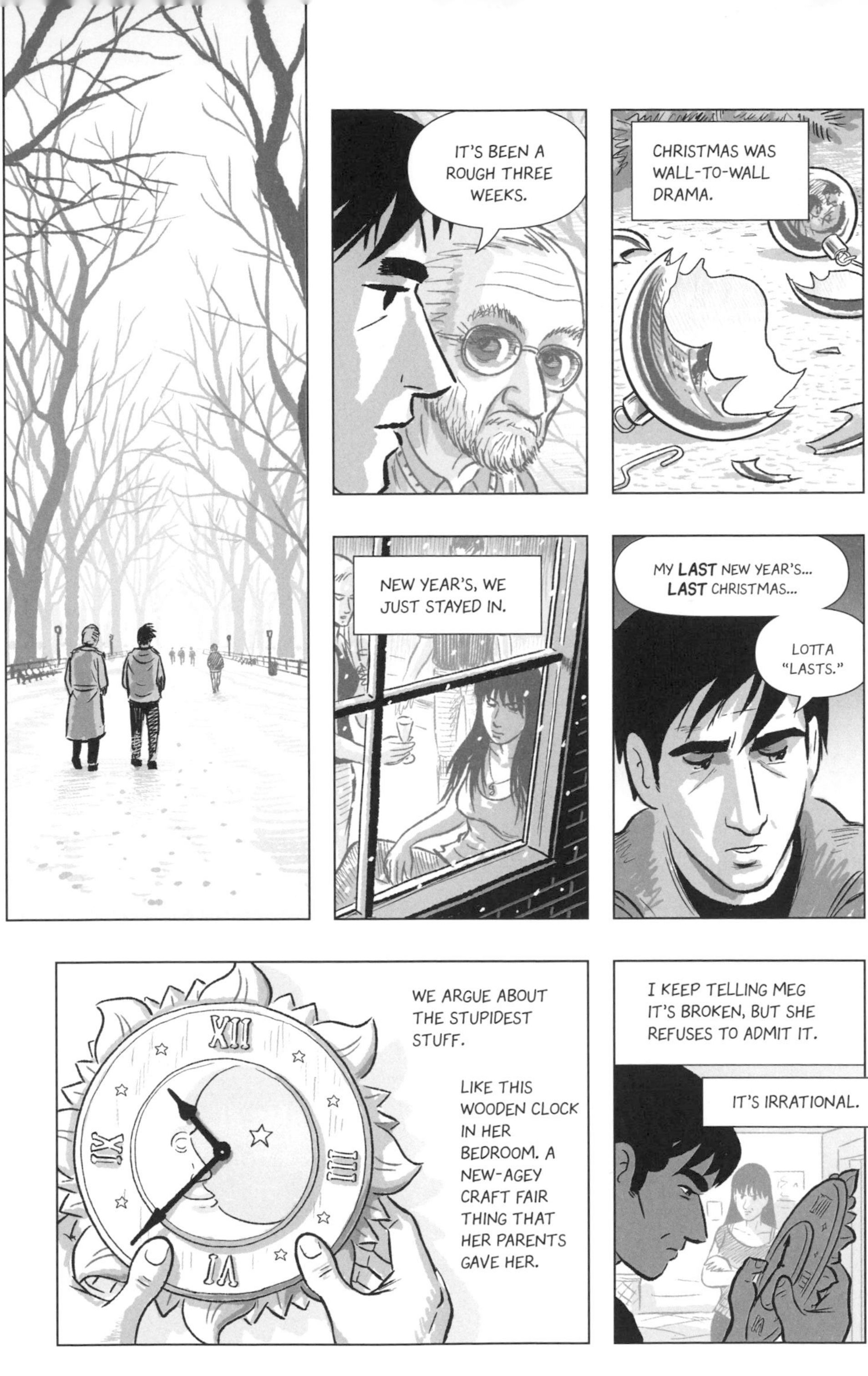

IT'S BEEN A ROUGH THREE WEEKS.
CHRISTMAS WAS WALL-TO-WALL DRAMA.
NEW YEAR'S, WE JUST STAYED IN.
MY **LAST** NEW YEAR'S... **LAST** CHRISTMAS...
LOTTA "LASTS."
WE ARGUE ABOUT THE STUPIDEST STUFF.
LIKE THIS WOODEN CLOCK IN HER BEDROOM. A NEW-AGEY CRAFT FAIR THING THAT HER PARENTS GAVE HER.
I KEEP TELLING MEG IT'S BROKEN, BUT SHE REFUSES TO ADMIT IT.
IT'S IRRATIONAL.

AND WORK...

WORK'S BEEN A **DISASTER.**

I KEEP STARTING NEW PIECES.

ABANDONING THEM...

SMASHING THEM...

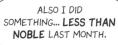

ALSO I DID SOMETHING... **LESS THAN NOBLE** LAST MONTH.

?

I'D OVERHEARD FINN BITCHING HOW HIS DAD THREATENED TO STOP SUBSIDIZING HIS ART "CAREER" IF THINGS DIDN'T GET SERIOUS; THEN SAYING ALL THESE SHITTY THINGS ABOUT OLLIE, CALLING HIM HIS "PET," MAKING FUN OF HIS CLOTHES...

DO NOT SIT ON ARTWORK

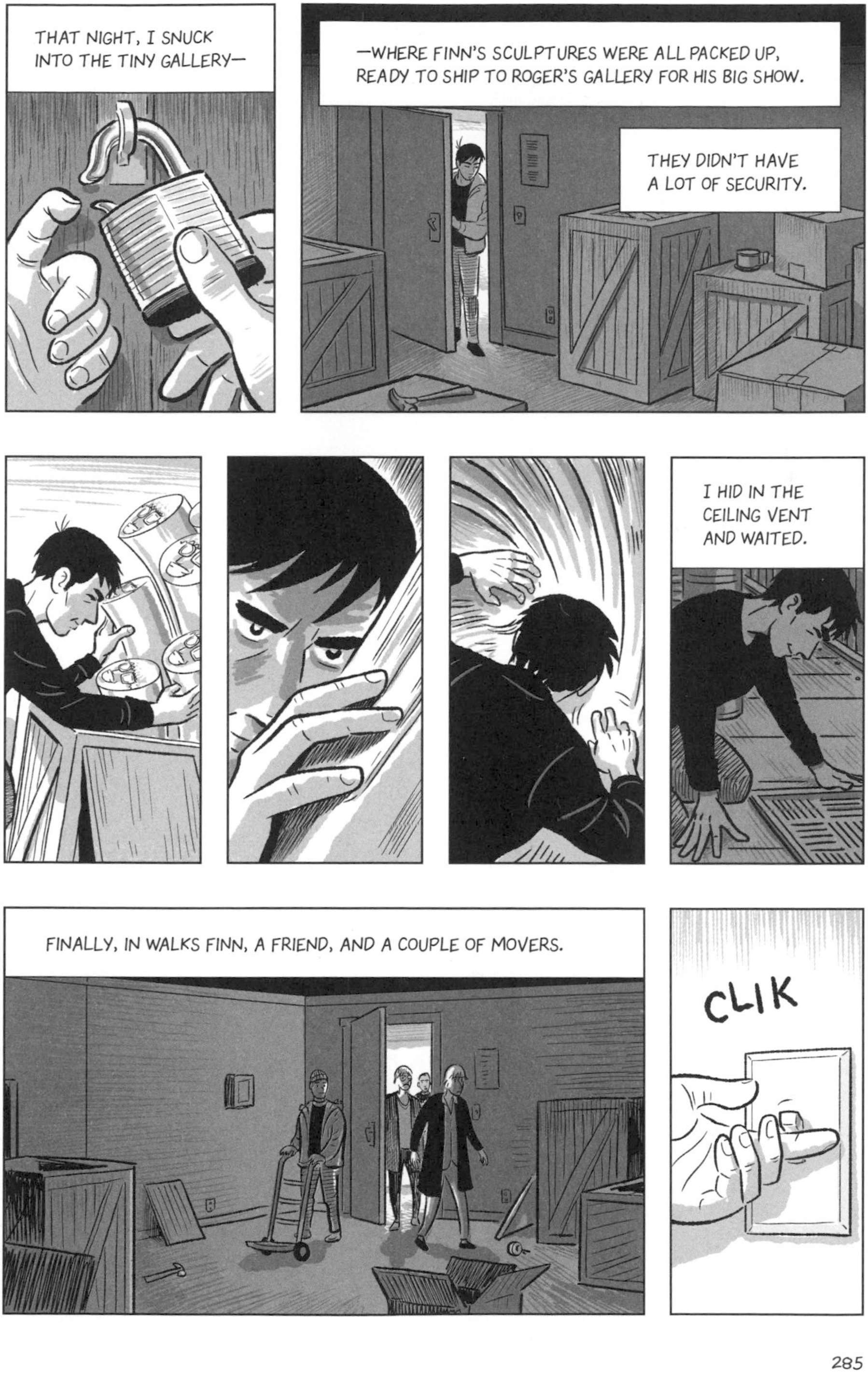
THAT NIGHT, I SNUCK INTO THE TINY GALLERY—
—WHERE FINN'S SCULPTURES WERE ALL PACKED UP, READY TO SHIP TO ROGER'S GALLERY FOR HIS BIG SHOW.
THEY DIDN'T HAVE A LOT OF SECURITY.
I HID IN THE CEILING VENT AND WAITED.
FINALLY, IN WALKS FINN, A FRIEND, AND A COUPLE OF MOVERS.
CLIK

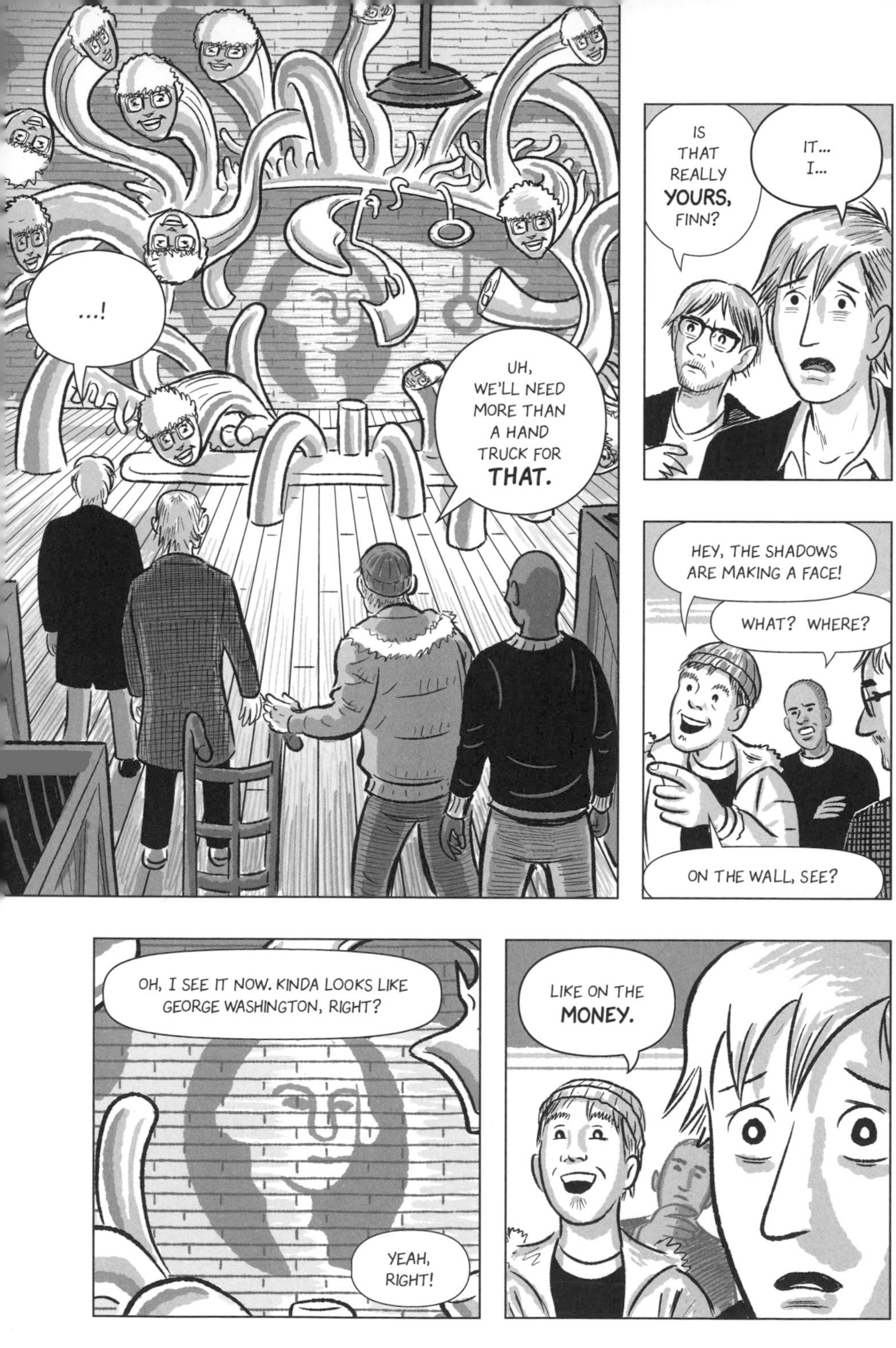
...!
UH, WE'LL NEED MORE THAN A HAND TRUCK FOR THAT.
IS THAT REALLY YOURS, FINN?
IT... I...
HEY, THE SHADOWS ARE MAKING A FACE!
WHAT? WHERE?
ON THE WALL, SEE?
OH, I SEE IT NOW. KINDA LOOKS LIKE GEORGE WASHINGTON, RIGHT?
YEAH, RIGHT!
LIKE ON THE MONEY.

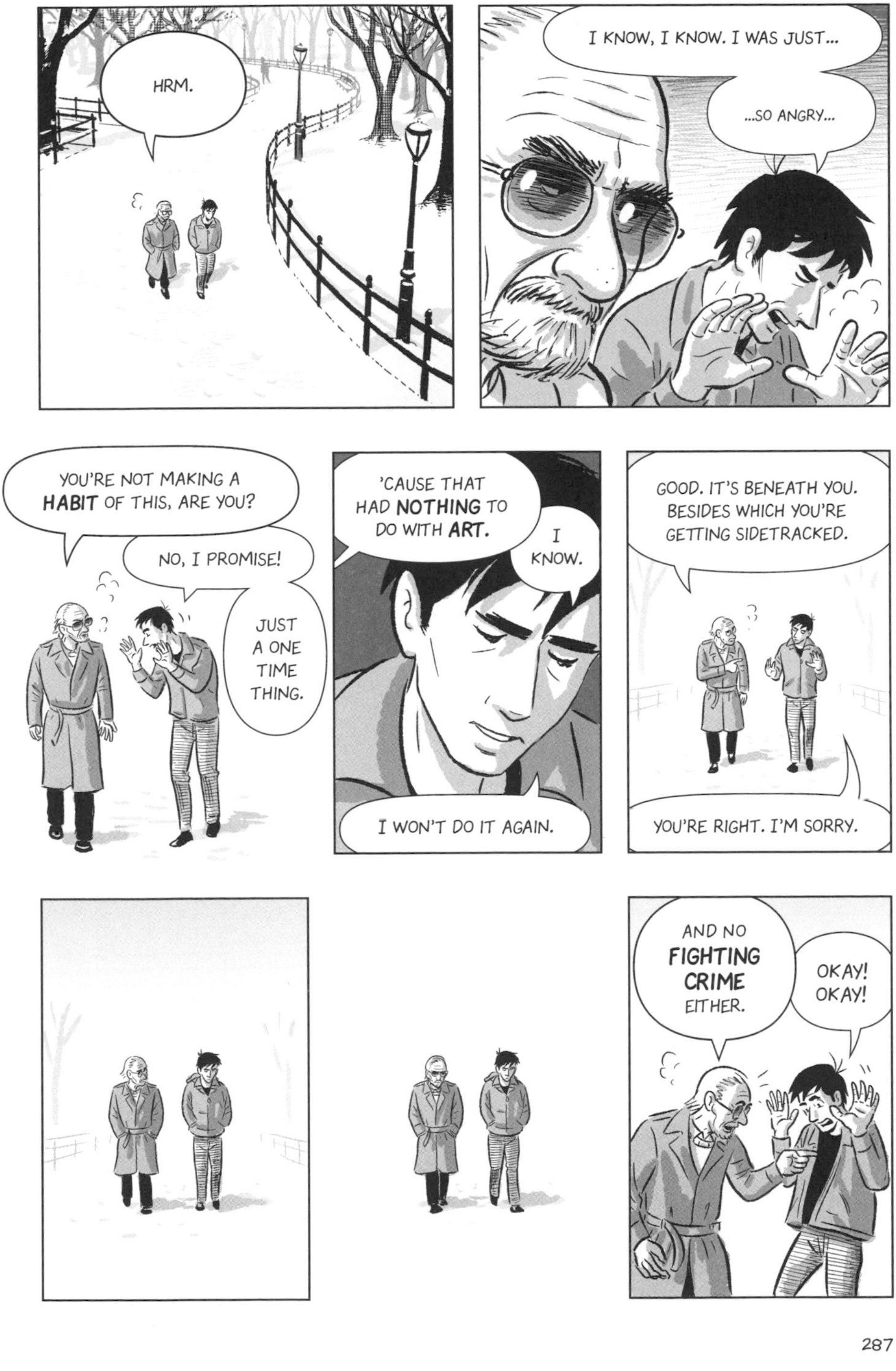
HRM.
I KNOW, I KNOW. I WAS JUST...
...SO ANGRY...
YOU'RE NOT MAKING A **HABIT** OF THIS, ARE YOU?
NO, I PROMISE!
JUST A ONE TIME THING.
'CAUSE THAT HAD **NOTHING** TO DO WITH **ART.**
I KNOW.
I WON'T DO IT AGAIN.
GOOD. IT'S BENEATH YOU. BESIDES WHICH YOU'RE GETTING SIDETRACKED.
YOU'RE RIGHT. I'M SORRY.
AND NO **FIGHTING CRIME** EITHER.
OKAY! OKAY!

THIS MORNING, MEG SEEMED **DIFFERENT.** LIKE MAYBE SHE'S COMING OUT OF IT.

GOD, I WISH I COULD JUST **TELL** HER ABOUT OUR **DEAL!**

YOU **CAN,** BUT YOU'D HAVE TO PAY THAT **PENALTY** YOU AND I DISCUSSED.

NO. NO. IT'S TOO MUCH.

THEN YOU'VE STILL GOT A SECRET BETWEEN YOU AND YOUR GIRL.

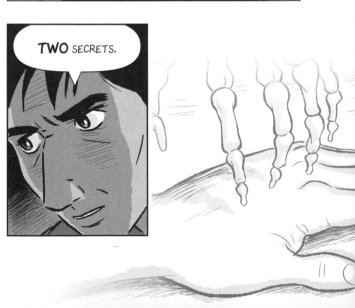

TWO SECRETS.

AND I'M KEEPING
THEM FROM
EVERYONE...

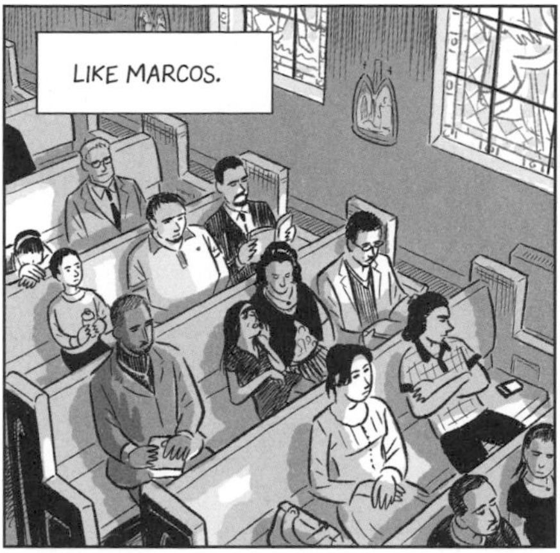
LIKE MARCOS.

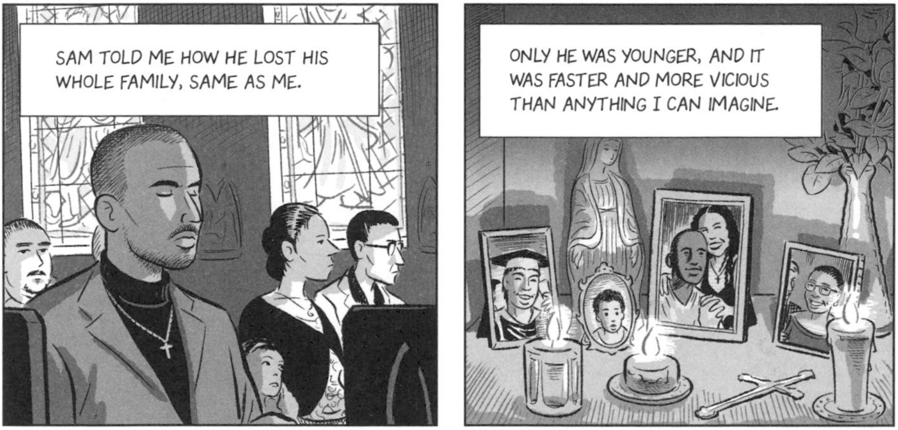
SAM TOLD ME HOW HE LOST HIS WHOLE FAMILY, SAME AS ME.
ONLY HE WAS YOUNGER, AND IT WAS FASTER AND MORE VICIOUS THAN ANYTHING I CAN IMAGINE.

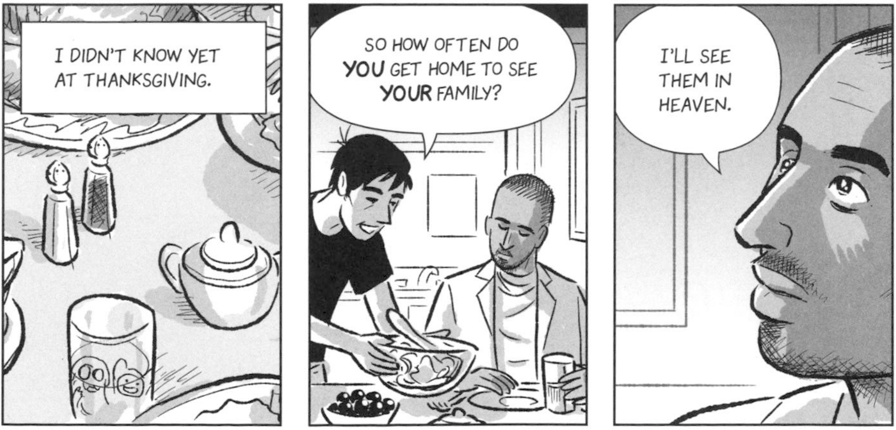
I DIDN'T KNOW YET AT THANKSGIVING.
SO HOW OFTEN DO YOU GET HOME TO SEE YOUR FAMILY?
I'LL SEE THEM IN HEAVEN.

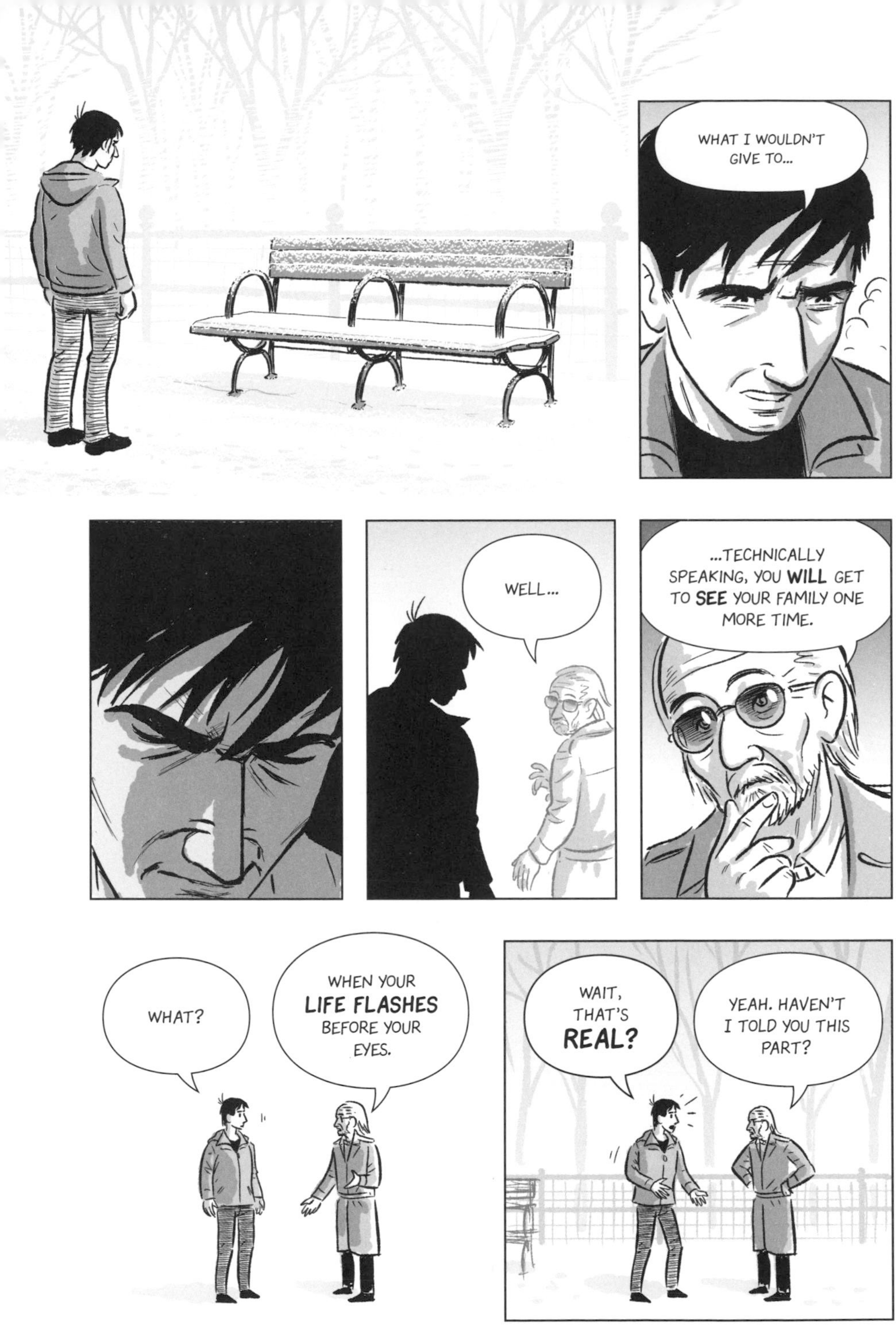
WHAT I WOULDN'T GIVE TO...
WELL...
...TECHNICALLY SPEAKING, YOU WILL GET TO SEE YOUR FAMILY ONE MORE TIME.
WHAT?
WHEN YOUR LIFE FLASHES BEFORE YOUR EYES.
WAIT, THAT'S REAL?
YEAH. HAVEN'T I TOLD YOU THIS PART?

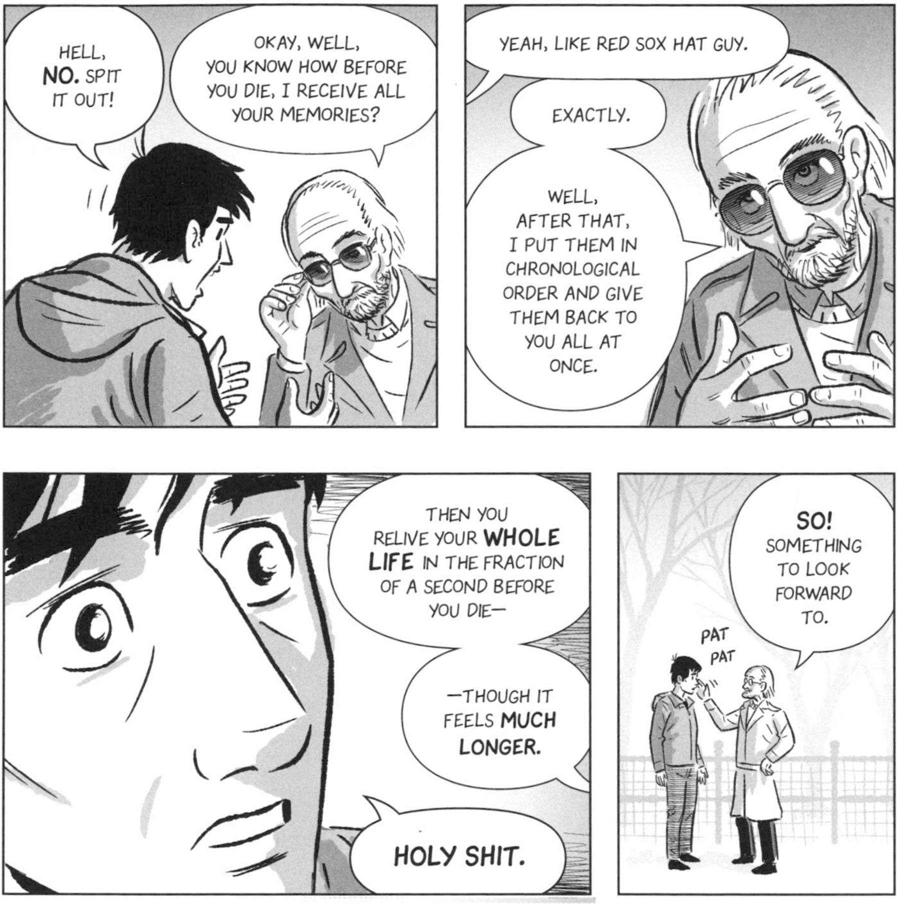
HELL, NO. SPIT IT OUT!
OKAY, WELL, YOU KNOW HOW BEFORE YOU DIE, I RECEIVE ALL YOUR MEMORIES?
YEAH, LIKE RED SOX HAT GUY.
EXACTLY.
WELL, AFTER THAT, I PUT THEM IN CHRONOLOGICAL ORDER AND GIVE THEM BACK TO YOU ALL AT ONCE.
THEN YOU RELIVE YOUR WHOLE LIFE IN THE FRACTION OF A SECOND BEFORE YOU DIE—
—THOUGH IT FEELS MUCH LONGER.
HOLY SHIT.
SO! SOMETHING TO LOOK FORWARD TO.
PAT PAT

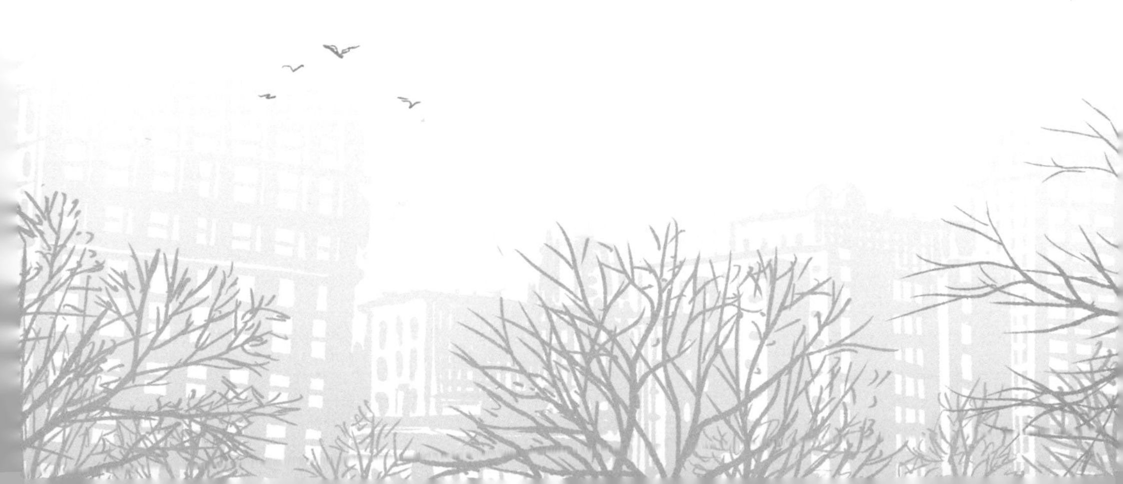

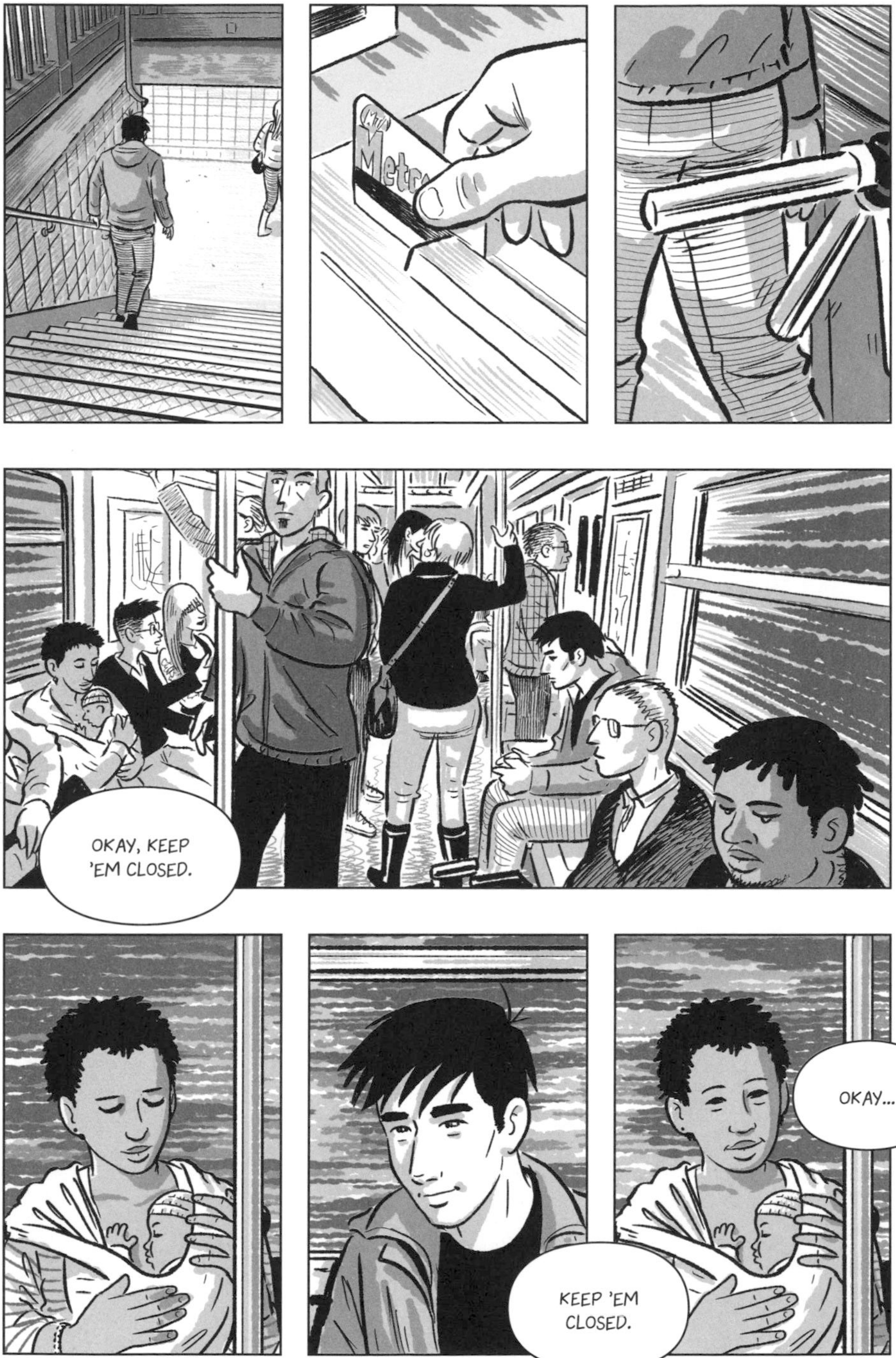
Metro
OKAY, KEEP 'EM CLOSED.
OKAY...
KEEP 'EM CLOSED.

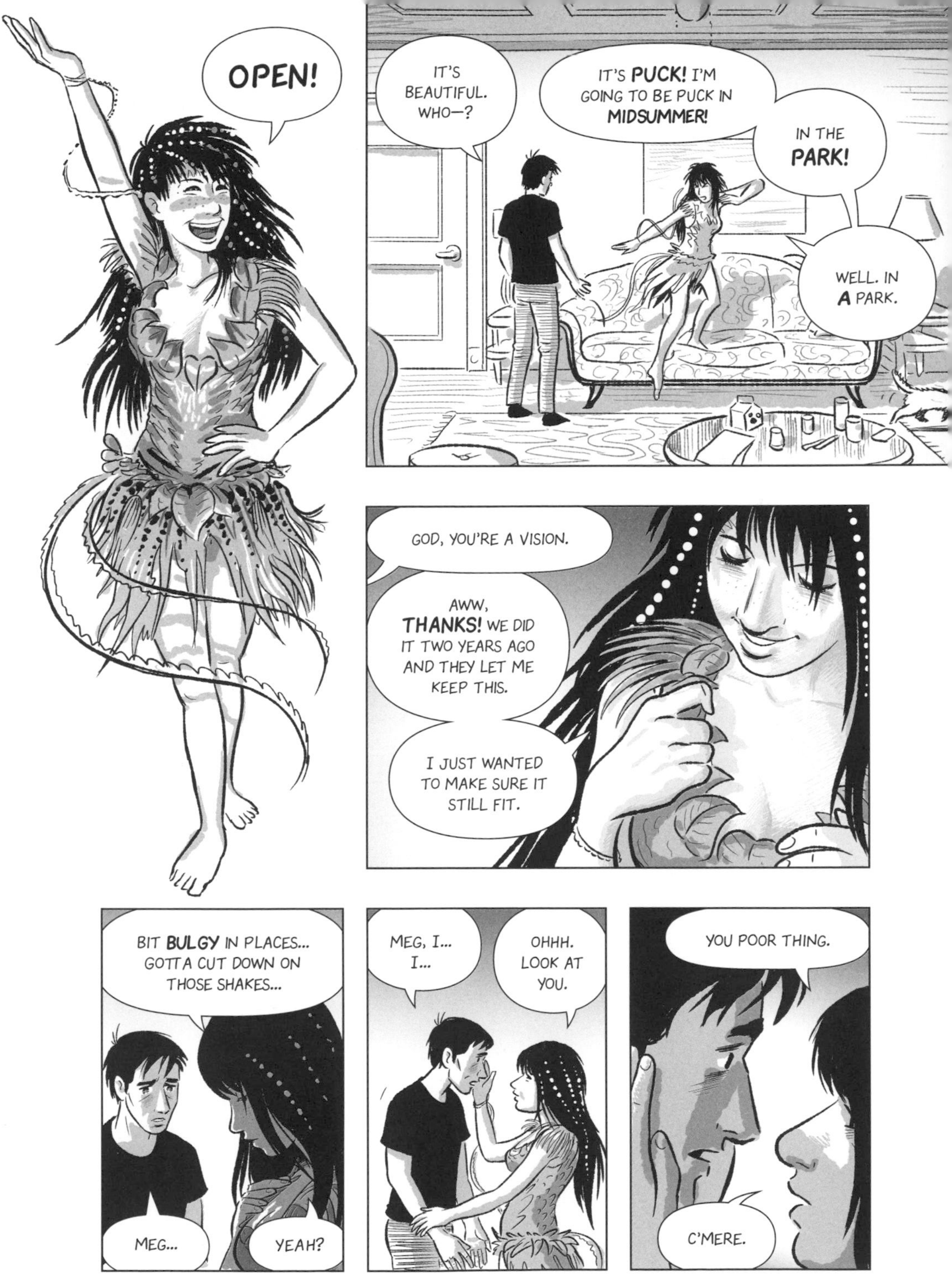
OPEN!
IT'S BEAUTIFUL. WHO—?
IT'S PUCK! I'M GOING TO BE PUCK IN MIDSUMMER!
IN THE PARK!
WELL. IN A PARK.
GOD, YOU'RE A VISION.
AWW, THANKS! WE DID IT TWO YEARS AGO AND THEY LET ME KEEP THIS.
I JUST WANTED TO MAKE SURE IT STILL FIT.
BIT BULGY IN PLACES... GOTTA CUT DOWN ON THOSE SHAKES...
MEG...
YEAH?
MEG, I... I...
OHHH. LOOK AT YOU.
YOU POOR THING.
C'MERE.

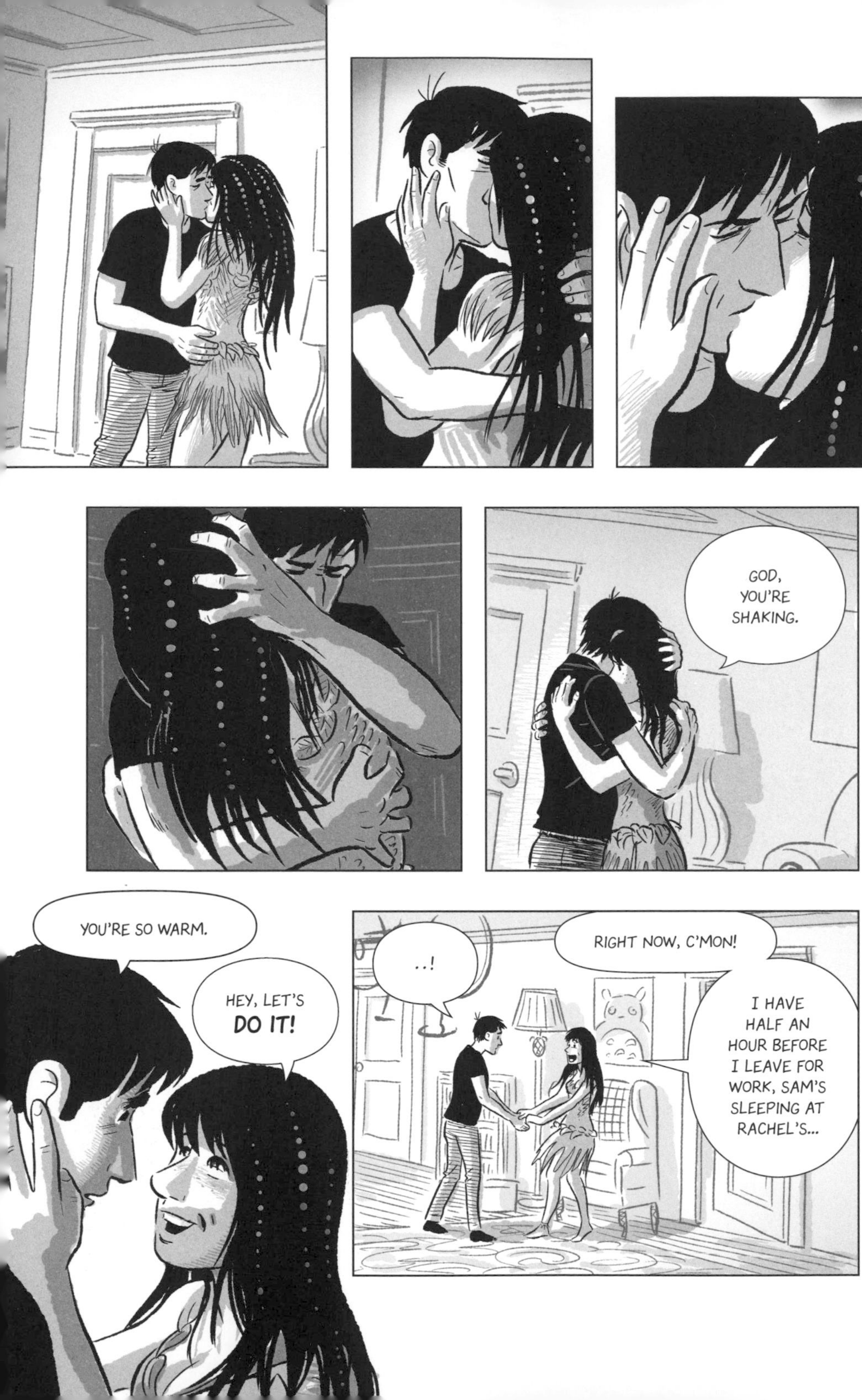
GOD, YOU'RE SHAKING.
YOU'RE SO WARM.
HEY, LET'S **DO IT!**
..!
RIGHT NOW, C'MON!
I HAVE HALF AN HOUR BEFORE I LEAVE FOR WORK, SAM'S SLEEPING AT RACHEL'S...

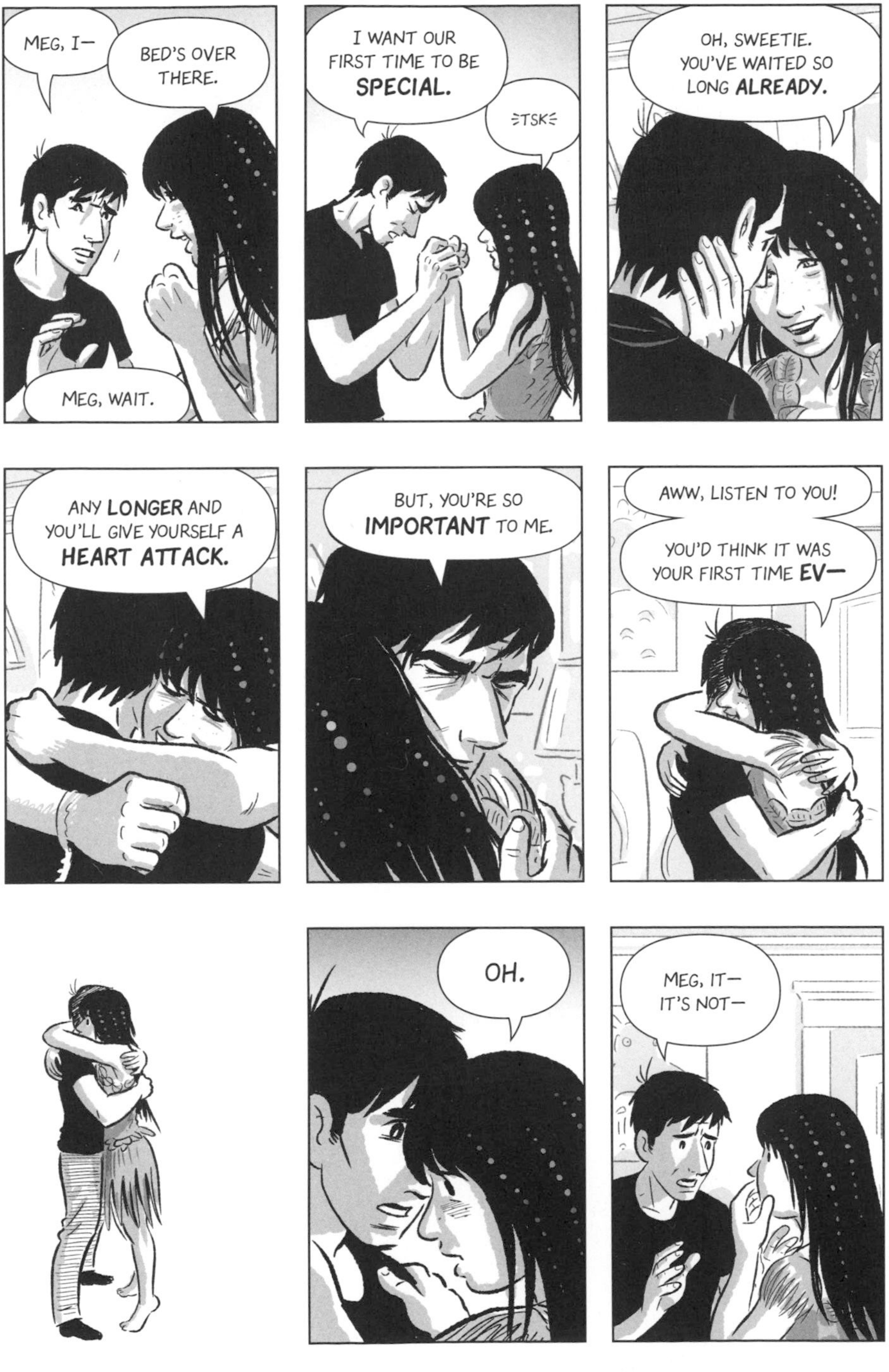
MEG, I—
BED'S OVER THERE.
MEG, WAIT.
I WANT OUR FIRST TIME TO BE SPECIAL.
TSK
OH, SWEETIE. YOU'VE WAITED SO LONG ALREADY.
ANY LONGER AND YOU'LL GIVE YOURSELF A HEART ATTACK.
BUT, YOU'RE SO IMPORTANT TO ME.
AWW, LISTEN TO YOU!
YOU'D THINK IT WAS YOUR FIRST TIME EV—
OH.
MEG, IT—
IT'S NOT—

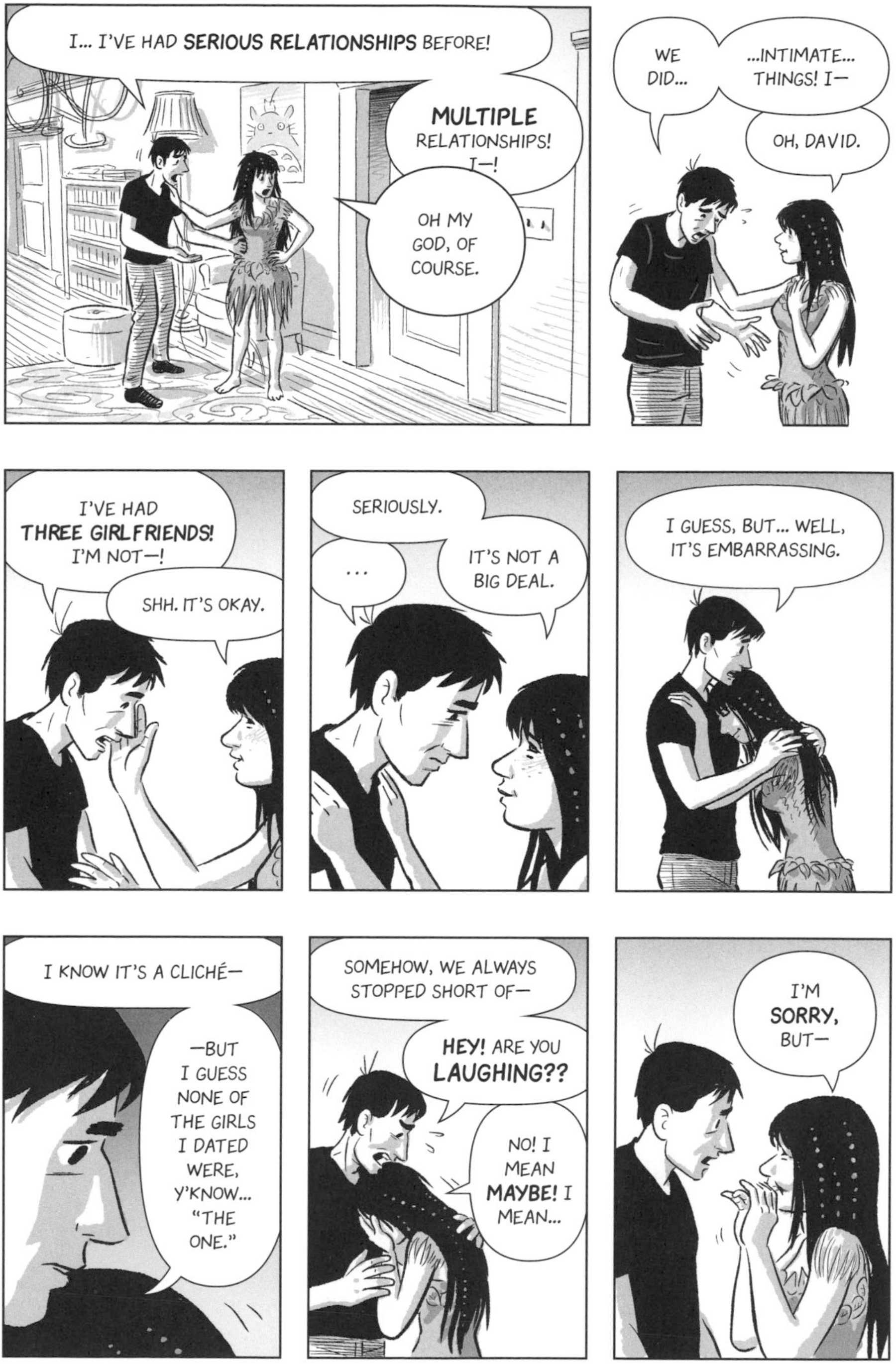
I... I'VE HAD **SERIOUS RELATIONSHIPS** BEFORE!
MULTIPLE RELATIONSHIPS! I—!
OH MY GOD, OF COURSE.
WE DID...
...INTIMATE... THINGS! I—
OH, DAVID.
I'VE HAD **THREE GIRLFRIENDS!** I'M NOT—!
SHH. IT'S OKAY.
SERIOUSLY.
...
IT'S NOT A BIG DEAL.
I GUESS, BUT... WELL, IT'S EMBARRASSING.
I KNOW IT'S A CLICHÉ—
—BUT I GUESS NONE OF THE GIRLS I DATED WERE, Y'KNOW... "THE ONE."
SOMEHOW, WE ALWAYS STOPPED SHORT OF—
HEY! ARE YOU **LAUGHING??**
NO! I MEAN **MAYBE!** I MEAN...
I'M **SORRY,** BUT—

IT EXPLAINS **SO MUCH.**

YEAH.

There's a flaw in my approach... or my methods, or my philosophy... Something basic, fundamental. There has to be!

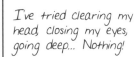

I've tried clearing my head, closing my eyes, going deep... Nothing!

What the hell is wrong with me? What am I missing?

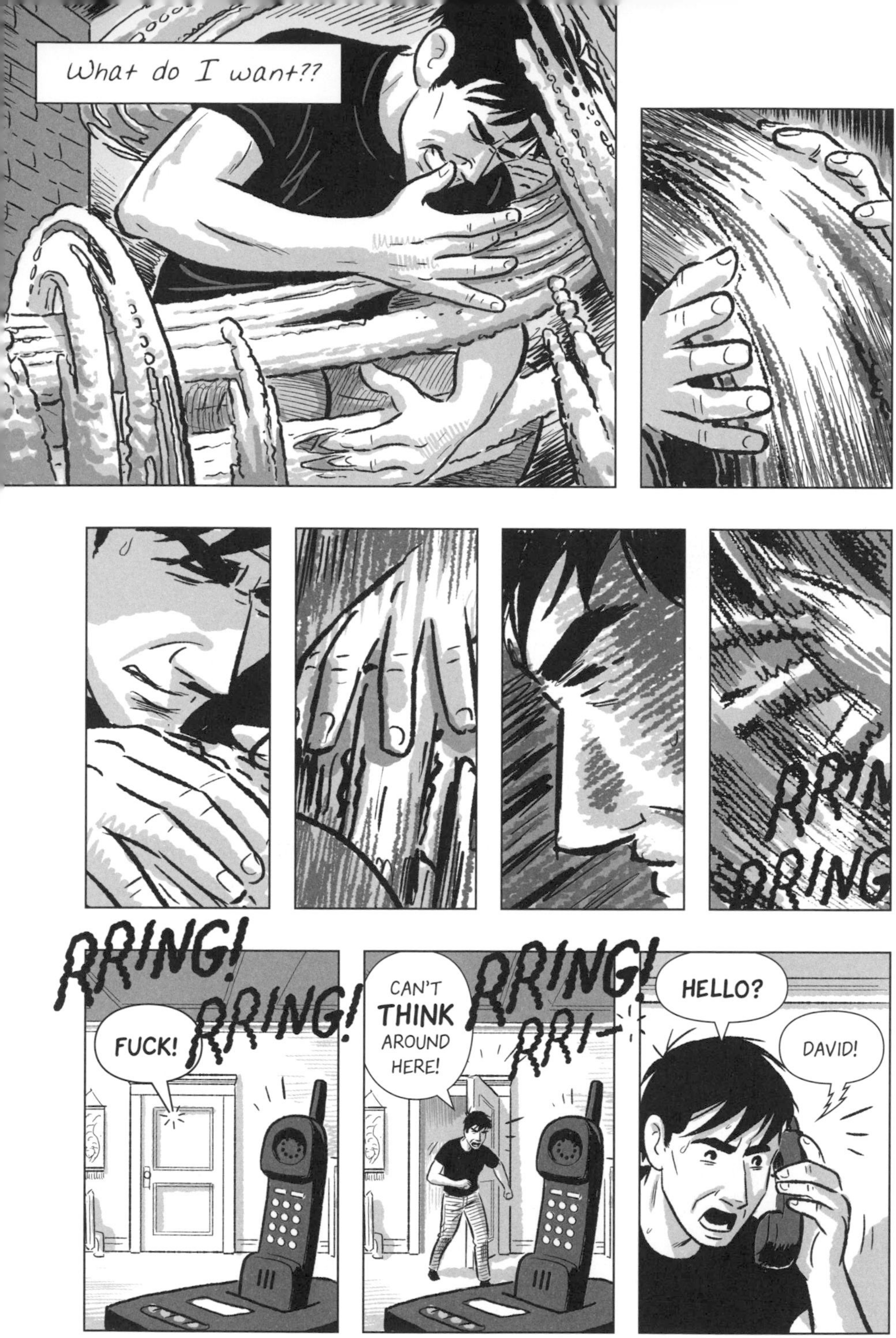
What do I want??
RRING
RRING
RRING!
FUCK!
RRING!
CAN'T THINK AROUND HERE!
RRING!
RRI–
HELLO?
DAVID!

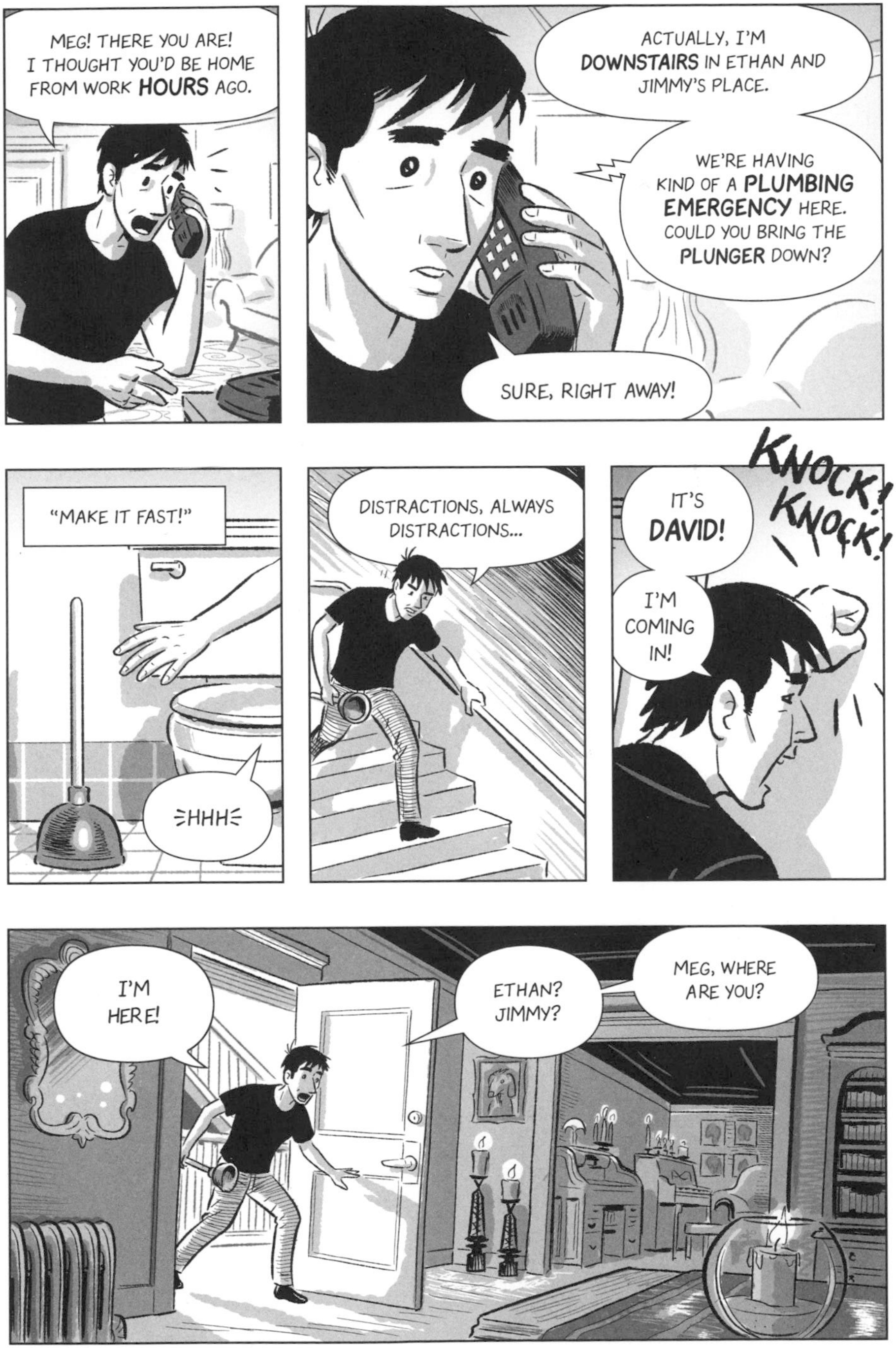
MEG! THERE YOU ARE! I THOUGHT YOU'D BE HOME FROM WORK HOURS AGO.
ACTUALLY, I'M DOWNSTAIRS IN ETHAN AND JIMMY'S PLACE.
WE'RE HAVING KIND OF A PLUMBING EMERGENCY HERE. COULD YOU BRING THE PLUNGER DOWN?
SURE, RIGHT AWAY!
"MAKE IT FAST!"
HHH
DISTRACTIONS, ALWAYS DISTRACTIONS...
KNOCK! KNOCK!
IT'S DAVID!
I'M COMING IN!
I'M HERE!
ETHAN? JIMMY?
MEG, WHERE ARE YOU?

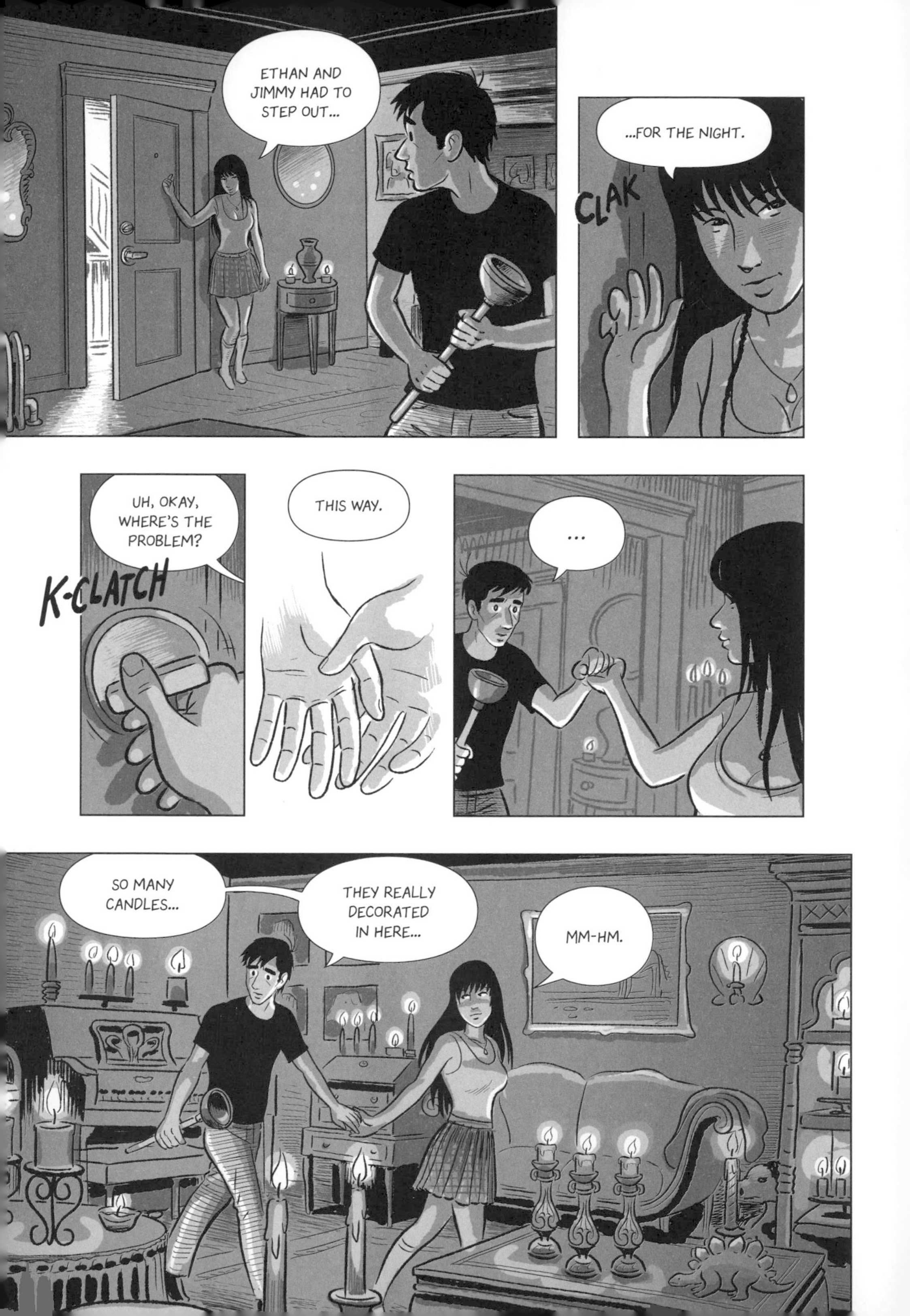
ETHAN AND JIMMY HAD TO STEP OUT...
...FOR THE NIGHT.
CLAK
UH, OKAY, WHERE'S THE PROBLEM?
K-CLATCH
THIS WAY.
...
SO MANY CANDLES...
THEY REALLY DECORATED IN HERE...
MM-HM.

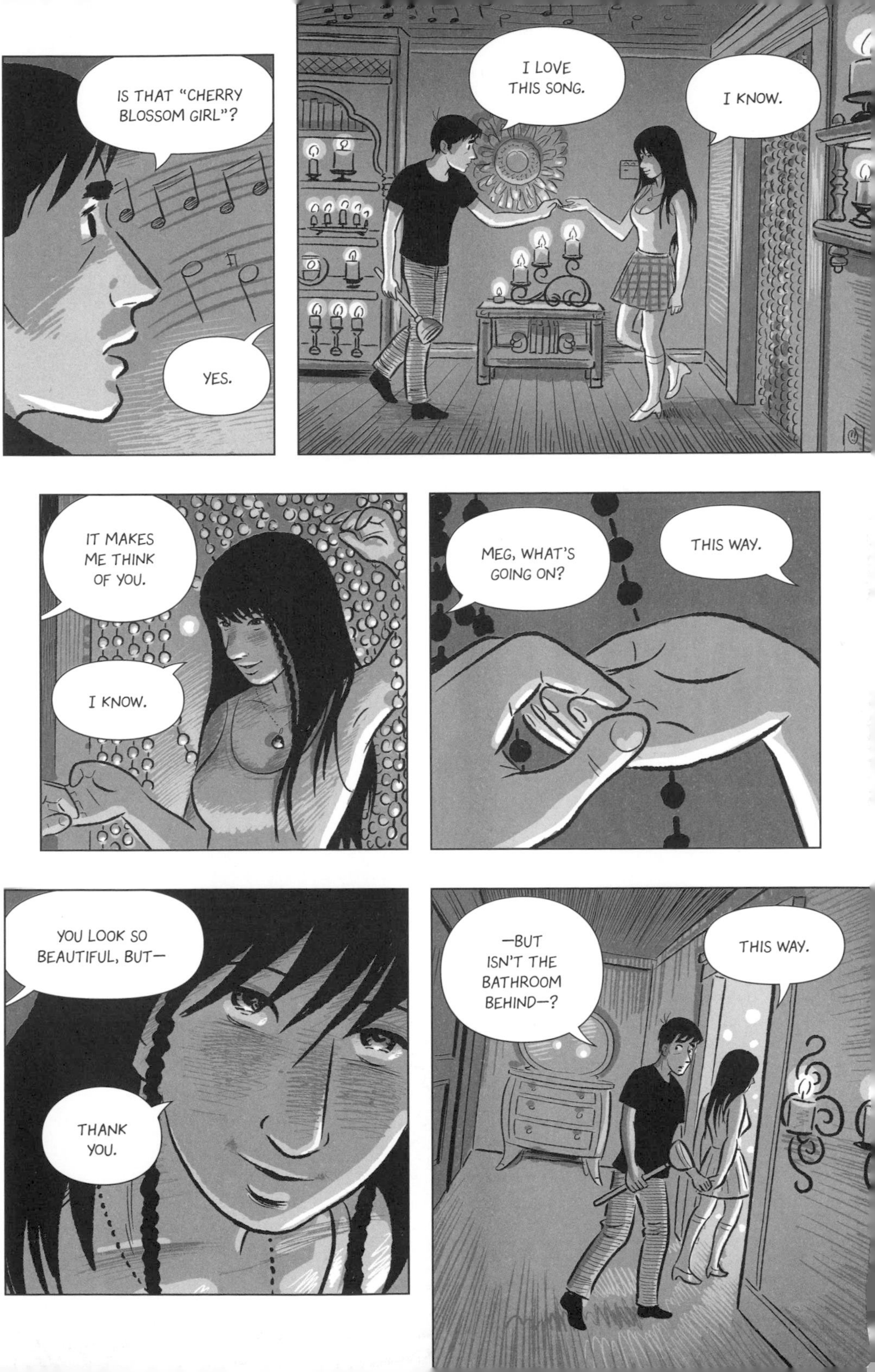
IS THAT "CHERRY BLOSSOM GIRL"?
YES.
I LOVE THIS SONG.
I KNOW.
IT MAKES ME THINK OF YOU.
I KNOW.
MEG, WHAT'S GOING ON?
THIS WAY.
YOU LOOK SO BEAUTIFUL, BUT—
THANK YOU.
—BUT ISN'T THE BATHROOM BEHIND—?
THIS WAY.

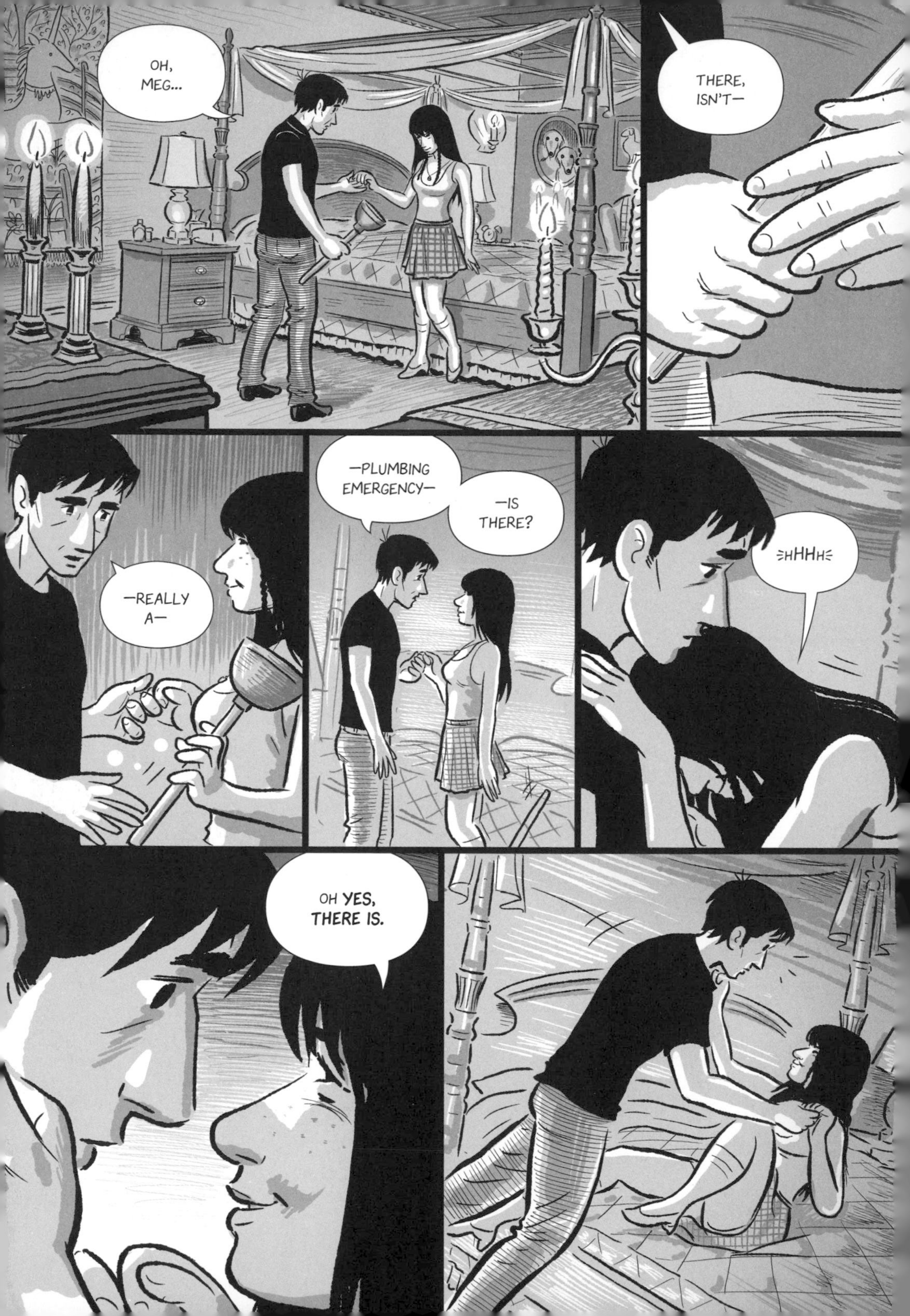
OH, MEG...
THERE, ISN'T—
—REALLY A—
—PLUMBING EMERGENCY—
—IS THERE?
≠HHHH≠
OH YES, THERE IS.

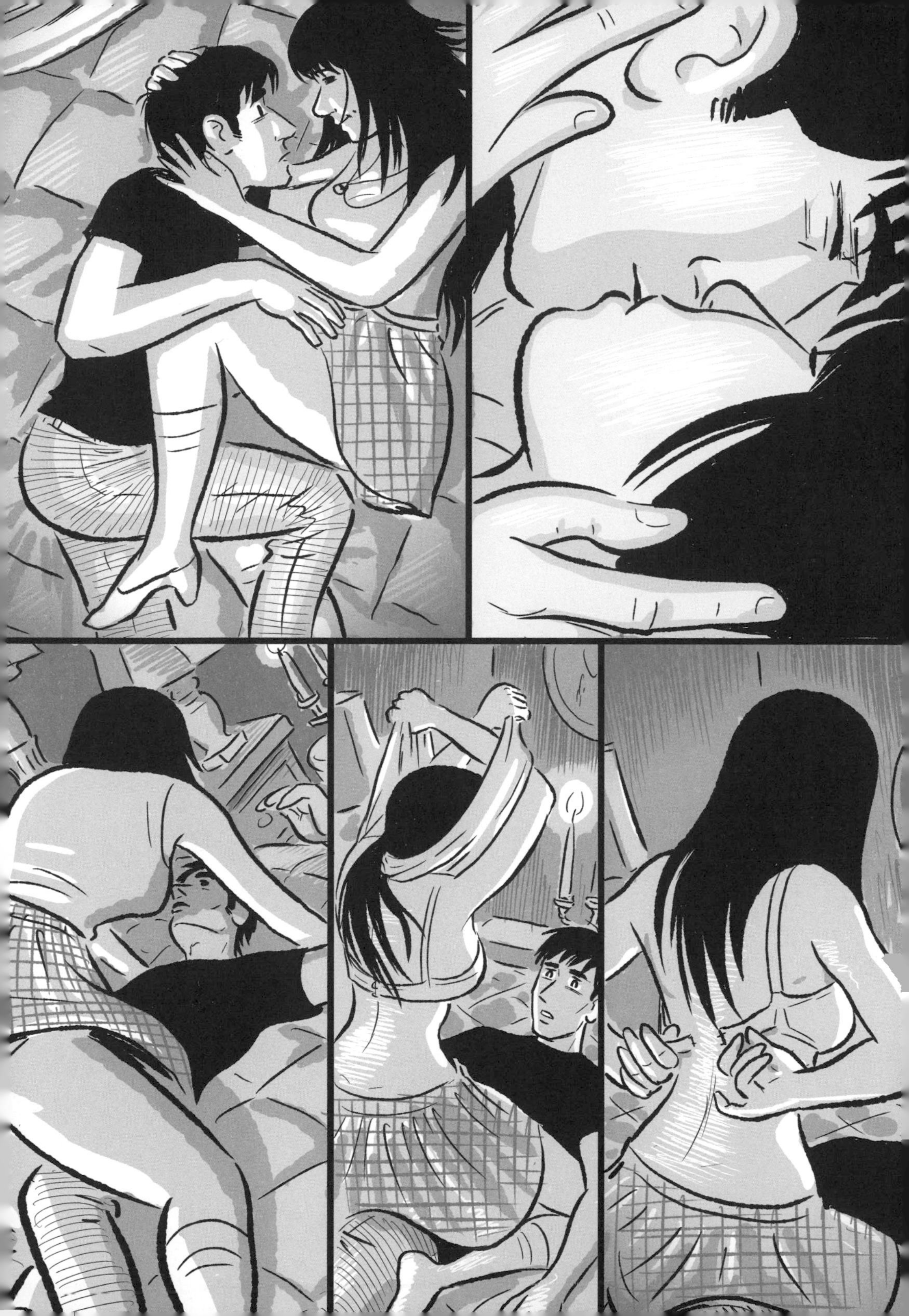

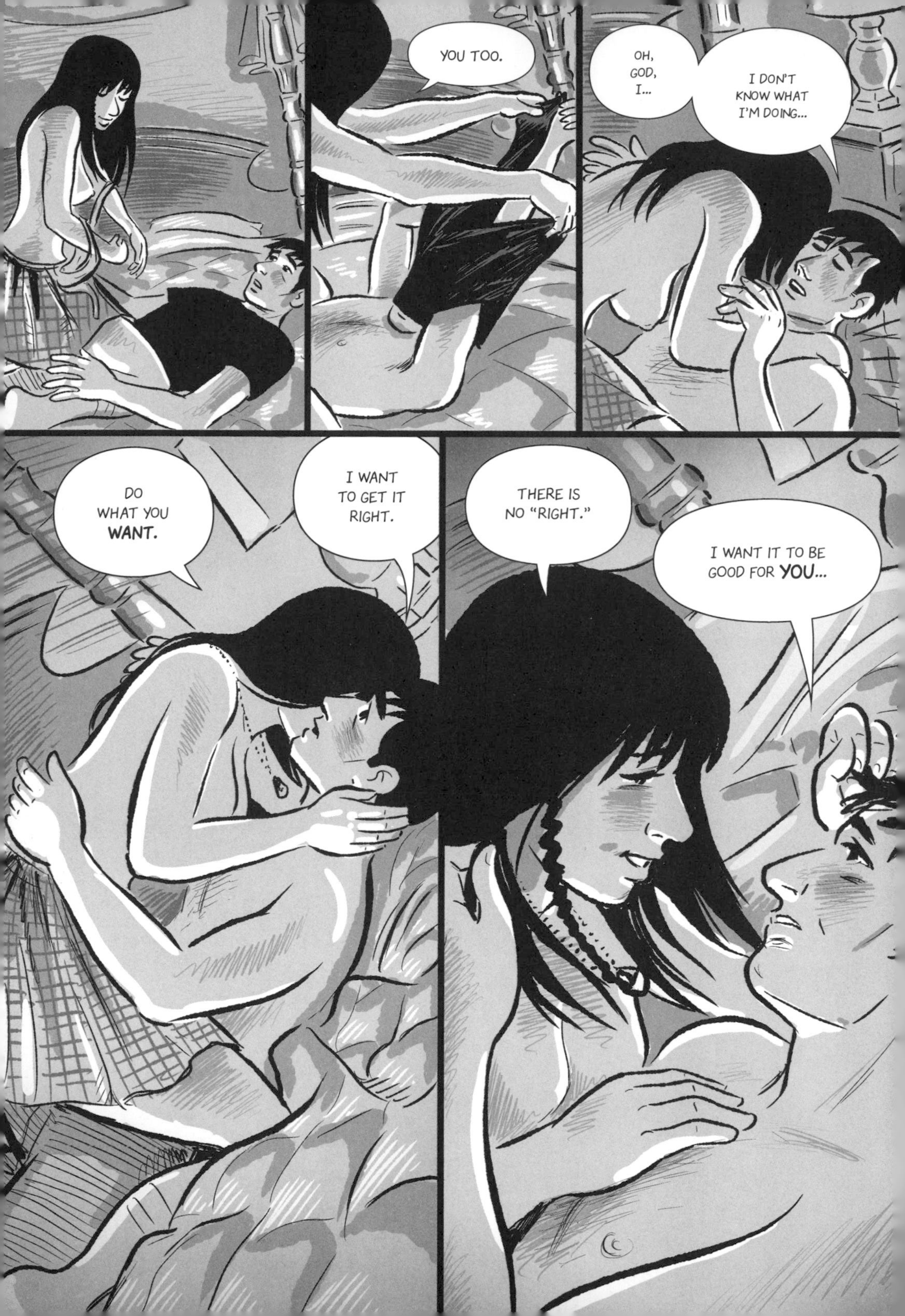
YOU TOO.
OH, GOD, I...
I DON'T KNOW WHAT I'M DOING...
DO WHAT YOU WANT.
I WANT TO GET IT RIGHT.
THERE IS NO "RIGHT."
I WANT IT TO BE GOOD FOR YOU...

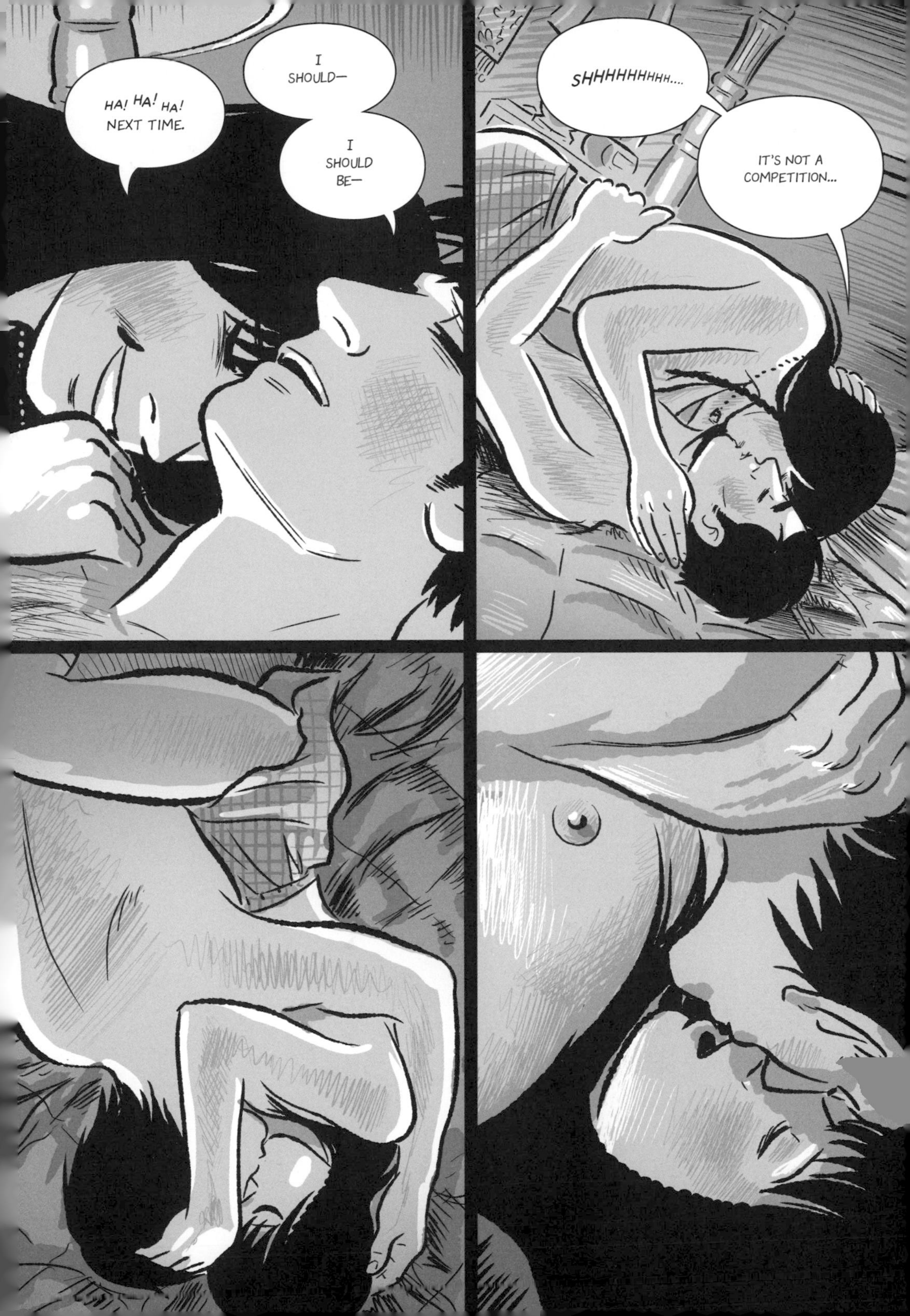
HA! HA! HA! NEXT TIME.
I SHOULD—
I SHOULD BE—
SHHHHHHHHH....
IT'S NOT A COMPETITION...

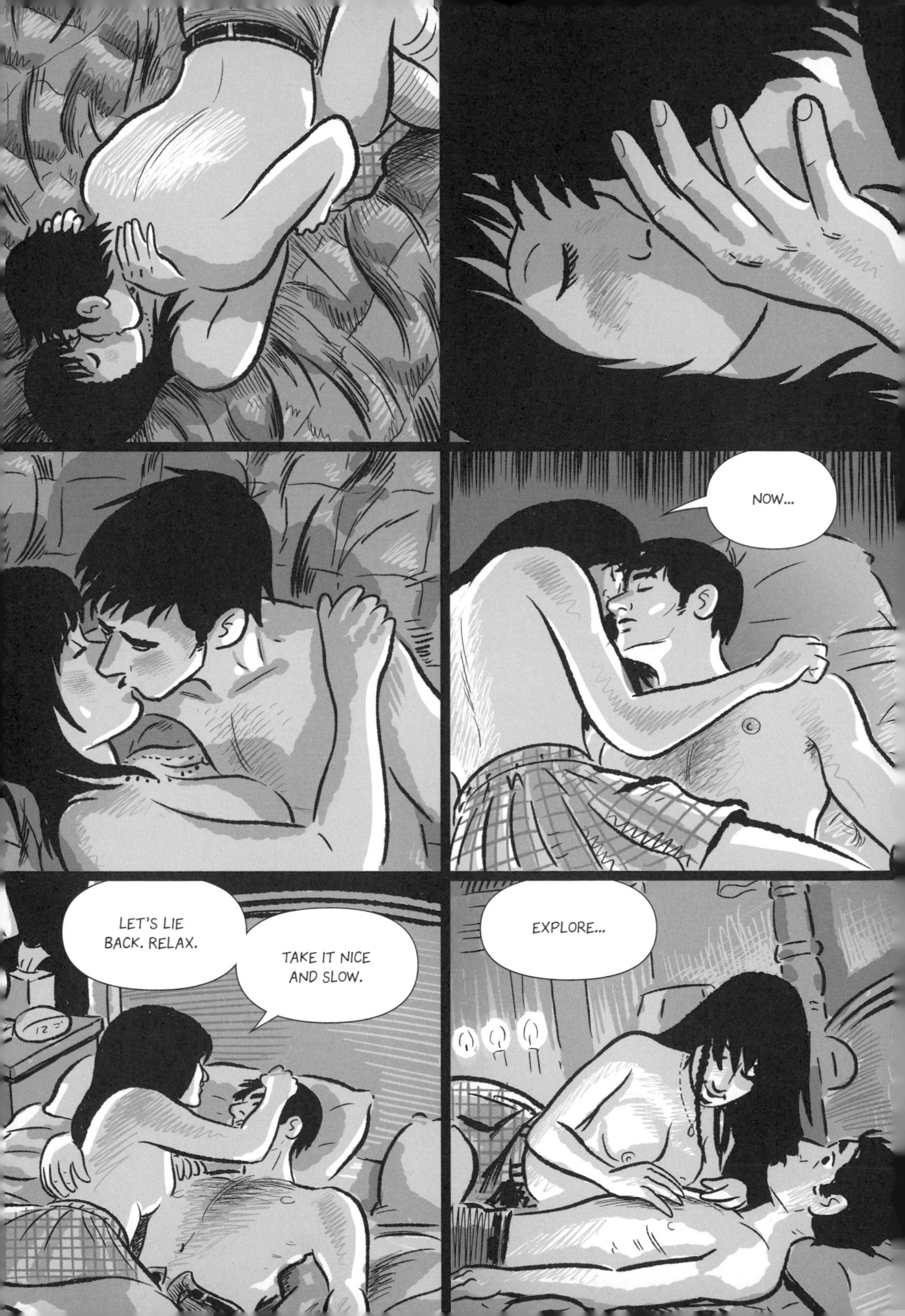
NOW...
LET'S LIE BACK. RELAX.
TAKE IT NICE AND SLOW.
EXPLORE...

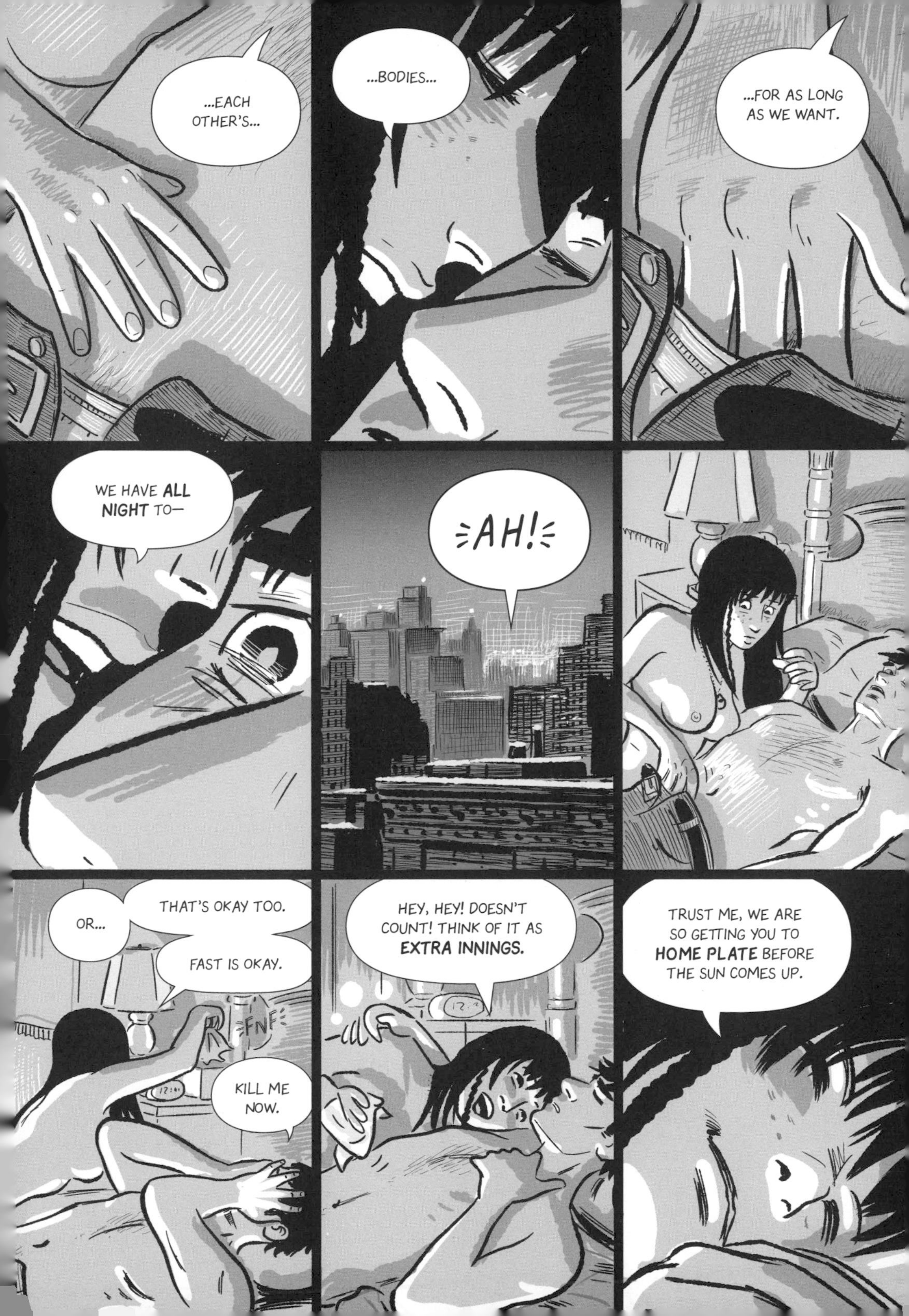
...EACH OTHER'S...
...BODIES...
...FOR AS LONG AS WE WANT.
WE HAVE **ALL NIGHT** TO—
AH!
OR...
THAT'S OKAY TOO.
FAST IS OKAY.
FNF
KILL ME NOW.
HEY, HEY! DOESN'T COUNT! THINK OF IT AS **EXTRA INNINGS.**
TRUST ME, WE ARE SO GETTING YOU TO **HOME PLATE** BEFORE THE SUN COMES UP.

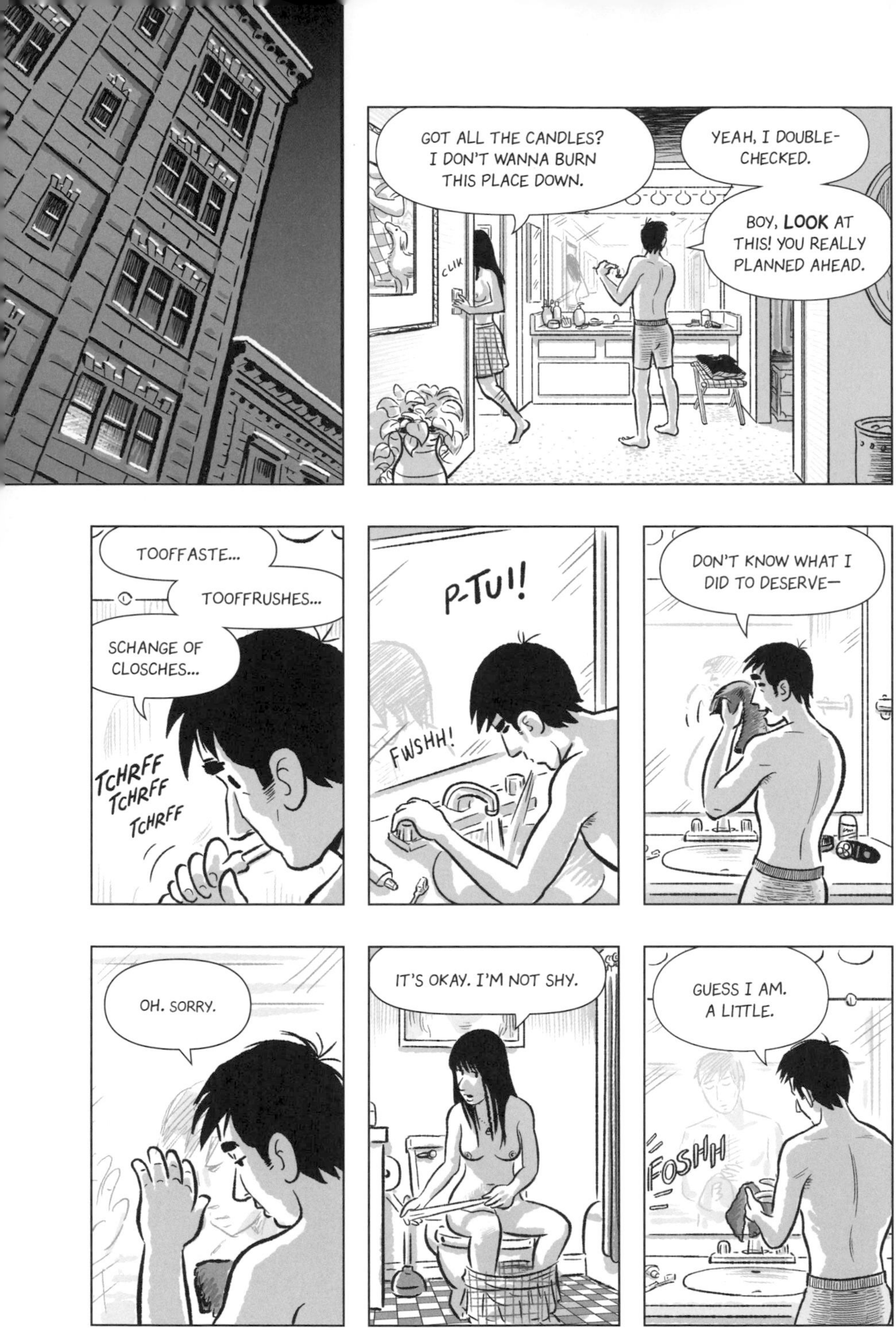
GOT ALL THE CANDLES? I DON'T WANNA BURN THIS PLACE DOWN.
YEAH, I DOUBLE-CHECKED.
BOY, **LOOK** AT THIS! YOU REALLY PLANNED AHEAD.
CLIK
TOOFFASTE...
TOOFFRUSHES...
SCHANGE OF CLOSCHES...
TCHRFF
TCHRFF
TCHRFF
P-TUI!
FWSHH!
DON'T KNOW WHAT I DID TO DESERVE—
OH. SORRY.
IT'S OKAY. I'M NOT SHY.
GUESS I AM. A LITTLE.
FOSHH

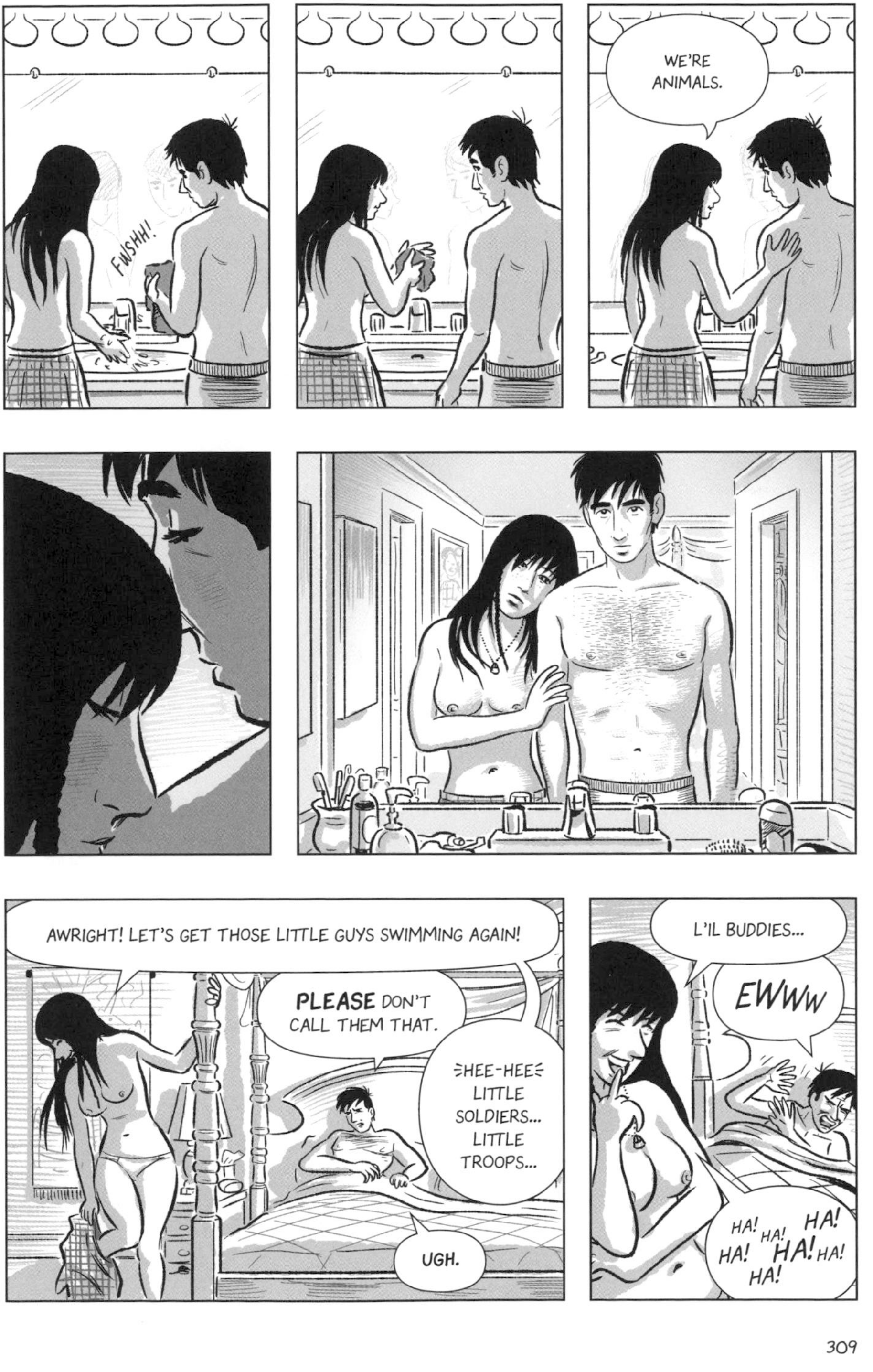
FWSHH!
WE'RE ANIMALS.
AWRIGHT! LET'S GET THOSE LITTLE GUYS SWIMMING AGAIN!
PLEASE DON'T CALL THEM THAT.
HEE-HEE LITTLE SOLDIERS... LITTLE TROOPS...
UGH.
L'IL BUDDIES...
EWWW
HA! HA! HA! HA! HA! HA! HA!

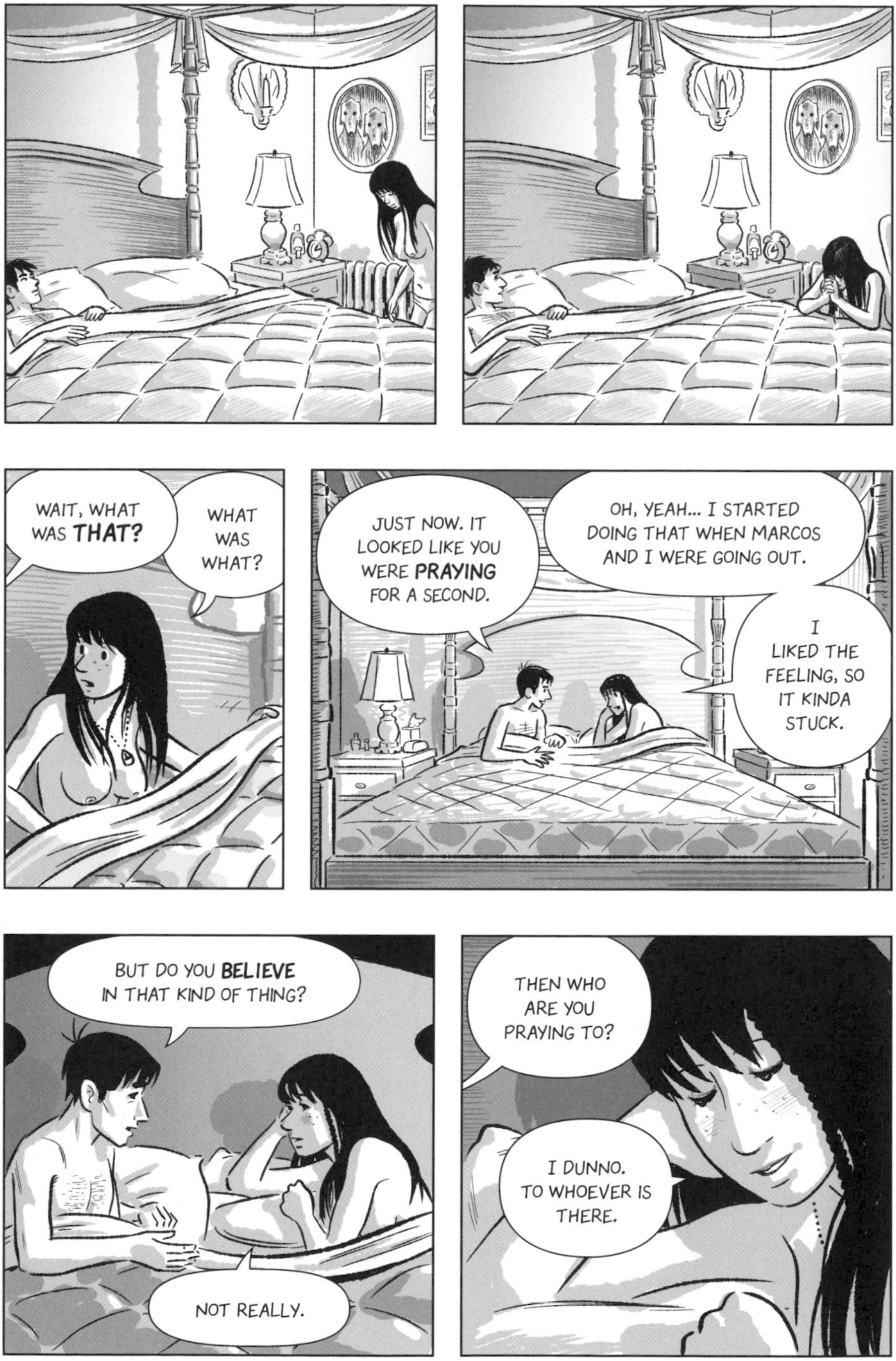
WAIT, WHAT WAS **THAT?**
WHAT WAS WHAT?
JUST NOW. IT LOOKED LIKE YOU WERE **PRAYING** FOR A SECOND.
OH, YEAH... I STARTED DOING THAT WHEN MARCOS AND I WERE GOING OUT.
I LIKED THE FEELING, SO IT KINDA STUCK.
BUT DO YOU **BELIEVE** IN THAT KIND OF THING?
NOT REALLY.
THEN WHO ARE YOU PRAYING TO?
I DUNNO. TO WHOEVER IS THERE.

WHAT IF **NOBODY** IS THERE?

THEN TO NOBODY.

OKAY, I'LL BITE. WHAT EXACTLY DO YOU **SAY**—

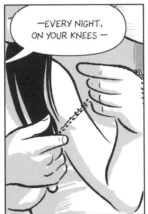

—EVERY NIGHT, ON YOUR KNEES —

—TO NO ONE IN PARTICULAR?

CLAK

"THANK YOU."

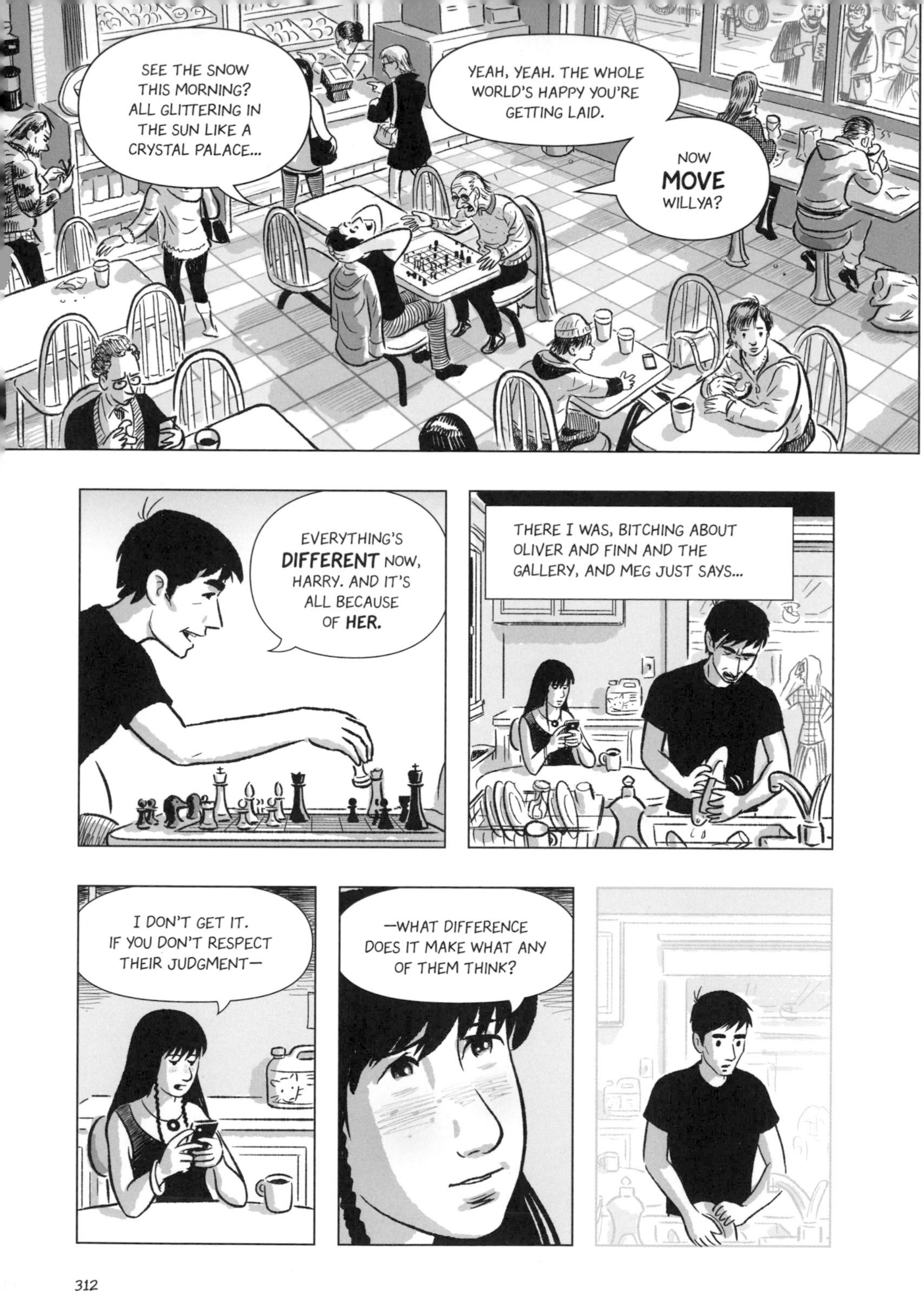
SEE THE SNOW THIS MORNING? ALL GLITTERING IN THE SUN LIKE A CRYSTAL PALACE...
YEAH, YEAH. THE WHOLE WORLD'S HAPPY YOU'RE GETTING LAID.
NOW **MOVE** WILLYA?
EVERYTHING'S **DIFFERENT** NOW, HARRY. AND IT'S ALL BECAUSE OF **HER.**
THERE I WAS, BITCHING ABOUT OLIVER AND FINN AND THE GALLERY, AND MEG JUST SAYS...
I DON'T GET IT. IF YOU DON'T RESPECT THEIR JUDGMENT—
—WHAT DIFFERENCE DOES IT MAKE WHAT ANY OF THEM THINK?

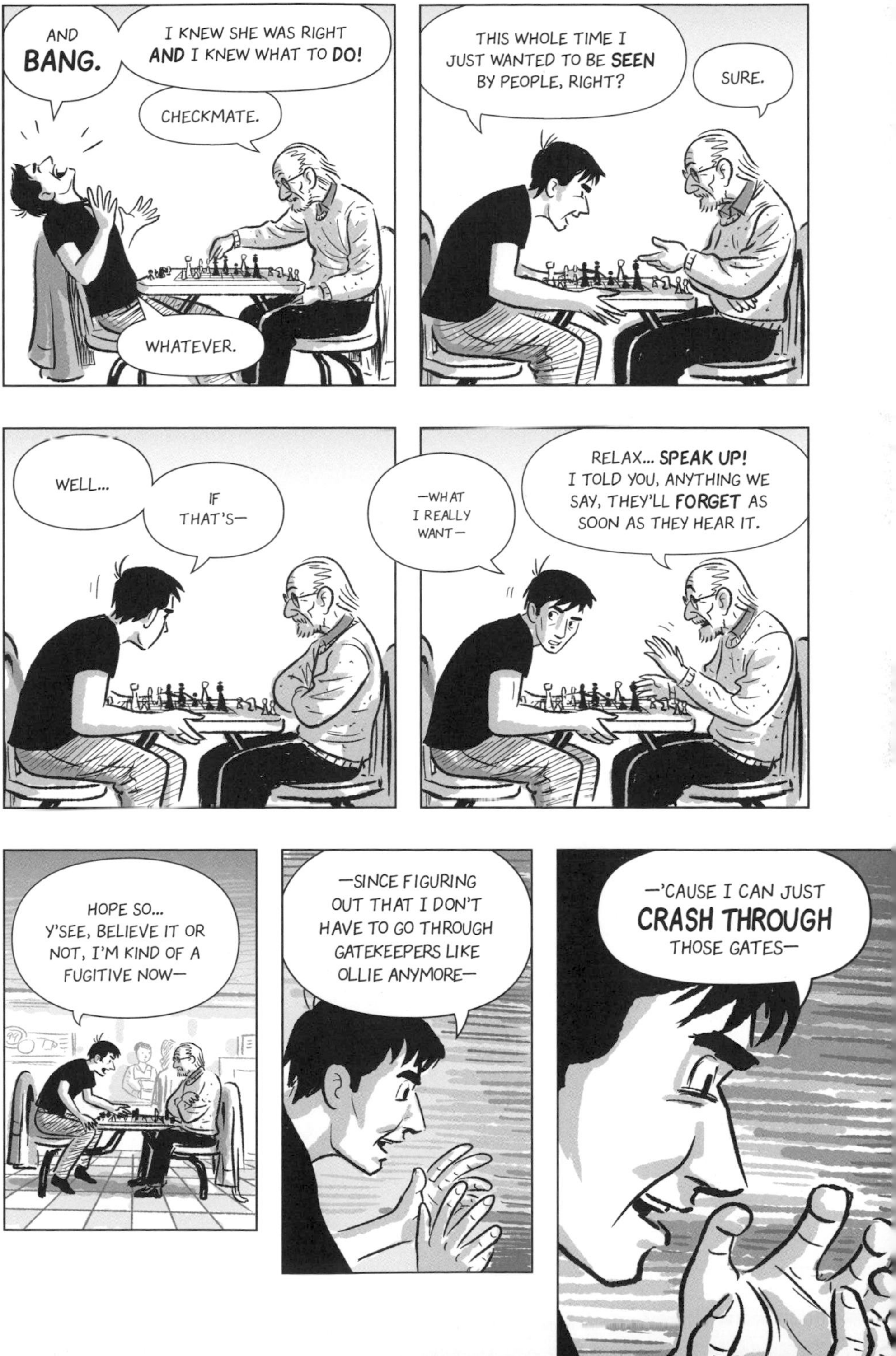
AND **BANG.**
I KNEW SHE WAS RIGHT **AND** I KNEW WHAT TO **DO!**
CHECKMATE.
WHATEVER.
THIS WHOLE TIME I JUST WANTED TO BE **SEEN** BY PEOPLE, RIGHT?
SURE.
WELL...
IF THAT'S—
—WHAT I REALLY WANT—
RELAX... **SPEAK UP!** I TOLD YOU, ANYTHING WE SAY, THEY'LL **FORGET** AS SOON AS THEY HEAR IT.
HOPE SO... Y'SEE, BELIEVE IT OR NOT, I'M KIND OF A FUGITIVE NOW—
—SINCE FIGURING OUT THAT I DON'T HAVE TO GO THROUGH GATEKEEPERS LIKE OLLIE ANYMORE—
—'CAUSE I CAN JUST **CRASH THROUGH** THOSE GATES—

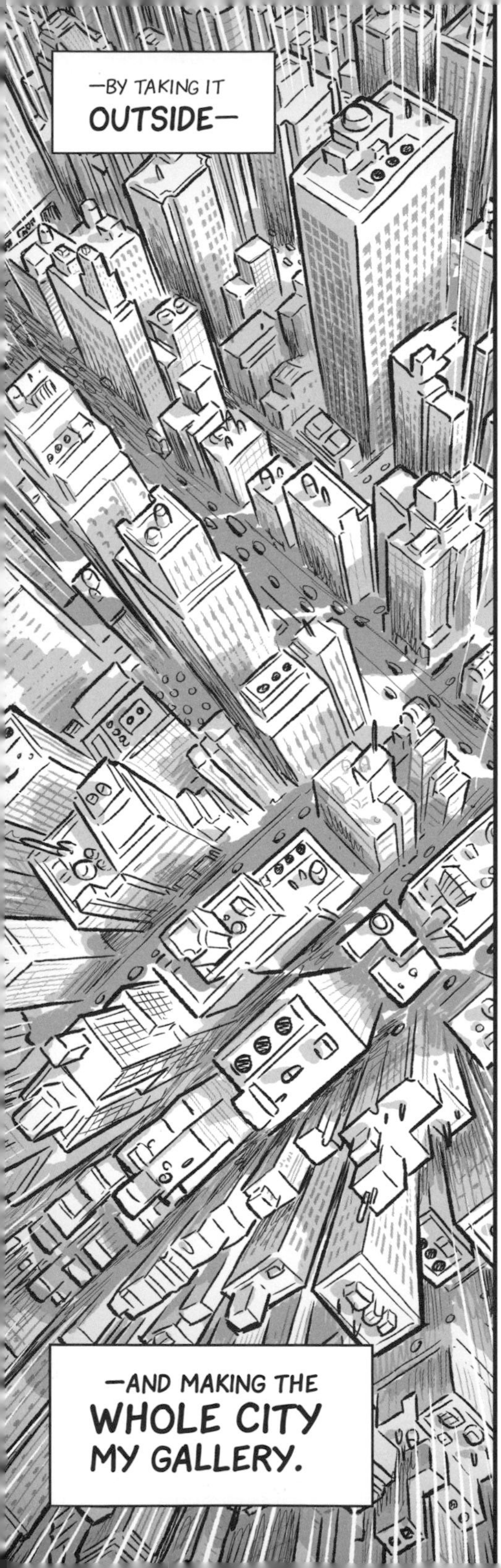
—BY TAKING IT
OUTSIDE—
—AND MAKING THE WHOLE CITY MY GALLERY.

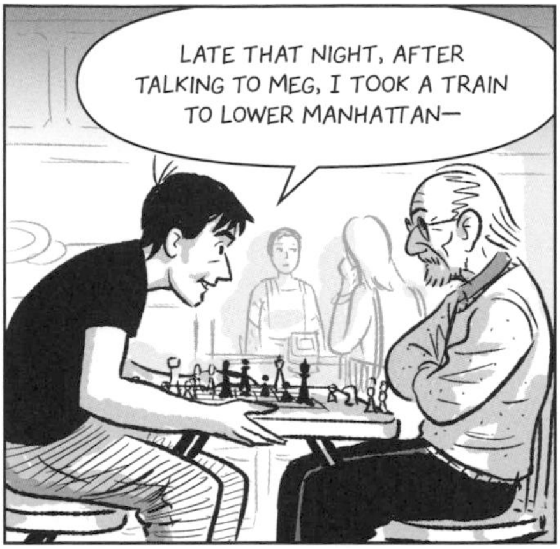
LATE THAT NIGHT, AFTER TALKING TO MEG, I TOOK A TRAIN TO LOWER MANHATTAN—

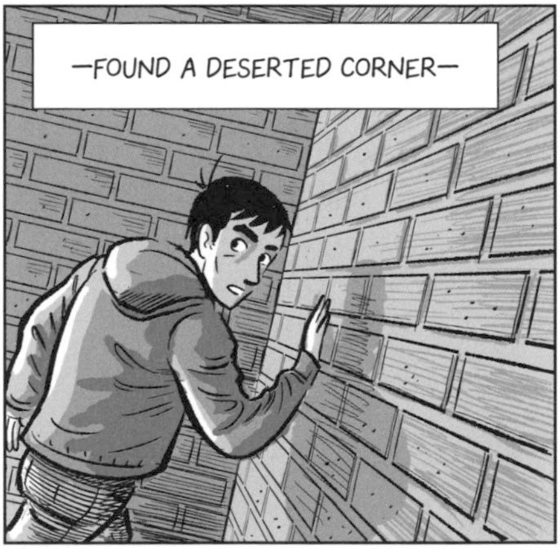
—FOUND A DESERTED CORNER—

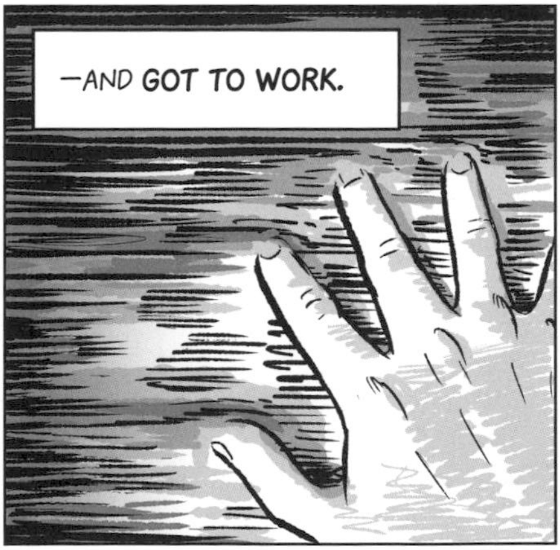
—AND GOT TO WORK.

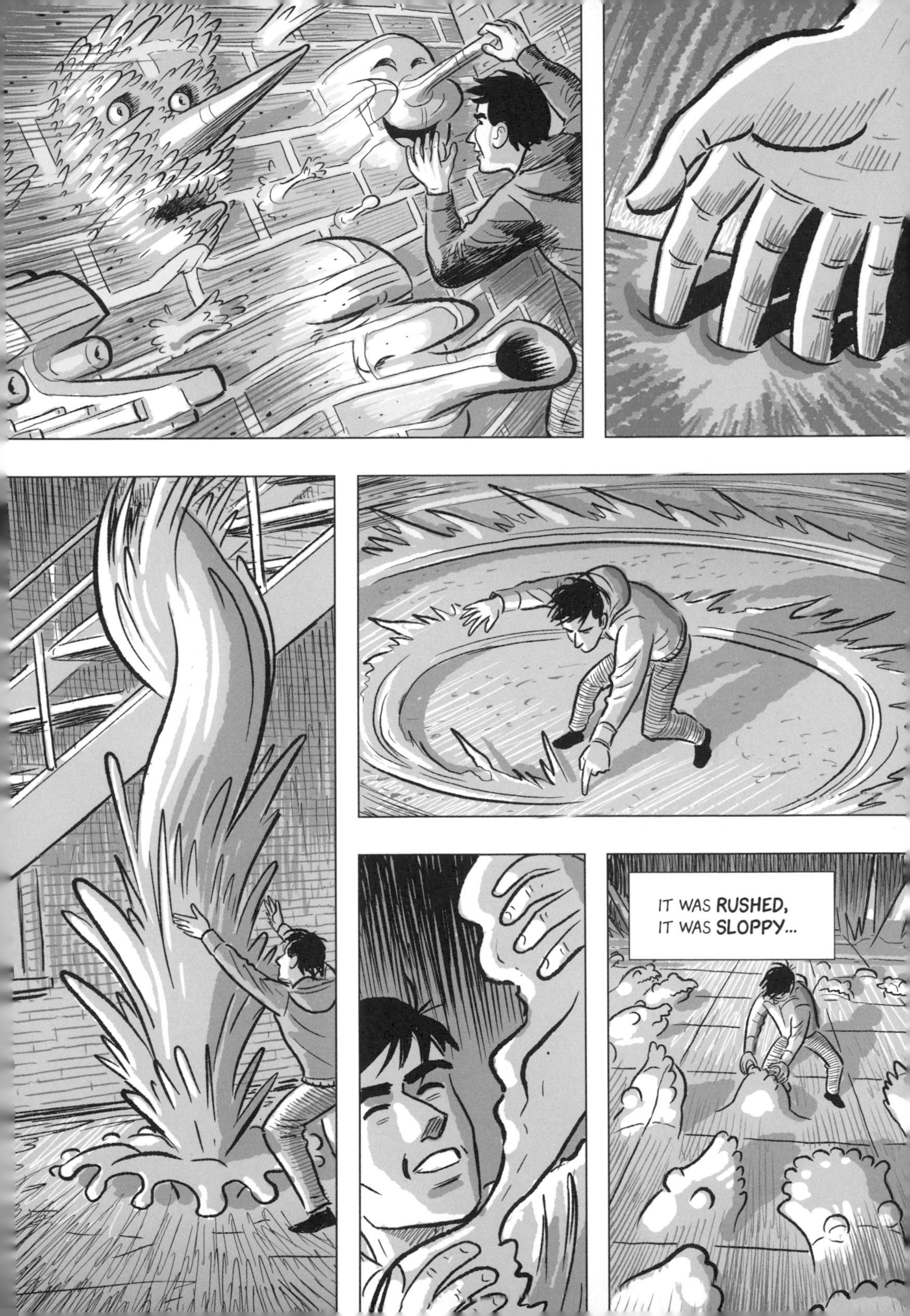
IT WAS RUSHED,
IT WAS SLOPPY...

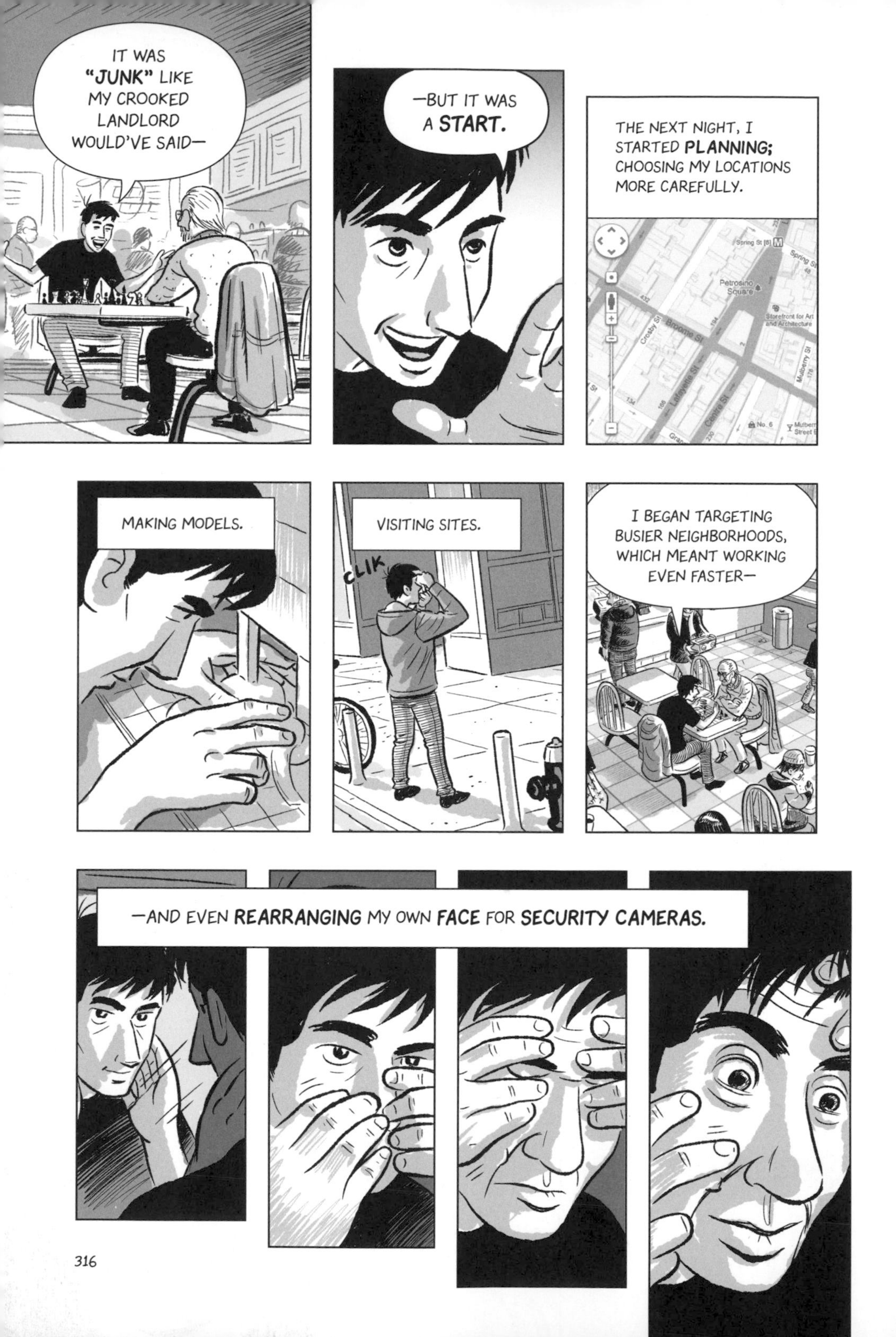
IT WAS "JUNK" LIKE MY CROOKED LANDLORD WOULD'VE SAID—
—BUT IT WAS A START.
THE NEXT NIGHT, I STARTED PLANNING; CHOOSING MY LOCATIONS MORE CAREFULLY.
Spring St
Petrosino Square
Storefront for Art and Architecture
Broome St
Crosby St
Lafayette St
Centre St
Mulberry St
No. 6
MAKING MODELS.
VISITING SITES.
CLIK
I BEGAN TARGETING BUSIER NEIGHBORHOODS, WHICH MEANT WORKING EVEN FASTER—
—AND EVEN REARRANGING MY OWN FACE FOR SECURITY CAMERAS.

IT'S STILL **RAW**, STILL **SLOPPY**—

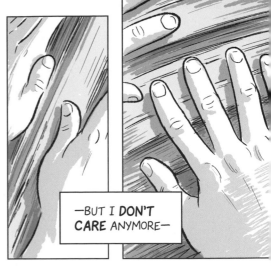

—BUT I **DON'T CARE** ANYMORE—

—'CAUSE AFTER **YEARS** OF BEING IGNORED—

—**BURIED** AND FORGOTTEN—

—UNDER A **MILLION TONS** OF **ROCK** AND **METAL**—

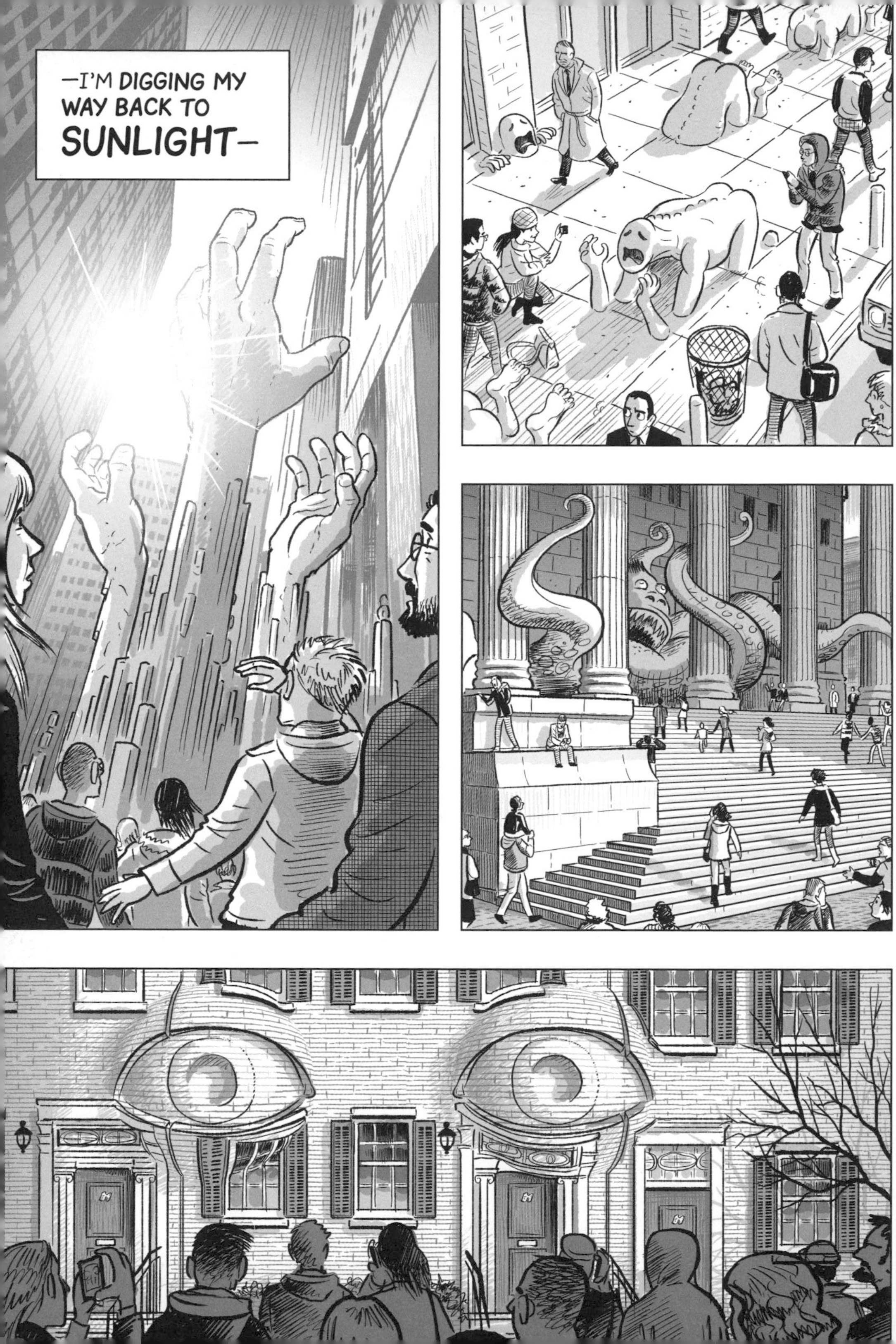
—I'M DIGGING MY WAY BACK TO SUNLIGHT—

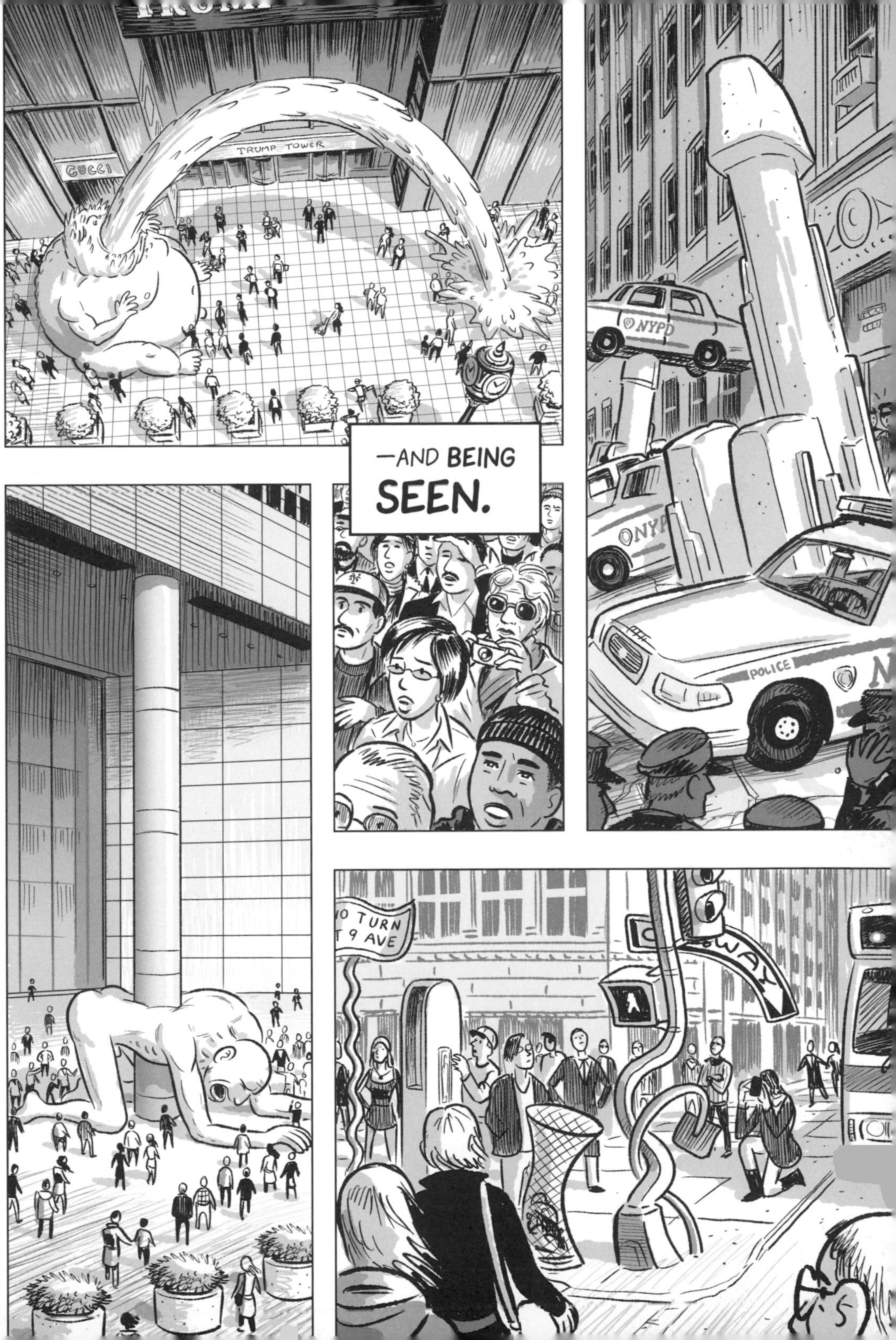
TRUMP TOWER
GUCCI
NYPD
—AND BEING SEEN.
POLICE
O TURN
T 9 AVE

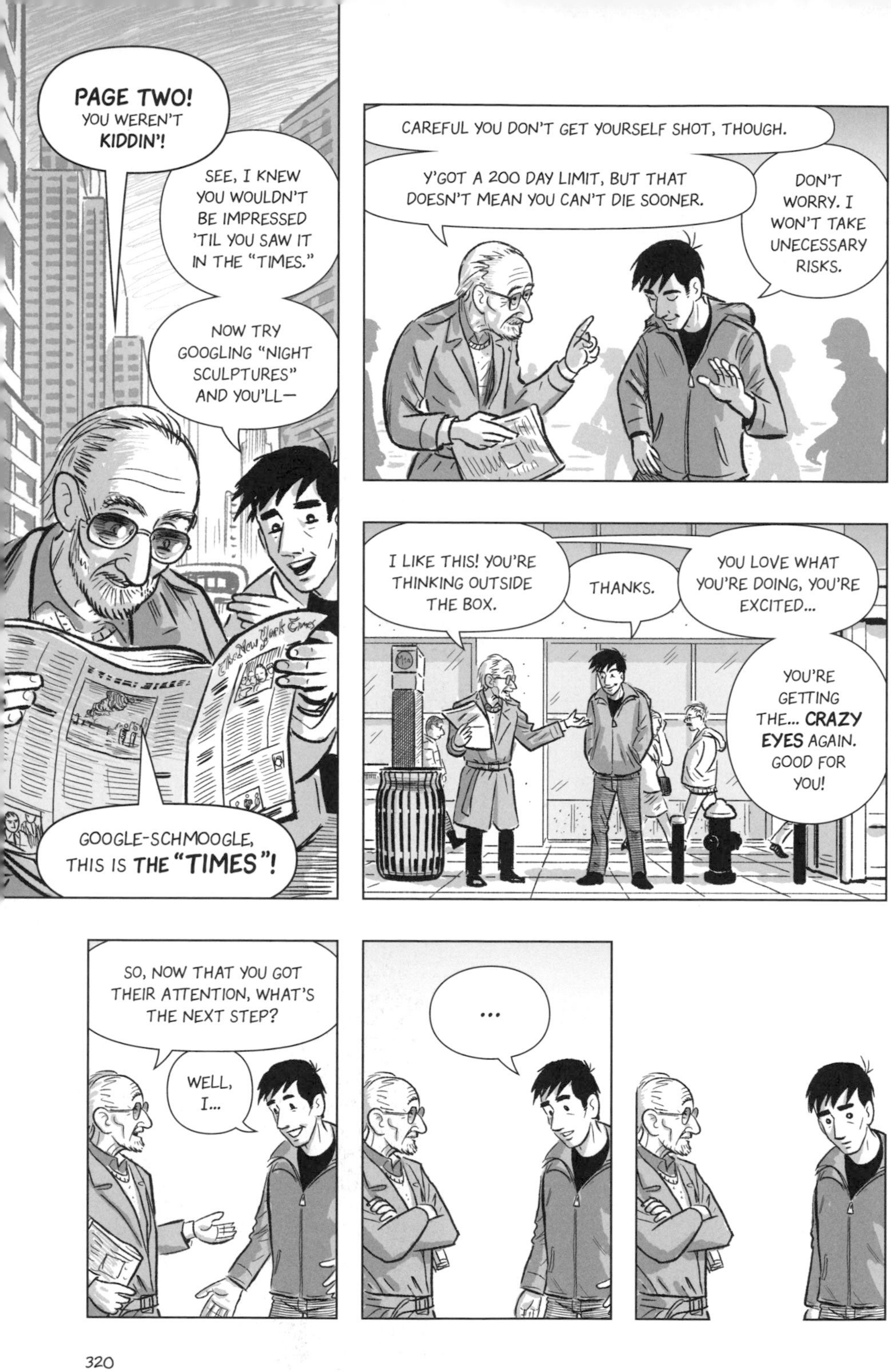
PAGE TWO! YOU WEREN'T KIDDIN'!
SEE, I KNEW YOU WOULDN'T BE IMPRESSED 'TIL YOU SAW IT IN THE "TIMES."
NOW TRY GOOGLING "NIGHT SCULPTURES" AND YOU'LL—
GOOGLE-SCHMOOGLE, THIS IS THE "TIMES"!
CAREFUL YOU DON'T GET YOURSELF SHOT, THOUGH.
Y'GOT A 200 DAY LIMIT, BUT THAT DOESN'T MEAN YOU CAN'T DIE SOONER.
DON'T WORRY. I WON'T TAKE UNECESSARY RISKS.
I LIKE THIS! YOU'RE THINKING OUTSIDE THE BOX.
THANKS.
YOU LOVE WHAT YOU'RE DOING, YOU'RE EXCITED...
YOU'RE GETTING THE... CRAZY EYES AGAIN. GOOD FOR YOU!
SO, NOW THAT YOU GOT THEIR ATTENTION, WHAT'S THE NEXT STEP?
WELL, I...
...

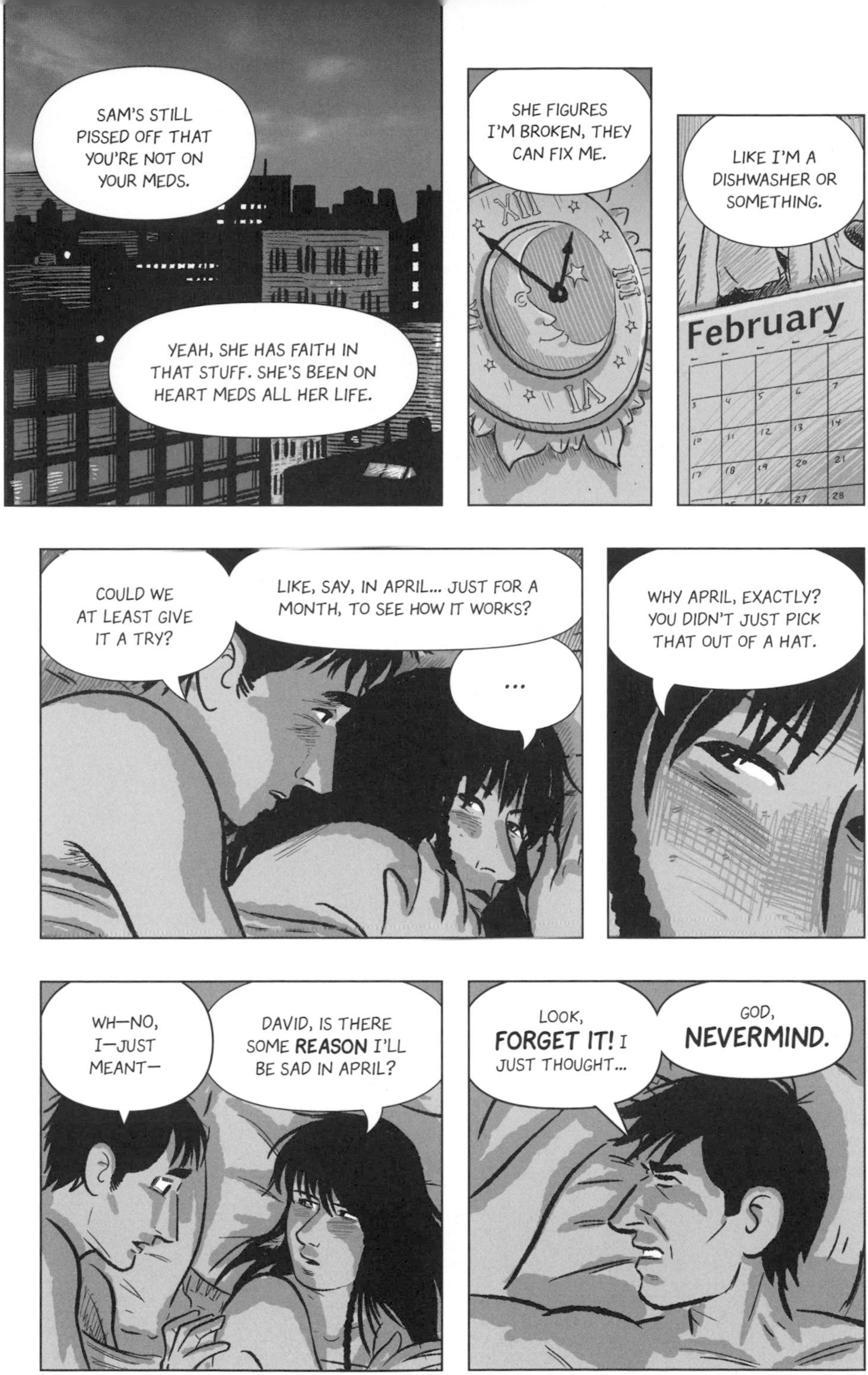
SAM'S STILL PISSED OFF THAT YOU'RE NOT ON YOUR MEDS.
YEAH, SHE HAS FAITH IN THAT STUFF. SHE'S BEEN ON HEART MEDS ALL HER LIFE.
SHE FIGURES I'M BROKEN, THEY CAN FIX ME.
LIKE I'M A DISHWASHER OR SOMETHING.
February
COULD WE AT LEAST GIVE IT A TRY?
LIKE, SAY, IN APRIL... JUST FOR A MONTH, TO SEE HOW IT WORKS?
...
WHY APRIL, EXACTLY? YOU DIDN'T JUST PICK THAT OUT OF A HAT.
WH—NO, I—JUST MEANT—
DAVID, IS THERE SOME **REASON** I'LL BE SAD IN APRIL?
LOOK, **FORGET IT!** I JUST THOUGHT...
GOD, **NEVERMIND.**

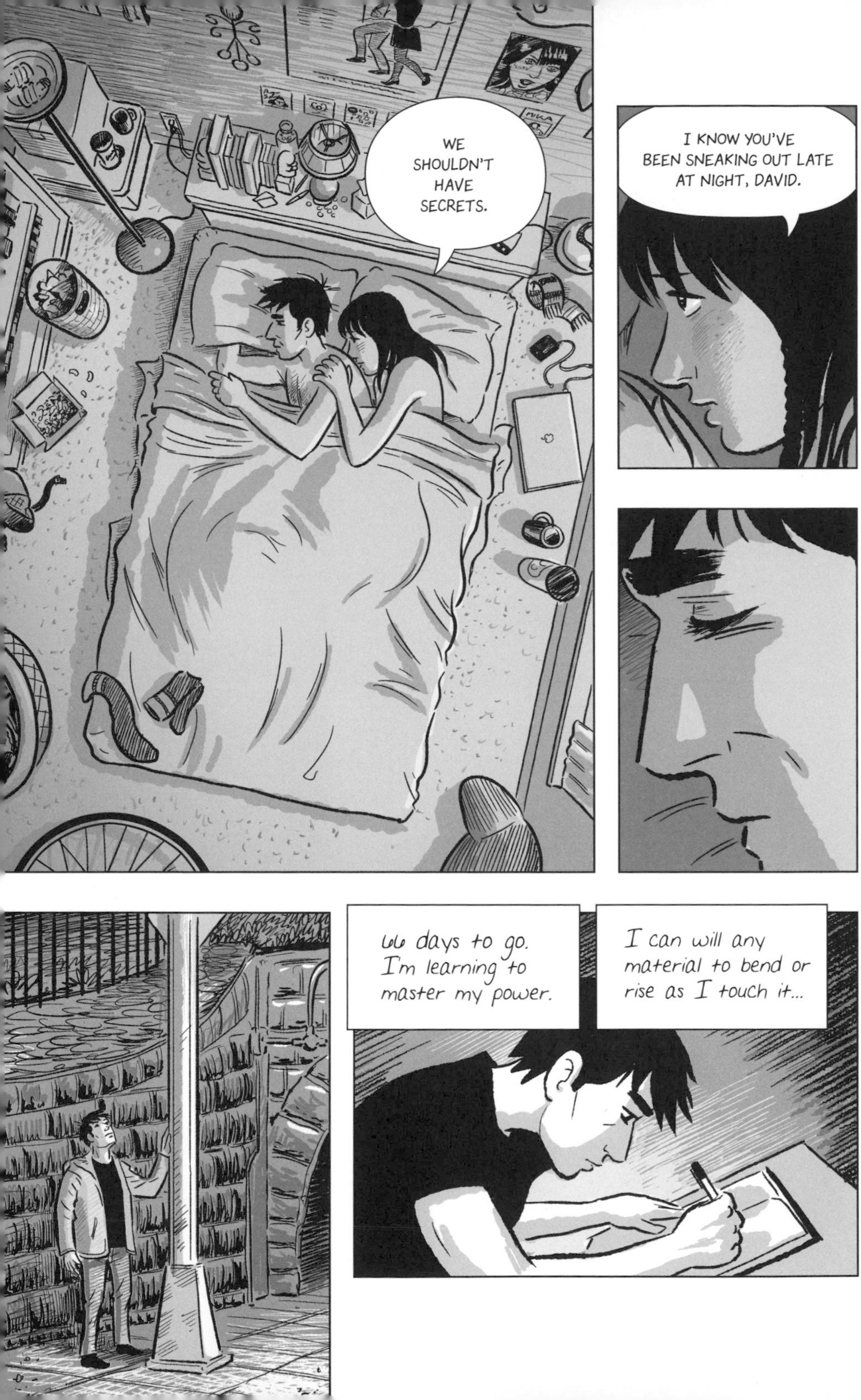
WE SHOULDN'T HAVE SECRETS.
I KNOW YOU'VE BEEN SNEAKING OUT LATE AT NIGHT, DAVID.
66 days to go. I'm learning to master my power.
I can will any material to bend or rise as I touch it...

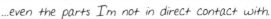
...even the parts I'm not in direct contact with.

I can feel it all from the inside, like an extension of my body.

And I'm getting faster, which has helped with the more public stuff.

599 Lexington, for example. Right across from Citicorp.

Here's how I did that one...

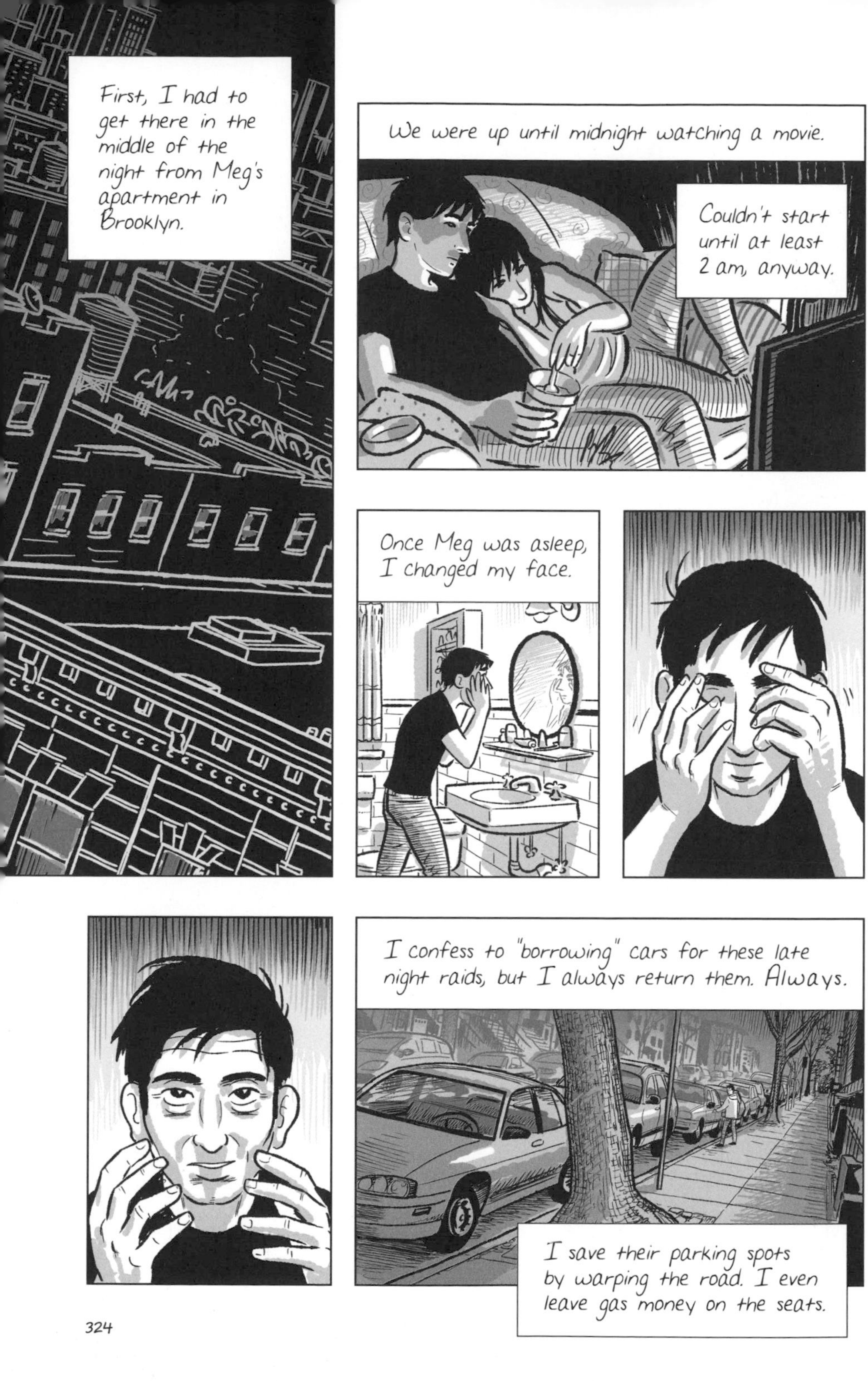
First, I had to get there in the middle of the night from Meg's apartment in Brooklyn.
We were up until midnight watching a movie.
Couldn't start until at least 2 am, anyway.
Once Meg was asleep, I changed my face.
I confess to "borrowing" cars for these late night raids, but I always return them. Always.
I save their parking spots by warping the road. I even leave gas money on the seats.

I look for old cars less likely to have sophisticated alarms or tracking.
Then I slip my own key slug in the locks—
—and "feel" my way through the tumblers.
So that night, I took my temporary wheels over the bridge and up the FDR to 53rd St.
W 52nd
6th Av
8th Ave
W 46th
E 47th
W 40th
E 39th
E 34th
5th Ave
E 30th
Park Ave S
E 23rd
E 14th
Avenue C
Bowery
E Houston
Hardly any traffic at 3 am.
I parked around the corner from my target.
First step: Keep security in.

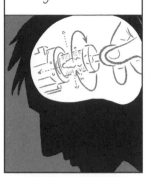

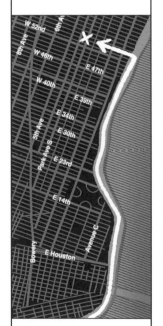

Then, as fast as I could, I snow-rolled huge chunks of the patio from all sides toward the column.

Not so much "pushing"—I'm not that strong—as willing it forward with my hands.

Took all of forty seconds.

Another three minutes to rough out the basic forms.

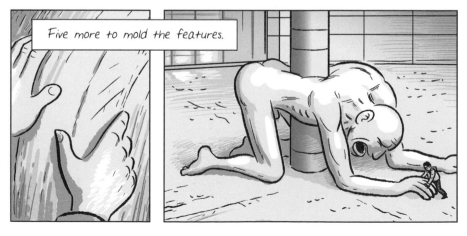

Five more to mold the features.

And I was off!

Six blocks away before I even heard the sirens.

Usually I'm the timid one...

I DUNNO. THIS NEIGHBORHOOD LOOKS KIND OF SKETCHY.

C'MON! IT'LL BE FUN! YOU WANNA LIVE FOREVER?

Yeah, I said I'd give my life for my art.

Still...

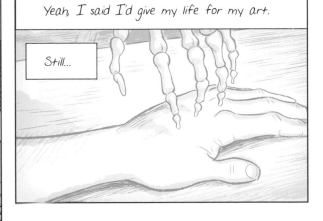

Is this the "art" I had in mind?

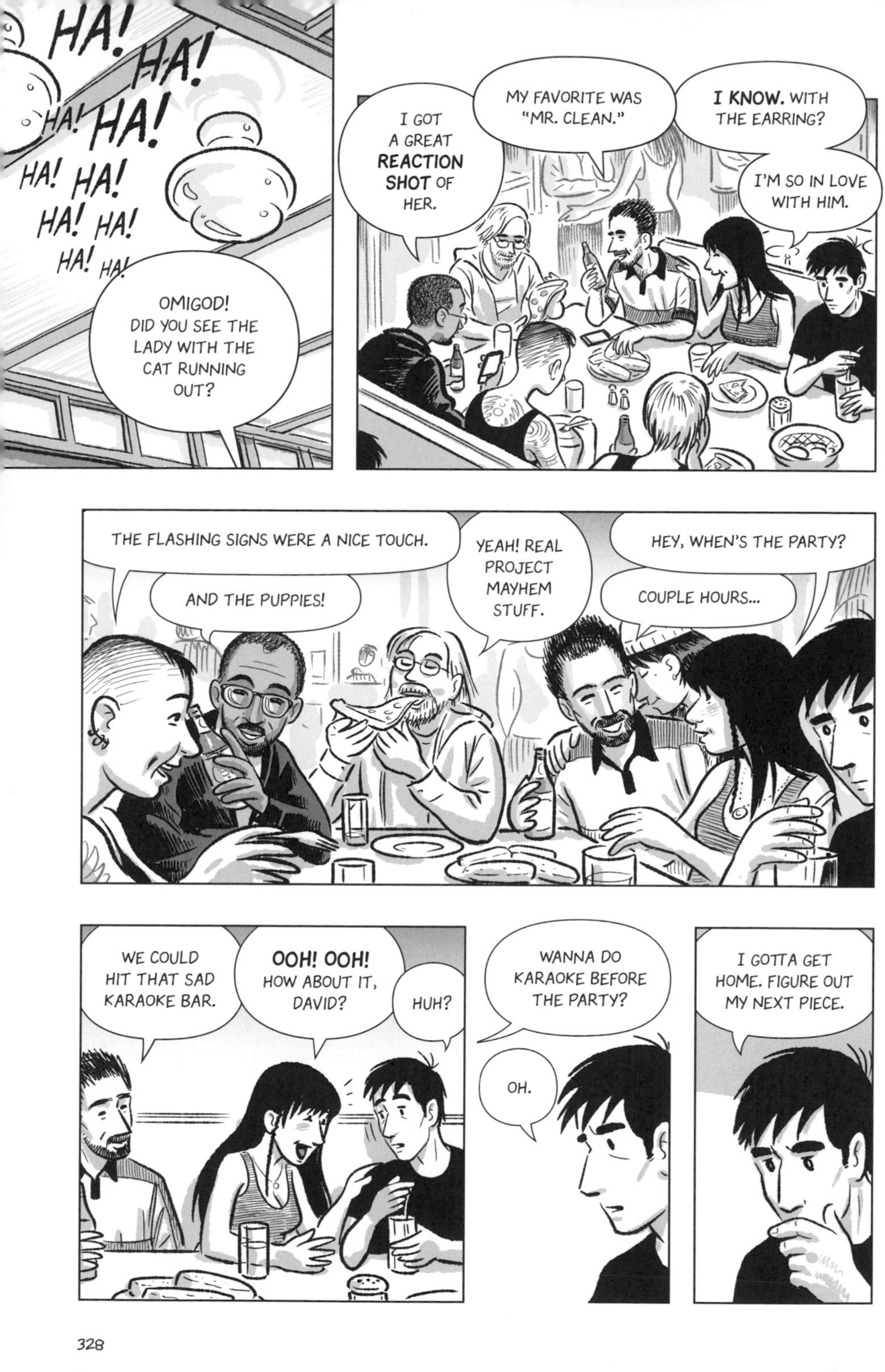
HA! HA! HA! HA! HA! HA! HA! HA! HA! HA!
OMIGOD! DID YOU SEE THE LADY WITH THE CAT RUNNING OUT?
I GOT A GREAT **REACTION SHOT** OF HER.
MY FAVORITE WAS "MR. CLEAN."
I KNOW. WITH THE EARRING?
I'M SO IN LOVE WITH HIM.
THE FLASHING SIGNS WERE A NICE TOUCH.
AND THE PUPPIES!
YEAH! REAL PROJECT MAYHEM STUFF.
HEY, WHEN'S THE PARTY?
COUPLE HOURS...
WE COULD HIT THAT SAD KARAOKE BAR.
OOH! OOH! HOW ABOUT IT, DAVID?
HUH?
WANNA DO KARAOKE BEFORE THE PARTY?
OH.
I GOTTA GET HOME. FIGURE OUT MY NEXT PIECE.

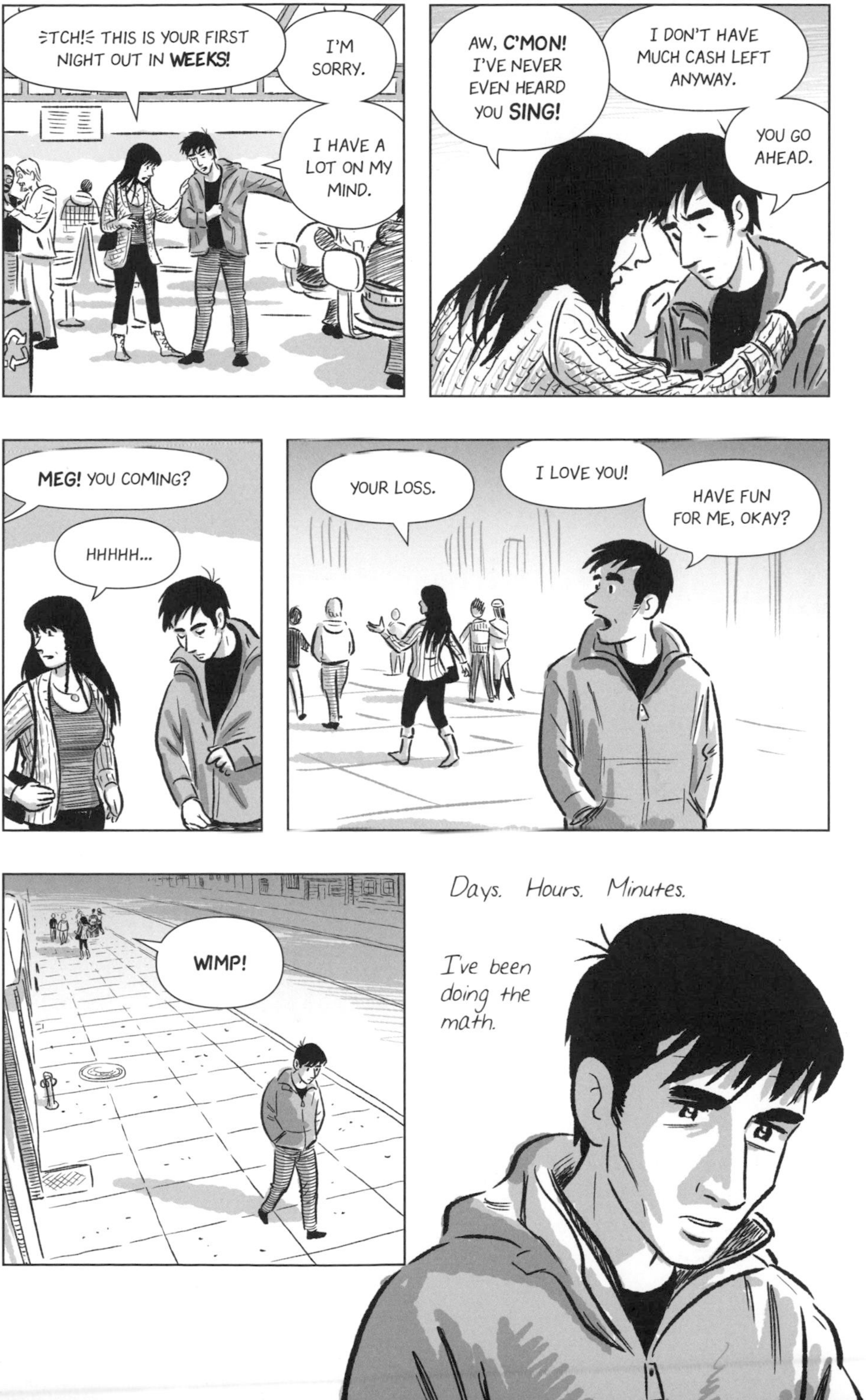
TCH! THIS IS YOUR FIRST NIGHT OUT IN WEEKS!
I'M SORRY.
I HAVE A LOT ON MY MIND.
AW, C'MON! I'VE NEVER EVEN HEARD YOU SING!
I DON'T HAVE MUCH CASH LEFT ANYWAY.
YOU GO AHEAD.
MEG! YOU COMING?
HHHHH...
YOUR LOSS.
I LOVE YOU!
HAVE FUN FOR ME, OKAY?
WIMP!
Days. Hours. Minutes.
I've been doing the math.

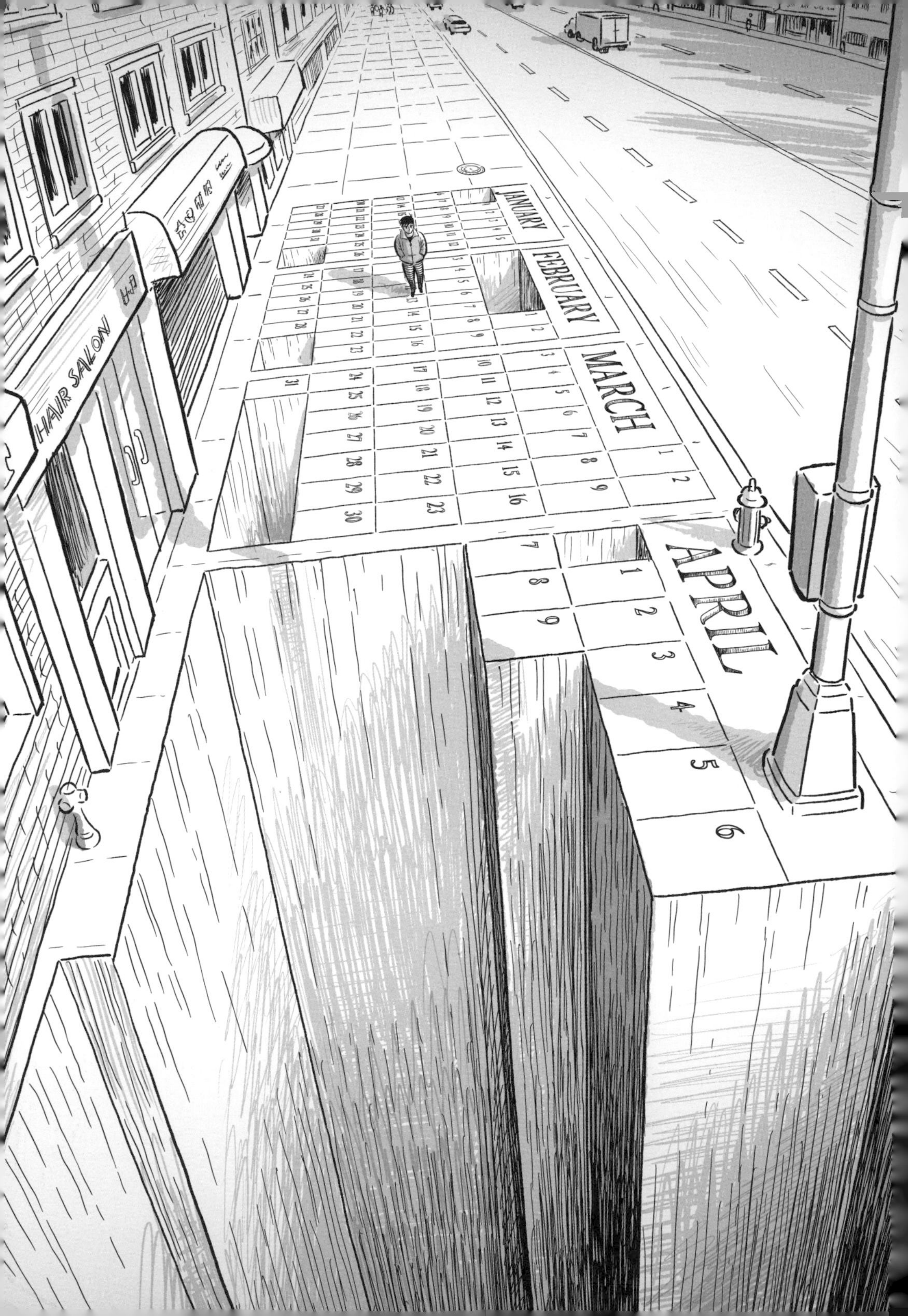
HAIR SALON
JANUARY
FEBRUARY
MARCH
APRIL

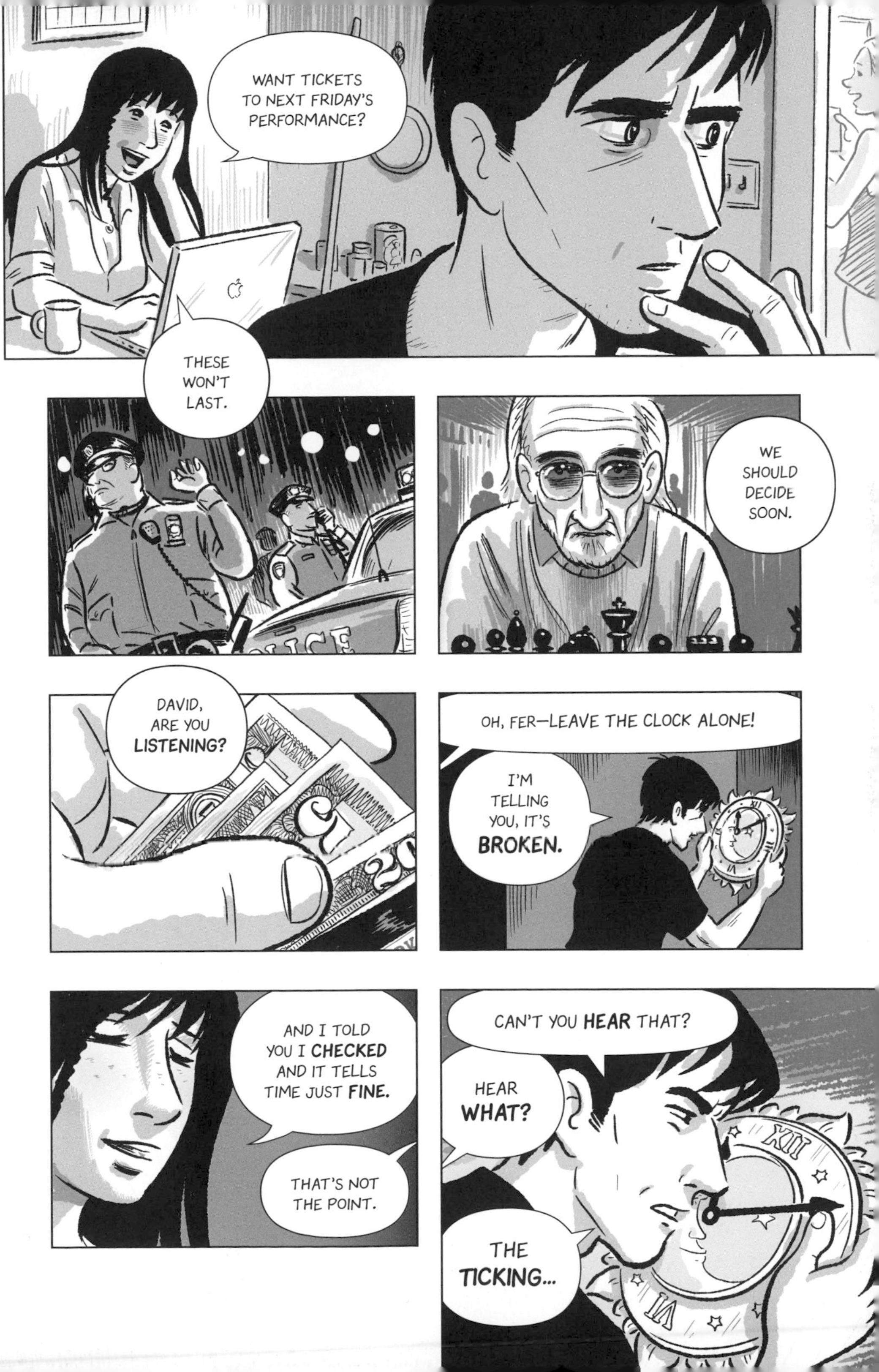
WANT TICKETS TO NEXT FRIDAY'S PERFORMANCE?
THESE WON'T LAST.
WE SHOULD DECIDE SOON.
DAVID, ARE YOU **LISTENING?**
OH, FER—LEAVE THE CLOCK ALONE!
I'M TELLING YOU, IT'S **BROKEN.**
AND I TOLD YOU I **CHECKED** AND IT TELLS TIME JUST **FINE.**
THAT'S NOT THE POINT.
CAN'T YOU **HEAR** THAT?
HEAR **WHAT?**
THE **TICKING...**

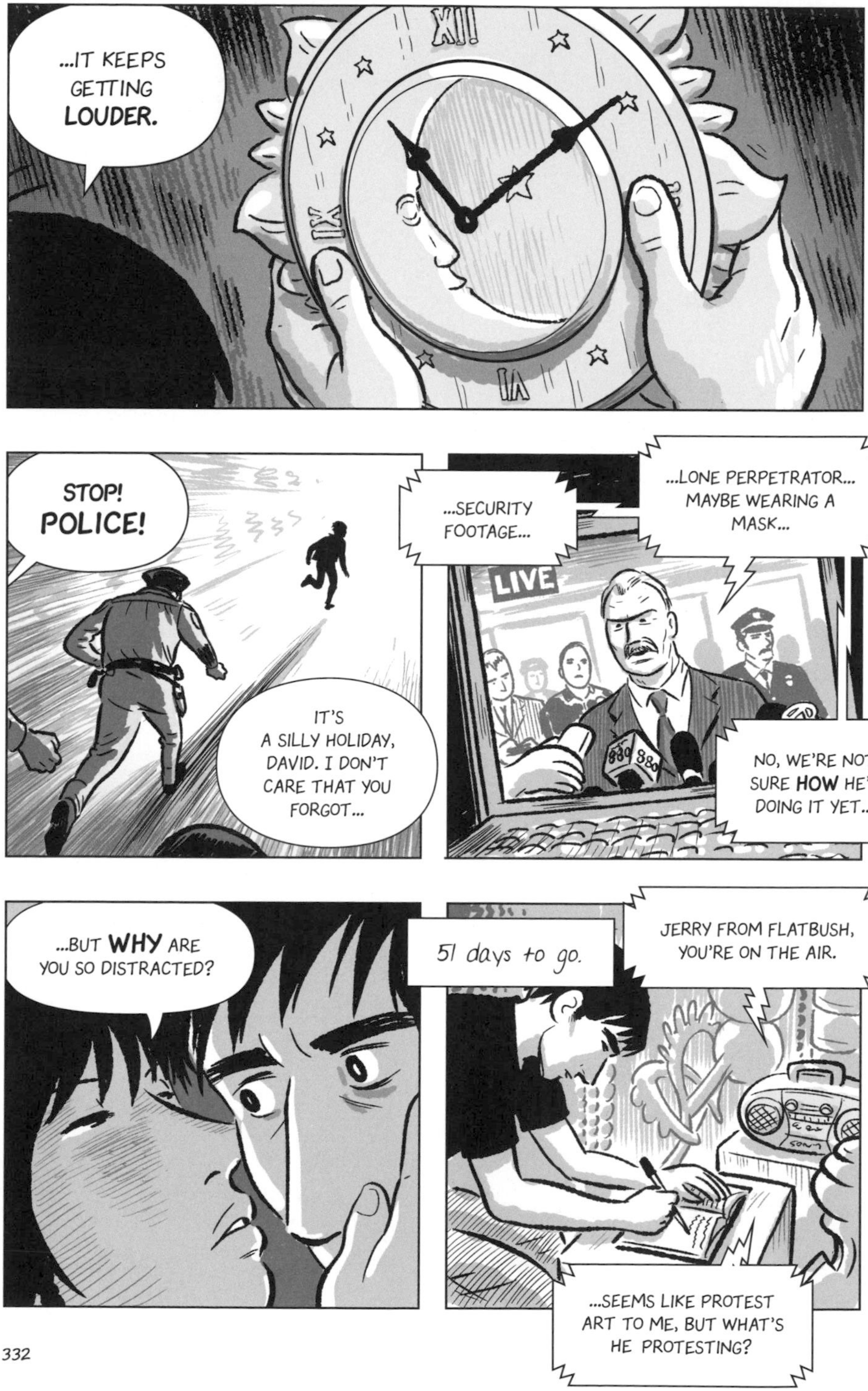
...IT KEEPS GETTING LOUDER.
STOP! POLICE!
IT'S A SILLY HOLIDAY, DAVID. I DON'T CARE THAT YOU FORGOT...
...SECURITY FOOTAGE...
...LONE PERPETRATOR... MAYBE WEARING A MASK...
LIVE
NO, WE'RE NOT SURE HOW HE'S DOING IT YET...
...BUT WHY ARE YOU SO DISTRACTED?
51 days to go.
JERRY FROM FLATBUSH, YOU'RE ON THE AIR.
...SEEMS LIKE PROTEST ART TO ME, BUT WHAT'S HE PROTESTING?

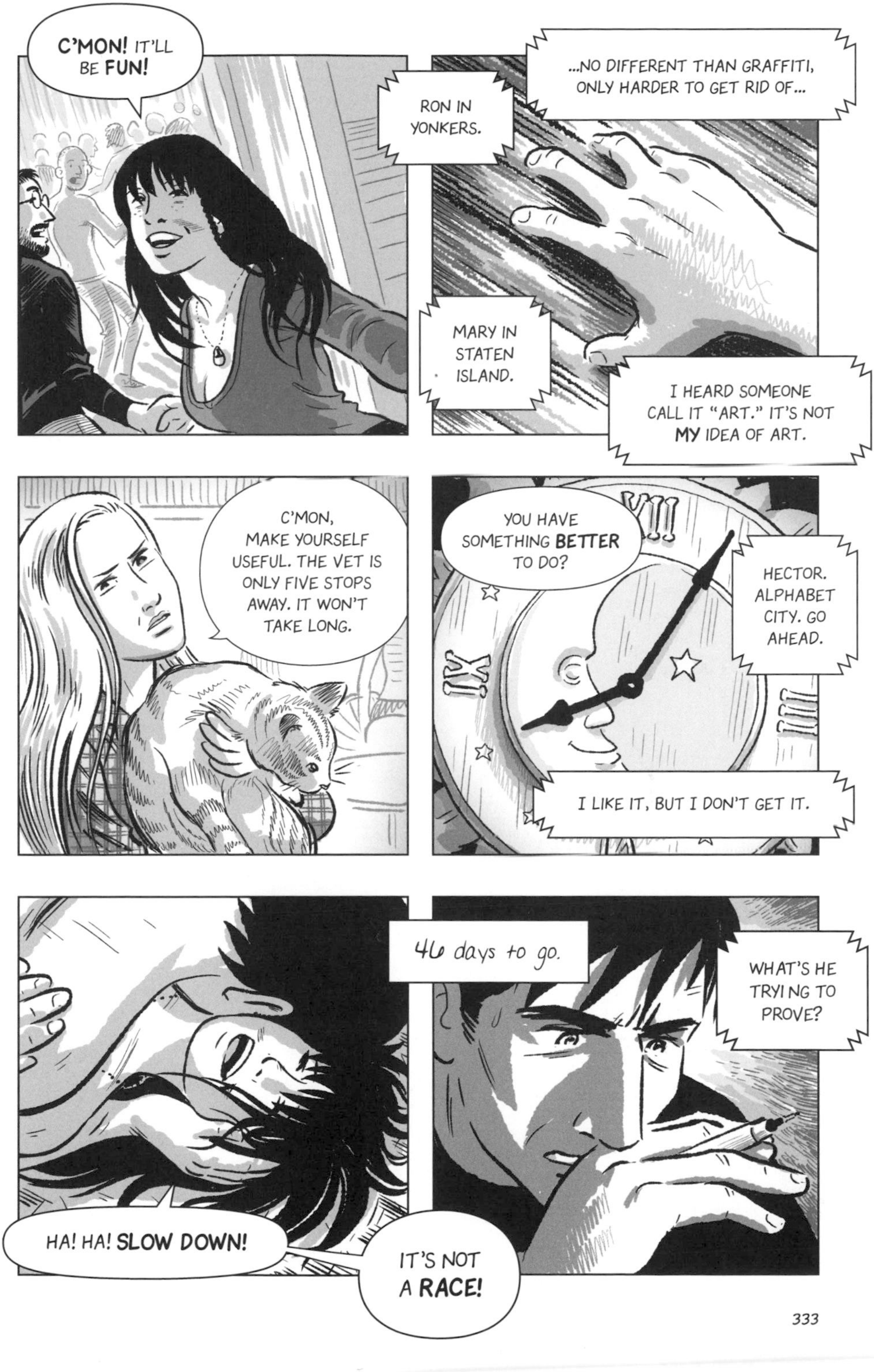
C'MON! IT'LL BE FUN!
RON IN YONKERS.
...NO DIFFERENT THAN GRAFFITI, ONLY HARDER TO GET RID OF...
MARY IN STATEN ISLAND.
I HEARD SOMEONE CALL IT "ART." IT'S NOT MY IDEA OF ART.
C'MON, MAKE YOURSELF USEFUL. THE VET IS ONLY FIVE STOPS AWAY. IT WON'T TAKE LONG.
YOU HAVE SOMETHING BETTER TO DO?
HECTOR. ALPHABET CITY. GO AHEAD.
I LIKE IT, BUT I DON'T GET IT.
46 days to go.
WHAT'S HE TRYING TO PROVE?
HA! HA! SLOW DOWN!
IT'S NOT A RACE!

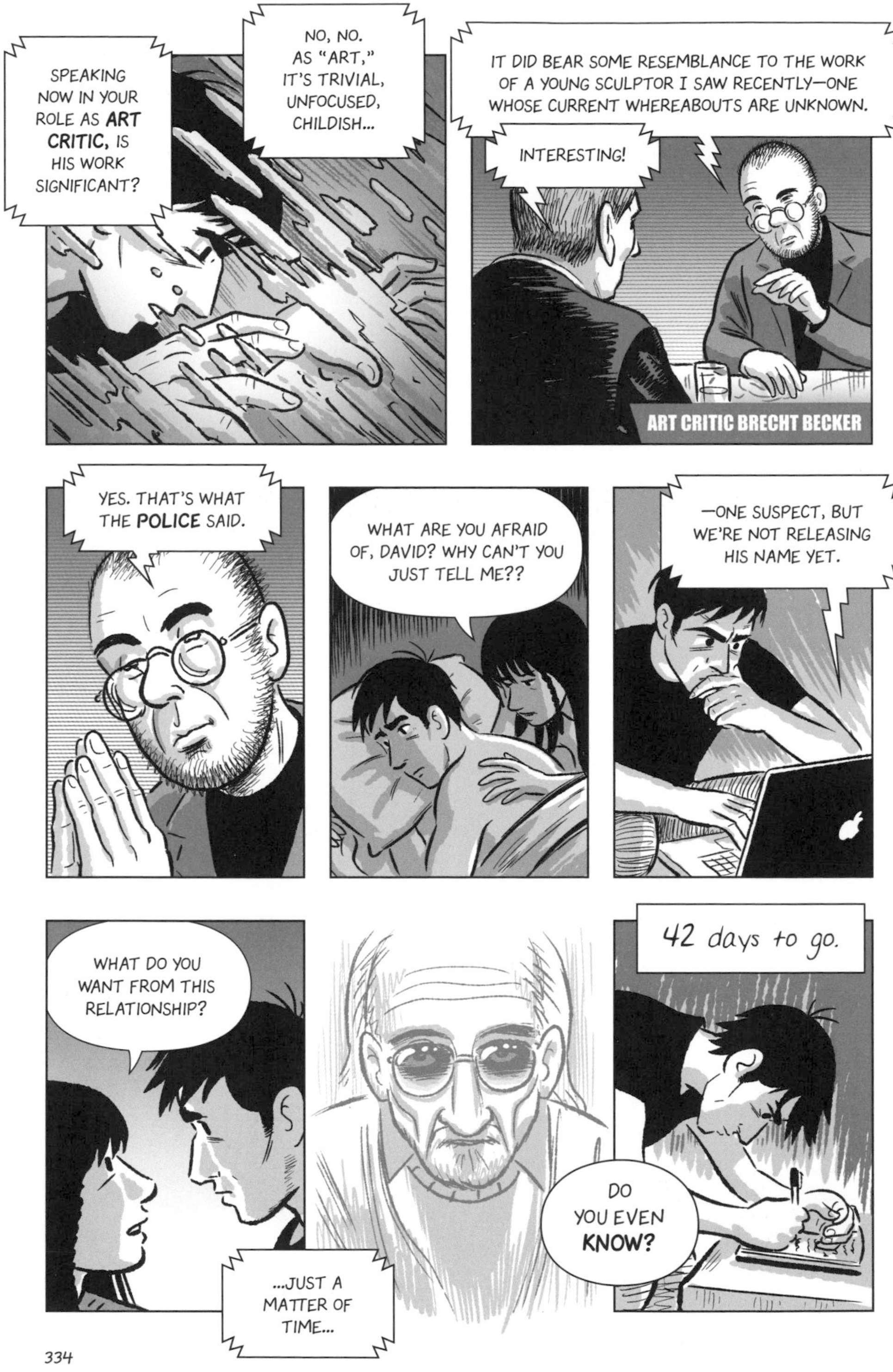
SPEAKING NOW IN YOUR ROLE AS **ART CRITIC,** IS HIS WORK SIGNIFICANT?
NO, NO. AS "ART," IT'S TRIVIAL, UNFOCUSED, CHILDISH...
IT DID BEAR SOME RESEMBLANCE TO THE WORK OF A YOUNG SCULPTOR I SAW RECENTLY—ONE WHOSE CURRENT WHEREABOUTS ARE UNKNOWN.
INTERESTING!
ART CRITIC BRECHT BECKER
YES. THAT'S WHAT THE **POLICE** SAID.
WHAT ARE YOU AFRAID OF, DAVID? WHY CAN'T YOU JUST TELL ME??
—ONE SUSPECT, BUT WE'RE NOT RELEASING HIS NAME YET.
WHAT DO YOU WANT FROM THIS RELATIONSHIP?
...JUST A MATTER OF TIME...
42 days to go.
DO YOU EVEN **KNOW?**

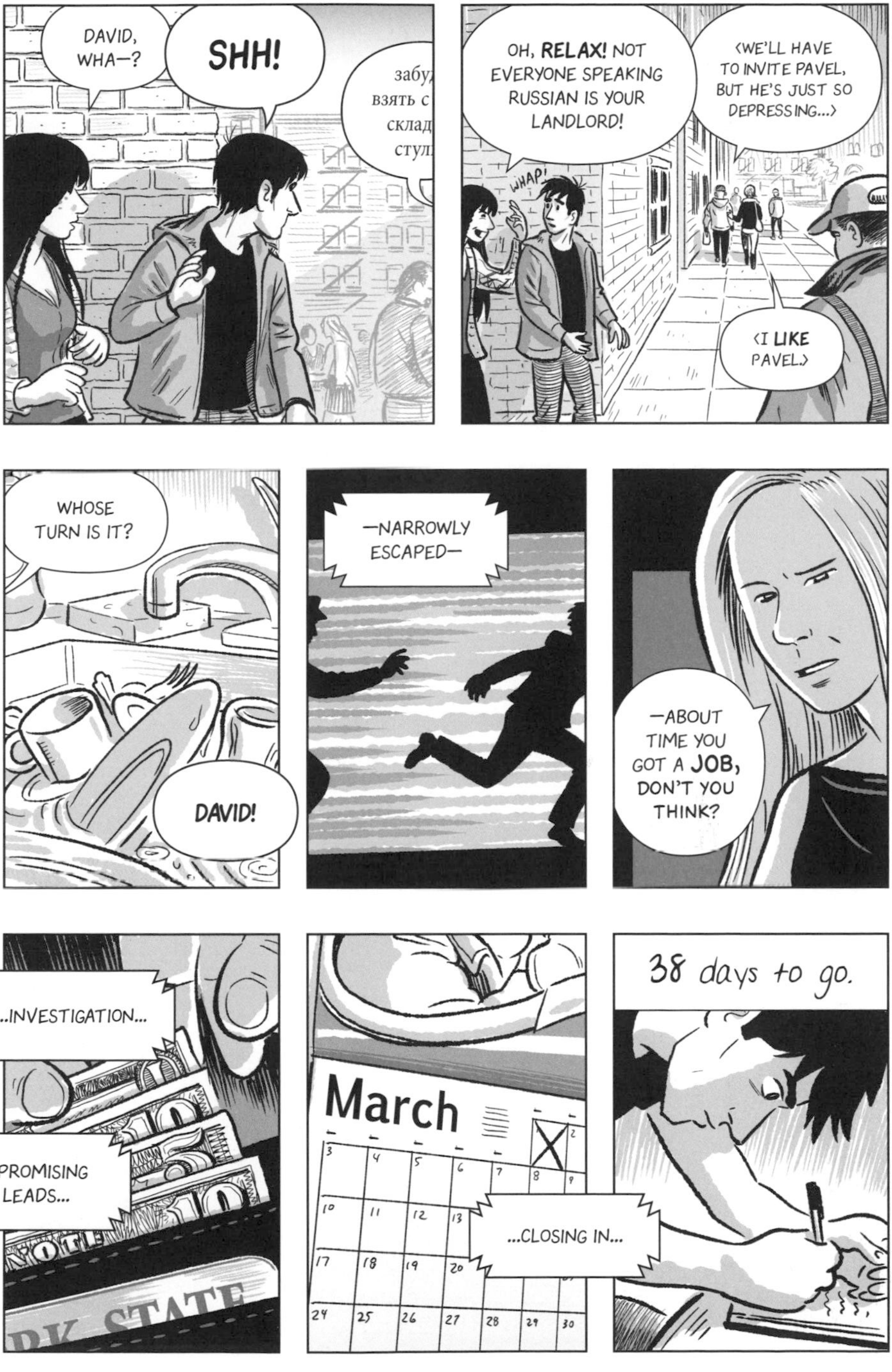
DAVID, WHA—?
SHH!
забуд
взять с
склад
стул
OH, RELAX! NOT EVERYONE SPEAKING RUSSIAN IS YOUR LANDLORD!
WHAP!
‹WE'LL HAVE TO INVITE PAVEL, BUT HE'S JUST SO DEPRESSING...›
‹I LIKE PAVEL.›
WHOSE TURN IS IT?
DAVID!
—NARROWLY ESCAPED—
—ABOUT TIME YOU GOT A JOB, DON'T YOU THINK?
...INVESTIGATION...
...PROMISING LEADS...
RK STATE
March
...CLOSING IN...
38 days to go.

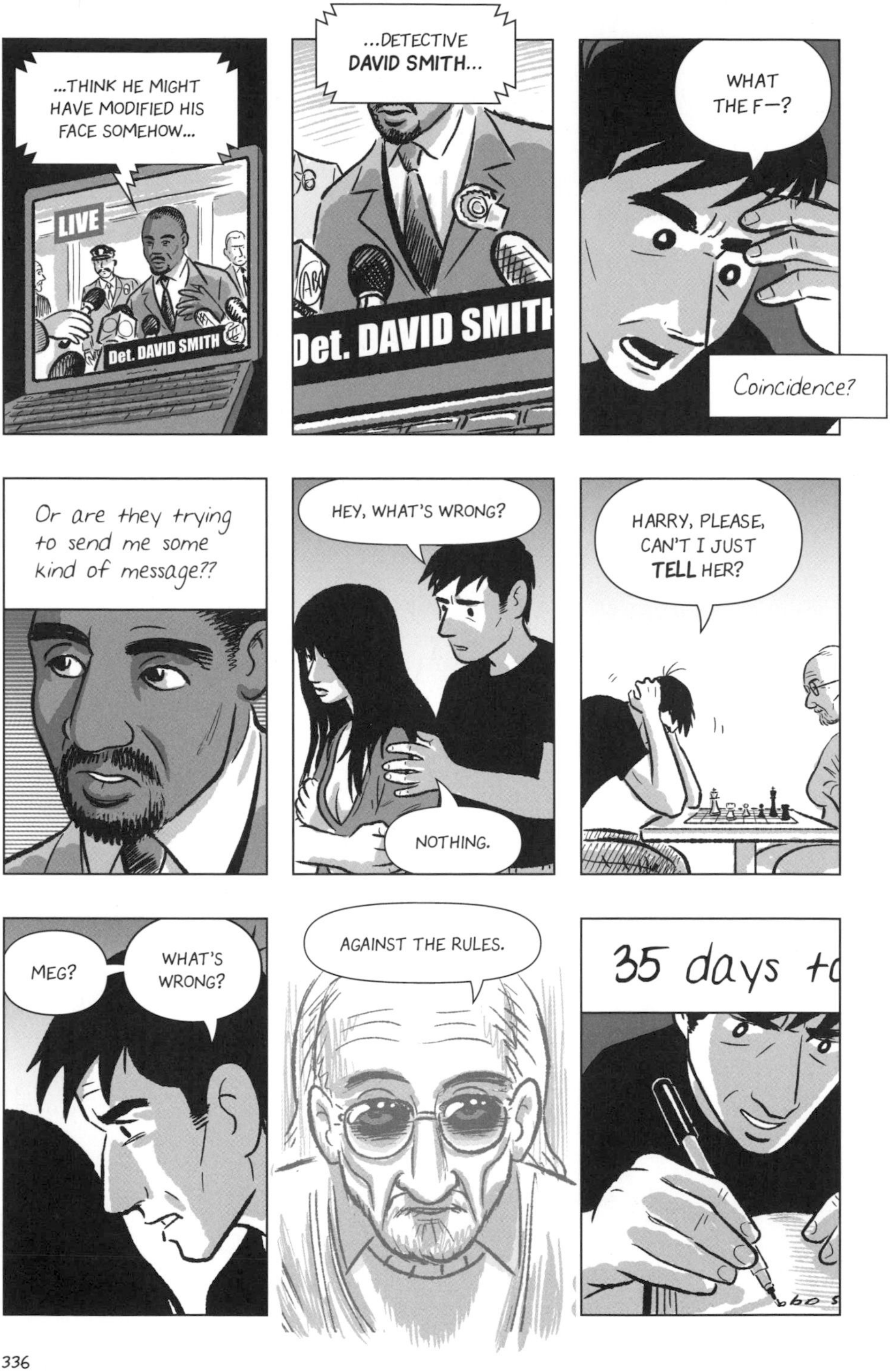
...THINK HE MIGHT HAVE MODIFIED HIS FACE SOMEHOW...
LIVE
Det. DAVID SMITH
...DETECTIVE DAVID SMITH...
Det. DAVID SMITH
WHAT THE F—?
Coincidence?
Or are they trying to send me some kind of message??
HEY, WHAT'S WRONG?
NOTHING.
HARRY, PLEASE, CAN'T I JUST TELL HER?
MEG?
WHAT'S WRONG?
AGAINST THE RULES.
35 days t

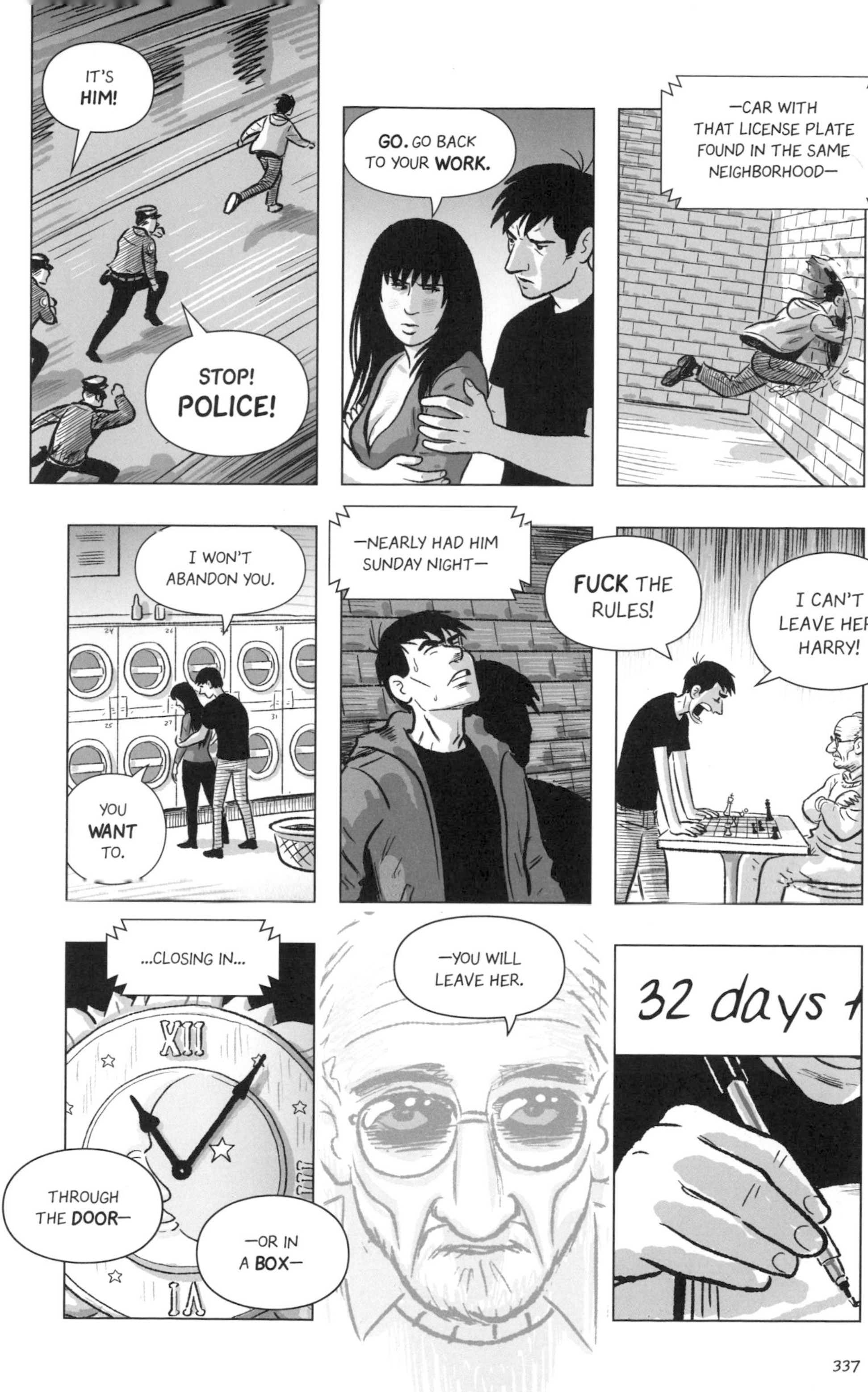
IT'S HIM!
STOP! POLICE!
GO. GO BACK TO YOUR WORK.
—CAR WITH THAT LICENSE PLATE FOUND IN THE SAME NEIGHBORHOOD—
I WON'T ABANDON YOU.
YOU WANT TO.
—NEARLY HAD HIM SUNDAY NIGHT—
FUCK THE RULES!
I CAN'T LEAVE HER, HARRY!
...CLOSING IN...
THROUGH THE DOOR—
—OR IN A BOX—
—YOU WILL LEAVE HER.
32 days

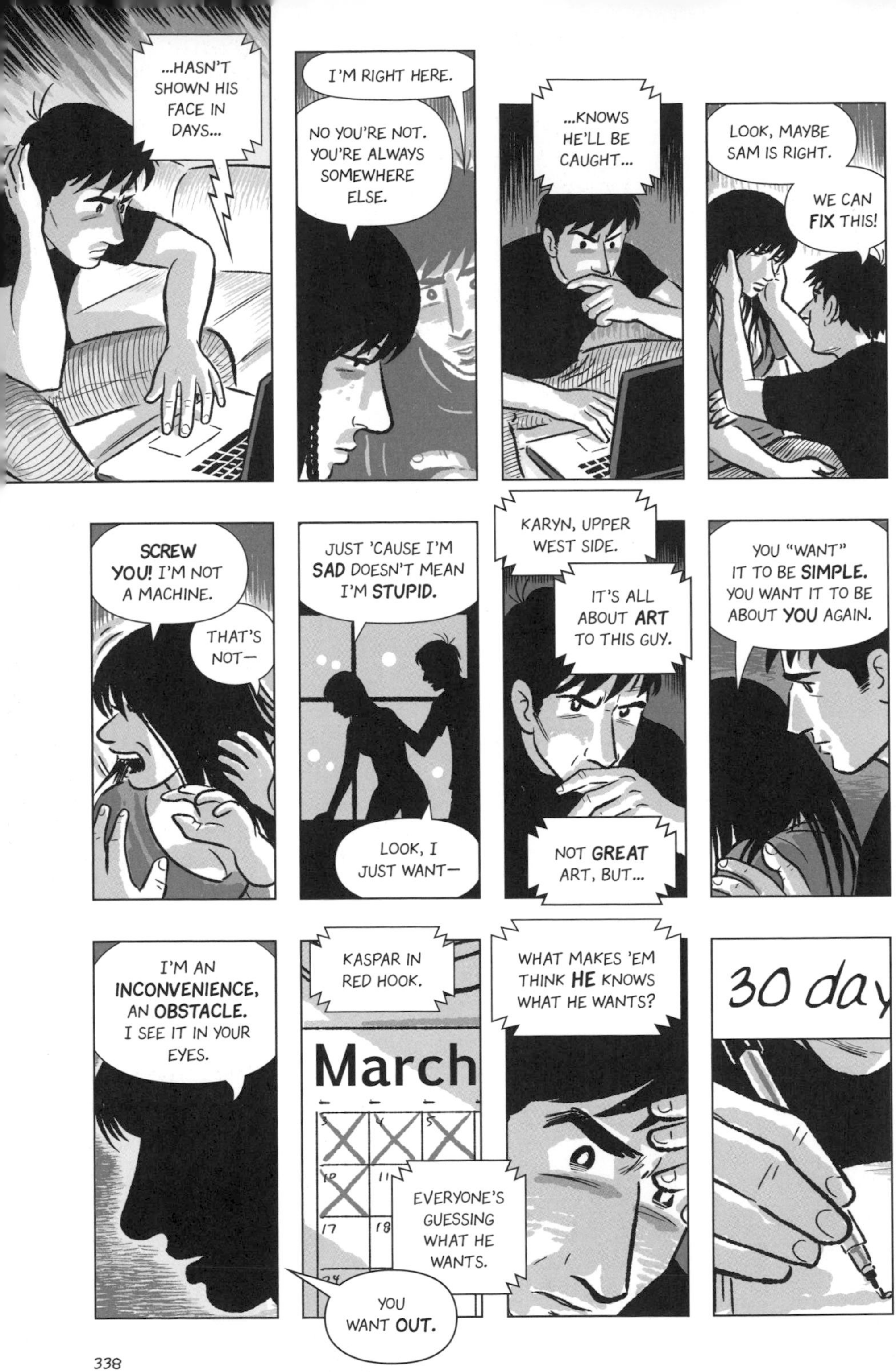
...HASN'T SHOWN HIS FACE IN DAYS...
I'M RIGHT HERE.
NO YOU'RE NOT. YOU'RE ALWAYS SOMEWHERE ELSE.
...KNOWS HE'LL BE CAUGHT...
LOOK, MAYBE SAM IS RIGHT.
WE CAN FIX THIS!
SCREW YOU! I'M NOT A MACHINE.
THAT'S NOT—
JUST 'CAUSE I'M SAD DOESN'T MEAN I'M STUPID.
LOOK, I JUST WANT—
KARYN, UPPER WEST SIDE.
IT'S ALL ABOUT ART TO THIS GUY.
NOT GREAT ART, BUT...
YOU "WANT" IT TO BE SIMPLE. YOU WANT IT TO BE ABOUT YOU AGAIN.
I'M AN INCONVENIENCE, AN OBSTACLE. I SEE IT IN YOUR EYES.
KASPAR IN RED HOOK.
March
EVERYONE'S GUESSING WHAT HE WANTS.
YOU WANT OUT.
WHAT MAKES 'EM THINK HE KNOWS WHAT HE WANTS?
30 day

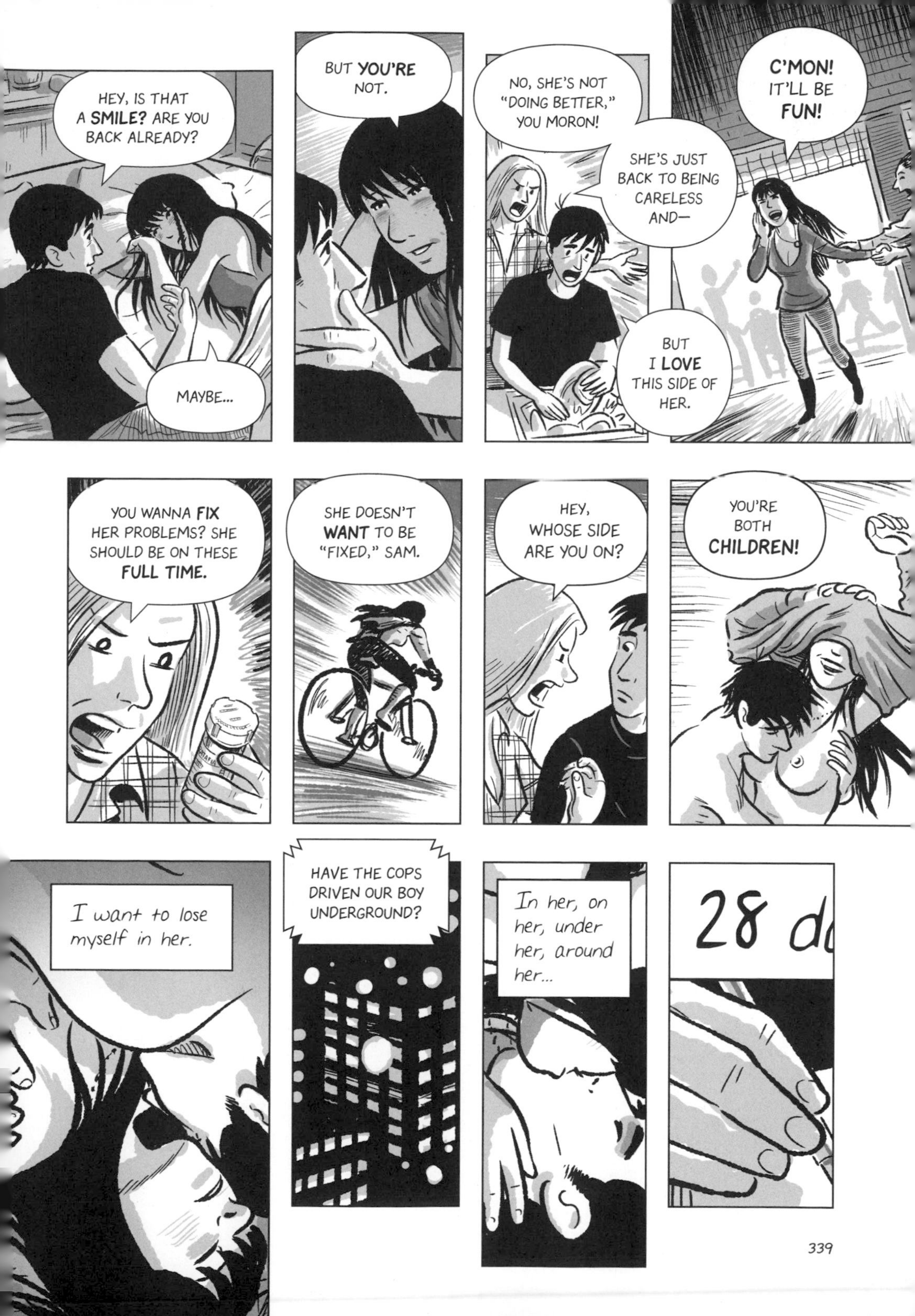
HEY, IS THAT A **SMILE?** ARE YOU BACK ALREADY?
MAYBE...
BUT **YOU'RE** NOT.
NO, SHE'S NOT "DOING BETTER," YOU MORON!
SHE'S JUST BACK TO BEING CARELESS AND—
BUT I **LOVE** THIS SIDE OF HER.
C'MON! IT'LL BE **FUN!**
YOU WANNA **FIX** HER PROBLEMS? SHE SHOULD BE ON THESE **FULL TIME.**
SHE DOESN'T **WANT** TO BE "FIXED," SAM.
HEY, WHOSE SIDE ARE YOU ON?
YOU'RE BOTH **CHILDREN!**
I want to lose myself in her.
HAVE THE COPS DRIVEN OUR BOY UNDERGROUND?
In her, on her, under her, around her...
28 d

...until I can't tell where I begin or end...

...until I can't remember my own name.

...CLOSING IN.

DAVID SM

JUST A MATTER OF **TIME.**

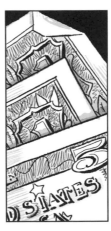

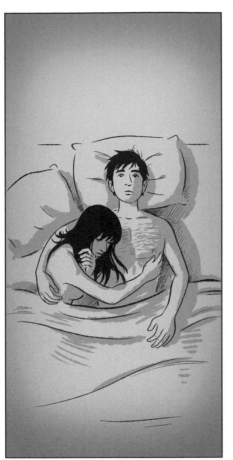

TIC -TIC -TIC -TIC -TIC -TIC

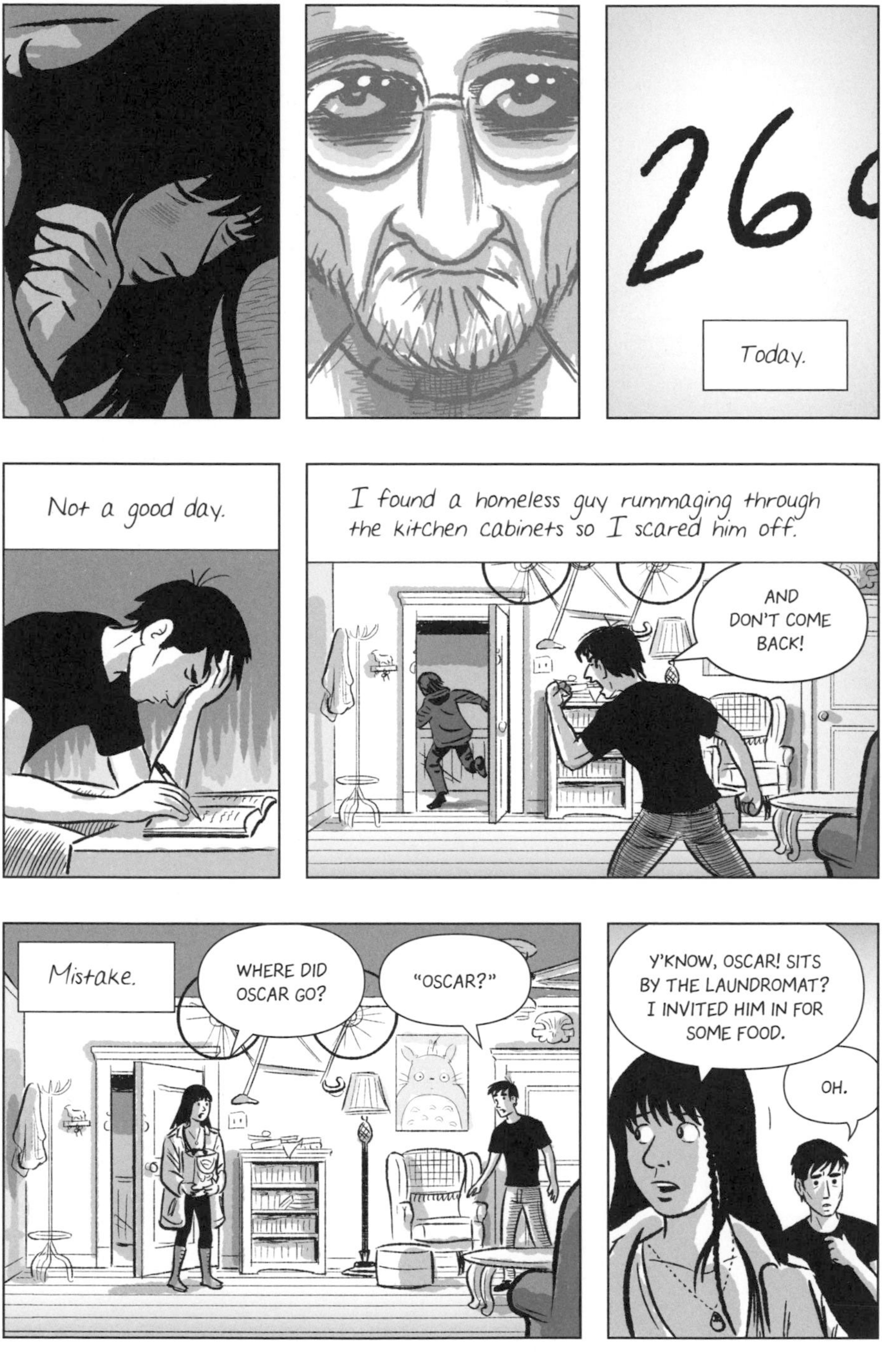
26
Today.
Not a good day.
I found a homeless guy rummaging through the kitchen cabinets so I scared him off.
AND DON'T COME BACK!
Mistake.
WHERE DID OSCAR GO?
"OSCAR?"
Y'KNOW, OSCAR! SITS BY THE LAUNDROMAT? I INVITED HIM IN FOR SOME FOOD.
OH.

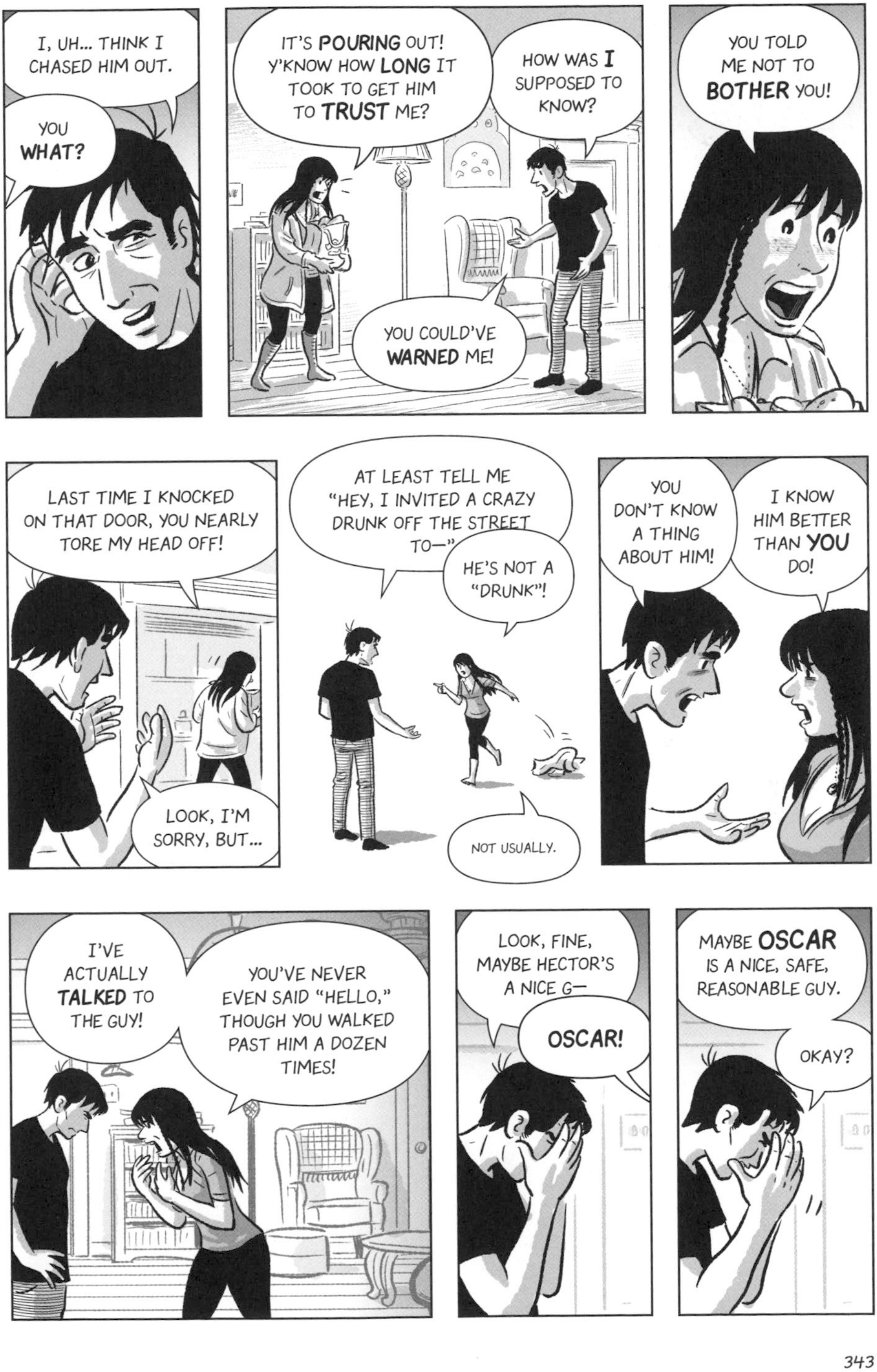
I, UH... THINK I CHASED HIM OUT.
YOU WHAT?
IT'S POURING OUT! Y'KNOW HOW LONG IT TOOK TO GET HIM TO TRUST ME?
HOW WAS I SUPPOSED TO KNOW?
YOU COULD'VE WARNED ME!
YOU TOLD ME NOT TO BOTHER YOU!
LAST TIME I KNOCKED ON THAT DOOR, YOU NEARLY TORE MY HEAD OFF!
LOOK, I'M SORRY, BUT...
AT LEAST TELL ME "HEY, I INVITED A CRAZY DRUNK OFF THE STREET TO—"
HE'S NOT A "DRUNK"!
NOT USUALLY.
YOU DON'T KNOW A THING ABOUT HIM!
I KNOW HIM BETTER THAN YOU DO!
I'VE ACTUALLY TALKED TO THE GUY!
YOU'VE NEVER EVEN SAID "HELLO," THOUGH YOU WALKED PAST HIM A DOZEN TIMES!
LOOK, FINE, MAYBE HECTOR'S A NICE G—
OSCAR!
MAYBE OSCAR IS A NICE, SAFE, REASONABLE GUY.
OKAY?

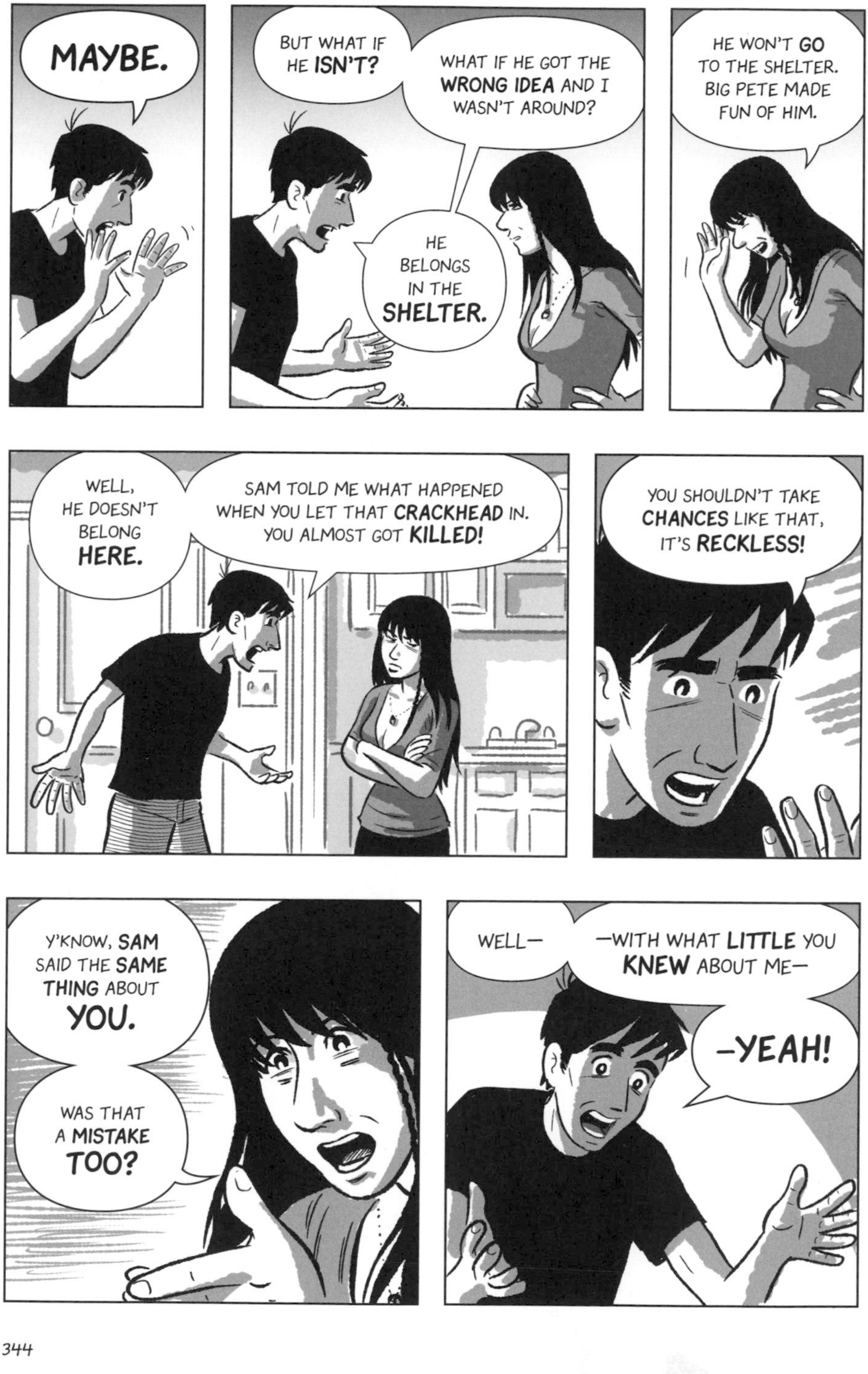
MAYBE.
BUT WHAT IF HE ISN'T?
WHAT IF HE GOT THE WRONG IDEA AND I WASN'T AROUND?
HE BELONGS IN THE SHELTER.
HE WON'T GO TO THE SHELTER. BIG PETE MADE FUN OF HIM.
WELL, HE DOESN'T BELONG HERE.
SAM TOLD ME WHAT HAPPENED WHEN YOU LET THAT CRACKHEAD IN. YOU ALMOST GOT KILLED!
YOU SHOULDN'T TAKE CHANCES LIKE THAT, IT'S RECKLESS!
Y'KNOW, SAM SAID THE SAME THING ABOUT YOU.
WAS THAT A MISTAKE TOO?
WELL—
—WITH WHAT LITTLE YOU KNEW ABOUT ME—
—YEAH!

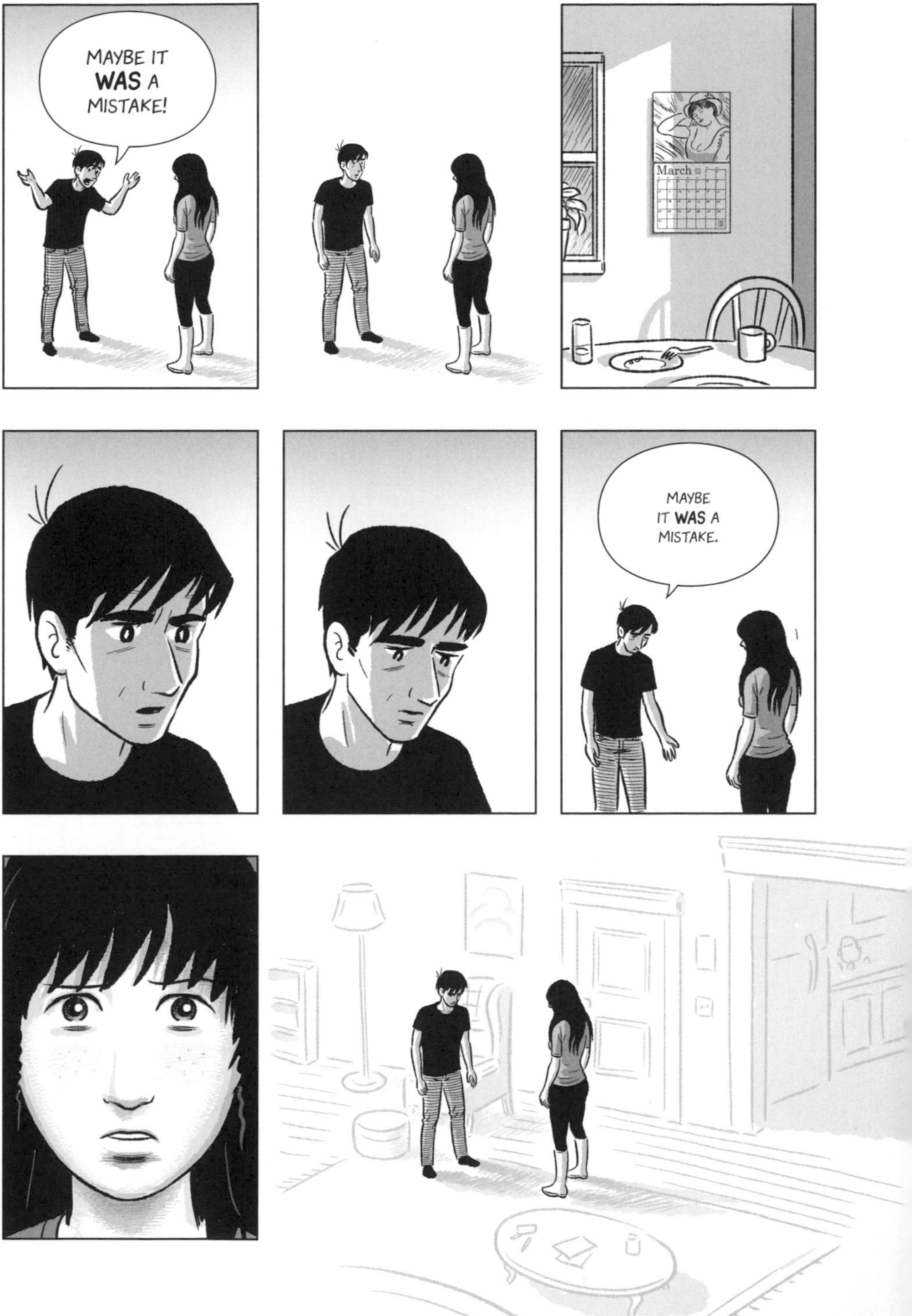
MAYBE IT **WAS** A MISTAKE!
March
MAYBE IT **WAS** A MISTAKE.

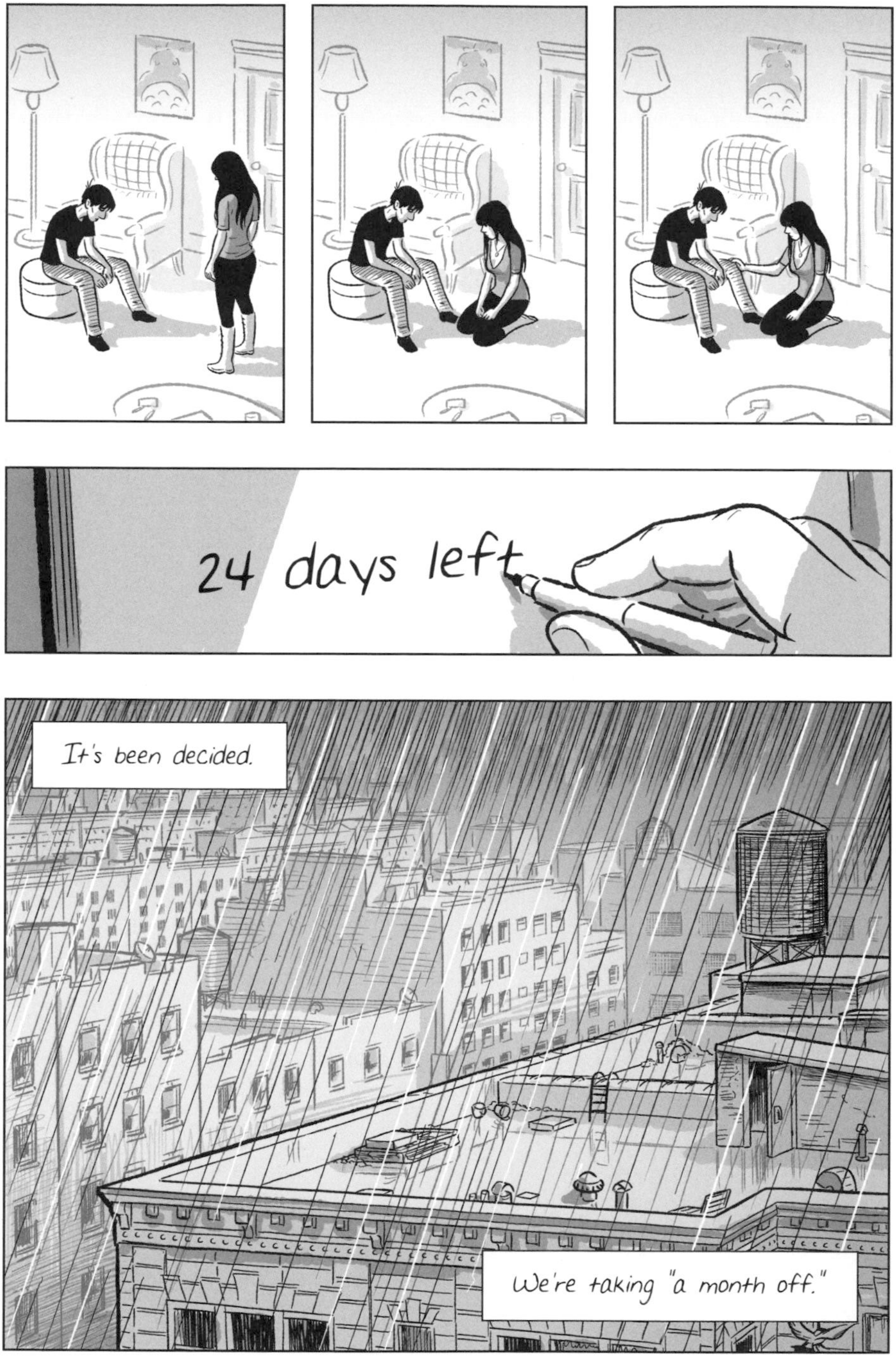
24 days left
It's been decided.
We're taking "a month off."

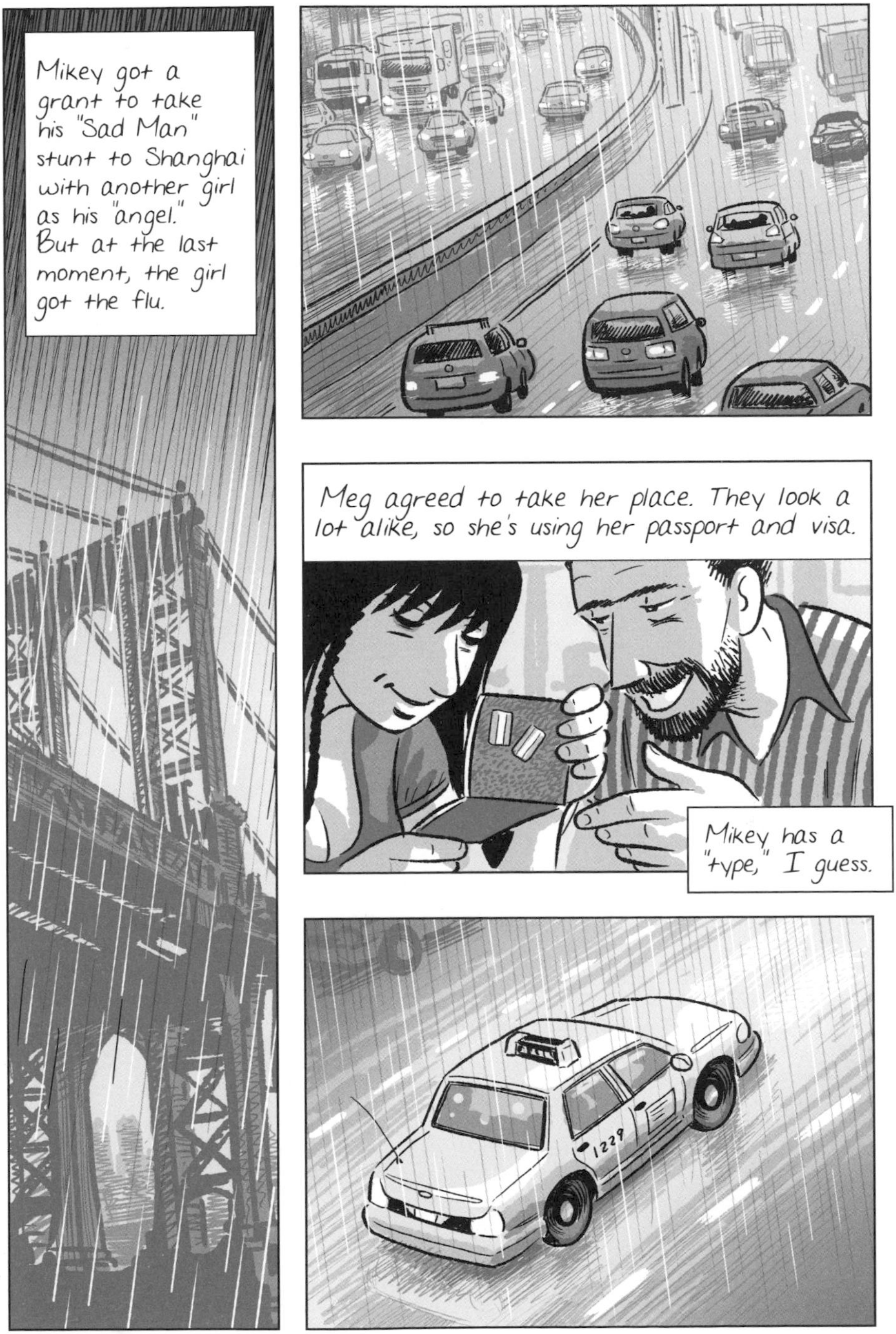

Mikey got a grant to take his "Sad Man" stunt to Shanghai with another girl as his "angel." But at the last moment, the girl got the flu.
Meg agreed to take her place. They look a lot alike, so she's using her passport and visa.
Mikey has a "type," I guess.
1229

The whole idea sounds crazy and dangerous to me, but that's Meg.

They'll train locals for most roles, but their tech guy, who's loaded, is joining them and going from there on an Asian backpacking trip—

—and he's got a super-nice apartment on the Upper West Side—

—which I get to house-sit for a month while he's gone.

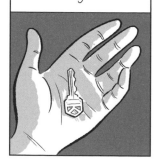

Meg figures we'll talk about whether or not we have a future together when the month is up.

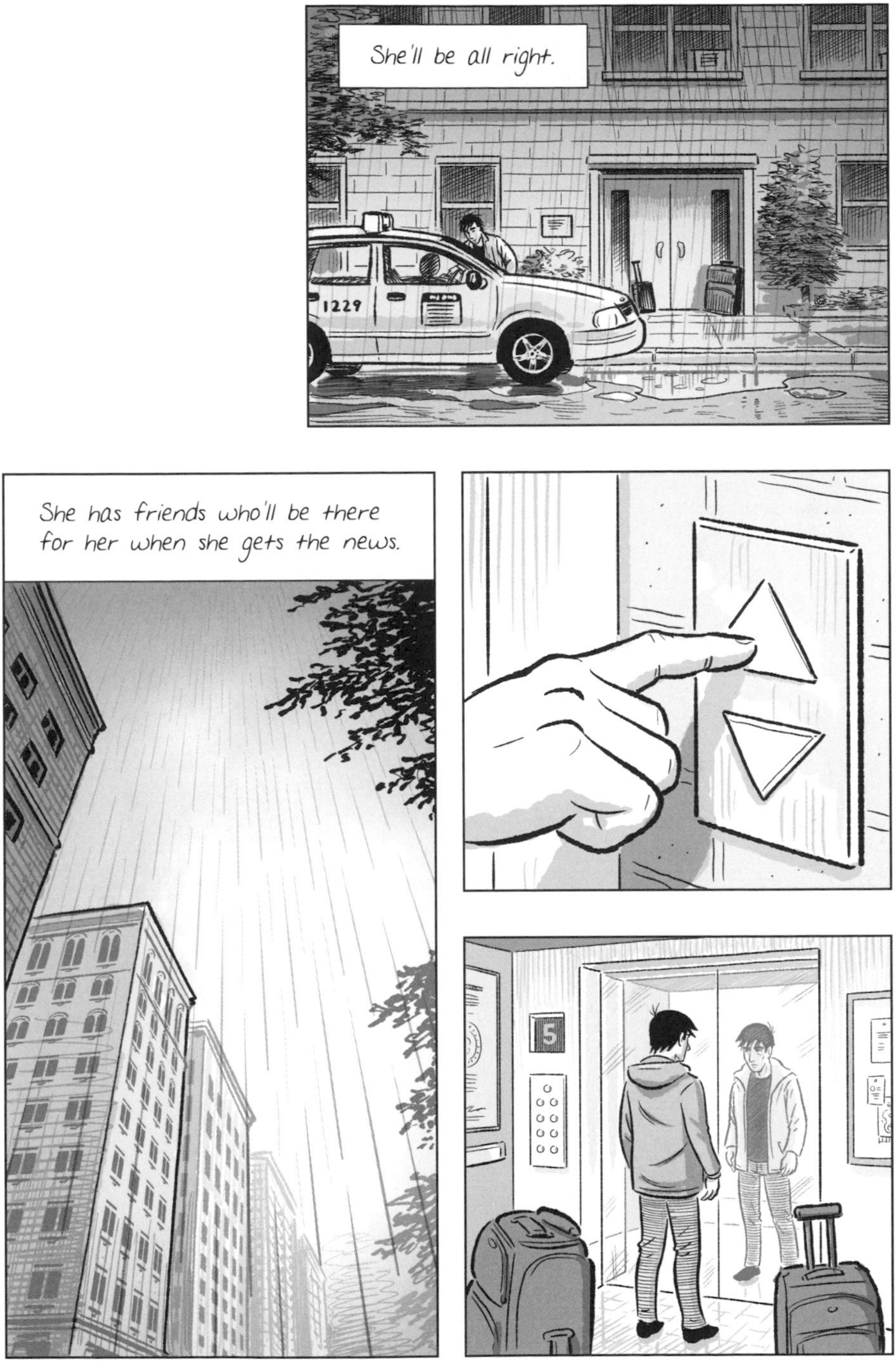
She'll be all right.
1229
She has friends who'll be there for her when she gets the news.
5

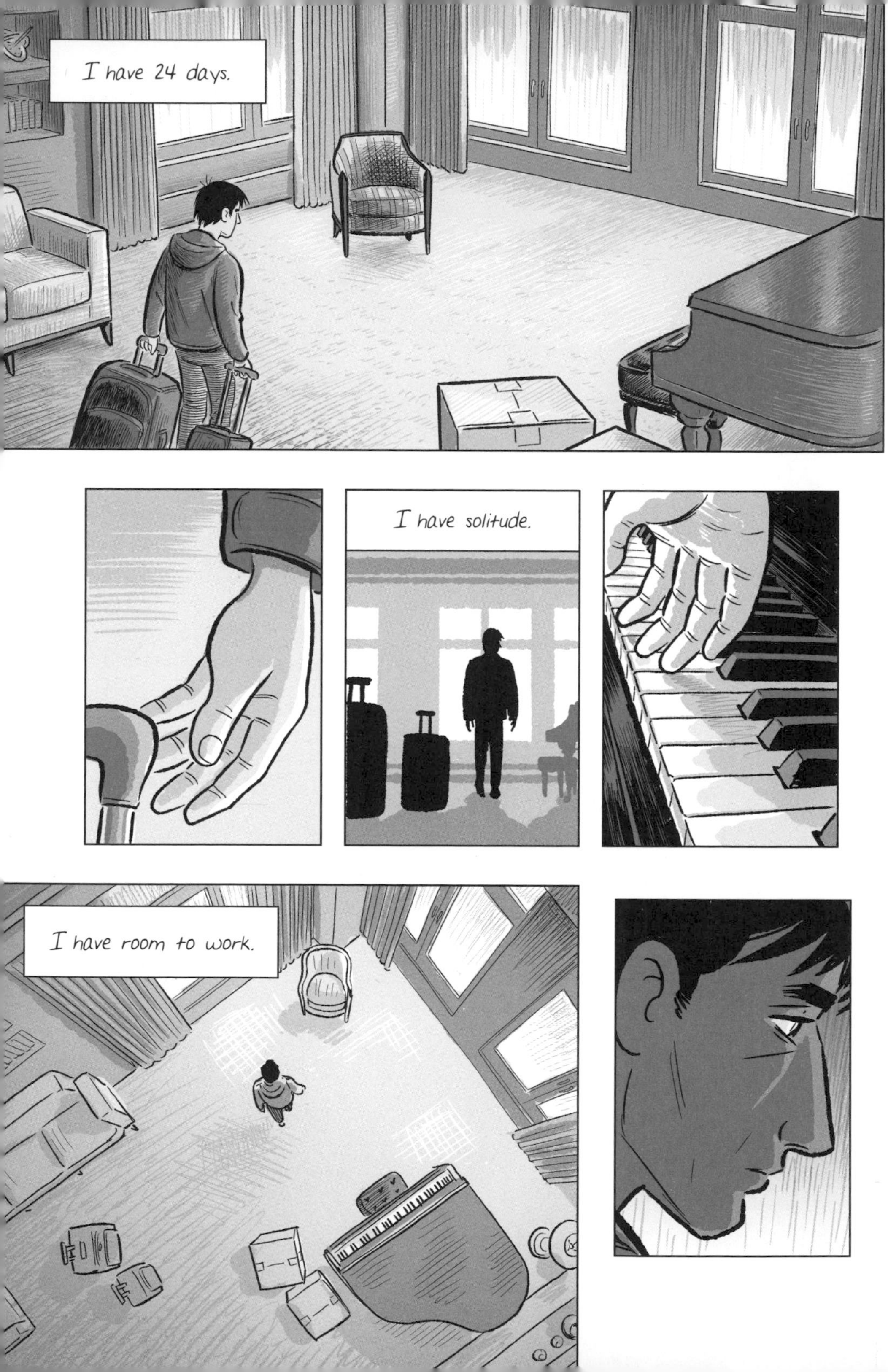
I have 24 days.
I have solitude.
I have room to work.

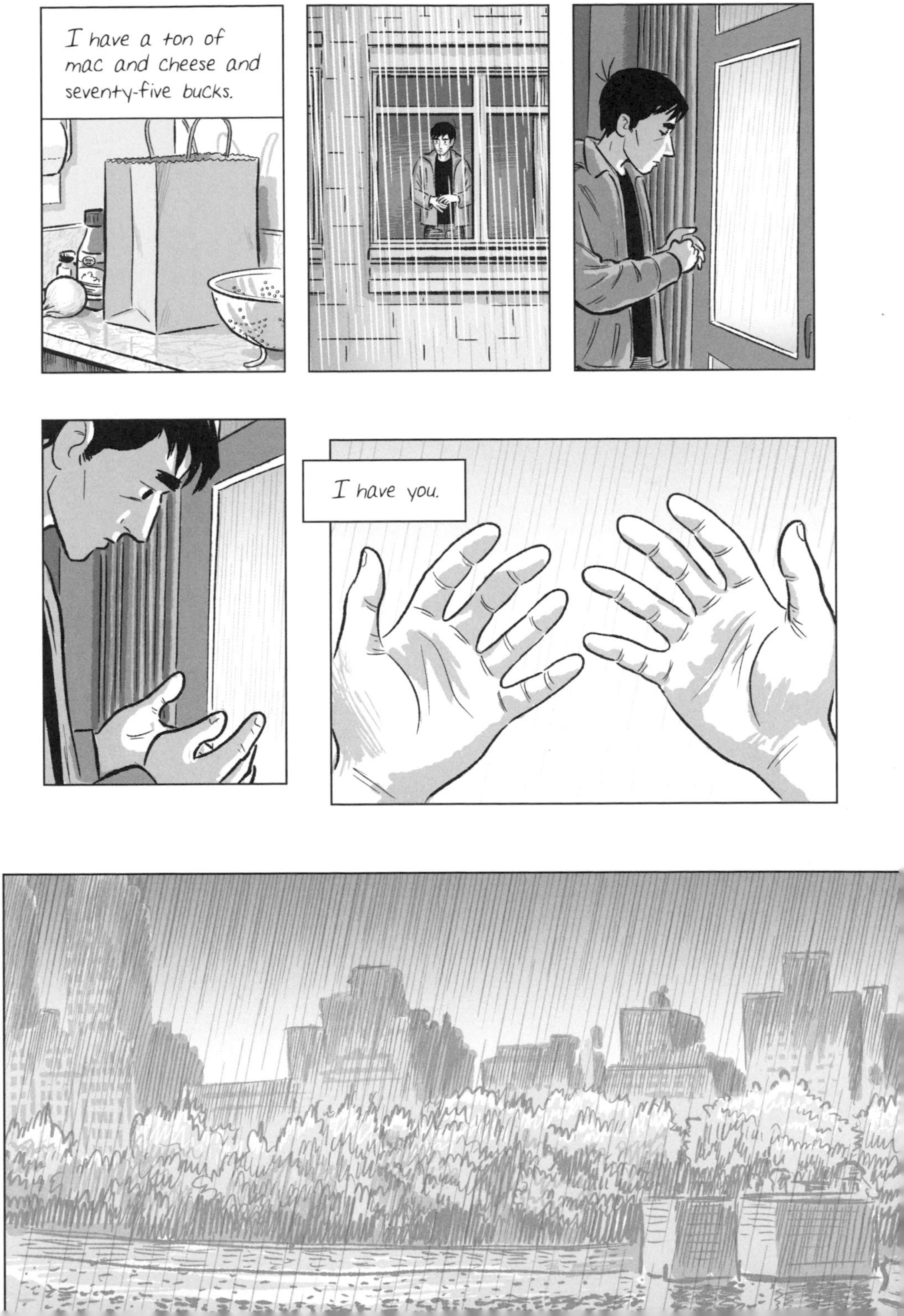
I have a ton of mac and cheese and seventy-five bucks.
I have you.

5.

THE ART OF DYING

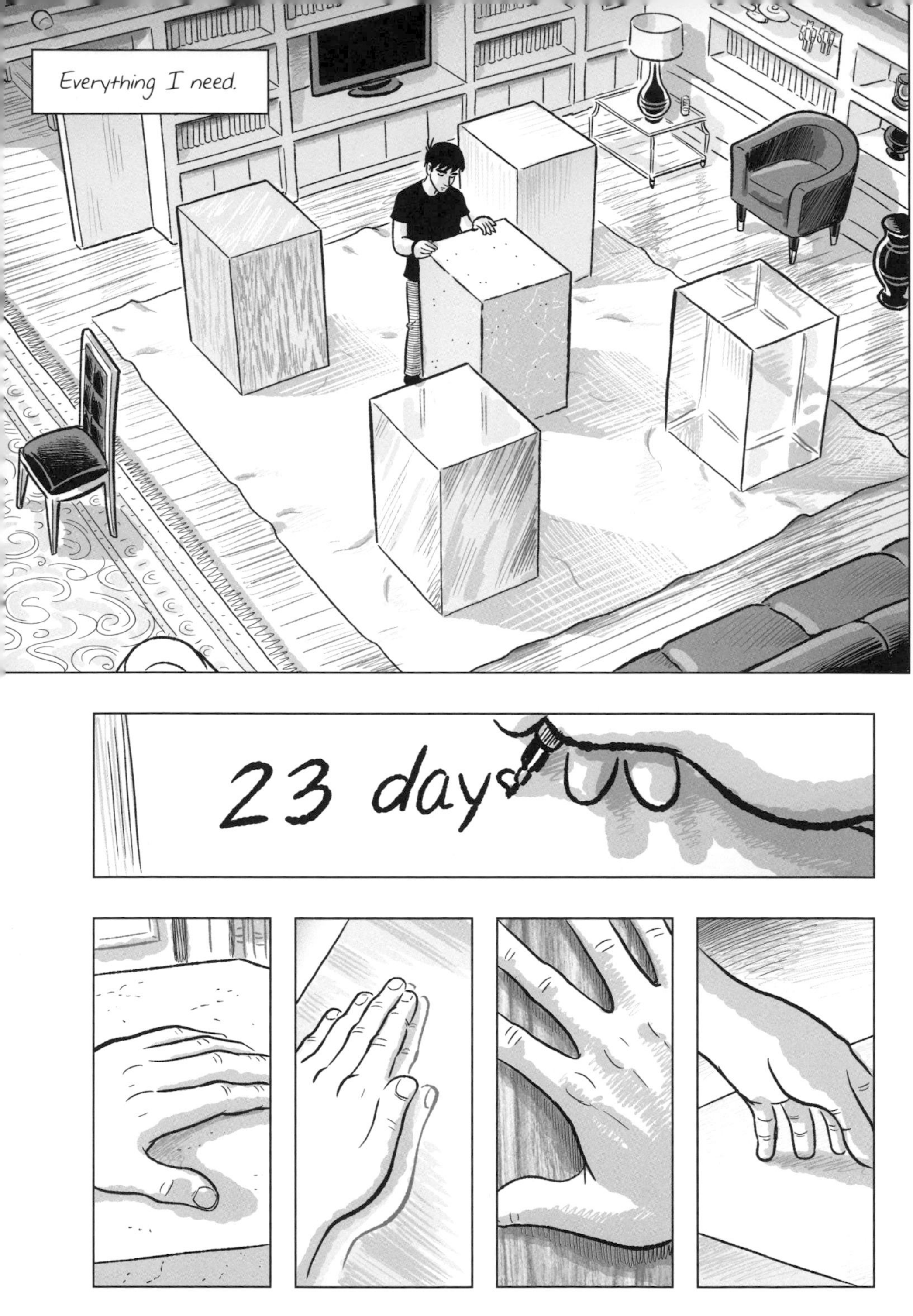
Everything I need.
23 days

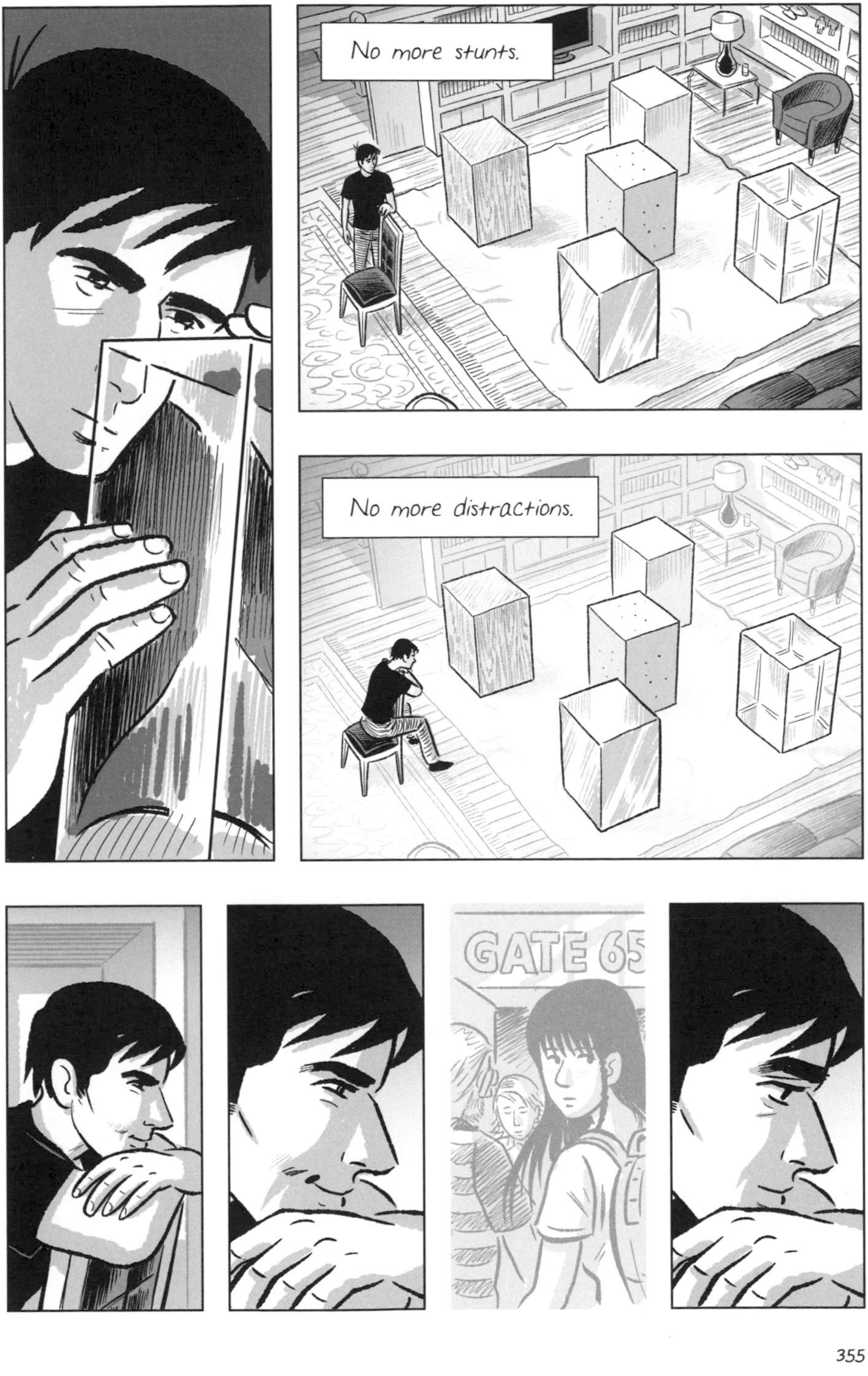
No more stunts.
No more distractions.
GATE 65

DAMMIT.

NOW, **LISTEN.**

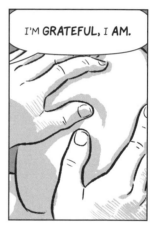

I'M **GRATEFUL, I AM.**

BUT **THIS** WAS THE RIGHT THING TO DO. I **KNOW** IT.

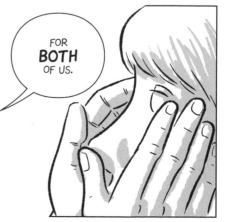

FOR **BOTH** OF US.

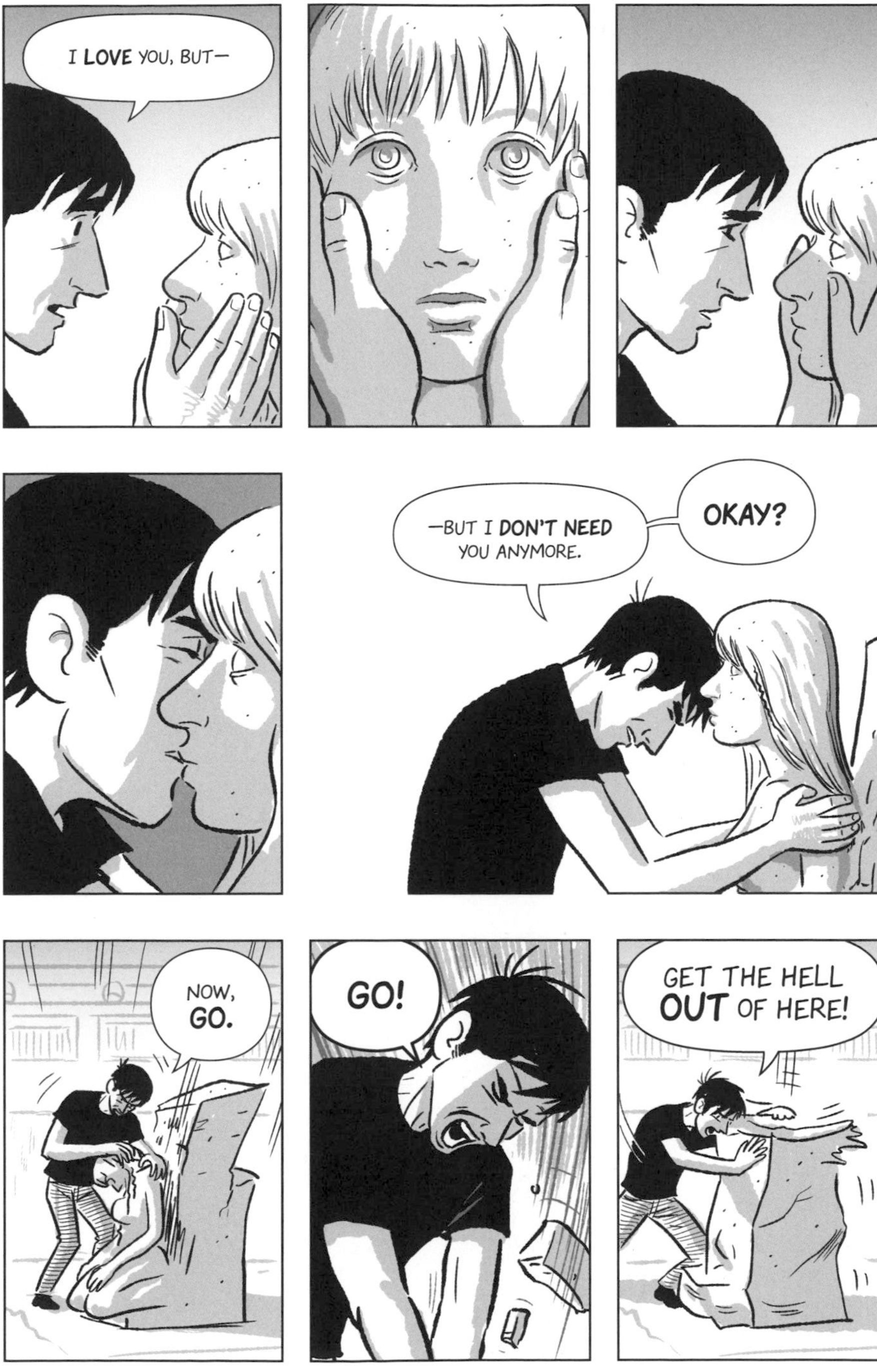
I **LOVE** YOU, BUT—
—BUT I **DON'T NEED** YOU ANYMORE.
OKAY?
NOW, **GO.**
GO!
GET THE HELL **OUT** OF HERE!

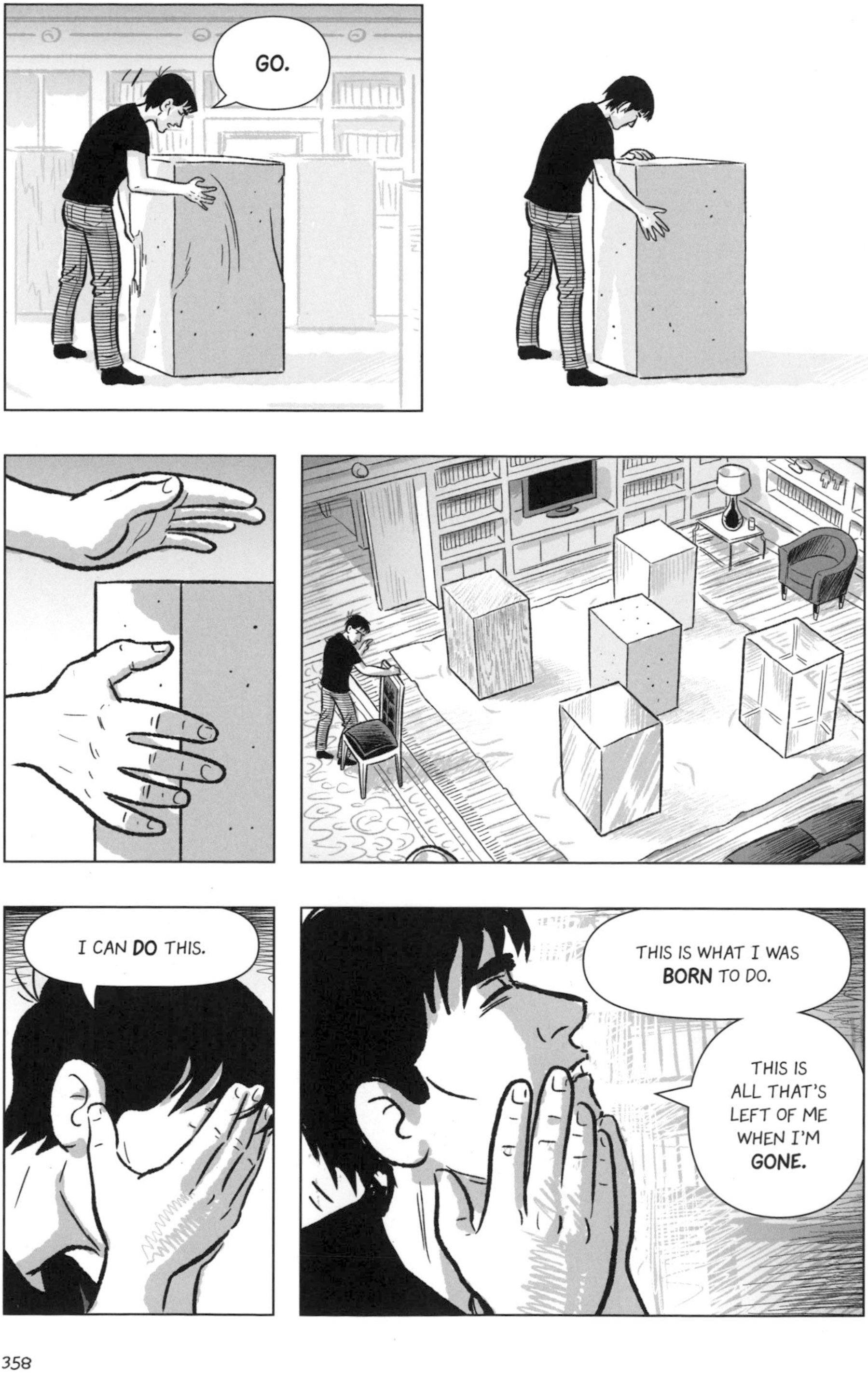
GO.
I CAN DO THIS.
THIS IS WHAT I WAS BORN TO DO.
THIS IS ALL THAT'S LEFT OF ME WHEN I'M GONE.

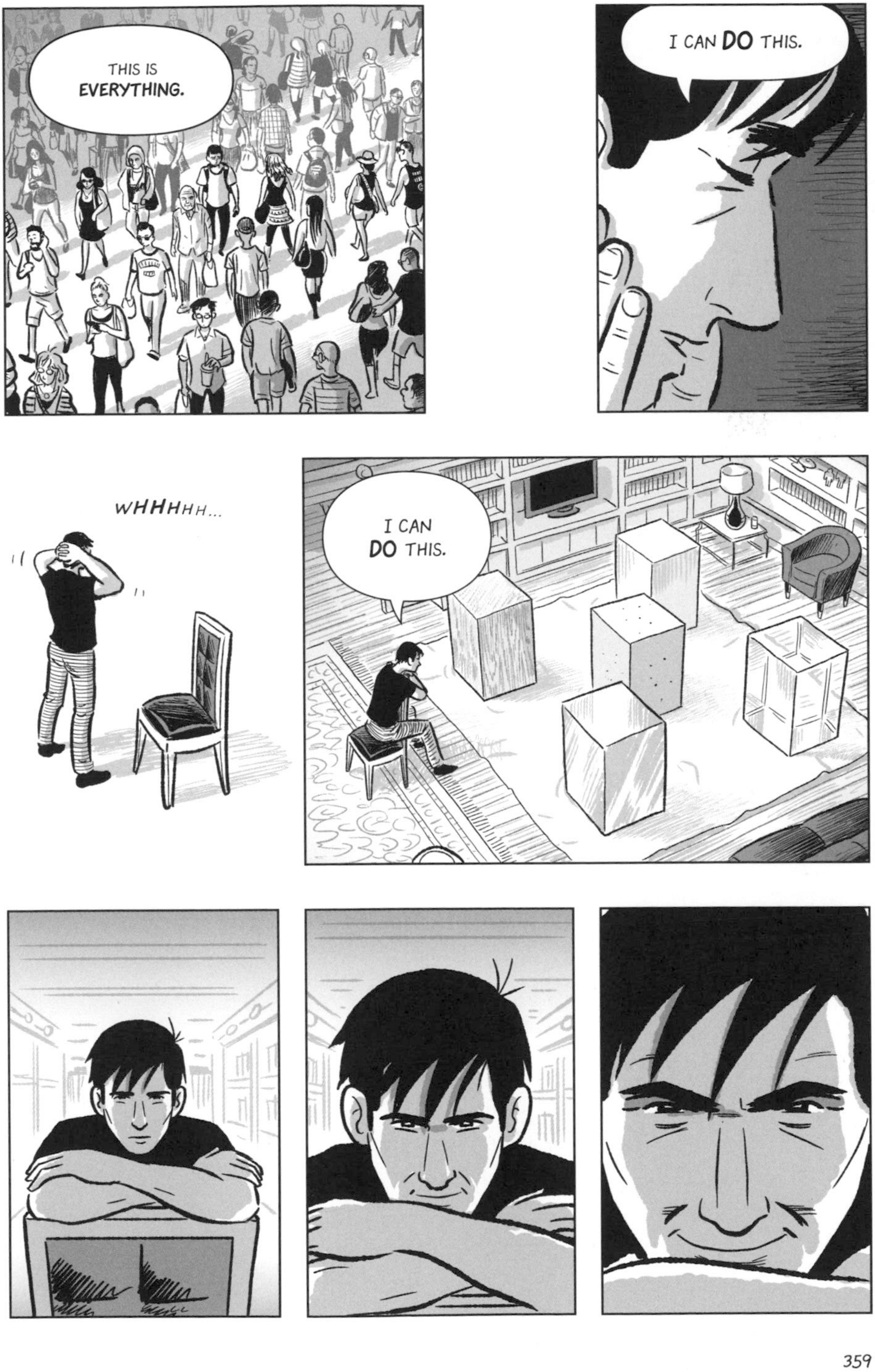
THIS IS EVERYTHING.
I CAN DO THIS.
WHHHHH...
I CAN DO THIS.

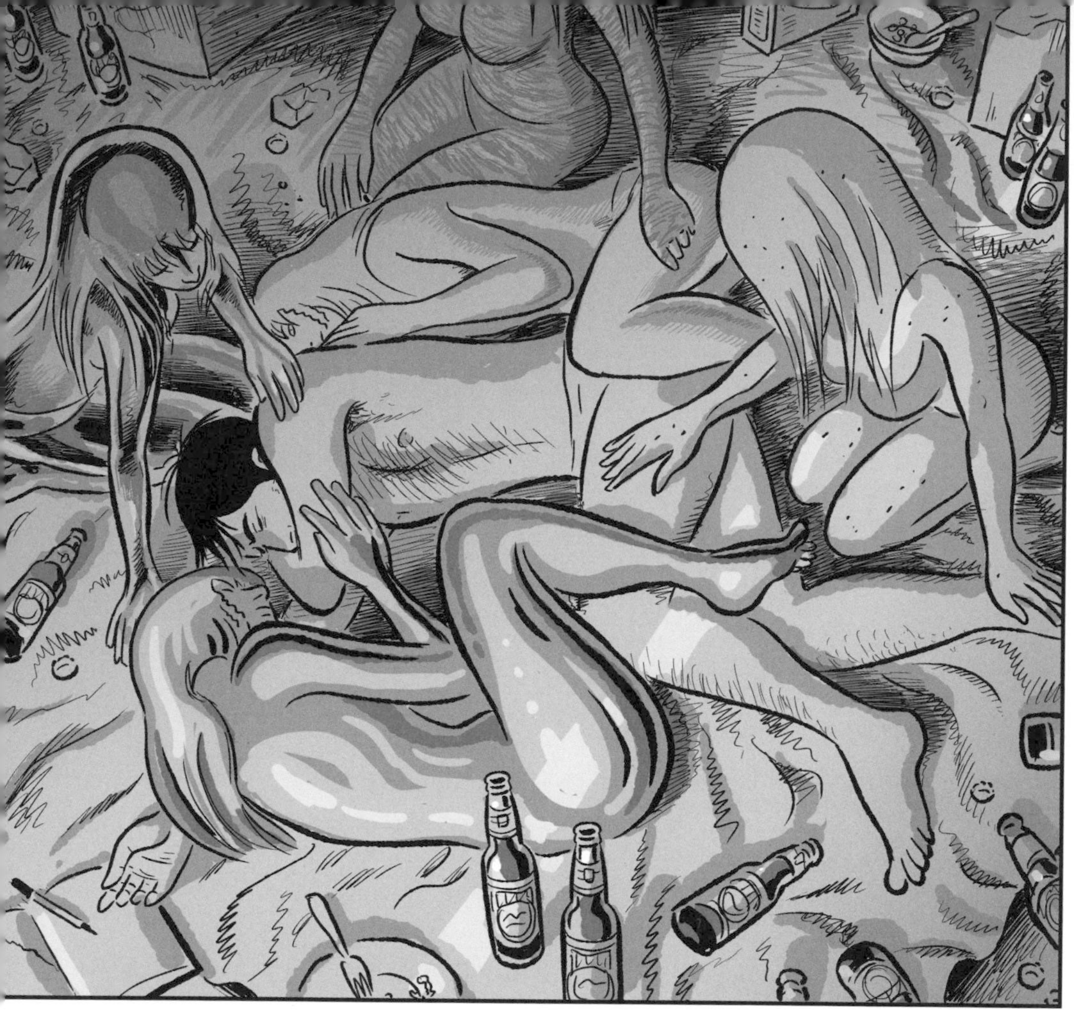

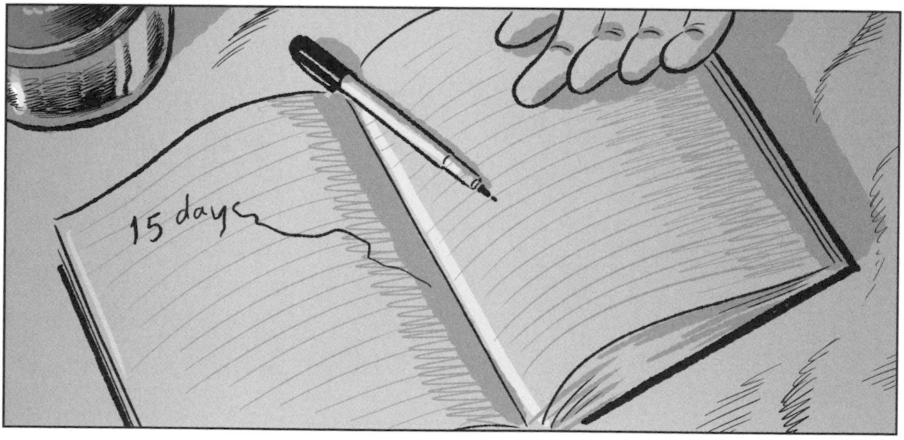
15 days

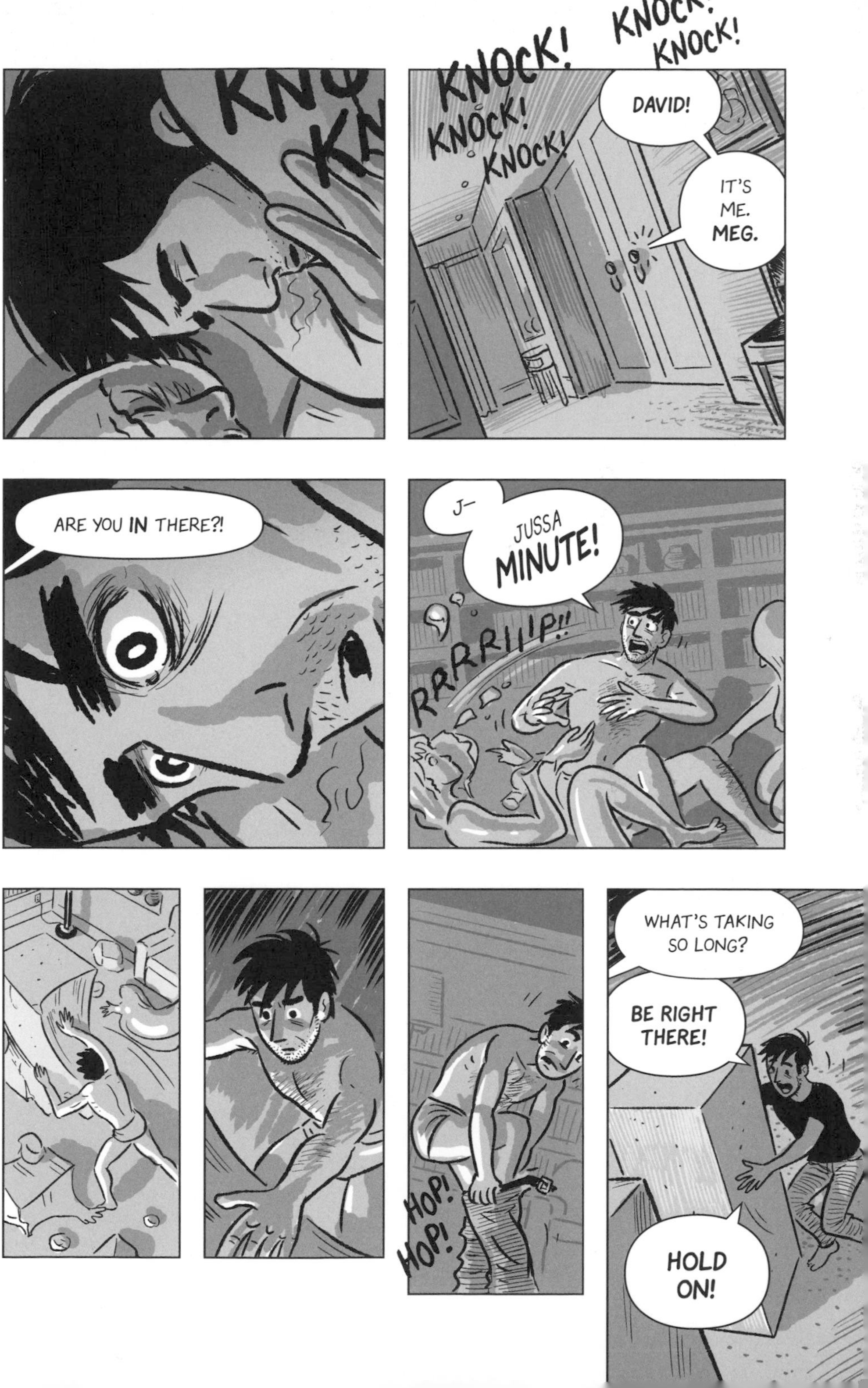
KNOCK! KNOCK! KNOCK!
KNOCK! KNOCK! KNOCK!
DAVID!
IT'S ME. MEG.
ARE YOU IN THERE?!
J—
JUSSA MINUTE!
RRRRIIIP!!
WHAT'S TAKING SO LONG?
BE RIGHT THERE!
HOP! HOP!
HOLD ON!

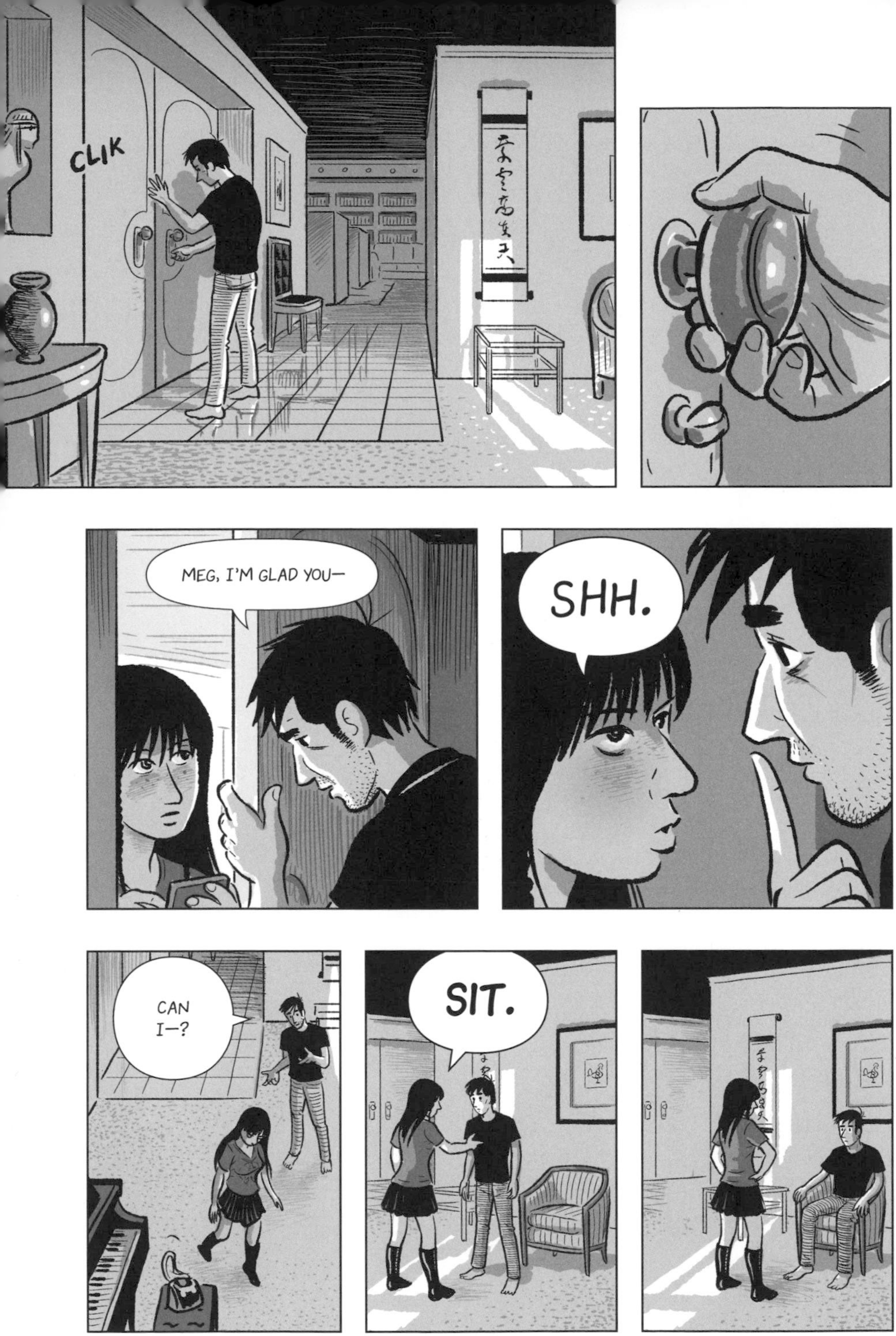
CLIK
MEG, I'M GLAD YOU—
SHH.
CAN I—?
SIT.

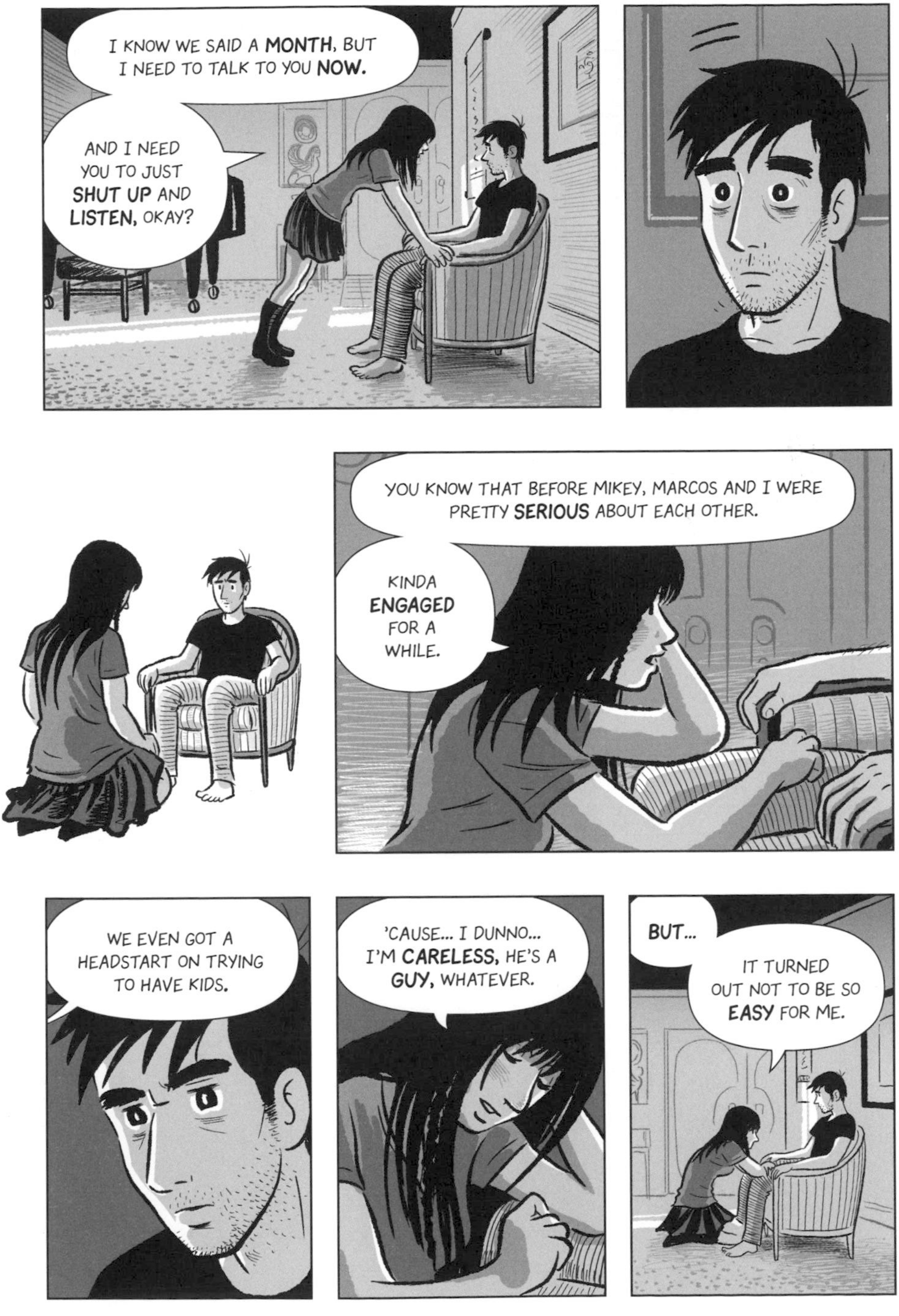
I KNOW WE SAID A MONTH, BUT I NEED TO TALK TO YOU NOW.
AND I NEED YOU TO JUST SHUT UP AND LISTEN, OKAY?
YOU KNOW THAT BEFORE MIKEY, MARCOS AND I WERE PRETTY SERIOUS ABOUT EACH OTHER.
KINDA ENGAGED FOR A WHILE.
WE EVEN GOT A HEADSTART ON TRYING TO HAVE KIDS.
'CAUSE... I DUNNO... I'M CARELESS, HE'S A GUY, WHATEVER.
BUT...
IT TURNED OUT NOT TO BE SO EASY FOR ME.

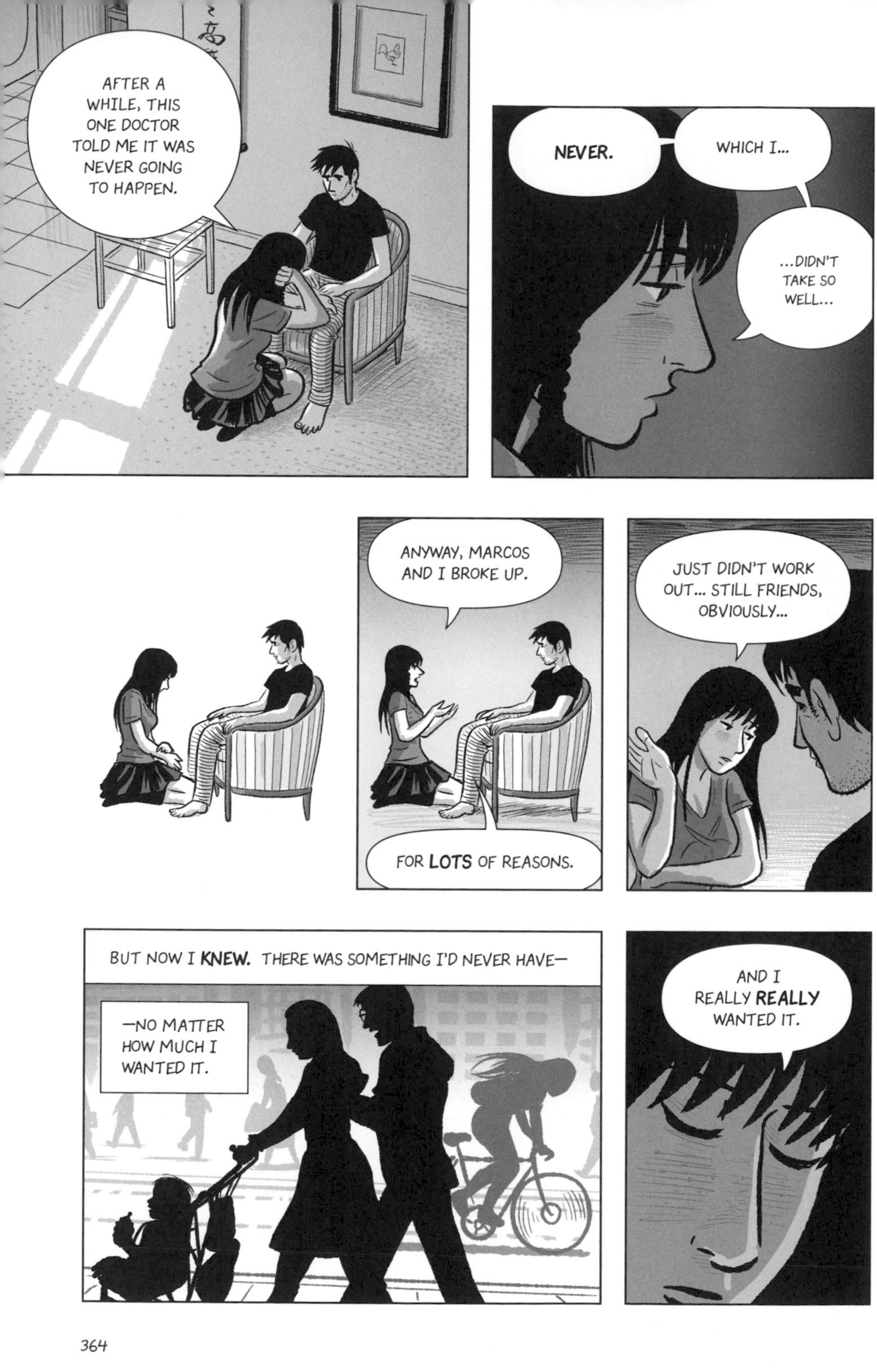

AFTER A WHILE, THIS ONE DOCTOR TOLD ME IT WAS NEVER GOING TO HAPPEN.
NEVER.
WHICH I...
...DIDN'T TAKE SO WELL...
ANYWAY, MARCOS AND I BROKE UP.
FOR LOTS OF REASONS.
JUST DIDN'T WORK OUT... STILL FRIENDS, OBVIOUSLY...
BUT NOW I KNEW. THERE WAS SOMETHING I'D NEVER HAVE—
—NO MATTER HOW MUCH I WANTED IT.
AND I REALLY REALLY WANTED IT.

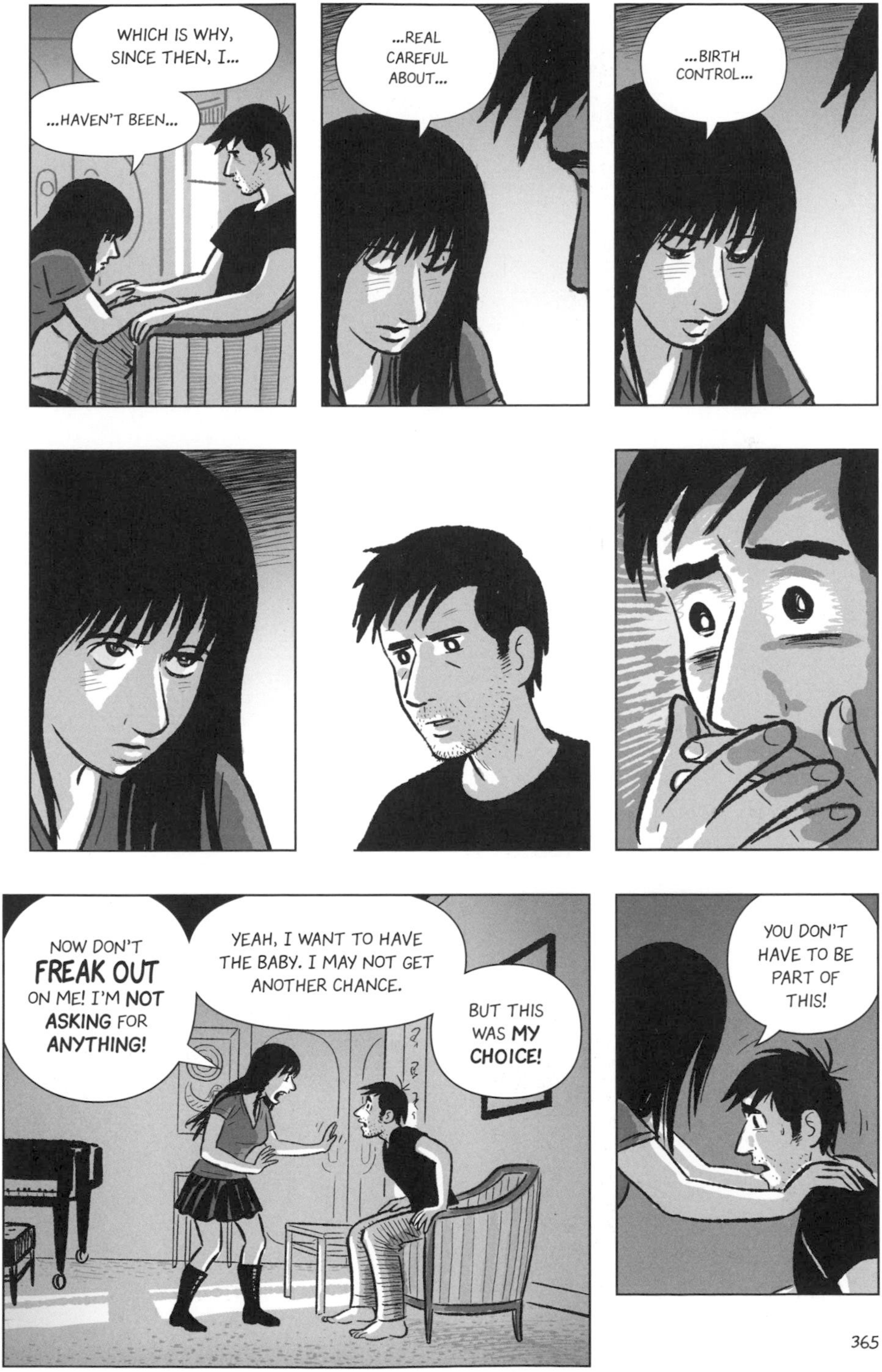

WHICH IS WHY, SINCE THEN, I...
...HAVEN'T BEEN...
...REAL CAREFUL ABOUT...
...BIRTH CONTROL...
NOW DON'T **FREAK OUT** ON ME! I'M **NOT ASKING** FOR **ANYTHING!**
YEAH, I WANT TO HAVE THE BABY. I MAY NOT GET ANOTHER CHANCE.
BUT THIS WAS **MY CHOICE!**
YOU DON'T HAVE TO BE PART OF THIS!

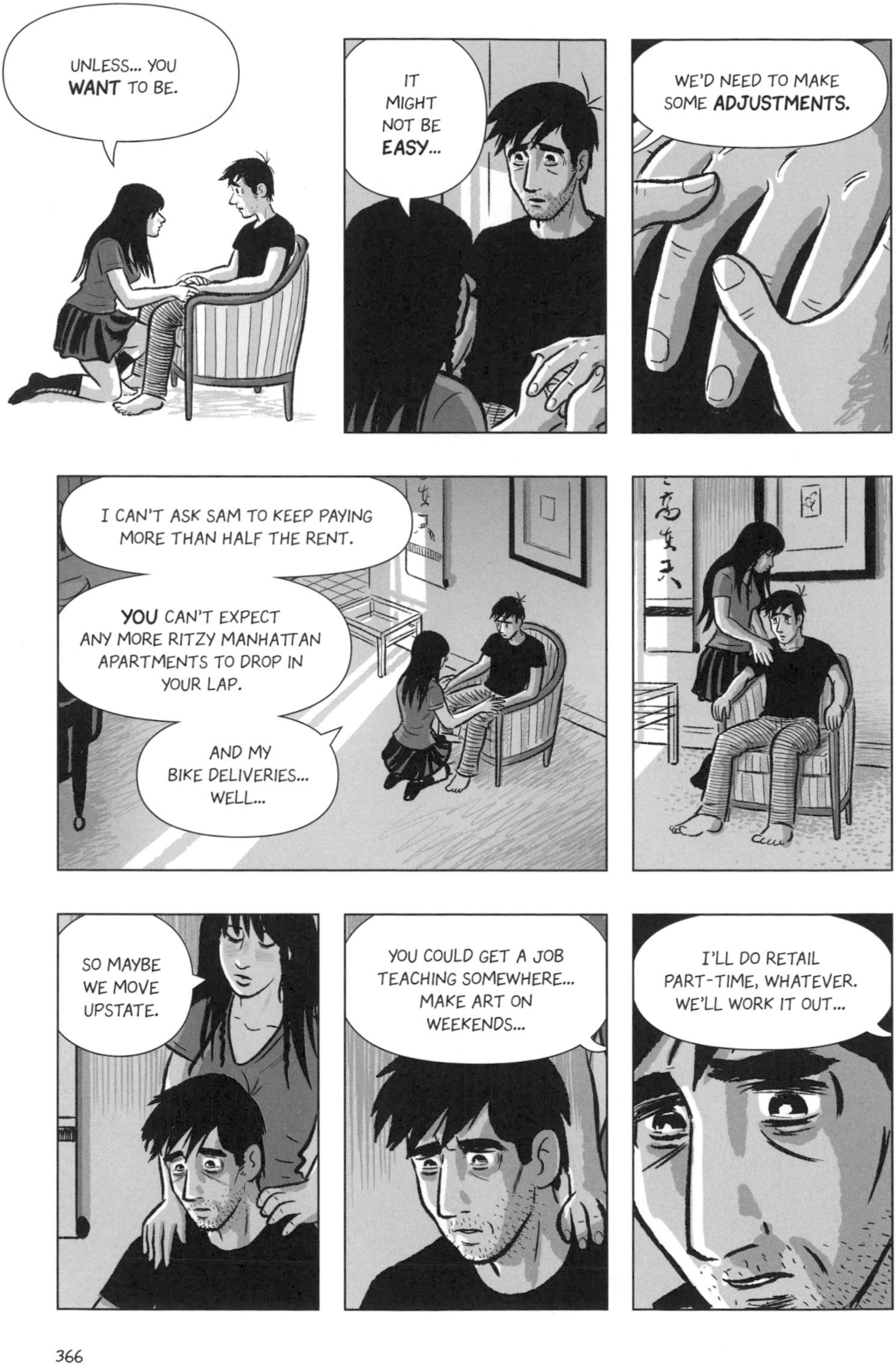
UNLESS... YOU **WANT** TO BE.
IT MIGHT NOT BE **EASY**...
WE'D NEED TO MAKE SOME **ADJUSTMENTS.**
I CAN'T ASK SAM TO KEEP PAYING MORE THAN HALF THE RENT.
YOU CAN'T EXPECT ANY MORE RITZY MANHATTAN APARTMENTS TO DROP IN YOUR LAP.
AND MY BIKE DELIVERIES... WELL...
SO MAYBE WE MOVE UPSTATE.
YOU COULD GET A JOB TEACHING SOMEWHERE... MAKE ART ON WEEKENDS...
I'LL DO RETAIL PART-TIME, WHATEVER. WE'LL WORK IT OUT...

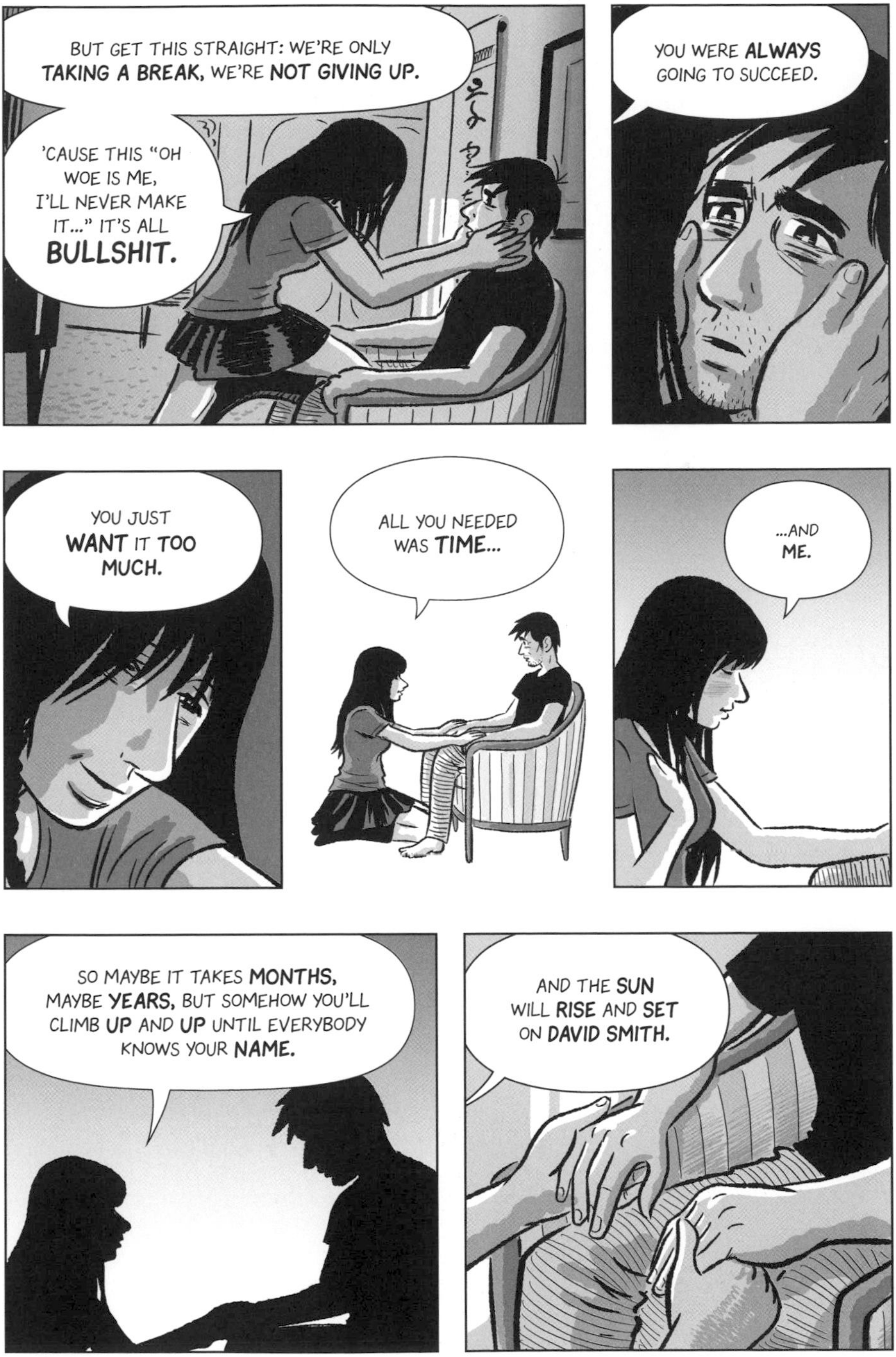
BUT GET THIS STRAIGHT: WE'RE ONLY TAKING A BREAK, WE'RE NOT GIVING UP.
'CAUSE THIS "OH WOE IS ME, I'LL NEVER MAKE IT..." IT'S ALL BULLSHIT.
YOU WERE ALWAYS GOING TO SUCCEED.
YOU JUST WANT IT TOO MUCH.
ALL YOU NEEDED WAS TIME...
...AND ME.
SO MAYBE IT TAKES MONTHS, MAYBE YEARS, BUT SOMEHOW YOU'LL CLIMB UP AND UP UNTIL EVERYBODY KNOWS YOUR NAME.
AND THE SUN WILL RISE AND SET ON DAVID SMITH.

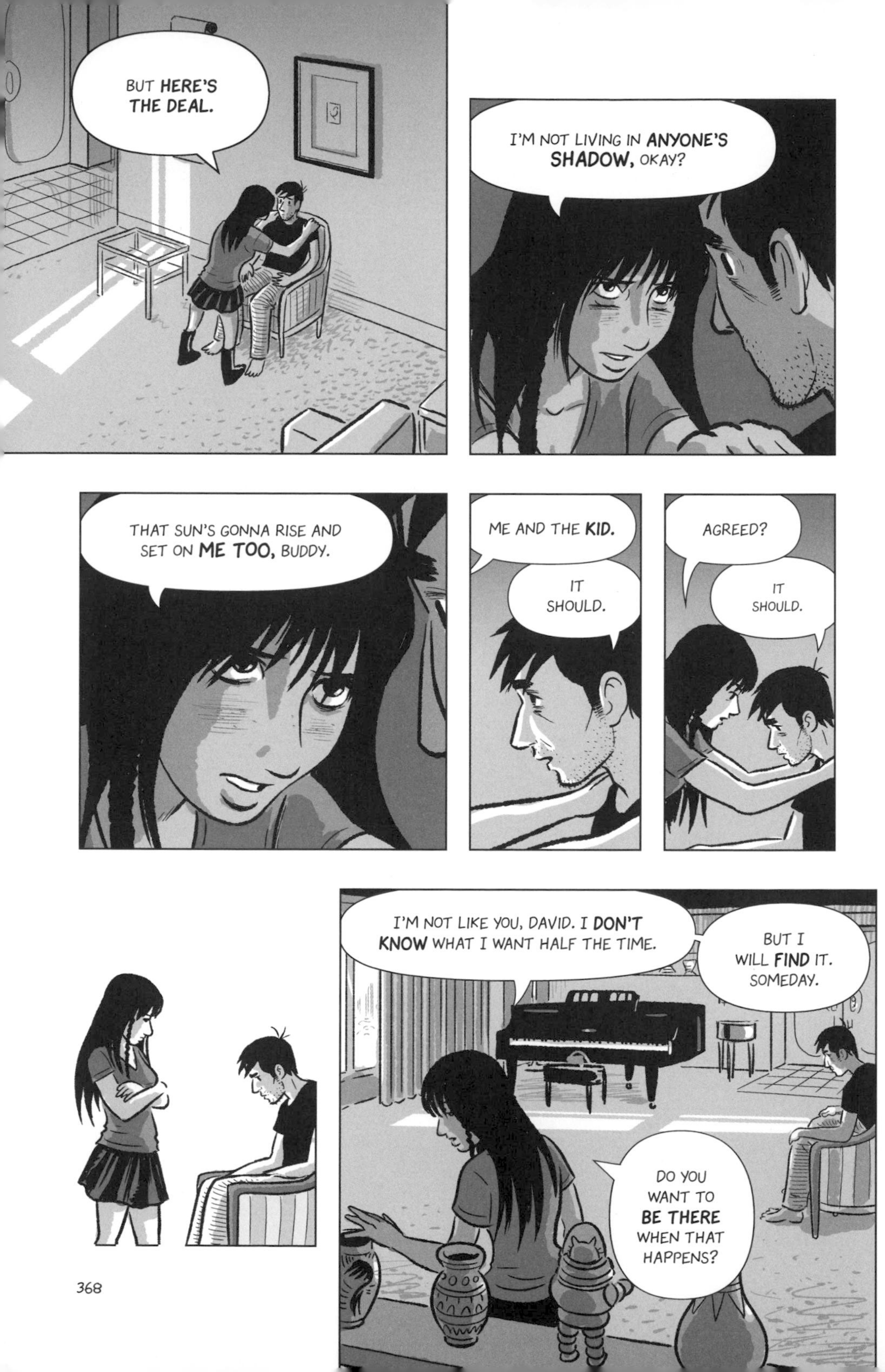
BUT **HERE'S THE DEAL.**
I'M NOT LIVING IN **ANYONE'S SHADOW,** OKAY?
THAT SUN'S GONNA RISE AND SET ON **ME TOO,** BUDDY.
ME AND THE **KID.**
IT SHOULD.
AGREED?
IT SHOULD.
I'M NOT LIKE YOU, DAVID. I **DON'T KNOW** WHAT I WANT HALF THE TIME.
BUT I WILL **FIND** IT. SOMEDAY.
DO YOU WANT TO **BE THERE** WHEN THAT HAPPENS?

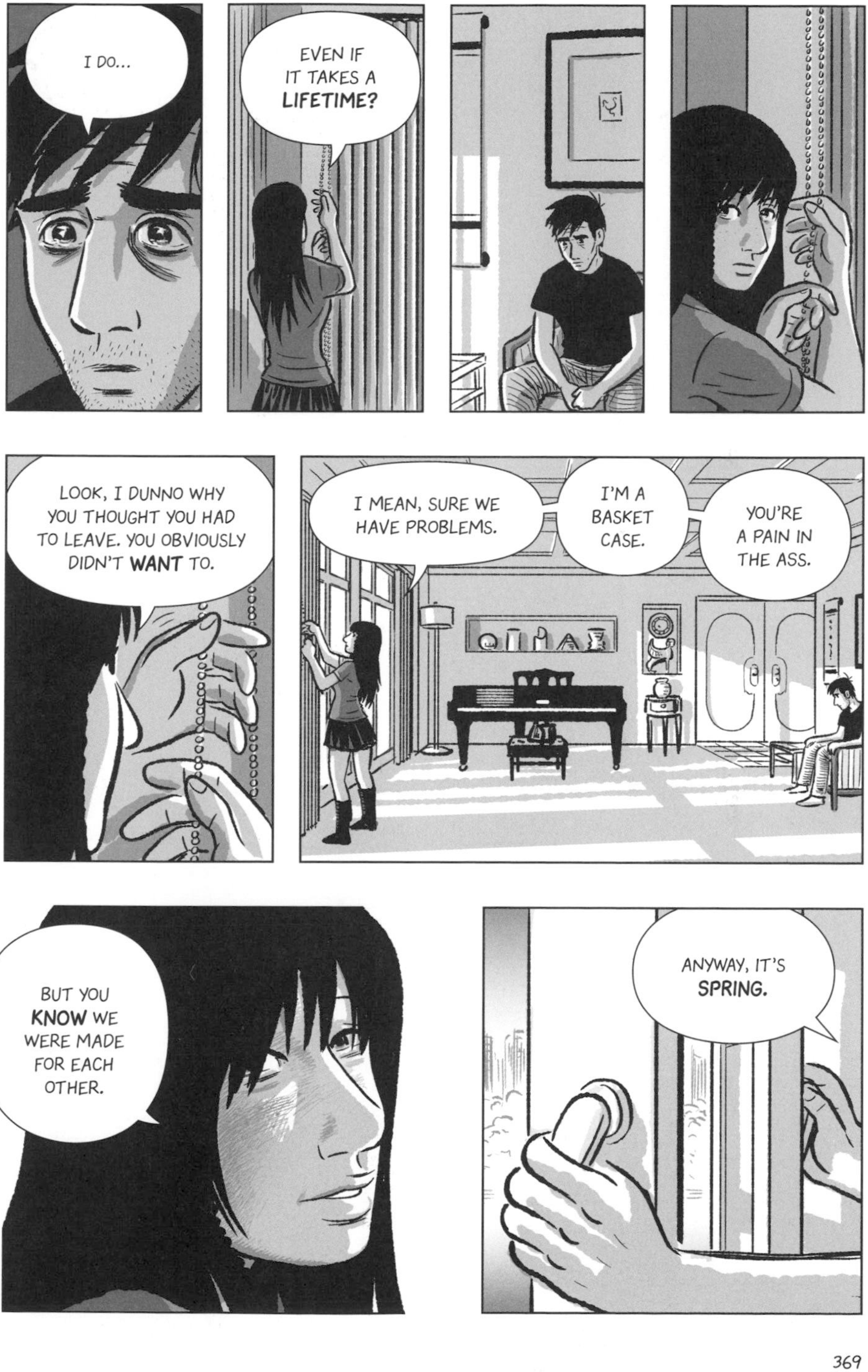
I DO...
EVEN IF IT TAKES A LIFETIME?
LOOK, I DUNNO WHY YOU THOUGHT YOU HAD TO LEAVE. YOU OBVIOUSLY DIDN'T WANT TO.
I MEAN, SURE WE HAVE PROBLEMS.
I'M A BASKET CASE.
YOU'RE A PAIN IN THE ASS.
BUT YOU KNOW WE WERE MADE FOR EACH OTHER.
ANYWAY, IT'S SPRING.

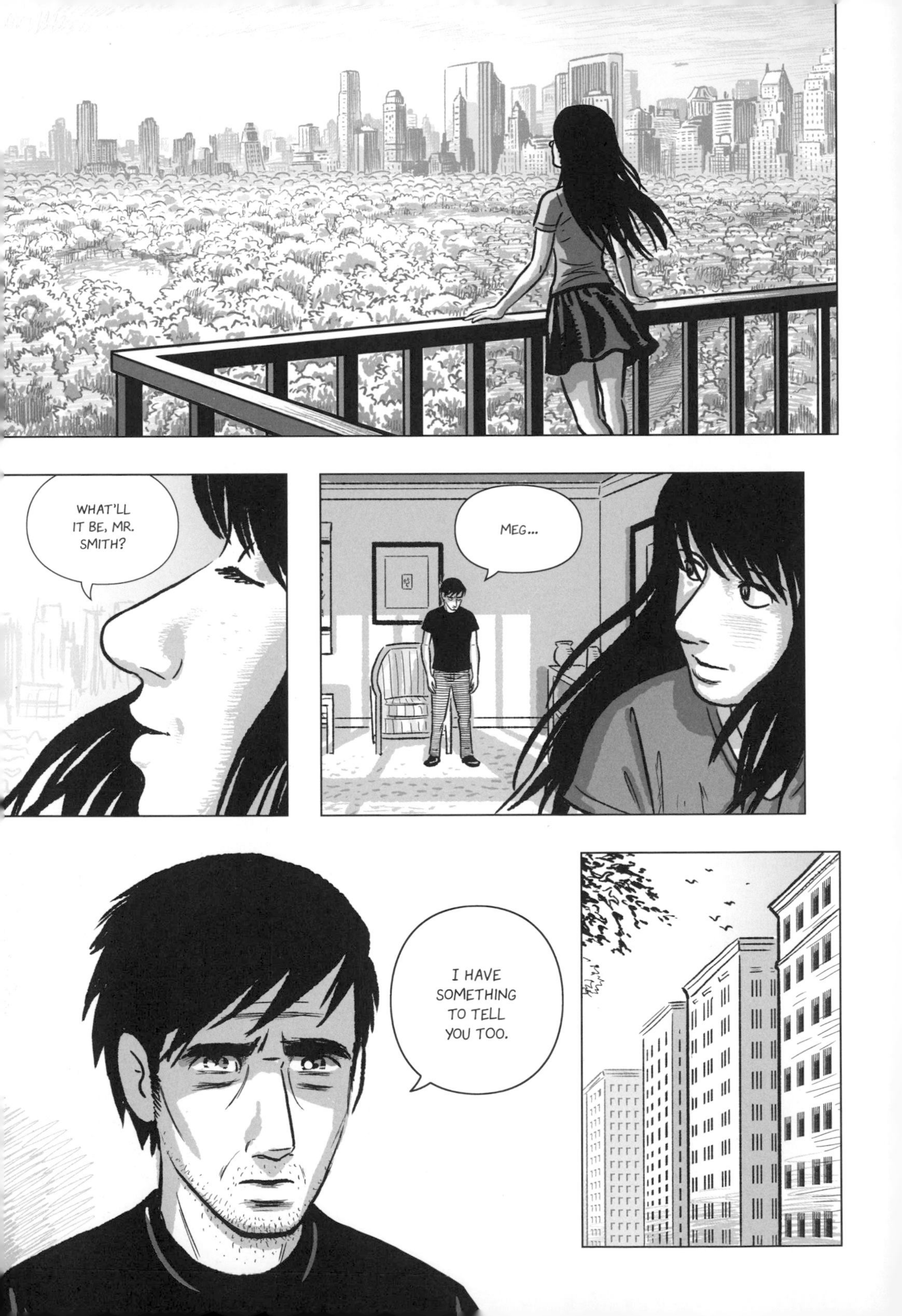
WHAT'LL IT BE, MR. SMITH?
MEG...
I HAVE SOMETHING TO TELL YOU TOO.

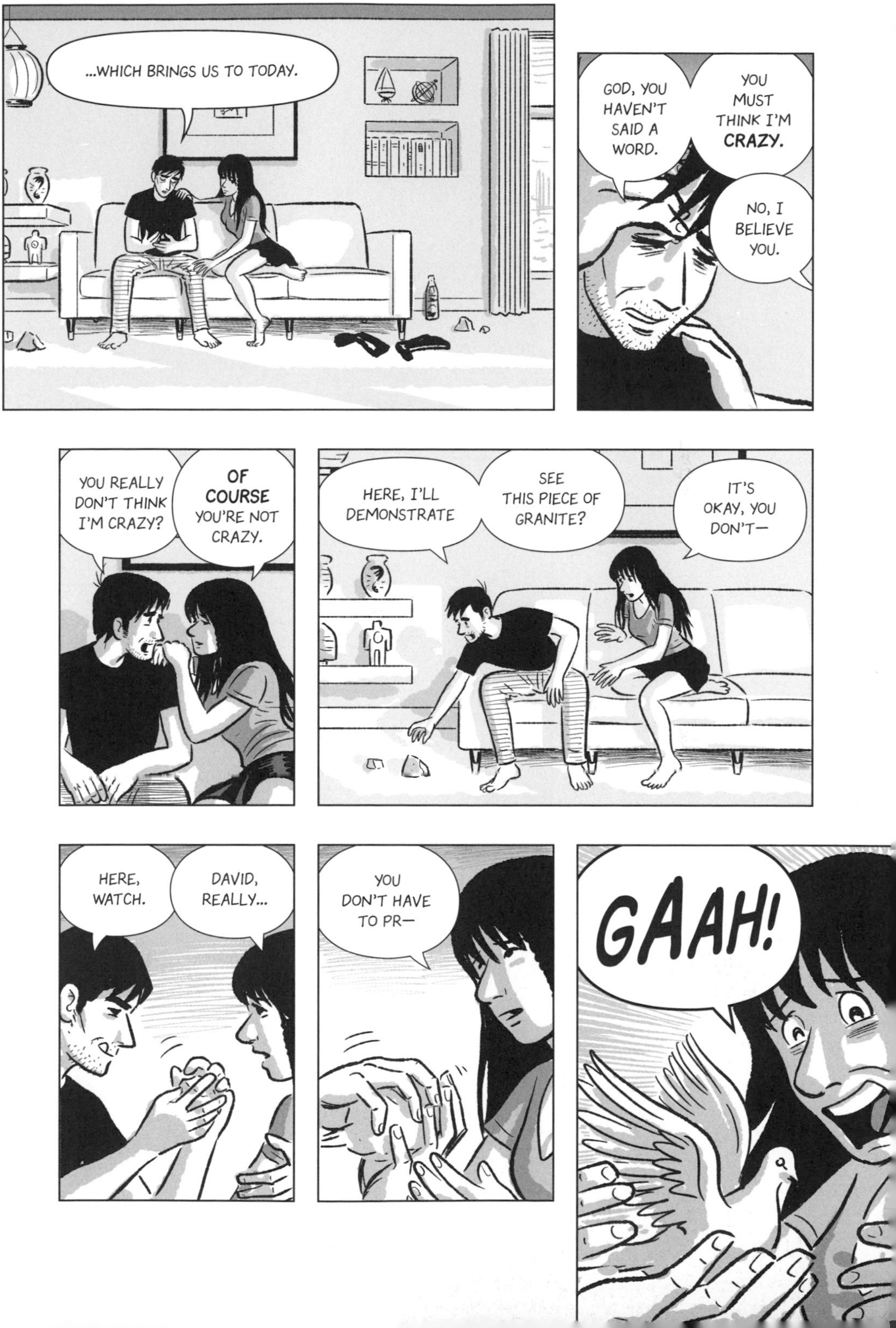
...WHICH BRINGS US TO TODAY.
GOD, YOU HAVEN'T SAID A WORD.
YOU MUST THINK I'M **CRAZY.**
NO, I BELIEVE YOU.
YOU REALLY DON'T THINK I'M CRAZY?
OF COURSE YOU'RE NOT CRAZY.
HERE, I'LL DEMONSTRATE
SEE THIS PIECE OF GRANITE?
IT'S OKAY, YOU DON'T—
HERE, WATCH.
DAVID, REALLY...
YOU DON'T HAVE TO PR—
GAAH!

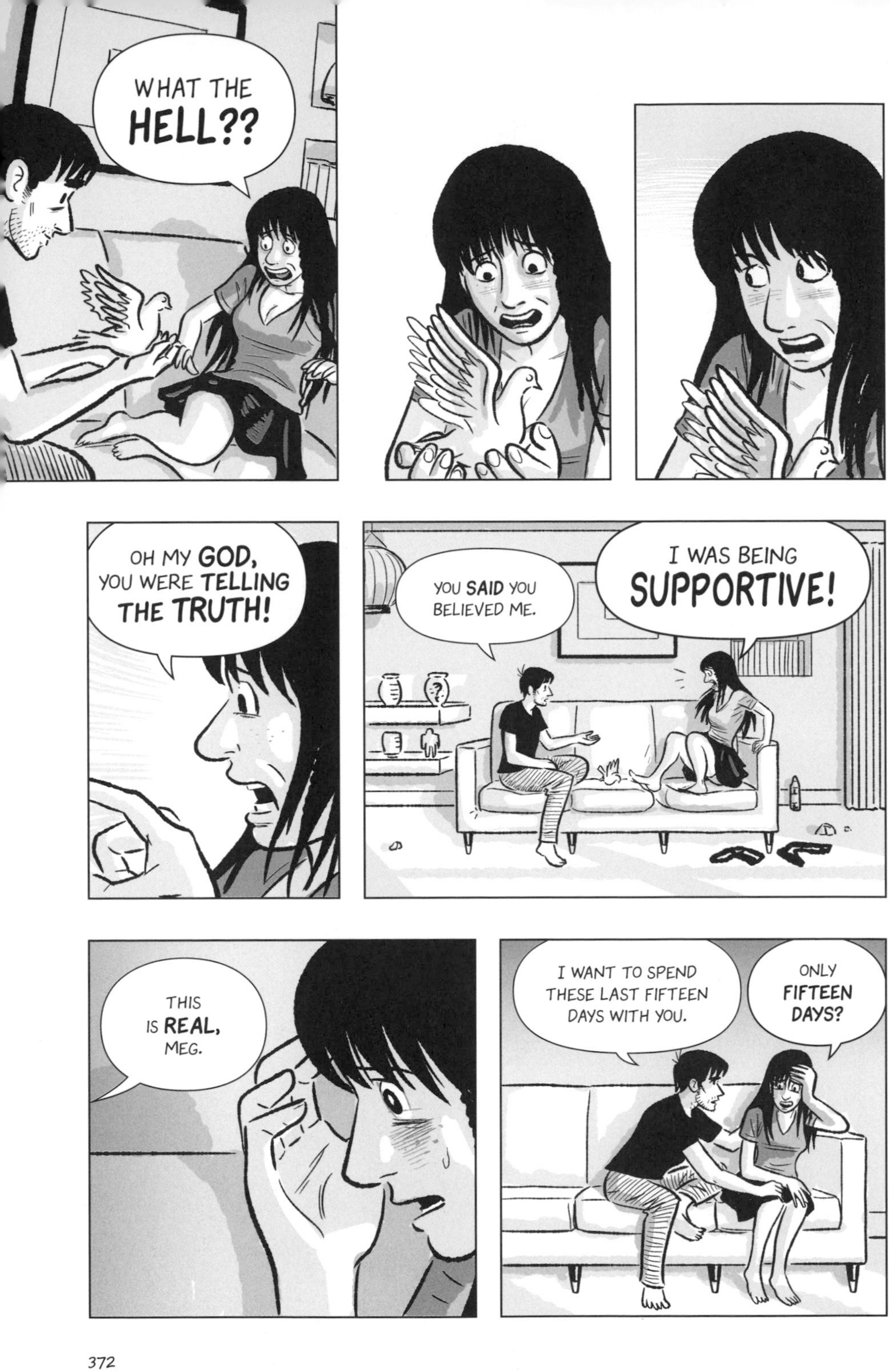
WHAT THE HELL??
OH MY GOD, YOU WERE TELLING THE TRUTH!
YOU SAID YOU BELIEVED ME.
I WAS BEING SUPPORTIVE!
THIS IS REAL, MEG.
I WANT TO SPEND THESE LAST FIFTEEN DAYS WITH YOU.
ONLY FIFTEEN DAYS?

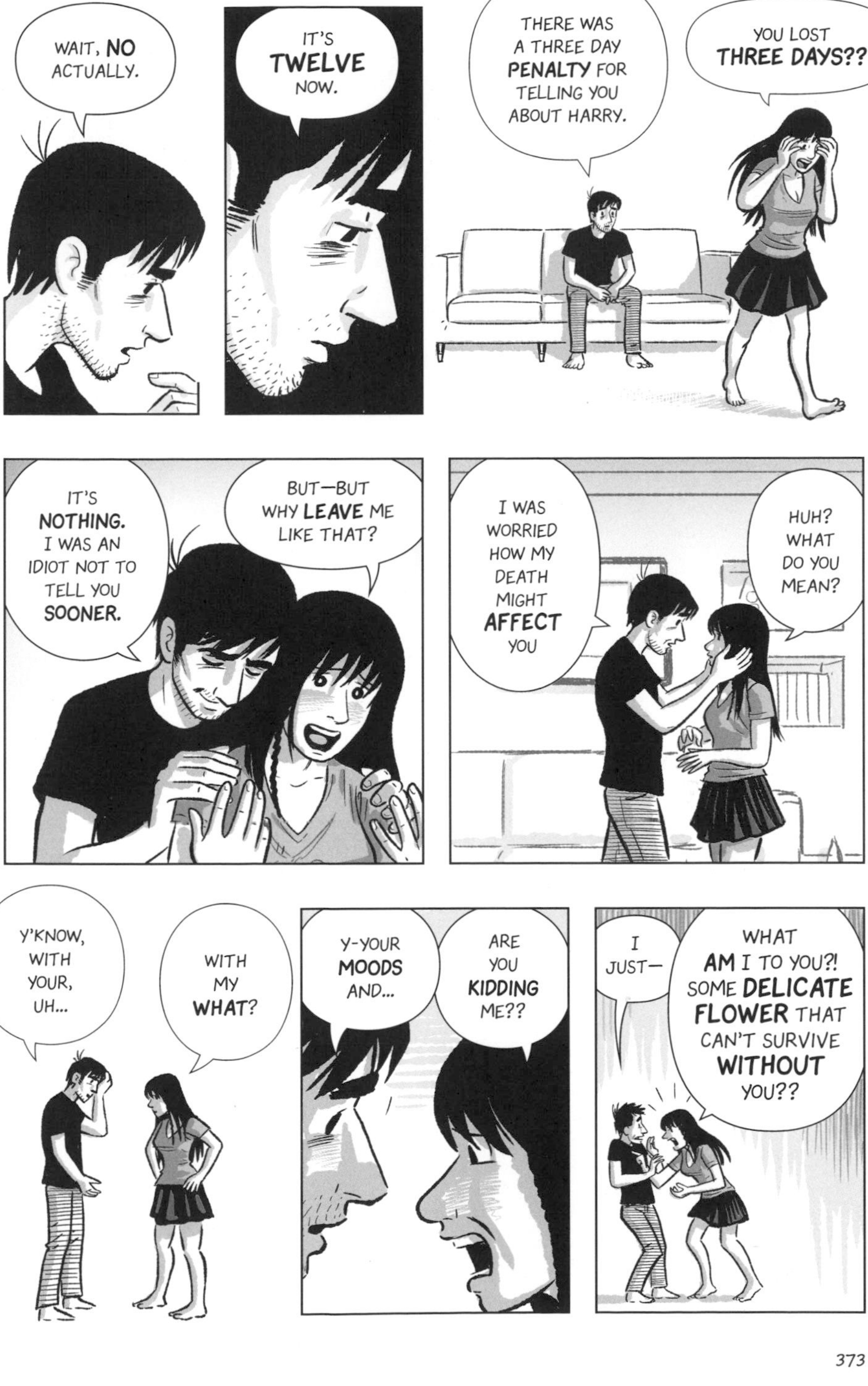
WAIT, **NO** ACTUALLY.
IT'S **TWELVE** NOW.
THERE WAS A THREE DAY **PENALTY** FOR TELLING YOU ABOUT HARRY.
YOU LOST **THREE DAYS??**
IT'S **NOTHING.** I WAS AN IDIOT NOT TO TELL YOU **SOONER.**
BUT—BUT WHY **LEAVE** ME LIKE THAT?
I WAS WORRIED HOW MY DEATH MIGHT **AFFECT** YOU
HUH? WHAT DO YOU MEAN?
Y'KNOW, WITH YOUR, UH...
WITH MY **WHAT**?
Y-YOUR **MOODS** AND...
ARE YOU **KIDDING** ME??
I JUST—
WHAT **AM** I TO YOU?! SOME **DELICATE FLOWER** THAT CAN'T SURVIVE **WITHOUT** YOU??

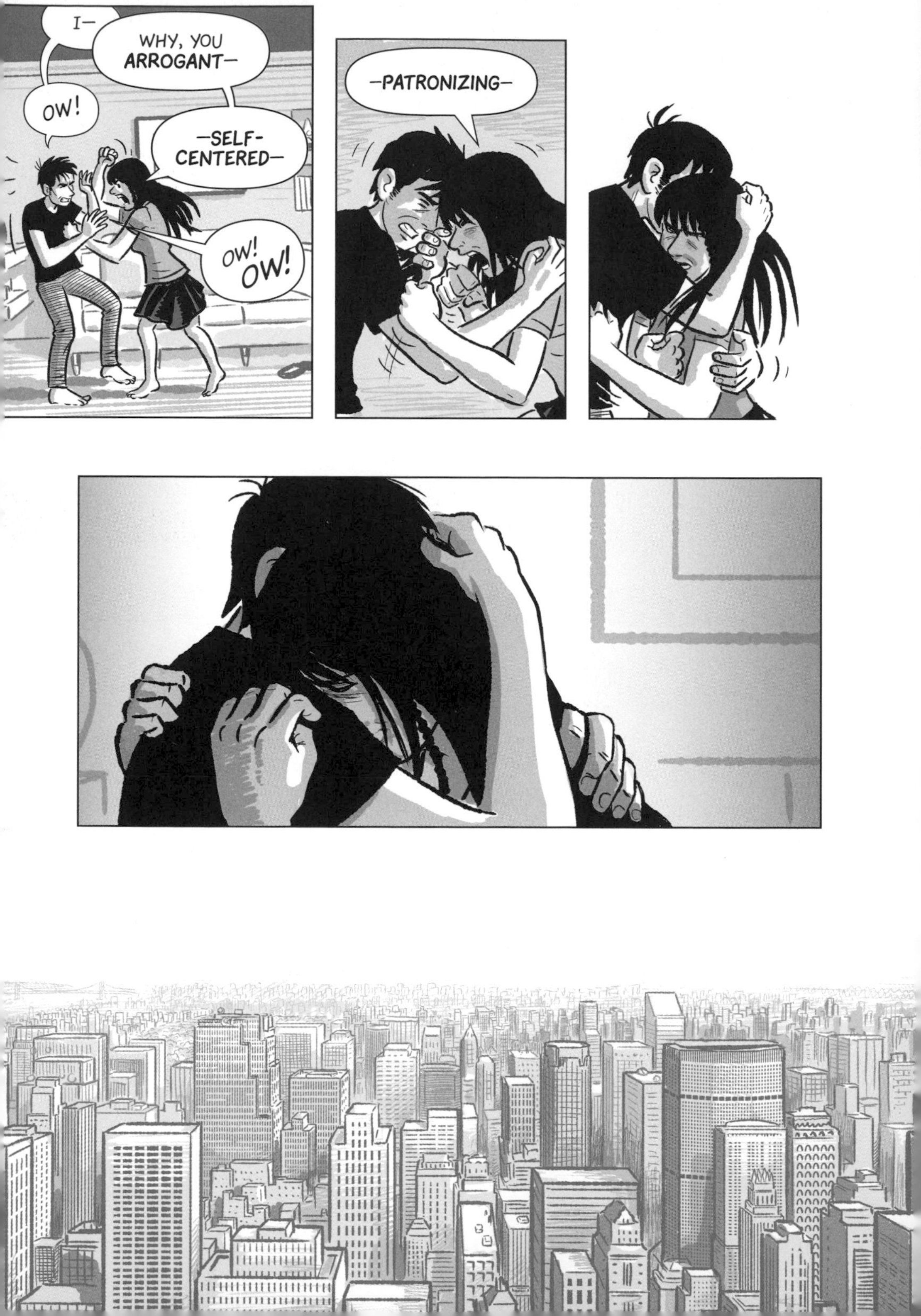
I—
WHY, YOU ARROGANT—
OW!
—SELF-CENTERED—
OW! OW!
—PATRONIZING—

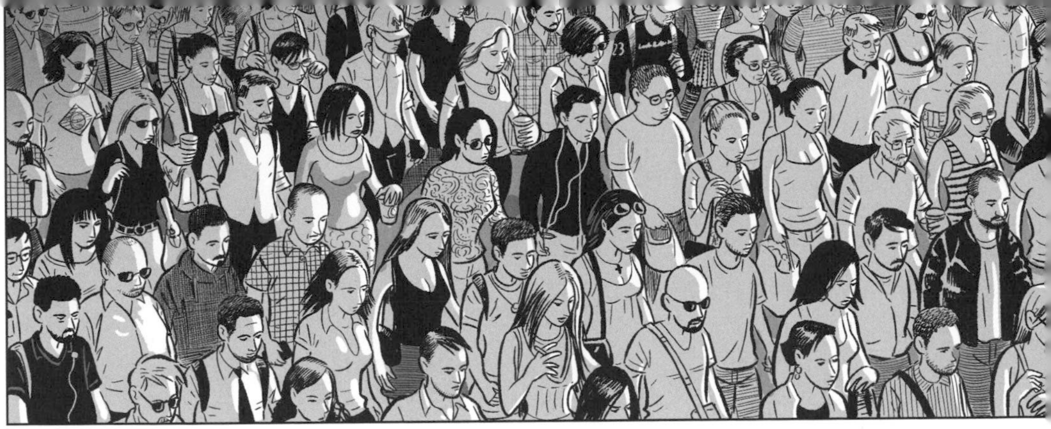

We all have a number.

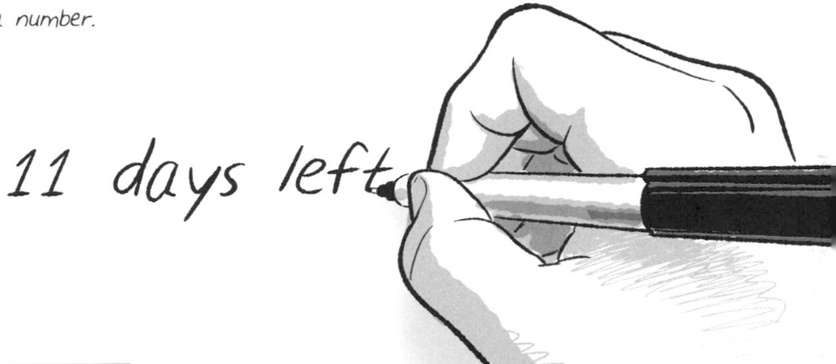

11 days left

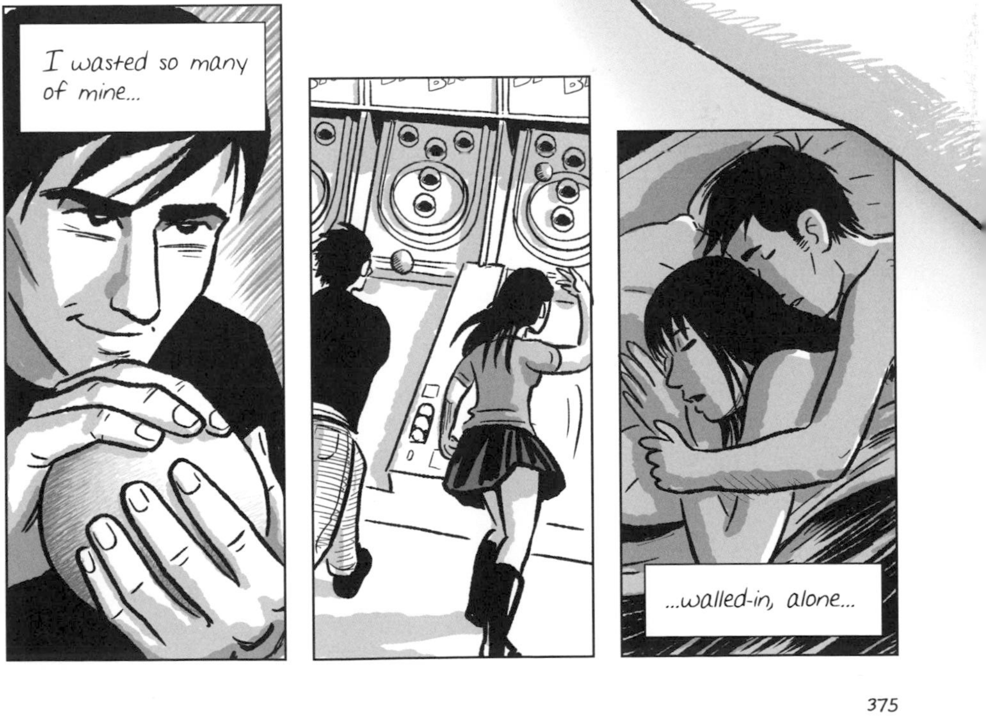

I wasted so many of mine...
...walled-in, alone...

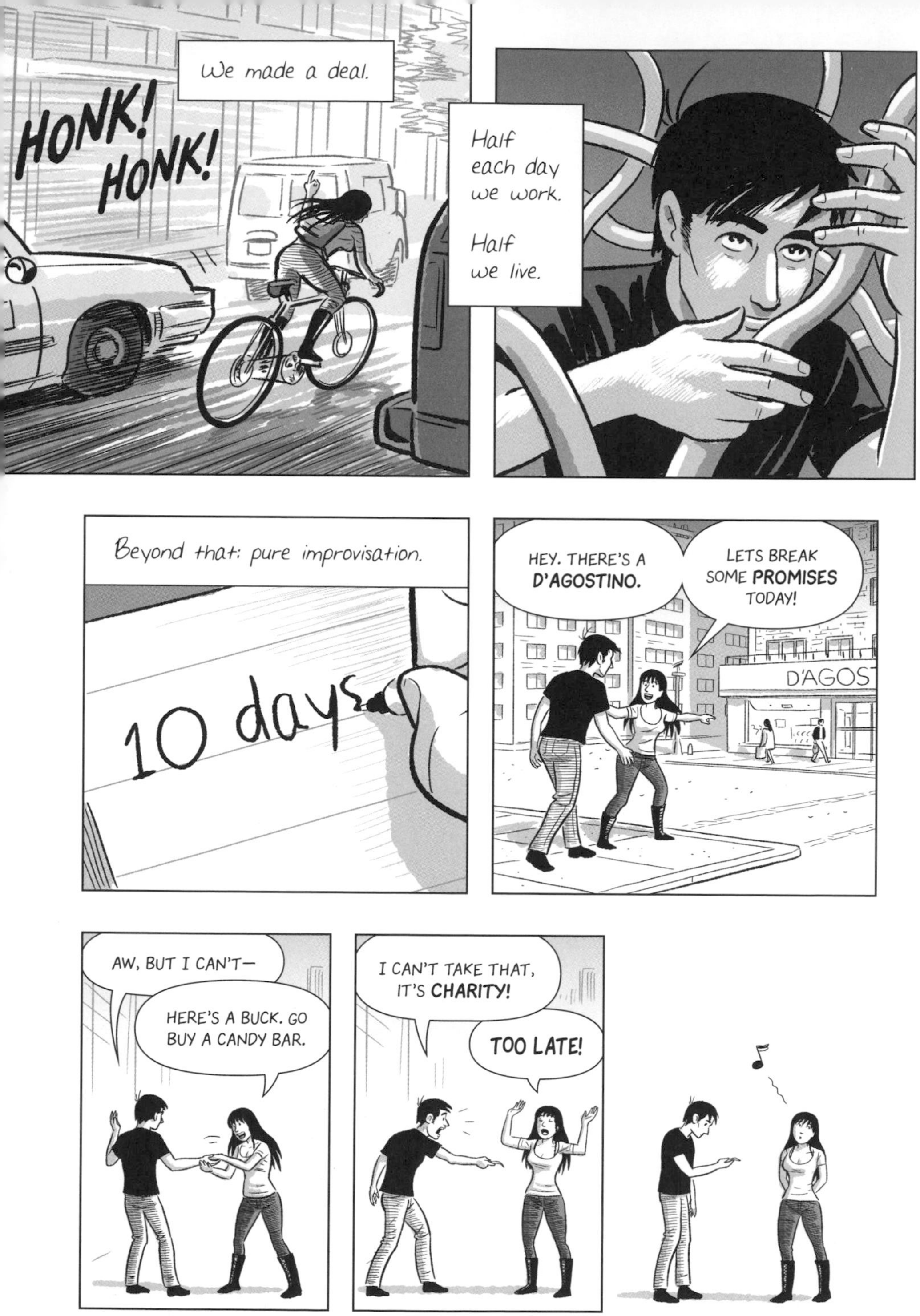
We made a deal.
HONK! HONK!
Half each day we work.
Half we live.
Beyond that: pure improvisation.
10 days
HEY. THERE'S A D'AGOSTINO.
LETS BREAK SOME PROMISES TODAY!
D'AGOST
AW, BUT I CAN'T—
HERE'S A BUCK. GO BUY A CANDY BAR.
I CAN'T TAKE THAT, IT'S CHARITY!
TOO LATE!

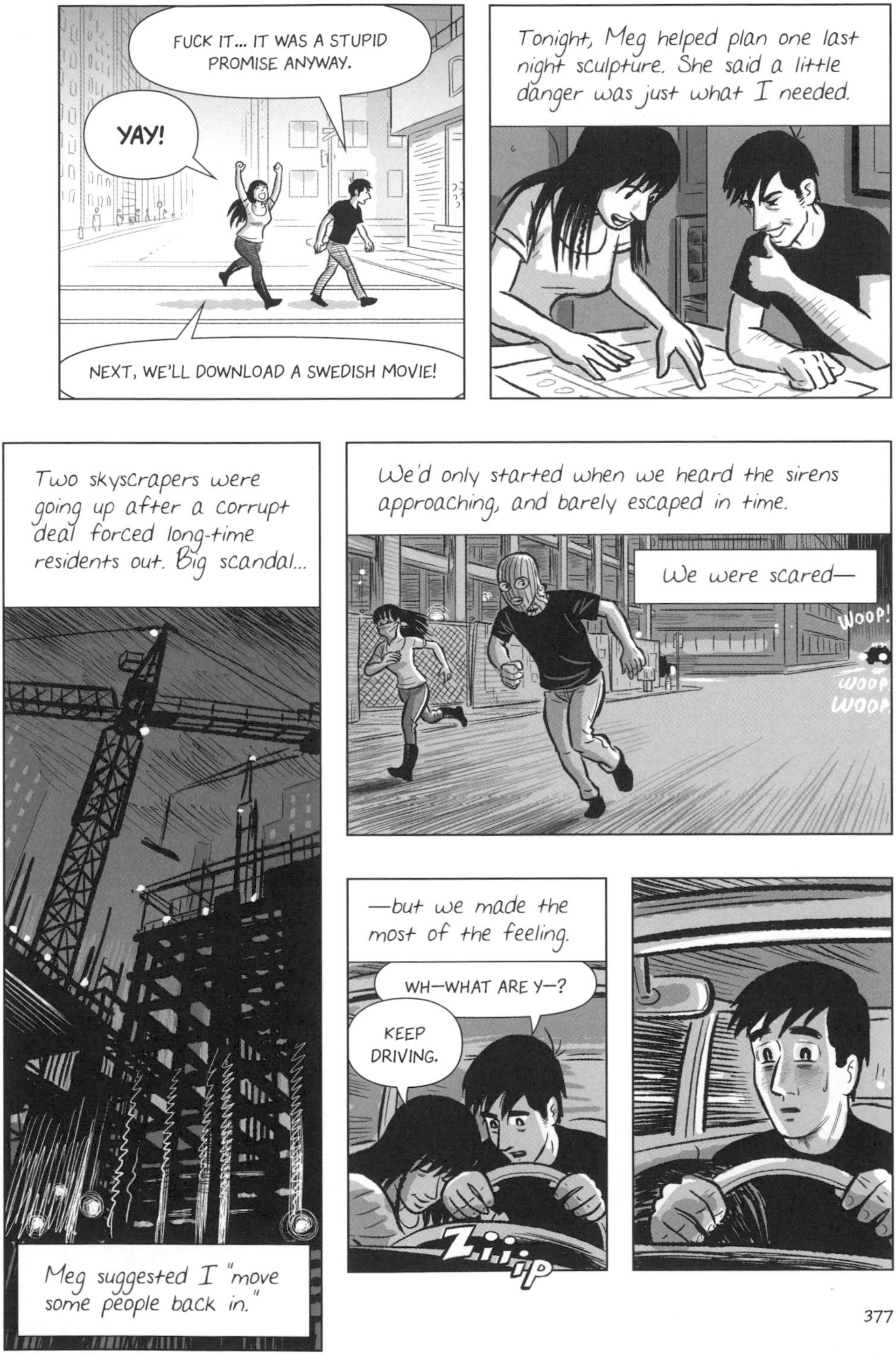
FUCK IT... IT WAS A STUPID PROMISE ANYWAY.
YAY!
NEXT, WE'LL DOWNLOAD A SWEDISH MOVIE!
Tonight, Meg helped plan one last night sculpture. She said a little danger was just what I needed.
Two skyscrapers were going up after a corrupt deal forced long-time residents out. Big scandal...
Meg suggested I "move some people back in."
We'd only started when we heard the sirens approaching, and barely escaped in time.
We were scared—
WOOP!
WOOP!
WOOP!
—but we made the most of the feeling.
WH—WHAT ARE Y—?
KEEP DRIVING.
Ziiip

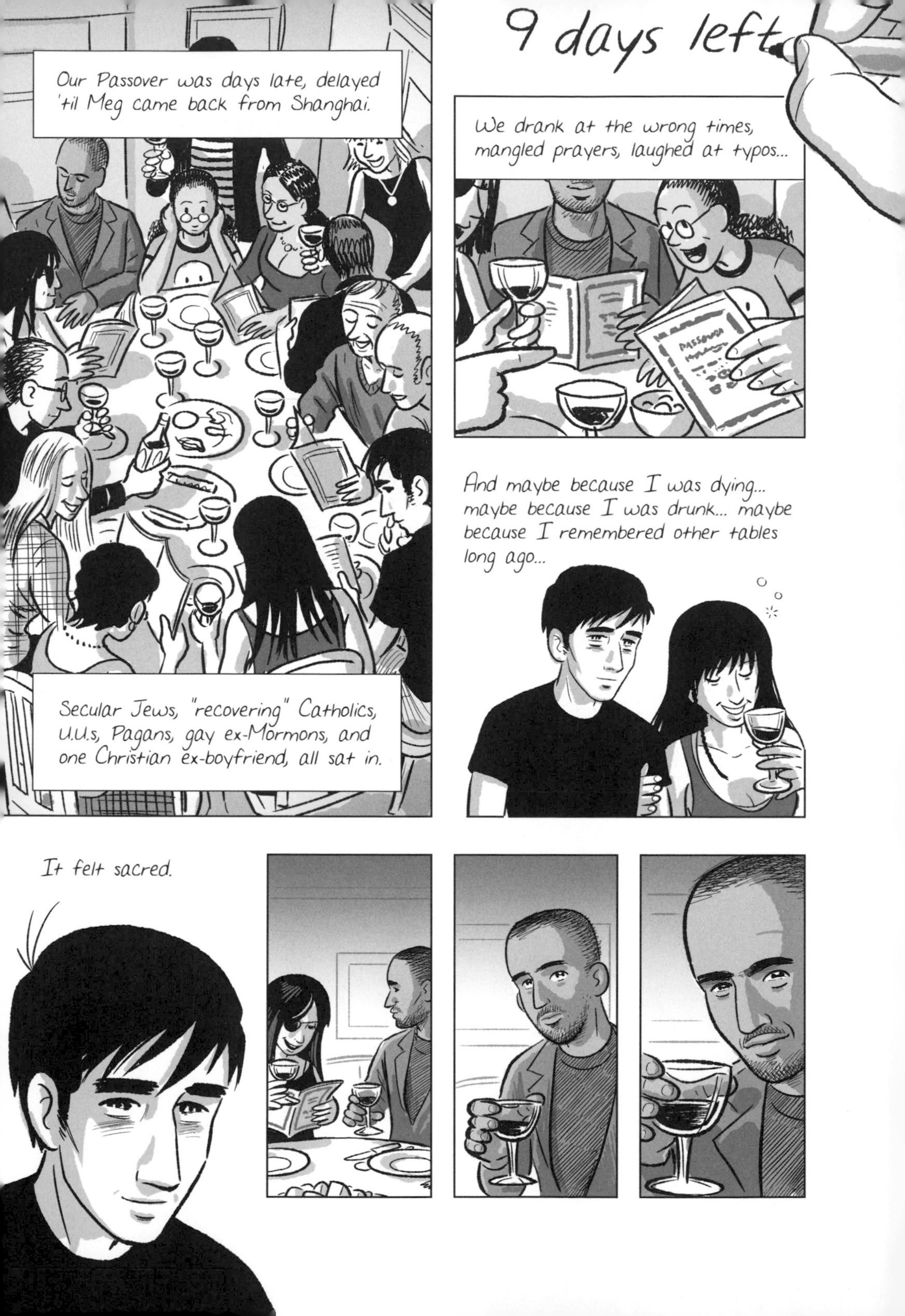
Our Passover was days late, delayed 'til Meg came back from Shanghai.
Secular Jews, "recovering" Catholics, U.U.s, Pagans, gay ex-Mormons, and one Christian ex-boyfriend, all sat in.
9 days left
We drank at the wrong times, mangled prayers, laughed at typos...
And maybe because I was dying... maybe because I was drunk... maybe because I remembered other tables long ago...
It felt sacred.

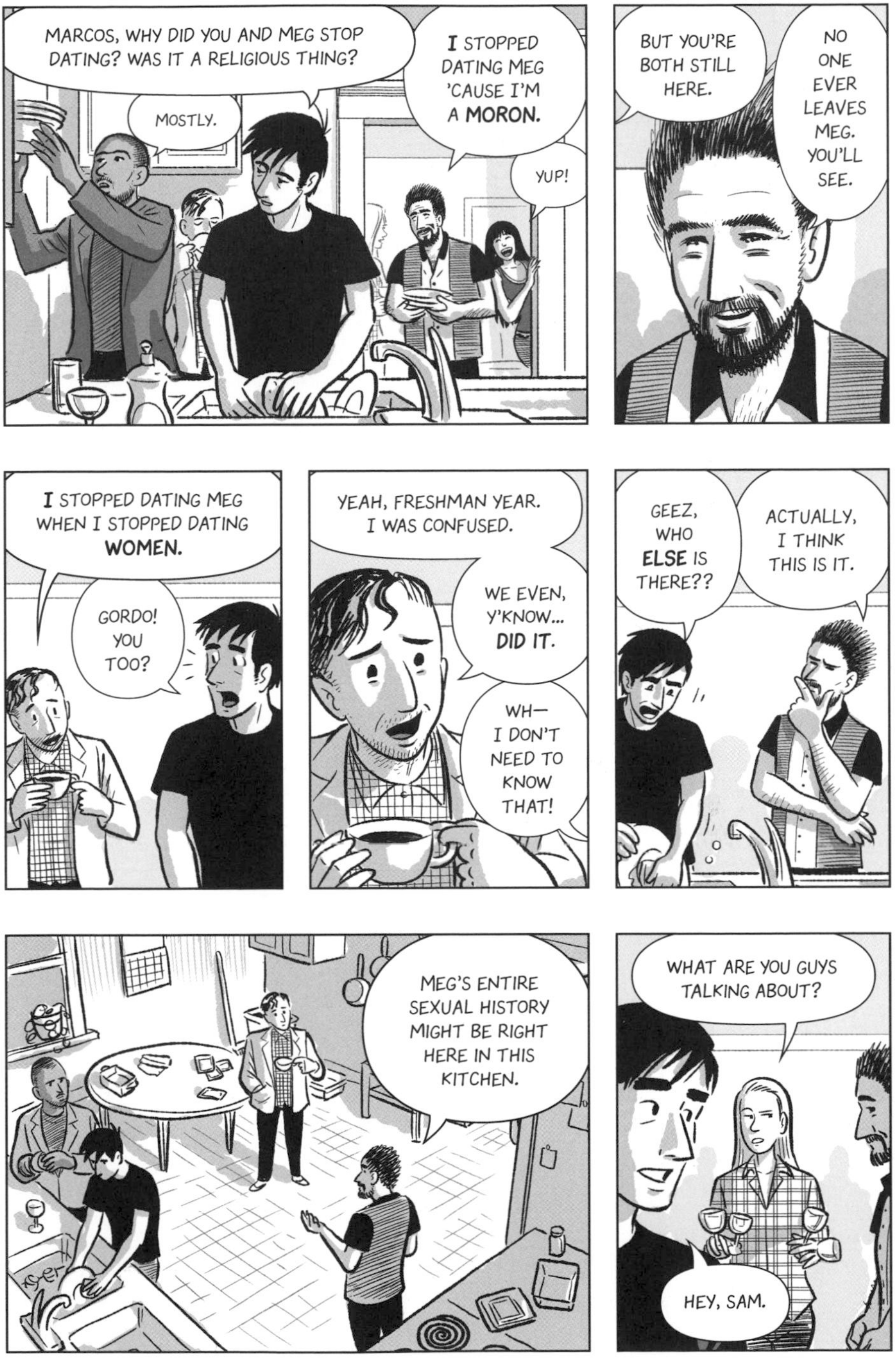
MARCOS, WHY DID YOU AND MEG STOP DATING? WAS IT A RELIGIOUS THING?
MOSTLY.
I STOPPED DATING MEG 'CAUSE I'M A MORON.
YUP!
BUT YOU'RE BOTH STILL HERE.
NO ONE EVER LEAVES MEG. YOU'LL SEE.
I STOPPED DATING MEG WHEN I STOPPED DATING WOMEN.
GORDO! YOU TOO?
YEAH, FRESHMAN YEAR. I WAS CONFUSED.
WE EVEN, Y'KNOW... DID IT.
WH— I DON'T NEED TO KNOW THAT!
GEEZ, WHO ELSE IS THERE??
ACTUALLY, I THINK THIS IS IT.
MEG'S ENTIRE SEXUAL HISTORY MIGHT BE RIGHT HERE IN THIS KITCHEN.
WHAT ARE YOU GUYS TALKING ABOUT?
HEY, SAM.

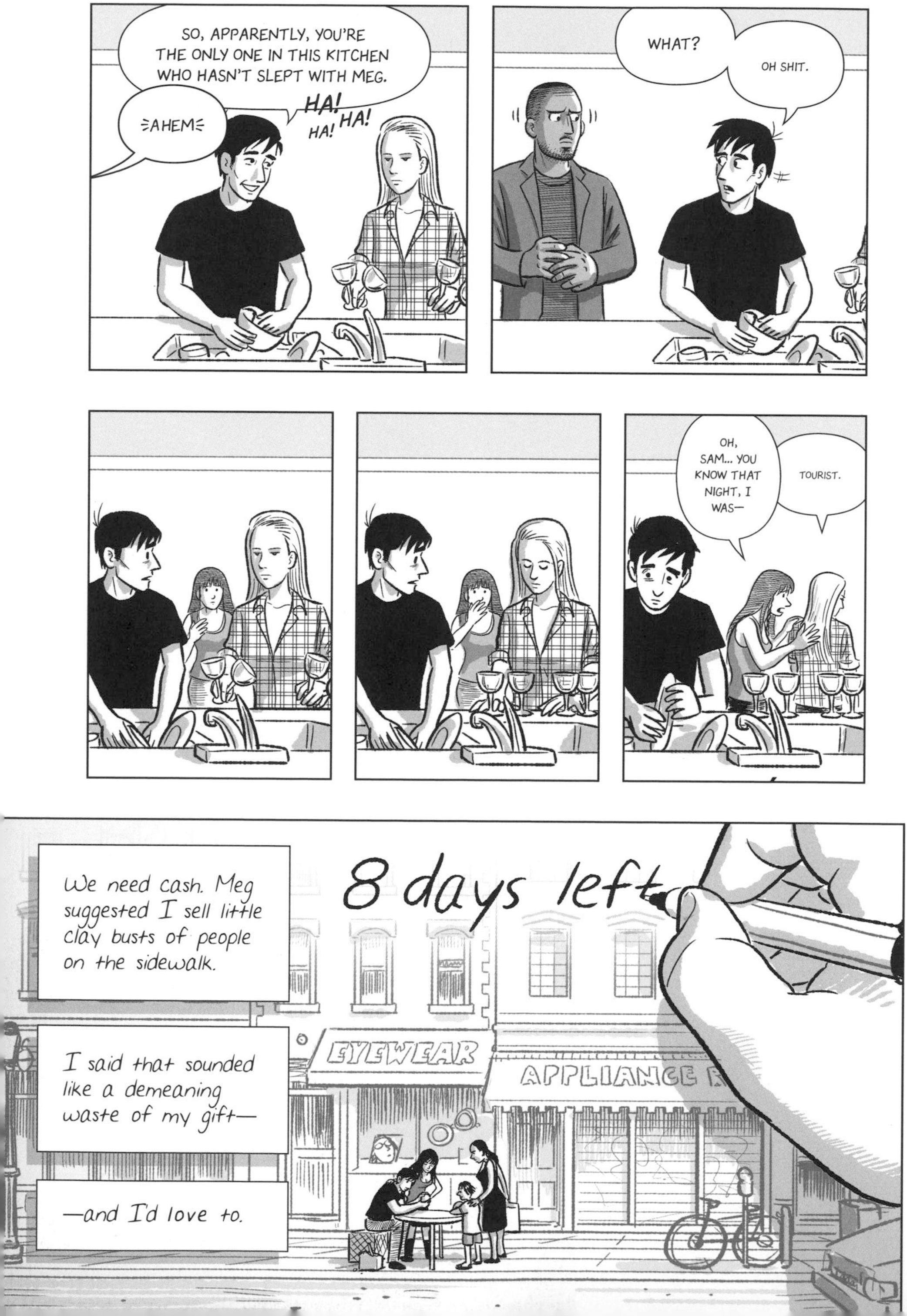
SO, APPARENTLY, YOU'RE THE ONLY ONE IN THIS KITCHEN WHO HASN'T SLEPT WITH MEG.
≡AHEM≡
HA! HA! HA!
WHAT?
OH SHIT.
OH, SAM... YOU KNOW THAT NIGHT, I WAS—
TOURIST.
8 days left
We need cash. Meg suggested I sell little clay busts of people on the sidewalk.
I said that sounded like a demeaning waste of my gift—
—and I'd love to.
EYEWEAR
APPLIANCE R

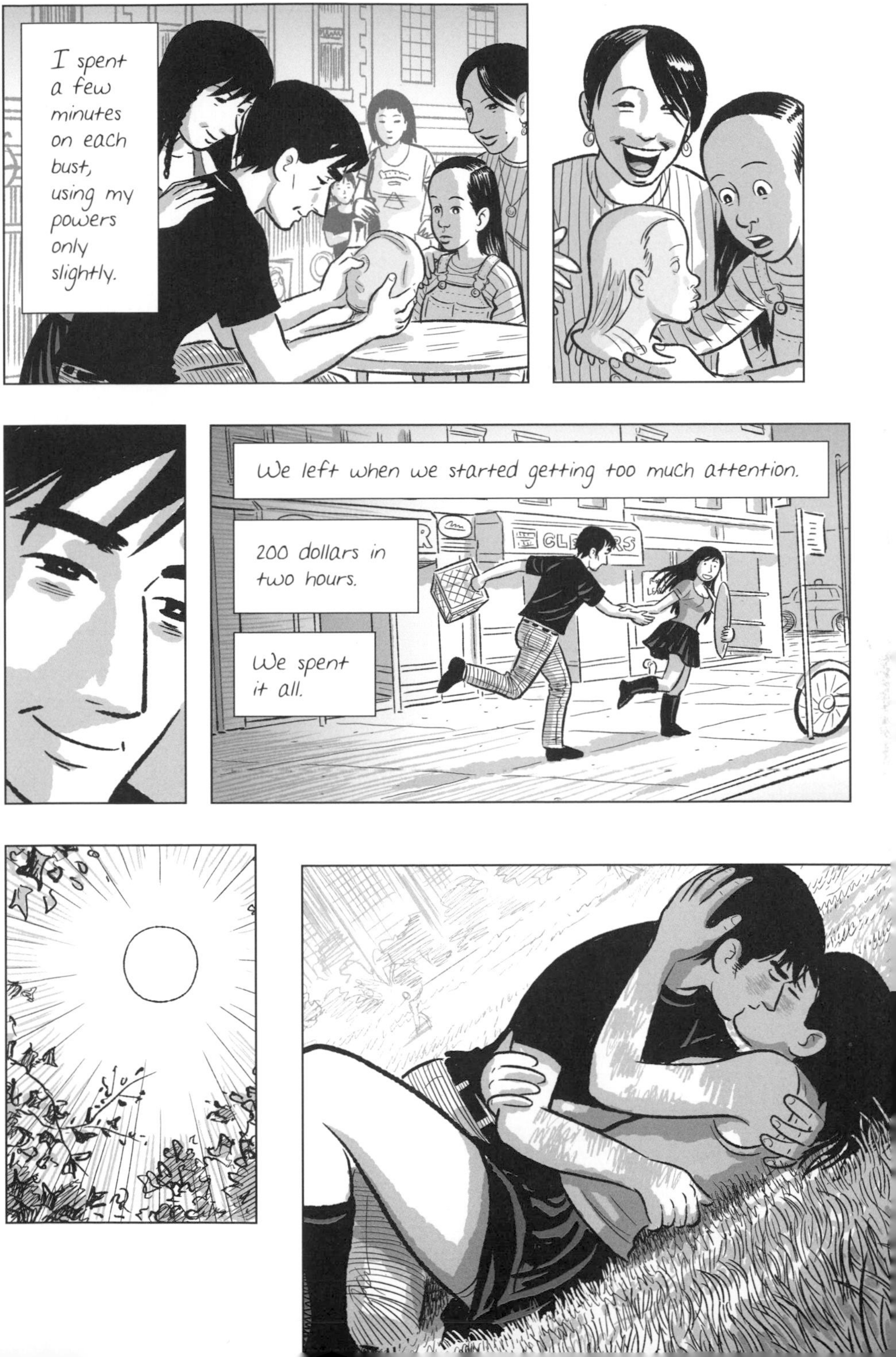
I spent a few minutes on each bust, using my powers only slightly.
We left when we started getting too much attention.
200 dollars in two hours.
We spent it all.

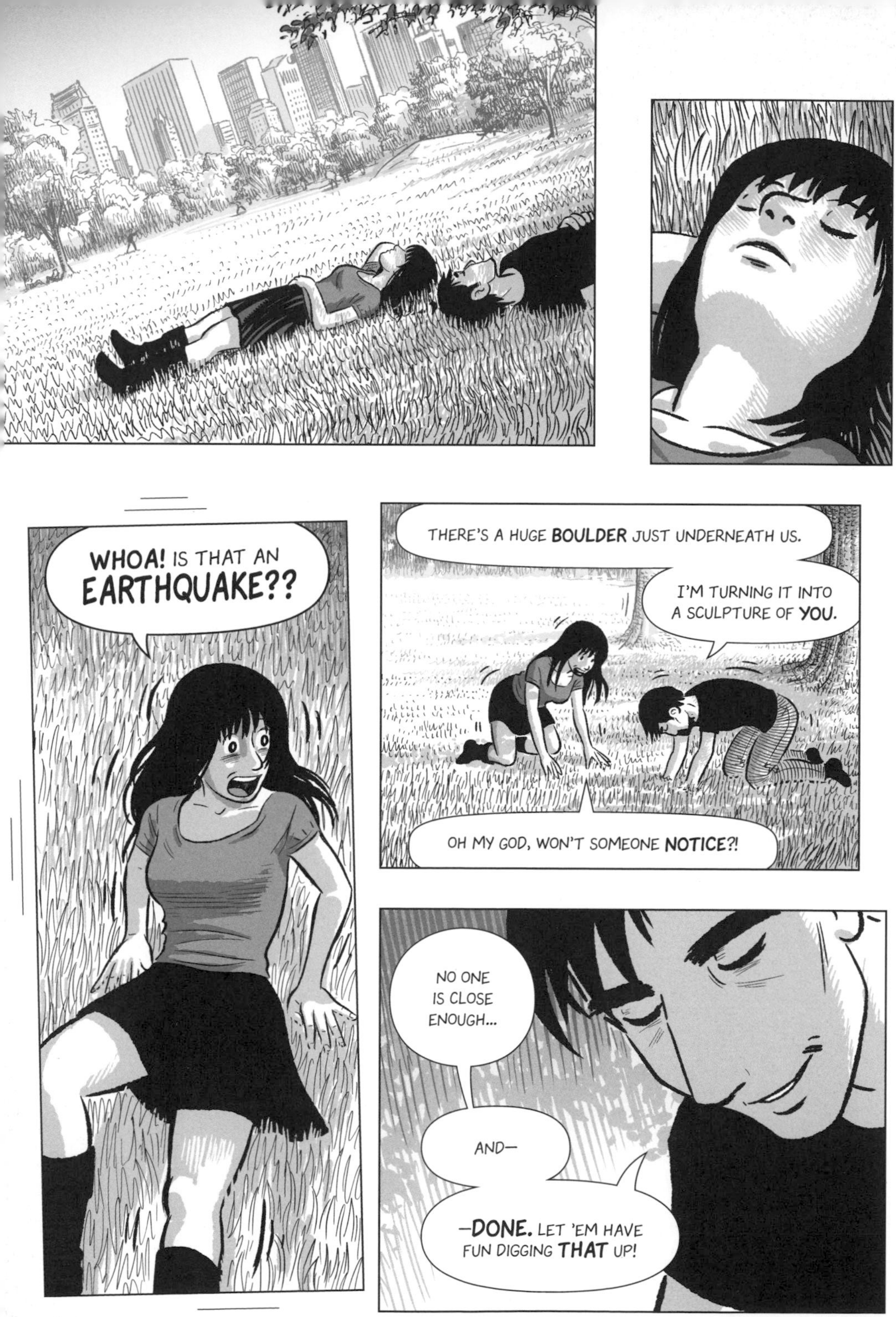
WHOA! IS THAT AN EARTHQUAKE??
THERE'S A HUGE BOULDER JUST UNDERNEATH US.
I'M TURNING IT INTO A SCULPTURE OF YOU.
OH MY GOD, WON'T SOMEONE NOTICE?!
NO ONE IS CLOSE ENOUGH...
AND—
—DONE. LET 'EM HAVE FUN DIGGING THAT UP!

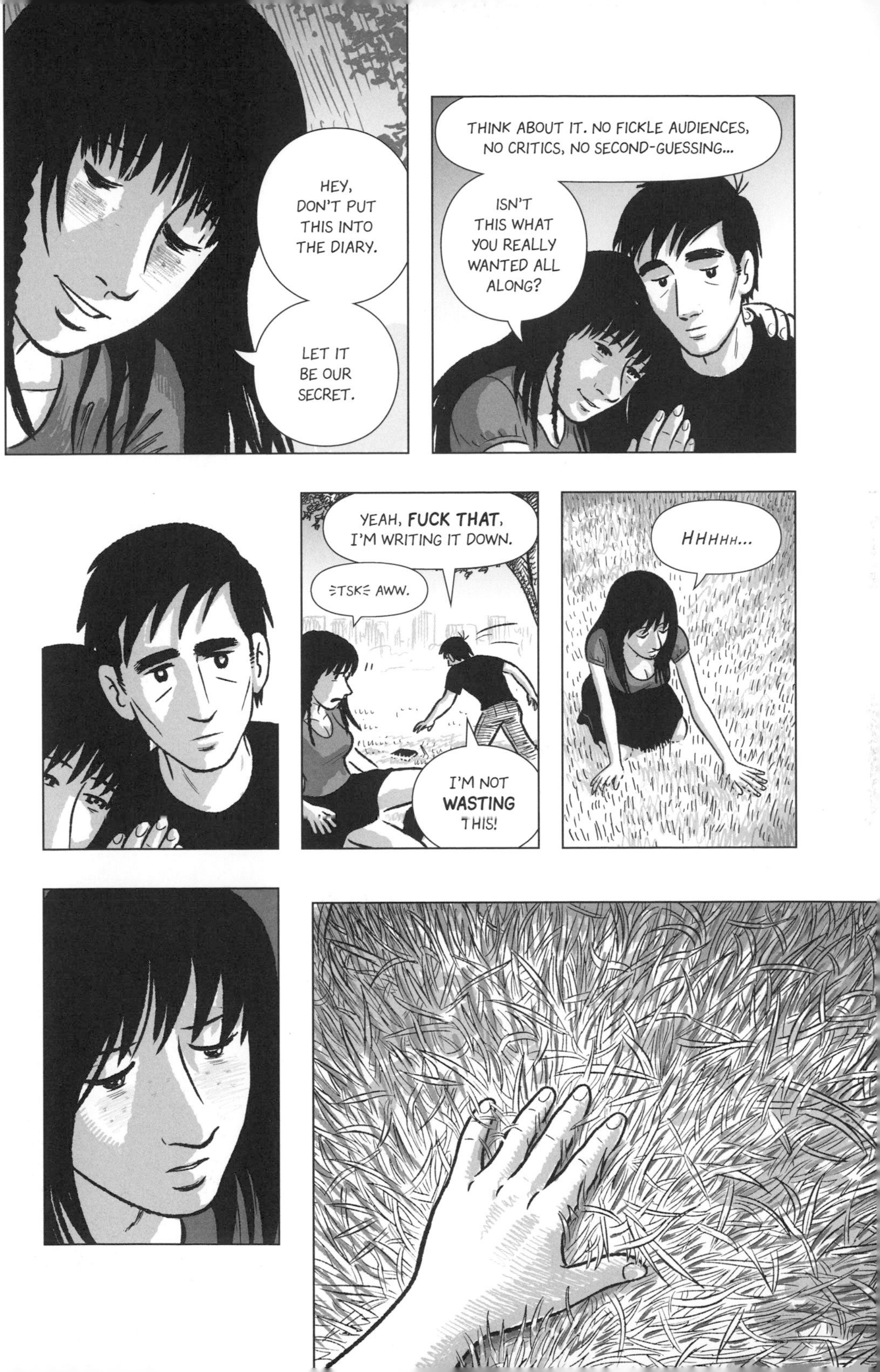
HEY, DON'T PUT THIS INTO THE DIARY.
LET IT BE OUR SECRET.
THINK ABOUT IT. NO FICKLE AUDIENCES, NO CRITICS, NO SECOND-GUESSING...
ISN'T THIS WHAT YOU REALLY WANTED ALL ALONG?
YEAH, **FUCK THAT**, I'M WRITING IT DOWN.
=TSK= AWW.
I'M NOT **WASTING** THIS!
HHHHH...

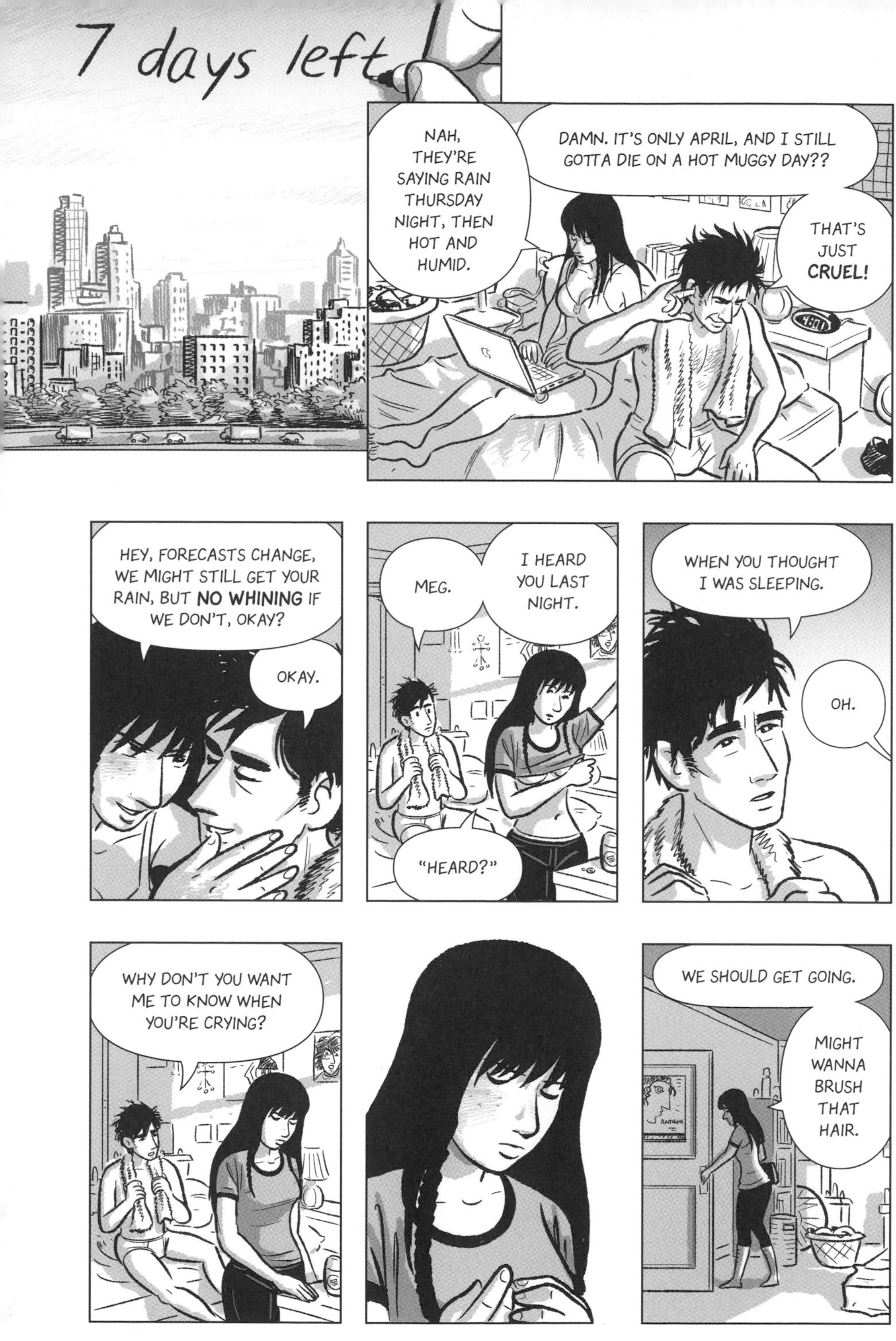

7 days left
NAH, THEY'RE SAYING RAIN THURSDAY NIGHT, THEN HOT AND HUMID.
DAMN. IT'S ONLY APRIL, AND I STILL GOTTA DIE ON A HOT MUGGY DAY??
THAT'S JUST **CRUEL!**
HEY, FORECASTS CHANGE, WE MIGHT STILL GET YOUR RAIN, BUT **NO WHINING** IF WE DON'T, OKAY?
OKAY.
MEG.
I HEARD YOU LAST NIGHT.
"HEARD?"
WHEN YOU THOUGHT I WAS SLEEPING.
OH.
WHY DON'T YOU WANT ME TO KNOW WHEN YOU'RE CRYING?
WE SHOULD GET GOING.
MIGHT WANNA BRUSH THAT HAIR.

MEG, COULD YOU HOLD HIM FOR A MINUTE?

I'D LOVE TO! C'MERE, SWEETIE.

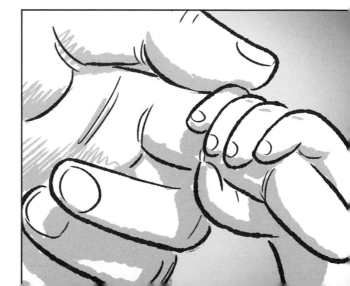

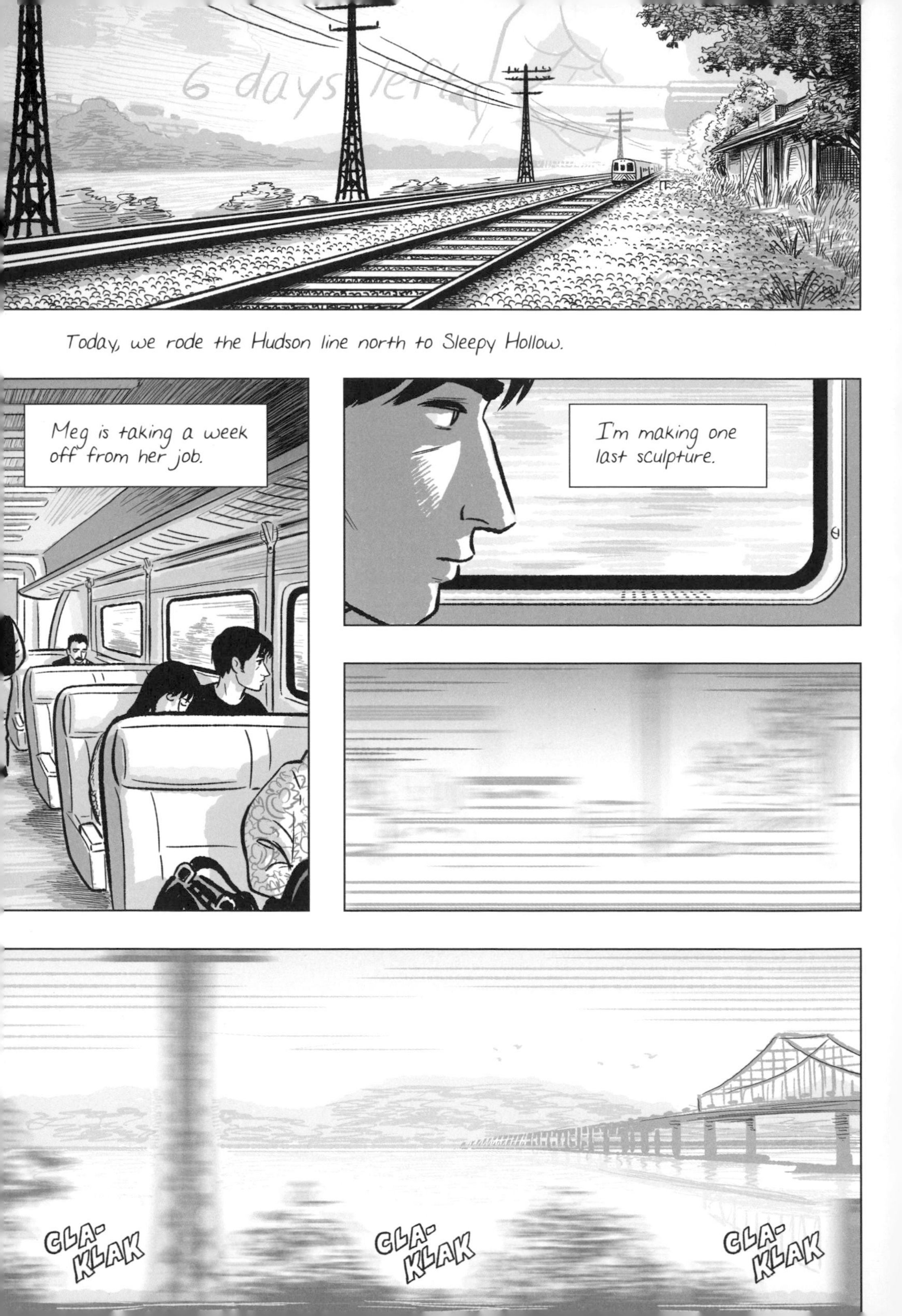
6 days left
Today, we rode the Hudson line north to Sleepy Hollow.
Meg is taking a week off from her job.
I'm making one last sculpture.
CLA-KLAK
CLA-KLAK
CLA-KLAK

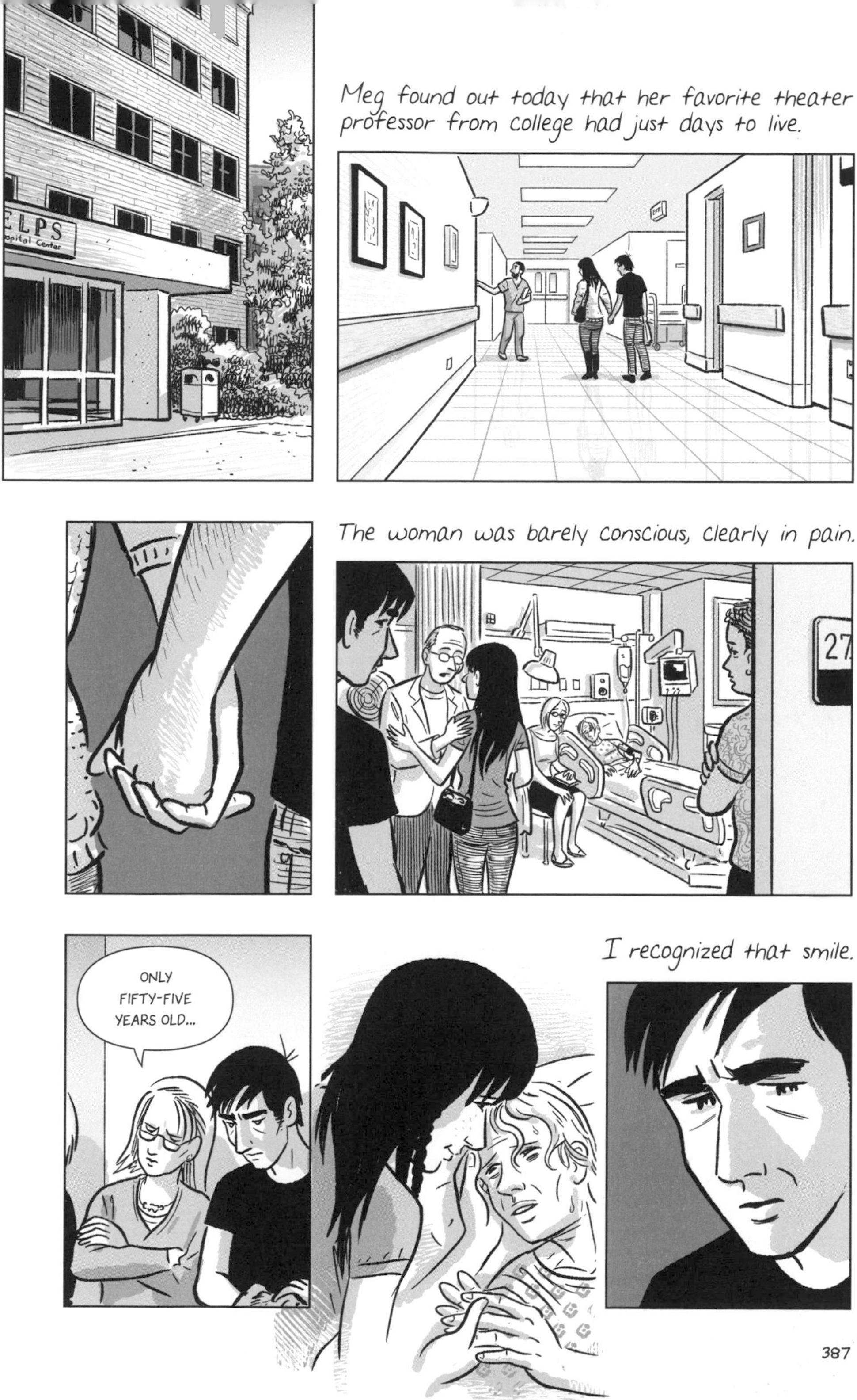

ELPS
Meg found out today that her favorite theater professor from college had just days to live.
The woman was barely conscious, clearly in pain.
27
ONLY FIFTY-FIVE YEARS OLD...
I recognized that smile.

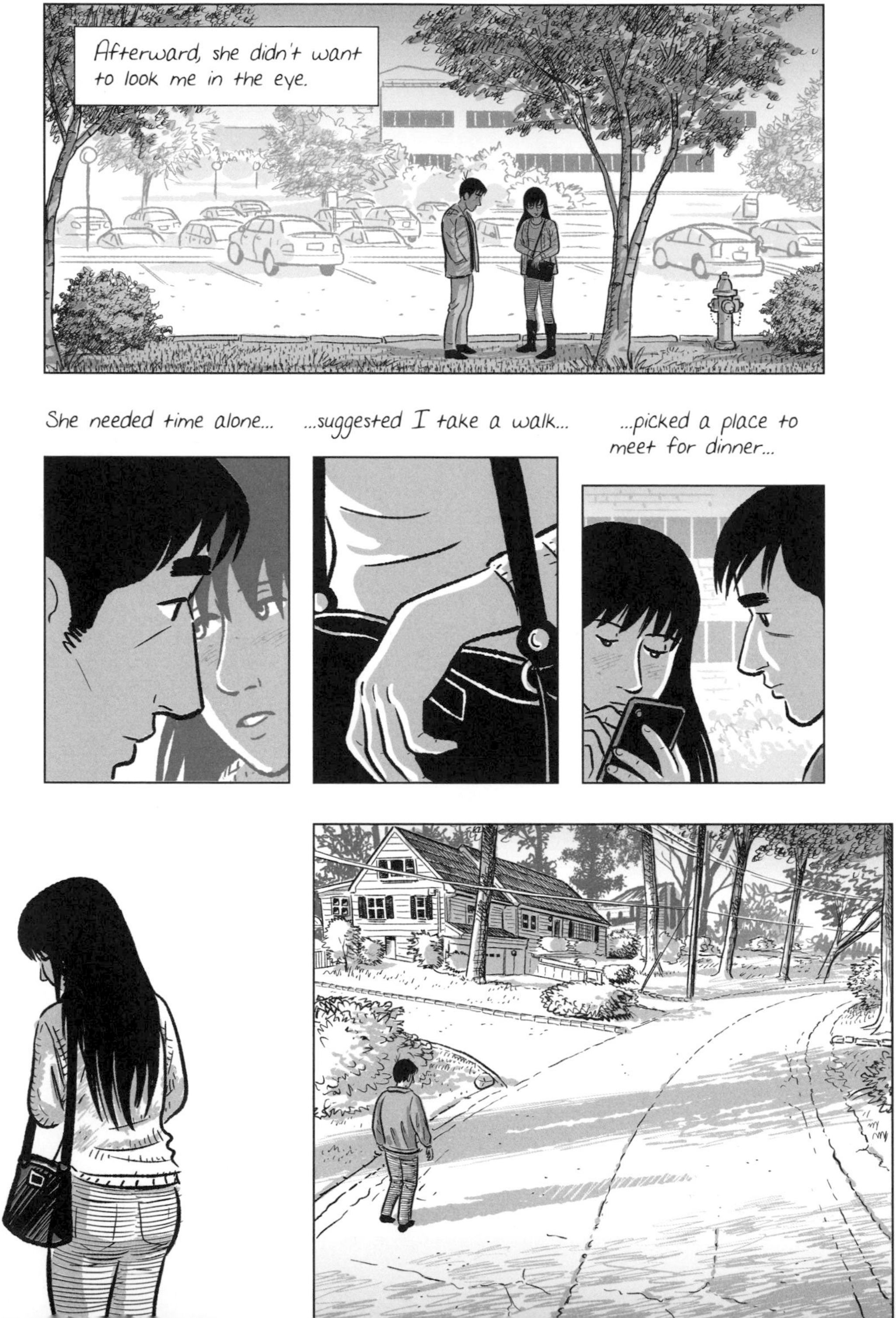
Afterward, she didn't want to look me in the eye.
She needed time alone...
...suggested I take a walk...
...picked a place to meet for dinner...

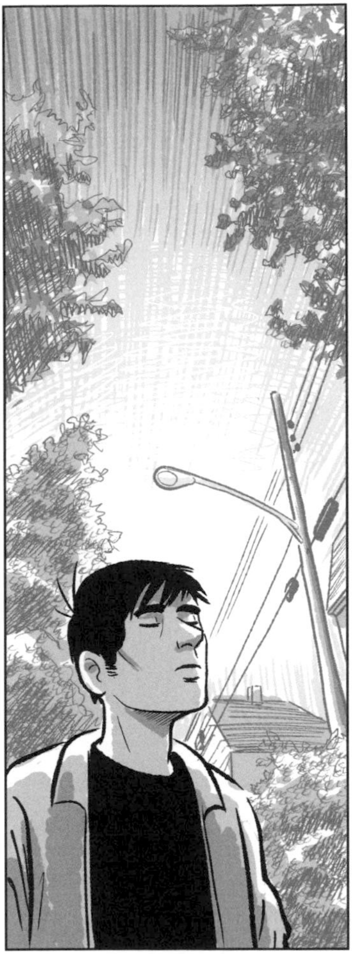

In parking lots, I kept noticing the painted lines.

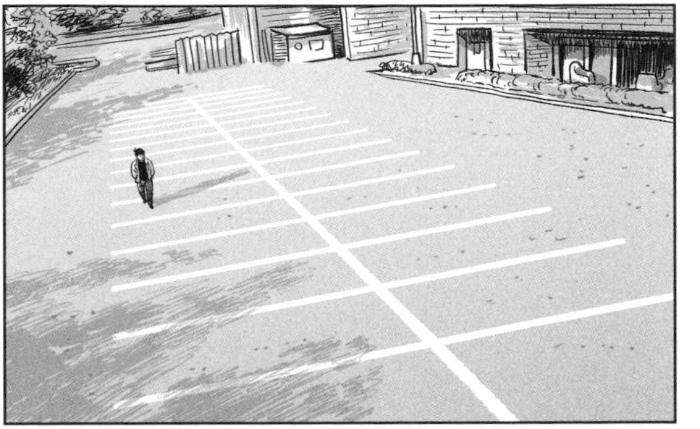

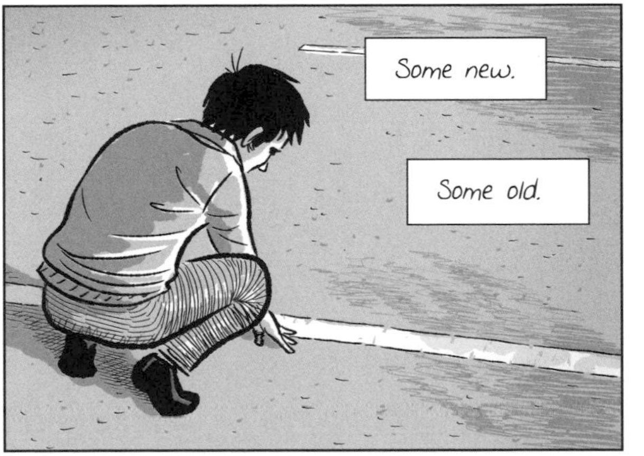
Some new.
Some old.

There wasn't much to the newest.

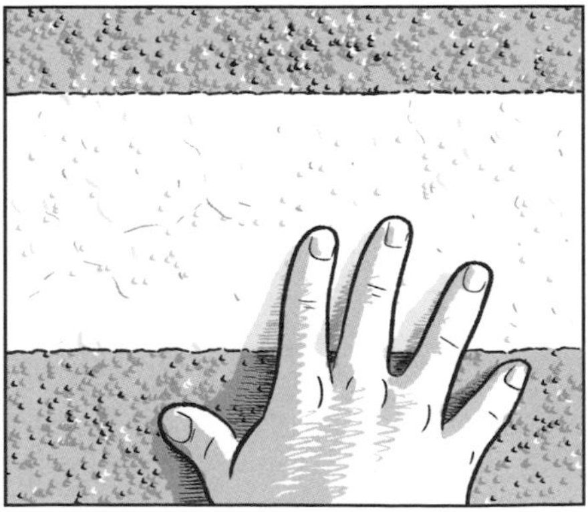

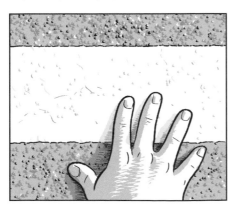

There wasn't much left of the oldest.

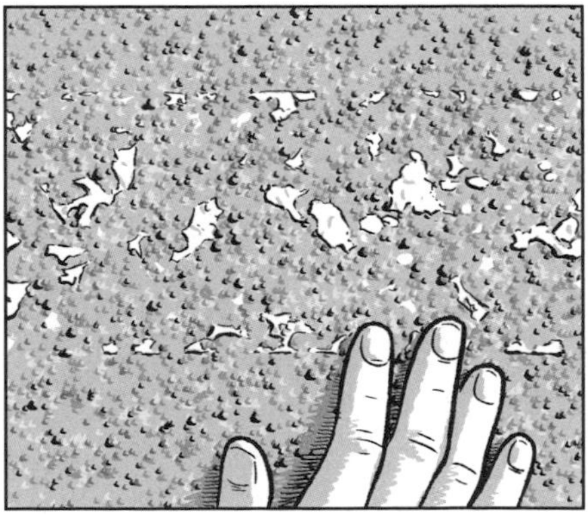

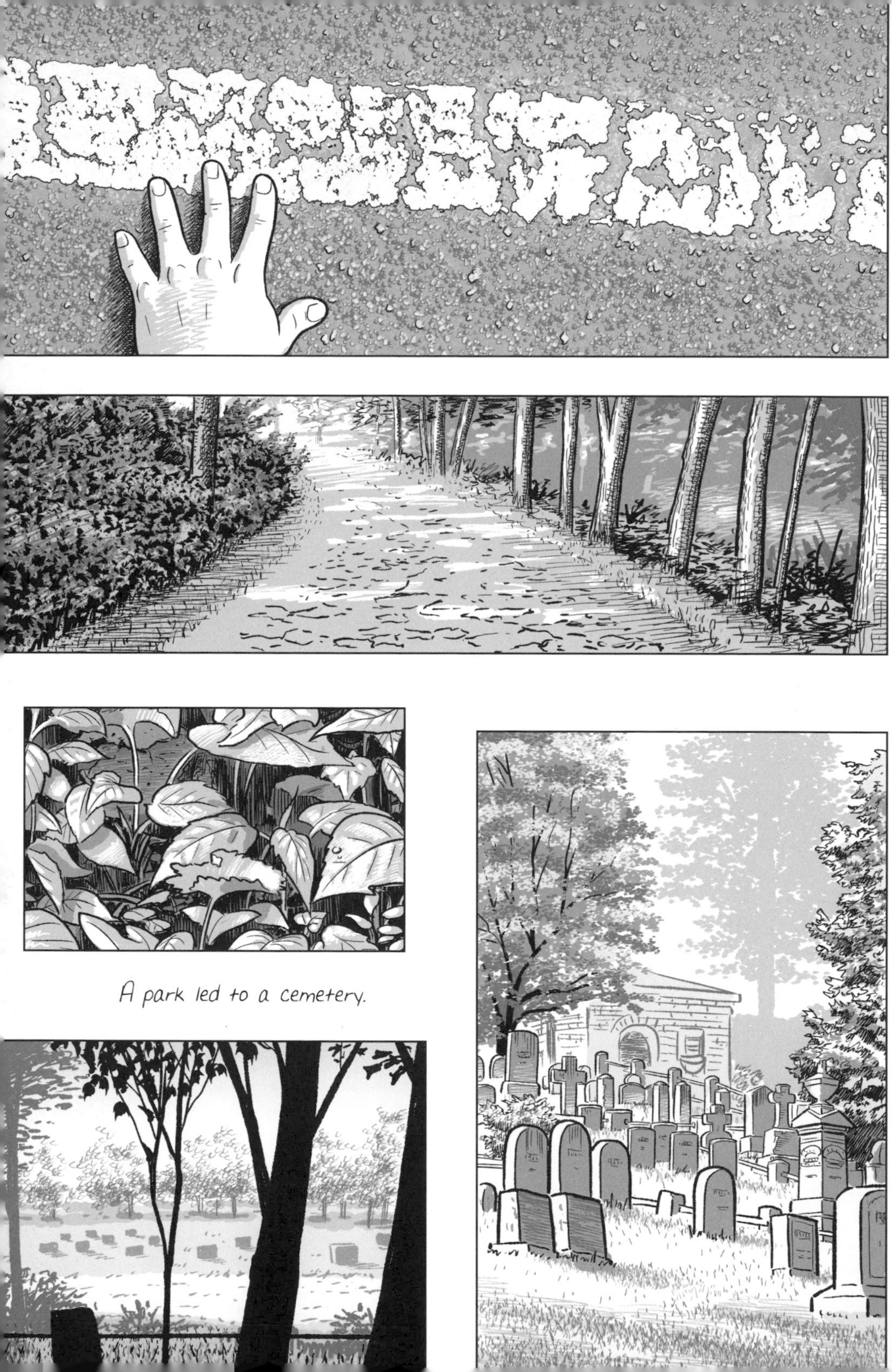
A park led to a cemetery.

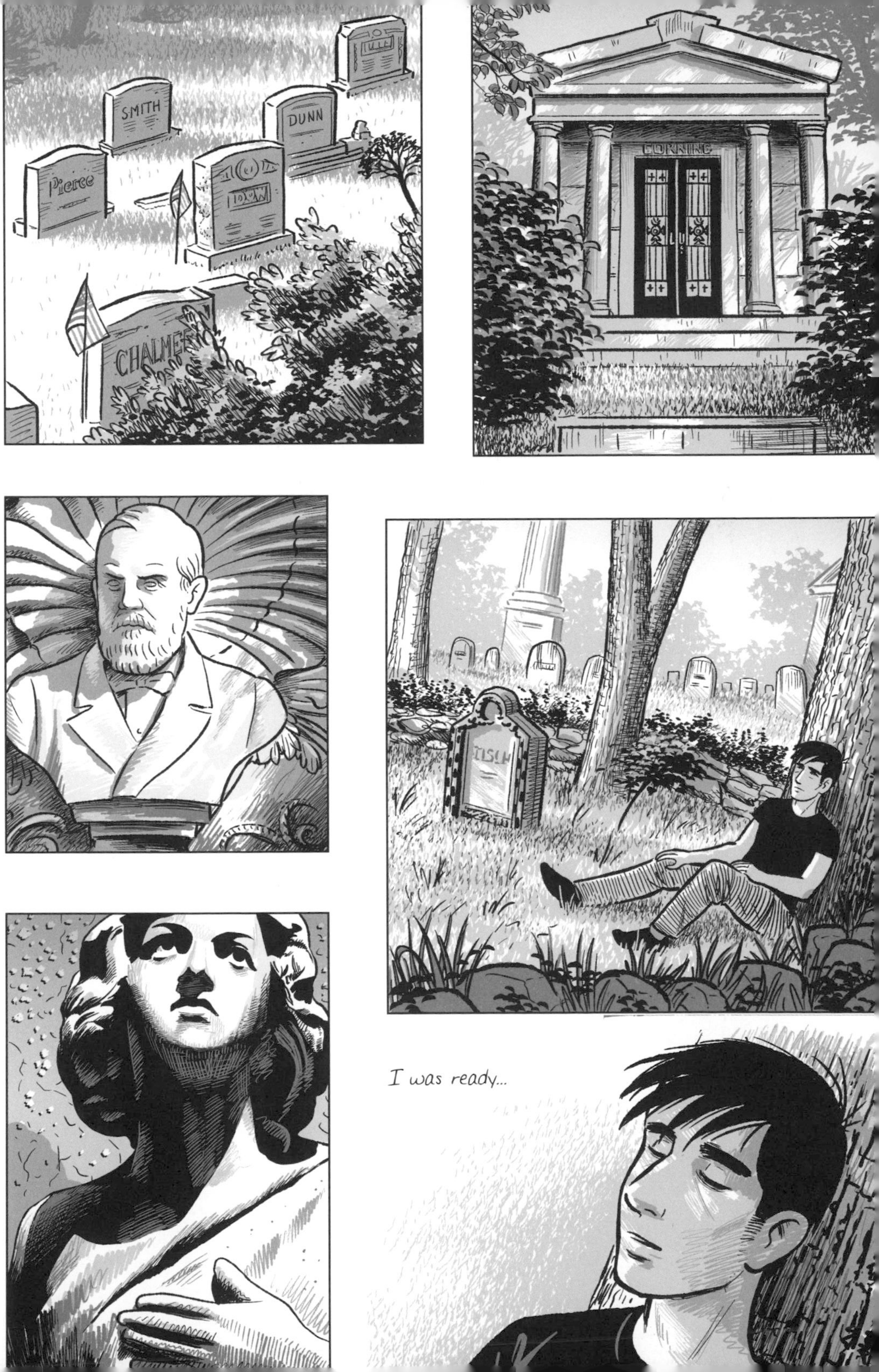
SMITH
DUNN
Pierce
CORNING
I was ready...

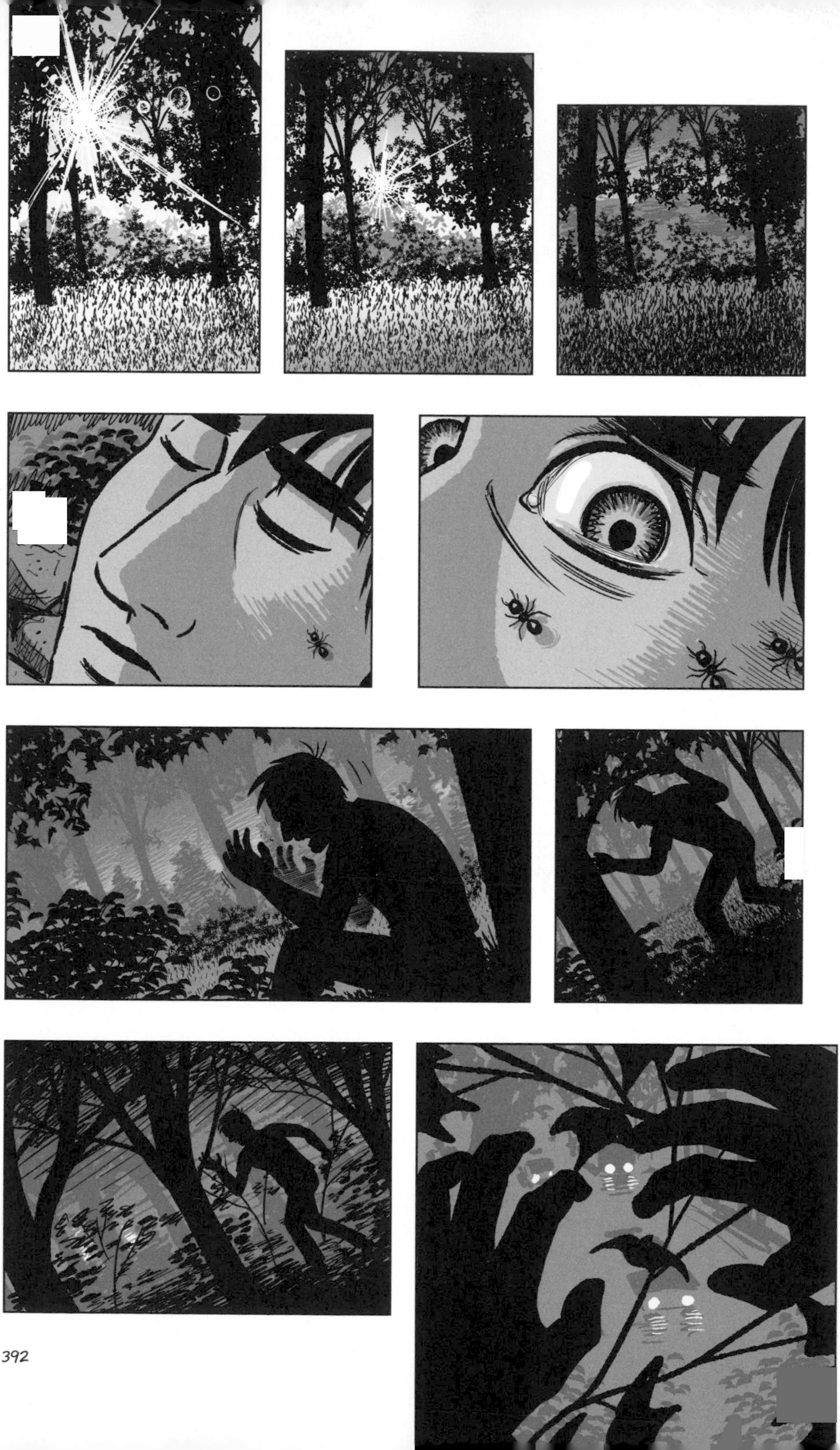

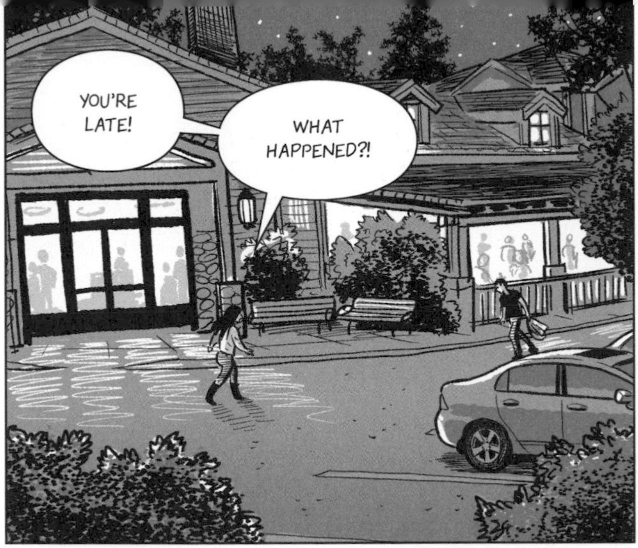
YOU'RE LATE!
WHAT HAPPENED?!

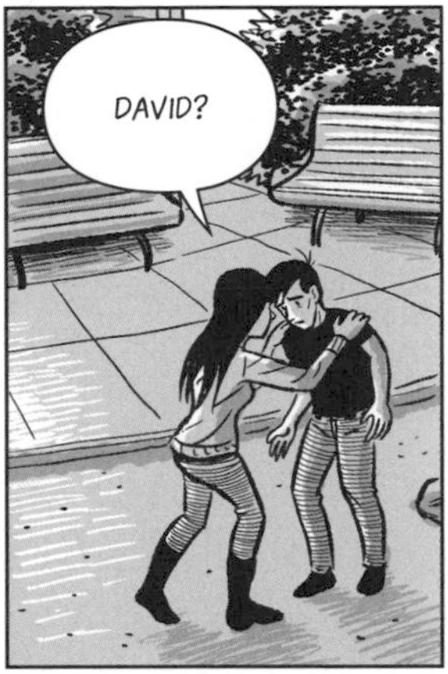
DAVID?

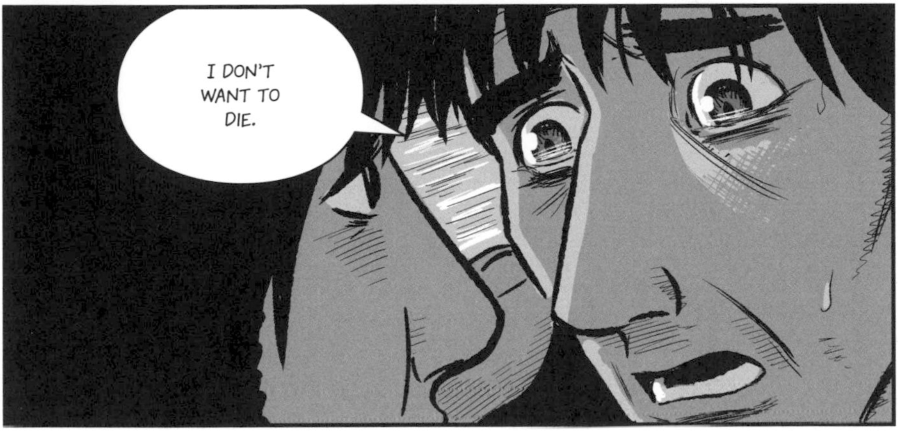
I DON'T WANT TO DIE.

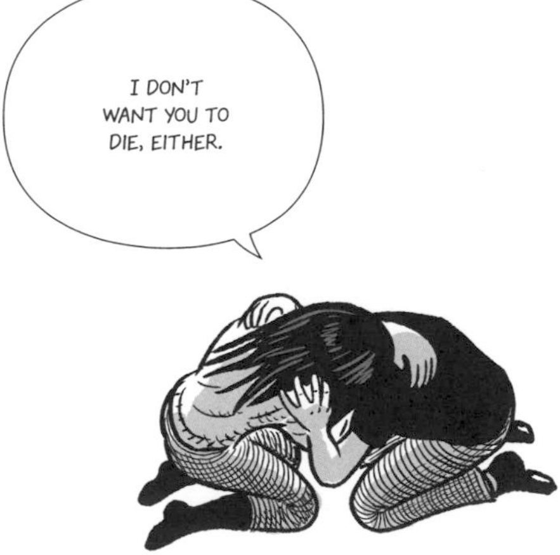
I DON'T WANT YOU TO DIE, EITHER.

5 days left.

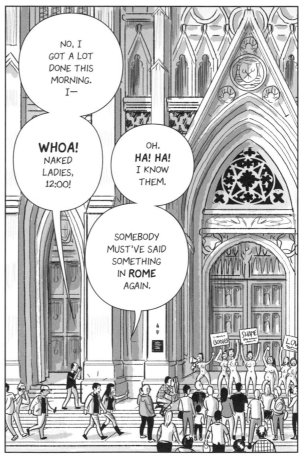

NO, I GOT A LOT DONE THIS MORNING. I—

WHOA! NAKED LADIES, 12:00!

OH. HA! HA! I KNOW THEM.

SOMEBODY MUST'VE SAID SOMETHING IN **ROME** AGAIN.

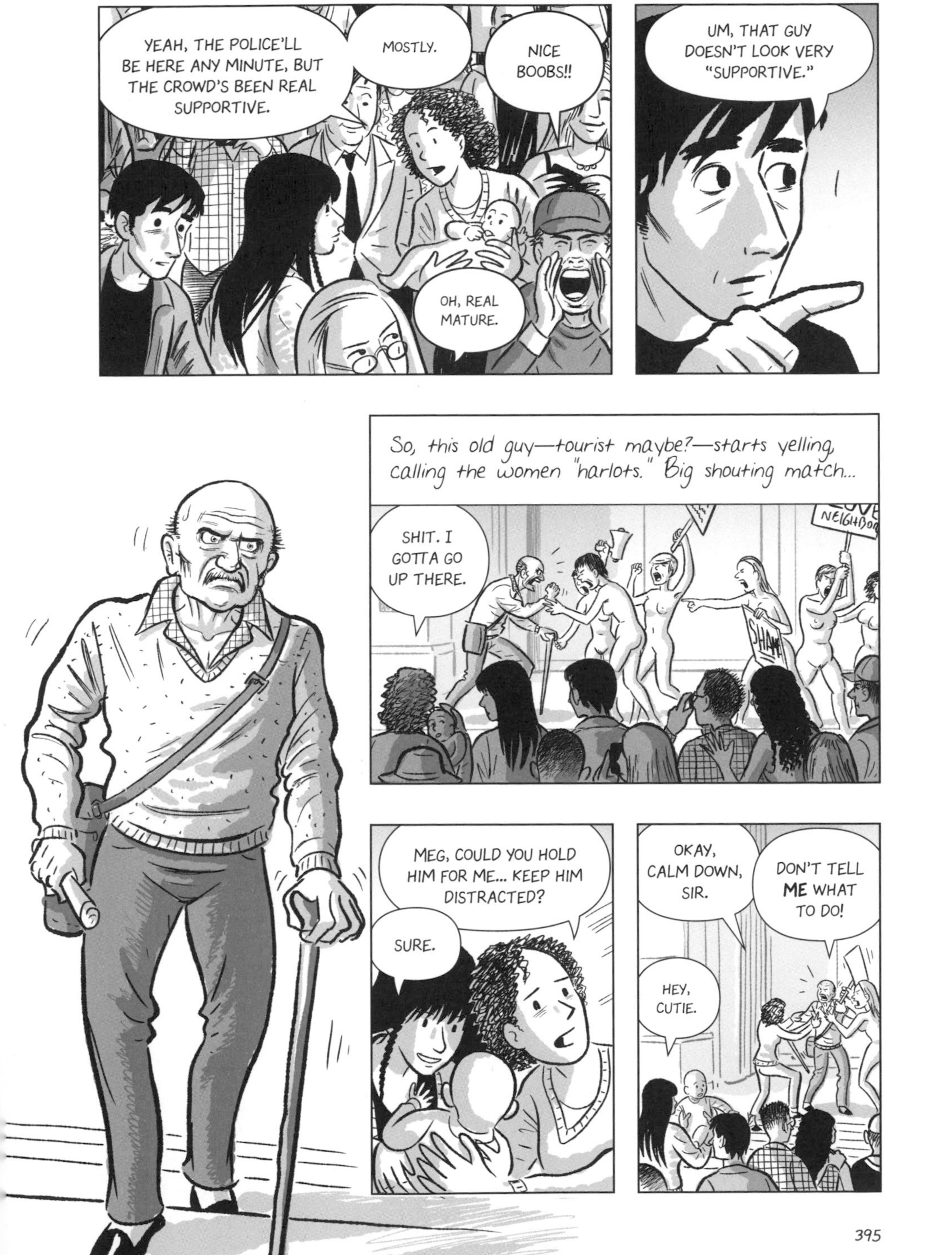
YEAH, THE POLICE'LL BE HERE ANY MINUTE, BUT THE CROWD'S BEEN REAL SUPPORTIVE.
MOSTLY.
NICE BOOBS!!
OH, REAL MATURE.
UM, THAT GUY DOESN'T LOOK VERY "SUPPORTIVE."
So, this old guy—tourist maybe?—starts yelling, calling the women "harlots." Big shouting match...
SHIT. I GOTTA GO UP THERE.
MEG, COULD YOU HOLD HIM FOR ME... KEEP HIM DISTRACTED?
SURE.
OKAY, CALM DOWN, SIR.
DON'T TELL ME WHAT TO DO!
HEY, CUTIE.

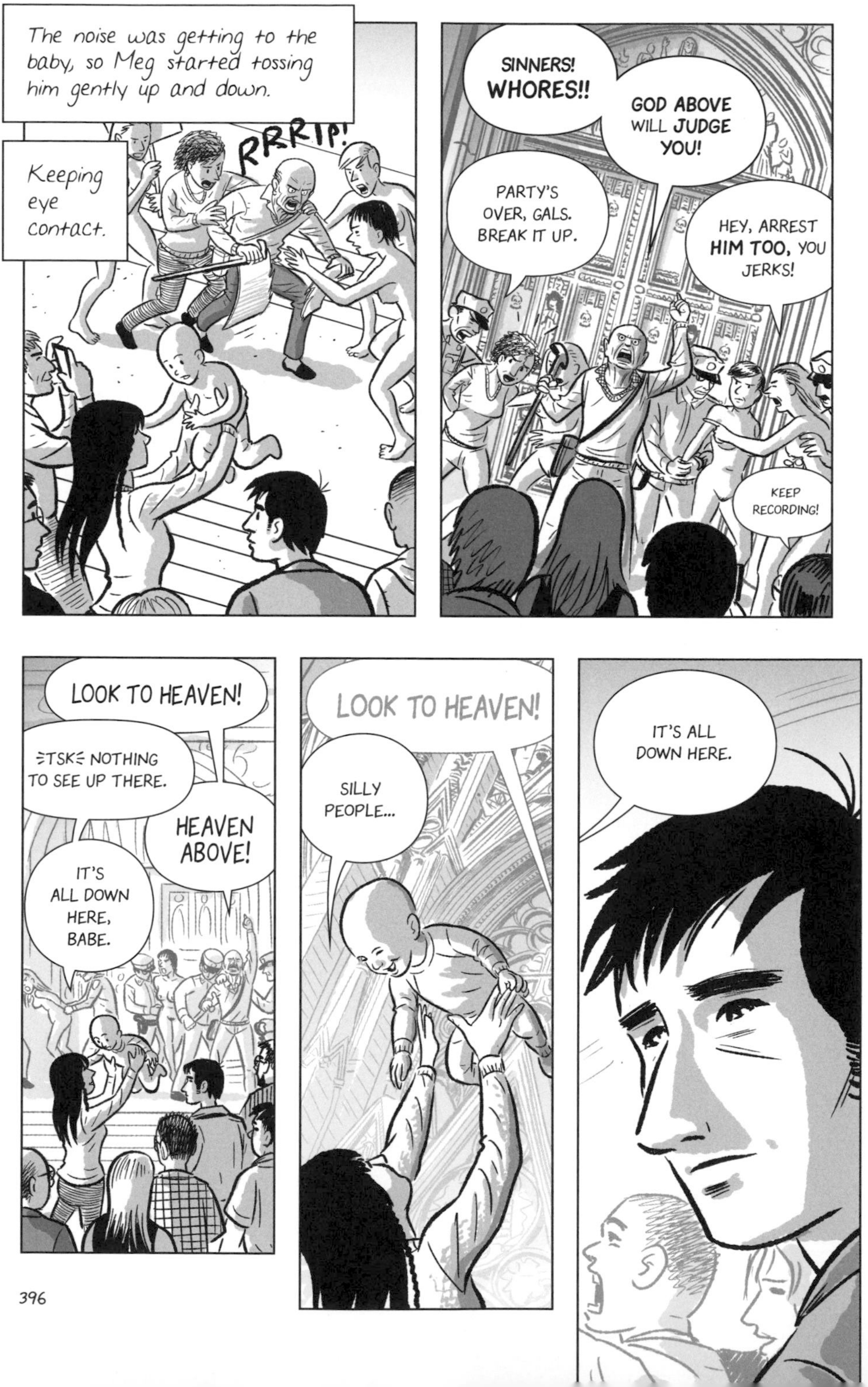
The noise was getting to the baby, so Meg started tossing him gently up and down.
RRRIP!
Keeping eye contact.
SINNERS! WHORES!!
GOD ABOVE WILL JUDGE YOU!
PARTY'S OVER, GALS. BREAK IT UP.
HEY, ARREST HIM TOO, YOU JERKS!
KEEP RECORDING!
LOOK TO HEAVEN!
TSK NOTHING TO SEE UP THERE.
HEAVEN ABOVE!
IT'S ALL DOWN HERE, BABE.
LOOK TO HEAVEN!
SILLY PEOPLE...
IT'S ALL DOWN HERE.

4 days left

I'll work 'til 4 pm at the other apartment.

I'll be done by tomorrow.

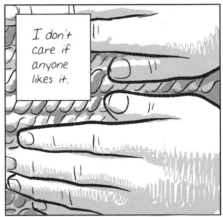

I don't care if anyone likes it.

Except her.

KNOCK! KNOCK!

COMING!

LEMME GRAB THE TICKETS.

I WAS THINK—

HELLO DAVID.

!

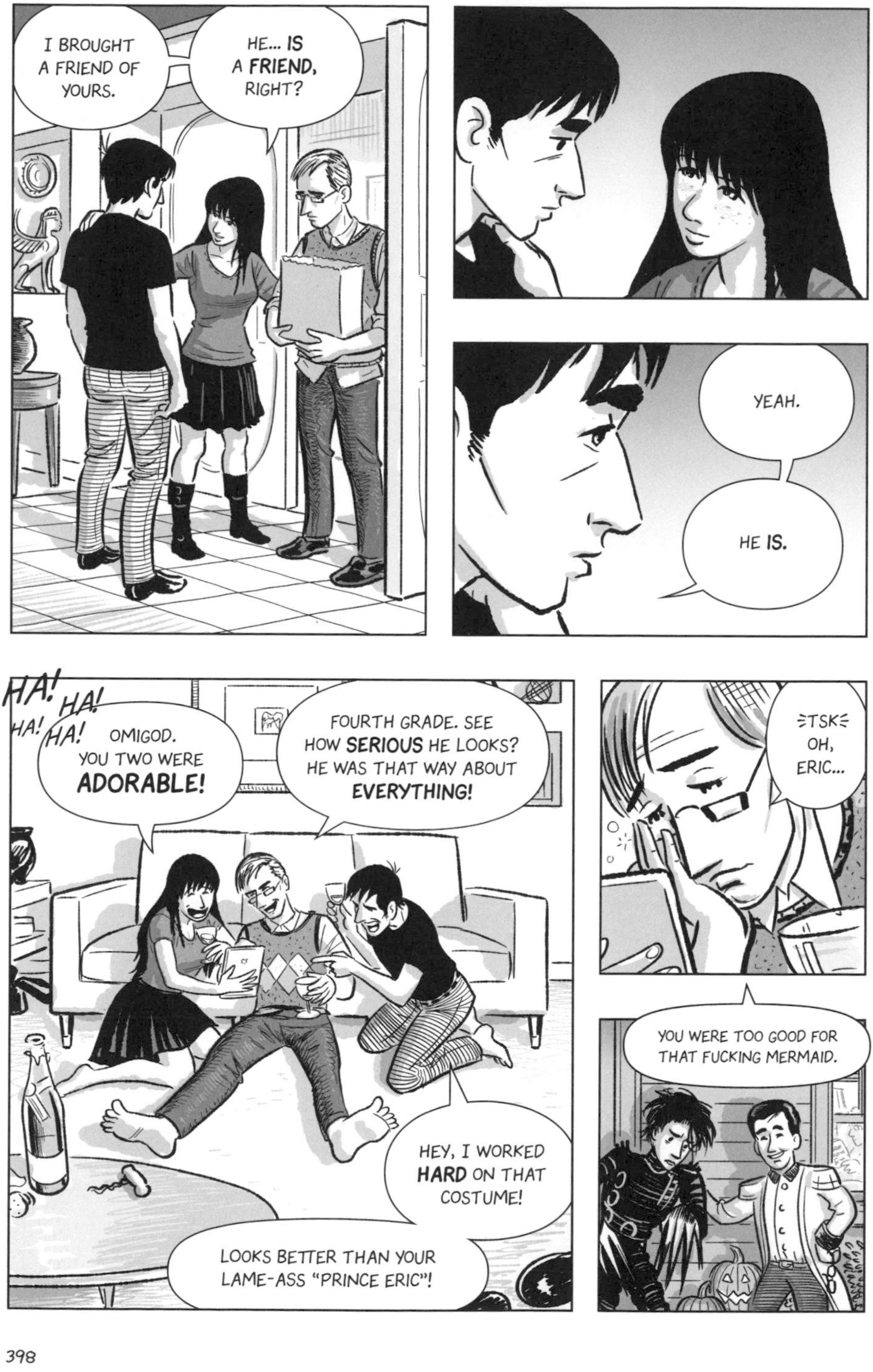
I BROUGHT A FRIEND OF YOURS.
HE... IS A FRIEND, RIGHT?
YEAH.
HE IS.
HA! HA! HA! HA!
OMIGOD. YOU TWO WERE ADORABLE!
FOURTH GRADE. SEE HOW SERIOUS HE LOOKS? HE WAS THAT WAY ABOUT EVERYTHING!
HEY, I WORKED HARD ON THAT COSTUME!
LOOKS BETTER THAN YOUR LAME-ASS "PRINCE ERIC"!
TSK OH, ERIC...
YOU WERE TOO GOOD FOR THAT FUCKING MERMAID.

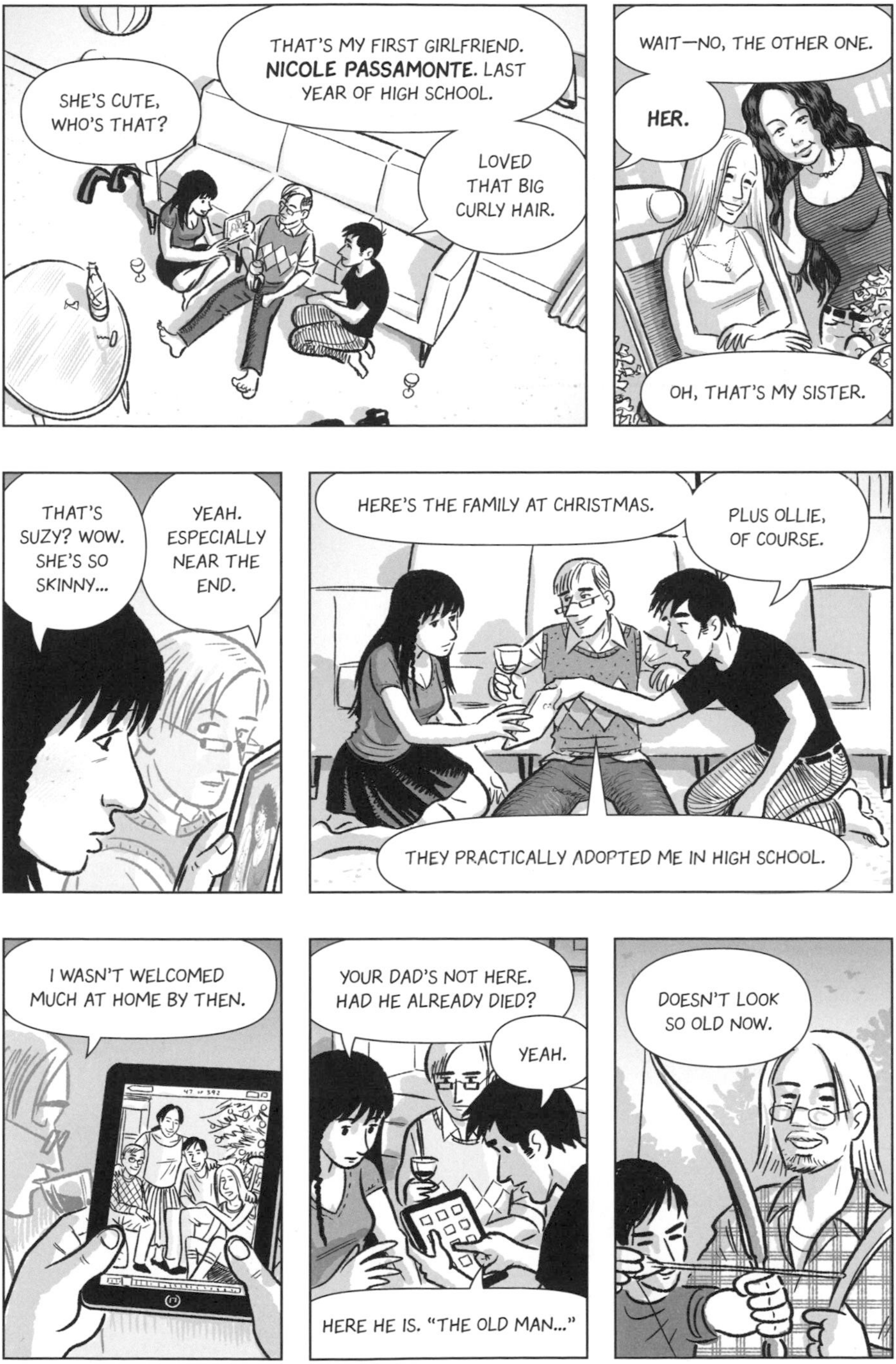
SHE'S CUTE, WHO'S THAT?
THAT'S MY FIRST GIRLFRIEND. **NICOLE PASSAMONTE**. LAST YEAR OF HIGH SCHOOL.
LOVED THAT BIG CURLY HAIR.
WAIT—NO, THE OTHER ONE.
HER.
OH, THAT'S MY SISTER.
THAT'S SUZY? WOW. SHE'S SO SKINNY...
YEAH. ESPECIALLY NEAR THE END.
HERE'S THE FAMILY AT CHRISTMAS.
PLUS OLLIE, OF COURSE.
THEY PRACTICALLY ADOPTED ME IN HIGH SCHOOL.
I WASN'T WELCOMED MUCH AT HOME BY THEN.
YOUR DAD'S NOT HERE. HAD HE ALREADY DIED?
YEAH.
HERE HE IS. "THE OLD MAN..."
DOESN'T LOOK SO OLD NOW.

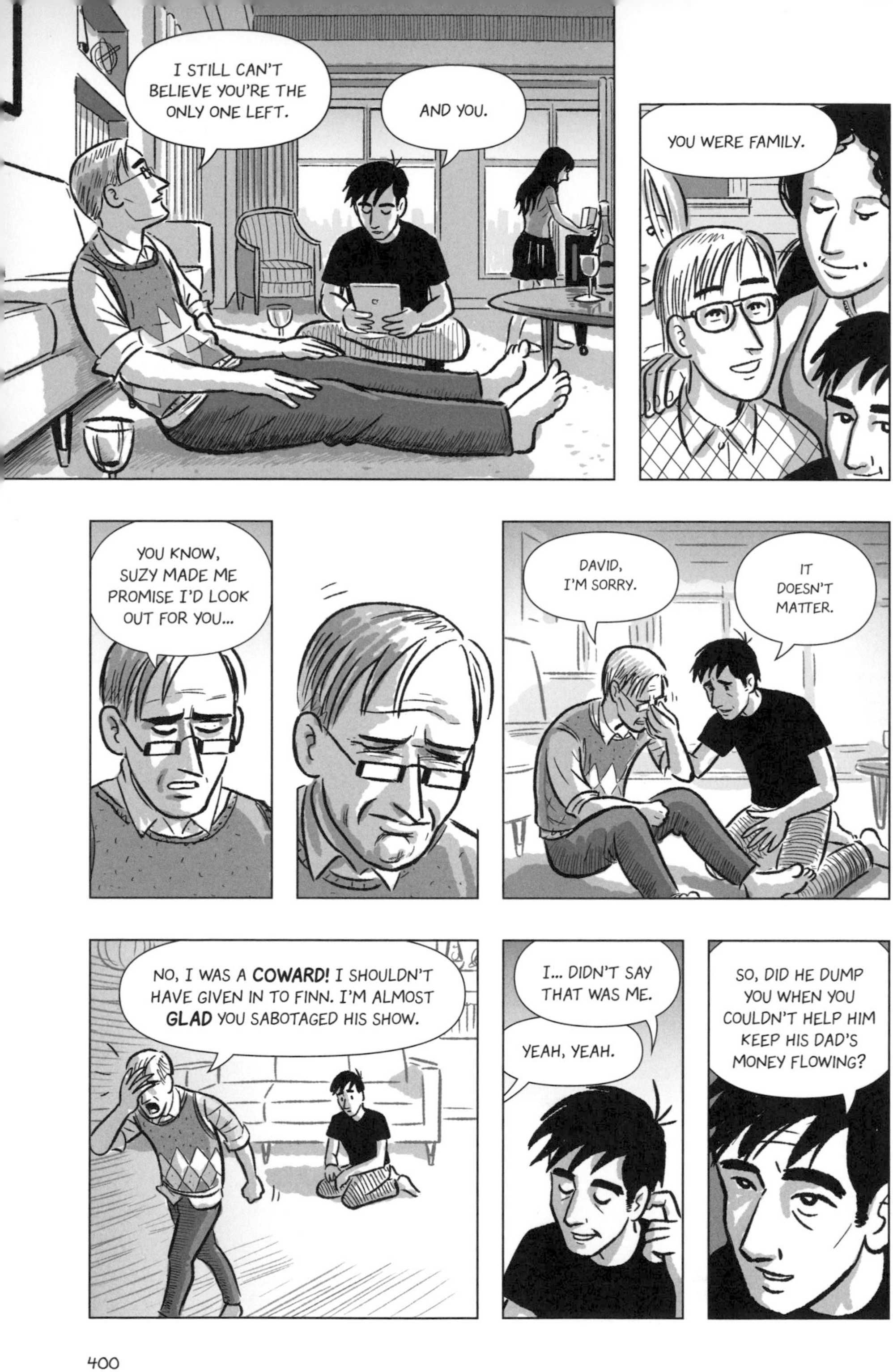
I STILL CAN'T BELIEVE YOU'RE THE ONLY ONE LEFT.
AND YOU.
YOU WERE FAMILY.
YOU KNOW, SUZY MADE ME PROMISE I'D LOOK OUT FOR YOU...
DAVID, I'M SORRY.
IT DOESN'T MATTER.
NO, I WAS A **COWARD!** I SHOULDN'T HAVE GIVEN IN TO FINN. I'M ALMOST **GLAD** YOU SABOTAGED HIS SHOW.
I... DIDN'T SAY THAT WAS ME.
YEAH, YEAH.
SO, DID HE DUMP YOU WHEN YOU COULDN'T HELP HIM KEEP HIS DAD'S MONEY FLOWING?

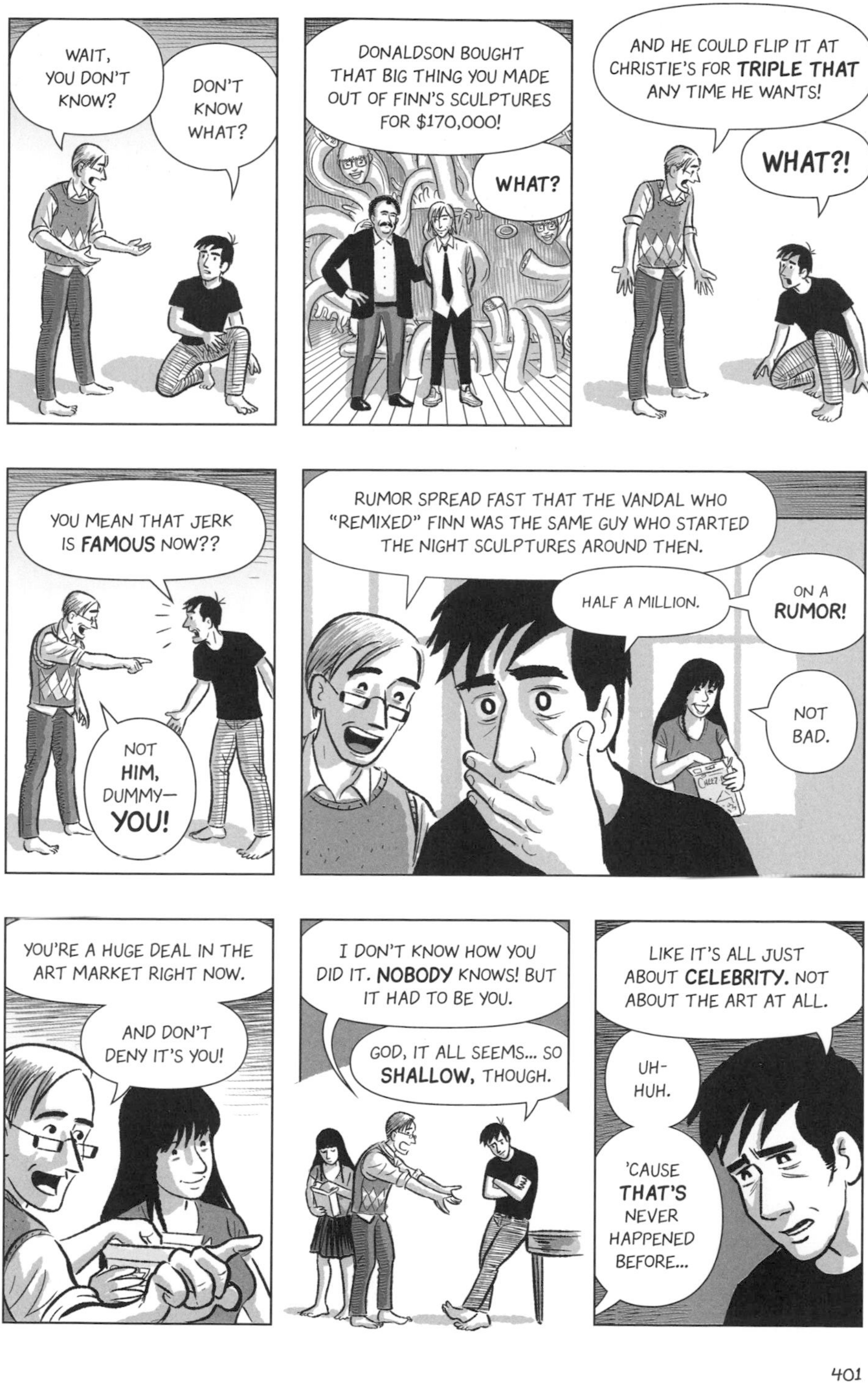
WAIT, YOU DON'T KNOW?
DON'T KNOW WHAT?
DONALDSON BOUGHT THAT BIG THING YOU MADE OUT OF FINN'S SCULPTURES FOR $170,000!
WHAT?
AND HE COULD FLIP IT AT CHRISTIE'S FOR **TRIPLE THAT** ANY TIME HE WANTS!
WHAT?!
YOU MEAN THAT JERK IS **FAMOUS** NOW??
NOT **HIM,** DUMMY— **YOU!**
RUMOR SPREAD FAST THAT THE VANDAL WHO "REMIXED" FINN WAS THE SAME GUY WHO STARTED THE NIGHT SCULPTURES AROUND THEN.
HALF A MILLION.
ON A **RUMOR!**
NOT BAD.
YOU'RE A HUGE DEAL IN THE ART MARKET RIGHT NOW.
AND DON'T DENY IT'S YOU!
I DON'T KNOW HOW YOU DID IT. **NOBODY** KNOWS! BUT IT HAD TO BE YOU.
GOD, IT ALL SEEMS... SO **SHALLOW,** THOUGH.
LIKE IT'S ALL JUST ABOUT **CELEBRITY.** NOT ABOUT THE ART AT ALL.
UH-HUH.
'CAUSE **THAT'S** NEVER HAPPENED BEFORE...

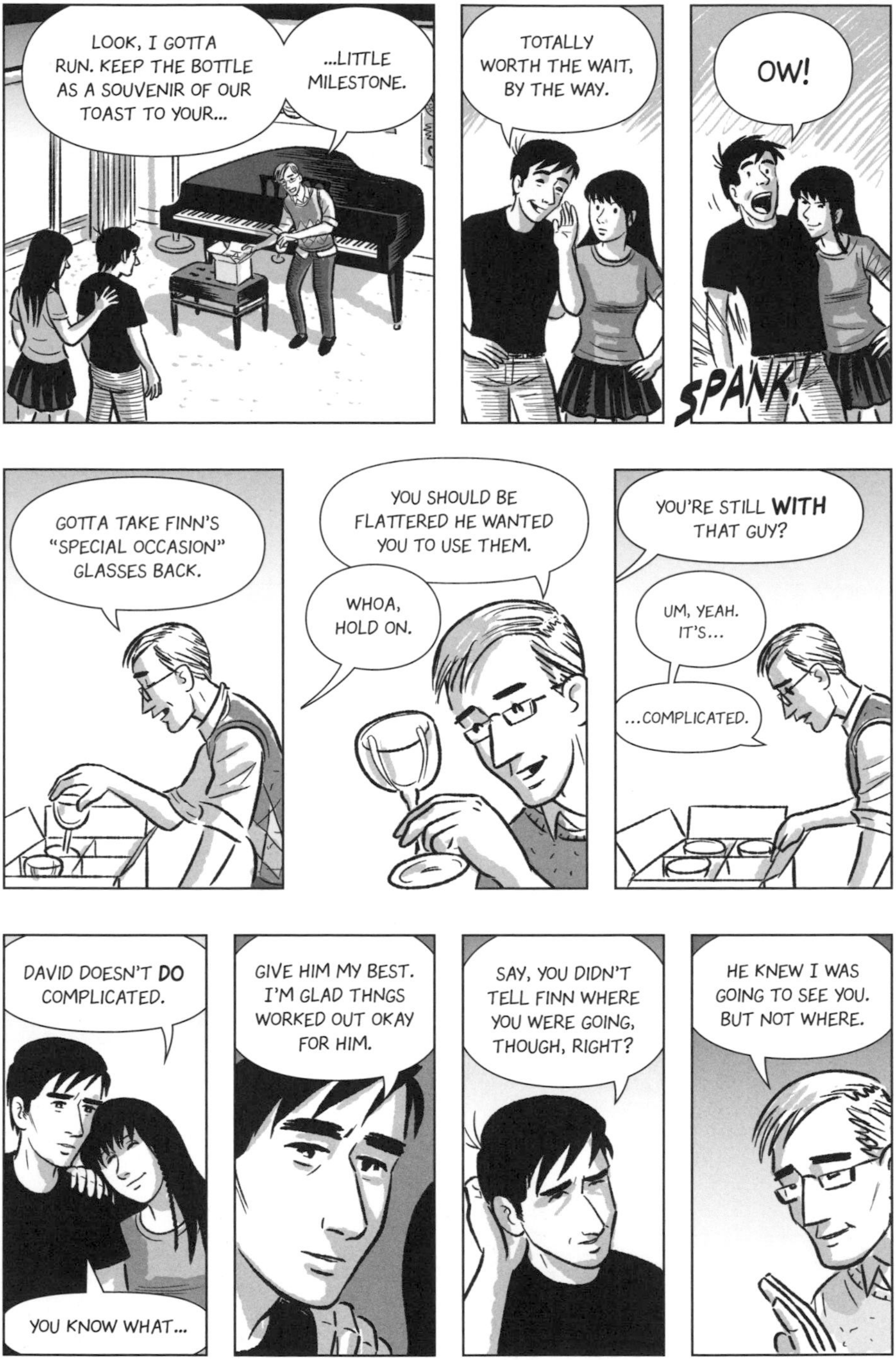
LOOK, I GOTTA RUN. KEEP THE BOTTLE AS A SOUVENIR OF OUR TOAST TO YOUR...
...LITTLE MILESTONE.
TOTALLY WORTH THE WAIT, BY THE WAY.
OW!
SPANK!
GOTTA TAKE FINN'S "SPECIAL OCCASION" GLASSES BACK.
YOU SHOULD BE FLATTERED HE WANTED YOU TO USE THEM.
WHOA, HOLD ON.
YOU'RE STILL **WITH** THAT GUY?
UM, YEAH. IT'S...
...COMPLICATED.
DAVID DOESN'T **DO** COMPLICATED.
YOU KNOW WHAT...
GIVE HIM MY BEST. I'M GLAD THNGS WORKED OUT OKAY FOR HIM.
SAY, YOU DIDN'T TELL FINN WHERE YOU WERE GOING, THOUGH, RIGHT?
HE KNEW I WAS GOING TO SEE YOU. BUT NOT WHERE.

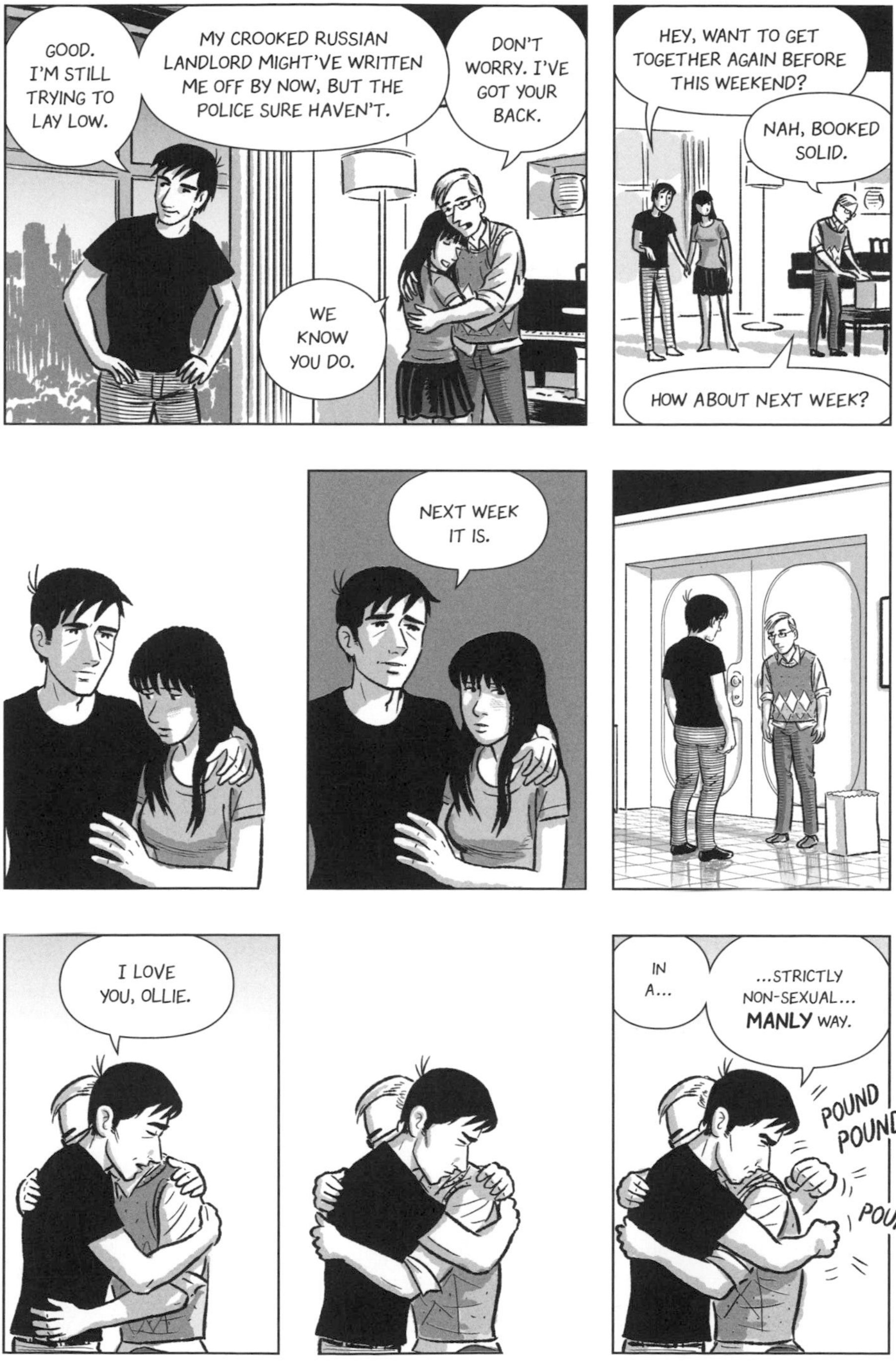

GOOD. I'M STILL TRYING TO LAY LOW.
MY CROOKED RUSSIAN LANDLORD MIGHT'VE WRITTEN ME OFF BY NOW, BUT THE POLICE SURE HAVEN'T.
DON'T WORRY. I'VE GOT YOUR BACK.
WE KNOW YOU DO.
HEY, WANT TO GET TOGETHER AGAIN BEFORE THIS WEEKEND?
NAH, BOOKED SOLID.
HOW ABOUT NEXT WEEK?
NEXT WEEK IT IS.
I LOVE YOU, OLLIE.
IN A...
...STRICTLY NON-SEXUAL... **MANLY** WAY.
POUND
POUND
POUND

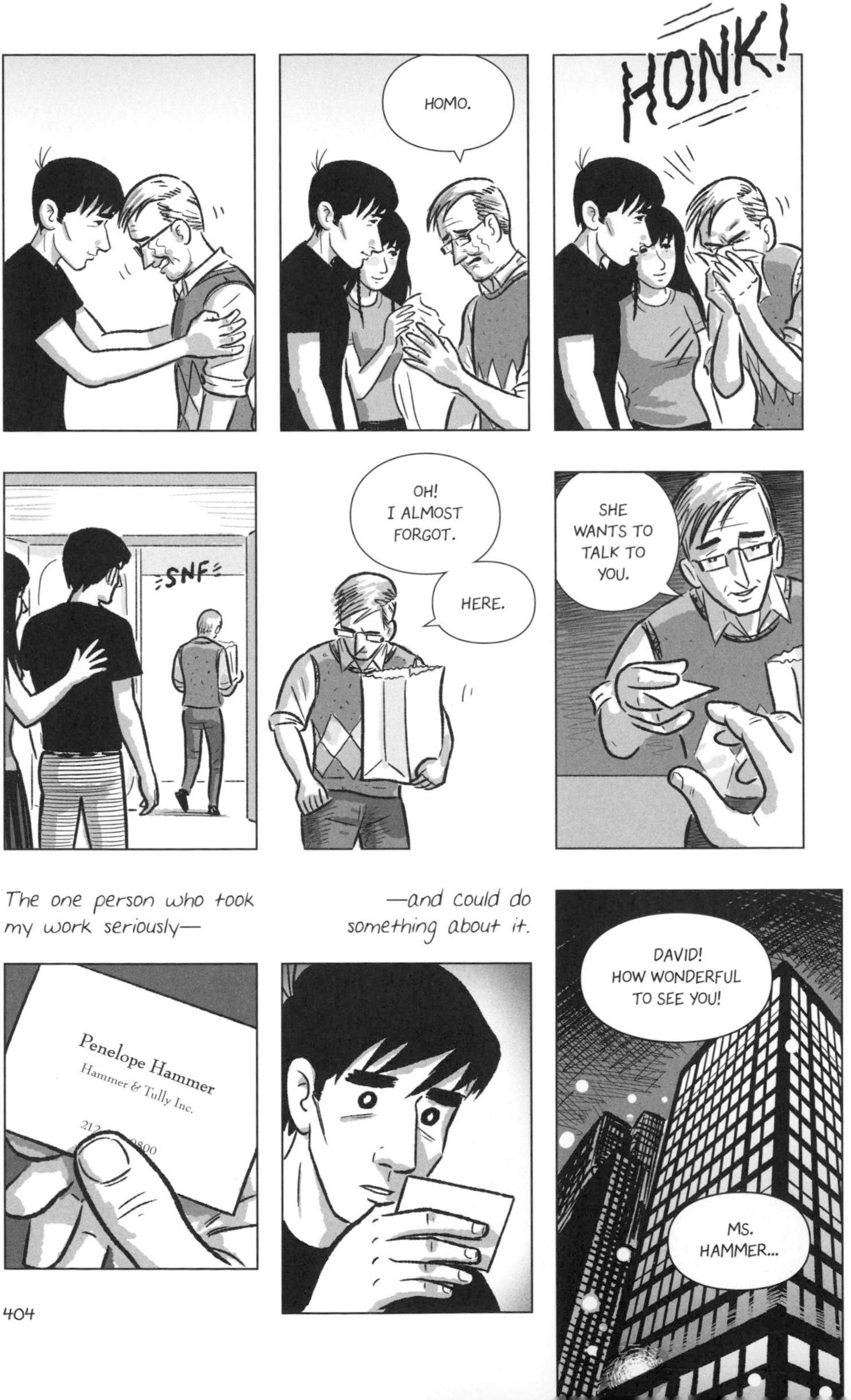
HONK!
HOMO.
SNF
OH! I ALMOST FORGOT.
HERE.
SHE WANTS TO TALK TO YOU.
The one person who took my work seriously—
—and could do something about it.
Penelope Hammer
Hammer & Tully Inc.
DAVID! HOW WONDERFUL TO SEE YOU!
MS. HAMMER...

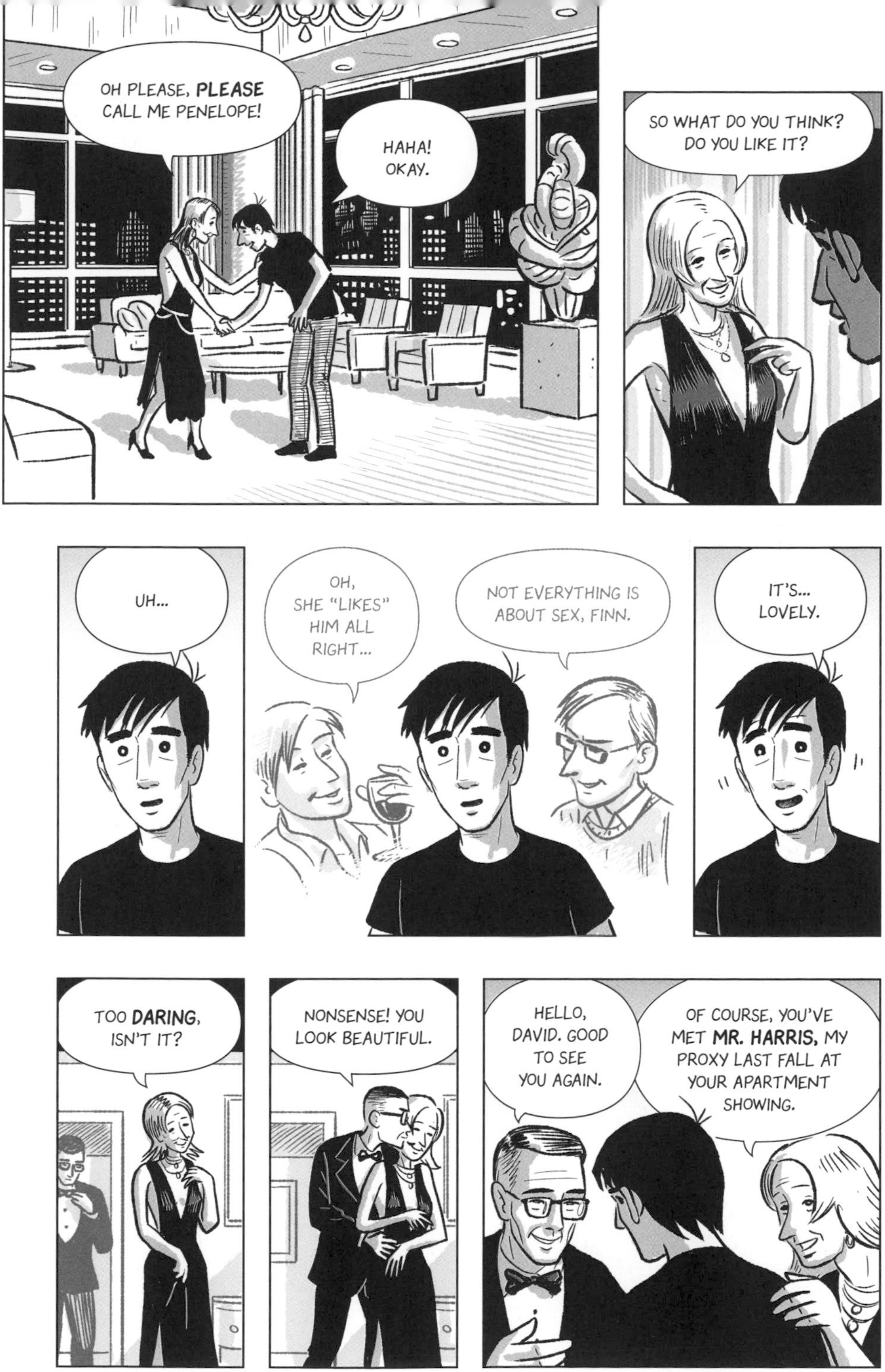
OH PLEASE, PLEASE CALL ME PENELOPE!
HAHA! OKAY.
SO WHAT DO YOU THINK? DO YOU LIKE IT?
UH...
OH, SHE "LIKES" HIM ALL RIGHT...
NOT EVERYTHING IS ABOUT SEX, FINN.
IT'S... LOVELY.
TOO DARING, ISN'T IT?
NONSENSE! YOU LOOK BEAUTIFUL.
HELLO, DAVID. GOOD TO SEE YOU AGAIN.
OF COURSE, YOU'VE MET MR. HARRIS, MY PROXY LAST FALL AT YOUR APARTMENT SHOWING.

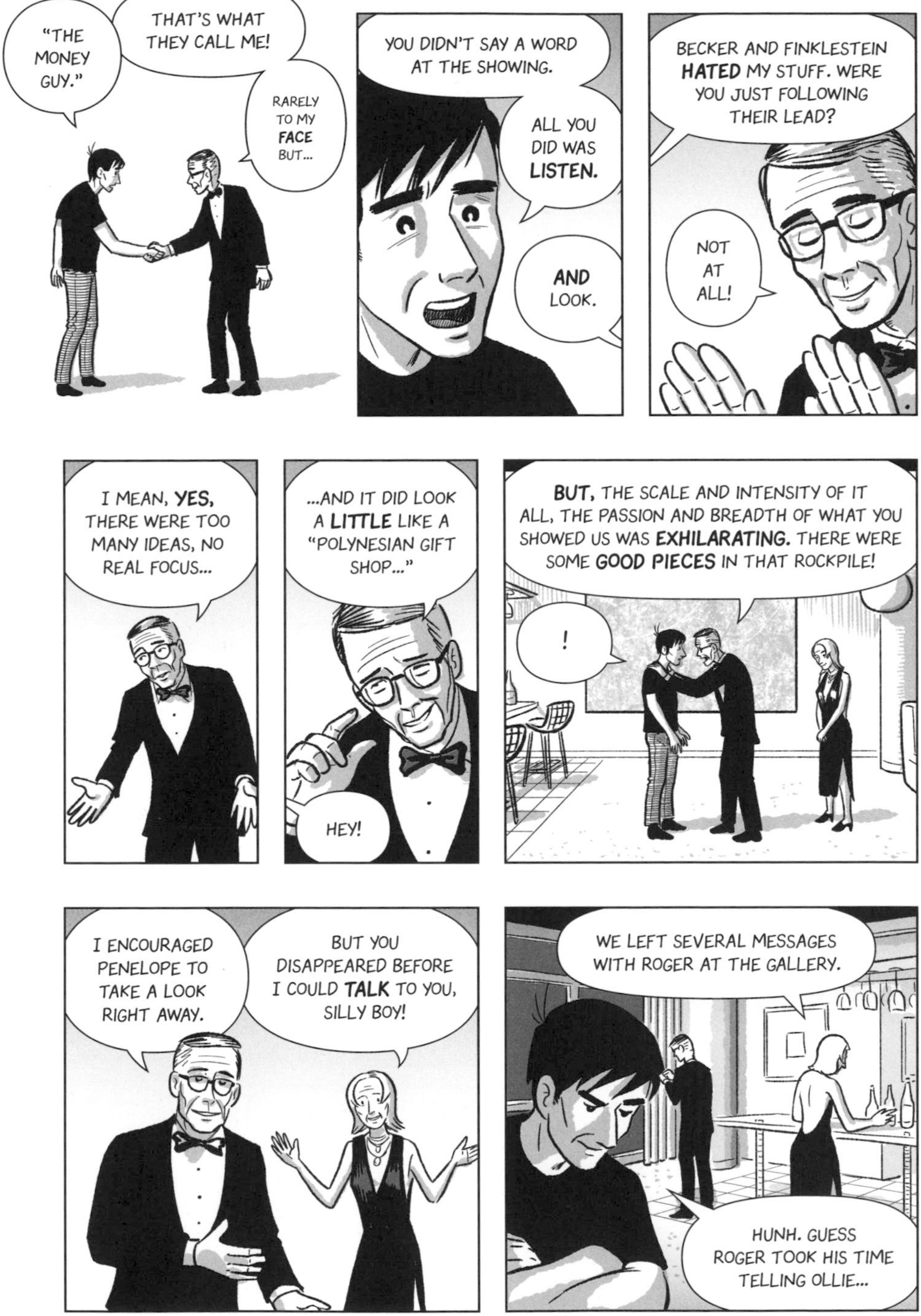
"THE MONEY GUY."
THAT'S WHAT THEY CALL ME!
RARELY TO MY **FACE** BUT...
YOU DIDN'T SAY A WORD AT THE SHOWING.
ALL YOU DID WAS **LISTEN.**
AND LOOK.
BECKER AND FINKLESTEIN **HATED** MY STUFF. WERE YOU JUST FOLLOWING THEIR LEAD?
NOT AT ALL!
I MEAN, **YES,** THERE WERE TOO MANY IDEAS, NO REAL FOCUS...
...AND IT DID LOOK A **LITTLE** LIKE A "POLYNESIAN GIFT SHOP..."
HEY!
BUT, THE SCALE AND INTENSITY OF IT ALL, THE PASSION AND BREADTH OF WHAT YOU SHOWED US WAS **EXHILARATING.** THERE WERE SOME **GOOD PIECES** IN THAT ROCKPILE!
!
I ENCOURAGED PENELOPE TO TAKE A LOOK RIGHT AWAY.
BUT YOU DISAPPEARED BEFORE I COULD **TALK** TO YOU, SILLY BOY!
WE LEFT SEVERAL MESSAGES WITH ROGER AT THE GALLERY.
HUNH. GUESS ROGER TOOK HIS TIME TELLING OLLIE...

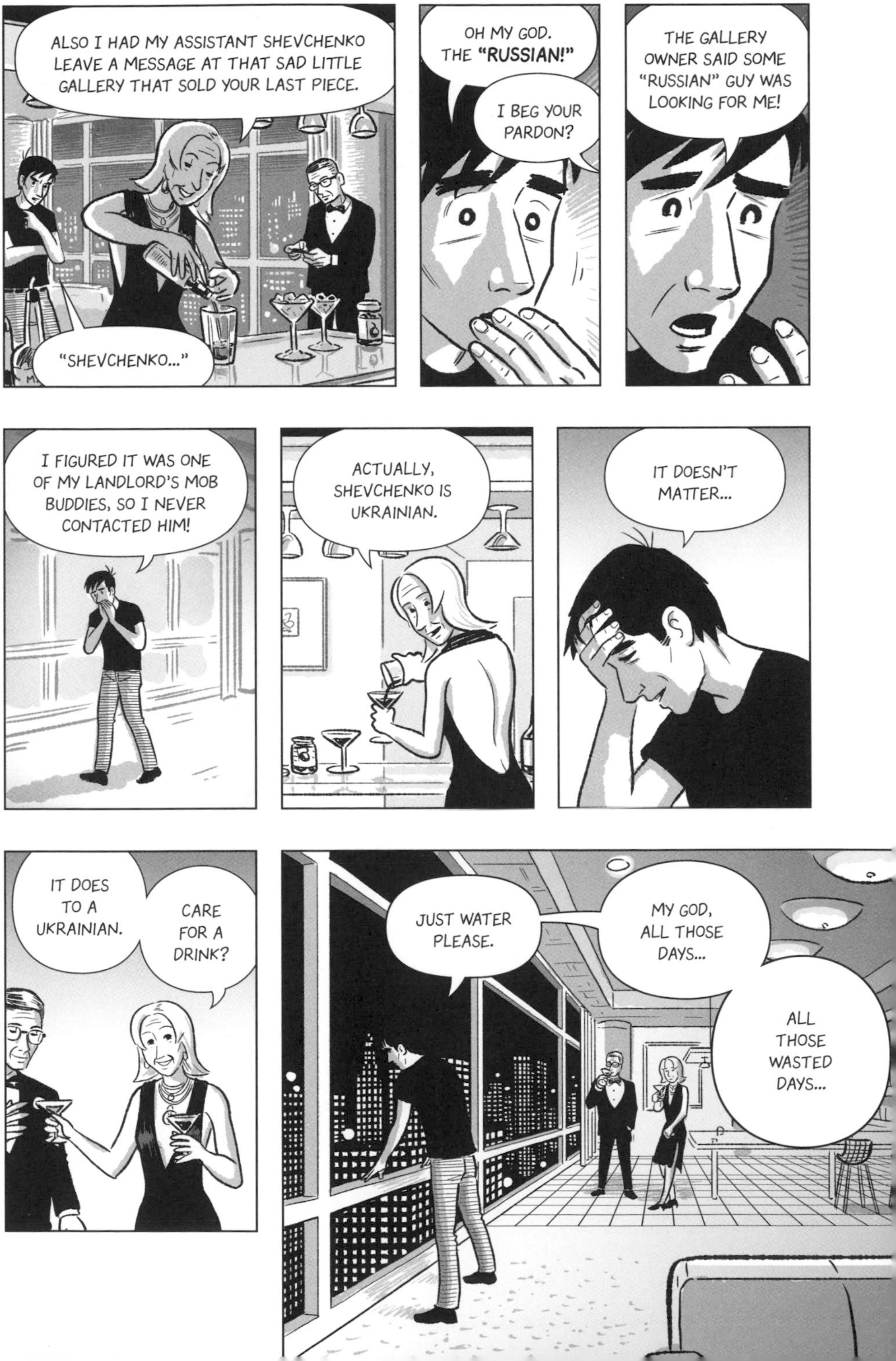
ALSO I HAD MY ASSISTANT SHEVCHENKO LEAVE A MESSAGE AT THAT SAD LITTLE GALLERY THAT SOLD YOUR LAST PIECE.
"SHEVCHENKO..."
OH MY GOD. THE **"RUSSIAN!"**
I BEG YOUR PARDON?
THE GALLERY OWNER SAID SOME "RUSSIAN" GUY WAS LOOKING FOR ME!
I FIGURED IT WAS ONE OF MY LANDLORD'S MOB BUDDIES, SO I NEVER CONTACTED HIM!
ACTUALLY, SHEVCHENKO IS UKRAINIAN.
IT DOESN'T MATTER...
IT DOES TO A UKRAINIAN.
CARE FOR A DRINK?
JUST WATER PLEASE.
MY GOD, ALL THOSE DAYS...
ALL THOSE WASTED DAYS...

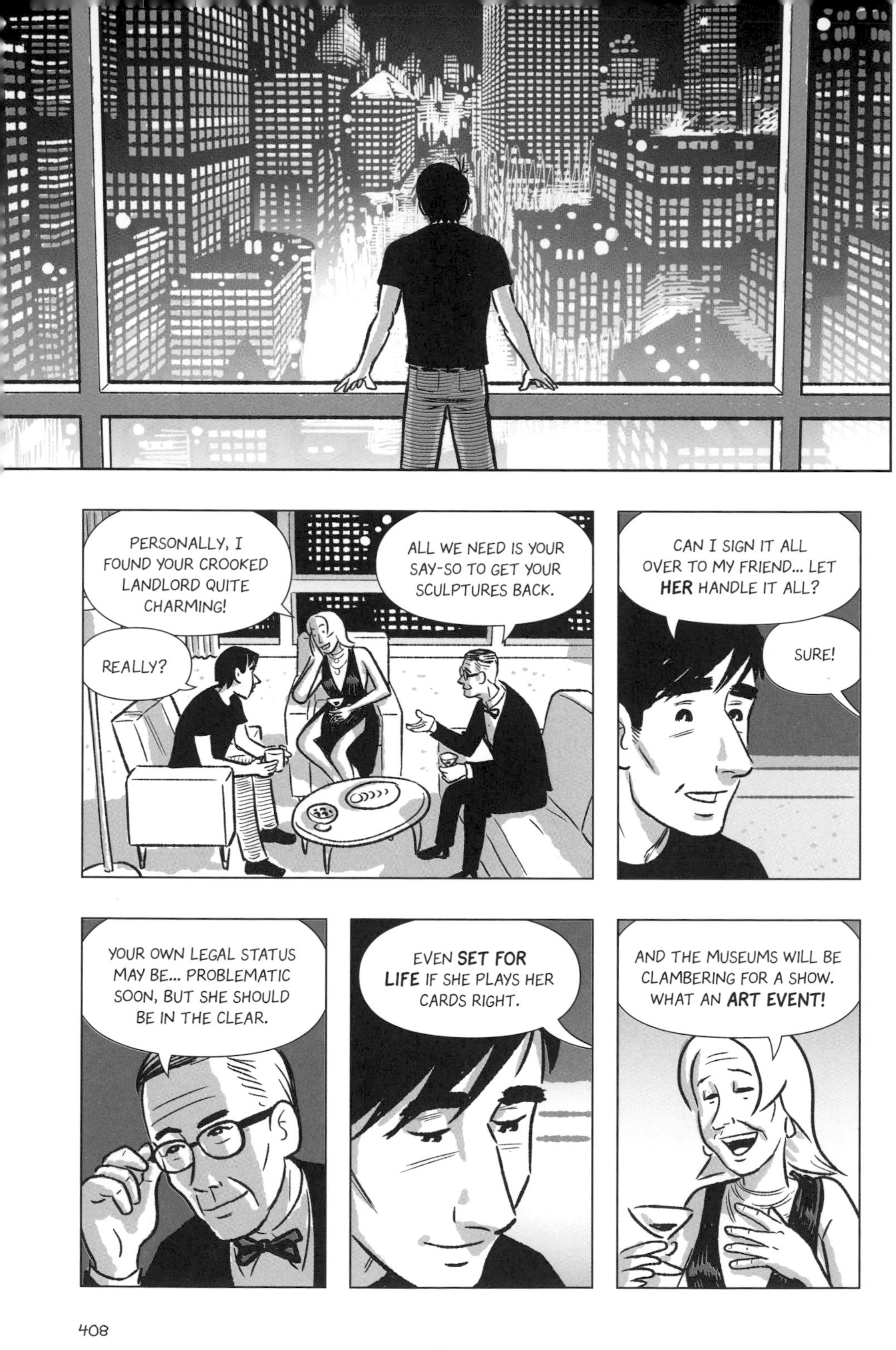
PERSONALLY, I FOUND YOUR CROOKED LANDLORD QUITE CHARMING!
REALLY?
ALL WE NEED IS YOUR SAY-SO TO GET YOUR SCULPTURES BACK.
CAN I SIGN IT ALL OVER TO MY FRIEND... LET **HER** HANDLE IT ALL?
SURE!
YOUR OWN LEGAL STATUS MAY BE... PROBLEMATIC SOON, BUT SHE SHOULD BE IN THE CLEAR.
EVEN **SET FOR LIFE** IF SHE PLAYS HER CARDS RIGHT.
AND THE MUSEUMS WILL BE CLAMBERING FOR A SHOW. WHAT AN **ART EVENT!**

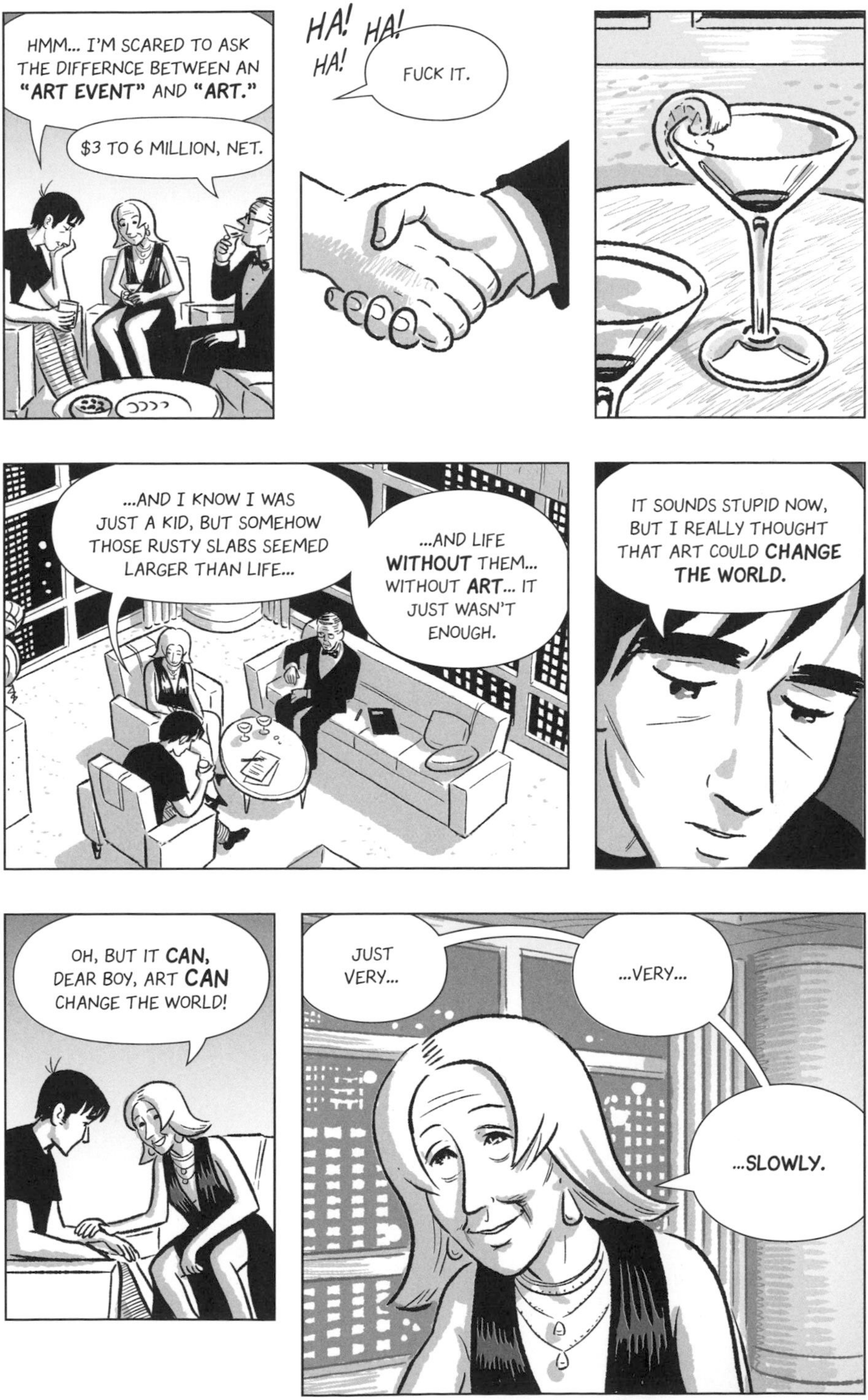
HMM... I'M SCARED TO ASK THE DIFFERNCE BETWEEN AN "ART EVENT" AND "ART."
$3 TO 6 MILLION, NET.
HA! HA! HA!
FUCK IT.
...AND I KNOW I WAS JUST A KID, BUT SOMEHOW THOSE RUSTY SLABS SEEMED LARGER THAN LIFE...
...AND LIFE WITHOUT THEM... WITHOUT ART... IT JUST WASN'T ENOUGH.
IT SOUNDS STUPID NOW, BUT I REALLY THOUGHT THAT ART COULD CHANGE THE WORLD.
OH, BUT IT CAN, DEAR BOY, ART CAN CHANGE THE WORLD!
JUST VERY...
...VERY...
...SLOWLY.

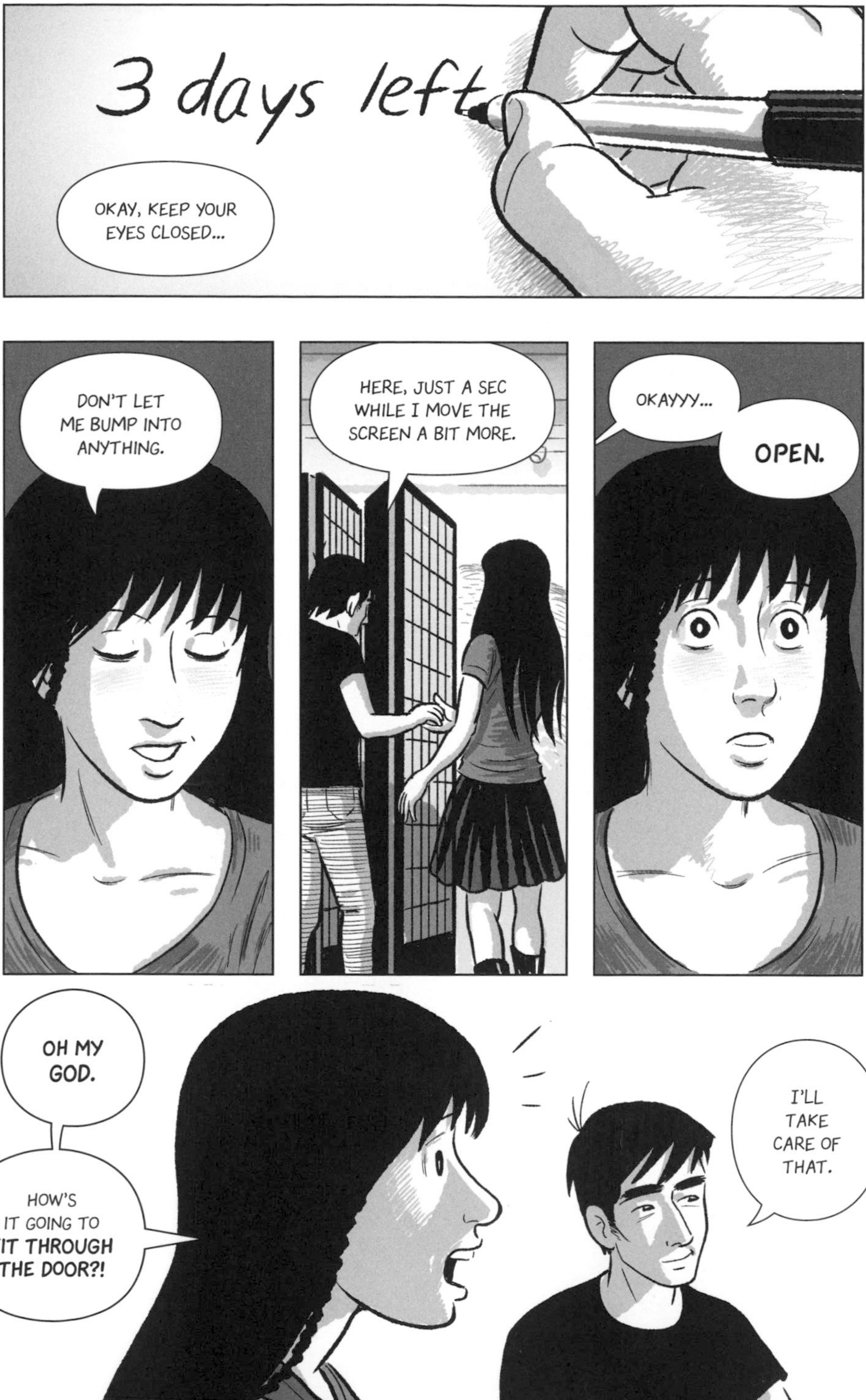
3 days left
OKAY, KEEP YOUR EYES CLOSED...
DON'T LET ME BUMP INTO ANYTHING.
HERE, JUST A SEC WHILE I MOVE THE SCREEN A BIT MORE.
OKAYYY...
OPEN.
OH MY GOD.
HOW'S IT GOING TO FIT THROUGH THE DOOR?!
I'LL TAKE CARE OF THAT.

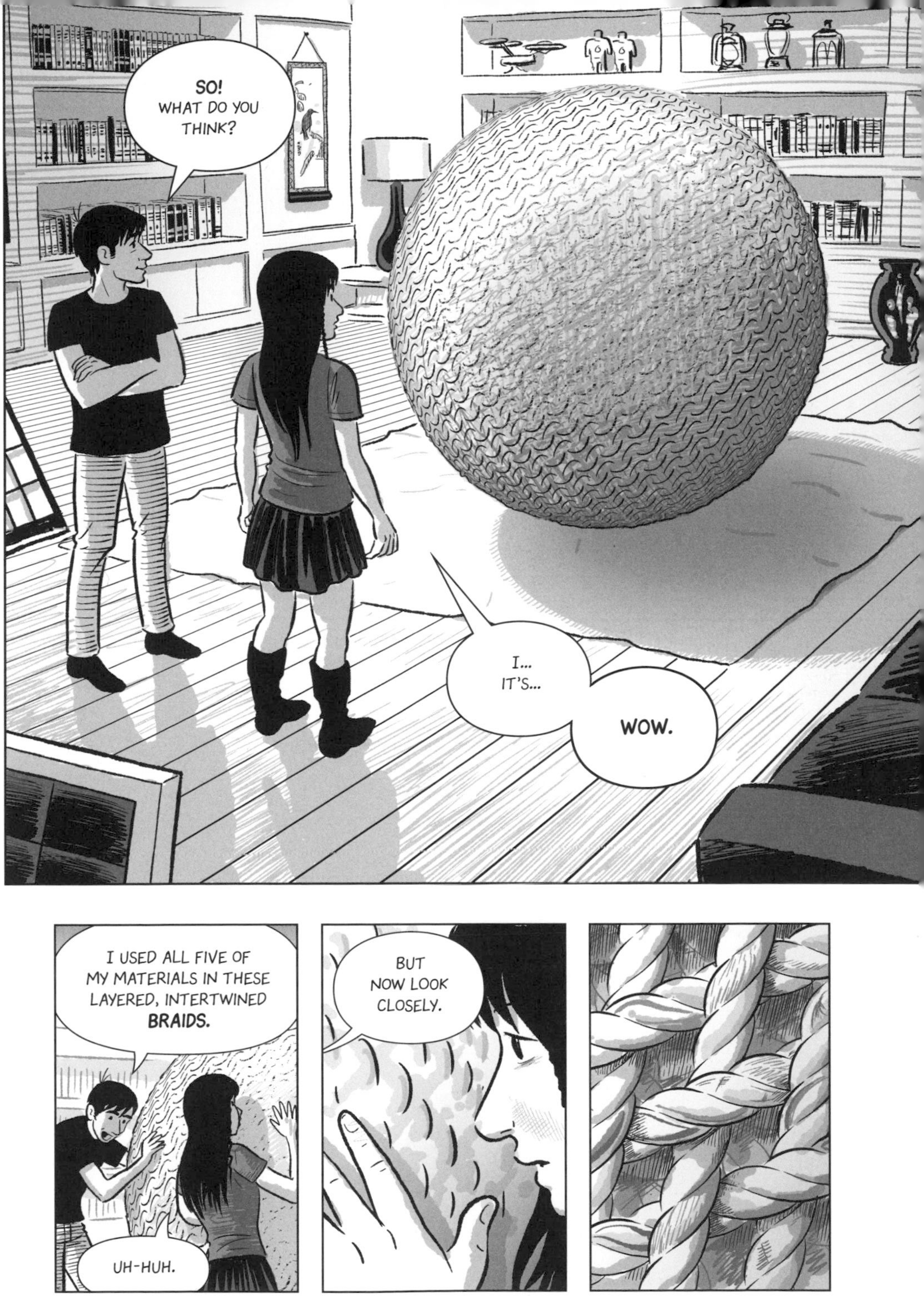
SO!
WHAT DO YOU THINK?
I... IT'S...
WOW.
I USED ALL FIVE OF MY MATERIALS IN THESE LAYERED, INTERTWINED **BRAIDS.**
UH-HUH.
BUT NOW LOOK CLOSELY.

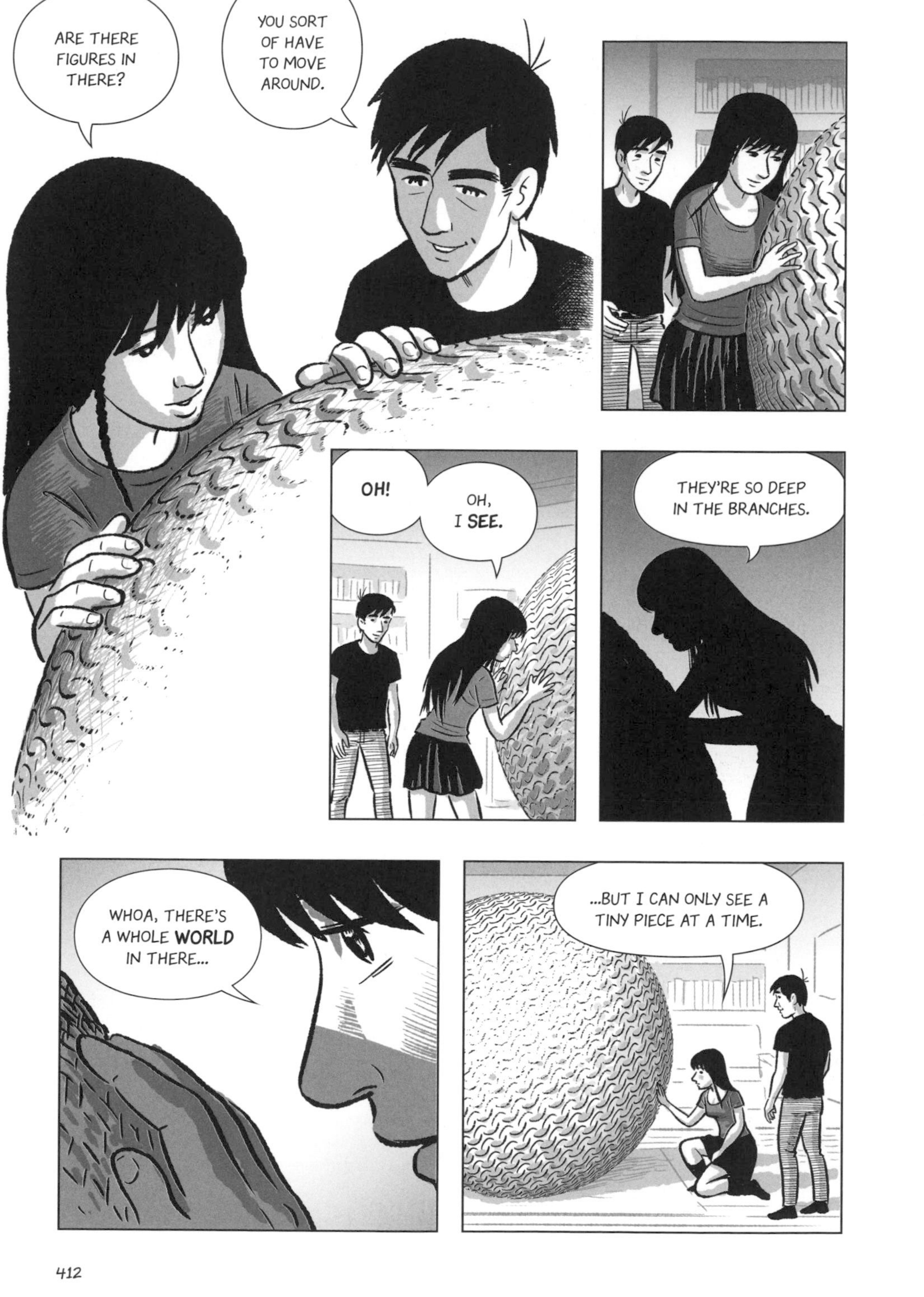
ARE THERE FIGURES IN THERE?
YOU SORT OF HAVE TO MOVE AROUND.
OH!
OH, I SEE.
THEY'RE SO DEEP IN THE BRANCHES.
WHOA, THERE'S A WHOLE WORLD IN THERE...
...BUT I CAN ONLY SEE A TINY PIECE AT A TIME.

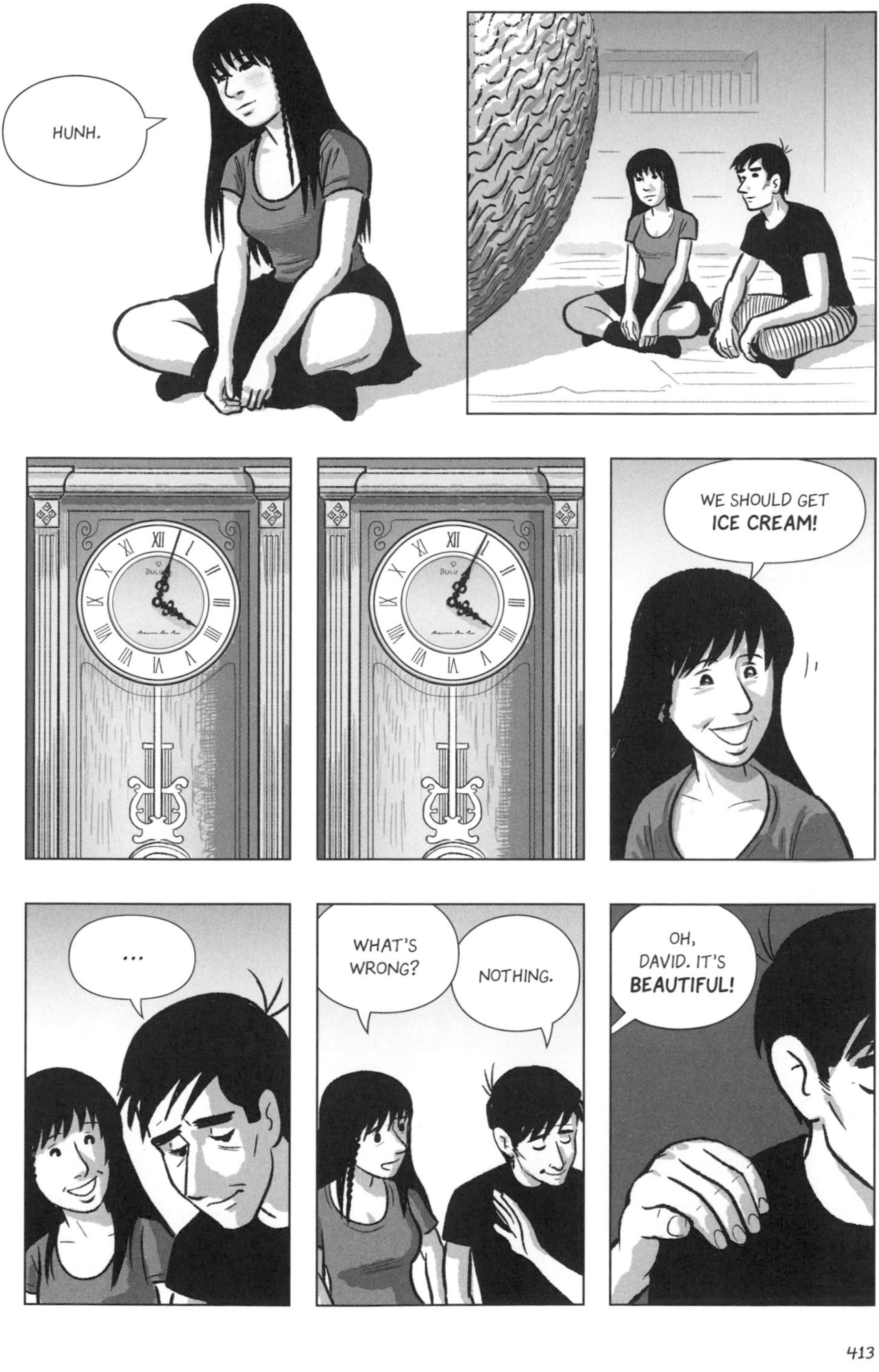
HUNH.
WE SHOULD GET ICE CREAM!
...
WHAT'S WRONG?
NOTHING.
OH, DAVID. IT'S BEAUTIFUL!

I **LOVE** IT! HONESTLY.

THING IS...

...I JUST REALLY FEEL LIKE *ICE CREAM* TODAY.

OKAY.

KNOCK! KNOCK!

OOH! IS THAT **HIM**?

THAT'S HIM! REMEMBER WHAT I TOLD YOU.

THAT I CAN ASK ANYTHING I WANT, BUT HE'LL ONLY **FRUSTRATE** ME?

EXACTLY.

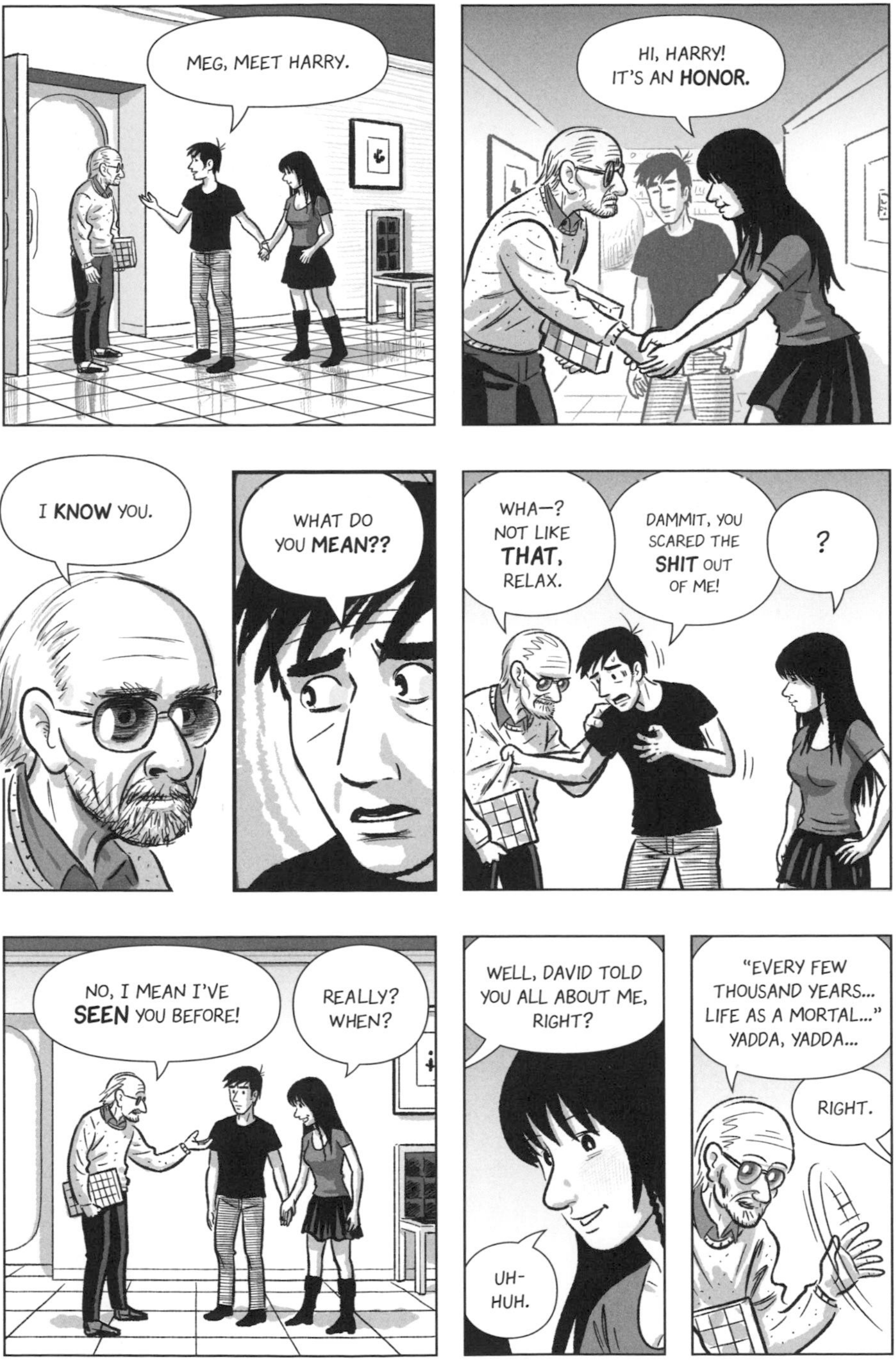
MEG, MEET HARRY.
HI, HARRY! IT'S AN **HONOR.**
I **KNOW** YOU.
WHAT DO YOU **MEAN??**
WHA—? NOT LIKE **THAT,** RELAX.
DAMMIT, YOU SCARED THE **SHIT** OUT OF ME!
?
NO, I MEAN I'VE **SEEN** YOU BEFORE!
REALLY? WHEN?
WELL, DAVID TOLD YOU ALL ABOUT ME, RIGHT?
UH-HUH.
"EVERY FEW THOUSAND YEARS... LIFE AS A MORTAL..." YADDA, YADDA...
RIGHT.

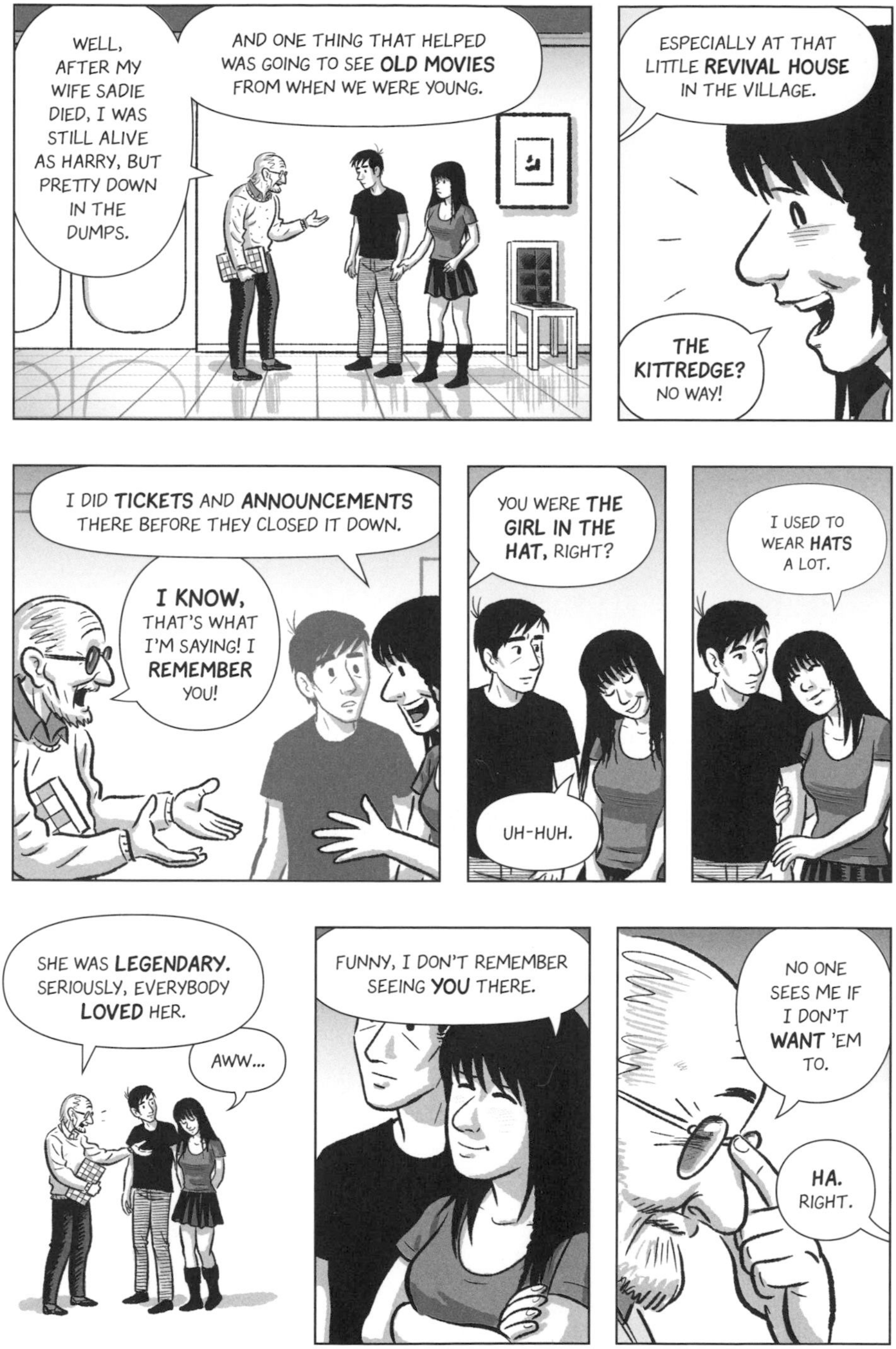
WELL, AFTER MY WIFE SADIE DIED, I WAS STILL ALIVE AS HARRY, BUT PRETTY DOWN IN THE DUMPS.
AND ONE THING THAT HELPED WAS GOING TO SEE **OLD MOVIES** FROM WHEN WE WERE YOUNG.
ESPECIALLY AT THAT LITTLE **REVIVAL HOUSE** IN THE VILLAGE.
THE KITTREDGE? NO WAY!
I DID **TICKETS** AND **ANNOUNCEMENTS** THERE BEFORE THEY CLOSED IT DOWN.
I KNOW, THAT'S WHAT I'M SAYING! I **REMEMBER** YOU!
YOU WERE **THE GIRL IN THE HAT,** RIGHT?
UH-HUH.
I USED TO WEAR **HATS** A LOT.
SHE WAS **LEGENDARY.** SERIOUSLY, EVERYBODY **LOVED** HER.
AWW...
FUNNY, I DON'T REMEMBER SEEING **YOU** THERE.
NO ONE SEES ME IF I DON'T **WANT** 'EM TO.
HA. RIGHT.

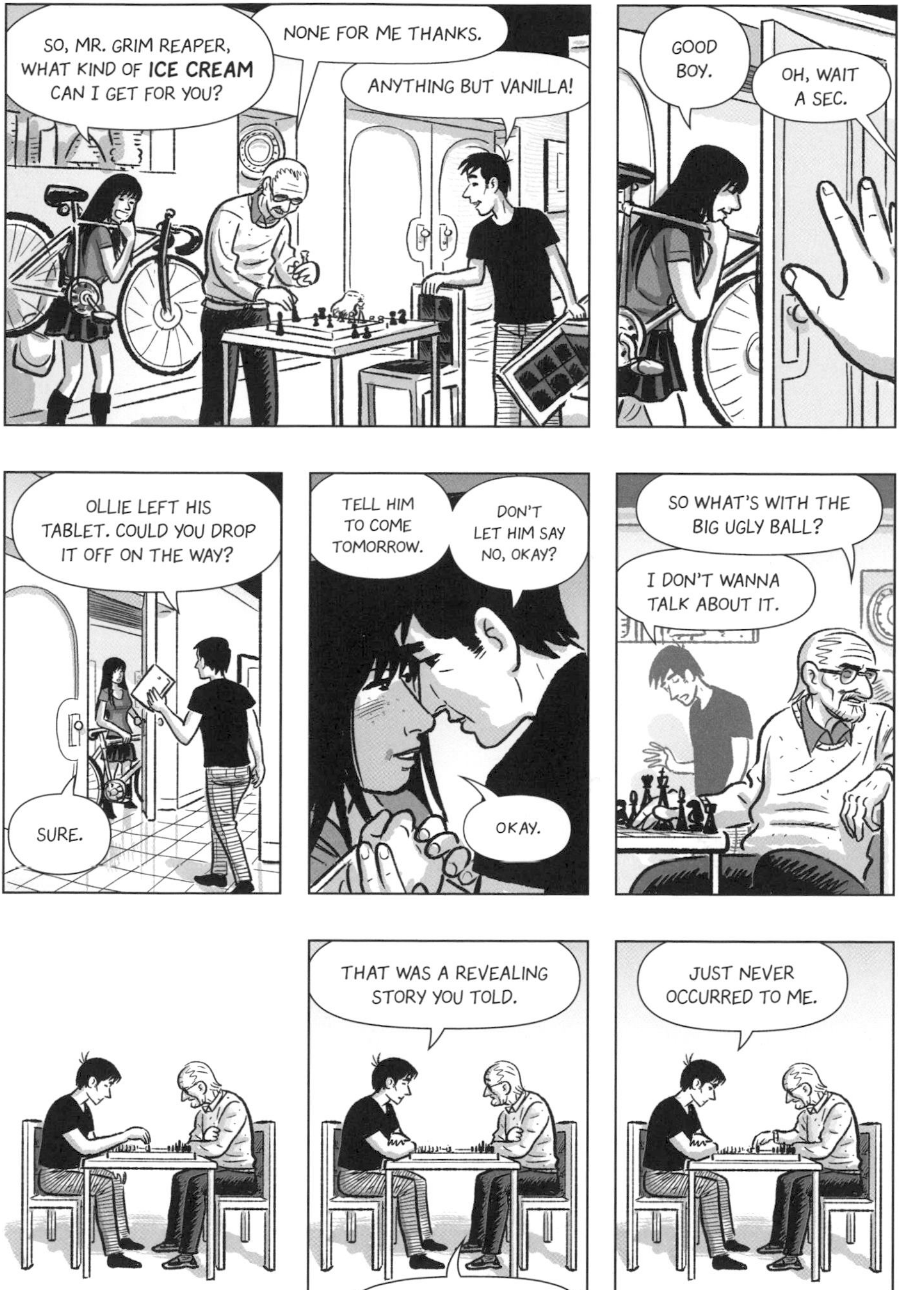
SO, MR. GRIM REAPER, WHAT KIND OF ICE CREAM CAN I GET FOR YOU?
NONE FOR ME THANKS.
ANYTHING BUT VANILLA!
GOOD BOY.
OH, WAIT A SEC.
OLLIE LEFT HIS TABLET. COULD YOU DROP IT OFF ON THE WAY?
SURE.
TELL HIM TO COME TOMORROW.
DON'T LET HIM SAY NO, OKAY?
OKAY.
SO WHAT'S WITH THE BIG UGLY BALL?
I DON'T WANNA TALK ABOUT IT.
THAT WAS A REVEALING STORY YOU TOLD.
YOU DIDN'T THINK I GOT DEPRESSED?
JUST NEVER OCCURRED TO ME.

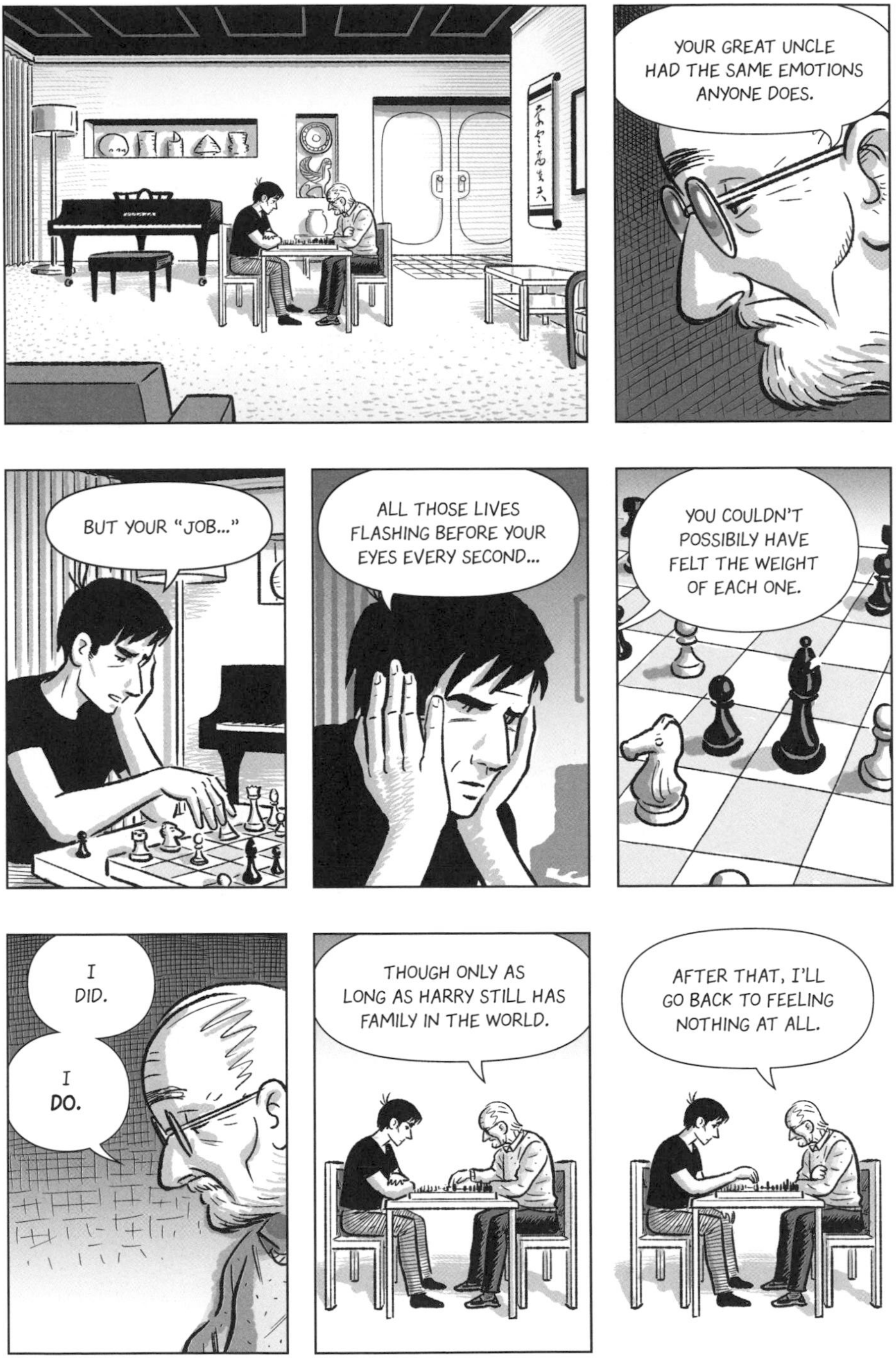
YOUR GREAT UNCLE HAD THE SAME EMOTIONS ANYONE DOES.
BUT YOUR "JOB..."
ALL THOSE LIVES FLASHING BEFORE YOUR EYES EVERY SECOND...
YOU COULDN'T POSSIBLY HAVE FELT THE WEIGHT OF EACH ONE.
I DID.
I DO.
THOUGH ONLY AS LONG AS HARRY STILL HAS FAMILY IN THE WORLD.
AFTER THAT, I'LL GO BACK TO FEELING NOTHING AT ALL.

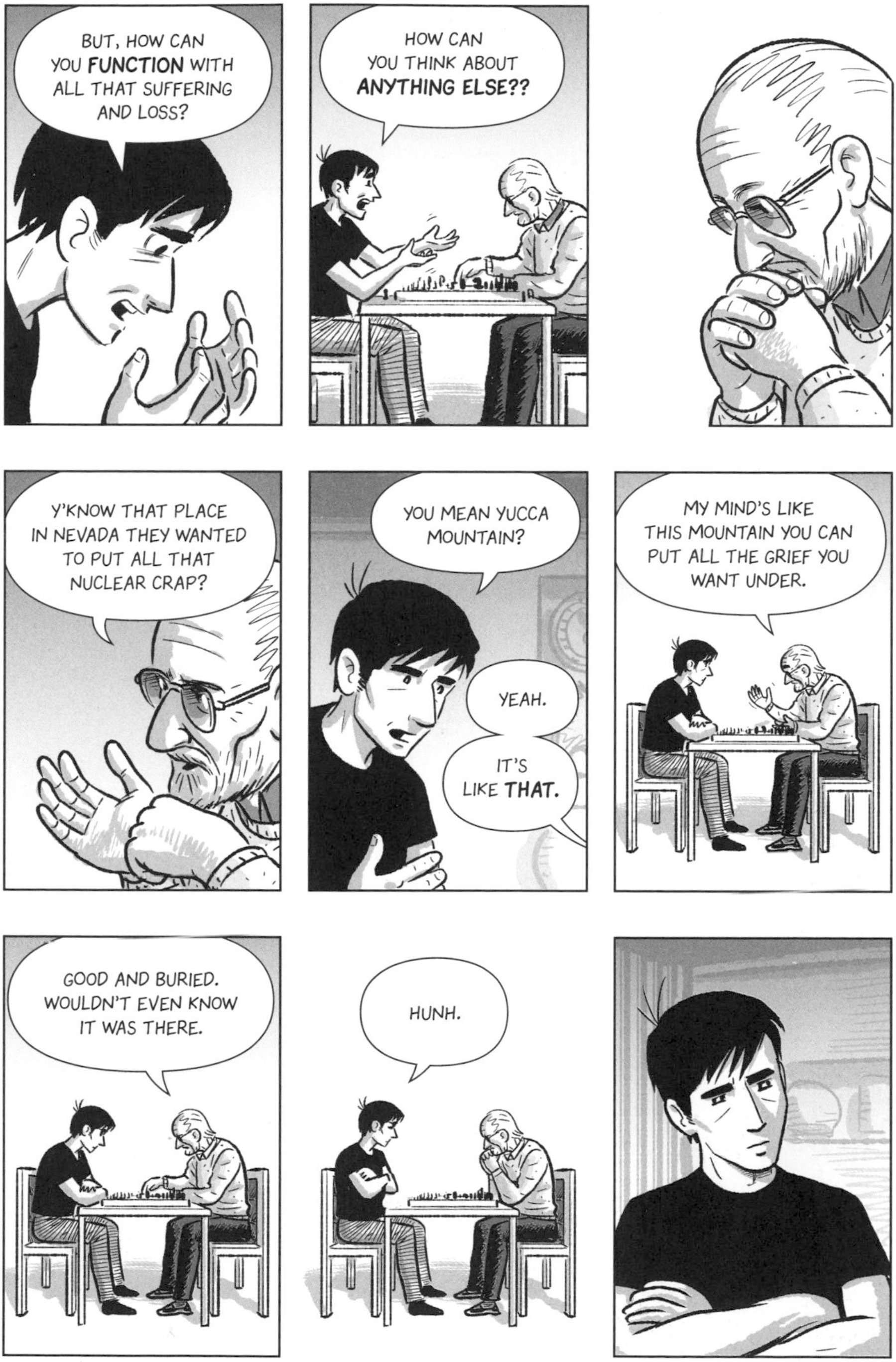
BUT, HOW CAN YOU FUNCTION WITH ALL THAT SUFFERING AND LOSS?
HOW CAN YOU THINK ABOUT ANYTHING ELSE??
Y'KNOW THAT PLACE IN NEVADA THEY WANTED TO PUT ALL THAT NUCLEAR CRAP?
YOU MEAN YUCCA MOUNTAIN?
YEAH.
IT'S LIKE THAT.
MY MIND'S LIKE THIS MOUNTAIN YOU CAN PUT ALL THE GRIEF YOU WANT UNDER.
GOOD AND BURIED. WOULDN'T EVEN KNOW IT WAS THERE.
HUNH.

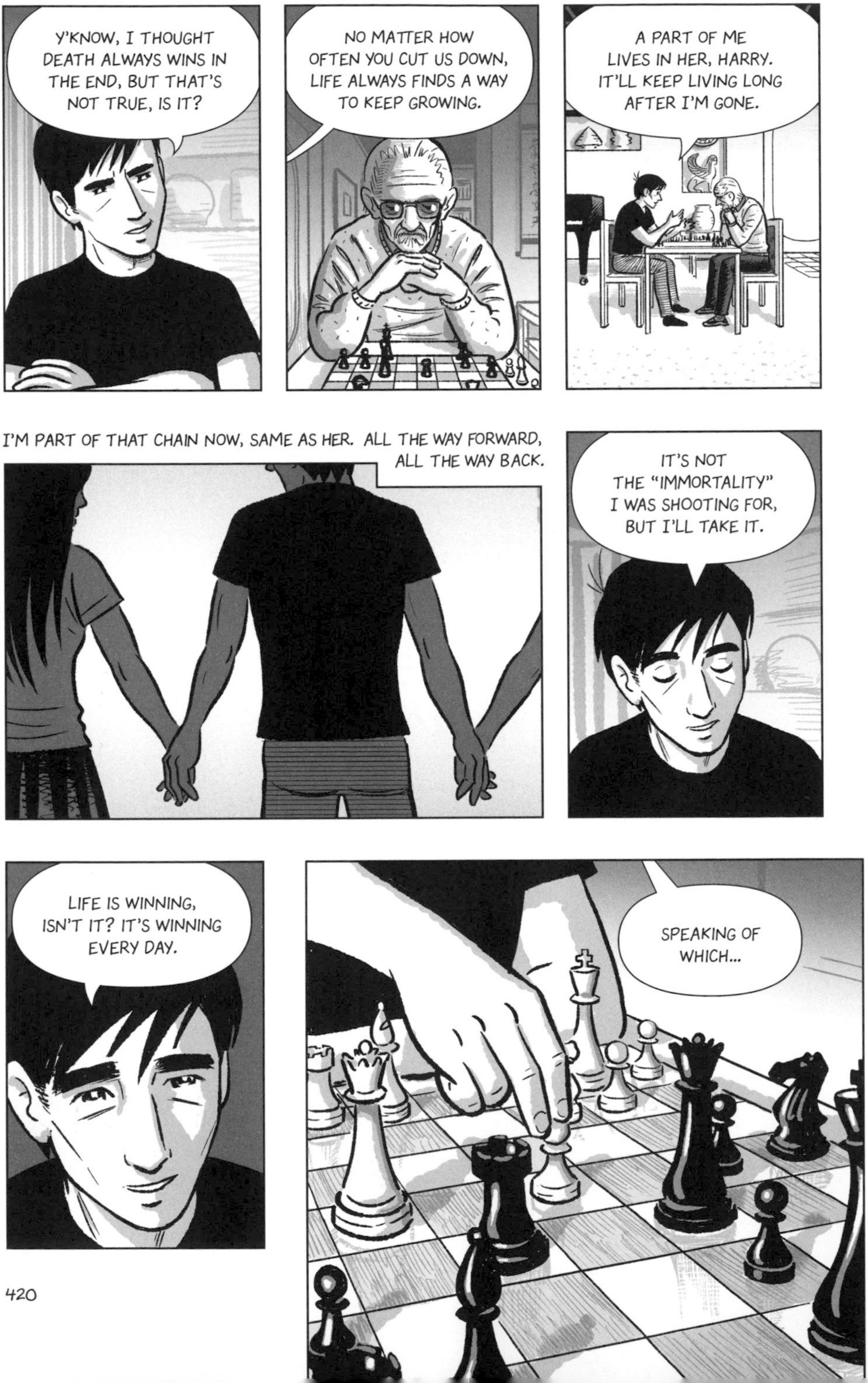
Y'KNOW, I THOUGHT DEATH ALWAYS WINS IN THE END, BUT THAT'S NOT TRUE, IS IT?
NO MATTER HOW OFTEN YOU CUT US DOWN, LIFE ALWAYS FINDS A WAY TO KEEP GROWING.
A PART OF ME LIVES IN HER, HARRY. IT'LL KEEP LIVING LONG AFTER I'M GONE.
I'M PART OF THAT CHAIN NOW, SAME AS HER. ALL THE WAY FORWARD, ALL THE WAY BACK.
IT'S NOT THE "IMMORTALITY" I WAS SHOOTING FOR, BUT I'LL TAKE IT.
LIFE IS WINNING, ISN'T IT? IT'S WINNING EVERY DAY.
SPEAKING OF WHICH...

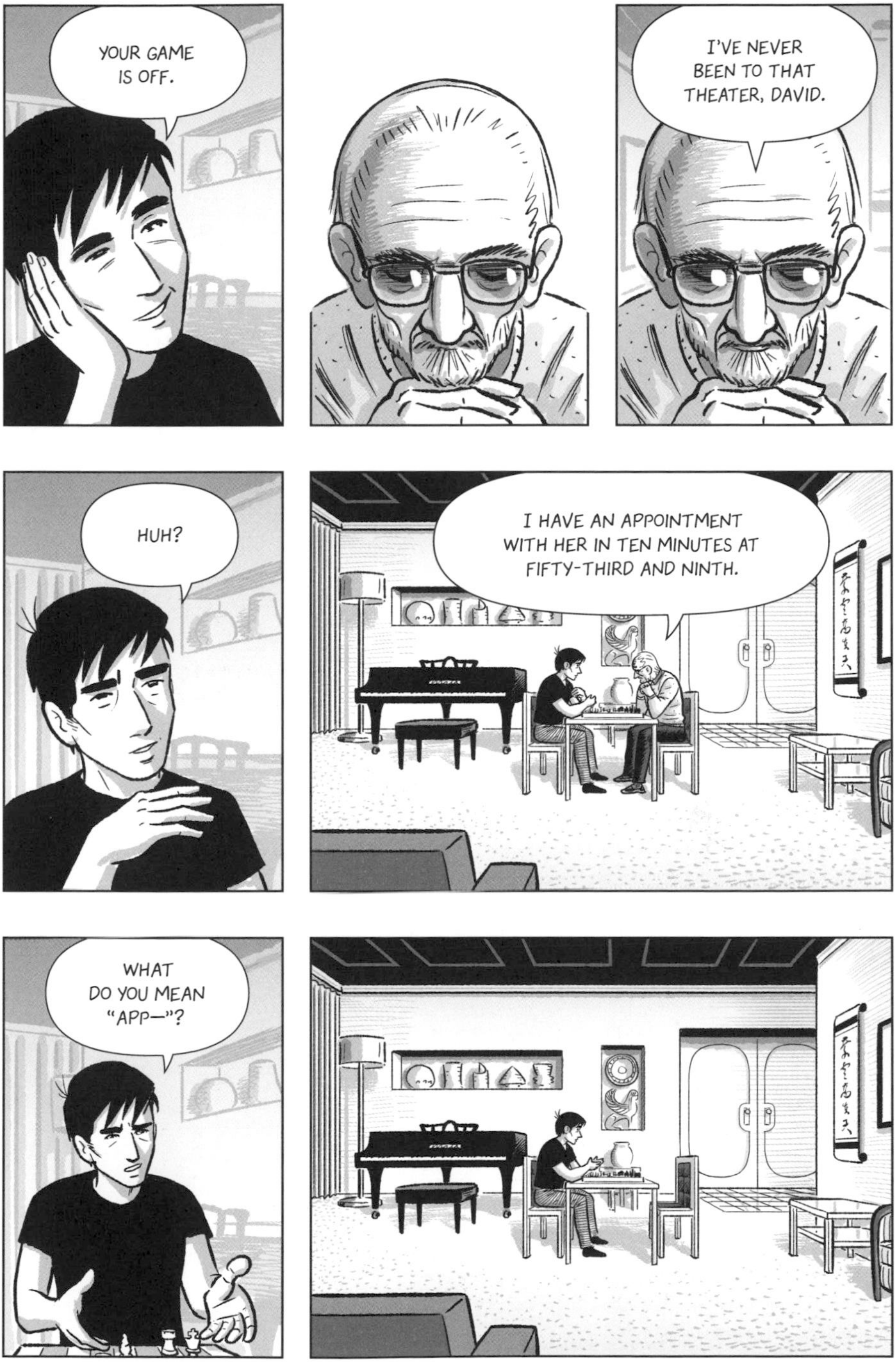
YOUR GAME IS OFF.
I'VE NEVER BEEN TO THAT THEATER, DAVID.
HUH?
I HAVE AN APPOINTMENT WITH HER IN TEN MINUTES AT FIFTY-THIRD AND NINTH.
WHAT DO YOU MEAN "APP—"?

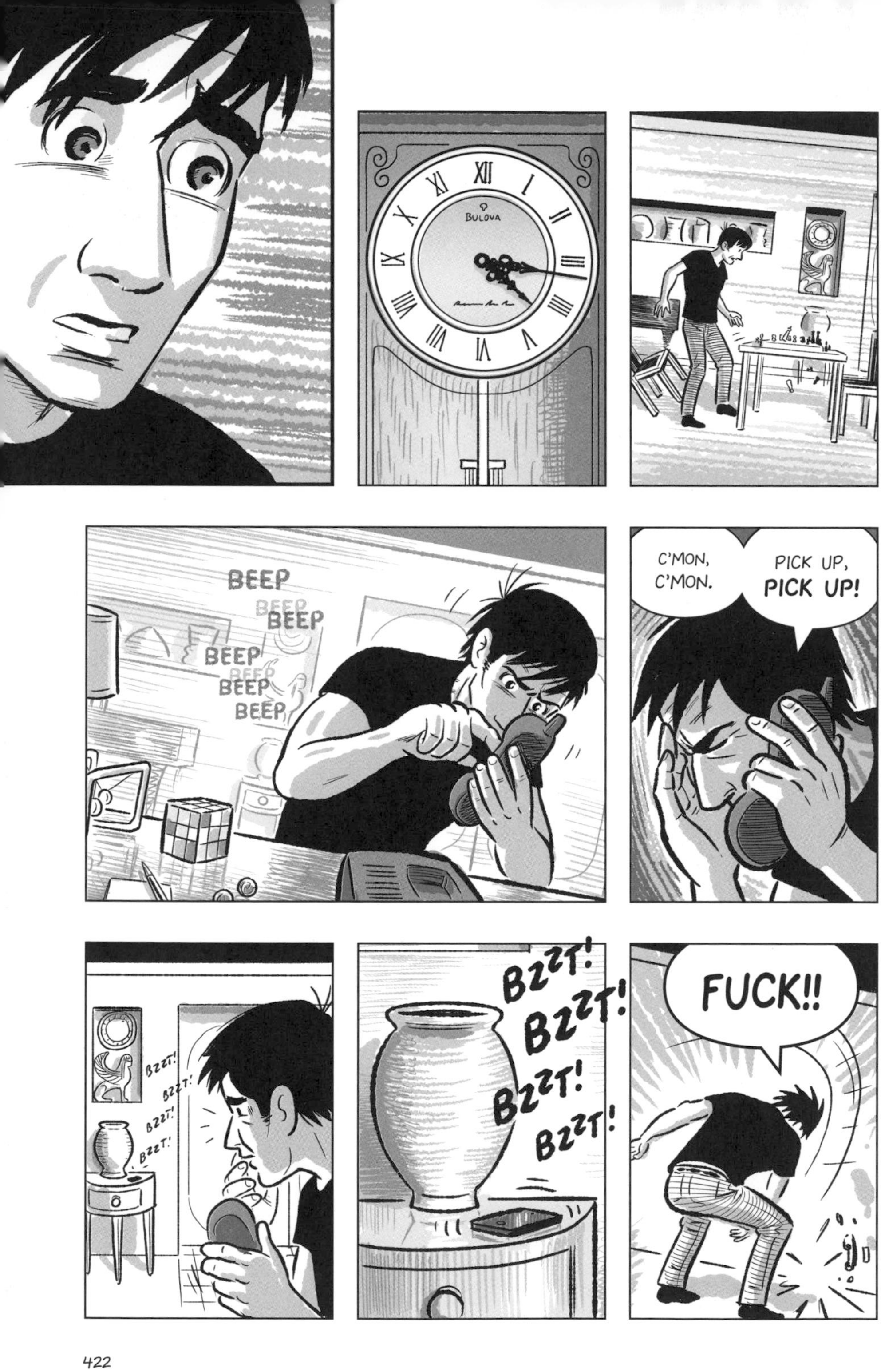
BULOVA
BEEP
BEEP
BEEP
BEEP
BEEP
BEEP
BEEP
BEEP
C'MON, C'MON.
PICK UP, PICK UP!
BZZT!
BZZT!
BZZT!
BZZT!
BZZT!
BZZT!
BZZT!
BZZT!
FUCK!!

BAMP!
BAMP!
BAMP!
BAMP!

POLICE. OPEN UP.

WE KNOW YOU'RE IN THERE, SMITH. **OPEN UP!**

NOT NOW.

NOT **NOW.**

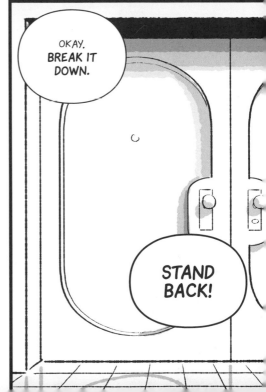

OKAY. BREAK IT DOWN.

STAND BACK!

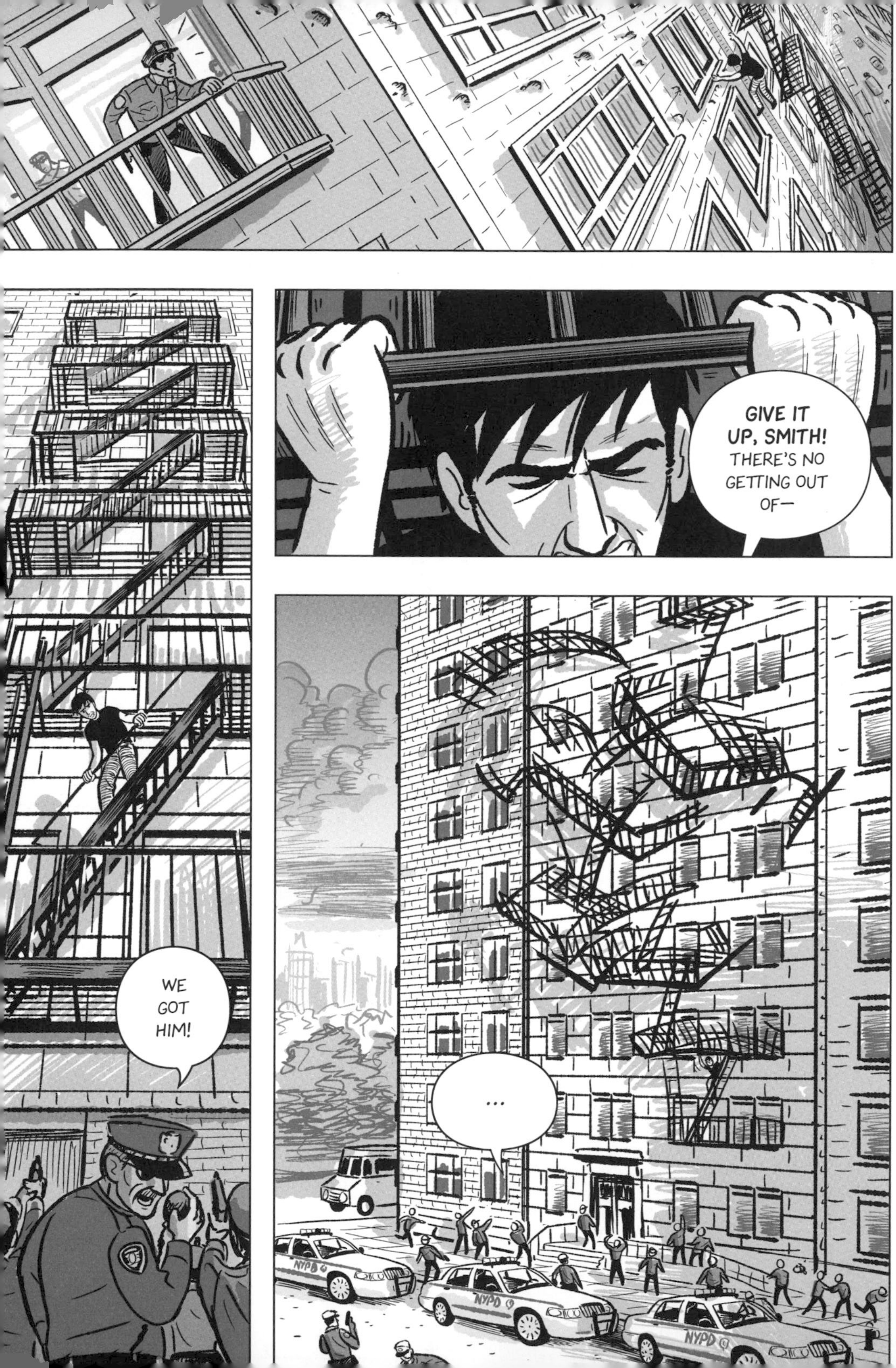
GIVE IT UP, SMITH! THERE'S NO GETTING OUT OF—
WE GOT HIM!
...

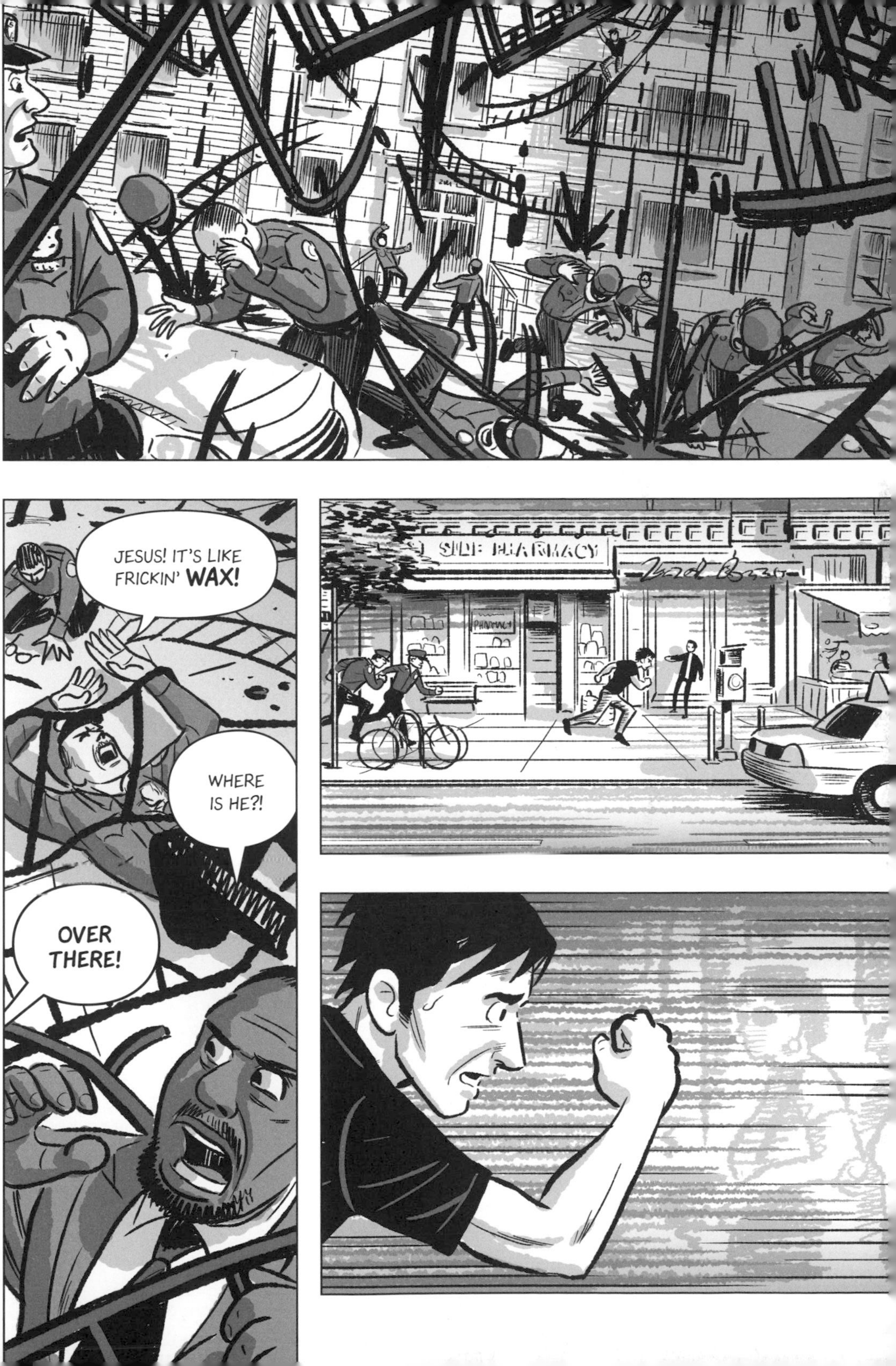
JESUS! IT'S LIKE FRICKIN' WAX!
WHERE IS HE?!
OVER THERE!

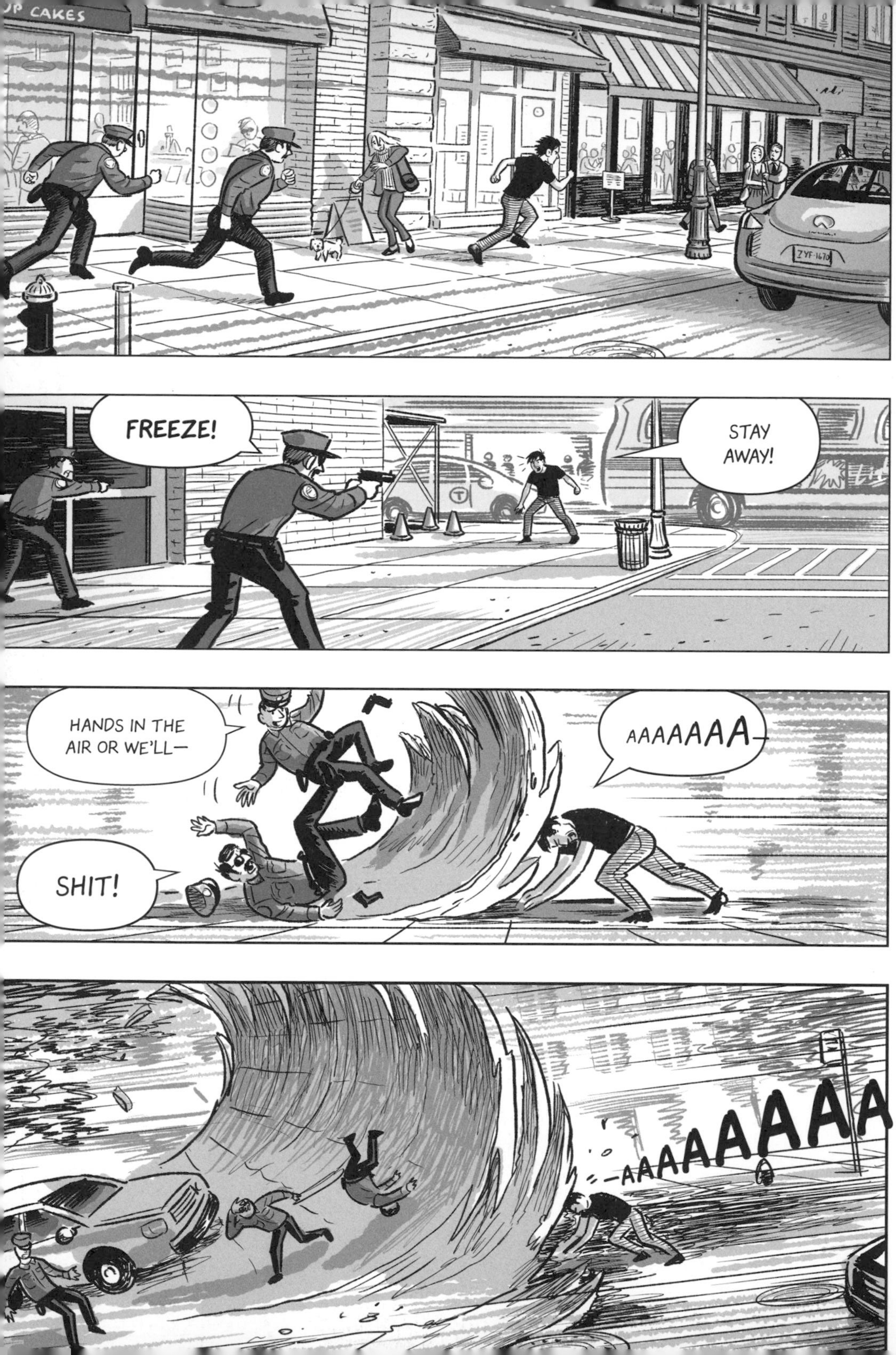
FREEZE!
STAY AWAY!
HANDS IN THE AIR OR WE'LL—
AAAAAAA—
SHIT!
—AAAAAAAAAA

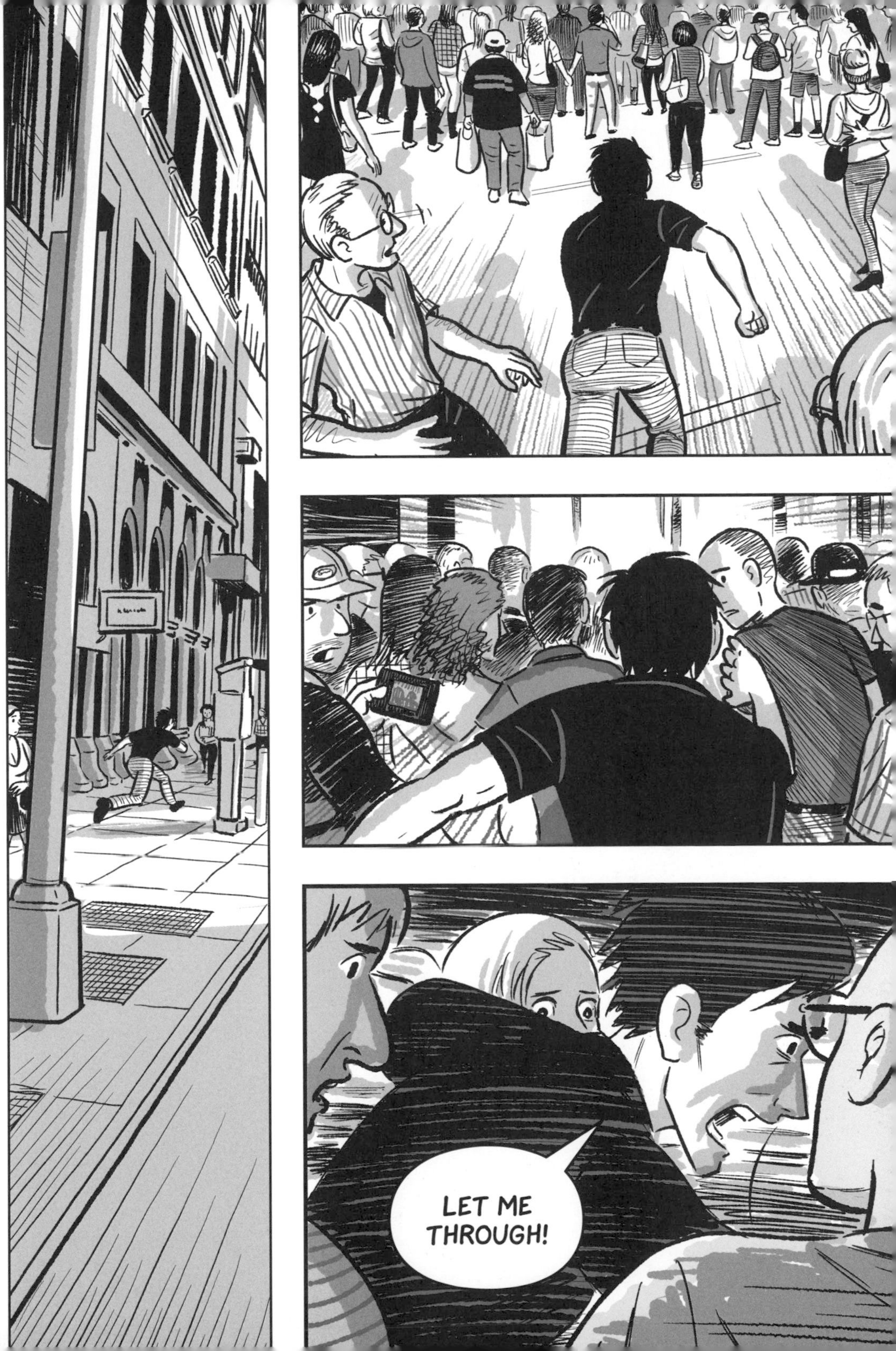
LET ME THROUGH!

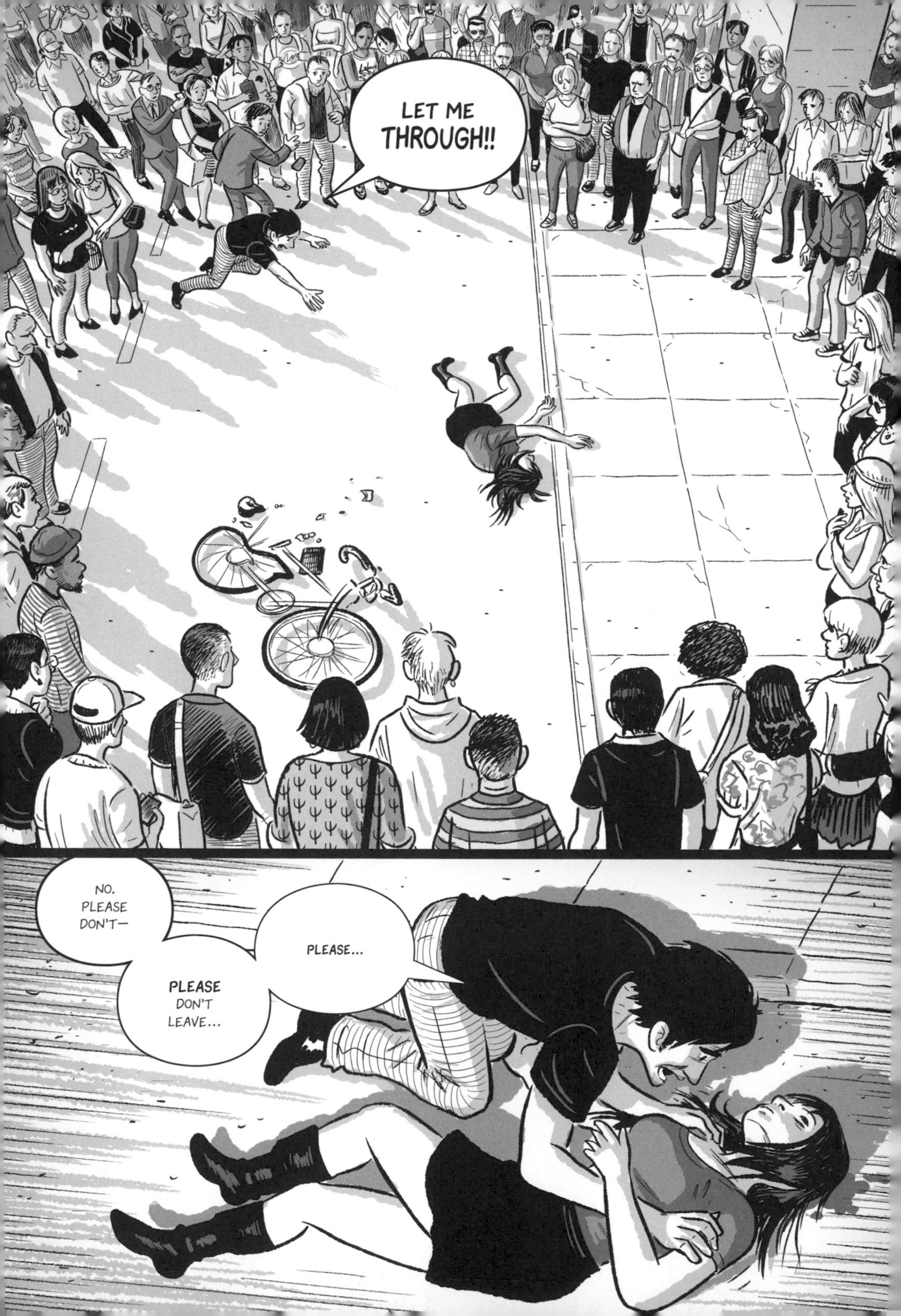
LET ME THROUGH!!
NO. PLEASE DON'T—
PLEASE...
PLEASE DON'T LEAVE...

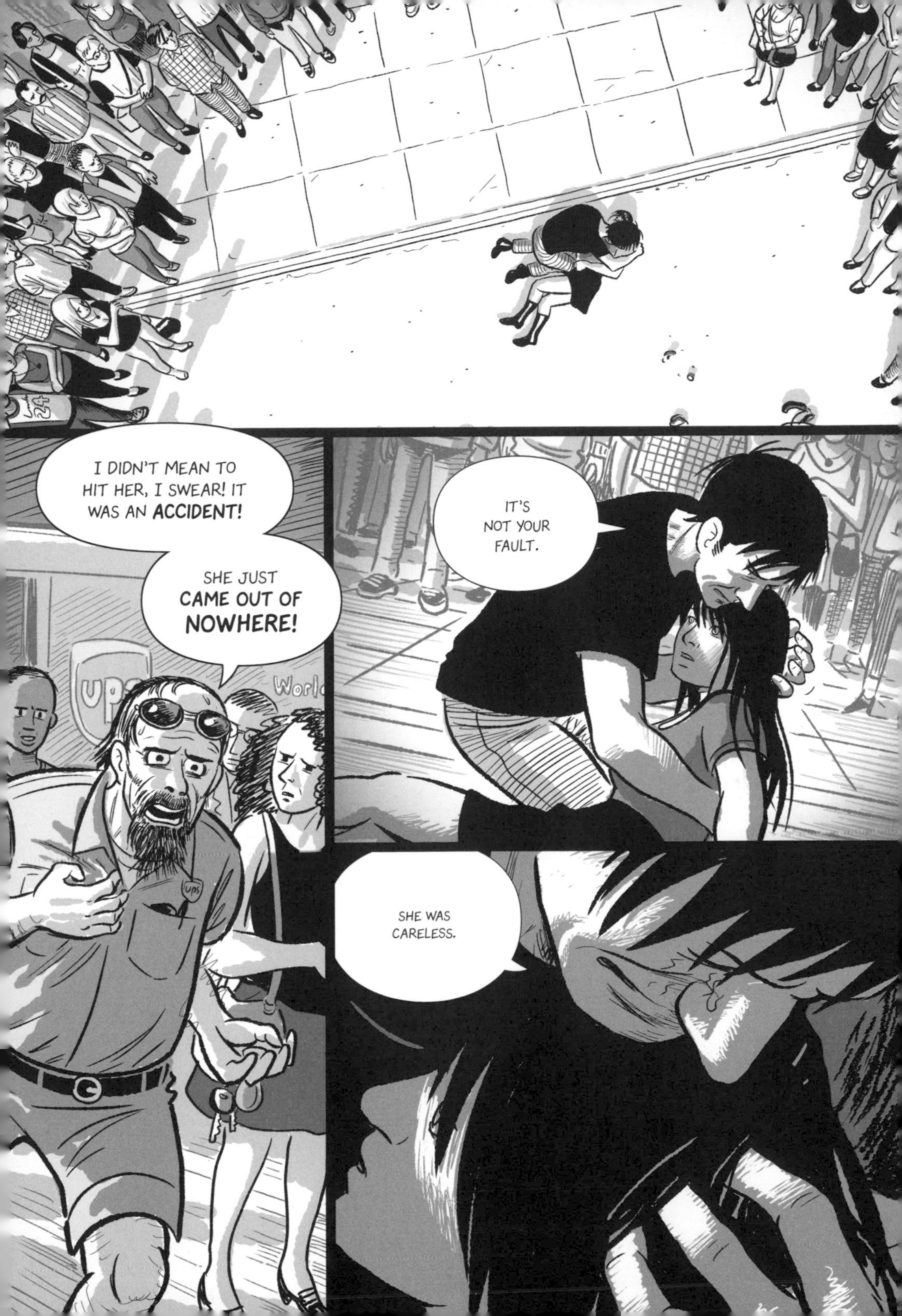
I DIDN'T MEAN TO HIT HER, I SWEAR! IT WAS AN **ACCIDENT!**
SHE JUST **CAME OUT OF NOWHERE!**
IT'S NOT YOUR FAULT.
SHE WAS CARELESS.

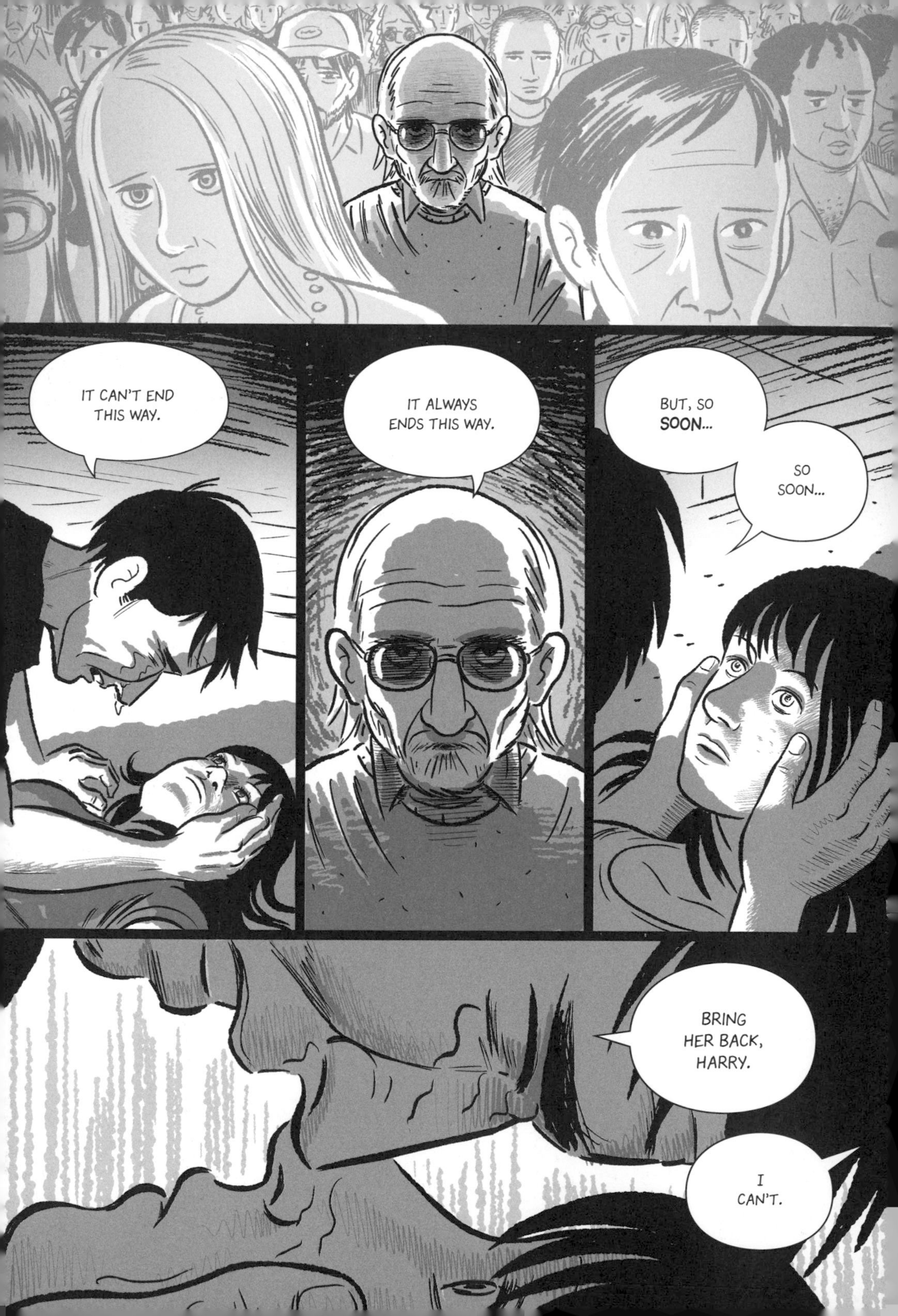
IT CAN'T END THIS WAY.
IT ALWAYS ENDS THIS WAY.
BUT, SO **SOON**...
SO SOON...
BRING HER BACK, HARRY.
I CAN'T.

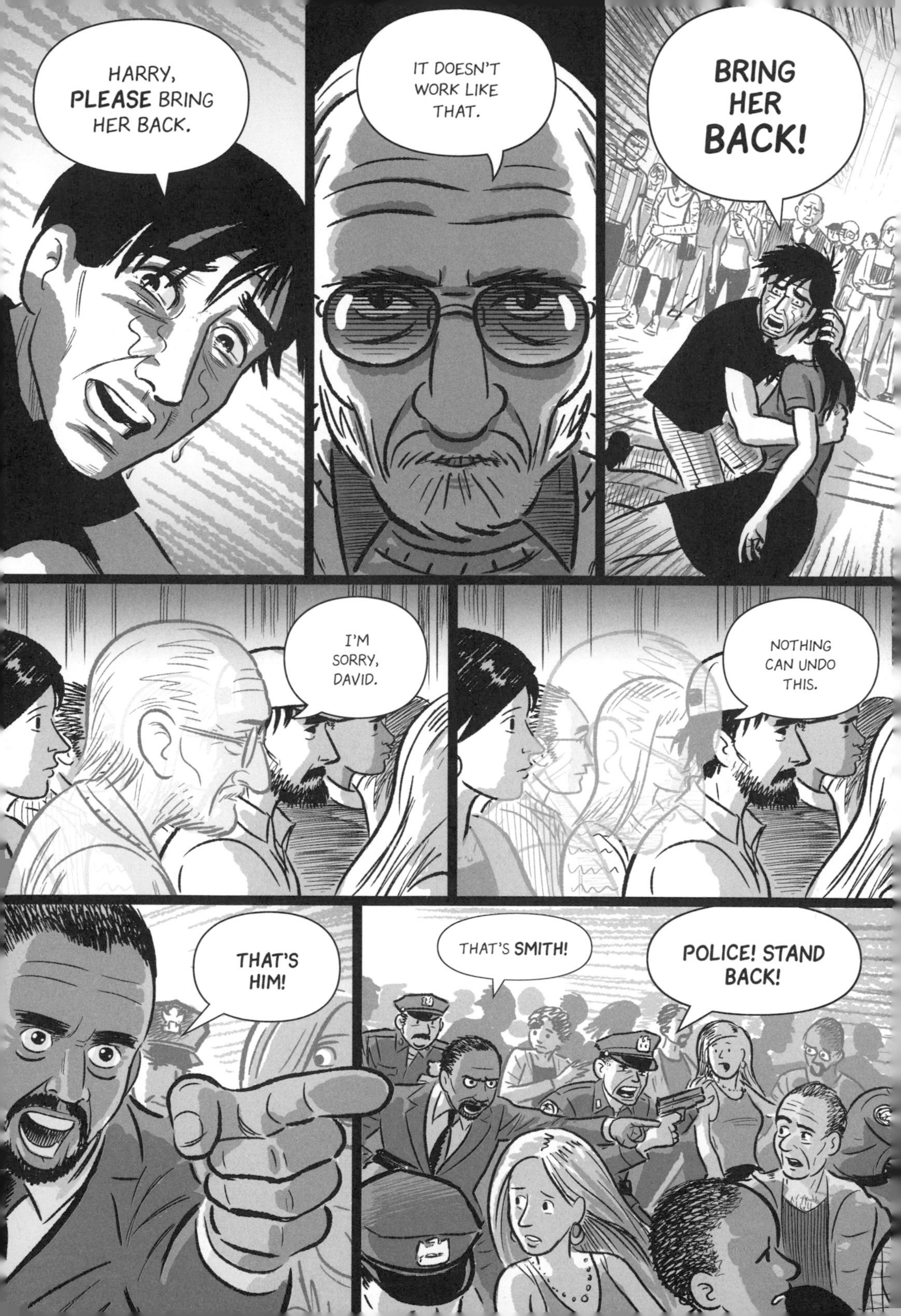
HARRY, **PLEASE** BRING HER BACK.
IT DOESN'T WORK LIKE THAT.
BRING HER BACK!
I'M SORRY, DAVID.
NOTHING CAN UNDO THIS.
THAT'S HIM!
THAT'S **SMITH!**
POLICE! STAND BACK!

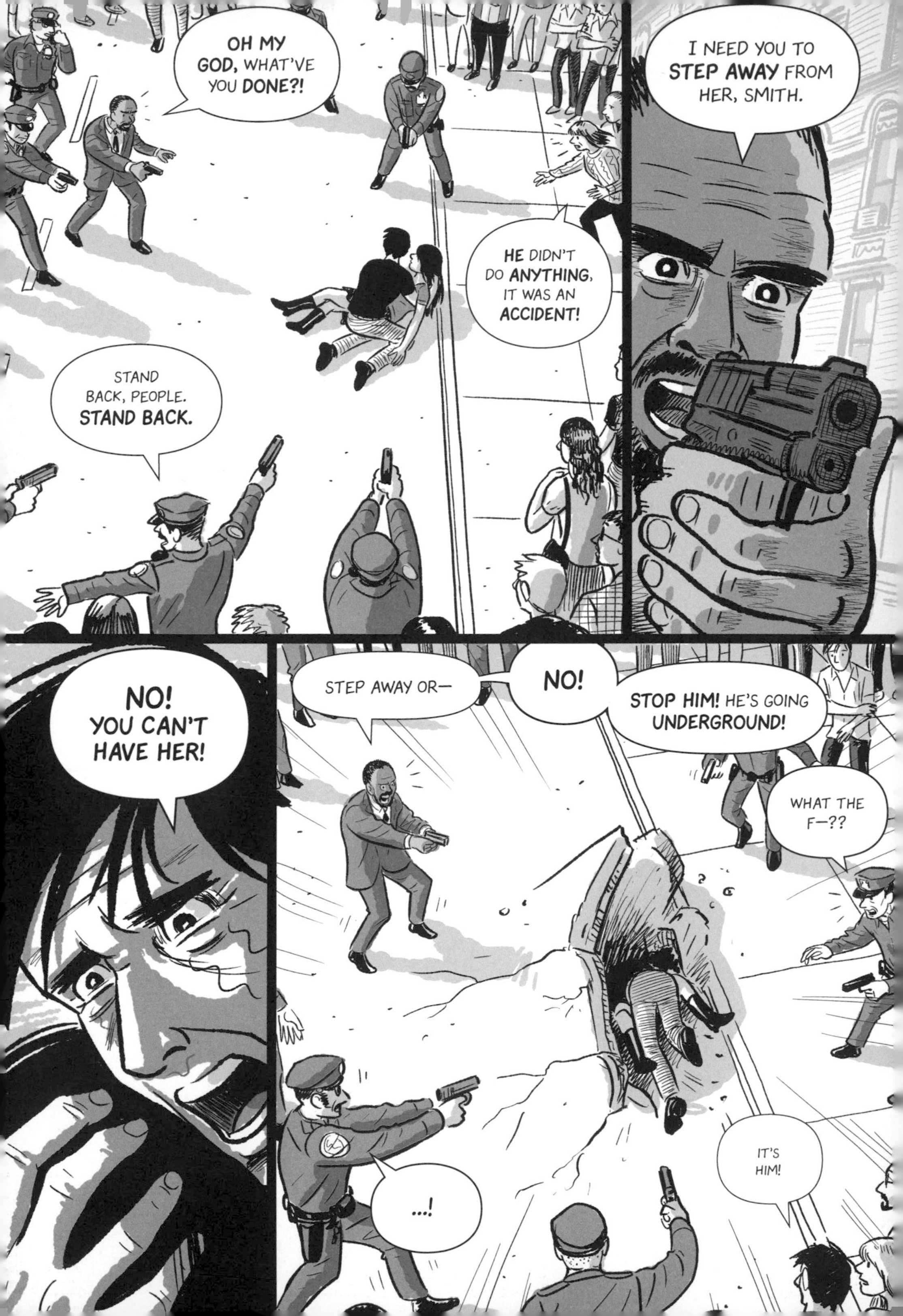
OH MY GOD, WHAT'VE YOU DONE?!
HE DIDN'T DO ANYTHING, IT WAS AN ACCIDENT!
STAND BACK, PEOPLE. STAND BACK.
I NEED YOU TO STEP AWAY FROM HER, SMITH.
NO! YOU CAN'T HAVE HER!
STEP AWAY OR—
NO!
STOP HIM! HE'S GOING UNDERGROUND!
WHAT THE F—??
...!
IT'S HIM!

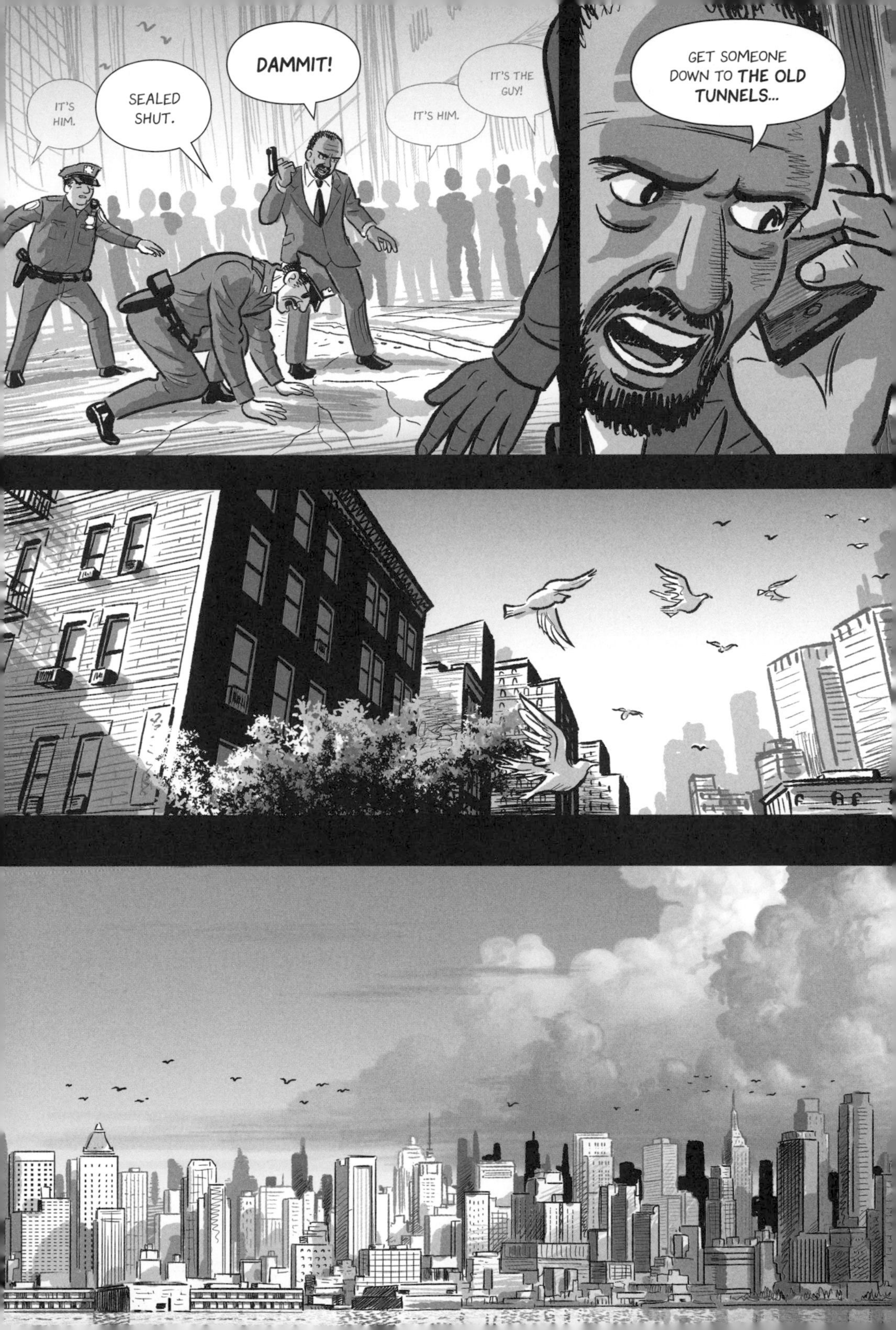
IT'S HIM.
SEALED SHUT.
DAMMIT!
IT'S HIM.
IT'S THE GUY!
GET SOMEONE DOWN TO THE OLD TUNNELS...

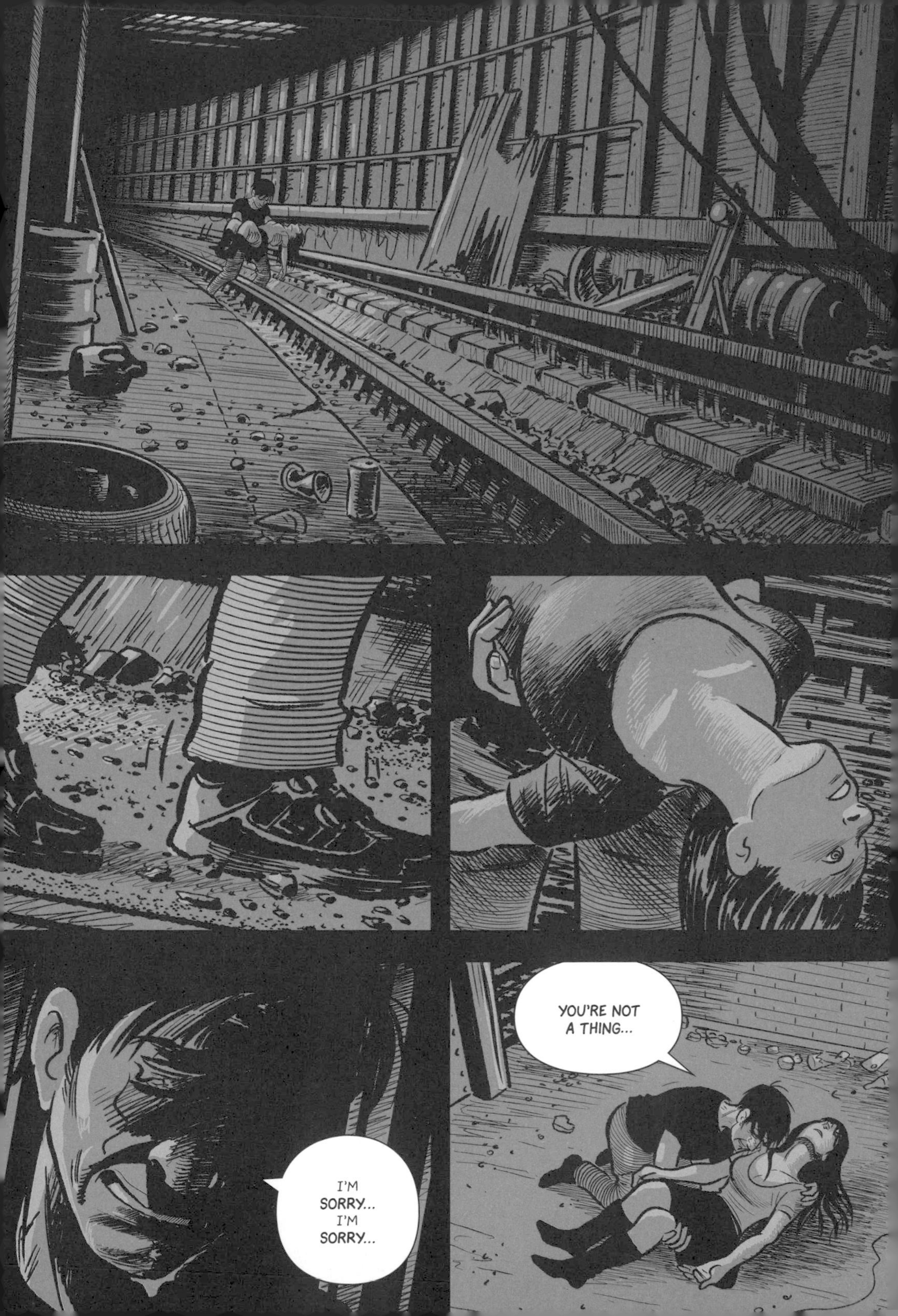
I'M SORRY... I'M SORRY...
YOU'RE NOT A THING...

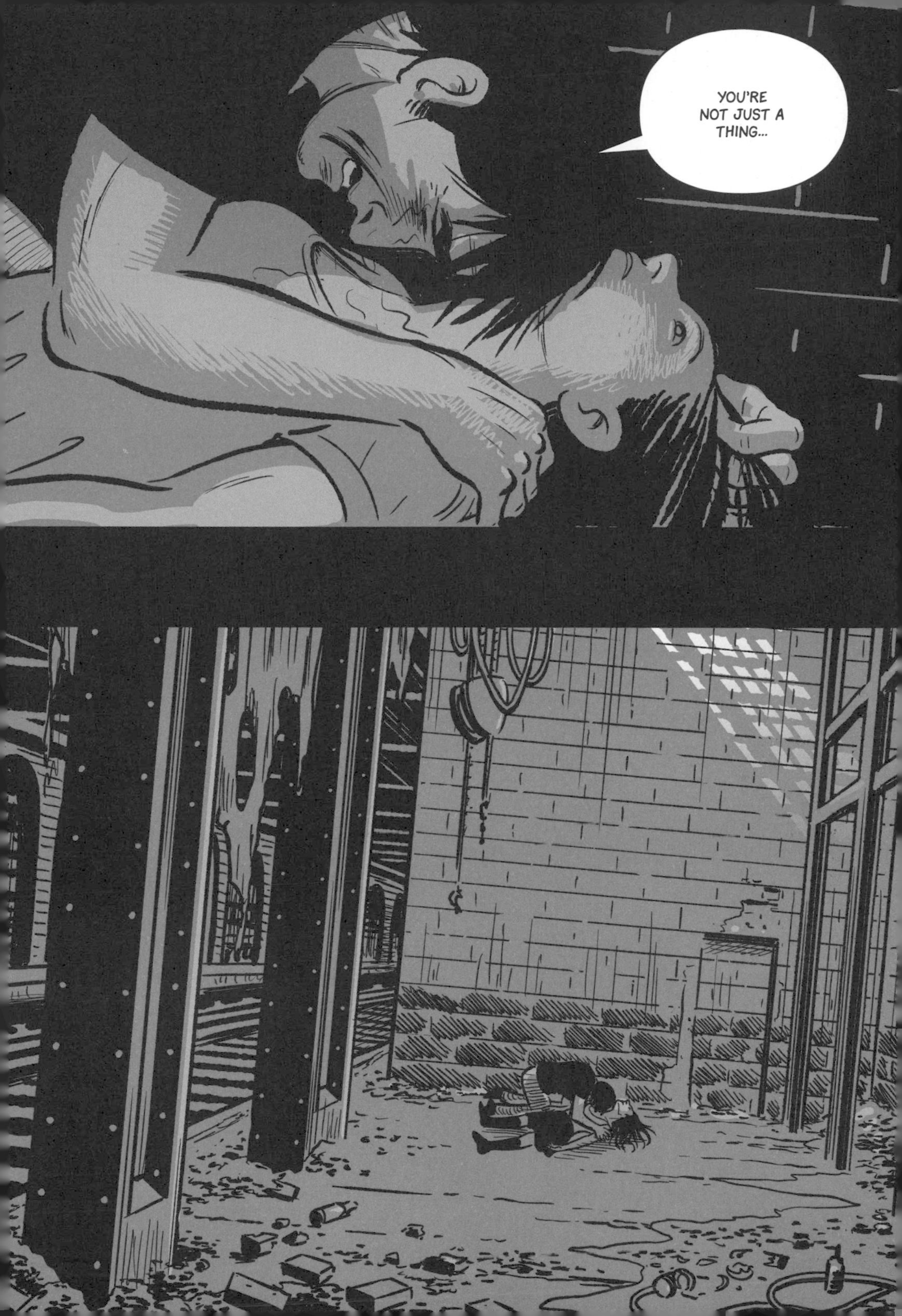
YOU'RE NOT JUST A THING...

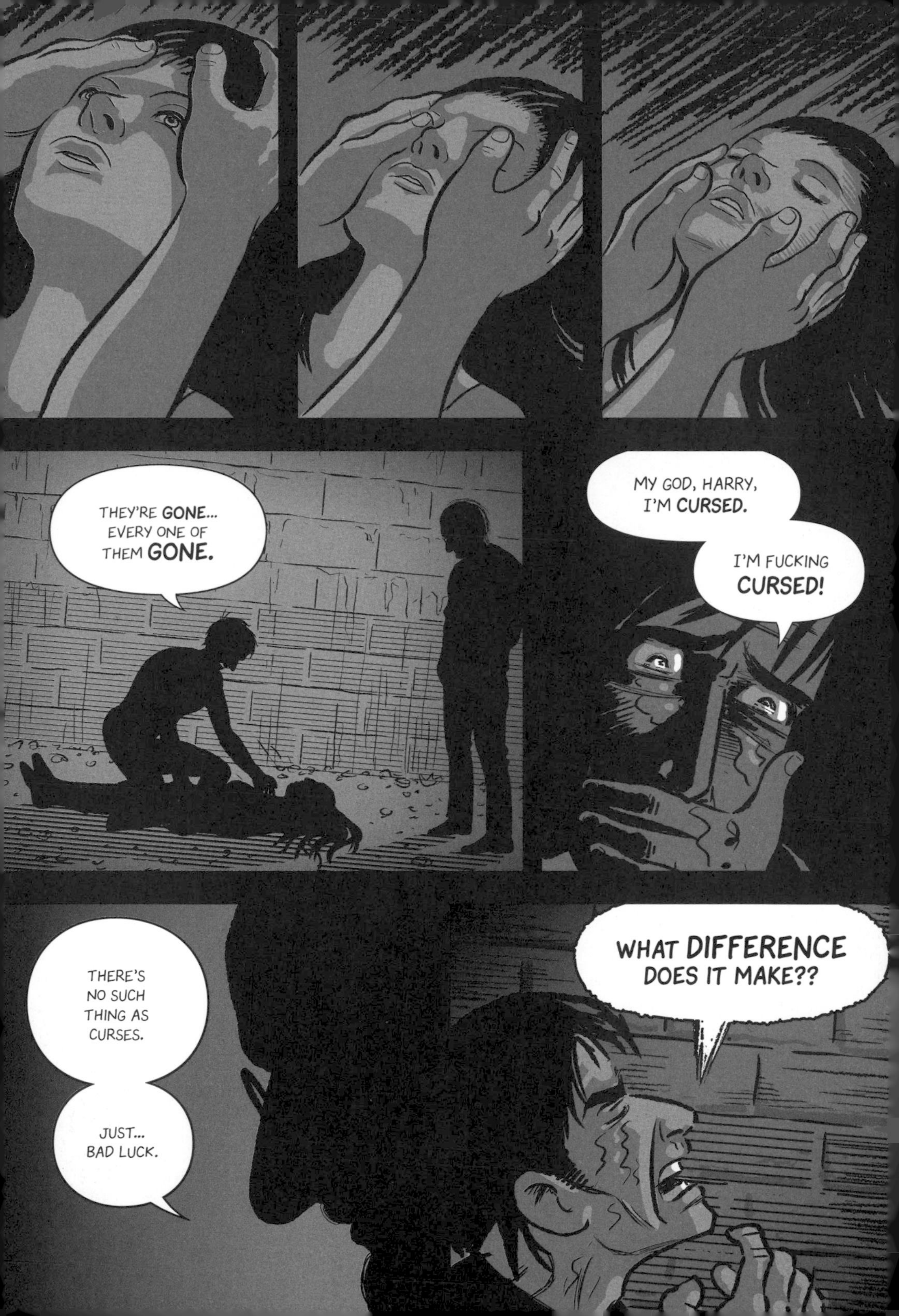
THEY'RE GONE... EVERY ONE OF THEM GONE.
MY GOD, HARRY, I'M CURSED.
I'M FUCKING CURSED!
THERE'S NO SUCH THING AS CURSES.
JUST... BAD LUCK.
WHAT DIFFERENCE DOES IT MAKE??

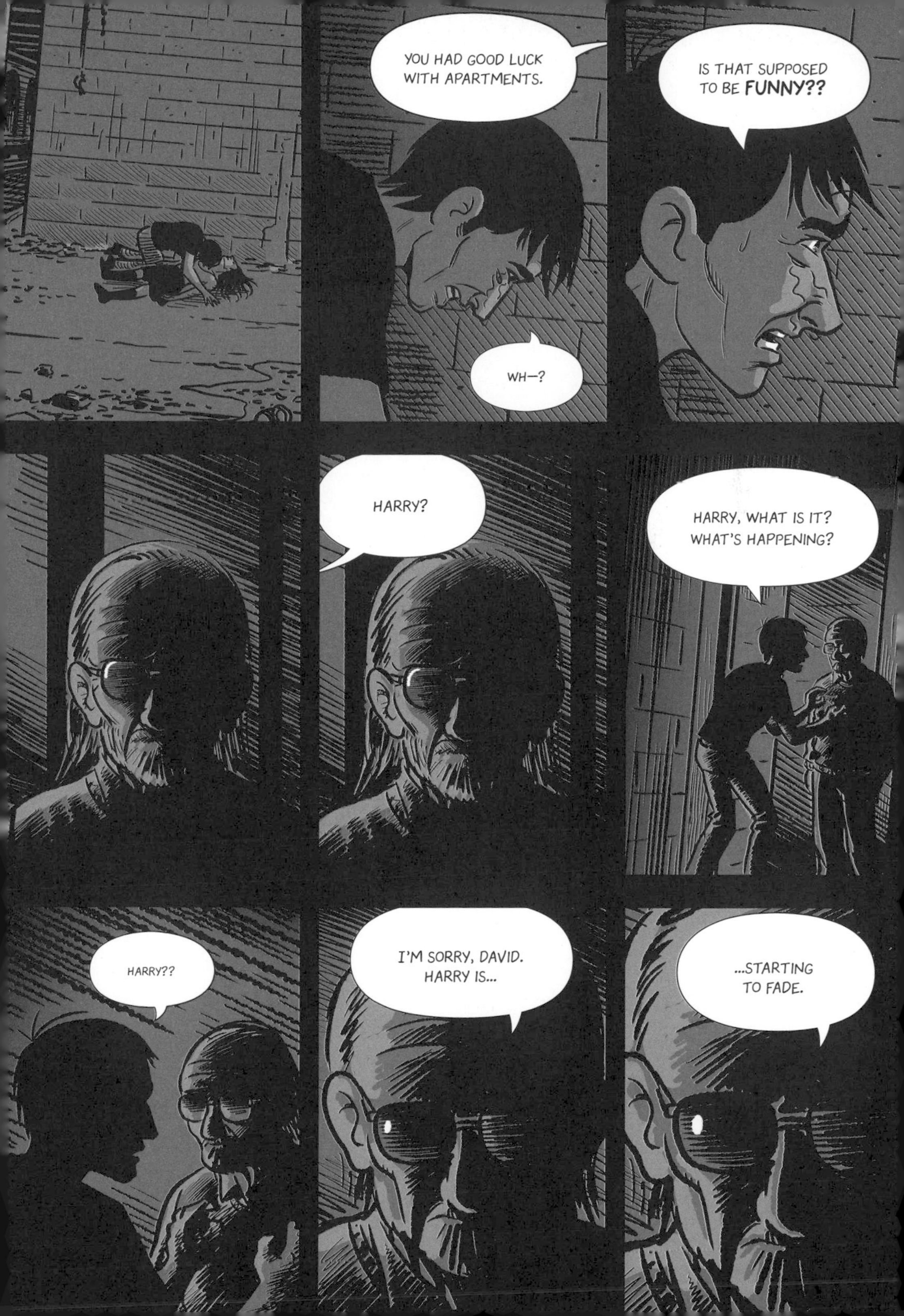
YOU HAD GOOD LUCK WITH APARTMENTS.
WH—?
IS THAT SUPPOSED TO BE **FUNNY??**
HARRY?
HARRY, WHAT IS IT? WHAT'S HAPPENING?
HARRY??
I'M SORRY, DAVID. HARRY IS...
...STARTING TO FADE.

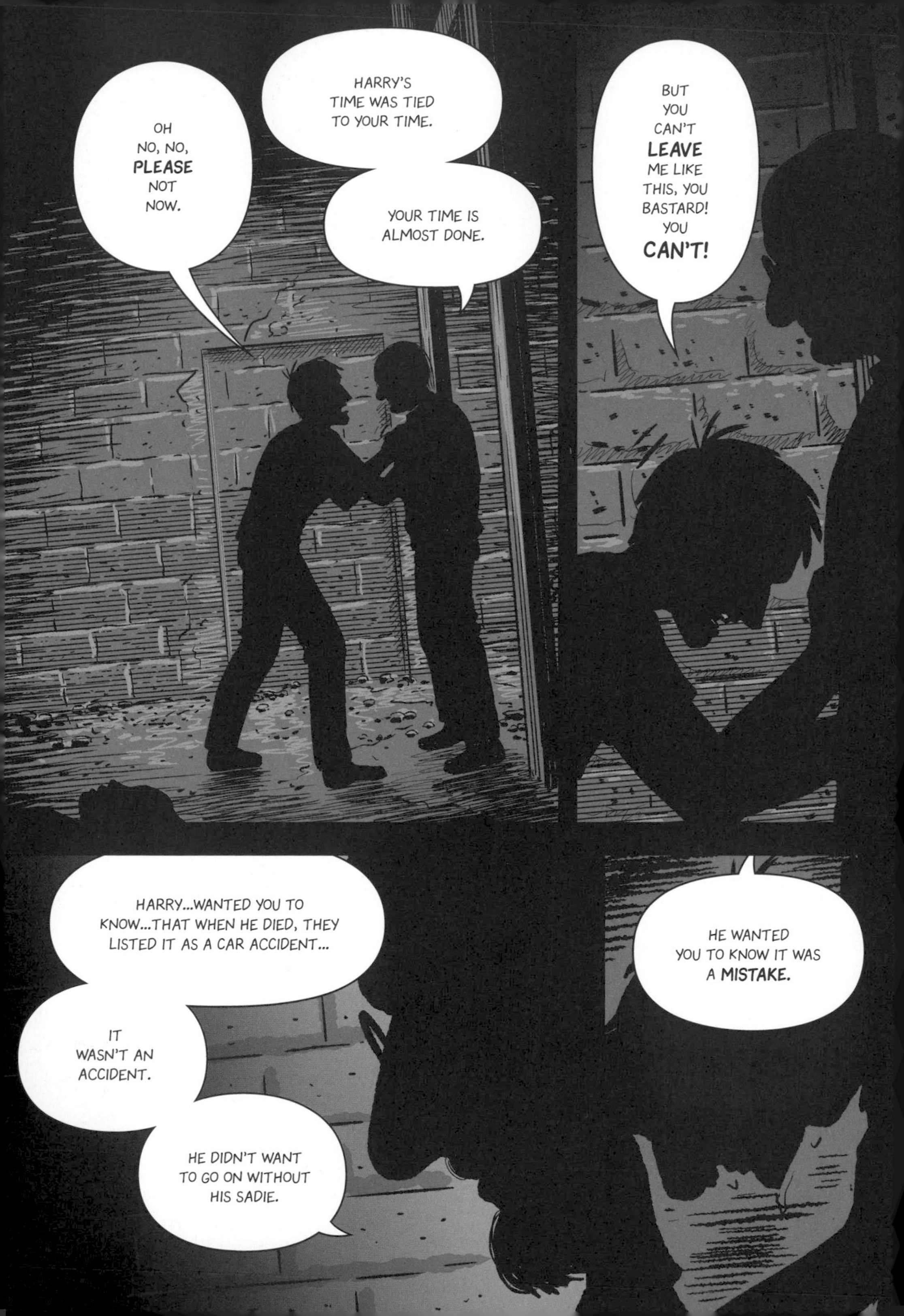
OH NO, NO, **PLEASE** NOT NOW.
HARRY'S TIME WAS TIED TO YOUR TIME.
YOUR TIME IS ALMOST DONE.
BUT YOU CAN'T **LEAVE** ME LIKE THIS, YOU BASTARD! YOU **CAN'T!**
HARRY...WANTED YOU TO KNOW...THAT WHEN HE DIED, THEY LISTED IT AS A CAR ACCIDENT...
IT WASN'T AN ACCIDENT.
HE DIDN'T WANT TO GO ON WITHOUT HIS SADIE.
HE WANTED YOU TO KNOW IT WAS A **MISTAKE.**

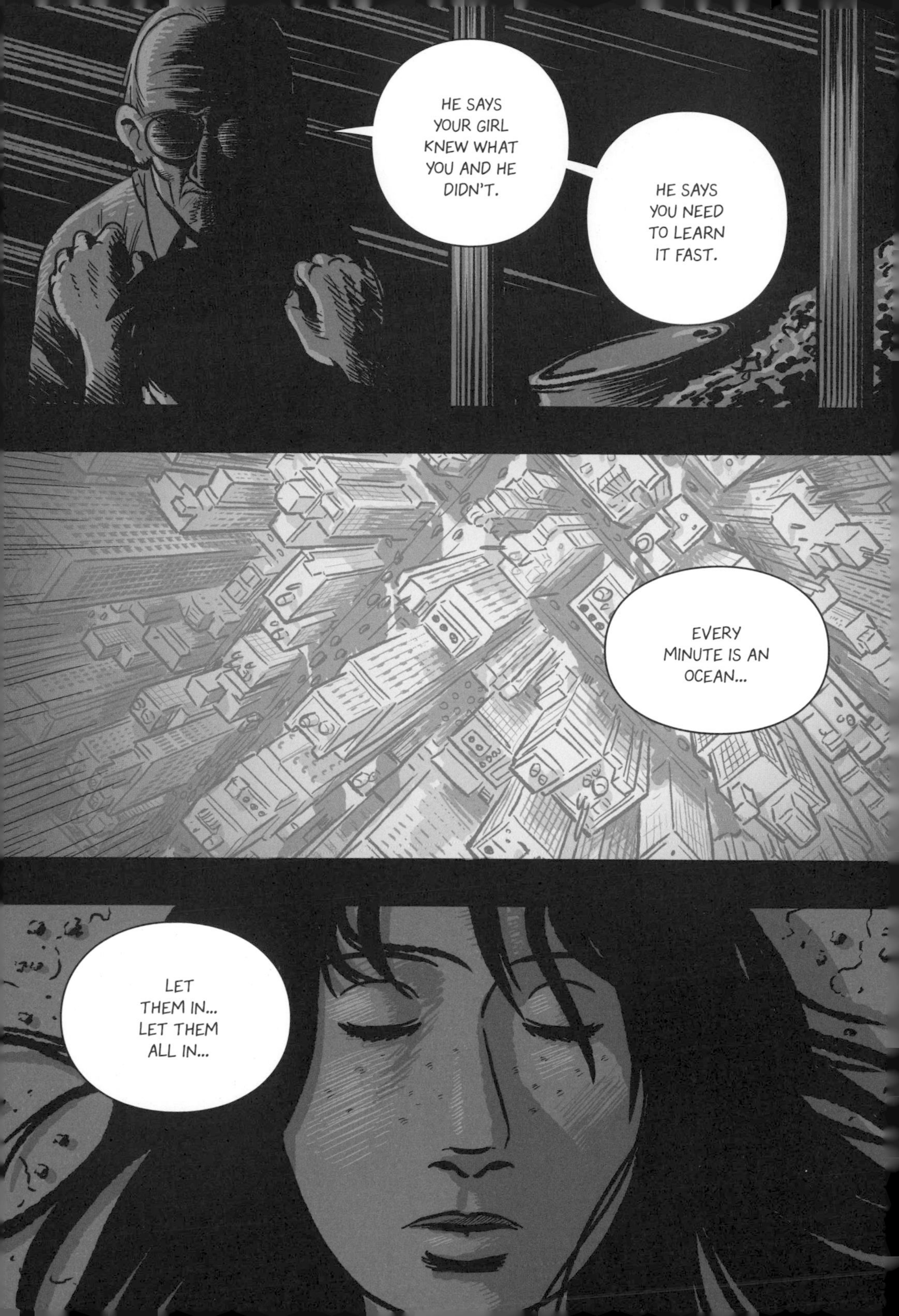
HE SAYS YOUR GIRL KNEW WHAT YOU AND HE DIDN'T.
HE SAYS YOU NEED TO LEARN IT FAST.
EVERY MINUTE IS AN OCEAN...
LET THEM IN... LET THEM ALL IN...

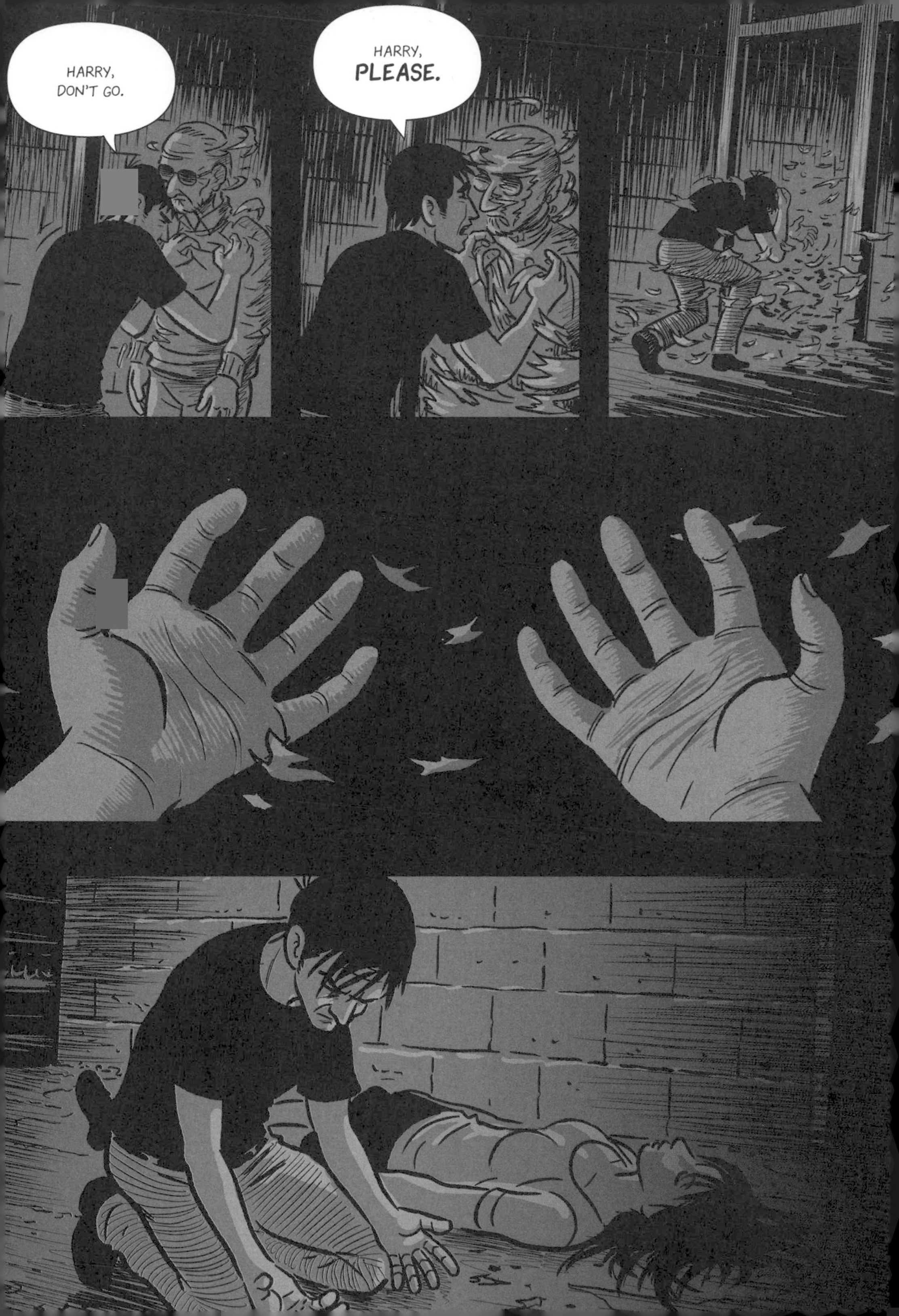
HARRY, DON'T GO.
HARRY, PLEASE.

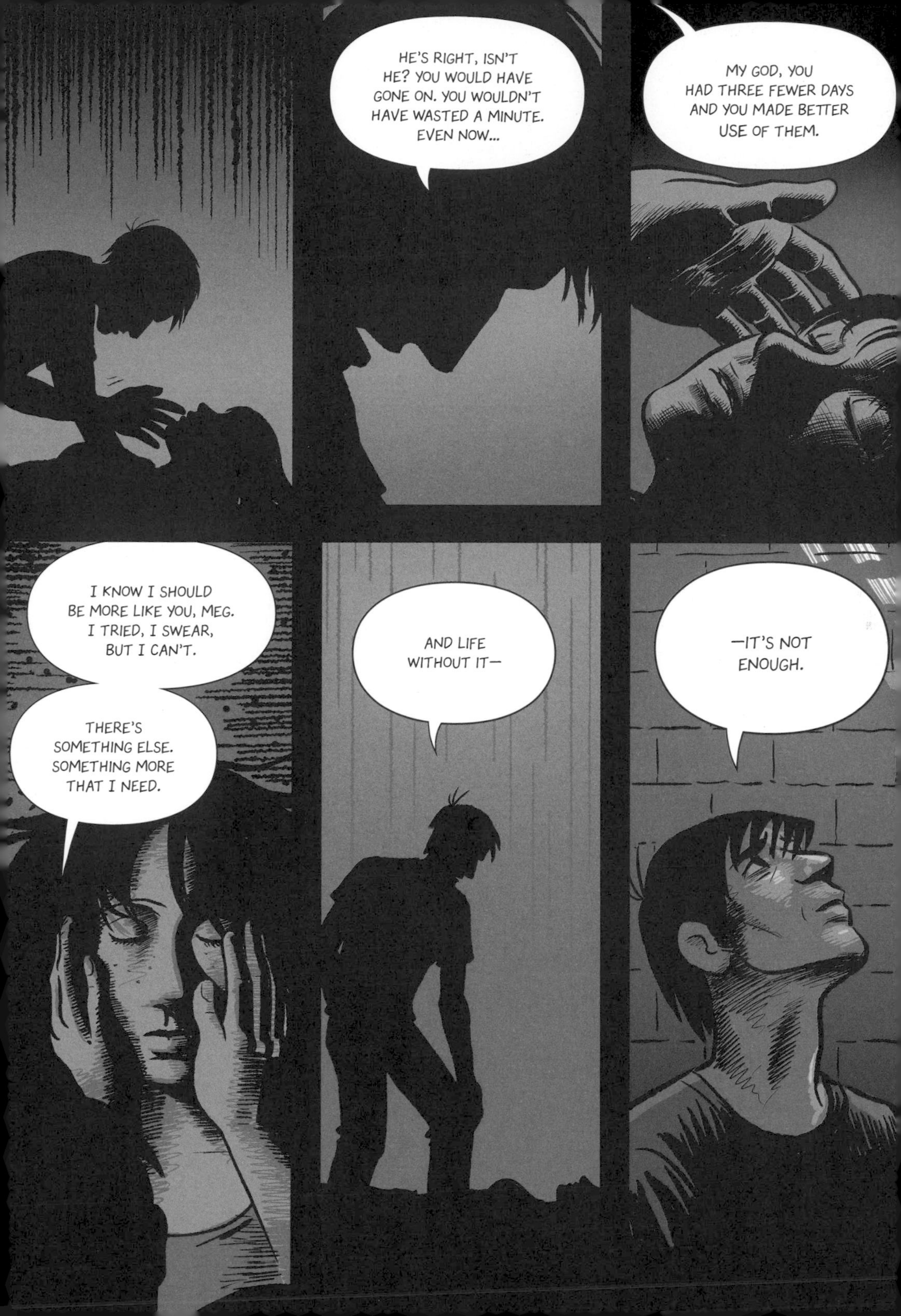
HE'S RIGHT, ISN'T HE? YOU WOULD HAVE GONE ON. YOU WOULDN'T HAVE WASTED A MINUTE. EVEN NOW...
MY GOD, YOU HAD THREE FEWER DAYS AND YOU MADE BETTER USE OF THEM.
I KNOW I SHOULD BE MORE LIKE YOU, MEG. I TRIED, I SWEAR, BUT I CAN'T.
THERE'S SOMETHING ELSE. SOMETHING MORE THAT I NEED.
AND LIFE WITHOUT IT—
—IT'S NOT ENOUGH.

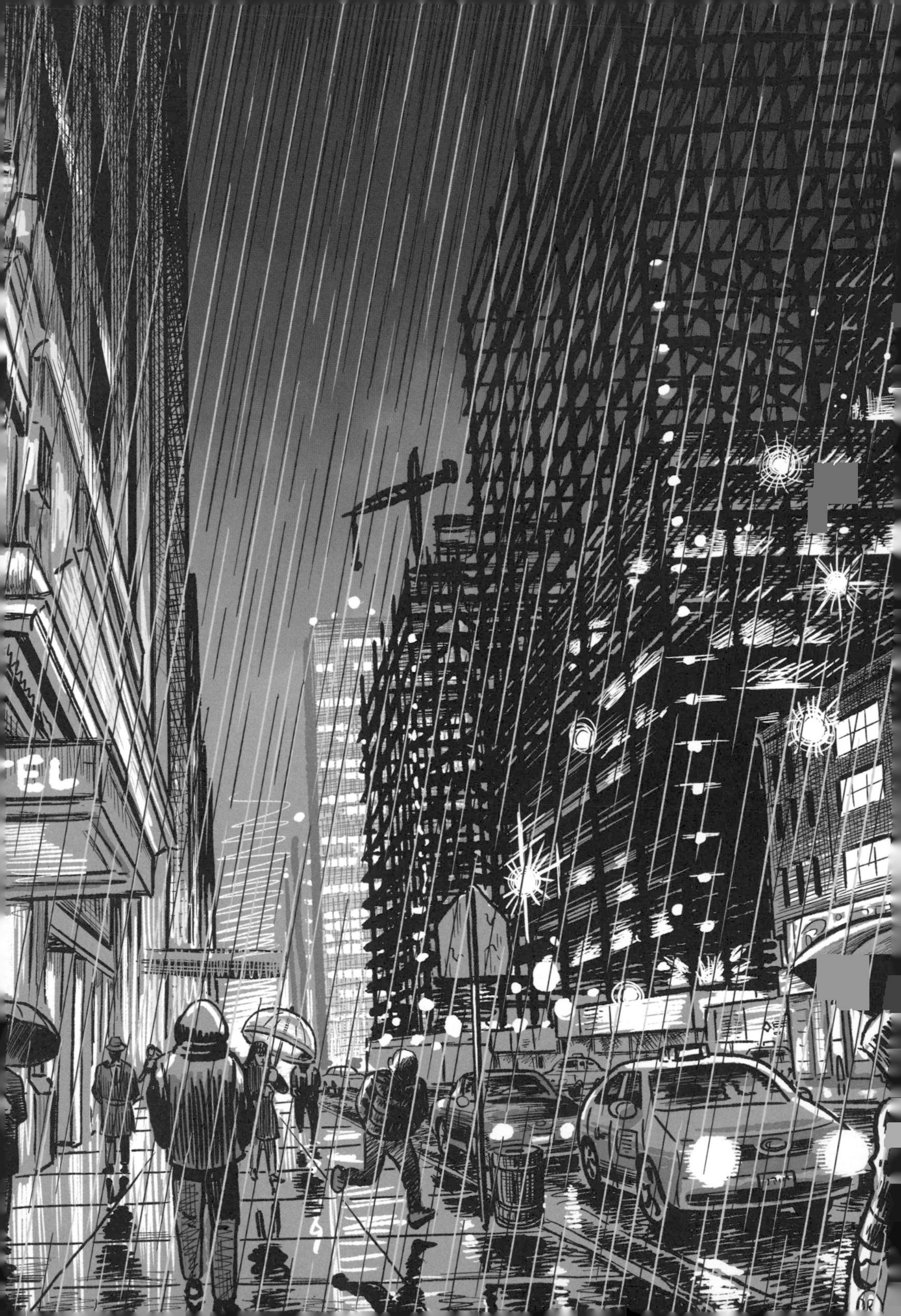

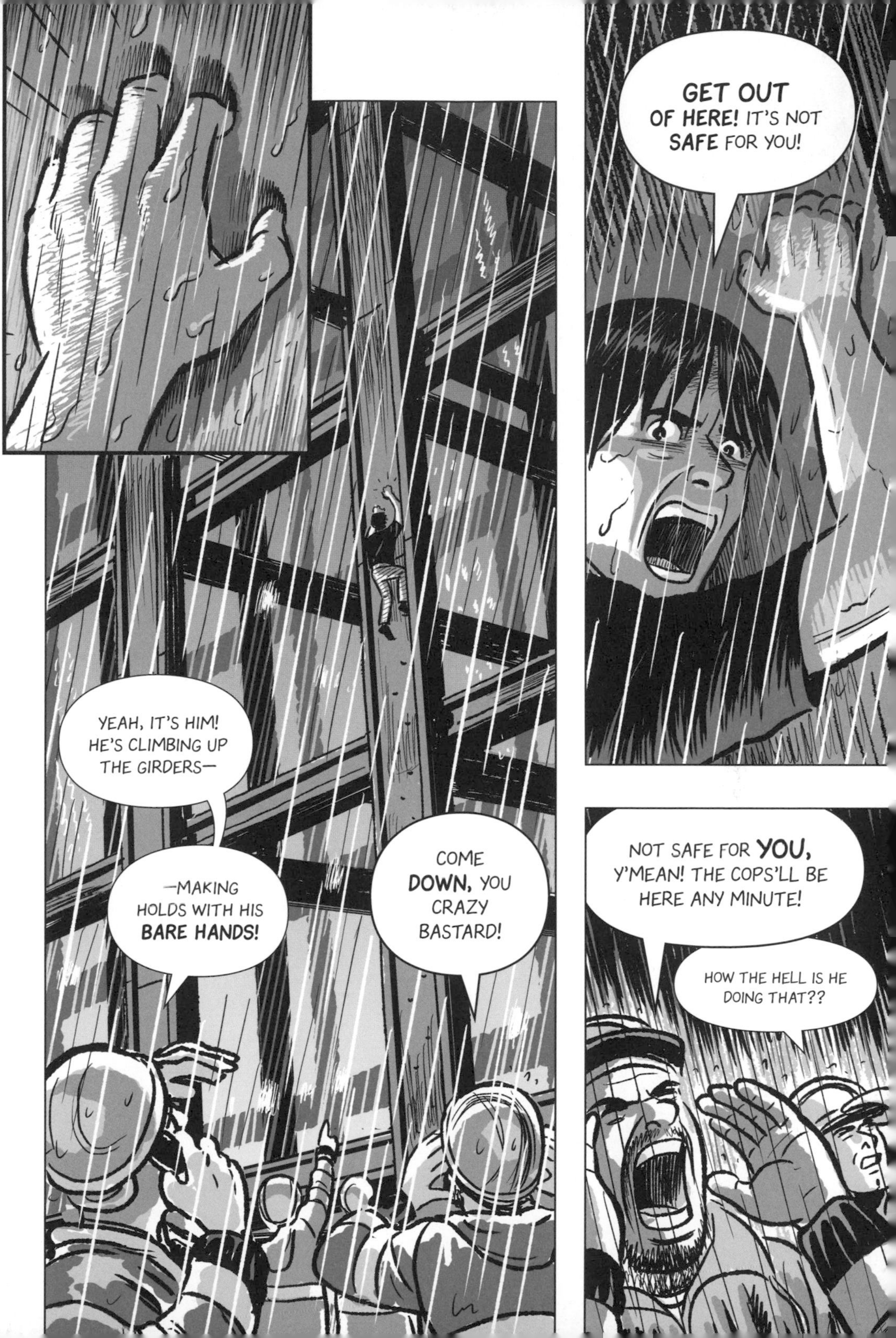
GET OUT OF HERE! IT'S NOT SAFE FOR YOU!
YEAH, IT'S HIM! HE'S CLIMBING UP THE GIRDERS—
—MAKING HOLDS WITH HIS BARE HANDS!
COME DOWN, YOU CRAZY BASTARD!
NOT SAFE FOR YOU, Y'MEAN! THE COPS'LL BE HERE ANY MINUTE!
HOW THE HELL IS HE DOING THAT??

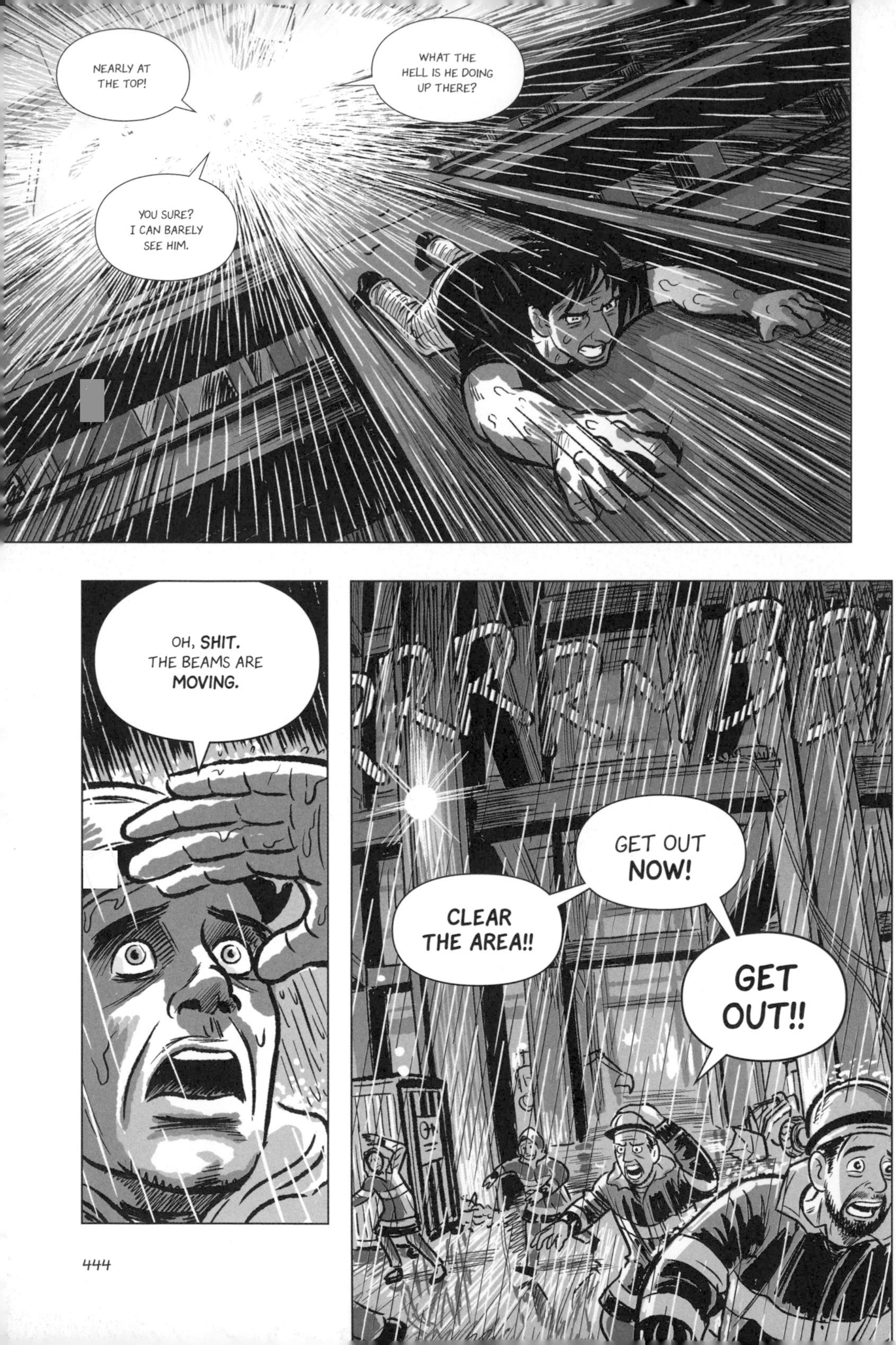
NEARLY AT THE TOP!
WHAT THE HELL IS HE DOING UP THERE?
YOU SURE? I CAN BARELY SEE HIM.
OH, SHIT. THE BEAMS ARE MOVING.
GET OUT NOW!
CLEAR THE AREA!!
GET OUT!!

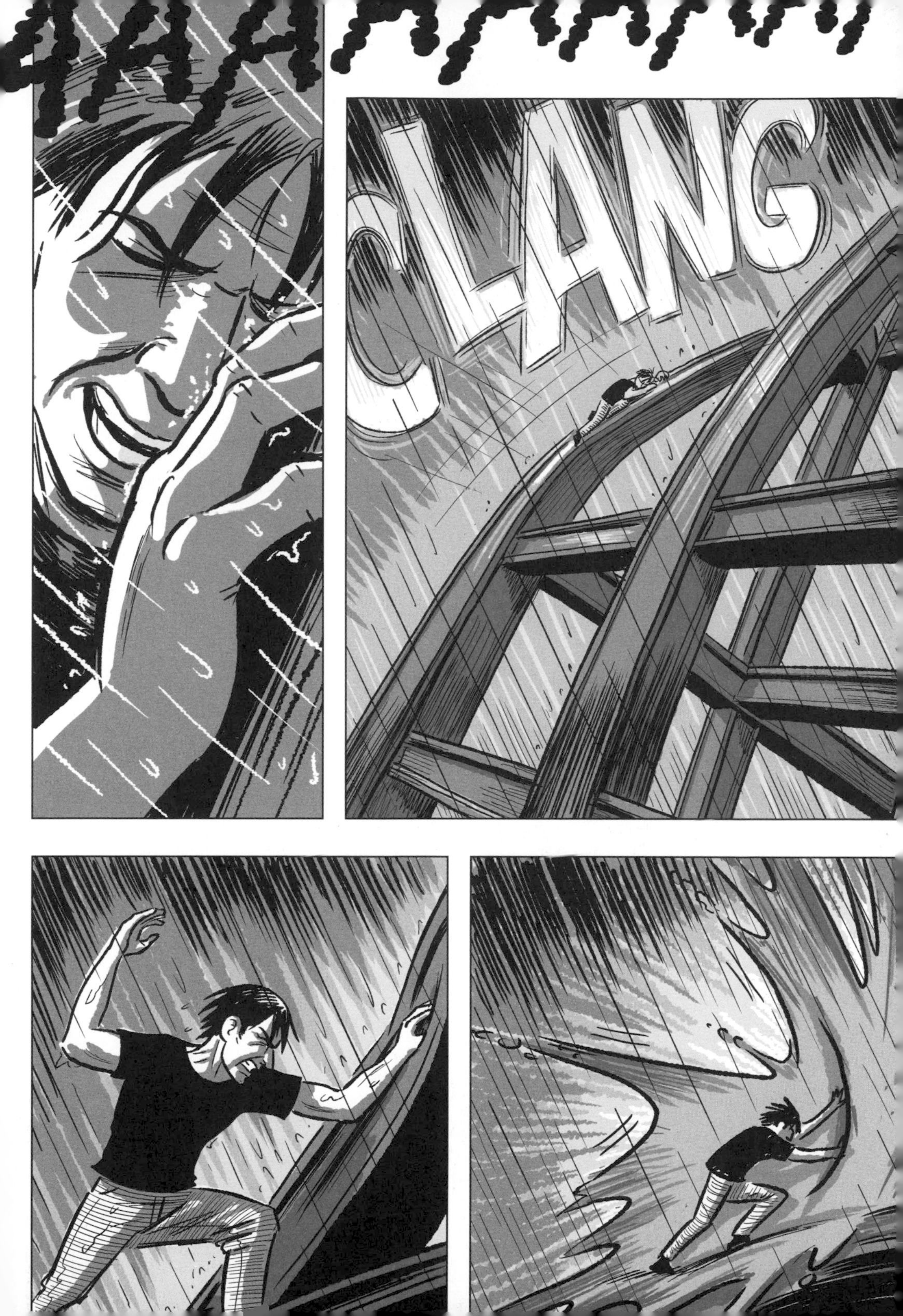
CLANG

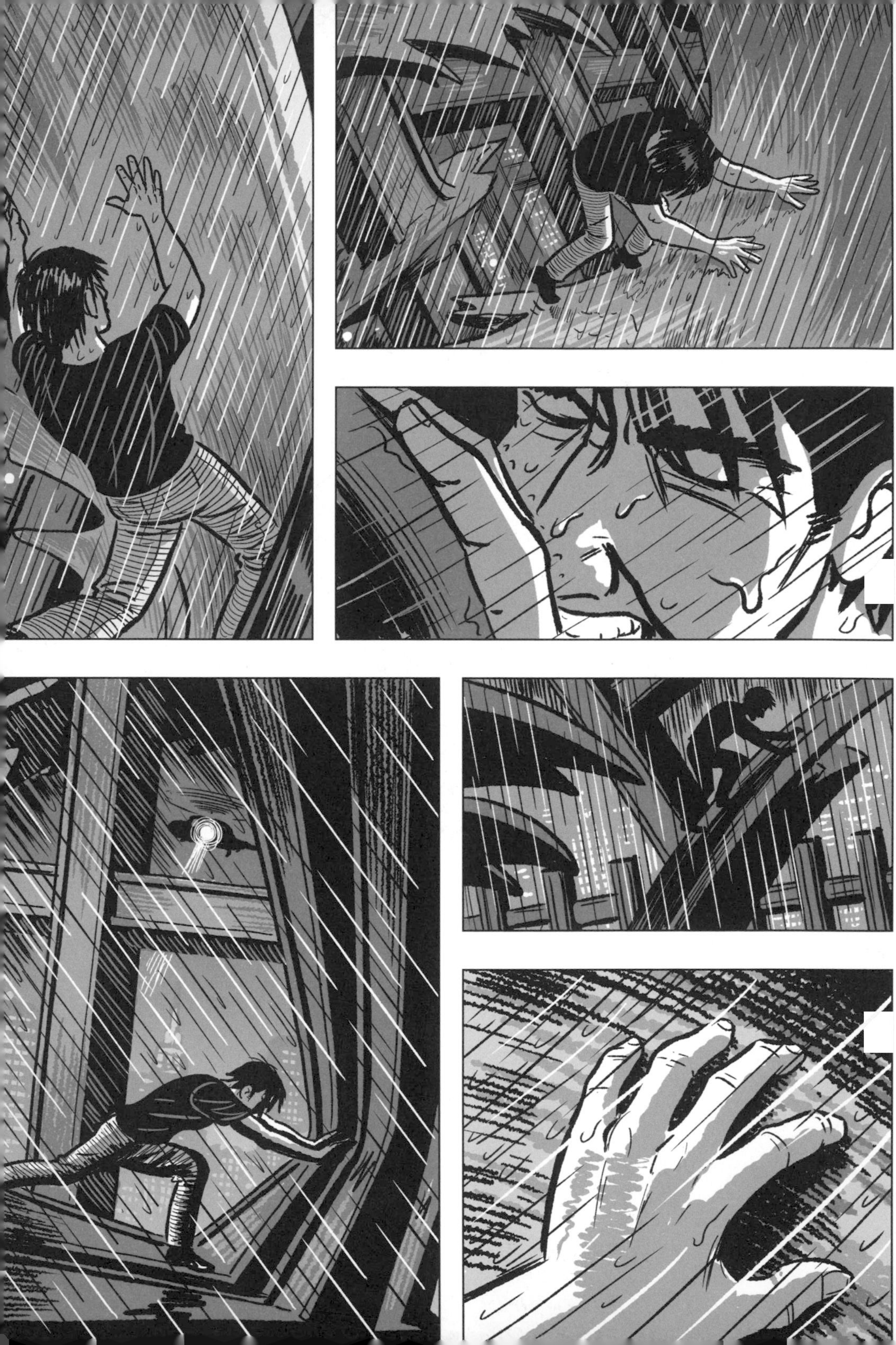

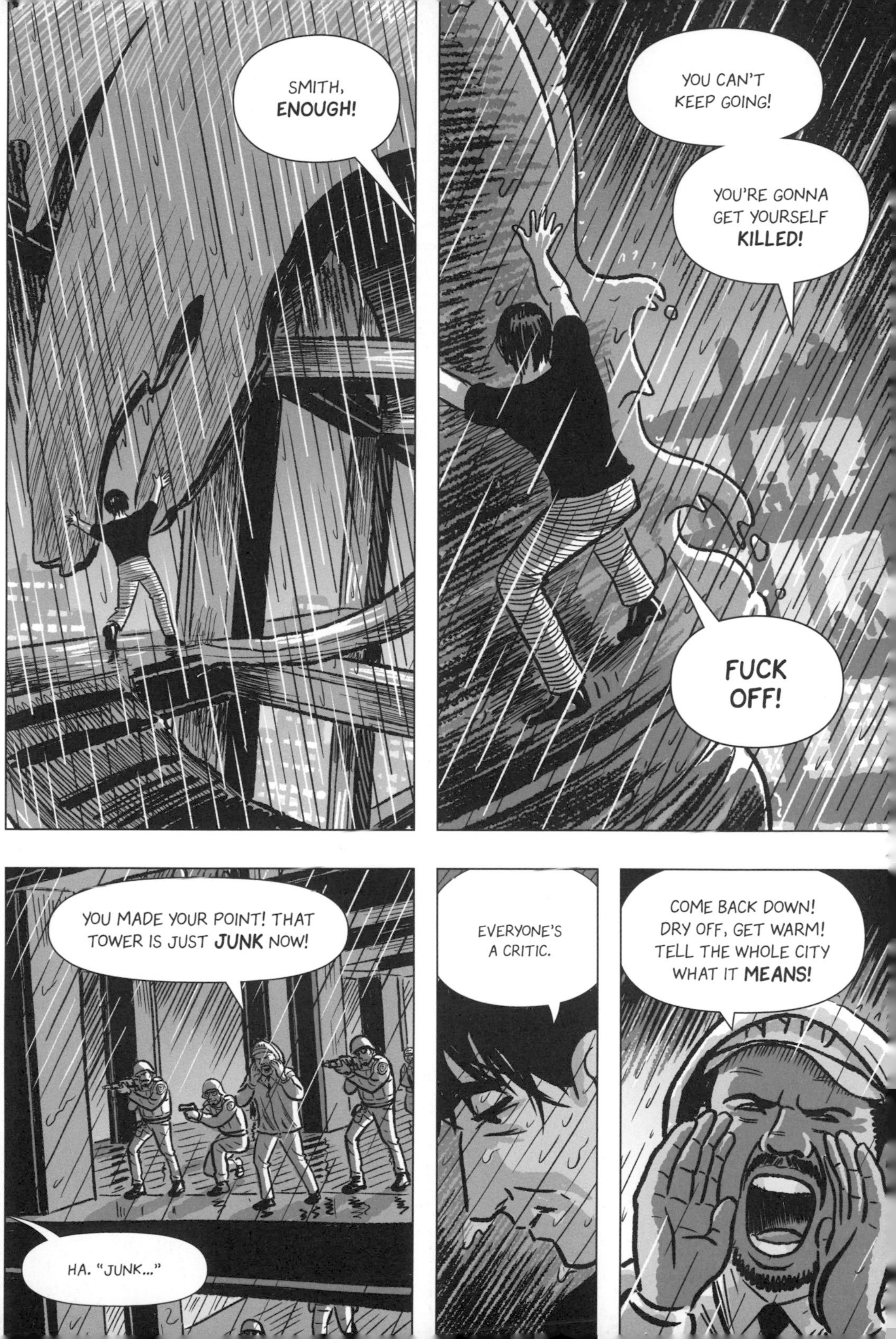
SMITH, ENOUGH!
YOU CAN'T KEEP GOING!
YOU'RE GONNA GET YOURSELF KILLED!
FUCK OFF!
YOU MADE YOUR POINT! THAT TOWER IS JUST JUNK NOW!
HA. "JUNK..."
EVERYONE'S A CRITIC.
COME BACK DOWN! DRY OFF, GET WARM! TELL THE WHOLE CITY WHAT IT MEANS!

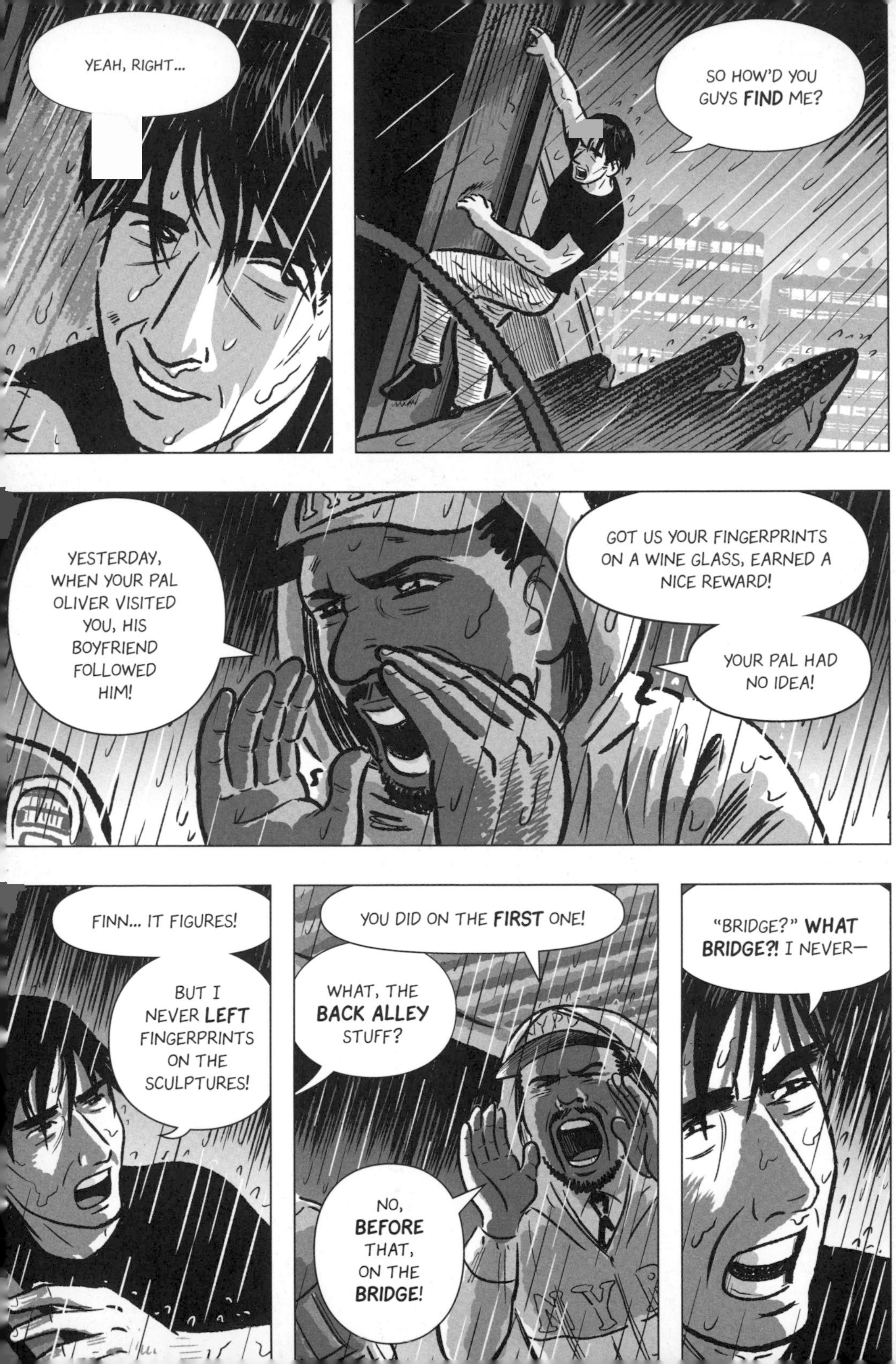
YEAH, RIGHT...
SO HOW'D YOU GUYS **FIND** ME?
YESTERDAY, WHEN YOUR PAL OLIVER VISITED YOU, HIS BOYFRIEND FOLLOWED HIM!
GOT US YOUR FINGERPRINTS ON A WINE GLASS, EARNED A NICE REWARD!
YOUR PAL HAD NO IDEA!
FINN... IT FIGURES!
BUT I NEVER **LEFT** FINGERPRINTS ON THE SCULPTURES!
YOU DID ON THE **FIRST** ONE!
WHAT, THE **BACK ALLEY** STUFF?
NO, **BEFORE** THAT, ON THE **BRIDGE**!
"BRIDGE?" **WHAT BRIDGE?!** I NEVER—

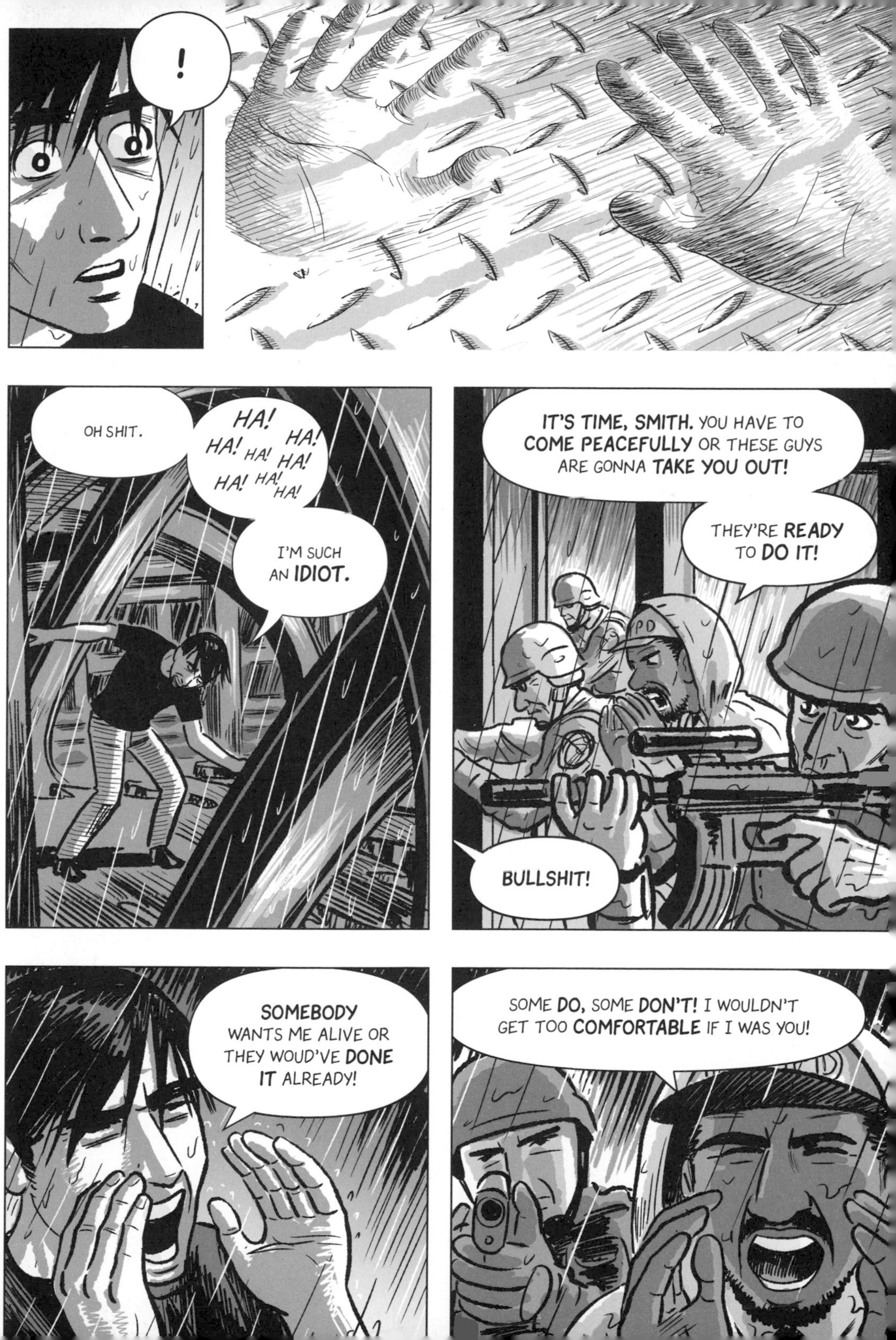
!
OH SHIT.
HA! HA! HA! HA! HA! HA! HA! HA!
I'M SUCH AN IDIOT.
IT'S TIME, SMITH. YOU HAVE TO COME PEACEFULLY OR THESE GUYS ARE GONNA TAKE YOU OUT!
THEY'RE READY TO DO IT!
BULLSHIT!
SOMEBODY WANTS ME ALIVE OR THEY WOUD'VE DONE IT ALREADY!
SOME DO, SOME DON'T! I WOULDN'T GET TOO COMFORTABLE IF I WAS YOU!

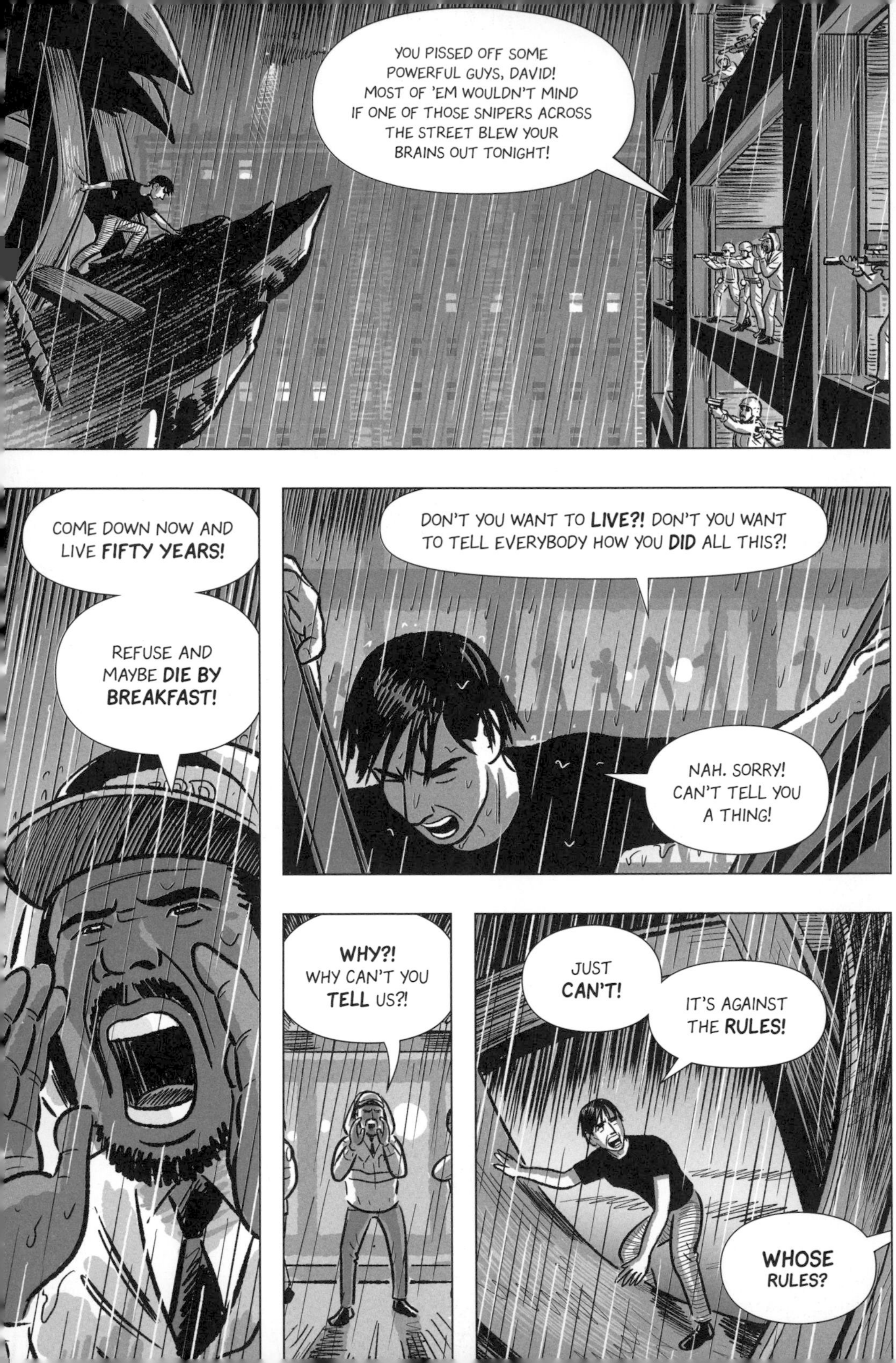
YOU PISSED OFF SOME POWERFUL GUYS, DAVID! MOST OF 'EM WOULDN'T MIND IF ONE OF THOSE SNIPERS ACROSS THE STREET BLEW YOUR BRAINS OUT TONIGHT!
COME DOWN NOW AND LIVE FIFTY YEARS!
REFUSE AND MAYBE DIE BY BREAKFAST!
DON'T YOU WANT TO LIVE?! DON'T YOU WANT TO TELL EVERYBODY HOW YOU DID ALL THIS?!
NAH. SORRY! CAN'T TELL YOU A THING!
WHY?! WHY CAN'T YOU TELL US?!
JUST CAN'T!
IT'S AGAINST THE RULES!
WHOSE RULES?

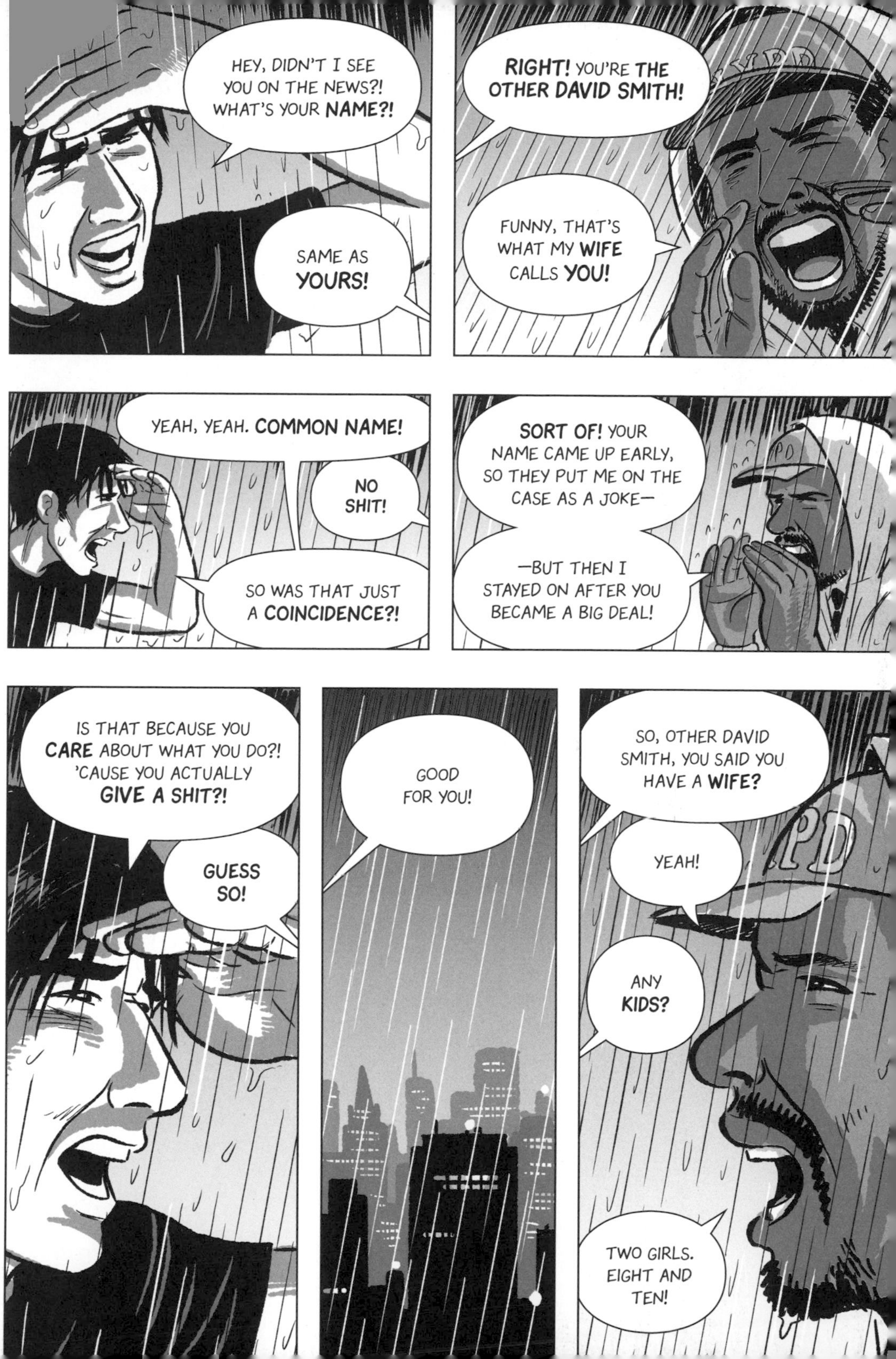
HEY, DIDN'T I SEE YOU ON THE NEWS?! WHAT'S YOUR NAME?!
SAME AS YOURS!
RIGHT! YOU'RE THE OTHER DAVID SMITH!
FUNNY, THAT'S WHAT MY WIFE CALLS YOU!
YEAH, YEAH. COMMON NAME!
NO SHIT!
SO WAS THAT JUST A COINCIDENCE?!
SORT OF! YOUR NAME CAME UP EARLY, SO THEY PUT ME ON THE CASE AS A JOKE—
—BUT THEN I STAYED ON AFTER YOU BECAME A BIG DEAL!
IS THAT BECAUSE YOU CARE ABOUT WHAT YOU DO?! 'CAUSE YOU ACTUALLY GIVE A SHIT?!
GUESS SO!
GOOD FOR YOU!
SO, OTHER DAVID SMITH, YOU SAID YOU HAVE A WIFE?
YEAH!
ANY KIDS?
TWO GIRLS. EIGHT AND TEN!

DO YOU TELL THEM HOW MUCH YOU **LOVE** THEM?

EVERY DAY, 'TIL THEY'RE **SICK** OF ME!

GOOD.

LISTEN, YOU HAVE **FIVE MINUTES** TO GET **OUT** OF HERE!

FIVE MINUTES UNTIL **WHAT?**

UNTIL I START USING THE REST OF MY **METAL.**

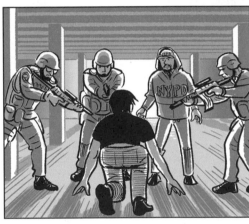

ALL RIGHT, **MOVE IT!**

EVERYBODY **OUT!**

NOW! **NOW!!**

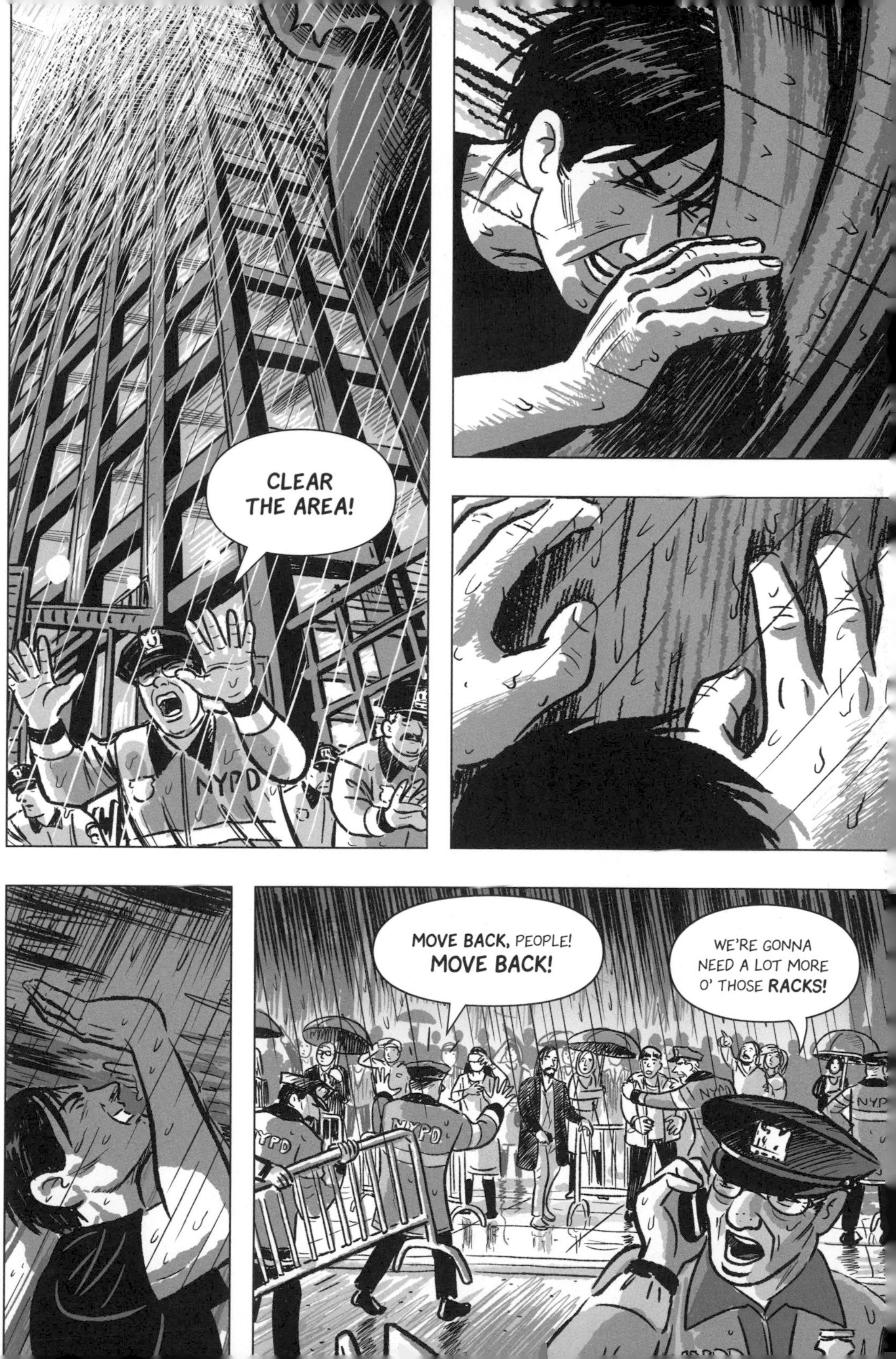
CLEAR THE AREA!
NYPD
NYPD
MOVE BACK, PEOPLE! MOVE BACK!
WE'RE GONNA NEED A LOT MORE O' THOSE RACKS!

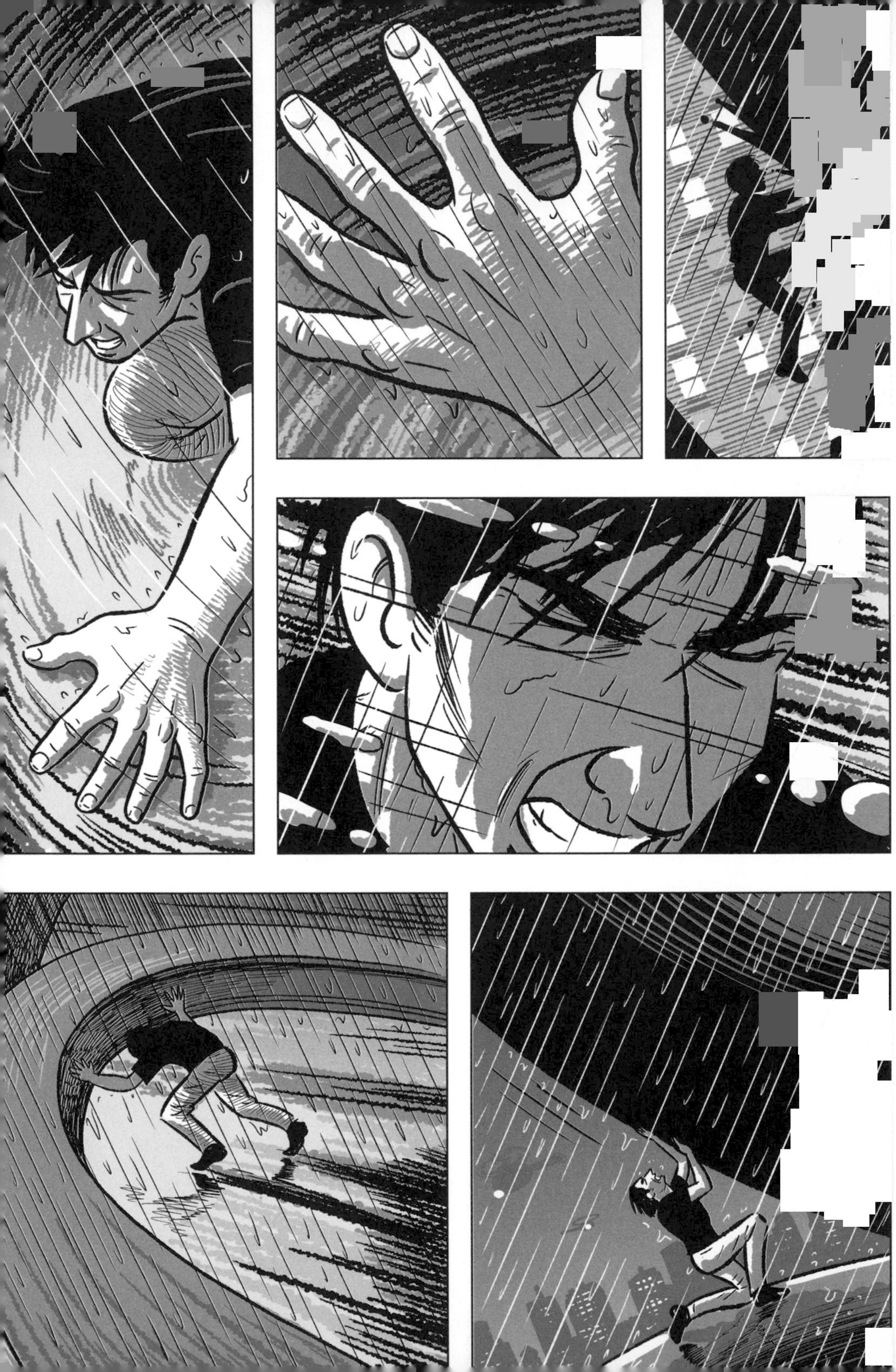

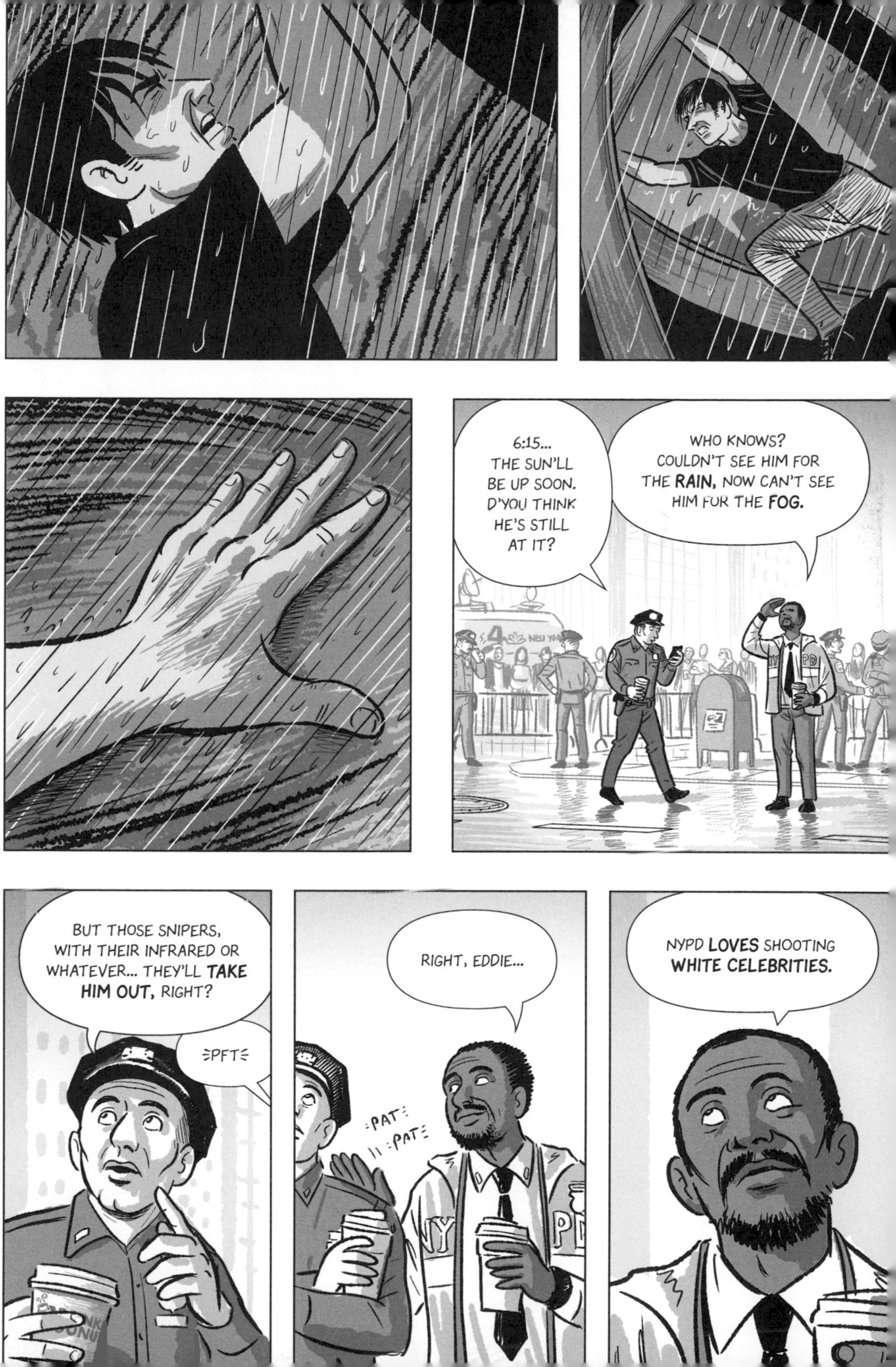
6:15... THE SUN'LL BE UP SOON. D'YOU THINK HE'S STILL AT IT?
WHO KNOWS? COULDN'T SEE HIM FOR THE RAIN, NOW CAN'T SEE HIM FOR THE FOG.
BUT THOSE SNIPERS, WITH THEIR INFRARED OR WHATEVER... THEY'LL TAKE HIM OUT, RIGHT?
PFT
RIGHT, EDDIE...
PAT
PAT
NYPD LOVES SHOOTING WHITE CELEBRITIES.

WELL... THE GUY'S STILL FORTY STORIES UP ON SLIPPERY METAL—

—RIGHT IN THE SIGHTS OF THREE DOZEN GUYS WITH ITCHY TRIGGER FINGERS—

—WHO'VE BEEN AWAKE TEN HOURS STRAIGHT, DRINKING GALLONS OF RED BULL...

HE'S NOT OUT OF THE WOODS YET.

NAAH... NOBODY'S GOING TO MAKE THAT CALL. NOBODY WANTS THE HASSLE.

SO... YOU FIGURE HE'S **SAFE?**

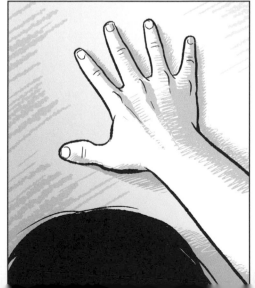

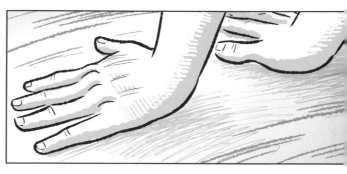

BANG!

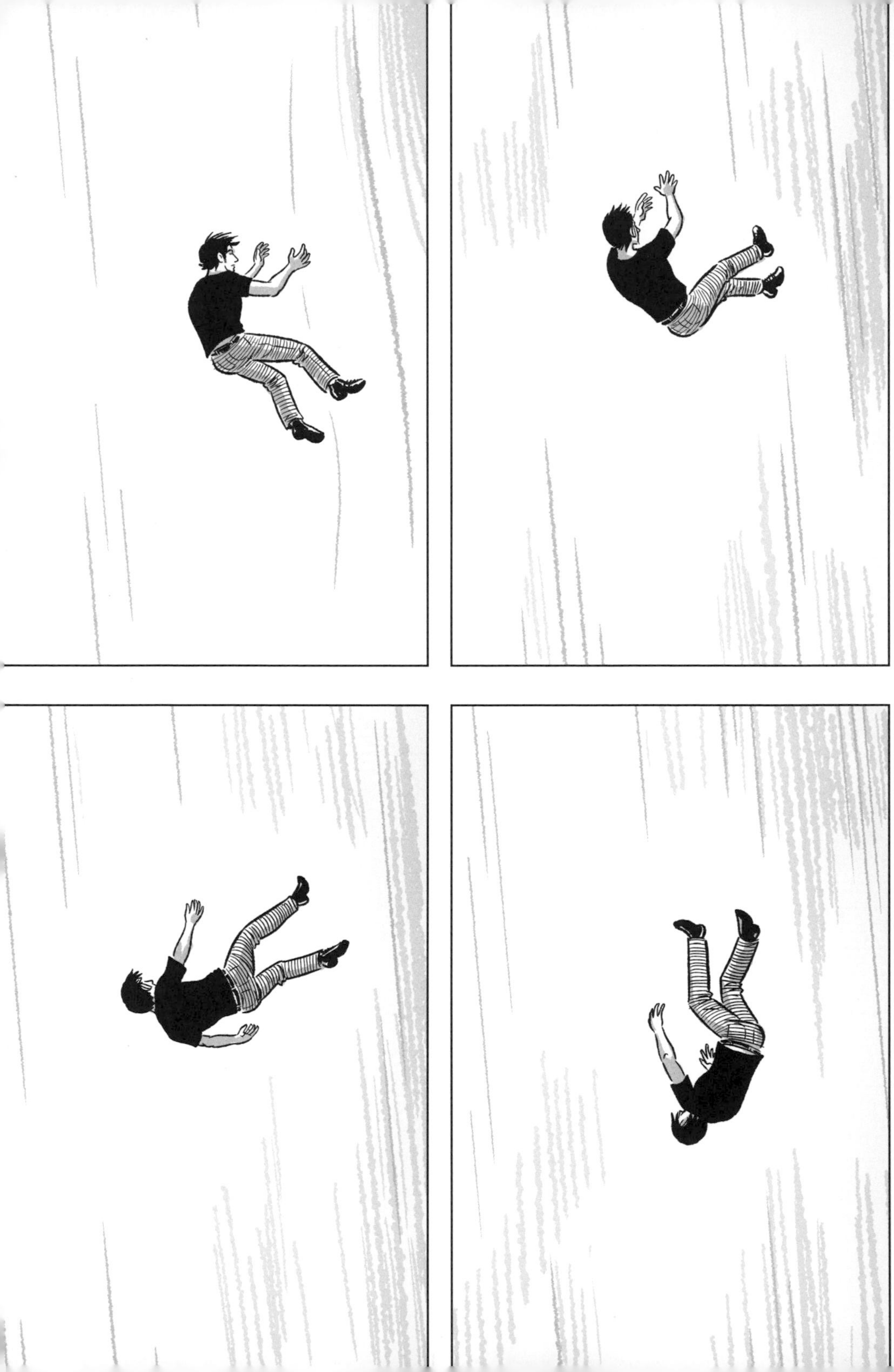

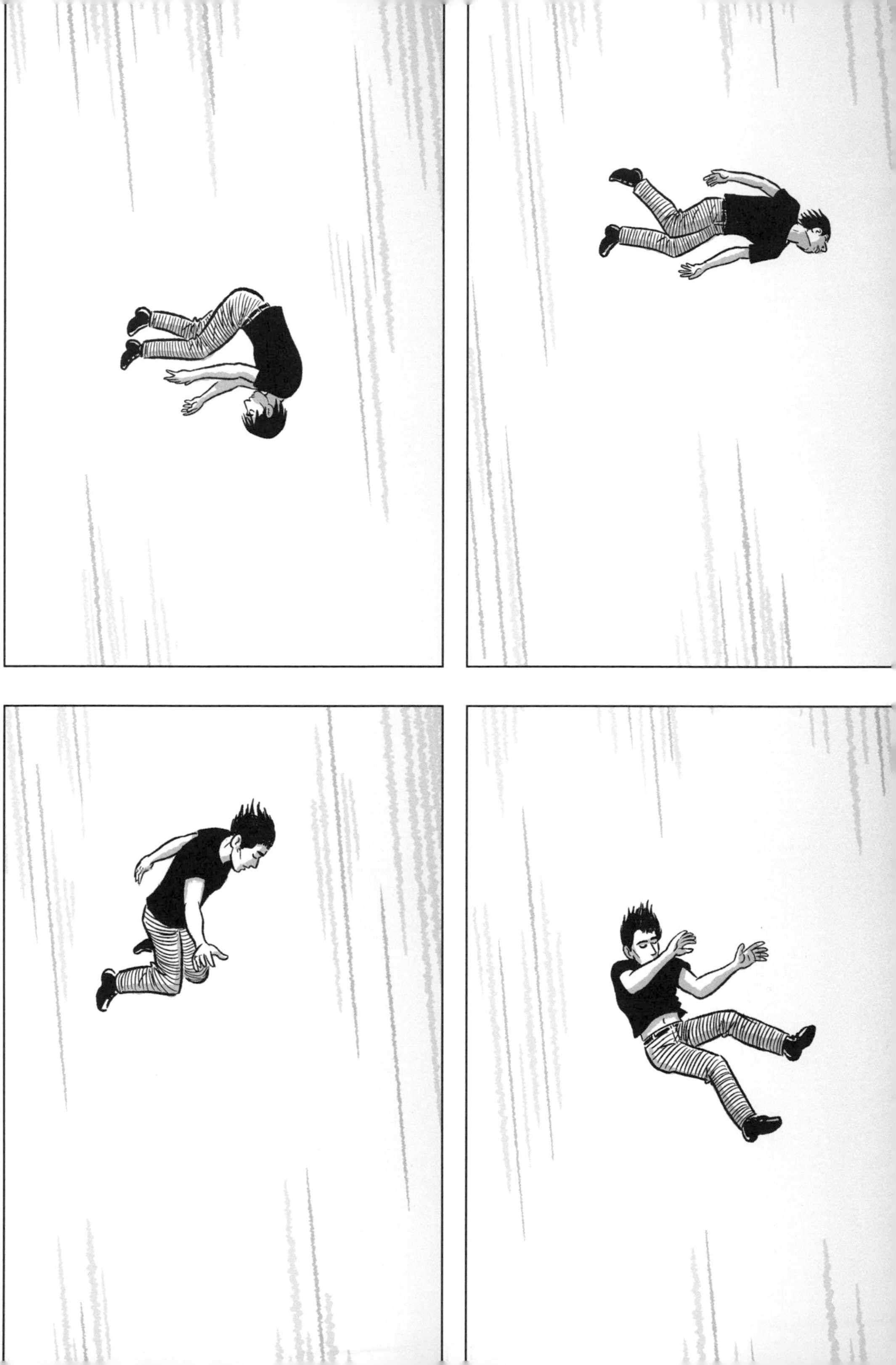

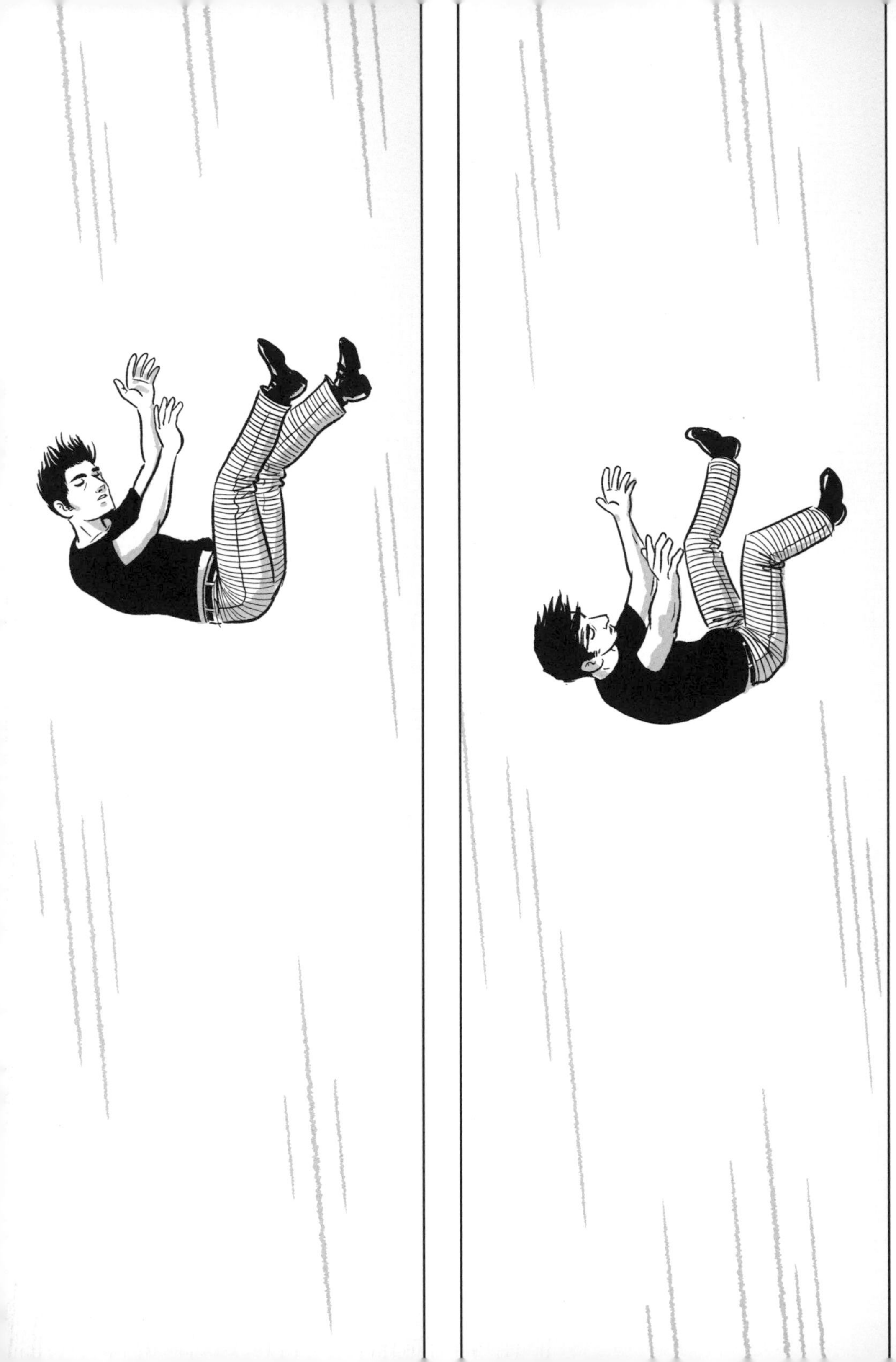

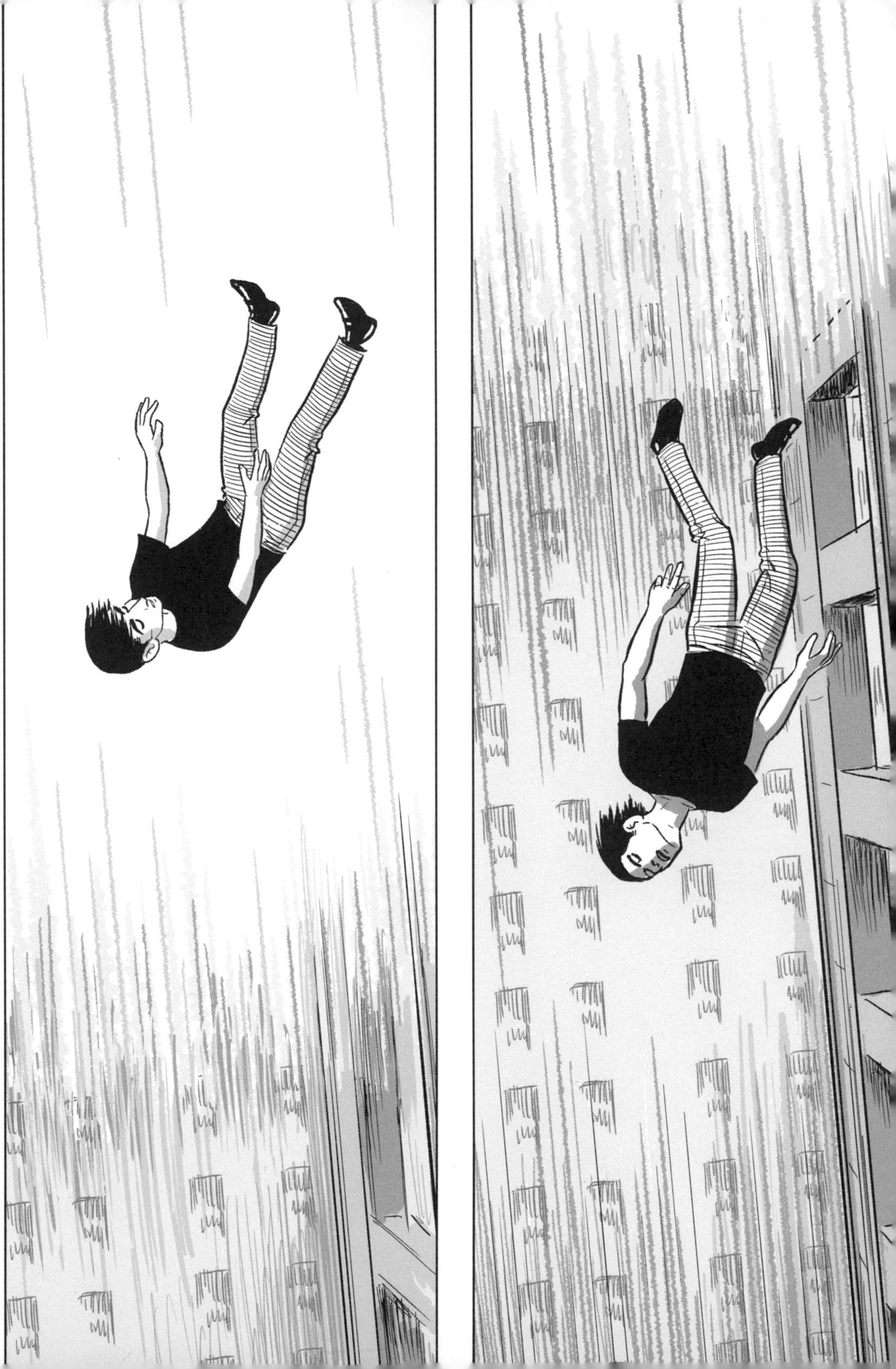

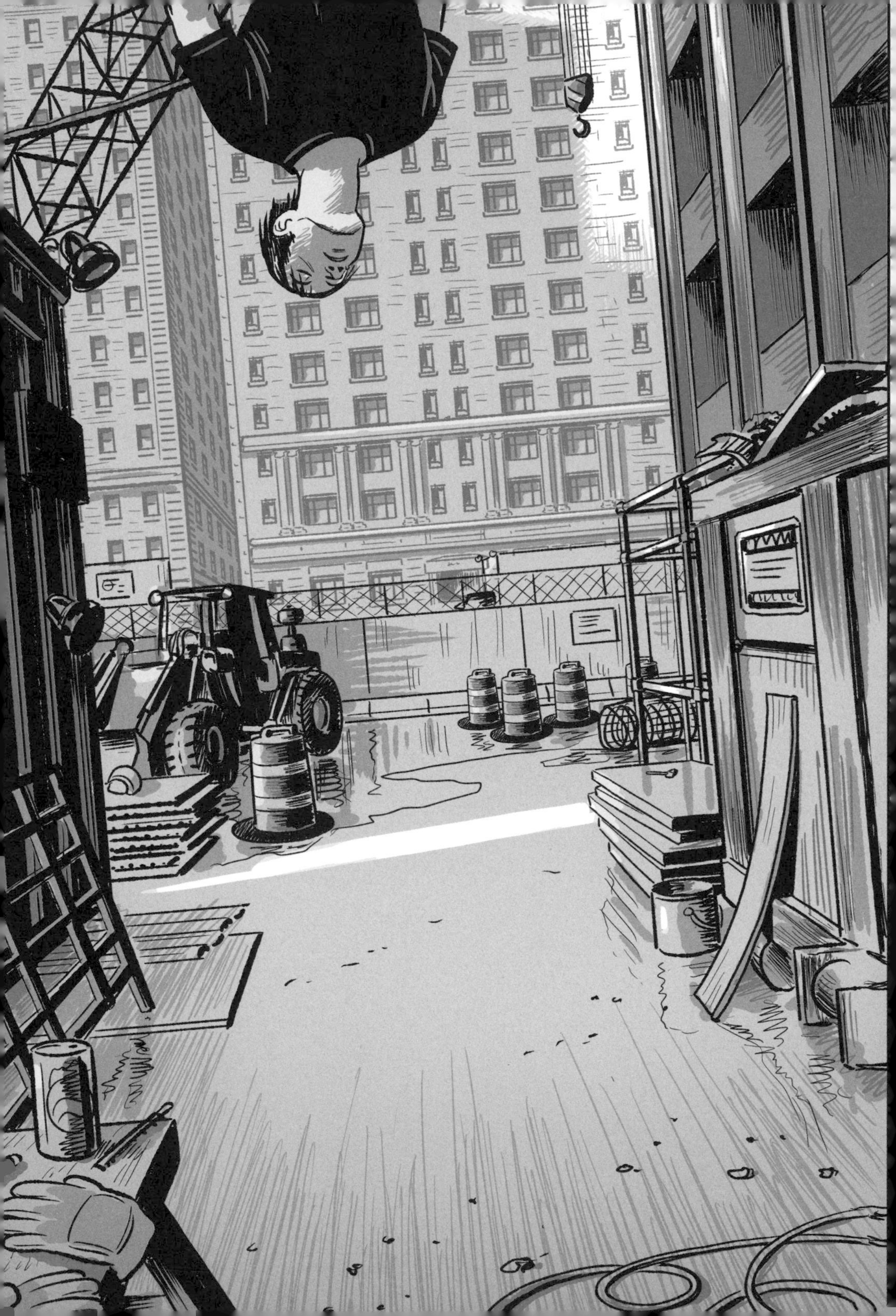

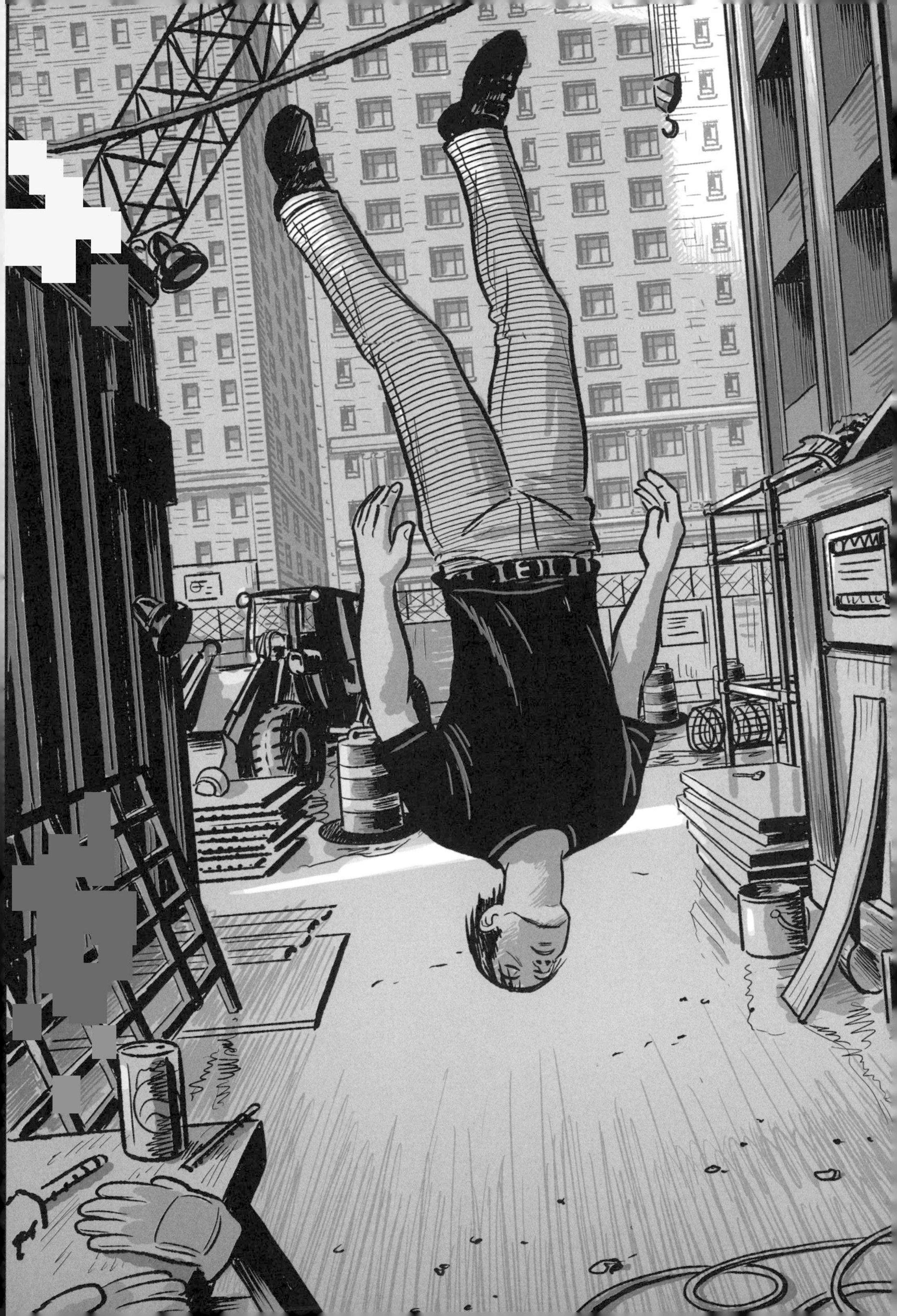

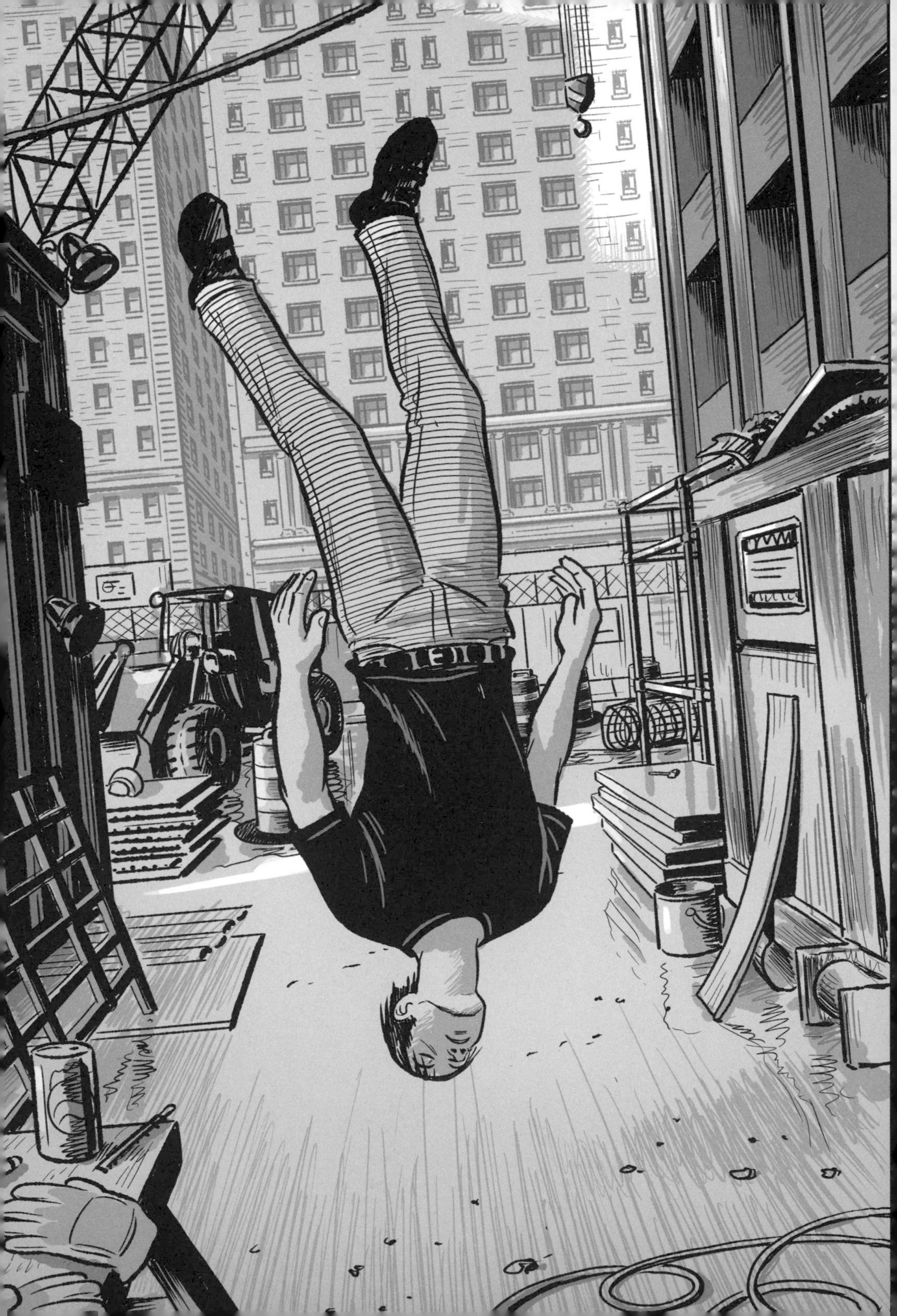

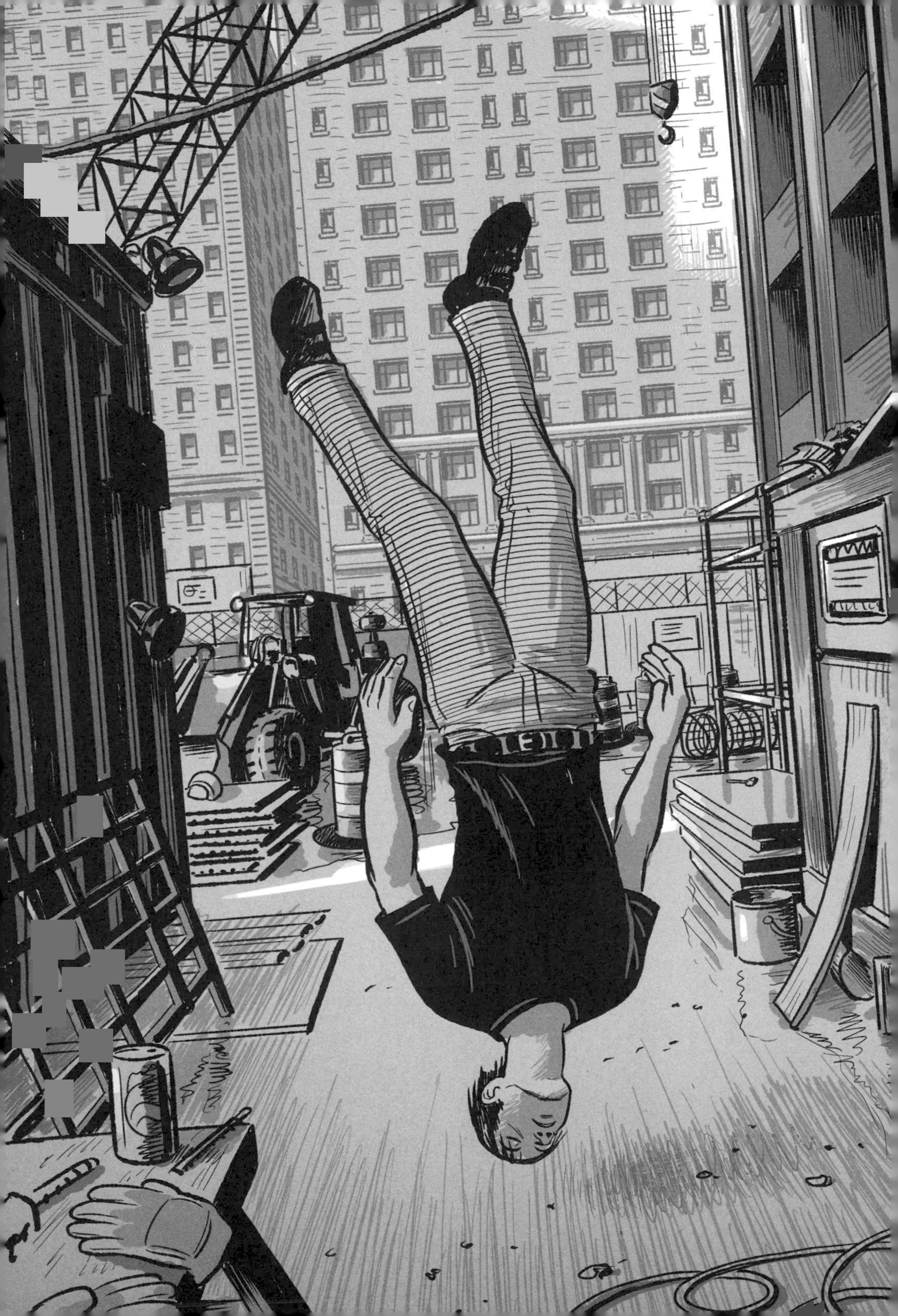

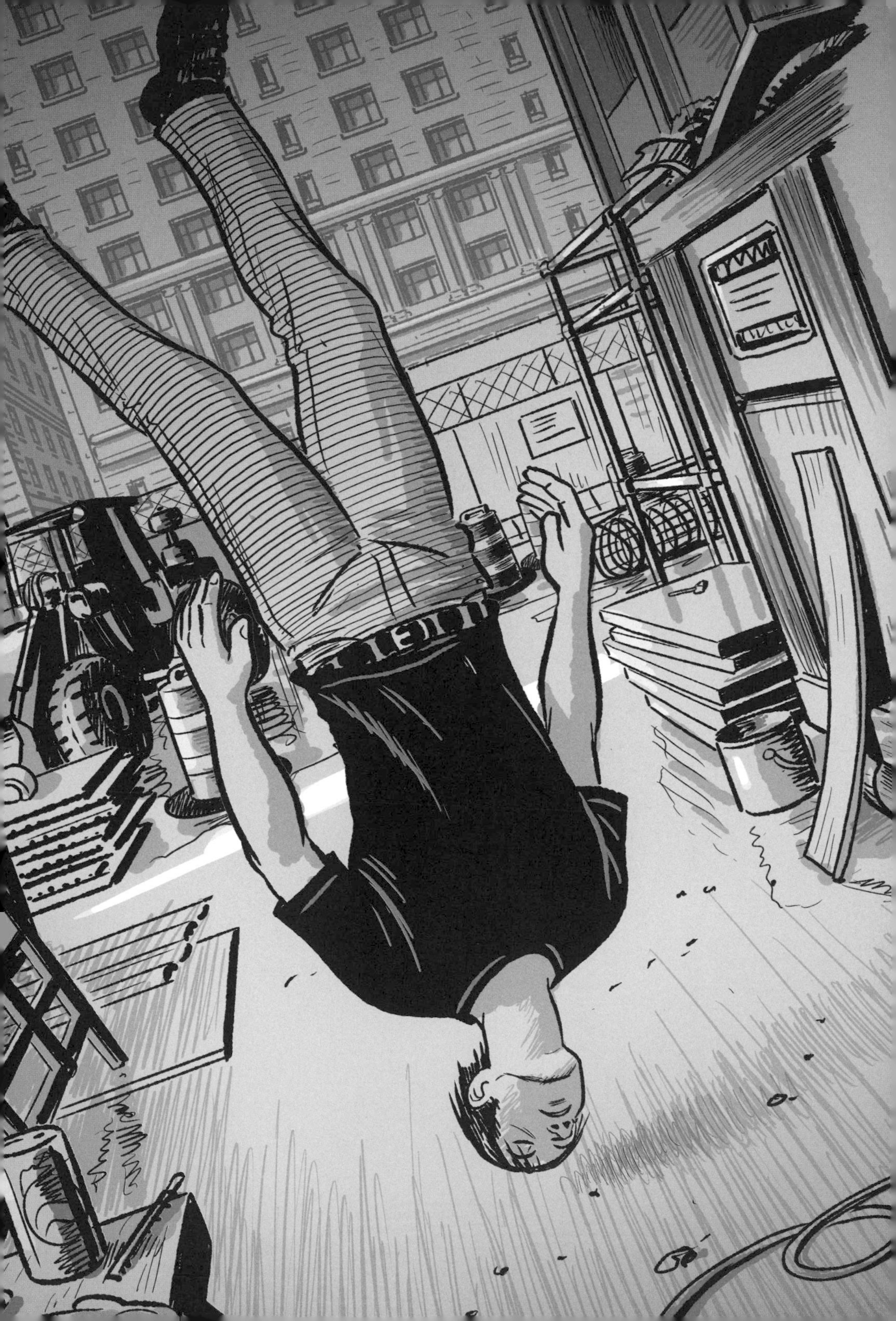

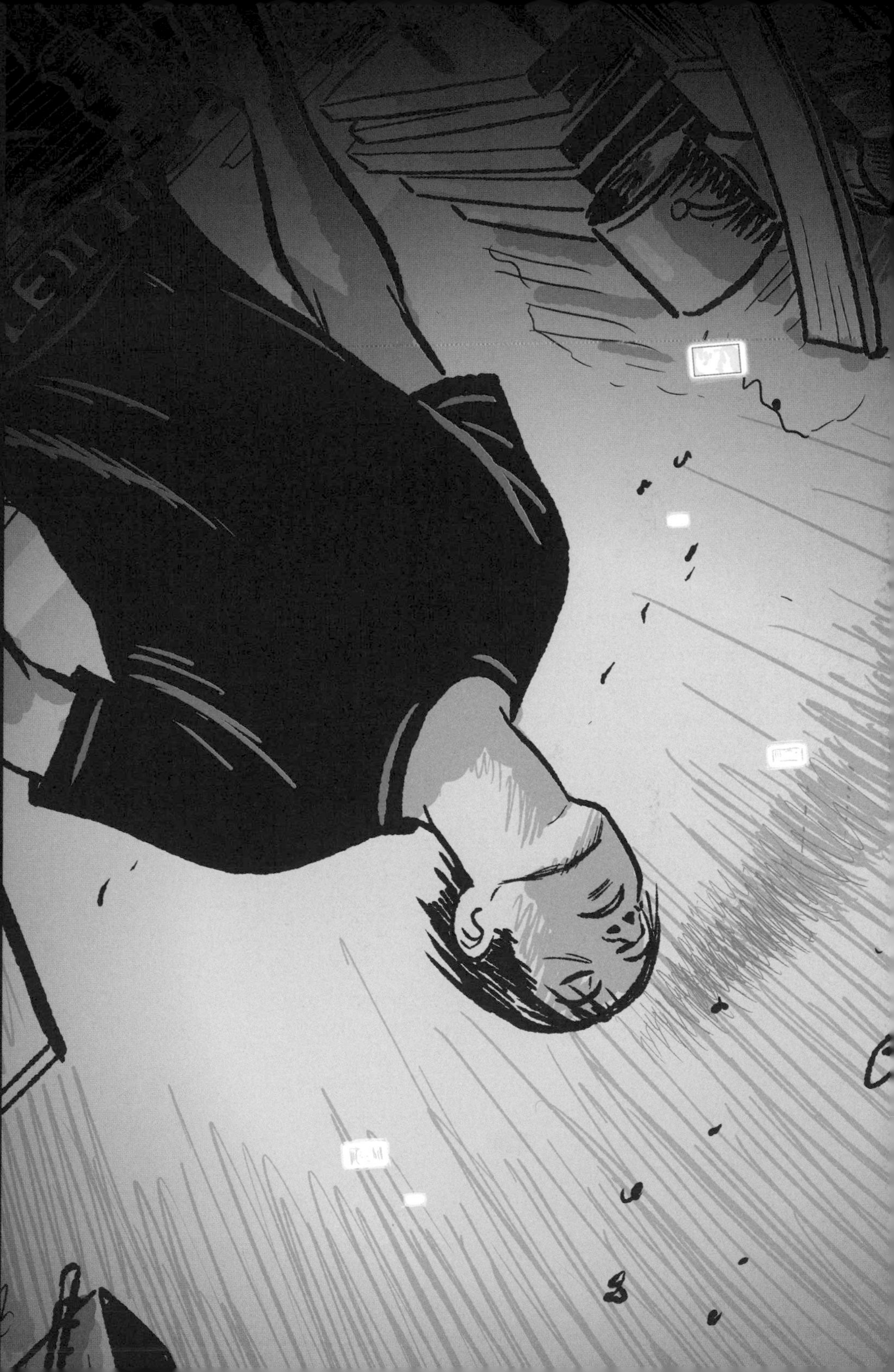

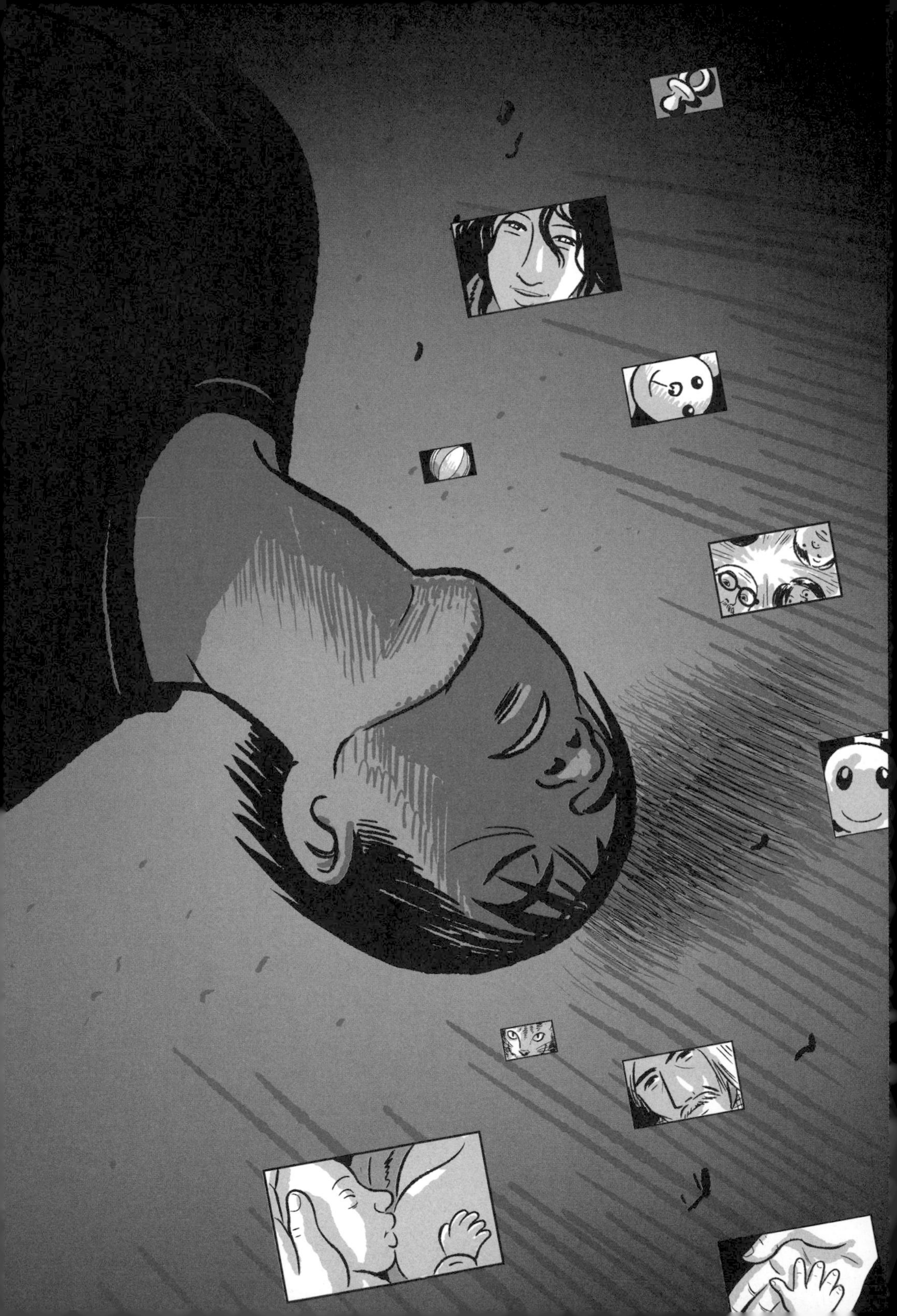

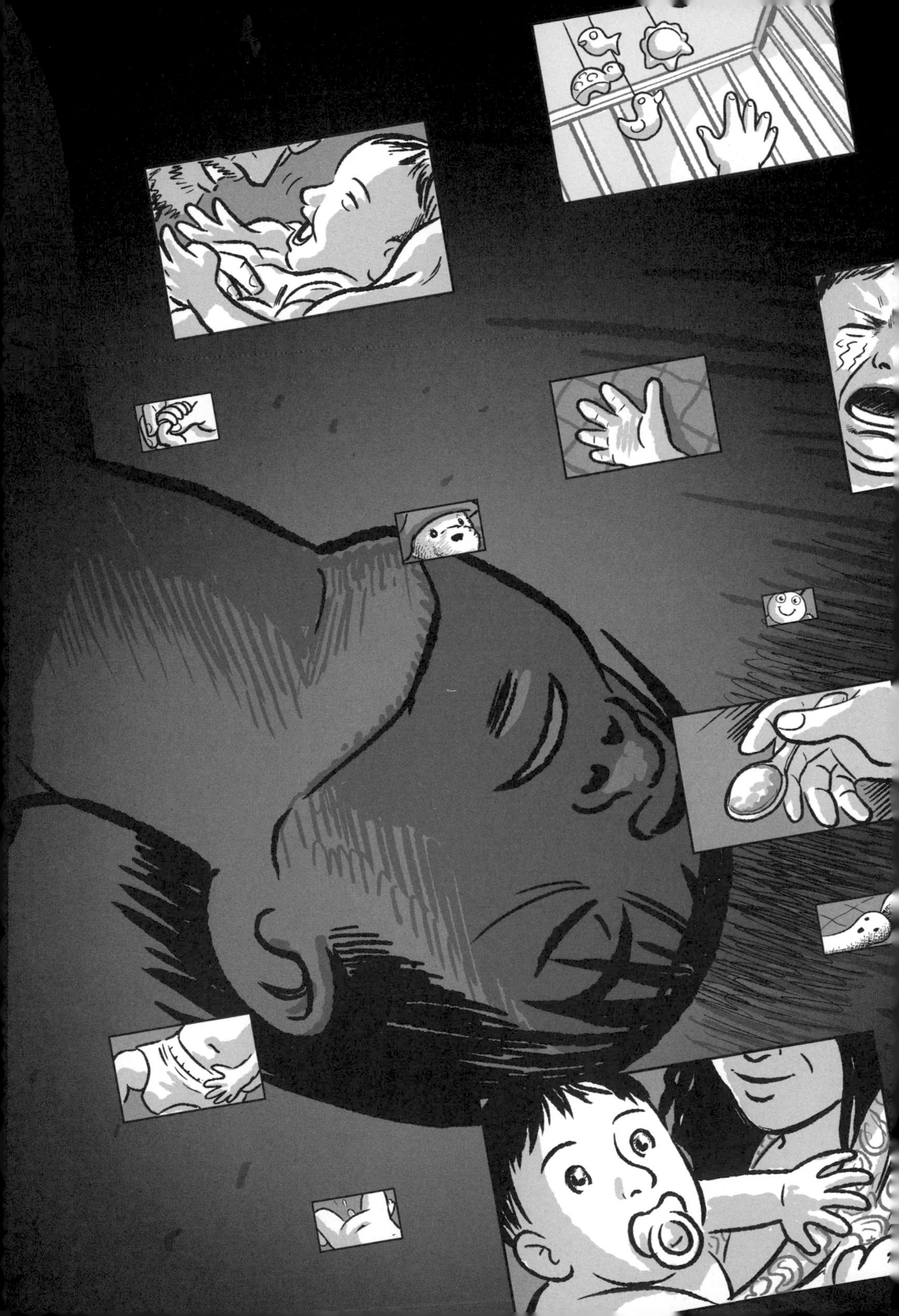

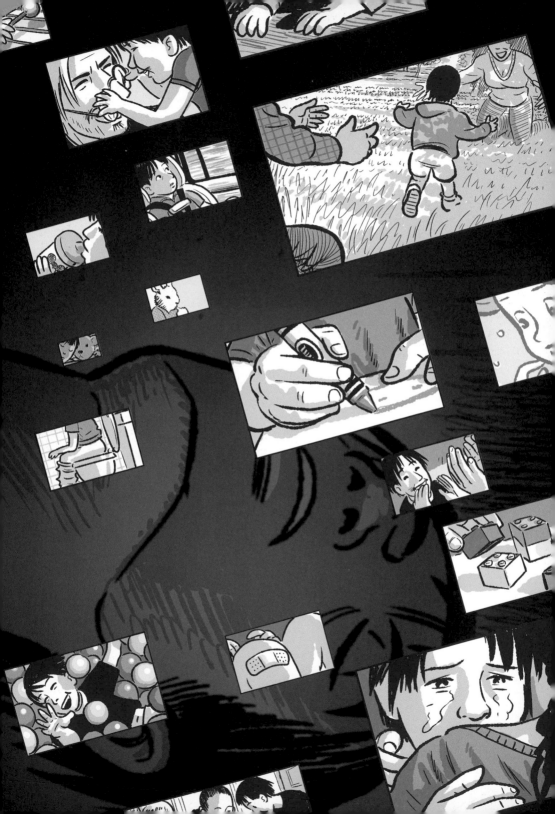

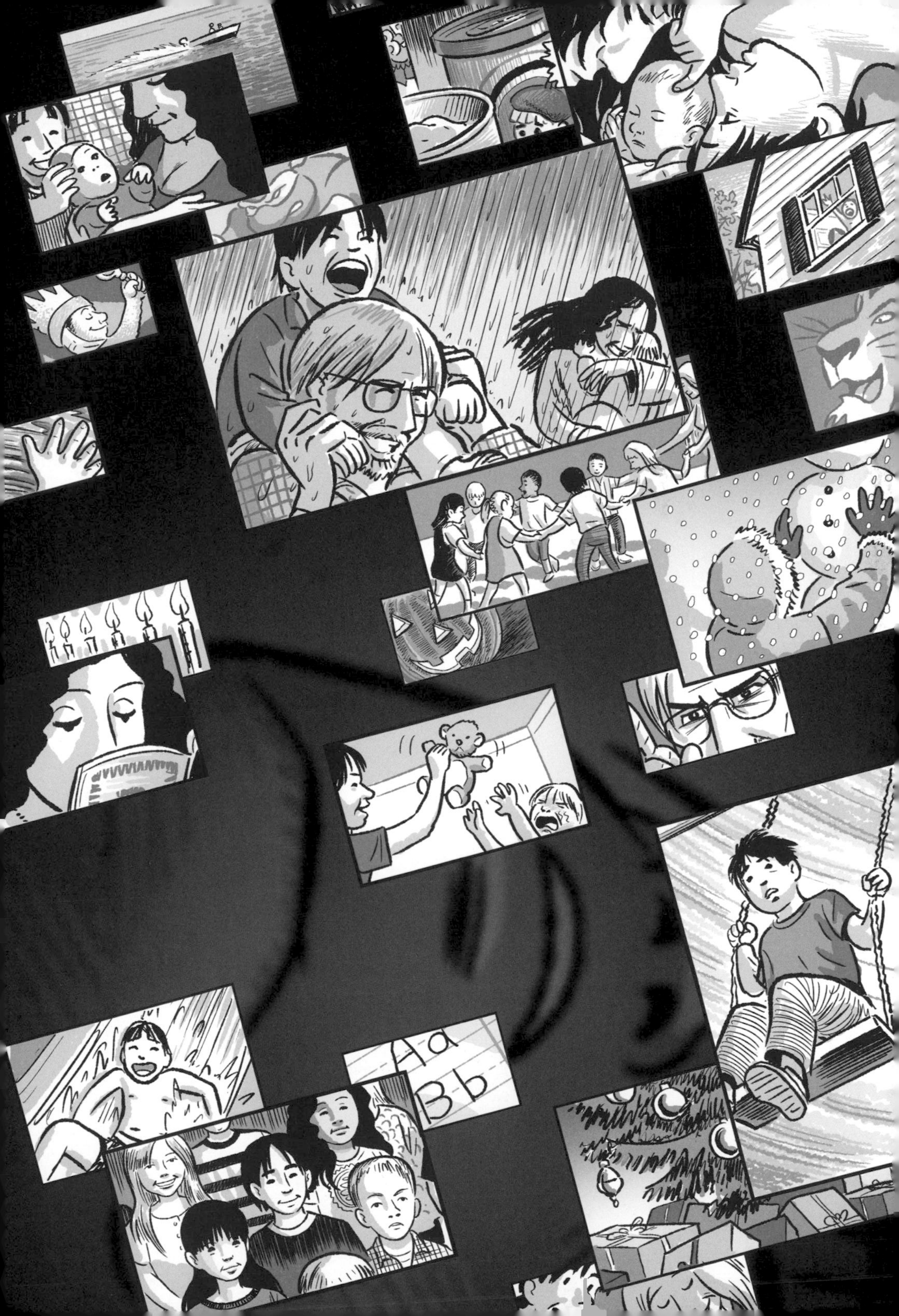
Aa
Bb

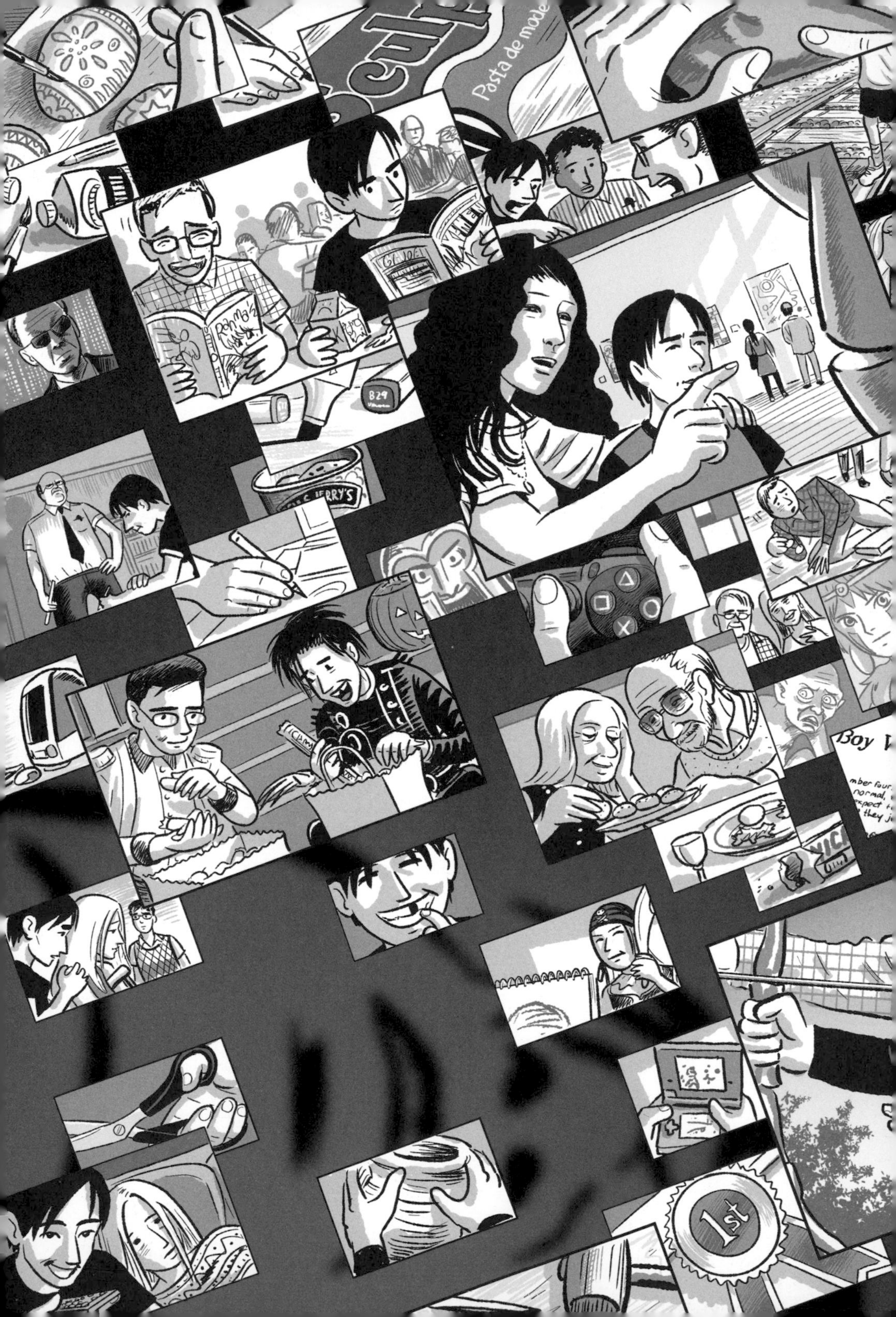
Pasta de mode
1st

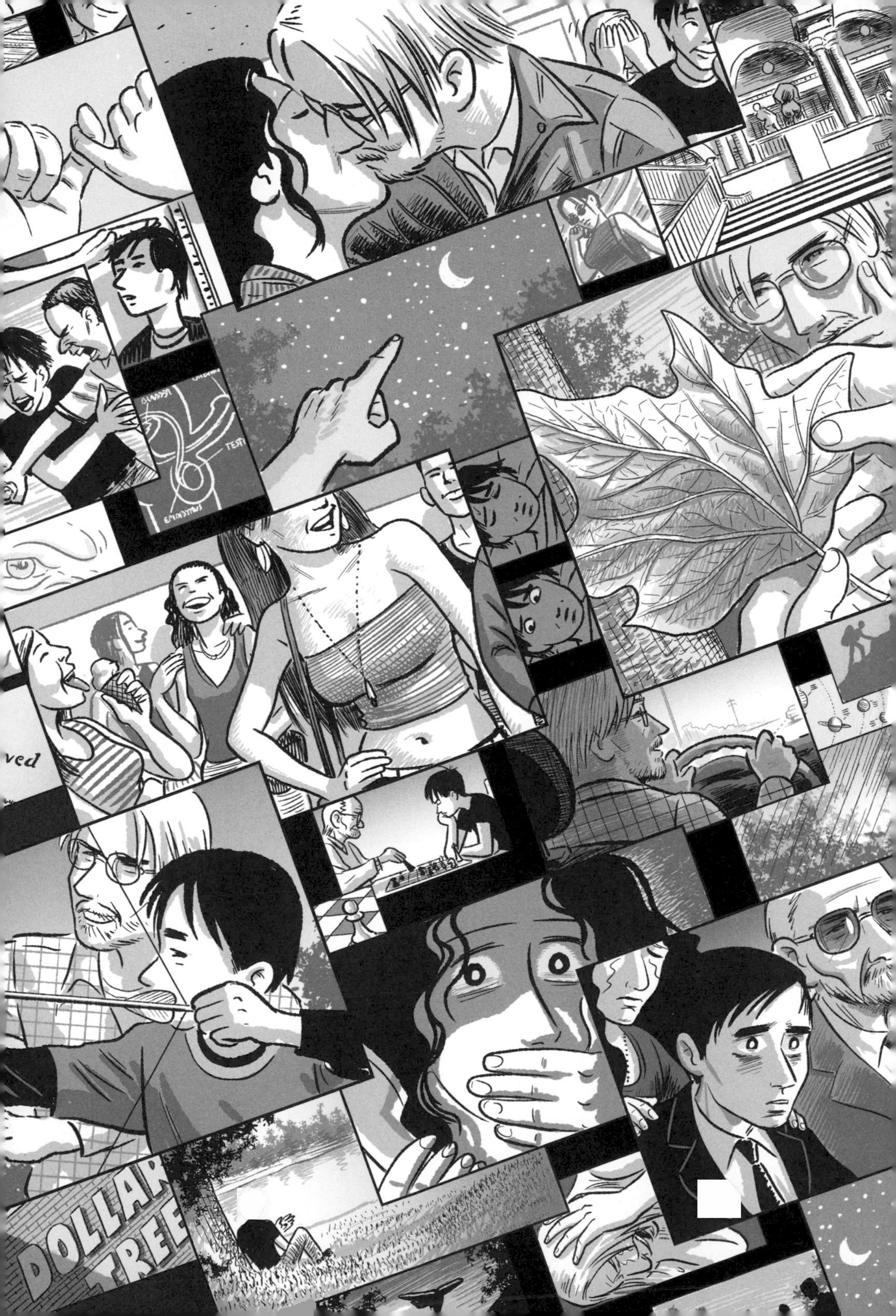
ved
DOLLAR
TREE

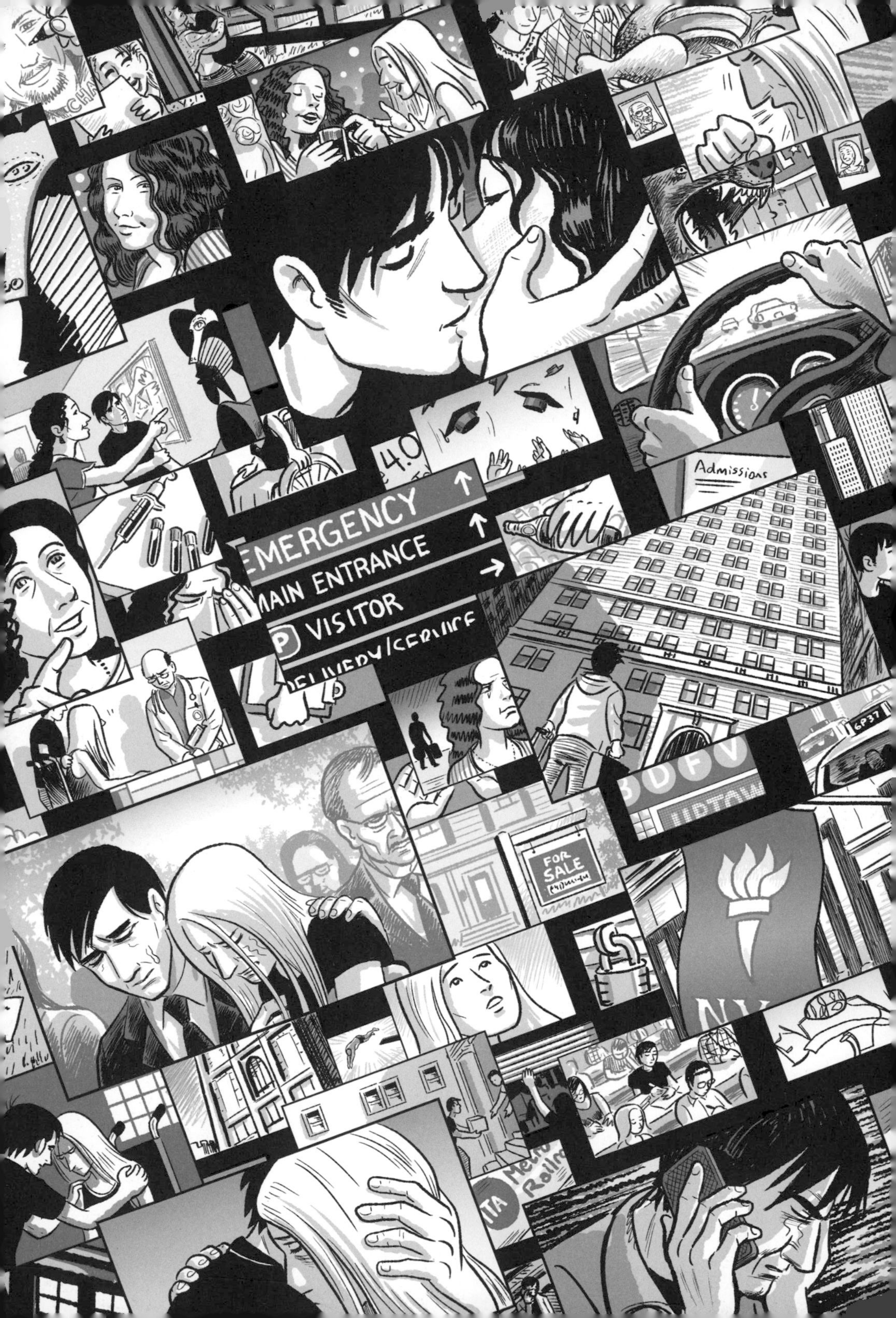
EMERGENCY
VISITOR
Admissions
FOR SALE

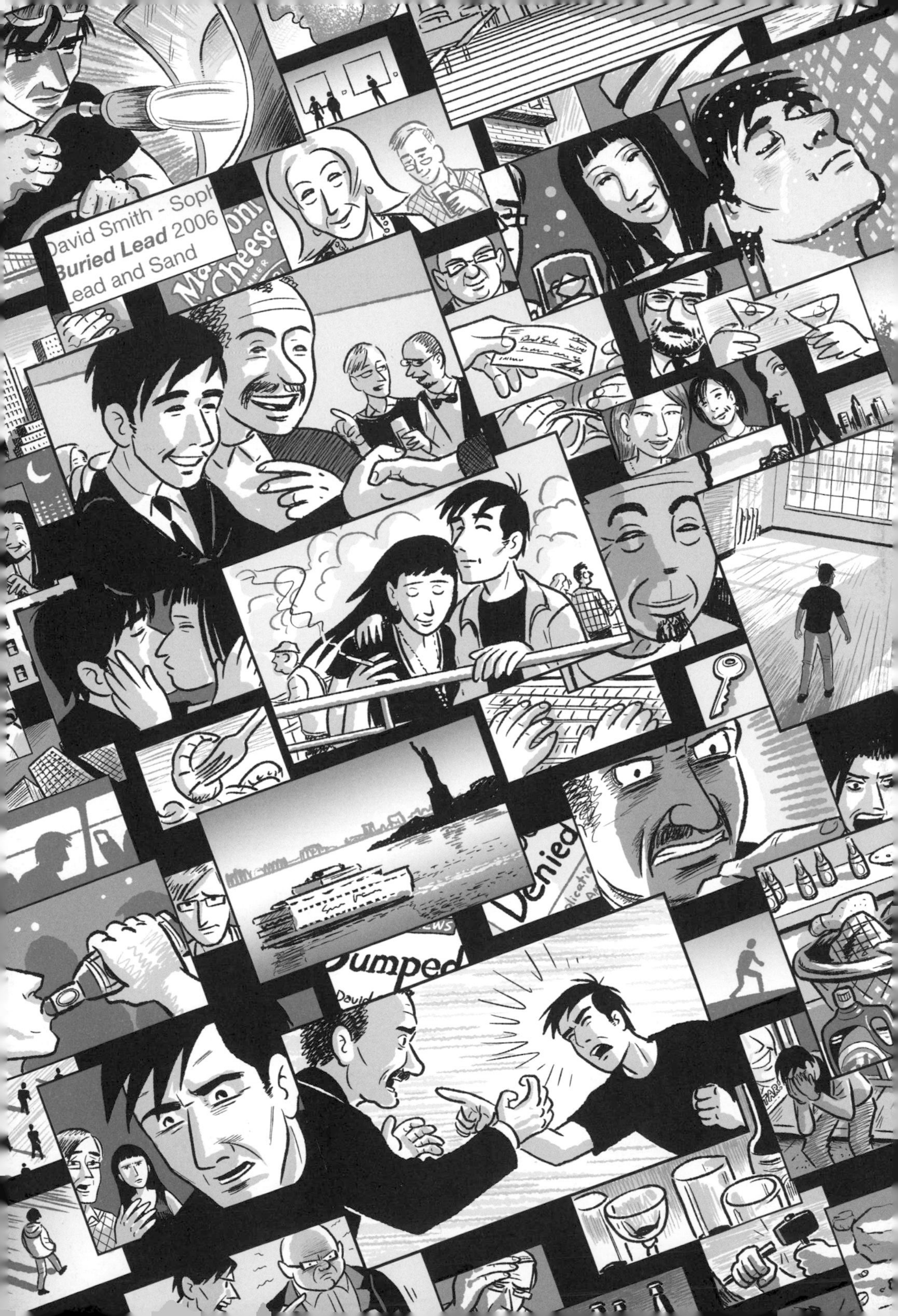

David Smith - Soph
Buried Lead 2006
Lead and Sand
Denied
Dumped

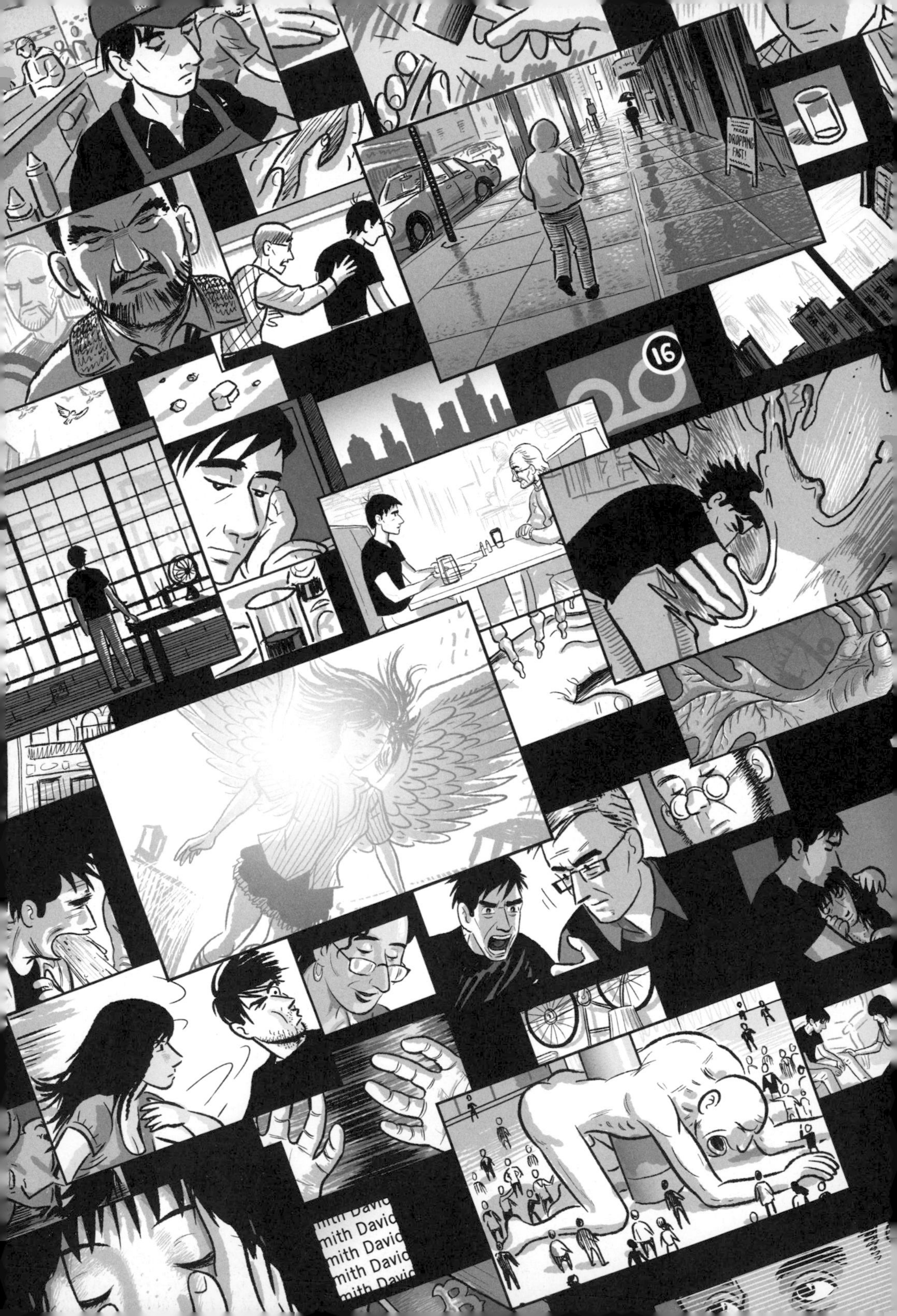
PRICES
DROPPING
FAST!
16
mith David
mith David
mith David
mith David
mith David

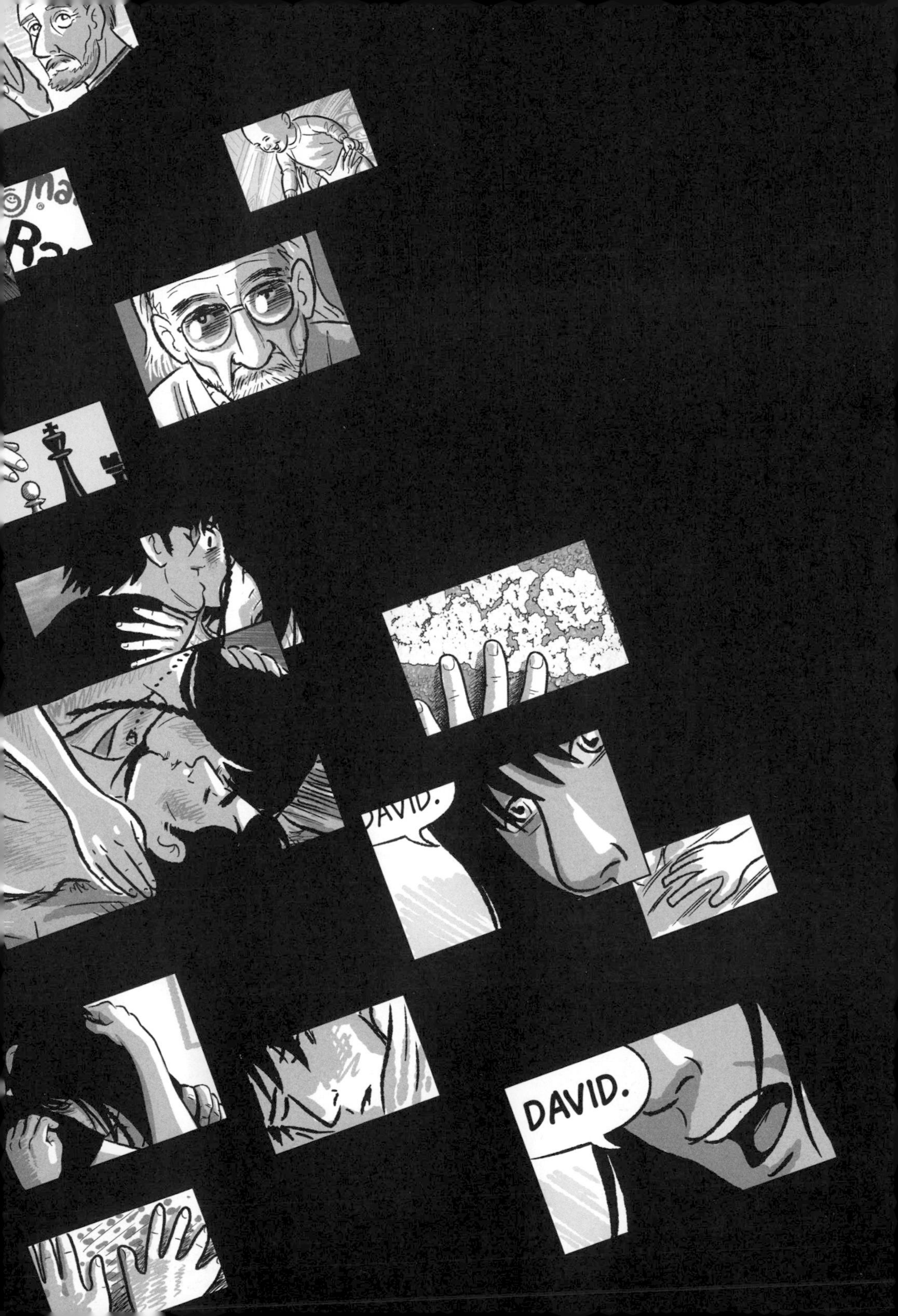
DAVID.
DAVID.

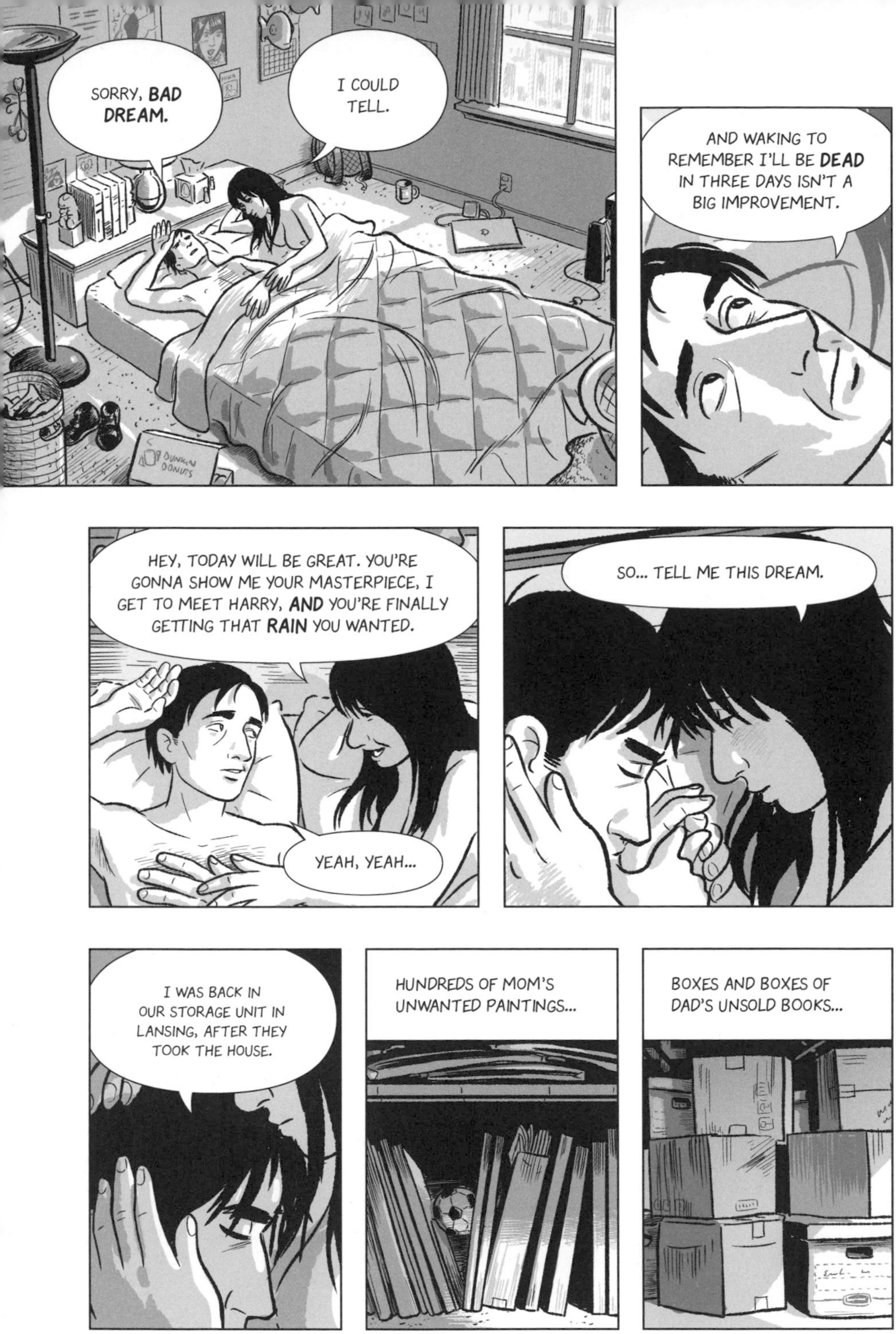
SORRY, BAD DREAM.
I COULD TELL.
DUNKIN DONUTS
AND WAKING TO REMEMBER I'LL BE DEAD IN THREE DAYS ISN'T A BIG IMPROVEMENT.
HEY, TODAY WILL BE GREAT. YOU'RE GONNA SHOW ME YOUR MASTERPIECE, I GET TO MEET HARRY, AND YOU'RE FINALLY GETTING THAT RAIN YOU WANTED.
YEAH, YEAH...
SO... TELL ME THIS DREAM.
I WAS BACK IN OUR STORAGE UNIT IN LANSING, AFTER THEY TOOK THE HOUSE.
HUNDREDS OF MOM'S UNWANTED PAINTINGS...
BOXES AND BOXES OF DAD'S UNSOLD BOOKS...

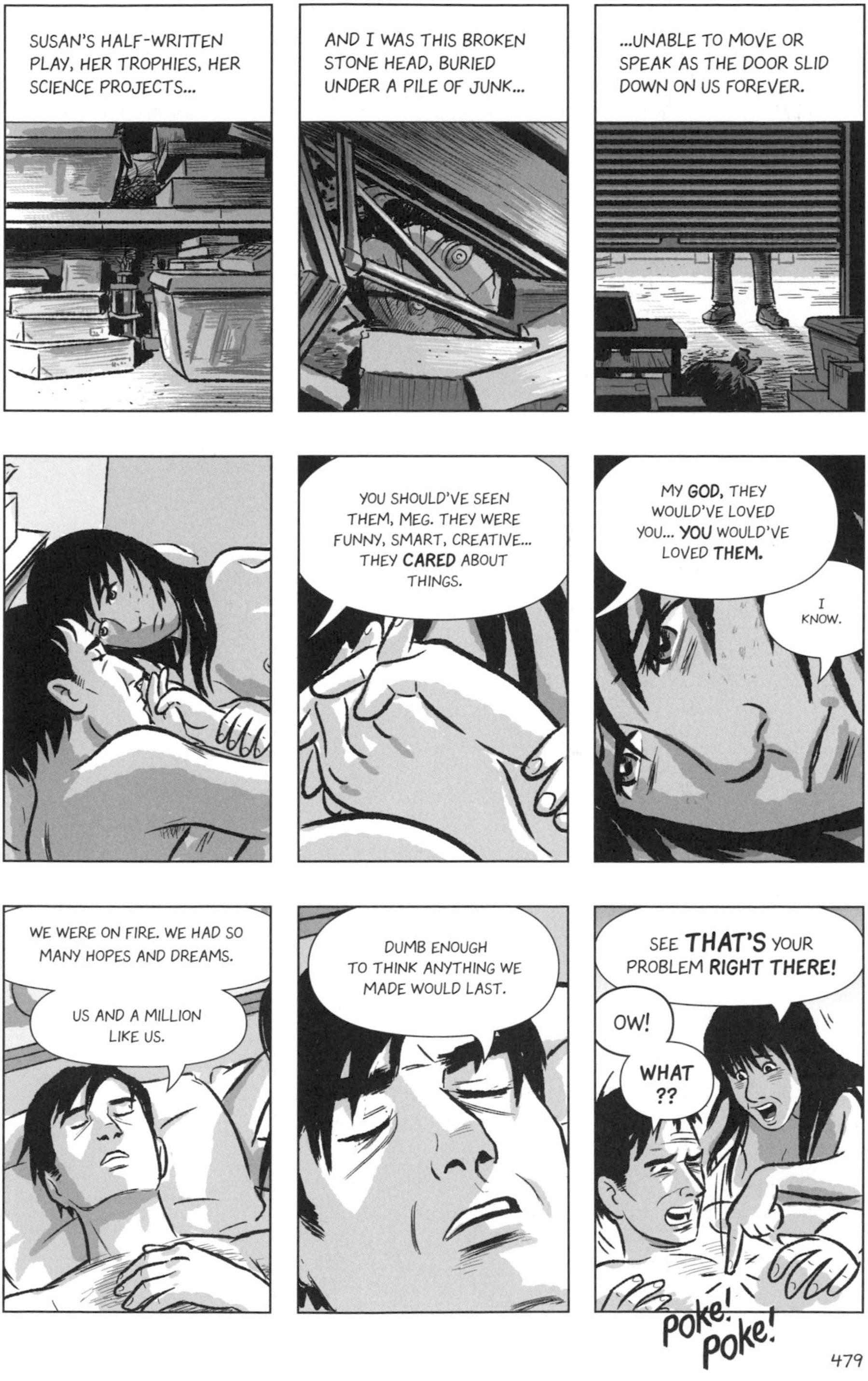
SUSAN'S HALF-WRITTEN PLAY, HER TROPHIES, HER SCIENCE PROJECTS...
AND I WAS THIS BROKEN STONE HEAD, BURIED UNDER A PILE OF JUNK...
...UNABLE TO MOVE OR SPEAK AS THE DOOR SLID DOWN ON US FOREVER.
YOU SHOULD'VE SEEN THEM, MEG. THEY WERE FUNNY, SMART, CREATIVE... THEY CARED ABOUT THINGS.
MY GOD, THEY WOULD'VE LOVED YOU... YOU WOULD'VE LOVED THEM.
I KNOW.
WE WERE ON FIRE. WE HAD SO MANY HOPES AND DREAMS.
US AND A MILLION LIKE US.
DUMB ENOUGH TO THINK ANYTHING WE MADE WOULD LAST.
SEE THAT'S YOUR PROBLEM RIGHT THERE!
OW!
WHAT ??
Poke! Poke!

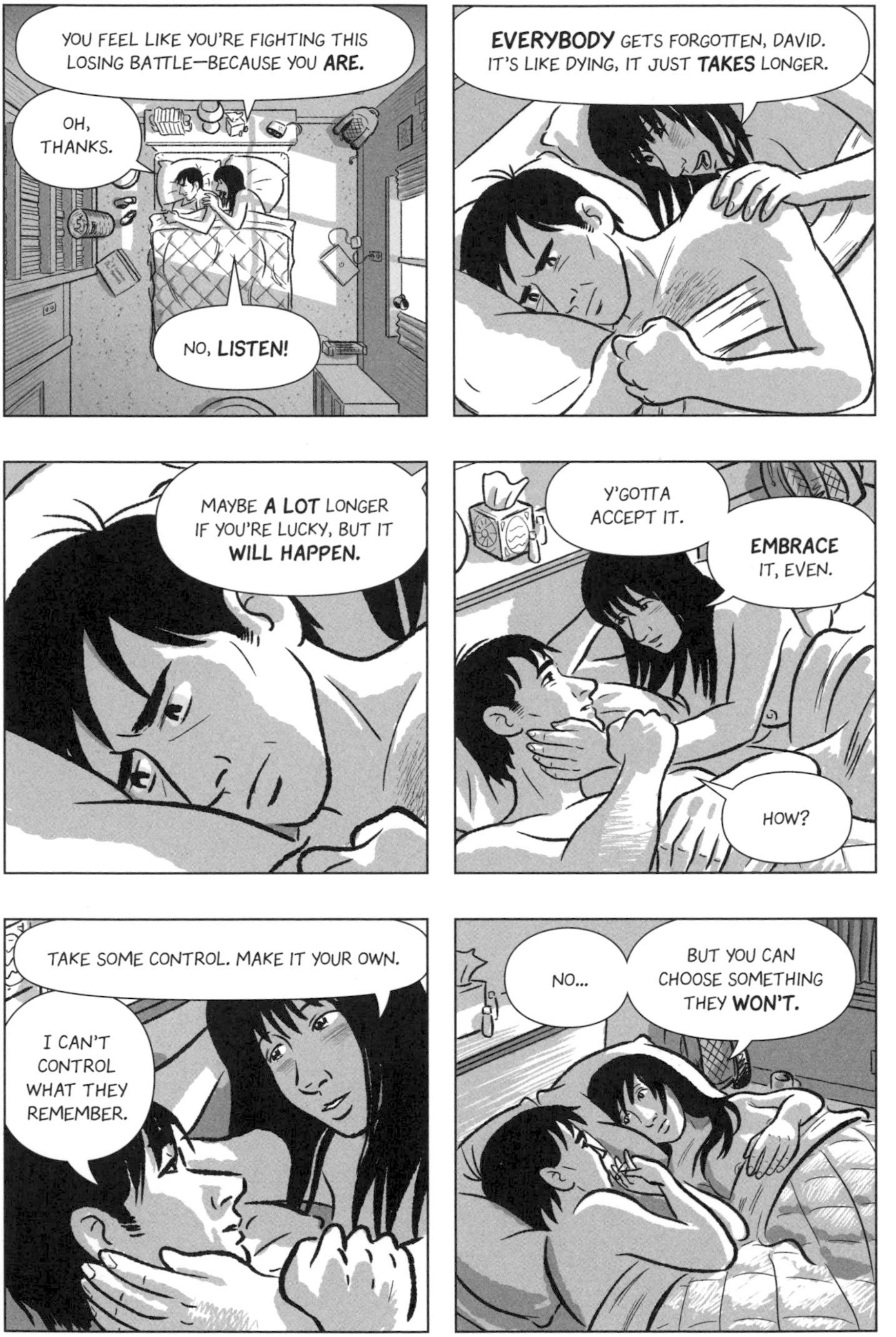

YOU FEEL LIKE YOU'RE FIGHTING THIS LOSING BATTLE—BECAUSE YOU **ARE.**
OH, THANKS.
NO, **LISTEN!**
EVERYBODY GETS FORGOTTEN, DAVID. IT'S LIKE DYING, IT JUST **TAKES** LONGER.
MAYBE **A LOT** LONGER IF YOU'RE LUCKY, BUT IT **WILL HAPPEN.**
Y'GOTTA ACCEPT IT.
EMBRACE IT, EVEN.
HOW?
TAKE SOME CONTROL. MAKE IT YOUR OWN.
I CAN'T CONTROL WHAT THEY REMEMBER.
NO...
BUT YOU CAN CHOOSE SOMETHING THEY **WON'T.**

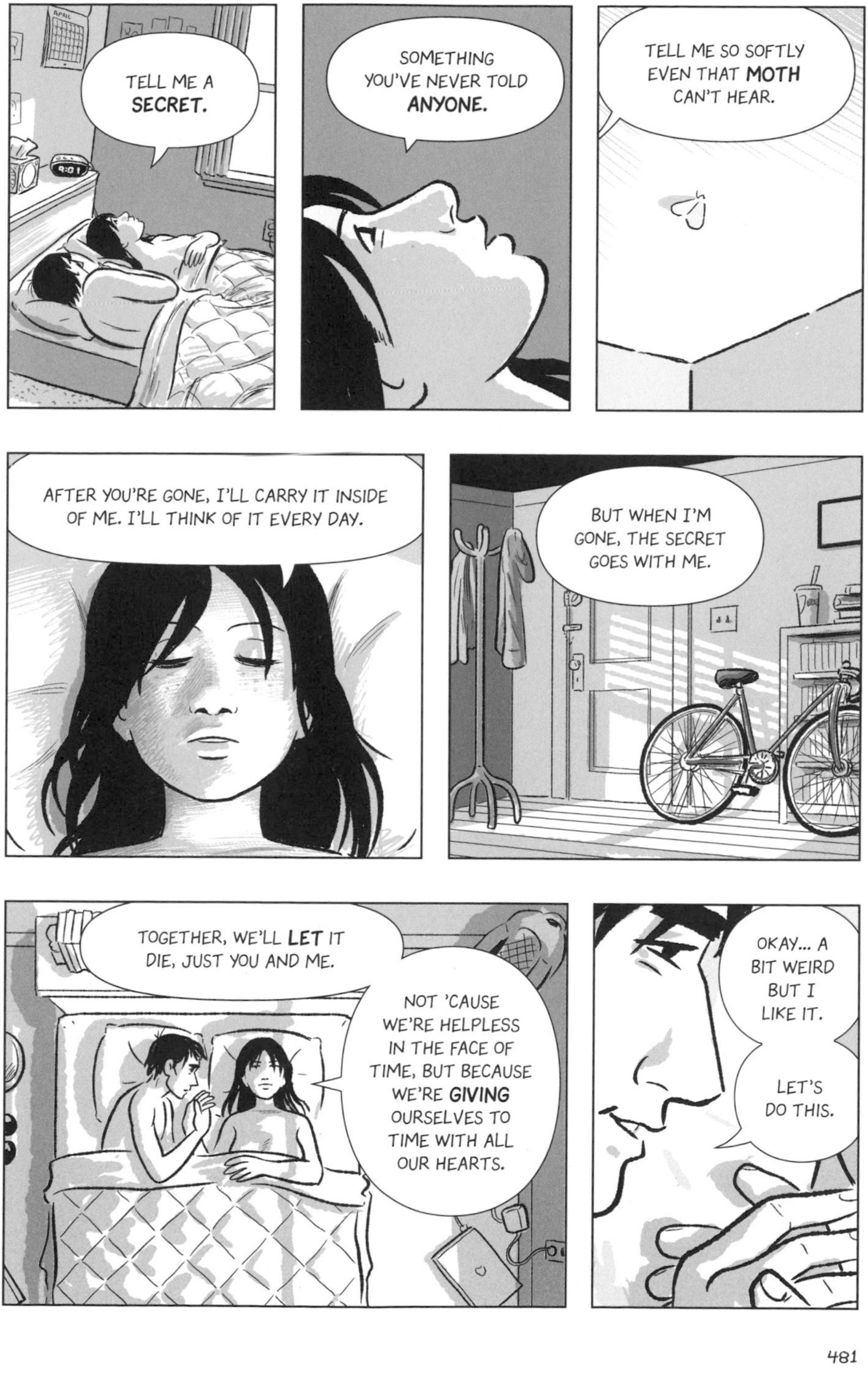
TELL ME A SECRET.
SOMETHING YOU'VE NEVER TOLD ANYONE.
TELL ME SO SOFTLY EVEN THAT MOTH CAN'T HEAR.
AFTER YOU'RE GONE, I'LL CARRY IT INSIDE OF ME. I'LL THINK OF IT EVERY DAY.
BUT WHEN I'M GONE, THE SECRET GOES WITH ME.
TOGETHER, WE'LL LET IT DIE, JUST YOU AND ME.
NOT 'CAUSE WE'RE HELPLESS IN THE FACE OF TIME, BUT BECAUSE WE'RE GIVING OURSELVES TO TIME WITH ALL OUR HEARTS.
OKAY... A BIT WEIRD BUT I LIKE IT.
LET'S DO THIS.

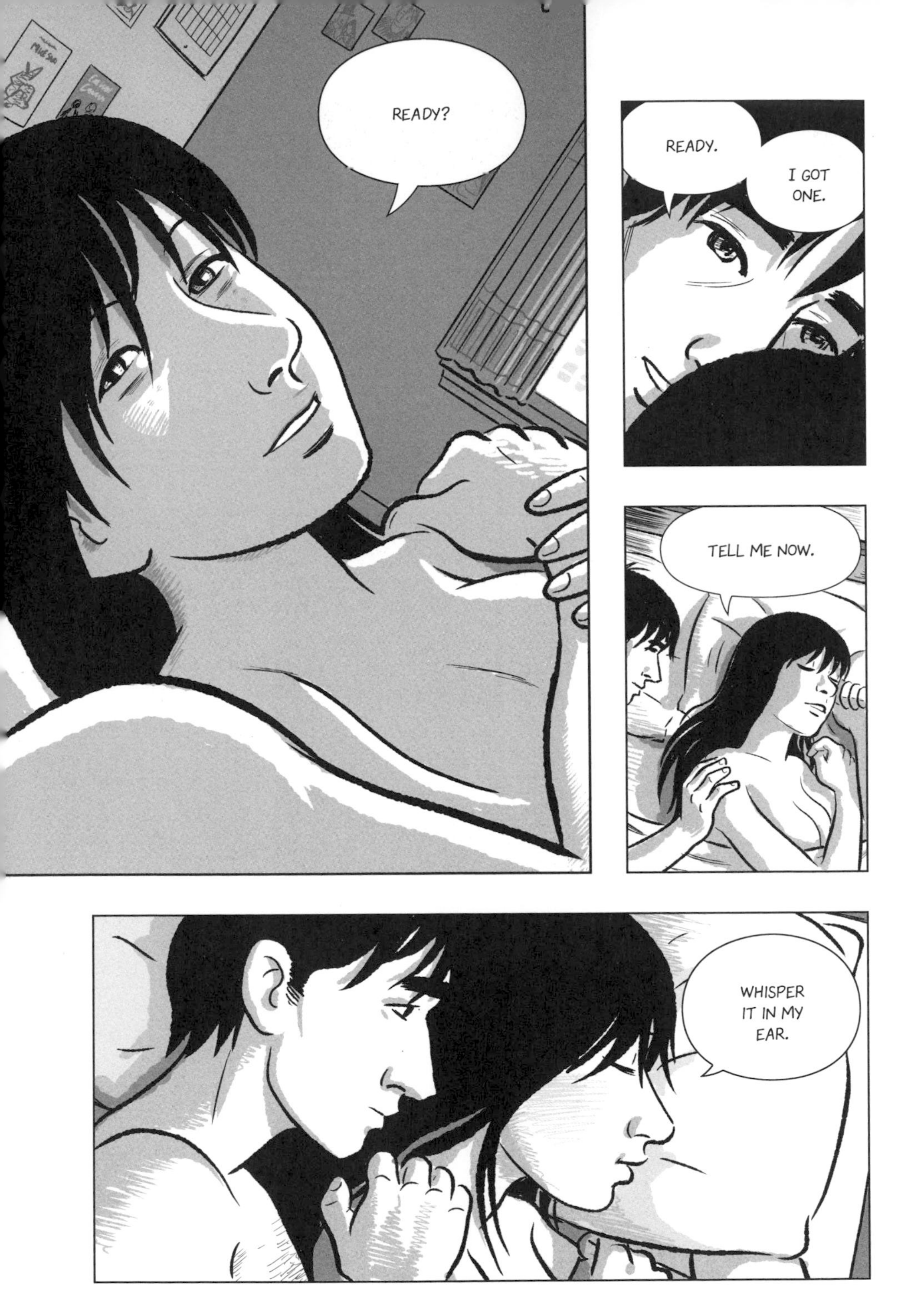
READY?
READY.
I GOT ONE.
TELL ME NOW.
WHISPER IT IN MY EAR.

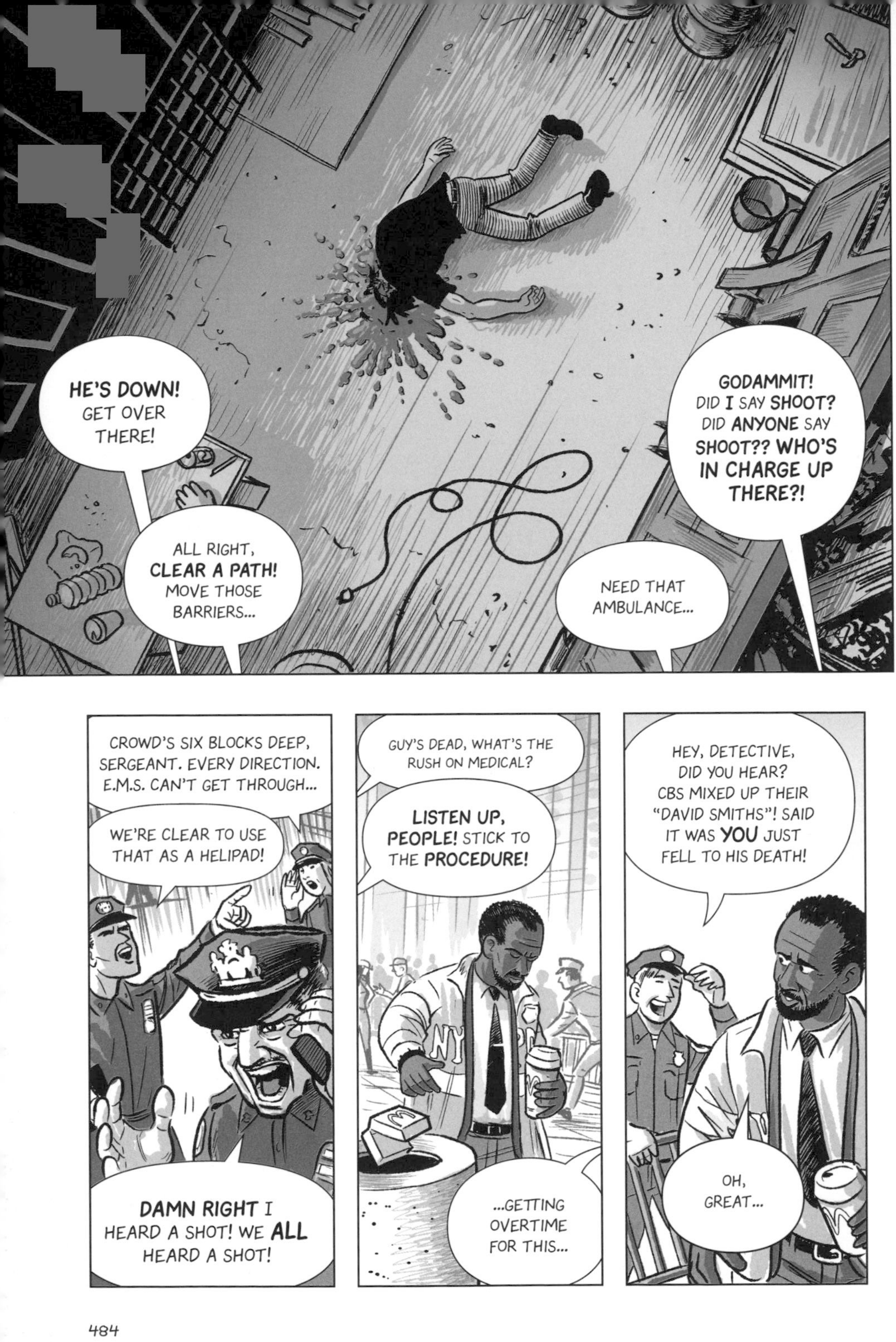
HE'S DOWN! GET OVER THERE!
ALL RIGHT, CLEAR A PATH! MOVE THOSE BARRIERS...
GODAMMIT! DID I SAY SHOOT? DID ANYONE SAY SHOOT?? WHO'S IN CHARGE UP THERE?!
NEED THAT AMBULANCE...
CROWD'S SIX BLOCKS DEEP, SERGEANT. EVERY DIRECTION. E.M.S. CAN'T GET THROUGH...
WE'RE CLEAR TO USE THAT AS A HELIPAD!
DAMN RIGHT I HEARD A SHOT! WE ALL HEARD A SHOT!
GUY'S DEAD, WHAT'S THE RUSH ON MEDICAL?
LISTEN UP, PEOPLE! STICK TO THE PROCEDURE!
...GETTING OVERTIME FOR THIS...
HEY, DETECTIVE, DID YOU HEAR? CBS MIXED UP THEIR "DAVID SMITHS"! SAID IT WAS YOU JUST FELL TO HIS DEATH!
OH, GREAT...

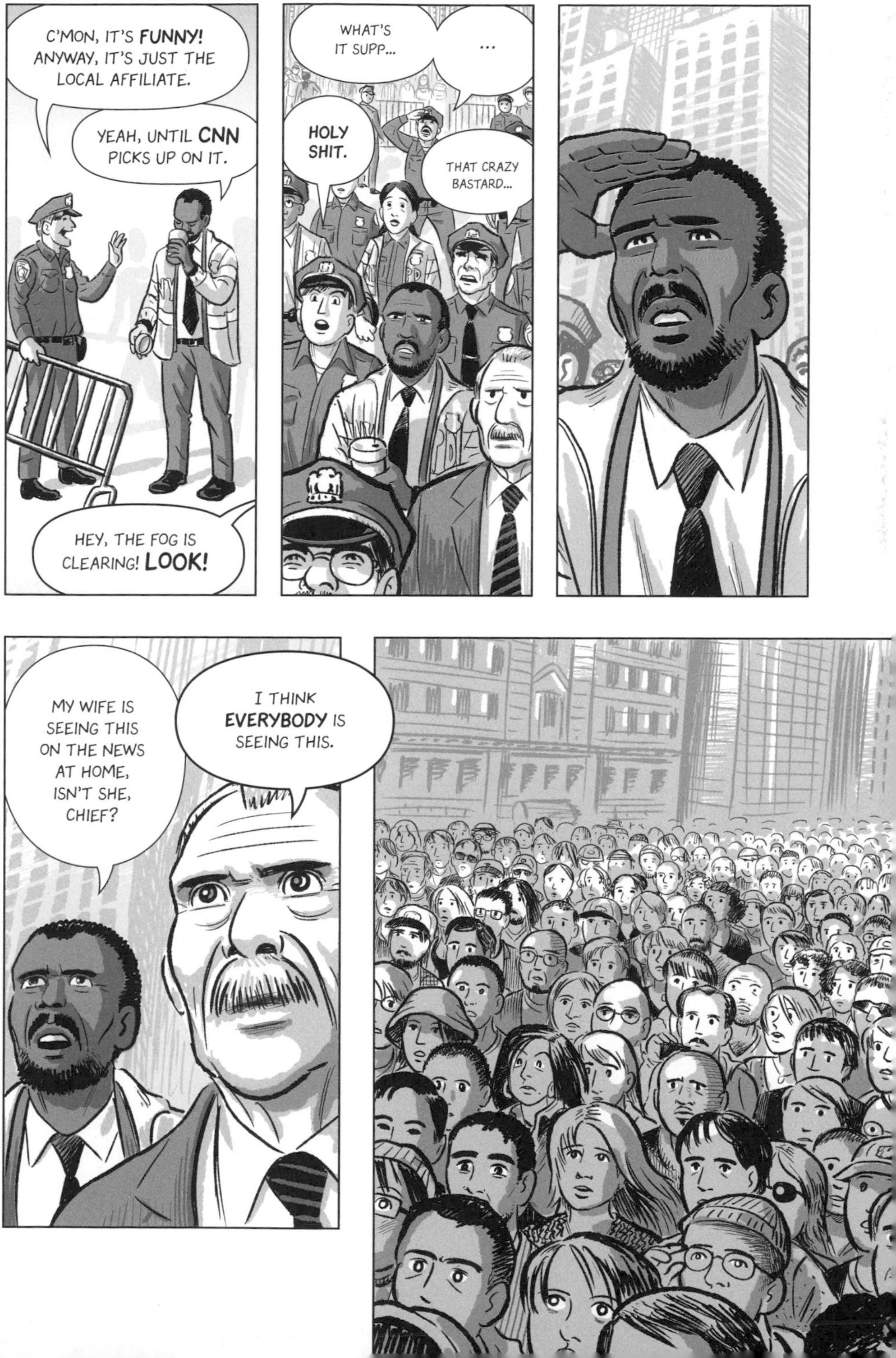
C'MON, IT'S FUNNY! ANYWAY, IT'S JUST THE LOCAL AFFILIATE.
YEAH, UNTIL CNN PICKS UP ON IT.
HEY, THE FOG IS CLEARING! LOOK!
WHAT'S IT SUPP...
...
HOLY SHIT.
THAT CRAZY BASTARD...
MY WIFE IS SEEING THIS ON THE NEWS AT HOME, ISN'T SHE, CHIEF?
I THINK EVERYBODY IS SEEING THIS.

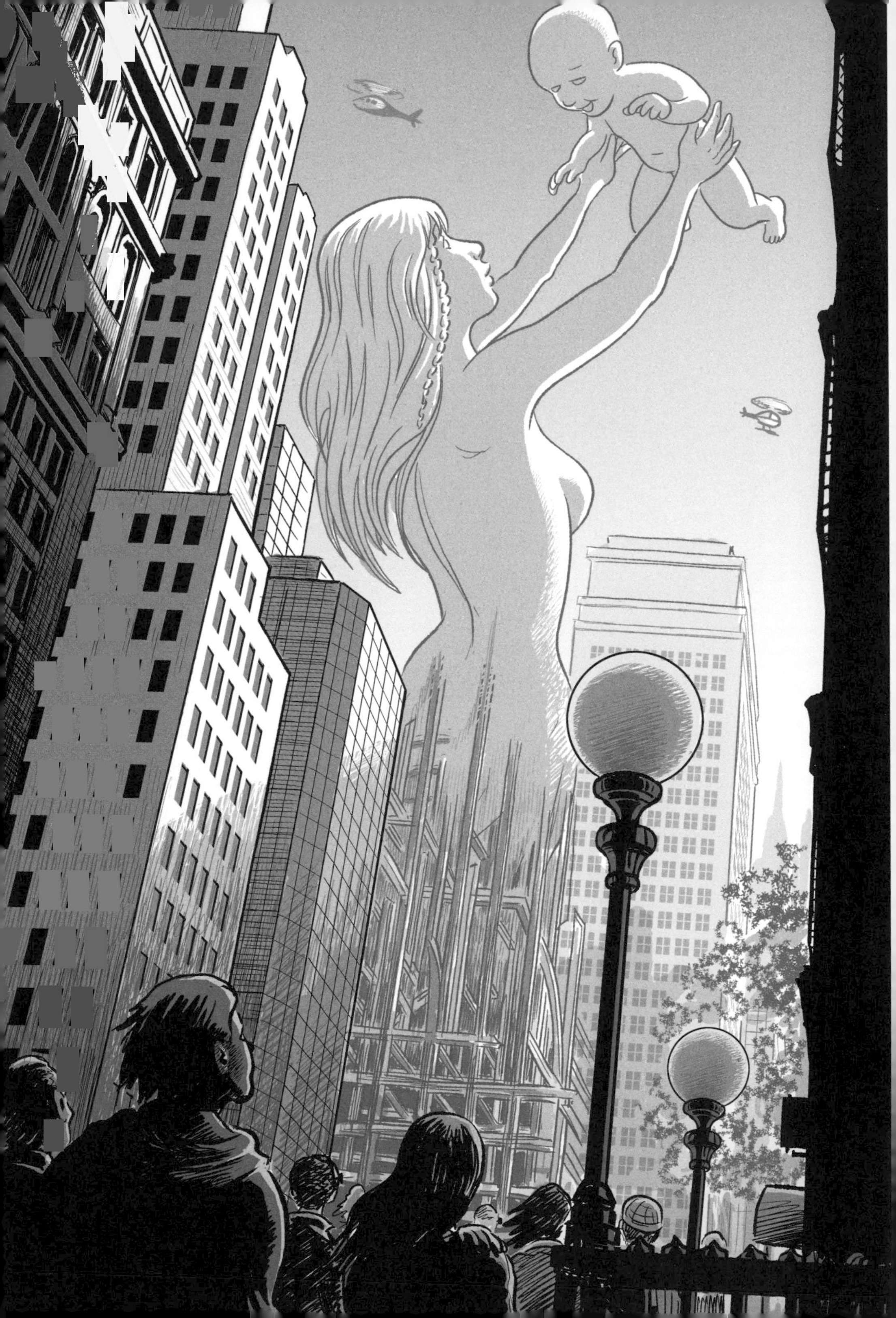

CNN.

YOU WERE RIGHT!

OH NO.

CHIEF, I GOTTA **CALL HOME.** TRACY'S GONNA THINK I'M **DEAD** IF SHE'S WATCHING THE **NEWS!**

CHIEF?

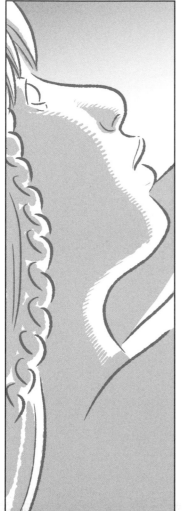

STILL ON THE CLOCK, SMITH. NO PERSONAL CALLS...

C'MON, SHE—

ZZT! BZZT!

CRAP, THAT'S HER NOW.

Y'KNOW WHAT, SCREW IT, I'M **TAKING** THIS.

BZZT! BZZT!

SUIT YOURSELF...

HEY.

IT'S ME.

DAVID!

OH, THANK GOD.

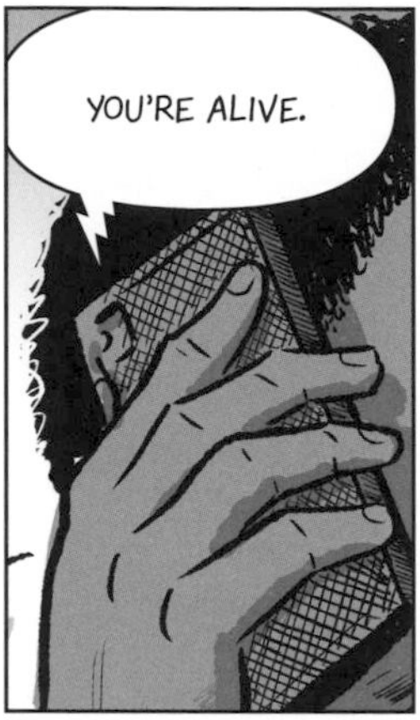
YOU'RE ALIVE.

Thank you . . .

To Mark Siegel, for keeping me on the right road, even when the road was barely a footpath; the best editor I could've hoped for in every respect; to the invincible Calista Brill, Colleen AF Venable, and Gina Gagliano of First Second; and to publisher Simon Boughton, who said yes when many would have said no, and thus made all the difference.

To agent supreme Judith Hansen for keeping me and my family safe, fed, and happy for over twenty years.

To my editorial kibitzers, Kurt Busiek, Larry Marder, Jenn Manley Lee, James Sturm, Vera Brosgol, and Ivy Ratafia, for helping my art and story suck less at every turn.

To the fearless Matthew Mercer and Jennifer Newman, who modeled for David and Meg and brought life and spontaneity into my usually stiff figure work. And to Lester Ratafia, my father-in-law, who modeled for David's Grand Uncle Harry. Les, you deserve a book of your own. Maybe one of these days.

To my phantom editors, Robert Weil and Charlie Kochman, who offered great advice while my book was still searching for its home. To Carol Pond, for preliminary proofreading and early comments, and to Alpha readers Lori Matsumoto, Kaitlyn Sudol, Lauren Girard, Robynne Blume, Holly Ratafia, daughter Sky, and to our friends at Macmillan and our publishers abroad, who offered some of my very first feedback and encouragement on the finished art and story as the book took its first baby steps into the sunlight.

To John Roshell of Comicraft, for designing our font, based on my hand lettering; available at ComicBookFonts.com if you want me lettering your next book for you.

To Keith Mayerson and Christine Zehner, who gave me some early impressions of the art scene in New York. In the end, this book was less about that community and more about the life and desires of my outsider protagonist, but if any of those few details ring false, blame me, not them.

To the Web itself, no joke, and all the photographers whose freely offered images taught me how to draw a thousand tiny details in my cartoon NYC, when my own ten thousand photos fell short.

To our many other models: Baby Godfrey (courtesy of Megan McDonough and Jim Byrnes), Tom Smith, Ayanna Gaines, Carol Pond, Krystal McCauley, Ivy, Winter, Sky, and the crowd of sweet, wonderful strangers who answered my plea and converged at our local mall to model for the pedestrian ring; boy, did we get some strange looks that day!

To DJ Lance Rock for being an awesome entertainer. My protagonist might not like the sculptures appropriating Lance's face, but I'm sure he likes Lance's own artistry just fine.

I'm sure I've forgotten someone, so for a fuller and more recently updated list, please visit scottmccloud.com/sculptor.

The "Girl in the Hat" is Ivy, whom I married in 1988, and who inspired the character of Meg well before that, during the seven years I was secretly in love with her.

Stories have their own physics, and I knew I'd need to let the gravity of this one pull my heroine whichever way it had to; even if it meant less and less of my wife on the page. We're an old, pudgy, middle-aged couple now, both of us. I'm less like David every day, she's less like the object of his affection. But, whenever my pen hit the screen, there she was just the same; in the hands and the voice and the freckles and the smile. Ivy.

As a family, we don't have much interest in gods and commandments. But we do love our traditions. Every winter, you'll find a menorah and a Christmas tree lighting up the living room. And there's one tradition from Ivy's side of the family that I'll confess to superstitiously using here as a kind of shield; it's a Jewish tradition regarding the naming of children.

Both our children's names carry the first initial of a deceased relative. It's said you should never pick your child's name from the names of the living, so you don't confuse the Angel of Death when the time comes. Ivy herself was named after Ivan, a great grandfather, gone before she was born, and she had three sisters and a brother whose names also followed the rule.

Her brother, Marcus, was the youngest, and was born healthy and on time, but each of his four older sisters had issues at birth.

Ivy was the oldest and was born a month early. Ivy's mother, Carol, smoked, like so many did in 1960, and that may have triggered the premature birth, and maybe her chronic battles with asthma too.

Holly was next. Born two and a half months premature only a year later, Holly was so tiny at birth, they say you could see the palm of her father's hand entirely around her head. After two and a half months in an incubator, she finally arrived home. When all the medical bills were finally paid two years later, the family celebrated with a "We own Holly" party.

Ivy's mother quit smoking. She took every precaution to ensure a healthy birth. Yet her next daughter, Pam, was born with Down syndrome. In the custom of the day, Pam was given over to an institution, but the decision never sat well with Carol and left scars that never fully healed.

So Carol began to smoke again, in despair and frustration. Again she conceived, again it was a girl, and again the baby was born prematurely; but this time, by four and a half months.

Ivy told me about this last premature birth when we were first married. As she remembered the story her mother told her, the doctors weren't hopeful, but they said that if the baby could last twenty-four hours, there was at least a slim chance she might make it in the long run.

So her parents waited the twenty-four hours to see if their baby could run out the clock. And they waited to give the baby her name. Twenty-four hours passed and the baby, against all odds, was still alive. So, with reason to hope, they chose a name, signed the papers, and made it official. And one hour later, the baby was gone.

The name they chose was Meg.

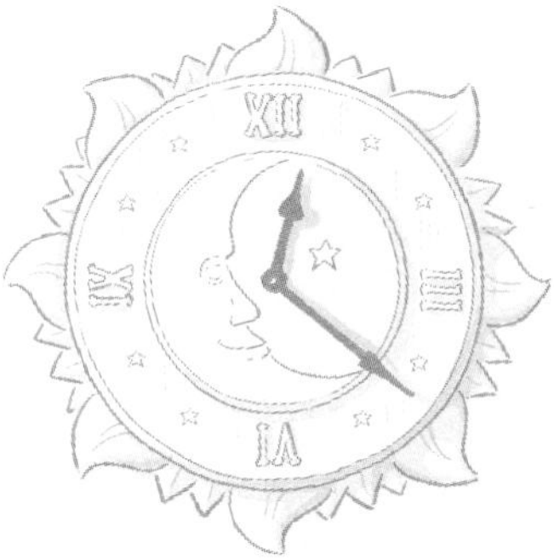
XII
III
VI
IX

FEB 2 0 2015

DATE DUE

		✐	